Assembly La... ...ogramming
for the IBM Systems 360 and 370 for OS and DOS

Assembly Language Programming
for the IBM Systems 360 and 370 for OS and DOS

Michael D. Kudlick

University of San Francisco

Second Edition

wcb

Wm. C. Brown Company Publishers
Dubuque, Iowa

Book Team

Robert B. Stern   Senior Editor
Nicholas Murray   Associate Developmental Editor
Mark E. Christianson   Designer
Lynne M. Meyers   Production Editor

wcb group

Wm. C. Brown   Chairman of the Board
Mark C. Falb   Executive Vice-President

wcb

Wm. C. Brown Company Publishers, College Division

Lawrence E. Cremer   President
David Wm. Smith   Vice-President, Marketing
E. F. Jogerst   Vice-President, Cost Analyst
David A. Corona   Assistant Vice-President, Production Development and Design
James L. Romig   Executive Editor
Marcia H. Stout   Marketing Manager
Marilyn A. Phelps   Manager of Design
William A. Moss   Production Editorial Manager
Mary M. Heller   Visual Research Manager

Second Printing, 1983

Printed in the United States of America   2-08166-02

To Elaine

Contents

Part Four
Directives

Part Five
Input/Output

Preface

In writing this textbook I have attempted to provide a thorough tutorial discussion of the topics that comprise problem-mode assembly language programming for the IBM Systems 360 and 370. This includes such fundamentals as base-displacement addressing, binary integer arithmetic, byte and bit manipulations, and subroutine linkage conventions, as well as the two-pass assembly process, floating-point and decimal arithmetic, conditional assemblies and macro definitions, and I/O programming.

Students using this text are expected to have completed one course in programming, on the order of an introductory FORTRAN course. Elementary concepts such as defining constants, reserving memory space, controlling loops, and processing arrays are explained with reference to allied concepts in FORTRAN; concepts with no immediate analogy in high-level languages (e.g., base-displacement addressing) are explained without assuming prior knowledge of these concepts by the students.

I have attempted to reinforce the students' understanding of the various topics through numerous examples, explanations, and programming solutions to problems. In addition, the student is frequently reminded of the important distinctions between assembly-time and run-time events, and of the interactions that take place among the Assembler, Loader, Operating System, user's program, and Central Processing Unit (CPU). The Summary and Exercises appearing at the end of each chapter and the sample problems (with complete programming solutions) that appear at the end of several of the chapters will, it is hoped, enhance the text's usefulness for students. References to related books and IBM manuals are given in Appendix G. Information summarizing the mnemonic instructions and directives, condition code settings, causes of run-time errors, and the EBCDIC and ASCII code schemes can be found in Appendixes A–F.

NEW TO THIS EDITION

In this second edition, all the features of the well-received earlier editions have been retained, and several additions have been made at the suggestion of reviewers and students. The additions are:

a. explanations of DOS/VS Assembly Language where there are differences from OS/VS;
b. chapter 22: an introductory chapter on VSAM programming;
c. expanded discussions of internal subroutines and DSECTs in chapter 9 and of packed-decimal operations in chapter 12;
d. clarifications of various topics throughout the text;
e. corrections of known first edition printing errors.

The DOS/VS explanations include the programming conventions and requirements (Section 2.3), elementary use of DTFCD, DTFPR, and related I/O macros (Section 2.4), an overview of I/O macros and parameters in chapter 19, sequential I/O in chapter 20, indexed sequential I/O in chapter 21 and VSAM I/O in chapter 22. The chapter on VSAM concentrates on fundamental concepts and techniques for defining, loading, and updating entry-sequenced and key-sequenced data sets for both OS/VS and DOS/VS.

TEXT ORGANIZATION

With the exception of the introductory chapters, the text's five parts may be covered in a number of different ways depending on the topics the instructor wishes to emphasize. Based on my own experience, I suggest the text be used in the following way in a one-semester course:

	chapters	sections covered in class	sections covered through reading and home study
Part One	1–3	all	—
Part Two	4–6	all	—
	7	7.1–7.7	7.8–7.9
	8–9	all	—
	10	—	all
Part Three	11	—	all
	12	all	—
	13	—	all
Part Four	14–15	—	all
	16	16.1–16.7	—
	17	17.1–17.6	17.7–17.9
Part Five	18–19	—	all
	20	20.1–20.4	20.5–20.11
	21	—	all
	22	—	all

There are perhaps three different approaches to the teaching of Assembly Language. They are not necessarily mutually exclusive, but given the constraints of time in a single semester, one of the approaches will probably dominate the other two. The first approach concentrates on the manner in which arithmetic processes are carried out. For this, chapters 1–5 and 11–13 form the heart of the course. The second approach concentrates on the manner in which nonarithmetic processes are carried out. For this, chapters 1–4, 7 and 8, and 18–22 are emphasized. The third approach uses Assembly Language as a means of introducing more systems-oriented topics. For this, chapters 1–10 and 14–17 are most helpful, especially chapters 9, 10, 16, and 17. The amount of emphasis given to any one chapter, regardless of the approach used, depends on the instructor as well as the capabilities of the students.

The three chapters in Part One include (1) the essentials of binary and hexadecimal integer arithmetic, (2) assembly language statement formats and their use in a simple program that reads and writes arbitrary text data, and (3) the seven types of instruction formats and the purpose and methods of using base-displacement addressing.

In Part Two, most of the elementary operations are discussed and illustrated. Chapter 4 introduces loop control and integer I/O techniques and shows how to obtain snaps of selected memory contents at run time. Chapter 5 covers binary integer arithmetic, including an explanation of two's complement arithmetic. Chapter 6 describes the techniques of defining run-time and assembly-time constants, of reserving memory space, and of assuring desired boundary alignments. Chapter 7 discusses byte manipulations, including the handling of variable-length strings; chapter 8 covers bit manipulations; and chapter 9 describes the subroutine linkage conventions and related topics. Chapter 10 explains the need for, and methods used by, a two-pass Assembler and includes a complete description of the object module and an introduction to the techniques of searching and sorting tables and of handling one-way lists such as the Assembler's cross-reference list.

The three chapters of Part Three deal with noninteger arithmetic. Chapter 11 briefly presents the rationale for decimal and floating-point hardware, chapter 12 describes the use of the decimal arithmetic instruction set and data formats, and chapter 13 describes the floating-point instruction set and data formats. In chapter 12, special emphasis is given to the problem of retaining sufficient accuracy through shifting, in the 360 as well as the 370, and to the problem of converting to and from EBCDIC format. In chapter 13, the emphasis is on the advantages and limitations of floating-point arithmetic, its similarities to and differences from fixed-point arithmetic, and the problem of converting to and from internal floating-point format.

Part Four, on the use of directives, begins with a discussion of the elementary directives in chapter 14, discusses control sections and related directives in chapter 15, introduces the concept of conditional assemblies in chapter 16, and demonstrates the usefulness and power of macros in chapter 17. A somewhat more extensive coverage of macros than is usually found in introductory texts is provided in chapter 17, in order to motivate advanced students to explore their capabilities.

The discussion of I/O programming in Part Five is, as far as I have been able to determine, more thorough than that found in any other introductory text on Assembly Language. Chapter 18 is primarily a description of the space and time constraints of using disks that are similar to the IBM 3330 system. Chapter 19 presents a comprehensive overview of the software facilities available for sequential and indexed sequential files through I/O macros. Chapter 20 illustrates how to create and maintain sequential files via QSAM, and chapter 21 does the same for indexed sequential files via QISAM and BISAM. Chapter 22 contains corresponding information for VSAM files.

Throughout the text, the approach taken in presenting the material is to illustrate all concepts and techniques with examples. These range in scope from simple demonstrations of the effects of individual instructions and directives to complete programs showing how instructions and directives are used in concert to produce desired results. I believe that one of the most effective methods of learning how to *write* assembly language programs is to *read* programs written by others. For this reason, a number of programs are included in the text.

Though I have attempted to cover many details and concepts, inevitably some have been omitted or passed over lightly. Therefore students are encouraged to seek additional information from reference manuals. In addition to compensating for those details that have not been adequately covered, this should have the beneficial effect of exposing students to the importance of using manuals at an early stage of the learning experience. For teachers, supplementary materials to accompany this text are available from the publisher in the form of an Instructor's Manual.

ACKNOWLEDGMENTS

The first edition of this book would not have been so well received were it not for the patience, encouragement, and wisdom of my editor, Robert Stern. The present edition has similarly benefited from Alan Apt's editorial assistance. I consider myself extremely fortunate to have had two such superb editors.

Many other persons have provided various suggestions that have helped me. My colleague George Ledin suggested the need for the approach I have used in this text. My former students Bruce Barton and Warren Chave have contributed a number of constructive criticisms and Mr. Barton provided invaluable assistance in the formulation of the VSAM chapter. It is also a pleasure once again to thank the prepublication reviewers of the first edition: their diligence and insights were exceptionally beneficial to me. Thus to Ken Danhoff of Southern Illinois University, John Forsythe of Michigan State University, Clinton Foulk of Ohio State University, Alfred Newhouse of the University of Houston, Udo Pooch of Texas A & M, and Alfred Weaver of the University of Virginia, I extend my sincerest appreciation for all the time, energy, and care they gave in reviewing my manuscripts. I am similarly indebted to Charles Downey of the University of Nebraska and Mondest C. Richards of Madison Area Technical College for providing very thoughtful and useful suggestions for incorporation into this second edition. And to Alan Canton and Louis Hatton I extend my gratitude for valuable explanations of basic DOS concepts. From all these persons and from daily contact with students using the text I have learned a great deal. Obviously, however, no blame is to be placed on any of these persons for inadequacies that appear in these pages.

Program testing was done on the University of San Francisco's computer system, a Univac Series 90 Model 90/60E. I owe many thanks to the former Director of USF's Computer Center, Michael Kelly, for his gracious and knowledgeable assistance, and to the continued support of the Center's staff. I also wish to thank my former secretary, Sarah Flowers, whose superb typing, editing, and organizational skills made preparation of the first edition much simpler than it otherwise would have been. I greatly missed her assistance in preparing the present edition; my one-fingered typing is not an appropriate substitute for her sure fingers.

PART
ONE

Fundamental Concepts

1
Computer System Concepts

The computer systems that we will be concerned with in this textbook, primarily the IBM 360 and 370 systems, consist of two broad categories of components: hardware and software. The term *hardware* refers to a computer system's electronic, electromagnetic, and electromechanical components: in short, its physical equipment. *Software* consists of the computer programs, procedures, rules, and documentation used in the operation of a computer system.

Broadly speaking, a program is a plan that specifies actions that may be taken and the conditions under which they are to be taken. We will use the terms *program* and *computer program* interchangeably to mean a sequence of actions and conditions written in such a way that they may either be processed directly by the hardware or be translated into a form that may be processed directly by the hardware. A program that can be processed directly by the hardware is known as a *machine language* program. A program that can be translated into machine language is said to be written in a computer *programming language*.

Assembly Language is a computer programming language. An assembly language program consists of statements that are processed by a program known as the Assembler. The statements are collectively called the *source code,* or *source module*. A significant portion of an assembly language program consists of statements that represent the detailed operations—known as *instructions*—which the hardware is capable of executing. Whereas programming languages such as FORTRAN and COBOL do not closely reflect the structure of a computer's hardware, Assembly Language does. For this reason, programming in Assembly Language is qualitatively different from programming in almost any other language.

1.1 ASSEMBLY LANGUAGE PROGRAMMING

When the Assembler processes a source module, it produces two things: an object module and a listing. The object module contains the numeric instructions and data formats that constitute the machine language representation of the source module statements. Thus one function of the Assembler is to translate source module statements into machine language. The listing produced by the Assembler is a printed record of the source module statements together with the information contained in the object module. A portion of such a listing is shown in figure 1.1. Not shown in figure 1.1, but also included in such listings, is information that is useful for analyzing program errors.

When submitting a source module to a computer system for processing, an assembly language programmer does not communicate directly with the hardware. Rather, the source module is literally the input data processed by the Assembler. As is illustrated in figure 1.2, another program, the Loader, processes the object module one step further in order to prepare it for execution by the hardware. This entails copying, or *loading,* the machine language version of the program into the main memory of the computer system.

It is useful at this point to emphasize that when a programmer's source module is being processed by the Assembler, it is the Assembler program that is being executed by the hardware, not the programmer's. The period of time during which this happens is known as *assembly time*. Similarly, when an object module is being processed by the Loader, it is the Loader program that is being executed, not the programmer's. This

Figure 1.1   Sample listing produced by an Assembler.

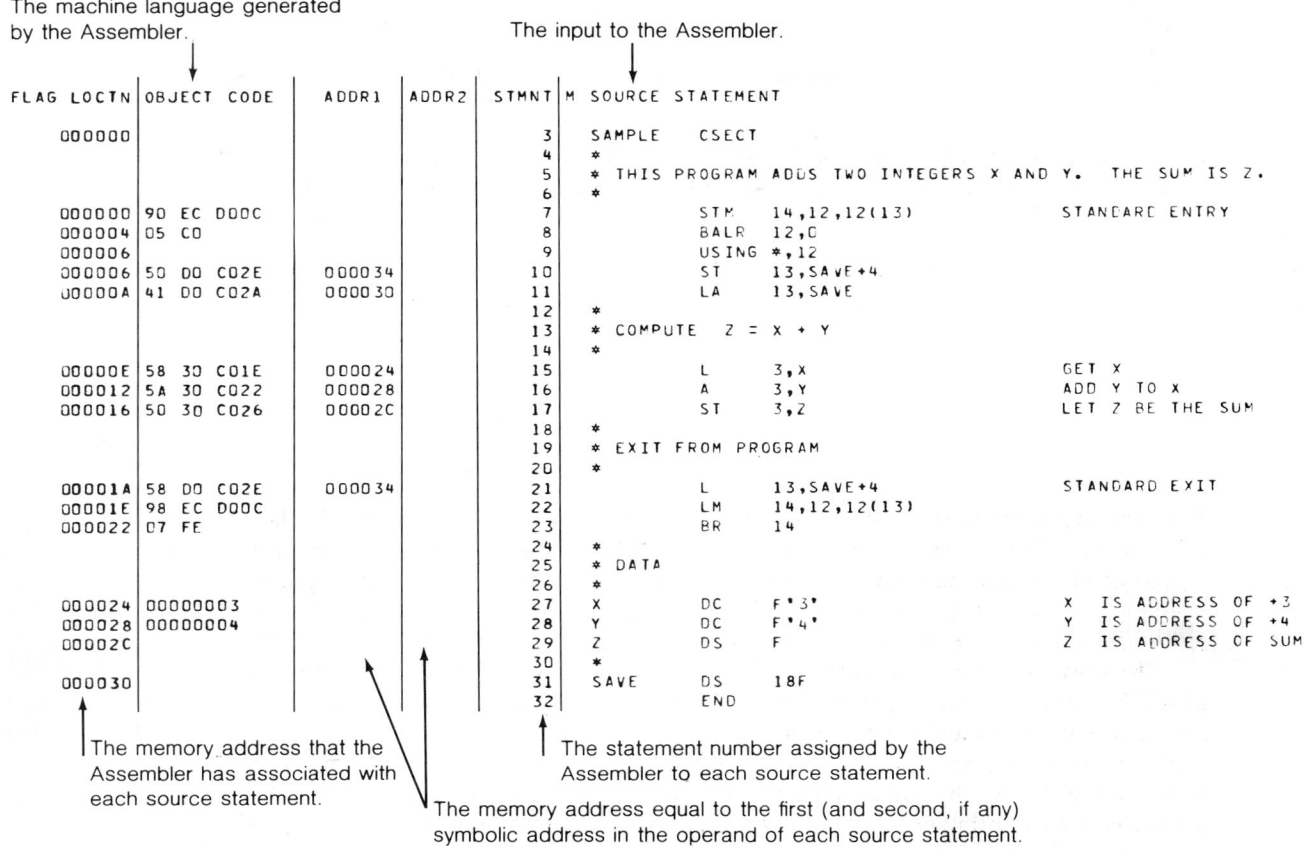

The machine language generated by the Assembler.

The input to the Assembler.

```
FLAG LOCTN OBJECT CODE    ADDR1  ADDR2  STMNT M SOURCE STATEMENT

     000000                          3   SAMPLE   CSECT
                                     4   *
                                     5   * THIS PROGRAM ADDS TWO INTEGERS X AND Y.  THE SUM IS Z.
                                     6   *
     000000 90 EC D00C               7            STM    14,12,12(13)          STANDARD ENTRY
     000004 05 C0                    8            BALR   12,0
     000006                          9            USING  *,12
     000006 50 D0 C02E      000034  10            ST     13,SAVE+4
     00000A 41 D0 C02A      000030  11            LA     13,SAVE
                                    12   *
                                    13   * COMPUTE  Z = X + Y
                                    14   *
     00000E 58 30 C01E      000024  15            L      3,X                   GET X
     000012 5A 30 C022      000028  16            A      3,Y                   ADD Y TO X
     000016 50 30 C026      00002C  17            ST     3,Z                   LET Z BE THE SUM
                                    18   *
                                    19   * EXIT FROM PROGRAM
                                    20   *
     00001A 58 D0 C02E      000034  21            L      13,SAVE+4             STANDARD EXIT
     00001E 98 EC D00C              22            LM     14,12,12(13)
     000022 07 FE                   23            BR     14
                                    24   *
                                    25   * DATA
                                    26   *
     000024 00000003               27   X         DC     F'3'                  X  IS ADDRESS OF +3
     000028 00000004               28   Y         DC     F'4'                  Y  IS ADDRESS OF +4
     00002C                        29   Z         DS     F                     Z  IS ADDRESS OF SUM
                                    30   *
     000030                        31   SAVE      DS     18F
                                    32            END
```

The memory address that the Assembler has associated with each source statement.

The statement number assigned by the Assembler to each source statement.

The memory address equal to the first (and second, if any) symbolic address in the operand of each source statement.

---

is known as *load time.* The programmer's program can be executed only after the Loader program has been executed. The period of time during which the programmer's program is being executed by the hardware is known as *run time;* while being executed, the program is said to be *running* in the computer.

Because some of the statements in a source module are specifically intended for use during assembly time and/or load time, and not during run time, the distinctions between assembly time, load time, and run time are of critical importance to the understanding of assembly language programming. An example of a statement used only at assembly time is the USING directive shown in figure 1.1.

In general, a source module statement may be a comment or may specify an instruction or a directive. Comment statements are identified by an asterisk in the first position of the statement; instructions and directives are specified by an operation code in one of the statement's fields. For example, the three statements

```
L     3,X
A     3,Y
ST    3,Z
```

in figure 1.1 specify the three instructions Load, Add, and Store, respectively; the statement

```
END
```

specifies a directive that identifies the statement as being the last one in the source module. The distinction between an instruction and a directive is that an *instruction* is a symbolic representation of a single machine language operation that will be executed by the hardware at run time, while a *directive* is a request to the

Figure 1.2   Relationship of Assembler and Loader.

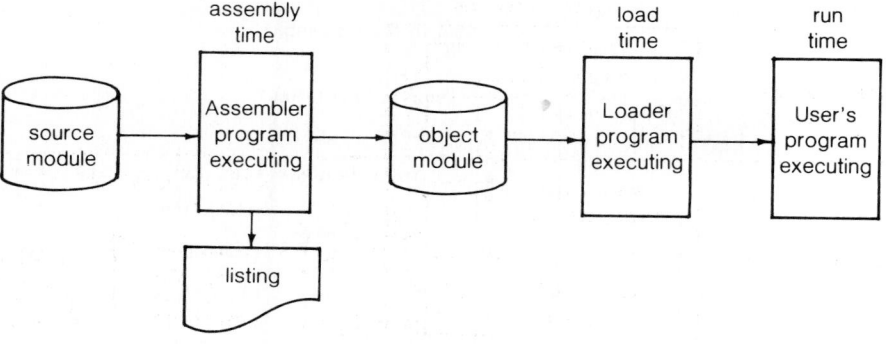

Assembler to perform some function other than translating instructions into machine language. Therefore, in your study of Assembly Language, it is important to learn the various capabilities provided by instructions and directives and how to specify them.

1.2   THE OPERATING SYSTEM

In addition to interacting with the Assembler and Loader programs, an assembly language programmer needs to become familiar with certain capabilities of the computer system's master control program. In the IBM 360 and 370, the master control program is more commonly known as the Operating System. This program manages the operation of the computer in such a way as to make it practicable for a number of users to efficiently utilize the computer's facilities without interfering with one another.

In many IBM 360 and 370 computers, the Operating System is known as *OS;* in others it is *DOS.* OS is essentially more complex and more versatile than DOS, having been designed for systems that cater to a larger variety of user needs than DOS. In this text, we will use the term *Operating System* to refer to both OS and DOS; however, we will delineate any differences that exist between OS and DOS Assembly Language. Except for these differences, which are primarily in the manner in which input and output operations are specified, programs written in IBM 360 or 370 Assembly Language use the same instructions and directives whether they are written for OS or DOS. However, since there are different versions of each of these operating systems, it is important to note that this text is oriented to the OS/VS and DOS/VS versions.

There are two mechanisms for communicating with the Operating System: (1) by means of job control language (JCL) statements and (2) by means of instructions. The principal functions of JCL statements are to identify the user and the user's accounting parameters, to initiate and terminate jobs, and to describe files and request certain activities related to files. In this context, a *job* is a unit of work such as assembling, loading, and running a program that is to be performed by the computer system; a *file* is a set of related data that is treated as a unit and is identified by name. Probably the most important function of instructions that communicate with the Operating System is to request that data be read from files and written to files at run time. The process of reading data is known as *input,* that of writing data as *output.*

Figure 1.3 indicates in a general way the processes that occur in order for output to take place. Every file to be processed by a program must be named on a JCL statement, and certain characteristics of that file must be described either by JCL statements or by data control (DCB or DTF) directives. The file must be "opened" at run time prior to its use and may then be written to in accordance with the specifications given when it was opened. When a file is opened, the Operating System collects the specifications of the file into a control area and allocates space for the anticipated output operations. When a write operation is performed, data is transferred from the user program area to the system output buffer and from there it is transferred to the file by the Operating System. A similar process takes place for input operations.

In a computer system in which many users can have access to the same facilities, each user's programs and data must be protected from being inadvertently or intentionally interfered with by other users' programs. Part of the function of the Operating System is to provide that protection, and for this reason it controls all input and output operations. But in order to ensure that no user program can bypass that control function,

Figure 1.3   Typical output processes.

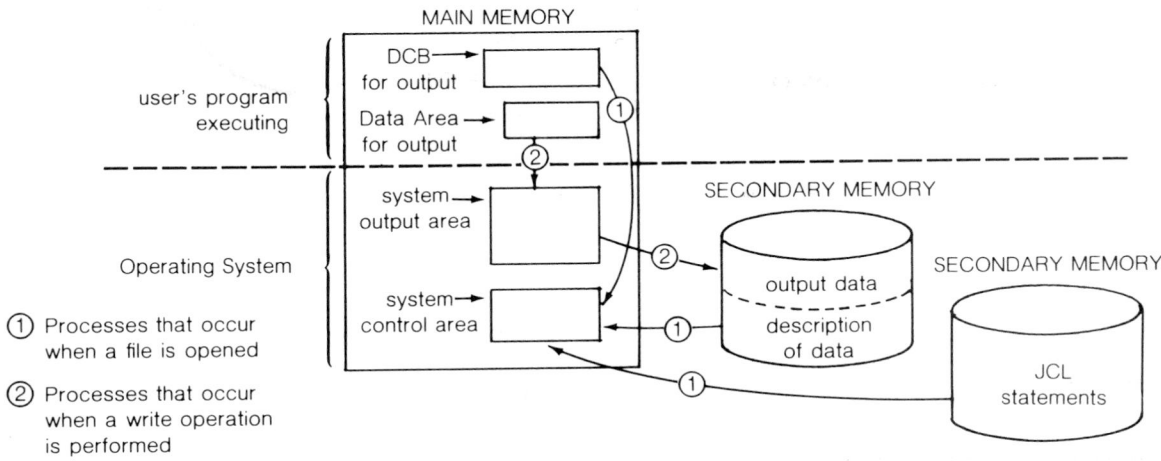

another degree of protection is provided by the hardware. When a user's program is being run, the hardware, or more precisely, the central processing unit (see next section), is in what is known as *problem mode;* this means that only those instructions that cannot be used to affect the system's integrity are allowed to be executed. When the Operating System is being run, the central processing unit is said to be in *supervisor mode,* in which all the instructions of the computer can be executed. Since input and output instructions are among those that can be used to affect system integrity, they can only be executed in supervisor mode and are therefore known as *privileged* instructions.

In the IBM 360 and 370 systems, there are some 180 executable instructions, of which about 30 are privileged. In the 3033 extension feature of the 370, there are also a dozen or so semiprivileged instructions used in the dual-address-space facility. These privileged and semi-privileged instructions will not be discussed in this text. Instead, attention will be focused on the 150 or so nonprivileged instructions and on the approximately fifty directives that can be used in Assembly Language.

1.3   HARDWARE

Assembly language programmers are forced, by the nature of the language, to become familiar with some aspects of a computer system's hardware. Chief among these are the machine language instructions and data formats, the methods of addressing information in main memory, and the manner in which arithmetic is accomplished. In this section, the functions of the principal hardware components are summarized, and some fundamental characteristics of two of these components, main memory and the central processing unit, are discussed.

The hardware can be represented in a general way by the diagram in figure 1.4. *Main memory* contains the Operating System and any other program that is being executed by the hardware. In addition, it contains data and control information required by the Operating System and the programs that are being executed. The *Central Processing Unit* (CPU) contains the electronics required to interpret and execute machine-language instructions, to control the transfer of data and programs into and out of main memory, and to detect various errors as they arise. The *input/output processors,* called data channels in IBM systems, contain the electronics required to transmit data between main memory and input/output devices, and between main memory and secondary memory. *Secondary, or auxiliary, memory* serves as storage space for programs when they are not being executed and for data. Secondary memory commonly consists of magnetic tapes, disks, and drums. *Input devices* generate signals required for the transmission of data into main memory from sources external to the computer system; common devices include card readers, terminals, and optical and magnetic ink character readers. *Output devices* receive signals transmitted from main memory for use outside the computer system; common devices include printers, terminals, card punches, and plotters.

Main memory consists of a large number of elements whose purpose is to store programs and data in such a way that the instructions can be executed, and the data operated on, by the CPU. The fundamental unit of information in main memory is the binary digit, or *bit,* which may be either a 0 or a 1. *All data and*

Figure 1.4   Relationship of hardware components.

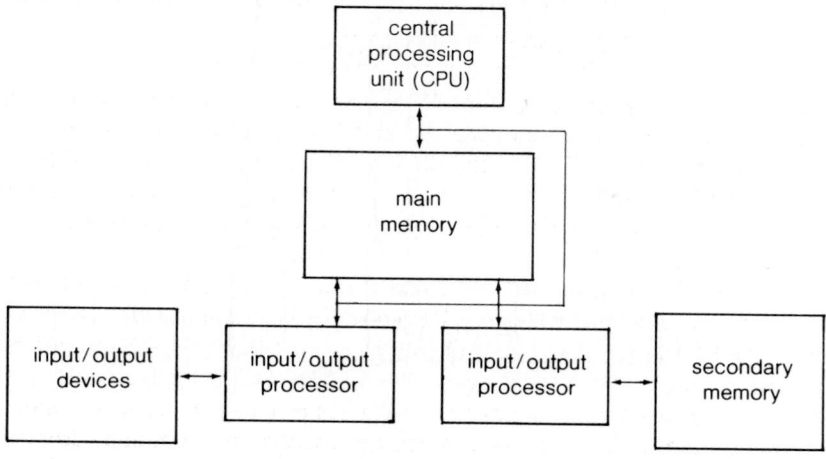

programs are represented as sequences of bits. In most computers some fixed number of bits is stored, accessed, and processed as a single unit of information. The term *byte* is used to denote a small number of consecutive bits, and the term *word* is generally used to denote a somewhat larger number of consecutive bits. In a unit of information consisting of k consecutive bits, the bits are usually numbered from 0 to $k-1$, starting at the high-order bit position:

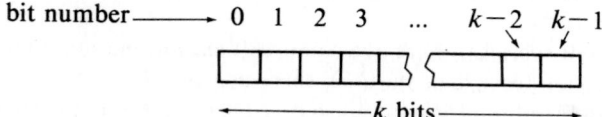

As shown, the high-order bit position is usually depicted as the left-most bit. It should be noted that with k bits, one can represent exactly 2^k different sequences of bits. For example, if $k = 2$, the four sequences are 00, 01, 10, and 11.

In the IBM 360 and 370 systems, a byte consists of 8 bits, and a word of 32 bits. Two other frequently used units are a half word, consisting of 16 bits (2 bytes), and a double word, consisting of 64 bits (8 bytes). A word is often called a *full word*, to distinguish it from half and double words. Each byte in main memory is said to occupy a location, or physical position, in memory, and each location is identified by a numeric name called its *address*. The set of all addresses in a main memory that contains N byte locations is the set of nonnegative integers $0,1,2,...,N-1$, as represented by this diagram:

In a one megabyte (*mega* means million) memory, there are approximately one million byte locations— $N = 2^{20} = 1,048,576$.

Each byte in the main memory of IBM 360 and 370 systems is characterized by two quantities: its address and the sequence of 8 bits contained in the byte. The latter are often called the *contents* of the byte. Similarly, one speaks of the contents of a word, of a half word, and of a double word. The address of these larger units is the address of their most significant byte, usually depicted in diagrams as the left-most byte. It should be noted, however, that in some computer systems individual bytes may not be addressable. In those systems, a word is usually the smallest addressable unit of information.

The CPU executes instructions that it obtains from main memory and, in doing so, frequently processes data that it also obtains from main memory. As has already been mentioned, the instructions and data are represented in machine language. This is a numeric language, the format and content of which usually differ considerably from one manufacturer's computer system to another's. The differences among various machine languages account for the differences among various Assembly Languages, since the format of the instructions and data represented in an Assembly Language is closely tied to that of machine language. Despite these differences, however, the general form of a machine language instruction can be depicted as follows:

opcode	operand

The sequence of bits in the opcode field identifies the particular instruction to be executed by the CPU, for example, add, compare, go-to. The bits in the operand field usually represent either the address of the data to be operated on by the instruction, or the data itself. In many instructions, two items of data are represented in the operand field, and in some instructions three are represented. These are known as two-address or three-address instructions, respectively. In go-to type instructions, the operand specifies the address of the next instruction to be executed.

Most CPU's execute only one instruction at a time. At any instant, the address of the next instruction to be executed is contained in a hardware element known as the *program location counter* (PC). In the IBM 360 and 370 systems, the PC is part of the program status word (PSW), which records various information about the instantaneous state of a running program. The address in the PC is initially set by the Operating System to refer to the first instruction in a program. But once program execution is under way, the address in the PC is controlled by the CPU as follows: When an instruction is obtained from memory, the CPU anticipates that the next instruction will be obtained from the next sequential location in memory. Therefore, it increments the address in the PC to refer to that location and then executes the instruction that was just fetched from memory.

When the executed instruction is anything other than a go-to type of instruction, the CPU uses the incremented PC address to fetch the next instruction upon completion of the current one. When the executed instruction is a go-to type of instruction, the address specified in that instruction's operand replaces the address in the PC, thereby changing the location of the next instruction from that which was anticipated by the CPU. In this way, the PC always contains the address of the next instruction that is to be fetched and executed by the CPU.

Thus, through the mechanism of the PC, program execution proceeds from one instruction to the next in the same logical sequence as that given in the source module.

In addition to fetching instructions and data directly from main memory, the CPU and main memory often are interfaced to one another through registers. *Registers* are special memory elements designed to provide faster access to data than is possible through main memory. Therefore, the use of registers contributes substantially to the speed with which a program can be executed. For this reason, most of the computations and comparisons performed by instructions use registers as well as main memory. But, because registers are more expensive than are main memory elements, there are far fewer registers than main memory locations in a computer system. One task of any program, therefore, is to copy data into and out of registers on an as-needed basis. Instructions specifically designed for this purpose are usually known as load and store instructions, respectively. In the three instructions of figure 1.1 mentioned earlier,

```
L       3,X
A       3,Y
ST      3,Z
```

the first instruction is a load instruction, the only purpose of which is to copy an integer into a register (Register 3 in this example) so that the addition specified by the second instruction can be performed in that register. The third instruction is a store instruction, the purpose of which is to copy the sum from the register into main memory, so that the register can then be used for other purposes. In FORTRAN, an assignment statement would look like this:

$$Z = X + Y$$

In Assembly Language, it is necessary to specify the detailed sequence of instructions needed to carry out the process.

1.4 REPRESENTATION OF DATA IN MEMORY

In a computer's memory, all data are represented as one or more sequences of bits. The bit sequences that are used generally depend on how the data are to be processed by the CPU.

One of the main processing distinctions is between arithmetic and nonarithmetic processes. Clearly, data that are to be used for arithmetic processes must be represented in such a way that the rules of arithmetic can be consistently and correctly applied to the data. Similarly, data used for nonarithmetic processes must be represented so that these processes can be carried out in a consistent manner. Usually the two sets of requirements are not compatible. Invariably, in a computer's memory, *a different representation is used for numbers that participate in arithmetic processes than is used for numbers that participate in nonarithmetic processes.* An example of a number used in an arithmetic process is the mathematical constant $\pi = 3.14159....$ An example of a number used in a nonarithmetic process is a telephone number, such as 555–1346.

Yet, all data that are transmitted between a computer's main memory and external input or output devices, such as card readers, printers, and terminals, are almost invariably transmitted in a form known as *character data.* This form is well suited for many nonarithmetic processes but is not well suited for arithmetic processes.

A *character* is any letter, digit, punctuation mark, or other symbol that can be represented on a punched card or typed on a keyboard. In the form of data representation known as character data, each character is represented as a sequence of bits in a code that uniquely identifies that character. Thus for purposes of data transmission, a number may be thought of as a sequence of one or more characters, each of which is represented in a unique code that is suitable for data transmission but not for arithmetic processes.

There are presently two main sets of character codes in widespread use. One is known as the American National Standard Code for Information Interchange (ASCII, usually pronounced *ask-ee*); the other is the Extended Binary-Coded Decimal Interchange Code (EBCDIC, pronounced *ebb-sid-ik*). EBCDIC is used in IBM devices and computer systems, as well as other computer systems; ASCII is used in terminals and computer systems not manufactured by IBM. *The two sets of codes are not the same.* EBCDIC is an 8-bit code, giving 256 possible character representations. ASCII is a 7-bit code, giving 128 possible character representations. For example, the digit "1" is represented as 0110001 in 7-bit ASCII but as 11110001 in 8-bit EBCDIC. The reader can ascertain other differences as well as similarities between the two schemes from the tables given in Appendix F.

In this text we will be concerned almost solely with the EBCDIC representations of characters. But whichever representation is used, one of the immediate problems the programmer has to face is that of translating input data from its character representation to the representation required in computer memory when the data is to be used in arithmetic processes. The programmer will also be faced with the reverse translation problem, to transmit arithmetic results from the computer's memory to an external device such as a printer or terminal. It must be emphasized that when a number is transmitted between memory and an external device, it is transmitted as character data—a sequence of digits, and possibly a plus or minus sign, punctuation marks, and/or a decimal point—each of which is represented in character form. This form is not used for the arithmetic processes of addition, subtraction, multiplication, and division in a computer system and is not even used to algebraically compare two numbers.

We will face these problems of translation in stages. First, we will consider only arithmetic processes involving integers. This discussion begins in the next section and continues, in various forms, through the first ten chapters. The representation and processing of numbers that are not integers will be dealt with in chapters 11, 12, and 13.

1.5 BINARY AND HEXADECIMAL INTEGERS

In the binary number system, only two digits are used in the representation of numbers: 0 and 1. With only two digits, the rules of arithmetic are especially simple and require much simpler electronics than if the decimal system were used.

From a programming standpoint, the methods used to represent binary integers and to compute arithmetic functions of them in computer systems must be thoroughly understood for two reasons: (1) calculations involving addresses are of critical importance in assembly language programming, and almost all such calculations are based on the binary system, and (2) the range of integers that can be represented in computer systems is not infinite and attempts to generate an integer whose value is outside the allowable range usually produce erroneous results.

In this section, we will show how to express an integer in the binary and hexadecimal number systems and how to convert an integer from its decimal system representation to either the binary or hexadecimal system. These operations are necessary for an understanding of the material to be covered in subsequent chapters.

Positional Notation

In a decimal integer such as 423, the position of each digit determines the value of the integer. Thus, the value of 423 is computed as

$$4 \times 10^2 + 2 \times 10^1 + 3 \times 10^0$$

In general, for a decimal integer consisting of k digits

$$d_0d_1d_2...d_{k-2}d_{k-1}$$

where d_n denotes any decimal digit (and below, b_n any binary digit, and h_n any hexadecimal digit), the value of the integer is computed as

$$d_0 \times 10^{k-1} + d_1 \times 10^{k-2} + d_2 \times 10^{k-3} + ... + d_{k-2} \times 10^1 + d_{k-1} \times 10^0$$

The representation $d_0d_1d_2...d_{k-2}d_{k-1}$ is said to use *positional notation* for the base 10.

Analogous to decimal integers, any nonnegative binary integer is a sequence of the binary digits 0 and 1 arranged in such an order that the position of each bit implies its value in the integer. For example, the positional value of each bit in the binary integer 10101 is computed as follows:

$$
\begin{array}{l}
1 \times 2^0 = 1 \\
0 \times 2^1 = 0 \\
1 \times 2^2 = 4 \\
0 \times 2^3 = 0 \\
1 \times 2^4 = 16
\end{array}
$$

The value of the binary integer 10101 is the sum of the positional values (represented here in the decimal system) of each bit:

$$16 + 0 + 4 + 0 + 1 = 21$$

In general, for a k-bit binary integer

$$b_0b_1b_2...b_{k-2}b_{k-1}$$

the value of the integer is computed as

$$b_0 \times 2^{k-1} + b_1 \times 2^{k-2} + b_2 \times 2^{k-3} + ... + b_{k-2} \times 2^1 + b_{k-1} \times 2^0$$

Binary numbers are therefore known as base 2 numbers. To avoid misinterpretation, they are often written with a subscript 2, as in 10101_2.

In the hexadecimal (base 16) system, there are sixteen digits, represented by the symbols 0,1,2,3,4,5,6,7,8,9,A,B,C,D,E, and F. The first ten symbols have their usual meaning; the remaining six—A through F—represent the values ten through fifteen when used as hexadecimal digits. In a hexadecimal integer, the value implied by each digit's position is a multiple of a power of sixteen, not of two as in binary or of ten as in decimal integers. For example, the positional values of the digits in the hexadecimal integer A423 is computed as follows:

$$
\begin{array}{lll}
3 \times 16^0 = & 3 & (16^0 = 1) \\
2 \times 16^1 = & 32 & (16^1 = 16) \\
4 \times 16^2 = & 1024 & (16^2 = 256) \\
10 \times 16^3 = & 40960 & (16^3 = 4096)
\end{array}
$$

The value of A423 is therefore $40960 + 1024 + 32 + 3 = 42019$ in decimal notation.

In general, for a k-digit hexadecimal integer

$$h_0h_1h_2...h_{k-2}h_{k-1}$$

Figure 1.5   Representations of integers.

name	decimal	binary	hexadecimal
zero	0	0000	0
one	1	0001	1
two	2	0010	2
three	3	0011	3
four	4	0100	4
five	5	0101	5
six	6	0110	6
seven	7	0111	7
eight	8	1000	8
nine	9	1001	9
ten	10	1010	A
eleven	11	1011	B
twelve	12	1100	C
thirteen	13	1101	D
fourteen	14	1110	E
fifteen	15	1111	F
sixteen	16	10000	10

the value of the integer is computed as

$$h_0 \times 16^{k-1} + h_1 \times 16^{k-2} + h_2 \times 16^{k-3} + \ldots + h_{k-2} \times 16^1 + h_{k-1} \times 16^0$$

Hexadecimal integers are often written with a subscript 16, and sometimes with a subscript x, as in $800_{16} = 800_x$.

It will prove worthwhile to gain complete familiarity with the representations of the first sixteen binary and hexadecimal integers shown in figure 1.5 since both the binary and hexadecimal forms will be used extensively in subsequent chapters. This use will include addition and subtraction of two binary integers, addition and subtraction of two hexadecimal integers, and conversion from binary to hexadecimal and vice versa.

Addition of two binary integers is a simple matter, since there are only four rules to learn: $0 + 0 = 0$, $0 + 1 = 1$, $1 + 0 = 1$, and $1 + 1 = 10$ (two, in binary). In the last rule, a carry of 1 is generated and must be added to the next higher-order digit sum, an operation that is analogous to the handling of carries in decimal addition. You should be able to verify that the following sums are correct:

```
   10110          10110          11111          11001
+   1100        +    11        +     1        + 11001
 100010          11001         100000         110010
```

Subtraction of two binary integers is also straightforward, since the only situation in which a borrow operation can arise is that of subtracting 1 from 0. As with decimal integers, subtraction of two binary integers is best done by subtracting the smaller from the larger integer. The following examples illustrate how subtraction is accomplished when the result is positive:

```
   10110          10110          10000          10010
-    101        -  1010        -     1        -  1101
  10001           1100           1111            101
```

Addition and subtraction of two hexadecimal integers requires some practice; it is an essential skill because it is used in address computations. In *addition* of two hexadecimal digits, the sum is a single digit if its value is less than sixteen; otherwise a carry of 1 is generated. In *subtraction,* a borrow of 10_x (sixteen, in hexadecimal) is necessary when the first digit is smaller than the second. The following examples illustrate these concepts. Note that all the integers here are in hexadecimal notation.

```
  4      4      A      B     10     18     DE      DE     40C     FFF
+ 6    + A    + 6    - 6    - 8    - 9    +C8    - C8    -  E    +  1
  A      E     10      5      8      F    1A6      16     3FE    1000
```

Conversion of Positive Integers from One Base to Another

The method for converting a positive integer from its representation in one base (the old base) to its representation in another (the new) depends on which number system the computations are performed in. When converting *from* decimal to another base, it is convenient to do the calculations in the decimal system, which, in this case, is the old base. When converting *to* decimal from another base, it is still convenient to calculate in the decimal system, which, in this case, is the new base. As we shall now see, calculating in the old base requires division; calculating in the new base requires multiplication.

Suppose that an integer J is represented in the decimal system as

$$d_0 d_1 d_2 ... d_{k-2} d_{k-1}$$

and that we wish to determine its binary representation

$$b_0 b_1 b_2 ... b_{m-2} b_{m-1}$$

The value of J can be computed in the decimal system (the old base) by either of these equations:

$$J = d_0 \times 10^{k-1} + d_1 \times 10^{k-2} + ... + d_{k-2} \times 10^1 + d_{k-1} \times 10^0 \qquad (1.1)$$

$$J = b_0 \times 2^{m-1} + b_1 \times 2^{m-2} + ... + b_{m-2} \times 2^1 + b_{m-1} \times 2^0 \qquad (1.2)$$

(Note that m is usually not equal to k.)

Since the d_j digits are known but the b_j are not, we know the value of J as given by Equation 1.1 and we can use this value to determine the b_j from Equation 1.2 by successive iterations, as follows.

We first divide by 2, producing an integer quotient and an integer remainder. Let the quotient be Q_1; the remainder is just b_{m-1}, i.e., the low-order digit in the binary representation of J.

$$\frac{J}{2} = b_0 \times 2^{m-2} + b_1 \times 2^{m-3} + ... + b_{m-2} \times 2^0 + \frac{b_{m-1}}{2} = Q_1 + \frac{b_{m-1}}{2}$$

We now obtain the next digit, b_{m-2}, by dividing Q_1 by 2.

$$\frac{Q_1}{2} = b_0 \times 2^{m-3} + b_1 \times 2^{m-4} + ... + b_{m-3} \times 2^0 + \frac{b_{m-2}}{2} = Q_2 + \frac{b_{m-2}}{2}$$

The process continues by dividing each successive integer quotient, Q_j, by 2 and collecting the integer remainders. When a quotient of 0 is obtained, the remainder will be the most significant digit b_0.

To illustrate, let $J = 18$ in decimal notation. Then

$$
\begin{aligned}
J/2 &= 9 + 0/2, &&\text{so } Q_1 = 9 \text{ and } b_{m-1} = 0 \\
Q_1/2 &= 4 + 1/2, &&\text{so } Q_2 = 4 \text{ and } b_{m-2} = 1 \\
Q_2/2 &= 2 + 0/2, &&\text{so } Q_3 = 2 \text{ and } b_{m-3} = 0 \\
Q_3/2 &= 1 + 0/2, &&\text{so } Q_4 = 1 \text{ and } b_{m-4} = 0 \\
Q_4/2 &= 0 + 1/2, &&\text{so } Q_5 = 0 \text{ and } b_{m-5} = 1 = b_0
\end{aligned}
$$

Thus the binary representation of 18_{10} is 10010_2.

It is perhaps simplest to perform the above operations as follows:

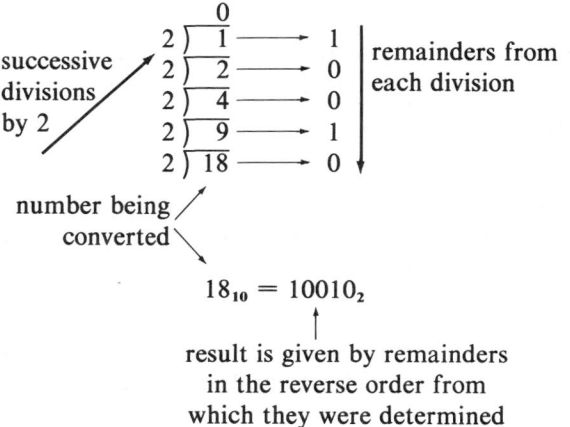

$$18_{10} = 10010_2$$

result is given by remainders
in the reverse order from
which they were determined

The process just described is not limited to conversions from decimal to binary. It can be used to convert from any base, P, to any other base, R, provided that the *the calculations are performed in the base P system.* Equations 1.1 and 1.2 must be replaced by their equivalent representations in the base P system. If we assume that the known base P representation is $p_0p_1p_2...p_{k-1}$ and that the desired base R representation is $r_0r_1r_2...r_{m-1}$, then the appropriate equations are

$$J = p_0 \times P^{k-1} + p_1 \times P^{k-2} + ... + p_{k-2} \times P^1 + p_{k-1} \times P^0 \tag{1.3}$$

$$J = r_0 \times R^{m-1} + r_1 \times R^{m-2} + ... + r_{m-2} \times R^1 + r_{m-1} \times R^0 \tag{1.4}$$

To begin the iteration procedure, divide Equation 1.4 by R, obtaining an integer quotient, Q_1, and an integer remainder, r_{m-1}. Then divide Q_1 by R to obtain Q_2 and r_{m-2}, and so forth. The calculations must be done in the base P system and are terminated when a zero quotient is obtained.

The reader can verify that if $P = 10$ (ten), and $R = 16$, then the conversion of the decimal integer $J = 18$ to the hexadecimal system proceeds as follows:

$$J/16 = 1 + 2/16, \quad \text{so } Q_1 = 1 \text{ and } r_{m-1} = 2$$

$$Q_1/16 = 0 + 1/16, \quad \text{so } Q_2 = 0 \text{ and } r_{m-2} = 1 = r_0$$

Thus the hexadecimal representation of 18_{10} is 12_{16}.

These methods are useful when converting by hand from the decimal system to any other system. But when converting from some other base to base 10, it makes sense to do the conversions in the new base (10). This is the method that we used when converting 10101_2 to 21_{10}, and $A423_{16}$ to 42019_{10}. In general we simply represent the value of the known integer in the new base, and calculate that value in the new base. Thus if the old base is P and the new base is R, and if the known integer J is represented in the base P system as $p_0p_1p_2...p_{k-1}$, then we represent each digit, p_j, as an integer in the base R system and calculate this expression:

$$\bar{p}_0 \times P^{k-1} + \bar{p}_1 \times P^{k-2} + ... + \bar{p}_{k-2} \times P^1 + \bar{p}_{k-2} \times P^0$$

Here, $\bar{p}_j$ is the representative of p_j in the base R system. For example, with J represented as $A423_{16}$, $P = 16$, $p_0 = A$, $p_1 = 4$, $p_2 = 2$, $p_3 = 3$. If $R = 10$ (ten), then $\bar{p}_0 = 10$, $\bar{p}_1 = 4$, $\bar{p}_2 = 2$, and $\bar{p}_3 = 3$ so that in the base 10 system, the hexadecimal integer $A423_{16}$ is represented as

$$10 \times 16^3 + 4 \times 16^2 + 2 \times 16^1 + 3 \times 16^0 = 42019_{10}$$

A useful method of performing this type of calculation is to group terms as follows:

$$[(10 \times 16 + 4) \times 16 + 2] \times 16 + 3 = 42019_{10}$$

Conversions between Binary and Hexadecimal Integers

Conversions between the hexadecimal and binary representations will frequently be required throughout this text. The binary system is simply too cumbersome to work with easily, and the hexadecimal system provides a useful and convenient substitute. Because the base 16 and base 2 systems are related by the equation $16 = 2^4$, *conversions between the two systems do not require use of the general procedures described earlier.* Instead, the following two rules are almost always used:

1. To convert from hexadecimal to binary, replace each hexadecimal digit with its equivalent four-bit binary representation.
2. To convert from binary to hexadecimal, replace every four consecutive binary digits by their equivalent hexadecimal digit, starting from the right-hand digit and adding zeroes on the left, if necessary.

The following examples demonstrate these rules. The reader should verify that the results obtained are equivalent to those that would be obtained using the general procedures described earlier. Note that spaces are used after each set of four binary digits to facilitate reading; they have no other purpose.

binary:	$\underbrace{0001}$	$\underbrace{0010}$		
hexadecimal:	1	2		
binary:	$\underbrace{0100}$	$\underbrace{0000}$		
hexadecimal:	4	0		
binary:	$\underbrace{1110}$	$\underbrace{0010}$	$\underbrace{0100}$	$\underbrace{1010}$
hexadecimal:	E	2	4	A
binary:	$\underbrace{1111}$	$\underbrace{1101}$	$\underbrace{1011}$	
hexadecimal:	F	D	B	

Thus, $10010_2 = 12_x$, $1000000_2 = 40_x$, $1110001001001010_2 = E24A_x$, and $111111011011_2 = FDB_x$.

One further example should serve to indicate why the substitution rules are valid. Consider this binary integer: 10101010011011. Applying the rules, we mark off groups of four binary bits from right to left, starting at the low-order bit, appending binary zeroes at the left, high-order end so that the last group also contains 4 bits: 0010 1010 1001 1011. Now we replace each group of 4 bits with its equivalent hexadecimal representation:

0010	1010	1001	1011
2	A	9	B

Notice that the value of the binary integer representation can be calculated as follows:

$$1 \times 2^{13} + 1 \times 2^{11} + 1 \times 2^9 + 1 \times 2^7 + 1 \times 2^4 + 1 \times 2^3 + 1 \times 2^1 + 1 \times 2^0$$

The value of the hexadecimal integer representation can similarly be calculated:

$$2 \times 16^3 + 10 \times 16^2 + 9 \times 16^1 + 11 \times 16^0$$

But since $16 = 2^4$, and

$$10 = 2^3 + 2^1$$
$$9 = 2^3 + 2^0$$
$$11 = 2^3 + 2^1 + 2^0$$

then the hexadecimal calculation is equivalent to the expression

$$2 \times (2^4)^3 + (2^3 + 2^1) \times (2^4)^2 + (2^3 + 2^0) \times (2^4)^1 + (2^3 + 2^1 + 2^0) \times (2^4)^0$$

and this reduces precisely to the expression given for the binary calculation.

1.6 SUMMARY

Computer systems consist of two broad classes of components, hardware and software. Some aspects of the structure of the hardware, particularly the main memory and the instructions that are executable by the CPU, are reflected in Assembly Language thereby making the language qualitatively different from almost all other programming languages. Among the concepts an assembly language programmer must be familiar with are the ways in which data are represented in memory for arithmetic and nonarithmetic processes; the organization of memory into bytes, words, and other units of information, each of which is accessed by means of its address; and the use of registers as an interface between the central processing unit and main memory. Important, too, are the distinctions between assembly time, load time, and run time, and the role of the Operating System in input and output operations.

The terminology used in conjunction with assembly language programming reflects its relationship to the hardware. One speaks of bits, bytes, words, addresses, registers, and so forth, because these entities have fundamental uses in Assembly Language. Definitions will be given whenever new terms are introduced, but you may also want to refer to the following dictionaries:

American National Dictionary for Information Processing. American National Standards Committee X3; Technical Report # X3/TR-1-77. Published by the Computer and Business Equipment Manufacturers Association, Washington, DC.

Data Processing Glossary. IBM Publication #GC20-1699. Obtainable from the IBM Data Processing Division, White Plains, NY.

Standard Dictionary of Computers and Information Processing. Martin H. Weik. Published by Hayden Book Co., Inc., Rochelle Park, NJ.

EXERCISES

1. The use of instructions and directives in Assembly Language has its counterpart in the use of executable and nonexecutable statements in high-level languages like FORTRAN and COBOL. Describe the fundamental distinction between executable and nonexecutable statements. In what way is this distinction related to the concepts of assembly time and run time as defined in chapter 1?

2. The distinction between the address of a memory location and the contents of that location exists in high-level languages as well as in Assembly Language. Explain this distinction in terms of either the FORTRAN assignment statement Z = X + Y or the corresponding COBOL assignment statement COMPUTE Z = X + Y.

3. Suppose that the title of a programming course is COMPUTER SCIENCE 102. Using the 8-bit EBCDIC codes given in Appendix F, write the EBCDIC character representation of the course name.

4. Assume that the 7-bit ASCII codes given in Appendix F are extended to 8 bits by appending a high-order bit of "1" to each code, so that, for example, the 7-bit code for the letter *A* (namely, 1000001) is extended to the 8-bit code 11000001. By extending each 7-bit ASCII code in this manner, write the 8-bit ASCII character representation of COMPUTER SCIENCE 102.

5. Assume that the 7-bit ASCII codes are extended to 8 bits by appending a high-order bit, which makes the number of 1's in each extended 8-bit code an even number. Using this scheme, for example, the 7-bit code for the letter *B* (1000010) becomes 01000010 while the 7-bit code for the letter *C* (1000011) becomes 11000011. The bit that is so appended is known as the parity bit. By extending each 7-bit ASCII code in this manner, write the 8-bit ASCII character representation of COMPUTER SCIENCE 102.

6. What is the EBCDIC character representation of each of the decimal integers given below? What is the binary number system representation of each of these decimal integers? What is the hexadecimal representation?

a.	0	**e.**	32	**i.**	31
b.	10	**f.**	64	**j.**	63
c.	49	**g.**	128	**k.**	4095
d.	102	**h.**	256	**l.**	255

7. State a rule that will allow you to determine whether an arbitrarily chosen binary integer is odd or even, without having to do any calculations. State a similar rule that will allow you to determine, without calculation, whether a given binary integer is exactly divisible by 4, by 8, and in general by 2^k for any positive integer k.

8. What is the hexadecimal representation of each of the following binary integers?

   a. 0100 0000

   b. 1111 1111

   c. 0101 1010

   d. 1110 1011 1100 1101

   e. 0010 0100 0110 1000

   f. 0011 1110 0000

9. What is the binary representation of each of the following hexadecimal integers? If each of these two-digit hexadecimal numbers is interpreted as the 8-bit EBCDIC code for a character, what character does it represent?

   a. 4E   **e.** 5D   **i.** F9
   b. 60   **f.** 40   **j.** C3
   c. 4B   **g.** 7D   **k.** 83
   d. 5C   **h.** 6B   **l.** 7A

10. Perform the indicated additions and subtractions using the rules of hexadecimal arithmetic:

a.	**b.**	**c.**	**d.**	**e.**
88C	EC0	6A	CB	DE4
+ 2A	− FF	+A6	−BC	+ 21C

11. In the base 8 number system (known as the octal system), there are only eight digits: 0,1,2,3,4,5,6,7. The value of an octal number such as 345_8 is computed in the decimal system as

$$3 \times 8^2 + 4 \times 8^1 + 5 \times 8^0 = 229_{10}$$

   a. Determine the octal system representations of the decimal integers 8 through 16.

   b. State a method of converting integers from the binary system to the octal system and vice versa that is analogous to the method of converting between the binary and hexadecimal systems. Prove that the method is equivalent to the general iterative procedures of Section 1.5.

   c. In some computer systems it is more useful to represent binary integers in the octal system than in the hexadecimal system. Under what conditions might this be done?

2

Fundamentals of the IBM 360 and 370 Assembly Language

In this chapter we describe the general format of Assembly Language statements for the IBM 360 and 370 computer systems, indicate how statements should be organized in a source module, and illustrate how input and output operations are written.

2.1 STATEMENT FORMATS

Each statement in a source module must be written in accordance with well-defined rules. The rules depend on the type and purpose of the statement, but the general format of all statements falls into one of two categories: (1) the format used for comment statements and (2) the format used for instructions and directives. In both cases, the general format is designed to accommodate the constraints imposed by eighty-column punched cards.

The eighty characters of a punched card are divided into four fields for the comment statement format, and six fields for the format of instructions and directives. Although the length and position of some fields may be varied, as will be seen, they are usually defined as shown in figure 2.1. The statements shown in figure 2.2 illustrate the use of these formats.

Comment Statement Format

The first position of a comment statement must contain an asterisk (∗). Comment statements may appear anywhere in a source module, and there may be any number of them. They are printed on the listing along with the other statements of the source module and therefore are used to provide a description of the purpose and techniques of the statements following the comments.

Positions 2 through 71 may contain any text desired by the programmer. The continuation field (position 72) is normally left blank. If not blank, the continuation field indicates that the comment's text is continued on the subsequent card or line of the source module, in the manner described in the next section for instructions and directives. The identification field (positions 73 through 80) is also used in the same manner as that for instructions and directives.

Format for Instructions and Directives

The two principal requirements in instructions and directives are these: (1) The first position must not contain an asterisk. It must either be blank, or be the first character of the name-field symbol (see below). (2) The opcode field must contain a string of from one to five characters that is a valid assembly language instruction or directive.

In addition, the information in each of the six fields is constrained by the requirements outlined in the following paragraphs.

Name Field. When the first character of the name field is not blank, the name field must consist of from one to eight characters followed by a blank. A name-field entry is called a *symbol,* and its purpose is to identify the statement so that the statement can be referred to by that symbol elsewhere in the source module.

Figure 2.1   Statement formats.

comment statement format:

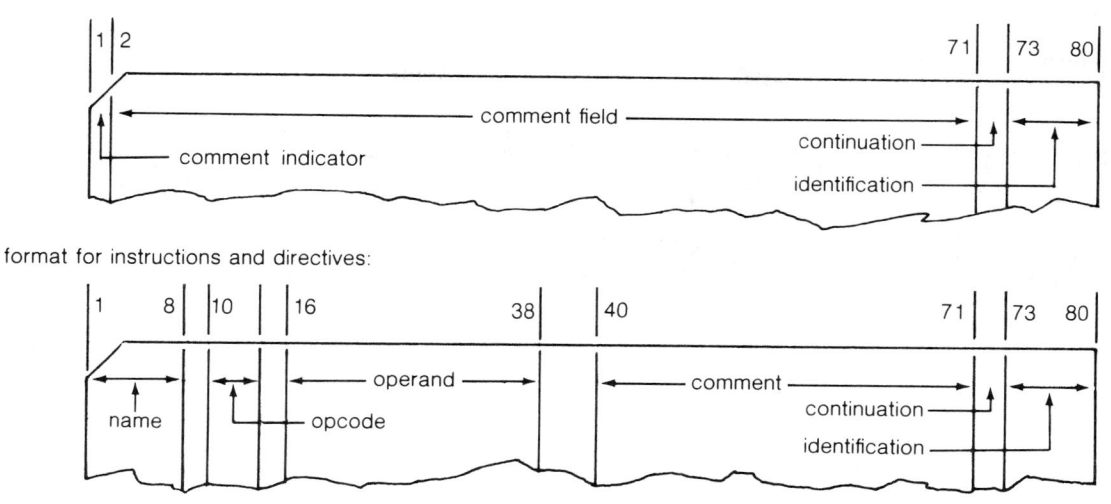

format for instructions and directives:

Except as discussed in chapters 16 and 17, the first character of a symbol must be a letter and the remaining characters, if any, must be letters or digits. No other characters are permitted. It should be noted that in the IBM 360 and 370 Assembly Language, the word *letter* is used to denote any of the twenty-six alphabetic characters *A* through *Z* and the three characters $ (dollar sign), # (number sign), and @ (at sign).

The following are examples of valid symbols:

> Q
> A101
> LOOP
> FOUND
> REP12A
> #1
> CONTINUE
> @HERE
> $###2

For the reasons stated, the following are examples of invalid symbols:

> 3   ⎫
> 101A   ⎬ first character not a letter
>
> F(1)   parentheses ⎫
> LOOP 1   blank   ⎬ not among
> LOOP .1   period   the allowable
> LOOP−1   hyphen   ⎭ characters
> ENCOUNTER   too many characters: maximum is 8

Opcode Field.   As mentioned earlier, the opcode field must contain a valid assembly language code of from one to five alphabetic characters that identifies one of the instructions or directives that exist in the language. An alphabetical summary of valid operation codes is given in Appendixes A, B, and E. The last character of the operation code must be followed by a blank.

Operand Field.   The format of the operand field depends on whether the opcode field designates an instruction or a directive, and it also depends on which instruction or directive is specified. But despite the fact that there are differences among operand formats, they all share two characteristics. First, unless the operand is blank, as it may be in some directives, it always consists of one or more subfields written without intervening

Figure 2.2   Assembly language statement examples.

```
 name      opcode      operand                         comment                  continuation  identification
 1        10      16                              40                             72            80

*          EVERY STATEMENT WITH AN ASTERISK IN THE FIRST POSITION                             ALP00010
*          IS A COMMENT STATEMENT.                                                            ALP00020
*                                                                                             ALP00030
*  THE OPERAND AND COMMENT FIELDS OF AN INSTRUCTION OR DIRECTIVE                               ALP00040
*  MAY BE CONTINUED ONTO THE FOLLOWING LINE BY PUTTING A NONBLANK                              ALP00050
*  CHARACTER IN POSITION 72, AS FOLLOWS:                                                       ALP00060
*                                                                                             ALP00070
LINE       DCB    DSORG=PS,MACRF=(PM),DDNAME=SYSPRINT,RECFM=FB,LRECL=132,       -ALP00080
                  BLKSIZE=4092                                                                 ALP00090
*                                                                                             ALP00100
*  NORMALLY CONTINUATION IS NOT REQUIRED, AS IN THESE STATEMENTS:                              ALP00110
*                                                                                             ALP00120
OUTER      L      4,=F'5'                     SET LINE COUNT TO 5                              ALP00130
*READ ONE CARD AND PRINT IT                                                                    ALP00140
INNER      GET    CARD,INAREA                 READ CARD INTO 'INAREA'                          ALP00150
           MVC    OUTAREA(80),INAREA          COPY DATA TO 'OUTAREA'                           ALP00160
           PUT    LINE,OUTAREA                WRITE CARD IMAGE ON PRINTER                      ALP00170
           BCT    4,INNER                     REPEAT READ/WRITE LOOP 5 TIMES                   ALP00180
*PRINT BLANK LINE                                                                              ALP00190
           MVC    OUTAREA(132),=132C' '       COPY 132 BLANKS TO 'OUTAREA'                     ALP00200
           PUT    LINE,OUTAREA                WRITE BLANK LINE ON PRINTER                      ALP00210
           B      OUTER                       REPEAT ENTIRE READ/WRITE PROCESS                 ALP00220
```

blanks. Every two adjacent subfields are separated by a comma, and a blank must immediately follow the last character of the last operand subfield. And second, blanks cannot be used indiscriminately within an operand. Use of a blank must follow prescribed rules that apply only to special cases such as text strings that are enclosed within apostrophes.

A few examples illustrating some of the varieties possible in operand fields were given in figure 2.2.

Comment Field.   The comment field may contain any information. The information in the comment field supplements the information specified in comment statements. It is usually a brief description of the purpose of the statement. Care must be taken, however, not to extend the comment field information into the continuation field. Examples of valid comment field entries were given in figure 2.2.

Continuation Field.   The operand and comment fields of a statement may in some cases contain more information than can fit on a single line of source code. In these cases the statement may be extended over two or more lines by means of the continuation field. If the continuation field contains any nonblank character, then the following line will be assumed to be a continuation of the line whose continuation field is nonblank.

When continuing a statement in this manner, each continuation line must begin in position 16, called the *continuing position*. In figure 2.2 the statement shown below consists of two lines, the second being a continuation of the first because of the nonblank character in position 72.

```
        position 16                                                        position 72
          |                                                                   |
LINE    DCB DSORG=PS,MACRF=(PM),DDNAME=SYSPRINT,RECFM=FB,LRECL=132,         -ALP00080
          BLKSIZE=4092
```

Identification Field.   The identification field may consist of any combination of letters, digits, and blank spaces. When the field is not all blank, its purpose is twofold: (1) to identify the source module in which the statement appears and (2) to record the sequential position of the statement within the source module.

The identification field contents is always printed on the listing, but otherwise it is ignored by the Assembler unless the ISEQ directive has been used to initiate sequence checking of statements. If an ISEQ directive has initiated sequence checking in the manner described in chapter 14, the Assembler compares the identification field contents of each line with the same field of the preceding line. With the exception that blank fields are ignored, the two fields must be in increasing sequence; otherwise a warning message is printed on the listing. An out-of-sequence condition does not affect the assembly of the source module in any other way.

2.2   STATEMENT FORMAT VARIATIONS

The field positions for the statement format defined in the preceding section are said to be in the *standard fixed format* of the IBM 360 and 370 Assembly Language. Position 1 of the standard fixed format is called the *beginning* position of a statement, position 71 is called the *ending* position, and position 16 is called the *continuing* position.

As previously stated, the beginning position is used for two purposes: (1) to distinguish a comment statement from statements containing instructions or directives and (2) as the first position of the name field. If the beginning position contains an asterisk, the statement is a comment statement. If the beginning position does not contain an asterisk, the statement is either an instruction or a directive. Any character other than an asterisk or blank in the beginning position of a statement is assumed to be the first character of a name-field symbol.

Other characteristics of standard fixed format include the following:

1. Any field that is omitted must be blank.
2. All nonblank fields must be left-justified within the field boundaries and be filled with trailing blanks.
3. Positions 9, 15, and 39 must be blank.
4. Information in the operand and/or comment fields of one line of a statement may be continued on the following line, provided that the continuation field contains a nonblank character. The information that is continued must begin in the continuing position.

These standard fixed format constraints may be overridden in one of two ways. One, the positions used for beginning, ending, and continuing a line may be redefined. This is done by means of the ICTL directive, which will not be discussed further until chapter 14. The second method utilizes the fact that in the IBM 360 and 370 Assembly Language, the opcode, operand, and comment fields need not begin in positions 10, 16, and 40, respectively; the information in any of these fields needs only to be separated by one or more blanks from the information in the immediately preceding field. This capability is called *free format.*

Free format can be used anywhere in a source module. It permits longer operands than can fit in the fixed positions 16 through 38; alternatively, it permits comments to be started before position 40. Another advantage is that it permits one to indent the opcode and operand fields and thereby emphasize the structure of the logic more clearly than if indentation were not employed. Figure 2.3 illustrates this for some of the statements that were given in figure 2.2. It should be noted, however, that whichever is used, standard fixed format or standard free format, the positions of the continuation and identification fields remain fixed in positions 72 and 73–80, respectively; and the beginning, ending, and continuing positions remain fixed in positions 1, 71, and 16, respectively.

2.3   SOURCE MODULE REQUIREMENTS

In this section the conventional requirements for writing source modules in IBM 360 and 370 Assembly Language are described. The requirements may vary somewhat among different computer installations, but those given here will probably be sufficient in most operating environments. Most of the statements provide an interface to the Operating System and other programs at run time, as will be explained in chapter 9. Two— the BALR instruction and the USING directive—have fundamental roles related to addressing within a program (see chap. 3).

There are two different sets of requirements: one for OS systems and one for DOS systems.

Figure 2.3   *Use of standard fixed and standard free formats.*

```
name     opcode  operand                         comment                      continuation  identification
1        10  16                                   40                           72            80
* PROGRAM LOGIC AND STRUCTURE CAN BE DEPICTED USING FREE FORMAT.               ALP01010
* IN OPCODE, OPERAND AND COMMENT FIELDS OF INSTRUCTIONS AND                    ALP01020
* DIRECTIVES AS IN THE FOLLOWING STATEMENTS:                                   ALP01030
*                                                                              ALP01040
OUTER    L   4,=F'5'                 SET LINE COUNT TO 5                        ALP01050
*                                                                              ALP01060
* INNER LOOP READS 5 CARDS ONE AT A TIME AND PRINTS EACH ONE                   ALP01070
*                                                                              ALP01080
INNER        GET   CARD,INAREA           READ CARD INTO 'INAREA'               ALP01090
             MVC   OUTAREA(80),INAREA    COPY DATA TO 'OUTAREA'                ALP01100
             PUT   LINE,OUTAREA          WRITE CARD DATA ON PRINTER            ALP01110
             BCT   4,INNER               REPEAT READ/WRITE LOOP                ALP01120
*                                                                              ALP01130
* OUTER LOOP PRINTS ONE BLANK LINE AFTER EVERY FIFTH DATA LINE                 ALP01140
*                                                                              ALP01150
         MVC   OUTAREA(132),=132C' '  COPY 132 BLANKS TO 'OUTAREA              ALP01160
         PUT   LINE,OUTAREA           WRITE BLANK LINE ON PRINTER              ALP01170
         B     OUTER                  REPEAT ENTIRE READ/WRITE PROCESS         ALP01180
```

Requirement 1. **Except for comment statements, which may be placed anywhere in a source module, the first statements of a source module should be these:**

In OS:

name field	opcode	operand
modname	CSECT	
↑	STM	14,12,12(13)
this symbol	BALR	12,0
used as name	USING	*,12
of the source	ST	13,SAVE+4
module	LA	13,SAVE

In DOS:

name field	opcode	operand
modname	CSECT	
	BALR	12,0
	USING	*,12
	LA	13,SAVE

Requirement 2. **The last executable statements of a source module should be these:**

In OS:

name field	opcode	operand
exitname	L	13,SAVE+4
↑	LM	14,12,12(13)
any valid	BR	14
symbol		

In DOS:

name field	opcode	operand
exitname	EOJ	

Requirement 3.   **The last statements of a source module should be these:**

<table>
<tr><th colspan="3">In OS:</th><th colspan="3">In DOS:</th></tr>
<tr><th>name field</th><th>opcode</th><th>operand</th><th>name field</th><th>opcode</th><th>operand</th></tr>
<tr><td>SAVE</td><td>DS</td><td>18F</td><td>SAVE</td><td>DS</td><td>9D</td></tr>
<tr><td></td><td>END</td><td></td><td></td><td>END</td><td></td></tr>
</table>

↑
this symbol
must be SAVE

Some of the statements given in Requirements 1–3 are directives, and some are instructions. Instructions are known as *executable statements* because they are translated into machine language by the Assembler and executed at run time by the hardware. Some directives, like EOJ in Requirement 2 for DOS, are also executable because they cause the Assembler to generate instructions. All other directives, including the CSECT, USING, and END directives previously mentioned, are called *nonexecutable* statements.

All executable statements, and those nonexecutable statements that define constants and data areas, are assembled into an object module which, as was indicated in chapter 1, is in a form that can be loaded into main memory and executed at run time. However, if the three requirements are followed and the object module size is greater than 4096 bytes, it may not run properly. Techniques for dealing with this situation will be described in chapter 9. None of the examples and exercises in the first eight chapters require object modules larger than 4096 bytes.

2.4   INPUT AND OUTPUT OPERATIONS

In this section the minimum IBM 360 and 370 assembly language requirements for reading and writing data in EBCDIC character format are summarized. This will provide for input from the input data stream and output to the printer. Methods of conversion to and from binary integer format will be described in chapter 4; other aspects of input/output operations will be more fully described in chapters 18 through 22.

Each file that is read or written from an assembly language program must be opened before any input or output operations are executed and closed after all such operations have been executed. Opening a file is achieved by the OPEN macro, and closing by the CLOSE macro. In addition, each file to be used must be described by a data control block (DCB) macro in OS systems and by a define-the-file (DTF) macro in DOS systems. To read data from the input data stream, we use the GET macro; to write it onto the printer, the PUT macro. The OPEN, CLOSE, GET, and PUT macros are directives that cause the Assembler to generate the instructions needed to request that the corresponding operations be performed by the Operating System. The areas of memory to be used for the input and output data must be reserved by the define storage (DS) directive.

Figure 2.4a and b contains the forms of these statements that should be sufficient for card input and printer output operations in most IBM 360 and 370 computer systems. Discussion of most of the details will be postponed until Part Five; however, assembly language programs that use these statements are shown in figure 2.5a and b. Each program may, at first sight, appear to be overwhelmingly complex. However, at this stage you are expected to understand only what it does and how it is organized, and not how it works. As can be seen, the two programs—one for OS and one for DOS—differ only in their input/output operations and in the three sets of required statements given in the preceding section. All other differences between OS and DOS Assembly Language are quite minor and will be discussed in subsequent chapters.

The program begins with a CSECT directive, a few comment statements to describe the purpose of the program, and the remaining required statements discussed previously. Disregarding the comment statements, which may appear anywhere in the program and do not affect the program's execution, the required statements are

<table>
<tr><th colspan="3">In OS:</th><th colspan="3">In DOS:</th></tr>
<tr><td>DEMO</td><td>CSECT</td><td></td><td>DEMO</td><td>CSECT</td><td></td></tr>
<tr><td></td><td>STM</td><td>14,12,12(13)</td><td></td><td>BALR</td><td>12,0</td></tr>
<tr><td></td><td>BALR</td><td>12,0</td><td></td><td>USING</td><td>*,12</td></tr>
<tr><td></td><td>USING</td><td>*,12</td><td></td><td>LA</td><td>13,SAVE</td></tr>
<tr><td></td><td>ST</td><td>13,SAVE+4</td><td></td><td></td><td></td></tr>
<tr><td></td><td>LA</td><td>13,SAVE</td><td></td><td></td><td></td></tr>
</table>

Figure 2.4a Card input and printer output statements: OS.

	name	opcode	operand	comment	continuation	identification
for card input:		OPEN	(CARD,(INPUT))			
			↳ symbol must be the same as that appearing in the DCB name-field			
		GET	CARD,INAREA			
			↳ symbol must be the same as that appearing in the name field of the DS statement that reserves the input area			
	FINISH	CLOSE	(CARD)			
	INAREA	DS	CL80	must be the name-field symbol in the instruction to be executed when there are no more cards to be read		
	CARD	DCB	DSORG=PS,MACRF=(GM),DDNAME=SYSIN,EODAD=FINISH,RECFM=FB,	—		
			LRECL=80,BLKSIZE=4080	must be the same as in the JCL statement //SYSIN DD *		
for printer output:		OPEN	(LINE,(OUTPUT))			
			↳ symbol must be the same as that appearing in the DCB name-field			
		PUT	LINE,OUTAREA			
			↳ symbol must be the same as that appearing in the name field of the DS statement that reserves the output area			
		CLOSE	(LINE)			
	OUTAREA	DS	CL132	must be the same as in the JCL statement //SYSPRINT DD SYSOUT=A		
	LINE	DCB	DSORG=PS,MACRF=(PM),DDNAME=SYSPRINT,RECFM=FB,LRECL=132,	—		
			BLKSIZE=4092			

Figure 2.4b Card input and printer output statements: DOS.

	name	opcode	operand	comment	continuation	identification
for card input:		OPEN	CARD			
			↳ symbol must be the same as that appearing in the DTFCD name field			
		GET	CARD,INAREA			
			↳ symbol must be the same as that appearing in the name field of the DS statement that reserves the input area			
	FINISH	CLOSE	CARD			
	INAREA	DS	CL80			
	INBUF	DS	CL80	must identify the system card reader		
	CARD	DTFCD	DEVADDR=SYSIPT,WORKA=YES,IOAREA1=INBUF,EOFADDR=FINISH,	—		
			DEVICE=2540	must be the name-field symbol in the instruction to be executed when there are no more cards to be read		
for printer output:		OPEN	LINE			
			↳ symbol must be the same as that appearing in the DTFPR name field			
		PUT	LINE,OUTAREA			
			↳ symbol must be the same as that appearing in the name field of the DS statement that reserves the output area			
		CLOSE	LINE			
	OUTAREA	DC	CL132' '			
	OUTBUF	DC	CL132' '			
	LINE	DTFPR	DEVADDR=SYSLST,WORKA=YES,IOAREA1=OUTBUF,BLKSIZE=132,	—		
			DEVICE=1403	must identify the system printer		

DEMO is the name chosen for the program. The identification fields are blank, but this does not affect the execution of the program at run time. Only the name field, the opcode field, and the operand field affect program execution.

Three more comment statements follow the aforementioned instructions. These statements describe the purpose of the ensuing two OPEN macros and provide blank lines for readability. The two OPEN macros identify the files by referring to the appropriate file description macros (the DCB in OS, and the DTF in DOS):

In OS:		*In DOS:*
OPEN	(CARD,(INPUT))	OPEN CARD
OPEN	(LINE,(OUTPUT))	OPEN LINE

At this point the main body of the program begins. It consists of a set of instructions that are repeated until all cards have been read and printed. The repetitions, called *loops,* are organized so that after every five cards have been read and printed, one blank line is printed to improve the output's readability. Thus a counter is needed to determine when each set of five cards has been read and printed. The counter is initialized by the L 4,=F'5' instruction, and reduced by the BCT 4,INNER instruction. (These instructions will be discussed further in chapter 4.) The entire set of six instructions is terminated when the GET statement reaches the end of the input card file. Note that the GET statement refers to the file being read and to the input area into which the data are placed, and that the PUT statement refers to the printer file and print data output area. The MVC instruction copies the data from the input area to the output area, which is analogous to a MOVE statement in COBOL, as shown here for both OS and DOS:

```
OUTER  L     4,=F'5'              SET LINE COUNT TO 5
  INNER      GET   CARD,INAREA     READ CARD INTO 'INAREA'
             MVC   OUTAREA(80),INAREA   COPY DATA TO 'OUTAREA'
             PUT   LINE,OUTAREA     WRITE CARD DATA ON PRINTER
             BCT   4,INNER          REPEAT READ/WRITE LOOP
       MVC   OUTAREA,=132C' '       COPY 132 BLANKS TO 'OUTAREA'
       PUT   LINE,OUTAREA           WRITE BLANK LINE ON PRINTER
       B     OUTER                  REPEAT ENTIRE READ/WRITE PROCESS
```

Execution of the aforementioned statements is terminated when an input end-of-file condition is detected by the Operating system. At this point, the Operating system transfers control to the instruction named FINISH, as is dictated in the OS program by the EODAD= parameter of the input file's DCB macro and in the DOS program by the EOFADDR= parameter of the DTF macro. The end-of-file routine closes the files and terminates the program with the required executable statements:

In OS:			*In DOS:*		
FINISH	CLOSE	(CARD)	FINISH	CLOSE	CARD
	CLOSE	(LINE)		CLOSE	LINE
EXIT	L	13,SAVE+4	EXIT	EOJ	
	LM	14,12,12(13)			
	BR	14			

The remaining statements in the program, not including the comment statements, describe the input and output files, reserve the input and output data areas, and conclude with the required statements mentioned in the preceding section.

You are encouraged to submit the program for assembly and execution on your computer system. In typing the statements, care must be taken to ensure that the information in the name field, opcode field, and operand field is exactly as shown in the figures. The values assigned to the DCB parameters DDNAME, LRECL, BLKSIZE, and RECFM in figure 2.5a (and to the corresponding DTF-parameter, BLKSIZE, in figure 2.5b) may not be compatible with those in use at your computer installation. Therefore it is advisable to have someone check these and to recommend alternatives if necessary. The values shown in the figures will be used throughout this text.

Figure 2.5a   Sample assembly language program: OS.

```
DEMO      CSECT
*
*  THIS PROGRAM READS CARDS FROM THE INPUT DATA STREAM
*    AND PRINTS THEM ON THE PRINTER.
*
*  ONE BLANK LINE IS PRINTED FOLLOWING EVERY FIFTH CARD
*
          STM    14,12,12(13)              STANDARD ENTRY TO PROGRAM
          BALR   12,0
          USING  *,12
          ST     13,SAVE+4
          LA     13,SAVE
*
*  OPEN INPUT CARD STREAM AND PRINTER FILES
*
          OPEN   (CARD,(INPUT))            OPEN CARD FILE
          OPEN   (LINE,(OUTPUT))           OPEN PRINT FILE
*
*  INITIALIZE LOOP COUNT FOR 5 LINES TO BE FOLLOWED BY ONE BLANK LINE
*
OUTER     L      4,=F'5'                   SET LINE COUNT TO 5
*
*  READ ONE CARD AND PRINT IT.   DO THIS 5 TIMES.
*
INNER        GET    CARD,INAREA            READ CARD INTO 'INAREA'
             MVC    OUTAREA(80),INAREA     COPY DATA TO 'OUTAREA'
             PUT    LINE,OUTAREA           WRITE CARD DATA ON PRINTER
             BCT    4,INNER                REPEAT READ/WRITE LOOP
*
*  PRINT BLANK LINE FOLLOWING EVERY FIFTH CARD.
*
          MVC    OUTAREA,=132C' '          COPY 132 BLANKS TO 'OUTAREA'
          PUT    LINE,OUTAREA              WRITE BLANK LINE ON PRINTER
          B      OUTER                     REPEAT ENTIRE READ/WRITE PROCESS
*
*  WHEN ALL CARDS HAVE BEEN READ AND PRINTED, TERMINATE THE PROGRAM.
*
FINISH    CLOSE  (CARD)                    CLOSE CARD FILE
          CLOSE  (LINE)                    CLOSE PRINT FILE
EXIT      L      13,SAVE+4                 STANDARD EXIT FROM PROGRAM
          LM     14,12,12(13)
          BR     14
*
*  DATA CONTROL BLOCKS FOR CARD INPUT AND PRINTER OUTPUT FILES.
*
CARD      DCB    DSORG=PS,MACRF=(GM),DDNAME=SYSIN,EODAD=FINISH,RECFM=FB,  -
                 LRECL=80,BLKSIZE=4080
LINE      DCB    DSORG=PS,MACRF=(PM),DDNAME=SYSPRINT,RECFM=FB,LRECL=132,  -
                 BLKSIZE=4092
*
*  AREAS RESERVED FOR INPUT CARD DATA AND OUTPUT PRINT DATA.
*
INAREA    DS     CL80          RESERVE 80 BYTES FOR CARD INPUT
OUTAREA   DC     CL132' '      RESERVE 132 BYTES FOR PRINT OUTPUT
*
*  REQUIRED STATEMENTS
SAVE      DS     18F
          END
```

Figure 2.5b   Sample assembly language program: DOS.

```
DEMO       CSECT
*
* THIS PROGRAM READS CARDS FROM THE INPUT DATA STREAM AND PRINTS THEM.
* ONE BLANK LINE IS PRINTED FOLLOWING EVERY FIFTH CARD.
*
           BALR   12,0                      STANDARD ENTRY TO PROGRAM
           USING  *,12
           LA     13,SAVE
* OPEN INPUT CARD STREAM AND PRINTER FILES
*
           OPEN   CARD                      OPEN CARD FILE
           OPEN   LINE                      OPEN PRINTER FILE
*
* INITIALIZE LOOP COUNT FOR 5 LINES TO BE FOLLOWED BY ONE BLANK LINE
*
OUTER      L      4,=F'5'                   SET LINE COUNT TO 5
*
* READ ONE CARD AND PRINT IT. DO THIS 5 TIMES.
*
INNER          GET     CARD,INAREA            READ CARD INTO 'INAREA'
               MVC     OUTAREA(80),INAREA     COPY DATA TO 'OUTAREA'
               PUT     LINE,OUTAREA           WRITE CARD DATA ON PRINTER
               BCT     4,INNER                REPEAT READ/WRITE LOOP
*
* PRINT BLANK LINE FOLLOWING EVERY FIFTH CARD.
*
           MVC    OUTAREA,=132C' '          COPY 132 BLANKS TO 'OUTAREA'
           PUT    LINE, OUTAREA             WRITE BLANK LINE ON PRINTER
           B      OUTER                     REPEAT ENTIRE READ/WRITE PROCESS
*
* WHEN ALL CARDS HAVE BEEN READ AND PRINTED, TERMINATE THE PROGRAM.
*
FINISH     CLOSE  CARD                      CLOSE CARD FILE
           CLOSE  LINE                      CLOSE PRINTER FILE
EXIT       EOJ                              STANDARD EXIT FROM PROGRAM
*
*  DTF'S FOR CARD INPUT AND PRINTER OUTPUT FILES
CARD       DTFCD  DEVADDR=SYSIPT,WORKA=YES,IOAREA1=INBUF,EOFADDR=FINISH,  -
                  DEVICE=2540
LINE       DTFPR  DEVADDR=SYSLST,WORKA=YES,IOAREA1=OUTBUF,BLKSIZE=132,    -
                  DEVICE=1403
* AREAS RESERVED FOR INPUT CARD DATA AND OUTPUT PRINTER DATA.
*
INAREA     DS     CL80          RESERVE 80 BYTES FOR CARD WORK AREA
INBUF      DS     CL80          RESERVE 80 BYTES FOR CARD BUFFER AREA
OUTAREA    DC     CL132' '      RESERVE 132 BYTES FOR PRINTER WORK AREA
OUTBUF     DC     CL132' '      RESERVE 132 BYTES FOR PRINTER BUFFER AREA
*
SAVE       DS     9D
           END
```

The following OS job control language (JCL) statements—or ones similar to these—will be required in conjunction with the DCB macros. These, too, should be checked for compatibility with the computer installation.

For card input:

```
//SYSIN    DD    *
```
identifies the input data stream

corresponds to the DDNAME=SYSIN
parameter used in the input DCB macro

For printer output:

```
//SYSPRINT    DD    SYSOUT=A
```
identifies the printer

corresponds to the DDNAME=SYSPRINT
parameter used in the output DCB macro

In most DOS systems, no JCL statements are required to identify the input data stream or the printer. You should, however, verify this with your DOS installation.

2.5 ASSEMBLY LISTINGS

As mentioned in chapter 1, the Assembler produces a listing of your program that shows the machine language together with your source language statements and indicates what (if any) errors have been detected during the assembly process. The appearance of the listing can be enhanced by using the following simple assembly language directives:

EJECT—starts a new page on the listing
TITLE—puts a title line at the beginning of each page
SPACE—inserts one or more blank lines on a page
PRINT NOGEN,NODATA—limits the amount of detail printed

It is easy to use these directives. Since their use can make the listing much more readable, you are advised to learn how to use them now by reading Sections 14.1 through 14.4 and by inserting the directives at appropriate places in the program of figure 2.6.

The listing also includes an index of the name-field symbols defined in the source module. This index, known as the *cross-reference* list (XREF), is very useful when debugging and modifying programs. It identifies the statement in which each symbol is defined and the statements in which each is used—i.e., where it appears in an operand field. The cross-reference list also gives the *value* of each symbol and the *length* of the instruction or data field that the symbol is associated with. If your installation's assembler does not always produce a cross-reference list, it is possible to request one with a JCL statement: // OPTION XREF in DOS, and // EXEC ASMFC,PARM=XREF(FULL) in OS. (Details are in the Assembler Programmer's Guide, IBM #GC33–4021 or –4024.)

2.6 SUMMARY

The format of an assembly language statement is designed to accommodate the constraints of an eighty-column punched card but can be varied somewhat within those constraints. In the standard format, the first character position is used to distinguish between comment statements and all other statements; an asterisk (∗) is used to denote a comment. The purpose of any statement that is not a comment is determined by the opcode field, which must contain a valid abbreviation of from one to five characters for an instruction or directive. The purpose of each instruction or directive is further defined by the information in its operand field. All instructions and directives may optionally include free-form comments following the operand. All statements may optionally include identification that can be used for checking the sequence of the statements. Statements whose operand or comments fields are too long to be contained on one card or line may be continued on the following card or line through appropriate use of the continuation field.

Certain instructions and directives are, by convention, required in every source module. These were described in Section 2.3. They provide an interface to the Operating System and other programs at run time and have important roles related to addressing.

To read data from the input data stream and print information on the printer, several things are required: certain attributes of the data must be described by a DCB or DTF macro and corresponding job control language DD statements; the input data stream must be opened before any data can be read at run time, and the printer must be opened before any data can be printed at run time; reading and printing are performed, respectively, by the GET and PUT macros; and the two files must be closed at completion of processing. In addition, an area must be reserved for the input data as well as the output data. All data read or written are in EBCDIC character form. The program in figures 2.6 and 2.7 will serve as a model for all input and output operations required until chapter 18.

The differences between OS and DOS Assembly Language are almost solely confined to statements that are used for input and output and to the required statements mentioned in Section 2.3. There are no differences in statement formats, and the other differences that do exist are quite minor ones, which do not affect any of the examples or programs that are given later in this text. Those minor differences will simply be pointed out at the appropriate places in the text.

EXERCISES

1. Determine what job control language (JCL) statements are required to assemble a source module at your computer installation, and use those statements to assemble the source module given in figure 2.5.

2. In conjunction with Exercise 1, determine what JCL statements are required to execute the object code produced by the Assembler, and use those statements to run the program whose source module is given in figure 2.5. NOTE: You will have to prepare some input data cards. There may be any number of them, and they may contain any information whatsoever because the program does not examine or manipulate any of the data; it only reads and prints it. It is recommended that you prepare at least ten data cards, in order to demonstrate the printer line-spacing provided by the program.

3. If you have reasonably inexpensive and frequent access to the computer, you may want to deliberately create some error situations to see how the Assembler responds. Several conditions that will cause assembly-time errors follow; i.e., errors that the Assembler will detect and note on the listing. Make the changes specified below to the source module of figure 2.5 and assemble the changed module using the JCL statements determined in Exercise 1. The error messages that will be printed on the listing are explained in IBM Publication GC33-4021, *OS/VS-VM/370 Assembler Programmer's Guide*.

   a. Delete and do not replace the following statements:

line#	statements		
21	OUTER	L	4,=F'5'
46	CARD	DCB	DSORG=PS,...
58		END	

   b. Insert the following statements anywhere in the module:

name field	opcode	operand
EXIT	B	FINISH
ERROR	BT	4,INNER
	LM	14,12
	MVC	OUTAREA,132C'
	L	3,X
12345	ST	13,SAVE+4

4. What assembly-time error would occur if, in addition to indenting the opcode and operand field as in lines 25 through 28 of figure 2.5, the name field of line 25 were also to be indented? Explain the reason for this error. If you cannot anticipate what it would be, then submit it for assembly as in Exercise 3.

5. Based on your understanding of the assembly language statement formats, deliberately generate some source module errors, incorporate them into the source module of figure 2.5, and submit the module for assembly to see how the Assembler responds. The errors should include mistakes in the name, opcode, operand, comment, and continuation fields. Is there any way to generate an invalid comment statement? Is there any way that a comment statement can cause an error in another statement or statements?

6. The constant 5 that controls the frequency with which blank lines are printed by the program in figure 2.5 is specified in the operand of the instruction in line 21:

$$\text{OUTER} \qquad \text{L} \qquad 4,=\text{F'5'}$$

What would be the effect at run time if the 5 were changed to a 1? What would be the effect if it were changed to a 0? (Try it!)

7. Some types of programming errors are not detected by the Assembler. Instead of causing assembly-time errors, they cause run-time errors. For example, such errors can cause execution of your program to be abnormally terminated, a situation known as an "abend." These types of errors are called *logic* errors. To see how the Operating System responds to a run-time error, assemble and run the program of figure 2.5 with the following statement deleted from the source module:

line#	statement
9	BALR 12,0

The reason that omission of this statement causes a run-time error will be explained in chapter 3.

8. There are a few directives that enable a programmer to gain some control over the appearance of the listing. Chief among these are the TITLE, EJECT, SPACE, and PRINT directives described in chapter 14. Read Sections 14.1 through 14.4 now, and experiment with use of these directives. Note particularly the effect of inserting the following directive immediately after line 1 of the source module in figure 2.5:

opcode	operand
PRINT	NOGEN

9. Without submitting a job for assembly, determine which of the following statements would, if inserted in the source module of figure 2.5 following line 1, cause an assembly-time error. Explain the reason for each error.

name field	opcode	operand
A#1	STM	14,12,12(13)
	BALR	
	USNIG	*,12
	ST	13,SAVE+$
	OPEN	(INAREA,(INPUT))
	GET	CARD,OUTAREA

3
Instructions and Addresses

Every machine language instruction contains two types of information: (1) a numeric opcode that identifies the purpose of the instruction and (2) an operand that identifies the information required for execution of the instruction.

Every assembly language instruction is a symbolic representation of a machine language instruction. The opcode and operand fields of an assembly language instruction correspond one for one to those of a machine language instruction. At assembly time, the Assembler translates each symbolic assembly language instruction into its numeric machine language representation. At run time, the translated instructions are executed by the central processing unit.

In this chapter we describe the formats of assembly language and machine language instructions and show how addresses are represented and processed at assembly time and at run time in the 360 and 370 computer systems. You may wish to review the processes of converting integers from decimal to binary and hexadecimal, especially the correspondences between the first sixteen integers, which was given in figure 1.5.

3.1 ADDRESSES

Each byte in memory is referred to by its address. A *memory address* is an unsigned integer in the range 0 through $2^n - 1$, where 2^n is the total number of bytes available in memory, i.e., the memory's capacity. The first byte in memory has address 0, the second address 1, the third 2, and so forth. Memory addresses are almost invariably written in hexadecimal notation, as in this diagram.

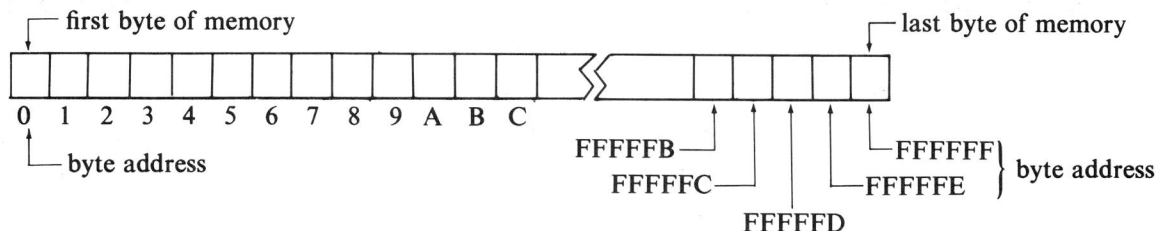

The address of the last byte in this diagram is $2^{24} - 1$, the largest allowable memory address in the IBM 360 and 370 computer systems. As a binary number, $2^{24} - 1$ is represented with 24 bits, all of which are 1's; therefore as a hexadecimal number it is represented with six digits, FFFFFF. In more familiar terms, $2^{24} = 16,777,216$—what is commonly known as a 16-megabyte memory.

The linear diagram above is not an especially useful way to represent memory, because bytes are very often grouped into units called full words, half words, and double words. A *full word* is any four consecutive bytes in which the address of the first byte is a number exactly divisible by four: 0, 4, 8, C, 10, 14, 18, 1C,.... In

Figure 3.1 *Schematic representation of memory.*

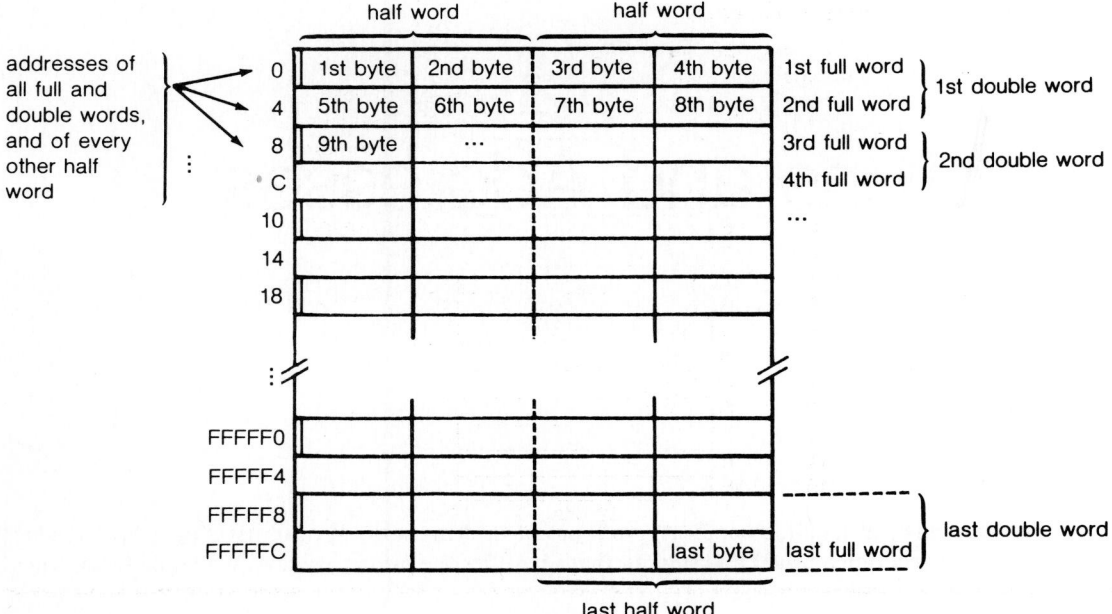

All addresses are shown in hexadecimal notation. In this notation, the low-order digit of a double-word address is either 0 or 8; that of a full-word address is 0, 4, 8, or C. Half-word addresses are even numbers ending in 0,2,4,6,8,A,C, or E.

a *half word,* the address of the first byte is exactly divisible by two; in a *double word,* by eight. The first byte of a full word is said to be at the full-word *boundary.* Half-word and double-word boundaries are at the beginning byte of each half and double word, respectively. Thus an alternative and more frequently used representation of memory is that shown in figure 3.1. The concept of boundaries is important because all machine language instructions must be aligned on a half-word boundary, and some data must be aligned on half-, full-, or double-word boundaries.

As mentioned in chapter 1, the execution of an instruction may require that data be in a register. There are 16 general-purpose registers in the IBM 360 and 370 systems, and each is referred to by an address that is an unsigned integer in the range from 0 through 15_{10} (fig. 3.2). Each register contains 32 bits (4 bytes), but neither the bits nor the bytes of a register are individually addressable. For purposes of discussion, the 32 bits in a register are numbered from 0 to 31. In diagrams, bit 0 is always shown at the left, bit 31 at the right. The left-most bits are the most significant, or high-order, bits of a register; the right-most bits are the least significant, or low-order, bits. The 32-bit quantity in a register is often called the *contents* of that register.

The information required for the execution of an instruction may be in a memory location, or it may be in a register. In either case, the address of that memory location or register is designated in the operand of the instruction. A register address is always represented by 4 bits in an instruction's operand. This is sufficient for all sixteen register addresses. But although a memory address may require up to 24 bits for its representation as a binary integer, only 16 bits are allocated for it in a machine language instruction. This is apparently insufficient, but the following fundamentally important scheme permits the 16 bits to refer to any one of the $2^{24}-1$ memory addresses.

The 16 bits that are used to represent a memory address do not represent a single integer; they represent two integers, each with a different purpose. One of the integers is 4 bits long and designates the address of a register known as the *base register.* The other integer is 12 bits long and represents an adjustment factor

Figure 3.2   Schematic diagram of the 16 general registers.

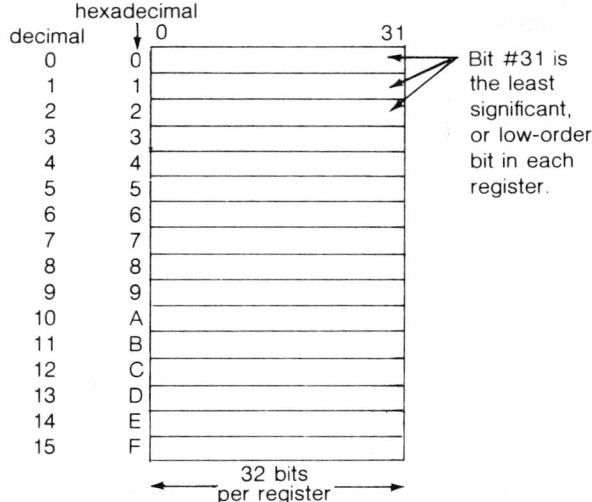

known as the *displacement*. This 16-bit representation of a memory address is known as the *base-displacement form* of that address. It will frequently be depicted like this:

B	D

where   B = base register address (4 bits)
                D = displacement (12 bits)

At run time, the base-displacement form of an address is translated by the central processing unit (CPU) into a 24-bit memory address. The memory address (M) is computed by the CPU from this formula:

$$M = \left\{ \begin{array}{l} \text{contents of} \\ \text{base register} \end{array} \right\} + \{\text{displacement}\}$$

Note that it is not the address of the base register that is added to the displacement, rather it is the contents of the register, more precisely, bits 8 through 31 of the register designated by that address, that is added. The quantity so added is known as the *base address* for memory address M. Both the base address and the displacement are always considered to be nonnegative integers, so that the resulting memory address is always a nonnegative integer, as it must be. M is known as the *effective address* generated from the base-displacement address.

There are two main reasons for the use of the base-displacement form rather than the full 24-bit memory address in an instruction. One is that it conserves space in the instruction. In other words, if space for a 24-bit address were available in each instruction, then most of the time this space would be only partly used, since most of the instructions in a program do not normally refer to addresses whose values require 24 bits. Most programs are simply not that big. If leading zeroes are disregarded, then the memory addresses used in most programs can be specified in fewer than 24 bits. The base-displacement form allows 16 bits to be used to refer to large addresses when they are needed but does not waste the space when it is not needed.

The other reason for the use of the base-displacement form is that when a program is loaded into memory by the Loader program, it is almost never assigned a starting address of 000000. Instead, it is assigned whatever address is available, depending on what memory locations are being used by other programs. Thus, a program which, when assembled, is assigned memory addresses from 000000 through 000500_{16}, may, when

Instructions and Addresses   31

loaded, be assigned addresses from 005000 through 005500_{16}. This is known as program relocation. When a relocated program is executed at run time, its instructions must refer to the addresses assigned by the Loader, not to the addresses assigned by the Assembler. All the Assembler-assigned addresses must be incremented by a constant factor, known as the relocation factor (005000_{16} in the example cited). The relocation factor can be a different number each time a program is loaded. But, since the base-displacement form of address is used in the operands of instructions, a program can be relocated simply by adding the relocation factor to the base address. Neither the B nor the D components of a base-displacement address needs to be changed. This greatly facilitates the process of program relocation.

In addition to the advantages just mentioned, there are two important constraints associated with the use of the base-displacement form of address. First, the base address must be large enough so that the corresponding displacement is not larger than FFF_{16}. If the displacement were larger than FFF_{16}, the displacement would not fit in the 12-bit displacement field. Second, the register chosen for use as the base register should ordinarily not be Register 0 since the IBM 360 and 370 hardware is designed to disregard the contents of Register 0 if that register is designated as the base register. If, however, Register 0 is the base register, then the base address is always assumed to be 000000.

3.2 INSTRUCTIONS

Each machine language instruction consists of a certain number of bytes. The number of bytes comprising an instruction is known as the instruction's *length*. In many computer systems, the length of all instructions is the same. In some computers, the length of an instruction depends on the type of instruction it is. We speak of a *variable-length* instruction set in the latter case and a *fixed-length* instruction set in the former. The IBM Systems 360 and 370 have a variable-length instruction set; some of its instructions occupy two consecutive bytes, some occupy four, and some occupy six.

The use of a variable-length instruction set, though apparently more complex than use of a fixed-length set, has one significant advantage: the number of bytes required for any instruction is just sufficient to provide only the information required in that instruction. This results in an overall saving of memory space in a program. In fixed-length sets, the length used for *all* instructions is the length needed by the instructions that contain the most information. This can result in unusable, hence wasted, memory space.

The address of an instruction is always the address of its first byte. Any two consecutive instructions in memory occupy consecutive locations. Thus, if we add the length of an instruction to its address, we obtain the address of the instruction immediately following it in memory.

One question that naturally arises is, How is the address of an instruction assigned? The answer is that it is assigned by the Assembler at assembly time. The Assembler maintains a counter, called the *memory location counter,* whose initial value is 0. When assembling an instruction, the Assembler assigns it an address whose value equals the value of the memory location counter. Before the next instruction is assembled, the Assembler increases the memory location counter by an amount equal to the length of the instruction that was just assembled.

$$\begin{Bmatrix} \text{memory} \\ \text{location} \\ \text{counter} \end{Bmatrix} = \begin{Bmatrix} \text{address} \\ \text{assigned} \\ \text{to an} \\ \text{instruction} \end{Bmatrix} = \begin{Bmatrix} \text{address} \\ \text{assigned to} \\ \text{preceding} \\ \text{instruction} \end{Bmatrix} + \begin{Bmatrix} \text{length of} \\ \text{preceding} \\ \text{instruction} \end{Bmatrix}$$

The value of the memory location counter maintained by the Assembler at assembly time is thus comparable to the value of the program location counter (PC) maintained by the CPU at run time.

When a machine language instruction refers to another instruction, as in a GO-TO type of instruction (known as a *branch* instruction), the address of the instruction to which the branch is to be made is specified in base-displacement form in the branch (B) instruction itself. In Assembly Language, the programmer need not specify the base-displacement form of an address. Instead, he or she can specify an address symbolically, by using the symbol defined in a statement's name field. The Assembler translates that symbol into its appropriate base-displacement form when assembling an instruction. For example, in the sequence

```
LOOP        ---     -------
            ---     -------
   B        LOOP
```

Figure 3.3 Machine language instruction formats.

instruction type	machine language instruction format	instruction length	
		no. of bytes	no. of bits
RR	opcode | R1 | R2 (0, 8, 12)	2	16
RX	opcode | R1 | X2 | B2 | D2 (0, 8, 12, 16, 20)	4	32
RS	opcode | R1 | R2 | B3 | D3 (0, 8, 12, 16, 20)	4	32
SI	opcode | I 2 | B1 | D1 (0, 8, 16, 20)	4	32
S	opcode | B1 | D1 (0, 16, 20)	4	32
SS₁	opcode | L | B1 | D1 | B2 | D2 (0, 8, 16, 20, 32, 36)	6	48
SS₂	opcode | L1 | L2 | B1 | D1 | B2 | D2 (0, 8, 12, 16, 20, 32, 36)	6	48

Note: For the RS format, the IBM reference manuals use R3 where we have used R2, and use B2 and D2 where we have used B3 and D3.

---

the Assembler translates the symbol LOOP specified in the operand of the B instruction into the base-displacement representation of the address of the instruction named LOOP. At the time that the instruction named LOOP was assembled, the Assembler assigned a value to LOOP equal to the address assigned to that instruction. That address was just the value of the memory location counter.

$$\left\{\begin{array}{c}\text{address assigned}\\\text{to a symbol}\end{array}\right\} = \left\{\begin{array}{c}\text{memory}\\\text{location}\\\text{counter}\end{array}\right\} = \left\{\begin{array}{c}\text{address assigned to}\\\text{instruction identified}\\\text{by that symbol}\end{array}\right\}$$

The Assembler maintains a list of all symbols defined in an assembly language program, together with the address values it has assigned to them. This list is known as the Assembler's *symbol table*. Whenever the Assembler processes a statement that contains a symbol in its name field, that symbol is entered into the symbol table, along with the value assigned to it. (Duplicate names, that is the same name on two different statements, are not allowed; they are flagged as multiply-defined symbols.) When the Assembler assembles a statement that contains a symbol in its operand field, it uses the value recorded for that symbol in its symbol table. The manner in which these processes are carried out will be discussed in chapter 10. For present purposes, the important thing to note is that in Assembly Language the programmer need not specify the numeric address of an instruction or data; he or she need only specify a symbolic address, i.e., the symbol whose value is equal to the numeric address.

Further discussion of assembly language statement formats is deferred until Section 3.4. The following section is a description of the machine language instruction formats upon which all assembly language instructions are based.

3.3   MACHINE LANGUAGE FORMATS

You will recall that machine language instructions on the IBM 360 and 370 are of variable length; some are 2 bytes long, some 4, and some 6. The length of an instruction, together with the type of information contained in the operand field of the instruction, constitute the instruction's *format*.

There are seven different instruction formats. These are known as the RR, RX, RS, SI, S, SS_1, and SS_2 formats. All seven are available on the 370, and all but the S format are available on the 360. Although the SS_1 and SS_2 formats are often referred to simply as *the* SS format, we will maintain the distinction between SS_1 and SS_2 since it is useful.

Each machine language instruction has one and only one format. For all instructions of a given format, the information required in the instruction is represented in the manner dictated by that format. The seven formats are illustrated in figure 3.3. They all have the following general structure:

```
 1 byte ┐              ┌ 1,3, or 5 bytes
        ↓              ↓
  ┌────────────┬──────────────────────┐
  │   opcode   │       operand         │
  └────────────┴──────────────────────┘
```

Each operand field contains either a register address, data, or a displacement. A displacement, denoted by D1, D2, or D3, is always immediately preceded by its associated base-register address, denoted by B1, B2, or B3. Together, the two constitute the base-displacement form of memory address that was previously discussed.

For the RS instruction format, we have departed from the notation convention used in IBM reference manuals. This departure allows us to refer to the second operand of assembly language RS instructions as R2, and to the third field in those instructions as D3(B3). For the other formats, the notation of figure 3.3 is consistent with that used in IBM reference manuals.

The following three examples illustrate the manner in which all but one of the fields occurring in a machine language instruction are specified at run time. The exception is the X2 field, which will be discussed separately. Note the following points in the examples:

1. The opcode field contains the 8-bit numeric code that identifies the instruction. A list of these codes is given in Appendix A.
2. The fields designated as R1 and R2 contain register addresses, 4 bits each. Data to be operated on by the instruction are obtained at run time from the designated registers.
3. The fields designated as D1, D2, and D3, 12 bits each, are paired with the corresponding B1, B2, and B3 fields, 4 bits each. Each pair is the base-displacement form of a memory address.
4. The field designated as I2 contains an 8-bit constant that is used as data in the execution of the instruction.
5. The field designated as L contains an 8-bit unsigned integer that represents the number of bytes to be operated on. The contents of the L field is one less than the actual number of bytes that it represents.

Example 1.   Add two integers (RR format)

The RR-type instruction for adding two integers has the opcode $1A_{16}$. Using figure 3.3, we find that the machine language format for RR-type instructions is as follows:

```
  ┌──────────┬────┬────┐
  │  opcode  │ R1 │ R2 │
  └──────────┴────┴────┘
```

If we choose Register 3 for R1 and Register 4 for R2, then the machine language instruction is this:

```
  ┌────┬────┬────┬────┐
  │ 1  │ A  │ 3  │ 4  │
  └────┴────┴────┴────┘
```

When executed at run time, this instruction will add the integer contained in the register whose address is 4 to the integer contained in the register whose address is 3. The result will be in Register 3.

Example 2.   Compare 2 bytes (SI format)

The SI-type instruction for comparing two bytes has the opcode 95_{16}. From figure 3.3, we find that the machine language format for SI-type instructions is as follows:

opcode	I2	B1	D1

Let us assume that the base-displacement form for a memory address in this instruction specifies Register 12 with a displacement of 32_{10}, so that the B1 field is C, and the D1 field is 020_{16}. Then, to compare the byte at that memory address with the 1-byte constant, 40_{16}, the machine language instruction is as follows:

9	5	4	0	C	0	2	0

Note that the 1-byte constant, 40_{16}, is contained in the I2 field of the instruction. Since these data are available to the CPU at the same time that it obtains the instruction, they are known as *immediate* data.

Example 3.   Compare five bytes (SS$_1$ format)

The SS$_1$-type instruction for comparing bytes at one memory location with those at another has the opcode $D5_{16}$. From figure 3.3, we find that the machine language format for SS$_1$-type instructions is as follows:

opcode	L	B1	D1	B2	D2

In an SS$_1$-compare instruction, one or more bytes beginning at the memory address whose base-displacement form is given in the B1, D1 fields are compared to the same number of bytes at the memory location whose base-displacement address is given in the B2,D2 fields. The number of bytes to be compared is specified in the L field of the instruction. When the contents of that field is 0, one byte is compared; when it is 1, two bytes are compared; and so forth. Since L is an 8-bit field, the maximum number of bytes that can be compared is 256.

Let us assume that the base-displacement address specified in the B1,D1 fields designates Register 12 with a displacement of 64_{10}, and that the base-displacement address specified in the B2,D2 fields designates Register 12 with a displacement of 200_{10}. To compare 5 bytes, the contents of the L field must be 4, so that under the assumptions just cited the machine language instruction is as follows:

D5	04	C	040	C	0C8

In SS$_2$-type instructions (not illustrated here), the fields designated as L1 and L2 serve the same purpose as the L field of an SS$_1$ instruction. They are byte counts. L1 is the number of bytes to be used starting at the memory address designated by B1,D1 ; L2, the number of bytes starting at B2,D2. L1 and L2 are 4-bit fields whose contents are in the range 0 through 15, representing counts of 1 through 16 bytes.

The only field not yet mentioned is X2 in the RX format. The register designated by the X2 field is known as the *index register*. RX-type instructions are said to be *indexed* instructions. This type of instruction permits an additional factor to be used in the computation of an effective address at run time. This factor, known simply as the *index*, provides the principal means by which subscripting of arrays (as in FORTRAN DO-loops) is accomplished in Assembly Language.

The CPU uses the X2 field at run time as follows. If the X2 field designates Register 0, then no indexing is performed. If the X2 field designates any register other than Register 0, then indexing is performed. The effective address is then computed by this formula:

$$\left\{ \begin{matrix} \text{effective} \\ \text{address} \end{matrix} \right\} = \left\{ \begin{matrix} \text{base} \\ \text{address} \end{matrix} \right\} + \{\text{displacement}\} + \{\text{index}\}$$

The index consists of bits 8 through 31 of the register designated by the X2 field and is considered to be an unsigned nonnegative binary integer, as are the other factors in this formula.

The examples discussed illustrate three important aspects of machine language instructions: (1) The position of the hex digits in an instruction, as well as the value of each digit, is crucial to a correct execution at run time. (2) There is no indication in an instruction that it *is* an instruction. In Example 3, the twelve hex digits D504C040C0C8 that constitute the instruction are indistinguishable from the same twelve digits that might be used to represent data. A similar statement could be made for any instruction. (3) Except for the I2 field in the SI-type instruction of Example 2, the data that an instruction operates on are not contained in the instruction. Instead, either they are contained in a register whose address is given in the instruction, or they are contained in a memory location whose address is represented in base-displacement form in the instruction.

The position and value of each hex digit in an instruction are determined by the Assembler when it translates an assembly language instruction into machine language. The translated instruction is often referred to as the *object code*. At run time, the CPU assumes that the object code is correct. If it is not, it is executed anyway, with the likelihood that the results will not be as intended by the programmer. Therefore considerable care must be taken when writing instructions in Assembly Language. Moreover, when an instruction is executed, the data to be operated on must already exist in the designated registers and memory locations. If this is not the case, the instruction will be executed anyway, and the results will very likely not be what was wanted. Failure to specify an instruction correctly and failure to ensure the correct placement of data are two common causes of run-time errors and invalid results.

We will see in the next section that there is a one-to-one correspondence between the fields required in a machine language instruction and those that are represented in an assembly language instruction. We will show how the operand format of each assembly language instruction is defined by the type of machine language instruction into which it is translated. Though often written symbolically rather than numerically, each operand format essentially mimics the format of the corresponding machine language instruction. For that reason, it is extremely useful, if not absolutely necessary, that you become familiar with the seven machine-language formats shown in figure 3.3.

3.4 ASSEMBLY LANGUAGE FORMATS

An assembly language instruction must specify the same information as that contained in the machine language instruction that it represents. Some of the fields in a machine language instruction must be explicitly represented in the assembly language instruction, while others can either be explicitly represented or implied.

The fields that must be explicitly represented are the opcode field, the R1 and R2 register address fields, and the I2 immediate data field. The fields that can be implied or explicit are the base-displacement fields, B1,D1, B2,D2, and B3,D3 , and the length fields, L, L1, and L2.

The opcode is represented symbolically by a mnemonic abbreviation consisting of from one to five alphabetic characters. The mnemonic abbreviation usually serves as a reminder of the name and purpose of the instruction. For example, B is the abbreviation for the Branch instruction. The mnemonic abbreviations that are available in the IBM 360 and 370 Assembly Language are summarized in Appendix A.

An assembly language instruction's *type* is defined to be the same as that of the machine language instruction that it represents. Thus, there are seven types of assembly language instructions: RR, RX, RS, SI, S, SS$_1$, and SS$_2$. As in machine language instructions, the opcode appearing in an assembly language instruction determines that instruction's type. The opcode also determines the instruction's operand format, although there may be more than one permissible format for a given type of instruction. The number of permissible formats is determined by the number of possible combinations of explicit and implicit fields in the operand. These are summarized in figure 3.4.

Explicit Formats

With one exception, the notation used in figure 3.4 for explicit formats is the same as that used in machine language instructions. The exception is that in Assembly Language the length field designators L, L1, and L2 represent the exact number of bytes that are to be operated on, whereas in machine language these designators represent one less than the exact number of bytes. The Assembler calculates the correct length for the machine language instruction at assembly time, so that the programmer can almost always ignore the difference of 1 when writing instructions. As examples of the use of explicit formats, the instructions illustrated in the preceding section are repeated (see Examples 1 through 3). These are followed by a discussion of the RX format. For the RX explicit format, there are three possibilities: X2 or B2 or both. Examples 4 through 5b use assumed values for the various fields.

Figure 3.4   Instruction format summary.

type	machine language instruction formats	assembly language operand formats	Notes
RR	`op │ R1 │ R2` (0 8 12)	explicit: R1,R2	
RX	`op │ R1 │ X2 │ B2 │ D2` (0 8 12 16 20 31)	explicit: R1,D2(X2,B2) R1,D2(,B2) R1,D2(X2) R1,D2 implicit: R1,S2(X2) R1,S2	1
RS	`op │ R1 │ R2 │ B3 │ D3` (0 8 12 16 20 31)	explicit: R1,R2,D3(B3) implicit: R1,R2,S3	2
SI	`op │ I2 │ B1 │ D1` (0 8 16 20 31)	explicit: D1(B1),I2 implicit: S1,I2	3
S	`op │ B1 │ D1` (0 16 20 31)	explicit: D1(B1) implicit: S1	
SS₁	`op │ L │ B1 │ D1 │ B2 │ D2` (0 8 16 20 32 36 47)	explicit: D1(L,B1),D2(B2) implicit: S1,S2 mixed: D1(L,B1),S2 S1(L),D2(B2) S1(L),S2 S1,D2(B2)	4,5
SS₂	`op │ L1 │ L2 │ B1 │ D1 │ B2 │ D2` (0 8 12 16 20 32 36 47)	explicit: D1(L1,B1),D2(L2,B2) implicit: S1,S2 mixed: D1(L1,B1),S2(L2) D1(L1,B1),S2 S1(L1),S2(L2) S1(L1),S2 S1,S2(L2) S1(L1),D2(L2,B2) S1,D2(L2,B2)	5,6

NOTES: 1. RX: When the index field X2 is omitted, it is assumed to be 0. An X2 field of 0 means no indexing.

2. RS: IBM manuals give R1,R3,D2(B2) where we have given R1,R2,D3(B3).

3. SI: The I2 field is one byte, used as immediate data.

4. SS₁: In machine language, the length field L is represented by a number that is one less than that used in Assembly Language.

5. SS₁,SS₂: Any of the length fields can be omitted in Assembly Language when a symbolic address is used. If so omitted, the Assembler uses the length-attribute of the corresponding symbol.

6. SS₂: In machine language the length fields L1 and L2 are represented by numbers that are one less than those used in the corresponding assembly language fields.

In Example 4, each field in the assembly language operand is assembled into the corresponding field in the machine language operand. In Example 5a the omission of the X2 field is indicated by the comma immediately following the left parenthesis: 4(,11). When X2 is omitted in this fashion, the Assembler assigns it a value of 0. In Example 5b, it is B2 that is omitted; this is indicated by the absence of a comma following the X2 field: 4(11). However, at run time the X2 and B2 fields are processed in exactly the same way in the calculation of the effective address. Consequently, *the two assembly language forms, D2(,B2) and D2(X2), have the same effect at run time.* The second form will often be used when omitting either X2 or B2.

Example 1. Add two integers (RR format)

machine language

op	R1	R2

1 A	3	4

Assembly Language

op   R1,R2

AR   3,4

Example 2. Compare 2 bytes (SI format)

machine language

op	I2	B1	D1

9 5	4 0	C	0 2 0

Assembly Language

op   D1(B1),I2

CLI   32(12),X'40'

Note that in Assembly Language, numbers are assumed to be in decimal notation unless otherwise indicated. X'...' denotes a hexadecimal number within the two delimiting apostrophes.

Example 3. Compare 5 bytes (SS₁ format)

machine language

op	L	B1	D1	B2	D2

D 5	0 4	C	0 4 0	C	0 C 8

Assembly Language

op   D1(L,B1),D2(B2)

CLC   64(5,12),200(12)

Example 4. Add two integers (RX format, X2 and B2 specified)

machine language

op	R1	X2	B2	D2

5 A	3	A	B	0 0 4

Assembly Language

op   R1,D2(X2,B2)

A   3,4(10,11)

Example 5a. Add two integers (RX format, X2 omitted)

machine language

Assembly Language

op   R1,D2(,B2)

A   3,4(,11)

Example 5b. Add two integers (RX format, B2 omitted)

machine language

Assembly Language

op   R1,D2(X2)

A   3,4(11)

There is one other important rule. When the B1, B2, or B3 field is specified in an explicit format, the corresponding D1, D2, or D3 field must not represent a memory address. Instead, it must represent a constant in the range 0 through 4095_{10}.

Implicit Formats

In the notation of figure 3.4, S1, S2, and S3 are used to indicate an address that is written in implicit form rather than in explicit base-displacement form. Use of implicit formats has a decided advantage over use of explicit formats: they are simpler to use, less error prone, and greatly facilitate the writing and modifying of source statements. Consequently, implicit formats are used frequently in assembly language programming.

The simplest implicit form of address consists of a statement name-field symbol. For example, this Add instruction,

$$A \qquad 3,Z$$

corresponds to the following implicit form for an RX-type instruction given in figure 3.4:

$$op \qquad R1,S2$$

In the Add instruction, the symbol Z is assumed to have been defined in the name field of some statement in the source module in which the Add occurs. The value of Z is an address, namely the address that the Assembler assigned to the statement in which Z was the name-field symbol. When assembling the machine language instruction corresponding to A 3,Z the Assembler generates the required base-displacement form of the address that is represented by Z. The programmer must not specify the displacement or the base register when using an implicit form of address.

The instructions shown in figure 3.5 illustrate a few of the other implicit forms of address. The phrase "symbolic address is Z" used in the explanation column of figure 3.5 means "the memory address that is equal to the value of the symbol Z." In each of the instructions, the implicit form of address is given by a statement-name symbol. In the last example of figure 3.5, the implicit format

$$op \qquad S1,S2$$

indicates that the length field L is implied, as in the instruction

$$CLC \qquad X,Z$$

The value of the implied length is assumed by the Assembler to be the number of bytes represented by the symbol X. This is known as the *length-attribute* of X and will be discussed further in chapter 6.

In all the examples of figure 3.5, the Assembler must generate the correct base-displacement form of a symbolic address. Thus, for the RX-type Add instruction

$$A \qquad 3,Z$$

the Assembler must generate a base register address for the B2 field and a displacement for the D2 field of the assembled machine language instruction. The machine language opcode for this Add instruction is 5A, so from figure 3.4 we see that the assembled instruction will have the following form:

5	A	3	0	?	?

$$\quad op \quad R1 \quad X2 \quad B2 \quad D2$$

The contents of the B2 and D2 fields must be such that the formula

$$\left\{ \begin{matrix} memory\ address \\ represented\ by\ Z \end{matrix} \right\} = \left\{ \begin{matrix} base \\ address \end{matrix} \right\} + \left\{ \begin{matrix} implied \\ displacement \end{matrix} \right\}$$

is satisfied. The base address in this formula is the contents of the base register that is implied by symbolic address Z. That register must be designated by the contents of the B2 field in the machine language instruction. The implied displacement must be calculated by the Assembler and represented in the D2 field of the instruction.

The question is, What should the B2 and D2 fields be, and what is the value of the base address, in order that the above formula be satisfied? The Assembler can determine the memory address represented by

Figure 3.5   Examples of implicit formats.

type	implicit format	instruction	explanation
RX	R1,S2	A 3,Z	Add the integer whose symbolic address is Z to the contents of Register 3.
RX	R1,S2(X2)	A 3,Z(5)	Add to Register 3 the integer whose address is the sum of the index in Register 5 and the symbolic address Z.
SI	S1,I2	CLI Z,X'40'	Compare the byte whose symbolic address is Z to the one-byte constant X'40', given as immediate data.
SS₁	S1(L),S2	CLC X(5),Z	Compare the five bytes at the location whose symbolic address is X to the five bytes whose symbolic address is Z.
SS₁	S1,S2	CLC X,Z	Compare the n bytes at the location whose symbolic address is X to the n bytes whose symbolic address is Z. Note: The value of n is implied and is the length attribute of X.

Z—the left-hand side of the above formula—by means of its symbol table, but how can it determine the quantities in the right-hand side of the equation? It appears that we have one equation and three unknowns: the base address, the implied base register designated by the B2 field, and the implied displacement in the D2 field. To resolve this situation, the following method must be used.

The programmer is required to specify the base address and the address of the implied base register by means of a USING directive. *The USING directive must occur before any statement in the source module that contains an operand for which an implied displacement must be calculated.* Its format is

opcode	operand
USING	A,R

where A represents the base address and R represents the implied base register.

Given this information, the Assembler can resolve the situation described. The implied displacement from the formula given above, can be written as follows:

$$\left\{ \begin{array}{l} \text{implied} \\ \text{displacement} \end{array} \right\} = \left\{ \begin{array}{l} \text{memory address} \\ \text{represented by Z} \end{array} \right\} - \left\{ \text{base address} \right\}$$

In general, whenever an implicit form of address is specified in the operand of an assembly language instruction, the Assembler uses the base address and the implied base register that are specified in the USING directive and computes the required implied displacement from the following formula:

$$\left\{ \begin{array}{l} \text{implied} \\ \text{displacement} \end{array} \right\} = \left\{ \begin{array}{l} \text{memory} \\ \text{address} \end{array} \right\} - \left\{ \begin{array}{l} \text{base} \\ \text{address} \end{array} \right\}$$

To return to our Add instruction,

$$A \qquad 3,Z$$

we are now entitled to assume that the memory address represented by Z is a known value, that the address of the implied base register is known, and that the base address is known. "Known," of course, means "known to the Assembler." Suppose, then, that the addresses just mentioned are as follows:

$$\text{memory address Z} = 80A_{16}$$
$$\text{implied base register} = C_{16}$$
$$\text{base address} = 6_{16}$$

The implied displacement can then be calculated from the previously mentioned formula:

$$\begin{array}{ll} \text{implied displacement} & = 80A - 6 \\ & = 804 \end{array}$$

The assembled instruction therefore becomes the following:

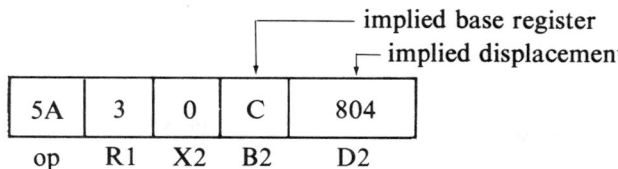

5A	3	0	C	804
op	R1	X2	B2	D2

The only constraint placed on the determination of the implied displacement is that the displacement must be a nonnegative integer in the range from 000 through FFF_{16} (0 through 4095_{10}). For this reason, it is always advisable to write programs that do not exceed 4096 bytes in length when assembled.

3.5   THE BALR-USING SEQUENCE   *Branch + link*

In the preceding section, we showed that in order to use the implicit form of address, the programmer must specify the base address and the implied base register in a USING directive, of the form

USING   A,R

where A represents the base address and R represents the implied base register. Given that information, the Assembler is able to calculate the implied displacement and generate the required base-displacement form of the address.

But what will happen at run time? At run time the computation of the effective address in RX, RS, SI, S, SS_1, and SS_2 instructions uses the base address that is in the base register:

$$\left\{ \begin{matrix} \text{effective} \\ \text{address} \end{matrix} \right\} = \left\{ \begin{matrix} \text{base address} \\ \text{in designated} \\ \text{base register} \end{matrix} \right\} + \{ \text{displacement} \}$$

Consequently, *there must be an instruction in the program that puts the base address into the implied base register at run time.* The instruction that is used for this purpose is the BALR instruction, an RR-type instruction. As shown in figure 3.4, the format of the BALR instruction is as follows:

opcode	operand
BALR	R1,R2

For the present purposes, we will use it with R1 = 12 and R2 = 0:

BALR   12,0

In this form, the BALR instruction, *when executed at run time,* places the address of the instruction that immediately follows the BALR into Register 12. Since the BALR's length is 2 bytes, the address placed into Register 12 is 2 plus the address of the BALR instruction itself. For example, if the address of the BALR 12,0 instruction is 0004, the address placed into Register 12 is 0006.

If in the USING directive we let R = 12 and A = {2 plus the address of the BALR instruction}, then the effective addresses computed for the RX, RS, SI, S, SS_1, and SS_2 instructions at run time will be identical with the effective addresses designated in those instructions at assembly time.

To specify the desired value of A and R in the USING directive, the programmer writes the BALR and USING statements in the following manner and in the following sequence:

BALR   12,0
USING   *,12

The asterisk symbol (*), when used in this manner, represents the value of the memory location counter that is maintained by the Assembler. As stated in Section 3.2, this value is equal to the address assigned to the preceding instruction, plus the length of that instruction. In other words, *it is the same as the address that the BALR instruction will place into Register 12 at run time.*

Throughout this book, Register 12 will be used as the implied base register. This is the standard base register convention in the IBM 360 and 370 systems. The reason for choosing Register 12 rather than any other register is this: Registers 1, 13, 14, and 15, which are used in the standard subroutine linkage convention (as will be described in chapter 9), ordinarily should not be used for any other purpose; Register 0 cannot be used, since its contents are disregarded by the IBM 360 and 370 hardware when it is used as a base register. By choosing Register 12, we have ten consecutive registers free for other use in the program.

Finally, it should be noted that no implicit forms of address may be used in the operands of statements that occur before the USING directive. If these forms were used, the Assembler could not calculate the implied displacement and would not know what register to use as the implied base register in those operands.

As an illustration of these concepts, consider the sequence of statements that are required at the beginning of each assembly language program:

```
NAME      CSECT
          STM      14,12,12(13)
          BALR     12,0
          USING    *,12
          ST       13,SAVE+4
          LA       13,SAVE
```

The Assembler initializes the memory location counter to 0 and then processes the statements one by one. The results can be depicted as shown below. Note that there is no opcode corresponding to a directive, only to an instruction.

assembly language statement		memory location counter	opcode	type	number of bytes	assembled object code	
NAME CSECT		0000	none	directive	0	none	
STM	14,12,12(13)	0000	STM = 90	RS	4	90ECD00C	(explicit)
BALR	12,0	0004	BALR = 05	RR	2	05C0	
USING	*,12	0006	none	directive	0	none	
ST	13,SAVE+4	0006	ST = 50	RX	4	50D0C---	(implicit)
LA	13,SAVE	000A	LA = 41	RX	4	41D0C---	(implicit)

The following observations summarize the results just depicted. First, before assembling a statement, the memory location counter is increased by the number of object code bytes (if any) required by the preceding statement. Then, the current value of the memory location counter is assigned to the name field symbol (if any) appearing in a statement, and to the symbol used to represent the memory location counter, namely the asterisk (*). Next, each instruction is translated into its appropriate machine language format, using the numeric equivalent of the mnemonic opcode. Operand fields given in explicit base-displacement form can be immediately translated, as in the STM instruction; but operands given implicitly, as in the ST instruction, cannot be translated until three things are known: the base address, the implied base register, and the value of the symbolic address. Fourth, the USING *,12 directive informs the Assembler that the base address is 0006 and that the base register is Register 12. And finally, to translate the ST instruction, the Assembler must calculate the implied displacement from the formula given earlier,

$$\left\{ \begin{array}{c} \text{implied} \\ \text{displacement} \end{array} \right\} = \left\{ \begin{array}{c} \text{memory address} \\ \text{represented} \\ \text{symbolically by} \\ \text{SAVE+4} \end{array} \right\} - \left\{ \begin{array}{c} \text{base address} \\ \text{in implied} \\ \text{base register} \end{array} \right\}$$

The base address is 0006, and the implied base register B2 is 12; but the memory address represented symbolically by SAVE+4 cannot be determined until the statement in which SAVE is the name-field symbol is processed. This statement is not shown above, but to complete the example let us assume that when it is processed the value assigned to SAVE is 500_{16}. Then the implied displacement will be

$$4FE = (500 + 4) - 0006$$

and the object code corresponding to the ST 13,SAVE+4 instruction will be as follows:

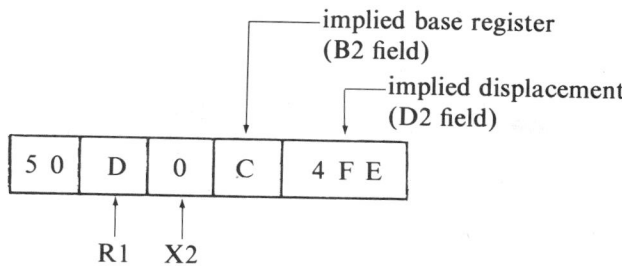

3.6   MNEMONIC OPCODES

The entire set of nonprivileged assembly language instructions is summarized in figure 3.6. We will describe in later chapters how to use these instructions. Through repeated usage they will become familiar to you; therefore, it is not necessary to begin learning them now.

Ultimately you will have to learn each instruction's mnemonic opcode and type (RR, RX, etc.). Together, the opcode and type dictate not only what operation is to be performed but also what kind of data is being operated on (binary, decimal, etc.) and whether the data are in memory or in registers.

The letters used in the opcodes are designed to help you remember each opcode and its purpose, as in *A* for Add and *B* for Branch. For this reason the opcodes are said to be *mnemonic,* from the Greek words meaning mindful and remember. For some instructions the type is easy to remember once the opcode is learned; for example, in most RR-type instructions the opcode ends in the letter *R*. For the others, however, learning the type will require frequent recourse to tables such as figure 3.6.

3.7   SUMMARY

Perhaps more than any other single fact, what makes Assembly Language qualitatively different from just about every other programming language is that *there is a one-to-one correspondence between the opcode and operand fields of a machine language instruction and those of an assembly language instruction.* Therefore, since in the IBM 360 and 370 systems there are seven different machine language instruction formats—RR, RX, RS, SI, S, SS₁, and SS₂—there are seven correspondingly different assembly language instruction formats.

Although in machine language all fields in an instruction contain binary numbers, in Assembly Language the fields are usually written symbolically or with decimal numbers. The Assembler translates the field representations into the binary formats required for execution at run time.

In each of the seven machine language formats, the opcode field occupies the first 8 bits. This means that there can be up to 256 ($=2^8$) different opcodes. As can be seen from the opcodes listed in Appendix A, there are in fact only about 150 nonprivileged opcodes. Some of the remaining 100 or so opcodes are privileged instructions that will not be discussed in this text; the others are not associated with hardware operations, i.e., they are invalid. In Assembly Language, the valid opcodes are represented mnemonically by codes of from one to five letters. In this text, their study will be undertaken in accordance with the functional categories depicted in figure 3.6.

The operand field of a machine language instruction specifies the data on which the instruction is to operate. The specification can take one of four forms:

1. the data itself (only in SI-type instructions)
2. the numeric address of a register containing the data
3. the numeric address of a memory location containing the data, the address being given in base-displacement form
4. the number of bytes (length) of the data at a memory location (given only in SS₁- and SS₂-type instructions)

Figure 3.6 Mnemonic opcode summary.

instruction category	general description	see section	mnemonic opcodes by instruction type						
			RR	RX	RS	SI	S	SS₁	SS₂
Branching and loop control	Unconditional branch	3.2;8.4	BR	B			(none)		
	Branch and link to subroutine	3.5;9.4	BALR BASR	BAL BAS					
	Conditional branch, depending on index	4.6			BXH BXLE				
	Conditional branch, depending on count	4.5	BCTR	BCT					
	Conditional branch, depending on condition code	5.4;5.5 7.4; 8.4; 12.5; 13.5	BCR BER BNER BLR BNLR BHR BNHR BZR BNZR BMR BNMR BPR BNPR BOR BNOR	BC BE BNE BL BNL BH BNH BZ BNZ BM BNM BP BNP BO BNO					
Binary integer operations	Add	5.3	AR ALR	A AH AL			(none)		
	Subtract	5.3	SR SLR	S SH SL					
	Multiply	5.3	MR	M MH					
	Divide	5.3	DR	D					
	Shift, with sign preserved	5.3;8.1			SRA SRDA SLA SLDA				
	Compare	5.5	CR	C CH					
	Test	5.4	LTR						
	Sign	5.6	LCR LNR LPR						
	Copy into register	5.2	LR	L LH	LM				
	Copy into memory	5.2		ST STH	STM				
	Convert decimal to binary	4.4;12.8		CVB					
	Convert binary to decimal	4.3;12.8		CVD					

			RR	RX	RS	SI	S	SS₁	SS₂
Decimal operations	Add	12.3			(none)				AP ZAP
	Subtract	12.3							SP
	Multiply	12.3							MP
	Divide	12.3							DP
	Shift	12.6							MVO
	Shift and round	12.5							SRP
	Compare	12.4							CP
	Copy	12.6						MVN MVZ	
	Convert zoned to packed	4.4;12.8							PACK
	Convert packed to zoned	4.3;12.8							UNPK
	Convert packed to EBCDIC	12.9						ED EDMK	

Figure 3.6 *continued*

instruction category	general description	see section	mnemonic opcodes by instruction type RR short	RR long	RR ext'd	RX short	RX long	RX ext'd	RS	SI	S	SS$_1$	SS$_2$
Floating-point operations	Add	13.7	AER AUR	ADR AWR	AXR	AE AU	AD AW		(none)				
	Subtract	13.7	SER SUR	SDR SWR	SXR	SE SU	SD SW						
	Multiply	13.7	MER	MDR	MXDR MXR	ME	MD	MXD					
	Divide	13.7	DER	DDR		DE	DD						
	Halve	13.7	HER	HDR									
	Round	13.7			LRER LRDR								
	Compare	13.5	CER	CDR		CE	CD						
	Test	13.5	LTER	LTDR									
	Sign	13.6	LCER LNER LPER	LCDR LNDR LPDR									
	Copy into register	13.4	LER	LDR		LE	LD						
	Copy into memory	13.4				STE	STD						

			RR	RX	RS	SI	S	SS$_1$	SS$_2$
Byte manipulations	Compare	7.3; 7.8	CLR CLCL	CL	CLM	CLI		CLC	
	Copy	7.2; 7.8	MVCL	IC STC	ICM STCM	MVI		MVC MVCIN	
	Translate	7.9						TR	
	Translate and test	7.9						TRT	
Bit manipulations	And	8.2	NR	N		NI		NC	
	Or	8.2	OR	O		OI		OC	
	Exclusive Or	8.2	XR	X		XI		XC	
	Test	8.3				TM	TS		
	Shift	8.1			SRL SRDL SLL SLDL				
Miscellaneous	Load address	4.5		LA					
	Execute	7.7		EX					
	Set program mask	11.4	SPM						
	No-op	6.4;8.4	NOPR	NOP					
	Supervisor call	19.4	SVC						
	Monitor call	---					MC		
	Store clock	---					STCK		
	Compare and swap	---			CS CDS				

These fields must also be specified in Assembly Language, though this is often done symbolically rather than numerically, and implicitly rather than explicitly. The correspondences between the operand fields of a machine language instruction and those of an assembly language instruction were given in figure 3.4. The choice of which operand format to use depends on the instruction's type. The functional summary of mnemonic opcodes in figure 3.6 and the alphabetical summary in Appendix A state each instruction's type. Without knowledge of an instruction's type or knowledge of how the operand must be specified for that type of instruction, a programmer cannot write an assembly language instruction correctly.

The use of base-displacement addressing in the IBM 360 and 370 systems requires that there be statements in each assembly language source module that specify the implied base register and base address to the Assembler and that cause the base address to be loaded into the implied base register at run time. The convention adopted for use in the 360 and 370 systems is that Register 12 be used for the implied base register. In this book we will adhere to this convention by employing the following two statements in the order given:

BALR	12,0
USING	*,12

The first of these satisfies the run-time requirement; the second satisfies the assembly time requirement. In satisfying the convention in this way, we are restricted to creating object modules whose size does not exceed 4096 bytes. In chapter 9 we will see how to circumvent this restriction. We will also see that Registers 1, 13, 14, and 15 have conventionally recognized purposes in calling subroutines. Because of these conventions and because the same registers are used by all input/output macros, programmers should avoid using these registers except in conjunction with subroutines and system macros. Registers 2 through 11 have no restrictions associated with their use.

EXERCISES

1. What is the difference in meaning between the phrase "the contents of a memory location" and the phrase "the address of a memory location"?

2. In the following assembly language ADD instruction, what is the purpose of the name-field symbol LOOP?

name field	opcode	operand
LOOP	A	3,X

In this instruction, what meaning does the Assembler attach to the number 3 in the operand?

3. Why is there no implicit form of operand in an assembly language RR-type instruction?

4. Analogous to the meanings of the symbols X, Y, and Z in the assembly language sequence

L	3,X
A	3,Y
ST	3,Z

what meanings should be attached to the variables X, Y, and Z in the FORTRAN assignment statement

$$Z = X + Y$$

5. The following questions pertain to the BALR-USING sequence:

BALR	12,0
USING	*,12

   a. What would be the effect at assembly time if the BALR instruction were omitted from this sequence?

   b. What would be the effect at assembly time if the USING directive were omitted from this sequence?

c. Why must the BALR instruction precede the USING directive as shown? Why couldn't the sequence be written in the reverse order, as

```
USING     *,12
BALR      12,0
```

and still achieve exactly the same purpose as the given sequence?

6. What is fundamentally incorrect about the following revision to the six statements required at the beginning of each source module, and why is it incorrect?

```
BOMB      CSECT
          STM       14,12,12(13)
          ST        13,SAVE+4
          LA        13,SAVE
          BALR      12,0
          USING     *,12
```

7. Assume that Register 12 has been designated as the implied base register by the BALR-USING sequence:

```
BALR      12,0
USING     *,12
```

Assume also that the address placed in Register 12 by the BALR 12,0 instruction is 000006. What implied displacements would be required to represent each of the following effective addresses in base-displacement form:

```
00012C
00FF2A
000006
00008E
001005
```

8. In an expression such as SAVE+4, which is used in the instruction

```
ST        13,SAVE+4
```

the Assembler determines the value of the symbol SAVE, adds 4 to that value, and generates the base-displacement address for the sum. Suppose that the value of SAVE is 000F4C, and suppose that Register 12 has been designated as the implied base register with base address 00001E. What is the base-displacement address corresponding to each of the operands in the following instructions:

a. L   5,4(1)   **d.** ST   6,SAVE(4)
b. ST   5,SAVE   **e.** L   11,SAVE+4(8)
c. L   6,SAVE+4   **f.** ST   11,SAVE−4

9. What base address always results from use of the convention that the first six statements in a source module be:

```
PROG      CSECT
          STM       14,12,12(13)
          BALR      12,0
          USING     *,12
          ST        13,SAVE+4
          LA        13,SAVE
```

Given this convention and resulting base address, what is the largest possible value of the symbol SAVE in a source module? What is the base-displacement form of address corresponding to that value of SAVE? In what way does this limit the size of an object module?

10. Suppose that, at load time, the Loader program places the object module into main memory beginning at address 02000_{16}. Assuming that the source module statements were written in accordance with the conventions stated in Exercise 9, what would be the memory addresses of the first four instructions in the program at run time? What would be the base address at run time? If the value of the symbol SAVE was 000248 at assembly time, what effective address would be represented at run time by the B2,D2 field of the assembled ST 13,SAVE+4 instruction?

11. Suppose that the contents of Registers 4, 5, and 6 are 000000, 000004, and 000008, respectively. Suppose also that the value of the symbol X is 00020A. What effective addresses would be represented by the second operand field of each of the following RX-type ADD instructions?

> A   8,X(4)
> A   8,X(5)
> A   8,X(6)

12. In some computer systems, the concept of base-displacement addresses is not employed. Instead, the memory address field of each instruction contains a single binary integer, which itself *is* the desired effective address. If in such a system the memory address field is 16 bits in length, what is the largest effective address that can be represented in an instruction? If in such a system the Assembler assigns addresses beginning at 0000 and the Loader places an object module into main memory beginning at address 0800, what would be required before that object module could be run?

13. From the summary given in figure 3.6 together with the names and properties of the instructions given in Appendix A, we can determine a few general characteristics of the mnemonic opcodes and the instructions they represent. For example, the opcodes of almost all RR-type instructions end in the letter R to remind us of their type; almost all operations on binary integers are either RR or RX instructions; and there is no single instruction that can be used to calculate a square root, or perform exponentiation, or compute more complicated mathematical functions. Missing from the summaries are any instructions that perform input or output, since, as was mentioned in chapter 1, these are all privileged instructions. What other patterns and general characteristics can you determine from these summaries?

PART
TWO

Fundamental Techniques

4

Elementary Operations:
Loops and Integer I/O

The manner in which registers are used for the computation of an effective address at run time was discussed in chapter 3. In this chapter, we will demonstrate some of the other uses of registers: for integer computations, array variable subscripts, and loop control.

The chapter begins with an explanation of how to add two integers. Next methods of defining integer constants and of reserving memory space for integers are described. In Section 4.3 the instructions required to translate the binary representation of nonnegative integers into a character representation that can be used for printed output are summarized. Section 4.4 covers the reverse translation process, character input to binary integer. Handling of negative integers is illustrated in the end-of-chapter exercises.

The important question of how loops may be initialized and controlled in Assembly Language is introduced in Sections 4.5 and 4.6. To demonstrate the use of loop-control techniques, we will show how to add two integer arrays. This also introduces the notions of subscripts and of memory allocation for one-dimensional arrays.

The chapter concludes with a brief discussion of some assembly language programming considerations.

4.1 ADDITION OF TWO BINARY INTEGERS

To add two binary integers in the IBM 360 and 370, the arithmetic must be done in a register. For example, to add the binary integers that are located at symbolic addresses X and Y, the programmer must decide which of the 16 registers to use, copy one of the integers into that register, and add the other integer to it. Using Register 3, the following two instructions will compute the sum of the two integers:

```
        L         3,X
        A         3,Y
```

The Load instruction L 3,X copies the integer that is at symbolic address X into Register 3. In doing so, it replaces whatever was previously in Register 3 but does not alter or erase the integer at X. The Add instruction A 3,Y adds the integer that is at symbolic address Y to the contents of Register 3. The sum replaces the integer that had been loaded into Register 3 by the previous instruction, but the number being added—the integer at symbolic address Y—is not changed.

Now, if we want to use Register 3 for any other purpose, we must first copy the sum out of that register because it may be replaced or altered by a subsequent instruction using that register. Therefore, the usual sequence for adding two binary integers is

```
        L         3,X
        A         3,Y
        ST        3,Z
```

The Store instruction ST 3,Z copies the sum into the memory location whose symbolic address is Z. In doing so, it replaces whatever was previously at that location but does not alter or erase the contents of Register 3. Once the sum is copied into a memory location, Register 3 can be used for other purposes.

In using the implicit form of address in each of the previous three RX-type instructions, namely

opcode   R1,S2

we have tacitly assumed that a base address and implied base register have been established in the program containing the instructions. This assumption is necessary in order to avoid having to use the explicit base-displacement form of address. The assumption also has one other consequence: In choosing a register for our computation, we were free to choose any register *except* the implied base register. Had we chosen the implied base register, Register 12, then a load instruction such as

L   12,X

would have replaced the base address with the integer that is at symbolic address X. The computation of the effective address in the execution of subsequent instructions would therefore probably have produced incorrect results. Consequently, in this text Register 12 will be used only as the implied base register. Similar considerations will cause us to avoid using Registers 0, 1, 13, 14, and 15 for computations.

4.2 BINARY INTEGER CONSTANTS AND MEMORY ALLOCATION

The example of the preceding section gives rise to two questions: How is integer data specified in an assembly language program, and how can memory space be reserved for results of calculations?

There are two methods for specifying binary integer constants. One is to define the constants by means of a directive designed for that purpose. The other is to specify the constants in the instructions that are to use them. The directive that is used to define an integer constant is the Define Constant (DC) directive, written in its simplest form as

name field	opcode	operand
{any symbol, or blank}	DC	F'x'

In the operand, the letter x denotes a signed or unsigned decimal integer. The Assembler converts that integer to its binary representation, and the symbol in the name field becomes the symbolic address of that integer. For example, if these statements were in an assembly language program,

```
X    DC    F'40'
Y    DC    F'-10'
```

then the Load and Add instructions of the previous section,

```
L    3,X
A    3,Y
```

would compute the sum of $+40$ and -10, i.e., $+30$.

Alternatively, the constants could be specified in the operand of the Load and/or Add instruction as

```
L    3,=F'40'
A    3,=F'-10'
```

In this case, there need be no corresponding DC directive. The Assembler generates the binary representation of the constant so specified, and assigns an address to it. The notation $=$F'x' where x denotes a signed or unsigned decimal integer is known as a *literal* constant. Other types of literal constants, and other forms of the DC directive, will be discussed in chapter 6.

To reserve memory space for the result of a calculation, we use the Define Storage (DS) directive. In its simplest form, it is written

name field	opcode	operand
{any symbol, or blank}	DS	F

In the operand, the letter *F* denotes that one full word is to be reserved. The symbol in the name field becomes the symbolic address of that word. To continue the example, we can now write these statements in an assembly language program:

```
              L      3,X
              A      3,Y
              ST     3,Z
              .
              .
              .
    X         DC     F'40'
    Y         DC     F'-10'
    Z         DS     F
```

The three dots indicate that there are other statements in the program between the ST instruction and the DC directive. Since the CPU cannot distinguish an instruction from data, do not intermix instructions with DC or DS directives. If there were no instructions following the ST that would ultimately terminate the program's execution at run time, then the CPU would, as it proceeded from one instruction to the next, attempt to execute data as though they were instructions! At best, the result would be undesirable; most likely, the program would be terminated due to an invalid instruction.

It is possible to use the DS directive to reserve more than one memory location, as would be needed for an array. We will see how to do this shortly. Other forms of the DS directive will be described in chapter 6.

4.3 PRINTING NONNEGATIVE INTEGERS

You will recall that the representation of integer data in memory is different from that used by most input and output devices. Integer data used for arithmetic purposes are represented in the binary number system, whereas all data transmitted between memory and most input and output devices are in character format. In the IBM 360 and 370 systems, the EBCDIC character format is used. This consists of a unique 8-bit code for each letter, digit, punctuation mark, and other symbol that can be typed at a keyboard, displayed at a terminal, or printed by a printer.

In producing a line of printed output, the hardware literally copies each line, character by character, from main memory to the printer device. This means that each line must be set up in memory in exactly the form in which it is to be transmitted to the printer. Therefore, *to print an integer that is represented in binary form in memory, it must first be converted to its character form.*

There is no single instruction in the IBM 360 or 370 systems that converts a binary integer to its representation as a decimal integer in character form. Instead, a sequence of instructions must be used. In this section, we present the instructions that are required to convert nonnegative integers to a form suitable for printing and discuss the manner in which the DC and DS directives can be used to allocate memory areas for the characters that are to be printed. A similar but slightly more complex procedure is used to convert negative integers; this will be discussed in Exercise 11 at the end of the chapter.

The conversion procedures to be discussed are the same whether you are using Assembly Language in OS or in DOS. The difference between the two systems is not in the conversion process but in the output process; namely, the use of OPEN, PUT, CLOSE, and DCB or DTF macros. Since this was already discussed in Section 2.4, we will confine our examples to OS output procedures.

Allocating a Memory Area

It is characteristic of virtually all printers that each printed line consists of a fixed number of print positions (the same number for each line), that each printed character—including blanks—may only be printed in a print position, and that no two characters may be printed in the same position of a given line. For the high-speed printers to which we restrict our attention, the number of print positions per line is 132.

Therefore, to allocate a memory area sufficient to accommodate any printed line, 132 bytes of memory must be reserved for the entire line. Some of these bytes must be allocated for the integers that are to be printed, others for any text that is also to be printed, and the remainder for blanks that fill out the line. Each such allocation will designate the print positions that are to be used.

To achieve the desired allocations, we will use the following four forms of the DC and DS directives:

1. To define the beginning and length of a printed line:

   LINE   DS   0CL132   The first operand character is zero.

2. To reserve space for an integer that consists of n characters, including one position for the sign:

   symbol   DS   CLn n is an unsigned decimal integer, and *symbol* is any valid name-field symbol.

3. To define text that is to be printed on the line:

   DC   C'...'   the three dots represent any text characters other than an apostrophe (') or an ampersand (&).

4. To assign m blanks to unused print positions:

   DC   CLm' ' m, an unsigned decimal integer, is the number of consecutive blanks to be printed; the apostrophes enclose a single blank.

As an example of the use of these directives, suppose we wanted to print the following line in order to see the result of the addition processes described earlier.

Then the directives to be used are those shown here:

```
LINE   DS   0CL132      DEFINE THE BEGINNING AND LENGTH OF THE LINE
       DC   CL7' '      DEFINE 7 CONSECUTIVE BLANKS
       DC   C'THE SUM IS '   DEFINE TEXT THAT IS TO BE PRINTED
SUM    DS   CL6         RESERVE 6 POSITIONS FOR THE INTEGER
       DC   CL108' '    DEFINE 108 CONSECUTIVE BLANKS
```

Except for the printing of leading zeroes, the following FORTRAN format statement will provide the same print position definitions:

FORMAT (7X, 'THE SUM IS ', I6, 108X)

In COBOL, a working storage definition for this print line might be

01	LINE.		
	02	FILLER	PICTURE X(7)	VALUE SPACES.
	02	FILLER	PICTURE X(11)	VALUE 'THE SUM IS '.
	02	SUM	PICTURE 9(6).	
	02	FILLER	PICTURE X(108)	VALUE SPACES.

It should be noted that in Assembly Language, as in FORTRAN and COBOL, the print positions are designated relative to the beginning of the line, by the sequence in which the information is specified and by the number of positions reserved for each item.

Conversion from Binary to Character Representation

Conversion of an integer from its representation in the binary number system to its representation as a sequence of decimal digits in character form is not a trivial process. For example, the binary integer representation of 12_{10} is

0000 0000 0000 0000 0000 0000 0000 1100

whereas its representation as the two digits 1 and 2 in character form is

$$\underbrace{1111\quad 0001}_{1}\qquad\underbrace{1111\quad 0010}_{2}$$

In the IBM 360 and 370 systems, there are instructions that enable the conversion to be done in two steps: (1) the binary integer is converted to its representation as a binary-coded decimal number by means of the Convert to Decimal (CVD) instruction, and (2) the binary-coded decimal representation is converted to its EBCDIC character representation by means of the Unpack (UNPK) instruction. This two-step process works for negative as well as nonnegative integers, but the manner in which the sign is handled is not entirely satisfactory in either case. Whether the binary integer being converted is negative or nonnegative, its sign is encoded into the low-order digit of the EBCDIC representation by the UNPK instruction.

For example, the binary representation of $+12_{10}$ would be converted not to the two characters 1 and 2, but to the characters 1 and B; the representation of -12_{10} would be converted to the characters 1 and K. The B represents the 2 encoded as $+2$, the K the 2 encoded as -2. In general, low-order digits (1,2,3,...,9) are encoded, respectively, as A,B,C,...,I for positive numbers and as J,K,L,...,R for negative numbers. A low-order zero digit is encoded as a left-brace { if the number is zero or positive, and as a right-brace } if it is negative. Since it is awkward to read numbers with their low-order digits encoded, instructions that supplement the CVD and UNPK instructions are used to decode the sign's representation.

There are a number of ways to resolve the sign problem. Some general solutions will be discussed in Sections 12.8 and 12.9. The representation known as binary-coded decimal, or packed decimal, will also be discussed at length in chapter 12. For present purposes, we will restrict our attention to the simplest case, that in which the numbers to be converted are either positive or zero. In this case, the conversion can be accomplished in four instructions, provided we impose the following conditions: *all nonnegative integers will be printed as ten-digit numbers, without punctuating commas, and with leading zeroes printed as zeroes. The sign will not be printed.*

For example, the number $+12$ would be printed as 0000000012, the number 123,456,789 would be printed as 0123456789, and the number 0 would be printed as 0000000000.

The sequence of four instructions required to convert a binary integer to the form just described is shown below and in figure 4.1. As can be seen from the figure, these instructions must be supplemented with three directives: one that defines the binary integer that is to be converted, one that allocates the 10-byte memory area required for the character form of the number, and one that reserves an area for the intermediate binary-coded decimal representation created by the CVD instruction.

There are a lot of details to learn, but it is not necessary at this point to know how the conversion instructions work. For now you only need to know how to write the required instructions and directives. A more detailed explanation will be given in chapter 12.

The four conversion instructions are:

```
L       5,Z             COPY THE BINARY INTEGER INTO A REGISTER
CVD     5,BCD           CONVERT IT TO BINARY-CODED DECIMAL FORM
UNPK    SUM,BCD         CONVERT THAT TO CHARACTER FORM
OI      SUM+9,X'F0'     ELIMINATE THE SIGN CODE IN LOW-ORDER DIGIT
```

It should be emphasized that these four instructions will convert *any* 32-bit nonnegative binary integer to the character form described provided that these procedures are followed:

1. The address of the binary integer must be specified in the second operand of the Load (L) instruction.
2. The address of the ten-byte memory area that is allocated for the character representation of the number must be specified in the first operand of the UNPK instruction.
3. The address of the *low-order digit* of the ten-byte character area must be specified in the first operand of the OI instruction.
4. The address of the area reserved for the intermediate binary-coded decimal representation must be specified in the second operand of both the CVD and the UNPK instructions.

Note that any register may be used by the L and CVD instructions, but the same register must be used by both instructions. Note also that in reserving an area for the intermediate binary-coded decimal representation, we have used a DS directive whose operand contains the single letter D. This reserves eight bytes on a double-word boundary, an alignment required in the IBM 360 but optional in the IBM 370.

Figure 4.1 Program to print the sum of two binary integers.

```
PRINTEX  CSECT
*
*    THIS PROGRAM WILL COMPUTE THE SUM OF TWO BINARY INTEGERS,
*     CONVERT THE SUM TO A 10-BYTE CHARACTER FORM SUITABLE FOR
*     PRINTING, AND PRINT THE RESULT.
*
*    THE CONVERSION PROCESS USED IS VALID ONLY FOR NONNEGATIVE
*     INTEGERS: I.E., THE SUM IN THIS PROCESS IS PRINTED AS A
*     10-DIGIT NUMBER WITHOUT PUNCTUATING COMMAS, WITH LEADING
*     ZEROES PRINTED AS ZEROES, AND WITH THE SIGN NOT PRINTED.
*
*    THE INTEGERS USED TO COMPUTE THE SUM ARE DEFINED WITHIN THE
*     PROGRAM: THEY ARE NOT READ AS INPUT DATA.
         STM    14,12,12(13)    STANDARD ENTRY
         BALR   12,0
         USING  *,12
         ST     13,SAVE+4
         LA     13,SAVE
*
         OPEN   (PRINTER,(OUTPUT))   OPEN THE PRINTER OUTPUT FILE
* ADD
         L      3,X             COMPUTE THE SUM OF THE INTEGERS GIVEN
         A      3,Y             AT SYMBOLIC ADDRESSES X & Y, AND
         ST     3,Z             STORE THE SUM AT SYMBOLIC ADDRESS Z.
* CONVERT
         L      5,Z             COPY THE SUM INTO REGISTER 5
         CVD    5,BCD           CONVERT IT TO BINARY-CODED DECIMAL FORM
         UNPK   SUM,BCD         CONVERT THAT TO CHARACTER (EBCDIC) FORM
         OI     SUM+9,X'F0'     ELIMINATE SIGN CODE IN LO-ORDER DIGIT.
* PRINT
         PUT    PRINTER,LINE    WRITE THE SUM, TOGETHER WITH TEXT, ONTO
* EXIT                          THE PRINTER.
         CLOSE  (PRINTER)
         L      13,SAVE+4       STANDARD EXIT
         LM     14,12,12(13)
         BR     14
*
* INTEGER CONSTANTS, AND AREA RESERVED FOR THEIR SUM
X        DC     F'437'          BINARY REPRESENTATION OF DECIMAL +437
Y        DC     F'562'          BINARY REPRESENTATION OF DECIMAL +562
Z        DS     F               BINARY SUM, TO BE CONVERTED TO EBCDIC
* AREA RESERVED FOR INTERMEDIATE BINARY-CODED DECIMAL REPRESENTATION
BCD      DS     D               8 BYTES RESERVED ON DOUBLE-WORD BOUNDARY
* AREA RESERVED FOR 132-BYTE PRINT LINE
LINE     DS     0CL132          BEGINNING AND LENGTH OF LINE
         DC     CL7' '            COLS  1 - 7    BLANK
         DC     C'THE SUM IS '         8 - 18    EXPLANATORY TEXT
SUM      DS     CL10                  19 - 28    10-BYTE SUM
         DC     CL104' '              29 - 132   BLANK
*
*   DATA CONTROL BLOCK FOR OUTPUT TO PRINTER
PRINTER  DCB    DSORG=PS,MACRF=(PM),DDNAME=SYSPRINT,RECFM=FB,         X
               LRECL=132,BLKSIZE=4092
* REQUIRED STATEMENTS:
SAVE     DS     18F
         END
```

4.4 READING NONNEGATIVE INTEGER INPUT DATA

As discussed, conversion from binary integer to character form is not a trivial process. Neither is the reverse conversion trivial. The reverse conversion is done as a two-step process in the IBM 360 and 370 systems. The PACK instruction converts from character form to binary-coded decimal, and the Convert to Binary (CVB) converts from binary-coded decimal to 32-bit binary integer form. The PACK-CVB sequence, the counterpart of the CVD-UNPK sequence used for printing, suffers the same limitation in its handling of the sign. Whereas negative as well as nonnegative integers may be converted, the PACK instruction assumes that the sign is encoded in the low-order digit of the character representation, using the same sign-encoding scheme that is used by the UNPK instruction.

At this stage, we will avoid these sign considerations as much as possible. Therefore, in this section we present the instructions and supplementary DC and DS directives that can be used to convert nonnegative integers from character form to 32-bit binary integer form. One method of handling negative integers will be described in Exercise 12 at the end of this chapter. We impose the conditions that *the character form of the decimal integer occupies exactly ten positions, right-justified with either leading zeroes or leading blanks. Its sign is omitted; it is assumed to be nonnegative.*

For example, either of these are acceptable forms for the decimal integer $+12_{10}$, the symbol ⌣ denoting one blank:

$$\text{⌣ ⌣ ⌣ ⌣ ⌣ ⌣ ⌣ ⌣ } 12 \qquad \text{or} \qquad 0000000012$$

but the following two forms are not acceptable under the above conditions:

$$\text{⌣ ⌣ ⌣ ⌣ ⌣ ⌣ ⌣ } +12 \qquad \qquad +0000000012$$

The instructions and directives used in the conversion procedures when reading integers are the same whether you use OS or DOS Assembly Language. It is only the input procedure—OPEN, GET, CLOSE, and DCB or DTF macros—that differs between OS and DOS. Since this was discussed in Section 2.4, we will restrict our examples to OS input procedures.

Allocating a Memory Area

In reading a line or card of input data, the hardware literally copies each line or card character by character from the input device into main memory. This means that an area of memory equal to the length of the line or card must be reserved for the data transmission. Although we will deal only with 80-column cards, you should recognize that the same principles hold for terminal line input.

Each column of a card may be thought of as a card character *position,* analogous to print line positions. Each of the 80 positions contains exactly one character, which may of course be a blank. We therefore reserve 80 bytes of memory for the entire card, allocate some of these bytes for the integers that are to be read, others for additional data that may be on the card, and the remainder for the blanks. Each such allocation will designate the card positions occupied by the data. We use the same forms of the DC and DS directives that were used for printer output.

For example, given the card format

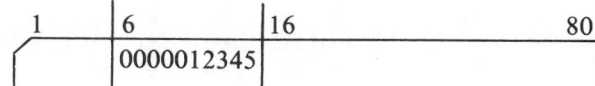

then the directives required to allocate the memory area for the card data can be written as shown below. Note that both of the DC directives could be DS directives without changing the meaning, since the data that are read from the card will replace the blanks defined by the DC's. But that is a relatively unimportant detail.

```
CARD    DS      0CL80       DEFINE BEGINNING AND LENGTH OF CARD
        DC      CL5' '      RESERVE 5 BYTES FOR UNUSED POSITIONS
INT     DS      CL10        10 BYTES FOR CHARACTER FORM OF INTEGER
        DC      CL65' '     65 BYTE POSITIONS FOR REMAINDER OF CARD
```

Conversion from Character Form to 32-Bit Binary Integer Form

Under the conditions imposed at the beginning of this section—namely that the character form of a decimal integer consist of exactly ten bytes, that the integer be nonnegative, that the sign not be represented, and that either leading zeroes or leading blanks may be used to the left of the most significant digit—only three instructions are required for the conversion to 32-bit binary integer form. These are:

```
PACK    BCD,INT    CONVERT FROM CHAR. FORM TO BINARY-CODED DECIMAL
CVB     5,BCD      CONVERT THAT TO 32-BIT BINARY IN REGISTER 5
ST      5,X        STORE THE BINARY FORM AT SYMBOLIC ADDRESS X
```

The symbolic address INT was defined by the DS directive given above.

```
INT    DS    CL10      RESERVE 10 BYTES FOR THE CHARACTER REPRESENTATION
```

The symbolic address BCD must be defined, as when performing the reverse conversion for output, as follows:

```
BCD    DS    D         RESERVE 8 BYTES ON A DOUBLE-WORD BOUNDARY
```

And the symbolic address X must be defined by a DS directive of the following form:

```
X      DS    F         RESERVE ONE FULL WORD FOR A 32-BIT BINARY INTEGER
```

It should be noted that these three instructions can be used to convert *any* decimal integer represented in character form under the previously mentioned conditions. The requirements are:

1. The address of the 10-byte memory area that is allocated for the input character representation of the number must be specified in the second operand of the PACK instruction.
2. The address of the area reserved for the intermediate binary-coded decimal representation of the number must be specified in the first operand of the PACK instruction and in the second operand of the CVB instruction.
3. The address of the area reserved for the binary integer must be specified in the second operand of the ST instruction.

Note that any register may be used by the CVB and ST instructions, but the same register must be used by both instructions.

A program that will read a card containing two nonnegative integers, compute their sum, and write the sum on the printer is given in figure 4.2. Note that only one GET macro is used; it reads the entire contents of the card. As in chapter 2, the card is assumed to be in the input data stream.

4.5 ADDITION OF INTEGER ARRAYS: THE BCT AND LA INSTRUCTIONS

Suppose there are two sets of integers, $\{X\}$ and $\{Y\}$, whose components are indicated by subscripts

$$X_1, X_2, X_3,...,X_n$$
$$Y_1, Y_2, Y_3,...,Y_n$$

In FORTRAN, we could add each corresponding pair of integers to produce a third set, $\{Z\}$, by means of a DO-loop such as

```
       DO   10   J = 1,N
             Z(J) = X(J) + Y(J)
  10         CONTINUE
```

In FORTRAN, the variable J can serve both as the loop-control variable and as the subscript. In Assembly Language, we frequently use separate variables for loop control and subscripts. Both subscripting and loop control are accomplished by means of registers: loop control is accomplished by counting the number of iterations using a counter in a register, and subscripting is accomplished by using an index register in RX-type instructions.

The simplest way to control the number of iterations in a loop is to determine how many iterations are desired, and either count up (by 1's) to that number or count down (again by 1's) to zero. These methods work even though the number of iterations may depend on the data, as it does in the FORTRAN DO-loop.

Figure 4.2　*Program to read two integers and print their sum.*

```
RDPRT      CSECT
*
*     THIS PROGRAM READS TWO NONNEGATIVE INTEGERS FROM A DATA CARD
*       THAT IS IN THE INPUT DATA STREAM, COMPUTES THEIR SUM, AND
*       PRINTS THE RESULT IN A SINGLE LINE ON THE PRINTER.
*
*     THE INPUT DATA IS ASSUMED TO BE REPRESENTED AS 10-BYTE UNSIGNED
*       DECIMAL INTEGERS, WITH EITHER LEADING ZEROES OR LEADING BLANKS.
*
*     THE SUM IS PRINTED AS A 10-BYTE UNSIGNED DECIMAL INTEGER, WITH
*       LEADING ZEROES PRINTED AS ZEROES.
*
           STM    14,12,12(13)     STANDARD ENTRY
           BALR   12,0
           USING  *,12
           ST     13,SAVE+4
           LA     13,SAVE
*
*     OPEN  INPUT AND OUTPUT FILES
           OPEN   (TRANS,(INPUT))      CARDS FROM INPUT DATA STREAM
           OPEN   (PRINTER,(OUTPUT))   PRINTER IS SYSOUT
*
*     READ ONE DATA CARD
           GET    TRANS,CARD           INPUT AREA IS 'CARD'
*
*     CONVERT EACH NUMBER TO 32-BIT BINARY
           PACK   BCD,INT1             FIRST INTEGER IS AT 'INT1'
           CVB    5,BCD                ITS 32-BIT BINARY INTEGER FORM IS
           ST     5,X                   STORED AT 'X'.
           PACK   BCD,INT2             SECOND INTEGER IS AT 'INT2'.
           CVB    5,BCD                ITS 32-BIT BINARY INTEGER FORM IS
           ST     5,Y                   STORED AT 'Y'.
*
*     COMPUTE THE SUM, AND STORE BINARY INTEGER RESULT AT 'Z'.
           L      3,X                  COMPUTE THE SUM OF THE INTEGERS GIVEN
           A      3,Y                  AT SYMBOLIC ADDRESSES X & Y, AND
           ST     3,Z                  STORE THE SUM AT SYMBOLIC ADDRESS Z.
*
*     CONVERT THE SUM TO UNSIGNED 10-BYTE CHAR. FORM WITH LEADING ZEROES.
           L      5,Z                  PUT THE SUM IN A REGISTER
           CVD    5,BCD                CONVERT IT TO BINARY-CODED DEC.
           UNPK   SUM,BCD              CONVERT THAT TO CHAR (EBCDIC)
           OI     SUM+9,X'F0'          ELIMINATE SIGN CODE
*
*     PRINT THE RESULT
           PUT    PRINTER,LINE
*
*     EXIT FROM PROGRAM
EOJ        CLOSE  (PRINTER)            CLOSE ALL FILES
           CLOSE  (TRANS)
           L      13,SAVE+4            STANDARD EXIT
           LM     14,12,12(13)
           BR     14
*
*     AREAS RESERVED FOR TWO BINARY INTEGERS AND THEIR SUM
X          DS     F                    BINARY REPRESENTATION OF INTEGER AT 'INT1'
Y          DS     F                    BINARY REPRESENTATION OF INTEGER AT 'INT2'
Z          DS     F                    SUM OF 'X' AND 'Y' INTEGERS
*
*     AREA RESERVED FOR INTERMEDIATE BINARY-CODED DECIMAL REPRESENTATION
BCD        DS     D                    SAME AREA USED FOR ALL CONVERSIONS
```

Figure 4.2 **continued**

```
*
*   AREA RESERVED FOR 80-BYTE INPUT CARD
CARD      DS      0CL80          BEGINNING AND LENGTH OF AREA
          DS      CL5            COLS  1 - 5  UNUSED
INT1      DS      CL10               6 - 15  FIRST 10-BYTE DECIMAL INTEGER
          DS      CL5               16 - 20  UNUSED
INT2      DS      CL10              21 - 30  SECOND 10-BYTE DECIMAL INTEGER
          DS      CL50              31 - 80  UNUSED
*
*   AREA RESERVED FOR 132-BYTE PRINT LINE
LINE      DS      0CL132             BEGINNING AND LENGTH OF LINE
          DC      CL7' '         COLS  1 - 7  BLANK
          DC      C'THE SUM IS '        8 - 18  EXPLANATORY TEXT
SUM       DS      CL10                 19 - 28  10-BYTE SUM
          DC      CL104' '             29 - 132 BLANK
*
*   DATA CONTROL BLOCKS FOR INPUT AND OUTPUT FILES
*
TRANS     DCB     DSORG=PS,MACRF=(GM),DDNAME=SYSIN,EODAD=EOJ,RECFM=FB,      X
                  LRECL=80,BLKSIZE=4080
PRINTER   DCB     DSORG=PS,MACRF=(PM),DDNAME=SYSPRINT,RECFM=FB,             X
                  LRECL=132,BLKSIZE=4092
*
*   REQUIRED STATEMENTS
*
SAVE      DS      18F
          END
```

In the IBM 360 and 370, there is one instruction especially suited to controlling the number of loop iterations by the method of "counting down by 1's." That is the Branch on Count (BCT) instruction. It is an RX-type instruction, for which we will use the implicit format

opcode	operand
BCT	R1,S2

When a BCT instruction is executed, two things take place *in this order:*

1. First, a $+1$ is algebraically subtracted from the register designated by the first operand, R1, and the result is placed into that register.
2. Then the result obtained is tested to see if it is zero. If it is not zero, a branch is made to the address designated by the second operand. But if the result is zero, no branch is made; instead, execution proceeds at the instruction that immediately follows the BCT.

For example, suppose that the location whose symbolic address is N contains the binary integer $+5$. Then, in the sequence

```
              L       4,N
LOOP          ---     ---
              ---     ---
              ---     ---
              BCT     4,LOOP
              ---     ---
```

the four instructions beginning with the statement named LOOP will be repeated five times. The first time the instruction at LOOP is executed, Register 4 will contain $+5$. Then the BCT instruction will reduce that value to $+4$, and branch back to the instruction at LOOP. The second time the BCT instruction is executed, it will reduce the value in Register 4 from $+4$ to $+3$, and again branch back to LOOP. The third time the value will be reduced from $+3$ to $+2$, the fourth time from $+2$ to $+1$, and the fifth time from $+1$ to 0. At this point the BCT instruction will no longer branch; instead, the instruction following the BCT will be executed.

Figure 4.3 Placement of arrays in memory.

The elements of each array are 32-bit integers. Consequently, each occupies one full word. Consecutive integers in each array are stored in consecutive full words. The size of each array is assumed to be 12 full words ($N = 12$), for purposes of illustration.

Similarly, if we suppose that the location whose symbolic address is N contains any positive binary integer, then in the previous illustration the four instructions will be repeated n times, where n denotes the value of the integer at address N. Thus, n serves as the loop-control variable, or *counter*, for the loop.

To illustrate how the FORTRAN DO-loop given earlier can be implemented in Assembly Language, we must introduce two further concepts: (1) the manner in which an array is stored in memory and (2) the manner in which its individual components can be accessed using index registers.

The components of an array are stored in consecutive memory locations, as depicted in figure 4.3. Since we are concerned only with binary integers at this time, each component occupies one full word, which we assume is located at a full-word boundary. Thus the address of any component in the array can be determined once the address of the first component is known. If the first component's address is Z, then the second component's is $Z+4$, the third one is at $Z+8$, and so forth. In general, the address of Z_J for $J = 1,2,...$ is given by the formula

$$\begin{Bmatrix} \text{address} \\ \text{of } Z_J \end{Bmatrix} = \begin{Bmatrix} \text{address} \\ \text{of } Z_1 \end{Bmatrix} + \{4*(J-1)\}$$

Thus, if the index $4*(J-1)$ is in an index register, say Register 5, then the following three instructions will compute the sum $Z_J = X_J + Y_J$:

```
L        3,X(5)
A        3,Y(5)
ST       3,Z(5)
```

In this sequence, we are using the indexed implicit format for RX-type instructions,

$$\text{opcode} \quad R1,S2(X2)$$

At run time, the effective address computed for each of these three instructions is

instruction		effective address	
L	3,X(5)	address of X +	index in Register 5
A	3,Y(5)	address of Y +	index in Register 5
ST	3,Z(5)	address of Z +	index in Register 5

As shown in figure 4.3, the address of X is identical to that of X_1, and similarly for Y and Z. Thus, using the assumption that the index in Register 5 is $4*(J-1)$, it follows that the effective address computed when the L 3,X(5) instruction is executed is the address of X_J; the effective address computed when the A 3,Y(5) instruction is executed is the address of Y_J; and the effective address computed when the ST 3,Z(5) instruction is executed is the address of Z_J. In other words, when Register 5 contains $4*(J-1)$, the three instructions compute the sum $Z_J = X_J + Y_J$.

To compute each of the sums Z_J for $J = 1,2,...,N$, we use a loop containing the three instructions, repeat the loop N times, and on each repetition ensure that the appropriate index $4*(J-1)$, namely $0,4,8,...,4*(N-1)$, is in Register 5. To ensure that Register 5 contains the appropriate index during each repetition of the loop, we use the Load Address (LA) instruction. We could also use an add instruction to increase the contents of an index register by +4 or by any other number. But the use of LA has become fairly common for this type of operation because the constant to be added is generally a small positive number and can be specified in the displacement field. LA is an RX-type instruction that places the effective address specified in its second operand into the register designated in its first operand.

opcode	operand	explanation
LA	R1,S2	the effective address represented in implicit form by S2 is placed into the register whose address is specified in the R1 field
LA	R1,S2(X2)	the effective address computed by adding the index that is in register X2 to the address represented by S2 is placed into the register specified in the R1 field
LA	R1,D2(X2,B2)	the effective address computed by adding the displacement D2 to the sum of the index from register X2 and the base address from register B2 is placed into register R1
LA	R1,D2	the effective address is equal to the displacement and replaces the contents of register R1

When an LA instruction is executed, the effective address replaces the quantity that was in the R1 register. However, the effective address is computed using the quantities that existed in the base and index registers just *before* the instruction is executed. Therefore the R1 field may designate the same register as either or both of the X2 and B2 fields without affecting the manner in which the effective address is computed.

These descriptions of the LA's execution can be summarized by the formula

$$\left\{ \begin{array}{l} \text{contents of} \\ \text{the register} \\ \text{designated by} \\ \text{the R1 field} \end{array} \right\} = \left\{ \begin{array}{l} \text{effective} \\ \text{address} \\ \text{represented by} \\ \text{S2 or B2,D2} \end{array} \right\} + \left\{ \begin{array}{l} \text{contents of} \\ \text{the register} \\ \text{designated by} \\ \text{the X2 field} \end{array} \right\} = \left\{ \begin{array}{l} \text{base} \\ \text{address} \end{array} \right\} + \{\text{displacement}\} + \{\text{index}\}$$

Note that the sum indicated by the right-hand side of this formula is just the second-operand address that is computed by the CPU when executing any RX-type instruction, as was explained in chapter 3. That is why the instruction's name is "Load *Address*." As in all such address computations, it is only bits 8 through 31 of the designated registers that participate in the addition; the result is a 24-bit nonnegative address. Therefore, bits 0 through 7 of the R1 register are set to 0's. For similar reasons, the value assumed for the index is zero if the X2 field designates Register 0, and the value assumed for the base address is zero if the B2 field designates Register 0.

As illustrations of these concepts, suppose that the following conditions existed at run time just prior to the execution of each of the LA instructions shown below:

$$\text{contents of Register 5} = 00000550_{16}$$
$$\text{contents of Register 6} = 00000040_{16}$$
$$\text{symbolic address W} = 00000400_{16}$$

Then, after execution of each of these instructions, the contents of the registers would be as indicated here:

		before execution		after execution	
		Reg 5	Reg 6	Reg 5	Reg 6
LA	5,W	00000550	00000040	00000400	00000040
LA	5,W(6)	00000550	00000040	00000440	00000040
LA	5,4(5)	00000550	00000040	00000554	00000040
LA	5,4(5,6)	00000550	00000040	00000594	00000040
LA	5,4	00000550	00000040	00000004	00000040

Note that LA 5,4(5) adds +4 to the contents of Register 5. Note also that LA 5,4 is equivalent to LA 5,4(0,0); if a register address is omitted in the base or index field of an explicit operand the Assembler assumes that the omitted address is zero. Thus the effective address in R1,D2 format is simply equal to the displacement, since at run time the CPU always ignores the contents of Register 0 when it is used as an index register or base register. The LA instruction can therefore be used in R1,D2 format to load a nonnegative integer constant (in the previous case, +4) into a register. But note that since a displacement cannot be negative or greater than 4095_{10}, the instruction LA 5,−4 is invalid, as is LA 5,8000.

Given these descriptions of the BCT and LA instructions, the sequence of assembly language instructions that can be used to compute the sums $Z_J = X_J + Y_J$ for $J = 1,2,...,N$ is shown in figure 4.4. Since we

Figure 4.4   Adding two arrays (see fig. 4.3).

```
* STATEMENTS TO ADD TWO SETS OF INTEGERS, X(J) + Y(J) = Z(J)
*
* INITIALIZATION OF LOOP CONTROL VARIABLE AND SUBSCRIPT
          L      4,N             1: REG 4 GETS LOOP CONTROL COUNTER
          L      5,=F'0'         2: REG 5 GETS INITIAL INDEX, 0
*
* COMPUTATION WITHIN LOOP
LOOP      L      3,X(5)          3: REG 3 GETS X(J)
          A      3,Y(5)          4: Y(J) ADDED TO X(J)
          ST     3,Z(5)          5: RESULT STORED IN Z(J)
*
* LOOP CONTROL MECHANISM
          LA     5,4(5)          6: ADD 4 TO INDEX
          BCT    4,LOOP          7: REPEAT TILL NO MORE TO DO
          .
          .
          .
* DIRECTIVES TO RESERVE MEMORY AREAS FOR THE ARRAYS
Z         DS     12F             12 WORDS FOR Z ARRAY
Y         DS     12F             12 WORDS FOR Y ARRAY
X         DS     12F             12 WORDS FOR X ARRAY
N         DC     F'12'           NUMBER OF COMPONENTS IN EACH ARRAY
```

Fundamental Techniques

Figure 4.5 Partial trace for statements of Figure 4.4. (N = 12)

			index in Reg 5 is used in the role of a subscript	effective memory address = address used to access the Jth elements of X, Y, and Z (see fig. 4.3)	loop-control counter in Reg 4 = the number of times the loop is still to be repeated
Initialization steps			Reg 5	effective address	Reg 4
	L	4,N	Put loop-control counter into Reg 4	--		12
	L	5,=F'0'	Put initial value of index into Reg 5	0		12
First time through the loop					
LOOP	L	3,X(5)	Copy X₁ from memory into Reg 3	0	70= X₁'s addr	12
	A	3,Y(5)	Compute X₁ + Y₁ in Reg 3	0	40= Y₁'s addr	12
	ST	3,Z(5)	Copy sum from Reg 3 to Z₁ in memory	0	10= Z₁'s addr	12
	LA	5,4(5)	Increase index in Reg 5 by 4	4		12
	BCT	4,LOOP	Decr loop count by 1, and go to LOOP	4		11
Second time through the loop					
LOOP	L	3,X(5)	Copy X₂ from memory into Reg 3	4	74= X₂'s addr	11
	A	3,Y(5)	Computé X₂ + Y₂ in Reg 3	4	44= Y₂'s addr	11
	ST	3,Z(5)	Copy sum from Reg 3 to Z₂ in memory	4	14= Z₂'s addr	11
	LA	5,4(5)	Increase index in Reg 5 by 4	8		11
	BCT	4,LOOP	Decr loop count by 1, and go to LOOP	8		10
Third time through the loop					
LOOP	L	3,X(5)	Copy X₃ from memory into Reg 3	8	78= X₃'s addr	10
	A	3,Y(5)	Compute X₃ + Y₃ in Reg 3	8	48= Y₃'s addr	10
	ST	3,Z(5)	Copy sum from Reg 3 to Z₃ in memory	8	18= Z₃'s addr	10
	LA	5,4(5)	Increase index in Reg 5 by 4	12		10
	BCT	4,LOOP	Decr loop count by 1, and go to LOOP	12		9

want the index to be the successive values $0,4,8,...,4*(N-1)$, it is initialized to 0 and incremented by 4. And since we want the sums to be computed in a loop that is repeated N times, the loop control counter is initialized to the number of components in the arrays and reduced by $+1$ after each repetition of the loop.

The first three repetitions of the loop are described in figure 4.5, assuming that the number of components in the arrays is 12 and that the addresses assigned to the arrays are as shown in figure 4.3. Subsequent repetitions would be executed in similar fashion.

It should be noted that the machine language instructions corresponding to the instructions in figure 4.5 do not change during the execution of the loop at run time. It is the effective addresses that change, due to the changes in the index. Since an instruction's execution is dependent on the value of the effective address, it will access different memory locations for different effective addresses. But since the instructions themselves are not changed, the same loop could be used many times during execution of a program, provided that the loop-control counter and the index are initialized each time the loop is used.

Finally, note that the DS directives in figure 4.4 reserve memory for the array data but that no data is specified. It is assumed that some other portion of the program read the data, converted it to binary form, and stored it in the arrays.

4.6 FURTHER ASPECTS OF LOOP CONTROL: THE BXH AND BXLE INSTRUCTIONS

Either the *B*ranch on Inde*x* *H*igh (BXH) or the *B*ranch on Inde*x* *L*ess Than or *E*qual (BXLE) instruction can be used to cause three things to happen during each iteration of a loop: (1) incrementing or decrementing the index, (2) counting the number of iterations of the loop, and (3) testing to see whether the loop should be repeated. BXH is usually used when an index, and hence an effective address, is to be *decreased* during each repetition of a loop; BXLE, when an effective address is to be *increased* during each iteration. But each is general enough to be used in either situation, and both are very useful in manipulating arrays. Neither instruction will be used in the examples given in this textbook, since their functions can readily be accomplished by the methods already illustrated, and they are not as simple to use as are the methods already cited. The following brief descriptions therefore serve merely as an illustration of the capabilities of these two instructions.

When either the BXH or BXLE instruction is executed, the index is incremented by a factor that is specified by one of the operands of the instruction. The factor can be either positive or negative. After the index is incremented, it is compared to some limit, which is also specified by one of the operands in the instruction. The BXH instruction branches if the new index is higher than the limit; the BXLE instruction branches if the new index is lower than or equal to the limit. Like the increment, the limit may be a positive or negative number. The address to which the BXH and BXLE instructions branch is specified in an operand field of the instruction.

Thus, there are four factors that must be specified by the operand fields of a BXH or BXLE instruction: the index, the increment, the limit, and the branch address. The first three of these must be in registers whose addresses are designated in the operand fields. The branch address must be specified in the operand. This is done in the following manner. Both BXH and BXLE are RS-type instructions, which may be written in one of two forms

	opcode	operand
explicit form:	BXH	R1,R2,D3(B3)
	BXLE	R1,R2,D3(B3)
implicit form:	BXH	R1,R2,S3
	BXLE	R1,R2,S3

The three operand fields have the same meanings in both instructions: R1 designates the register that contains the *index*; R2 designates the register that contains the *increment*; and S3 and D3(B3) specify the *branch address*. The *limit,* (the number to which the index is compared after it has been incremented) *must be in an odd-numbered register* whose address depends on the R2 field. If the R2 field designates an odd-numbered register, then the limit is in that register; in this case, the limit and the increment are one and the same. If the R2 field designates an even-numbered register, then the limit is in the odd-numbered register whose address is one more than that designated by the R2 field. For example, if R2 designates Register 3, then both the increment and the limit are in Register 3; but if R2 designates Register 4, then the increment is in Register 4 and the limit is in Register 5.

Since three of the four quantities required for execution of the BXH and BXLE instructions must be in registers, it should be clear that before the loop iterations are begun, the index, increment, and limit must be placed into the registers. As an example, consider the following sequence of statements that could be used to compute the sums $Z_J = X_J + Y_J$ discussed earlier.

```
        L       7,LIMIT     ◄──── Load the limit into Register 7.
        L       6,INCR      ◄──── Load the increment into Register 6.
        L       5,=F'0'     ◄──── Initialize the index to be 0, in Register 5.
LOOP    L       3,X(5)  ⎫
        A       3,Y(5)  ⎬   ◄──── Same as in figure 4.4.
        ST      3,Z(5)  ⎭
        BXLE    5,6,LOOP    ◄──── Add the increment that is in Register 6 to the
                                  index that is in Register 5, and compare the re-
                                  sult to the limit that is in Register 7. If the new
                                  index is less than or equal to the limit, then branch
                                  to symbolic address LOOP; if it is more than the
                                  limit, do not branch.
```

In this sequence, it is assumed that the location whose symbolic address is INCR contains the constant 4, corresponding to the increment of 4 in the instruction LA 5,4(5) given in figure 4.4. It is also assumed that the location whose symbolic address is LIMIT contains the limit factor $4*(N-1)$, where N is the number of components in each of the arrays. Note that under these conditions, the above sequence accomplishes the same purpose as the sequence given in figure 4.4.

4.7 SOME PROGRAMMING CONSIDERATIONS

The computer programs that we shall be considering in this text have the overall structure depicted by the diagram

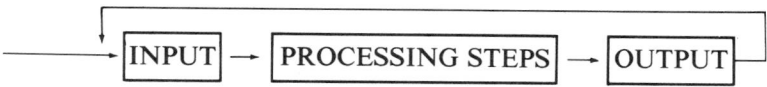

The meaning of this diagram is that each program obtains data from its input operations, processes those data to produce some output results, and then repeats the procedure. This iterative procedure is repeated until either there are no more data to be obtained, or until a processing step determines that no more processing is required.

In Assembly Language, the programmer must specify not only the processing steps but must also define all constants that are to be used at run time as well as reserve memory areas for all input and output data. In addition, the programmer must describe all the files that are to be used for input and output and indicate what is to be done when there are no more input data. It is good practice to separate all statements that constitute instructions and associated comments for input, processing, and output from those that constitute data, data areas, file descriptions, and comments associated with these.

Getting Started

Given what may seem to be a bewilderingly complex set of instructions and directives, the beginning assembly language programmer may well ask some fundamental questions at this point. For example, how does one decide what the processing steps should be for the solution to a given problem? Having decided the steps, in what order should they be carried out, and what should be the interrelationships among them? How are they to be coded in Assembly Language? How can the processing steps be expressed so that they are relatively easy to modify when it is necessary to accommodate new or previously unforeseen requirements?

There is no surefire formula for deciding what processing steps are needed to arrive at a programming solution to a problem or how best to represent them in Assembly Language. But there are certain ways of approaching a problem that may prove more fruitful than others. One way to think about technical problems in general, and a methodology for thinking about solving them, is described in G. Polya's book, *How to Solve It* (Princeton University Press, 1973). A collection of papers and a bibliography relevant to programming in particular is contained in *Tutorial on Software Design Techniques*, edited by Peter Freeman and Anthony Wasserman (IEEE Computer Society, 1976). Perhaps of overriding importance in following the guidelines given in these books is the following set of principles:

1. *You must understand the problem for which a programming solution is desired.* This means not only understanding the technical aspects of the problem but also the manner in which the solution is to be used so that the results can be presented in a useful manner. To do this you must know what results are expected, what input data will be provided, and what tools are available for solving the problem, e.g., formulas, existing solution procedures for all or part of the problem, and the capabilities and limitations of the programming language to be used.

2. *Before beginning to devise a programming solution to a problem, you must know how to solve the problem without a computer system.* This does not necessarily mean solving it but knowing *how* to solve it if there were sufficient time to do so.

A time-honored (and perhaps the best) way to determine how to solve a problem is to depict the solution by means of a flow diagram. This should be done *before* attempting to write the solution in a programming language, because once into the details of a programming solution, it is easy to lose sight of some aspects of the problem and/or solution and to fail to take them into account. In addition, a programmer can overlook similarities in various aspects of the solution that make the program easier to write and modify later, if necessary. For this reason, we will employ flow diagrams fairly often in this text. When not employed in the text, you may benefit from preparing your own diagram from the programming solution that is presented in order to better understand the logic used in the solution.

An alternative and more concise way to represent a solution procedure before coding it in Assembly Language is to write the solution in a suitable high-level language. We will sometimes write a portion of a solution as a set of FORTRAN statements as a means of specifying the solution procedure. You may find this approach useful for other programming problems. Any suitable high-level language can be used for this purpose.

The more programs you write, the better your understanding will be of the capabilities and limitations of Assembly Language. It is also helpful to study programs written by other persons. For these reasons, a number of programs are included in the text, and a number of programming problems are included in the exercises at the end of the chapter.

Detecting Errors

Errors in the logic of a procedure, as well as errors in the use of instructions and data constants, are often not detected until a program is run. However, many errors can be anticipated and corrected before running a program, by thinking through a programming solution instruction by instruction, mentally mimicking the way the CPU processes the instructions at run time. For this task, it is useful to have some systematic way of recording the expected actions of the CPU. One such method was illustrated in figure 4.5; similar techniques will be discussed in subsequent chapters. It is also extremely useful to design data that will test as many as possible of the different types of conditions that a program is expected to encounter at run time. Since it is not feasible to test every possible data condition that may arise, you should attempt to reduce the complexity of the solution's logic and thereby reduce the likelihood that there will be errors in logic. One means of achieving this is to reduce the number of interconnections among processing steps, by making each step have just one point at which it is entered and one from which it is exited. This is one of the cardinal rules of writing well-structured programs. In practice, this principle leads to the use of subroutines and macros and to a sharp reduction in the number of unconditional branches that might otherwise be used.

Despite all precautions, you may still find yourself with run-time programming errors that need to be unraveled and corrected. For this task the *memory dump* is an indispensable aid. The memory dump is a printing of the contents of a program's memory and registers and related information at the time an error occurred. Instructions on how to read memory dumps may be found in a number of sources, among them Rindfleisch's *Debugging System 360/370 Programs Using OS and VS Storage Dumps* (Prentice-Hall, 1976) and the IBM *Debugging Guide* manual (GC24–5093). An explanation of the numeric code that is printed on a memory dump to identify the immediate cause of a run-time error may be found in the IBM *System Messages* manual (GC38–1001). A summary of the run-time error conditions that are detectable by the CPU and that will generally cause program termination is given in Appendix D.

In addition to a memory dump, it is often useful when debugging an assembly language program to print selected portions of memory while a program is running and before an error occurs. This type of memory print is known as a snapshot, or *snap,* and is obtained in OS by the SNAP macro and in DOS by the PDUMP macro. The idea is to insert a SNAP or PDUMP macro into the source module at places where you would like to have the contents of the registers and/or selected memory locations printed at run time.

SNAP   The following summary shows the essential aspects of using SNAP and will prove satisfactory for most debugging needs. Figure 4.7 shows how to interpret the information that is printed by the SNAP macro. A complete discussion of the SNAP macro may be found in the IBM *Supervisor Services and Macro Instructions* manual (GC24–5103).

1. Before the first SNAP is executed, we must open the SNAP data set by using the OPEN macro

```
OPEN   (snapdcb,(OUTPUT))
```

where "snapdcb" is the name of the associated DCB macro described below.

2. Wherever we wish a snap of registers and memory locations, the following macro should be inserted:

name field	opcode	operand
{any symbol,} or blank	SNAP	DCB=snapdcb,ID=k,PDATA=(PSW,REGS),STORAGE=(s1,s2)

where   ID=k $(0 \leq k \leq 127)$ will be used to identify the snap on the snap listing
PDATA=(PSW,REGS) will cause printing of the PSW and all register contents
STORAGE=(s1,s2) will cause printing of memory contents between the symbolic addresses s1 and s2 inclusive.

It should be noted that the three parameters, ID=, PDATA=, and STORAGE=, may be given in any order, and any of them may be omitted. The DCB= parameter may not be omitted. The example in figure 4.7 shows one use of SNAP with PDATA omitted and one with it included.

3. As part of the program termination procedure, we should close the SNAP output file by using the CLOSE macro:

```
CLOSE   (snapdcb)
```

4. Among the constants and data areas, we must include the DCB macro that describes the SNAP output file, as follows[1]:

```
snapdcb   DCB   DSORG=PS,RECFM=VBA,MACRF=(W),BLKSIZE=1632,LRECL=125,   X
                DDNAME=snapdd
```

The name-field symbol 'snapdcb' must be the same as that used in the OPEN, SNAP, and CLOSE macros shown previously. The DDNAME= parameter must identify the following JCL statement in the execution step:

```
//snapdd   DD   SYSOUT=A
```

Note: When executing the OPEN, CLOSE, or SNAP macros, Register 13 must contain the address of the SAVE area. Execution of any of these macros may alter the contents of Registers 0, 1, 14, and 15, but all other register contents will remain intact. The use of PRINT NOGEN, as shown in figure 4.6, suppresses printing of the source and object code that is produced by the Assembler when it processes the macros. This makes the assembly listing easier to read and less lengthy than if PRINT NOGEN were not used (see chap. 14).

PDUMP   In DOS, run-time snapshots of memory and register contents are obtained via the PDUMP macro, which may be written in any of four ways:

opcode	operand
PDUMP	s1,s2
PDUMP	(r1),(r2)
PDUMP	(r1),s2
PDUMP	s1,(r2)

In each case, the first operand designates the starting memory address for the snapshot, and the second one designates the ending address. The ending address should not be less than the starting address.

When a parenthesized operand field (r1) or (r2) is used, the corresponding memory address is in a register. The address of that register is what is enclosed in the parentheses. When parentheses are not used, then we just specify a symbolic address s1 or s2, as illustrated below. In all four cases, the contents of all registers are always printed.

For example, the purpose of the SNAP macro shown in figure 4.6 can be achieved by either of these two forms of PDUMP:

```
PDUMP      SNAPTEST,SAVE
LA         5,SAVE
PDUMP      SNAPTEST,(5)
```

The PDUMP output is always placed on the SYSLST printer file. No JCL, DTF, or other I/O statements are required unless SYSLST is a disk file. If it *is* a disk file, then a SYSLST DTF is required, and an OPEN macro must immediately follow each execution of PDUMP. For further details, see IBM publication #GC33–5373, *DOS/VS Supervisor and I/O Macros.*

---

1. Before using the SNAP macro, you should verify that the LRECL= and BLKSIZE= values given in the DCB macro are the same as those required at the computer installation being used.

Figure 4.6 Example of use of SNAP macro.

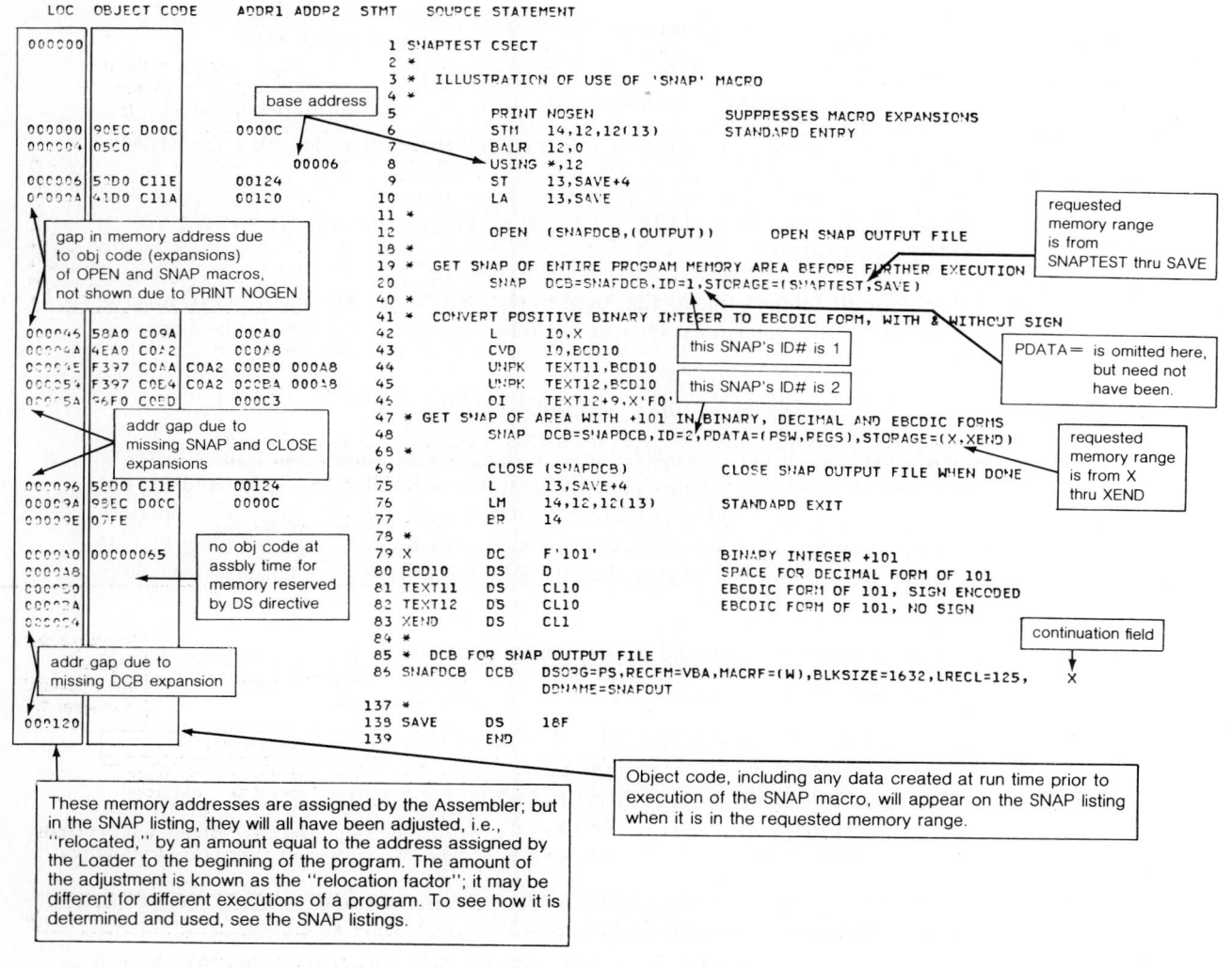

Object code, including any data created at run time prior to execution of the SNAP macro, will appear on the SNAP listing when it is in the requested memory range.

These memory addresses are assigned by the Assembler; but in the SNAP listing, they will all have been adjusted, i.e., "relocated," by an amount equal to the address assigned by the Loader to the beginning of the program. The amount of the adjustment is known as the "relocation factor"; it may be different for different executions of a program. To see how it is determined and used, see the SNAP listings.

4.8 SUMMARY

The instruction we will use to count the number of iterations of a loop in the IBM 360 and 370 systems is Branch on Count (BCT). Each time the BCT is executed, it subtracts +1 from the counter, and if the resulting new count is not zero, the BCT will branch to the effective address specified in its second operand. If the new counter is zero, the BCT will not branch.

Subscripting can be achieved through index registers because of the manner in which an index register participates in the formation of an effective address at run time. To simplify the process, a systematic scheme is used to store each array's data in memory, as is illustrated in figure 4.3 for one-dimensional integer arrays. The instruction we will use to increment the index is the Load Address (LA) instruction. Together, the LA and BCT instructions will be the heart of the loop-control mechanisms used in this text.

An alternative method of controlling the number of loop iterations and achieving the effect of subscripting involves use of either the Branch on Index High (BXH) or Branch on Index Less Than or Equal (BXLE) instructions. These instructions combine the iteration-counting and index-incrementing operations into a single operation. Consequently, their use requires slightly different loop initialization steps than does the LA-BCT pair.

Figure 4.6 *continued*

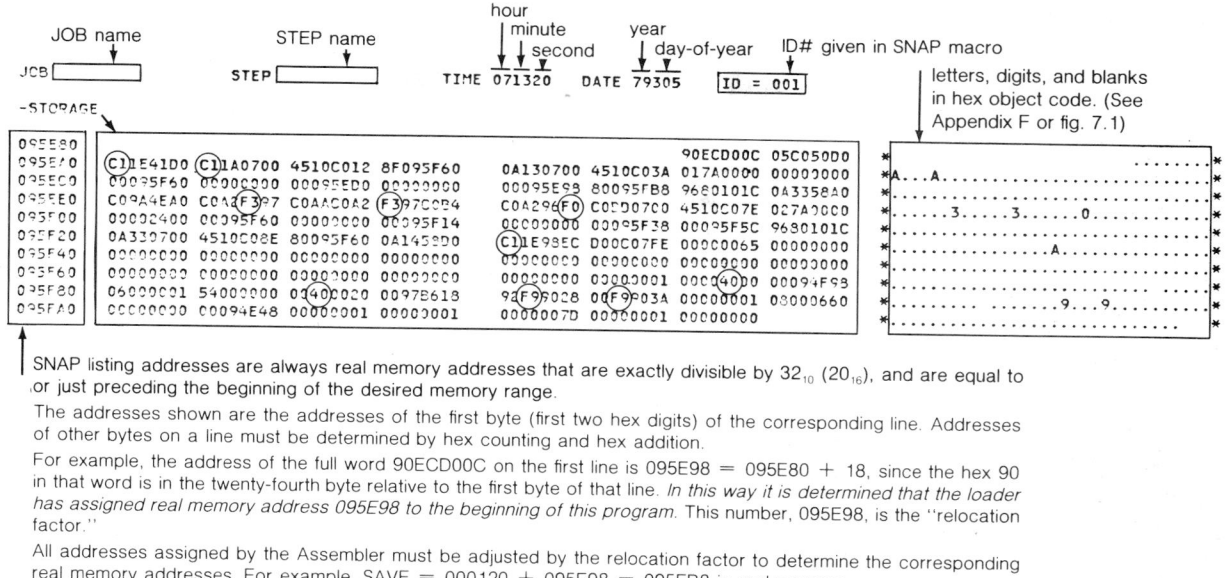

SNAP listing addresses are always real memory addresses that are exactly divisible by 32_{10} (20_{16}), and are equal to or just preceding the beginning of the desired memory range.

The addresses shown are the addresses of the first byte (first two hex digits) of the corresponding line. Addresses of other bytes on a line must be determined by hex counting and hex addition.

For example, the address of the full word 90ECD00C on the first line is 095E98 = 095E80 + 18, since the hex 90 in that word is in the twenty-fourth byte relative to the first byte of that line. *In this way it is determined that the loader has assigned real memory address 095E98 to the beginning of this program.* This number, 095E98, is the "relocation factor."

All addresses assigned by the Assembler must be adjusted by the relocation factor to determine the corresponding real memory addresses. For example, SAVE = 000120 + 095E98 = 095FB8 in real memory.

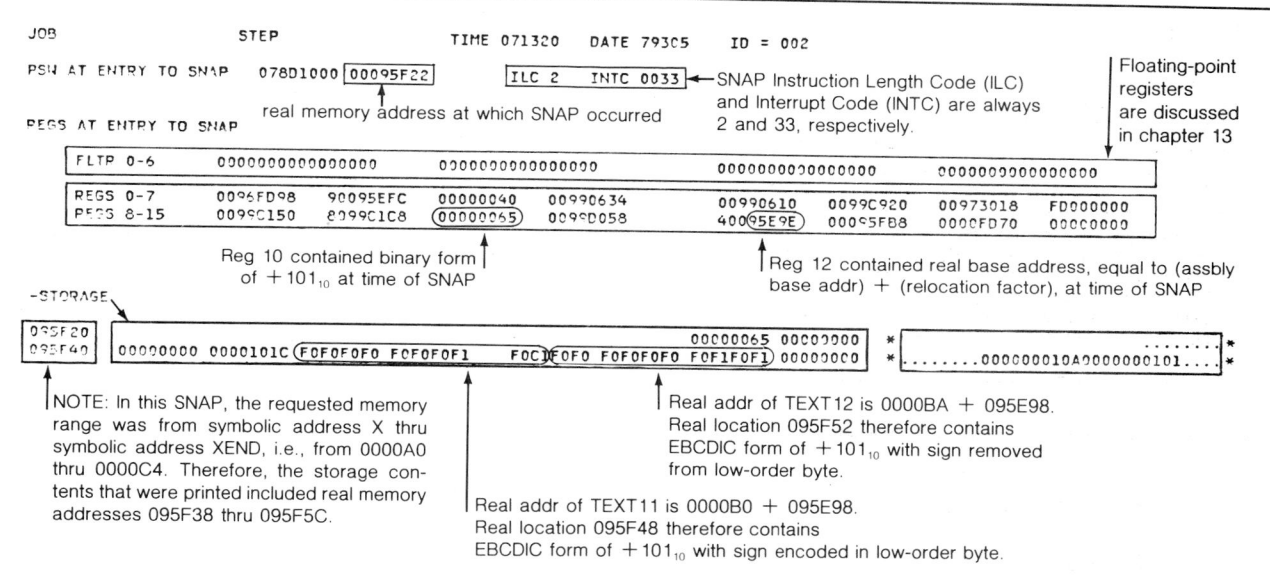

The character representation of integers is always used when they are printed, displayed at terminals, or read from cards or terminals. Since this representation cannot be used for arithmetic processes—there being no instructions to do so—integer input must be converted to binary, and integer output must be converted from binary. Two sets of instructions simplify the conversion processes considerably: PACK and CVB for converting from character to binary integer representation, and CVD and UNPK for converting from binary integer to character representation. Since neither pair's handling of the sign is entirely satisfactory, additional instructions are used to compensate.

In this chapter we have shown how to convert positive integers from character to binary format (and vice versa) under certain simple conditions. A procedure for converting negative as well as positive integers from character to binary format is given in Exercise 12 at the end of this chapter, and a more general procedure is given at the end of Section 12.8. Similarly, a procedure that converts integers from binary to character format is given in Exercise 11, and others are given at the end of Section 12.9.

SAMPLE PROBLEM
AND SOLUTION

PROBLEM STATEMENT

Write a program that will read input data cards containing class enrollments in the format described below and print all the input data followed by a line giving the total enrollment in all classes.

The input data card format is this:

> columns 1–6 : course i.d.
> 10–50: course name
> 55–64: number of students enrolled

SOLUTION PROCEDURE

The procedure requires that for each input data card that is read, the number of enrolled students be converted to binary integer format and added to a cumulative tally. After having read and printed all input data cards and having accumulated all the enrollments in the tally, the tally must be converted to its EBCDIC representation and printed.

Note that the tally cannot be printed until the end-of-data portion of the program is entered. This is done when the Operating System, in responding to the input GET macro, detects that there are no more data cards. It then transfers control not to the instruction following the GET macro but to the instruction whose symbolic address is specified by the EODAD= parameter in the input DCB macro. It is at that point that the tally is converted to EBCDIC and printed.

Figure 4.7a **Overview of sample problem solution procedure.**

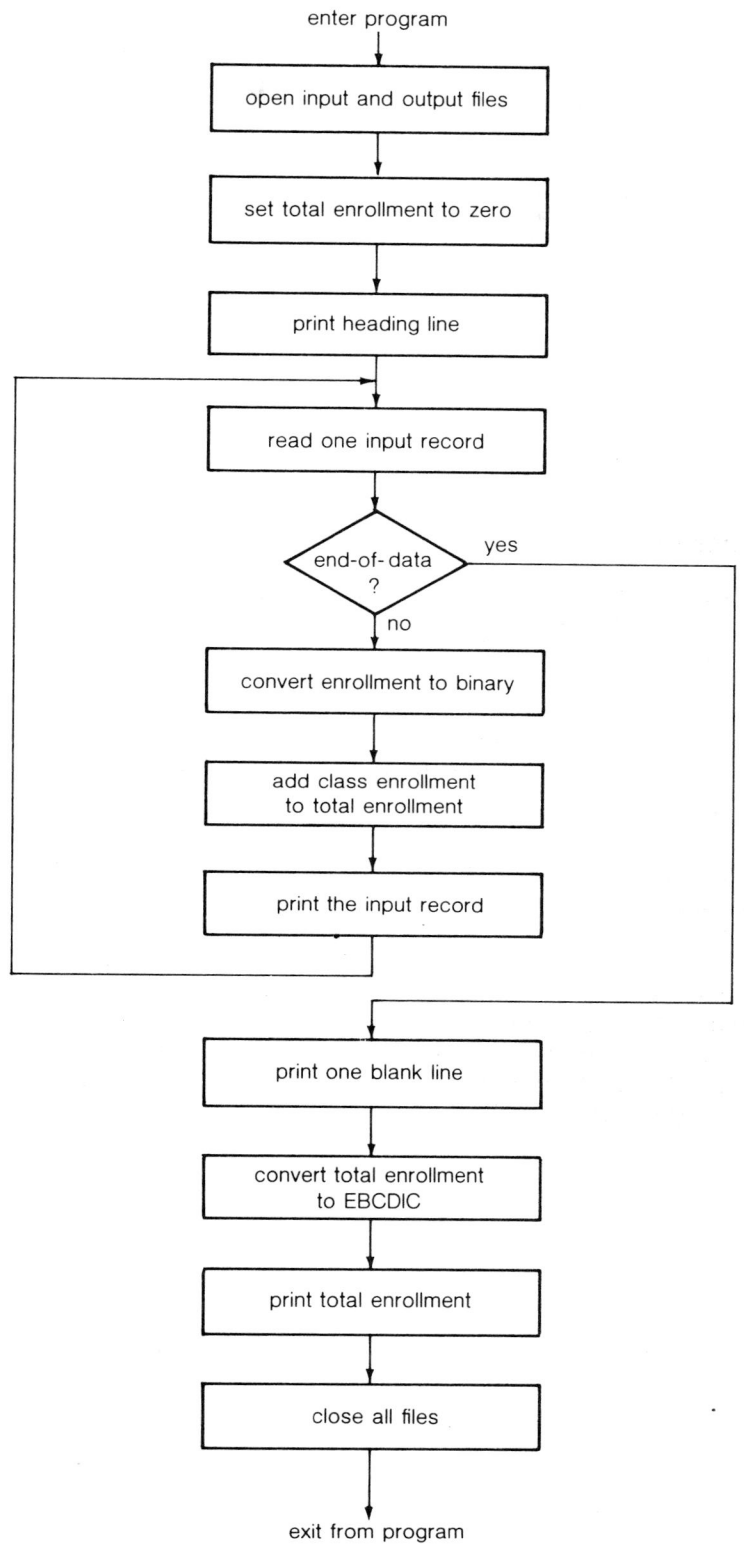

Figure 4.7b   Solution to sample problem.

```
FLAG LOCTN OBJECT CODE     ADDR1  ADDR2  STMNT M SOURCE STATEMENT

     000000                           3 SPCH4     CSECT
                                      4 *
                                      5 * SPCH4 READS INPUT DATA CARDS CONTAINING CLASS ENROLLMENTS
                                      6 *   IN THE FORMAT DESCRIBED BELOW, AND PRINTS EACH INPUT DATA
                                      7 *   CARD, THE LAST CARD BEING FOLLOWED BY A PRINTED LINE GIVING
                                      8 *   THE TOTAL ENROLLMENT IN ALL CLASSES.
                                      9 *
                                     10 * INPUT DATA IS IN TEXT (EBCDIC CHARACTER) FORM, AS FOLLOWS
                                     11 *     COLS  1-6    COURSE I.D.
                                     12 *          10-50   COURSE NAME
                                     13 *          55-64   NUMBER OF STUDENTS ENROLLED
                                     14 *     OTHER COLUMNS ARE UNUSED.
                                     15 *
     000000 90 EC D00C               16           STM    14,12,12(13)          STANDARD ENTRY
     000004 05 C0                    17           BALR   12,0
     000006                          18           USING  *,12
     000036 50 D0 C3FE        000404 19           ST     13,SAVE+4
     00000A 41 D0 C3FA        000400 20           LA     13,SAVE
                                     21 *
                                     22 * INITIALIZE TOTAL ENROLLMENT
                                     23 *
     00000E 58 60 C442        000448 24           L      6,=F'0'
     000012 50 60 C0D6        0000DC 25           ST     6,ENROLLED
                                     26 *
                                     27 * OPEN INPUT AND OUTPUT FILES
                                     28 *
     000016                          29           OPEN   (SYSIN,(INPUT))       INPUT IS 'SYSIN' DATA STREAM
     000022                          35           OPEN   (SYSPRNT,(OUTPUT))    OUTPUT IS 'SYSOUT' PRINTER

                                     41 *   DOS *******
                                     42 *           OPEN   SYSIN
                                     43 *           OPEN   SYSPRNT
                                     44 ***************

                                     45 *
                                     46 * PRINT HEADING LINE FOR START OF OUTPUT
                                     47 *
     00002E                          48           PUT    SYSPRNT,HEADING
                                     53 *
                                     54 * MAIN PROCESSING LOOP ...
                                     55 *       READS ONE INPUT CARD
                                     56 *       CONVERTS COURSE ENROLLMENT TO BINARY INTEGER
                                     57 *       ADDS COURSE ENROLLMENT TO TOTAL ENROLLMENT
                                     58 *       PRINTS THE CARD
                                     59 *       WHEN END-OF-DATA OCCURS, CONTROL TRANSFERS TO 'EOD'
                                     60 *
     00003C                          61 LOOP      GET    SYSIN,INAREA          GET INPUT CARD INTO INPUT AREA
                                     66 *
     00004A F2 79 C0CAC110 000000 000116 67       PACK   BCD,DATA              CONVERT INPUT DATA TO DECIMAL
     000050 4F 60 C0CA        000000 68           CVB    6,BCD                 CONVERT DECIMAL TO BINARY
     000054 50 60 C0D2        0000D8 69           ST     6,BINARY               AND SAVE IT IN MEMORY
                                     70 *
     000058 58 60 C0D6        0000DC 71           L      6,ENROLLED            GET TOTAL ENROLLMENT
     00005C 5A 60 C0D2        0000D8 72           A      6,BINARY              ADD COURSE ENROLLMENT TO TOTAL
     000060 50 60 C0D6        0000DC 73           ST     6,ENROLLED             AND RETURN NEW TOTAL TO MEMORY
                                     74 *
     000064 D2 4F C134C0DA 00013A 0000E0 75       MVC    OUTLINE,INAREA        COPY INPUT DATA TO OUTPUT AREA
     00006A                          76           PUT    SYSPRNT,OUTAREA       PUT OUTPUT LINE ONTO PRINTER FILE
     000078 47 F0 C036        00003C 81           B      LOOP                  BRANCH BACK TO GET NEXT CARD
                                     82 *
                                     83 * WHEN END-OF-DATA IS SENSED BY 'GET', CONTROL IS TRANSFERRED HERE
                                     84 *
     00007C                          85 EOD       PUT    SYSPRNT,BLANKS        PRINT ONE BLANK LINE
                                     90 *
     00008A 58 60 C0D6        0000DC 91           L      6,ENROLLED            GET TOTAL ENROLLMENT
     00008E 4E 60 C0CA        0000D0 92           CVD    6,BCD                 CONVERT TOTAL TO DECIMAL
     000092 F3 97 C272C0CA 000278 000000 93       UNPK   TOTAL,BCD              AND THEN TO EBCDIC (TEXT)
     000098 96 F0 C27B        000281 94           OI     TOTAL+9,X'F0'         REMOVE SIGN CODE
                                     95 *
     00009C                          96           PUT    SYSPRNT,TOTALS        PRINT TOTAL LINE
                                    101 *
                                    102 * TERMINATION OF PROGRAM
                                    103 *
     0000AA                         104           CLOSE  (SYSIN)
     0000B6                         110           CLOSE  (SYSPRNT)
     0000C2 58 D0 C3FE        000404 116          L      13,SAVE+4             STANDARD EXIT
     0000C6 98 EC D00C               117          LM     14,12,12(13)
     0000CA 07 FE                    118          BR     14

                                    119 *   DOS *******
                                    120 *           CLOSE SYSIN
                                    121 *           CLOSE SYSPRNT
                                    122 *           EOJ
                                    123 ***************

                                    124 *
                                    125 *
                                    126 * DATA AREAS AND CONSTANTS
                                    127 *
```

Figure 4.7b   *continued*

```
FLAG LOCTN OBJECT CODE      ADDR1 ADDR2  STMNT M SOURCE STATEMENT

      000000                                128    BCD      DS     D             DECIMAL COURSE ENROLLMENT
      0000D8                                129    BINARY   DS     F             BINARY COURSE ENROLLMENT
      0000DC                                130    ENROLLED DS     F             BINARY TOTAL ENROLLMENT
                                            131    *
                                            132    * INPUT CARD AREA
                                            133    *
      0000E0                                134    INAREA   DS     0CL80         DEFINITION OF INPUT AREA ...
      0000E0                                135    ID       DS     CL6           COLS 1-6    COURSE I.D.
      0000E6                                136             DS     CL3                7-9    UNUSED
      0000E9                                137    NAME     DS     CL41               10-50  COURSE NAME
      000112                                138             DS     CL4                51-54  UNUSED
      000116                                139    DATA     DS     CL10               55-64  ENROLLMENT
      000120                                140             DS     CL16               65-80  UNUSED
                                            141    *
                                            142    * OUTPUT LINE AREA
                                            143    *
      000130                                144    OUTAREA  DS     0CL132        DEFINITION OF OUTPUT AREA ...
      000130 4040404040404040               145             DC     CL10' '       COLS 1-10   BLANKS
      00013A                                146    OUTLINE  DS     CL80               11-90  SPACE FOR INPUT CARD
      00018A 4040404040404040               147             DC     CL42' '            91-132 BLANKS
                                            148    *
                                            149    * BLANK LINE FOR OUTPUT
                                            150    *
      0001B4                                151    BLANKS   DS     0CL132        DEFINITION OF BLANK LINE ...
      0001B4 4040404040404040               152             DC     CL132' '      COLS 1-132  BLANKS
                                            153    *
                                            154    * LINE FOR TOTALS
                                            155    *
      000238                                156    TOTALS   DS     0CL132        DEFINITION OF TOTAL LINE ...
      000238 4040404040404040               157             DC     CL54' '       COLS 1-54   BLANKS
      00026E E3D6E3C1D340407E               158             DC     CL10'TOTAL   ='    55-64  TOTAL = (FOR INFO)
      000278                                159    TOTAL    DS     CL10               65-74  TOTAL ENROLLMENT
      000282 4040404040404040               160             DC     CL58' '            75-132 BLANKS
                                            161    *
                                            162    * HEADING LINE
                                            163    *
      0002BC                                164    HEADING  DS     0CL132        DEFINITION OF HEADING LINE ...
      0002BC 4040404040404040               165             DC     CL10' '       COLS 1-10   BLANKS
      0002C6 40C94BC44B40                   166             DC     CL6' I.D.'         11-16  I.D. HEADING
      0002CC 404040                         167             DC     CL3' '             17-19  BLANKS
      0002CF 40C3D6E4D9E2C540               168             DC     CL41' COURSE NAME' 20-60  COURSE NAME HEADING
      0002F8 40404040                       169             DC     CL4' '             61-64  BLANKS
      0002FC C5D5D9D6D3D3D4C5               170             DC     CL10'ENROLLMENT'   65-74  ENROLLMENT HEADING
      000306 4040404040404040               171             DC     CL58' '            75-132 BLANKS
                                            172    *
                                            173    *
                                            174    * DCB'S FOR INPUT AND OUTPUT FILES
                                            175    *
      000340                                176    SYSIN    DCB    DSORG=PS,MACRF=(GM),DDNAME=SYSIN,EODAD=EOD,       X
                                            177                    RECFM=FB,LRECL=80,BLKSIZE=4080
                                            229    *
      0003A0                                230    SYSPRNT  DCB    DSORG=PS,MACRF=(PM),DDNAME=SYSPRINT,              X
                                            231                    RECFM=FB,LRECL=132,BLKSIZE=4092              \
                                            283    *  DOS  *******
                                            284    *SYSIN    DTFCD DEVADDR=SYSIPT,WORKA=YES,IOAREA1=INBUF,EOFADDR=EOD,  X
                                            285                    DEVICE=2540
                                            286    *SYSPRNT DTFPR DEVADDR=SYSLST,WORKA=YES,IOAREA1=OUTBUF,BLKSIZE=132,  X
                                            287    *               DEVICE=1403
                                            288    *
                                            289    *INBUF    DS     CL80
                                            290    *OUTBUF   DC     CL132' '
                                            291    ***************
                                            292    *
                                            293    * SAVE AREA
                                            294    *
      000400                                295    SAVE     DS     18F
                                            296    *  DOS  *******
                                            297    *SAVE     DS     9D
                                            298    ***************
                                            299    * LITERALS
      000448 00000000                       301                    =F'0'
                                            302             END
```

Figure 4.7b continued

CROSS-REFERENCE

SYMBOL	LEN	VALUE	DEFN	REFERENCES				
BCD	00008	0000D0	00128	00067	00068	00092	00093	
BINARY	00004	0000D8	00129	00069	00072			
BLANKS	00084	0001B4	00151	00087				
DATA	0000A	000116	00139	00067				
ENROLLED	00004	0000DC	00130	00025	00071	00073	00091	
EOD	00004	00007C	00086	00198				
HEADING	00084	0002BC	00164	00050				
ID	00006	0000E0	00135					
INAREA	00050	0000E0	00134	00063	00075			
LOOP	00004	00003C	00062	00081				
NAME	00029	0000E9	00137					
OUTAREA	00084	000130	00144	00078				
OUTLINE	00050	00013A	00146	00075				
SAVE	00004	000400	00295	00019	00020	00116		
SPCH4	00001	000000	00003					
SYSIN	00004	000340	00177	00033	00062	00108		
SYSPRNT	00004	0003A0	00231	00039	00049	00077	00086	00097	00114
TOTAL	0000A	000278	00159	00093	00094			
TOTALS	00084	000238	00156	00098				

EXERCISES

1. What is the main advantage gained by storing the elements of an array in consecutive locations in memory?

2. Suppose that in figure 4.4, Statement 6,

$$LA \quad 5,4(5)$$

is replaced by this statement:

$$LA \quad 5,8(5)$$

What would be the effect on the computations at run time?

3. Assume that for the statements shown in figure 4.4, the following conditions are true:

> base address = 00006
> base register = 12
> symbolic address LOOP = 500_x
> symbolic address N = 800_x

Using the values of the symbolic addresses for X, Y, and Z given in figure 4.3, what is the machine language representation of the instructions given in figure 4.4?

4. Show how to change the program segment of figure 4.4 so that instead of computing $Z_j = X_j + Y_j$ for $J = 1,2,...,N$, it computes $Z_j = X_j + 8$.

5. Show how to change the program segment of figure 4.4 so that instead of computing $Z_j = X_j + Y_j$ for $J = 1,2,...,N$, it computes $Z_j = X_j + Y_j$ for $J = 2,4,...,N$ (assume that N is an even number).

6. Show how to change the program segment of figure 4.4 so that instead of computing $Z_j = X_j + Y_j$ for $J = 1,2,...,N$ it computes $Z_j = X_j + Y_j$ for $J = N,N-1,N-2,...,1$. Do this using the same register for both the loop-control variable and the array index.

7. Suppose there are fifty input data cards, each with a positive integer in columns 1–10 (right-justified). Write an assembly language program that will read the fifty integers into an array and then print them in the reverse order from that in which they were read.

8. Use the same input data as in Exercise 7. Write an assembly language program that will print them two per line as follows: the first and twenty-sixth integers on the first line, the second and twenty-seventh on the second line, and so on up to the twenty-fifth and fiftieth on the last line.

9. Write an assembly language program that will print the positive integers $+1, +2,..., +9, +10$ and the negative integers $-1, -2,..., -10$. The integers should be converted to character form by just three instructions similar to these:

```
L      5,Z
CVD    5,BCD
UNPK   SUM,BCD
```

The OI instruction given in Section 4.3 has been omitted so that you can observe the effect of the UNPK instruction on the low-order digit of positive and negative integers. Note that, as in Section 4.3, the symbolic address SUM is the address of the integer in its character form, ready for printing; and the symbolic address Z is the address of the integer in its 32-bit binary form.

10. Repeat Exercise 9, except that the conversions from binary integer to character form should be done by these four instructions for both the positive and the negative integers:

```
L      5,Z
CVD    5,BCD
UNPK   SUM,BCD
OI     SUM+9,X'F0'
```

The purpose of including the OI instruction for negative as well as positive integers is to demonstrate its effect: it eliminates the code used for the sign in the low-order digit position. From the table of EBCDIC characters given in Appendix F, we can see what is happening: the code used to represent a +1 is changed from 1100 0001 (the letter *A*) to 1111 0001 (the digit 1); the code used to represent a −1 is changed from 1101 0001 (the letter *J*) to 1111 0001; and similarly for the other codes. The OI instruction performs the Boolean "or" function and is described in Section 8.2.

11. The following eight instructions can be used to convert a 32-bit binary integer to its representation as a decimal integer in EBCDIC character form. The sign is represented by a blank if the integer is positive or zero and by a dash (the familiar minus sign) if the integer is negative. Ten bytes are used for the character representation: the left-most byte is used for the sign, and the remaining 9 bytes for the digits. Zeroes are not suppressed. The notation is the same as that given in Section 4.3.

```
* CONVERT FROM BINARY TO EBCDIC
          L        5,Z              COPY AN INTEGER INTO REGISTER 5.
          CVD      5,BCD            CONVERT IT TO BINARY-CODED DECIMAL.
          UNPK     SUM,BCD          CONVERT THAT TO EBCDIC (10 BYTES).
          MVI      SUM,X'40'        ASSUME IT'S NONNEG, AND PUT A BLANK
          LTR      5,5              (X'40') IN 1ST POSITION. THEN TEST:
          BNM      NONNEG           IF NONNEGATIVE, LEAVE SIGN BLANK.
          MVI      SUM,X'60'        IF NEGATIVE, PUT DASH (X'60') IN.
NONNEG    OI       SUM+9,X'F0'      ELIMINATE SIGN CODE IN LO-ORDER DIGIT.
```

Repeat Exercise 9, using these eight instructions to convert each integer. The LTR and BNM instructions are discussed in Section 5.4; they enable the sign of the integer to be determined. The MVI instruction is discussed in Section 7.2; it copies 1 byte from its immediate data field into the byte whose address is given in its first operand.

12. The following six instructions can be used to convert a decimal integer from its 10-byte EBCDIC representation to its 32-bit binary integer representation. If the decimal integer is positive or zero, its sign must be represented by a blank in the left-most character position. If the integer is negative, its sign must be represented by a dash (the minus sign) in the left-most character position. Leading zeroes may be present or suppressed. The notation is the same as that given in Section 4.4.

```
* CONVERT FROM EBCDIC TO BINARY
          PACK     BCD,INT          CONVERT FROM EBCDIC TO BINARY-CODED DECIMAL.
          CVB      5,BCD            CONVERT THAT TO 32-BIT BINARY INTEGER.
          CLI      INT,X'60'        SEE IF LEFT-MOST BYTE WAS A DASH (X'60').
          BNE      NODASH           IF NOT, ACCEPT SIGN AS CONVERTED.
          LNR      5,5              IF SO, FORCE INTEGER TO BE NEGATIVE.
NODASH    ST       5,X              STORE 32-BIT INTEGER.
```

Write an assembly language program that will read exactly five input data cards, each containing an integer in columns 1–10 in the format described. Use the above six instructions to convert them to 32-bit binary representation, and compute their sum. Print the sum after converting it to EBCDIC with the instructions from Exercise 11.

5

Integer Arithmetic

The term *integer arithmetic* includes several types of instructions that operate on full-word and half-word binary numbers: copying data into and out of a register; addition, subtraction, multiplication, and division of two binary integers; changing sign, and generating the absolute value of a binary integer; testing for a positive, negative, or zero numeric result; and comparing two binary integers algebraically. The reason for emphasizing the word *binary* is that there are two other types of numeric data: packed decimal numbers and floating point numbers. Each of these requires its own set of arithmetic instructions, different from those required for binary integers. Packed decimal arithmetic will be discussed in chapter 12, floating point arithmetic in chapter 13.

There are two general characteristics of the binary integer arithmetic instructions:

1. Almost all the instructions operate on two integers. One of the integers must be in a register, and the other must be either in a register or in memory, depending on the instruction. The instructions that require that both integers being operated on be in registers are recognizable by their opcodes, which end in the letter *R:* AR, SR, MR, DR, CR.
2. On the IBM 360, almost all the instructions require that the data that are in memory be aligned on full-word boundaries when being operated on. Those that don't require full-word alignment require half-word alignment. The latter are all recognizable by their opcodes, which end in the letter *H:* LH, STH, AH, SH, MH, CH. On the IBM 370, neither full-word nor half-word alignment is necessary; byte alignment is all that is required. However, the 370's performance may be degraded if the data are not aligned the way they must be on the 360.

Section 5.1 discusses the method used to represent binary integers in the IBM 360 and 370 systems. This is followed by several sections that describe the various instructions that operate on integers and two sections (5.7 and 5.8) of examples that illustrate how these instructions can be used in programs. It should be noted that although we are restricting our discussions to integers, the instructions described in this chapter can be used to process numbers other than integers, i.e., mixed numbers. To do so, the mixed numbers must be represented as integers, with an implied but fixed position of the decimal point. For this reason, the more general term used for the instructions described in this chapter is *fixed point* arithmetic. A brief summary of the methods of using binary integers to represent mixed numbers is given in chapter 11.

5.1 TWO'S COMPLEMENT ARITHMETIC

Representation of Binary Integers

Using the notation of chapter 1, we will let b_n represent the nth bit in a binary integer, so that each integer can be represented as $b_0b_1b_2...b_{k-1}$, where b_0 is used to designate the sign bit: $b_0 = 0$ for positive integers and $b_0 = 1$ for negative integers. The number of bits, k, determines the maximum value that a binary integer may have in a computer: $(2^{k-1} - 1)$. In the IBM 360 and 370 systems, k may be either 32 or 16; the former are full-word integers, the latter are half-word integers. Without loss of generality we will write $b_0b_1b_2...b_{k-1}$ for the binary representation of an integer and understand that k is the same for all integers being discussed.

Two main methods are used for the representation of integers in computer systems. One is known as the sign-magnitude form, the other as the two's complement form. The two's complement form, which has certain advantages over the sign-magnitude form, is used in the IBM 360 and 370 systems.

In the sign-magnitude form, bits b_1 through b_{k-1} represent the absolute value, or magnitude, of the integer, and bit b_0 represents the sign. To illustrate, we take $k = 4$ for simplicity; then 2^4 integers can be represented as follows:

decimal	binary	decimal	binary
+0	0000	−0	1000
+1	0001	−1	1001
+2	0010	−2	1010
+3	0011	−3	1011
+4	0100	−4	1100
+5	0101	−5	1101
+6	0110	−6	1110
+7	0111	−7	1111

The value of each integer $b_0b_1b_2b_3$ can be computed as

$$(1 - 2b_0) \times \{b_1 \times 2^2 + b_2 \times 2^1 + b_3 \times 2^0\}$$

For example, $1101_2 = (1 - 2 \times 1) \times \{1 \times 2^2 + 0 \times 2^1 + 1 \times 2^0\} = -1 \times \{4 + 1\} = -5_{10}$.

To perform arithmetic on two integers that are in sign-magnitude form, we must process the sign bit in a separate manner from the magnitude bits. In *addition,* we must determine whether the signs of the two integers are the same or different and proceed according to the rules of algebra. In *subtraction,* we change the sign of the second factor, and then proceed as in addition. In both addition and subtraction, the result may be too large to be represented in k bits. This is known as *overflow* and causes an erroneous result. For example, with $k = 4$

decimal	binary	
4	0100	no overflow:
+ (−5)	+ 1101	the smaller magnitude is subtracted
−1	1001	from the larger when the signs are not the same

decimal	binary	
−4	1100	
+ (−5)	+ 1101	
−9	1001	overflow:
	⌐_____	the carry out of the high-order digit
		is lost, and the result is in error

Of course, a larger value than $k = 4$ is usually used, but overflow always occurs when an attempt is made to generate a result whose magnitude exceeds $(2^{k-1} - 1)$, whatever value is used for k. However, the disadvantages of using sign-magnitude form do not lie in the problem of overflow. The main disadvantages are the need to process the sign bit separately and the need to determine which of the two factors in additions and subtractions is larger when their signs are different. Another, but lesser, disadvantage is that the number 0 is represented in two forms, +0 and −0. *The use of the two's complement form eliminates all these problems except that of overflow.* The overflow problem is inherent in all methods that use a fixed number of bits to represent an integer.

In two's complement form, the leading bit is still used for the sign, but it participates in arithmetic operations as though it represented the value $-b_0 \times 2^{k-1}$. The remaining bits represent the magnitude of nonnegative integers, as is done in the sign-magnitude form. But the negative form of an integer is obtained by reversing the value of each bit and adding +1 to the result. The process of bit reversal—0 becomes 1, and 1 becomes 0—is known as *complementing* the bit. The maximum positive value that can be represented is $2^{k-1} - 1$; the minimum negative value is -2^{k-1}. The number zero is always represented with its sign bit $b_0 = 0$.

For example, with $k = 4$, the largest positive integer is $2^3 - 1 = 7$, and the smallest negative integer is $-2^3 = -8$. The integers 0 through 7 are represented as in sign-magnitude format:

decimal	binary
0	0000
+ 1	0001
+ 2	0010
+ 3	0011
+ 4	0100
+ 5	0101
+ 6	0110
+ 7	0111

The representations of the negative integers -1 through -7 are obtained by complementing the positive binary integers, and adding $+1$ as shown here:

integer	0001	0010	0011	...	0110	0111
complement	1110	1101	1100	...	1001	1000
+1	+ 0001	+ 0001	+ 0001	...	+ 0001	+ 0001
result:	1111	+ 1110	1101	...	1010	1001

The remaining 4-bit representation, 1000, is -8, since the sign bit in general must represent the value $-b_0 \times 2^{k-1}$. The negative integers, therefore, are represented as

decimal	binary
− 1	1111
− 2	1110
− 3	1101
− 4	1100
− 5	1011
− 6	1010
− 7	1001
− 8	1000

The value of each positive or negative (or zero) integer $b_0b_1b_2b_3$ can be computed as

$$-b_0 \times 2^3 + b_1 \times 2^2 + b_2 \times 2^1 + b_3 \times 2^0$$

For example, $1011_2 = -1 \times 2^3 + 0 \times 2^2 + 1 \times 2^1 + 1 \times 2^0 = -8 + 2 + 1 = -5_{10}$.

It should be noted that the negative of a negative integer is represented properly by the above method, except that $+8$, i.e., $-(-8)$, cannot be represented in 4 bits.

For integers represented by k bits, $b_0b_1b_2...b_{k-1}$, the methods illustrated above are essentially the same. The value of a k-bit integer is computed as

$$J = -b_0 \times 2^{k-1} + b_1 \times 2^{k-2} + ... + b_{k-2} \times 2^1 + b_{k-1} \times 2^0$$

When the integer is positive, then $b_0 = 0$, and this reduces to the familiar expression for evaluating positive integers. When the integer is negative in two's complement form, the above expression for J also gives its value, for $-J$ is then positive, and

$$-J = +b_0 \times 2^{k-1} - b_1 \times 2^{k-2} - ... - b_{k-2} \times 2^1 - b_{k-1} \times 2^0.$$

But by writing $-J = (2^{k-1} - J) - 2^{k-1}$, and noting that

$$2^{k-1} = 1 + 2^{k-2} + 2^{k-3} + ... + 2^1 + 2^0$$

the expression for $-J$ can be rewritten as

$$-J = 1 + \left\{ -(1-b_0) \times 2^{k-1} + (1-b_1) \times 2^{k-2} + ... + (1-b_{k-1}) \times 2^0 \right\}.$$

The value within braces $\{...\}$ is the value of the bit-for-bit complement of the representation we started with, $b_0b_1b_2...b_{k-1}$. Consequently, the expression for $-J$ represents the algorithm previously given for computing the two's complement, and the expression for J is therefore valid for evaluating both positive and negative k-bit integers represented in two's complement form.

Figure 5.1   *Two's complement integers in IBM 360 and 370 systems.*

full-word integers		half-word integers	
-2^{31}	1000 0000 0000 0000 0000 0000 0000 0000		
$-2^{31} + 1:$	1000 0000 0000 0000 0000 0000 0000 0001		
$-2^{31} + 2:$	1000 0000 0000 0000 0000 0000 0000 0010	-2^{15}	1000 0000 0000 0000
	... ...	$-2^{15} + 1:$	1000 0000 0000 0001
$-2:$	1111 1111 1111 1111 1111 1111 1111 1110		...
$-1:$	1111 1111 1111 1111 1111 1111 1111 1111	$-1:$	1111 1111 1111 1111
$0:$	0000 0000 0000 0000 0000 0000 0000 0000	$0:$	0000 0000 0000 0000
$+1:$	0000 0000 0000 0000 0000 0000 0000 0001	$+1:$	0000 0000 0000 0001
$+2:$	0000 0000 0000 0000 0000 0000 0000 0010		...
	... ...	$2^{15} - 2:$	0111 1111 1111 1110
$2^{31} - 2:$	0111 1111 1111 1111 1111 1111 1111 1110	$2^{15} - 1:$	0111 1111 1111 1111
$2^{31} - 1:$	0111 1111 1111 1111 1111 1111 1111 1111		

The name *two's complement* is due to the fact that the negative of a k-bit integer $b_0b_1b_2...b_{k-1}$ is the representation obtained by subtracting the $(k+1)$-bit integer $0b_0b_1b_2...b_{k-1}$ from 2^k, as can be readily verified. For this reason, the name *two's complement* is also often used to designate the representation of a negative integer.

In the IBM 360 and 370 systems, the range of numbers that can be represented as full-word integers ($k = 32$) is from -2^{31} through $2^{31} - 1$; that for half-word integers ($k = 16$) is from -2^{15} through $2^{15} - 1$. This is illustrated in figure 5.1.

Clearly, all the integers that can be represented in a half word can also be represented in a full word. Moreover, *a half-word representation is converted to the full-word representation of the same integer by copying its sign into each of the 16 high-order bits of the full word, and copying the low-order bits of the half word, one by one, into the corresponding low-order bits of the full word.* For example:

	full word								half word			
$-4:$	1111	1111	1111	1111	1111	1111	1111	1100	1111	1111	1111	1100
$2^{15}-4:$	0000	0000	0000	0000	0111	1111	1111	1100	0111	1111	1111	1100

The reason that the sign bit must be copied, or *propagated,* in this manner is that the additional bits must contribute a net value of zero to the value of the integer, while the new high-order bit must become the sign bit. In general, to change from an m-bit representation $b_0b_1b_2...b_{m-1}$ to an equivalent k-bit representation with $k > m$, the new form is

$$\underbrace{b_0b_0b_0...b_0}b_0b_1b_2...b_{m-1}$$
$$\uparrow\!\!\text{---}k-m\text{ bits}$$

The value of the new representation may be computed as $J = K + L$, where L is the value of the low-order m bits,

$$L = b_0 \times 2^{m-1} + b_1 \times 2^{m-2} + ... + b_{m-1} \times 2^0$$

and K is the value of the $k-m$ high-order bits,

$$K = b_0 \times \{-2^{k-1} + 2^{k-2} + ... + 2^{m+1} + 2^m\}$$

The value contributed by the term in braces $\{...\}$ is -2^m, so that

$$J = K + L = -b_0 \times (2^m - 2^{m-1}) + b_1 \times 2^{m-2} + ... + b_{m-1} \times 2^0$$
$$= -b_0 \times 2^{m-1} + b_1 \times 2^{m-2} + ... + b_{m-1} \times 2^0$$

Since this is just the value of the original m-bit integer $b_0b_1b_2...b_{m-1}$, the propagation of the sign bit has not altered that value.

Integer Arithmetic

When integers are represented in two's complement form, the operations of addition, subtraction, multiplication, and division are much simpler than when sign-magnitude form is used. All bits participate in the arithmetic. The sign bit contributes a value of $-b_0 \times 2^{k-1}$, and the remaining bits contribute values $b_j \times 2^{k-j-1}$ for $j = 1, 2, ..., k-1$. Except when overflow occurs, the sign of the result is algebraically correct. We will illustrate how arithmetic is performed with $k = 4$, since the methods carry over without change for larger values of k.

When adding or subtracting two 4-bit integers, the result must be a 4-bit integer. If the value of the result exceeds $2^3 - 1$ or is less than -2^3, it cannot be represented in 4 bits. This situation is known as overflow, and the 4-bit representation of the result is incorrect. As examples of the addition and subtraction processes, we have

$+6$	0110	-6	1010	$+5$	0101	-5	1011
$+ (+1)$	0001	$+ (-1)$	1111	$+ (+6)$	0110	$+ (-6)$	1010
	0111		1 1001		0 1011		1 0100
	no overflow		no overflow		overflow		overflow

Note that in all cases the sum is computed as though these were unsigned 4-bit integers, and the carries into and out of the sign bit position are examined to determine whether there is overflow. The rule for determining overflow is this: *if the carry into the sign bit from position b_1 is different from the carry out of the sign bit position, then there is overflow.* Otherwise, there is no overflow. When two negative numbers cause overflow, the resulting representation is positive; when two positive numbers cause overflow, the result is negative. Addition of two numbers with opposite signs cannot cause overflow.

That the carry rule stated above detects overflow situations correctly depends in part on the fact that the sum of two binary digits can at most produce a carry of 1. This can occur only when both digits are 1's, or when at least one of them is 1 and a carry from the previous digit is added to their sum: $1 + 0 + (carry) = 10$, $1 + 1 + (carry) = 11$. The rule also depends on two other properties of binary integers that are represented in two's complement form: (1) If P is positive, then its high-order numeric bit b_1 is a 1 if and only if $P \geq \frac{1}{2} (2^{k-1} - 1)$; (2) if N is negative, then its high-order numeric bit b_1 is a 1 if and only if $N \geq -\frac{1}{2} (2^{k-1})$.

Using these properties, the correctness of the carry rule can be demonstrated by considering the three cases cited below.

Case 1. Adding two positive integers, P_1 and P_2

Since the sign bits in both integers are both 0's, there can be no carry out of b_0. Moreover, there is a carry out of b_1 if and only if $P_1 + P_2 > (2^{k-1} - 1)$.

Case 2. Adding two negative integers, N_1 and N_2

Since the sign bits in both integers are both 1's, there will always be a carry out of b_0. Moreover, there is a carry out of b_1 if and only if $N_1 + N_2 \geq -(2^{k-1})$.

Case 3. Adding a positive integer, P, and a negative integer, N

Since the sum must always be correctly representable in k-bit two's complement form, the sign of the sum must be the same as the sign of whichever integer is larger in magnitude. But since the sign bit of P is a 0 and that of N is a 1, the sign of the sum will be negative if there is no carry out of b_1 (and thus no carry out of the sign bit) and positive if there is a carry out of b_1 (and thus also a carry out of the sign bit).

In multiplication of two integers, the product may contain more significant bits than either of the two factors. The largest possible product of two k-bit integers is $(-2^{k-1}) \times (-2^{k-1}) = 2^{2k-2}$, which requires $2k-1$ bits. To allow for this, most computers generate a $2k$-bit product when multiplying k-bit integers. In doing so, each of the two factors is considered to be extended on the left with as many copies of the sign bit as are needed to generate the $2k$-bit product. As demonstrated earlier, this does not change the value of either factor. Since there can be no overflow when a $2k$-bit product is generated, the correct representation for the product is assured.

For $k = 4$, we illustrate the above concepts with the following examples:

$$
\begin{array}{rr}
+6 & 0110 \\
\times (+2) & 0010 \\
\hline
0000\ 1100 \\
\underbrace{} \\
+12
\end{array}
\qquad
\begin{array}{rr}
+6 & 0110 \\
\times (-2) & 1110 \\
\hline
1111\ 0100 \\
\underbrace{} \\
-12
\end{array}
\qquad
\begin{array}{rr}
-3 & 1101 \\
\times (+6) & 0110 \\
\hline
1110\ 1110 \\
\underbrace{} \\
-18
\end{array}
\qquad
\begin{array}{rr}
-3 & 1101 \\
\times (-6) & 1010 \\
\hline
0001\ 0010 \\
\underbrace{} \\
+18
\end{array}
$$

To verify that these are the correct 8-bit representations of the products, we can carry out the multiplications by hand rather easily, since the multiplication table is simply $1 \times 1 = 1$, $1 \times 0 = 0 \times 1 = 0 \times 0 = 0$. But since the sign bit b_0 participates in k-bit arithmetic operations as though it represented the value $-b_0 \times 2^{k-1}$, then with $k = 4$ the sign bit represents the value -2^3, i.e., -8. To account for this in 4-bit hand calculations, we must propagate the sign bit four positions to the left before doing the calculations. For example:

$$
\begin{array}{rr}
-3 & 1111|1101 \\
\times (+6) & \times \quad 0000|0110 \\
\hline
& 111111010 \\
& 11111101 \\
\text{discarded} \longrightarrow 101|&11101110 \\
\hline
& -18
\end{array}
\qquad
\begin{array}{rr}
-3 & 1111|1101 \\
\times (-6) & \times \qquad 1111|1010 \\
\hline
& 111111010 \\
& 111111010 \\
& 11111101 \\
& 11111101 \\
& 11111101 \\
& 11111101 \\
\hline
\text{discarded} \longrightarrow 11110111|&00010010 \\
& +18
\end{array}
$$

It should be noted that even though a $2k$-bit product is generated, there might be only k or fewer significant bits in the product. There are, of course, not many situations in which this can occur when $k = 4$, but, for larger k, products will often be developed containing fewer than k significant bits. This means that the product can still be represented in the same fixed number of bits used for other integers, a decided advantage when programming. If $k = 8$, then all products in the range from -128 through $+127$ can be represented in 8 bits; if $k = 16$, the range is $-32,768$ through $+32,767$; and if $k = 32$, the range is $-2,147,483,648$ through $2,147,483,647$, i.e., -2^{31} through $2^{31} - 1$.

In the IBM 360 and 370, we can multiply two 32-bit integers and obtain a 64-bit product, using either of two instructions designed for this purpose. There is also an instruction for multiplying two 16-bit integers to produce a 32-bit product, but one of the factors must first be extended to 32 bits. We shall see how this is done when the multiply instructions are discussed later in this chapter.

Turning to division, we note that the result of dividing two integers K and L can be written as

$$
\frac{K}{L} = Q + \frac{R}{L}
$$

where the quotient, Q, and the remainder, R, are both integers. For example, in decimal arithmetic

$$
\frac{7}{4} = 1 + \frac{3}{4}
$$

and the same division problem could be represented in 4-bit notation as

$$0100 \overline{)\,0111} \begin{array}{l} \underline{0001} \longleftarrow \text{integer quotient } Q \\ \underline{0100} \\ 0011 \longleftarrow \text{integer remainder } R \end{array}$$

However, in two's complement arithmetic division of two k-bit integers, we cannot in general develop a k-bit quotient and a k-bit remainder. What is required is that the dividend, K, be represented by $2k$ bits. The following examples illustrate this for $K = -7$, $L = 4$, and $k = 4$.

$$0100 \overline{)\,1001} \begin{array}{l} \underline{0001} \longleftarrow Q \neq -1 \\ \underline{0100} \\ 0101 \longleftarrow R \neq -3 \end{array}$$

only k bits are
retained after each
intermediate
calculation

$$0100 \overline{)\,11111001} \begin{array}{l} \underline{1111} \longleftarrow Q = -1 \\ \underline{0100} \\ 10110 \\ \underline{0100} \\ 00100 \\ \underline{0100} \\ 00001 \\ \underline{0100} \\ 1101 \longleftarrow R = -3 \end{array}$$

The quotient is represented in 4 bits (in general, in k bits) with its proper algebraic sign. The remainder is also a k-bit integer; its sign is the same as that of the dividend. It should be noted that it is possible to generate a quotient that is too large to be represented in k bits. This will occur if the original k-bit dividend is -2^{k-1} and the divisor is -1; in this situation the quotient $+2^{k-1}$ could not be represented in k bits. It could also occur in other situations, since the dividend that is used in the division process is $2k$ bits, while the divisor is only k bits.

In the IBM 360 and 370 systems, we can divide a 64-bit dividend by a 32-bit divisor, using either of two instructions designed for this purpose. These instructions will be described later in this chapter.

5.2 COPYING DATA TO AND FROM A REGISTER

Since almost all the instructions considered in this chapter require that the data be in a register in order to be operated on, it is necessary to use instructions that copy data into a register prior to performing the desired arithmetic operations and to use instructions that copy the results from the register into memory after the operations are completed.

To copy data into a register, we use a *LOAD* instruction. To copy data out of a register, we use a *STORE* instruction.

The LOAD instructions are

opcode	meaning	type
L	copy a full word from memory into a register	RX
LH	copy a half word from memory into a register	RX
LM	copy from 1 to 16 consecutive full words from consecutive memory locations into consecutively numbered registers	RS
LR	copy a full word from one register into another	RR

Since the half-word LOAD instruction (LH) copies a half word (2 bytes) from memory into a full-word area—a register—its effect is slightly different from the other LOAD instructions. The same applies to the half-word STORE instruction (STH). The differences will be illustrated in Examples 3a, 3b, and 4.

The STORE instructions are

opcode	meaning	type
ST	copy a full word from a register into memory	RX
STH	copy a half word from a register into memory	RX
STM	copy from 1 to 16 full words from consecutively numbered registers into consecutive memory locations	RS

From these two lists, it can be seen that, with one exception, the LOAD and STORE instructions are paired. The exception is LR, for which a counterpart STORE instruction would be meaningless. The pairings are

L
ST   } copy a full word

LH
STH   } copy a half word

LM
STM   } copy from 1 to 16 consecutive full words

In each LOAD and STORE instruction, the operand field that designates where the data are copied *from* is called the *source operand*. The field that designates where the data are copied *to* is called the *destination operand*. Data from the source always replace the data that existed at the destination. But the source data itself is not changed when one of these instructions is executed.

In summary, three instructions copy data from memory to a register, three corresponding instructions copy data from a register to memory, and one instruction copies data from register to register. This is illustrated in the following table and in Examples 1 through 7.

instruction	operand	source field	destination field
L	R1,D2(X2,B2)	D2(X2,B2)	R1
LH	R1,D2(X2,B2)	D2(X2,B2)	R1
LM	R1,R2,D3(B3)	D3(B3)	R1 thru R2
ST	R1,D2(X2,B2)	R1	D2(X2,B2)
STH	R1,D2(X2,B2)	R1	D2(X2,B2)
STM	R1,R2,D3(B3)	R1 thru R2	D3(B3)
LR	R1,R2	R2	R1

In the examples, the data that exist at the source and destination are shown in hexadecimal notation with values that are assumed to exist *before* the instruction is executed, and with the values that would exist *after* the instruction is executed. The examples are not related to one another, except that the value of the symbol A is assumed to be 1000 (in hex) in each example.

Example 1.

				Register 3		memory address 1000
L	3,A	{	before execution:	0246 0357		0001 0010
			after execution:	0001 0010		0001 0010

Example 2.

				Register 4		memory address 1000
ST	4,A	{	before execution:	0123 0456		0ABC 0DEF
			after execution:	0123 0456		0123 0456

Example 3a.

			Register 5	memory address 1000
LH	5,A	before execution:	0159 0260	4321
		after execution:	0000 4321	4321

Note that although only a half word is loaded into Register 5, the entire content of that register is replaced. The half word is loaded into the right-hand half of the register—the so-called *low-order* half of the register—and the left-hand half of the register is replaced by all zeroes. (However, see the next example.)

Example 3b.

			Register 5	memory address 1000
LH	5,A	before execution:	0159 0260	9876
		after execution:	FFFF 9876	9876

As in Example 3a, a half word is loaded into the low-order (right-hand) half of Register 5, but the left-hand half is replaced by all F's (not zeroes as in Example 3a). The rule for the left-hand portion of the register, whenever the LH is used, is: The sign bit of the half word that is loaded is *copied into each bit* of the left-hand portion of the register. This is called propagating the sign bit to the left.

In the hexadecimal number 4321 = 0100 0011 0010 0001, the sign bit is 0, so 4321 is extended to the full-word integer 00004321.

In the hexadecimal number 9876 = 1001 1000 0111 0110, the sign bit is 1, so 9876 is extended to the full-word integer FFFF9876.

This rule for the LH instruction guarantees that an integer's sign and value will be the same in a 32-bit representation as it is in a 16-bit representation.

Example 4.

			Register 6	memory address 1000
STH	6,A	before execution:	0123 0246	0ABC
		after execution:	0123 0246	0246

Note that only the low-order 16-bits are copied from a register by the STH instruction.

Example 5.

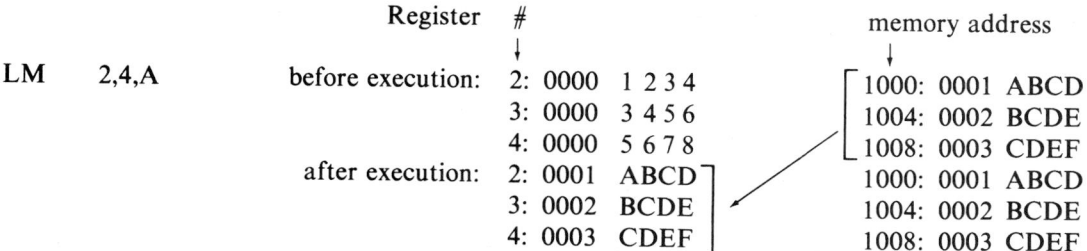

LM	2,4,A	before execution:	Register #		memory address	
			2: 0000 1 2 3 4		1000: 0001 ABCD	
			3: 0000 3 4 5 6		1004: 0002 BCDE	
			4: 0000 5 6 7 8		1008: 0003 CDEF	
		after execution:	2: 0001 ABCD		1000: 0001 ABCD	
			3: 0002 BCDE		1004: 0002 BCDE	
			4: 0003 CDEF		1008: 0003 CDEF	

In the LM instruction, the destination is registers R1 thru R2 inclusive. Here, R1 = 2, and R2 = 4.

Example 6.

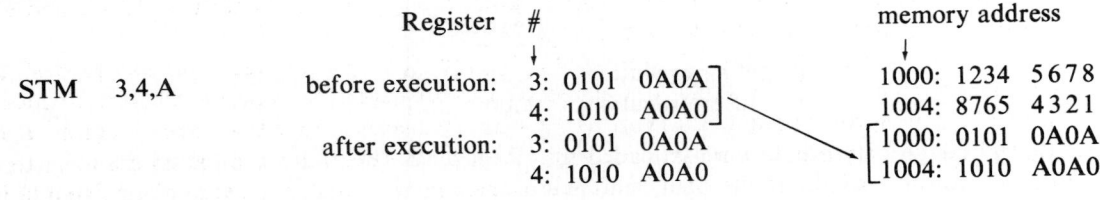

	Register #			memory address
STM 3,4,A	before execution:	3: 0101 0A0A		1000: 1234 5678
		4: 1010 A0A0		1004: 8765 4321
	after execution:	3: 0101 0A0A		1000: 0101 0A0A
		4: 1010 A0A0		1004: 1010 A0A0

Example 7.

		Reg 3	Reg 4
LR 3,4	before execution:	ABCD EF00	1234 5678
	after execution:	1234 5678	1234 5678

Recall that in all LOAD instructions, the source is the second operand; the destination is the first operand. Thus, in this example, the number in Register 4 is copied into Register 3.

5.3 ADDITION, SUBTRACTION, MULTIPLICATION, DIVISION

The instructions for these four operations all operate on two binary integers; therefore they all require two operand fields. The number that is addressed by the second operand field is combined with the number addressed by the first field. The result *replaces* the number addressed by the first field.

In the descriptions that follow, we will use this notation:

V_1 = the number whose address is specified by the *first* operand field of the instruction

V_2 = the number whose address is specified by the *second* operand field of the instruction.

Addition

There are five binary integer addition instructions: A, AL, AR, ALR, and AH.

opcode	meaning	type
A	ADD	RX
AL	ADD LOGICAL	RX
	Both A and AL add the full word V_2 to the full word V_1. V_2 is in memory, V_1 in a register. The result replaces V_1. The distinction between A and AL is discussed below.	
AR	ADD REGISTERS	RR
ALR	ADD LOGICAL REGISTERS	RR
	Both AR and ALR add the full word V_2 to the full word V_1. V_1 and V_2 are in registers. The result replaces V_1. The distinction between AR and ALR is discussed below.	
AH	ADD HALF WORD	RX
	Adds half word V_2 to full word V_1. V_2 is in memory, V_1 in a register. The result, a full word, replaces V_1.	

The result of an A, AR, and AH instruction is a 32-bit integer. If there is no overflow, i.e., if the sum is within the range from -2^{31} though $2^{31}-1$, the sum is correctly represented as a positive, negative, or zero quantity. However, if an overflow occurs during an addition, the 32-bit result cannot and does not represent the true sum. Remember that in two's complement addition, overflow occurs if the carry out of the sign bit position is different from the carry out of the high-order numeric bit position.

When an overflow occurs during an A, AR, or AH instruction, execution of the program may be interrupted by the hardware, and the program may be terminated by the Operating System. The only way to prevent such a hardware interruption is by means of the program mask, a capability of the IBM 360 and 370 systems that will be discussed further in chapter 11.

In the AL and ALR instructions, the quantities V_1, V_2, and $V_1 + V_2$ are treated as *unsigned* 32-bit integers. Thus bit b_0 of each quantity is not a sign bit; instead, it is the high-order numeric bit, with positional value $b_0 \times 2^{32}$. When an overflow occurs during an AL or ALR instruction, execution of the program is not interrupted by the hardware. Instead, execution proceeds with the next instruction in the program.

A hardware indicator known as the *condition code* records the nature of the result of all five add instructions. The meaning of the condition code that is recorded depends on which add instruction was executed, as shown in the following table.

instruction	condition code and its meaning			
	0	1	2	3
A, AR, AH	result was zero	result was negative	result was positive	overflow occurred
AL, ALR	result was zero with no carry out of the sign bit position	result was not zero with no carry out of the sign bit position	result was zero with a carry out of the sign bit position	result was not zero with a carry out of the sign bit position

Since there are only a few problems in which AL or ALR is used, they will not be considered further in this text.

In Examples 1 through 4 and in the rest of this chapter, we will often specify the second operand as a *literal constant*, recognizable by an equal sign (=). For example:

=F'10' specifies a full-word integer, +10 (0000000A in hex)
=H'8' specifies a half-word integer, +8 (0008 in hex)

Similarly, =F'−10' and =H'−8' specify full- and half-word negative integers. Note that in this notation, the integer is written in the decimal system; the Assembler translates this to its binary representation.

Example 1.   64 + 10 = 74

	Reg 3		=F'10'	
before execution:	0000	0040	0000	000A
after execution:	0000	004A	0000	000A

$+74_{10}$

A   3,=F'10'

full-word literal constant, V_2
address of the register containing V_1

Example 2.   4096 + (−1) = 4095

	Reg 5		Reg 6	
before execution:	FFFF	FFFF	0000	1000
after execution:	FFFF	FFFF	0000	0FFF

$+4095_{10}$

AR   6,5

address of register containing V_2
address of register containing V_1

Example 3.   80 + 8 = 88

				Reg 10		=H'8'
AH	10,=H'8'		before execution:	0000	0050	0008
			after execution:	0000	0058	0008

$+88_{10}$

half-word literal constant V_2
address of register containing V_1

Example 4.   80 + (−8) = 72

				Reg 10		=H'−8'
AH	10, =H'−8'		before execution:	0000	0050	FFF8
			after execution:	0000	0048	FFF8

When the AH instruction is executed, the half-word integer V_2 is extended to 32 bits just prior to the addition, without changing the representation of V_2 in memory. As discussed earlier, the extension of a half-word integer to a 32-bit integer is done by propagating the sign bit into the 16 high-order bits, so that, for example, 0008 becomes 00000008 and FFF8 becomes FFFFFFF8.

Subtraction

There are five binary integer subtraction instructions: S, SL, SR, SLR, and SH.

opcode	meaning	type
S	SUBTRACT	RX
SL	SUBTRACT LOGICAL	RX
	Both S and SL subtract the full word V_2 from the full word V_1. V_2 is in memory, V_1 in a register. The result replaces V_1. The distinction between S and SL is discussed below.	
SR	SUBTRACT REGISTERS	RR
SLR	SUBTRACT LOGICAL REGISTERS	RR
	Both SR and SLR subtract the full word V_2 from the full word V_1. V_1 and V_2 are in registers. The result replaces V_1. The distinction between SR and SLR is discussed below.	
SH	SUBTRACT HALF WORD	RX
	Subtracts half word V_2 from full word V_1. V_2 is in memory, V_1 in a register. The result, a full word, replaces V_1.	

In the S, SR, and SH instructions, the quantities V_1, V_2, and $V_1 - V_2$ are signed integers, and two's complement arithmetic is performed. If overflow occurs, execution may be interrupted and the program terminated. In the SL and SLR instructions, V_1, V_2, and $V_1 - V_2$ are treated as *unsigned* integers: bit b_0 is the high-order numeric bit, with positional value $b_0 \times 2^{32}$, and overflow does not cause program interruption.

The condition code is set for each subtract instruction as indicated in the following table.

instruction	condition code and its meaning			
	0*	1	2	3
S, SR, SH	result was zero	result was negative	result was positive	overflow occurred
SL, SLR	---	result was not zero with no carry out of the sign bit position	result was zero with a carry out of the sign bit position	result was not zero with a carry out of the sign bit position

*Condition code 0 is never set during an SL or SLR instruction due to the manner in which subtraction is performed by the hardware.

Compared to the S, SR, and SH instructions, there are not many problems for which SL and SLR are used. Consequently, the two logical subtracts will not be considered further in this text.

Example 1.   **64 − 10 = 54**

			Reg 3		= F'10'
S	3, = F'10'	before execution:	0000	0040	0000 000A
		after execution:	0000	0036	0000 000A

Example 2.   **4096 − (−1) = 4097**

			Reg 5		Reg 6
SR	6,5	before execution:	FFFF	FFFF	0000 1000
		after execution:	FFFF	FFFF	0000 1001

Example 3.   **8 − 80 = −72**

			Reg 10		= H'80'
SH	10, = H'80'	before execution:	0000	0008	0050
		after execution:	FFFF	FFB8	0050

In half-word subtraction, as in half-word addition, the second factor, V_2, is extended to 32 bits by propagating its sign bit into the 16 high-order bits. The CPU does this without affecting the representation of V_2 in memory.

Multiplication

There are three binary integer multiply instructions: M, MR, and MH. The M and MR instructions work similarly to one another, while the MH works somewhat differently.

In the M and MR instructions, V_1 must always be in an odd-numbered register. The product is a 64-bit signed integer that occupies two consecutive registers. These two registers are called an even-odd register pair, because the first of them is an even-numbered register and the second is the next consecutively addressed register. The following diagram shows the relationship of the registers that contain V_1 and its product with V_2.

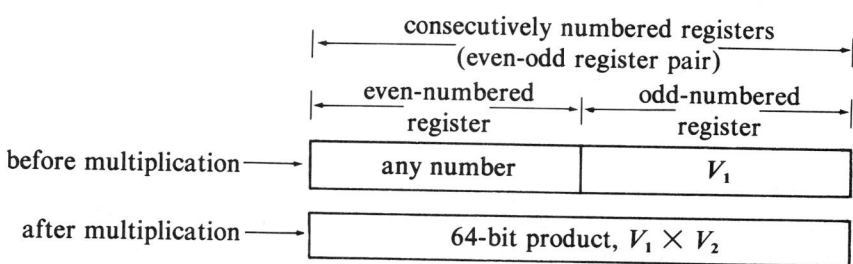

opcode	meaning	type
M	MULTIPLY Multiply V_1 by V_2. V_2 is a full word in memory. V_1 is a full word in an *odd*-numbered register. Result is a 64-bit double word, replacing the contents of the even-odd register pair that contained V_1.	RX
MR	MULTIPLY REGISTERS Multiply V_1 by V_2. V_2 is a full word in a register. V_1 is a full word in an *odd*-numbered register. Result is a 64-bit double word, replacing the contents of the even-odd register pair that contained V_1.	RR

In both the M and the MR instructions, the first operand must specify the address of the even-numbered register of the even-odd pair containing V_1. Examples 1 and 2 illustrate this.

Example 1. **Multiply 2×3; $V_1 = 2$ and $V_2 = 3$**

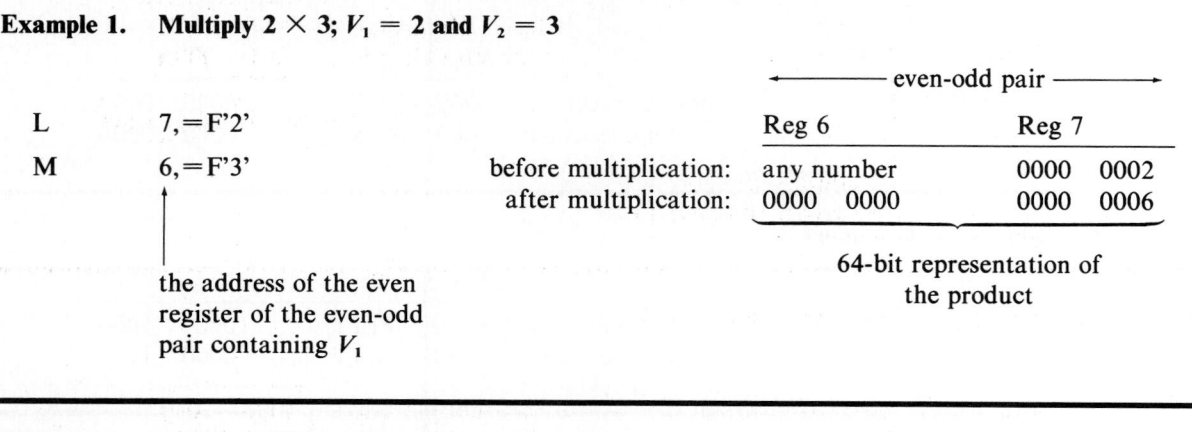

			even-odd pair	
			Reg 6	Reg 7
L	7,=F'2'			
M	6,=F'3'	before multiplication:	any number	0000 0002
		after multiplication:	0000 0000	0000 0006

the address of the even register of the even-odd pair containing V_1

64-bit representation of the product

Example 2. **Multiply $65{,}536 \times 65{,}536$ (i.e., $2^{16} \times 2^{16}$)**

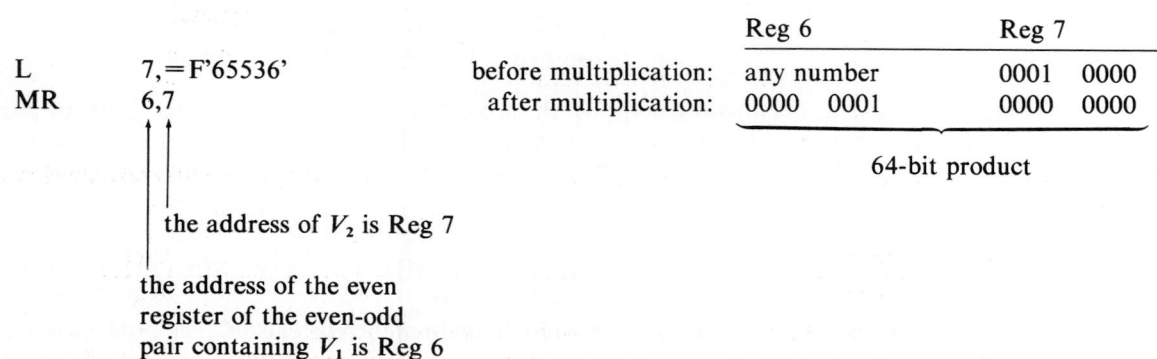

			even-odd pair	
			Reg 6	Reg 7
L	7,=F'65536'	before multiplication:	any number	0001 0000
MR	6,7	after multiplication:	0000 0001	0000 0000

the address of V_2 is Reg 7

64-bit product

the address of the even register of the even-odd pair containing V_1 is Reg 6

Note that $V_1 = V_2$ and both are in the same register, yet the two register addresses in the MR instruction are different. This example illustrates one method of multiplying a number by itself.

In Example 1, all the significant bits of the product, together with its sign, can be contained in the low-order 32 bits, that is, in the odd-numbered register. The high-order 32 bits are all nonsignificant, they do not contribute to the value of the product. In Example 2, the high-order 32 bits contain some significant bits. This is because the value of the product $2^{16} \times 2^{16} = 2^{32}$ is greater than $2^{31} - 1$ and so cannot be contained within 31 bits. *This is not considered an overflow;* the program is not interrupted. It is the responsibility of the programmer to know whether a product might exceed $2^{31} - 1$ (or be less than -2^{31}); if it will, there must be appropriate provisions in the program to ensure that the high-order significant bits are not lost. Alternatively, the programmer may want to use floating-point numbers, since the maximum allowable floating-point number is 2^{252} (approximately 10^{75}), rather than $2^{31} - 1$. Floating-point numbers are discussed in chapter 13.

Because the MH instruction does not require that an even-odd register pair be used, it is simpler to use than the M or MR instructions. *Any* register can be used for V_1, and the address of V_1 specifies the register that contains it. However, because the product generated by MH is always a 32-bit number—31 bits for numeric value, 1 bit for sign—MH should not be used if the product could exceed $2^{31} - 1$ or be less than -2^{31}. If the product's value lies outside the range of a 32-bit number, the most significant bits are lost *and there is no overflow.* The MH instruction is summarized by the following description and examples.

opcode	meaning	type
MH	MULTIPLY HALF WORD Multiply V_1 by V_2. V_2 is a half word in memory. V_1 is a full word in any register. Result replaces V_1.	RX

Example 3.   Multiply 2 × 5, for a half word, 5.

				Reg 7
L	7,=F'2'	before multiplication:	0000	0002
MH	7,=H'5'	after multiplication:	0000	000A

correct 32-bit product

the address of V_1 is
the register containing it.

Example 4.   Multiply 2^{30} × 2^4, for a half word, 2^4

				Reg 7
L	7,=F'1073741824'	before multiplication:	4000	0000
MH	7,=H'16'	after multiplication:	0000	0000

incorrect
product

most significant bits are lost

Division

There are two binary integer division instructions, D and DR. (Note that there is no half-word division instruction.)

opcode	meaning	type
D	DIVIDE Divide V_1 by V_2. V_2 is a full word in memory. V_1 is a double word in an even-odd register pair. Result replaces V_1 (see below).	RX
DR	DIVIDE REGISTERS Divide V_1 by V_2. V_2 is a full word in a register. V_1 is a double word in an even-odd register pair. Result replaces V_1.	RR

In the D and DR instructions, V_1 is a 64-bit integer and must always be in an even-odd register pair. Its position is specified by the even register of the pair.

The result of an integer division consists of two signed integers: an integer quotient, Q, and an integer remainder, R, defined as

$$\frac{V_1}{V_2} = Q + \frac{R}{V_2}.$$

The sign of the quotient is determined by the rules of algebra. The sign of the remainder is the same as that of the dividend, V_1, except when $R = 0$ and $V_1 < 0$. (The sign bit of a zero remainder is always 0, as is that of a zero quotient.) For example, if $V_1 = 150$ and $V_2 = 40$, then $Q = 3$ and $R = 30$. If $V_1 = -150$ and $V_2 = 40$, then $Q = -3$ and $R = -30$. If $V_1 = -120$ and $V_2 = 40$, then $Q = -3$ and $R = 0$. The quotient

Q replaces the low-order half of V_1 (i.e., Q replaces the contents of the odd-numbered register), and the remainder, R, replaces the high-order half of V_1. The following diagram illustrates this:

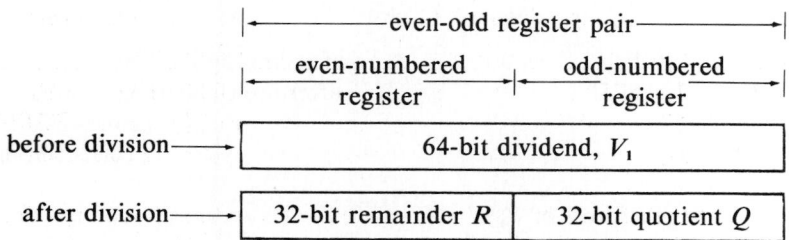

These concepts are illustrated in Examples 1 and 2.

Example 1.   Divide 7 by 2; $V_1 = 7$, $V_2 = 2$

```
L        9, = F'7'
L        8, = F'0'
D        8, = F'2'
```

the address of V_1 is the even-numbered register

	Reg 8	Reg 9
	$\longleftarrow$ V_1 $\longrightarrow$	
before division:	0000 0000	0000 0007
after division:	0000 0001	0000 0003
	remainder +1	quotient +3

Example 2.   Divide 150 by -40; $V_1 = +150$, $V_2 = -40$

```
L        9, = F'150'
L        8, = F'0'
L        10, = F'-40'
DR       8,10
```

address of V_2
address of V_1

	Reg 8	Reg 9	Reg 10
	$\longleftarrow$ V_1 $\longrightarrow$		$\longleftarrow$ V_2 $\longrightarrow$
before division:	0000 0000	0000 0096	FFFF FFD4
after division:	0000 001E	FFFF FFFD	FFFF FFD4
	remainder +30	quotient -3	

In both examples, the dividend, V_1, was a positive number. Changing it from a full-word 32-bit integer to a double-word 64-bit integer posed no special problem; the high-order half of the even-odd register pair was simply set to zero. When V_1 is negative, or, more generally, when its sign is not known in advance by the programmer, care must be taken to ensure that the sign bit is extended into each of the bits of the even-numbered register. The situations in Case 1 and 2 illustrate this.

Case 1. V_1 is positive or zero

decimal number	hexadecimal 32-bit representation				hexadecimal 64-bit representation			
0	00	00	00	00	0000	0000	0000	0000
12	00	00	00	0C	0000	0000	0000	000C
32,767	00	00	7F	FF	0000	0000	0000	7FFF
2,147,483,647	7F	FF	FF	FF	0000	0000	7FFF	FFFF

Case 2. V_1 **is negative**

decimal number	hexadecimal 32-bit representation				hexadecimal 64-bit representation			
−12	FF	FF	FF	F4	FFFF	FFFF	FFFF	FFF4
−32,767	FF	FF	8 0	01	FFFF	FFFF	FFFF	8001
−2,147,483,647	8 0	0 0	0 0	01	FFFF	FFFF	8000	0001

In the IBM 360 and 370, the correct 64-bit representation can be obtained by means of the *arithmetic double-word right-shift instruction,* SRDA. This is done in two steps: (1) the 32-bit dividend is placed into the even-numbered register and (2) the SRDA instruction is used to arithmetically shift the integer from the even-numbered register into the odd-numbered register of the pair. When the SRDA instruction is executed, it causes the sign bit of the even-numbered register to be copied into each of the bit positions vacated by the shifted quantity. Note that the shift is to the *right:* one begins by placing V_1 into the *even*-numbered register, and after execution of the shift it is properly represented as a 64-bit quantity. The required form of the SRDA instruction is as follows:

SRDA   R1,32

number of positions to be shifted

address of the even-numbered register that contains V_1

Other properties and uses of the SRDA instruction will be discussed in chapter 8.

For Examples 1 and 2, the SRDA instruction would be used like this:

To divide 7 by 2:

L	8,=F'7'
SRDA	8,32
D	8,=F'2'

To divide 150 by −40:

L	8,=F'150'
SRDA	8,32
D	8,=F'−40'

Example 3 illustrates what is taking place. The DR instruction is used for the division.

Example 3.   Divide −150 by +40; $V_1 = -150$ **and** $V_2 = +40$

			Reg 6	Reg 7	Reg 8
L	6,=F'−150'	after loading:	FFFFFF6A	any number	any number
SRDA	6,32	after shifting:	FFFFFFFF	FFFFFF6A	any number
L	8,=F'40'	after loading:	FFFFFFFF	FFFFFF6A	00000028
DR	6,8	after dividing:	FFFFFFE2	FFFFFFFD	00000028
			remainder	quotient	divisor
			−30	−3	40

address of V_2
address of V_1

After shifting, Registers 6 and 7, the even-odd register pair, contain the correct representation of the 64-bit dividend, −150. After dividing, the high-order and low-order portions of the dividend have been replaced by the remainder and the quotient, respectively.

There are two other precautions to observe when using either of the two divide instructions. First, division by zero ($V_2 = 0$) is not valid. If attempted, the program is automatically interrupted by the hardware and terminated by the Operating System. And, second, a divide instruction that attempts to generate a quotient larger than $2^{31}-1$ or smaller than -2^{31} is not valid. The program is interrupted by the hardware and terminated by the Operating System. Each of these situations is known as a *fixed-point divide exception.*

5.4   CONDITIONAL BRANCHES

It is frequently necessary, and quite easy, to determine whether the result of an add, subtract, multiply, or divide instruction is positive, negative, or zero. This is done by determining the setting of the condition code via conditional branch instructions.

As mentioned in the discussion of the add instructions, the condition code is a number stored in a hardware indicator to record the nature of a result. This is done whenever an add or subtract instruction is executed. The meaning of the number that is stored in the condition code indicator, that is, the meaning of the condition code itself, depends on what instruction was executed. In the IBM 360 and 370 systems, more than half of the available instructions generate conditions that are recorded in the condition code indicator. Since there is only one condition code indicator used during the execution of a program, *the condition code is changed each time an instruction that sets it is executed.* In other words, the condition code reflects only the result of the most recently executed code-setting instruction.

A list of all the nonprivileged instructions that set the condition code, together with the corresponding meanings of the codes, is given in figure 8.5a (see chap. 8). Included in this list, of course, are the add and subtract instructions. But notably missing are the multiply and divide instructions. We will learn how to deal with this discrepancy shortly.

There are six RX-type conditional branch instructions that can be used to determine whether the condition code is set to reflect a zero, a positive, or a negative result. The assembly language opcodes for these instructions are

opcode	meaning
BZ	Branch if result was zero
BNZ	Branch if result was not zero
BM	Branch if result was minus (i.e., negative)
BNM	Branch if result was not minus (i.e., was positive or zero)
BP	Branch if result was positive
BNP	Branch if result was not positive (i.e., was negative or zero)

Unlike other RX instructions, these six conditional branch instructions are written with only one operand field, for reasons that will be explained in chapter 8. The single operand designates the address of the instruction to which a branch is to be made if the condition being tested is true. If the condition being tested is *not* true, then no branch is made; instead, execution of the program continues with the instruction that immediately follows the conditional branch instruction. A simple example should serve to illustrate this capability:

```
       L     3,X          copy an integer from symbolic address X into Register 3
       S     3,=F'7'      subtract +7 from Register 3
       BZ    ZERO         branch to symbolic address ZERO if the result was zero
       BP    POS          branch to symbolic address POS if it was positive

       ⋮                  } section of the program that is executed
                          } when the difference computed above was negative

POS    ⋮                  } section of the program that is executed
                          } when the difference was positive

ZERO   ⋮                  } section of the program that is executed
                          } when the difference was zero
```

Note that the test for a positive result is independent of the test for a zero result, and vice versa. This is because there is a separate condition code setting for a positive result and for a zero result—and for a negative result, as well. *The conditional branch instructions themselves do not set the condition code; they merely test it.* Therefore, the setting that resulted from the subtract instruction in the example cited exists not only when the BZ instruction is executed but also when the BP instruction is executed. The setting of the condition code remains unchanged until an instruction that changes it is executed. The generally accepted practice is to follow a code-setting instruction with one or more conditional branch instructions whenever one wants to determine the nature of a result. This practice avoids the possibility that another code-setting instruction will be executed before the intended conditional branches.

In the preceding section, the meanings of the condition codes for the A, AR, and AH add instructions and the S, SR, and SH subtract instructions were given. From these, it may be seen that any of the six conditional branch instructions may be used to determine the nature of the result following one of the six add or subtract instructions. But it is a design property of the IBM 360 and 370 systems that none of the multiply or divide instructions set the condition code. So the question is, How can we determine whether the result of a multiply or divide instruction is positive, negative, or zero? The answer lies in the use of another instruction, Load and Test Register (LTR).

The LTR instruction is an RR-type instruction. Its format is as follows:

opcode	operand
LTR	R1,R2

The purpose of the LTR instruction is to set the condition code according to the contents of a register—zero, positive, or negative. Once set by this instruction, the condition code, and thus the nature of the number that was tested, can be determined via a conditional branch instruction. The LTR works as follows: the number in the register designated by the second operand (R2) is copied into the register designated by the first operand (R1), and the condition code is set according to whether the number that was copied is zero, positive, or negative. R1 and R2 may designate the same register.

The following two examples illustrate the use of LTR to determine whether a product is zero, negative, or positive.

If we know that the product is within the range of a 32-bit integer, then we can test it as follows:

```
L      7,V1    R7 = MULTIPLICAND
M      6,V2    R6 & R7 = 64-BIT PRODUCT
LTR    7,7     TEST LOW-ORDER 32 BITS OF PRODUCT
BM     NEG     BRANCH IF PRODUCT WAS NEGATIVE
BZ     ZRO     BRANCH IF ZERO
B      POS     BRANCH IF POSITIVE
```

If the range of the product is not known, the test is a little more complex, since the LTR only allows testing the contents of one register at a time:

```
L      7,V1    R7 = MULTIPLICAND
M      6,V2    R6 & R7 = 64-BIT PRODUCT
LTR    6,6     TEST HIGH-ORDER 32 BITS OF PRODUCT
BM     NEG     <0 IF HI-ORDER NEGATIVE.
BNZ    POS     >0 IF HI-ORDER NOTNEG,NOTZRO:
LTR    7,7     ELSE,MUST TEST LO-ORDER 32 BITS
BNZ    POS     >0 IF LOW-ORDER NOT ZERO,
BZ     ZRO     =0 IF LOW-ORDER IS ZERO.
```

In this sequence, a negative product will cause a branch to location NEG, a positive product will cause a branch to POS, and a product of zero will cause a branch to ZRO; however, no distinction is made for products outside the range of 32-bit integers.

For division, the sign of the quotient can be determined as follows:

```
L      6,V1    R6 & R7 = DIVIDEND
SRDA   6,32    SHIFT TO ENSURE PROPER SIGN
D      6,V2    R6 = REMAINDER,R7 = QUOTIENT
LTR    7,7
BM     NEG     BRANCH IF QUOTIENT NEGATIVE
BZ     ZRO     BRANCH IF QUOTIENT ZERO
B      POS     OTHERWISE IT'S POSITIVE
```

The nature of the remainder can be determined in similar fashion.

5.5 COMPARING INTEGERS

Any binary integer can be algebraically compared to any other binary integer without having to subtract one from the other. One of the two integers being compared must be in a register; the other can either be in a register or in a memory location, depending on the compare instruction that is used. *Neither integer is changed by a compare instruction.*

There are three algebraic compare instructions for binary integers: C, CR, and CH. To describe these instructions, we will continue to use the notation introduced earlier:

V_1 = the integer whose address is specified by the first operand of the instruction
V_2 = the integer whose address is specified by the second operand of the instruction.

opcode	meaning	type
C	COMPARE Compares V_1 to V_2. V_1 is in a register; V_2 is a 32-bit integer in a memory location.	RX
CR	COMPARE REGISTERS Compares V_1 to V_2. Both V_1 and V_2 are in registers.	RR
CH	COMPARE HALF WORD Compares V_1 to V_2. V_1 is in a register; V_2 is a 16-bit integer in a memory location.	RX

In algebraic comparisons, the two quantities, V_1 and V_2, are compared as signed 32-bit integers, and the rules of algebra are used: V_1 is considered to be less than V_2 if there is a positive integer N such that $V_1 + N = V_2$. For the half-word comparison CH, V_2 is expanded to 32 bits for purposes of the comparison but is not altered in its memory location. The expansion, performed by propagating the sign bit of V_2 into the high-order 16 bits of a 32-bit word, takes place in a register that is unavailable to programmers.

Each execution of a compare instruction sets the condition code as indicated in the following table:

instruction	condition code and its meanings			
	0	1	2	3
C, CR, CH	$V_1 = V_2$	$V_1 < V_2$	$V_1 > V_2$	- - -

In order to determine the result of a comparison, we can use one of the following six RX-type conditional branch instructions:

opcode	meaning	
BE	Branch if V_1 equals V_2	$V_1 = V_2$
BNE	Branch if V_1 is not equal to V_2	$V_1 \neq V_2$
BL	Branch if V_1 is less than V_2	$V_1 < V_2$
BNL	Branch if V_1 is not less than V_2	$V_1 \geq V_2$
BH	Branch if V_1 is higher than V_2	$V_1 > V_2$
BNH	Branch if V_1 is not higher than V_2	$V_1 \leq V_2$

The use of these instructions is analogous to that of the six arithmetic conditional branch instructions described in the previous section. Each of these six instructions is written with only one operand field. That field designates the address of the instruction to which a branch is made if the condition being tested is true. If the condition being tested is *not* true, then no branch is made; instead, execution of the program continues with the instruction that immediately follows the conditional branch instruction.

Examples 1 through 3 serve to illustrate the use of the compare and conditional branch instructions. As with the arithmetic conditional branch instructions, the instructions used here do not set the condition code; they merely test it.

Example 1. Algebraic comparison of two 32-bit binary integers, one of which is in a register, the other in memory

L	3,X	copy an integer from symbolic address X into Register 3
C	3,=F'9'	compare Register 3's contents to +9
BE	EQUAL	branch to symbolic address EQUAL if the integers were equal
BH	HIGH	branch to symbolic address HIGH if the contents of Register 3 were algebraically greater than +9

$\qquad\qquad$ ⋮ $\qquad\qquad\Big\}$ section of the program that is executed when the contents of Register 3 were algebraically less than +9

HIGH $\qquad$ ⋮ $\qquad\qquad\Big\}$ section of the program that is executed when the contents of Register 3 were algebraically greater than +9

EQUAL $\qquad$ ⋮ $\qquad\qquad\Big\}$ section of the program that is executed when the contents of Register 3 were equal to +9

Example 2. Algebraic comparison of two 32-bit integers, both of which are in registers

L	3,X	copy an integer from symbolic address X into Register 3
L	4,=F'9'	copy the integer +9 into Register 4
CR	3,4	compare the contents of Register 3 to that of Register 4
BNH	LE	branch to symbolic address LE if Register 3's contents
B	GT	were not greater than Register 4's; otherwise branch to symbolic address GT

LE $\qquad$ ⋮ $\qquad\qquad\Big\}$ section of the program that is executed when Register 3's contents were not greater than Register 4's

GT $\qquad$ ⋮ $\qquad\qquad\Big\}$ section of the program that is executed when Register 3's contents were greater than Register 4's

Example 3. Algebraic comparison of two integers, one a 32-bit integer in a register, the other a 16-bit integer in memory

L	5,X	copy an integer from symbolic address X into Register 3
CH	5,=H'−1'	compare the contents of Register 5 to −1
BNE	NEQ	branch to symbolic address NEQ if the two integers were not equal

$\qquad\qquad$ ⋮

$\qquad\qquad$ ⋮ $\qquad\qquad\Big\}$ section of program that is executed when the two integers were equal

NEQ $\qquad$ ⋮ $\qquad\qquad\Big\}$ section of the program that is executed when the two integers were not equal

5.6 CHANGING SIGN AND GENERATING ABSOLUTE VALUES

Use of the instructions described here makes it easy for programmers to deal with two's complement representation when an integer's sign must be changed or made positive or negative. The three instructions in this group are all RR-type instructions, so that in each instruction both operand fields must specify register addresses. As before, we use the notation V_1 and V_2 to describe the effect of the instructions.

opcode	meaning	type
LCR	LOAD COMPLEMENT FROM REGISTER Copies the negative of V_2—i.e., its two's complement —into the register occupied by V_1; the result replaces V_1	RR
LPR	LOAD POSITIVE ABSOLUTE VALUE FROM REGISTER Copies the positive absolute value of V_2 into the register occupied by V_1; the result replaces V_1.	RR
LNR	LOAD NEGATIVE ABSOLUTE VALUE FROM REGISTER Copies the negative absolute value of V_2 into the register occupied by V_1; the result replaces V_1.	RR

Each of the three instructions sets the condition code as indicated in the following table. Consequently, the nature of the result may be determined by use of the conditional branch instructions BZ, BNZ, BM, BNM, BP, and BNP.

	condition code and its meanings			
instruction	0	1	2	3
LCR	result was zero	result was negative	result was positive	overflow occurred
LPR	result was zero	- - -	result was positive	overflow occurred
LNR	result was zero	result was negative	- - -	- - -

The occurrence of overflow, illustrated in Examples 2 and 5, usually causes the hardware to interrupt execution of the program, with consequent termination by the Operating System. This can be prevented by use of the "program mask," as will be discussed in chapter 11.

Example 1.

			Reg 3
LCR	3,3	before execution:	FFFFFFFA
		*after execution:	00000006

* When both register addresses are the same, the result replaces the number that was in that register before execution of the LCR.

Example 2.

			Reg 3	Reg 4
LCR	3,4	before execution:	87654321	80000000
		*after execution:	80000000	80000000

* The two's complement of -2^{31} is still -2^{31}. The number $+2^{31}$ cannot be represented in 32 bits. Therefore, when $V_2 = -2^{31}$, the LCR instruction generates an overflow error condition.

Example 3.

				Reg 4	Reg 5
LPR	5,4	before execution:		FFFFFFFA	000000AB
		after execution:		FFFFFFFA	00000006

Example 4.

				Reg 4	Reg 5
LPR	4,5	before execution:		FFFFFFFA	000000AB
		*after execution:		000000AB	000000AB

* The positive absolute value of a positive number is that positive number.

Example 5.

				Reg 7	Reg 8
LPR	8,7	before execution:		80000000	12345678
		*after execution:		80000000	80000000

* The positive absolute value of -2^{31} cannot be represented in 32 bits. When $V_2 = -2^{31}$, execution of an LPR instruction generates an overflow error condition.

Example 6.

				Reg 4	Reg 5
LNR	4,5	before execution:		FFFFFFFA	000000AB
		after execution:		FFFFFF55	000000AB

Example 7.

				Reg 4	Reg 5
LNR	5,4	before execution:		FFFFFFFA	0 0 0 0 0 0 A B
		*after execution:		FFFFFFFA	F F F F F F F A

* The negative absolute value of a negative number is that negative number. However, it should be noted that the negative absolute value of 0 (zero) is 0. In the IBM 360 and 370 systems, the binary integer representations of -0 and $+0$ are the same, that is, all bits in the representation are zeroes.

5.7 INTEGER ARITHMETIC EXAMPLES

In the following programs, and in those of all subsequent chapters, the technique of indexing and loop control described in chapter 4 is used. The best way to understand these programs, and the best way to learn how the instructions work together to produce the desired result, is to manually trace the execution of each program, statement by statement. This requires patience and a systematic method of recording the results of each instruction. The first example is traced in detail to illustrate the concept. For the others, only the important aspects are summarized; you may trace them for your own experience.

The problems to be considered are:

1. Compute the sum of N integers.
2. Compute the average value of N integers.
3. Multiply each integer in an array by a constant.
4. Count the number of positive integers that occur in an array of N integers.
5. Replace each integer in an array by its absolute value.
6. Determine the largest and the smallest integers in an array of N integers.

Solutions to these problems, shown in figures 5.2 through 5.7, are explained in the discussion of the examples. Since it is assumed that the statements shown in the figures represent part of a larger program, the CSECT, END, and BALR-USING base-register statements are not included.

The programming solutions given for each problem are valid for any integers that do not cause overflow, but no data are included in the solutions. Instead, memory space for the data is reserved by means of the DS directive. This directive has an effect similar to that of a FORTRAN DIMENSION statement: Space is reserved, but no data are placed in that space by the directive. Use of the DS directive will be described in the next chapter; for the purposes of the present chapter, all that is required is to understand the meaning of a DS directive in this form:

name field	opcode	operand
X	DS	nF

This statement reserves n consecutive full words, each on a full-word boundary, and assigns the address of the first word that is reserved to the symbol X; n can be any unsigned decimal integer. If n is omitted, its value is assumed to be 1.

The reason for excluding data from the solutions is to emphasize that the solutions are not dependent on any particular data. For the solutions to be run in a computer system, however, you would have to add statements whose purpose is to place data into the reserved memory areas. This could be done by reading the data and converting it to binary integer format, as discussed in chapter 4. The sample program given at the end of this chapter provides a further illustration of the techniques required to do this.

Example 1. Compute the sum of N integers
(See fig. 5.2.)

The solution shown in figure 5.2 is valid for any N integers, for N between 1 and 100 inclusive. The limit of 100 is set by the operand in Statement 14, which reserves 100 full words for the integers. The lower limit of 1 is set by the loop-control mechanism of the program—in particular, the BCT instruction in Statement 9—which requires that there be at least one integer in the array.

The program begins with three loop-initialization instructions. The Load Address (LA) instruction of Statement 2 puts the address of the first integer—symbolic address ARRAY, defined by Statement 14—into Register 8. During each iteration of the loop, Register 8 will contain the address of the integer that is to be added to the sum during that iteration. The Load (L) instruction of Statement 3 puts the count of the number of integers in the array into Register 9. This count will determine how many iterations of the loop will be performed at run time. The Subtract Register (SR) instruction of Statement 5 puts a zero into Register 10, by subtracting whatever number was in that register from itself. Register 10 is initialized to zero because it will be used to accumulate the sum during each loop iteration.

Following these loop initialization instructions, the loop is executed N times. Each time it is executed a different integer component of the array is added to the sum in Register 10. The possibility that an addition would generate a number outside the range of allowable full-word integers (greater than $2^{31}-1$ or less than -2^{31}) is not considered; it is assumed that this will not happen, but, if it did, the program would be terminated by the Operating System because of an overflow error condition.

Execution of the loop proceeds as follows. The Add (A) instruction of Statement 6 adds the integer whose address is in Register 8 to the sum being accumulated in Register 10. The Load Address (LA) instruction of Statement 8 increases the address in Register 8 by the constant 4 given in its displacement field.

This is done as preparation for the next loop iteration; an increase of 4 adjusts the address to the next integer in the array, as shown in this diagram:

The Branch on Count (BCT) instruction of Statement 9 determines whether the loop should be repeated. The BCT reduces the count that is in Register 9 by +1, and, if the reduced count is not zero, the BCT branches to the instruction whose symbolic address is ADD. If the reduced count *is* zero, the BCT instruction does not branch, thereby terminating the loop. As explained in Chapter 4, this technique of loop control depends on the fact that the initial loop-control counter, in this case, the number of integers in the array, is at least 1.

A different array component is added to the sum in Register 10 during each iteration of the loop. When the loop-control counter in Register 9 is finally reduced to zero, the loop is terminated with the total sum of the array's integers in Register 10. At this point, the Store (ST) instruction of Statement 11 copies the sum from Register 10 into a memory location for subsequent use by other portions of the program (not shown).

In order to trace the execution of the program, let us assume the following addresses have been assigned, and that the data are as shown:

symbolic address	numeric address	number stored at that address	
		hex	decimal
N	500	0000 0003	3
ARRAY	504	0000 000A	10
	508	FFFF FFF2	−14
	50C	0000 000C	12

Figure 5.2   Compute sum of N integers.

```
 1      * INITIALIZATION
 2      START    LA      8,ARRAY     R8 = ADDR OF FIRST INTEGER
 3               L       9,N         R9 = NUMBER OF INTEGERS
 4               SR      10,10       R10 = SUM BEING ACCUMULATED
 5      * COMPUTE SUM
 6      ADD      A       10,0(8)     ADD CURRENT INTEGER TO R10
 7      * LOOP CONTROL
 8               LA      8,4(8)      R8 = ADDR OF NEXT INTEGER
 9               BCT     9,ADD       DECR # INTEGERS BY 1 & REPEAT
10      * SAVE FINAL RESULT
11               ST      10,SUM      COPY ACCUMULATED SUM INTO MEMORY
                 .
                 .
                 .
12      SUM      DS      F           FULL WORD FOR FINAL SUM
13      N        DS      F           FULL WORD FOR NO. OF INTEGERS
14      ARRAY    DS      100F        100 FULL WORDS FOR ARRAY
                 .
                 .
                 .
```

In other words, the assumptions are that there are three integers in the array, that the array begins at address 504, and that the integers stored in the array are 0000000A, FFFFFFF2, and 0000000C. The trace is as follows (underlined numbers indicate changes to previous numbers in the respective registers).

	statement	Reg 8	Reg 9	Reg 10
initialization	#2	000504		
	#3	000504	00 00 00 03	
	#4	000504	00 00 00 03	00 00 00 00
first iteration	#6	000504	00 00 00 03	00 00 00 0A
	#8	000508	00 00 00 03	00 00 00 0A
	#9	000508	00 00 00 02	00 00 00 0A
second iteration	#6	000508	00 00 00 02	FF FF FF FC
	#8	00050C	00 00 00 02	FF FF FF FC
	#9	00050C	00 00 00 01	FF FF FF FC
third iteration	#6	00050C	00 00 00 01	00 00 00 08
	#8	000510	00 00 00 01	00 00 00 08
	#9	000510	00 00 00 00	00 00 00 08

At this point, the loop-control counter in Register 9 has been reduced to zero by the BCT in Statement 9, so there is no branch to continue the loop. Instead, the sum 00000008 in Register 10 is stored into symbolic address SUM, which is numeric address 4FC, since SUM just precedes N in memory (see fig. 5.2).

Example 2. Compute the average of N integers
(See fig. 5.3.)

This solution is a modification of the previous one, since to compute the average it is necessary to first determine the sum. The modification consists of Statements 11.1 through 11.7.

To compute the average, the sum must be divided by the number of integers, N. The divide instruction requires that the dividend be a 64-bit integer in a pair of consecutively numbered registers, the first of which must be an even-numbered register. This means that for the divide instruction of Statement 11.3, namely D 10,N, Registers 10 and 11 must contain the dividend as a 64-bit binary integer, and symbolic memory location N must contain the divisor as a 32-bit binary integer. As discussed earlier, the SRDA instruction in Statement 11.2 generates the appropriate representation of the 64-bit dividend.

When the division instruction is executed, the 64-bit dividend is replaced by two 32-bit quantities, the quotient and the remainder. Remember that the remainder always has the same sign as the dividend (unless the remainder is zero), whereas the sign of the quotient is determined by the rules of algebra. Also remember that both the remainder and the quotient are integers. As an illustration, consider four simple cases: 12/3, 12/(−3), 13/3, and (−13)/3.

divisor	dividend		remainder	quotient
	Reg 10	Reg 11	Reg 10	Reg 11
0000 0003	0000 0000	0000 000C	0000 0000	0000 0004
FFFF FFFD	0000 0000	0000 000C	0000 0000	FFFF FFFC
0000 0003	0000 0000	0000 000D	0000 0001	0000 0004
0000 0003	FFFF FFFF	FFFF FFF3	FFFF FFFF	FFFF FFFC

In chapters 12 and 13, other methods for performing arithmetic calculations will be described. Those methods allow integers and mixed numbers in all calculations, and, in particular, they allow a quotient to be computed as a mixed number rather than by generating a separate integer remainder. However, the use of those methods requires different instructions and different representations of data.

Figure 5.3 *Compute the average of N integers.*

```
              .
              .
              .
 1      * INITIALIZATION
 2      START   LA     8,ARRAY          STATEMENTS #1 - #11 AND
 3              L      9,N              #12 - #14 ARE IDENTICAL
 4              SR     10,10            TO THOSE IN FIG. 5.2
 5      * COMPUTE SUM
 6      ADD     A      10,0(8)
 7      * LOOP CONTROL
 8              LA     8,4(8)
 9              BCT    9,ADD
10      * SAVE FINAL RESULT
11              ST     10,SUM
11.1    * COMPUTE AVERAGE             FIRST, CREATE SIGNED DOUBLE-WORD
11.2            SRDA   10,32             DIVIDEND IN EVEN-ODD REG PAIR
11.3            D      10,N            THEN DIVIDE BY NO. OF INTEGERS
11.4            ST     11,QUOTIENT     SAVE INTEGER QUOTIENT Q
11.5            ST     10,REMNDR       SAVE INTEGER REMAINDER R
              .
              .
              .
11.6    QUOTIENT DS    F               FULL-WD FOR Q
11.7    REMNDR   DS    F               FULL-WD FOR R
12      SUM      DS    F
13      N        DS    F
14      ARRAY    DS    100F
              .
              .
              .
```

Example 3. Multiply each integer in an array by a constant
(See fig. 5.4.)

The heart of this solution is the following three-instruction sequence:

```
        MULT    L      11,0(8)
                MR     10,5
                ST     11,0(8)
```

The first operand of the MR instruction designates the even-odd register pair that contains the 32-bit multiplicand and will contain the 64-bit product. The second operand of the MR designates the 32-bit multiplier. The multiplier is placed into Register 5 by Statement 4; the multiplicand is placed into Register 11 by Statement 6. The product replaces the multiplicand, via Statement 7.

The solution given in figure 5.4—in particular, Statement 8—assumes that the magnitude of each product will not require more than 32 bits. A product requiring more than 32 bits would be generated whenever the two factors, multiplicand and multiplier, were such that the product exceeded $2^{31}-1$ or was less than -2^{31}.

Figure 5.4   Multiply each integer in an array by a constant.

```
        .
        .
        .
 1   * INITIALIZATION
 2           LA      8,ARRAY              R8 = ADDR OF FIRST INTEGER
 3           L       9,N                  R9 = NUMBER OF INTEGERS
 4           L       5,CONSTANT           R5 = MULTIPLIER, A CONSTANT
 5   * COMPUTE PRODUCT =  CURRENT INTEGER X CONSTANT . . . PRODUCT < 2**31
 6   MULT    L      11,0(8)               R11=MULTIPLICAND=CURRENT INTEGER
 7           MR     10,5                  R11 X R5 = PRODUCT IN R10 & R11
 8           ST     11,0(8)               REPLACE INTEGER BY PRODUCT
 9   * LOOP CONTROL
10           LA      8,4(8)               R8 = ADDR OF NEXT INTEGER
11           BCT     9,MULT               DECR # INTEGERS BY 1 & REPEAT
        .
        .
        .
12   N         DS    F                    SPACE FOR NO. OF INTEGERS
13   CONSTANT  DS    F                    SPACE FOR CONSTANT MULTIPLIER
14   ARRAY     DS    50F                  SPACE FOR 50-INTEGER ARRAY
        .
        .
        .
```

Figure 5.5   Count the number of positive integers in an array.

```
 1   * INITIALIZATION
 2           LA      8,ARRAY              R8 = ADDR OF FIRST INTEGER
 3           L       9,N                  R9 = NUMBER OF INTEGERS
 4           SR     10,10                 R10 = COUNT OF POSITIVE INTEGERS
 5   * DETERMINE WHICH INTEGERS ARE POSITIVE, AND COUNT THOSE
 6   POSCHK   L      11,0(8)              R11 GETS CURRENT INTEGER
 7           LTR    11,11                 LTR ESTABLISHES SIGN CONDITION
 8           BNP    LOOPCTL               IF NOT POSITIVE, DON'T COUNT IT
 9           A      10,=F'1'              ELSE, ADD 1 TO COUNT IN R10
10   * LOOP CONTROL
11   LOOPCTL  LA      8,4(8)              R8 = ADDR OF NEXT INTEGER
12           BCT     9,POSCHK             DECR # INTEGERS BY 1 & REPEAT
13           ST     10,POSCTR             SAVE COUNT OF POSITIVE INTEGERS
        .
        .
        .
14   POSCTR   DS    F                     SPACE FOR NO. POS INTEGERS
15   N        DS    F                     SPACE FOR NO. OF INTEGERS
16   ARRAY    DS    200F                  SPACE FOR 200-INTEGER ARRAY
```

Example 4.   Count the number of positive integers in an array
          (See fig. 5.5.)

The heart of this solution is given by the following three statements:

```
        POSCHK        L        11,0(8)
                      LTR      11,11
                      BNP      LOOPCTL
```

To determine whether an integer is positive, use either the BP or BNP conditional branch instructions, as in Statement 8. Since all conditional branch instructions depend on the most-recent result or, more precisely, on the most recent setting of the condition code, it is necessary to set the condition code before using a conditional branch instruction. It is a property of the design of the IBM 360 and 370 computer systems that the Load (L) instruction does not set the condition code, whereas the Load and Test Register (LTR) instruction does. Therefore the LTR is used in Statement 7 to set the condition code depending on whether the integer that had just been loaded via L 11,0(8) is positive, negative, or zero. This enables the BNP instruction following the LTR instruction to correctly determine whether that integer is not positive, i.e., is zero or negative.

Figure 5.6 *Replace integers by their absolute values.*

```
1    * INITIALIZATION
2           LA    8,ARRAY              R8 = ADDR OF FIRST INTEGER
3           L     9,N                  R9 = NUMBER OF INTEGERS
4    * REPLACE EACH INTEGER BY ITS (POSITIVE) ABSOLUTE VALUE
5    ABSVAL L     10,0(8)              R10 = CURRENT INTEGER
6           LPR   10,10                LPR GENERATES POS. ABS. VAL.
7           ST    10,0(8)              REPLACE CURRENT INTEGER
8    * LOOP-CONTROL
9           LA    8,4(8)               R8 = ADDR OF NEXT INTEGER
10          BCT   9,ABSVAL             DECR # INTEGERS BY 1 & REPEAT
                  .
                  .
                  .
11   N      DS    F
12   ARRAY  DS    200F
                  .
                  .
                  .
```

Example 5. **Replace integers by their absolute values**
(See fig. 5.6.)

This solution is similar to that of figure 5.5. Statement 6, the LPR instruction, generates the positive absolute value of the integer that was placed into Register 10 by Statement 5. Statement 7 copies the positive absolute value into the memory location that had been occupied by the original integer. It should be noted that the solution assumes that none of the integers is equal to -2^{31}; if any integers were equal to -2^{31}, its positive absolute value, $+2^{31}$, would be outside the range of integers that can be represented in 32 bits and the LPR instruction would cause an overflow.

Example 6. **Determine the algebraically largest and smallest integers in an array**
(See figs. 5.7 and 5.8.)

One way to solve this problem is to arrange all the integers in order, from the smallest to largest. The desired result would then be obtained by choosing the first and last integers in the rearranged set. Such a procedure, known as *sorting,* is not necessary for this problem. Instead, the following simpler technique is used.

Each integer in the array is examined, one by one. Each time an integer is examined, it is compared to the largest integer of all those previously examined. If the integer is larger than the currently largest integer, it clearly must replace the largest integer of all those examined so far. If the integer being examined is *not* larger than the currently largest integer, it is compared to the currently smallest integer to see if it is smaller than it. After all integers have been examined in this way, the two desired results will have been established without having rearranged the integers. The technique just outlined is illustrated in the flow diagram of figure 5.7 (numbers by the boxes correspond to the statements in figure 5.8).

Note that in the initialization steps, the first array entry is used to establish the initial values of the current largest and smallest integers. This is preferable to attempting to estimate these initial values, since by not estimating, the procedure remains independent of the data in the array. Note also that the current largest and smallest integers are held in registers until all integers in the array have been examined. This makes it easy for the program to compare and replace them.

Figure 5.7 *Diagram for Figure 5.8.*

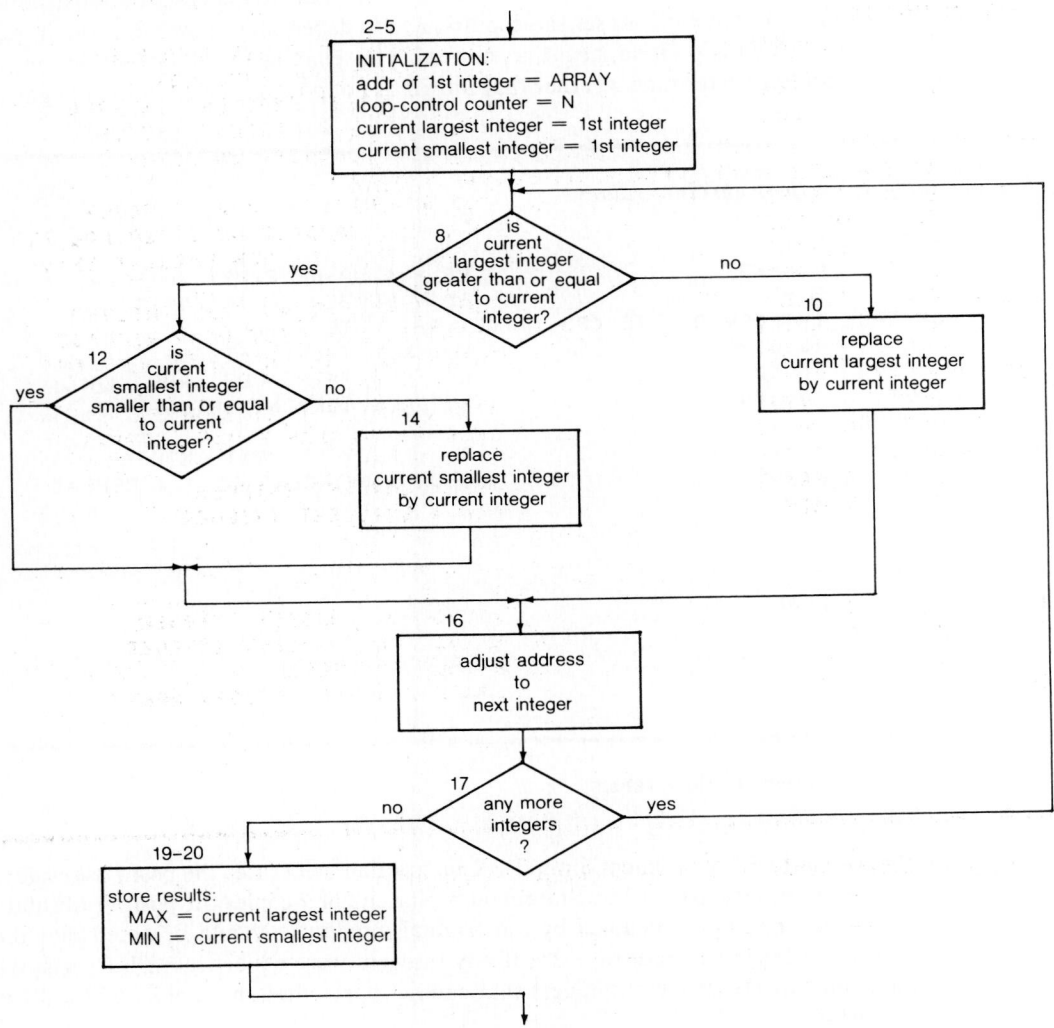

5.8 TWO-DIMENSIONAL ARRAYS

A two-dimensional array consisting of *M* rows and *N* columns is stored in memory according to the pattern shown in figure 5.9. The components of the array, assumed to be full-word integers, are stored consecutively, column by column. The last component of any column, *K*, is followed immediately by the first component of column $K+1$, for $K = 1,2,..., N-1$. This is known as *column-major* form. The address of the full-word integer in the Jth row and Kth column of an array, A, stored in column-major form is

$$\{\text{address of A(J,K)}\} = \{\text{address of A(1,1)}\} + \{4*(J-1)\} + \{4*M*(K-1)\}.$$

When processing a two-dimensional array in FORTRAN, it is usually necessary to use two subscript variables in nested DO-loops. For example, to set each component of a two-dimensional integer array, A, to zero in FORTRAN, it is common practice to write statements like these:

```
        DO   20   J=1,M
        DO   10   K=1,N
        A(J,K) = 0
10      CONTINUE
20      CONTINUE
```

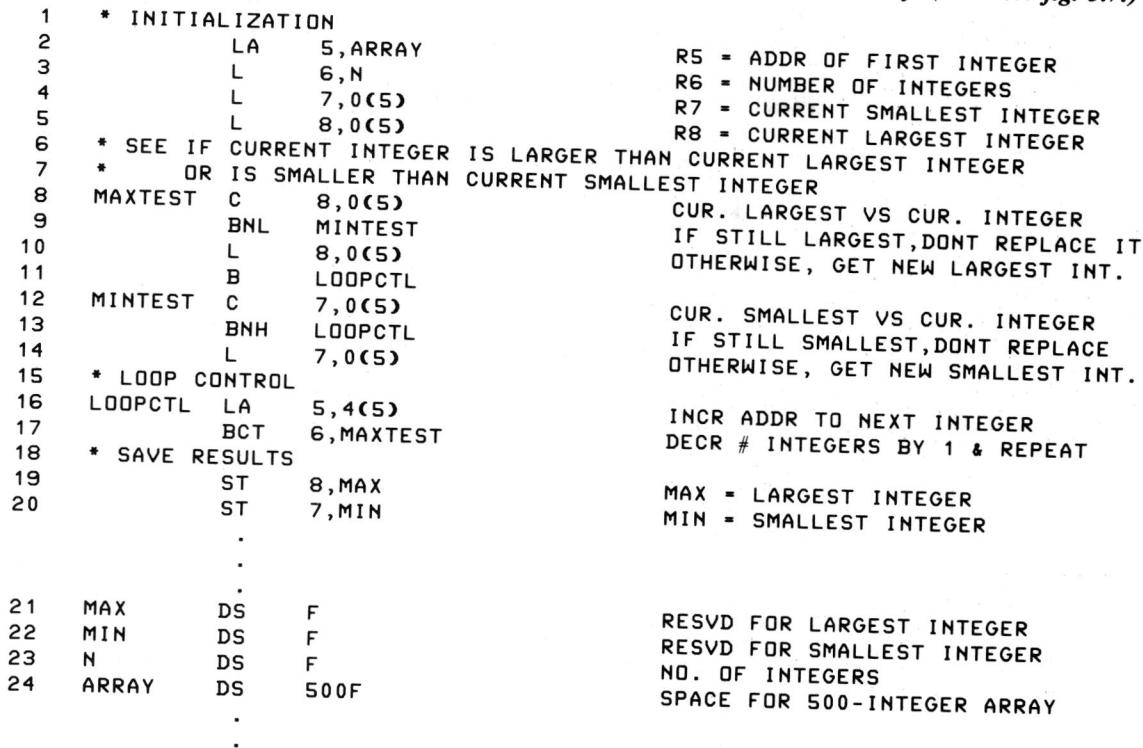

Figure 5.8 *Determine the algebraically largest and smallest integers in an array. (See also fig. 5.7.)*

```
1       * INITIALIZATION
2               LA      5,ARRAY             R5 = ADDR OF FIRST INTEGER
3               L       6,N                 R6 = NUMBER OF INTEGERS
4               L       7,0(5)              R7 = CURRENT SMALLEST INTEGER
5               L       8,0(5)              R8 = CURRENT LARGEST INTEGER
6       * SEE IF CURRENT INTEGER IS LARGER THAN CURRENT LARGEST INTEGER
7       *     OR IS SMALLER THAN CURRENT SMALLEST INTEGER
8       MAXTEST C       8,0(5)              CUR. LARGEST VS CUR. INTEGER
9               BNL     MINTEST             IF STILL LARGEST,DONT REPLACE IT
10              L       8,0(5)              OTHERWISE, GET NEW LARGEST INT.
11              B       LOOPCTL
12      MINTEST C       7,0(5)              CUR. SMALLEST VS CUR. INTEGER
13              BNH     LOOPCTL             IF STILL SMALLEST,DONT REPLACE
14              L       7,0(5)              OTHERWISE, GET NEW SMALLEST INT.
15      * LOOP CONTROL
16      LOOPCTL LA      5,4(5)              INCR ADDR TO NEXT INTEGER
17              BCT     6,MAXTEST           DECR # INTEGERS BY 1 & REPEAT
18      * SAVE RESULTS
19              ST      8,MAX               MAX = LARGEST INTEGER
20              ST      7,MIN               MIN = SMALLEST INTEGER
                        .
                        .
                        .
21      MAX     DS      F                   RESVD FOR LARGEST INTEGER
22      MIN     DS      F                   RESVD FOR SMALLEST INTEGER
23      N       DS      F                   NO. OF INTEGERS
24      ARRAY   DS      500F                SPACE FOR 500-INTEGER ARRAY
                        .
                        .
                        .
```

Figure 5.9 *Memory allocation for M × N array in column-major form.*

Figure 5.10   Set an M × N array to zero.

```
*     STATEMENTS TO SET EACH COMPONENT OF AN M × N ARRAY TO ZERO
*       ARRAY NAME  IS   A
*       A   CONTAINS   FULL-WORD   INTEGERS
*
*     NUMBER OF ROWS ASSUMED STORED AT SYMBOLIC ADDRESS   M
*     NUMBER OF COLUMNS ASSUMED STORED  AT SYMBOLIC ADDRESS   N
*
*     INITIALIZATION OF OUTER LOOP CONTROL VARIABLE (REGISTER 6)
*       AND INDEX   (REGISTER 7)
*
          L     6,N           R6 = NUMBER OF COLUMNS FOR OUTER LOOP CTL
          LA    7,0           R7 = INDEX FOR ACCESSING COMPONENTS
          L     8,=F'0'       R8 = ZERO, TO BE STORED INTO ARRAY  A
*
*     BEGIN OUTER LOOP BY INITIALIZING INNER LOOP CONTROL VARIABLE
OUTER     L     9,M           R9 = NUMBER OF ROWS FOR INNER LOOP CONTROL
*       INNER LOOP SETS EACH COMPONENT OF A COLUMN TO ZERO
INNER     ST    8,A(7)        STORE 0 INTO CURRENT ROW OF CURRENT COL.
          LA    7,4(7)        INCREASE INDEX TO NEXT COMPONENT
          BCT   9,INNER       COUNT DOWN # ROWS REMAINING IN COLUMN
          BCT   6,OUTER       COUNT DOWN # COLUMNS REMAINING IN A
          .
          .
          .
M         DS    F             RESERVED FOR # ROWS
N         DS    F             RESERVED FOR # COLUMNS

A         DS    (20*20)F      SPACE FOR UP TO   20 × 20   ARRAY
```

Figure 5.11   Sum the diagonal components of an M × M array.

```
*     STATEMENTS TO SUM UP THE DIAGONAL COMPONENTS OF AN   M × M   ARRAY
*
*     ARRAY  A   CONTAINS FULL-WORD INTEGERS
*
*     NUMBER OF ROWS AND COLUMNS ASSUMED STORED AT SYMBOLIC ADDRESS   M
*
*     INITIALIZATION OF LOOP CONTROL VARIABLE (REGISTER 6)
*
          L     6,M           R6 = NUMBER OF ROWS AND COLUMNS
*
*     COMPUTE   4*M   FOR USE AS PART OF INDEX   4+4*M
*
          L     5,=F'4'       R5 IS ODD-NUMBERED REGISTER FOR MULTIPLY
          MR    4,6           R4 AND R5 CONTAIN PRODUCT 4*M
*     ASSUME  4*M  IS  LESS THAN  2**31
*       SO THAT CORRECT REPRESENTATION OF 4*M IS IN REGISTER 5
*       AND INITIAL VALUE OF SUM (ZERO) IS IN R4
*
*     INITIALIZE INDEX TO ZERO (REGISTER 8)
          LA    8,0           R8 = INDEX TO ACCESS A(J,J)
*     LOOP TO ACCUMULATE SUM OF DIAGONAL COMPONENTS IN   REGISTER 4
*
TRACE     A     4,A(8)        R4 = SUM + A(J,J)
          LA    8,4(8,5)      INCR INDEX BY 4 + 4*M, WHERE R5 = 4*M
          BCT   6,TRACE       COUNT DOWN # ROWS
*
*     STORE SUM AT SYMBOLIC ADDRESS 'ISUM'
*
          ST    4,ISUM
          .
          .
          .
M         DS    F             RESERVED FOR # ROWS AND COLUMNS
ISUM      DS    F             RESERVED FOR SUM OF DIAGONAL COMPONENTS
A         DS    (30*30)F      SPACE FOR UP TO 30 × 30 ARRAY
```

In Assembly Language, we must also use two nested loops, but as with one-dimensional arrays it is convenient to separate the loop-control variables from the index needed to successively address each component. The statements in figure 5.10 illustrate how the problem of setting each component to zero might be programmed in Assembly Language. A similar procedure can be used to add the corresponding components of two arrays.

When the number of rows equals the number of columns, the address formula given previously shows that the difference between the address of any two consecutive diagonal components A(J,J) and A(J+1,J+1) is $4 + 4*M$, where $M = N =$ number of rows and columns. Therefore, to sum up the diagonal components of an M$\times$M array, as in this FORTRAN sequence

$$
\begin{array}{ll}
 & \text{ISUM} = 0 \\
 & \text{DO} \quad 20 \quad \text{J}=1,\text{M} \\
 & \text{ISUM} = \text{ISUM} + \text{A(J,J)} \\
20 & \text{CONTINUE}
\end{array}
$$

we need simply start with A(1,1) and increment the index by an amount equal to $4 + 4*M$ for each iteration of the loop. The statements in figure 5.11 illustrate how this might be accomplished in Assembly Language. As in previous examples, it is assumed that there will be no overflow.

5.9   SUMMARY

The instructions discussed in this chapter are summarized in figure 5.12, except for the arithmetic shift instruction (SRDA), which will be described in Section 8.1, and the instructions for converting between binary integer and text format, which will be described in Section 12.8.

The instructions treat all binary data as integers. We have therefore referred to them as "integer arithmetic" instructions. It should be noted that they are also known as "fixed-point" arithmetic instructions, since, in general, they can be used to process noninteger data, as will be discussed briefly in chapter 11. A binary integer in the IBM 360 and 370 systems is usually represented and processed as a 32-bit quantity, including one bit for its algebraic sign. However, the division instructions require that the dividend be 64 bits, and two of the multiply instructions generate 64-bit products. Also, 16-bit integers can be processed by using the half-word instructions LH, STH, AH, SH, MH, and CH. In all cases, two's complement arithmetic is employed. Other methods of representing and processing numeric data, noningegers as well as integers, will be discussed in chapters 11 through 13.

Each of the integer arithmetic instructions operates on either one or two quantities, one or both of which must be in registers. Consequently, included among the instructions are some that copy data from memory into a register, others that copy data from a register into memory, and still others that copy data from one register to another. Among the latter are instructions that will change a number's sign (LCR), create its positive or negative absolute value (LPR, LNR), and test to see if a number is zero, positive, or negative (LTR). The result of the LTR test can be determined by means of one of the conditional branch instructions, e.g., BZ, BP, or BM.

Two integers may be algebraically compared without altering either integer by means of the C, CR, and CH instructions. The result of the comparison can be determined by one of the conditional branch instructions, e.g., BE, BH, or BL.

The addition, subtraction, multiplication, and division instructions each operate on two integers. Arithmetic combinations of more than two integers must be programmed as appropriate sequences of these four fundamental operations. There is no instruction that will raise an integer to an arbitrary power.

Three types of error conditions can arise during execution of certain binary arithmetic instructions. These are known as fixed-point overflow, fixed-point divide, and specification errors. The situations that can cause these errors and the instructions in which they can occur are summarized in Appendix D. The occurrence of a fixed-point divide or a specification error will result in the program's being interrupted and terminated. Unless specifically prohibited by the Set Program Mask (SPM) instruction, this will also happen if fixed-point overflow occurs (described in chap. 11).

In the IBM 360, it is imperative that 32-bit integers be aligned on full-word memory boundaries and that 16-bit integers be aligned on half-word boundaries. In the 370, this is not required; but the 370's arithmetic operations are faster on integers that are so aligned than they are on integers that are not.

Figure 5.12 Summary of integer arithmetic instructions.

opcode	name	type	section	condition codes	summary of action taken
A	Add	RX	5.3	0,1,2,3	V_1 replaced by V_1+V_2
AH	Add Half Word	RX	5.3	0,1,2,3	V_1 replaced by V_1+V_2; V_2 is a half word
AL	Add Logical	RX	5.3	0,1,2,3	V_1 replaced by V_1+V_2; overflow ignored
ALR	Add Logical Registers	RR	5.3	0,1,2,3	V_1 replaced by V_1+V_2; overflow ignored
AR	Add Registers	RR	5.3	0,1,2,3	V_1 replaced by V_1+V_2
C	Compare	RX	5.5	0,1,2,3	$V_1:V_2$
CH	Compare Half Word	RX	5.5	0,1,2,3	$V_1:V_2$; V_2 is a half word
CR	Compare Registers	RR	5.5	0,1,2,3	$V_1:V_2$
D	Divide	RX	5.3		$V_1/V_2=Q+R/V_2$; R_1 replaced by R, and R_1+1 by Q
DR	Divide Registers	RR	5.3		$V_1/V_2=Q+R/V_2$; R_1 replaced by R, and R_1+1 by Q
L	Load	RX	5.2		V_1 replaced by V_2
LCR	Load Complement from Registers	RR	5.6	0,1,2,3	V_1 replaced by $-V_2$
LH	Load Half Word	RX	5.2		V_1 replaced by V_2; V_2 is a half word
LM	Load Multiple	RS	5.2		$R_1,R_1+1,\ldots$ replaced by $V_2,\ldots$ (up to 16 consecutive words)
LNR	Load Negative Absolute Value	RR	5.6	0,1	V_1 replaced by $-ABS(V_2)$
LPR	Load Positive Absolute Value	RR	5.6	0,2,3	V_1 replaced by $+ABS(V_2)$
LR	Load Registers	RR	5.2		V_1 replaced by V_2
LTR	Load and Test Registers	RR	5.6	0,1,2,3	V_1 replaced by V_2
M	Multiply	RX	5.3		bits 0–63 of R_1 and R_1+1 replaced by $V_1\times V_2$
MH	Multiply Half Word	RX	5.3		bits 0–31 of R_1 replaced by $V_1\times V_2$; V_2 is a half word
MR	Multiply Registers	RR	5.3		bits 0–63 of R_1 and R_1+1 replaced by $V_1\times V_2$
S	Subtract	RX	5.3	0,1,2,3	V_1 replaced by V_1-V_2
SH	Subtract Half Word	RX	5.3	0,1,2,3	V_1 replaced by V_1-V_2; V_2 is a half word
SL	Subtract Logical	RX	5.3	1,2,3	V_1 replaced by V_1-V_2; overflow ignored
SLR	Subtract Logical Registers	RR	5.3	1,2,3	V_1 replaced by V_1-V_2; overflow ignored
SR	Subtract Registers	RR	5.3	0,1,2,3	V_1 replaced by V_1-V_2
ST	Store	RX	5.2		V_2 replaced by V_1
STH	Store Half Word	RX	5.2		V_2 replaced by bits 16–31 of R_1; V_2 is a half word
STM	Store Multiple	RS	5.2		$V_2,\ldots$ replaced by $V_1,\ldots$ (up to 16 consecutive words)

Note: V_1 denotes the quantity whose address is specified by the first operand
V_2 denotes the quantity whose address is specified by the second operand
R_1 denotes the register specified in the first operand

Meanings of the condition codes are summarized in the indicated sections, and in Fig. 8.5a

SAMPLE PROBLEM AND SOLUTION

PROBLEM STATEMENT

Write a program that will read employee time cards, each card containing two clock times in hours and minutes in the format described below. For each time card, the program is to compute and print the elapsed time, together with the given input data.

The two clock times are assumed to be within 24 hours of one another but not necessarily on the same day. They represent the time an employee's work started and the time it ended. The earlier time is in columns 20–23, and the later time in columns 30–33; both times are given in so-called military format (e.g., 11:30 A.M. = 1130, 11:30 P.M. = 2330).

Each line of printed output should contain the given input data together with the elasped time in hours and minutes, as in these examples:

start time	stop time	elapsed hrs	mins
0830	1700	08	30
1700	2400	07	00
2000	0330	07	30
0330	2000	16	30

SOLUTION PROCEDURE

The procedure depends on being able to treat each clock time as two two-digit integers and on being able to convert each two-digit integer to its binary integer representation. Once that is done for each of the four two-digit integers, we can assume that they are symbolically defined as follows:

$$HH = \text{stopping hour, } MM = \text{stopping minute}$$
$$hh = \text{starting hour, } mm = \text{starting minute}$$

The decisions that govern how to compute the elapsed time are depicted in the accompanying flow diagram. Note that the underlying assumption that the elapsed time is less than 24 hours means that we do not need any dates associated with the times. But the assumption that the work may start on one day and end on the next means that the stopping time may be numerically smaller than the starting time. The procedure recognizes this, and accounts for it by adding 24 hours to the stop time.

Figure 5.13a   Overview of sample problem solution procedure.

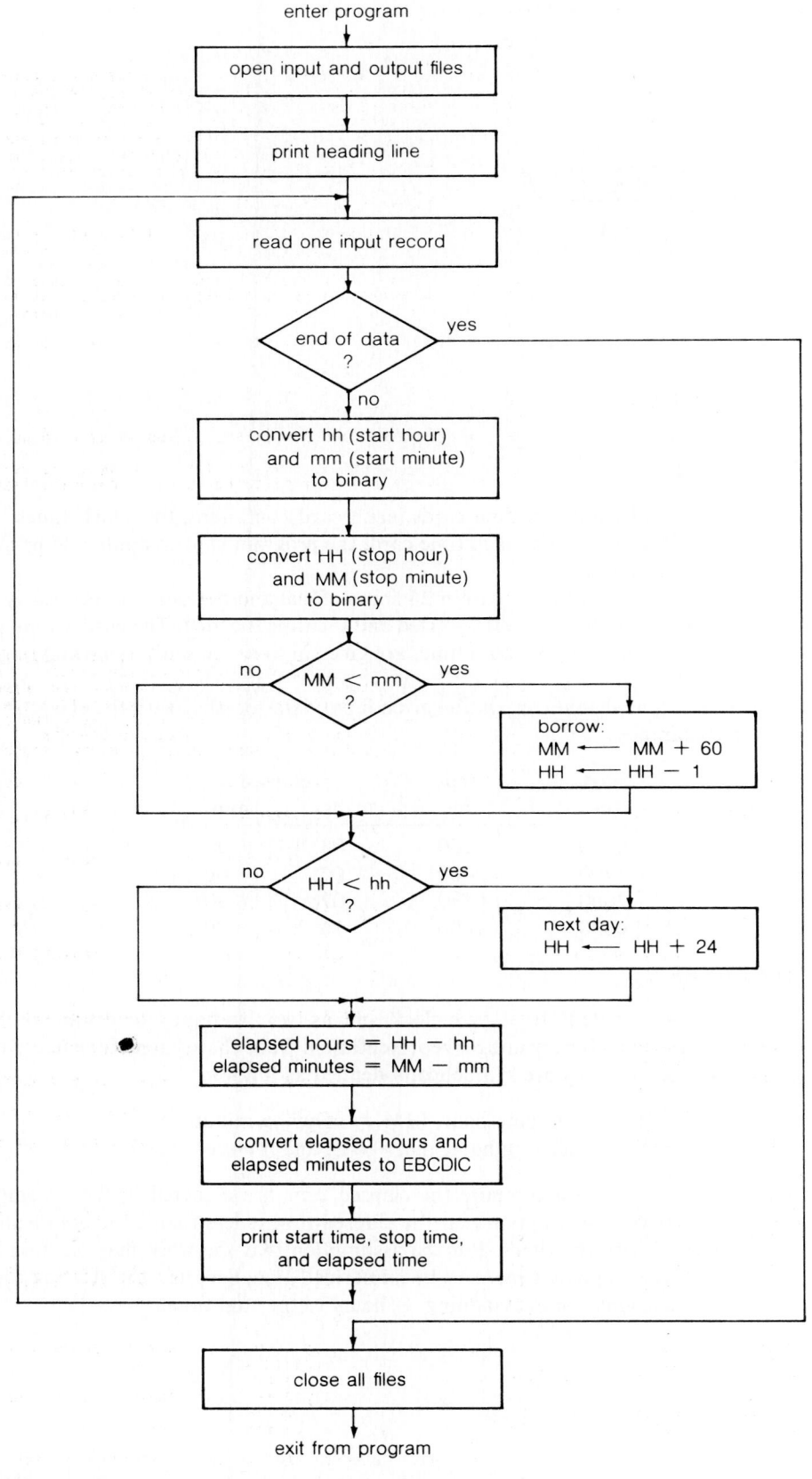

Figure 5.13b *Solution to sample problem.*

```
FLAG LOCTN OBJECT CODE    ADDR1 ADDR2 STMNT M SOURCE STATEMENT

     000000                             3  SPCH5    CSECT
                                        4  *
                                        5  * SPCH5   READS INPUT DATA CARDS CONTAINING EMPLOYEE 'TIME CARDS'.
                                        6  *    EACH CARD CONTAINS THE CLOCK TIMES FOR START AND
                                        7  *    TERMINATION OF A WORK SHIFT FOR ONE EMPLOYEE.
                                        8  *    THE PROGRAM COMPUTES THE ELAPSED WORK TIME
                                        9  *    (IN HOURS AND MINUTES) FOR THAT EMPLOYEE, AND PRINTS
                                       10  *    THE GIVEN START AND STOP TIMES TOGETHER WITH THE ELAPSED TIME.
                                       11  *    IT DOES THIS FOR AS MANY INPUT CARDS AS THERE ARE.
                                       12  *
                                       13  *    THE INPUT DATA FORMAT IS AS FOLLOWS
                                       14  *
                                       15  *         COLS  20-23    HHMM    START TIME, IN HOURS AND MINUTES
                                       16  *               30-33    HHMM    STOP TIME, IN HOURS AND MINUTES
                                       17  *
                                       18  * ALL TIMES ARE MILITARY TIMES   0000 = MIDNIGHT; 2359 = 11 59 PM
                                       19  * THE ELAPSED TIME IS ASSUMED TO BE LESS THAN 24 HOURS, BUT
                                       20  *    THE STOP TIME MAY OCCUR ON THE DAY FOLLOWING THE START TIME.
                                       21  *
     000000 90 EC 000C                 22           STM   14,12,12(13)       STANDARD ENTRY
     000004 05 C0                      23           BALR  12,0
     000006                            24           USING *,12
     000036 50 D0 C35E      000364     25           ST    13,SAVE+4
     00000A 41 D0 C35A      000360     26           LA    13,SAVE
                                       27  *
                                       28  * OPEN INPUT AND OUTPUT FILES, AND PRINT HEADING LINE.
                                       29  *
     00000E                            30           OPEN  (SYSIN,(INPUT))     INPUT IS 'SYSIN' DATA STREAM
     00001A                            36           OPEN  (SYSPRNT,(OUTPUT))  OUTPUT IS 'SYSOUT' PRINTER

                                       42  * DOS *******
                                       43  *         OPEN  SYSIN
                                       44  *         OPEN  SYSPRNT
                                       45  ***************

     000026                            46           PUT   SYSPRNT,HEADING
                                       51  *
                                       52  * MAIN PROCESSING LOOP ...
                                       53  *       READS ONE INPUT CARD
                                       54  *       CONVERTS START HOUR AND START MINUTE TO BINARY INTEGERS
                                       55  *       CONVERTS STOP HOUR AND STOP MINUTE TO BINARY INTEGERS
                                       56  *       COMPUTES ELAPSED TIME IN HOURS AND MINUTES
                                       57  *       CONVERTS ELAPSED HOURS AND ELAPSED MINUTES TO TEXT (EBCDIC)
                                       58  *       PRINTS THE START AND STOP TIMES, AND ELAPSED HRS & MINS
                                       59  *       REPEATS THE LOOP UNTIL END-OF-DATA
                                       60  *       WHEN END-OF-DATA IS REACHED, THE PROGRAM IS TERMINATED.
                                       61  *
     000034                            62  LOOP     GET   SYSIN,INAREA                 GET AN INPUT CARD
                                       67  *
     000042 F2 71 C122C155 000128 00015B  68        PACK  BCD,STARTHR      CONVERT START HOUR TO BINARY
     000048 4F 30 C122      000128     69           CVB   3,BCD
     00004C 50 30 C12A      000130     70           ST    3,STARTHH
     000050 F2 71 C122C157 000128 00015D  71        PACK  BCD,STARTMIN     CONVERT START MINUTE TO BINARY
     000056 4F 30 C122      000128     72           CVB   3,BCD
     00005A 50 30 C12E      000134     73           ST    3,STARTMM
     00005E F2 71 C122C15F 000128 000165  74        PACK  BCD,STOPHR       CONVERT STOP HOUR TO BINARY
     000064 4F 30 C122      000128     75           CVB   3,BCD
     000068 50 30 C132      000138     76           ST    3,STOPHH
     00006C F2 71 C122C161 000128 000167  77        PACK  BCD,STOPMIN      CONVERT STOP MINUTE TO BINARY
     000072 4F 30 C122      000128     78           CVB   3,BCD
     000076 50 30 C136      00013C     79           ST    3,STOPMM
                                       80  *
                                       81  * ADJUST START AND STOP TIMES FOR BORROWING AND FOR NEXT DAY IF NEED BE
                                       82  *
     00007A 58 60 C136      00013C     83           L     6,STOPMM         SEE IF STOP MIN LESS THAN START MIN
     00007E 59 60 C12E      000134     84           C     6,STARTMM
     000082 47 B0 C094      00009A     85           BNL   NOBORROW         BRANCH IF BORROW NOT NECESSARY
                                       86  *
     000086 5A 60 C3A2      0003A8     87           A     6,=F'60'         TO BORROW, ADD 60 MINS TO STOPMM
     00008A 50 60 C136      00013C     88           ST    6,STOPMM
     00008E 58 60 C132      000138     89           L     6,STOPHH         AND SUBT 1 HOUR FROM STOPHH
     000092 5B 60 C3A6      0003AC     90           S     6,=F'1'
     000096 50 60 C132      000138     91           ST    6,STOPHH
                                       92  *
     00009A 58 60 C132      000138     93  NOBORROW L     6,STOPHH         SEE IF STOP HOUR LESS THAN START HOUR
     00009E 59 60 C12A      000130     94           C     6,STARTHH
     0000A2 47 B0 C0A8      0000AE     95           BNL   ELAPSED          BRANCH IF BOTH HOURS ARE IN SAME DAY
                                       96  *
     0000A6 5A 60 C3AA      0003B0     97           A     6,=F'24'         IF STOP HOUR IS IN NEXT DAY,
     0000AA 50 60 C132      000138     98           ST    6,STOPHH              INCREASE IT BY 24 HOURS
                                       99  *
                                      100  * COMPUTE ELAPSED TIME
                                      101  *
     0000AE 58 60 C132      000138    102  ELAPSED  L     6,STOPHH         COMPUTE ELAPSED HOURS
     0000B2 5B 60 C12A      000130    103           S     6,STARTHH
     0000B6 50 60 C13A      000140    104           ST    6,ELAPSHH
     0000BA 58 60 C136      00013C    105           L     6,STOPMM         COMPUTE ELAPSED MINUTES
     0000BE 5B 60 C12E      000134    106           S     6,STARTMM
     0000C2 50 60 C13E      000144    107           ST    6,ELAPSMM
                                      108  *
                                      109  * CONVERT ELAPSED TIME TO EBCDIC (TEXT) FORM FOR PRINTING
                                      110  *
```

Figure 5.13b continued

```
FLAG LOCTN OBJECT CODE      ADDR1  ADDR2  STMNT M SOURCE STATEMENT

    0000C6 58 60 C13A       000140        111        L       6,ELAPSHH
    0000CA 4E 60 C122       000128        112        CVD     6,BCD
    0000CE F3 17 C1ECC122 0001F2 000128   113        UNPK    ELAPSHR,BCD      ELAPSHR IS 2-DIGIT FIELD
    0000D4 96 F0 C1ED         0001F3      114        OI      ELAPSHR+1,X'F0'
    0000D8 58 60 C13E       000144        115        L       6,ELAPSMM
    0000DC 4E 60 C122       000128        116        CVD     6,BCD
    0000E0 F3 17 C1EFC122 0001F5 000128   117        UNPK    ELAPSMIN,BCD     ELAPSMIN IS 2-DIGIT FIELD
    0000E6 96 F0 C1F0         0001F6      118        OI      ELAPSMIN+1,X'F0'
                                          119      *
                                          120      * PRINT START TIME, STOP TIME, AND ELAPSED TIME, AND GO GET NEXT CARD.
                                          121      *
    0000EA D2 4F C19CC142 0001A2 000148   122        MVC     OUTLINE,INAREA     MOVE INPUT CARD TO OUTPUT LINE AREA
    0000F0                                123        PUT     SYSPRNT,OUTAREA
    0000FE 47 F0 C02E       000034        128        B       LOOP
                                          129      * WHEN END-OF-DATA IS REACHED, CONTROL IS TRANSFERRED HERE
                                          130      *
    000102                                131 EOD    CLOSE   (SYSIN)
    00010E                                137        CLOSE   (SYSPRNT)
    00011A 58 D0 C35E       000364        143        L       13,SAVE+4                    STANDARD EXIT
    00011E 98 EC D00C                     144        LM      14,12,12(13)
    000122 07 FE                          145        BR      14

                                          146      *  DOS  *******
                                          147      *EOD    CLOSE SYSIN
                                          148      *       CLOSE SYSPRNT
                                          149      *       EOJ
                                          150      ***************

                                          151      *
                                          152      * CONSTANTS AND DATA AREAS
                                          153      *
    000128                                154 BCD      DS    D              SPACE FOR DECIMAL FORM OF HRS & MINS
    000130                                155 STARTHH  DS    F              START HOUR IN BINARY
    000134                                156 STARTMM  DS    F              START MINUTE IN BINARY
    000138                                157 STOPHH   DS    F              STOP HOUR IN BINARY
    00013C                                158 STOPMM   DS    F              STOP MINUTE IN BINARY
    000140                                159 ELAPSHH  DS    F              ELAPSED HOURS IN BINARY
    000144                                160 ELAPSMM  DS    F              ELAPSED MINUTES IN BINARY
                                          161      *
                                          162      * INPUT CARD AREA
                                          163      *
    000148                                164 INAREA   DS    0CL80          DEFINITION OF INPUT AREA ...
    000148                                165          DS    CL19           COLS 1-19    UNUSED
    00015B                                166 STARTHR  DS    CL2            20-21        START HOUR
    00015D                                167 STARTMIN DS    CL2            22-23        START MINUTE
    00015F                                168          DS    CL6            24-29        UNUSED
    000165                                169 STOPHR   DS    CL2            30-31        STOP HOUR
    000167                                170 STOPMIN  DS    CL2            32-33        STOP MINUTE
    000169                                171          DS    CL47           34-80        UNUSED
                                          172      *
                                          173      * OUTPUT PRINT AREA
                                          174      *
    000198                                175 OUTAREA  DS    0CL132         DEFINITION OF OUTPUT AREA ...
    000198 4040404040404040               176          DC    CL10' '        COLS 1-10    BLANKS
    0001A2                                177 OUTLINE  DS    CL80           11-90        CARD INPUT DATA
    0001F2                                178 ELAPSHR  DS    CL2            91-92        ELAPSED HOURS
    0001F4 40                             179          DC    CL1' '         93           BLANK
    0001F5                                180 ELAPSMIN DS    CL2            94-95        ELAPSED MINUTES
    0001F7 4040404040404040               181          DC    CL37' '        96-132       BLANKS
                                          182      *
                                          183      * HEADING LINE FOR BEGINNING OF PRINTED OUTPUT
                                          184      *
    00021C                                185 HEADING  DS    0CL132         DEFINITION OF HEADING ...
    00021C 4040404040404040               186          DC    CL26' '        COLS 1-26    BLANKS
    000236 E2E3C1D9E340E3C9               187          DC    CL11'START TIME'  27-37     START TIME HEADING
    000241 E2E3D6D740E3C9D4               188          DC    CL11'STOP TIME'   38-48     STOP TIME HEADING
    00024C 4040404040404040               189          DC    CL42' '        49-90        BLANKS
    000276 C5D3C1D7E2C5C440               190          DC    CL12'ELAPSED TIME' 91-102   ELAPSED TIME HEADING
    000282 4040404040404040               191          DC    CL30' '        103-132      BLANKS
                                          192      * DCB'S FOR INPUT AND OUTPUT FILES
                                          193      *
    0002A0                                194 SYSIN    DCB   DSORG=PS,MACRF=(GM),DDNAME=SYSIN,EODAD=EOD,             X
                                          195                RECFM=FB,LRECL=80,BLKSIZE=4080
    000300                                247
                                          248 SYSPRNT  DCB   DSORG=PS,MACRF=(PM),DDNAME=SYSPRINT,                   X
                                          249                RECFM=FB,LRECL=132,BLKSIZE=4092

                                          301      *  DOS  *******
                                          302      *SYSIN    DTFCD DEVADDR=SYSIPT,WORKA=YES,IOAREA1=INBUF,EOFADDR=EOD, X
                                          303      *               DEVICE=2540
                                          304      *SYSPRNT DTFPR DEVADDR=SYSLST,WORKA=YES,IOAREA1=OUTBUF,BLKSIZE=132, X
                                          305      *               DEVICE=1403
                                          306      *
                                          307      *INBUF    DS    CL80
                                          308      *OUTBUF   DC    CL132' '
                                          309      ***************

                                          310      *
                                          311      * SAVE AREA
```

Figure 5.13b   continued

```
FLAG LOCTN OBJECT CODE    ADDR1 ADDR2  STMNT M SOURCE STATEMENT

                                        312  *
     000360                             313  SAVE     DS      18F

                                        314  *  DOS  *******
                                        315  *SAVE    DS      9D
                                        316  ***************

                                        317  * LITERALS
     0003A8 0000003C                    319                   =F'60'
     0003AC 00000001                    320                   =F'1'
     0003B0 00000018                    321                   =F'24'
                                        322           END
```

CROSS-REFERENCE

```
SYMBOL    LEN   VALUE  DEFN    REFERENCES

BCD       00008 000128 00154   00068  00069  00071  00072  00074  00075  00077  00078  00112  00113  00116  00117
ELAPSED   00004 0000AE 00102   00095
ELAPSHH   00004 000140 00159   00104  00111
ELAPSHR   00002 0001F2 00178   00113  00114
ELAPSMIN  00002 0001F5 00180   00117  00118
ELAPSMM   00004 000144 00160   00107  00115
EOD       00004 000104 00133   00216
HEADING   00084 00021C 00185   00048
INAREA    00050 000148 00164   00064  00122
LOOP      00004 000034 00063   00128
NOBORROW  00004 00009A 00093   00085
OUTAREA   00084 000198 00175   00125
OUTLINE   00050 0001A2 00177   00122
SAVE      00004 000360 00313   00025  00026  00143
SPCH5     00001 000000 00003
STARTHH   00004 000130 00155   00070  00094  00103
STARTHR   00002 00015B 00166   00068
STARTMIN  00002 00015D 00167   00071
STARTMM   00004 000134 00156   00073  00084  00106
STOPHH    00004 000138 00157   00076  00089  00091  00093  00098  00102
STOPHR    00002 000165 00169   00074
STOPMIN   00002 000167 00170   00077
STOPMM    00004 00013C 00158   00079  00083  00088  00105
SYSIN     00004 0002A0 00195   00034  00063  00135
SYSPRNT   00004 000300 00249   00040  00047  00124  00141
```

EXERCISES

1. Suppose that Registers 2 and 3 and symbolic memory location X contain the following hexadecimal integers:

Register 2:	0000A000
Register 3:	FFFF6000
Location X:	00000002

What integers exist in Registers 2 and 3 after each of the following instructions is executed? Assume that, for each instruction, the integers given above exist just prior to the execution of that instruction.

a. A	2,X	**d.** D	2,X	**h.** MR	2,3
b. S	3,X	**e.** AR	2,3	**i.** DR	2,3
c. M	2,X	**f.** AR	3,2	**j.** SH	3,X
		g. SR	3,2		

2. Suppose that Registers 2, 3, and 4 and symbolic memory locations X, X+4, and X+8 contain the following hexadecimal integers:

Register 2:	0000A000	Location X:	02040608
Register 3:	FFFF6000	Location X+4:	0A0B0C0D
Register 4:	00000000	Location X+8:	FFFFFFFF

What integers exist in Registers 2, 3, and 4 and at addresses X, X+4, and X+8 after each of the following instructions is executed? Assume that for each instruction, the integers given above exist just prior to the execution of that instruction.

a. LM	2,4,X	**d.** LNR	3,4	**h.** LTR	3,3
b. LCR	3,4	**e.** LR	2,4	**i.** LH	3,X+4
c. STM	3,4,X	**f.** LPR	4,3	**j.** STH	3,X+8
		g. LR	4,2		

3. Suppose that Registers 8 and 9 and symbolic memory locations Y and Y+4 contain the following hexadecimal integers:

Register 8:	00000123	Location Y:	0000A000
Register 9:	FFFFF123	Location Y+4:	FFFF6000

What condition—high, equal, or low—results from each of the following compare instructions? Assume that for each instruction, the integers given above exist just prior to execution of that instruction.

a. CR	8,9	**c.** CH	8,Y+4	**e.** C	9,Y
b. C	8,Y	**d.** CR	9,8	**f.** CH	9,Y+4

4. The Load Multiple (LM) and Store Multiple (STM) instructions each have the following property: if the address of the register designated by the R2 field is less than that designated by the R1 field, the registers that participate in the execution of the instruction are R1, R1+1,...,15, 0, 1,...,R2. For example, in the instruction

$$STM \quad 14,12,12(13)$$

the contents of registers 14,15,0,1,...,12 are stored in the 15 consecutive full words beginning at the address designated by the third operand field 12(13). Given this property of the LM and STM instructions, what can be said about the contents of all 16 registers immediately after execution of the following standard program exit sequence?

```
L        13,SAVE+4
LM       14,12,12(13)
BR       14
```

Note: In each of the following problems, you should create appropriate test data and include instructions that write the results on the printer using the techniques described in chapter 4.

5. Write an assembly language program that will divide each of the integers in a one-dimensional array, L, by an integer constant, K. The integer quotient of each division should replace the dividend L(J); the integer remainder from each division should be stored in the corresponding position, M(J), of the one-dimensional integer array, M. The following FORTRAN segment illustrates the computations that are to be performed:

```
          DIMENSION L(100),M(100)
          N = ...
          K = ...
            ⋮
          DO 10 J = 1,N
          IQUO = L(J)/K
          IREM = L(J) − IQUO * K
          L(J) = IQUO
          M(J) = IREM
10        CONTINUE
```

Your solution should be valid for any integers, N and K, provided that $1 \le N \le 100$, and $-2^{31} \le K \le 2^{31}-1$, with $K \ne 0$.

6. Write an assembly language program to determine how many integers in a one-dimensional array, M, are greater than some given integer, K. In FORTRAN, this might be accomplished as follows:

```
          DIMENSION M(200)
          LM = ...
          K = ...
            ⋮
          J = 0
          DO 10 N = 1,LM
          IF ( M(N) .GT. K ) J = J + 1
10        CONTINUE
```

7. Write an assembly language program segment that will copy each of the integers from a two-dimensional array, L, into a two-dimensional array, M. In FORTRAN, this segment might be accomplished as follows:

```
          DIMENSION L(25,25),M(25,25)
          LM = ...
            ⋮
          DO 20 J = 1,LM
          DO 10 K = 1,LM
          M(J,K) = L(J,K)
10        CONTINUE
20        CONTINUE
```

8. Write an assembly language program segment to determine how many integers in a two-dimensional array, M, are less than some given integer, K. In FORTRAN, this segment might be accomplished as follows:

```
         DIMENSION M(50,50)
         LM = ...
         K = ...
            ⋮
         N = 0
         DO 10 J1 = 1,LM
         DO 20 J2 = 1,LM
         IF ( M(J1,J2) .LT. K ) N = N+1
20       CONTINUE
10       CONTINUE
```

9. Write an assembly language program segment that will put any arbitrary set of 25 integers into ascending numerical sequence. The segment can use the logic illustrated in this FORTRAN sequence:

```
         DIMENSION M(100)
         N = 25
            ⋮
         DO 20 J = 1,N−1
         DO 10 K = J,N
         IF ( M(J) .LE. M(K) ) GOTO 10
         L = M(J)
         M(J) = M(K)
         M(K) = L
10       CONTINUE
20       CONTINUE
```

10. Write a program segment that will multiply any two full-word integers together, and determine whether the product exceeds $+2^{31}-1$, is less than -2^{31}, or is in the range -2^{31} to $+2^{31}-1$.

If the product exceeds $+2^{31}-1$, the program should substitute $+2^{31}-1$ for the product.

If the product is less than -2^{31}, the program should substitute -2^{31} for the product.

If the product is in the range -2^{31} to $+2^{31}-1$, the program should not substitute any integer for the product.

11. Write a program segment that will calculate the scalar product of two one-dimensional integer arrays, M and N, each consisting of K components. The scalar product is formed by summing the products of corresponding components, as shown in this FORTRAN segment:

```
         DIMENSION M(10),N(10)
         K = 10

            ⋮

         ISUM = 0
         DO 10 J = 1,K
         ISUM = ISUM + M(J)*N(J)
10       CONTINUE
```

12. Write a program segment that will calculate the product of two M×M integer arrays, M and N. The product is itself an M×M array, MN, each component MN(J,K) being the scalar product of the Jth row of M and the Kth column of N, as shown in this FORTRAN segment:

```
            DIMENSION M(10,10),N(10,10),MN(10,10)
            MNSIZE = 10
               ⋮
            DO 30 J = 1,MNSIZE
            DO 20 K = 1,MNSIZE
            MN(J,K) = 0
            DO 10 L = L,MNSIZE
            MN(J,K) = MN(J,K) + M(J,L)*N(L,K)
10          CONTINUE
20          CONTINUE
30          CONTINUE
```

13. The sum of the first N positive integers, $1 + 2 + 3 + ... + N$, which can be written as Σn, is $N \cdot (N+1)/2$. The sum of their squares, Σn^2, is $N \cdot (N+1) \cdot (2N+1)/6$; and the sum of their cubes, Σn^3, is $N^2 \cdot (N+1)^2/4$.

   a. Using the above formulas, write a set of assembly language statements that will compute each of the three sums for any given integer, N.

   b. Modify your solution to Exercise 13a so that it will compute any one (but only one) of the three sums, the sum to be computed being determined by a parameter, K: If $K = 1$, compute the sum of the integers; if $K = 2$, compute the sum of their squares; and if $K = 3$, the sum of their cubes.

   c. What is the largest integer, N, for which the sum of the cubes can be represented as a 32-bit binary integer (including sign)? Modify your solutions to Exercises 13a and 13b so that they print an appropriate message when a sum is too large to be represented in 32 bits.

14. Write a set of assembly language statements that will compute the factorial function of N for any positive integer, N. (The factorial function of a positive integer, N, is the product of the first N integers, $1 \times 2 \times 3 \times ... \times N$, commonly written as $N!$) Modify your solution so that it prints an appropriate message when $N!$ exceeds 32 bits. What is the smallest N for which this is the case? How might $N!$ be calculated for integers greater than this using binary integer arithmetic?

15. Suppose there is a one-dimensional array, A, consisting of no more than 100 full-word integers. Write the assembly language statements that will create another integer array, B, that consists of all the integers in A but stored in reverse order. For example, if A consists of the five integers $-1, 2, 3, -4, 5$, then B would consist of the five integers $5, -4, 3, 2, -1$.

16. The concept of the transpose of an M×M array, A, is simply that each component of the transposed array, B, is obtained from the array A by the following rule: B(J,K) = A(K,J) for each pair of subscripts, K and J. In FORTRAN, the transpose of an array, A, can be created like this:

```
            DO 20 K=1,M
            DO 10 J=1,M
            B(J,K) = A(K,J)
10          CONTINUE
20          CONTINUE
```

Write a set of assembly language statements that will create the transpose of an M×M integer array, A. Your program should work correctly for any M such that $M \leq 30$.

6
Constants and Data Areas

An assembly language programmer can specify two categories of constants in a source module: constants to be used by the program at run time, and constants to be used by the Assembler at assembly time.

Run-time constants can be specified in two ways: (1) as defined constants, specified by means of the DC directive or (2) as value-based constants, specified either by use of "literals" or by use of "self-defining terms."

An *assembly-time constant* is represented by a symbol whose value is the value of the constant. There are two main classes of such symbols: (1) symbols that are part of the Assembly Language itself and (2) symbols that are defined by the EQU directive.

In addition to the distinction between assembly-time constants and run-time constants, all constants are classified as being either relocatable or absolute. An *absolute* constant is one that is independent of any factor affecting, or affected by, the location of a program in memory. A *relocatable* constant is one that depends on the location of a program in memory.

Every assembly language constant consists of an algebraic expression containing one or more terms. A term is the smallest element of the language that can be used to represent a distinct and separate value. Each term that appears in an expression is itself either absolute or relocatable: it is relocatable if, and only if, it is a symbol used to represent a memory address; otherwise it is absolute. The integer $+1$ used to increment a counter is an example of an absolute term. An example of a relocatable term is any symbol used as the symbolic address of an instruction.

A constant consisting of a single term is relocatable if that term is relocatable; under all other conditions, it is absolute. A constant consisting of an algebraic combination of absolute and relocatable terms is considered to be either absolute, relocatable, or invalid according to the following rules:

1. Any algebraic combination of two absolute terms is an absolute constant. In addition, the difference between two relocatable terms is an absolute constant.
2. If an absolute term is added to or subtracted from a relocatable term, the result is a relocatable constant.
3. A unary plus or minus operator may be used to emphasize or change the sign of an absolute or relocatable term without changing the nature of that term.
4. Constants formed in accordance with the previous three rules may themselves be algebraically combined to form another constant. The rules used to combine terms are also used to combine constants: the resulting constant is either absolute or relocatable.
5. No other algebraic combination of absolute or relocatable terms or constants is permitted. If such combinations are used, the result is an invalid constant; in particular, the sum, product, or quotient of two relocatable terms or constants is an invalid constant.

The distinction between absolute and relocatable terms and constants is important because the value of a relocatable term or constant may be different at run time than it is at assembly time since it depends on where the Loader places a program in memory. The value of an absolute term or constant is the same at run time as at assembly time since it is independent of the location of a program in memory.

To illustrate these rules, let R, S, and T be nonnegative relocatable constants, and let A, B, and C be any absolute constants.

valid absolute constants:	$-A, A+B, A-B, A*B, A/B, (A+B)/C, R-S$
valid relocatable constants:	$R+A, R-A, R+(S-T), R-(S-T), -R$
invalid constants:	$R+S, R*S, R/S, R+(S-A)$

6.1   RUN-TIME CONSTANTS

Run-time constants occupy memory locations when a program is being executed. Like all other information in memory, run-time constants are represented by sequences of bits. However, the length of the bit sequence and the combination of bits used to represent a constant depend on the type of constant involved.

For example, the integer constant $+3$ is represented differently from the floating-point constant $+3$, and both are different from the text character 3 that might occur, say, in a telephone number. The integer $+3$ is represented like this:

$$0000 \quad 0000 \quad 0000 \quad 0000 \quad 0000 \quad 0000 \quad 0000 \quad 0011$$

the floating-point representation of $+3$ is

$$0100 \quad 0001 \quad 0011 \quad 0000 \quad 0000 \quad 0000 \quad 0000 \quad 0000$$

and the character representation of 3 is

$$1111 \quad 0011$$

The representation of a constant in memory contains no indication of the type of constant it is. A constant's type is implied by context only. When a constant is used at run time, the type of use to which it is put must necessarily be in agreement with the type of constant it is, otherwise invalid results may occur.

In the IBM 360 and 370 Assembly Language, there are seven principal types of run-time constants. Some of these may also be represented in FORTRAN and COBOL, though the terminology is different in these languages (fig. 6.1). In Assembly Language, the seven types of run-time constants are:

1. text, or "characters"
2. binary integers, either full-word or half-word
3. floating-point numbers, either single-precision, double-precision, or extended precision
4. decimal numbers, also called packed-decimal numbers and binary-coded decimal numbers
5. hexadecimal digits
6. binary digits
7. addresses, either full-word or half-word

Figure 6.1   Data type terminology.

Assembly Language	FORTRAN	COBOL
Text	enclosed in quotes	USAGE IS DISPLAY
Binary integers	INTEGER (full-word integer)	USAGE IS COMPUTATIONAL
Floating-point		
single-precision	REAL	USAGE IS COMPUTATIONAL-1
double-precision	DOUBLE-PRECISION	USAGE IS COMPUTATIONAL-2
Decimal	--	USAGE IS COMPUTATIONAL-3
Hexadecimal	--	--
Binary digits	--	--
Addresses	program names	program names
	variable names	elementary, group, and record names
	statement labels	paragraph and section names

Defined Constants

The Define Constant (DC) directive causes the Assembler to generate an appropriate machine language representation of one or more constants. These constants can be specified in a variety of ways: as decimal numbers, hexadecimal numbers, binary numbers, character data, and, in a few cases, as symbols that the Assembler translates into their numeric equivalances. Each specification of a constant must be preceded by a type code identifying the form in which the constant is being specified. And each specification is subject to certain rules governing the size and other characteristics of the data and determining the machine language representation that will be generated.

Each use of a DC directive is written as a single assembly language statement, with the same fields as other statements: name field, opcode, operand, comments, continuation, and identification. As with other statements, the comments, continuation, and identification fields may optionally be blank. The name field, opcode, and operand have the following general form in a DC directive:

name field	opcode	operand
{ any symbol or blank }	DC	{ one or more subfields, separated by commas }

Each subfield in the operand has up to four components, two of which are required and two of which are optional:

DC operand subfield components

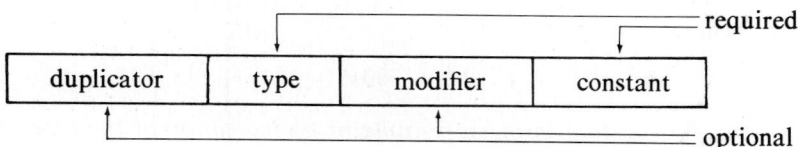

The components are written in the order depicted in the diagram, without any separation between them. For example,

DC   2FS10'3'

When one or both optional components are omitted, no indication is made of their omission:

DC   F'3'

There can be more than one subfield in a DC operand, and more than one constant in a subfield, as these examples indicate:

DC	F'3',F'4'	two subfields, separated by a comma
DC	F'3,4'	two constants in a subfield, separated by a comma

The two required subfield components—type and constant—have provisions that allow an assembly language programmer to specify every representation of data that is possible in the IBM 360 and 370 computer systems. A list of the permissible type codes, and some information pertinent to their meanings, is given in figure 6.2.

When a symbol is used in the name field of a DC directive statement, that symbol becomes the symbolic address of the first constant that occurs in the operand of the statement. As such, the symbol can be used in instructions to refer to the constant, as, for example:

```
        L      5,FCON
FCON    DC     F'3'
```

Figure 6.2 Types of constants for DC directive.

type code	meaning	see also	examples	comments	alignment
C	text, or "characters"	Chapter 7	C'ABC:123'	Each character is converted to its 8-bit EBCDIC representation. The characters are stored in consecutive bytes.	byte
F	binary integer (full word)	Chapter 5,6	F'3' F'—3'	The number is converted to its 32-bit binary integer representation (including sign). Maximum number = 2,147,483,647	full-word
H	binary integer (half word)		H'3' H'—3'	The number is converted to its 16-bit binary integer representation (including sign). Maximum = 32,767	half-word
E	floating-point (short form)	Chapter 13	E'3' E'—3.5'	The number is converted to its floating-point representation. Maximum approximately 7.2×10^{75}; accuracy about seven digits.	full-word
D	floating-point (long form)		D'3' D'—3.5'	Maximum approx. 7.2×10^{75}, with about 16-digit accuracy.	double-word
L	floating-point (extended form)		L'3' L'—3.5'	Maximum approx. 7.2×10^{75}, with about 32-digit accuracy.	double-word
P	decimal numbers (packed form)	Chapter 12	P'3.5' P'—3'	Each digit is converted to a 4-bit binary integer. Maximum, 31 digits. Decimal point is ignored, e.g., P'3.5' is same as P'35'.	byte
Z	decimal numbers (zoned form)		Z'3' Z'—3.5'	Each digit is converted to its 8-bit EBCDIC representation. Maximum, 16 digits. Decimal point is ignored, as in P-type constants.	byte
X	hexadecimal	Chapter 8	X'12AC'	Each digit must be one of the 16 hexadecimal digits, and is represented by an equivalent 4-bit binary number. Decimal point not allowed.	byte
B	bit sequence	Chapter 8	B'11001'	The bits are represented as given, 8 bits per byte.	byte
A	address	Chapter 9	A(SYMBOL)	Value of the symbol as a binary integer.	full-word
V			V(SYMBOL)	Space reserved for an external address.	
Y S Q	address	--		These three types of address constants are not discussed in this text.	

Here, the Load instruction L 5,FCON will, at run time, copy the binary representation of the decimal integer +3 into Register 5, as was discussed in the preceding chapter.

The *duplicator* designates how many consecutive representations of the constant or constants are to be generated by the Assembler. If the duplicator is omitted, its value is assumed to be 1. For example:

DC	F'3'	generates one representation of the integer +3
DC	2F'3'	generates two consecutive representations of +3

The duplicator may also be written as an arithmetic expression enclosed in parentheses; this expression may include symbols, provided that they were defined in statements prior to their use in the duplicator. For example,

DC	(8*16)F'3'	generates 128 consecutive representations of $+3$
DC	(N)F'3'	generates N consecutive representations of $+3$, if the value of N had been previously defined.

The *modifier*, when present, can consist of from one to three factors. These are known as the length modifier, the scale modifier, and the exponent modifier. If more than one of these factors is present in a modifier, they must be written in the order just stated.

The purpose of the length modifier (Ln) is to specify that n bytes of memory are to be used for the representation of the constant. If n is larger than the number of bytes the constant would ordinarily require, the constant may be extended (*padded*) on the left or right by the Assembler, depending on the constant's type. If n is smaller than what would ordinarily be required, the Assembler will truncate the constant on the left or right, depending on its type. For example, with $n = 1$,

DC	FL1'3'	generates a 1-byte binary integer representation of $+3$.

The scale modifier (Sn) specifies that the constant is to be multiplied by 2^n or by 16^n before its binary representation is generated by the Assembler. The factor 2^n is used for F- and H-type constants; in this case, n must be in the range of from -187 through $+346$. The factor 16^n is used for D-, E-, and L-type constants: $0 \leq n \leq 14$ for D and E, and $0 \leq n \leq 28$ for L. For example, with $n = 10$:

DC	FS10'3'	generates a full-word binary integer representation of $3 \times 2^{10} = 3072$.

The exponent modifier (En) specifies that an H-, F-, D-, E-, or L-type constant is to be multiplied by 10^n before its representation is generated by the Assembler. In this case, n must be in the range of from -85 through $+75$. For example, with $n = 5$,

DC	FE5'3'	generates a full-word binary integer representation of $3 \times 10^5 = 300,000$.

F- and H-type constants are always specified as signed or unsigned decimal integers, *without commas or decimal points*. In the absence of a length modifier, an F-type constant generates a full-word binary integer. The constant must, therefore, be in the range of from -2^{31} through $2^{31}-1$, i.e., $-2,147,483,648$ through $+2,147,483,647$. Similarly, in the absence of a length modifier, an H-type constant generates a half-word binary integer. Such a constant must be in the range of from -2^{15} through $2^{15}-1$, i.e., $-32,768$ through $+32,767$.

Unless a length modifier is specified, F-type constants are aligned on full-word boundaries and H-type constants are aligned on half-word boundaries. If a length modifier is specified, alignment is on a byte boundary. The scale and exponent modifiers do not affect the boundary alignments.

Examples of the use of a DC directive for F- and H-type constants are shown in figure 6.3. These examples do not include the use of modifiers; we leave that to you as an exercise. Examples of most of the other types of constants will be given in subsequent chapters.

Value-based Constants

The use of value-based constants allows a programmer to specify a constant in an operand without having to define that constant elsewhere in the program. There are two types of value-based constants that can be used to create data for use at run time: literals and self-defining terms.

Literals. A *literal* is a symbolic representation of a constant to which the Assembler assigns an address. When a single constant is needed in the operand of certain instructions, the programmer can use a literal to designate that constant without having to define the constant with a DC directive. The following three statements illustrate this:

Statement 1	FCON	DC	F'1'
Statement 2		L	5,FCON
Statement 3		L	5,=F'1'

Figure 6.3 *Specifying constants for full- and half-word data.*

```
FLAG LOCTN OBJECT CODE      ADDR1   ADDR2  STMNT M SOURCE STATEMENT
                                           4   * FULL-WORD CONSTANTS
                                           5   *                          NUMBER OF BYTES
      000000 0000000A                      6          DC     F'10'        4
      000004 FFFFFFF6                      7          DC     F'-10'       4
      000008 0000000A                      8          DC     2F'10'       2 X 4
             0000000A
      000010 FFFFFFF6                      9          DC     2F'-10'      2 X 4
             FFFFFFF6
      000018 0000000A0000000A             10          DC     F'10,10'     1 X (4 + 4)
      000020 0000000A0000000A             11          DC     2F'10,10'    2 X (4 + 4)
             0000000A0000000A
      000030 0000000A                     12          DC     F'10',F'10'  4 + 4
      000034 0000000A
      000038 0000000A                     13          DC     3F'10',2F'10'   3 X 4  +  2 X 4
             0000000A
             0000000A
      000044 0000000A
             0000000A
      00004C 7FFFFFFF                     14          DC     F'2147483647'   4
      000050 80000000                     15          DC     F'-2147483648'  4

                                          16   * IF NUMBER OUTSIDE RANGE, CONSTANT IS INCORRECT
      000054 7FFFFFFF                     17          DC     F'-2147483649'  (LESS THAN  -2**31 )
      000058 80000000                     18          DC     F'2147483648'   (EXCEEDS  2**31 - 1 )

                                          19   * HALF-WORD CONSTANTS
      00005C 000A                         20          DC     H'10'        2
      00005E FFF6                         21          DC     H'-10'       2
      000060 000A                         22          DC     2H'10'       2 X 2
             000A
      000064 FFF6                         23          DC     2H'-10'      2 X 2
             FFF6
      000068 000A000A                     24          DC     H'10,10'     1 X (2 + 2)
      00006C 000A000A                     25          DC     2H'10,10'    2 X (2 + 2)
             000A000A
      000074 000A                         26          DC     H'10',H'10'  2 + 2
      000076 000A
      000078 000A                         27          DC     3H'10',2H'10'   3 X 2  +  2 X 2
             000A
             000A
      00007E 000A
             000A
      000082 7FFF                         28          DC     H'32767'     2
      000084 8000                         29          DC     H'-32768'    2

                                          30   * IF NUMBER OUTSIDE RANGE, CONSTANT IS INCORRECT
      000086 7FFF                         31          DC     H'-32769'    (LESS THAN  -2**15 )
      000088 8000                         32          DC     H'32768'     (EXCEEDS  2**15 - 1 )
```

At run time, the second and third statements would produce exactly the same result. Each would load the full-word binary integer +1 into Register 5. However, Statement 2 requires that Statement 1 be included; Statement 3 does not require Statement 1. The operand =F'1' is a literal designating the constant +1.

When the Assembler processes Statement 3, it generates the binary integer representation of +1, assigns an address to it, and creates the appropriate base-displacement form of its address in the assembled Load instruction. It does this in response to the presence of the F-type literal, =F'1'. As may be inferred, the format of a literal is, with one major exception, nearly identical to that of an operand in a DC directive. The exception is the presence of the equals sign (=), which must precede the subfields as shown here:

format of a literal

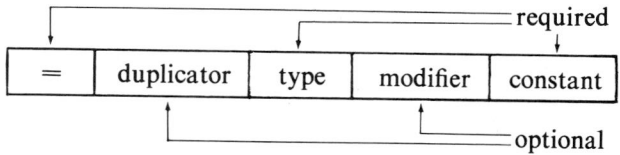

Thus, in Statement 3 above, the literal =F'1' does not include the two optional fields.

In addition to the mandatory presence of the equals sign, there are a few other differences, all minor, between the format of a literal and that of an operand in a DC directive. The most important of these is that one cannot specify more than one operand in a literal. For example, =F'1',F'2' is not valid. Except for these differences, all the rules for forming an operand in a DC directive also apply to literals and any of the data type codes listed in figure 6.2 can be used in the specification of a literal.

Certain restrictions govern the use of literals. These derive from the fact that the Assembler assigns a memory address to each literal and substitutes the base-displacement form of that address in the instruction in which the literal is used. The restrictions are: literals cannot be used to designate a register address in any instruction, to specify the immediate data or mask fields in any instruction, or to specify the length fields (L, L1, or L2) in any instruction. *They can, however, be specified in the second operand of any Load, Add, Subtract, Multiply, Divide, and Move instruction that is not an RR or SI instruction.* Literals can also be specified in the second operand of most Compare instructions and of a few other instructions to be covered in chapter 12. Note in particular that a literal should not be used as the second operand in a Store instruction nor as the destination of other copy-type operations.

The reason for these restrictions is twofold. First, as was mentioned, the Assembler places the address of a literal, not the constant that it represents, into a machine language instruction. Length fields, mask fields, immediate data fields, and register addresses cannot be represented by memory addresses. Second, when the same literal is used more than once in a program, as for example in the instructions

```
L        5,=F'2'
M        4,=F'2'
```

only one representation of that literal is created by the Assembler, and the assembled instructions referring to that literal will all contain the same memory address. Therefore, if we were to store or otherwise copy data into the memory area reserved by the Assembler for the literal, the execution of the other instructions that refer to the literal could be adversely affected.

Despite what may seem like a rather lengthy list of restrictions, literals are exceptionally useful, for their use removes the necessity to define a constant via a DC directive when that constant is needed for the operand of an instruction.

Self-defining Terms. A *self-defining* term is an absolute constant that can be written in one of four ways: as a decimal integer, a binary integer, a hexadecimal integer, or a sequence of text characters. The formats for writing self-defining terms are shown in figure 6.4. Although the notation used for self-defining terms is similar to that used for literals, sometimes causing problems for beginning programmers, the distinction between the two is of critical importance. In contrast to the use of literals in instructions, the use of self-defining terms has the following property: when a self-defining term is used in an instruction, the Assembler substitutes the binary representation of that term, *not* its address. The Assembler distinguishes a self-defining term from a literal by the absence or presence of an equal sign.

As can be seen from figure 6.4, self-defining decimal integers are not written in the F-notation that is used with literals. This is because they are used so extensively in source modules. For example, in the statement

```
L     5,FCON
```

the 5 is a self-defining decimal integer. The Assembler substitutes its 4-bit binary representation, 0101, when it assembles the Load instruction.

Self-defining terms are frequently used to specify the immediate data fields in instructions, as well as the mask fields, length fields, and register addresses. For example, consider the SI instruction Compare Logical Immediate (CLI):

Assembly Language		machine language			
opcode	D1(B1),I2	opcode	I2	B1	D1
CLI	0(8),C'Z'	95	E9	8	000

The immediate data field, the I2 field, is specified in this CLI instruction as the self-defining term C'Z'. This term represents the text character Z. In machine language, the binary representation used to represent the Z in the assembled instruction is the EBCDIC code for Z, 1110 1001, which in hexadecimal notation is E9. (See fig. 7.1 for the EBCDIC codes for all the printable characters.) It would be incorrect to write CLI 0(8),=C'Z' since a literal cannot be specified in the immediate data field of any instruction. Specifying a self-defining term causes the Assembler to generate the binary representation of that term, not its address.

Figure 6.4 *Types of self-defining terms.*

type of term	method of representation	comments	examples
decimal integer	unsigned decimal integer	maximum, OS: $2^{31}-1$ DOS: $2^{24}-1$	3 12
binary integer	B'⌣' binary digits	maximum, OS: 32 bits DOS: 24 bits	B'0001' B'11' B'1011'
hexadecimal integer	X'⌣' hexadecimal digits	maximum, OS: 8 hex digits DOS: 6 hex digits	X'4A' X'6D' X'4100'
sequence of text characters	C'⌣' text characters	maximum, OS: 4 chars. DOS: 3 chars.	C'Z' C'CAT' C'A=B'

Note: Two of the text characters that can be used in a C-type term require special treatment: the apostrophe (') and the ampersand (&). Two consecutive apostrophes and two consecutive ampersands must be written in the character sequence whenever one apostrophe or one ampersand is wanted, e.g., in the term C'&&', the two ampersands represent one ampersand.

6.2 ASSEMBLY-TIME CONSTANTS

Assembly-time constants do not occupy memory locations in a user's program, i.e., they are not in memory when a program is being executed. Instead, their values can be used by the Assembler as part of the assembly process, when generating instructions and defined constants and when processing directives.

There are two main classes of assembly-time constants: those represented by symbols that are part of the Assembly Language itself, and those represented by user-defined symbols. The most important symbol that is part of the Assembly Language and is used as an assembly-time constant is the memory location symbol, an asterisk (∗). User-defined symbols that are to be used as assembly-time constants must be defined by means of the EQU directive.

Memory Location Symbol

In chapter 3, we saw that when the Assembler generates the object code corresponding to an instruction or defined constant, it assigns a memory address to that code. In general, the Assembler associates a memory address with each source-language statement that it processes. The memory address associated with a statement is determined by the following formula:

$$\left\{\begin{matrix} \text{address associated} \\ \text{with a statement} \end{matrix}\right\} = \left\{\begin{matrix} \text{address associated} \\ \text{with the preceding} \\ \text{statement} \end{matrix}\right\} + \left\{\begin{matrix} \text{number of bytes} \\ \text{generated or reserved} \\ \text{by preceding statement} \end{matrix}\right\}$$

In this formula, the address associated with the first statement of a program is 0000.

The memory address associated with a statement is, with a few exceptions (such as the EQU to be described in the following section), the value that the Assembler assigns to the symbol appearing in the name field of that statement. In addition, this value is always assigned to another symbol, the memory location symbol. Thus, *the value of the memory location symbol depends on the statement in which it is used.* In the IBM 360 and 370 Assembly Language, the memory location symbol is always represented by a single character, the asterisk (∗). The asterisk can be used in the operand field of most instructions and in the operand field of some directives. However, it cannot be used in the name field of any statement. Its most frequent and perhaps most important use is in the EQU and USING directives.

Consider the following sequence of statements, the statements required at the beginning of every source module:

```
SUB    CSECT
       STM      14,12,12(13)
       BALR     12,0
       USING    *,12
       ST       13,SAVE+4
       LA       13,SAVE
```

Let us assume that the Assembler associates memory address 0000 with the CSECT directive. This assumption determines the memory addresses associated with all subsequent statements shown. It, therefore, also determines the value assigned to the memory location symbol * appearing in the operand of the USING directive.

The value assigned to the symbol SUB is 0000, since that is the address that is associated with the CSECT directive. The CSECT directive, like most other directives, does not cause any bytes to be generated or reserved in the object module. Therefore, the address associated with the statement following the CSECT directive, namely with the STM instruction, is also 0000. Since the STM instruction is an RS-type instruction, 4 bytes are generated for it. Consequently, the address associated with the statement following the STM, namely the BALR instruction, is 0004. Two bytes are generated by the BALR instruction (an RR-type instruction), so that the memory address associated with the USING directive that follows it is 0006. This example can be summarized as follows:

source language statement		address associated with the statement	generated object code	number of bytes generated
SUB	CSECT	0000	none	none
	STM 14,12,12(13)	0000	90ECD00C	4
	BALR 12,0	0004	05C0	2
	USING *,12	0006	none	none
	ST 13,SAVE+4	0006	50D0C---	4
	LA 13,SAVE	000A	41D0C---	4

Since the address associated with the USING directive is 0006, the value of the memory location symbol * appearing in the operand of that USING directive is also 0006. In other words, the following two statements are interchangeable:

```
              USING        *,12
```

and

```
     HERE     USING        HERE,12
```

The memory location symbol * is therefore a convenient shorthand notation that can be used in a statement's operand field to represent the address associated with that statement. In terms of the definitions given at the beginning of this chapter, the memory location symbol is a relocatable constant.

Equivalence Constants

The concept of equivalence constants allows a programmer to define a value for a symbol and use that symbol whenever he or she wishes to employ that value in the operand of a source language statement. The value of the symbol is defined by means of the Equivalence (EQU) directive.

The symbol being defined is placed in the name field of the EQU statement; the value of the symbol is the value of the operand field of that statement. Once it is defined, the symbol can be used in the operand of any subsequent statement in the program. However, its value cannot be changed by any other statement in the program.

A major reason for using the EQU directive is to provide an easy means of changing the value of an assembly-time constant whenever the program is reassembled. No matter how many times that symbol is used in the program, the only statement that needs to be changed in order to change its value is the EQU statement that defines it.

There are other important reasons for using the EQU directive. The required value may not be known by the programmer when writing the program; the required value is too tedious to compute by hand; the required value would change if a change is made in the program; or the required value is easier to use symbolically than numerically. Moreover, all uses of a symbol defined by an EQU directive will appear in the cross-reference listing produced by the Assembler. These concepts are illustrated in the discussions and examples that follow.

The general format of the EQU directive is the same as that of any other directive: name field, opcode field, operand field, comment field, continuation field, and identification field. But, unlike the DC directive that defines a run-time constant, *the EQU does not cause any bytes to be generated in the object module.* Instead, the constant defined by an EQU directive is used by the Assembler at assembly time.

To illustrate one use of the EQU directive, consider the example used in the preceding subsection, modified to include an EQU:

```
SUB     CSECT
        STM       14,12,12(13)
        BALR      12,0
BASE    EQU       *
        USING     BASE,12
        ST        13,SAVE+4
        LA        13,SAVE
```

The memory address associated with each statement is determined by the formula given earlier:

$$\left\{ \begin{array}{c} \text{address associated} \\ \text{with a statement} \end{array} \right\} = \left\{ \begin{array}{c} \text{address associated} \\ \text{with the preceding} \\ \text{statement} \end{array} \right\} + \left\{ \begin{array}{c} \text{number of bytes} \\ \text{generated or reserved} \\ \text{by preceding statement} \end{array} \right\}$$

Thus, the memory address associated with the EQU statement is 0006, as the following summary indicates.

source language statement			address associated with the statement	generated object code	number of bytes generated
SUB	CSECT		0000	none	none
	STM	14,12,12(13)	0000	90ECD00C	4
	BALR	12,0	0004	05C0	2
BASE	EQU	*	0006	none	none
	USING	BASE,12	0006	none	none
	ST	13,SAVE+4	0006	50D0C--	4
	LA	13,SAVE	000A	41D0C--	4

Since the memory address associated with the EQU statement is 0006, the value of the memory location symbol is also 0006. Therefore the value of the operand in the EQU directive is 0006. But since the value assigned to the symbol in the name field of any EQU directive is always equal to the value of the operand in that directive, the value of the symbol BASE is 0006. In the example, the value of BASE happens to coincide with the value of the address associated with the EQU statement. But, because the operand in an EQU statement can include any symbol defined in statements preceding that EQU statement, and since the symbols in the operand can be combined algebraically, this need not always be the case. This is shown in some of the following examples.

Example 1.   Value not known in advance by programmer

```
HERE     EQU     *
```

The symbol HERE is assigned the current value of the memory location symbol. This value is not known in advance by the programmer. Note that HERE is a relocatable constant since it represents a memory address.

Example 2.   Value too tedious to compute by hand

```
MSG1        DC     C'SAMPLE USE OF THE EQU.'
TLNG1       EQU    *-MSG1
```

The symbol TLNG1 is assigned the value computed by subtracting the value that was assigned to the symbol MSG1 from the current value of the memory location symbol. This value will be exactly equal to the number of bytes reserved by the above DC directive, namely 22. Use of the EQU removes the tedium of having to count the number of characters should the message length be needed as a value elsewhere in the program. If the text message is changed by the programmer, the value of TLNG1 will automatically be changed when the program is reassembled. Note that TLNG1 is an absolute constant, since it equals the difference of two relocatable constants.

Example 3.   Value can change if program is changed

```
TABLE2      DC     F'1'
            DC     F'2'
            DC     F'3'
            DC     F'4'
            DC     F'5'
TLNG2       EQU    *-TABLE2
```

The value of TLNG2 is 20. This is the number of bytes reserved for the above table of integers (4 bytes per integer). Although it is easy enough for a programmer to compute the value 20, it is advantageous to let the Assembler compute it using the EQU directive. Then, if statements are added to or deleted from the TABLE2 table, for example when modifying or correcting a program, the value of TLNG2 will be recomputed by the Assembler. The following illustrates this:

```
TABLE2      DC     F'1'
            DC     F'2'
            DC     F'3'
            DC     F'4'
            DC     F'5'
            DC     F'6'           NEW STATEMENT ADDED
TLNG2       EQU    *-TABLE2       NOW THE VALUE OF TLNG2 IS 24
```

Example 4.   Value used symbolically

```
STATUS      DS     CL1            CARD READER STATUS BYTE
OFF         EQU    X'00'          READER IS OFF
ON          EQU    X'FF'          READER IS ON
```

To illustrate the use of these three statements, assume that the byte reserved for the symbol STATUS records the fact of whether or not a card reader connected to the computer is "off" (without power) or "on." Then, elsewhere in a program, we can determine that card reader's status before attempting to use it, by means of a compare instruction such as

```
CLI    STATUS,ON
BE     POWERON
```

This is equivalent to writing

```
CLI    STATUS,X'FF'
BE     POWERON
```

but the use of ON has two advantages: (1) each use of ON will be recorded in the cross-reference listing by the Assembler and (2) a change can be made to the value of ON without having to change any statements in the program except the EQU that defines ON. Since the cross-reference listing can be of significant help in debugging or modifying programs and since it does not include references to self-defining terms such as X'FF', it is good practice to use symbols that are equated to self-defining terms. Moreover, if the need to record status information other than the ON/OFF status indicated here arose, it would be a simple matter to do so if EQU's were being used, and not so simple if they were not. For example,

```
STATUS    DS    CL1           CARD READER STATUS BYTE
OFF       EQU   X'00'         READER IS OFF
ON        EQU   X'0F'         READER IS ON BUT NOT IN USE
INUSE     EQU   X'FF'         READER IS ON AND BEING USED
```

Now the CLI instruction given earlier to test the card reader's status *does not have to be changed* to reflect the change in meaning of the symbol ON, for now

```
CLI   STATUS,ON
BE    POWERON
```

is equivalent to

```
CLI   STATUS,X'0F'
BE    POWERON
```

If the symbolic definition ON had not been used, the CLI instruction, and all other instructions in the program that were testing for X'FF' under the previous definition, would have had to be changed to test for X'0F'. This might have required a tedious and error-prone set of changes. As it is, only the EQU had to be changed.

Example 5. Use of symbolic register addresses and symbolic displacements

Example 4 showed two advantages of symbolically defining self-defining terms. Similar advantages can be gained from symbolically defining the addresses of the general registers and the values of displacement constants. As an example, suppose OFFSET is defined by EQU

```
OFFSET    EQU    12
```

and suppose the 16 general register addresses are defined symbolically, as shown in figure 6.5. Then the following two instructions are equivalent:

```
STM    14,12,12(13)
```

and

```
STM    R14,R12,OFFSET(R13)
```

Figure 6.5   Symbolic register addresses

```
R0     EQU    0
R1     EQU    1
R2     EQU    2
R3     EQU    3
R4     EQU    4
R5     EQU    5
R6     EQU    6
R7     EQU    7
R8     EQU    8
R9     EQU    9
R10    EQU    10
R11    EQU    11
R12    EQU    12
R13    EQU    13
R14    EQU    14
R15    EQU    15
```

At first glance this may not appear to be of much use. But the symbolic register addresses and all their uses in a source module are printed in the cross-reference listing by the Assembler. So, of course, are the symbolic displacement constants. Since no uses of the self-defining decimal integers 0,1,2,3,... are printed in the cross-reference listing, the advantages gained from the use of symbols should be clear at this point: with symbols, it is easy to determine whether (and where) a given register and/or displacement is used in a program. This, in turn, can be of significant help in debugging a program, and it can make program modification less prone to error than it would be without symbolic constants.

Example 6.   Invalid use of EQU

```
SPLNG     EQU    *-SPCHAR
SPCHAR    DC     C'@#$%c&&*()+-=:;?/,.'
```

This EQU is an invalid attempt to define SPLNG as the number of characters in the SPCHAR constant. A valid definition would be

```
SPCHAR    DC     C'@#$%c&&*()+-=:;?/,.'
SPLNG     EQU    *-SPCHAR
```

The reason the first is invalid and the second is not is that *all symbols appearing in the operand of an EQU directive must have been defined prior to their appearance in that operand.* The reason for this restriction will be explained in the discussion of two-pass assemblers in chapter 10. (It should also be noted that if the first definition of SPLNG above *was* valid, the value of SPLNG would then be zero.)

Example 7.   Relocatable versus absolute constants

A memory-address field of an instruction operand is in implicit form if and only if it is a relocatable constant or a literal.

```
      L     4,Y     IMPLICIT: USES IMPLIED BASE REGISTER
      LA    5,Y       "         "         "
      LA    6,W       "         "         "
      LA    7,Z     EXPLICIT: SAME AS LA 7,4(0,0)
      L     8,Z       "         "       L  8,4(0,0)
      ...
Y     DC    F'4'    Y IS A RELOCATABLE CONSTANT (A SYMBOLIC ADDRESS)
Z     EQU   4       Z IS AN ABSOLUTE CONSTANT
W     EQU   Y       W IS A RELOCATABLE CONSTANT (EQUAL TO AN ADDR)
```

Note that the instruction L 8,Z would load the contents of the location whose address is 000004; i.e., it does *not* load the *value* of Z, it loads the *contents* of Z. On the other hand, the LA 7,Z instruction loads the value of Z as discussed in Section 4.5.

6.3   DATA AREAS

The Define Storage (DS) directive is used to reserve an area of memory for future data. This directive causes a designated amount of memory space to be reserved in the program but does not place any data into the reserved area.

When using the DS directive, we must specify how much memory space is to be reserved as well as the type of boundary alignment that is required for the data that will eventually be placed in the area. The area that is reserved may be subdivided into smaller areas of varying length, and each of the subdivisions may be assigned symbolic addresses. The entire area and/or any subdivision of the area may be duplicated. The duplication process reserves consecutive areas or subdivisions with the same characteristics as the original.

The manner in which the DS directive is used in conjunction with instructions will be described in subsequent chapters. In this section, attention is focused on the DS directive itself: (1) general format, (2) examples, and (3) subdivisions.

General Format

The DS directive consists of the same fields as other assembly language directives: name, opcode, operand, comments, continuation, and identification. The general format of the name, opcode, and operand fields is

name	opcode	operand
$\begin{cases} \text{a symbol,} \\ \text{or blank} \end{cases}$	DS	$\begin{cases} \text{one or more subfields,} \\ \text{separated by commas} \end{cases}$

Each operand subfield of a DS directive can contain from one to four components, arranged as shown below without any intervening blanks or other separators:

DS operand subfield components

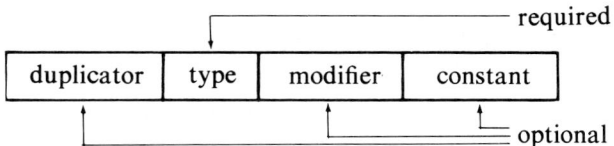

As an example of this arrangement, the following DS directive will reserve two consecutive 8-byte areas, each aligned on a byte boundary, with the first byte of the first area having the symbolic address DATE:

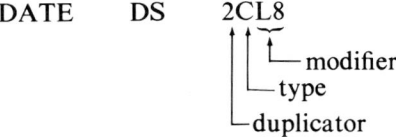

Other examples will be given later.

It should be apparent that the operand format of the DS directive is identical to that of the DC directive, except that the required and the optional subfield components are different. But, aside from this, there are important differences in the ways in which the subfield components are interpreted.

Constant. Since the DS directive does not cause any data to be placed in memory, the constant is not required. However, we may wish to specify a constant for either of two reasons. First, for documentation purposes the specification of a typical constant indicates on the listing the kind of data that will occupy the area at run time. Second, if a typical constant is specified without specifying a length modifier, the Assembler will compute the length of the area as being equal to the number of bytes that would be required for that typical constant. Thus, the example given previously for two consecutive 8-byte areas would have the same effect as the DS directive

$$\text{DATE} \qquad \text{DS} \qquad 2\text{C'06/07/80'}$$

Modifier. The only modifier allowed in a DS directive is the length modifier. This may be written either as Ln where n is a nonnegative, unsigned decimal integer or as L(x) where x is any valid arithmetic expression whose value is a nonnegative decimal integer and an absolute rather than relocatable constant.

The value of n or x is the number of bytes—the length—reserved for the area that is associated with the symbol appearing in the name field. Thus in the first example given earlier, the length of the area associated with DATE is 8. It can also be stated as the *length-attribute* of DATE is 8. Note that although the amount of space reserved is 16 bytes, for two consecutive 8-byte areas, only the length of the first of these areas is associated with the symbol DATE. Figure 6.6 shows the relationship of the length modifier to the constant and type components of a DS operand.

The length attribute of a symbol has the following importance: *if a programmer omits a length field when specifying a symbolic address in an SS$_1$ or SS$_2$ instruction, the Assembler uses the length attribute of*

Figure 6.6 *Boundary alignment and length of an area as a function of type, modifier, and constant.*

length modifier	type code	constant	boundary alignment	length
length modifier is used in the operand	any valid type code	either no constant, or any valid constant	byte boundary	determined via length modifier
length modifier is not used in the operand	B, C, P, X, or Z	any valid constant	byte boundary	determined via constant
		no constant	byte boundary	1
	H or Y	either no constant, or any valid constant	half-word boundary	2
	E or F A, Q, or S	either no constant, or any valid constant	full-word boundary	4
	D or L	either no constant, or any valid constant	double-word boundary	8

that symbol for the omitted length-field specification. Thus, for the definition of DATE given above, the following two instructions are equivalent to one another:

```
        MVC     DATE(8),=C'06/07/80'
        MVC     DATE,=C'06/07/80'     { length omitted, so
                    ┣━━━━━━━━━━━━━━━━   length attribute of DATE
DATE    DS      2CL8                   is used by Assembler
```

Type.   The only required subfield component in a DS directive's operand is *type*. Any type code shown in figure 6.2 may be specified in a DS directive. The type code determines the boundary alignment of the first byte of the reserved area unless the length modifier is specified. If the length modifier is specified, then alignment is on a byte boundary, irrespective of the type code. In the absence of a length modifier, the type code also determines the length of the area and the length attribute of the symbol associated with the area (fig. 6.6).

Duplicator.   The optional duplicator component of a DS operand is used to specify the number of consecutive areas to be reserved. When the duplicator is omitted, its value is assumed to be 1. When present, it must be written either as an unsigned nonnegative decimal integer or as (x), where x is any valid arithmetic expression whose value is a nonnegative decimal integer; x must be an absolute constant.

If the duplicator's value is 0 (zero), no memory space is reserved, but the alignment and length attribute of the area are determined as shown in figure 6.6. This fact is used as a means of defining subdivisions within an area.

Examples.   The examples that follow illustrate the relationships among the type, modifier, and constant components of a DS operand, which are given in figure 6.6. They also illustrate one other rule, that for determining the total number of bytes reserved for a memory area. The total number of bytes reserved may be called the *size* of an area and is computed by multiplying the duplicator by the area's length attribute:

$$
\left\{\begin{array}{c} \text{size of} \\ \text{memory area} \\ \text{in number} \\ \text{of bytes} \end{array}\right\} = \{\text{duplicator}\} \times \left\{\begin{array}{c} \text{length attribute of} \\ \text{memory area} \\ \text{in number} \\ \text{of bytes} \end{array}\right\}
$$

If the duplicator is not present in an operand, its value is assumed to be 1. Note that although the size and length attribute of an area are equal when the duplicator is 1, *the size and length attribute are conceptually different aspects of an area.* Of course, when the duplicator is not 1, the size and length attribute are numerically different as well. For brevity, we will use the word *length* instead of *length attribute* when no ambiguity exists.

Example 1. One full-word area

EG1   DS   F

Duplicator not present, so assumed value is 1.
Length modifier not present, so length is 4, determined by type code F; alignment is on a full-word boundary.
Size = Duplicator × Length = 1 × 4 = 4 bytes.

Example 2. Two 3-byte areas

EG2   DS   2CL3

Duplicator is 2.
Length modifier specifies that length is 3; alignment is on a byte boundary.
Size = Duplicator × Length = 2 × 3 = 6 bytes.

Example 3. Eighty 1-byte areas

EG3   DS   80C

Duplicator is 80.
Length modifier not present, no constant specified; thus length is 1, determined by type code C. C gives byte-boundary alignment.
Size = Duplicator × Length = 80 × 1 = 80 bytes

Example 4. One 80-byte area

EG4   DS   CL80

Duplicator is 1 (by omission).
Length modifier specifies that length is 80; alignment is on a byte boundary.
Size = Duplicator × Length = 1 × 80 = 80 bytes.

Example 5. Double-word areas

EG5   DS   4D

Duplicator is 4.
Length modifier not present, so length is 8, determined by type code D; alignment is on a double-word boundary.
Size = Duplicator × Length = 4 × 8 = 32 bytes.

Example 6. No space reserved

EG6   DS   0H

Duplicator is 0 (zero).
Length modifier not present, so length is 2, determined by type code H; alignment is on a half-word boundary.
Size = Duplicator × Length = 0 × 2 = 0 bytes.

Subdivisions

It is sometimes desirable to define areas within an area. In COBOL, this facility is provided through the technique of group items. In FORTRAN, the EQUIVALENCE statement is used. In Assembly Language, the following procedure is used.

Suppose we want to reserve an 8-byte area for a calendar date, in the form month/day/year where month, day, and year are each 2 bytes, e.g., 06/07/83. Suppose also that the entire calendar date area is to be given the name DATE, and that the month, day, and year subfields are to be given the names MONTH, DAY, and YEAR, respectively. To accomplish this, we use a duplication factor of zero for the overall area

```
DATE     DS    0CL8      8 BYTES FOR DATE, BUT NONE RESERVED
MONTH    DS    CL2       2 BYTES FOR MONTH
         DS    C         1 BYTE FOR /
DAY      DS    CL2       2 BYTES FOR DAY
         DS    C         1 BYTE FOR /
YEAR     DS    CL2       2 BYTES FOR YEAR
```

The length attribute of DATE is 8, so that it can be used to refer to the 8 bytes beginning at the address assigned to DATE. But the size of the area associated with DATE is zero. *Therefore, both DATE and MONTH will be assigned the same address.* This appears in memory as

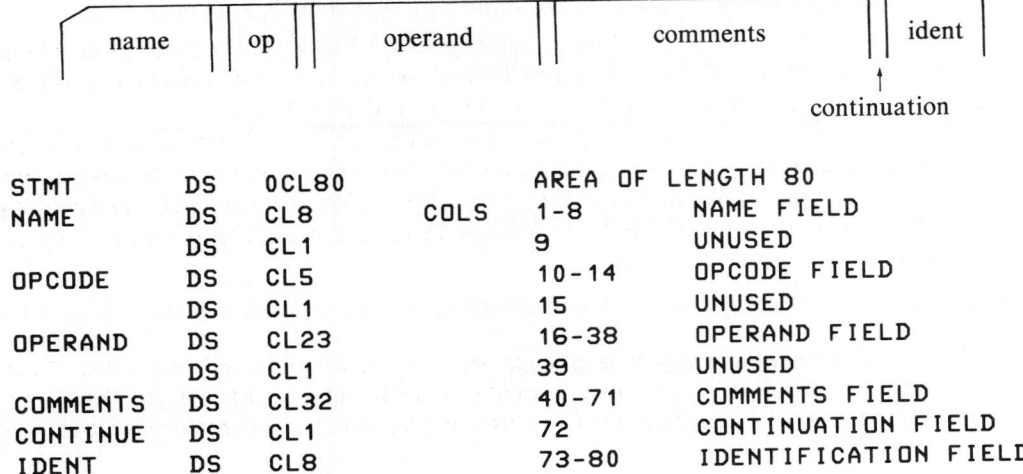

The result is that both DATE and MONTH refer to the same byte position. But DATE is associated with an 8-byte field, whereas MONTH is associated with a 2-byte field.

These subdivisions could be defined in a COBOL data division by the statements

```
01    DATE.

      02    MONTH    PICTURE    XX.
      02    FILLER   PICTURE    X.
      02    DAY      PICTURE    XX.
      02    FILLER   PICTURE    X.
      02    YEAR     PICTURE    XX.
```

As another example of subdividing an area, the statements given below will assign symbolic addresses to each of the data fields shown in the card diagram and also assign the symbolic address STMT with length attribute 80 to the entire area:

```
STMT     DS    0CL80            AREA OF LENGTH 80
NAME     DS    CL8       COLS   1-8       NAME FIELD
         DS    CL1              9         UNUSED
OPCODE   DS    CL5              10-14     OPCODE FIELD
         DS    CL1              15        UNUSED
OPERAND  DS    CL23             16-38     OPERAND FIELD
         DS    CL1              39        UNUSED
COMMENTS DS    CL32             40-71     COMMENTS FIELD
CONTINUE DS    CL1              72        CONTINUATION FIELD
IDENT    DS    CL8              73-80     IDENTIFICATION FIELD
```

6.4 BOUNDARY ALIGNMENTS

As was shown in figure 6.6, boundary alignment, which assures that a constant or memory area begins at a half-word, full-word, or double-word address, is always performed by the Assembler when an H-, F-, D-, or related type of constant or data area is defined without a length modifier. However, full-word, half-word, and double-word boundary alignment is often needed for data constants or data areas even when the data is byte-oriented data, such as characters, bits, and decimal numbers. For these types of data, the Assembler will not provide the desired alignment unless it is explicitly designated in the program. If the desired alignment is not explicitly designated, the Assembler provides only the alignments shown in figure 6.6. A method for explicitly designating the desired data alignment is described in the material that follows.

In addition to data alignment, it is occasionally necessary to align an instruction on a full-word or double-word boundary. The Assembler ensures that each instruction is aligned on a half-word boundary, but, when full-word or double-word alignment is desired, the programmer must use the conditional no-op (CNOP) directive.

Data Alignment

The most straightforward way to force alignment to the desired boundary for any constant or data area is to immediately precede the DC or DS directive that defines it with one of these three statements:

```
DS      0H
DS      0F
DS      0D
```

The DS 0H statement forces alignment of the following data constant or data area to be on a half-word boundary; DS 0F forces it to a full-word boundary; and DS 0D forces it to a double-word boundary.

For example, the statement

```
DC      X'80000000'
```

does not guarantee alignment of the hexadecimal constant X'80000000' on a full-word boundary; it only guarantees alignment on a byte boundary. If alignment on a full-word boundary is desired, this pair of statements will guarantee it:

```
DS      0F
DC      X'80000000'
```

Similarly, the following pair guarantees alignment of the packed-decimal constant P'2.84' on a double-word boundary:

```
DS      0D
DC      P'2.84'
```

And this pair guarantees alignment of the memory area CARD on a half-word boundary:

```
        DS      0H
CARD    DS      CL84
```

There are thus two ways in which half-word, full-word, and double-word alignment can take place: (1) through use of the H-, F-, or D-type codes in a DC or DS statement, as shown in the preceding sections of this chapter; or (2) by forcing alignment with duplication factors of 0 (zero), as shown above.

One small fact should be noted: whenever alignment takes place, the Assembler may leave some memory bytes unused in order to place a constant or data area at the next available boundary of the desired type. The unused byte positions are included in the memory of the program in which they occur, but no data are placed in these positions. The statements of figure 6.7a, together with the corresponding diagram of figure 6.7b, illustrate these concepts.

Instruction Alignment

Because there should ordinarily not be any unused bytes between two consecutive instructions, the method used to force alignment of constants or data areas should ordinarily not be used to force alignment of instructions. When the hardware finishes execution of any instruction other than a branch instruction, it obtains

Figure 6.7a *Illustration of forced and natural alignment.*

```
LOCTN OBJECT CODE SOURCE STATEMENT

001000                         DS    0F        FORCE ALIGNMENT TO FULL-WD BDY
001000 80              A        DC    X'80'     1-BYTE CONSTANT
001004 00000001        B        DC    F'1'      4-BYTE CONST, ON FULL-WD BDY
001008                 C        DS    CL25      25 BYTES RESERVED
001028                         DS    0D        FORCE ALIGNMENT TO DBL-WD BDY
001028 F1F2F3          D        DC    X'F1F2F3' 3-BYTE CONST
00102C 0002            E        DC    H'2'      2-BYTE CONST, ON HALF-WD BDY
001030                 F        DS    18F       18 FULL WORDS RESERVED
001078 C5D5C4          G        DC    C'END'    3-BYTE CONST, ON BYTE BDY
00107B FF              H        DC    X'FF'     1-BYTE CONST, ON BYTE BDY
```

Figure 6.7b *Memory allocation for statements of Figure 6.7a.*

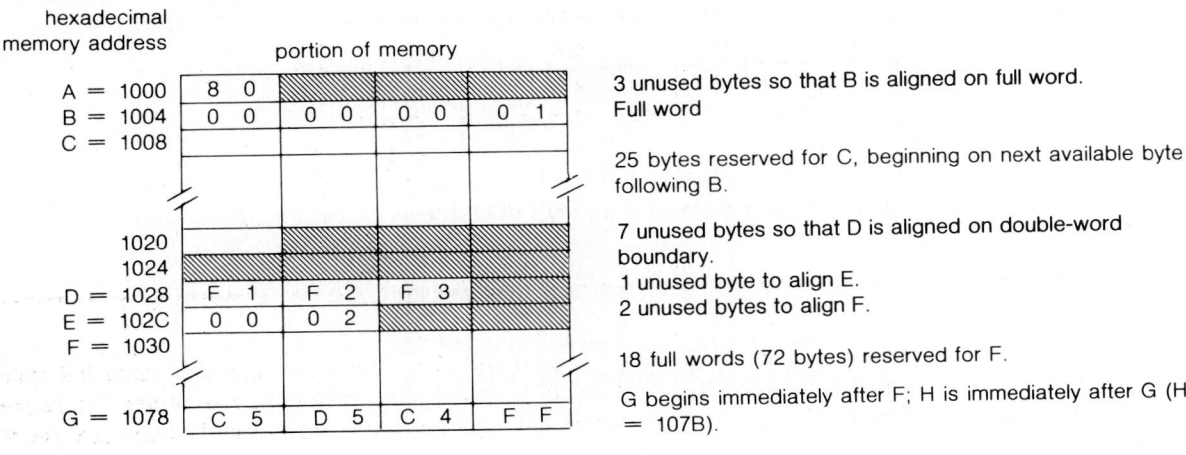

its next instruction from the byte positions immediately following the just completed instruction. If these byte positions are unused—do not contain an instruction—the hardware nevertheless assumes that there *is* an instruction in those byte positions and attempts to execute whatever is there. The result may be that the program terminates due to an opcode error or it continues after executing an instruction that was not intended to be executed.

If the alignment of instructions is left entirely to the Assembler, no unused bytes will be generated between instructions. This is because the length of each instruction is always either 2, 4, or 6 bytes, and the Assembler aligns each instruction on the half-word boundary immediately following the preceding instruction. However, if the programmer wishes to align certain instructions on full-word or double-word boundaries, the CNOP directive can be used to ensure that there will be no unused bytes that could cause such an error.

The CNOP directive causes the Assembler to generate the number of RR-type "no-op" instructions needed to increase the value of the memory location counter to a full-word or double-word boundary or to any other half-word boundary within a double word. No-op instructions are instructions that when executed do not cause any action to be taken by the hardware except the normal incrementing of the program location counter. RR-type no-op instructions occupy 2 bytes each, as do all other RR instructions. The object code generated for an RR no-op is 0700 (hex).

The format of the CNOP directive is this:

name field	opcode	operand
{ any symbol, } { or blank }	CNOP	*b,w*

Figure 6.8   *Operands of the CNOP directive.*

b,w   meaning

0,4   align next instruction on a full-word boundary
2,4   align next instruction on the 2nd half word of a full word

0,8   align next instruction on a double-word boundary
2,8   align next instruction on the 2nd half word of a double word
4,8   align next instruction on the 3rd half word of a double word
6,8   align next instruction on the 4th half word of a double word

Note: $w=4$ refers to a full word (address exactly divisible by four)
         $w=8$ refers to a double word (address exactly divisible by eight)
         b is the number of bytes beyond the full- or double-word boundary at which alignment is to take place.

The values of b and w determine the type of alignment desired and, therefore, determine how many RR-type no-op instructions—represented mnemonically as NOPR 0—will be generated by the Assembler. There are six permissible pairs of values for b,w as shown in figure 6.8. The following examples illustrate the use of CNOP.

Example 1.

Suppose that in the following source language statements, we wish to ensure that the BALR 12,0 instruction is aligned on a double-word boundary:

```
SUB     CSECT
        STM     14,12,12(13)
        BALR    12,0
        USING   *,12
        ST      13,SAVE+4
        LA      13,SAVE
```

As shown earlier (see Section 6.2), the address of the memory location associated with the BALR 12,0 instruction is 0004 (assuming, as always, that the CSECT directive begins the program at address 0000). But 0004 is not a double-word boundary since it is not exactly divisible by eight. To ensure that the BALR 12,0 instruction is aligned on a double-word boundary, the following statements are required:

```
SUB     CSECT
        STM     14,12,12(13)
        CNOP    0,8
        BALR    12,0
        USING   *,12
        ST      13,SAVE+4
        LA      13,SAVE
```

The effect of the CNOP 0,8 directive in this sequence is

source language statement		address associated with the statement	generated object code	number of bytes generated
SUB	CSECT	0000	none	none
	STM 14,12,12(13)	0000	90ECD00C	4
	CNOP 0,8	0004	07000700	4
	BALR 12,0	0008	05C0	2
	USING *,12	000A	none	none
	ST 13,SAVE+4	000A	50D0C---	4
	LA 13,SAVE	000E	41D0C---	4

The effect of the CNOP 0,8 in this sequence is two-fold: (1) the BALR 12,0 instruction is aligned on a double-word boundary and (2) to achieve this alignment without leaving unused memory bytes between the STM and BALR instructions, the Assembler generated two NOPR 0 instructions, shown in the object code as 07000700.

Example 2.

If, instead of desiring to force alignment of the BALR 12,0 instruction to a double-word boundary, we desire simply a full-word alignment, the appropriate statements and their effect would be

source language statement		address associated with the statement	generated object code	number of bytes generated
SUB	CSECT	0000	none	none
	STM 14,12,12(13)	0000	90ECD00C	4
	CNOP 0,4	0004	none	none
	BALR 12,0	0004	05C0	2
	USING *,12	0006	none	none
	ST 13,SAVE+4	0006	50D0C---	4
	LA 13,SAVE	000A	41D0C---	4

The BALR 12,0 instruction is seen to be aligned on a full-word boundary, but the Assembler did not need to generate a NOPR 0 instruction to achieve this. Consequently, none were generated.

6.5 SUMMARY

Every constant that appears in an assembly language source module statement is either a relocatable constant or an absolute constant and is either a run-time or an assembly-time constant. A relocatable constant is one whose value depends on the location of a program in main memory. For example, all symbols used to represent memory addresses, including the memory location symbol *, are relocatable constants. An absolute constant is one whose value is independent of any factor affecting or affected by the location of a program in memory. For example, all self-defining terms are absolute constants. Certain algebraic combinations of absolute and relocatable constants yield relocatable constants, other combinations yield absolute constants, and still others are invalid.

A run-time constant is one whose value is represented in memory at the time a program is being executed or run. For example, all data generated by a DC directive are run-time constants. An assembly-time constant is one whose value is not represented in memory when a program is being run but is available for use by the Assembler when a source module is being assembled. For example, all constants defined by the EQU directive are assembly-time constants.

The length of the bit sequence and the combination of bits used to represent a run-time constant depends on three factors: (1) the constant's type, as specified by the type-code in a DC operand, a literal, or a self-defining term; (2) the modifier in a DC operand or literal; and (3) the value that is specified. In addition, the memory address assigned to a run-time constant generated by a literal or DC directive depends on the type of boundary alignment indicated in the constant. If a length modifier is used in the specification of the constant, alignment is simply on the byte boundary corresponding to the current value of the memory location counter. If no length modifier is specified, alignment is dictated by the type code, as indicated in figure 6.6.

Memory areas may be reserved for use at run time by means of the DS directive. The operand of the DS directive is identical in format to that of the DC directive; but, unlike the DC directive, the DS directive does not cause the Assembler to generate constants. The amount of memory space and the type of boundary alignment is determined from the operand of a DS directive, and the address of the first byte reserved is assigned to the name-field symbol (if any) in that directive.

To force the Assembler to align a defined constant or reserved memory area on a boundary other than that dictated by the type code or length modifier, you can precede the DC or DS directive with a DS directive whose duplicator is zero and whose type code specifies the desired alignment. Thus, DS 0D would force the memory location counter to be adjusted to the next double-word boundary if it were not already at such a boundary. Similarly, DS 0H and DS 0F can be used to force half- and full-word boundary alignment, respectively. Whenever the memory location counter is adjusted to force alignment, there may be one or more unused bytes in the resulting object module.

Unlike a defined constant or a reserved memory area, an instruction is always assembled on a half-word boundary. If necessary, the Assembler adjusts the memory location counter accordingly. To force the alignment of an instruction to be on one of the two half-word boundaries in a full word or on one of the four half-word boundaries in a double word, the CNOP directive is used. When this is done, bytes that would otherwise be unused are filled with RR-type no-op instructions, i.e., instructions that do not alter any register or memory contents and that do not branch.

EXERCISES

1. What is the fundamental difference between a DC and a DS directive? What other differences and similarities exist between these two directives?

2. What is the fundamental difference between the following two directives:

```
X       DC      X'40'
Y       EQU     X'40'
```

Is X a relocatable or an absolute symbol? What about Y? State the reasons for your answers.

3. Consider the purpose and effect of the following directives. How do they differ? How are they similar?

```
D       DC      X'0001'
E       DC      H'0001'
```

4. Assume that the address assigned to the symbol DATA in the following set of statements is 000500_{16}. What address would the Assembler assign to each of the other name-field symbols if this sequence appeared in a source module exactly as shown?

```
DATA    DS      F
MSG1    DC      C'PROBLEM #4'
MSG2    DS      2F
MSG3    DC      X'0087000041'
MSG4    DC      CL132
```

5. Write an appropriate DS or DC directive for each of the following requirements:

a. Define an area of memory that contains 200 blanks.
b. Define an area of memory that contains 200 bytes of binary zeroes.
c. Reserve an area of memory for a one-dimensional integer array consisting of at most 100 components.
d. Reserve an area of memory for a two-dimensional integer array consisting of at most 20 rows and 30 columns.
e. Reserve 18 consecutive full words, with the symbolic address of the first of these being SAVE.
f. Reserve 132 bytes beginning on a double-word boundary.

6. What DC and/or DS directives are required to achieve the same purpose as these COBOL data division statements?

```
01   HEADING.
     02   FILLER      PICTURE   X(50)      VALUE SPACES.
     02   FILLER      PICTURE   X(50)      VALUE 'YEAR-END REPORT'.
     02   FILLER      PICTURE   X(6)       VALUE 'PAGE'.
     02   PAGE        PICTURE   9999.
     02   FILLER      PICTURE   X(22)      VALUE SPACES.
```

7. Convert each of the following two sets of assembly language statements into machine language, giving the address associated with each statement as well as the object code (in hex) corresponding to each instruction and defined constant. Assume that, in each case, the address to be assigned to the symbol TEST is 000000.

a.	TEST	CSECT		b.	TEST	CSECT	
		STM	14,12,12(13)			STM	14,12,12(13)
		BALR	12,0			BALR	12,0
		USING	*,12			USING	*,12
		ST	13,SAVE+4			ST	13,SAVE+4
		LA	13,SAVE			LA	13,SAVE
		L	5,CON5			LA	8,AREA
		MH	5,Z			L	9,CON5
	*				LOOP	MVC	0(5,8),PATTERN
		ST	5,P			LA	8,5(8)
		L	13,SAVE+4			BCT	9,LOOP
		LM	14,12,12(13)			L	13,SAVE+4
		BR	14			LM	14,12,12(13)
	CON5	DC	F'5'			BR	14
	CON6	DC	F'6'		CON5	DC	F'5'
	P	DS	F		PATTERN	DC	X'0102030405'
	Z	DC	H'20'		AREA	DS	5CL5
	SAVE	DS	18F		SAVE	DS	18F
		END				END	

8. What object code would be generated for each of these DC directives?

   a. DC   FS10'2'
   b. DC   FE2'10'
   c. DC   4X'4'
   d. DC   XL4'4'
   e. DC   F'2',F'100'
   f. DC   F'2,100'
   g. DC   4XL4'4'
   h. DC   80CL80' '

9. What is the relationship between the length modifier specified in a DC or DS directive and the length field in the operand of an SS_1 or SS_2 instruction when that length field is implied? What length-field contents would be assembled for this SS_1 instruction,

$$\text{MVC} \qquad \text{PRINTER,CARD}$$

for each of the following pairs of DS directives?

   a. PRINTER   DS   132C
      CARD   DS   80C

   b. PRINTER   DS   CL132
      CARD   DS   CL80

c.
PRINTER	DS	2CL60
CARD	DS	CL80

d.
PRINTER	DS	0CL132
CARD	DS	0CL80

10. In addition to the use of the exponent modifier (En) following the type code in a DC directive, we can specify a power of ten by which a constant is to be multiplied through use of the exponent notation *following* the constant. For example, DC F'1E5' is equivalent to DC F'100000'. The difference between use of the exponent notation as a modifier and its use following a constant is that the modifier applies to all the constants specified in a given operand subfield, whereas, when it follows a constant, the exponent applies only to that constant. If both are specified, their algebraic sum is the exponent that is applied. The sum must be in the range of from -85 through 75. For example,

DC   FE5'2E2,3E$-$1,4E0'

specifies constants of 2×10^7, 3×10^4, and 4×10^5, respectively. What decimal constants are specified by each of these DC directives?

a. DC   F'1E2'
b. DC   FE3'2E4,4E2,1E$-$3'
c. DC   HS3'1E3,2E2'
d. DC   FE6'5',F'6E7'

11. Suppose there is a set of input data cards in which each card contains the name, ID, and course grades for a student in the following format: student name in columns 1–25, student ID in columns 30–38, course ID's in columns 40–45, 50–55, 60–65, and 70–75, with corresponding course grades in columns 46–49, 56–59, 66–69, and 76–79. Write a sequence of directives that will reserve an area of memory for an input card and assign symbolic addresses to each of its fields.

12. Draw a diagram similar to that of figure 6.7b to represent the memory allocations that would result from the following set of directives. Assume that the address assigned to the symbol AREAS is 000EF4.

AREAS	DS	0F
A1	DC	CL5'X'
A2	DC	XL5'C'
A3	DC	F'12'
A4	DC	2H'12'
A5	DS	11CL11
A6	DS	3D
A7	DS	0H
A8	DS	CL80

What is the length attribute of each of the symbols in these statements?

13. Suppose that the results of a questionnaire are recorded on a set of input data cards. The questionnaire consisted of six questions, each requiring a *yes, no,* or *undecided* response. The responses are coded as integers, 0 = no, 1 = yes, and 2 = undecided, card columns 12,24,36,48,60,72 being used for questions 1,2,3,4,5,6, respectively. Write an assembly language program that will read all the input cards; calculate the number of *yes, no,* and *undecided* responses to each question; and print the results in a suitably readable format.

14. Write an assembly language program that will calculate and print the integers 2^n through 10^n for $n = 1,2,...,9$. Each line of output should contain all the integers calculated for a given n.

7
Byte and String Manipulations

As discussed previously, the word *byte* refers to any addressable 8-bit quantity. In the IBM EBCDIC code scheme, many of the 256 possible 8-bit quantities are used to represent characters that can be typed or displayed at a terminal or printer. The printable characters in the EBCDIC code scheme are shown in figure 7.1.

A sequence of bytes is called a *string*. Sometimes the terms *character string* or *text string* are used to emphasize that the bytes represent printable characters. The number of bytes in a string is called the *string length*. Thus, the terms *byte manipulations* and *string manipulations* are essentially interchangeable; both refer to the following types of operations on one or more consecutive bytes: copying bytes, comparing two sequences of bytes, and searching a sequence of bytes for the occurrence of specific values. In this chapter, the instructions used to accomplish these operations will be described and illustrated with several examples.

Byte-manipulation instructions have three general characteristics. (1) All byte-manipulation instructions operate on two strings. One of the strings is always in memory; the other may be in memory or in a register, depending on the instruction itself. (2) All byte-manipulation instructions require that the number of bytes being operated on—the length of the strings—be specified either explicitly or implicitly. (3) All the byte-manipulation instructions described in this chapter treat bytes as 8-bit nonalgebraic quantities: the high-order bit is not considered to be a sign bit but is treated in the same way as the other bits.

7.1 CHARACTER CONSTANTS

To define a data constant as a sequence of characters, we use the C data-type code. This code may be used in the DC directive, in literals, and in self-defining terms. The C code requires that each character be specified just as it would be written (including the blank character), with two exceptions: (1) to specify an apostrophe (') we must write two consecutive apostrophes ('') so that the Assembler can distinguish the specified apostrophes from the delimiting apostrophes and (2) to specify an ampersand (&) we must write two consecutive ampersands (&&).

One byte is always allotted for each specified character. The maximum number of characters that can be specified for a single DC or literal constant is 256; for self-defining terms, the maximum is four characters.

Figure 7.2 illustrates the usual methods of specifying constants as character sequences. It also illustrates what happens in two special situations: truncation and padding.

When the length modifier Ln specifies *fewer* bytes than are needed to contain the binary representation of the data constant given in a C-type DC directive, the Assembler deletes characters from the right. It accepts only the number of characters specified in the length modifier. This is called *truncation* on the right.

When the length modifier Ln specifies *more* bytes than are needed to contain the binary representation of the data constant given in a C-type DC directive, the Assembler adds blank characters on the right to fill the length that was specified. This is called *padding* with blanks.

Figure 7.1 *Printable characters in the EBCDIC code scheme. (Note: Each 8-bit EBCDIC code is shown as a two-digit hexadecimal number.)*

SPECIAL GRAPHIC CHARACTERS

hex code	character symbol & name	hex code	character symbol & name	hex code	character symbol & name	hex code	character symbol & name	hex code	character symbol & name
40	blank space	50	& ampersand	60	– hyphen	79	` grave accent	A1	~ tilde
4A	¢ cent sign	5A	! exclamation	61	/ slash	7A	: colon	C0	{ left brace
4B	. period	5B	$ dollar	6A	¦ vertical bars	7B	# number sign	CC	∫ hook
4C	< less-than	5C	* asterisk	6B	, comma	7C	@ commercial at	CE	⊤ fork
4D	(left paren	5D	) right paren	6C	% percent	7D	' apostrophe	D0	} right brace
4E	+ plus	5E	; semicolon	6D	_ underline	7E	= equals	E0	\ reverse slash
4F		logical OR	5F	¬ logical NOT	6E	> greater than	7F	" quotation mark	EC	⊓ chair
				6F	? question mark			FA		long vertical bar

LOWERCASE ALPHABET

hex		hex		hex	
81	a	91	j		
82	b	92	k	A2	s
83	c	93	l	A3	t
84	d	94	m	A4	u
85	e	95	n	A5	v
86	f	96	o	A6	w
87	g	97	p	A7	x
88	h	98	q	A8	y
89	i	99	r	A9	z

UPPERCASE ALPHABET

hex		hex		hex	
C1	A	D1	J		
C2	B	D2	K	E2	S
C3	C	D3	L	E3	T
C4	D	D4	M	E4	U
C5	E	D5	N	E5	V
C6	F	D6	O	E6	W
C7	G	D7	P	E7	X
C8	H	D8	Q	E8	Y
C9	I	D9	R	E9	Z

DECIMAL DIGITS

hex	
F0	0
F1	1
F2	2
F3	3
F4	4
F5	5
F6	6
F7	7
F8	8
F9	9

Figure 7.2 *Character constants and data areas.*

```
FLAG LOCTN OBJECT CODE     ADDR1 ADDR2  STMNT M SOURCE STATEMENT

                                          5   * CHARACTER CONSTANTS, VIA 'DC'
     000000 C1                             6         DC      3C'A'       1 'A' REPEATED 3 TIMES
            C1
            C1
     000003 C1C1C1                         7         DC      C'AAA'      1 SET OF 3 A'S
     000006 C14DC2C5E3                     8         DC      C'A BET'    1 5-BYTE CONSTANT
                                           9   * SELF-DEFINING TERMS
     00006F                               10   E1    EQU     C'?'     ONE BYTE, HEX 6F
     00007D                               11   E2    EQU     C''''    ONE APOSTROPHE = HEX 7D
     0000C1                               12   E3    EQU     C'A'     ONE BYTE, HEX C1

                                          13   * RESERVING DATA AREAS FOR CHARACTERS, ALIGNED ON
                                          14   * BYTE BDY UNLESS PRECEDING  DS  SAYS OTHERWISE.
     00000B                               15         DS      CL77
     000058                               16         DS      CL2
     00005A                               17         DS      OH       ON HALF-WORD BOUNDARY
     00005A                               18         DS      CL40
     000084                               19         DS      OF       ON FULL-WORD BOUNDARY
     000084                               20         DS      133C
     000110                               21         DS      OD       ON DOUBLE-WD BOUNDARY
     000110                               22   X     DS      CL20

                                          23   * TRUNCATION ON THE RIGHT TO FIT LENGTH
     000124 C1C2                          24         DC      CL2'ABCD'   1 CONST, LENGTH = 2 BYTES
     000126 E7                            25         DC      3CL1'XYZ'   3 CONSTS, EACH OF LNG = 1
            E7
            E7

                                          26   * PADDING ON THE RIGHT WITH BLANKS
     000129 C1C240                        27         DC      CL3'AB'     1 CONST, LENGTH = 3 BYTES
     00012C E740                          28         DC      2CL2'X'     2 CONSTS, EACH OF LNG = 2
            E740

                                          29   * LITERALS
     000130 D2 00 C110C140 000110 000140  30         MVC     X(1),=C'&&'  ONE AMPERSAND (&) = HEX 50
     000136 D2 01 C110C141 000110 000141  31         MVC     X(2),=C'ZZ'  TWO Z'S  ( Z = HEX E9 )
                                          32         LTORG
     000140 50
     000141 E9E9
```

7.2 COPYING BYTES

There are two sets of byte-copying instructions: (1) those that copy bytes from memory into a register or from a register into memory, and (2) those that copy bytes from one area of memory to another area of memory. The former are called INSERT and STORE instructions, respectively; the latter are called MOVE instructions. (Strictly speaking, the word MOVE is a slight misnomer, since it implies erasure of the bytes from their original position. The MOVE instructions would be more accurately named COPY, since they produce a duplicate of the original byte string without erasing the original. However, the name MOVE is preserved for historical reasons.)

Copying Bytes to and from Registers

opcode	meaning	type
IC	**INSERT CHARACTER** Copies 1 byte from memory into the 8 right-most bits of a register, without altering the other bits in that register.	RX
STC	**STORE CHARACTER** Copies 1 byte—the 8 right-most bits of a register—into memory.	RX
ICM	**INSERT CHARACTERS UNDER MASK** Copies N bytes, $N \le 4$, from memory into a register. The number of bytes copied and their relative positions in the register are specified in the second operand of the instruction.	RS
STCM	**STORE CHARACTERS UNDER MASK** Copies N bytes, $N \le 4$, from a register into memory. The number of bytes copied and their relative position in the register are specified in the second operand of the instruction.	RS

Note that the ICM and STCM instructions are available on the IBM 370 but not on the IBM 360. The letter M in these instructions refers to the fact that the second operand of the ICM and STCM constitutes a *mask* rather than a register address or a length. In these two instructions the mask is a 4-bit field that has a dual purpose. First, the number of bytes that are inserted or stored is equal to the number of 1's in the 4-bit mask. And second, the relative position of the bytes in the register is determined by the relative position of the 1's in the mask, the correspondence being from left to right, one for one.

In the examples that follow, it is assumed that symbolic address A is 1000 (hex). The examples are not necessarily related to one another.

Example 1.

			Reg 6	memory location 1000
IC	6,A	before execution:	01 23 AB CD	E1 E2 E3 E4
		after execution:	01 23 AB E1	E1 E2 E3 E4

As in the LOAD instructions, the source field in an INSERT instruction is designated by the second operand, the destination by the first.

Example 2.

		Reg 6	memory location 1000
STC 6,A	before execution:	01 23 AB CD	E1 E2 E3 E4
	after execution:	01 23 AB CD	CD E2 E3 E4

In all STORE instructions, the source field is designated by the first operand, the destination by the second.

Example 3.

This mask is 1010 in binary. Its meaning is: 2 bytes are inserted, since there are two 1's in the mask; the relative byte positions *in the register* are the first and third, as shown in the diagram.

Example 4.

This mask is given in binary rather than hex. Its meaning is: 3 bytes are stored, since there are three 1's in the mask; the relative byte positions *in the register* are the second, third, and fourth, as shown in the diagram.

Copying Bytes from One Area of Memory to Another

opcode	meaning	type
MVI	MOVE IMMEDIATE Copies 1 byte *from* I2 field of MVI instruction *to* memory location designated by first operand.	SI
MVC MVCIN	MOVE CHARACTERS MOVE INVERSE Copies L bytes, $L \leq 256$, *from* memory location designated by second operand *to* memory location designated by first operand. (L = value of length field in first operand.)	SS_1 SS_1
MVCL	MOVE CHARACTERS LONG Copies L bytes, $L \leq 2^{24}$, *from* memory location designated by bits 8–31 of the general register specified in the second operand *to* memory location designated by bits 8–31 of the general register specified in the first operand. (L = value of length field associated with the first operand.)	RR

Note that the MVCL and MVCIN instructions are available on the IBM 370 but not the 360. A discussion of MVCL will be presented in Section 7.8.

In the examples of MVI and MVC that follow, it is assumed that symbolic address A is 1000 (hex), and that B is 2000 (hex).

Example 1.

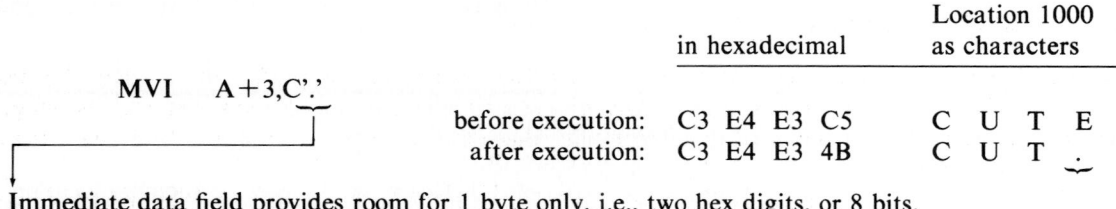

		in hexadecimal	Location 1000 as characters
	before execution:	C3 E4 E3 C5	C U T E
	after execution:	C3 E4 E3 4B	C U T .

Immediate data field provides room for 1 byte only, i.e., two hex digits, or 8 bits.

Example 2.

		Location 2000 as characters	Location 1000 as characters
MVC B(4),A			
	before execution:	P O R T	T A L K
	after execution:	T A L K	T A L K

Length field specifies how many bytes are to be copied.

Example 3.

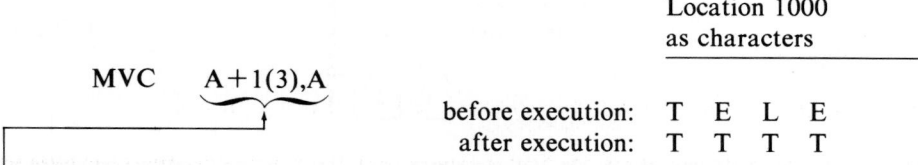

		Location 1000 as characters
MVC A+1(3),A		
	before execution:	T E L E
	after execution:	T T T T

Sending field 1000–1002 overlaps receiving field 1001–1003. What happens is the following. First, a byte is copied from 'A' to 'A+1', i.e., from address 1000 to address 1001, with the result that the character E at 1001 is replaced by the character T copied from 1000. Then, since the second of the three bytes in the sending field is at 1001, the character T is copied from 1001 to 1002, replacing the L that was there. Finally, the T is copied from 1002 to 1003, with the result shown above: TTTT has replaced TELE.

MVCIN (Move Inverse)

The MVCIN instruction is available as a special feature rather than as a standard instruction on most IBM 370 systems. As in the MVC instruction, MVCIN can copy from 1 to 256 bytes from one location to another. The sending location's address is specified in the second operand field, and the receiving location's address and length are specified in the first operand field. However, MVCIN differs from MVC in two important respects: (1) the first operand address in MVCIN designates the *right*-most byte of the receiving location (not the left-most byte); and (2) in the receiving location the left-to-right sequence of bytes is reversed from what it was in the sending location.

For example, if as in the MVC instruction of Example 2 above these are the *sending* location's bytes for MVCIN,

T A L K   second operand designates the address of this byte then the *receiving* location's bytes will be these:

K L A T   ⌐————first operand designates
                     the address of this byte

Using the notation of Example 2, the MVCIN that would accomplish this is MVCIN B+3(4),A. Obviously, the MVCIN is useful only in situations—such as the use of special input/output devices—that require reversal of the normal character sequence.

7.3 COMPARING BYTES

In comparing any two bytes, the contents of each byte are treated as unsigned 8-bit numbers. An unsigned quantity such as a byte contents is called a *logical* quantity, whereas signed quantities such as integers are *arithmetic* quantities. To emphasize this distinction, all byte comparison instructions begin with the letters CL, meaning *Compare Logical*.

The smallest byte contents is 0000 0000; the largest is 1111 1111 (FF in hex notation). Any of the 256 possible 8-bit patterns is allowed in a byte. In the IBM Systems 360 and 370, the correspondence between bytes and characters given by the EBCDIC coding scheme determines whether one character is greater than or less than another character. For example, A is less than B since an A is represented as 1100 0001, which is less (numerically) than the representation of a B, namely 1100 0010. Notice that the blank (0100 0000) is less than any other printable character.

In comparing two byte strings of equal length, the comparison starts at the left-hand (high-order) end of each string and proceeds byte by byte to the right, comparing the bytes from corresponding positions, until one of two situations occurs: (1) either two bytes (one from each string) are found to be unequal or (2) the strings are exhausted and all pairs of bytes are found to be equal.

In the first situation, the relative value of the first pair of unequal bytes determines which string is the greater and which the lesser. In the second situation, the strings are considered equal. These two situations are illustrated in Examples 1–3.

Example 1.

First string: WILY
Second string: WARD

Result: First string is greater than the second string, since I is greater than A.

Example 2.

First string: STRIPE
Second string: STRUNG

Result: First string is less than the second string, since I is less than U.

Example 3.

First string: VALUE
Second string: VALUE

Result: Both strings are equal, since each corresponding pair of bytes is equal.

There are six instructions in the IBM Systems 360 and 370 that compare byte strings. In all but one of these, the two strings must be of equal length, i.e., consist of an equal number of bytes. The exception, the CLCL instruction, permits comparison of unequal-length strings by momentarily filling, or padding, the shorter string with a pad character designated by the second operand of the instruction.

The six byte-comparison instructions fall naturally into two groups: (1) instructions in which one of the strings must be in a register and (2) instructions in which both of the strings are in memory locations.

Comparing Bytes When One of the Strings Is in a Register

opcode	meaning	type
CL	COMPARE LOGICAL Compares two 4-byte strings: *first string* is in the register designated by the first operand. *Second string* is in the memory location designated by the second operand.	RX
CLR	COMPARE LOGICAL REGISTERS Compares two 4-byte strings: *first string* is in the register designated by the first operand. *Second string* is in the register designated by the second operand.	RR
CLM	COMPARE LOGICAL UNDER MASK Compares two N-byte strings, $N \leq 4$: *first string* is in the register designated by the first operand. *Second string* is in the memory location designated by the second operand.	RS

Note that the CLM instruction is available on the IBM 370 but not on the IBM 360. The letter M in this instruction refers to the fact that the second operand is a *mask*. The CLM mask functions in a manner similar to that in the ICM and STCM instructions discussed previously: the number of 1's in the mask is the number of bytes that are compared, and the relative position of the 1's determines which bytes in the register are used in the comparison.

Comparing Bytes When Both Strings Are in Memory Locations

opcode	meaning	type
CLI	COMPARE LOGICAL IMMEDIATE Compares two 1-byte strings: *first string* is in the memory location designated by the first operand. *Second string* is in the immediate data field of the instruction itself.	SI
CLC	COMPARE LOGICAL CHARACTERS Compares two N-byte strings, $N \leq 256$: *first string* is in the memory location designated by the first operand. *Second string* is in the memory location designated by the second operand. (N = value of length field in first operand)	SS$_1$
CLCL	COMPARE LOGICAL CHARACTERS LONG Compares two possibly unequal-length strings, maximum length $= 2^{24} - 1$: *first string* is in the memory location designated by bits 8–31 of the general register specified in the first operand. *Second string* is in the memory location designated by bits 8–31 of the general register specified in the second operand.	RR

Note that the CLCL instruction is available on the IBM 370 but not the IBM 360. A discussion of the CLCL is presented in Section 7.8.

	condition code and its meaning			
instruction	0	1	2	3
CL,CLC,CLCL, CLI,CLM,CLR	first string equal to second string	first string less than second string	first string greater than second string	---

All the compare instructions mentioned up to this point set the condition code as shown in the table above. This provides the means by which the result of a comparison can be determined, as discussed in the next section.

7.4 DETERMINING THE RESULT OF A STRING COMPARISON

Whichever compare instruction is used, the result of the comparison may be determined by means of a conditional branch instruction. The same conditional branch instructions used in determining the result of an algebraic comparison are used in determining the result of a string comparison. If V_1 denotes the string whose address is specified by the first operand in a compare instruction, and V_2 the string specified by the second operand, then the six RX-type conditional branch instructions can be used as follows:

opcode	meaning	
BE	Branch if V_1 equals V_2	$V_1 = V_2$
BNE	Branch if V_1 is not equal to V_2	$V_1 \neq V_2$
BL	Branch if V_1 is less than V_2	$V_1 < V_2$
BNL	Branch if V_1 is not less than V_2	$V_1 \geq V_2$
BH	Branch if V_1 is higher than V_2	$V_1 > V_2$
BNH	Branch if V_1 is not higher than V_2	$V_1 \leq V_2$

As discussed in chapter 5, each of these six instructions is written with only one operand field. That field designates the address of the instruction to which a branch is made if the condition being tested is true. If the condition is *not* true, then no branch is made; instead, execution of the program continues with the instruction that immediately follows the conditional branch instruction. Examples illustrating the use of the conditional branch instructions with string comparisons are given in the sections that follow.

7.5 STRING-PROCESSING EXAMPLES

The byte-manipulation instructions described in the preceding sections are sufficient to enable many string processing problems to be programmed efficiently in Assembly Language. From a problem-solving standpoint, the key aspect of these instructions is that they allow a programmer to deal with strings of arbitrary length, provided their length is known at the time the program is written. The examples considered in this section illustrate this. However, if a string's length is not known at the time a program is written, the solutions presented here would not be valid. This type of problem will be discussed in Sections 7.7 and 7.8.

Consider the following elementary but typical string-handling tasks:

1. Fill an area of memory with blank spaces.
2. Search a string for all occurrences, if any, of the exclamation point character "!"; replace each occurrence with the period ".".
3. Search a string for the first occurrence of either a blank or a comma, and determine how many characters in the string preceded the first blank or comma that was found.
4. Compare an arbitrary 5-byte string with the value "END   " (the letters *E N D* followed by two blanks) to see if it is equal to it or not.
5. Compare an arbitrary 5-byte string with each of the three 5-byte strings "END   ", "STOP ", "FINIS" and determine which, if any, of these it is equal to.

The assembly language statements to perform each of these tasks are given in figures 7.3 through 7.7 and are explained in the examples that follow. In all of these examples, it is assumed that the statements shown represent part of a program, not the whole program. Consequently, the CSECT, END, and BALR-USING base register statements are not shown.

Example 1.   Fill an area with blanks
(See figure 7.3)

To fill an area of memory with blanks, two things must be known: (1) the address of the area and (2) the number of bytes in the area, i.e., the area's length. The address can be written either symbolically or in base-displacement form. The area's length, an unsigned integer, can be written symbolically or numerically, or can be omitted and implied by the length attribute of the area.

Figure 7.3 *Fill an area with blanks.*

```
1                MVI    CARD,C' '              PUT A BLANK INTO FIRST BYTE
2         *                                    OF AREA NAMED 'CARD'
3                MVC    CARD+1(79),CARD        PROPAGATE BLANK INTO REMAINING
4         *                                    79 POSITIONS OF 'CARD' AREA
                        .
                        .
                        .
5    CARD    DS    CL80                         RESERVE 80 BYTES FOR CARD
                        .
                        .
                        .
```

The simplest method of filling an area with blanks is to define one area that always contains blanks and copy that to the area that is to be filled. For the definitions of CARD and BLANKS given,

CARD	DS	CL80	LENGTH ATTRIBUTE OF 'CARD' IS 80
BLANKS	DC	CL80' '	80 BLANK CHARACTERS

either of the following two MVC instructions will copy 80 blanks into the area named CARDS:

MVC	CARD(80),BLANKS	EXPLICIT LENGTH FIELD
MVC	CARD,BLANKS	LENGTH FIELD IMPLIED

In figure 7.3, a different method is used. This illustrates the concept of *destructive overlap*, created by an MVC when two conditions exist simultaneously: (1) the sending area designated by the second operand *overlaps* the receiving area designated by the first operand, and (2) the first byte of the receiving area is *within* the sending area.

Destructive Overlap

In figure 7.3, Statement 5 defines the area, giving it a symbolic name and a size of 80 bytes. Statements 1 and 3 utilize the destructive overlap concept as follows: Statement 1 puts a blank into the first byte of the area; Statement 3 causes that blank to be propagated into the remaining bytes of the area. This propagation is a form of destructive overlap.

A trace of the execution of the two instructions in figure 7.3 shows the following sequence of events:

MVI moves blank into first byte.

MVC propagates first byte in 79 distinct steps, successively replacing the sending area bytes, one at a time, before they are copied into the receiving area.

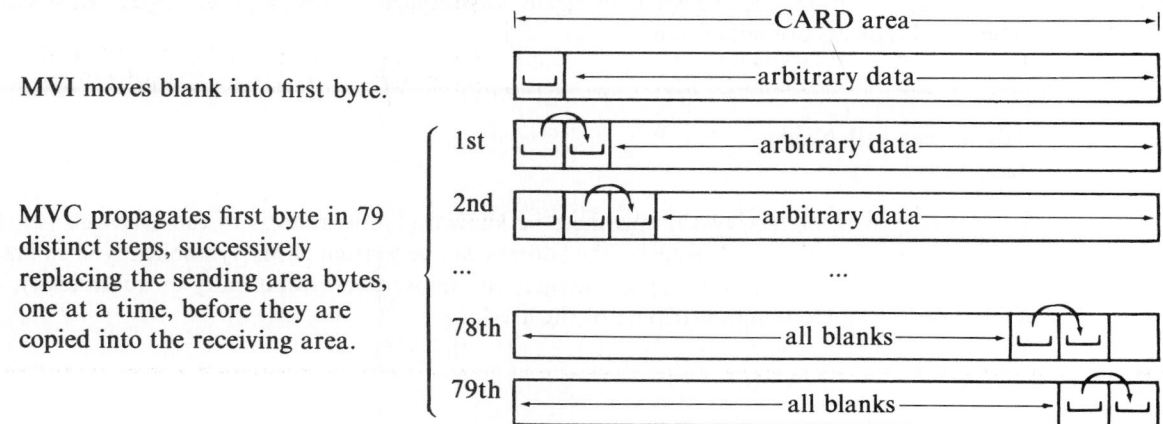

Two things should be noted. First, whereas the method of propagation illustrated here can be useful, it can also be disastrous if the programmer is unaware of the destructive overlap potential of the sending and receiving fields. Thus, each use of the MVC must be carefully planned. Second, if the first byte of the receiving area is *not* within the sending area, destructive overlap cannot occur. If, in this situation, the two areas partially overlap, they are said to overlap nondestructively. This is illustrated by this diagram:

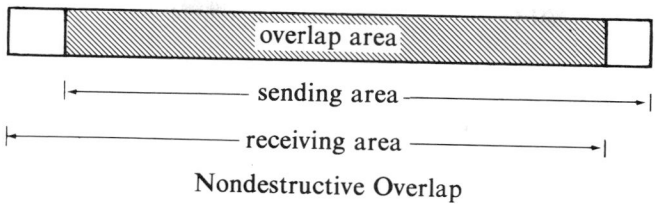

Nondestructive Overlap

Example 2. Replace exclamation points with periods
(See fig. 7.4)

In this solution, each repetition of the loop examines one byte of the string; the address of the byte being examined is in Register 4, initialized to the beginning (left-end) of the string by Statement 2 and incremented to the next consecutive byte by Statement 9. The number of loop repetitions, i.e., the loop-control counter, is the string length, defined by Statements 12 and 13. Statement 3 initializes the loop-control counter, placing the string length into Register 5. The BCT instruction in Statement 10 reduces the loop-control counter by one; if the result of this reduction is not zero, the BCT branches to the statement named COMPARE to continue the search. When the counter reaches zero, no branch is made and the search is terminated.

Statements 5 and 6 determine whether the byte whose address is in Register 4 is an exclamation point or not. Since only one byte is being examined, the CLI instruction is used. Its first operand, 0(4), is in base-displacement form D1(B1) and means "a displacement of zero bytes beyond the address given in Register 4." (This phrase is usually stated as "zero beyond 4.") In other words, Statement 4 compares the byte whose address is in Register 4 with the exclamation point in the immediate data field of the CLI. Statement 5 determines what the result of that comparison is: when the result is equal, that is, when an exclamation point is found, no branch occurs. The BNE only branches when the result of the comparison is not equal.

Statement 7 is executed whenever an exclamation point is found. It moves (copies) a period from its immediate data field to the same location, designated as 0(4), at which the exclamation point is found, thereby replacing the exclamation point.

Figure 7.4 ***Replace exclamation points with periods.***

```
 1     *  INITIALIZATION
 2     START    LA    4,STRING        R4=ADDR OF FIRST BYTE OF STRING
 3              LA    5,LENGTH        R5=LENGTH OF STRING
 4     * SEARCH FOR ALL EXCLAMATION POINTS
 5     COMPARE  CLI   0(4),C'!'       COMPARE CURRENT BYTE TO '!'
 6              BNE   NEXT            IF NOT EQUAL, ATTEMPT NEXT BYTE
 7              MVI   0(4),C'.'       IF EQUAL, REPLACE IT WITH '.'
 8     * LOOP CONTROL
 9     NEXT     LA    4,1(4)          R4=ADDR OF NEXT BYTE OF STRING
10              BCT   5,COMPARE       DECR STR LNG BY 1,REPEAT LOOP
11     * END OF PROCEDURE
                 .
                 .
                 .
12     STRING   DC    C'TEST! WILL IT WORK? YES!'
13     LENGTH   EQU   *-STRING
                 .
                 .
                 .
```

Statement 13 illustrates a useful way to let the Assembler calculate the length of a string: the Assembler calculates the difference of two addresses—the address of the byte following the last byte of the string, minus the address of the first byte of the string—and assigns this value to the symbol LENGTH. (The EQU pseudo-op and the memory location symbol * were described in chapter 6.)

Example 3. **Find first comma or blank in a string and compute length**
(See fig. 7.5.)

This solution is similar to that of Example 2. The differences are that: (1) the search is terminated *either* when a comma or blank is found *or* when there are no more bytes to be examined, and (2) when the search is terminated, the number of bytes that precede the first comma or blank is calculated and stored in the location named POSIT. Note that it always requires at least two types of statements to examine a string: the first is a comparison, the second is a conditional branch determining the results of the comparison.

Statements 13 and 14 calculate the number of bytes that precede the first comma or blank in the string. For the sample string of Statement 17, this number is four; i.e., the program finds the blank following the D in FIND. However, the program shown will work for *any* string, provided its address is STRING and that it consists of at least 1 byte. For example,

sample string	string length	number of bytes preceding the first comma or blank
C'DEAR JOHN,'	10	4 (blank in 5th position)
C'DEARJOHN,'	9	8 (comma in 9th position)
C' DEAR JOHN,'	11	0 (blank in 1st position)
C'DEARJOHN'	8	8 (no blank or comma found)

Since it is inconceivable that any string would have a length for which the binary representation would require more than 15 bits ($2^{15} = 32,768$), only a half word was reserved for the computed value stored in POSIT. Thus, in Statement 16, the half-word store instruction STH is used in conjunction with the half word reserved by Statement 19.

Figure 7.5 Find first comma or blank, and compute length.

```
1     * INITIALIZATION
2     START     LA    4,STRING        R4=ADDR OF FIRST BYTE OF STRING
3               LA    5,LENGTH        R5=LENGTH OF STRING
4     * SEARCH FOR FIRST BLANK OR COMMA
5     COMPARE   CLI   0(4),C','       COMPARE CURRENT BYTE TO COMMA
6               BE    DONE            IF COMMA, TERMINATE SEARCH
7               CLI   0(4),C' '       IF NOT, COMPARE TO BLANK
8               BE    DONE            IF BLANK, TERMINATE SEARCH
9     * LOOP CONTROL
10              LA    4,1(4)          R4=ADDR OF NEXT BYTE OF STRING
11              BCT   5,COMPARE       DECR STR LNG BY 1,REPEAT LOOP
12    * COMPUTE NUMBER OF BYTES PRECEDING THE BLANK OR COMMA
13    DONE      LA    4,LENGTH        ORIGINAL LENGTH MINUS REMAINING
14              SR    4,5              LENGTH IS RESULT DESIRED
15    * END OF PROCEDURE
16    EXIT      STH   4,POSIT         R4=LENGTH UP TO COMMA OR BLANK
                .
                .
                .
17    STRING    DC    C'FIND COMMA, OR BLANK'
18    LENGTH    EQU   *-STRING        ASSBLR COMPUTES #BYTES IN STRING
19    POSIT     DS    H               HALF-WORD FOR PTR TO ' ' OR ','
                .
                .
                .
```

Figure 7.6   Compare 5-byte string to C'END   '

```
1              CLC    COMMAND(5),STRING        COMPARE 5-BYTE STRINGS
2              BE     FOUND                    BRANCH IF EQUAL
               .
               .
               .
3   STRING  DS    CL5                          5-BYTE AREA RESERVED FOR STRING
4   COMMAND DC    CL5'END'                     'END' IS PADDED ON RIGHT
               .
               .
               .
```

Example 4.   Compare 5-byte string to C'END   '
          (See fig. 7.6)

Since both strings are in memory and are of length greater than four, the CLC instruction is used. If the string lengths were greater than 256, or if the strings were of unequal length, the CLCL instruction would have to be used instead of the CLC.

Figure 7.7   Compare 5-byte string with strings in a table.

```
1   * INITIALIZATION
2   START    LA    4,TABLE            R4=ADDR OF FIRST ENTRY IN TABLE
3            LA    5,ENTRIES          R5=NUMBER OF ENTRIES
4   * COMPARE STRING TO EACH ENTRY (STRING LENGTH IS 5)
5   LOOK     CLC   0(5,4),STRING      COMPARE CURRENT ENTRY TO STRING
6            BE    EXIT               TERMINATE PROCEDURE WHEN FOUND
7   * LOOP CONTROL
8            LA    4,5(4)             IF NOT FOUND, ADV TO NEXT ENTRY
9            BCT   5,LOOK             DECR #ENTRIES BY 1,REPEAT LOOP
10  * END OF PROCEDURE                WHEN SEARCH IS COMPLETE,EITHER
11           SR    4,4                R4=0 IF NOT FOUND IN TABLE, OR
12  EXIT     ST    4,POSIT            R4=ADDR OF ENTRY THAT WAS FOUND
               .
               .
               .
13  STRING   DS    CL5               5-BYTE AREA RESERVED FOR STRING
14  TABLE    DC    CL5'END'          TABLE WITH 3 5-BYTE ENTRIES
15           DC    CL5'FINIS'
16           DC    CL5'STOP'
17  ENTRIES  EQU   (*-TABLE)/5       ASSBLR COMPUTES NO.ENTRIES
18  POSIT    DS    F                 FULL-WD FOR ADDR OF FOUND ENTRY
               .
               .
               .
```

Example 5.   Compare 5-byte string with strings in a table
          (See fig. 7.7)

A *table* is a set of related items stored in memory. In the case at hand, each of the items is a 5-byte string; the strings are stored consecutively in memory. An item in a table is almost always called a table *entry*, the terminology used in figure 7.7.

The number of entries in a table depends on two things: the length of each entry and the amount of space available for the table. In figure 7.7, there are three entries, given by Statements 14 through 16. But, instead of using the number three in the program, Statement 17 lets the Assembler calculate the number and assign it to the symbol ENTRIES. In this way, if the programmer wanted to insert more entries, he or she would not have to change any of the statements in the program, not even Statement 17.

Statements 5, 8, and 12 require comment. Statement 5 compares the 5-byte string located at the current table-entry address given in Register 4 with the 5-byte string located at the symbolic address STRING. Statement 8 increments the table-entry address in Register 4 by five (the length of each table entry) so that the second iteration of the loop will examine the second entry, and the third iteration will examine the third entry. This is illustrated in the diagram.

address in Reg 4:				+1	+2	+3	+4
1st iteration:	TABLE	→	E	N	D		
2nd iteration:	TABLE + 5	→	F	I	N	I	S
3rd iteration:	TABLE + 10	→	S	T	O	P	`

The search is terminated when a match is found *or* when no match is found and there are no more entries to be examined. In the first case, the address of the matching entry is stored in symbolic location POSIT for possible future use. If no match is found, a zero is stored in POSIT to indicate "no match." Other actions would be equally valid. The point is that some action is advisable to indicate, for subsequent portions of the program, what the result of the search is. Since an address of zero cannot be the address of any table entry within a program, the use of zero for "no match" is unambiguous. In this type of programming technique, the symbolic location POSIT is called a *flag* or *switch*.

POSIT requires at least 3 bytes because addresses are 24-bit numbers in the IBM Systems 360 and 370. A full word was reserved for POSIT so that the straightforward store instruction ST could be used in Statement 12. Alternatively, 3 bytes could have been reserved for POSIT and the STCM instruction used to select the low-order (right-most) 3 bytes from Register 4, as follows:

```
EXIT    STCM    4,B'0111',POSIT
         .
         .
         .
POSIT   DS      CL3             3 BYTES FOR ADDR OF FOUND ENTRY
```

This is an illustration of a situation that arises again and again in assembly language programming: we must select an instruction that is compatible with the type and length of the data being operated on, and we must be certain that the data area is properly aligned in memory and of sufficient size for the instruction that is selected.

7.6 SUBSTRING OPERATIONS

In some types of programming applications, it is necessary to process strings that exist within other, larger strings. The smaller strings are known as *substrings* of the larger ones, as in this example:

```
                               ┌──────── string of length 7
                          'ABCDEFG'
                          └──────── substring of length 4
```

We frequently need to be able to determine if a given substring, say S, exists within some string T. Among the operations we may wish to perform on S are those of deleting each occurrence of S from T; replacing S by another string, S1; or of inserting a string, S2, immediately following S in T. For example, suppose we are given these definitions of T, S, S1, and S2:

T:	'A NOT SO TYPICAL STRING NAMED T'
S:	'NOT SO '
S1:	'VERY '
S2:	'UNUSUAL BUT RATHER '

Then, each of the three operations named previously can be illustrated as follows:

1. Deleting S from T would yield a new string, TNEW (say):

TNEW: 'A TYPICAL STRING NAMED T'

2. Replacing S in T by S1 would yield this new string:

TNEW: 'A VERY TYPICAL STRING NAMED T'

3. Inserting S2 immediately following S in T would give this:

TNEW: 'A NOT SO UNUSUAL BUT RATHER TYPICAL STRING NAMED T'

Figure 7.8 is a flow diagram summarizing the sequence of steps required for each of these three string-editing operations. An obvious point to note is that each operation—delete, replace, insert—can change the length of the string being edited. A perhaps not so obvious observation is that the CLC and MVC instructions are not well designed for these types of problems because the length fields in the CLC and MVC instructions must be specified at assembly time. For these types of problems, this would mean that different-length substrings S, S1, and S2 could not be processed at run time by the same MVC and CLC instructions. For example, if we had written the following sequence of statements:

```
        . . . . .
        LA      3,N           R3 = NUMBER OF ITERATIONS OF LOOP
        SH      3,=H'6'              TO SEARCH FOR 7-CHAR SUBSTR IN T
        LA      2,T           R2 = ADDR OF CURRENT SUBSTR IN T
        LA      1,S           R1 = ADDR OF SUBSTRING S
LOOP    CLC     0(7,1),0(2)         COMPARE 7 BYTES OF S TO SUBSTR IN T
        BE      EQUAL               BRANCH WHEN SUBSTRING S FOUND IN T
NOTEQ   EQU     *             BEGIN UPDATING TO NEXT CHARACTER POSITION
        .
        .
        .
EQUAL   EQU     *             BEGIN STRING EDITING FUNCTION
        . . . . . .
S       DC      C'NOT SO '
T       DC      C'A NOT SO TYPICAL STRING NAMED T'
N       EQU     *-T           LENGTH OF STRING NAMED T
```

both the length of string T and the length of substring S are, so to speak, "baked in" to the program. Once assembled, the program will not run for any other lengths of S and T than those shown.

We do not need any new techniques to remove the dependence on the length of the string T: we can simply replace the statements defining T and its length by the two statements

```
T       DS      CL256         SPACE RESERVED FOR MAX LENGTH STRING T
N       DS      H             SPACE RESERVED FOR LENGTH OF T
```

and replace the statement that initializes the loop-control counter with this one:

```
        LH      3,N           R3 = NUMBER OF ITERATIONS OF LOOP
```

But the problem is, how can we remove the dependence on the length of the substring S? In the above sequence of statements, this dependence shows itself in two forms. First, the number of comparisons required to search for a substring of length M is obtained by subtracting $M-1$ from the length of the string being examined. This is illustrated by the following diagram, in which $M = 7$ and the length of T = 31, so that the number of comparisons is $31 - (7 - 1) = 25$:

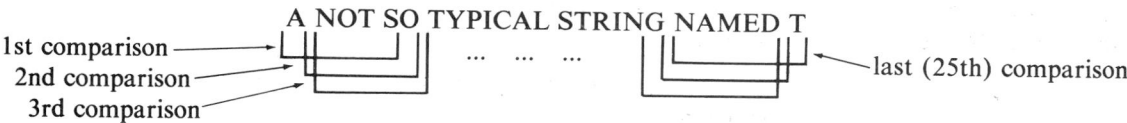

The second, and more critical, way in which the dependence on the length of substring S shows itself in the sequence of statements is in the length field of the CLC instruction:

```
LOOP    CLC     0(7,1),0(2)   COMPARE 7 BYTES OF S TO SUBSTR IN T
```

Figure 7.8 *Overview of string-editing procedures DELETE, REPLACE, and INSERT.*

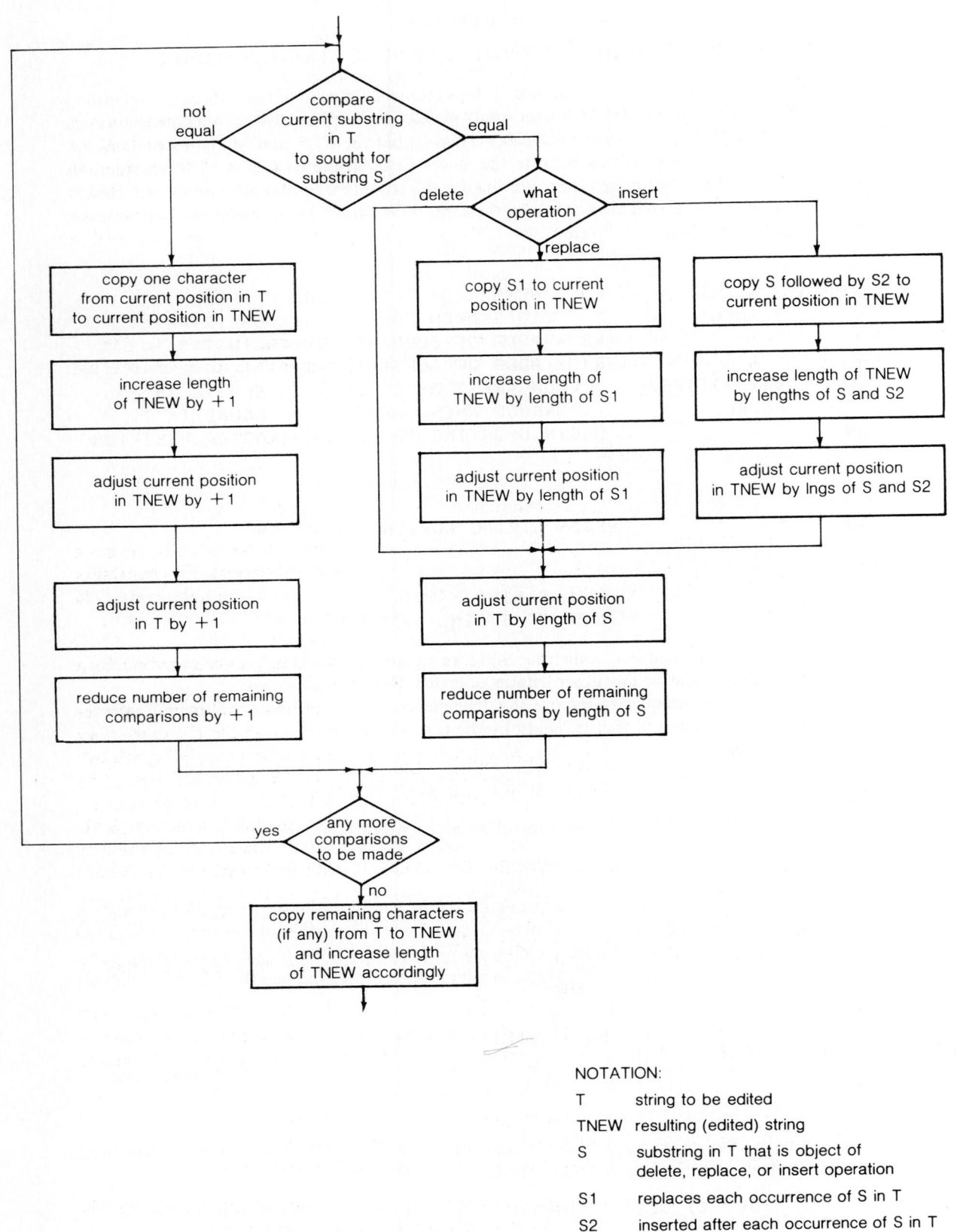

NOTATION:

T	string to be edited
TNEW	resulting (edited) string
S	substring in T that is object of delete, replace, or insert operation
S1	replaces each occurrence of S in T
S2	inserted after each occurrence of S in T

Substituting a symbol for the numeric length will not remove the dependence:

```
LOOP    CLC    0(M,1),0(2)
         .
         .
S       DC     C'NOT SO '
M       EQU    *-S              LENGTH OF STRING NAMED S
```

Dependence is still "baked in" at assembly time because the symbol M, like the self-defining term 7, can have only one value at assembly time. So the question remains: how can we remove the dependence on the length of substring S in such a way that a single sequence of statements can be used to examine an arbitrary string T for the occurrence of an arbitrary substring S without having to reassemble the statements for each different string T and substring S? The answer is to be found in the use of other instructions: the Execute (EX) instruction, described in Section 7.7; and the CLCL and MVCL instructions, described in Section 7.8.

7.7 THE EXECUTE INSTRUCTION

The Execute (EX) instruction is an RX-type instruction. When executed at run time, it causes the CPU to execute another instruction, called the "target" instruction, located at the address given in the second operand field of the EX instruction. Its format is

opcode	operand
EX	R1,D2(X2,B2)

address of target instruction designated by second operand

One of the main uses of the EX instruction depends on its capability for effectively but not actually changing the second byte (bits 8–15) of the target instruction before the target instruction is executed. This capability makes it possible to vary the length field contents of SS_1 and SS_2 instructions and to vary the mask field contents in certain RS and SI instructions. The following specifications govern use of the EX instruction:

1. The target instruction can be any valid instruction except an EX instruction.

2. When the target instruction is executed by the EX, it is executed just as though it were located where the EX itself is located, with one additional characteristic (see specification 3).

If the target instruction is anything other than one of the conditional or unconditional branch instructions, then, after the target instruction is executed by the EX, the instruction following the EX in memory will be the next one performed by the CPU. If the target instruction is a conditional branch, the branch will be made if the condition being tested is true. If the condition being tested is not true, the branch will not be made and the instruction following the EX will be the next one performed by the CPU. If the target instruction is an unconditional branch, the branch will be made. If the target is a branch and link instruction (BAL or BALR, to be discussed further in chap. 9), the address placed into the register designated by the first operand field of these instructions will be the address of the instruction that follows the EX, *not* the address of the instruction following the BAL or BALR. Similarly, if the target instruction is a supervisor call instruction (SVC, to be discussed in chap. 19), the address transmitted to the Operating System will be the address of the instruction following the EX, *not* the address of the instruction following the SVC.

3. The register designated by the first operand of the EX instruction plays a special role, depending on whether it is Register 0 or some other general register.

If the register designated by the first operand of an EX instruction is Register 0, that register is not used in the execution of the EX instruction. If the register designated by the first operand is any general register *other than* Register 0, the target instruction is executed as though its second byte contained the result of the Boolean OR operation

$$\left\{ \begin{array}{c} \text{bits } 24\text{--}31 \\ \text{of designated} \\ \text{register} \end{array} \right\} \quad \text{OR} \quad \left\{ \begin{array}{c} \text{second byte} \\ \text{of target} \\ \text{instruction} \end{array} \right\} = \left\{ \begin{array}{c} \text{effective contents} \\ \text{of second byte} \\ \text{of target instruction} \end{array} \right\}$$

Neither the contents of the designated register nor the contents of the target instruction are changed by this operation. The Boolean OR is carried out by the CPU in a register unavailable to programmers.

In this context, the Boolean OR is *an operation on pairs of bits:* bit 24 of the register operates on bit 8 of the target, bit 25 operates on bit 9 of the target, and so forth up to bit 31 operating on bit 15 of the target. *If both bits of a pair are '0', the resulting bit is a '0'; otherwise, the resulting bit is a '1'.* The following examples illustrate this:

bits 24–31 of register		bits 8–15 of target		resulting bits
00001111	OR	00110011	=	00111111
00001100	OR	00110011	=	00111111
00001111	OR	00000000	=	00001111
00001100	OR	00000000	=	00001100

The last two examples illustrate an important, frequent use of the EX instruction: *if the second byte of the target instruction contains all 0's, then the result of the OR operation will always be just the contents of bits 24–31 of the designated register.*

With the EX instruction, we can now resolve the problem posed in the preceding section: how to remove the dependence of a CLC instruction and, by analogy, of a MVC instruction, on the length field assembled into that instruction. Remember that in the preceding section we presented a sequence of assembly language statements that included the following compare instruction:

```
LOOP      CLC    0(7,1),0(2)    COMPARE 7 BYTES OF S TO SUBSTR IN T
```

where Register 1 contained the address of the current substring in the string T and Register 2 contained the address of a 7-byte string S. Now, if we assume that the length of S is stored as a half-word binary integer at symbolic address M, we can replace the compare instruction with the following statements:

```
          LH     4,M            R4 = LENGTH OF S, MINUS 1
          SH     4,=H'1'        (ONE LESS THAN LENGTH IS NEEDED FOR EX)
LOOP      EX     4,COMPARE      COMPARE S TO SUBSTRING IN T
          .
          .
          .
M         DS     H              SPACE FOR LENGTH OF S
COMPARE   CLC    0(0,1),0(2)    LENGTH FLD OF ZERO FOR EX INSTRUCTION
```

There are two important points to be noted. First, *it is necessary that the length that is placed into the register for use by the EX instruction be one less than the length desired.* This is because in machine language, the length-field content of an SS_1 or SS_2 instruction is always one less than the actual length; a machine language length of L corresponds to an actual length of $L+1$, so that an 8-bit length field can represent the 2^8 possible lengths 1,2,3,...,256 rather than 0,1,2,...,255, and, similarly, a 4-bit length field represents the 2^4 possible lengths 1,2,3,...,16 rather than 0,1,...,15.

Second, *the target instruction should be removed from the sequence of instructions that includes the EX instruction;* i.e., the target may be considered as a kind of data on which the EX operates.

Using the above five statements instead of the single CLC demonstrated previously, the EX instruction will cause a string of arbitrary length (not exceeding 256 bytes) to be compared to a substring in T. For example, if the length of S is 7, then, when the EX is executed bits 24–31 of Register 4 will contain 00000110, i.e., a binary 6 ($= 7 - 1$), so that the CLC instruction is executed *as though* it were written as CLC 0(7,1),0(2).

As a further illustration of the capabilities of the EX instruction, figure 7.9 shows a set of statements that will delete all occurrences of an arbitrary string, S (of length less than or equal to 256 bytes), from an arbitrary string, T. The processing logic is as given in figure 7.8 for the 'DELETE' operation.

As noted, the main restriction on the arbitrariness of the length field when the EX instruction is used as above is that the length be less than or equal to 256. This is because the length fields in MVC and CLC instructions are similarly restricted; the EX is designed to operate within this restriction. When a length field is greater than 256 bytes, then there are two alternatives available: we can use a sequence of EX's (with a corresponding sequence of MVC's or CLC's) so that all the bytes are accounted for; or we can use the MVCL or CLCL instructions. The latter instructions are not available on the IBM 360, only on the IBM 370. They will be discussed in the next section.

Figure 7.9   *The string-editing DELETE operation. (See also fig. 7.8.)*

```
                .
                .
                .
* THE FOLLOWING STATEMENTS CAN BE USED TO DELETE EACH OCCURRENCE OF AN
*  ARBITRARY-LENGTH SUBSTRING  S  FROM ANOTHER STRING  T .  THE RESULT
*  IS STORED AT SYMBOLIC ADDRESS 'TNEW' .
* THE LENGTH OF  T  IS GIVEN AS A HALF-WORD BINARY INTEGER AT  'N' .
* THE LENGTH OF  S  IS A HALF-WORD BINARY INTEGER AT  'M' .
* THE LENGTH OF THE RESULTING STRING  'TNEW'  DEPENDS ON THE NUMBER OF
*  OCCURRENCES OF  S  IN  T .  THIS LENGTH IS COMPUTED AND STORED AS
*  A HALF-WORD BINARY INTEGER AT  'NN' .
* THE GIVEN STRINGS  S  AND  T  ARE NOT ALTERED.  THEIR LENGTHS ARE
*  RESTRICTED TO BE LESS THAN OR EQUAL TO 256 , AND GREATER THAN 0 .

* INITIALIZATIONS
              LA    1,S            R1 = ADDR OF  S
              LA    2,T            R2 = ADDR OF CURRENT POSITION IN  T
              LA    9,TNEW         R9 = ADDR OF CUR. POSITION IN  TNEW
              LH    10,=H'0'       R10 = COMPUTED LNG OF  TNEW (INITIALLY 0)
              LH    3,N            R3  = NUMBER OF COMPARISONS REMAINING TO
              SH    3,M                  BE MADE. INITIALLY, EQUAL TO
              AH    3,=H'1'              N - ( M - 1 )
              BNP   MOVE                 IF N < M THEN MAKE NO COMPARISONS
              LH    4,M            R4  = LENGTH OF  S , MINUS 1
              SH    4,=H'1'              +1  IS SUBTRACTED FOR EX INSTR

* COMPARE   S  TO SUBSTRING OF SAME LENGTH IN  T
LOOP          EX    4,COMPARE          COMPARISON  OF   M  BYTES
              BE    EQUAL              BRANCH IF SUBSTRING  S  IS FOUND
NOTEQUAL      MVC   0(1,9),0(2)    COPY ONE CHAR FROM  T  TO  TNEW
              AH    10,=H'1'       INCR LNG OF  TNEW  BY  +1
              LA    9,1(9)         ADJ CUR POSIT IN  TNEW  BY  +1
              LA    2,1(2)         ADJ CUR POSIT IN   T   BY  +1
              BCT   3,LOOP         REDUCE #REMAINING COMPARISONS BY  +1
              B     MOVE           IF NO MORE COMPARISONS, GO COPY REST OF T

* DELETE OPERATION AVOIDS MOVING  S  FROM  T  TO  TNEW
EQUAL         AH    2,M            ADJ CUR POSITION IN  T  BY LENGTH OF  S
              SH    3,M            REDUCE # REMAINING COMPARISONS BY LNG OF S
              BP    LOOP           IF MORE COMPARISONS REMAIN, DO THEM

* COPY REMAINING CHARACTERS (IF ANY) FROM  T  TO  TNEW
MOVE          LA    5,T            COMPUTE # CHARACTERS REMAINING IN  T , BY
              AH    5,N                 SUBTRACTING CUR. POSIT. IN T FROM ADDR
              SR    5,2                 OF FIRST BYTE BEYOND  T
              BNP   NOMORE         NO MORE CHARS IF  S  OCCUPIED LAST  M
              AR    10,5                BYTES OF  T .  OTHERWISE, INCR LNG OF
              SH    5,=H'1'             TNEW, AND PREPARE TO MOVE REMAINING
              EX    5,MOVEX             CHARS TO  TNEW  VIA  EX  INSTR
NOMORE        STH   10,NN          STORE COMPUTED LENGTH OF  TNEW
                .
                .
                .
T             DS    CL256          SPACE FOR MAX LENGTH  T   STRING
S             DS    CL256          SPACE FOR MAX LENGTH  S   STRING
TNEW          DS    CL256          SPACE FOR MAX LENGTH  TNEW STRING
N             DS    H              SPACE FOR LENGTH OF  T  ( 0<LNG≤256 )
M             DS    H              SPACE FOR LENGTH OF  S  ( 0<LNG≤256 )
NN            DS    H              SPACE FOR LENGTH OF  TNEW
* FOLLOWING ARE TARGET INSTRS FOR   EX  INSTRUCTIONS IN ABOVE PROCEDURE
COMPARE       CLC   0(0,1),0(2)    R1=ADDR OF S; R2= CUR POSIT IN T
MOVEX         MVC   0(0,9),0(2)    R9= CUR POSIT IN TNEW; R2 = POSIT IN T
```

7.8 THE CLCL AND MVCL INSTRUCTIONS

The Compare Logical Characters Long (CLCL) and Move Logical Characters Long (MVCL) are so named because, in both of these instructions, the number of bytes operated on is not restricted to be less than or equal to 256, as is the case in the CLC and MVC instructions. In CLCL and MVCL, the number of bytes can be from 0 to $2^{24}-1$. Since the latter number is one less than the maximum number of addressable bytes in main memory, there is no real length restriction at all. To accommodate such a numeric range, CLCL and MVCL were designed as RR-type instructions. The following descriptions explain how the contents of the designated registers are interpreted in each of these instructions.

CLCL

For its execution, the CLCL instruction utilizes two even-odd pairs of registers. As discussed earlier, an even-odd register pair is two consecutively numbered registers in which the address of the first register is an even number and that of the second an odd number. An even-odd register pair is specified by its even-numbered register address. For the CLCL instruction, one register pair contains the address and length of one of the strings to be compared, while the other register pair contains the address and length of the other string. Moreover, for the CLCL instruction the lengths of the two strings need not be the same. To compensate for strings of unequal length, a padding character must be in one of the registers at the time of execution. The padding character is used during execution to temporarily lengthen the shorter string so that it is the same length as the longer one during the comparison. This lengthening, done in a register unavailable to the programmer, does not alter the strings in memory. Most often, the padding character is chosen to be a blank (X'40') if the strings contain nothing but printable characters, or a binary zero (X'00') for arbitrary strings. These choices will ensure that the shorter string will be less than the longer string, if it is not equal to it.

The format of the CLCL instruction and the meaning attached to the even-odd register pairs are as follows:

<u>opcode</u>   <u>operand</u>

CLCL   R1,R2   (both R1 and R2 are even-numbered registers)

Clearly, the string addresses and lengths as well as the padding character must be loaded into the registers before the CLCL is executed. The result of the comparison may be tested in the usual manner by one of the conditional branch instructions: the string specified by the first operand field (R1) is determined to be equal, less than, or greater than the string specified by the second operand field. For example, consider the following EBCDIC strings, and assume that the padding character is X'00':

first string	second string	result of comparison
EQ	EQU	1st < 2nd
ABCD	ABC	1st > 2nd
102400	1024	1st > 2nd

In the third example, the strings are not equal because the padding character is a binary zero (X'00') not an EBCDIC zero (X'F0'). Note, however, that if we compare the two hexadecimal strings X'1024' and X'102400', the strings would be considered equal if the padding character were X'00'.

By using the CLCL instruction, we can resolve the problem posed at the end of Section 7.6: how to avoid having a string's length being "baked-in" to a program at assembly time so that it cannot be altered at run time. For, the CLCL can be used to compare two arbitrary strings as follows:

```
        LA      2,S             PUT ADDR OF 1ST STRING IN EVEN # REG
        L       3,M             PUT LENGTH OF 1ST STR IN NEXT ODD # REG
        LA      4,T             PUT ADDR OF 2ND STR IN EVEN # REG
        LR      5,3             USE LNG OF 1ST STR, WITH PAD CHAR = X'00'
        CLCL    2,4             COMPARE STR SPECIFIED IN R2 & R3
                                  WITH STR SPECIFIED IN R4 & R5
        .
        .
        .
S       DS      CL1000          SPACE FOR UP TO 1000-BYTE STRING
T       DS      CL2000          SPACE FOR UP TO 2000-BYTE STRING
M       DS      F               SPACE FOR LENGTH OF STRING S
```

In these statements, the space reserved for the two strings depends on the problem in which the strings occur. There is no restriction other than memory size. Similarly, in order to accommodate any allowable length, the space reserved for the string length is a full word. If we wanted to compare two strings of unequal length, we would replace the LR 5,3 instruction with L 5,N where N is the symbolic address of the full word whose content is the second string's length. If we wanted to use a padding character other than X'00', we could follow the LR 5,3 or L 5,N instruction with ICM 5,X'8',PAD where PAD is the symbolic address of the desired padding character.

One other characteristic of the CLCL instruction's execution significantly affects the way in which the instruction must be used in loops: *the contents of the two pairs of registers are altered during the execution of the instruction.* If the result of the comparison is that the two strings are not equal, the length and address fields of each register pair identify the bytes that caused the unequal result. In this case, the two lengths are decreased by the number of bytes that were equal, and the addresses point to the first unequal bytes in the respective strings. (If the two strings were unequal in *length,* the length field of the shorter operand is set to zero and the address field of the shorter operand is increased by the length of that operand.) Similarly, if the result of the comparison is that the two strings are equal, including the padding character, if necessary, both length fields are set to zero and the addresses are incremented by the corresponding lengths. In all cases, bits 0–7 of the even-numbered registers are set to zero, and bits 0–7 of the odd-numbered registers (and hence the padding character) are unchanged. Further details are given in the IBM 370 *Principles of Operation* manual (GA22–7000). One consequence of the register alterations just described is that if the CLCL is to be used in a loop, the length fields must be reloaded before each execution of the CLCL, and, depending on the locations of the strings being compared, the address fields may also have to be reloaded into the registers.

MVCL

The MVCL instruction, like the CLCL instruction, utilizes two even-odd pairs of registers during its execution. The format of MVCL and the meaning of the contents of the register-pairs are similar to those of the CLCL:

opcode   operand

MVCL   R1,R2   (both R1 and R2 designate even-numbered registers)

The number of bytes specified by the length field in Register R1+1 is copied into the receiving field, beginning at the address designated in Register R1. The bytes are copied from the sending field, starting from the address designated in Register R2. If the sending-field length is less than the receiving-field length, the remaining bytes of the receiving field are filled with the padding character. If the receiving-field length is specified as zero, no bytes are copied.

The contents of the two pairs of registers are altered during the execution of a MVCL instruction, as follows: at the completion of execution, the length field in Register R1+1 is zero and the address in Register R1 has been incremented by the original length in R1+1. The length field in Register R2+1 has been decreased by the number of bytes copied from the receiving field and the address in Register R2 has been incremented by the same amount. Bits 0–7 of the even-numbered registers are set to zero; bits 0–7 of the two odd-numbered registers (and hence the padding character) are unchanged. One consequence of these register-content changes is that if the MVCL is to be used in a loop, the length fields (and possibly the address fields) will have to be reloaded into the respective registers before each execution of MVCL. Further details of the execution of the MVCL can be found in the IBM 370 *Principles of Operations* manual (GA22–7000).

One other point deserves mention before concluding this discussion: *no bytes are copied if the sending and receiving fields overlap destructively.* Instead, condition code 3 is set and the situation may be detected with the Branch on Overlap (BO) conditional branch instruction. The conditions defining destructive overlap were described in Section 7.5; a complete discussion of the condition code will be found in Section 8.4.

It should be clear from this discussion that the MVCL instruction can be used instead of the combination of EX and MVC whenever it is desirable to postpone specification of a field length until run time. Details of how to accomplish this are left as an exercise.

7.9 THE TR AND TRT INSTRUCTIONS

The Translate (TR) and Translate and Test (TRT) instructions are specifically designed to help reduce the size and running time of programs that perform the following types of recurring string operations: (1) replacing some, but not necessarily all, bytes in a string with other predetermined bytes, and (2) searching a string from left to right for the first occurrence of any one of some predetermined set of bytes.

The TR instruction can be used in any situation where it is desirable to *replace* certain bytes in a string with other bytes. For example, it can be used to replace all exclamation points with periods, all commas with semicolons, and all other punctuation characters with question mark characters; change all lowercase letters in a string to uppercase letters; and translate a string from the EBCDIC codes in which it is represented to some other code scheme, such as ASCII.

The TRT instruction can be used in any situation where we want to *find* one of a number of different characters in a string. For example, it can be used to find the first occurrence of any punctuation character; find the first occurrence of any mathematical operator + − * / ; or find the first occurrence of a nonprinting character, i.e., a character that does not produce a symbol on a printer or terminal.

The discussion that follows describes how the TR and TRT instructions can be used for tasks similar to those mentioned.

General Description

Both the TR and TRT instructions operate on two strings. For purposes of discussion, one of the two strings is called the *argument* string and the other is called the *function* string. The bytes in the argument string are generally not known to the programmer, for it is the bytes in the argument string that are replaced by the action of the TR and searched by the action of the TRT. The bytes of the function string *are* known to the programmer; the programmer defines them in such a way as to cause the desired result to be achieved by the TR or TRT instructions. This will be illustrated in the discussion that follows.

In the TR and TRT instructions, the argument string and its length are designated by the first operand and the function string is designated by the second operand. However, the length of the function string, which is usually 256 bytes, is not specified in either instruction. Both the TR and TRT instructions are SS$_1$-type instructions:

opcode	operand
TR	D1(L,B1),D2(B2)
TRT	D1(L,B1),D2(B2)

argument   function
string   string

Each of the two instructions works on the following principles. The CPU examines each of the bytes of the argument string one by one, from left to right. Immediately after examining a byte of the argument string, and before examining the next byte in that string, the CPU selects one of the bytes in the function string. The position of the byte that is selected depends on the value of the argument byte that was just examined.

In the TR instruction, the function byte that is selected replaces the argument byte that was just examined. Then the next argument byte (if any) is examined. If there are no more argument bytes to be examined, the execution of the TR instruction is terminated.

In the TRT instruction, the selected function byte is tested to see if it is either X'00' or not X'00'. If the selected function byte is not X'00', a copy of that byte is inserted into bit positions 24–31 of Register 2, the address of the corresponding argument byte is inserted into bit positions 8–31 of Register 1, execution of the instruction is terminated, and a condition code is set. *Condition code 1 is set* if one or more argument bytes still remain to be examined when the nonzero function byte is found; *condition code 2 is set* when no more argument bytes remain to be examined when the nonzero function byte is found.

If a function byte selected during the execution of a TRT instruction is X'00', no further action is taken with that byte. Instead, the next argument byte (if any) is examined. If there are no more argument bytes to be examined, the execution of the TRT instruction is terminated *and condition code 0 is set.*

The condition code setting generated by a TRT instruction can be determined by following the TRT instruction with a conditional branch instruction, as described in Section 8.4. For example, if FN2 is the table defined in figure 7.11 and ARG2 is the symbolic address of any 8-byte string, then the following sequence will find the leftmost math operator (if any) in the ARG2 string:

```
* BRANCH TO 'NONE' IF NO MATH OPERATOR IS FOUND IN 'ARG2'
* BRANCH TO 'MORE' IF A MATH OPERATOR IS FOUND IN ANY BYTE OF 'ARG2'
*  EXCEPT THE LAST (RIGHTMOST) BYTE
* BRANCH TO 'ONE' IF THE LEFTMOST OPERATOR FOUND IS IN THE LAST
*  (RIGHTMOST) BYTE OF 'ARG2'
*
         TRT   ARG2(8),FN2   LOOK FOR A MATH OPERATOR IN 'ARG2'
         BC    8,NONE        BRANCH IF NONE FOUND
         BC    4,MORE        BRANCH IF FOUND PRIOR TO LAST BYTE
         BC    2,ONE         BRANCH IF FOUND ONLY IN LAST BYTE
```

In both the TR and TRT instructions, the CPU determines the position of the function byte that is to be selected by adding the 8-bit value of the corresponding argument byte to the address of the beginning of the function string:

$$\left\{ \begin{array}{c} \text{position, or} \\ \text{address, of} \\ \text{the function byte} \\ \text{to be selected} \end{array} \right\} = \left\{ \begin{array}{c} \text{address of} \\ \text{the first byte} \\ \text{of the function} \\ \text{string} \end{array} \right\} + \left\{ \begin{array}{c} \text{8-bit value} \\ \text{of the} \\ \text{corresponding} \\ \text{argument byte} \end{array} \right\}$$

For example, if the function string begins at location 1004 (hex) and the argument byte that was just examined is X'5A', the position of the function byte that is selected is computed to be $1004 + 5A = 105E$. Whenever an argument byte is a X'5A', the address of the function byte that is selected will be 5A bytes beyond the beginning of the function string. Another way of expressing this is to say that the first byte of the function string is selected if the corresponding argument byte is X'00', the second byte is selected if the argument byte is X'01', the third if the argument byte is X'02' and so forth. Thus an argument byte of X'FF', i.e., the largest possible byte, will cause the 256th byte to be selected from the function string. Since the programmer, in general, does not know what bytes will be in the argument string, it is always advisable to make the function string 256 bytes long.

The remaining question is, what should the bytes in a function string be? The answer depends on which instruction—TR or TRT—is used and for what specific purpose the instruction is to be used.

Function String for TR Instruction

The function string for the TR instruction consists of 256 bytes, chosen as follows: for each byte of the argument string that is to be replaced, the position in the function string corresponding to that argument-byte value must contain the byte that is to replace that argument byte. For any byte of the argument string that is not to be replaced, the position in the function string corresponding to that argument-byte value must contain a duplicate of the byte that caused that position to be selected.

Figure 7.10   Function string to replace lowercase letters with uppercase letters. (See also fig. 7.1.)

```
*    FUNCTION STRING USED WITH  TR  INSTRUCTION TO REPLACE ALL LOWERCASE
*    LETTERS IN AN ARGUMENT STRING WITH UPPERCASE LETTERS, WITHOUT
*    ALTERING THE OTHER BYTES IN THE ARGUMENT STRING.
*
FN1        DS       0CL256     DEFINE BEGINNING & LENGTH OF FUNCTION STRING.

*   FIRST 129 BYTES,  X'00'  THROUGH X'80'
           DC       X'00,01,02,03,04,05,06,07,08,09,0A,0B,0C,0D,0E,0F'
           DC       X'10,11,12,13,14,15,16,17,18,19,1A,1B,1C,1D,1E,1F'
           DC       X'20,21,22,23,24,25,26,27,28,29,2A,2B,2C,2D,2E,2F'
           DC       X'30,31,32,33,34,35,36,37,38,39,3A,3B,3C,3D,3E,3F'
           DC       X'40,41,42,43,44,45,46,47,48,49,4A,4B,4C,4D,4E,4F'
           DC       X'50,51,52,53,54,55,56,57,58,59,5A,5B,5C,5D,5E,5F'
           DC       X'60,61,62,63,64,65,66,67,68,69,6A,6B,6C,6D,6E,6F'
           DC       X'70,71,72,73,74,75,76,77,78,79,7A,7B,7C,7D,7E,7F,80'

*   130TH  THRU   138TH  BYTES REPLACE LOWERCASE  A THRU I
*                               WITH  UPPERCASE   A THRU I
           DC       X'C1,C2,C3,C4,C5,C6,C7,C8,C9'

*   139TH THRU 145TH BYTES,  X'8A' THRU X'90'
           DC       X'8A,8B,8C,8D,8E,8F,90'
*   146TH  THRU   154TH  BYTES REPLACE LOWERCASE  J THRU R
*                               WITH  UPPERCASE   J THRU R
           DC       X'D1,D2,D3,D4,D5,D6,D7,D8,D9'

*   155TH THRU 162ND BYTES,  X'9A' THRU X'A1'

           DC       X'9A,9B,9C,9D,9E,9F,A0,A1'

*   163RD  THRU   170TH  BYTES REPLACE LOWERCASE  S THRU Z
*                               WITH  UPPERCASE   S THRU Z
           DC       X'E2,E3,E4,E5,E6,E7,E8,E9'

*   REMAINING 86 BYTES,  X'AA' THRU X'FF'
           DC       X'AA,AB,AC,AD,AE,AF'
           DC       X'B0,B1,B2,B3,B4,B5,B6,B7,B8,B9,BA,BB,BC,BD,BE,BF'
           DC       X'C0,C1,C2,C3,C4,C5,C6,C7,C8,C9,CA,CB,CC,CD,CE,CF'
           DC       X'D0,D1,D2,D3,D4,D5,D6,D7,D8,D9,DA,DB,DC,DD,DE,DF'
           DC       X'E0,E1,E2,E3,E4,E5,E6,E7,E8,E9,EA,EB,EC,ED,EE,EF'
           DC       X'F0,F1,F2,F3,F4,F5,F6,F7,F8,F9,FA,FB,FC,FD,FE,FF'
```

For example, if we wanted to change all lowercase letters in a string to uppercase letters, without changing any of the other characters in the string, the function string would consist of the 256 EBCDIC codes X'00', X'01', ...X'FF', except for the following (see fig. 7.1): the 130th through 138th bytes (corresponding to lowercase a = X'81' through lowercase i = X'89') would be the representations of uppercase A through I, namely X'C1', X'C2',...,X'C9'; the 146th through 154th bytes (lowercase j through r) would be the representations of uppercase J through R, namely X'D1', X'D2',...,X'D9'; and the 163rd through 170th bytes (lowercase s through z) would be the representations of uppercase S through Z, namely X'E2', X'E3',...,X'E9'. Figure 7.10 shows how the function string could be defined. It begins at symbolic address FN1 and occupies 256 consecutive bytes. If we assume that the argument string—the one whose lowercase letters are to be changed to uppercase letters—is located at symbolic address ARG1 and consists of 30 characters, then the following single TR instruction will accomplish the desired result:

```
TR   ARG1(30),FN1
```

before execution: ARG1   DC   C'This is a 30-character string'
after execution: ARG1   DC   C'THIS IS A 30-CHARACTER STRING'

Figure 7.11   Function string to search for occurrences of mathematical operators $+$, $-$, $*$, and $/$.

```
*    FUNCTION STRING FOR USE WITH  TRT  INSTRUCTION TO SEARCH FOR
*    OCCURRENCES OF ANY ONE OF THE FOUR MATHEMATICAL OPERATORS
*             +    ( X'4E')
*             -    ( X'60')
*             *    ( X'5C')
*             /    ( X'61')
*
FN2       DS    0CL256    DEFINE BEGINNING & LENGTH OF FUNCTION STRING
*  FIRST 78 BYTES ARE  X'00'
          DC    78X'00'
*  79TH BYTE IS  X'4E', FOR THE PLUS SIGN
          DC    X'4E'
*  80TH THRU 92ND BYTES ARE  X'00'
          DC    13X'00'
*  93RD BYTE IS  X'5C', FOR THE ASTERISK
          DC    X'5C'
*  94TH THRU 96TH BYTES ARE  X'00'
          DC    3X'00'
*  97TH AND 98TH BYTES ARE X'60', X'61'  FOR THE MINUS AND SLASH
          DC    X'60,61'
*  REMAINING 158 BYTES ARE X'00'
          DC    158X'00'
```

Function String for TRT Instruction

The function string for the TRT instruction consists of 256 bytes, chosen as follows: for each byte of the argument string that is to cause the search to stop, the position in the function string corresponding to that argument-byte value must contain a nonzero byte. For each byte of the argument string that is not to cause the search to stop, the position in the function string corresponding to that argument-byte value must contain X'00'.

For example, if we wanted to search for the first occurrence of any one of the four mathematical operators $+$, $-$, $*$, $/$, then all bytes in the function string should be X'00' *except these four:* the 79th byte, corresponding to C'$+$' = X'4E'; the 93rd byte, corresponding to C'$*$' = X'5C'; the 97th byte, corresponding to C'$-$' = X'60'; and the 98th byte, corresponding to C'$/$' = X'61'. Figure 7.11 shows how the function string for this example could be defined. It begins at symbolic address FN2 and occupies 256 consecutive bytes. If we assume that the argument string is located at symbolic address ARG2 and consists of 8 bytes:

```
ARG2   DC   C'A=X+Y**2'
```

then the following single TRT instruction will determine the position of the first occurrence of a mathematical operator in the ARG2 string:

```
TRT ARG2(8),FN2
```

Neither string is altered by the TRT instruction, but Registers 1 and 2 and the condition code are altered. To illustrate this, suppose the following conditions exist before the TRT is executed.

	location 1004								Reg 1	Reg 2	condition code
hex →	C1	7E	E7	4E	E8	5C	5C	F2	12 34 56 78	87 65 43 21	0
chars →	A	=	X	+	Y	*	*	2			

After execution of the TRT instruction the following conditions would exist.

Further Observations

Two further observations may be helpful. First, since at assembly time the programmer generally does not know the lengths of the argument strings that will be processed at run time, he or she usually uses the EX instruction in conjunction with TR and TRT. For the example of the TRT instruction illustrated in the previous section, the following statements would be more generally useful.

```
         LA    4,ARG2        R4 = ADDR OF START OF ARG STRING
         LH    5,LARG2       R5 = LENGTH OF ARG STRING
LOOP     SH    5,=H'1'       SUBTRACT +1 FOR 'EX' INSTR
         EX    5,TRTFN2      TRT FOR ARG STRING VIA 'FN2'
         BZ    NONE          BRANCH IF NO MATH OPERATOR FOUND
         .                   process the operator whose address is in Reg 1
         .
         .
         LA    5,0(5,4)      R5 = ADDR OF LAST BYTE IN ARG STRING
         SR    5,1           R5 = LNG OF REMAINDER OF ARG STRING
         BZ    NOMORE        BRANCH IF NO MORE ARG BYTES TO EXAMINE
         LA    4,1(1)        R4 = ADDR OF START OF REMAINING ARG STRING
         B     LOOP          GO EXAMINE REMAINING ARG STRING
         .
         .
         .
ARG2     DS    CL256         SPACE FOR MAX LNG ARG STRING
LARG2    DS    H             SPACE FOR ACTUAL LNG OF ARG STRING
TRTFN2   TRT   0(0,4),FN2    TRT FOR ANY STRING USING 'FN2'
FN2      DS    0CL256        START & LENGTH OF FUNCTION STRING FOR
                             MATHEMATICAL OPERATORS
         .
         .
         .
```

Note that this sequence depends on two properties of the TRT instruction: (1) the TRT sets condition code 0 if no argument-string bytes match any of the nonzero function-string bytes, and (2) the TRT sets Register 1 (bits 8–31) equal to the address of the first argument-string byte found that matches a nonzero function byte. The first property is used by the BZ NONE instruction, as will be explained further in Section 8.4; the second property is used by the SR 5,1 instruction to compute the number of bytes remaining to be examined by the TRT instruction, and by the LA 4,1(1) instruction to determine the address at which the TRT is to begin its next search. Thus, the combination of EX and TRT can be used in a loop to find, successively, all occurrences of a mathematical operator in the given argument string.

The second observation concerns the tedium of preparing a function string such as the one in figure 7.10. In some cases the tedium can be relieved by creating the function string at run time; in other cases, a macro that will cause the Assembler to generate the desired function string at assembly time can be defined. Macros are discussed in chapter 17. Here we merely wish to point out that with an appropriately defined macro named FN, we could create the function string of figure 7.10 with the following seven statements:

name field	opcode	operand			
FN1	FN	X'00',X'80'	FIRST 129 BYTES, X'00' THROUGH X'80'		
	FN	X'C1',X'C9'	130TH	THRU	138TH
	FN	X'8A',X'90'	139TH	THRU	145TH
	FN	X'D1',X'D9'	146TH	THRU	154TH
	FN	X'9A',X'A1'	155TH	THRU	162ND
	FN	X'E2',X'E9'	163RD	THRU	170TH
	FN	X'AA',X'FF'	171ST	THRU	256TH

Alternatively, we could create the function string of figure 7.10 by means of a run-time procedure such as this one:

```
* CREATE FUNCTION STRING TO REPLACE LOWERCASE LETTERS
*   IN AN ARGUMENT STRING WITH UPPERCASE LETTERS.
* 'LOOP' SETS THE  (N+1)ST BYTE TO THE HEX REPRESENTATION OF N,
        LH    2,=H'255'              FOR N = 255,254,253,..., 2,1.
LOOP    STC   2,FN1(2)    EFFECTIVE ADDR CALCULATED VIA INDEX REG 2.
        BCT   2,LOOP                AT CONCLUSION OF LOOP, INITIALIZE
        MVI   FN1,X'00'          FIRST BYTE TO X'00'.
        MVC   FN1+129(9),=C'ABCDEFGHI'   130TH-138TH BYTES (A-I)
        MVC   FN1+145(9),=C'JKLMNOPQR'   146TH-154TH BYTES (J-R)
        MVC   FN1+162(8),=C'STUVWXYZ'    163RD-170TH BYTES (S-Z)
        .
        .
        .
FN1     DS    CL256       RESERVE 256 BYTES FOR FUNCTION STRING TO
*                         REPLACE LOWERCASE LETTERS WITH UPPERCASE
*                         LETTERS. CONTENTS CREATED AT 'LOOP'.
```

It should be clear that such a run-time procedure will find its greatest utility when the large majority of function bytes can be generated via a loop. Moreover, it should be adequately documented, as should the area reserved for the function string itself, to avoid any doubt about the purpose of the procedure and the contents of the function string.

7.10 SUMMARY

The byte and string manipulation instructions discussed in this chapter are summarized in figure 7.12. With but one exception, these instructions involve the operations of copying and/or comparing byte strings. The exception is the Execute (EX) instruction, which has been included here because of its frequent use in enabling variable-length strings to be operated on.

The instructions that copy bytes fall into two categories: (1) those that copy bytes to or from a register, and (2) those that copy bytes from one main memory location to another. In the first category are the IC, ICM, STC, and STCM instructions; in the second are the MVI, MVC, and MVCL instructions.

The instructions that compare byte strings also fall into two categories: (1) those in which one or both strings are in registers (CL, CLM, CLR), and (2) those in which both strings are in memory locations (CLI, CLC, CLCL). The result of any of these comparisons may be determined by use of a conditional-branch instruction: the string designated by the first operand of a compare instruction will always be equal to, less than, or greater than the string designated by the second operand.

The Translate (TR) and Translate and Test (TRT) instructions are specially designed for two particular types of string-searching operations. TR examines each byte of a string and, depending on its value, either replaces it with some predetermined byte or leaves it unchanged. TRT examines each byte of a string from left to right and stops the search when it finds the first occurrence of any one of some predetermined set of values. The TR is aptly named, since it translates any given string into a (possibly) different string. The TRT

Figure 7.12   **Summary of byte manipulation instructions.**

opcode	name	type	section	condition codes	summary of action taken
CL	Compare Logical	RX	7.3	0,1,2	$V_1:V_2$ (compares 4 bytes)
CLC	Compare Logical Characters	SS_1	7.3	0,1,2	$V_1:V_2$ (compares L bytes, $L \leq 256$)
CLCL	Compare Logical Characters Long	RR	7.8	0,1,2	$V_1:V_2$ (compares L bytes with padding, $L \leq 2^{24} - 1$)
CLI	Compare Logical Immediate	SI	7.3	0,1,2	V_1:I2 (compares 1 byte to I2 field)
CLM	Compare Logical under Mask	RS	7.3	0,1,2	$V_1:V_2$ (compares 0 to 4 bytes, via M1 field)
CLR	Compare Logical Registers	RR	7.3	0,1,2	$V_1:V_2$ (compares 4 bytes)
EX	Execute	RX	7.7		executes target instr; uses bits 24–31 of $R1$ if $R1 \neq 0$
IC	Insert Character	RX	7.2		bits 24–31 of $R1$ replaced by V_2
ICM	Insert Characters under Mask	RS	7.2	0,1,2	selected bytes of $R1$ replaced by V_2, via M1 field
MVC	Move Characters	SS_1	7.2		L bytes of V_1 replaced by V_2, $L \leq 256$
MVCIN	Move Inverse	SS_1	7.2		L bytes of V_1 ($L \leq 256$) replaced by V_2 in reverse sequence
MVCL	Move Characters Long	RR	7.8	0,1,2,3	L bytes of V_1 replaced by V_2 + padding, $L \leq 2^{24} - 1$
MVI	Move Immediate	SI	7.2		V_1 replaced by I2 field
STC	Store Character	RX	7.2		V_2 replaced by bits 24–31 of $R1$
STCM	Store Characters under Mask	RS	7.2		V_2 replaced by selected bytes of $R1$, via M1 field
TR	Translate	SS_1	7.9		L bytes of V_1 replaced by selected bytes of V_2
TRT	Translate and Test	SS_1	7.9	0,1,2	L bytes of V_1 searched via string V_2

Note: The meanings of the condition codes for individual instructions are summarized in figure 8.5a. In the action summaries given V_1 denotes the quantity whose address is specified by the first operand of an instruction, and V_2 denotes the quantity whose address is specified by the second operand of an instruction.

is not so aptly named, since no translation takes place; instead, the condition under which its search is terminated is reflected in the condition code and the contents of Registers 1 and 2, as described in Section 7.9.

The EX instruction provides a means of varying the quantity in the length fields of SS_1 and SS_2-type instructions. This permits strings whose lengths are not known until run time to be processed by the MVC, CLC, TR, and TRT instructions, provided that the lengths do not exceed 256 bytes. Use of the EX instruction also enables the immediate data field of SI-type instructions, such as MVI, CLI, and TM (the latter to be discussed in chap. 8), to be varied at run time. In all cases, the instruction that is executed via EX is not changed in memory; instead, its length or immediate data field (bits 8–15) is modified in a register not available to programmers.

The instructions summarized are used primarily for nonarithmetic operations such as determining the contents of a string, searching for a particular substring within a given string, replacing one string with another, and inserting or deleting a string within another string. The need for these types of operations arises whenever text must be processed, for example, when printing messages and when performing the operations inherent in text-editing systems.

SAMPLE PROBLEM
AND SOLUTION

PROBLEM STATEMENT

Write a program that will read student Grade Point Average (GPA) data and compute and print a distribution of GPA's by giving the total number of students for which data were read and the number of students whose GPA's lie in one of each of these eight ranges: 0.00–0.99, 1.00–1.49, 1.50–1.99, 2.00–2.49, ..., 3.50–3.99, and exactly 4.00. We assume that each input card contains the GPA of one student in columns 30–33, including a decimal point in column 31. The range of GPA's is assumed to be from 0.00 to 4.00; anything outside this range is counted as an error.

SOLUTION PROCEDURE

The procedure, as outlined in figure 7.13a, is to read each data card, determine the appropriate range for the GPA given on that card, and add +1 to the counter that is defined for that range. When end-of-data is reached, all the counters are converted to EBCDIC format and printed, one per line, with an accompanying text message that identifies the range corresponding to that counter. After all the counters have been printed, the total number of students is also printed, the total having been obtained by counting the number of input data cards that were read.

Figure 7.13a Overview of sample problem solution procedure.

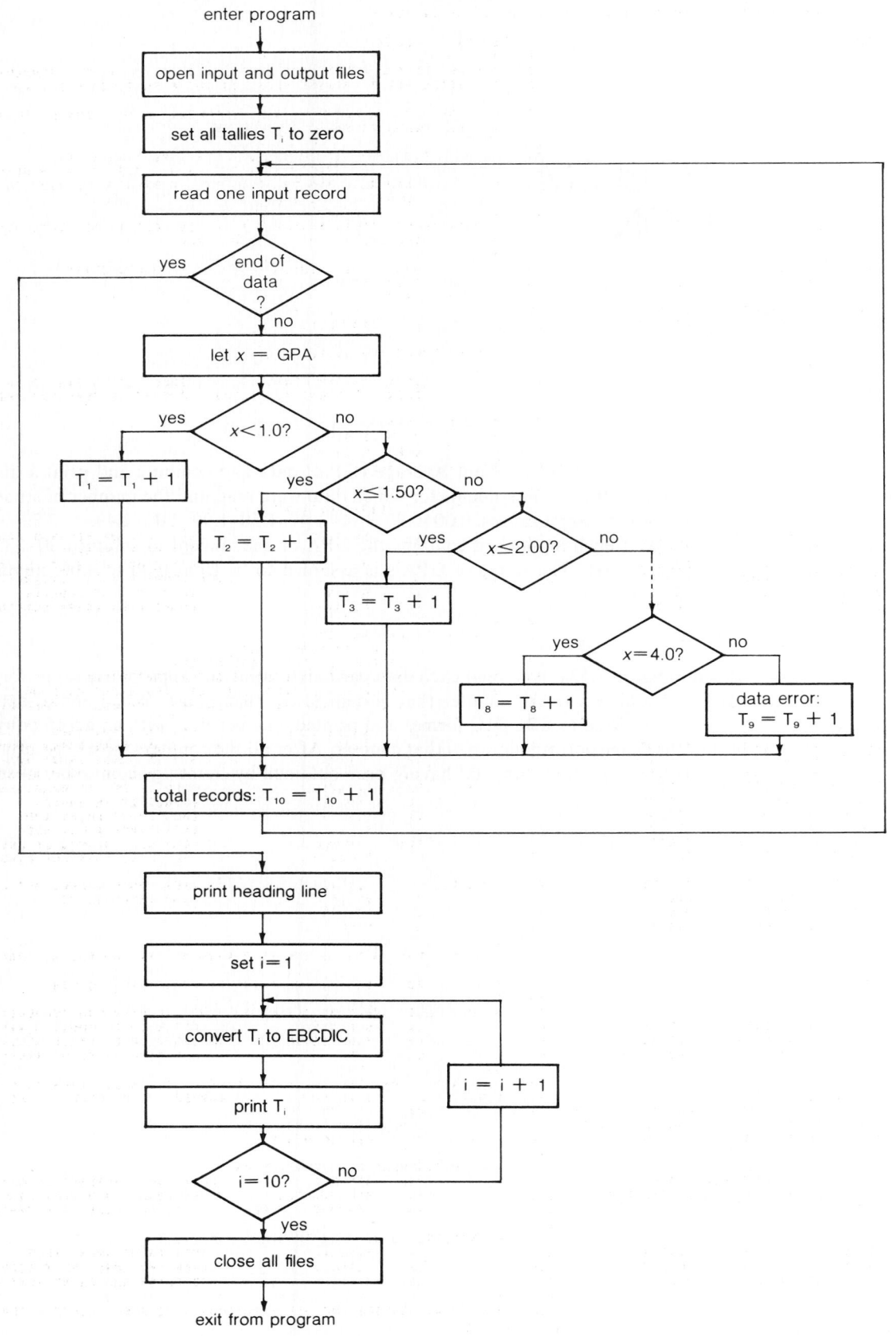

Figure 7.13b   Solution to sample problem.

```
FLAG LOCTN OBJECT CODE    ADDR1  ADDR2  STMNT M SOURCE STATEMENT

    000000                                  3  SPCH7     CSECT
                                            4  *
                                            5  * SPCH7   READS INPUT DATA CARDS, EACH CONTAINING A STUDENT
                                            6  *    GRADE POINT AVERAGE (GPA) IN THE FORMAT GIVEN BELOW.
                                            7  *
                                            8  *    THE PROGRAM COMPUTES A DISTRIBUTION OF ALL GPA'S, IN THE
                                            9  *    FOLLOWING RANGES ...
                                           10  *
                                           11  *        0.00-0.99, 1.00-1.49, 1.50-1.99, 2.00-2.49,
                                           12  *                   2.50-2.99, 3.00-3.49, 3.50-3.99, 4.00-4.00
                                           13  *    AND ALSO ANY GPA OUTSIDE THE RANGE 0.00-4.00 IS
                                           14  *        COUNTED AS INVALID.
                                           15  *
                                           16  * EACH INPUT RECORD CONTAINS A GPA IN COLS 30-33, INCLUDING
                                           17  *        THE DECIMAL POINT, E.G.   2.49
                                           18  *
  000000 90 EC D00C                        19            STM    14,12,12(13)        STANDARD ENTRY
  000004 05 C0                             20            BALR   12,0
  000006                                   21            USING  *,12
  000006 50 D0 C40E       000414           22            ST     13,SAVE+4
  00000A 41 D0 C40A       000410           23            LA     13,SAVE
                                           24  *
                                           25  * OPEN INPUT AND OUTPUT FILES
                                           26  *
  00000E                                   27            OPEN   (SYSIN,(INPUT))      INPUT IS 'SYSIN' DATA STREAM
  00001A                                   33            OPEN   (SYSPRNT,(OUTPUT))   OUTPUT IS 'SYSOUT' PRINTER

                                           39  * DOS *******
                                           40  *      OPEN   SYSIN
                                           41  *      OPEN   SYSPRNT
                                           42  ***************

                                           43  *
                                           44  * INITIALIZE DISTRIBUTION COUNTERS
                                           45  *
  000026 41 50 C132       000138           46            LA     5,DISTR             GET ADDR OF COUNTER ARRAY
  00002A 58 60 C106       00010C           47            L      6,N                 GET SIZE OF ARRAY
  00002E 58 70 C452       000458           48            L      7,=F'0'             GET ZERO FOR INITIALIZATIONS
  000032 50 75 0000       000000           49  INIT      ST     7,0(5)              JTH COUNTER = 0,  J=1,2,...,N
  000036 41 55 0004       000004           50            LA     5,4(5)              INCR TO NEXT COUNTER
  00003A 46 60 C02C       000032           51            BCT    6,INIT              COUNT DOWN ARRAY COMPONENTS
                                           52  *
                                           53  * MAIN PROCESSING LOOP ...
                                           54  *        READS AN INPUT CARD
                                           55  *        DETERMINES THE RANGE OF GPA
                                           56  *        ADDS +1 TO THE COUNTER FOR THAT RANGE
                                           57  *        REPEATS THE PROCEDURE FOR EACH INPUT CARD UNTIL END-OF-DATA
                                           58  *        WHEN END-OF-DATA IS REACHED, CONTROL IS TRANSFERRED TO 'EOD'
                                           59  *
  00003E                                   60  LOOP      GET    SYSIN,INAREA        GET AN INPUT CARD
  00004C 41 50 C132       000138           65            LA     5,DISTR             SET UP COUNT ARRAY ADDRESS
  000050 41 60 C10A       000110           66            LA     6,RANGE             SET UP RANGE ARRAY ADDRESS
  000054 58 70 C106       00010C           67            L      7,N                 GET SIZE OF COUNT ARRAY
  000058 D5 03 C20D6000   000213           68  COMP      CLC    GPA,0(6)            COMPARE GPA TO RANGE IN ARRAY
  00005E 47 40 C06C       000072           69            BL     COUNTIT             BRANCH IF IN RANGE.
  000062 41 55 0004       000004           70            LA     5,4(5)              INCR COUNT ARRAY ADDR
  000066 41 66 0004       000004           71            LA     6,4(6)              INCR RANGE ARRAY ADDR
  00006A 46 70 C052       000058           72            BCT    7,COMP              COMP NEXT RANGE, IF ANY
  00006E 41 50 C132       000138           73            LA     5,DISTR             ELSE IT IS 'OUTSIDE RANGE'

  000072 58 A5 0000       000000           74  COUNTIT   L      10,0(5)             WHEN RANGE KNOWN, GET COUNTER
  000076 5A A0 C456       00045C           75            A      10,=F'1'            AND INCREASE IT.
  00007A 50 A5 0000       000000           76            ST     10,0(5)
  00007E 47 F0 C038       00003E           77            B      LOOP
                                           78  *
                                           79  * WHEN END-OF-DATA IS SENSED DURING 'GET', CONTROL IS TRANSFERRED HERE.
                                           80  *
  000082                                   81  EOD       PUT    SYSPRNT,HEADING     PRINT HEADING LINE
                                           86  *
                                           87  * INITIALIZE ARRAY ADDRESSES AND LOOP COUNTER FOR CONVERSION TO EBCDIC
  000090 41 50 C132       000138           88            LA     5,DISTR             GET ADDR OF COUNT ARRAY
  000094 41 60 C15A       000160           89            LA     6,RANGEMSG          GET ADDR OF RANGE MESSAGE ARRAY
  000098 58 70 C106       00010C           90            L      7,N                 GET SIZE OF COUNT ARRAY
                                           91  *
                                           92  * 'CONVT' LOOP CONVERTS EACH COUNTER TO ECBDIC, THEN PRINTS IT & RANGE
  00009C 58 A5 0000       000000           93  CONVT     L      10,0(5)             CONVERT  JTH  COUNT TO EBCDIC TEXT
  0000A0 4E A0 C0F2       0000F8           94            CVD    10,BCD
  0000A4 F3 97 C0FAC0F2   000100 0000F8    95            UNPK   EBCDIC,BCD
  0000AA 96 F0 C103       000109           96            OI     EBCDIC+9,X'F0'
                                           97  *
                                           98  * PRINT CURRENT DISTRIBUTION DATA
  0000AE D2 0E C2456000   00024B           99            MVC    MSG,0(6)            COPY RANGE MESSAGE TO OUTPUT LINE
  0000B4 D2 09 C254C0FA   00025A 000100   100            MVC    AMOUNT,EBCDIC       COPY COUNT TO OUTPUT LINE
  0000BA                                  101            PUT    SYSPRNT,OUTAREA     PRINT ONE LINE WITH RANGE & COUNT
                                          136  *
                                          107  * INCREASE TO NEXT DISTR RANGE AND COUNT
  0000C8 41 55 0004       000004          108            LA     5,4(5)              INCR COUNT ARRAY ADDR
  0000CC 41 66 000F       00000F          109            LA     6,15(6)             INCR RANGEMSG ARRAY ADDR
  0000D0 46 70 C096       00009C          110            BCT    7,CONVT             GO CONVT AND PRINT NEXT LINE, IF ANY
                                          111  *
                                          112  * WHEN ALL RANGES AND DISTRIBUTIONS HAVE BEEN PRINTED, TERMINATE.
```

Figure 7.13b continued

```
FLAG LOCTN OBJECT CODE     ADDR1  ADDR2  STMNT M SOURCE STATEMENT

     000004                           113          CLOSE (SYSIN)
     0000DE                           119          CLOSE (SYSPRNT)
     0000EA 58 D0 C40E        000414  125          L     13,SAVE+4          STANDARD EXIT
     0000EE 98 EC D00C                126          LM    14,12,12(13)
     0000F2 07 FE                     127          BR    14

                                      128   *   DOS  *******
                                      129   *         CLOSE SYSIN
                                      130   *         CLOSE SYSPRNT
                                      131   *         EOJ
                                      132   ***************

                                      133   *
                                      134   * CONSTANTS AND DATA AREAS
                                      135   *
     0000F8                           136   BCD      DS    D          DECIMAL FORM OF DISTR COUNTER
     000100                           137   EBCDIC   DS    CL10       TEXT FORM OF DISTR COUNTER
                                      138   * TABLES FOR RANGES AND DISTRIBUTIONS
                                      139   *
     00010C 0000000A                  140   N        DC    F'10'      NUMBER OF RANGES IN TABLE
                                      141   *
     000110 F04BF0F0                  142   RANGE    DC    CL4'0.00'    NOT  0.00-4.00   = DISTR(1)
     000114 F14BF0F0                  143            DC    CL4'1.00'    0.00-0.99        = DISTR(2)
     000118 F14BF5F0                  144            DC    CL4'1.50'    1.00-1.49        = DISTR(3)
     00011C F24BF0F0                  145            DC    CL4'2.00'    1.50-1.99        = DISTR(4)
     000120 F24BF5F0                  146            DC    CL4'2.50'    2.00-2.49        = DISTR(5)
     000124 F34BF0F0                  147            DC    CL4'3.00'    2.50-2.99        = DISTR(6)
     000128 F34BF5F0                  148            DC    CL4'3.50'    3.00-3.49        = DISTR(7)
     00012C F44BF0F0                  149            DC    CL4'4.00'    3.50-3.99        = DISTR(8)
     000130 F44BF0F1                  150            DC    CL4'4.01'    EQUAL TO 4.00    = DISTR(9)
     000134 00000000                  151            DC    XL4'0000'  DUMMY FOR TOTALS  = DISTR(10)
                                      152   *
     000138                           153   DISTR    DS    10F        SPACE FOR 10 DISTRIBUTION COUNTS
                                      154   *
                                      155   * RANGE MESSAGE TABLE FOR OUTPUT PRINT LINES  (SEE 'RANGE' TABLE ABOVE)
                                      156   *
     000160 D5D6E340F04BF0F0          157   RANGEMSG DC    CL15'NOT 0.00-4.00'
     00016F F04BF0F060F04BF9          158            DC    CL15'0.00-0.99'
     00017E F14BF0F060F14BF4          159            DC    CL15'1.00-1.49'
     00018D F14BF5F060F14BF9          160            DC    CL15'1.50-1.99'
     00019C F24BF0F060F24BF4          161            DC    CL15'2.00-2.49'
     0001AB F24BF5F060F24BF9          162            DC    CL15'2.50-2.99'
     0001BA F34BF0F060F34BF4          163            DC    CL15'3.00-3.49'
     0001C9 F34BF5F060F34BF9          164            DC    CL15'3.50-3.99'
     0001D8 F44BF0F040404040          165            DC    CL15'4.00'
     0001E7 4040E3D6E3C1D3E2          166            DC    CL15'  TOTALS'
                                      167   *
                                      168   * INPUT CARD AREA
                                      169   *
     0001F6                           170   INAREA   DS    0CL80      DEFINITION OF INPUT AREA ...
     0001F6                           171            DS    CL29       COLS 1-29  UNUSED
     000213                           172   GPA      DS    CL4          30-33    GPA AS  X.XX
     000217                           173            DS    CL47         34-80    UNUSED
                                      174   *
                                      175   * OUTPUT PRINT AREA
                                      176   *
     000246                           177   OUTAREA  DS    0CL132     DEFINITION OF OUTPUT AREA ...
     000246 4040404040                178            DC    CL5' '     COLS 1-5   BLANKS
     00024B                           179   MSG      DS    CL15         6-20     SPACE FOR RANGE MESSAGE
     00025A                           180   AMOUNT   DS    CL10         21-30    SPACE FOR DISTR COUNT
     000264 40404040404040           181            DC    CL102' '     31-132   BLANKS
                                      182   *
                                      183   * HEADING LINE
                                      184   *
     0002CA                           185   HEADING  DS    0CL132     DEFINITION OF HEADING LINE ...
     0002CA 4040404040404040          186            DC    CL10' '    COLS 1-10  BLANKS
     0002D4 D9C1D5C7C54040 40          187            DC    CL10'RANGE'  11-20    RANGE HEADING
     0002DE C3D6E4D5E3404040          188            DC    CL10'COUNT '  21-30    COUNT  HEADING
     0002E8 40404040404040 40         189            DC    CL102' '      31-132   BLANKS
                                      190   * DCB'S FOR INPUT AND OUTPUT FILES
                                      191   *
     00034E                           192   SYSIN    DCB   DSORG=PS,MACRF=(GM),DDNAME=SYSIN,EODAD=EOD,     X
                                      193                  RECFM=FB,LRECL=80,BLKSIZE=4080
     0003B0                           245   SYSPRNT  DCB   DSORG=PS,MACRF=(PM),DDNAME=SYSPRINT,            X
                                      246                  RECFM=FB,LRECL=132,BLKSIZE=4092

                                      298   *  DOS  *******
                                      299   *SYSIN    DTFCD DEVADDR=SYSIPT,WORKA=YES,IOAREA1=INBUF,EOFADDR=EOD,  X
                                      300   *               DEVICE=2540
                                      301   *SYSPRNT  DTFPR DEVADDR=SYSLST,WORKA=YES,IOAREA1=OUTBUF,BLKSIZE=132,  X
                                      302   *               DEVICE=1403
                                      303   *
                                      304   *INBUF    DS    CL80
                                      305   *OUTBUF   DC    CL132' '
                                      306   ***************

                                      307   *
     000410                           308   SAVE     DS    18F        SAVE AREA
```

Figure 7.13b continued

```
                              309   *  DOS *******
                              310   *SAVE    DS    9D
                              311   ***************
 000458 00000000             312   * LITERALS
 00045C 00000001             314                        =F'0'
                              315                        =F'1'
                              316          END
```

CROSS-REFERENCE

SYMBOL	LEN	VALUE	DEFN	REFERENCES			
AMOUNT	0000A	00025A	00180	00100			
BCD	00008	0000F8	00136	00094	00095		
COMP	00006	000058	00068	00072			
CONVT	00034	00009C	00093	00110			
COUNTIT	00004	000072	00074	00069			
DISTR	00004	000138	00153	00046	00065	00073	00088
EBCDIC	0000A	000100	00137	00095	00096	00100	
EOD	00004	000082	00082	00214			
GPA	00004	000213	00172	00068			
HEADING	00084	0002CA	00185	00083			
INAREA	00050	0001F6	00170	00062			
INIT	00004	000032	00049	00051			
LOOP	00004	00003E	00061	00077			
MSG	0000F	00024B	00179	00099			
N	00004	00010C	00140	00047	00067	00090	
OUTAREA	00084	000246	00177	00103			
RANGE	00004	000110	00142	00066			
RANGEMSG	0000F	000160	00157	00089			
SAVE	00004	000410	00308	00022	00023	00125	
SPCH7	00001	000000	00003				
SYSIN	00004	000350	00193	00031	00061	00117	
SYSPRNT	00004	000380	00246	00037	00082	00102	00123

EXERCISES

1. Suppose that a character constant is defined by

CON   DC   C'ASSEMBLY'

What condition—high, low, or equal—would result from execution of each of the following compare instructions:

  a. CLI   CON,C'C'
  b. CLI   CON,C' '
  c. CLC   CON,=C'ASSEMBLE'
  d. CLC   CON(5),=C'EMBLY'

2. Suppose that a character constant is defined by

             DS   0F
SYMBOL   DC   CL10'CONSTANT'

Describe the result that would be produced by execution of each of the following instructions:

  a. IC   4,SYMBOL
  b. ICM   5,X'9',SYMBOL
  c. L   6,SYMBOL
  d. MVC   SYMBOL+1(9),SYMBOL
  e. MVI   SYMBOL,C' '
  f. MVC   SYMBOL,=10C' '

3. Write an assembly language program that will read a set of input data cards and print them one card per line, with a blank character separating card columns 4 and 5, 8 and 9, 12 and 13, and so on. For example, a card like this

```
/ ABCDEFGHIJKLMNOPQRSTUVWXYZ                           //
```

would be printed like this

```
/ ABCD EFGH IJKL MNOP QRST UVWX YZ                     //
```

4. Write an assembly language program that will read a set of input data cards and print only those cards that contain an asterisk (∗) in card column 1.

5. Write an assembly language program that will read a set of input data cards and print only those cards that contain no characters other than letters, digits, and blanks.

6. Write an assembly language program that will read a set of input data cards that consist of assembly language statements, and print the statements one per line except as follows: any statement that contains the directive SPACE in its opcode field should not be printed. In its place, the program should print n consecutive blank lines where the value of n is specified as an unsigned decimal integer in the statement's operand field. Assume that $1 \leq n \leq 9$; also assume that all input statements are in standard fixed format.

7. Write an assembly language program in accordance with the same criteria as those given in Exercise 6, except that the input statements may be in free format (see Section 2.2 for a definition of free format).

8. Suppose there is a set of input data cards that describe characteristics of persons you know, as follows: In each card, columns 1–10 contain someone's first name, columns 11–20, 21–30, and 31–40 contain three one-word characteristics that describe that person. For example,

3rd card	BILL	STRONG	QUIET	SMART
2nd card	JAN	SMART	OUTGOING	POPULAR
1st card	AL	POPULAR	TALL	STRONG

Write an assembly language program that will read all the data cards and print a record of all the different characteristics that appear in the input, together with the names of those persons described by a characteristic. Each characteristic should appear only once in the printed output. For example, if the input consisted of only the above three cards, the output would consist of these lines:

POPULAR	AL	JAN
TALL	AL	
STRONG	AL	BILL
SMART	JAN	BILL
OUTGOING	JAN	
QUIET	BILL	

9. Write an assembly language program that will read a set of input data cards that contains any arbitrary text, and perform the following task: count the number of occurrences of each letter of the alphabet, and the number of occurrences of each of these pairs of consecutive letters: EI, IE, OU, TH. Print the results in some appropriate format.

10. Assume that there is a string of n characters ($1 \leq n \leq 256$) at symbolic address T, and that the value of n is given as a half-word binary integer at symbolic address N. Write assembly language statements that could be used to replace each occurrence of the three-character string C'###' with the three characters C'...'.

11. Assume that there is a set of input data cards and that all but the first contain any arbitrary text. Assume that the first card contains a string, S, beginning in column 13, and that the length of S is given as an unsigned decimal integer, right-justified, in columns 1–12. Incorporate the statements of figure 7.9 into a program that deletes all occurrences of S from the text in each of the input cards and prints the results. Each line of output should correspond to an input card.

12. Analogous to the program statements of figure 7.9, write a set of statements that will perform the string-editing REPLACE operation depicted for arbitrary strings in figure 7.8. Then, incorporate these statements into a program that will replace a given string, S, with another given string, S1, in text that is read as input data cards, as in Exercise 11. Print the resulting text, one line per input card.

13. Suppose there is an arbitrary string at address STR, whose length is given as a half-word binary integer at address N. Write a set of assembly language statements that will examine this string one character at a time, left to right, and perform the following deletion operation: for each occurrence of the EBCDIC backspace character (X'16'), delete that character *and the one preceding it* before examining the next character in the string. (The string may contain several consecutive backspaces, such as might be created when correcting text typed at a terminal.)

For example, if we let a back-arrow ← denote the backspace character, then, if the given string is

A FEWW ← ERTOR←←←RORS

the resulting string would be

A FEW ERRORS

14. Suppose there is a 10-byte string that represents an integer in EBCDIC code. Write a set of assembly language statements that will examine this string, one character at a time, left to right, and replace all leading zeroes by blanks. Write a program that calculates and prints the numbers 2^n through 5^n for $n = 1, 2, ..., 10$ in the tabular form shown below, with leading zeroes replaced by blanks.

2	3	4	5
4	9	16	25
8	27	64	125
. .	. . .	. . .	. . . .
256	6561	65536	390625
512	19683	262144	1953125
1024	59049	1048576	9765625

15. Modify your program solution to Exercise 14 so that the results are printed with appropriate punctuating commas. For example, the last line (for $n = 10$) would be printed

1,024	59,049	1,048,576	9,765,625

(Note: The ED and EDMK instructions described in Section 12.9 provide an easier solution to the problems of suppressing leading zeroes and providing punctuating commas than solutions based solely on the instructions described in chaps. 4 through 7.)

16. Analogous to the program statements of figure 7.9, write a set of statements that will perform the string-editing INSERT operation depicted for arbitrary strings in figure 7.8. Then, incorporate these statements into a program that will insert a given string, S2, after each occurrence of another given string, S, in text that is read as input data cards. Print the resulting text, one line per input card. The two strings, S and S2, together with their lengths, can be read from the first input data card.

17. Define a function string that could be used by the TR instruction to translate any argument string of up to 256 characters from EBCDIC code to ASCII code. EBCDIC characters that have no representation in the ASCII scheme might be translated into the question mark (?) character or some other appropriate character.

18. Define a function string that could be used by the TRT instruction to find occurrences of left and right parentheses in any argument string. Then write an assembly language program that uses the TRT and your function string to determine how many left parentheses there are in a given string, whether the number of left parentheses is the same as the number of right parentheses, and what the deepest level of nested pairs of parentheses is.

19. Rework Exercise 5, using the TRT instruction with an appropriate function string to determine whether a card should be printed or not.

8
Bit Manipulations

The term *bit manipulations* includes several types of instructions that operate on one or more consecutive bits: (1) shifting a bit sequence to the right or left, (2) altering individual bits, (3) testing individual bits, and (4) testing the condition code.

Since bits are not individually addressable by a base-displacement address (the smallest unit of addressable information being a byte), the bits that are operated on must be *selected* from within one or more bytes. Except for the shift instructions, the selection is accomplished by means of a *mask*, a sequence of 4, 8, or 32 consecutive bits that are matched one for one to the sequence of bits from which the selected bits are chosen. The manner in which the selection takes place, and the result of the selection process, depends on the instruction being used. In shift instructions, either 32 or 64 bits are always selected.

Analogous to the concept of a byte or character string, a sequence of consecutive bits is often called a *bit string*. To avoid confusion with the word *string* in its meaning of a sequence of bytes, the full phrase *bit string* is usually used to refer to a sequence of bits.

To define a data constant as a sequence of bits, we can use the *B*, the *C*, or the *X* data-type code. These may be used in the DC directive, in literals, and in self-defining terms. The *B* code requires that the bits be specified in binary notation; the *X* requires hexadecimal notation, 4 bits for each hex digit; the *C* code requires character notation, 8 bits per character as has been seen.

One byte is always used for each consecutive 8 bits. If an integral multiple of 8 bits is not specified, the left-most byte used by the bit sequence is padded on the left with binary zeroes. The maximum number of bytes that can be specified for a single DC or literal constant is 256; for self-defining terms, the maximum is 4 bytes.

Figure 8.1 illustrates the methods of specifying constants as bit sequences.

To reserve data areas for bit sequences, we can use the B, X, or C data-type codes in the DS directive. However, only an integral multiple of bytes can be reserved, no matter what code is used.

8.1 SHIFTING BITS

The 32 bits in a general register and the 64 bits in an even-odd pair of general registers can be simultaneously shifted to the right or to the left by means of the RS-type shift instructions described in this section. There are no instructions available to shift a bit string in memory; all shifting takes place in registers.

There are two categories of shift instructions: arithmetic and logical. In *arithmetic* shifts, the sign bit of the register or register-pair is treated differently from the other bits, and the condition code will be set to reflect the nature of the result. In *logical* shifts, the sign bit is treated in the same manner as all other bits, and the condition code is not set.

Arithmetic Shift Instructions

There are two pairs of arithmetic shift instructions. One pair is used for shifting the 32 bits in a single register, and the other pair is used for shifting the 64 bits in a double register. In each pair, one of the instructions is used when shifting right, and the other when shifting left. All four instructions are RS-type instructions, but instead of the usual RS operand format—R1,R2,D3(B3)—the second operand, R2, is not written in Assembly

Figure 8.1 'B' and 'X' constants.

```
FLAG LOCTN OBJECT CODE     ADDR1  ADDR2   STMNT M SOURCE STATEMENT

                                            5    * DEFINED CONSTANTS                      COMMENTS
000000 0F0F                                 6            DC    B'111100001111'   0000 1111 0000 1111
000002 F0                                   7            DC    B'11110000'       1111 0000
000003 0F                                   8            DC    B'1111'           0000 1111
000004 07                                   9            DC    B'111'            0000 0111
000005 03                                  10            DC    B'11'             0000 0011
000006 01                                  11            DC    B'1'              0000 0001
000007 FFFF                                12            DC    X'FFFF'           1111 1111 1111 1111
000009 0FFF                                13            DC    X'FFF'            0000 1111 1111 1111
00000B FF                                  14            DC    X'FF'             1111 1111
00000C 0F                                  15            DC    X'F'              0000 1111

                                           16    * EQU CONSTANTS
000001                                     17    E1      EQU   B'1'              0000 0001
000003                                     18    E2      EQU   B'11'             0000 0011
000007                                     19    E3      EQU   B'111'            0000 0111
00000F                                     20    E4      EQU   B'1111'           0000 1111
00001F                                     21    E5      EQU   B'11111'          0001 1111
00003F                                     22    E6      EQU   B'111111'         0011 1111
00007F                                     23    E7      EQU   B'1111111'        0111 1111
0000FF                                     24    E8      EQU   B'11111111'       1111 1111
000100                                     25    E9      EQU   B'100000000'      0000 0001 0000 0000

                                           26    * SELF-DEFINING TERMS
00000E 95 01 C066          000066          27            CLI   L0,B'1'           0000 0001
000012 95 01 C066          000066          28            CLI   L0,X'1'           0000 0001
000016 95 03 C066          000066          29            CLI   L0,B'11'          0000 0011
00001A 95 11 C066          000066          30            CLI   L0,X'11'          0001 0001
00001E 95 E9 C066          000066          31            CLI   L0,B'11101001'    1110 1001
000022 95 E9 C066          000066          32            CLI   L0,X'E9'          1110 1001
000026 95 E9 C066          000066          33            CLI   L0,C'Z'           1110 1001

                                           34    * LITERALS
00002A D2 00 C066C060 000066 000060        35            MVC   L0,=B'1'          0000 0001
000030 D2 00 C066C060 000066 000060        36            MVC   L0,=X'1'          0000 0000
000036 D2 00 C066C061 000066 000061        37            MVC   L0,=B'11'         0000 0011
00003C D2 00 C066C062 000066 000062        38            MVC   L0,=X'11'         0001 0001
000042 D2 00 C066C063 000066 000063        39            MVC   L0,=B'1111'       0000 1111
000048 D2 00 C066C063 000066 000063        40            MVC   L0,=X'F'          0000 1111
00004E D2 00 C066C063 000066 000063        41            MVC   L0,=X'0F'         0000 1111
000054 D2 00 C066C064 000066 000064        42            MVC   L0,=X'F0'         1111 0000
00005A D2 00 C066C065 000066 000065        43            MVC   L0,=X'FF'         1111 1111
                                           44            LTORG
000060 01
000061 03
000062 11
000063 0F
000064 F0
000065 FF

000066                                     45    L0      DS    XL1
```

Language and is not used in machine language. The first field, R1, designates the register or register pair whose contents are to be shifted. The second field, D3(B3), specifies the number of positions to be shifted. *The number of positions shifted, N, is the value of the low-order 6 bits of the effective address designated by the D3(B3) field.* N is always considered to be non-negative. Therefore its value is in the range $0 \leq N \leq 63$. (If $N = 0$, the instruction is executed but no shift occurs.)

The four arithmetic shift instructions are

opcode	meaning	type
SRA	SHIFT RIGHT SINGLE ARITHMETIC	RS
SLA	SHIFT LEFT SINGLE ARITHMETIC	RS

The 32-bit quantity in the register designated by the first operand is arithmetically shifted right (or left) N bit positions.

opcode	meaning	type
SRDA	SHIFT RIGHT DOUBLE ARITHMETIC	RS
SLDA	SHIFT LEFT DOUBLE ARITHMETIC	RS

The 64-bit quantity in the even-odd register pair designated by the first operand is arithmetically shifted right (or left) N bit positions. The first operand must designate the even-numbered register of the register pair.

The arithmetic shift instructions have the following properties:

1. When the contents of a register or register pair are shifted N bits to the *right*, the N right-most bits are lost, and the sign bit (bit 0) that existed before the shift began is inserted into each of the N left-most vacated positions, i.e., into bit positions 1 through N. The sign bit itself remains unchanged.

2. When the contents of a register or register pair are shifted N bits to the *left*, zeroes are inserted into the N right-most vacated positions, the N left-most bits (not including the sign bit) are lost, and condition code 3—the overflow indicator—is set if a bit value different from that of the sign bit was among those that were lost. The sign bit itself remains unchanged.

3. If the overflow indicator is not set as the result of an arithmetic shift instruction, condition code 0, 1, or 2 is set depending on the resulting single- or double-register contents—zero, negative, or positive.

There are several consequences of these properties. In the single-register shifts, SRA and SLA, all arithmetic bits (bits 1–31) will be lost if $N \geq 31$. When $N \geq 31$ for SRA, the sign bit replaces bits 1–31; when $N \geq 31$ for SLA, a 0-bit replaces bits 1–31. In the double-register shifts, SRDA and SLDA, the sign bit is bit 0 of the even-numbered register; all the other bits, numbered from 1–63, are arithmetic bits. Therefore, in double-register shifts all arithmetic bits will be lost only when $N = 63$; they are replaced by the sign bit in right shifts and by a 0-bit in left shifts.

Because of the special handling given to the sign bit, it follows that a left shift of N positions multiplies the number in the register or register-pair by 2^N, preserving the correct algebraic sign for the product. The result will be correct unless the left shift generates an overflow condition. It also follows that a right shift of N positions divides the number in the register or register pair by 2^N, preserving the correct algebraic sign for the quotient but discarding the remainder. For positive numbers, shifting right to divide by 2^N gives the same quotient as ordinary division. For example, $(+7)/2 = 3$, and $+7$ shifted right one place is also 3. But for negative numbers, shifting right can give a quotient different from that of division. For example, $(-7)/2 = -3$, whereas -7 shifted right one place is -4. In other words, truncation is towards minus infinity, not towards zero as in division.

Finally, it should be noted that, since the condition code is set by the arithmetic shift instructions, the conditional branch instructions can be used to determine whether the result was zero, negative, or positive unless there was an overflow. If an arithmetic left shift causes an overflow, the program will be interrupted and terminated by the Operating System unless the Set Program Mask (SPM) instruction is used to prohibit interruption (see Section 11.4). In the latter case, the Branch on Overflow (BO) conditional branch instruction can be used to detect the overflow condition.

The examples that follow and those in figures 8.2a through 8.2c illustrate these properties of arithmetic shifts.

Figure 8.2a   Arithmetic shifts of a 32-bit positive number.

Figure 8.2b **Arithmetic shifts of a 32-bit negative number.**

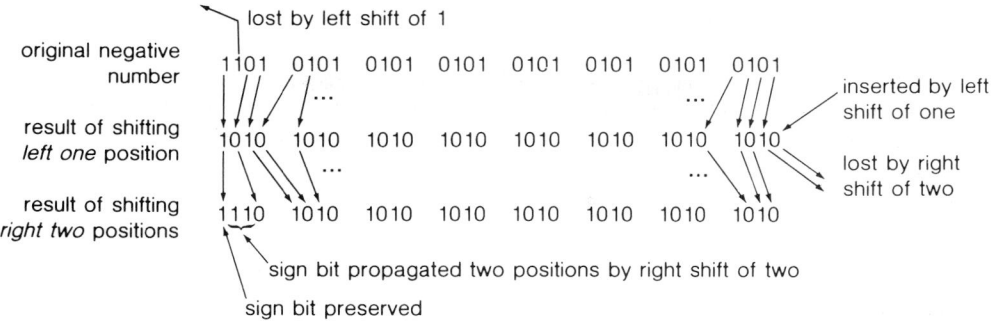

Fig. 8.2c **Arithmetic shifts of a 64-bit negative number.**

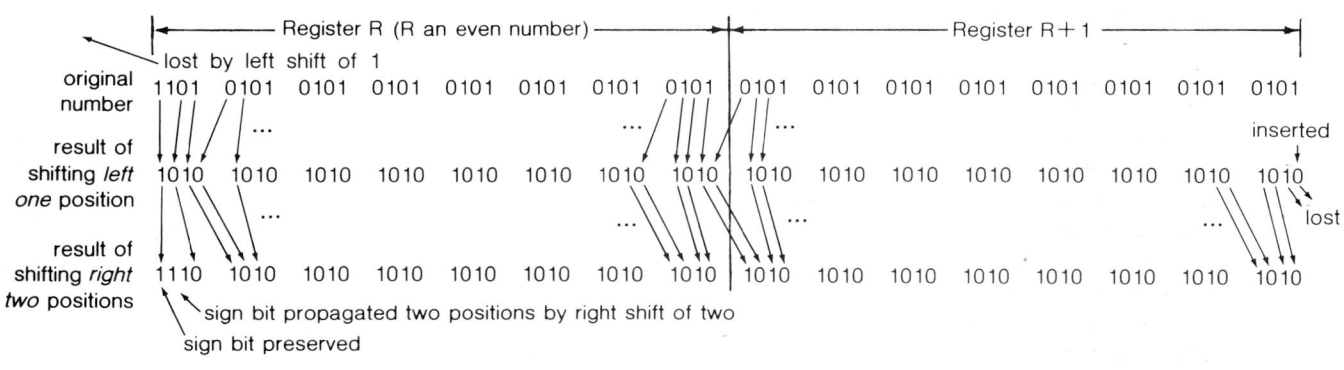

Example 1. **Result is zero**

Example 2. **Negative result**

Example 3.   Overflow generated

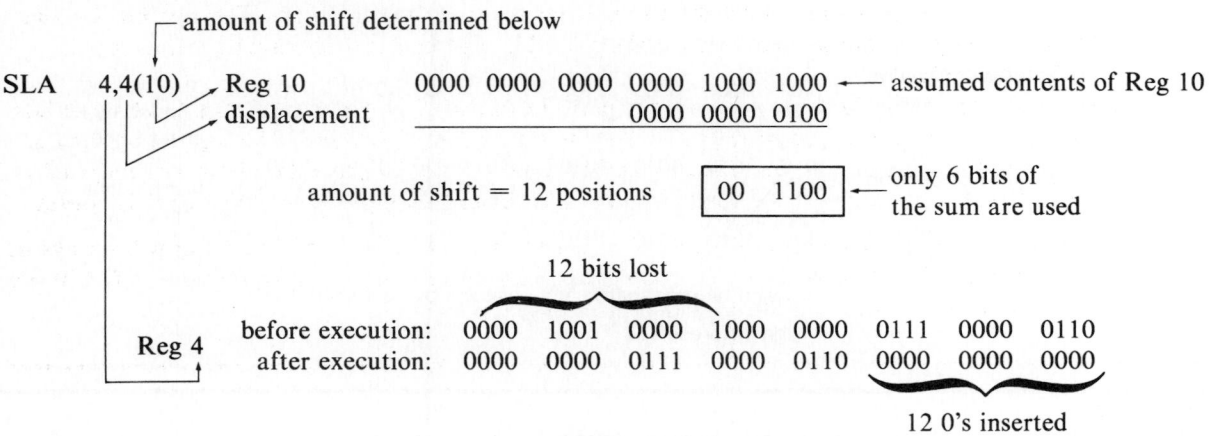

amount of shift determined below

SLA   4,4(10)   Reg 10   0000 0000 0000 0000 1000 1000 ⟵ assumed contents of Reg 10

displacement   0000 0000 0100

amount of shift = 12 positions | 00   1100 | ⟵ only 6 bits of
                                                      the sum are used

12 bits lost

Reg 4   before execution: 0000 1001 0000 1000 0000 0111 0000 0110
         after execution: 0000 0000 0111 0000 0110 0000 0000 0000

12 0's inserted

Example 4.   Positive result

shift 3 positions

SRDA   8,3

Register pair 8 and 9   ⟵ Reg 8 ⟶   ⟵ Reg 9 ⟶

before (in hex):   1A 1B 1C 1D   1E 1F 10 11
after (in hex):   03 43 63 83   A3 C3 E2 02

Example 5.   Overflow generated

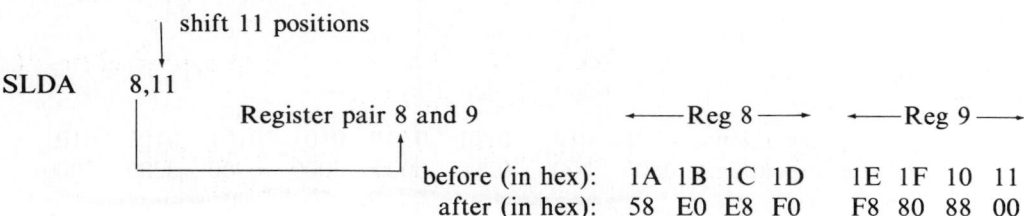

shift 11 positions

SLDA   8,11

Register pair 8 and 9   ⟵ Reg 8 ⟶   ⟵ Reg 9 ⟶

before (in hex):   1A 1B 1C 1D   1E 1F 10 11
after (in hex):   58 E0 E8 F0   F8 80 88 00

Logical Shifts

Logical shifts are used in conjunction with other bit- and byte-manipulation instructions to separate or join sequences of bits. Like arithmetic shifts, there are four logical shift instructions, two for single-register shifts and two for double-register shifts. The register address and the number of positions to be shifted are specified in the same way as for arithmetic shifts. The four instructions are

opcode	meaning	type
SRL	SHIFT RIGHT SINGLE LOGICAL	RS
SLL	SHIFT LEFT SINGLE LOGICAL	RS
	The 32-bit quantity in the register designated by the first operand is logically shifted right (or left) N bit positions.	
SRDL	SHIFT RIGHT DOUBLE LOGICAL	RS
SLDL	SHIFT LEFT DOUBLE LOGICAL	RS
	The 64-bit quantity in the even-odd register pair designated by the first operand is logically shifted right (or left) N bit positions. The first operand must designate the even-numbered register of the register pair.	

The logical shift instructions have the following properties:

1. When the contents of a register or register pair are shifted N bits to the *right*, the N right-most bits are lost, and zeroes are inserted into the N left-most vacated positions. The sign bit position (bit 0) is treated in the same manner as the other bit positions; it is not propagated as it is in arithmetic shifts.

2. When the contents of a register or register pair are shifted N bits to the *left*, the N left-most bits are lost, and zeroes are inserted into the N right-most vacated positions. The sign bit position is treated in the same manner as the other bit positions; an overflow condition is never generated.

3. Regardless of the nature of the result of a logical shift instruction, the condition code is not set.

Since vacated positions at the right or left ends are always filled with zeroes, the result will always be zero in single-register shifts if the number of bits shifted exceeds 31. But a double-register shift will not necessarily produce a result of zero, since N is always less than 64.

Example 1.

```
                  | shift 5 positions
                  ↓
SRL    3,5
                                                                              5 bits lost
         Reg 3  before execution:  1111  1111  1111  1111  1111  1111  1010  0100
                 after execution:  0000  0111  1111  1111  1111  1111  1111  1101

                                   5 0's inserted
```

Example 2.

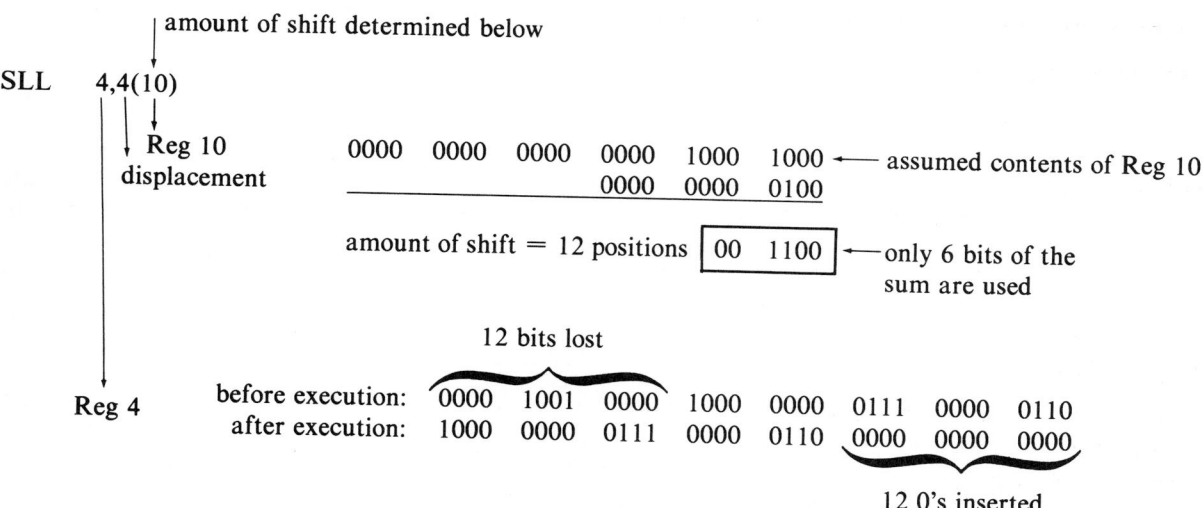

```
                    | amount of shift determined below
                    ↓
SLL    4,4(10)

          | Reg 10      0000  0000  0000  0000  1000  1000  ←── assumed contents of Reg 10
          ↓ displacement                  0000  0000  0100
                        _____

          amount of shift = 12 positions  | 00  1100 |  ←── only 6 bits of the
                                                          sum are used

                                   12 bits lost
                            ⌢‾‾‾‾‾‾‾‾‾‾‾‾‾‾‾‾⌢
         before execution:  0000  1001  0000  1000  0000  0111  0000  0110
 Reg 4   after execution:   1000  0000  0111  0000  0110  0000  0000  0000
                                                        ⌣_____⌣
                                                           12 0's inserted
```

Example 3.

```
                | shift 3 positions
                ↓
SRDL  8,3

             Register pair 8 and 9              ←── Reg 8 ──→    ←── Reg 9 ──→
                            before (in hex):   1A  1B  1C  1D   1E  1F  10  11
                            after (in hex):    03  43  63  83   A3  C3  E2  02
```

Example 4.

shift 11 positions

SLDL 8,11

Register pair 8 and 9

	←——Reg 8——→	←——Reg 9——→
before (in hex):	1A 1B 1C 1D	1E 1F 10 11
after (in hex):	D8 E0 E8 F0	F8 80 88 00

8.2 ALTERING BITS

Some assembly language programs use the individual bits in a bit string to represent status information. This type of information can be used to control the flow of a program and to keep a succinct record of events that occur during the execution of a program. For example, the status of a file could be recorded in this bit string:

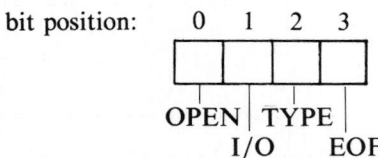

bit position: 0   1   2   3

OPEN | TYPE

I/O   EOF

Each bit in this bit string has a value of 0 or 1. These values could imply the status of a file as follows:

bit	value		meaning
OPEN bit	0	=	file not opened
	1	=	file opened
I/O bit	0	=	if opened, file is used for input only
	1	=	if opened, file is used for output only
TYPE bit	0	=	sequential file
	1	=	indexed sequential file
EOF bit	0	=	file has not reached end-of-file
	1	=	file has reached end-of-file

A single bit is often not enough for a given situation. In that case, two or more bits can be used. Because there are only two possibilities in each case, a single bit is sufficient for the OPEN and EOF situations. But two bits each for the I/O and TYPE information would allow four possibilities for these entities:

bit position: 0   1   2   3   4   5

OPEN   EOF

I/O   TYPE

These bits could have the following meanings:

bit	value		meaning
OPEN bit	0	=	file not opened
	1	=	file opened
I/O bits	00	=	no meaning
	01	=	opened for input only
	10	=	opened for output only
	11	=	opened for input and output
TYPE bits	00	=	none of the standard types
	01	=	sequential
	10	=	indexed sequential
	11	=	direct
EOF bit	0	=	not yet end-of-file
	1	=	end-of-file

Figure 8.3a   The Boolean OR operation.

mask bit	target bit	resulting bit	
0	0	0	} mask bit = 0
0	1	1	target bit *unchanged*
1	0	1	} mask bit = 1
1	1	1	target bit *set to 1*

Figure 8.3b   The Boolean AND operation.

mask bit	target bit	resulting bit	
0	0	0	} mask bit = 0
0	1	0	target bit *reset to 0*
1	0	0	} mask bit = 1
1	1	1	target bit *unchanged*

Figure 8.3c   The Boolean EXCLUSIVE-OR operation.

mask bit	target bit	resulting bit	
0	0	0	} mask bit = 0
0	1	1	target bit *unchanged*
1	0	1	} mask bit = 1
1	1	0	target bit *reversed*

In general, n consecutive bits will provide for 2^n possible meanings. By using bits instead of bytes or larger units to record status information, programmers can be frugal in their use of available memory space.

Then the problem becomes the ability to alter and test the values of individual bits or bit strings. The instructions that *alter* bits are the Boolean operations OR, AND, and EXCLUSIVE-OR; these are described in the following. There are two instructions that *test* bits on the IBM Systems 360 and 370, the Test Under Mask (TM) and Test and Set (TS) instructions. These are described in Section 8.3.

The Boolean operations, OR, AND, and EXCLUSIVE-OR have three characteristics in common:

1. They operate on two bit strings, each of the same length.
2. Only one of the bit strings, the *target*, is altered. The other bit string, the *mask*, selects the individual bits that are to be altered in the target bit string. Each bit in the mask that is a "1" selects the correspondingly positioned bit in the target, regardless of whether that target bit is a "0" or a "1."
3. The mask bit string is matched, bit for bit, with the target bit string: each bit in the mask operates on the corresponding bit in the target.[1] The sign bit is not given any special treatment.

The Boolean OR operation *sets* the selected target bits to 1, regardless of what the previous values of those bits were. Bits not selected by the mask are not changed.

The Boolean AND operation *preserves* the value of the selected target bits and *resets* the remaining bits to zero, regardless of what the previous values of those bits were.

1. In the IBM Systems 360 and 370, the emphasis on mask and target bit strings is valid because the result always replaces the target. Bits in the target bit string are selected and altered *in place*. However, in many electronic applications of the Boolean operations, the result does not replace the target; instead, it is generated as a separate quantity. In these instances, the use of the mask and target nomenclature is not appropriate; there are simply two operands that obey the rules of combination given in figures 8.3a through 8.3c.

The Boolean EXCLUSIVE-OR operation *reverses* the value of the selected target bits: if a selected bit was 0, it is set to 1; if it was 1, it is reset to 0. Bits not selected by the mask are not changed.

These three operations are depicted in figures 8.3a through 8.3c.

There are four OR instructions, four AND instructions, and four EXCLUSIVE-OR instructions on the IBM Systems 360 and 370. Within each set of four, the instructions are distinguished by the length and location of the mask and target bit strings. Figure 8.4 summarizes these distinctions.

The bit string resulting from an OR, AND, or EXCLUSIVE-OR operation is considered to be either zero or nonzero, and the condition code is set accordingly. No distinction is made between positive and negative results. Thus the only conditional branch instructions that should be used following Boolean instructions are BZ, BZR, BNZ, and BNZR.

Example 1.

|target operand
|↓ mask operand

OR   5,6

before execution:
Reg 6 = 1111 1111 1111 1111 0000 0000 0000 0000
Reg 5 = 0101 0101 0101 0101 0101 0101 0101 0101

after execution:
Reg 5 = 1111 1111 1111 1111 0101 0101 0101 0101
                 set to 1's   unchanged

Example 2.

|target operand
|↓ mask operand

NR   5,6

before execution:
Reg 6 = 1111 1111 1111 1111 0000 0000 0000 0000
Reg 5 = 0101 0101 0101 0101 0101 0101 0101 0101

after execution:
Reg 5 = 0101 0101 0101 0101 0000 0000 0000 0000
                 unchanged   set to 0's

Figure 8.4   Boolean instructions on IBM systems 360 and 370.

opcode	op-name	op-type	location of MASK	location of TARGET	length of mask and target
O N X	OR AND EXCLUSIVE-OR	RX	in full-word memory location designated by second operand	in register designated by first operand	32 bits
OR NR XR	OR Registers AND Registers EXCLUSIVE-OR Regs.	RR	in register designated by second operand	in register designated by first operand	32 bits
OI NI XI	OR Immediate AND Immediate EXCLUSIVE-OR Immed.	SI	in immediate data field (second operand)	in 1-byte memory location designated by first operand	8 bits
OC NC XC	OR Characters AND Characters EXCLUSIVE-OR Chars.	SS₁	in L-byte* memory location designated by second operand	in *L*-byte* memory location designated by first operand	8 × L bits*

*The value of L is specified in the length-field of the first operand: $1 \le L \le 256$

Example 3.

```
       | target operand
   ↓   ↓ mask operand
XR   5,6
```

before execution:	Reg 6	=	1111	1111	1111	1111	0000	0000	0000	0000
	Reg 5	=	0101	0101	0101	0101	0101	0101	0101	0101
after execution:	Reg 5	=	1010	1010	1010	1010	0101	0101	0101	0101

each bit reversed   unchanged

8.3   TESTING BITS

Two instructions test individual bits to determine whether their values are 0 or 1. Both of these test the bits of a byte in memory. In the IBM Systems 360 and 370, there is no instruction that tests individual bits in a bit string whose length is greater than eight; but this can be accomplished by using Boolean operations, as will be shown. The instructions testing individual bits should not be confused with the *byte compare* instructions (CL, CLR, CLI, CLM, CLC, CLCL). The latter compare the values of two byte strings; the former determine whether individually selected bits are 0 or 1.

The two instructions that test individual bits in a byte are (1) Test Under Mask (TM) and (2) Test and Set (TS). TM is the more generally useful of the two. It tests up to 8 bits at once, without altering the bits that are tested. TS tests only 1 bit—the high-order or "sign" bit of a byte—and then sets all the bits in the tested byte to 1. Its use is restricted to certain special situations, which will be described shortly.

Test Under Mask

The TM instruction tests any subset of the 8 bits in a byte. The byte whose bits are tested—the target byte—can be located in any addressable memory position. The bits to be tested in the target byte are selected by a 1-byte mask located in the immediate data field of the TM instruction.

The TM is an SI-type instruction:

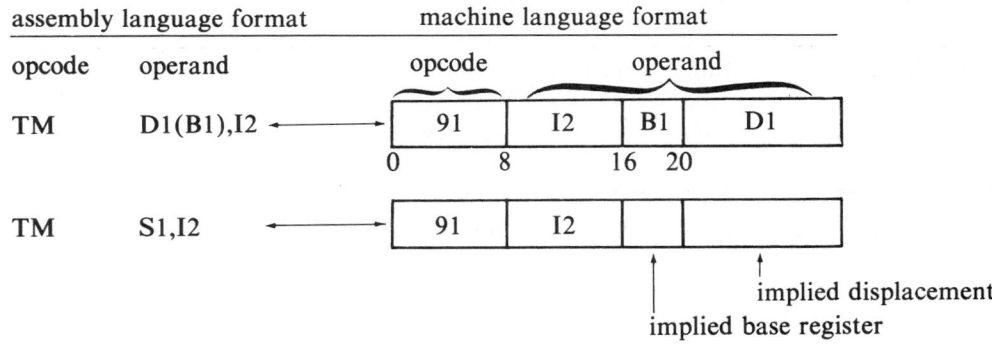

The 8 bits in the I2 mask field correspond, one-for-one, left-to-right, with the 8 bits in the target byte (addressed by the first operand field). Each 1-bit in the mask causes the corresponding bit in the target byte to be selected for testing. Each 0-bit in the mask causes the corresponding bit in the target byte *not* to be selected for testing.

The result of the TM instruction can be determined by means of conditional branch instructions:

        BZ Branch if Zeroes
           branches if all tested bits are 0's, or if all *mask* bits are 0's

        BO Branch if Ones
           branches if all tested bits are 1's

        BM Branch if Mixed Zeroes and Ones
           branches if some tested bits are 0's and the other tested bits are 1's

Examples of the use of the TM are given following the next section.

Test and Set

The TS instruction tests the high-order, or "sign," bit of a byte in memory; after testing that bit, it replaces the entire byte with 1's (B'11111111'). Thus, the TS behaves as though it were two consecutive instructions built into one:

TM   BYTE,B'10000000'

MVI   BYTE,B'11111111'

The TS is an S-type instruction: it requires only a single operand field. As shown below, no mask is necessary because the TS always tests the high-order bit of a byte.

The result of the test made by the TS instruction can be determined by means of conditional branch instructions:

BZ Branch if Zero

branches if the tested bit had a value of 0

BNZ Branch if Not Zero

branches if the tested bit had a value of 1

The unusual nature of the TS instruction, i.e., the fact that after it tests the high-order bit it sets all the bits in the bytes to 1's, is specifically designed for multiprogramming and multiprocessing systems in which two or more programs are contending for use of a nonshareable component of the computer system. Such a component, also called a nonshareable computer system *resource,* could be a printer, a terminal, a portion of memory, and so forth. A computer system resource is said to be nonshareable if only one program can use it at a time.

It is a common practice for the program that controls the use of a nonshareable resource to do so by utilizing one bit or byte to record the instantaneous status of the resource, similar to the file status bits mentioned earlier. The most important status information with which we are concerned is whether the nonshareable resource is in use or not. This could be recorded as

STATUS-BYTE: value 0 = not in use

value 1 = in use

The TS instruction permits such a status byte to be tested and then immediately set to the "in-use" mode, so that no other program can gain access to that byte while its status is being tested by the first program. This is necessary for the following reason: if, instead of a TS instruction, a program used the two-instruction sequence TM followed by MVI, another program could gain access to that byte during the instant between the completion of the TM and the beginning of the MVI's execution. The second program would then find that byte set to 0 (not in use) even though the first program was about to set it to 1 (in use). Both programs might then attempt to use the nonshareable resource simultaneously without being aware of one another's actions. This would violate the integrity of the computer system. Use of the TS instruction can prevent this from happening.

Example 1.

TM   ALPHA,X'F0'

mask byte

designates address
of target byte

mask byte =   1111   0000
assumed target byte =   1010   1111

Result of TM: some tested bits are 0's, others are 1's

Example 2.

TM   ALPHA,X'0F'

mask byte =   0000   1111
assumed target byte =   1010   1111

Result of TM: all tested bits are 1's

Example 3.

TM   ALPHA,B'01010000'

mask byte =   0101   0000
assumed target byte =   1010   1111

Result of TM: all tested bits are 0's

Example 4.

TS   ALPHA

	byte at ALPHA	
before execution:	0111	1111
after execution:	1111	1111

Result of TS: tested bit was 0

Example 5.

TS   ALPHA

	byte at ALPHA	
before execution:	1000	0000
after execution:	1111	1111

Result of TS: tested bit was 1

8.4 THE CONDITION CODE

The condition code is a hardware indicator that records the nature of the result of certain instructions. Since the indicator consists of only two bits, only four possible conditions can be recorded. These are known as the *condition code settings:*

$$00 = \text{Condition Code } 0$$
$$01 = \text{Condition Code } 1$$
$$10 = \text{Condition Code } 2$$
$$11 = \text{Condition Code } 3$$

The specific meaning of each of these four condition code settings depends on the instruction that generated the condition. Not all of the instructions available on the IBM Systems 360 and 370 cause the condition code to be set, but more than half of them do. The condition code is always set to one of its four possible values whenever one of the code-setting instructions is executed. However, the condition code is not affected by any of the instructions that are not code-setting instructions.

The setting of the condition code can be examined and its value determined by two instructions designed for this purpose: (1) Branch on Condition (BC), and (2) Branch on Condition via Register (BCR). *Both of these instructions are conditional branch instructions.* The setting of the condition code when either of these instructions is executed determines whether or not a branch is made. More precisely, the bits in a 4-bit mask field within the BC and BCR instruction determine which setting or settings of the condition code will cause a branch. The mask field occupies bits 8–11 of a machine language BC and BCR instruction. Each of the 4 bits in the mask field denotes a different one of the four possible settings of the condition code:

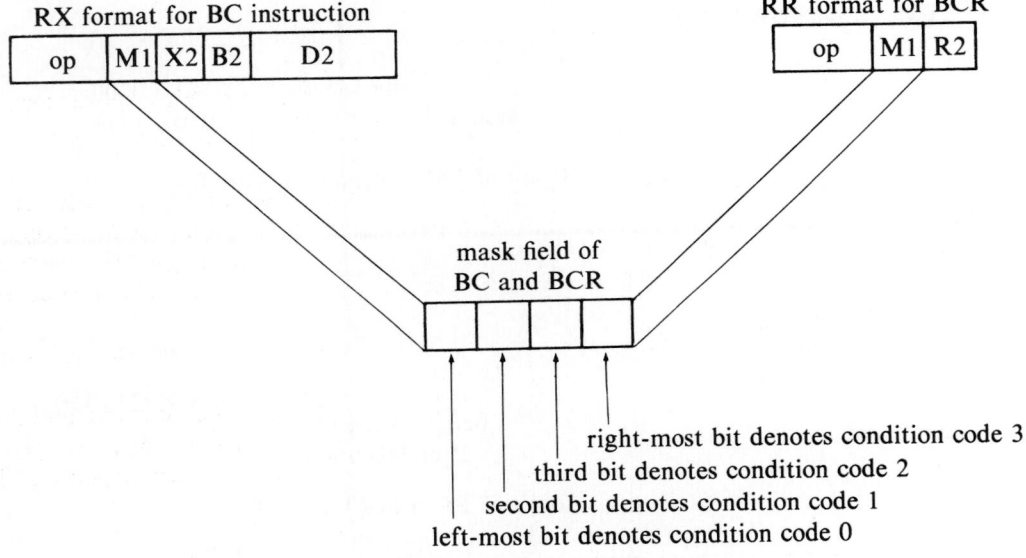

When any of these bits is set to the value 1, the corresponding condition code setting will cause the BC and BCR instructions to branch. For example:

mask field	meaning
1000	if the condition code is 0, the BC and BCR will branch
1100	if the condition is either 0 or 1, the BC and BCR will branch
1010	if the condition code is either 0 or 2, the BC and BCR will branch
0011	if the condition code is either 2 or 3, the BC and BCR will branch
1111	whatever the condition code setting is, the BC and BCR will branch (thereby constituting an unconditional branch)
0000	whatever the condition code setting is, the BC and BCR will not branch (thereby constituting a so-called "no-op," or no operation, instruction).

Any of the sixteen possible 4-bit mask-field contents is allowed. Each has a precise meaning, as indicated by the preceding examples and (later) in figures 8.6a and 8.6b.

In previous sections, it was stated that the nature of the result of certain instructions, for example, *compare* instructions, *arithmetic* instructions, *Boolean* instructions, and so forth, could be determined by means of conditional branch instructions such as BE, BH, BL, BZ, BP, BM, and their negative counterparts BNE, BNH, BNL, BNZ, BNP, BNM. Now a more precise statement can be made: each conditional branch instruction just mentioned is a variation of the BC instruction. The variations are created by different values of the mask field and are often called *extended mnemonic opcodes* since they are all based on the same actual opcode, namely that of the BC.

Extended mnemonic opcodes are used so that we need not remember the appropriate mask field. For example, the instruction

BE   FOUND

is identical to the instruction

BC   8,FOUND

The first operand in the BC instruction is the mask-field value:

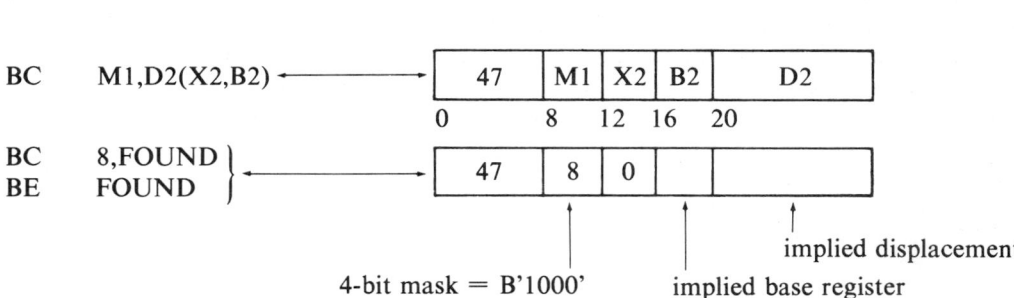

However, as shown, a mask field of B'1000' means that condition code 0 causes a branch. So the immediate question is, what does condition code 0 mean? *The meaning of each condition code setting depends on the instruction that caused the code to be set.* Figure 8.5a summarizes the meanings of the condition code settings for all nonprivileged instructions. (Some privileged instructions also set the condition code, but they are not discussed in this text.)

Figure 8.5a shows that condition code 0 is set by any compare instruction when the two quantities being compared are equal: BC 8,FOUND is identical to BE FOUND.

Figure 8.5b shows that none of the multiply or divide instructions sets the condition code, and that none of the logical shift instructions sets the condition code. To determine whether the result of a multiply, divide, or logical shift is positive, negative, or zero, we must therefore use the Load and Test Register (LTR) instruction. For logical shifts, the determination could be made like this:

```
SLL     4,8      SHIFT REG 4 CONTENTS LEFT 8 BITS
LTR     4,4      SEE IF THE RESULT OF THE SHIFT IS ZERO
BZ      ZERO
```

The complete set of correspondences between the extended mnemonic conditional branch instructions and the BC instruction is shown in figure 8.6a. Note that the unconditional branch B is actually a BC that *always* branches; similarly, the no-op instruction NOP is a BC that *never* branches.

The BC is an RX-type instruction. Its counterpart, the BCR, is an RR-type instruction. In the BC instruction, the second operand designates the address of the instruction to which the branch is to be made if the condition code is set to one of the values selected by the mask:

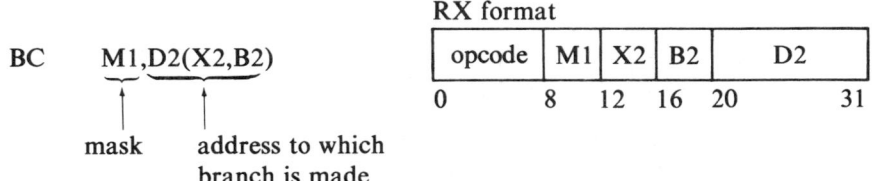

Figure 8.5a *Condition code settings for nonprivileged instructions.*

	instruction		condition code setting depends on the instruction and its result			
			condition code 0	condition code 1	condition code 2	condition code 3
INTEGER OPERATIONS	Add Subtract	A, AR, AH S, SR, SH	result is 0	result is negative	result is positive	operation generated an overflow
	Add Subtract	AL,ALR SL,SLR	result is 0, with no carry (AL, ALR only)	result is not 0, with no carry	result is 0, with carry	result is not 0, with carry
	Compare	C, CR, CH	both operands are equal	first operand less than second	first operand greater than second	---
	Load	LCR LNR LPR LTR	result is 0 result is 0 result is 0 result is 0	result is negative result is negative --- result is negative	result is positive --- result is positive result is positive	overflow generated --- overflow generated ---
	Shift	SLA, SLDA SRA, SRDA	result is 0 result is 0	result is negative result is negative	result is positive result is positive	overflow generated ---
BYTE OPERATIONS	Insert	ICM	all inserted bits 0, or all mask bits 0	1st inserted bit is 1	1st inserted bit is 0 but not all are 0	---
	Compare	CL, CLR CLC,CLI	both operands are equal	first operand less than second	first operand greater than second	---
		CLCL	operands are equal, or have zero lengths	first operand less than second	first operand greater than second	---
		CLM	bytes selected are equal or mask bits are all 0	first operand field less than second	first operand field greater than second	---
	Copy	MVCL	first operand length equals second operand's	first operand length less than second	first operand length greater than second	destructive overlap (no bytes copied)
	Translate	TRT	all argument bytes tested; all function bytes 0	one or more argument bytes not tested	search stopped on last argument byte	---
BIT OPERATIONS	AND OR EXCL-OR	N,NC,NI,NR O,OC,OI,OR X,XC,XI,XR	result is 0 result is 0 result is 0	result is not 0 result is not 0 result is not 0	--- --- ---	--- --- ---
	Test	TM	all selected bits 0 or all mask bits 0	some sel. bits are 0 and some bits are 1	---	all selected bits are 1's
		TS	left-most bit of tested byte is 0	left-most bit of tested byte is 1	---	---
DECIMAL	Add Subtract	AP, ZAP SP	result is 0	result is negative	result is positive	operation generated an overflow
	Compare	CP	both operands are equal	first operand less than second	first operand greater than second	---
	Shift	SRP	result is 0	result is negative	result is positive	overflow generated
FLOATING POINT	Add	AE,AER,AD, ADR,AU,AUR, AW,AWR,AXR	mantissa of result is 0	result is negative	result is positive	---
	Subtract	SE,SER,SD, SDR,SU,SUR, SW,SWR,SXR	mantissa of result is 0	result is negative	result is positive	---
	Load	LCER,LCDR LNER,LNDR LPER,LPDR LTER,LTDR	result mantissa is 0 result mantissa is 0 result mantissa is 0 result mantissa is 0	result is negative result is negative --- result is negative	result is positive --- result is positive result is positive	--- --- --- ---
	Compare	CE, CER CD, CDR	both operands are equal	first operand less than second	first operand greater than second	---
MISCELLANEOUS	Compare and swap	CS, CDS	compared operands equal, second one is replaced	compared operands not equal, first is replaced	---	---
	Set pgm mask	SPM	(the condition code is set to the value of bits 2 and 3 of the designated register)			
	Store clock	STCK	clock in set state	clock in not-set state	clock in error state	clock in stopped state or not-operational
	Editing	ED, EDMK	last edited field is 0	last edited field is negative	last edited field is positive	---

Branches	Branch and Link	BAL	BALR	BAS	BASR			
	Branch on Condition	BC	BCR					
	Branch on Count	BCT	BCTR					
	Branch on Index	BXH	BXLE					
Integer operations	Multiply	M	MR	MH				
	Divide	D	DR					
	Load	L	LM	LH				
	Store	ST	STM	STH				
Byte operations	Copy	IC	STC	STCM	MVC	MVI	MVCIN	
	Translate	TR						
Bit operations	Shift Logical	SRL	SRDL					
		SLL	SLDL					
Decimal operations	Multiply	MP						
	Divide	DP						
	Copy	MVN	MVO	MVZ				
Floating-point operations	Multiply	ME	MER	MD	MDR	MXD	MXDR	MXR
	Divide	DE	DER	DD	DDR			
	Halve	HER	HDR					
	Round	LRER	LRDR					
	Load	LE	LER	LD	LDR			
	Store	STE	STD					
Miscellaneous operations	Decimal-binary conv.	CVB	CVD					
	Decimal-EBCDIC conv.	PACK	UNPK					
	Execute	EX						
	Load address	LA						
	Monitor call	MC						
	Supervisor call	SVC						

In the BCR instruction, the second operand field designates a register address, not a memory address. The designated register must contain the address of the instruction to which the branch is to be made if the condition code is set to one of the values selected by the mask:

The BCR gets its name, Branch on Condition via Register, from the fact that the branch is made to the address contained in the designated register. There is one exception, however: if the designated register is zero, no branch is made regardless of the contents of the mask field M1.

An extended mnemonic conditional branch instruction is defined for most of the sixteen possible mask fields of the BCR instruction. These are summarized in figure 8.6b. Although not discussed in preceding chapters, an RR-type conditional branch may be used in any situation in which its corresponding RX-type branch would be used. One of the most important instructions in this group is the unconditional branch, Branch via Register (BR). The BR is used to return from a subroutine to a calling program, as will be discussed in the next chapter. The instruction BCR with M1=0 is the counterpart of the BC with M1=0: both are no-op instructions. The BCR no-op, written mnemonically as NOPR, is the instruction that is generated by the CNOP directive discussed at the end of chapter 6.

Figure 8.6a RX-type conditional branch instructions.

extended mnemonic	equivalent BC	mask bits	condition codes designated by mask bits
BE	BC 8,	1000	0
BNE	BC 7,	0111	1, 2, and 3
BL	BC 4,	0100	1
BNL	BC 11,	1011	0, 2, and 3
BH	BC 2,	0010	2
BNH	BC 13,	1101	0, 1, and 3
BZ	BC 8,	1000	0
BNZ	BC 7,	0111	1, 2, and 3
BM	BC 4,	0100	1
BNM	BC 11,	1011	0, 2, and 3
BP	BC 2,	0010	2
BNP	BC 13,	1101	0, 1, and 3
BO	BC 1,	0001	3
BNO	BC 14,	1110	0, 1, and 2
NOP	BC 0,	0000	none
B	BC 15,	1111	0, 1, 2, and 3
--	BC 12,	1100	0 and 1
--	BC 3,	0011	2 and 3
--	BC 10,	1010	0 and 2
--	BC 5,	0101	1 and 3
--	BC 9,	1001	0 and 3
--	BC 6,	0110	1 and 2

Figure 8.6b RR-type conditional branch instructions.

extended mnemonic	equivalent BCR	mask bits	condition codes designated by mask bits
BER	BCR 8,	1000	0
BNER	BCR 7,	0111	1, 2, and 3
BLR	BCR 4,	0100	1
BNLR	BCR 11,	1011	0, 2, and 3
BHR	BCR 2,	0010	2
BNHR	BCR 13,	1101	0, 1, and 3
BZR	BCR 8,	1000	0
BNZR	BCR 7,	0111	1, 2, and 3
BMR	BCR 4,	0100	1
BNMR	BCR 11,	1011	0, 2, and 3
BPR	BCR 2,	0010	2
BNPR	BCR 13,	1101	0, 1, and 3
BOR	BCR 1,	0001	3
BNOR	BCR 14,	1110	0, 1, and 2
NOPR	BCR 0,	0000	none
BR	BCR 15,	1111	0, 1, 2, and 3
--	BCR 12,	1100	0 and 1
--	BCR 3,	0011	2 and 3
--	BCR 10,	1010	0 and 2
--	BCR 5,	0101	1 and 3
--	BCR 9,	1001	0 and 3
--	BCR 6,	0110	1 and 2

8.5 BIT MANIPULATION EXAMPLES

The bit manipulation instructions described in the preceding sections provide capabilities needed in a variety of problems and situations. For example:

1. Shift instructions, in addition to their obvious use as a succinct method of multiplying and dividing by powers of two, enable a program to separate and link adjacent bit strings.
2. Boolean instructions enable a program to isolate bits, to set individual bits to 0 or 1, and to reverse the setting of bits.
3. The TM instruction provides an easy method for testing the values of individual bits, thereby facilitating the use of status indicators and switches.
4. The BC and BCR operations underlie the conditional branch instructions, without which decisions could not be made by programs.

The four examples that follow illustrate how these capabilities are used in conjunction with other instructions.

Figure 8.7 *Definitions for a file-status byte.*

```
 1   * FILE STATUS INFORMATION
 2   FILESTAT DC    B'00000000'    FILE STATUS INITIALLY 0'S
 3   OPEN     EQU   B'10000000'    BIT 0     0=CLOSED, 1=OPEN
 4   IO       EQU   B'01100000'    BIT 1,2   FOR I/O STATE:
 5   IOIN     EQU   B'00100000'              01=INPUT ONLY
 6   IOOUT    EQU   B'01000000'              10=OUTPUT ONLY
 7   IOINOUT  EQU   B'01100000'              11=INPUT & OUTPUT
 8   TYPE     EQU   B'00011000'    BIT 3,4   FOR FILE TYPE
 9   TYPSAM   EQU   B'00001000'              01=SEQTL (SAM)
10   TYPISAM  EQU   B'00010000'              10=INDEXED (ISAM)
11   TYPBDAM  EQU   B'00011000'              11=DIRECT (BDAM)
12   EOF      EQU   B'00000100'    BIT 5     0=NOT EOF, 1=EOF
```

Example 1. Use of a status byte
(See fig. 8.7.)

Suppose that the instantaneous status of a file is to be recorded in a single status byte, as follows:

bit name	bit position within byte	value of bits		meaning
OPEN	0	0	=	file is closed
		1	=	file is opened
IO	1,2	00	=	no meaning
		01	=	opened for input only
		10	=	opened for output only
		11	=	opened for input and output
TYPE	3,4	00	=	none of the standard types
		01	=	sequential
		10	=	indexed sequential
		11	=	direct
EOF	5	0	=	not yet end-of-file
		1	=	end-of-file

Schematically, this can be represented as

bit position:	0	1	3	5	6
bit meaning:	OPEN	IO	TYPE	E O F	

In a program, it can be defined as in figure 8.7. The definition requires a number of statements; one virtue of this is that the status byte is fully documented within the program in which it is defined.

Note that a whole byte is used for the status information, even though there are two unused bits in the byte. This serves two purposes: (1) it leaves a little room for defining other status bits at a later time, and (2) it facilitates use of the bit manipulation instructions that can only address a whole byte.

Note also that the EQU directive is used to assign *names* to the bits and to the various states, and that the DC directive gives a name to the status byte and sets its initial value. All names used in a program are listed in the cross-reference table produced by the Assembler; therefore, the use of names for the status bits and for the various states facilitates any debugging and modifying that might have to be done.

Several situations arise in connection with the use of such a status byte. Using the definitions of figure 8.7, some of them could be handled in the following manner:

1. When the file is opened,

```
OI    FILESTAT,OPEN        SET OPEN BIT TO '1'
```

2. If the file is opened as an indexed sequential file,

```
OI      FILESTAT,TYPISAM      SET ISAM BIT TO '1'
```

3. If it is necessary to determine whether the file is opened for output or input,

```
        TM      FILESTAT,IOOUT      SEE IF OUTPUT BIT IS '1'
        BO      OUTPUT              BRANCH IF IT IS '1'
        TM      FILESTAT,IOIN       SEE IF INPUT BIT IS '1'
        BO      INPUT               BRANCH IF IT IS '1'
        . . . . . . . . . . . . . . . . . . . .
OUTPUT  EQU     *                   file is opened for output
        .
        .
INPUT   EQU     *                   file is opened for input
        .
        .
```

4. If it is necessary to determine whether the file is opened both for input and for output,

```
        TM      FILESTAT,IOINOUT    TEST I/O BITS
        BO      BOTH                BRANCH IF BOTH ARE 1's
```

5. If it is necessary to reset the "open" status bit to zero, indicating the file has been closed,

```
        NI      FILESTAT,X'FF'-OPEN    SET OPEN BIT TO '0'
```

In all cases, the Assembler substitutes the value of the symbol that is used for each status bit. For example, based on the definitions of figure 8.7, the following three statements are equivalent to one another:

```
        TM      FILESTAT,IOIN
        TM      FILESTAT,B'00100000'
        TM      FILESTAT,X'20'
```

In Situation 5, to reset a bit to zero, the mask must be set up so that all bits are preserved (unchanged) except the one to be reset. The operand X'FF'-OPEN has the value B'01111111'. The result of this value ANDed to the file-status byte value is that all bits in the file-status byte are preserved except the OPEN bit, bit 0. That one is set to 0. The operand X'FF'- {any mask} always reverses each bit of an 8-bit mask. We can see from the example that such a reversal is precisely what is needed to reset a bit.

Example 2.   Use of a status word
(See fig. 8.8.)

Sometimes 8 bits are not enough to represent the status of a situation. In such cases, we use either several bytes in the manner described in the previous section, or a full word or several full words. To use full words, the techniques of setting, testing, resetting, and inverting status bits can be handled as follows.

Suppose that a full word is used to record the status of up to 32 terminals connected to the computer. Each bit corresponds to a terminal, the bits are numbered from left to right 0, 1, 2, 3,...,31, and these numbers correspond to the terminal numbers. Each bit records the state of one terminal: if bit N is a 0, then terminal N is not in use; if bit N is a 1, then terminal N is being used.

Testing or Resetting Bit N.   In order to test or reset the Nth bit in the status word, that word can be placed into a register and the Nth bit isolated from the other bits. The isolation is achieved by SHIFT and AND instructions (see figure 8.8):

```
        LH      2,BITN        R2=VALUE OF N
        L       3,STATUS      R3=STATUS WORD
        SLL     3,0(2)        MOVE BIT N TO POSITION 0
        N       3,PATTERN     SET ALL BUT BIT #0 TO '0'.
```

Figure 8.8 *Test the value of the Nth bit in a word.*

```
1    * THIS SET OF STATEMENTS TESTS THE NTH BIT OF A STATUS WORD
2    * (N IS BETWEEN 0 AND 31, INCLUSIVE)
3    *
4    * IF THE BIT'S VALUE IS 0, CONTROL GOES TO STMT NAMED ''OFF''
5    * IF THE BIT'S VALUE IS 1, CONTROL GOES TO STMT NAMED ''ON.''
6    *
7    * THE STATUS WORD IS LOCATED AT STMT NAMED ''STATUS''
8    *
9    *
10            LH       2,BITN         R2=VALUE OF N (BIT POSITION)
11            L        3,STATUS       R3=WORD CONTAINING BIT TO TEST
12            SLL      3,0(2)         MOVE BIT TO POSITION 0
13            N        3,PATTERN      ISOLATE TESTED BIT
14            BZ       OFF            RESULT=0 IF TESTED BIT WAS 0
15            B        ON
                .
                .
                .
16   BITN     DS       H             HALF WORD FOR N (BIT POSITION)
17   STATUS   DS       F             FULL WORD FOR STATUS BITS
18   PATTERN  DC       X'80000000'   BIT 0 OF PATTERN IS A 1
                .
                .
                .
```

It is assumed that BITN is the half-word location that has the value of N, that STATUS is the location of the status word, and that PATTERN is a location that contains a 1-bit in position 0 and 0-bits everywhere else:

```
                 PATTERN   DC   X'80000000'
```

The amount of the left-shift is in Register 2; that is what the operand 0(2) of the SLL instruction produces. For example, if $N=8$, then SLL 3,0(2) is interpreted as though it were SLL 3,8. The effect of the left-shift is to move bit N into position 0 of Register 3. (Recall that N is in the range 0–31; if N is 0, then SLL 3,0(2) causes no shift.) Once bit N is in position 0, it is isolated by the AND instruction using the PATTERN word. At this point, bit N is in a known position. It can easily be tested, reset, set, or inverted.

To test bit N after it has been isolated by this procedure, we follow the AND instruction with a conditional branch instruction as shown in Statement 14 of figure 8.8.

To reset bit N to 0, the procedure of figure 8.8 can be replaced by these seven statements:

```
     LH       2,BITN      R2= VALUE OF N
     L        3,STATUS    R3= WORD CONTAINING BIT TO TEST
     SLL      3,0(2)      MOVE BIT TO POSITION #0
     N        3,PATTERN   ISOLATE TESTED BIT
     SRL      3,0(2)      MOVE BIT BACK TO POSITION #N
     X        3,STATUS    FORCE BIT #N TO BE 0, AND PUT
     ST       3,STATUS    RESULT BACK INTO STATUS WORD
```

Setting or Inverting Bit N. To illustrate how to set and invert a bit in a word, we once again use the areas and the constant defined in figure 8.8.

To set bit N to 1, these five statements are sufficient:

```
     LH       2,BITN      R2=VALUE OF N
     L        3,PATTERN   R3='1' IN POSITION #0
     SRL      3,0(2)      MOVE '1' TO POSITION #N
     O        3,STATUS    'OR' THE STATUS BITS INTO R3,
     ST       3,STATUS    PUT RESULT BACK INTO STATUS WORD
```

Bit Manipulations   197

To invert bit *N*, from 0 to 1 or vice versa, these five statements suffice:

```
LH      2,BITN      R2=VALUE OF N
L       3,PATTERN   R3='1' IN POSITION #0
SRL     3,0(2)      MOVE '1' TO POSITION #N
X       3,STATUS    REVERSE BIT #N, PRESERVE OTHERS
ST      3,STATUS    PUT RESULT BACK INTO STATUS WORD
```

Trace these four situations for two different cases: (1) in which the *N*th bit is originally 0, and (2) in which it is originally 1.

Example 3.   Convert hex digits to EBCDIC codes
(See fig. 8.9.)

To print a hex digit on an IBM terminal or line printer, the digit must be represented in the EBCDIC character scheme. Each EBCDIC code requires 8 bits, whereas a hex digit requires only 4. Thus a full word of hex digits requires two words of EBCDIC bytes. This is shown in the accompanying diagrams, together with the EBCDIC code for each hex digit.

In this example, the goal is to convert a sequence of eight arbitrary hex digits into their EBCDIC codes. The program in figure 8.9 does this. Two things should be noticed in this solution: the use of the double logical left shift in Statement 13 to isolate a hex digit in a register, and simultaneously position the next hex digit for its eventual isolation; and (2) the use of the LA instruction in Statement 14 to compute the address of the correct EBCDIC byte, based on the numeric value of the hex digit.

The techniques used are illustrated by the trace given below, which assumes that the hex digits to be converted are X'C0F9A6B4'. The other assumptions are merely address assumptions, namely:

$$RESULT = 4020, \qquad EBCDIC = 4028$$

The program will work, however, for any hex digits and any valid addresses.

In the trace, the values shown are those that exist immediately *after* Statement 15 is executed during each iteration of the loop:

contents of registers shown in hex

iteration	Reg 2	Reg 3	Reg 6	Reg 7	Reg 8	bytes moved to RESULT
1st	4020	8	0000000C	0F9A6B40	4034	C3
2nd	4021	7	00000000	F9A6B400	4028	C3 F0
3rd	4022	6	0000000F	9A6B4000	4037	C3 F0 C6
4th	4023	5	00000009	A6B40000	4031	C3 F0 C6 F9
5th	4024	4	0000000A	6B400000	4032	C3 F0 C6 F9 C1
6th	4025	3	00000006	B4000000	402E	C3 F0 C6 F9 C1 F6
7th	4026	2	0000000B	40000000	4033	C3 F0 C6 F9 C1 F6 C2
8th	4027	1	00000004	00000000	402C	C3 F0 C6 F9 C1 F6 C2 F4

Figure 8.9 *Convert eight hex digits to EBCDIC codes.*

```
           .
           .
           .
1   * THIS SET OF STATEMENTS GENERATES EIGHT CONSECUTIVE BYTES IN
2   * EBCDIC CODE FORMAT CORRESPONDING TO EIGHT CONSECUTIVE HEX DIGITS.
3   *
4   * THE HEX DIGITS ARE ASSUMED TO BE IN THE FULL WORD NAMED ''DIGITS''
5   * THE EBCDIC BYTES ARE PLACED IN THE AREA NAMED ''RESULT.''
6   *
7           LA    1,EBCDIC         R1=ADDR OF EBCDIC CODE TABLE
8           LA    2,RESULT         R2=ADDR OF FIRST RESULT BYTE
9           L     3,=F'8'          R3=LOOP-CONTROL COUNTER
10          L     7,DIGITS         R7=HEX DIGITS
11  * GENERATE AN EBCDIC BYTE
12  NEXT    LH    6,=H'0'          R6 IS CLEARED, THEN NEXT HEX
13          SLDL  6,4                DIGIT IS SHIFTED INTO IT, AND
14          LA    8,0(6,1)           IS USED TO COMPUTE ADDR OF
15          MVC   0(1,2),0(8)        CORRESPONDING EBCDIC CODE.
16  * LOOP-CONTROL
17          LA    2,1(2)           ADJUST ADDR TO NEXT RESULT BYTE
18          BCT   3,NEXT           REPEAT TILL EIGHT DIGITS DONE
           .
           .
           .
19  DIGITS  DS    F                HEX DIGITS (FULLWORD) TO BE CONV
20  RESULT  DS    CL8              AREA FOR RESULT BYTES
21  EBCDIC  DC    C'0123456789ABCDEF'  EBCDIC CODES FOR HEX DIGITS
           .
           .
           .
```

The number in Register 8 that is computed by Statement 14,

$$LA \qquad 8,0(6,1)$$

is the address of the 8-bit EBCDIC code that corresponds to the hex digit in Register 6. For example, in the first iteration the hex digit is C. The LA instruction adds this to the number in Register 1, i.e., it adds it to the address of the beginning of the EBCDIC code table, 4028, and thereby generates the address of the desired 8-bit code: 4028 + C = 4034.

Example 4.   Translate from decimal to binary integer
            (See fig. 8.10.)

When data enter a computer's memory from an I/O device such as a terminal or card reader, they are stored in the format in which the device transmitted them. For IBM devices, this format is the EBCDIC code scheme. If the data are numeric, they must be translated into their appropriate internal format—binary integer, floating-point, or packed-decimal—before they can be used in arithmetic calculations. This example shows one way to translate a positive decimal integer from its EBCDIC representation to its internal binary integer format.

To understand the concepts involved, recall that a decimal integer's value is determined by means of the positional notation method:

$$1358 = 1 \times 10^3 + 3 \times 10^2 + 5 \times 10^1 + 8 \times 10^0$$
$$= 1000 \quad + 300 \quad + 50 \quad + 8$$

Figure 8.10 *Translating a nonnegative integer from EBCDIC to binary.*

```
         .
         .
         .
1    * THIS SET OF STATEMENTS TRANSLATES A NONNEGATIVE INTEGER
2    * FROM ITS EBCDIC REPRESENTATION TO ITS FULL-WORD BINARY REPRESENTATION
3    *
4    *
5    * THE EBCDIC REPRESENTATION IS ASSUMED TO BE EIGHT BYTES LONG, RIGHT-
6    *   JUSTIFIED, BEGINNING AT SYMBOLIC ADDRESS  ''INT10.''  IT MAY HAVE
7    *   LEADING ZEROES OR LEADING BLANKS
8    *
9    * THE RESULTING BINARY REPRESENTATION WILL BE STORED AT  'INT2'.
10   *
11   *     INITIALIZATION
12             LA     2,INT10X        R2 = ADDR OF LOW-ORDER BYTE
13             LA     3,P10           R3 = ADDR OF TABLE OF  10**N
14             LH     4,=H'8'         R4 = MAX # DIGITS TO BE TRANSLATED
15             LH     5,=H'0'         R5 = ACCUMULATED RESULT (INITIALLY ZERO)
16   *
17   NEXT      CLI    0(2),X'F0'      IF CURRENT BYTE VALUE NOT BETWEEN
18             BL     DONE            0 AND 9 (IN EBCDIC) THEN A LEADING
19             CLI    0(2),X'F9'      BLANK HAS BEEN REACHED.
20             BH     DONE
21   *                               MULTIPLY CURRENT DIGIT BY 10**N :
22             IC     7,0(2)            PUT EBCDIC DIGIT INTO ODD-NUMBERED
23             N      7,PATTERN         REGISTER, AND REMOVE ITS ZONE BITS.
24             M      6,0(3)          THEN MPY BY CURRENT POWER OF  10,  AND
25             AR     5,7             ADD PRODUCT TO RESULT IN REG 5.
26   *
27             SH     2,=H'+1'        FOR LOOP CONTROL, ADJUST BYTE ADDRESS
28             AH     3,=H'+4'        TO NEXT DIGIT, AND TABLE ADDR TO NEXT
29             BCT    4,NEXT          10**N;  THEN REPEAT UP TO EIGHT TIMES.
30   *
31   DONE      ST     5,INT2          SAVE RESULTING BINARY INTEGER
                 .
                 .
                 .
32   INT2      DS     F               BINARY INTEGER RESULT (FULL WORD)
33   INT10     DS     CL8             EIGHT EBCDIC DIGITS, RIGHT-JUSTIFIED
34   INT10X    EQU    *-1             ADDR OF LEAST SIGNIFICANT EBCDIC DIGIT
35   PATTERN   DC     X'0000000F'     MASK PRESERVES RIGHT-MOST FOUR BITS
36   *
37   P10       DC     F'1,10,100,1000'       TABLE OF POWERS OF 10,  I.E.
38             DC     F'1E4,1E5,1E6,1E7'     10**N  FOR  N = 0,1,2,...,7
                 .
                 .
                 .
```

In EBCDIC format, the number 1358 is represented as a 4-byte binary quantity whose hex representation is

and whose binary representation is

1111 0001	1111 0011	1111 0101	1111 1000

To convert this to a binary integer, these steps must be followed:

1. The so-called *zone bits* 1111 of the EBCDIC scheme must be removed for each digit.
2. The remaining bits of each digit, i.e., the bits that represent each digit in binary form, must be multiplied by the appropriate power of 10.
3. Each of the products in Step 2 must be added together to form the binary integer result.

For the number 1358, this works as follows:

Step 1: $\underbrace{1111\ 0001}$ $\underbrace{1111\ 0011}$ $\underbrace{1111\ 0101}$ $\underbrace{1111\ 1000}$

                0001   0011   0101   1000

Step 2: Since $10^3 = 0011\ 1110\ 1000$ in binary
$10^2 = 0110\ 0100$ in binary
$10^1 = 1010$ in binary
$10^0 = 0001$ in binary

then, for the number 1358,

$1 \times 10^3 = 0001 \times 0011\ 1110\ 1000 = 0011\ 1110\ 1000 = \text{3E8 in hex}$
$3 \times 10^2 = 0011 \times 0110\ 0100 = 0001\ 0010\ 1100 = \text{12C in hex}$
$5 \times 10^1 = 0101 \times 1010 = 0011\ 0010 = \text{32 in hex}$
$8 \times 10^0 = 1000 \times 0001 = 1000 = \text{8 in hex}$

Step 3: The resulting binary integer is the sum of the products just formed, namely 0101 0100 1110, or 54E in hex.

This three-step procedure forms the basis for the programming solution in figure 8.10. However, there is one main difference between the program's design and the three steps: the program does the three steps for each digit in turn, *accumulating* the sum of Step 3 as it goes, and processing the digits from *right to left* (low-order to high-order). A maximum of eight digits is allowed; the program stops when it reaches this limit or when it finds a nondigit character such as a blank in the EBCDIC representation.

Let us illustrate how the program works, with a trace for the number 1358. We make the following address assumption:

$$\text{INT10} = 4000_{16}$$

All other addresses shown in the trace can be derived from this one. In the trace, the numbers shown are those that exist *immediately after Statement 25 is executed* during each iteration of the loop.

contents of registers shown in hexadecimal

iteration	Reg 2	Reg 3	Reg 4	Reg 5	Reg 6	Reg 7
1st	4007	400C	8	0000 0008	0	0000 0008
2nd	4006	4010	7	0000 003A	0	0000 0032
3rd	4005	4014	6	0000 0166	0	0000 012C
4th	4004	4018	5	0000 054E	0	0000 03E8

At this point the program has completed its calculations, the result being in Register 5.

There are several things to notice about the program:

1. The number 1358 is assumed to exist in symbolic location INT10, i.e., memory location 4000, like this:

40	40	40	40	F1	F3	F5	F8

The program, however, will work equally well for any positive integer that contains no more than 8 digits.

2. The digits are processed right to left, so the initial address in Register 2, namely 4007, is the address of the right-most digit. This address is decreased by 1 in Statement 27, once during each iteration of the loop. This decrease allows the right-to-left processing.

3. Statement 22 places the current EBCDIC digit in Register 7, and Statement 23 removes all but the low-order 4 bits from Register 7.

4. Statement 24 multiplies the low-order 4 bits of the current digit by the appropriate power of 10, as was done in the hand calculations of Step 2. Statement 24 gets the appropriate power of 10 from the table located at symbolic address P10; this table is accessed via Register 3.
5. Statement 25 adds the result of the multiplication to the sum being accumulated in Register 5.

Because we frequently need to convert a number from EBCDIC format to binary integer format, the instruction set of the IBM 360 and 370 systems contains two instructions designed for this purpose. These are the PACK and CVB instructions, which were briefly introduced in chapter 4 and will be discussed more extensively in chapter 12. Correspondingly, we can perform the reverse translation from binary integer to EBCDIC format with the CVD instruction, in conjunction with either the UNPK, the ED, or the EDMK instructions. See chapter 12 for the necessary details.

8.6 SUMMARY

The instructions classified as bit-manipulation instructions are summarized in figure 8.11. Since individual bits are not addressable in the IBM 360 and 370 systems, all but two of the instructions must specify the address of a register and/or memory location that contains the bits to be operated on. The two exceptions are the BC and BCR instructions. In these, the bits that are tested are not explicitly addressed; instead they are always understood to be the two condition code bits.

The eight shift instructions are distinguished from one another by the direction of the shift (right or left), the length and location of the quantity being shifted (32 bits in any general register, or 64 bits in an even-odd pair of registers), and the manner in which the sign bit and the result are handled (arithmetically or logically). *Logical shifts* are useful in separating and linking bit strings, as in the examples of figures 8.8 and 8.9. Logical shifts treat the sign bit the same as any other bit and do not set the condition code. *Arithmetic shifts* are useful in situations where the sign bit must be propagated, for example in extending a full-word integer to a double-word representation; they are also useful as a means of multiplying or dividing by powers of two. Arithmetic right shifts cause the sign bit to be propagated to the right; arithmetic left shifts compare the sign bit (bit 0) to each bit shifted out of bit position 1 and set the condition code to 3 (overflow) if any such pair of bits is unequal. Except in the case of overflow, arithmetic shifts set the condition code to 0, 1, or 2, depending on whether the result is zero, negative, or positive, respectively.

The Boolean instructions OR, AND, and EXCLUSIVE-OR allow individual bits to be set to 1, reset to 0, or inverted. The address of the register or memory location containing the bits must be specified in the instruction, and the bits to be set or reset must be selected by a mask field. The mask field is in a general register when an RR-type Boolean instruction is used; it is in a memory location when an RX- or SS_1-type Boolean instruction is used; and it is in the immediate data field for SI-type instructions. Boolean instructions are especially useful for the control of bits that represent the occurrence of events or other status information.

Of the two bit-testing instructions Test Under Mask (TM) and Test and Set (TS), the TM is more frequently used because it allows the setting of one or more bits in a byte to be tested. The TS tests only the left-most bit of a byte, and, unlike the TM, it sets all the bits in that byte to 1's. Both TM and TS set the condition code, so that the result of the test can be determined by a conditional branch instruction.

The BC and BCR instructions test the current setting of the condition code and branch if the setting matches one of the settings designated in the mask field of the instruction. Since the condition code records the nature of the result of the most recently executed code-setting instruction, as defined in figure 8.5, the BC and BCR instructions provide the means by which conditional branches (IF-type instructions) are executed at run time. The so-called extended mnemonic opcodes—BE, BER, BZ, BZR, etc.—are nothing but convenient abbreviations, as it were, of particular BC or BCR instructions. It is the mask field contents, not the machine language opcode, that distinguish one RX- or RR-type extended mnemonic instruction from another.

Figure 8.11 **Summary of bit manipulation instructions.**

opcode	name	type	section	condition codes	summary of action taken
BC	Branch on Condition	RX	8.4		branches to addr of V_2, if cond. codes selected by M1
BCR	Branch on Condition via Register	RR	8.4		branches to addr in R1, if cond. codes selected by M1
N	AND	RX	8.2	0,1	V_1 replaced by AND of V_1 and V_2 (32 bits)
NC	AND Characters	SS$_1$	8.2	0,1	V_1 replaced by AND of V_1 and V_2 (L bytes, $L \leq 256$)
NI	AND Immediate	SI	8.2	0,1	V_1 replaced by AND of V_1 and I2 (1 byte)
NR	AND Registers	RR	8.2	0,1	V_1 replaced by AND of V_1 and V_2 (32 bits)
O	OR	RX	8.2	0,1	V_1 replaced by OR of V_1 and V_2 (32 bits)
OC	OR Characters	SS$_1$	8.2	0,1	V_1 replaced by OR of V_1 and V_2 (L bytes, $L \leq 256$)
OI	OR Immediate	SI	8.2	0,1	V_1 replaced by OR of V_1 and I2 (1 byte)
OR	OR Registers	RR	8.2	0,1	V_1 replaced by OR of V_1 and V_2 (32 bits)
SLA	Shift Left Single Arithmetic	RS	8.1	0,1,2,3	V_1 arithmetically shifted left N bits, $N \leq 31$
SLDA	Shift Left Double Arithmetic	RS	8.1	0,1,2,3	V_1 arithmetically shifted left N bits, $N \leq 63$
SLDL	Shift Left Double Logical	RS	8.1		V_1 logically shifted left N bits, $N \leq 63$
SLL	Shift Left Single Logical	RS	8.1		V_1 logically shifted left N bits, $N \leq 31$
SRA	Shift Right Single Arithmetic	RS	8.1	0,1,2	V_1 arithmetically shifted right N bits, $N \leq 31$
SRDA	Shift Right Double Arithmetic	RS	8.1	0,1,2	V_1 arithmetically shifted right N bits, $N \leq 63$
SRDL	Shift Right Double Logical	RS	8.1		V_1 logically shifted right N bits, $N \leq 63$
SRL	Shift Right Single Logical	RS	8.1		V_1 logically shifted right N bits, $N \leq 31$
TM	Test under Mask	SI	8.3	0,1,3	tests bits in V_1 selected by M1 mask field
TS	Test and Set	S	8.3	0,1	tests high-order bit of V_1 and sets all V_1 bits to 1
X	EXCLUSIVE-OR	RX	8.2	0,1	V_1 replaced by EXCL-OR of V_1 and V_2 (32 bits)
XC	EXCLUSIVE-OR Characters	SS$_1$	8.2	0,1	V_1 replaced by EXCL-OR of V_1 and V_2 (L bytes, $L \leq 256$)
XI	EXCLUSIVE-OR Immediate	SI	8.2	0,1	V_1 replaced by EXCL-OR of V_1 and I2 (1 byte)
XR	EXCLUSIVE-OR Registers	RR	8.2	0,1	V_1 replaced by EXCL-OR of V_1 and V_2 (32 bits)

Note: V_1 denotes the quantity whose address is specified via the first operand of the instruction; V_2 denotes the quantity whose address is specified via the second operand.

SAMPLE PROBLEM
AND SOLUTION

PROBLEM STATEMENT

Write a program that will read an arbitrary number of input data cards, and print an encoded version of them, one line per data card. The encoded version is to be obtained by interchanging the high-order four bits in each EBCDIC character with the low-order four bits of that character, and then inverting each of the four new high-order bits. For example, the letter 'A' is represented as hexadecimal C1 (1100 0001) in the input data and would be encoded to hexadecimal EC (1110 1100) since X'C1' becomes X'1C' when the high- and low-order bits are interchanged, and then the four new high-order bits, 0001, when inverted become 1110.

This encoding scheme has the advantage of being simple to implement and of being invertible; it has the disadvantage of being exceptionally easy to decipher.

SOLUTION PROCEDURE

The procedure for each input data card that is read is to encode each character in a register, using the SHIFT, OR, and EXCLUSIVE-OR instructions, and then move the encoded character to its appropriate position in the output line area. When all the characters of a given input data card have been encoded and moved to the output area, the line is printed.

Note that some of the encoded characters may not be among those that are printable, as described in figure 7.1 of the preceding chapter. In that case, the printer or terminal will most likely print a blank in the character's stead. Some printers, however, will not print anything (i.e., the unprintable character will be treated as a null character), and some printers will not accept the unprintable character, causing the program to be terminated with an output data error. You will have to determine what the response of your printer or terminal is by running the program solution given in figure 8.12b.

Figure 8.12a *Overview of sample problem solution procedure.*

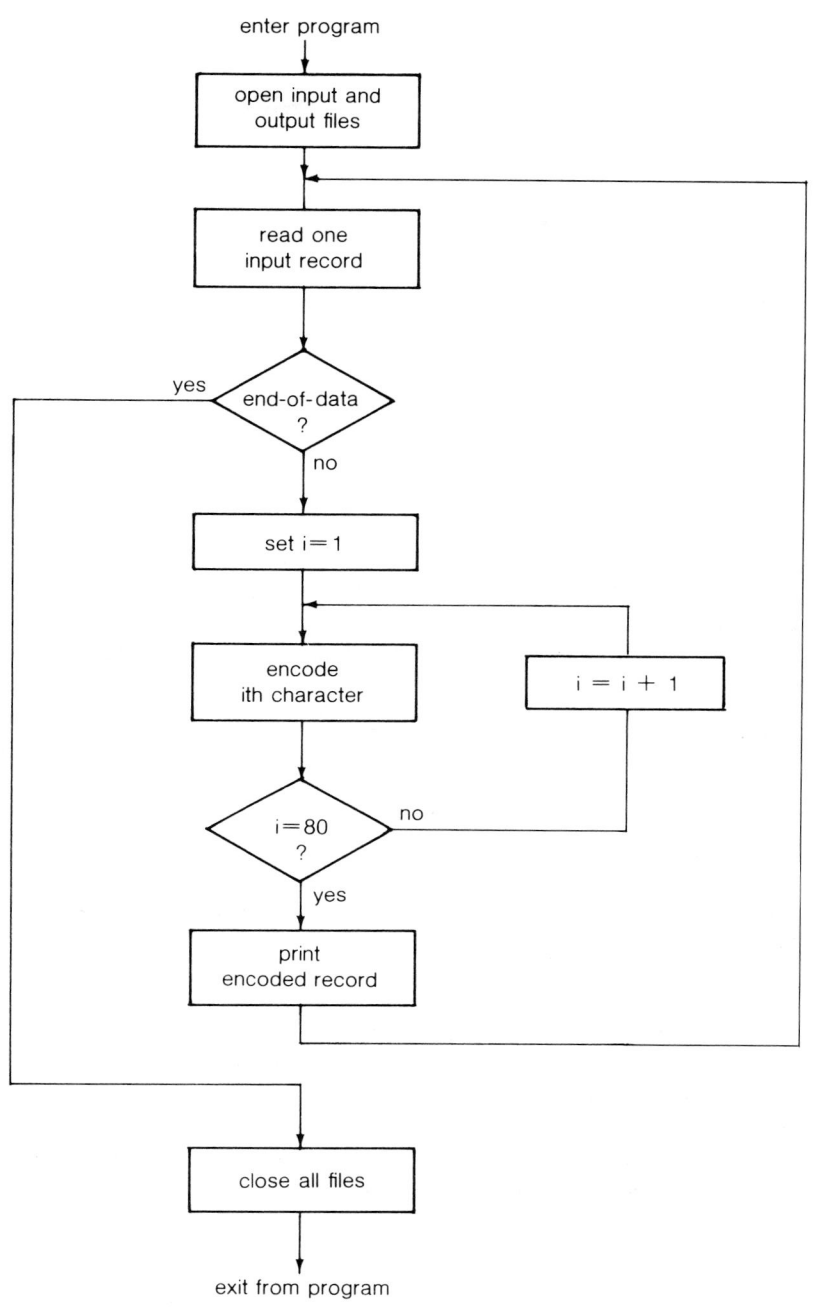

Figure 8.12b Solution to sample problem.

```
FLAG LOCTN OBJECT CODE     ADDR1  ADDR2  STMNT M SOURCE STATEMENT

     000000                              3      SPCH8    CSECT
                                         4      *
                                         5      * SPCH8   READS AN ARBITRARY NUMBER OF INPUT DATA CARDS
                                         6      *    AND PRINTS AN ENCODED VERSION OF THEM, ONE CARD PER LINE.
                                         7      *
                                         8      *    THE ENCODED VERSION IS OBTAINED BY INTERCHANGING THE HIGH-ORDER
                                         9      *    FOUR BITS WITH THE LOW ORDER FOUR BITS OF EACH EBCDIC CHARACTER
                                        10      *    AND THEN INVERTING EACH OF THE FOUR NEW HIGH-ORDER BITS.
                                        11      *
                                        12      *    E.G., THE LETTER 'A' IS X'C1' AND WOULD BECOME X'EC',
                                        13      *    SINCE X'C1' IS FIRST TRANSFORMED TO X'1C', AND
                                        14      *    THEN THE '1' (B'0001') IS TRANSFORMED INTO 'E' (B'1110').
                                        15      *
     000000 90 EC D00C                  16               STM   14,12,12(13)       STANDARD ENTRY
     000004 05 C0                       17               BALR  12,0
     000006                             18               USING *,12
     000006 50 D0 C22E      000234      19               ST    13,SAVE+4
     00000A 41 D0 C22A      000230      20               LA    13,SAVE
                                        21      *
                                        22      * OPEN INPUT AND OUTPUT FILES
                                        23      *
     00000E                             24               OPEN  (SYSIN,(INPUT))    INPUT IS 'SYSIN' DATA STREAM
     00001A                             30               OPEN  (SYSPRNT,(OUTPUT)) OUTPUT IS 'SYSOUT' PRINTER

                                        36      *  DOS  *******
                                        37      *        OPEN  SYSIN
                                        38      *        OPEN  SYSPRNT
                                        39      ****************

                                        40      *
                                        41      * MAIN PROCESSING LOOP ...
                                        42      *        READS AN INPUT DATA CARD
                                        43      *        TRANSFORMS IT AS DESCRIBED IN COMMENTS ABOVE
                                        44      *        WRITES THE TRANSFORMED DATA ONTO PRINTER FILE
                                        45      *        CONTINUES READING, TRANSFORMING, AND WRITING TILL END-OF-DATA
                                        46      *        END-OF-DATA ROUTINE IS AT 'EOD', JUST TO TERMINATE PROGRAM.
                                        47      *
     000026                             48      LOOP     GET   SYSIN,INAREA       GET AN INPUT DATA CARD
                                        53      *
     000034 41 50 C096      00009C      54               LA    5,INAREA           INITIALIZE CHARACTER ADDRESS
     000038 58 60 C272      000278      55               L     6,=F'80'           INITIALIZE CHARACTER COUNT
                                        56      *
                                        57      * TRANSFORM EACH INPUT CHARACTER ONE AT A TIME
                                        58      *
     00003C 58 80 C276      00027C      59      TRANS    L     8,=F'0'            CLEAR R8 TO ZEROS
                                        60      *
     000040 43 85 0000      000000      61               IC    8,0(5)             R8 BITS 24-31 GET EBCDIC BITS 0-7.
     000044 88 80 0004      000004      62               SRL   8,4                RIGHT SHIFT PUTS EBCDIC BITS 0-3 INTO
                                        63      *                                 R8 BITS 28-31 AND 0'S INTO R8 BITS 24-27
                                        64      *
     000048 43 95 0000      000000      65               IC    9,0(5)             R9 BITS 24-31 GET EBCDIC BITS 0-7.
     00004C 89 90 0004      000004      66               SLL   9,4                LEFT SHIFT PUTS EBCDIC BITS 4-7 INTO
                                        67      *                                 R9 BITS 24-27 AND 0'S INTO R9 BITS 28-31
                                        68      *
     000050 16 89                       69               OR    8,9                R8 BITS 24-27 GET EBCDIC BITS 4-7 FROM R9.
                                        70      *
     000052 42 85 0000      000000      71               STC   8,0(5)             STORE REPLACES EBCDIC BITS 0-3 & 4-7
                                        72      *                                 WITH EBCDIC BITS 4-7 & 0-3, RESPECTVLY.
                                        73      *
     000056 97 F0 5000                  74               XI    0(5),X'F0'         INVERT NEW EBCDIC BITS 0-3 IN MEMORY
                                        75      *
     00005A 41 55 0001      000001      76               LA    5,1(5)             INCR TO NEXT CHAR
     00005E 46 60 C036      00003C      77               BCT   6,TRANS            REPEAT TILL NO MORE CHARS
                                        78      *
                                        79      * COPY INPUT DATA TO OUTPUT LINE AND PRINT IT
                                        80      *
     000062 D2 4F C0F0C096 0000F6 00009C 81             MVC   OUTLINE,INAREA
     000068                             82               PUT   SYSPRNT,OUTAREA
     000076 47 F0 C020      000026      87               B     LOOP
                                        88      *
                                        89      * END-OF-DATA TRANSFERS CONTROL HERE TO TERMINATE PROGRAM.
                                        90      *
     00007A                             91      EOD      CLOSE (SYSIN)
     000086                             97               CLOSE (SYSPRNT)
     000092 58 D0 C22E      000234      103              L     13,SAVE+4          STANDARD EXIT
     000096 98 EC D00C                  104              LM    14,12,12(13)
     00009A 07 FE                       105              BR    14

                                        106     *  DOS  *******
                                        107     *EOD      CLOSE SYSIN
                                        108     *        CLOSE SYSPRNT
                                        109     *        EOJ
                                        110     ****************

                                        111     *
                                        112     * INPUT CARD AREA
                                        113     *
     00009C                             114     INAREA   DS    0CL80              INPUT AREA DEFINITION ...
     00009C                             115              DS    CL80               COLS 1-80  INPUT CARD
```

Figure 8.12b   *continued*

```
                                        116   *
                                        117   * OUTPUT PRINT AREA
                                        118   *
      0000EC                            119   OUTAREA  DS    0CL132              OUTPUT AREA DEFINITION ...
      0000EC  40404040404040404040      120            DC    CL10' '             COLS 1-10   BLANKS
      0000F6                            121   OUTLINE  DS    CL80                      11-90   INPUT DATA
      000146  40404040404040            122            DC    CL42' '                   91-132  BLANKS
                                        123   *
                                        124   *
                                        125   * DCB'S FOR INPUT AND OUTPUT FILES
                                        126   *
      000170                            127   SYSIN    DCB   DSORG=PS,MACRF=(GM),DDNAME=SYSIN,EODAD=EOD,        X
                                        128            RECFM=FB,LRECL=80,BLKSIZE=4080
                                        180   *
      0001D0                            181   SYSPRNT  DCB   DSORG=PS,MACRF=(PM),DDNAME=SYSPRINT,               X
                                        182            RECFM=FB,LRECL=132,BLKSIZE=4092
                                        234   *  DOS  *******
                                        235   *SYSIN    DTFCD DEVADDR=SYSIPT,WORKA=YES,IOAREA1=INBUF,EOFADDR=EOD,  X
                                        236   *          DEVICE=2540
                                        237   *SYSPRNT DTFPR DEVADDR=SYSLST,WORKA=YES,IOAREA1=OUTBUF,BLKSIZE=132,  X
                                        238   *          DEVICE=1403
                                        239   *
                                        240   *INBUF    DS    CL80
                                        241   *OUTBUF   DC    CL132' '
                                        242   ***************
                                        243   *
                                        244   * SAVE AREA
                                        245   *
      000230                            246   SAVE     DS    18F
                                        247   *  DOS  *******
                                        248   *SAVE     DS    9D
                                        249   ***************
                                        250   * LITERALS
      000278  00000050                  252                  =F'80'
      00027C  00000000                  253                  =F'0'
                                        254            END
```

CROSS-REFERENCE

```
SYMBOL    LEN    VALUE   DEFN    REFERENCES

EOD       00004  00007C  00093   00149
INAREA    00050  00009C  00114   00050  00054  00081
LOOP      00004  000026  00049   00087
OUTAREA   00084  0000EC  00119   00084
OUTLINE   00050  0000F6  00121   00081
SAVE      00004  000230  00246   00019  00020  00103
SPCH8     00001  000000  00003
SYSIN     00004  000170  00128   00028  00049  00095
SYSPRNT   00004  0001D0  00182   00034  00083  00101
TRANS     00004  00003C  00059   00077
```

EXERCISES

1. What would be the contents of Registers 6 and 7 after each of the following shift instructions was executed? Assume that *before* each instruction is executed, the contents of Registers 6 and 7 are as follows:

   Reg 6: X'01234567'   Reg 7: X'89ABCDEF'

a.	SRA	6,4	**e.**	SLA	6,6	**i.**	SLDL	6,63
b.	SRA	7,8	**f.**	SLDA	6,6	**j.**	SRDL	6,63
c.	SRL	6,4	**g.**	SLL	6,8	**k.**	SLL	7,31
d.	SRL	7,8	**h.**	SLDL	6,8	**l.**	SRDA	6,32

2. Assume that before each of the following instructions is executed, the contents of the memory location whose symbolic address is Y is as follows:

$$Y \quad DC \quad X'0189'$$

What would be the contents of location Y after each of the following instructions was executed?

a. NI	Y,X'F0'	**e.** XC	Y,=X'0189'	**i.** NC	Y,=X'FFFF'
b. NI	Y,X'00'	**f.** OC	Y,=X'0189'	**j.** OC	Y,=X'FFFF'
c. OI	Y,X'F0'	**g.** NC	Y,=X'FF00'	**k.** XC	Y,=X'FFFF'
d. OI	Y,X'0F'	**h.** XC	Y,=X'FF00'	**l.** XI	Y,X'89'

3. Suppose that, as in chapter 5, we represent the kth bit in a register with the symbol b_k, $k = 0,1,2,...,31$, where b_0 represents the sign bit. Then the contents of a register can be represented as $b_0b_1b_2...b_{31}$. Write a sequence of instructions that will interchange bits $b_0b_1... b_n$ of a register with bits $b_{n+1}b_{n+2}...b_{31}$, for any n such that $0 \leq n \leq 30$. For example, if the register contents exist as

$$0000\ 0001\ 0010\ 0011\ 0100\ 0101\ 0110\ 0111$$

and if $n = 15$, then the resulting register contents would be

$$0100\ 0101\ 0110\ 0111\ 0000\ 0001\ 0010\ 0011$$

4. It is sometimes desirable to convert a byte string to some other byte string, in such a manner that reconversion to the original string is possible. This is known as *encoding* the original string, the reconversion being *decoding*. Assume that an arbitrary byte string (of length less than or equal to 256 bytes) exists at the memory location whose symbolic address is STR. The string's length is stored as a half-word integer at location LNG.

For each of the following encoding schemes, write a sequence of instructions that will replace the string at STR with its encoded version. Also, for each of the schemes write a sequence of instructions that will decode the encoded version of a string.

   a. Interchange bits 0–3 of each byte with bits 4–7 of that byte.
   b. Shift the entire string right 4 bits, with the original right-most 4 bits becoming the new left-most 4 bits.
   c. Generate the bit-by-bit complement of each byte in the string.
   d. For each 4 consecutive bytes in the string, generate the complement of just those bits whose relative positions correspond to the 1's in an arbitrary full-word integer. If when the string's length is divided by 4, the remainder is $N \neq 0$, then use the first N bytes of the integer to encode the last N bytes of the string.
   e. For each K consecutive bytes in the original string, generate the complement of just those bits whose relative positions correspond to the 1's in an arbitrary K-byte string. If, when the original string's length is divided by K, the remainder *is* $N \neq 0$, use the first N bytes of the arbitrary K-byte string to encode the last N bytes of the original string.

5. Write a sequence of instructions that will determine the relative position, k ($k = 0,1,2,...,31$), of the left-most 1-bit in any nonzero full-word integer, and store the result as a 1-byte nonnegative integer whose value is $4*k$. For example, if the arbitrary full-word integer is

$$0000\ 0001\ 0010\ 0011\ 0100\ 0101\ 0110\ 0111$$

then $k = 7$, and the 1-byte result is 0001 1100.

6. Rewrite the program statements given in figure 8.10 so that if the value of the decimal integer $d_0d_1d_2...d_7$ (where d_n is a decimal digit) is

$$d_0 \times 10^7 + d_1 \times 10^6 + ... + d_6 \times 10^1 + d_7 \times 10^0$$

then your conversion algorithm computes this value by effectively grouping terms and performing the arithmetic as follows:

$$(...((d_0 \times 10 + d_1) \times 10 + d_2) \times 10 + ... + d_6) \times 10 + d_7$$

7. Suppose there exists an arbitrary bit string of 1024 bits (32 full words) at the memory location whose symbolic address is BITS. Write assembly language statements that can be used to search this bit string for all occurrences of a 4-bit string given (right-justified) in location PAT, and replace each occurrence with a 4-bit string of all 0's.

8. Suppose, as in Exercise 7, that an arbitrary 1024-bit string exists at symbolic address BITS. Write the assembly language statements that can be used to replace each occurrence of m consecutive 0's—for any m such that $8 \leq m \leq 256$—with 16 bits, the first 8 of which are all 0's, and the last 8 of which are the binary representation of $m-1$. For example, if the original string consisted of 1024 0's, the resulting string would consist of just 64 bits, as follows:

$$00000000 \quad 11111111 \quad 00000000 \quad 11111111 \quad 00000000 \ldots 11111111$$

9. Suppose that a bit string has been transformed by the procedure described in Exercise 8, and that the transformed string is at symbolic address NEWBITS, its length (in numbers of bits) being stored as a half-word integer at symbolic address NEWLNG. Write the assembly language statements that can be used to recreate the original bit string from the transformed string.

10. In the IBM 360 and 370 systems, main memory addresses that end in three hex zeroes are said to define a page boundary. A main memory page consists of 4096 ($=1000_{16}$) consecutive bytes, beginning at a page boundary. Since main memory addresses consist of 24 bits, each page is identified by the high-order 12 bits of its page boundary address. This quantity is known as the page number. If there are $4 \times N \times 2^{10}$ bytes of main memory, then there are N pages of main memory ($N = 1,2,\ldots,4096$).

   Suppose that $N = 1024$—a 4 megabyte main memory—and suppose that an N-bit string has been defined so that there is a one-to-one correspondence between bits of the string and pages of main memory, bit k corresponding to page k. Suppose also that when bit k is a 0, page k is not in use at the moment, and that when k is a 1, page k is in use by some program.

   a. Write the assembly language statements that will count the number of pages that are not in use at any given moment.
   b. Write assembly language statements that will change the status bit for page k to "in use," for any k such that $0 \leq k \leq 1023$.
   c. Write assembly language statements that will change the status bit for page k to "not in use."
   d. Write assembly language statements that will determine the largest page number, m, such that page m is not in use.

11. In the terminology of Exercise 10, suppose that instead of an N-bit string that records the status of each main memory page as being "in use" or "not in use," there is an N-byte string that records the status of each memory page, one byte per page. Assume that the bits of each page-status byte have the following meaning:

Bit 0	0 = "not in use,"	1 = "in use"
Bit 1	0 = "system page,"	1 = "user page"
Bit 2	0 = "read-only page,"	1 = "writeable page"
Bit 3	(not used for any purpose)	
Bits 4–7	4-bit priority number, 0000–1111_2	

   a. Write the assembly language statements that will count the number of user pages with priority number greater than eight that are not in use at any given moment.
   b. Write assembly language statements that will determine the largest page number, m, such that page m is a "read-only user page" that has a priority number greater than eight and is not in use.
   c. Write assembly language statements that will determine the number of user pages that are read-only and the number that are writeable.
   d. Write assembly language statements that will determine how many in-use pages exist for each of the sixteen possible priority numbers.

9
Subroutines

A *subroutine* is a set of statements written to perform some task at the request of a computer program. Although subroutine statements may be contained within the requesting program, they need not be. In the former case, we speak of an *internal* subroutine, in the latter, of an *external* subroutine. Alternate names used to denote the concept of a subroutine are subprogram and procedure. In this text, we will use the term *subroutine*, the prefix *sub-* meaning "subordinate to the requesting program," and the word *routine* being synonymous with the idea of a "method of performing a commonly needed task."

What might constitute a commonly needed task? This very brief list indicates the variety, generality, and scope of subroutines.

1. *Numeric calculations,* such as computing the square root of any positive number, finding the solution to a system of linear algebraic equations, and computing the mean value and standard deviation of an arbitrary set of numbers
2. *String manipulations,* such as finding and correcting all instances of a misspelled word in a paragraph or inserting a word or phrase at a particular point in a sentence
3. *Data conversions,* such as converting an integer from its internal binary representation to a form suitable for printing in decimal notation, with leading zeroes replaced by blanks
4. *Form conversions,* such as converting an arbitrary set of numeric data into a bar graph or into a two-dimensional *x-y* plot

A subroutine, which always produces specific results for specific data, is usually written in such a way that it is capable of producing results for a wide range of data values. Therefore, we can say that *a subroutine is a general programming solution to a specific problem.* Through use of subroutines, we can divide a problem into a number of manageably small and related sub-problems, each with its own programming solution.

The primary purpose of this chapter is to explain the requirements for interfacing a program to a subroutine and to explain how these requirements are conventionally programmed in Assembly Language in the IBM 360 and 370 systems. The discussion will be oriented to external subroutines. Terminology and the linkage requirements are described in Sections 9.1 and 9.2; the linkage conventions used with external subroutines in the IBM 360 and 370 are described in Section 9.3. Reasons for the use of the conventions are summarized in Section 9.4, and further aspects of the use of subroutines are given in Section 9.7. Internal subroutines are discussed briefly in Section 9.5, and the techniques of establishing more than one implied base register are in Section 9.6.

9.1 TERMINOLOGY AND LINKAGE REQUIREMENTS

Since only closed subroutines will be discussed in this chapter, we should, at the outset, distinguish between closed and open subroutines. A *closed* subroutine is one written in such a way that a single copy of it is all that is required, no matter how many places it is used in a program. An *open* subroutine, in contrast, is one that must be inserted at each place it is used in a program.

Figure 9.1 *Calling and called programs.*

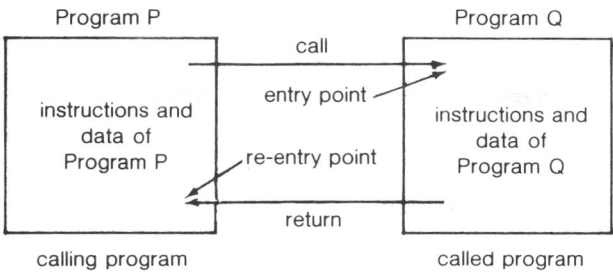

Figure 9.2 *Sequence of called programs.*

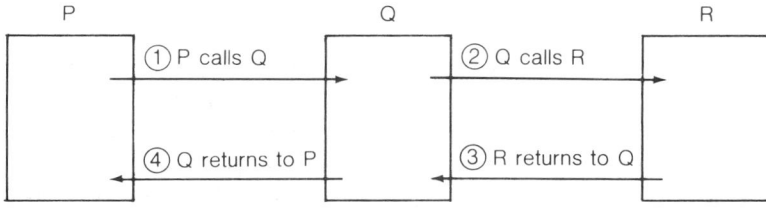

When a program requests that a subroutine perform a task, it is said to *call* that subroutine. The program making the request is known as the *calling program,* whereas the subroutine requested to perform the task is known as the *called program.* The address of the first instruction executed by a subroutine when it is called is known as the subroutine's *entry point.* Correspondingly, the address of the instruction to which a subroutine branches when it returns to a calling program is known as the calling program's *reentry point.*

These concepts are depicted in figure 9.1. There is no restriction on the number of times one program may call another, nor is there any restriction on the number of different places within a program from which a call may be made to another program. In addition, a called program may, in turn, call another program. If it does so, it becomes the calling program for that encounter. However, a called program normally returns to the program that called it. For example, in the sequence of figure 9.2, P calls Q and, before it returns to P, Q calls R; after R returns to Q, Q can return to P.

Since a closed subroutine can be called from any number of different places within a program, there needs to be some mechanism by which the calling program can specify the appropriate reentry point to which the subroutine will return. Moreover, since each subroutine is assumed to be written as a general solution to a particular problem, there needs to be some mechanism by which the calling program can specify the data that the subroutine is to operate on and the memory areas that are to be used for the results. These last two types of information—the data and the areas for the results—are the values of the subroutine's *parameters,* i.e., the values of the variables that must be specified when the subroutine is called, without which the subroutine cannot perform its task satisfactorily. The calling program is said to *pass* the values of the parameters to the subroutine.

It should be noted that the parameter values must be passed in the exact order the subroutine expects to receive them. Moreover, the data must be of the type expected by the subroutine—integer, character data, etc.—and the areas reserved for the results must be consistent with the type and number of results. In short, the design of a subroutine determines the nature of the information that is passed to that subroutine. The programmer cannot write a program to call a subroutine unless he or she knows the number and types of data and results to specify, and the order in which to specify them. The programmer usually determines these things by reading the documentation about the subroutine.

We may summarize the discussion by saying that, in order to call a closed subroutine, certain requirements must be met. These requirements are known as the *linkage requirements,* since they are what is needed to interface, or link, a calling program to a called program. The linkage requirements are: (1) passing the values of the parameters, (2) passing the address of the reentry point, and (3) branching to the entry point.

Figure 9.3   Memory addresses assigned by the Assembler.

The mechanism by which these requirements are met is known as the *calling sequence,* a set of statements in the calling program that fulfill the requirements. In many computer systems, the calling sequence has been standardized, especially for calls to external subroutines. The standard calling sequence in the IBM 360 and 370 Assembly Language, together with standard procedures to be followed within subroutines, will be described in Section 9.3. These standards, known as the *linkage conventions*, depend on certain addressing considerations.

9.2   ADDRESSING AND ADDRESS CONSTANTS

Two facts about the execution of computer programs should be abundantly clear at this point: (1) whenever data is to be obtained from or placed into memory, the address of the memory location of that data must be specified via the operand of the instruction; and (2) whenever one instruction is to branch to another instruction, the address of the new instruction must be specified via the operand of the branch instruction.

In machine language, a memory address is an unsigned integer that denotes the number of bytes from the beginning of the real, hardware main memory of the computer. The beginning of real main memory is a particular byte designated by the hardware designers as having an address of zero. However, a programmer is rarely concerned with real memory and real memory addresses. Instead, his or her concern is primarily with the set of memory addresses assigned to a program by the Assembler. These addresses will ultimately be transformed, or mapped, into real memory addresses by the combined actions of the Operating System and the CPU, but, until that happens, they do not refer to physical locations in main memory. Therefore, although two programs may be assigned the same memory addresses at assembly time, there will be no conflict when they are run because their respective addresses can be mapped into different real memory addresses.

The distinction between the set of addresses assigned at assembly time and the set of real memory addresses into which these are mapped is important because it enables programmers to write programs independent of one another without worrying about memory address conflicts. For example, if Program P has an instruction that, when assembled, branches to memory address 000500, that means address 000500 in Program P, and that particular address is independent of address 000500 in any other program. Nor is it necessarily address 000500 in real memory.

We can say that the addresses assigned to a program at assembly time are *internal* to that program. We can also say that addresses that are internal to one program are *external* to all other programs. Figure 9.3 shows the addresses assigned to two programs, Program P and Program Q, that were assembled separately from one another. The Assembler assigned addresses beginning at zero for each program; all addresses assigned in Q are external to those assigned in P (and vice versa). This obviously means that if an instruction in Q branches to address 10, that instruction refers to address 10 in Q only, not to address 10 in P. Clearly, some addresses in Q conflict with (are identical with) some addresses in P.

Figure 9.4 Memory addresses in a load module.

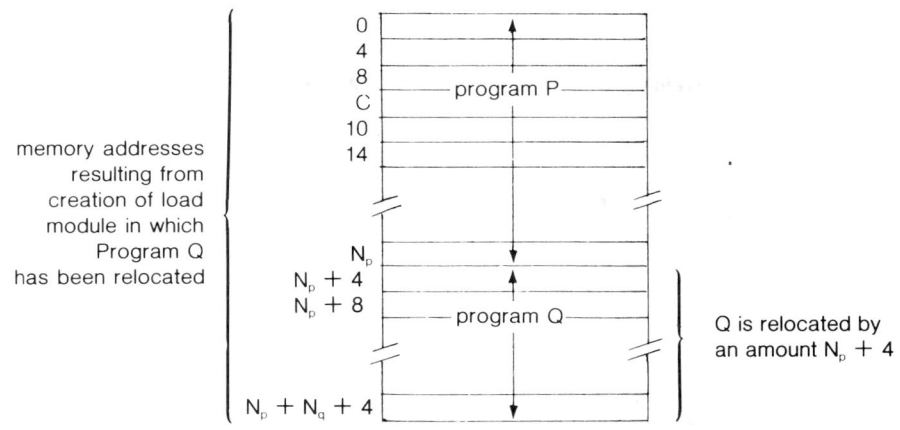

Now, suppose Q is a subroutine, and suppose that when P is running, P wants to request that Q perform calculations using P's data. The linkage requirements listed at the end of the previous section give rise to these questions:

1. How does Q gain access to the data and result areas that are in the calling program, P?
2. How can P specify the entry point in subroutine Q in order to branch to it at run time?
3. How will Q specify the reentry point in order to return to the calling program, P, at run time?

It should be clear that the answer to each question involves external addresses: Q needs the addresses of P's data, of P's result areas, and of the instruction in P to which it should return when it finishes its calculations. Also, P needs the address of the first instruction in Q, in order to branch to it.

But, as was pointed out, some of the addresses of Q and P are identical. How, for example, can address 000000 in Q be distinguished from address 000000 in P? The answer is, it can't. In order for P and Q to be able to communicate information to one another, their addresses must not be in conflict. Some mechanism is required to ensure that, when an address is specified at run time in either Program P or Subroutine Q, the CPU will be able to determine to which of the two programs that address refers. One of the mechanisms most commonly used for this purpose is provided by the Linkage Editor program.

The Linkage Editor program has an intermediary role between the Assembler and the Loader. It produces what is known as a *load module,* a combination of all the object modules required to run a given program, such as Program P. In the load module, there are no address conflicts: each object module has been relocated by an amount just sufficient to render its addresses distinct from those of all the other object modules in that load module. A simple case is depicted in figure 9.4, in which it is assumed that in order for Program P to run, only Subroutine Q and no other subroutine is required. Thus, the load module consists of both P and Q, with Q relocated as shown. In order to run Program P, it is the load module consisting of P together with its subroutine Q that is loaded. Loading P's object module alone is insufficient; loading both P's and Q's object modules could produce address conflicts between P and Q. Because all address conflicts and all references from P to Q (and vice versa) have been resolved in the load module, it is the load module that is loaded.

Having briefly outlined why address conflicts are resolved by the Linkage Editor, we will now learn how a program, such as P, can specify the entry point of Q (an external address) at assembly time so that the appropriate branch from P to Q's entry point will be assembled. When the Assembler assembles the branch instruction, it does not, indeed cannot, include the assembled entry-point address in that branch instruction. It leaves this task to the Linkage Editor. When the Linkage Editor creates the load module, it will, in effect, complete the assembled branch instruction and thereby *bind* the subroutine to the calling program.

In the IBM 360 and 370 systems, references from any program to an external program are accomplished by means of "external address constants." An *external address constant* symbolically specifies an address that is in some other program than the one in which it is specified. The letter V is used to denote an external address constant; it may appear either in the operand of a DC directive or as a literal, as in

```
DC        V(symbol)
L         15,=V(symbol)
```

The parentheses, which are required, are used instead of apostrophes. The *symbol* enclosed in parentheses is the symbolic address of an entry point in another program. Its value, as mentioned, is determined by the Linkage Editor, not by the Assembler. The Assembler will, however, reserve a full word for each V-type constant and inform the Linkage Editor of it. The details of how this is done are not important at this point; they will be discussed in chapter 10. What is important is that, *through the V-type constant, a program can refer symbolically to the entry point of another program*. It is this facility that enables a program to branch to a subroutine's entry point.

9.3 LINKAGE CONVENTIONS

The conventions used to satisfy the linkage requirements in the IBM 360 and 370 systems are divided very naturally into two groups: (1) those that are used in the calling program and (2) those that are used in the called program. The conventions used in these programs are intimately related, of course, and constitute the interface between the two programs.

To the set of three linkage requirements described in Section 9.1, a fourth requirement is added in IBM systems and in many other computer systems. This is the requirement that the data contained in the registers at the time a call is made to a subroutine *be preserved by the subroutine* so that upon return to the calling program the registers have the same contents as when the subroutine was entered. The manner in which this is done is prescribed by the linkage conventions. (The usefulness of this requirement from a programming standpoint should be evident since it is simpler not to have to save and restore register contents in the calling program.)

An overview of the standard linkage conventions in the IBM 360 and 370 systems is provided in figure 9.5. Refinements and extensions will be discussed shortly, but, from the standard set of conventions, we can observe the following:

1. Every program, be it a called or calling program, begins and ends its execution in the same manner.
2. The values of the parameters and the addresses of the result areas are passed indirectly through Register 1.
3. The conventions dictate how certain registers shall be used when calling or returning from a subroutine.
4. Certain registers may be used to pass results back to the calling program.

Beginning and Ending Execution: The SAVE Areas

As shown in figure 9.5, every assembly language subroutine begins with a sequence of statements like this:

```
X         CSECT                      ESTABLISH NAME OF PROGRAM
          STM      14,12,12(13)      SAVE REGISTERS 14,15,0,1,2,...,12
          BALR     12,0              ESTABLISH BASE ADDRESS IN REG 12
          USING    *,12
          ST       13,SAVE+4         SAVE CALLER'S SAVE AREA ADDRESS
          LA       13,SAVE           LOAD OWN SAVE AREA ADDRESS
```

Similarly, the last three instructions executed by a subroutine at run time are defined by these statements:

```
          L        13,SAVE+4         RESTORE CALLER'S SAVE AREA ADDRESS
          LM       14,12,12(13)      RESTORE CALLER'S REGS 14,15,0,...,12
          BR       14                BRANCH TO ADDRESS GIVEN IN REG 14
```

And, supplementing these statements is the definition of SAVE, as follows:

```
SAVE      DS       18F               RESERVE 18 CONSECUTIVE FULL WORDS
```

Figure 9.5 *Standard linkage conventions in IBM 360 and 370 systems.*

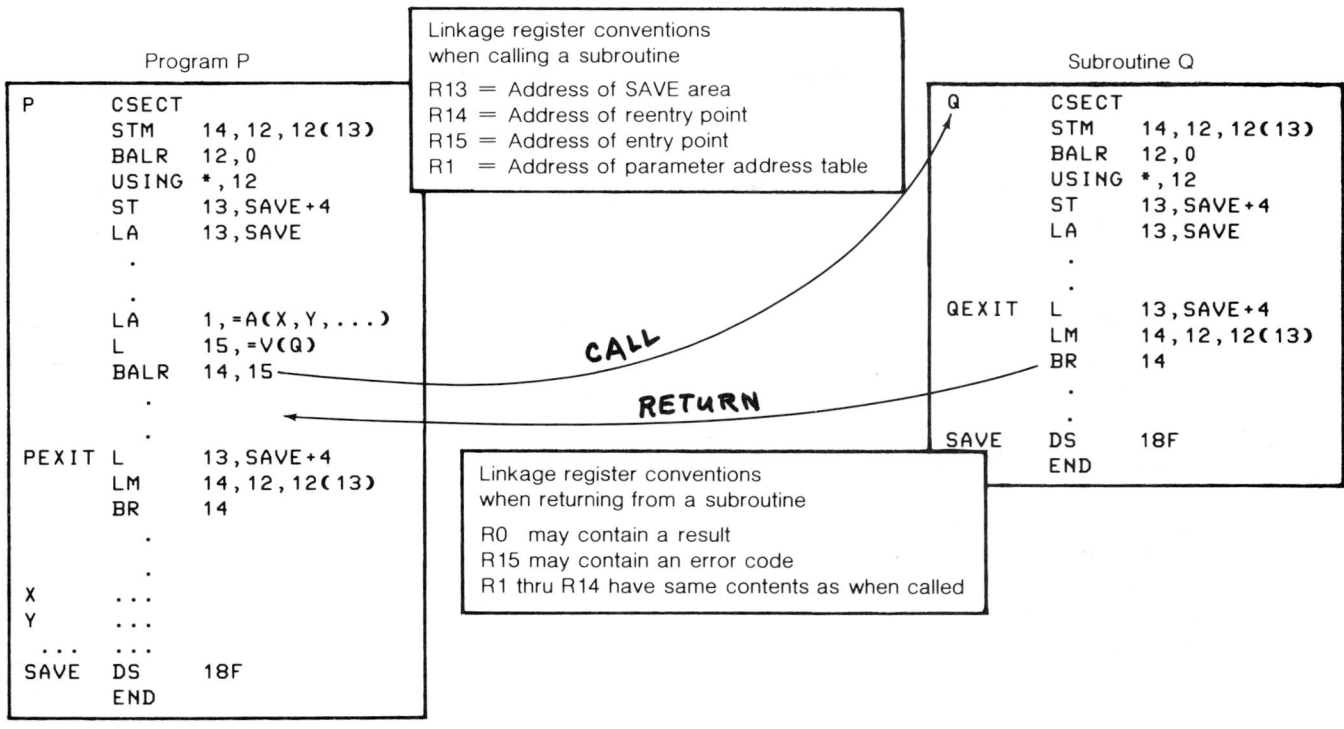

Note: You will recall from Section 2.3 that these requirements are the same as those required in OS for *all* programs, whether or not they are subroutines. In DOS, the requirements for subroutines are as shown above with but one difference: the SAVE area must begin on a double-word boundary:

```
SAVE          DS          9D              'DOS' SAVE AREA = 18 FULLWDS ON DBLWD BDY
```

From figure 9.5, we see that one of the conventions used when calling a subroutine is to have the address of the calling program's SAVE area in Register 13. Thus, when Subroutine Q begins execution, its STM instruction stores the contents of Registers 14,15,0,1,2,...,12 into the calling program's SAVE area, specifically, beginning at the fourth word (twelfth byte) of that area. It then stores the address of the calling program's SAVE area in its own (Q's) SAVE area via the ST 13,SAVE+4 instruction. It does this for two reasons. First, the calling program's SAVE area address must be saved somewhere, because Subroutine Q must be able to use Register 13 for its *own* SAVE area address whenever it calls another program or executes a system input/output or other macro. Second, since the contents of Register 13 must be saved and since they will be needed when restoring the other register contents, they had better be saved in an area from which they can be recovered prior to returning to the calling program. There are only three alternatives: save Register 13's contents in another register, save them in the calling program's memory area, or save them in Q's own memory area. The first alternative is unsatisfactory since it would preempt a register from further use. The second alternative is unsatisfactory since it would require that yet another address be saved by Subroutine Q—namely, the address where Register 13's contents were stored in the calling program. So the only satisfactory alternative is to store the calling program's SAVE area address in Q's own memory area. Then it is accessible through a base address internal to Q and can easily be recovered. By convention, the second word of Q's own SAVE area is used to store the address of the calling program's SAVE area (fig. 9.6).

Figure 9.7a depicts the contents of the SAVE areas of three programs: Program P, Subroutine Q (called by P), and Subroutine R (called by Q). This illustrates the manner in which the areas are used under the standard linkage conventions described previously. However, the standard linkage convention has one further

Figure 9.6 Format of Register SAVE area.

The description shown here is for the SAVE area in Program P after P calls Program Q, and before it calls another program. It is assumed that P was called by Program X. If P were a main program, X would be the Operating System (see also Figs. 9.7a and 9.7b).

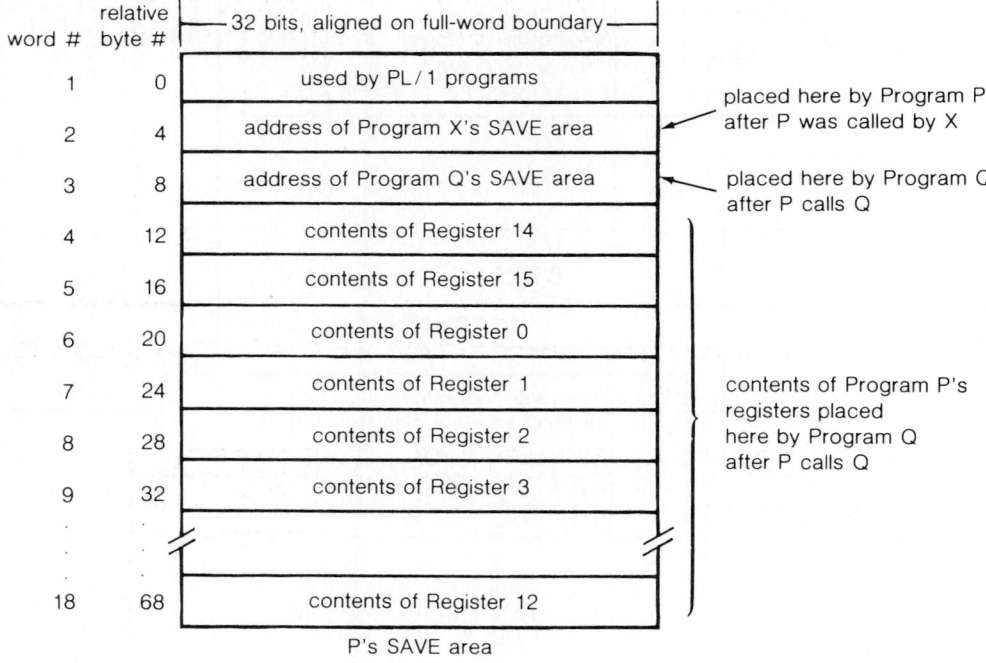

P's SAVE area

refinement, as illustrated in figure 9.7b: the third word of each calling program's SAVE area contains the address of the SAVE area in the program that it has called. This is put there by the called program, through the sequence of statements at the beginning of the called program:

```
STM     14,12,12(13)    SAVE REGS 14,15,0,1,...,12 IN CALLER'S AREA
BALR    12,0            ESTABLISH BASE ADDRESS IN REG 12
USING   *,12
ST      13,SAVE+4       SAVE CALLER'S SAVE AREA ADDRESS IN OWN AREA
LR      2,13            COPY CALLER'S ADDR TO REG 2 FOR SUBSEQ STORE
LA      13,SAVE         LOAD OWN SAVE AREA ADDRESS
ST      13,8(2)         SAVE OWN SAVE AREA ADDR IN CALLER'S AREA
```

One advantage to having both SAVE area addresses stored in this fashion is that it can be of assistance during debugging sessions. However, we will employ only the standard convention of figures 9.5 and 9.7a. The complete convention and various aspects of its use are fully described in *OS/VS1 Supervisor Services and Macro Instructions* (IBM Publication GC24–5103) and in *DOS/VS Supervisor and I/O Macros* (GC33–5373).

Passing Values of Parameters

Assuming that the contents of Register 13 had been correctly set to the address of the SAVE area at the beginning of a program's execution and had not been changed from that value, the conventional calling sequence in the IBM 360 and 370 systems consists of these instructions (see fig. 9.5):

```
LA      1,=A(X,Y,...)
L       15,=V(Q)
BALR    14,15
```

The first instruction enables the values of the parameters to be passed to the subroutine. It works as follows: The literal constant $=A(X,Y,...)$ is a table of address constants, similar in format to the V-type address constant required for external addresses, but with the difference that the list of one or more symbols enclosed in parentheses in the A-type address constant *all represent addresses internal to the program*. The three dots simply indicate that there may be more symbols included; their number depends, as has been mentioned, on the requirements of the subroutine. For any given A-type constant, the Assembler creates a table of full-word addresses, one word for each symbol specified in the constant. This is shown in figure 9.8; the table consists of consecutive full words, in which bits 8–31 of each word contain the address assigned to the corresponding symbol by the Assembler and bits 0–7 of each word are 0's.

Thus, what is passed to the subroutine is the address of the table: not the values of the parameters, not the addresses of the parameters, but the address of a table that contains the addresses of the parameters. It is worth noting that it does not matter how many or what type of data or results must be exchanged between calling and called program; the calling sequence enables all situations to be handled with a single address, namely the address of the parameter address table. It is also worth noting that the order in which the parameter addresses must appear in this table is dictated by the subroutine's design; it is not a decision that can be made by the calling program.

Corresponding to each symbol listed in the A-type literal operand, there must be a statement defining that symbol. This statement will usually be either a DC or DS directive, i.e., it will either define the symbol as the symbolic address of a constant defined at assembly time or as the symbolic address of a memory area whose data is to be supplied at run time. In either case, the subroutine needs the address at run time in order to obtain the data from the calling program's memory or to store the results in that memory. Therefore, one of the first instructions that the subroutine will execute after it has stored the register contents and the caller's SAVE area address is one that will obtain one or more parameter addresses from the table.

Figure 9.8   Passing parameter addresses through Register 1.

For example, to copy the first parameter address into Register 2, this instruction is sufficient:

        L   2,0(1)

To copy the first two parameter addresses into Registers 2 and 3, respectively, these two instructions can be used:

        L   2,0(1)
        L   3,4(1)

or this single instruction can be used:

        LM   2,3,0(1)

The significance of this technique is that, without having specified its parameters as external addresses at assembly time, for example, without specifying them as V-type constants, the subroutine has, at run time, obtained the external memory addresses of data and/or result areas in the calling program. The technique works no matter how large or small the calling program is, no matter where in its memory the table of parameter addresses is, and no matter where the data and/or result areas are. Thus, the subroutine is truly independent of the calling program. All that is required is that the linkage conventions be followed and that the calling program specify the correct number, type, and order of the parameters.

To illustrate these concepts, consider the subroutine VABS in figure 9.9 and the skeletal calling program accompanying it. The subroutine's purpose, as shown in the figure, is to replace each component of an integer array with its absolute value. Although the comments in the subroutine refer to an array named K and to its size, the variable N, there is, in fact, no directive or operand that specifies K or N. Indeed, in the calling program, the variable names are M and MN, respectively. This makes no difference. What the subroutine needs in order to complete its task is the address of the array and the number of components in it. In accordance with the linkage convention, this information is obtained as follows: the calling program's instruction LA 1,=A(M,MN) puts the address of the parameter address table into Register 1. In this case, the parameter address table consists of two addresses, in this order:

                address assigned to M
                address assigned to MN

Figure 9.9   Illustration of linkage conventions.

```
P       CSECT                              VABS      CSECT
        STM   14,12,12(13)                 *
        BALR  12,0                         *  SUBROUTINE VABS(K,N) REPLACES EACH COMPONENT OF THE INTEGER
        USING *,12                         *    ARRAY  K  WITH ITS ABSOLUTE VALUE.   'N'  IS THE NUMBER
        ST    13,SAVE+4                    *  OF COMPONENTS IN   K .
        LA    13,SAVE                      *
        .                                            STM   14,12,12(13)     SAVE CALLER'S REGS 14,15,0,1,...,12
        .                                            BALR  12,0             ESTABLISH BASE ADDRESS IN REG 12
        .                                            USING *,12
        LA    1,=A(M,MN)  )                          ST    13,SAVE+4        SAVE CALLER'S SAVE AREA ADDRESS
        L     15,=V(VABS) } CALL                     LA    13,SAVE          LOAD SUBR'S SAVE AREA ADDRESS
        BALR  14,15       )                 *
        .                                  *  OBTAIN PARAMETERS FROM CALLING PROGRAM
        .                                  *
        .                                            LM    7,8,0(1)         R7 = ADDRESS OF ARRAY  K
        L     13,SAVE+4                              L     9,0(8)           R8 = ADDRESS OF PARAMETER N
        LM    14,12,12(13)                 *                               R9 = N
        BR    14                           *  COMPUTE ABSOLUTE VALUES
        .                                  *
        .                                  LOOP      L     5,0(7)           R5 = K(J), J=1,2,...,N
        .                                            LPR   5,5              R5 = ABS(K(J))
M       DS    100F                                   ST    5,0(7)           K(J) = ABS(K(J))
MN      DC    F'100'                       *
SAVE    DS    18F                          *  LOOP CONTROL
        END                                          LA    7,4(7)           INCR ADDR TO NEXT COMPONENT
                                                     BCT   9,LOOP           REPEAT IF STILL MORE COMPONENTS
                                           *  EXIT FROM SUBROUTINE
                                                   ( L     13,SAVE+4        RESTORE CALLER'S SAVE AREA ADDR.
                                           RETURN  { LM    14,12,12(13)     RESTORE REGS 14,15,0,1,2,...,12
                                                   ( BR    14               BRANCH TO RE-ENTRY POINT
                                           *
                                           SAVE      DS    18F              SUBROUTINE'S SAVE AREA
                                                     END
```

The subroutine's instruction LM 7,8,0(1) copies the first of these two parameter addresses into Register 7 and the second into Register 8. This is followed by the instruction L 9,0(8), which loads Register 9 with the contents of the word whose address is in Register 8, i.e., with the size of the array. At this point, the subroutine has all the information it needs to complete its task.

Branching to and Returning from a Subroutine

The branch to a subroutine and the subroutine's branch back to the calling program both depend on the properties of the Branch and Link via Register (BALR) instruction. The primary property, as its name implies, is its ability to establish the necessary link between subroutine and calling program, namely the reentry point. Generally, the properties of the BALR instruction are these:

opcode	operand	type
BALR	R1,R2	RR

When the BALR instruction is executed, a branch is made to the address contained in bits 8–31 of the register designated by the R2 field, unless that register is Register 0. If R2 designates Register 0, no branch is made. Regardless of whether or not R2 designates Register 0, execution of the BALR instruction places the address of the BALR instruction *plus two* into bits 8–31 of the R1 register. (Execution of the BALR instruction also copies certain data from the program status word into bits 0–7 of the R1 register: bits 0–1 = the instruction length code; bits 2–3 = the condition code; bits 4–7 = the program mask. The contents of the R1 register are not changed, however, until either the address to which the BALR branches is obtained from the R2 register, or it is determined that the R2 register is Register 0. Some models of the IBM 370 include the instruction BASR, Branch and Save via Register, as an alternative to BALR. The only difference between BASR and BALR is that BASR puts X'00' into bits 0–7 of the R1 register instead of the instruction length code, condition code, and program mask.)

For example, suppose the address of a BALR 12,0 instruction is 005432_{16}. When this instruction is executed, 005434 will be placed into bits 8–31 of Register 12, but no branch will be made. However, if, instead

Figure 9.10 *Linkage conventions with error codes.*

```
P       CSECT                        VABS        CSECT
        STM     14,12,12(13)         *
        BALR    12,0                 * SUBROUTINE VABS(K,N) REPLACES EACH OF  N  INTEGERS IN
        USING   *,12                 *   THE ARRAY  K  WITH ITS ABSOLUTE VALUE.    A CODE IS
        ST      13,SAVE+4            *   RETURNED IN REGISTER 15 AS FOLLOWS:
        LA      13,SAVE              *            REG 15 = 0  IF  N  IS POSITIVE
                                     *            REG 15 = 4  IF  N  NOT POSITIVE
          .                          *
          .                                      STM     14,12,12(13)     SUBROUTINE ENTRY PROCEDURE
          .                                      BALR    12,0
        LA      1,=A(M,MN)                       USING   *,12
        L       15,=V(VABS)                      ST      13,SAVE+4
        BALR    14,15                            LA      13,SAVE
        LTR     15,15                *                           GET PARAMETERS AND TEST  N
        BZ      OK                               LM      7,8,0(1)         R7 = ADDRESS OF ARRAY  K
BAD     ...                                      L       9,0(8)           R9 = N
                                                 LTR     9,9              TEST  N  TO SEE IF IT'S POSITIVE
OK      ...                                      BNP     ERR              IF NOT, SET ERROR CODE AND EXIT.
                                                 LH      15,=H'0'         IF POSITIVE, SET RETURN INDICATOR.
        L       13,SAVE+4           *                           COMPUTE ABSOLUTE VALUES
        LM      14,12,12(13)        LOOP         L       5,0(7)           R5 = K(J), J=1,2,...,N
        BR      14                               LPR     5,5              R5 = ABS(K(J))
          .                                      ST      5,0(7)           K(J) = ABS(K(J))
          .                         *                           LOOP CONTROL
          .                                      LA      7,4(7)           INCR ADDR TO NEXT COMPONENT
                                                 BCT     9,LOOP           REPEAT IF STILL MORE COMPONENTS
M       DS      100F                *                           EXIT FROM SUBROUTINE
MN      DC      F'100'              EXIT         L       13,SAVE+4        RESTORE CALLER'S SAVE AREA ADDR.
SAVE    DS      18F                              L       14,12(13)        RESTORE REG 14 BUT NOT REG 15
        END                                      LM      0,12,20(13)      RESTORE REGS 0,1,2,...,12
                                                 BR      14               BRANCH TO RE-ENTRY POINT
                                     *                           ERROR DETECTED
                                     ERR         LH      15,=H'4'         SET RETURN CODE TO  4
                                                 B       EXIT             EXIT WITHOUT PROCESSING ARRAY DATA
                                     *                           SUBR REGISTER SAVE AREA
                                     SAVE        DS      18F
                                                 END
```

of BALR 12,0, the instruction at 005432 was BALR 14,15, then its execution would cause a branch to whatever address was in Register 15 and would also cause 005434 to be placed into bits 8–31 of Register 14.

Thus it should be clear that in the IBM 360 and 370 systems, the combined effect of the two instructions

```
        L       15,=V(Q)
        BALR    14,15
```

is that the BALR 14,15 simultaneously branches to the entry point designated by the literal =V(Q) and places the reentry point address into Register 14. In other words, the reentry point is at the instruction that immediately follows the BALR instruction.

Note that since the contents of Register 14 are saved by the subroutine, then in the sequence of instructions that constitutes the return from the subroutine, namely

```
        L       13,SAVE+4
        LM      14,12,12(13)
        BR      14
```

the BR 14 instruction branches to the reentry point that was established by the calling program's BALR 14, 15. That address is not known at assembly time, of course; it is not known until the subroutine is called at run time.

Passing Results Back to the Calling Program

As in high-level languages, results from assembly language subroutines are almost invariably passed back to the calling program via one or more of the parameters specifically understood to be result variables. Although the results replaced the data in the 'VABS' subroutine of figure 9.9, this need not have been the case. The subroutine could have been designed so that the resulting array was separate from the original array; this would have meant that three parameters would have been required, not two.

Figure 9.11   Restoring registers when returning from a subroutine.

to restore all registers:

```
      L    13,SAVE+4
      LM   14,12,12(13)
      BR   14
```

to restore all but register 15:

```
      L    13,SAVE+4
      L    14,12(13)
      LM   0,12,20(13)
      BR   14
```

to restore all but register 0:

```
      L    13,SAVE+4
      LM   14,15,12(13)
      LM   1,12,24(13)
      BR   14
```

to restore all but registers 0 and 15:

```
      L    13,SAVE+4
      L    14,12(13)
      LM   1,12,24(13)
      BR   14
```

However, there are two situations in which results may be passed back via registers rather than parameters: (1) when the result consists entirely of a single quantity, such as would be produced for a mathematical function, the linkage conventions permit the result to be passed back via Register 0; and (2) when the subroutine is designed to detect errors in the parameters (for example a request to compute the square root of -1 would not be acceptable to most square root routines) the linkage conventions permit an error code to be returned via Register 15.

As a matter of principle, all programs should include instructions that detect and reject invalid data. This is even more important for subroutines than for main programs. A programmer using a subroutine written by someone else, should not be expected to have to deal with invalid results that come up due to invalid data. Consider, for example, the VABS subroutine of figure 9.9. This subroutine does not test the value of N, the number of components in the array; it assumes this value will be positive. What would happen if the calling program unwittingly passed a negative or zero value of N? At best the subroutine would get hung up in a long loop, due to the way the BCT instruction works. Worse things could happen, however, especially if during this long loop the address in Register 7 was incremented to a point where the Load and Store sequence disrupted some instructions in the program. The subroutine also fails to test any integer whose absolute value is being computed. Thus, if any integer were exactly equal to -2^{31}, the LPR instruction would cause an overflow with probable program termination.

Figure 9.10 shows how the VABS subroutine might be rewritten to detect and process an invalid value of N: it returns a code in Register 15 indicating whether the value of N was valid or not. (Detection and processing of a potential overflow situation is left as an exercise.) Note that once the decision to return some quantity in either Register 0 or Register 15 is made, the standard sequence for returning to the calling program has to be amended. The act of restoring the calling program's Register 0 and/or Register 15 contents would void the result and/or code that had been placed in those registers by the subroutine. Consequently, there are four cases to be considered when returning from a subroutine: (1) restore all registers, (2) restore all but Register 0, (3) restore all but Register 15, and (4) restore all but Registers 0 and 15. Figure 9.10 illustrates the use of one of these and also illustrates how the calling program might be programmed to determine whether the subroutine accepted or rejected its data. Figure 9.11 gives the sequences of instructions required to handle each of the four return situations mentioned. The displacements in the various LM instructions are derived from the format of the SAVE area (see fig. 9.6).

Call by Reference vs. Call by Value

As we have seen, the parameter addresses passed to the subroutine point to—i.e., *refer* to—memory locations in the calling program. Some of those locations contain data the subroutine is to operate on (its *input*) and the others contain the results (*output*) of the subroutine's operations. A calling sequence that passes addresses of data instead of data values is known as a *call by reference*. Other types of calling sequences are possible, one of the most common being *call by value*. In a call-by-value sequence, data values rather than addresses are passed to the subroutine.

There are certain advantages and disadvantages to each method; we will briefly mention two. A more complete discussion is in James L. Peterson's book, *Computer Organization and Assembly Language Programming* (Academic Press, 1978).

The main advantage of call by reference is that it can easily be adapted for use with any type or amount of data. Whatever the data—large arrays, character strings, complex data structures—a single address gives the data's location and another may point to its length or other descriptive information. Another advantage is that a single uniform method is used whether a calling program is passing data to the subroutine or is receiving the subroutine's output data.

Clearly this advantage of call by reference can be a corresponding disadvantage of call by value. For example, it would be quite cumbersome if not utterly unworkable to pass all the values of a large array rather than its address. The values would have to be passed either through the registers or in some memory area or file common to both the calling and called programs; otherwise the subroutine would not be able to gain access to the data.

Yet there are cases where call by value is justified. This occurs when there is a single value (or just a few values) to be passed. The calling program can use registers to pass input data to the subroutine, and the subroutine can pass its results back to the calling program in similar fashion. A good example of this is a subroutine that computes the square root of a number: there is only one input and one output data value.

In simple situations the appeal of call by value is usually outweighed by its lack of generality. That is why call by reference is used in the IBM linkage conventions.

9.4 COMMENTS ON THE LINKAGE CONVENTIONS

There are several reasons for the use of conventional methods of interfacing to external subroutines. Among the most important are

1. A subroutine written by one person can be called by a program written by someone else. If the subroutine's method of return is clear to both persons, neither has to investigate the details of the other's program.
2. The passing of parameters is done in a single consistent manner, whether the data and results are integers, characters, or of any other type or length.
3. If all compilers generate the same standard code for the equivalent of the subroutine call and return operations, then programs written in FORTRAN, COBOL, and other high-level languages can be interfaced to one another and to assembly language programs.
4. Benefits 1–3 are increased in importance when a person wishes to transfer a program from one computer installation to another, if the same conventional methods are used at both sites.

This is not to say that every external subroutine conforms to the conventions, or that every compiler produces code that conforms to the conventions. But it is a goal worth striving toward. To determine the differences between the conventions and code produced by any given compiler, it is necessary to read the relevant documentation, e.g. an IBM Programmer's Guide, for that compiler. To determine the differences between the conventions and the code used in another assembly language program, it may be necessary to obtain a listing of that program.

As previously discussed, each external subroutine must establish its own implied base register and not rely on the base register established in a calling program. The reason for this is that no external address will, at run time, be compatible with the implied displacements generated by the Assembler. However, part of the convention is that the calling program pass the entry-point address to the subroutine in Register 15. For this reason, some programmers establish Register 15, rather than Register 12, as the base register in a subroutine. This proves unsatisfactory in two important situations: (1) when the subroutine calls another subroutine, and (2) when the subroutine returns an error code in Register 15. As a general rule, therefore, Register 15 should not be used as the base register.

Registers 0, 1, 13, 14, and 15 are known as the *linkage registers*. This is because they are used in fixed ways as part of the subroutine linkage conventions and because they are used in fixed ways when system macro instructions are executed. System macro instructions, such as the I/O macros OPEN, CLOSE, GET, and PUT, result in calls either to subroutines provided from the system subroutine library as an extension of the Operating System capabilities, or as calls directly to the Operating System itself. In either case the linkage registers are used by system macros to pass information in a manner virtually identical to that of the subroutine linkage conventions. In particular, all system macros depend on there being a register-save-area address in Register 13. For this reason it is good practice to load the save area address into Register 13 as part of the instruction sequence that begins program execution and not change the contents of Register 13 thereafter.

9.5 INTERNAL SUBROUTINES

There are several disadvantages connected with the use of external subroutines that can be avoided by the use of internal subroutines. Remember the difference between internal and external subroutines: external subroutines are assembled separately from any other program, whereas internal subroutines are assembled as part of another program and are considered internal to that program. The major disadvantages of external subroutines are these: (1) If the subroutine requires only a few instructions to achieve its purpose, there is a relatively large amount of overhead in the number of statements required to write it as an external subroutine, and in the number of instructions that must be executed at run time just to call it and return from it. (2) If the subroutine's task is such that a large number of parameters must be passed to it, then it becomes unwieldly to write the subroutine or its calling sequence.

Internal subroutines can be used to avoid both of these difficulties. The first difficulty can be avoided by simply relaxing some of the conventions for calls and returns; and the second can be avoided simply because an internal subroutine has access to the same memory areas as all other portions of the program do, so that it may not be necessary to pass many parameters. (The concept of calling an internal subroutine is analogous to the COBOL PERFORM verb and the GOSUB verb in the BASIC Language. Both of these call portions of the program in which they reside, and those portions have access to the same variables as do the rest of the program statements.)

To call an internal subroutine in Assembly Language, the instructions that should be used, if the entry point's symbolic address is SUBR, are either these two

```
        L       15,=A(SUBR)
        BALR    14,15
```

or this one

```
        BAL     14,SUBR
```

It is simpler to use the single BAL instruction. Notice, however, that, if we use the Load/BALR sequence, the address constant is an A-type constant, not a V-type constant. This is due to the fact that the subroutine's symbolic address is an internal address, not an external one.

The Branch and Link (BAL) instruction is the RX-type counterpart of the BALR instruction. Like the BALR instruction, execution of the BAL instruction places the address of the instruction following it into bits 8–31 of the register whose address is specified in the R1 field. But since BAL is an RX instruction, this link address is *four* plus the address of the BAL instruction, not two plus that address. And unlike the BALR instruction, the BAL *always* branches to the address specified by the second operand. In short, the instruction BAL 14,SUBR branches to the subroutine entry point and causes the reentry point address to be placed into Register 14. (Some models of the IBM 370 include the instruction BAS, Branch and Save, as an alternative to BAL. Analogous to the BASR/BALR pair mentioned earlier, the only difference between BAS and BAL is that BAS puts X'00' into bits 0–7 of the R1 register, whereas BAL puts the instruction length code in bits 0–1, the condition code in bits 2–3, and the program mask in bits 4–7 of the R1 register.)

An example of the use of the BAL instruction is shown in figure 9.12. The internal subroutine in that figure has the same purpose as the VABS subroutine discussed earlier, but does not follow all the linkage conventions. Another example is an internal subroutine that will determine whether a 2-digit month (whose address is passed in Register 2) is valid. If it is, the address of that month's three-letter abbreviation is returned in Register 15. If it isn't, a zero is returned.

```
* CALLED VIA BAL   14,MMCONV WITH ADDR OF 2-DIGIT MONTH IN R2
MMCONV   LA  15,MMTBL         R15 = ADDR OF 3-LETTER/2-DIGIT PAIR
         LH  10,=H'12'        R10 = # PAIRS TO BE SEARCHED
MMCONV1  CLC 3(2,15),0(2)     LOOK FOR GIVEN 2-DIGIT MONTH IN TABLE
         BE  MMCONVX          BRANCH EQUAL WHEN FOUND
         LA  15,5(15)         ELSE, INCR TO NEXT TABLE ENTRY
         BCT 10,MMCONV1       KEEP LOOKIN'
         SR  15,15            GIVE 'INVALID' INDICATOR
MMCONVX  BR  14               RETURN TO CALLER
* TABLE OF 2-DIGIT MONTHS AND CORRESPONDING ABBREVIATIONS
MMTBL    DC  C'JAN01FEB02MAR03APR04MAY05JUN06'
         DC  C'JUL07AUG08SEP09OCT10NOV11DEC12'
```

Figure 9.12 Example of use of BAL instruction. (See also fig. 9.9.)

```
MAIN        CSECT
            STM     14,12,12(13)
            BALR    12,0
            USING   *,12
            ST      13,SAVE+4
            LA      13,SAVE

              .
              .

            LA      1,=A(M,MN)
            BAL     14,VABS         CALL INTERNAL 'VABS' FOR ARRAY   M
            LA      1,=A(P,PN)
            BAL     14,VABS         CALL INTERNAL 'VABS' FOR ARRAY   P

              .
              .

            L       13,SAVE+4
            LM      14,12,12(13)
            BR      14              EXIT FROM MAIN PROGRAM
*
VABS        LM      7,8,0(1)        INTERNAL SUBROUTINE VABS
            L       9,0(8)            REPLACES EACH COMPONENT IN AN
VABSLOOP    L       5,0(7)            INTEGER ARRAY WITH ITS ABS VALUE
            LPR     5,5
            ST      5,0(7)
            LA      7,4(7)
            BCT     9,VABSLOOP
            BR      14              RETURN TO CALLER
*
M           DS      100F            SPACE FOR A 100-COMPONENT ARRAY
MN          DS      F               SPACE FOR SIZE OF ARRAY   M
P           DS      50F             50-COMPONENT ARRAY
PN          DS      F               SIZE OF ARRAY   P
SAVE        DS      18F             REGISTER SAVE AREA
            END
```

Internal subroutines can also provide a top-down structure in Assembly Language, similar to the use of COBOL's PERFORM verb. For example:

```
TOPDOWN   CSECT
          STM     14,12,12(13) STANDARD ENTRY
          BALR    12,0
          USING   *,12
          ST      13,SAVE+4
          LA      13,SAVE
* OVERALL LOGIC
          BAL     14,PREPWORK   PERFORM INITIALIZATIONS
          BAL     14,MAINWORK   PERFORM MAIN PROCESSING
          BAL     14,CLEANUP    PERFORM CLOSING DETAILS
* EXIT FROM PROGRAM
          L       13,SAVE+4    STANDARD EXIT
          LM      14,12,12(13)
          BR      14
            . . .
```

In the above, the PREPWORK, MAINWORK, and CLEANUP symbols denote the beginning of sections of the source module that can be similarly structured with BAL instructions to other internal subroutines.

Figure 9.13 *Example of the USING directive.*

```
                        MAIN     CSECT
                                 STM    14,12,12(13)
                                 BALR   12,0
                                 USING  *,12,11,10
                        - - - - - - - - - - - - - - - -
                        BASE0    L      11,BASE1
                                 L      10,BASE2
                                 B      BEGIN
  range of   exactly    BASE1    DC     A(BASE0+4096)
  Reg 12     4096       BASE2    DC     A(BASE0+8192)
             bytes      BEGIN    ST     13,SAVE+4
                                 LA     13,SAVE
                                          .
                                          .
                                          .
                        - - - - - - - - - - - - - - - -
  range of   exactly                      .
  Reg 11     4096                          .
             bytes                         .

                        - - - - - - - - - - - - - - - -
                                          .
  range of   up to                        .
  Reg 10     4096
             bytes      SAVE     DS     18F
                                 END
```

9.6 MULTIPLE BASE REGISTERS

Sometimes use of internal subroutines rather than external ones leads to program sizes exceeding 4096 bytes. In such cases, more than one implied base register may have to be used in order that all implicit operands can be correctly represented in base-displacement form by the Assembler. The problem, of course, is that every displacement must be less than or equal to $4095_{10} = \mathrm{FFF}_{16}$. If there is only one implied base register, then, by the conventions we have been using, the implied base address will be 000006; thus, the largest address that could be specified in base-displacement form would be $000006 + \mathrm{FFF} = 001005_{16} = 4101_{10}$. This is slightly larger than 4096, but certainly not enough larger to eliminate the problem. With more than one implied base register, we could use one of these with a base address of 000006; another with a base address of 001006; a third, if necessary, with a base address of 002006; and so forth. It is a fairly simple matter to establish more than one implied base register, and, once that has been done, the Assembler will choose the base register whose base address requires the smallest implied displacement for each implicit operand. Thus, different operands may be represented in base-displacement form with different implied base registers.

To establish more than one implied base register, each register and its base address must be designated via a USING directive to fulfill the assembly-time requirements. For each such register, there must also be an instruction placing the appropriate base address in that register at run time. This is identical to the requirement for a single implied base register, but the method of accomplishing it is somewhat different. The BALR 12,0 instruction is insufficient by itself. One method is shown in figure 9.13; it relies on a property of the USING directive summarized in figure 9.14. That property means, for example, that this single directive,

```
                 USING      *,12,11,10
```

Figure 9.14 The USING directive.

opcode	operand
USING	$B_0, R_0, R_1, R_2, ..., R_n$

where B_0 and the R_k's are defined and related as follows:
B_0 = symbol whose value is assumed by the Assembler to be the base address in Register R_0.
R_k = address of any one of the general registers.

The *base address* in Register R_k and the *range* of R_k are assumed by the Assembler to be related to those of Register R_0 as follows:

register	base address	range
R_0	B_0	B_0 through $B_0 + 4095$
R_1	$B_1 = B_0 + 4096$	B_1 through $B_1 + 4095$
R_2	$B_2 = B_0 + 8192$	B_2 through $B_2 + 4095$
.	.	.
R_n	$B_n = B_0 + 4096 \cdot n$	B_n through $B_n + 4095$

is equivalent to these three consecutive directives,

```
USING    *,12
USING    *+4096,11
USING    *+8192,10
```

In each of these operands, the symbol $*$ is the memory location symbol, not the multiplication operator.

This property of the USING directive makes it easy to satisfy the assembly-time requirement. To satisfy the run-time requirement we must be a bit more careful as demonstrated by the statements in figure 9.13.

To use implicit addressing at all, we must designate at least one implied base register and base address, and each implicit address must, at run time as well as at assembly time, be in the range of at least one of the implied base registers. In figure 9.13 the implicit addresses SAVE+4 and SAVE are in the range of base register 10 only, due to the USING directive. So before the respective ST and LA instructions can be executed at run time, the base address that corresponds to the USING declaration must be loaded into base register 10. The rule is that *when an instruction is executed at run time, any base address required for its execution must already be in the appropriate base register.* We can also apply this rule to the two load instructions that follow the USING directive in figure 9.13 and thereby see why the two respective address constants must be in the range of base register 12.

Once an implied base register is declared by a USING directive, the Assembler will use it as needed until a subsequent DROP directive specifies that register. The purpose of the DROP directive is simply to inform the Assembler that a register previously declared by a USING directive is no longer to be used for implicit addresses. By judicious combinations of USING and DROP directives we can therefore reduce the number of registers committed to base addresses at any one time. The format of the DROP directive is

opcode	operand
DROP	$R_0, R_1, ..., R_n$

where the operand contains a list of one or more register addresses. An example and further discussion of the DROP and USING directives is given in chapter 10.

9.7 TOPICS FOR FURTHER STUDY

Related to the use of subroutines are several techniques for allowing symbolic references between separately assembled modules. Among these are the following: (1) external addresses: ENTRY, EXTRN, (2) common addresses: COM, and (3) dummy addresses: DSECT.

Figure 9.15 Illustration of ENTRY and EXTRN directives.

```
MAIN    CSECT                          identifies entry point
        EXTRN  VABS                    in another
        STM    14,12,12(13)            source module
         .
         .
         .                             A-type constant
         .                             used when
        L      15,=A(VABS)             external symbol
        BALR   14,15                   identified
         .                             via EXTRN
         .
         .                             CSECT automatically
                                       defines SUB1
                                       to be an entry point
SUB1    CSECT
        ENTRY  VABS                    ENTRY defines VABS
VABS    EQU    SUB1                    to be an additional
        STM    14,12,12(13)            entry point;
         .                             in this example,
         .                             VABS is identical
         .                             to SUB1, but in
                                       general that is
                                       not necessary.
```

External Addresses: ENTRY, EXTRN

As has been shown, the V-type address constant is used to symbolically reference an external address, i.e., an address that is defined outside the program in which it is referenced. In order for that to be possible, the external address must be an *entry point* of the program in which it is defined. In the examples, the entry point has identified the first instruction to be executed in a subroutine, i.e., it has always been the symbol appearing in the name field of a subroutine's CSECT directive. In addition to symbols defined by a CSECT directive, any other symbol defined in a source module can be referenced by V-type constants from a different source module. For this to be accomplished, the module in which the symbol is *defined* must include an ENTRY statement whose operand contains the symbol. The ENTRY statement essentially declares that the symbol or symbols in its operand field can be referenced by a V-type constant in another program. ENTRY is a directive, not an instruction. No memory locations are reserved for this directive in the object module.

Under two conditions we can reference an external address by means of an A-type constant instead of using a V-type constant to reference an external address. First, the external symbol referred to in the A-type constant must not appear in the name field of any statement within the program that is referencing it as an external address. And second, the external symbol referred to in the A-type constant must appear in the operand field of an EXTRN directive in the same program in which it is referenced as an external address. In other words, the EXTRN directive essentially declares that the symbol or symbols in its operand field represent external addresses. When EXTRN is used to identify an external symbol, the symbol is referenced with an A-type constant; when EXTRN is not used, the symbol is referenced with a V-type constant. No memory locations are reserved for an EXTRN statement. Figure 9.15 illustrates the ENTRY and EXTRN directives.

Common Addresses: COM

When a programmer subdivides a large program into two or more modules, one of these modules constitutes the main program, the program in which the major logic decisions are made, and the others are subroutines. As has been pointed out, there are several advantages to such a modular approach, but sometimes there is also an added problem: it may happen that two or more of the modules must refer to many of the same constants and memory areas. This could mean that many parameters have to be passed from one program to another, creating a programming burden. To avoid this, an area of memory common to all the programs can be defined. Parameters, data, and results can be stored into and loaded from this area by any of the programs, *as though the area were internal to each program.* By using this technique, we can avoid passing parameters and using V-type or EXTRN/A-type constants.

Figure 9.16   Illustration of COM.

```
MAIN      CSECT
          STM     14,12,12(13)
          BALR    12,0
          USING   *,12
          ST      13,SAVE+4
          LA      13,SAVE
          L       11,=A(COMMON)
          USING   COMMON,11
            .
            .
            .
          L       15,=V(ABS)
          BALR    14,15
            .
            .
            .
SAVE      DS      18F

          COM
COMMON    DS      0F
N         DS      F
K         DS      100F
            .
            .
            .
          END
```

```
ABS       CSECT
          STM     14,12,12(13)
          BALR    12,0
          USING   *,12
          ST      13,SAVE+4
          LA      13,SAVE
          L       11,=A(COMMON)
          USING   COMMON,11
          L       7,=F'0'
          L       8,N
LOOP      L       5,K(7)
          LPR     5,5
          ST      5,K(7)
          LA      7,4(7)
          BCT     8,LOOP
          L       13,SAVE+4
          LM      14,12,12(13)
          BR      14
SAVE      DS      18F

          COM
COMMON    DS      0F
N         DS      F
K         DS      100F
            .
            .
            .
          END
```

identical statements

To use this technique, each source module must include a set of identical statements describing the organization of data in the common memory. This set of statements begins with the COM directive and usually contains only DS directives. The order of the DS directives, the amount of storage that each reserves, and the name-field symbols in each statement must be identical in each source module. At execution time, any of the programs can use these symbols to place data into the common memory for it and the other programs to use. The only requirement is that each source module designate an implied base register whose purpose is to provide addressability for the symbols in the common memory. The Assembler must be informed of this through the USING directive, and the base address must be loaded at run time before instructions that symbolically referred to the common memory are executed. This is illustrated in figure 9.16.

It should be noted that, although the area of memory defined by a COM directive is external to all the programs that use it at run time, it is made to appear to be internal to each program through the use of identical symbols (fig. 9.16). Because of this, it is sometimes difficult to determine the cause of programming errors involving the use of common memory.

Dummy Addresses: DSECT

The major reason that one program, Program *A*, passes a parameter to another program, Program *B*, is that the memory area in *A*, which is addressed by that parameter, becomes accessible to *B*. Now, it may happen that there are several subareas within that area; for example, fields within a personnel record or columns within an array. How can *B* gain access to each subarea? One way would be for *A* to pass a separate parameter for each subarea, but that would be awkward. Another, much better way, would be for *B* to reference each subarea in terms of its distance, or displacement, from the beginning of the area that the subareas belong to. This is easy to do, since the address of the beginning of the area is passed to *B* as a parameter. The use of the DSECT directive allows the displacements to be symbolic rather than numeric. Symbolic displacements provide greater flexibility and result in fewer programming errors than do numeric displacements.

DSECT defines the beginning of a *dummy section*. A dummy section is not translated into machine language data or instructions and therefore occupies no memory space at run time. Instead, the statements within a dummy section are used solely as symbolic descriptions of the logical structure of a memory area.

Symbols defined within a dummy section can be used at assembly time to process data from any memory area that has the same logical structure as is described by the dummy section. The reason for this is as follows.

A relocatable symbol defined in the name field of a dummy section statement is assigned a value relative to the beginning of the dummy section. Moreover, the Assembler always assigns the value 000000 to the beginning of a dummy section. When a dummy section symbol is used in the operand of an instruction, the Assembler does not use the implied base register or base address of the section in which the instruction appears. Instead, it uses the dummy section's implied base register and base address. This, in turn, requires that there be a USING directive and an appropriate load-type instruction that establishes an implied base register and base address for the dummy section and that these appear in the section containing the instruction.

But since a dummy section occupies no memory space at run time, the fundamental question is, "What address should be used as the base address for a dummy section?" Not surprisingly, there are two aspects to the answer: one applies to assembly-time processing, the other to run-time processing.

At *assembly time,* the USING directive should specify the name of the dummy section (the name-field symbol of the DSECT directive) in its base-address field, and it should specify a register other than 0, 1, 12, 13, 14, or 15 as the implied base register. This establishes a base address of zero, and an implied base register that is not in conflict with other register usage. For example, see the USING DAREA,11 directive in figure 9.17. In that figure, the base-displacement address field of the assembled CLI OTCODE,C'X' instruction will refer to Register 11, with a displacement of 032_{16}. This is because OTCODE is defined as byte position

Figure 9.17 Illustration of DSECT.

An 80-byte area within the calling program is described by a dummy section within the "PAYROLL" subroutine, so that instructions in the subroutine can symbolically refer to fields within the calling program's memory area.

The address of the actual area is passed as a parameter. The Load (L) instruction in the subroutine places that parameter into a register, and the following USING directive informs the Assembler that that register is to be used as the implied base register for symbols in the dummy section.

the instruction
CLI   OTCODE,C'X'
is equivalent to
CLI   50(11),C'X'

50_{10}, relative to the beginning of the dummy section, and the base address (DAREA) is zero since DAREA is at the beginning of the dummy section. Thus the Assembler translates the CLI instruction as though it were addressing a byte in the dummy section.

But note what happens at *run time* for the programs in figure 9.17. The address of the beginning of the area named AREA is passed from the calling program to the subroutine in the conventional manner, and the called subroutine loads that address into the same register that had been declared as the implied base register for the dummy section. Therefore when the assembled CLI instruction is executed at run time, the effective address computed by the CPU for symbolic address OTCODE is not 000032_{16}, but 032_{16} plus the address in Register 11. In other words, it is the real memory address of a byte in the calling program, namely the byte that is in the fiftieth position beyond the beginning of the area named AREA. Thus the CPU processes the CLI instruction as though it were addressing a byte in the calling program, even though it was not assembled that way.

Further study of figure 9.17 will reveal the three-fold advantage gained from the use of dummy sections:

1. The elements in the area named AREA can be referred to symbolically even though their addresses are not known at assembly time and even though they are not part of the PAYROLL subroutine that refers to them.
2. If a change is made to the logical structure of AREA, that change must also be made to the dummy section, but no such change has to be made to instructions that refer to dummy section symbols: all that is required is a reassembly of the modules.
3. Although the dummy section of figure 9.17 describes just one employee record, the LA 11,DLNG(11) instruction that increments the run-time base address permits each entry in a table of identically structured employee records to be processed symbolically.

The distinction between addresses assigned at assembly time and those used at run time is obviously of crucial importance to the understanding of the DSECT directive. Further examples of the use of DSECT will be given in chapters 10, 15, 20, and 21.

9.8 SUMMARY

A subroutine is a set of statements that constitute a programming solution to a particular problem; it may be used any number of times by one or more computer programs. Subroutines may be either internal to the programs that call them, or external to those programs. If external, they need not be written in the same language as the programs that use them. A program uses a subroutine by means of a specially adapted sequence of statements known as the "calling sequence." This sequence satisfies the linkage requirements of branching to the subroutine's entry point, of designating the reentry point of the calling program, and of passing to the subroutine the parameters that it was designed to process.

Each computer system usually has a conventional method of calling and returning from external subroutines. These almost always include a method of saving the contents of registers so that the calling program will remain unaffected by the subroutine's use of registers. In the IBM 360 and 370 systems, the conventions require that upon entry to a subroutine, Register 1 must contain the address of a parameter address table, Register 13 the address of the calling program's register save area, Register 14 the reentry address, and Register 15 the entry address. Upon return from a subroutine, the contents of the registers must be the same as when the subroutine was entered, except that Register 0 may contain a result and Register 15 may contain an error code. The subroutine returns to the reentry address specified by the calling program.

Internal and external subroutines both have advantages and disadvantages. Internal subroutines have the advantage of sharing the same set of symbolic and real memory addresses as the portion of the program that calls them, so that it may be unnecessary to pass as many parameters as with external subroutines. It may also be convenient to relax the linkage requirements and thereby reduce the overhead associated with calling and returning. The use of internal subroutines may result in an object module longer than 4096 bytes; this could require the use of more than one base register, thereby reducing the number of registers available for general use.

An advantage of external subroutines is that they can be written and tested separately from other portions of an overall programming solution, can be used in the solution of more than one problem without having to be rewritten or reassembled, and can even be written in languages different from those used in the programs that call them or are called by them.

EXERCISES

1. What would be the effect at run time in a subroutine that began its execution with the instructions corresponding to these statements:

   a.

   ```
   A       CSECT
           STM     14,12,12(13)
           BALR    12,0
           USING   *,12
           LA      13,SAVE
   ```

   b.

   ```
   B       CSECT
           BALR    12,0
           USING   *,12
           STM     14,12,12(13)
           ST      13,SAVE+4
           LA      13,SAVE
   ```

   c.

   ```
   C       CSECT
           USING   *,15
           STM     14,12,12(13)
           ST      13,SAVE+4
           LA      13,SAVE
   ```

2. What would be the effect at run time if a subroutine ended its execution with the instructions corresponding to these statements:

   a.

   ```
   LM      14,12,12(13)
   L       13,SAVE+4
   BR      14
   ```

   b.

   ```
   L       13,SAVE+4
   LM      12,14,12(13)
   BR      14
   ```

   c.

   ```
   LA      13,SAVE+4
   LM      14,12,12(13)
   BR      14
   ```

3. There are two IBM system macros that can be used to simplify the process of saving and restoring registers. These are the SAVE and RETURN macros, described in the *OS/VS1 Supervisor Services and Macro Instructions* manual, #GC24–5103. Using this manual or simply by experimenting with the SAVE and RETURN macros, determine the expansion that is generated for each of the following statements:

   a. SAVE   (14,12)
   b. SAVE   (14,12),,*
   c. SAVE   (12,14)
   d. RETURN (14,12)
   e. RETURN (14,12),RC=15
   f. RETURN (14,12),RC=(15)
   g. RETURN (14,12),T,RC=0
   h. SAVE   (14,12),T

4. Write an internal subroutine that will convert a 32-bit binary integer to its EBCDIC character representation. Make whatever assumptions seem reasonable about the format of the result.

5. Write an internal subroutine that will convert a 32-bit binary integer to its EBCDIC character representation in accordance with the requirements of the FORTRAN FORMAT specification Iw for any decimal integer $w \le 16$. This means that the character representation should contain exactly w characters, with leading zeroes suppressed, no punctuating commas, and a sign included only if the integer is negative. When negative, the sign is to be placed immediately to the left of the most significant digit.

6. Write an internal subroutine that will convert a decimal integer from its n-byte EBCDIC representation to its representation as a 32-bit binary integer. The subroutine should permit the EBCDIC representation to contain leading blanks as well as leading zeroes and a sign (plus, minus, or omitted) to the left of the left-most significant digit.

7. Write an external subroutine that will print the contents of the sixteen general registers in hexadecimal notation, in a suitably readable format (similar to that which appears in a memory dump).

8. Referring to the string-editing operations depicted in figure 7.8, what parameters would have to be passed to a subroutine that performed the DELETE operation? To a subroutine that performed the INSERT operation? The REPLACE operation? Write three external subroutines, one for each of the three string-editing operations of figure 7.8.

9. Write an external subroutine named MATMPY that will compute the product of an MxN array and an NxK array (in that order), the result being an MxK array. Assume that the arrays are integer arrays and that the product is computed as in this FORTRAN subroutine:

```
            SUBROUTINE MATMPY (JA,M,N,JB,K,JC)
            DIMENSION JA(50,50),JB(50,50),JC(50,50)
            DO 40 KROW = 1,M
            DO 30 KCOL = 1,K
            JC(KROW,KCOL) = 0
            DO 20 KK = 1,N
            JC(KROW,KCOL) = JC(KROW,KCOL) + JA(KROW,KK)*JB(KK,KCOL)
      20    CONTINUE
      30    CONTINUE
      40    CONTINUE
            RETURN
            END
```

10. Write an internal subroutine that, for any given 32-bit binary integer J, will determine the largest value of n such that J can be expressed as an integral multiple of 2^n. For example, if $J = 1024$, then $n = 10$ since $J = 1 \times 2^{10}$. If $J = 1025$, then $n = 0$. The subroutine should return the value of n as a binary integer in Register 0.

11. a. Write an external subroutine that will print the contents of memory from address A$-a$ to address B, where A and B are specified as parameters, and a is calculated by the subroutine so that $a < 8$ and A$-a$ is a double-word boundary. The memory contents should be printed in hexadecimal notation, in a suitably readable format (similar to that which appears in a memory dump).

    b. Modify your Exercise 11a subroutine so that A$-a$ is exactly divisible by 32, and $a<32$. The first line printed should contain blanks instead of the contents of locations A$-a$, A$-a+1$,..., A-1.

    c. Modify your Exercise 11b subroutine so that it will also print the contents of the sixteen general registers that are passed to it. It can do this by calling the external subroutine written as the solution to Exercise 7.

    d. Modify your Exercise 11c solution so that it will print the memory contents, the register contents, or both, depending on the value of a parameter passed to the subroutine.

12. Each of the following questions pertain to the example in figure 9.13, which shows one method of establishing more than one implied base register.

    a. What would be incorrect about replacing these five statements,

```
        BASE0       L           11,BASE1
                    L           10,BASE2
                    B           BEGIN
        BASE1       DC          A(BASE0+4096)
        BASE2       DC          A(BASE0+8192)
```

with these two statements,

```
        BASE0       L           11,=A(BASE0+4096)
                    L           10,=A(BASE0+8192)
```

    b. What would be incorrect about deleting the five statements mentioned in Exercise 12a without replacing them; in other words, just having these statements at the beginning of the module:

```
        MAIN        CSECT
                    STM         14,12,12(13)
                    BALR        12,0
                    USING       *,12,11,10
                    ST          13,SAVE+4
                    LA          13,SAVE
```

    c. By what sequences of statements other than those shown in figure 9.13 could three implied base registers be correctly established?

13. Write a main program (not a subroutine) that will copy all the components of a 50×50 two-dimensional integer array A into another 50×50 integer array B. Explain why more than one implied base register is needed. How many implied base registers would be needed if this were a subroutine rather than a main program? How many implied base registers would be needed if this were a main program and the arrays were 30×30 instead of 50×50?

10
Assembler Concepts

The purpose of this chapter is to provide some understanding of the processes that take place when a source module is assembled. We begin by explaining the need for a two-pass Assembler and then describe several of the concepts and techniques used in an Assembler. The discussion is totally oriented to the IBM 360 and 370 Assemblers, though a number of simplifying assumptions have been made. Thus, the chapter essentially constitutes a conceptual, not a detailed, description of those Assemblers.

Some of the data structures for representing information about source module statements and machine language are discussed in detail: the symbol table, the object module tables, and cross-reference lists. In addition, an overview of the Assembler's Pass 1 and Pass 2 processing logic and a brief description of table-searching and table-sorting techniques used in an Assembler have been included.

10.1 INTRODUCTORY CONCEPTS

In simple terms, the assembly process can be depicted by the diagram of figure 10.1. The machine language representation of the source module is produced by the Assembler and stored in an object module, where it is available to the Loader program and/or the Linkage Editor. In addition to the object module, the Assembler produces a listing that correlates the source and object module contents and provides certain diagnostic information.

Let us consider the source statements in figure 10.2. We can begin to appreciate the processes by which the transformation from source to object module takes place, by pretending to *be* the Assembler. As the Assembler, we must process the source statements one by one, in the order of their occurrence. Therefore, to save time, we should attempt to get all the information we possibly can from one reading of each statement (i.e., from one pass through the entire set of statements). At this point, it might help to review the address concepts and instruction formats presented in chapter 3. We can then proceed in the following manner.

Figure 10.1   Assembler input and output.

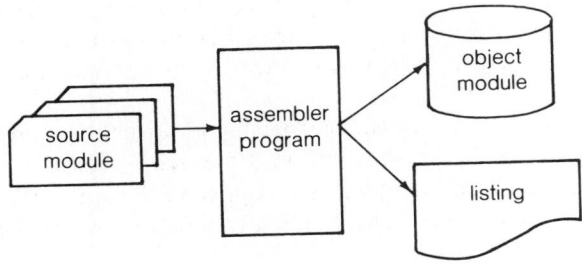

Figure 10.2 Creating object code.

#	label	op	operand	addr	object code		addr	object code	
1	MAIN	CSECT		0000			0000		
2		STM	14,12,12(13)	0000	90EC	D00C	0000	90EC	D00C
3		BALR	12,0	0004	05C0		0004	05C0	
4		USING	*,12	0006			0006		
5		ST	13,SAVE+4	0006	50D0	----	0006	50D0	C02A
6		LA	13,SAVE	000A	41D0	----	000A	41D0	C026
7	*								
8		L	3,X	000E	5830	----	000E	5830	C01E
9		A	3,=F'8'	0012	5A30	----	0012	5A30	C072
10		ST	3,Y	0016	5030	----	0016	5030	C022
11	*								
12		L	13,SAVE+4	001A	58D0	----	001A	58D0	C02A
13		LM	14,12,12(13)	001E	98EC	D00C	001E	98EC	D00C
14		BR	14	0022	07FE		0022	07FE	
15	*								
16	X	DC	A(N)	0024	----	----	0024	0000	0074
17	Y	DS	F	0028			0028		
18	*								
19	SAVE	DS	18F	002C			002C		
20	*								
21	LAST	EQU	*	0074			0074		
22	N	EQU	LAST-MAIN	0074			0074		
23		END		0078	0000	0008	0078	0000	0008

source code	object code end of Pass 1	object code end of Pass 2

Before processing the first statement, we set our memory location counter (MLC) to zero. The first statement, a CSECT directive, gives the name of the control section. Since it is the first CSECT with that name, we assign the value of MLC to MAIN. The second and third statements can be translated into object code immediately, since both contain valid mnemonic instructions and since neither contains symbols in the operand field. The address assigned to each statement is obtained by increasing MLC by an amount that depends on the preceding statement. Since the CSECT results in no object code or memory space being reserved, the STM instruction will be assigned to address 0000, and since the STM requires 4 bytes, the BALR is assigned to address 0004.

The USING directive is a note to the Assembler that Register 12 should be used as the implied base register and that the base address in Register 12 is the current value of MLC; this value was obtained from the address of the previous instruction plus its length; $0004 + 2 = 0006$.

The next six instructions pose a problem: although we can assign addresses to those instructions (since we know the length of each one), and although we can translate the mnemonic instruction code into machine language, *we cannot create the machine language corresponding to the second operand field* because we do not yet know the value of the symbols SAVE, X, and Y. Nor have we assigned an address to the literal =F'8' appearing in Statement 9. This is a consequence of having to process the statements one at a time, in the order of their occurrence. We can see immediately that we will have to return to these six statements and others, e.g., Statement 16, after we have obtained the necessary information. Therefore, we proceed with the remaining statements, assigning addresses to symbols and to literals and taking any other action dictated by directives that we process.

For example, the DC directive in Statement 16 requires the allocation of four bytes beginning on a full-word boundary, but we can't assemble the constant until the value of N is known. The DS directives of Statements 17 and 19 require the allocation of one and eighteen full words, respectively. The two EQU directives define values for the symbols LAST and N. Finally, when we reach the END directive, we assign addresses to any literals in the literal pool.

At the completion of our first pass through the source statements, we have compiled the following information (see the middle column of fig. 10.2):

literals	address
=F'8'	00078

symbol	value
LAST	00074
MAIN	00000
N	00074
SAVE	0002C
X	00024
Y	00028

base register	base address
12	00006

To complete the transformation to object code, we must make a second pass over the source statements using this information. In doing so, we shall have to calculate the implied displacements to use in the base-displacement form of addresses in the operands of instructions. As discussed previously, this is done according to the formula

$$\left\{ \begin{array}{c} \text{implied} \\ \text{displacement} \end{array} \right\} = \left\{ \begin{array}{c} \text{desired} \\ \text{address} \end{array} \right\} - \left\{ \begin{array}{c} \text{base} \\ \text{address} \end{array} \right\}$$

You should verify that the object code given in the right-hand column of figure 10.2 is consistent with the information given here.

To recapitulate, the constraint that each statement must be processed in the order of its occurrence, plus the fact that some symbols will be used in operand fields before they are defined, has led us to make two passes over the source statements. In the first pass, our main function was to determine and remember the values of all symbols and to assign addresses to literals. In the second pass, our main function was to complete the transformation from source code to object code, using the information that was gathered in the first pass. To perform these two passes, we also needed certain reference information: the hexadecimal opcode and instruction format and length corresponding to each mnemonic instruction code, and the definition of each directive. As we will learn in the next section, this information must also be available to the Assembler during the assembly process.

There is one other observation to be made. Suppose that in the source statements of figure 10.2, we reverse Statements 21 and 22, so that instead of the sequence

21	LAST	EQU	*
22	N	EQU	LAST-MAIN

we have the following statements 21' and 22'

21'	N	EQU	LAST-MAIN
22'	LAST	EQU	*

If this were done, we would be unable to compute the value of LAST-MAIN when Statement 21' is processed in Pass 1, since the value of LAST will not be defined until Statement 22' is processed. Thus, the value of N would not be known at the end of Pass 1. As a consequence, when Statement 16—X DC A(N)—is processed in Pass 2, we will be unable to translate its operand into object code. To determine the value of N and to complete the translation of Statement 16, we would have to wait until Statement 21' was processed in Pass 2.

There are several ways to avoid this apparent dilemma. The simplest, and the one used in most Assemblers, including that of the IBM 360 and 370, is simply to forbid a sequence such as the one represented by Statements 21' and 22': all symbols in the operand of an EQU directive are required to be defined in statements preceding that EQU, as was done in figure 10.2. Thus, if the source module contains no errors, the value of all symbols will be known at the end of Pass 1 and all instructions and constants will be translatable in Pass 2.

10.2 FUNDAMENTALS OF THE ASSEMBLY PROCESS

The outline presented in Section 10.1 illustrates the need for a two-pass Assembler. But the outline differs in two essential ways from the sequence of steps taken in an Assembler. First, the Assembler does not attempt to generate any object code in Pass 1, not even for instructions or constants where this could be done. This is because it is simpler, from a design and implementation standpoint, to generate all the object code in Pass 2. Second, the Assembler does not process the original source module in Pass 2. Instead, it processes an augmented version of that source module, produced by Pass 1. This intermediate file, as it is often called, contains not only the source statements but also some of the information determined by Pass 1: information about the opcode and the MLC associated with each statement.

Nevertheless, for the Assembler to carry out the types of processes outlined in Section 10.1, it needs descriptions of the instructions and directives and it must be able to determine and remember the values of symbols, the identities and addresses of literals, and the base register and base address. It also must be prepared to handle multiple base registers, external symbols, arithmetic expressions in operands, and other aspects of Assembly Language. To do these things it must be able to store and process a variety of types of information.

One of the principal information-handling techniques used by an Assembler is based on the concept of a table. A *table* is simply a collection of data arranged in some orderly fashion so that the data items are relatively easy to locate and process. The data items are organized into a number of subcollections called *entries*, all of which usually contain the same types of items. One of the items, called a *key*, is used to identify each entry. The value of each key is often distinct from that of all other keys in the table, so that the identity is unique.

Figure 10.3 shows how the table that describes instructions will be defined for our descriptions of the assembly process. Each entry, shown as a single line of the table, consists of 8 bytes that are unevenly divided

Figure 10.3   Opcode table format.

Figure 10.4 *Directive table format.*

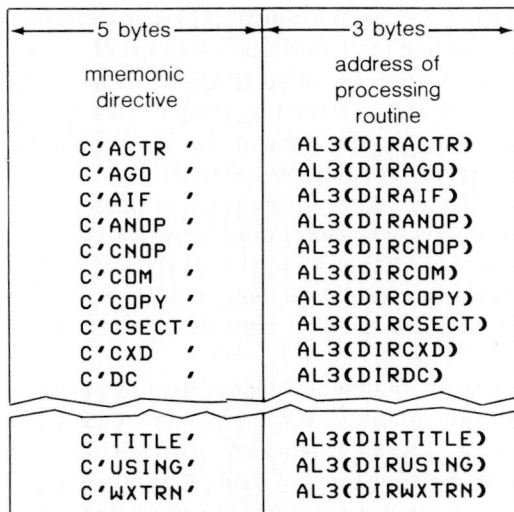

mnemonic directive	address of processing routine
C'ACTR '	AL3(DIRACTR)
C'AGO '	AL3(DIRAGO)
C'AIF '	AL3(DIRAIF)
C'ANOP '	AL3(DIRANOP)
C'CNOP '	AL3(DIRCNOP)
C'COM '	AL3(DIRCOM)
C'COPY '	AL3(DIRCOPY)
C'CSECT'	AL3(DIRCSECT)
C'CXD '	AL3(DIRCXD)
C'DC '	AL3(DIRDC)
C'TITLE'	AL3(DIRTITLE)
C'USING'	AL3(DIRUSING)
C'WXTRN'	AL3(DIRWXTRN)

into five items, or *fields*. The key field is the mnemonic instruction code; entries are in ascending sequence by the values of this field. The other fields provide information that the Assembler will need to process an instruction: the machine language opcode, the instruction's type and length, the 4-bit mask defining conditional branch instructions such as BE, and a few other pieces of information described by 1-bit flags. The information in a table is represented as concisely as possible in order to conserve memory space. However, since it would be impracticable to have an entry's length be other than an integral multiple of bytes and inefficient from a processing standpoint if we did not align counters, addresses, etc., on appropriate boundaries, the table formats presented here represent an attempt at a reasonable compromise between memory and processing efficiency.

Figure 10.4 shows the table that will be used to process directives. Because of the diversity of operand formats in directives, the table simply contains the address of a routine within the Assembler that processes each directive. Like the opcode table of figure 10.3, the directive table can be used to determine whether a given character string represents a valid directive, and, if it does, what should be done with it. But, unlike the opcode table, the action to be taken is decentralized; each directive has its own processing routine.

The opcode and directive tables are examples of tables in which all the entries are known in advance, so to speak, so that the information in each entry can be coded in the source module of the Assembler itself. By placing the entries in key sequence, the process of finding an entry, which is required each time a statement is processed by the Assembler, can be made more efficient.

The Assembler also needs tables in which the entries are not known until assembly time. Among these are the symbol table, the literal table, and the base register table. Since the entries in these tables depend on the statements processed by the Assembler, they must be created and inserted at assembly time. Before discussing these tables, it might prove useful to summarize where we are heading.

As demonstrated, the assembly process depends on information represented in tables. Some of these tables are generated as part of the Assembler source module, some at assembly time. The Assembler itself operates in two phases, or passes: the primary function of the first pass is to determine the values of symbols; the primary function of the second pass is to produce the object code. The second pass relies on information generated in the first pass, and both passes rely on the opcode and directive tables, as well as on the source module statements.

This interdependence is depicted in figure 10.5. The arrowheads indicate the direction in which information is transferred. For example, Pass 1 creates the symbol table by transferring information into it, and Pass 2 uses that information. In the next section we will describe the contents of the Assembler's tables in more detail. Following that, the activities in Pass 1 and Pass 2 will be examined; first in overview fashion, then to see how information might be inserted into and retrieved from the tables, how the symbol table can be sorted into sequence at the end of Pass 1, and how the object module and cross reference information is compiled.

Figure 10.5   Assembler table and file usage.

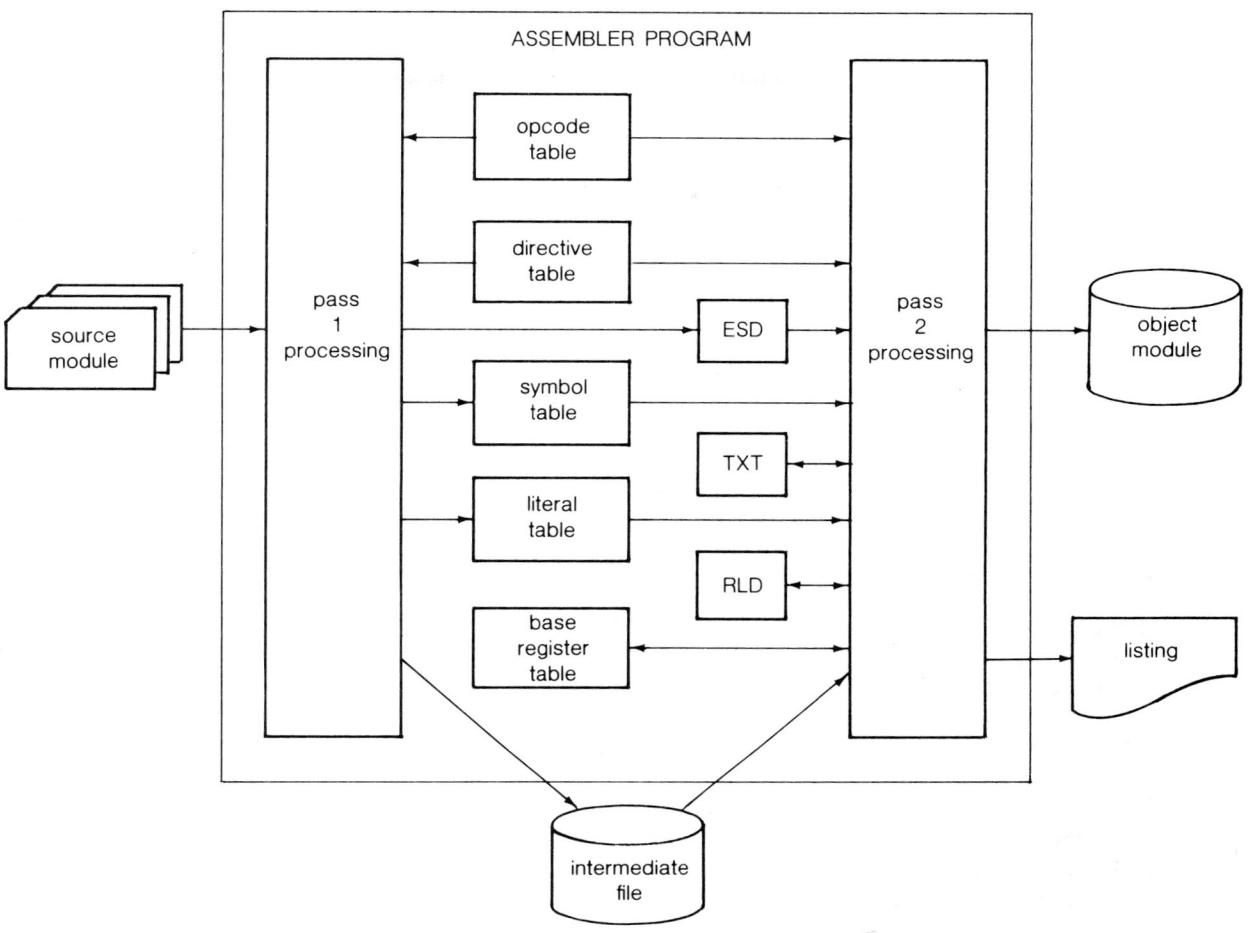

Even at this stage of the discussion, it should be clear that the Assembler is a complex program. If it is written in Assembly Language, it will require tens of thousands of statements to adequately handle all the potential situations that could occur in a user's source module. In addition to the nearly 150 instruction codes and 7 instruction formats with implied or explicit lengths and base registers, there are 15 data type codes and nearly 50 directives in the IBM 360 and 370 Assembly Language. Arithmetic expressions must be analyzed, macros (see chapter 17) expanded, control sections segregated, errors detected, and a listing and object module created. Further, since the Assembler is a frequently used program, its design and implementation must use memory space and processing time efficiently.

It is therefore simply not practicable to describe in one chapter all the processes that take place in an Assembler. Consequently, we will impose four major simplifications in order to concentrate on a few underlying principles:

1. We will consider only ten of the most frequently used directives, and will not consider macro processing at all. The ten directives are CSECT, DSECT, ENTRY, EXTRN, USING, DROP, DC, DS, EQU, END.

2. We will consider only five of the data type codes: C-, X-, F-, A-, and V- and will exclude any discussion of exponent and scale factors in F-type constants.

3. We will not discuss the procedures involved in translating operand expressions such as SAVE+4.

4. We will not be concerned with the process of creating a listing but will focus attention on the creation of the object module instead.

10.3 ASSEMBLER TABLES

In this section, we will describe a few of the principal tables used by an Assembler: the symbol table, the literal table, the base register table, and the intermediate file. The ESD, TXT, and RLD tables used for the creation of the object module (see fig. 10.5) will be discussed in Section 10.6.

Note that although the descriptions given here are meant to be accurate in their portrayal of the kinds of information contained in the tables, they are not necessarily accurate in terms of field size or position within an entry, or even in terms of all the fields that might be in an entry. These details depend on design considerations that will not be discussed in this chapter.

The Symbol Table

An entry is made in the symbol table (see fig. 10.6) in Pass 1 for each symbol that occurs in the name field of an instruction or directive. An entry is also made in Pass 1 for each symbol that occurs in the operand of an EXTRN directive. At the end of Pass 1, the entries are sorted into ascending order by the key field values. Duplicates (multiply-defined symbols) are kept in the table so that they can be reported in the cross-reference portion of the listing and flagged as errors.

As indicated in figure 10.6, each entry contains several fields: the symbol itself, its value, its length attribute, the number assigned by the Assembler to the statement in which the symbol was defined, and a number identifying the control section in which the statement appeared. In addition, each entry contains information characterizing the symbol as being relocatable or absolute.

Except for external symbols and symbols defined by an EQU directive, the *value of a symbol* is the address of the instruction, constant, or data area for which it has been defined. The value of a symbol defined by an EQU directive is the value of the operand in that directive. The value of an external symbol is arbitrarily set to zero, since it is the Loader or Linkage Editor, not the Assembler, that must determine that value.

The *length attribute of a symbol* is the number of bytes in the object code that are identified by that symbol. This clearly depends on the statement in which the symbol is defined. If a symbol is defined in the name field of an instruction, its length attribute is the instruction's length. If a symbol is defined in the name field of a DC or DS directive, its length attribute is either the number of bytes explicitly represented in the length modifier Ln, or, in the absence of a length modifier, it is the number of bytes implied by the constant or data type code. (For most other directives, the length attribute is arbitrarily set to 0 or 1; in these cases, its value is unimportant.) The Assembler inserts a symbol's length attribute into the length field of an SS_1 or SS_2 machine language instruction whenever the corresponding source language operand references that symbol but does not include an explicit length-field specification.

Each symbol's value (and, by definition, the symbol itself) is always considered to be either relocatable or absolute. The word *relocatable* means that the value of the symbol is a function of the starting memory address of the object code being assembled. When the Loader or Linkage Editor assigns a starting memory address to the object code, that starting address is added to all relocatable addresses in order to make it possible for the object code to be executed in that area of memory. Correspondingly, the word *absolute* in this context means that the value of the symbol is not dependent on the starting address assigned by the Loader or Linkage Editor. *The only absolute symbols are those defined by an EQU directive whose operand value is absolute. All other symbols are relocatable.*

The Assembler assigns a number, the *statement number,* to each statement that it processes. This number makes it easy to identify statements in the cross-reference portion of a listing. The Assembler also assigns a *control section number,* or i.d., to each separate control section in a source module. This number is used by the Assembler to determine which base register is eligible for use in the base-displacement address calculation for a symbol. Both these numbers are inserted into the symbol table at the time a symbol is defined.

The Literal Table

A literal is entered into this table (see fig. 10.7) when it is obtained from an instruction's operand field in Pass 1. Since the number of bytes in each entry depends on the number of characters in the literal string, each entry includes its length. There are no duplicates. If two instructions specify the same literal in exactly the same way, there will be only one entry for that literal in the table. (In the terminology of earlier chapters, the literal table is identical to the literal *pool*.)

Addresses are assigned to any literals in the table when an END directive is processed and also when the LTORG directive is processed (see chap. 15). In the IBM 360 and 370 systems, the first address assigned to a literal is always on a double-word boundary. The addresses are assigned in the following order: first, to

Figure 10.6   Symbol table format.

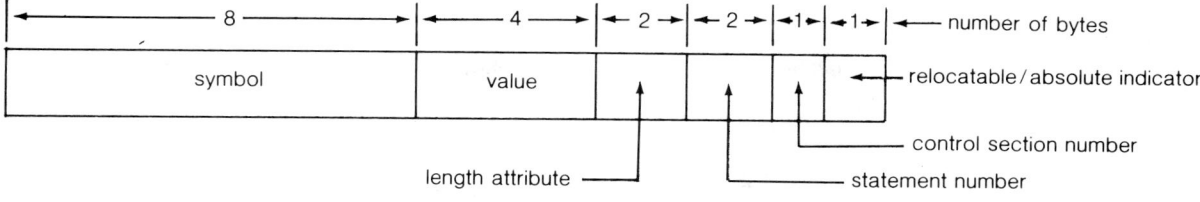

Figure 10.7   Literal table format.

Figure 10.8   Base-register table format.

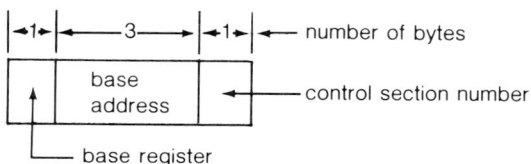

all literals whose assembled lengths are a multiple of eight; next, to all whose assembled lengths are a multiple of four but not of eight; third, to those whose assembled lengths are a multiple of two but not four; and, last, to all remaining literals. This hierarchy removes the need to adjust address values (and possibly leave unused bytes) for the proper boundary alignment each time an address is assigned to a literal.

The Base-Register Table

The entries in this table (see fig. 10.8) reflect the information obtained from the USING and DROP directives. As discussed in chapter 9, the general format of these directives is

> USING   base-address, base-register-1, base-register-2,...
> DROP   base-register-1, base-register-2,...

To allow for the designation of symbolic base registers and symbolic base addresses, entries are not made in this table until Pass 2. (This differs from the scheme used in Section 10.1.) There is one entry per base register. A USING directive causes an entry to be made in the table for each base register designated in its operand; a DROP directive causes entries to be deleted.

To compute a base-displacement address corresponding to a relocatable symbolic address, the Assembler chooses the base register whose base address is in the same control section as the symbolic address, and whose value is closest to but not greater than the value of the symbolic address. If there are no addressing errors in the source module, this procedure guarantees that the displacement will be as small as possible but nonnegative.

Figure 10.9 Intermediate file format.

The Intermediate File

A file is essentially a table in which all the entries either cannot fit or need not be in main memory at the same time. Since file processing will be discussed in Part Five, we need only note here that each entry in the intermediate file (fig. 10.9) is created in Pass 1 and used in Pass 2. The sequence of the entries is the same as that of the statements in the source module.

As illustrated in figure 10.9, each entry contains a copy of a source module statement plus some additional information determined in Pass 1. This includes the value of the MLC at the time the statement was processed, the address of the opcode or directive table entry corresponding to the mnemonic instruction code in the source statement, and a summarization of the statement's type. This information is included in order to eliminate the need to repeat the process of determining it in Pass 2; this saves some processing time in Pass 2.

The statement type byte in an intermediate file entry illustrates a technique often used to represent information: 1-bit indicators whose status (1 or 0) indicates a true or false condition. For example, if the statement is a comment, the first bit (labeled as lowercase *c*) will be set to 1; the other bits are irrelevant. If the statement is not a comment, then the first bit will be set to 0, and one of the other bits will be set to 1 (the remaining bits being set to 0). The second bit will be 1 if the statement is a macro, the third if it is a directive, the fourth if an instruction, and the right-most bit if the opcode is undecipherable. The setting of these bits can easily be tested in Pass 2 by means of the TM instruction.

10.4 ASSEMBLER TABLE EXAMPLE

To illustrate the ideas presented in the previous section, we will describe the contents of the Assembler tables that would result from the assembly of the source module shown in figure 10.10. (The statements in the source module do not constitute a meaningful program; they are for illustrative purposes only.)

All the tables except the base-register table are created in Pass 1. For each statement that is processed in Pass 1, the following procedures take place:

1. The current value of the MLC, adjusted if necessary for boundary alignment requirements, is assigned to the name-field symbol (if any), and that symbol is entered into the symbol table along with the other information that characterizes that symbol.
2. Directives that affect the value of the MLC are processed just enough so that the new MLC can be computed. This includes not only DC and DS directives, but also CSECT and DSECT directives. (There is a separate MLC maintained for each reference control section, as discussed in chap. 15.) It should be noted that in Statement 34 of figure 10.10—ARRAY2 DS (N)F—the value of N is required in Pass 1 in order that the number of full words, and thus the number of assembled bytes, can be determined. For this reason, a symbol must be defined before it is used in the duplicator field of a DC or DS directive's operand.
3. For instructions, the operand is scanned for the presence of a literal, and whenever one is found it is entered into the literal table along with its string length (provided it is not already there).
4. When the END directive is processed, the symbol table is sorted into sequence and addresses are assigned to literals.

Figure 10.10   Sample source module.

```
 1          MAIN      CSECT
 2          MAINLINE  STM    14,12,12(13)
 3                    BALR   12,0
 4                    USING  *,12
 5                    ST     13,SAVE+4
 6                    LA     13,SAVE
 7          *
 8                    ENTRY  MAINLINE
 9                    EXTRN  ARRAY1
10          *
11                    LA     1,=A(ARRAY1,ARRAY2)
12                    L      15,=V(SUBR)
13                    BALR   14,15
14          *
15                    USING  ARRAYFLD,DUMMYREG
16                    LA     DUMMYREG,ARRAY2
17                    MVC    A1,=C'ABC'
18                    MVC    A3,ZEROES
19                    DROP   DUMMYREG
20          *
21                    L      13,SAVE+4
22                    LM     14,12,12(13)
23                    BR     14
24          *
25          ARRAYFLD  DSECT
26          A1        DS     CL3
27          A2        DS     CL4
28          A3        DS     CL5
29          A4        DS     CL2
30          A5        DS     C
31          MAIN      CSECT
32          *
33          N         EQU    15
34          ARRAY2    DS     (N)F
35          SAVE      DS     18F
36          DUMMYREG  EQU    11
37          ZEROES    DC     15X'00'
38                    END
```

Note that the symbol and literal tables for the source module of figure 10.10 are as shown in figure 10.11. Note also that all the symbol values and length attributes are known; if this were not the case, undefined symbols would be detected in Pass 2.

In Pass 2, each statement is processed again, this time using the copy in the intermediate file. Each instruction is assembled into machine language by substituting the values for symbols in the operand fields and by using the instruction format given in the opcode table. Constants defined by DC directives are assembled in accordance with the rules governing the various type codes, including padding, truncation, duplication, conversion to machine language, and so forth. The DS, EQU, and EXTRN directives are effectively skipped over (they are of course printed on the listing), since all the information provided by them was obtained and utilized in Pass 1. The CSECT and DSECT directives determine the control section that is being assembled. When a USING directive is processed, an appropriate entry is made in the base-register table, and when a DROP directive is processed an appropriate entry is deleted.

For example, when Statement 4—USING ∗,12—is processed, the following entry is made in the base-register table:

base register	base address	control section
12	000006	1

Figure 10.11 Symbol and literal tables (for the source module in fig. 10.10).

Symbol Table

symbol	value (hex)	length attribute	statement number (decimal)	control section	rel/abs flag
ARRAYFLD	000000	1	25	2	R
ARRAY1	000000	1	9	1	R
ARRAY2	000034	4	34	1	R
A1	000000	3	26	2	R
A2	000003	4	27	2	R
A3	000007	5	28	2	R
A4	00000C	2	29	2	R
A5	00000E	2	30	2	R
DUMMYREG	00000B	1	36	1	A
MAIN	000000	1	1	1	R
MAINLINE	000000	4	2	1	R
N	00000F	1	33	1	A
SAVE	000070	4	35	1	R
ZEROES	0000B8	1	37	1	R

Literal Table

string length (hex)	address (hex)	assembled length (hex)	literal string
0011	0000C8	0008	=A(ARRAY1,ARRAY2)
0008	0000D0	0004	=V(SUBR)
0007	0000D4	0003	=C'ABC'

This entry remains in the table and is used by the Assembler to determine the base-displacement addresses in subsequent operands, until one of three events is detected: (1) the END directive is processed, thereby terminating Pass 2 except for the assembling of literals; (2) another USING directive for the same base register is processed, thereby causing the previous entry to be replaced by a new entry; or (3) a DROP directive for that base register is processed, thereby causing the previous entry to be deleted from the table.

When Statement 15—USING ARRAYFLD,DUMMYREG—is processed, the values of the base-address and base-register symbols in the USING operand are determined from the symbol table, and an entry is added to the base-register table so that it now contains

base register	base address	control section
12	000006	1
11	000000	2

Now when an instruction is processed, the Assembler must decide which base register to use. For example, when Statement 18—MVC A3,ZEROES—is processed, the Assembler determines from the symbol table that A3 is in control section 2, and ZEROES is in control section 1. From the base-register table, it finds that Register 11 governs control section 2, and Register 12, control section 1. It then computes the implied displacements as follows:

$$\left\{ \begin{array}{c} \text{implied} \\ \text{displacement} \\ \text{for A3} \end{array} \right\} = \left\{ \begin{array}{c} \text{value} \\ \text{of A3} \end{array} \right\} - \left\{ \begin{array}{c} \text{base address} \\ \text{in Register 11} \end{array} \right\}$$

$$= \quad 000007 \quad - \quad 000000$$

$$\left\{ \begin{array}{c} \text{implied} \\ \text{displacement} \\ \text{for ZEROES} \end{array} \right\} = \left\{ \begin{array}{c} \text{value} \\ \text{of ZEROES} \end{array} \right\} - \left\{ \begin{array}{c} \text{base address} \\ \text{in Register 12} \end{array} \right\}$$

$$= \quad 0000B8 \quad - \quad 000006$$

Figure 10.12   Assembly listing for Figure 10.10.

```
FLAG LOCTN OBJECT CODE      ADDR1  ADDR2  STMNT M SOURCE STATEMENT

     003000                              3  MAIN     CSECT
     000000 90 EC D00C                   4  MAINLINE STM   14,12,12(13)
     000004 05 C0                        5           BALR  12,0
     000006                              6           USING *,12
     000006 50 D0 C06E        000074      7           ST    13,SAVE+4
     00000A 41 D0 C06A        000070      8           LA    13,SAVE
                                         9  *
     000000                             10           ENTRY MAINLINE
                                        11           EXTRN ARRAY1
                                        12  *
     00000E 41 10 C0C2        0000C8     13           LA    1,=A(ARRAY1,ARRAY2)
     000012 58 F0 C0CA        0000D0     14           L     15,=V(SUBR)
     000016 05 EF                       15           BALR  14,15
                                        16  *
     000000                             17           USING ARRAYFLD,DUMMYREG
     000018 41 B0 C02E        000034     18           LA    DUMMYREG,ARRAY2
     00001C D2 02 B000C0CE  000000 0000D4 19           MVC   A1,=C'ABC'
     000022 D2 04 B007C0B2  000007 0000B8 20           MVC   A3,ZEROES
                                        21           DROP  DUMMYREG
                                        22  *
     000028 58 D0 C06E        000074     23           L     13,SAVE+4
     00002C 98 EC D00C                  24           LM    14,12,12(13)
     000030 07 FE                       25           BR    14
                                        26  *
     000000                             27  ARRAYFLD DSECT
     000000                             28  A1       DS    CL3
     000003                             29  A2       DS    CL4
     000007                             30  A3       DS    CL5
     00000C                             31  A4       DS    CL2
     00000E                             32  A5       DS    C
     000032                             33  MAIN     CSECT
                                        34  *
     00000F                             35  N        EQU   15
     000034                             36  ARRAY2   DS    (N)F
     000070                             37  SAVE     DS    18F
     00000B                             38  DUMMYREG EQU   11
     000088 00                         39  ZEROES   DC    15X'00'
     0000C8 0000000000000034           40
     0000D0 00000000
     0000D4 C1C2C3
                                        41           END
```

In addition, since MVC is an SS₁ instruction and since no length field is specified in the source statement, the Assembler substitutes the length attribute of A3, which it obtains from the Symbol Table, reduced by +1 for machine language. Thus the assembled instruction is created as follows:

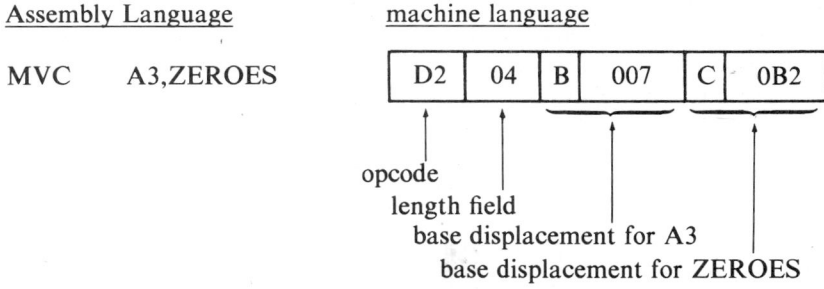

The DROP directive in Statement 19 causes the entry for Register 11 to be removed from the base-register table. If any subsequent instruction referred to a symbol in control section 2, the Assembler would report an "addressability error," i.e., an error in which the base-displacement address cannot be calculated due to lack of a base register for control section 2.

Figure 10.12 is the listing that would be produced for the figure 10.10 source module. Pretend once more to be the Assembler, this time using the symbol table, literal table, and base-register table as described, and verify that the object code shown on the listing is consistent with the descriptions provided in this section. Note that, although there are two occurrences of the CSECT directive, both with the name-field symbol MAIN, this does not result in MAIN being multiply-defined. The first CSECT defines the beginning of control section MAIN, while the second defines the resumption of that section and, consequently, a resumption of the addresses assigned in that section. The second CSECT thus permits the Assembler to switch from assembling the dummy section ARRAYFLD back to assembling the control section MAIN. Further discussion of this concept can be found in Section 15.1.

10.5 ASSEMBLER PROCESSING LOGIC

Based on the discussion and simplifications presented in the preceding sections, the overall processing logic of Pass 1 and Pass 2 can be summarized in flow diagram form (figs. 10.13 and 10.14). The diagrams are virtually identical to the descriptions already given, except for the processes associated with creating the object module and cross-reference information. The latter will be discussed in Section 10.9, after some characteristics of table processing have been presented. The object module is described in Section 10.6.

The principal ideas in Pass 1 processing shown in figure 10.13 are

1. Comment statements are processed by simply putting an appropriate entry on the intermediate file.
2. Instructions must be aligned on a half-word boundary; literals and name-field symbols must be placed in the appropriate tables; and the MLC must be increased by the instruction length.
3. Each directive has separate processing requirements. Some, like USING and DROP, are not processed at all except to put the statements in which they occur on the intermediate file. The CSECT, DSECT, EXTRN, and ENTRY directives contain information that must be placed in the ESD table for use in the creation of the object module. The DC and DS directives affect the MLC in two ways: (1) through the boundary alignment that may be required for the constant or data area and (2) through the increase due to the size of the constant or data area. Most directives will include a name-field symbol that must be entered into the symbol table, but in the EXTRN directive it is the operand symbols that are entered into the symbol table so that they may be referred to by A-type address constants.

The principal ideas in Pass 2 processing depicted in figure 10.14 are

1. Since there is sufficient information in the intermediate file to describe the statement type, the opcode and directive tables need not be searched.
2. Each instruction requires extensive processing that depends on its type, e.g., RR, RX. This processing is summarized in the right-hand portion of the flow diagram. After the object code has been created, it is not immediately written onto the object module but instead is placed in the TXT table. This is because each TXT entry may contain more than one assembled instruction or constant.
3. Of the ten directives under consideration, only four require special processing: END, DC, USING, and DROP. In particular, it should be noted that even though the DS directive causes the MLC to be changed during Pass 1 processing, it does not cause any object code to be generated during Pass 2. For this reason, you should not assume that an area reserved by a DS will contain blanks, or zeroes, or whatever, at the start of program execution.
4. The listing is created in Pass 2, one line at a time, as each statement is processed. The cross-reference information is accumulated by putting the operand symbols in a cross-reference table to be printed at the end of Pass 2. Address constants created by DC directives and literals are accumulated in the RLD table to be written on the object module at the end of Pass 2.

10.6 THE OBJECT MODULE

An object module is a file containing four types of entries: External Symbol Dictionary (ESD) entries, which identify each control section, entry point, and external reference; Text (TXT), or object code entries, which consist of the machine language instructions and data; Relocation Dictionary (RLD) entries, which describe each A- and V-type address constant; and an END entry, which specifies the address of the first instruction to be executed at run time.

The reason that there is more than just object code (TXT) data in an object module is to provide the Loader and Linkage Editor programs with the information they need to link together external subroutines and to relocate the object code into whatever main memory area is allocated by the Operating System.

The process of relocation does not alter the manner in which the object code is executed, but it does involve increasing each A- and V-type constant by a nonnegative integer, known as the *relocation factor*. For example, if the object code corresponding to the source module of figure 10.10 were loaded into memory location 4000_x, then, at run time, the address of ARRAY2 would be 004034_x, not 000034_x as it was at assembly time. Therefore, the address constant defined by the literal =A(ARRAY1,ARRAY2) would have

Figure 10.13   Pass 1 processing logic summary.

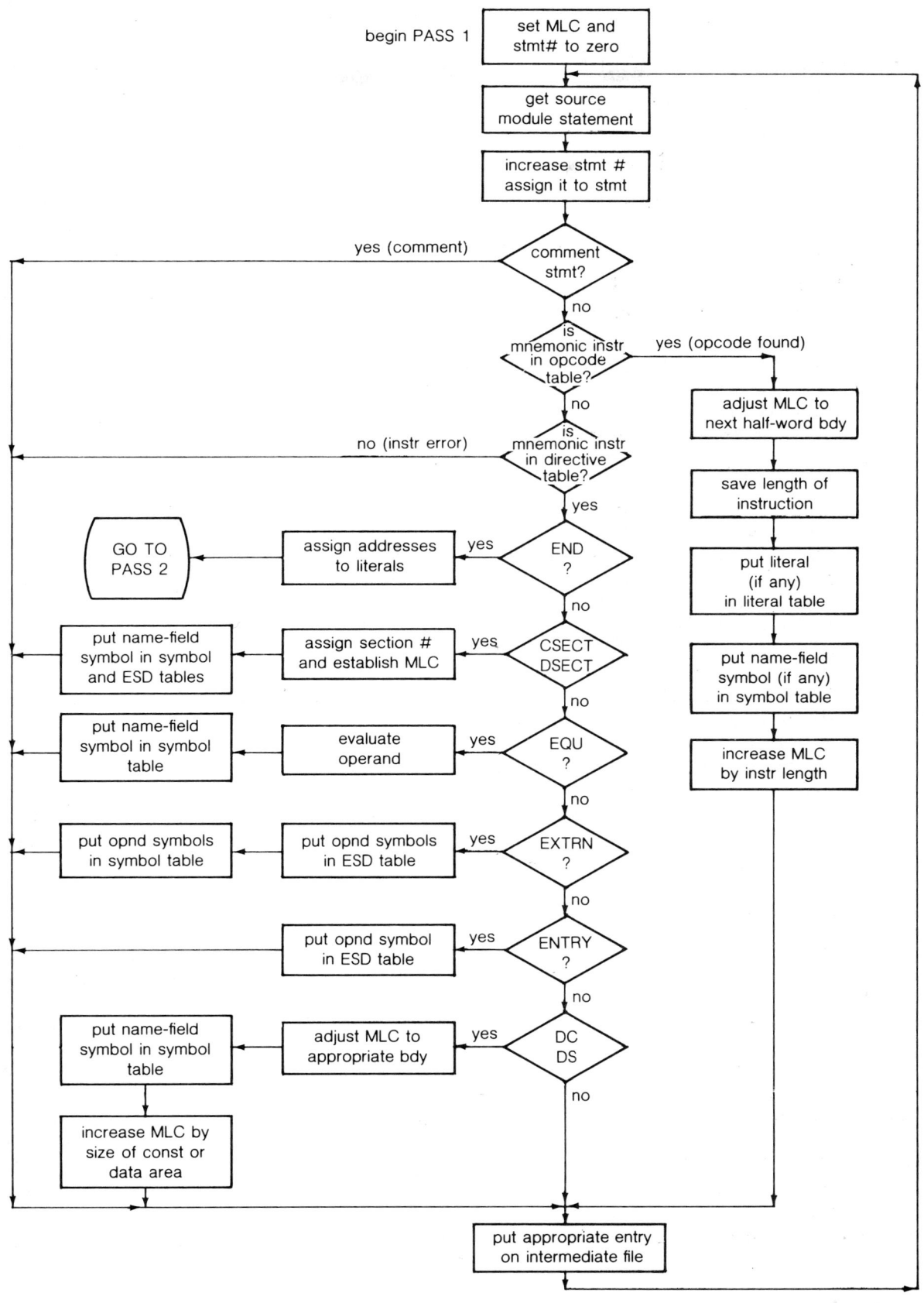

begin PASS 1

set MLC and stmt# to zero

get source module statement

increase stmt # assign it to stmt

comment stmt?

yes (comment)

no

is mnemonic instr in opcode table?

yes (opcode found)

adjust MLC to next half-word bdy

save length of instruction

put literal (if any) in literal table

put name-field symbol (if any) in symbol table

increase MLC by instr length

no

is mnemonic instr in directive table?

no (instr error)

yes

END ?

yes

assign addresses to literals

GO TO PASS 2

no

CSECT DSECT

yes

assign section # and establish MLC

put name-field symbol in symbol and ESD tables

no

EQU ?

yes

evaluate operand

put name-field symbol in symbol table

no

EXTRN ?

yes

put opnd symbols in ESD table

put opnd symbols in symbol table

no

ENTRY ?

yes

put opnd symbol in ESD table

no

DC DS

yes

adjust MLC to appropriate bdy

put name-field symbol in symbol table

increase MLC by size of const or data area

no

put appropriate entry on intermediate file

Figure 10.14   Pass 2 processing logic summary.

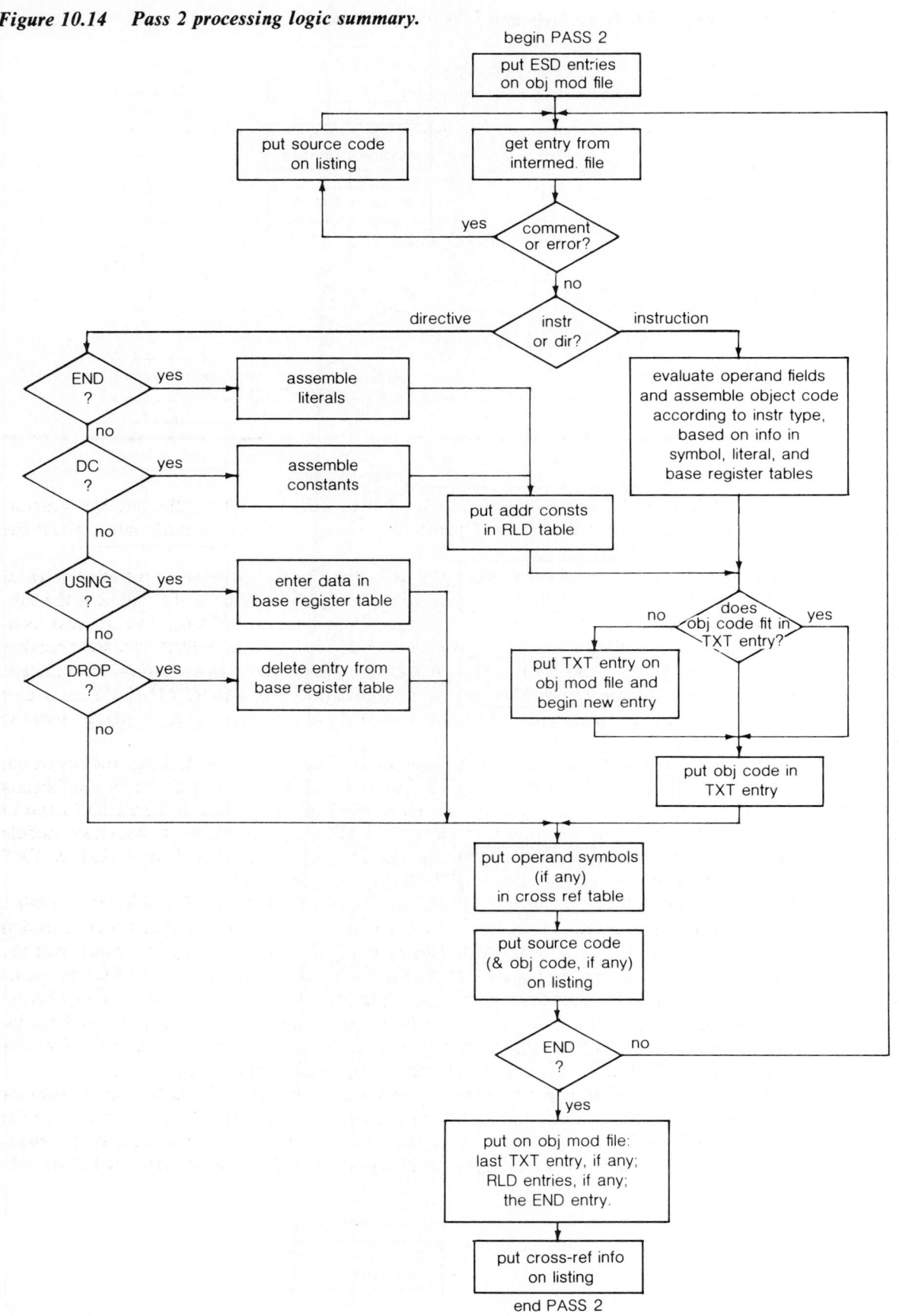

Figure 10.15 **Overview of ESD, TXT, RLD, and END entry formats.**

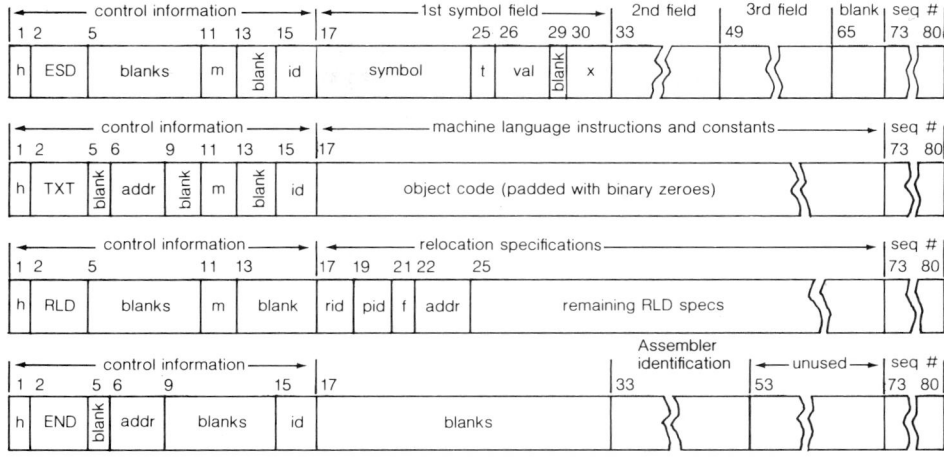

to be increased by 4000ₓ in order to be consistent with the run-time address. 4000ₓ is the relocation factor. The Loader obtains the relocation factor from the Operating System; it obtains the information about the literal address constant from the RLD entries.

The process of linking subroutines together requires that each address constant referring to an external symbol be replaced with the memory address with which that symbol is associated. For example if the subroutine named SUBR in figure 10.10 were loaded into memory location 6000ₓ, the address constant =V(SUBR) would be replaced with the binary representation of 006000ₓ. Similarly, if there were another program that referred to ours by a V-type constant, say =V(MAIN), then, in that program, the constant would be replaced by 004000ₓ, since that is the address associated with the symbol MAIN. The Loader obtains the information it needs about external references, control section names, and entry points from the ESD entries.

Although there are a number of other considerations in the processes of loading, linking, and relocation that will not be discussed in this text, the brief descriptions given should serve as a rationale for the formats of the ESD, TXT, and RLD entries. These formats are presented in summary form in figure 10.15 and in detail in figures 10.16a–10.16d. The examples presented in the detailed figures represent the object module formats for the same source module we discussed previously (see fig. 10.12). You should verify that the TXT data of figure 10.16b corresponds to the object code in the listing in figure 10.12.

Perhaps the main concept to be noted is that of the External Symbol Dictionary Identification Number (ESDID). As pointed out in the discussion of the symbol table entries, the Assembler assigns a control section number to each control section in the source module. This makes it simple to correlate a symbol with the control section in which it is defined, for purposes of choosing a base register and base address from the base-register table. A similar numbering technique is used in the object module. In fact, it is the same numbering technique just mentioned but extended to include not only control sections but also external references. ESDID's are assigned sequentially, in the order in which the control section names and external references occur in the source module. The ESDID of each such symbol is represented in the ESD entries.

In TXT entries, the ESDID of the control section to which the object code belongs is given in positions 15 and 16. In figure 10.16c, there are three TXT entries, each containing a portion of the object code in the control section whose ESDID is 0001ₓ, which, as may be seen from the first ESD entry in figure 15.16a, is the ESDID of MAIN. Thus, the two-byte ESDID serves as a kind of shorthand for the 8-byte symbol C'MAIN'.

Figure 10.16a ESD explanation and example.

Figure 10.16b TXT explanation and example.

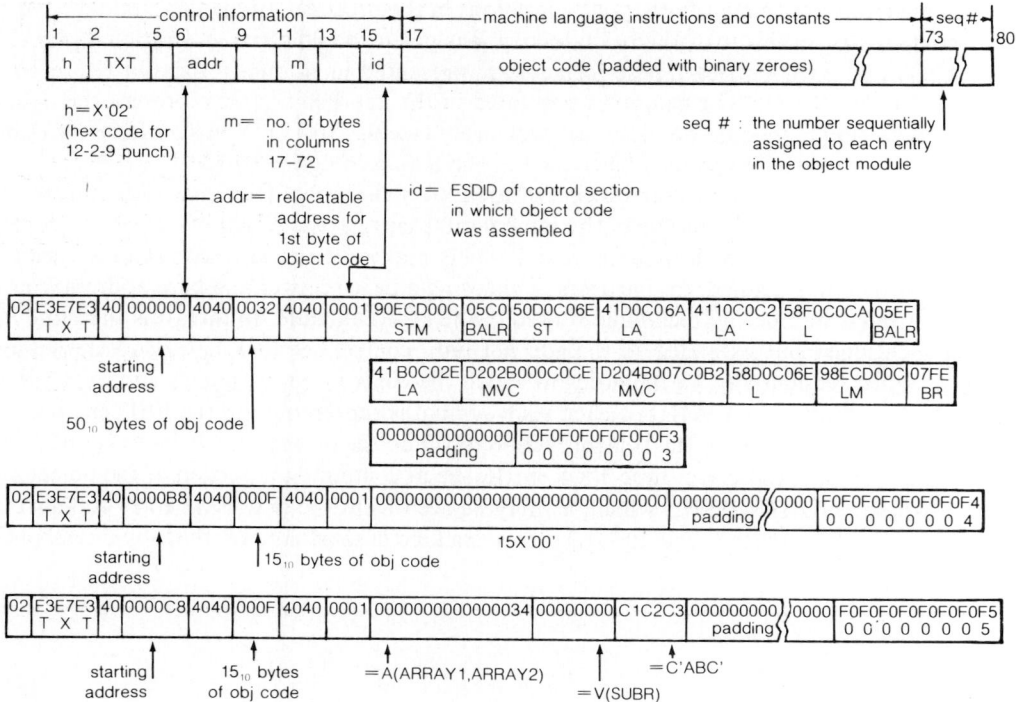

Figure 10.16c   RLD explanation and example.

Figure 10.16d   END explanation and example.

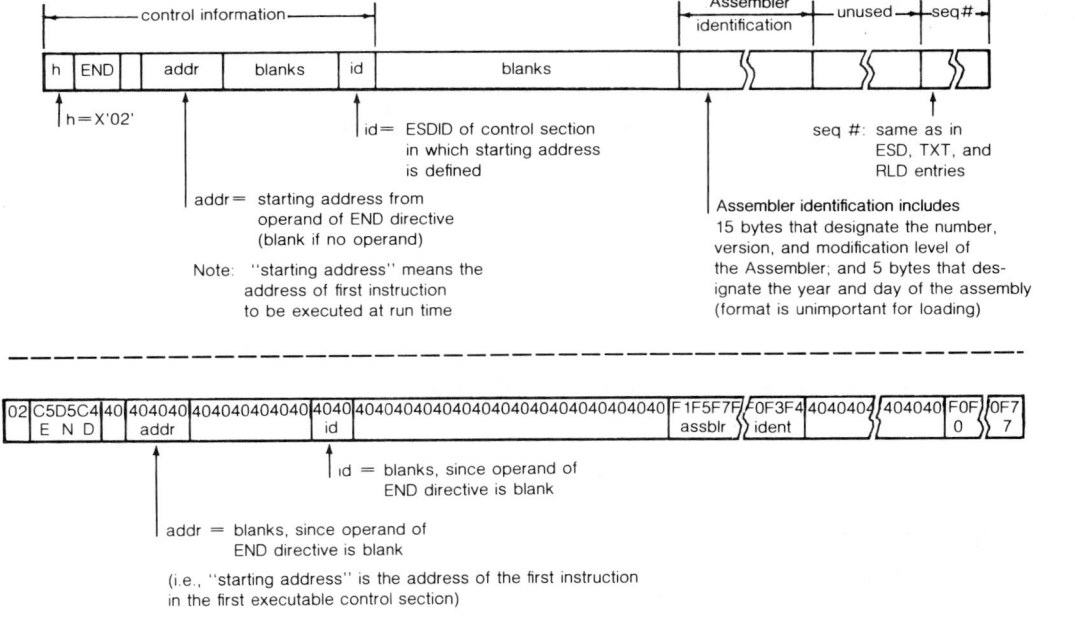

In RLD entries, it is not only necessary to identify the control section in which an A- or V-type constant occurs but also to identify the address of that constant, the symbol used to create it, and whether that symbol is an external or internal symbol. Referring to figure 10.16c, we see that this information is coded as follows:

rid	pid	f	addr

where

rid	=	ESDID of the symbol
pid	=	ESDID of the control section in which the symbol occurs
f	=	indicators describing the length of the constant, whether it is negative or positive, and whether the following constant has the same or different "rid" and "pid" numbers
addr	=	address of the constant

The "rid" number leads back to an ESD entry, where further information about that symbol may be found. For example, for the address constant =A(ARRAY1), we have, in the above format,

0002	0001	0C	0000C8

meaning that this constant is at address $0000C8_x$ in the control section whose ESDID is 0001_x, that it is defined further in the ESD field for ESDID 0002_x, and that the constant is 4 bytes long, positive, and not followed by another RLD field for the same symbol. Referring back to figure 10.16a, we find that ESDID 0002_x identifies the symbol ARRAY1, an external symbol whose value therefore must be determined by the Loader or Linkage Editor.

Further discussion of the object module and the manner in which it is processed by the Loader and Linkage Editor will not be pursued.

10.7 TABLE SEARCHING

In the preceding discussions of the Assembler, the role of tables was seen to be fundamental. The problem we now wish to touch upon is that of determining by what processing technique a sought-for table entry can be found. The most obvious solution is to examine each entry in turn, starting at the first one, until the desired entry is found. This is known as a *linear search* procedure (fig. 10.17). Linear searching has the advantage of being simple to implement; it has the disadvantage of being time-consuming if there are a large number of entries in the table.

Figure 10.17   Linear search procedure for table with M entries.

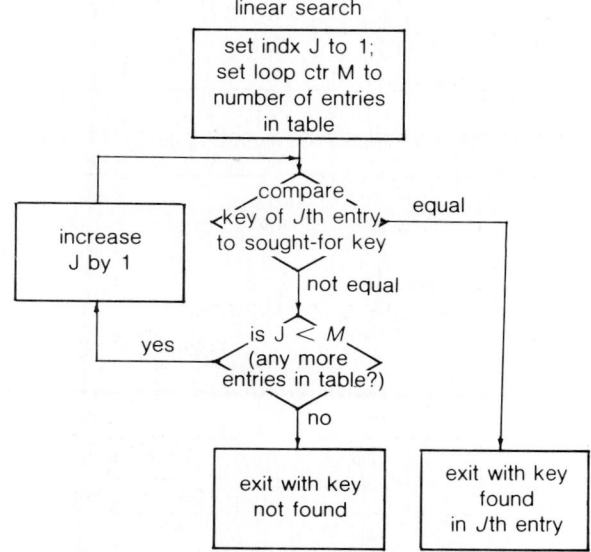

If many searches have to be made through a table, a linear search will require that half the entries, on the average, be examined. If there are N entries, the average search time will be $A(N/2)$, where the constant A is a function of the speed of the computer and of the number and type of instructions used in each iteration of the search procedure. If the entries are not in sequence, every entry would have to be examined to determine that the sought-for entry is not in the table. If the entries are in sequence, the search could be terminated at the point beyond which the sought-for entry could not occur.

It may be helpful to visualize the linear search technique by imagining oneself searching through a small dictionary or glossary for a particular word and its definition. Starting at the first word, you would eventually come to a word beyond which the word being sought could not occur. This, of course, is a consequence of the fact that the words are in alphabetical sequence. Obviously, you would not use a linear search to look for a word in a dictionary, because a faster method is available. You would start looking somewhere near where the word is expected to occur, and work forward or backward, perhaps reversing direction several times in the process, until you found the word or were certain it wasn't there. A similar technique, known as the *binary search technique,* has long been used in searching tables in computer memory.

Simply stated, the binary search technique involves starting at the middle of the table, not the beginning, and proceeding in the following manner. First, we determine, by comparing the search key to the key of the middle entry, whether the sought-for entry is in the first half or the last half of the table. Then, when the appropriate area is determined, we examine the middle entry of *that* half, to determine which of the two halves of that half is the appropriate area in which to look further. The process continues in this way, with further subdivisions into smaller and smaller halves, until the entry is either found or not found.

It can be shown that on the average the search time using the binary search technique will be $B(\log_2 N)$, where B is some constant. The technique is depicted in figure 10.18. It is somewhat more complex than a linear search; consequently, the constant B will be somewhat larger than A for a given computer system. A

Figure 10.18 Binary search procedure for table with M entries.

Figure 10.19   Comparison of N/2 with Log₂N.

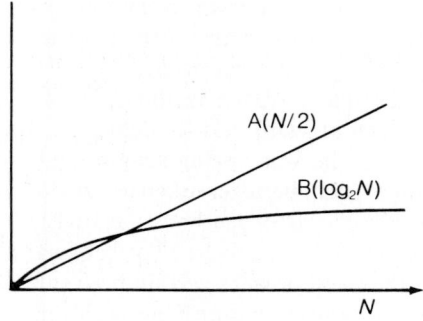

comparison of $B(\log_2 N)$ and $A(N/2)$ is described by the curves in figure 10.19, so that for reasonably large N, a binary search is to be preferred. For example, if $B = 10 \times A$, then the cutover point will be approximately $N = 150$. If $B = 5 \times A$, the cutover is approximately $N = 50$.

Suppose that $B = 5A$, i.e., that each iteration in the binary search takes five times as much processing time as an iteration in the linear search. Then, by calculating the ratio $\dfrac{B(\log_2 N)}{A(N/2)}$, we see that, if $N = 100$, the average table search time using the binary technique will be half as long as that using the linear technique; if $N = 500$, it will take one fifth the time; if $N = 1000$, one tenth the time. If, as in the Assembler, hundreds if not thousands of table searches must be made each day, the appropriate choice of search technique can yield large dividends in terms of reduced processing time.

To search a table by any method, the values of several variables must be known: the number of entries in the table, the size (number of bytes) of each entry, the position and length of the key field in each entry, and the key of the sought-for entry. From a programming standpoint, it is clearly desirable that the size of all entries be the same and the length of the key field be the same in each entry. However, this is not always possible. It depends on the table. For example, in the opcode table each entry is 8 bytes long, and the key occupies the first 5 bytes of each entry; but in the literal table, the length of each entry depends on the length of the literal string, and that string is itself the key of each entry. The opcode table entries are said to be *fixed-length,* the literal entries *variable-length.* Similar terminology is used to describe the keys.

Since in a program such as the Assembler there are several tables to be searched, it is convenient to have a single subroutine that will search any table. The subroutine should be general enough to handle any values of the variables mentioned above, and it must be programmed to return one of two results: (1) the address of the sought-for entry if it is found, or (2) an indication that it wasn't found. The subroutine in figure 10.20 is a binary search routine that satisfies most of the requirements discussed. The constraints are that the entries and keys be fixed-length and that the key length be less than or equal to 256 bytes. The first constraint makes the programming simpler; the key-length constraint allows us to use the CLC instruction (via the EX instruction) for the key comparisons. The routine closely follows the processing logic depicted in figure 10.18.

If the keys are of variable length, as in the literal table, or if their length exceeds 256 bytes, it might be more convenient to use the CLCL instruction discussed in Section 7.8. This instruction allows strings of virtually arbitrary length to be compared; the two strings being compared need not have the same length. As an exercise, you should alter the binary search routine of figure 10.20 so that it utilizes the CLCL instruction and could thereby be used to search a table such as the literal table.

The comprehensive analysis and comparison of linear, binary, and other search techniques given in Donald E. Knuth's *The Art of Computer Programming, vol. 3: Sorting and Searching* (Addison Wesley, 1973) is recommended for those who wish further details of these techniques.

```
BISRCH    CSECT
*
* BINARY SEARCH SUBROUTINE, ENTERED WITH CALL BISRCH(TBL,M,L,KP,KL,SK)
*      WHERE   TBL = ADDRESS OF FIRST ENTRY IN TABLE TO BE SEARCHED
*              M   = NUMBER OF ENTRIES IN TABLE
*              L   = LENGTH OF EACH ENTRY (NUMBER OF BYTES)
*              KP  = RELATIVE POSITION OF ENTRY KEY (0=1ST BYTE OF ENTRY)
*              KL  = LENGTH OF KEY (NUMBER OF BYTES)
*              SK  = ADDR OF KEY OF SOUGHT-FOR ENTRY
* IF SOUGHT-FOR ENTRY IS FOUND, ITS ADDRESS IS RETURNED IN REG 15
* IF SOUGHT-FOR ENTRY IS NOT FOUND, A ZERO IS RETURNED IN REG 15
*
* USES FOLLOWING INDEXES:
*         LOWPT  = RELATIVE POSITION OF THE LOWEST ENTRY IN THAT
*                  'HALF' OF THE TABLE CURRENTLY BEING EXAMINED
*          HIPT  = REL POSITION OF HIGHEST ENTRY IN CURRENT HALF
*                  OF TABLE
*         MIDPT  = REL POSITION OF MID-ENTRY IN CURRENT HALF OF
*                  TABLE (INTEGER PORTION OF (LOWPT+HIPT)/2  )
*
* USES FOLLOWING SYMBOLIC REGISTER ADDRESSES:
TBL       EQU    1              REG 1 (TEMPORARY) ADDR OF 1ST TABLE ENTRY
KPA       EQU    1              REG 1 = KPA, ADDR OF KEY IN 1ST ENTRY
M         EQU    2              REG 2 = M, # ENTRIES IN TBL
L         EQU    3              REG 3 = L, LENGTH OF EACH ENTRY
KP        EQU    4              REG 4 = KP, REL BYTE POSITION OF KEY
KL        EQU    5              REG 5 = KL, LENGTH OF KEY
SK        EQU    6              REG 6 = SK, ADDR OF SOUGHT-FOR KEY
LOWPT     EQU    7              REG 7 = POSITION OF LOWEST ENTRY IN THIS HALF
HIPT      EQU    8              REG 8 = POSITION OF HIGHEST ENTRY, THIS HALF
MIDPT     EQU    9              REG 9 = POSITION OF MID-ENTRY IN THIS HALF
X         EQU    10             REG 10= SCRATCH REGISTER
CUR       EQU    11             REG 11= ADDR OF KEY OF CURRENT MID-ENTRY
BASE      EQU    12             REG 12= BASE REGISTER FOR SUBROUTINE
*
          STM    14,12,12(13)   STANDARD ENTRY
          BALR   BASE,0
          USING  *,BASE
          ST     13,SAVE+4
          LA     13,SAVE
*
          LM     TBL,SK,0(1)    GET PARAMETERS FROM CALLER
          L      M,0(M)         # ENTRIES IN TABLE
          LTR    M,M            SEE IF TABLE IS EMPTY
          BNP    NOTFOUND       IF SO, CAN'T FIND SOUGHT-FOR ENTRY
          L      L,0(L)         LENGTH OF EACH ENTRY
          L      KP,0(KP)       REL BYTE POSITION OF KEY
          AR     TBL,KP         COMPUTE ADDR OF KEY IN 1ST ENTRY
          L      KL,0(KL)       LENGTH OF KEY
          SH     KL,=H'1'       SUBTRACT 1 FOR EXECUTE INSTRUCTION
*
          LH     LOWPT,=H'1'    INITIALIZE LOWPT TO FIRST ENTRY
          LR     HIPT,M         INITIALIZE HIPT TO LAST ENTRY
*
*
* COMPUTE INDEX OF MID-ENTRY, AND ADDRESS OF MID-ENTRY'S KEY
LOOP      LA     MIDPT,0(LOWPT,HIPT)   MIDPT=(LOWPT+HIPT)/2
          SRA    MIDPT,1        (RIGHT-SHIFT 1 BIT TO DIVIDE BY 2)
          LR     CUR,MIDPT      ADDR OF MID-ENTRY'S KEY EQUALS
          SH     CUR,=H'1'      ADDR OF 1ST ENTRY'S KEY, PLUS
          MR     X,L            L*(MIDPT-1)
          AR     CUR,KPA
*
```

Figure 10.20   continued

```
        * COMPARE KEY OF SOUGHT-FOR ENTRY TO KEY OF MID-ENTRY
                EX      KL,COMPARE       COMPARE KEYS
                BH      UPPER            H1 MEANS LOOK IN UPPER HALF
                BL      LOWER            LO MEANS LOOK IN LOWER HALF
                B       .FOUND           EQ MEANS IT'S FOUND
        *
        * SET HIPT = MIDPT-1      IF SOUGHT-FOR KEY MUST BE IN LOWER HALF
        LOWER   SH      MIDPT,=H'1'
                LR      HIPT,MIDPT
                B       MORE
        *
        * SET LOWPT = MIDPT+1     IF SOUGHT-FOR KEY MUST BE IN UPPER HALF
        UPPER   AH      MIDPT,=H'1'
                LR      LOWPT,MIDPT
        *
        * SEE IF THERE ARE AT LEAST TWO ENTRIES THAT HAVEN'T BEEN EXAMINED
        MORE    CR      HIPT,LOWPT       IS  HIPT>LOWPT ?
                BH      LOOP             IF SO, CONTINUE SEARCHING
                BE      ONEMORE          IF EQUAL, THERE'S ONE MORE ENTRY TO BE
                B       NOTFOUND            EXAMINED; OTHERWISE, IT'S NOT FOUND.
        *
        * EXAMINE SOLE REMAINING ENTRY
        ONEMORE LR      CUR,MIDPT        COMPUTE ADDR OF REMAINING ENTRY'S KEY
                SH      CUR,=H'1'
                MR      X,L
                AR      CUR,KPA
                EX      KL,COMPARE       COMPARE KEYS
                BE      FOUND
        *
        * SOUGHT-FOR KEY NOT IN TABLE, SO RETURN  0  IN REG 15.
        NOTFOUND SR     15,15
                B       EXIT
        *
        * SOUGHT-FOR ENTRY FOUND IN TABLE, SO RETURN ADDR OF ENTRY IN REG 15.
        FOUND   LR      15,CUR           ADDR OF ENTRY IS ADDR OF KEY IN THAT
                SR      15,KP            ENTRY, MINUS POSITION OF KEY
        *
        * EXIT FROM SUBROUTINE
        EXIT    L       13,SAVE+4
                L       14,12(13)        PRESERVE CONTENTS OF REG 15
                LM      0,12,20(13)
                BR      14
        *
        * COMPARE INSTRUCTION FOR EXECUTE INSTR.
        COMPARE CLC     0(0,SK),0(CUR)
        *
        SAVE    DS      18F
                END
```

10.8   SORTING TABLES

Sorting involves rearrangement of entries into some prescribed order. The rearrangement is usually physical, much like the physical rearrangement of personal canceled checks into check number sequence, or the rearrangement of a deck of cards into sequence within each suit. Clearly, any rearrangement that places entries into some prescribed order must be based on some property of each entry. In sorting, this property is invariably the value of one or more fields in the entry. For example, the entries in the Assembler's opcode table are in sequence by the mnemonic instruction code. But if the entries in the symbol table were not sorted into sequence based on the alphanumeric symbols that constitute the key field of each entry, then symbol table searching would not be as efficient as it could be.

We mention table sorting in the title of this section to emphasize that all the entries that are to be sorted can fit in main memory throughout the sorting process. This is commonly known as *internal* sorting—internal to main memory. When the number of entries is so large that only a portion can be in main memory at one time, the rest being in secondary memory, the process is known as *external* sorting. Since external sorting must involve input and output, it entails considerations that are qualitatively different from those in internal sorting. We will restrict our discussions to internal sorting.

Many studies have been made to devise fast sorting algorithms. Knuth discusses five major internal sorting techniques and describes some two dozen algorithms. But as Knuth points out, this "is only a fraction of the algorithms that have been devised so far." The main reason for the existence of so many algorithms is the importance of using one that is in some sense best suited to the data and the computer system. *There is no known best way to sort an arbitrary set of data in an arbitrarily chosen computer system.* The best way for a given situation would be one that used the least amount of time and the least amount of memory space. This will certainly depend on the computer and on the instructions used in the algorithm on that computer, and it will also depend on the data—how many entries are to be sorted and how badly out of sequence (or how nearly in sequence) they are when the sort is begun.

Let us illustrate a simple sorting procedure, known as *straight insertion,* by considering the symbol table that would exist at the end of Pass 1 for the sample source module of figure 10.10. To simplify the discussions, we will adopt the notation and terminology used in Knuth's book:

Let R_j denote the jth entry, or *record,* in the table

Let K_j denote the key field in record R_j

Assume that there are N entries or records in the table

Then the straight insertion technique can be summarized as follows: Assume that $1 < j \leq N$, and that records $R_1,...,R_{j-1}$ have been sorted. We now compare the jth key K_j to the keys preceding it in the table, in the following order: K_{j-1}, $K_{j-2},...,K_1$. When we discover a key, K_i, such that $K_j \geq K_i$, the record R_j is inserted between records R_i and R_{i+1}. To make this insertion, the records R_{i+1}, $R_{i+2},...,R_{j-1}$ are moved back one position in the table.

Figure 10.21 illustrates the procedure for our symbol table; figure 10.22a is a flow diagram depicting the steps in the procedure. Note that the comparison and moving operations are interleaved to avoid another loop. Note also that very little temporary memory space is required: the records are sorted "in place", so to speak. Finally, note from figure 10.21 that when a record is already in its correct position for a given j, all the comparisons must be made (the computer having no other way to determine that the record is in its proper

---

Figure 10.21   Symbol table sorted by straight insertion. (The original table is given in the order of occurrence in fig. 10.10.)

i	j=2 original table	j=3	j=4	j=5	j=6	j=7	j=8	j=9	j=10	j=11	j=12	j=13	j=14	j=15	sorted table
1	MAIN	MAIN	ARRAY1	ARRAYFLD	ARRAYFLD	ARRAYFLD	ARRAYFLD	ARRAYFLD	ARRAYFLD	ARRAYFLD	ARRAYFLD	ARRAYFLD	ARRAYFLD	ARRAYFLD	ARRAYFLD
2	MAINLINE	MAINLINE	MAIN	ARRAY1	ARRAY1	ARRAY1	ARRAY1	ARRAY1	ARRAY1	ARRAY1	ARRAY1	ARRAY1	ARRAY1	ARRAY1	ARRAY1
3	ARRAY1	ARRAY1	MAINLINE	MAIN	A1	A1	A1	A1	A1	A1	A1	ARRAY2	ARRAY2	ARRAY2	ARRAY2
4	ARRAYFLD	ARRAYFLD	ARRAYFLD	MAINLINE	MAIN	A2	A2	A2	A2	A2	A2	A1	A1	A1	A1
5	A1	A1	A1	A1	MAINLINE	MAIN	A3	A3	A3	A3	A3	A2	A2	A2	A2
6	A2	A2	A2	A2	A2	MAINLINE	MAIN	A4	A4	A4	A4	A3	A3	A3	A3
7	A3	A3	A3	A3	A3	A3	MAINLINE	MAIN	A5	A5	A5	A4	A4	A4	A4
8	A4	A4	A4	A4	A4	A4	A4	MAINLINE	MAIN	MAIN	MAIN	A5	A5	A5	A5
9	A5	A5	A5	A5	A5	A5	A5	A5	MAINLINE	MAIN	MAIN	MAIN	MAIN	DUMMYREG	DUMMYREG
10	MAIN	MAIN	MAIN	MAIN	MAIN	MAIN	MAIN	MAIN	MAIN	MAINLINE	MAINLINE	MAIN	MAIN	MAIN	MAIN
11	N	N	N	N	N	N	N	N	N	N	N	MAINLINE	MAINLINE	MAIN	MAIN
12	ARRAY2	ARRAY2	ARRAY2	ARRAY2	ARRAY2	ARRAY2	ARRAY2	ARRAY2	ARRAY2	ARRAY2	ARRAY2	N	N	MAINLINE	MAINLINE
13	SAVE	SAVE	SAVE	SAVE	SAVE	SAVE	SAVE	SAVE	SAVE	SAVE	SAVE	SAVE	SAVE	N	N
14	DUMMYREG	DUMMYREG	DUMMYREG	DUMMYREG	DUMMYREG	DUMMYREG	DUMMYREG	DUMMYREG	DUMMYREG	DUMMYREG	DUMMYREG	DUMMYREG	DUMMYREG	SAVE	SAVE
15	ZEROES	ZEROES	ZEROES	ZEROES	ZEROES	ZEROES	ZEROES	ZEROES	ZEROES	ZEROES	ZEROES	ZEROES	ZEROES	ZEROES	ZEROES

Figure 10.22a *Algorithm for straight insertion sort for a table with N records.*

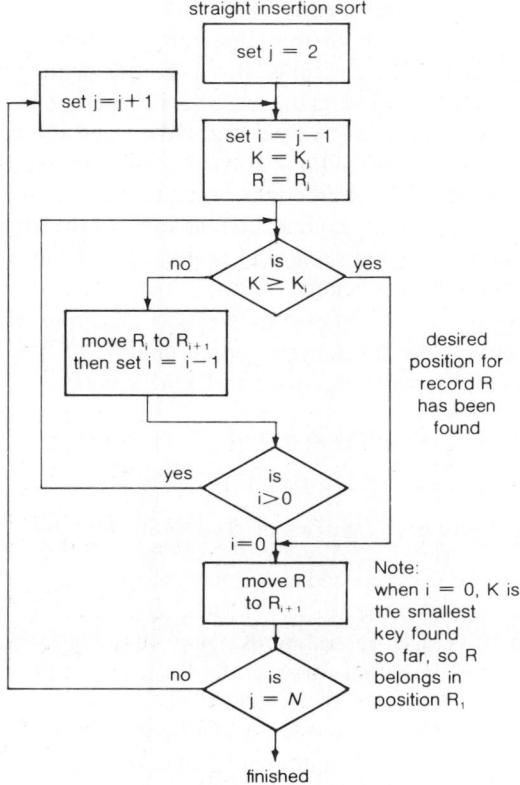

position) although no records are moved. For simplicity, only the keys K_i are shown in figure 10.21. In actuality, the entire record containing each key would be moved as appropriate. The subroutine in figure 10.22b illustrates this; it uses the algorithm of figure 10.22a to sort any table that contains fixed-length entries.

The straight insertion technique moves records one position at a time. This is satisfactory from the standpoint of overall processing time only if the records are nearly in their final position or if, as in figure 10.21, there are relatively few records to be sorted. The technique would be rather slow under other conditions. Consequently, a number of variations of the straight insertion technique have been developed to reduce the number of comparisons and/or to reduce the amount of data movement. Several of these techniques are described in Knuth's book. In addition to the straight insertion technique, Knuth investigated four other categories of techniques, each with their own set of algorithms. These may be summarized in a simplified fashion as follows:

1. *Exchange* techniques, which interchange pairs of entries that are out of order until no more such pairs exist in the table.
2. *Selection* techniques, which search first for the smallest (or largest) entry, then for the next smallest (or largest), and so on.
3. *Merge* techniques, which combine two or more already sequenced subsets of entries to produce a new sequenced subset and continue in this way until all the sequenced subsets have been merged into one, which is the final sorted table.
4. *Distribution* techniques, in which a portion of each key is examined and the entries separated (or distributed) into subsets, one for each different value of the key portion being examined. A different portion of the key is then used and the process repeated, maintaining the order of the entries that was established by the previous distribution. The process continues in this way until the final portion of the key has been examined. The final subset produced consists of all the entries in sequence.

Of course, these summaries convey only the broadest differences among the techniques. Further discussion of these techniques is beyond the scope of this text.

```
STSORT    CSECT
*
*   STRAIGHT INSERTION SORT SUBROUTINE STSORT(TBL,N,L,KP,KL)
*       WHERE TBL = ADDRESS OF FIRST ENTRY IN TABLE TO BE SORTED
*             N   = NUMBER OF ENTRIES IN THE TABLE
*             L   = LENGTH OF EACH ENTRY (NUMBER OF BYTES)
*             KP  = RELATIVE POSITION OF ENTRY KEY (0=1ST POSITION)
*             KL  = LENGTH OF KEY (NUMBER OF BYTES)
*
*   THIS ROUTINE ASSUMES THE PARAMETERS SATISFY THESE CONSTRAINTS:
*     N>0,  0<L≤256,  0≤KP≤256,  0≤KP+KL≤256.
*   THE ENTRIES ARE SORTED 'IN PLACE', I.E., THE SORTED ENTRIES
*     REPLACE THE ORIGINAL UNSORTED ENTRIES.
*   'STSORT' USES THE FOLLOWING SYMBOLIC REGISTER ADDRESSES:
*   (NOTE THAT THE USE OF REGS 1-5 MATCHES THE SEQUENCE OF PARAMS)
*
TBL       EQU     1             REG 1 = ADDR OF 1ST TABLE ENTRY
N         EQU     2             REG 2 (TEMPORARY) = # ENTRIES IN TBL
NADDR     EQU     2             REG 2 = ADDR OF LAST TABLE ENTRY
L         EQU     3             REG 3 = L, LENGTH OF EACH ENTRY
KP        EQU     4             REG 4 = KP, RELATIVE BYTE POSITION OF KEY
KLX       EQU     5             REG 5 = KL-1, ONE LESS THAN KEY LENGTH
KL        EQU     KLX
LX        EQU     6             REG 6 = L-1, ONE LESS THAN ENTRY LENGTH
RI        EQU     7             REG 7 = ADDR OF RECORD 'I'
KI        EQU     8             REG 8 = ADDR OF KEY IN RECORD 'I'
RI1       EQU     9             REG 9 = ADDR OF RECORD 'I+1'
RJ        EQU     10            REG 10= ADDR OF RECORD 'J'
KJ        EQU     11            REG 11= ADDR OF KEY IN 'RECJ' TEMP AREA
XEVEN     EQU     10            REG 10= (TEMP) EVEN# REG FOR COMPUTING (N-1)*L
XODD      EQU     11            REG 11= (TEMP) ODD #      ''               ''
*
          STM     14,12,12(13)  ENTRY TO SUBR
          BALR    12,0
          USING   *,12
          ST      13,SAVE+4
          LA      13,SAVE
          LM      TBL,KL,0(1)   GET PARAMS IN REG 1 THRU 5
*
*   INITIALIZATIONS
          L       N,0(N)        N = NUMBER OF ENTRIES
          C       N,=F'1'
          BNH     FINIS         IF 'N' NOT GREATER THAN 1, DON'T SORT
          L       L,0(L)        L = ENTRY LENGTH
          LR      LX,L          LX= L-1  FOR 'EX' INSTRUCTION
          SH      LX,=H'1'
          LR      XODD,N
          SH      XODD,=H'1'        COMPUTE  (N-1)*L  IN REG 'XODD'
          MR      XEVEN,L           NADDR = (N-1)*L + ADDR OF TABLE
          LA      NADDR,0(XODD,TBL)     = ADDR OF LAST TBL ENTRY
          L       KP,0(KP)      KP= RELATIVE KEY POSITION IN ENTRY
          L       KLX,0(KL)     KL= KEY LENGTH
          SH      KLX,=H'1'     KLX = KL-1  FOR 'EX' INSTRUCTION
          LA      RJ,0(L,TBL)   RJ= ADDR OF JTH ENTRY
*                               INITIALLY, J = 2
*
*
*   MAIN LOOP FOR COMPARING RECDS, AND MOVING THEM WHEN NECESSARY
*
MAINLOOP  EX      LX,MOVEJ      MOVE JTH RECD TO TEMP AREA
          LA      KJ,RECDJ(KP)  KJ = ADDR OF KEY IN TEMP AREA
          LR      RI,RJ         RI = ADDR OF ITH RECD
          SR      RI,L          INITIALLY, I = J-1
*
COMPLOOP  LA      RI1,0(L,RI)   RI1 = ADDR OF (I+1)ST RECD
```

Figure 10.22b   continued

```
                LA    KI,0(KP,RI)       KI = ADDR OF KEY IN ITH RECD
                EX    KLX,COMPARE       IS JTH RECD > OR = ITH RECD ?
                BNL   COMPYES           IF SO, BRANCH TO 'COMPYES'
                EX    LX,MOVEI          ELSE, MOVE ITH RECD TO (I+1)ST
                SR    RI,L              BACK UP TO (I-1)ST RECD
                CR    RI,TBL            IS THIS THE ZEROTH RECD ?
                BNL   COMPLOOP          IF NOT, REPEAT THE COMPARE/MOVE LOOP
                LR    RI1,TBL           IF I=0, SET RI1 = ADDR OF 1ST ENTRY
         *
         * IF JTH RECD GREATER THAN ITH, OR IF 'I' HAS BEEN REDUCED TO ZERO,
         COMPYES EX   LX,MOVE           MOVE JTH RECD FROM TEMP TO (I+1)ST
                AR    RJ,L              INCR TO (J+1)ST RECD
                CR    RJ,NADDR          WAS JTH RECD THE NTH (LAST) RECD ?
                BNH   MAINLOOP          IF NOT, GO DO NEXT PASS WITH J = J+1
         *
         FINIS   L    13,SAVE+4
                LM    14,12,12(13)      EXIT FROM SUBR
                BR    14
         *
         MOVEI   MVC  0(0,RI1),0(RI)    MOVE ITH RECD TO (I+1)ST
         MOVEJ   MVC  RECDJ(0),0(RJ)    MOVE JTH RECD TO TEMP AREA
         MOVE    MVC  0(0,RI1),RECDJ    MOVE JTH RECD FROM TEMP TO (I+1)ST
         COMPARE CLC  0(0,KJ),0(KI)     COMPARE JTH RECD (IN TEMP AREA) TO ITH
         *
         RECDJ   DS   CL256       TEMP SPACE FOR MAX LENGTH JTH RECORD
         SAVE    DS   18F         REGISTER SAVE AREA
                END
```

10.9   CROSS-REFERENCES

The task of producing cross-reference information for a source module requires some mechanism for remembering the statement numbers of all statements in which the symbol appears in an operand field, in order that they can be printed at the end of Pass 2.

One way to meet this requirement would be to have one cross-reference table for each symbol. But this poses two immediate problems: (1) how many tables should there be and (2) how much space should be reserved for each table? We don't know how many tables there should be, because we don't know how many symbols there will be in a given source module until that module is processed. Nor do we know how much space to reserve for each table since we don't know ahead of time how many references there will be to each symbol in a source module. It would be a waste of memory space to make each table big enough to hold all the expected cross-references to a symbol; some symbols will clearly never be referenced, others may be referenced only a few times, and some may be referenced many times. We need a scheme that will accommodate these differences and uncertainties without undue waste of memory space.

One such scheme would be to reserve space for just one table, instead of having one table for each symbol. This space must be large enough to hold the totality of all cross-references in the source module. We could then allocate the space at assembly time by adding each new cross-reference entry to the then current end of the table, much as we would add a symbol table entry to the end of the symbol table. To identify the symbol to which each cross-reference entry pertains, it would seem logical to reserve 8 bytes in each entry for that symbol, similar to the definition of a symbol table entry. However, we can avoid doing this, and thereby save even more space, by using the concept of a list.

A *list* is a set of entries that may be scattered in memory, instead of being consecutive as in a table. Each list entry contains at least one field that is used in locating another entry of the list. The content of this field is known as a *pointer,* since it points to the location of an entry. The pointer can be an address or any other number that can be used in calculating an address.

Figure 10.23   *Cross-reference list structure and example.*

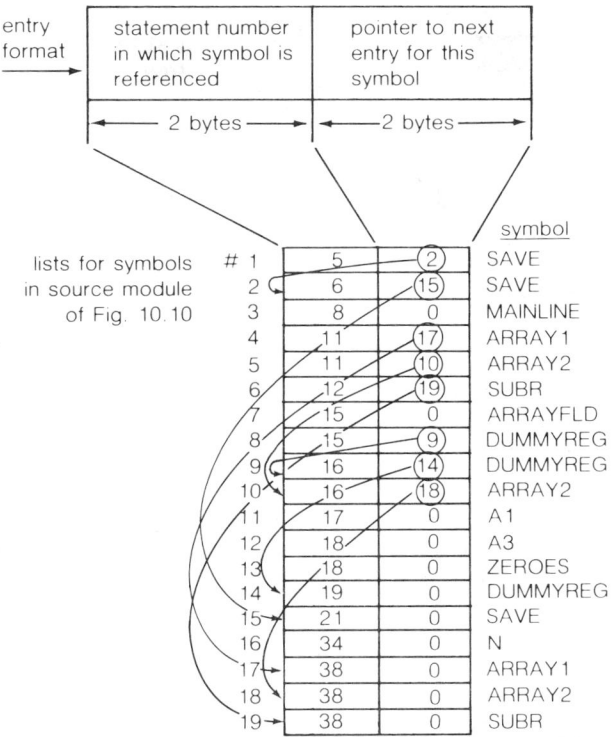

The list structure we have in mind for the cross-reference table is illustrated in figure 10.23. The entries are shown in the order in which they would be placed there in Pass 2 of the Assembler when the intermediate file corresponding to figure 10.10 is processed. The structure has these properties. Each entry consists of two fields of 2 bytes each: a statement number field that identifies the statement in which the cross-reference occurs and a pointer field that identifies the next entry in the structure that contains a cross-reference for the same symbol. (If the pointer is zero, there are no more entries in the structure for that symbol.) If we know where the first entry for a given symbol is located in the structure, we can find the other entries for that symbol by using the pointer in each entry to locate the next entry. Moreover, since the entries on a given list were added in the order in which they were discovered in Pass 2, they are in statement number sequence and need not be sorted before printing.

For example, the entries for the symbol SAVE are in positions 1, 2, and 15 of the structure. The entry in position 1 corresponds to the reference made in Statement 5—ST 13,SAVE+4; the entry in position 2 corresponds to the reference in Statement 6—LA 13,SAVE; and the entry in position 15 corresponds to the reference in Statement 21—L 13,SAVE+4. Between position 2 and position 15, a number of references to other symbols occurred; these were assigned to consecutively available positions in the structure.

Clearly, the problems that now need to be resolved in order to use this scheme in the Assembler are

1. Where is the first entry for a given symbol located?
2. When adding a new entry to a given list (for example, when adding the entry in position 15 for the symbol SAVE), how would we find the previous last entry on that list in order to replace its "zero" pointer with a pointer to the new entry (e.g., how would we find that 15 should be placed in the pointer field of position 2 when we add the reference to SAVE that occurs in Statement 21)?
3. When adding a new entry to a given list, how do we determine which position in the structure to use for that new entry?

For the first two problems, it is convenient to provide the information in the symbol table itself. This requires a change to the symbol table entry format, as follows. Instead of the format that was defined in figure 10.5,

symbol	value	length attr	stmnt #	ctl sect	rel/ abs

we define the following format:

Each of the last three fields is 2 bytes long. The content of the last field does not change after the first cross-reference for that symbol is added to the list structure. The content of the other two fields changes each time a cross-reference for the symbol is added in Pass 2.

For example, after Statement 6 of the source module has been processed in Pass 2, the symbol table entry for SAVE would be this:

symbol	value	length attr	stmnt #	ctl sect	rel/ abs	ref ctr	last entry	first entry
SAVE	000070	4	35	1	R	2	2	1

After Statement 21 has been processed in Pass 2, the symbol table entry for SAVE would be this:

symbol	value	length attr	stmnt #	ctl sect	rel/ abs	ref ctr	last entry	first entry
SAVE	000070	4	35	1	R	3	15	1

We still need a mechanism for determining where to place each new entry in the cross-reference list structure. The mechanism for this is quite simple. In conjunction with the cross-reference table area, two fields are defined to control the information that is placed in that area: (1) a quantity that specifies the maximum number of entries that may be placed in the table, and (2) a pointer to the last-used entry position in the table. The maximum prevents the Assembler from exceeding the capacity of the cross-reference area; if a source module has more references than this maximum allows, the assembly must be aborted and the user must segment the module into two or more modules before reassembly. The pointer is initially set to 0 and is increased each time a cross-reference entry is added to the structure.

Let us assume that the Assembler has determined the address of the symbol table entry for a symbol that has been referenced in the operand of a source module statement. Then, to make an entry in the cross-reference table, the following procedure may be used:

1. The pointer to the next available position in the cross-reference area is determined.
2. If the reference counter field in the symbol table entry is zero, this is the first cross-reference for that symbol. Therefore, the pointer to the next available position is placed in both the first and last entry pointer fields, the reference counter is set to 1, and an entry is made in the cross-reference area with a pointer of 0.

3. If the reference counter in the symbol table entry is not zero, the pointer to the last cross-reference entry for that symbol tells the Assembler where to insert the new pointer in the list. The new entry is added in the first available position, and *its* pointer field is set to 0. Both the reference counter and the last entry pointer fields in the symbol table entry are updated accordingly.

The subroutine in figure 10.24 illustrates one method of implementing this procedure. Note that the cross-reference control data (maximum number of entries, pointer to last-used entry position) is maintained in the first position of the cross-reference table.

The structure described for the cross-reference data is known as a *one-way list,* since the pointers always point to the *next* entry on the list, not to the previous or any other entry. In addition, the structure is known as a first-in, first-out (FIFO) list, because we start at the first entry that was made when retrieving entries from the list. A FIFO list is a queue of entries, the last entry on the queue being the last one to be retrieved for further processing, such as printing the cross-reference information.

The concept and use of lists is one of the fundamental mechanisms for structuring data in computer memories. The use of pointers allows us to break free of the essentially linear constraint imposed by the physical organization of memory and to interrelate data that need not be stored in consecutive locations of memory. List entries may contain more than one pointer: a pointer back to the previous entry, a pointer to the first and/or last entry, pointers to entries on other lists. Each such pointer allows a relationship to be represented without requiring that the two entries be adjacent in memory or that they belong to the same table or file. The study of these techniques is not within the scope of this text; the reader may find that Donald Knuth's *The Art of Programming, vol I: Fundamental Algorithms* provides a good starting point for further study.

Figure 10.24   Cross-reference list maintenance subroutine.

```
CROSSREF   CSECT
*
*    SUBROUTINE  CROSSREF(XREFTBL,SYMBOL,STMT#)
*    APPENDS A CROSS REF ENTRY TO THE CROSS REF TABLE.
*    PARAMS = ADDR OF BEGINNING OF CROSS REF TABLE
*           = ADDR OF SYMBOL TABLE ENTRY TO WHICH CROSS REF APPLIES
*           = ADDR OF NEW CROSS REF STMT #
*    RETURNS   0  IN  R15  IF CROSS REF (XREF) ADDED SUCCESSFULLY
*              4  IN  R15  IF XREF TBL WAS FULL AND NO CROSS REF ADDED.
*
           STM    14,12,12(13)        ENTRY TO SUBR
           BALR   12,0
           USING  *,12
           ST     13,SAVE+4
           LA     13,SAVE
*                            PARAMS...
           LM     2,4,0(1)             R2 = ADDR OF CROSS REF TABLE
*                                      R3 = ADDR OF SYMBOL TBL ENTRY
*                                      R4 = ADDR OF CROSS REF STMT #
*
           USING SYMENTRY,3    R3 =BASE REG FOR SYMBOL TABLE DSECT
           USING STKENTRY,11   R11=BASE REG FOR CROSS REF DSECT
           LR     11,2
*
           LH     8,STKPTR       SEE IF CROSS REF TBL IS FULL
           CH     8,STKMAX
           BNL    STKFULL        BRANCH IF IT'S FULL.
           AH     8,=H'1'        OTHERWISE,
           STH    8,STKPTR        UPDATE PTR TO NEXT AVAILABLE ENTRY
*
```

Figure 10.24   continued

```
               LH       9,REFCTR              SEE IF THIS IS FIRST REF FOR SYMBOL
               LTR      9,9
               BNZ      NOTFIRST              BRANCH IF OTHER REFS ALREADY EXIST
               STH      8,REF1ST     ELSE, SET PTR TO 1ST CROSS REF TBL ENTRY,
               STH      8,REFLAST             AND TO LAST ENTRY (THE SAME ENTRY).
               MVC      REFCTR,=H'1'          ALSO, SET COUNT OF CROSS REFS TO 1.
               B        NEWENTRY              THEN GO MAKE NEW ENTRY IN XREF TBL.
     *
     NOTFIRST  AH       9,=H'1'               UPDATE # CROSS REFS FOR THIS SYMBOL.
               STH      9,REFCTR
               LH       10,REFLAST   R10= PTR TO PREV LAST CROSS REF.
               STH      8,REFLAST             STORE PTR TO NEW REF IN SYMB TBL.
     *
     * COMPUTE  (ADDR OF XREF ENTRY) = (ADDR OF XREF TBL) + ( 4*PTR ),
     *    THE FACTOR '4' BECAUSE EACH XREF ENTRY IS 4 BYTES.
     *
               SLL      10,2         R10 = 4*PTR  = INDEX TO PREV LAST CROSS REF.
               LA       11,0(10,2)   R11 = ADDR OF PREV LAST CROSS REF.
               STH      8,NEXTREF    STORE PTR TO NEW REF IN PREV REF.
     *
     NEWENTRY  SLL      8,2          R8  = INDEX TO NEW CROSS REF.
               LA       11,0(8,2)    R11 = ADDR OF NEW CROSS REF.
               MVC      NEXTREF,=H'0'    SET NEW REF'S FWD PTR TO ZERO.
               MVC      STMTREF,0(4)     SET NEW REF'S STMT# FIELD VIA REG 4.
               LH       15,=H'0'         SET RETURN CODE 'O.K.'
     *
     REFXIT    L        13,SAVE+4        EXIT FROM SUBR
               L        14,12(13)
               LM       0,12,20(13)      DON'T RESTORE R15
               BR       14
     *
     STKFULL   LH       15,=H'4'         SET ERR CODE WHEN XREF TBL IS FULL
               B        REFXIT
     *
     *   DATA AREAS AND DSECTS
     *
     SAVE      DS       18F              REGISTER SAVE AREA
     *
     SYMENTRY  DSECT                     , DSECT FOR SYMBOL TABLE ENTRY ...
     SYMNAME   DS       CL8          BYTES 0-7    SYMBOL
     SYMVALUE  DS       CL4                8-11   SYMBOL VALUE
     SYMLNG    DS       CL2                12-13  LENGTH ATTRIBUTE
     SYMDEFN   DS       CL2                14-15  STMT# WHERE DEFINED
     SYMSECT   DS       CL1                16     SYMBOL'S SECTION#
     SYMTYPE   DS       CL1                17     REL/ABS INDICATOR
     REFCTR    DS       H                  18-19  CROSS REF COUNT
     REFLAST   DS       H                  20-21  PTR TO LAST XREF ENTRY
     REF1ST    DS       H                  22-23  PTR TO 1ST XREF ENTRY
     *
     STKENTRY  DSECT                     , DSECT FOR CROSS REF TBL STRUCTURE
     *                             TYPICAL XREF ENTRY . . .
     STMTREF   DS       H           BYTES 0-1    STMT# THAT REF'D SYMBOL
     NEXTREF   DS       H                 2-3    PTR TO NEXT XREF IN TBL
     *                             FIRST ENTRY ONLY . . .
     STKMAX    EQU      STMTREF          1ST HALF-WORD HAS MAX # XREF ENTRIES
     STKPTR    EQU      NEXTREF          2ND HALF-WD POINTS TO LAST USED ENTRY
     *                                   (ASSUMING STKPTR = 0 INITIALLY)
               END
```

10.10 SUMMARY

The assembly process we have described is typical of that used in many computer systems, particularly the IBM 360 and 370 systems. It requires two passes over the source module statements and depends on mechanisms that permit reasonably efficient processing of information.

The first pass assigns addresses to all instructions, constants, and data areas and thereby also assigns values to name-field symbols. The second pass generates the object module and the listing. If there were only one pass, it would be impracticable to assemble source statements in which the operand referred to symbols that had not yet been defined. Even with two passes, the operands of a few directives, most notably EQU, are restricted to already defined symbols and to self-defining terms.

The mechanisms for processing information are based on the concepts of tables and lists. These data structures consist of entries (also known as records) that are usually subdivided into a number of fields. The contents of one or more fields in an entry serve to identify that entry; the contents of other fields describe certain characteristics of whatever the entry represents. In a table, the addresses of the entries can be inferred once the address of the first entry is known (or at worst they can be calculated from it). This is so because table entries are stored in consecutive locations in memory. In a list, the entries are not necessarily stored in consecutive memory locations. Consequently, an explicit representation of each entry's address is required. This representation, often called a pointer, must be available in order to process an entry. In the cross-reference list described in this chapter, the pointer to each entry other than the first was stored in the entry logically preceding that entry. Other schemes, not discussed in this chapter, are also possible.

The principal Assembler tables and lists covered in this chapter are the opcode and directive tables, the symbol, literal, and base-register tables; the object-module tables (ESD, TXT, RLD, END), and the cross-reference list. In addition, the intermediate file, consisting of the source-module statements and certain information about these statements determined in Pass 1, was described. The content of two of these tables—the opcode and directive tables—is known at the time the Assembler program is written. The entries in these two tables are thus "built into" the Assembler. The entries in the other data structures mentioned must be determined at assembly time. The intermediate file and the symbol, literal, and ESD tables are created in Pass 1; the base-register, cross-reference, and remaining object module tables are created in Pass 2.

The Assembler may have to search one or more tables in order to complete the processing of a given source-module statement. One of the most efficient and frequently used methods of table searching is known as the binary search technique. In this technique, the middle table entry is the first one examined, to determine which half of the table to search further. Then the middle entry of that half is examined to further restrict the search domain, and so forth until the sought-for entry is either found or not found. Use of this technique requires that the entries be in sequence, and that the field controlling the sequence be the same as the field used in the search. Built-in tables, such as the opcode and directive tables, can be created in sequence and are thus directly amenable to the binary search technique. Tables that are created, such as the symbol table, might not be created in the sequence needed for searching. In such a case, the entries must be sorted before a binary search can be used. One method of sorting—straight insertion—was summarized in this chapter. It is one of the simpler methods of sorting. Many other sorting methods have been devised; their relative merits depend in large part on the characteristics of the data and of the computer system. There is no known best method to be used under all conditions.

EXERCISES

1. Compared to the two-pass assembly process described in this chapter, what would be the disadvantage of having a one-pass assembly instead? What would be the advantage of having a three-pass assembly?

2. Explain why entries are not made in the base-register table until Pass 2 (as shown in the diagram of fig. 10.8 and the accompanying text).

3. Why is it that no object code is generated by the Assembler when it processes an EQU directive (see, for example, fig. 10.2)?

4. Which of the symbols in the source module of figure 10.2 are relocatable and which are absolute constants? Except for the entry that would be made in the symbol table for the relocatable constants of figure 10.2, is there any other way in which they would be processed differently from the absolute constants? Would the address constant of Statement 16 in figure 10.2 be considered a relocatable constant or an absolute constant? Why?

5. If an assembly language program is large enough to warrant use of two or more implied base registers in a single control section, by what rule would the Assembler most likely choose one of those registers when creating the base-displacement form of address corresponding to an implicit operand?

6. In chapter 14, we will discuss how the OPSYN directive may be used to define a new opcode that is synonymous with (has the same properties as) an existing opcode, and how it may be used to remove an opcode from the set of allowable opcodes. In the context of the discussions in the present chapter, explain how these two functions of the OPSYN directive might be implemented in the Assembler. Would the implementation of the OPSYN directive be part of Pass 1 processing, Pass 2 processing, or both?

7. Suppose that you wanted to provide a new directive in Assembly Language, call it OPDEF, whose purpose would be to allow a programmer to define an entirely new instruction opcode. For example, if you had an Assembler for the IBM 360, you might use the OPDEF directive to define the instruction opcodes such as CLCL, MVCL, and the other IBM 370 instructions so that the 360 Assembler could be used to assemble 370 programs. In the context of the discussions in this chapter, explain how the OPDEF directive might be implemented in the Assembler. Would the implementation be part of Pass 1 processing, Pass 2 processing, or both?

8. What would be the contents of the object module for the source code shown in figure 10.2? Write your answer in the same form as that shown in figures 10.16a–10.16d.

9. From figure 10.14, it can be seen that entries are placed in an object module in the following order: (1) all the ESD entries, (2) all the TXT entries, (3) the RLD entries, and (4) the END entry. What is the minimum number of each type of entry that can occur in an object module? From the standpoint of the Linkage Editor program, what advantage is gained by having the entries in the order just described, and not in some other order?

10. Based on figure 10.17, write an assembly language subroutine that will perform a linear search of a table of M entries subject to the following criteria:

   a. Each entry in the table has the fixed-length symbol table entry format shown in figure 10.5.

   b. The search key is an 8-byte symbol to be matched against the symbol field in each entry.

   c. The subroutine should return the address of the entry in Register 15 if the entry is found, and a full-word zero in Register 15 if the entry is not found. The table entries should not be assumed to be in any particular sequence. The number of entries in the table should be permitted to be any integer M such that $M \geq 0$.

11. Modify your subroutine solution to Exercise 10 so that if the sought-for entry is not found, it adds an entry to the end of the table. The entry to be added must be provided by the calling program and the subroutine must increase the caller's entry-count M by $+1$ and return the address of the newly inserted entry in Register 15.

12. What modifications should be made to your subroutine solution to Exercise 10 if

    a. The symbol table entries are in ascending sequence by key field?

    b. No symbol occurs more than once in the table?

13. Modify your solution to Exercise 10 so that your subroutine can search a table all of whose entries have the same fixed length, L, and a key field of length KL, and in which the key field in each entry begins in byte position KP relative to the beginning of the entry. The integers L, KL, and KP are to be passed as parameters to your subroutine, and each can be assumed to be in the range from 1 to 256. As in Exercise 10, the number of entries in the table should be permitted to be any nonnegative integer M, and the key field should be assumed to be an EBCDIC string.

14. Write an assembly language program that will read input data consisting of assembly language source-module statements, and create a symbol table according to these criteria: Your program should assign a statement number to each statement it processes and create an entry to be added to the symbol table for each statement that contains a valid name-field entry. The entry should be in the format of figure 10.5, although all but the symbol and statement number fields will be blank. The symbol table should be created using your subroutine solution to Exercise 11. After all input statements have been processed, print the contents of the symbol table.

15. Modify the assembly language subroutine of figure 10.22b so that it is tailored to the format of the symbol table given in figure 10.5. In other words, your subroutine should assume that the table being sorted consists of fixed-length entries of length L = 18, key length KL = 8, and key position KP = 0. The number of entries in the table is a parameter that must be passed to your subroutine. The symbol table entries should be sorted "in place" as in figure 10.22b, i.e., at each stage of the sorting process the partially sorted entries should occupy the same area of memory that was occupied by the original, unsorted entries.

16. Modify your solution to Exercise 14 so that after printing the symbol table it calls your sort subroutine of Exercise 15 and then prints the sorted symbol table.

17. Draw a flow diagram describing the processing that must take place in order that an entry may be made for a given symbol reference in the cross-reference list structure of figure 10.23. Your description should be consistent with the discussions of Section 10.9 regarding the revisions to the symbol table entry format and be general enough to be applicable to any symbol and any cross-reference entry. (Hint: See fig. 10.24.)

18. Draw a flow diagram that describes the processes that must take place in order that all the cross-reference entries for a given symbol may be removed from the list structure of figure 10.23 and printed as on a cross-reference listing.

19. Write a subroutine that will accomplish the task described in Exercise 18.

PART
THREE

Noninteger Arithmetic

11
Introductory Concepts

Problems that involve computations with mixed numbers—numbers that may contain both an integer portion and a fractional portion—are almost invariably programmed in FORTRAN or some other high-level language rather than in Assembly Language. Nevertheless, an understanding of how these computations are handled at the assembly language or machine language level is important for at least two reasons: (1) to enable programmers to understand the limitations inherent in computer arithmetic when mixed numbers are processed, and (2) to enable programmers to solve arithmetic problems on computers that have no appropriate high-level language.

In the IBM 360 and 370 systems, and in virtually all other present-day computer systems, the position of the decimal point in arithmetic operations is not explicitly represented. Its position is implied. This poses no serious problem when handling integers, since the decimal point's position is always to the right of the right-most digit and it would be superfluous to represent it explicitly. Even with integers, however, the lack of an explicit decimal point poses somewhat of a problem in division; the solution is to represent the result in two parts: an integer quotient and an integer remainder. With mixed numbers, the lack of a decimal point is more serious; we can't ignore the decimal point, since its position determines the value of a number. We cannot, for example, add two numbers such as 0.15 and 1.5 unless we can align the decimal points before doing the addition.

There are two principal hardware solutions to this problem. One is known as floating-point arithmetic, the other as decimal (or packed-decimal) arithmetic. In floating-point arithmetic, the hardware aligns the position of the decimal point during the execution of instructions. In decimal arithmetic, all numbers are represented as integers and the programmer has the responsibility of aligning the implied decimal point positions in every arithmetic operation. Because of its added complexity and cost, floating-point hardware and decimal hardware are not available on some computers. However, both are available on the IBM 360 and 370 systems.

Before discussing the instructions required for utilizing these hardware capabilities, the following introductory concepts are presented: methods of converting mixed numbers from one base to another, problems inherent in the use of mixed numbers in computer systems, and methods for preventing certain numerical errors from terminating a program in the IBM 360 and 370.

11.1 A QUESTION OF ACCURACY

The fractional portion of a mixed decimal number can be represented as a sequence of decimal digits, d_j, preceded by a decimal point, as follows:

$$0 . d_1 d_2 d_3 ...$$

Except for the representation of some rational fractions p/q (where p and q are both integers, and $p < q$), the fractional portion must be truncated to whatever accuracy is desired. When performing arithmetic with pencil and paper, we always have the option of including as many digits to the right of the decimal point as we wish. In computer systems, increasing the number of digits beyond the capacity of a word usually requires additional hardware, additional software, or both. Even then there is an upper limit to how many digits can be incorporated, so that what results is the representation of a rational fraction that only approximates the desired number.

For example, when we write 0.33333... we understand that we can write as many three's as we please in order to better approximate the rational fraction ⅓. But in computer systems, a fixed upper limit on the number of digits that can be accommodated is imposed by the hardware and software. If the limit is six, then our best approximation would be 0.333333. Further, if during the course of a computation we were to attempt to compute the quantity $(A-B)*C$, where $C=30$ and $A-B = 1/10,000,000$, the correct result of 0.000003 would be incorrectly represented as 0.000000, since to six places the value of $A-B$ is 0.000000. If the same $(A-B)*C$ were multiplied by another factor, D, the result would be zero *no matter what the value of D is*. Note that the exact value of $(A-B)*C$ required only six digits to the right of the decimal point, yet, because of the sequence in which it was computed, it could not be represented accurately. Worse, the result of subsequent calculations such as $(A-B)*C*D$ could be greatly in error.

It is not the purpose of this textbook to discuss methods for handling such problems; this falls under the topic of numerical analysis. But you should be aware that the problems exist and should consult a numerical analysis text for further information (see references in Section 11.5).

11.2 CONVERSION FROM ONE BASE TO ANOTHER

In base 10, the value of the decimal fraction represented as

$$0 . d_1 d_2 d_3 ... d_m$$

may be computed as

$$d_1 \times 10^{-1} + d_2 \times 10^{-2} + ... + d_m \times 10^{-m}.$$

In base P, the value of the fraction consisting of the base digits p_j,

$$0 . p_1 p_2 p_3 ... p_k$$

can be computed as

$$p_1 \times P^{-1} + p_2 \times P^{-2} + ... + p_k \times P^{-k}.$$

For example, in base 2, the representation 0.110011 has the value

$$1 \times 2^{-1} + 1 \times 2^{-2} + 0 \times 2^{-3} + 0 \times 2^{-4} + 1 \times 2^{-5} + 1 \times 2^{-6}$$

$$= \frac{1}{2} + \frac{1}{4} + 0 + 0 + \frac{1}{32} + \frac{1}{64}$$

$$= \frac{51}{64}$$

To convert from the representation of a fraction in one base, P, to another base, Q, the required calculations depend on whether they are done in the base P system (the old base) or in the base Q system (the new base). We would ordinarily like to perform the calculations in whichever system is the easiest to manipulate.

To convert a base P representation, $0 . p_1 p_2 p_3 ... p_k$, to a base Q representation, $0 . q_1 q_2 q_3 ... q_m$, calculations in the base P system are performed iteratively. The value of the number can be expressed either in the old system as

$$J = p_1 \times P^{-1} + p_2 \times P^{-2} + ... + p_k \times P^{-k}$$

or in the new system as

$$J = q_1 \times Q^{-1} + q_2 \times Q^{-2} + ... + q_m \times Q^{-m}.$$

Therefore the iteration proceeds as follows:

$$\begin{aligned}
\text{Let} \quad N_1 &= Q \times J &&= q_1 + q_2 \times Q^{-1} + q_3 \times Q^{-2} + ... + q_m \times Q^{-m+1} \\
N_2 &= Q \times (N_1 - q_1) &&= q_2 + q_3 \times Q^{-1} + ... + q_m \times Q^{-m+2} \\
N_3 &= Q \times (N_2 - q_2) &&= q_3 + q_4 \times Q^{-1} + ... + q_m \times Q^{-m+3}
\end{aligned}$$

and so forth. Note that the quantity $N_i - q_i$ that appears in the calculation of N_{i+1} is simply the fractional portion of N_i. In other words, the ith step of the iteration procedure produces a number, N_i, whose integer portion is q_i and whose fractional portion, $N_i - q_i$, is used in the next step. In general, the number of digits, q_i, that are determined by this process depends on the accuracy that is desired.

For example, to convert the number one-half from its decimal representation 0.5 to its binary representation, we have P=10 and Q=2, and

$$N_1 = 2 \times 0.5 = 1.0, \text{ so } q_1 = 1, \text{ and } N_1 - q_1 = 0.$$

Thus, $N_2 = N_3 = ... = N_j = 0$ for all $j > 1$. The binary representation of one-half is thus 0.1_2.

However, to convert the number one-tenth from its decimal representation 0.1_{10} to its binary representation, we find

$$\begin{aligned}
N_1 &= 2 \times 0.1 = 0.2, \text{ so } q_1 = 0, \text{ and } N_1 - q_1 = 0.2 \\
N_2 &= 2 \times 0.2 = 0.4, \text{ so } q_2 = 0, \text{ and } N_2 - q_2 = 0.4 \\
N_3 &= 2 \times 0.4 = 0.8, \text{ so } q_3 = 0, \text{ and } N_3 - q_3 = 0.8 \\
N_4 &= 2 \times 0.8 = 1.6, \text{ so } q_4 = 1, \text{ and } N_4 - q_4 = 0.6 \\
N_5 &= 2 \times 0.6 = 1.2, \text{ so } q_5 = 1, \text{ and } N_5 - q_5 = 0.2
\end{aligned}$$

At this point, notice that $N_5 - q_5 = N_1 - q_1$, so the binary representation of one-tenth is a never ending sequence of bits, 0.0001100110011001100 11....

When converting a base P representation, $0 . p_1 p_2 p_3 ... p_k$, to a base Q representation, $0 . q_1 q_2 q_3 ... q_m$, calculations in the base Q system are most easily performed as follows. Let $J = 0 . p_1 p_2 p_3 ... p_k$, and define the integer K by the equation $J = K \times P^{-k}$. In other words, K is the integer represented by the digits $p_1 p_2 p_3 ... p_k$. We can convert K to the base Q system by the methods used for conversion of integers (as described in chap. 1) and then divide the result by P^k, doing the computations in the base Q system.

For example, to convert 0.110011_2 to its equivalent decimal representation, we have P=2, Q=10, and

$$J = 110011_2 \times (2^{-6})_{10}.$$

But,

$$\begin{aligned}
110011_2 &= 1 \times 2^5 + 1 \times 2^4 + 0 \times 2^3 + 0 \times 2^2 + 1 \times 2^1 + 1 \times 2^0 \\
&= 32 + 16 + 0 + 0 + 2 + 1 \\
&= 51_{10}
\end{aligned}$$

and $2^{-6} = 1/64$. Thus, in the base 10 system the number 0.110011_2 is represented as $51/64 = 0.796875_{10}$.

Similarly, to convert $0.C1_{16}$ to its decimal representation, we have P=16, Q=10, and

$$J = C1_{16} \times (16^{-2})_{10}.$$

But,

$$\begin{aligned}
C1_{16} &= 12 \times 16^1 + 1 \times 16^0 \\
&= 193_{10}.
\end{aligned}$$

Thus in the base 10 system the number $0.C1_{16}$ is represented as $(193)_{10} \times (16^{-2})_{10}$, i.e.,

$$\frac{193}{16^2} = \frac{193}{256} = 0.75390625_{10}.$$

11.3 REPRESENTATION OF MIXED NUMBERS

Binary Representation

One way to represent mixed numbers in a 32-bit word is to let a certain number of low-order bits be used for the fractional portion and the remaining high-order bits for the sign and integer portion. For example, if we choose 12 bits for the fractional portion, then a 32-bit word could be considered to represent a mixed number in the following fashion:

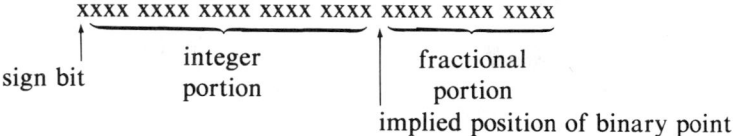

Using this scheme to represent the decimal number 1.5, we would have

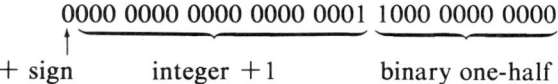

With twelve bits for the fractional portion in a 32-bit word, the magnitude of the smallest fraction that can be represented is 2^{-12} (approximately 2×10^{-4}) and that of the largest integer is $2^{19}-1$ (i.e., about 5×10^{5}). Thus, neither the range of numbers nor the accuracy that can be attained for fractions is very great, and we can increase one only at the expense of the other.

It should be noted that if we use the integer arithmetic instructions to process mixed numbers represented by the above scheme in the IBM 360 and 370 systems, the implied position of the binary point would have to be explicitly adjusted via arithmetic shift instructions to retain the desired accuracy in multiplication or division. To illustrate this, let us continue the previous example and suppose that we wish to multiply 1.5_{10} by 1.5_{10}. Since the representation of 1.5 is indistinguishable from the integer representation of 3×2^{11}, the integer multiply instruction would yield the following 32-bit product of 1.5×1.5, namely the representation of 9×2^{22}:

$$0000 \ 0010 \ 0100 \ 0000 \ 0000 \ 0000 \ 0000 \ 0000$$

To recover the desired representation of 2.25 we would have to shift the integer product right 12 bits (or divide it by 2^{12}), the correct result being

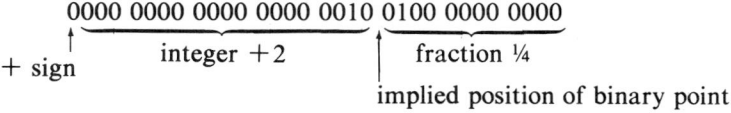

Thus we see that the integer arithmetic instructions can be used to perform arithmetic on mixed numbers, provided that shifting is employed. There are, however, two limitations: (1) we cannot easily provide for both a wide range of numbers and a sufficient degree of accuracy in a fixed number of bits, e.g. in a full word of 32 bits; and (2) unless there are a sufficient number of bits for the fractional portion, fractions such as one-tenth will be represented with relatively poor accuracy due to the incommensurability of the decimal and binary systems. (For example, one-tenth would be represented in this scheme as

$$\underset{\substack{\uparrow \\ + \text{ sign}}}{0000} \ \underbrace{0000 \ 0000 \ 0000 \ 0000}_{\text{integer } 0} \ \underbrace{0001 \ 1001 \ 1010}_{\text{fraction one-tenth, rounded to twelve bits}}$$

But, $.0001 \ 1001 \ 1010_2 = .1000 \ 9765 \ 625_{10}$, clearly a poor approximation.) To overcome these limitations, the decimal method and floating-point method of representing mixed numbers is more commonly employed.

Decimal Representation

This method employs the decimal number system in the hardware. In the IBM 360 and 370 systems, this is done with a method of representation known as packed-decimal format. In this format, integers and mixed numbers are represented as decimal (not binary) integers. Each decimal digit is represented by 4 bits in what is known as the binary-coded decimal, or BCD, code scheme: 0, 1, 2,..., 9 are represented, respectively, as 0000, 0001, 0010, ..., 1001. A mixed number, F, is represented as the integer $N = F \times 10^n$, where n is the number of digits to the right of the decimal point in F. For example, the number 1.5 might be represented by the integer $N = 15 = 1.5 \times 10^1$, and the number 0.1 by the integer $N = 1 = 0.1 \times 10^1$. The factor 10^n is called the *scale factor*. Different scale factors may be used for different numbers.

The sign of a number in the packed-decimal format is represented by 4 bits, 1100 for plus and 1101 for minus. The sign bits are placed to the right of the low-order digit. For example, the product of $(+1.5) \times (-1.5)$ would be the product of these numbers:

$$(0001\ 0101\ 1100) \times (0001\ 0101\ 1101)$$
$$(\ 1\quad 5\quad +\ )\quad (\ 1\quad 5\quad -\ )$$

the result being (0000 0010 0010 0101 1101), namely the representation of 0225$-$, or -2.25×10^2. Notice that the representation of the product is obtained by treating the two factors as decimal numbers and performing the arithmetic using the rules of the decimal number system. This is done by the hardware in the IBM 360 and 370 systems. Notice also that there is no problem of incommensurability, for decimal fractions are represented as decimal integers and there need be no approximation that wouldn't also be made with pencil and paper. The only restriction is that no packed-decimal number may consist of more than thirty-one decimal digits.

As will be discussed in chapter 12, a set of instructions explicitly designed for decimal arithmetic is used to process packed-decimal numbers. These include add, subtract, multiply, divide, compare, and shift instructions. Shifting, i.e., effectively multiplying or dividing by powers of ten, enables us to make explicit adjustments of the position of the implied decimal point so that numbers with different scale factors can be arithmetically combined.

Floating-point Representation

Perhaps the most common method of representing mixed numbers in computers is known as the floating-point method. In this method, numbers are represented and processed as a fraction times a scale factor. The method is conceptually similar to that of scientific notation, where for example 1.5 can be written as 0.15×10^1. But in floating-point format, unlike scientific notation, the complete scale factor is not represented; only its exponent is represented. Moreover, the base of the scale factor is usually a power of two, say 2^m, rather than ten. We will first consider a base of 2 (i.e., $m = 1$), and then a base of $2^4 = 16$. The latter base is employed in the IBM 360 and 370 systems, the former in some other computer systems.

With a scale factor base of 2, the fraction is represented with n bits, e.g., $b_1 b_2 b_3 \ldots b_n$, its value being $b_1 \times 2^{-1} + b_2 \times 2^{-2} + b_3 \times 2^{-3} + \ldots + b_n \times 2^{-n}$. For example, since $0.15 \times 10^1 = 0.15 \times 1.25 \times 2^3 = 0.1875 \times 2^3$, and since $0.1875_{10} = 0.0011_2$, the decimal number 1.5 would be represented in floating-point format by the equivalent of $(0.0011)_2 \times 2^3$, the fraction bits being $b_1 b_2 b_3 \ldots b_n = 0011000\ldots0$, and the exponent being 3. The base of the scale factor 2^3—the 2 itself—would not be represented explicitly; its value would be implied in all computations.

In a k-bit word, the sign, exponent, and fraction bits are often arranged as follows:

The sign bit represents the sign of the fraction, not the sign of the exponent. Thus, if we assume that $k = 32$ with $p = 7$ and $n = 24$, we might expect that $(0.0011) \times 2^3$ would be represented in floating-point format as

However, this is not quite the way it's done, for two reasons. First, there must be a provision for representing negative exponents. Second, the two leading zeroes in the fraction are in a sense "wasted," since we can write $(0.0011) \times 2^3 = (0.11)_2 \times 2^1$. In other words, leading zeroes can be absorbed into the exponent, thereby providing additional bit positions for increased accuracy. This may be of no consequence for a number such as 0.0011, which is the exact equivalent of 0.1875, but it *is* of some consequence for a number such as 0.000110011001100110011...which must be truncated to an approximate representation of one-tenth. Thus, the generally preferred form of a fraction is with its leading bit nonzero (unless of course the number is exactly zero). This is known as the *normalized form* of the fraction.

Turning to the problem of the exponent's sign, how might a negative exponent be represented? One way of course is to use the first exponent bit as its sign bit and to represent the exponent in sign-magnitude form, e.g., 0000011 for $+3$ and 1000011 for -3. Another way is to represent the exponent in p-bit two's complement form, e.g., (with $p = 7$) 0000011 for $+3$ and 1111101 for -3. A third way is to represent an exponent m by an unsigned binary integer, $q + m$. This is known as *excess-q notation*. For a 7-bit exponent, $q = \frac{1}{2} \times 2^7$; for a p-bit exponent, $q = \frac{1}{2} \times 2^p$. Thus, in 7 bits $q = 64$; the exponent $+3$ would be represented as $64 + 3 = 67_{10} = 1000011_2$, and the exponent -3 would be $64 + (-3) = 61_{10} = 0111101_2$. The advantage of this latter method over the sign-magnitude and two's complement methods is that the exponent is always represented by a nonnegative integer and its sign is implied, not explicit. Adjustments of an exponent required for normalizing a fraction and for doing arithmetic on two floating-point numbers therefore need not be concerned with the sign of the exponent.

Now the remaining question is, what should be the number of bits allotted for the exponent portion of a floating-point number? Clearly, the more bits, the greater the range of numbers that can be represented. But in a k-bit word, we must have $k = p + n + 1$, where p is the number of exponent bits and n the number of fraction bits. Clearly, the larger p is, the smaller n—and hence the accuracy—will be. If k is large, then both p and n can be reasonably large so that both range and accuracy can be of acceptable size. But in the IBM 360 and 370 systems $k = 32$, not an especially large word length. For accuracy to about six decimal digits, we need an n of at least 24, leaving $p = 7$. But with a scale factor base of 2, a 7-bit exponent gives a range of from 2^{-64} to 2^{63} for the scale factor, not an especially large range since $2^{63} \approx 10^{19}$. In the IBM 360 and 370 systems, this limitation is overcome as follows.

The number of exponent bits is seven, but the base of the scale factor is 16 ($= 2^4$), not 2. Thus the range of the exponents is from 16^{-64} to 16^{63}, i.e., from 2^{-256} to 2^{252}. This is comfortably large enough to handle the vast majority of computational needs, since $2^{252} \approx 10^{76}$. Note that with a scale factor base of 16, the fraction bits must be treated as hexadecimal fractions rather than binary fractions. In other words, the 24 bits allotted for the fraction are treated as six hexadecimal digits. For example, the representation of the number 1.5 can be determined as follows:

$$0.15 \times 10^1 = 0.15 \times 0.625 \times 16^1 = 0.09375 \times 16^1$$
$$\text{but since } 0.09375_{10} = 0.18_{16}$$
$$\text{then } 0.15 \times 10^1 = 0.18_{16} \times 16^1$$

Thus, in the floating-point format of the IBM 360 and 370 systems, 1.5 is represented as

$$0\ 1000001\ 0001\ 1000\ 0000\ 0000\ 0000\ 0000$$

+ sign, fraction $= 0.18_{16}$, $41_{16} = 65_{10} = 64 + 1$, i.e., 16^1

This is the normalized form of the fraction, even though the leading bit is zero, the reason being that as a hexadecimal fraction the leading *digit* is not zero. Thus, we are back to the "wasted bits," so to speak. But we have gained considerably in the range of numbers that can be represented. To provide for more accuracy when needed, the floating-point format in the IBM 360 and 370 systems can be processed either as a full word, a double word, or a quadruple word. These three possibilities are known as single-precision, double-precision, and extended-precision, respectively. The double-precision form provides slightly more than twice the accuracy of single-precision, and the extended-precision format provides twice the accuracy of the double-precision format. In all three cases, however, the exponent occupies only 7 bits, is represented in excess-64 notation, and corresponds to a power of 16.

To summarize briefly: in all floating-point formats, in whatever computer system is being used, the principle of separating the order of magnitude of a number from its significant digits—similar to scientific notation—allows a wider range of numbers to be represented in a fixed number of bits than any other method in use. This, together with the fact that the hardware performs all the adjustments of exponents when two floating-point numbers are arithmetically combined, makes the use of this format attractive for a large class of problems.

As will be shown in chapter 13, a set of instructions explicitly designed for floating-point arithmetic is used to process floating-point numbers. These include add, subtract, multiply, divide, and compare instructions, as well as instructions that test and/or change the sign of a floating-point number. Normalization of fractions is accomplished during the execution of most instructions; there are no shift instructions to normalize a fraction.

11.4 OVERFLOW, UNDERFLOW, AND SIGNIFICANCE ERRORS: SPM

As in integer arithmetic, arithmetic with mixed numbers may produce a result that cannot be represented in the number of bits allowed. If the magnitude of the number is too large for the range permitted, the condition is called *overflow*. If the magnitude of the number is too small for the range (but not 0), the condition is called *underflow*. In floating-point addition and subtraction, if the resulting fraction is 0 but the exponent isn't, all significant bits have been lost and the condition is termed a *significance* error.

In the IBM 360 and 370 systems, the occurrence of any of these conditions normally causes program interruption:

1. Overflow in fixed-point operations (integer arithmetic and arithmetic left shifts)
2. Overflow in packed-decimal operations
3. Underflow in floating-point operations
4. Significance error in floating-point operations

When a program is interrupted, control of the CPU is given to the Operating System and the program's execution is usually terminated. In order to prevent interruption in any of these situations, the SPM (Set Program Mask) instruction must be executed at some point *before* the arithmetic operation is executed.

The SPM instruction sets the condition code and a 4-bit program-mask field. It is an RR-type instruction in which only the R1 field is specified:

opcode	operand
SPM	R1

Bits 2 through 7 of the register designated by the R1 field are used to *replace* the 2-bit condition code and the 4-bit program mask that exist in the program status word. Bits 2 and 3 pertain to the condition code, bits 4 through 7 to the program mask. Bits 0, 1, and 8–31 of the register are ignored during execution of the SPM instruction, and the entire contents of the register are unchanged by the instruction. Bits 2 through 7 have the meaning shown in this diagram:

If a mask bit is set to 0, the program will not be interrupted when the corresponding error condition arises. If it is set to 1, the program will be interrupted when that error arises. *All mask bits are set each time the SPM is executed.* If the SPM is not executed in a program, the initial settings of these mask bits—established by the Operating System—will prevail.

11.5 SUMMARY

In most computer systems, the representation and processing of noninteger quantities demands special consideration. This may take the form of software to simulate noninteger arithmetic even though the quantities are represented as integers, or it may take the form of hardware and associated software instructions that are separate and distinct from the facilities for operating on integers. One of the problems posed by noninteger arithmetic operations in computer systems is the incommensurability of the decimal and binary number systems: there can be a loss of accuracy when a fixed number of bits is used to represent noninteger decimal numbers in the binary system, no matter how many bits are used. Another problem arises from the need to align the decimal point positions of two numbers before they may be added or subtracted and to ensure that a sufficient number of digit positions to the right and/or left of the decimal point are reserved for arithmetic results. Yet a third problem is due to the fact that there must be some realistic upper limit on the number of bits used to represent numbers, whether they be integers or mixed numbers: the more of these bits used for the fractional portion of a number, the less that can be used for the integer portion, and vice versa. Too severe a restriction on the number of integer bits may reduce the range of representable numbers below acceptable limits.

One of the commonly implemented methods of dealing with these problems is that of floating-point format. Conceptually this format is similar to the use of scientific notation in hand calculations. Each number in floating-point format—integer or noninteger—is represented in a fixed number of bits that consist of three components: a fraction, which represents the most significant digits of the number; an exponent, which represents the power to which some fixed integer base is raised; and a sign, which represents the algebraic sign of the fraction. The product of two factors, the fraction and the base raised to the power represented by the exponent, represents the magnitude of the floating-point number; the sign of the fraction is the sign of that number. In all calculations, the fraction is considered to be a number from 0 to 1 (including 0 but not 1); it is scaled to its appropriate magnitude by increasing or decreasing the exponent. In the IBM 360 and 370, the exponent is in excess-64 notation. This means that the quantity 64_{10} must be subtracted from the exponent to obtain the integer power of 16 that it represents.

As will be discussed in chapter 13, a special set of instructions and registers is available in the IBM 360 and 370 systems to facilitate the processing of floating-point numbers. Many other computer systems have similar instruction sets. The use of these instructions eliminates the need for the programmer to align decimal point positions prior to or following a calculation. This is done by the hardware. The principle of separating the order of magnitude of a number from its significant digits allows for a wide range of numbers to be represented in a relatively small number of bits, while providing for a fixed number of significant digits in each number.

An alternative method of dealing with the problems posed by noninteger arithmetic is embodied in the number format known as packed-decimal representation. This format, and associated instructions, is available on the IBM 360 and 370 systems. In it, all numbers are represented as decimal integers (each digit being represented in 4-bit binary-coded decimal form), and all calculations are performed according to the rules of decimal arithmetic. Numbers with up to thirty-one significant digits can be represented. However, as will be discussed in chapter 12, the position of the decimal point is not represented. Instructions that explicitly handle decimal point alignment must be used whenever necessary to ensure correct results.

In all methods of representing numbers, a calculation may produce a result that is too large for the range of numbers that can be accommodated. When this happens, the condition known as *overflow* usually results in interruption of program execution. In using floating-point format, two other error conditions can arise. One, known as *underflow,* occurs when the magnitude of a result is too small (but not zero) to be represented; the other, a *significance* error, occurs when all significant bits of a sum or difference are zero but the exponent is not. As with overflow, the occurrence of either of these two conditions usually results in program interruption. However, program interruption can be prevented in the IBM 360 and 370 systems by use of the SPM instruction. When the SPM is used, it is up to the user's program to detect the error and take appropriate action. The conditions for which SPM can be used are overflow in fixed-point arithmetic, overflow in packed-decimal arithmetic, underflow, and significance errors. Overflow in floating-point operations always results in program interruption.

For further study of numerical analysis, you may wish to consult:

Conte, S.D., and deBoor, Carl. *Elementary Numerical Analysis: An Algorithmic Approach*. New York: McGraw Hill, 1972.

Forsythe, George E. *Computer Methods for Mathematical Computations*. Englewood Cliffs, N.J.: Prentice-Hall, 1977.

McNeary, Samuel S. *Introduction to Computational Methods for Students of Calculus*. Englewood Cliffs, N.J.: Prentice-Hall, 1973.

Nievergelt, Jurg, et al. *Computer Approaches to Mathematical Problems*. Englewood Cliffs, N.J.: Prentice-Hall, 1974.

Spencer, Donald D. *Computer Science Mathematics*. Indianapolis: Bobbs-Merrill, 1976.

EXERCISES

1. Convert the following decimal numbers to a 32-bit binary representation in which the low-order 12 bits represent the fraction:

   a. 3.125   **d.** 0.99   **g.** 0.333333

   b. 0.03125   **e.** 0.999   **h.** 0.75390625

   c. 31.25   **f.** 0.9999   **i.** 7539.0625

2. Convert the following numbers from base 2 or base 16 (as indicated) to base 10:

   a. 0.111_2 **d.** 0.01010101_2 **g.** 0.01110111_2

   b. $0.E_{16}$ **e.** 8.6_{16} **h.** 0.1110111_2

   c. $0.AA_{16}$ **f.** 0.86_{16} **i.** $3.B8_{16}$

3. What is the 7-bit excess-64 exponent that represents the power of 16 in each of the following terms:

   a. 16^3 **d.** 16^{30} **g.** 16^{60}

   b. 16^{-3} **e.** 16^{-30} **h.** 16^{-60}

   c. 16^2 **f.** 16^{-2} **i.** 16^0

4. Each of the following is the hexadecimal representation of a floating-point number in the IBM 360 and 370 systems. What is the representation of that number in scientific notation in the decimal system?

   a. 40400000   **d.** 40800000   **g.** C0333333

   b. C1C20000   **e.** 41100000   **h.** 00000001

   c. 3F3F0000   **f.** 46000001   **i.** 7FFFFFFF

5. Whenever we compute a number in floating-point format, the calculation may cause an exponent overflow error condition or an exponent underflow error condition. If we write that number as

$$a \times 16^b$$

   with $16^{-1} \leq a < 1$, what determines the smallest positive value of b for which exponent overflow would occur? What is that value in the IBM 360 and 370 systems? (Note that if B is a value of b for which exponent overflow will occur, $B + n$ for all positive n is also such a value.)

6. In the notation of Exercise 5, with $16^{-1} \leq a < 1$, what determines the algebraically largest value of b for which exponent underflow will occur? What is that value in the IBM 360 and 370 systems?

7. One major difference between the packed-decimal method of representing numbers and the floating-point method of representing numbers is that in the former the scale factor is implied, not explicitly represented, whereas in the latter, the scale factor is represented. What are some of the consequences of this difference from a programming standpoint?

8. Imagine a computer system in which the floating-point representation is based on the decimal system instead of the binary or hexadecimal system, i.e., each digit of the fraction is represented in 4-bit BCD code, the base of the scale factor is ten, and all computations are performed in accordance with the rules of decimal arithmetic. How might the exponent be represented in order to allow a range of positive numbers from approximately 10^{-99} to 10^{99}?

12

Packed-decimal Operations

In addition to the *binary* integer arithmetic operations described in chapters 4 and 5, the IBM Systems 360 and 370 provide a capability for *decimal* integer arithmetic. It is based on a representation of numbers called *packed-decimal* format. Constants can be defined for this format by the DC directive and by literals, and there is a set of instructions that perform decimal arithmetic and that convert numbers between EBCDIC character format and packed-decimal format.

There are two main reasons for the use of packed-decimal format:

1. To reduce the amount of memory space that would be required in EBCDIC format to store simple integers, such as inventory part numbers and telephone numbers.
2. To provide a method of processing decimal fractions without the loss of accuracy that could occur if they were processed as binary numbers.

The reduction in memory space is the reason this format is called "packed." As will be seen, two digits can be stored in a byte with packed format rather than the one digit per byte that EBCDIC requires.

However, it is the consideration of accuracy that dictates the use of packed-decimal operations when performing calculations in banking and related business applications, as the following discussion illustrates.

In the decimal system, fractions are represented in terms of negative powers of ten, as this example illustrates:

$$\text{three-fourths} \; = \; 0.75 \; = \; 7 \times 10^{-1} + 5 \times 10^{-2}$$
$$= \; 7/10 + 5/100$$

In the binary system, fractions are represented in terms of negative powers of two:

$$\text{three-fourths} \; = \; .11 \; = \; 1 \times 2^{-1} + 1 \times 2^{-2}$$
$$= \; \tfrac{1}{2} + \tfrac{1}{4}$$

The problem this presents is not in converting from one representation to the other but rather the possible loss of accuracy in converting from a decimal fraction to a binary fraction. This is because the set of numbers expressible in a finite number of binary digits is not in one-to-one correspondence with the set of numbers expressible in a finite number of decimal digits.

For example, consider the fraction 1/10 (one-tenth). In the decimal system, this is

$$\text{one-tenth} \; = \; 0.1 \; = \; 1 \times 10^{-1}$$

In the binary system, however, this is a never ending sequence of bits:

$$\text{one-tenth} \; = \; .000110011001100110011...$$
$$= \; 1 \times 2^{-4} + 1 \times 2^{-5} + 1 \times 2^{-8} + 1 \times 2^{-9} + ...$$

As a consequence, we obtain different results when, for example,we multiply 1/10 by ten in the decimal system and in the binary system. In the decimal system, $10 \times 0.1 = 1.0$. In the binary system, this is

$$(1010) \times (0.00011001100110011...)$$
$$= .1111111111...$$

i.e., not quite 1.0. In problems involving a large number of calculations, this type of discrepancy may lead to cumulative rounding errors that may not be tolerable, particularly in banking and related business applications.

The use of packed-decimal operations can avoid these errors. Nevertheless, since the decimal arithmetic instructions operate only on integers, it is necessary to represent fractions and mixed numbers as integers with an implied decimal point position. For example, 1.43 would be represented and processed as 143. It is up to the programmer to properly account for the decimal point's implied position. We shall indicate how this is done after describing the directives and instructions that are used to define and process packed-decimal integers. (It should be noted that in IBM COBOL, packed-decimal format is specified by the clause USAGE IS COMPUTATIONAL-3. This format is not readily available to FORTRAN programmers.)

12.1 DATA FORMATS

In the data formats referred to as packed-decimal in IBM terminology, and more generally as binary-coded decimal (BCD) format, each of the ten decimal digits is represented by 4 bits:

decimal digit	packed-decimal representation
0	0000
1	0001
2	0010
3	0011
4	0100
5	0101
6	0110
7	0111
8	1000
9	1001

As should be obvious, these 4-bit representations are simply those of the respective digits in the binary number system. However, they are manipulated as *decimal* digits during all arithmetic operations. For example, the number 10 (ten) is represented as two digits (8 bits), not as a binary ten (4 bits). The following examples illustrate this difference.

decimal	packed decimal	binary integer
10	0001 0000	1010
32	0011 0010	100000
432	0100 0011 0010	110110000
5432	0101 0100 0011 0010	1010100111000

The maximum number of digits allowable in a packed-decimal number is thirty-one. This gives a range of $-10^{31}+1$ through $10^{31}-1$. Since each digit requires 4 bits, the maximum packed-decimal number requires 16 bytes.

Note that the binary integer format generally requires fewer bits to represent a value than does the packed-decimal format. For example, with 32 bits, the maximum packed-decimal number is 10^7-1, whereas the maximum binary integer is $2^{31}-1$, or approximately 2.1×10^9. Although less economical in bits, packed-decimal accuracy is more suitable for some applications than binary, especially when dealing with fractions.

The sign of a packed-decimal number is always represented by 4 bits (not by one bit, as in binary numbers). These 4 bits always occupy the right-most bit positions in the low-order byte, as follows:

decimal	packed decimal			
+325	0011	0010	0101	1100
	3	2	5	C
−789	0111	1000	1001	1101
	7	8	9	D

(sign bits point to the right-most byte: C and D)

The plus sign + is almost always represented by 1100 (X'C') and the minus sign by 1101 (X'D'). The hardware also accepts X'A', X'E', and X'F' for plus and X'B' for minus, but the preferred codes, X'C' and X'D', are generated by all arithmetic and shift instructions in accordance with the rules of algebra.

There is one additional observation to be made: each packed-decimal number is always represented in an integral number of bytes. The number of bytes required depends on the number of digits. If N is the number of digits, then the number of bytes is $\frac{N+1}{2}$ if N is odd, and $\frac{N+2}{2}$ if N is even. (This rule includes allowance for the bits required for the sign, which are stored in the right half of the right-most byte.) For example,

decimal number	number of digits	packed decimal (in hex)	number of bytes
+2	1	2C	1
−32	2	032D	2
+432	3	432C	2
+5432	4	05432C	3
−65432	5	65432D	3
−765432	6	0765432D	4

Note that when the number of digits is even, a leading 0 (zero) is supplied to fill the left-most byte. Note also that the sign bits serve as a delimiter for a packed-decimal number: that is, the sign bit identifies the byte position of the low-order digit.

In Assembly Language, packed-decimal constants are distinguished from other constants by the letter P. For example, DC P'5' defines a 1-byte packed-decimal representation of the decimal integer +5. Figure 12.1 illustrates a few other typical P-type constants. There are several observations to be made:

1. In the DC directive, the only permissible modifier for P-type constants is the length modifier, Ln. The value of n is the number of *bytes,* not digits, and must be less than or equal to sixteen.
2. In P-type constants, padding is always on the left with zeroes. Truncation is also always at the left and can result in a loss of the most significant digits.
3. Truncation can always be avoided by a reasonable choice of the length modifier Ln or by omitting the length modifier.

To reserve data areas for packed-decimal data, we can use the P-type operand with a length modifier or the P-type operand with a typical value to imply the length. For example,

```
AREA1   DS   PL5              RESERVES 5 BYTES
AREA2   DS   P'+123456789'    RESERVES 5 BYTES
```

In both methods, alignment is always on a byte boundary.

12.2 INSTRUCTION FORMATS

Unlike the operations on binary integers described in chapter 5, the operations on packed-decimal numbers do not take place in registers; they take place in main memory. There are four categories of packed-decimal operations:

1. Arithmetic—add, subtract, multiply, divide, shift-and-round
2. Comparison of two numbers
3. Copying a number from one memory location to another
4. Conversion to and from packed-decimal format

Figure 12.1 *Defining packed-decimal constants.*

```
FLAG LOCTN OBJECT CODE      ADDR1  ADDR2  STMNT M SOURCE STATEMENT

     000000 325C                       5          DC     P'+3.25'        DECIMAL POINT IGNORED

     000002 000000325C                 6          DC     PL5'+325'       PADDING ON LEFT SINCE LNG L = 5
                                       7 *                               EXCEEDS NUMBER OF BYTES RE-
                                       8 *                               QUIRED FOR THE CONSTANT

     000007 5C                         9          DC     PL1'+325'       TRUNCATION ON LEFT SINCE
                                      10 *                               L = 1 IS LESS THAN NUMBER
                                      11 *                               OF BYTES REQD FOR CONSTANT.

     000008 120C                      12          DC     2P'1.20'        TWO CONSECUTIVE COPIES OF
            120C
                                      13 *                               +120 (PLUS ASSUMED IN AB-
                                      14 *                               SENCE OF MINUS SIGN.)

     00000C 034D567C                  15          DC     P'-34,567'      MULTIPLE OPERANDS ALLOWED IN 'DC'

     000010                           16 X        DS     PL8
     000018 F8 22 C010C048 000010 000048   17     ZAP    X(3),=P'1258'
     00001E F8 22 C010C04B 000010 00004B   18     ZAP    X(3),=P'-1258'
     000024 F8 00 C010C04E 000010 00004E   19     ZAP    X(1),=P'-1'
     00002A F8 00 C010C04F 000010 00004F   20     ZAP    X(1),=P'+1'
     000030 F8 11 C010C050 000010 000050   21     ZAP    X(2),=P'+0.1'
     000036 F8 11 C010C052 000010 000052   22     ZAP    X(2),=P'15'     NOTE FROM LITERAL TABLE THAT
     00003C F8 11 C010C052 000010 000052   23     ZAP    X(2),=P'1.5'    P'15', P'1.5'  AND  P'0.15'
     000042 F8 11 C010C052 000010 000052   24     ZAP    X(2),=P'0.15'   ARE ONE AND THE SAME LITERAL.

                                      25 * P-TYPE LITERALS ARE ALIGNED ON BYTE BOUNDARY

     000048 01258C
     00004B 01258D
     00004E 1D
     00004F 1C
     000050 001C
     000052 015C
```

All but two of the instructions in these categories are either SS_1-type or SS_2-type instructions. In SS_1-type instructions there are two operand fields; each field specifies the memory address of the data being operated on and the length of each data item is specified in the first operand:

$$D1(L,B1),D2(B2) \qquad \text{[SS}_1\text{ operand]}$$
$$\text{with } 1 \leq L \leq 256$$

In SS_2-type instructions, there are also two operand fields that specify the memory addresses of data items, but the length of each item is specified separately in each operand:

$$D1(L1,B1),D2(L2,B2) \qquad \text{[SS}_2\text{ operand]}$$
$$\text{with } 1 \leq L1 \leq 16$$
$$1 \leq L2 \leq 16$$

Thus, one critical factor in packed-decimal operations is the length of each data item. In the IBM 360 and 370 systems, *this length is always specified in number of bytes, not digits.* So, unlike binary integers, which are always 2 or 4 bytes long, a packed-decimal number can consist of from 1 to 16 bytes. Programmers must therefore assure that each number's length is correctly specified each time it is referred to in an instruction. This can be done either explicitly or implicitly. When an implicit operand is used (see fig. 3.4), the length field in the operand can be omitted provided that the corresponding data length is correctly specified in a DC or DS directive. When omitted, the length is said to be implied and the Assembler inserts the data length when it translates the operand into machine language.

12.3 ARITHMETIC OPERATIONS

In this section, we will discuss the five packed-decimal arithmetic operations

Zero and Add Packed (ZAP)
Add Packed (AP)
Subtract Packed (SP)
Multiply Packed (MP)
Divide Packed (DP)

The section concludes with a discussion of the decimal overflow, decimal divide, and data error conditions.

All five instructions are of SS₂-type format. Each instruction requires two operands, and each operand designates the address and length of a packed-decimal number in memory. The result of each arithmetic operation replaces the number specified by the first operand. Thus, the first operand is the destination; the second is the source.

Zero and Add Packed

ZAP   D1(L1,B1),D2(L2,B2)

address and length (in bytes) of source

address and length (in bytes) of destination

Zero and Add Packed (ZAP) copies a packed-decimal number from one memory location to another, after filling the destination area with zeroes. The destination can be of greater length than the number copied from the source field. This makes it possible to extend a number on the left with zeroes in preparation for any of the other arithmetic operations. Such an extension can avoid the possibility of overflow.

When $L1 > L2$, the result in the destination area will contain at least $L1-L2$ bytes of leading zeroes. If $L1 < L2$, and if there is not enough room in the destination area to accommodate all the significant digits of the number in the source field, a decimal overflow occurs (condition code 3 is set). In all other cases, the condition code is set according to whether the result is zero, negative, or positive.

Example 1.

			A	B
ZAP	B(8),A(4)	before execution:	0023456C	any 8 bytes
		after execution*:	0023456C	00000000 0023456C

*$L1-L2 = 4 =$ number of bytes of leading zeroes.

Example 2.

			A	B
ZAP	B(2),A(4)	before execution:	0023456C	any 2 bytes
		after execution*:	0023456C	456C

*$L1 < L2$ and loss of significant digits causes decimal overflow.

Example 3.

			A	B
ZAP	B(3),A(4)	before execution:	0023456C	any 3 bytes
		after execution*:	0023456C	23456C

*Although $L1 < L2$, there is no decimal overflow since no significant digits were lost.

Add Packed

AP   D1(L1,B1),D2(L2,B2)

When this instruction is executed, the number whose address and length are specified by the second operand is algebraically added to the number whose address and length are specified by the first operand. The sum replaces the number specified by the first operand, and the condition code is set to 0, 1, or 2 when the sum is zero, negative, or positive, respectively. However, the number of byte positions, L1, must be large enough to contain all the significant digits of the result and its sign. If not, an overflow error condition occurs, condition code 3 is set, and the program may be automatically interrupted and terminated.

Example 1.

			X1	Y1
AP	X1(3),Y1(2)	before execution:	03214C	010C
		after execution:	03224C	010C

Example 2.

			X2	Y2
AP	X2(2),Y2(3)	before execution:	099C	00001C
		after execution:	100C	00001C

Example 3.

			X3	Y3
AP	X3(2),Y3(3)	before execution:	999C	00001C
		after execution*:	000C	00001C

*A carry out of the high-order digit causes an overflow error condition.

Example 4.

			X4	Y4
AP	X4(3),Y4(3)	before execution:	00123D	00123C
		after execution*:	00000C	00123C

*A result of zero is always positive.

Subtract Packed

SP   D1(L1,B1),D2(L2,B2)

When this instruction is executed, the number whose address and length are specified by the second operand is algebraically subtracted from the number whose address and length are specified by the first operand. The resulting difference replaces the number specified by the first operand, and the condition code is set to 0, 1, or 2 according to whether the difference is zero, negative, or positive.

As in packed-decimal additions, there is one precaution to observe: *the number of byte positions, L1, must be large enough to contain all the significant digits of the result and its sign.* If not, an overflow error condition occurs, condition code 3 is set, and the program may be automatically interrupted and terminated.

Example 1.

			X1	Y1
SP	X1(3),Y1(2)	before execution:	03214C	010C
		after execution:	03204C	010C

Example 2.

			X2	Y2
SP	X2(2),Y2(3)	before execution:	099D	00001C
		after execution:	100D	00001C

Example 3.

			X3	Y3
SP	X3(2),Y3(3)	before execution:	999D	00001C
		after execution*:	000D	00001C

*A carry out of the high-order digit causes an overflow error condition.

Example 4.

			X4	Y4
SP	X4(3),Y4(3)	before execution:	00123D	00123D
		after execution*:	00000C	00123D

*A result of zero is always positive.

Multiply Packed

$$\text{MP} \quad \underbrace{\text{D1(L1,B1)}}_{\text{multiplicand}},\underbrace{\text{D2(L2,B2)}}_{\text{multiplier}}$$

When this instruction is executed, the number whose address and length are specified by the first operand is multiplied by the number whose address and length are specified by the second operand. The resulting product, its sign determined by the rules of algebra, replaces the multiplicand in memory, *but the condition code is not set*. However, the Compare Packed (CP) instruction can be used to determine the sign of the product.

Due to the fact that the number of significant bytes in the product is the sum of the number of significant bytes in the multiplier and multiplicand, there are several precautions to observe.

1. $L2 < L1$: the number of bytes in the multiplier must be less than the number of bytes in the multiplicand.
2. $1 \le L2 \le 8$: the number of bytes in the multiplier must not exceed 8.
3. In order that there will always be enough room to contain the product, whatever its value might be, the multiplicand (the number specified by the first operand) must have at least *L2* bytes of high-order zeroes.

When these precautions are observed, there will be no product overflow and no specification error (see discussion of errors at end of this section). Moreover, the leading digit of the product will always be zero.

Example 1.

			V1	W1
MP	V1(4),W1(2)	before execution:	0000999C	999D
		after execution:	0998001D	999D

Example 2.

	V2	W2
MP V2(3),W2(2) before execution:	00999C	999D
after execution*:	98001D	999D

*Overflow error condition: not enough high-order zeroes in V2.

Example 3.

	V3	W3
MP V3(2),W3(2) before execution:	012C	012C
after execution*:	012C	012C

*The operation is not carried out since L2 is not less than L1.

Example 4.

	V4
MP V4(4),V4+2(2) before execution:	0000256D
after execution*:	0065536C

*A number can be multiplied by itself if all the precautions discussed are observed. In this example, the second operand address and length denote the last 2 bytes of V4, namely 256D, while the first operand address and length denote the entire field, 0000256D.

Divide Packed

$$DP \quad \underbrace{D1(L1,B1)}_{\text{dividend}},\underbrace{D2(L2,B2)}_{\text{divisor}}$$

When this instruction is executed, the number whose address and length are specified by the first operand is divided by the number whose address and length is specified by the second operand. The result consists of two components: (1) Q, the integer quotient, of length L1-L2 *bytes;* and (2) R, the integer remainder, of length L2 bytes. The quotient and the remainder are stored side-by-side as packed-decimal integers in the memory location that had been occupied by the dividend, as indicated in this diagram:

The sign of the quotient is determined by the rules of algebra; the sign of the dividend is the same as that of the remainder even if the remainder is zero. The condition code is not set by the DP instruction, so the nature of the quotient—zero, negative, or positive—must be determined by a separate test (for example, via the compare instruction, CP).

In order to avoid any error condition that could interrupt the program, several precautions must be observed.

1. L2 < L1: the number of digits in the divisor must be less than the number of digits in the dividend, including leading zeroes.
2. $1 \leq L2 \leq 8$: the number of digits in the divisor must be less than sixteen.

3. The number of significant digits in the quotient must be smaller than the number of digits that can be stored in the L1-L2 bytes allowed for the quotient. This will always be the case if the dividend—the number specified by the first operand—has at least L2 bytes of leading zeroes.

4. The value of the divisor must not be zero.

Example 1.

			V1	W1
			—	—
DP	V1(4),W1(2)	before execution:	0000999C	998D
		after execution:	001D001C	998D

L1-L2 = 2 = length of quotient   remainder

Example 2.

			V2	W2
			—	—
DP	V2(4),W2(1)	before execution:	0000999C	3C
		after execution:	00333C0C	3C

L1-L2 = 3 = length of quotient   remainder

Example 3.

			V3	W3
			—	—
DP	V3(2),W3(1)	before execution:	999C	3C
		after execution:	999C	3C

L1-L2 = 1 = insufficient length for the quotient 333C, an error condition known as *divide exception.*

Example 4.

			V4	W4
			—	—
DP	V4(2),W4(3)	before execution:	999C	00003C
		after execution:	999C	00003C

L1-L2 = −1 = an impossible length for the quotient, an error condition known as *specification exception.*

Error Situations

Several types of error situations can be detected during execution of a packed-decimal arithmetic instruction:

1. *Decimal overflow* occurs when the length of the result of an AP, SP, SRP, or ZAP instruction is too long to fit into the number of bytes specified in the first operand. (Leading zeroes cannot cause overflow; only significant digits can.)

2. *Data exception* occurs in any of four situations:
   a. the sign or digit codes of a packed-decimal number are invalid
   b. the operands of AP, SP, MP, DP, or CP overlap without having identical right-most bytes
   c. the operands of ZAP overlap with the right-most byte of the second operand to the right of that of the first operand
   d. the first operand of an MP instruction does not have a sufficient number of high-order zeroes.

3. *Specification exception* occurs when the operand lengths of an MP or DP instruction are incompatible. Either the multiplier or divisor exceeds fifteen digits and sign (i.e., L2 > 8), or the multiplier or divisor has the same number or more digits than the multiplicand or dividend (i.e., L2 ≥ L1).

4. *Divide exception* occurs when the quotient would be too large for the operand field, as would be the case in an attempt to divide by zero.

When one of these errors is detected, execution of the program is interrupted by the hardware and terminated by the Operating System. The only exception is that interruptions due to decimal overflow can be prevented by resetting the appropriate program mask bit to zero, as discussed in chapter 11. Whether or not the decimal overflow interrupt has been prohibited by the SPM instruction, the occurrence of decimal overflow causes condition code 3 to be set so that it may be detected by a subsequent Branch on Overflow (BO) instruction.

Combined Multiply and Divide Example

Suppose we want to compute $(a \cdot b)/c$. We first need to determine how many bytes should be allocated for $a \cdot b$ and for $(a \cdot b)/c$, in order to assure that the answer is correctly represented. This depends on the number of bytes in each of the factors a, b, and c, which we can assume are as follows:

factor	number of bytes
a	k
b	m
c	p

The rules for the multiply instruction MP require that the multiplier contain no more than 8 bytes, that the number of bytes in the multiplicand exceed that of the multiplier, and that the product contain no more than thirty-one significant digits (16 bytes). We will therefore assume that b is the multiplier with $m \leq 8$ and that $k + m \leq 16$. We can then satisfy all the rules for MP by putting a in a multiplicand field that is $k + m$ bytes long. For example, if $a = 999$ in a 2-byte field and $b = 9$ in a 1-byte field, then $k = 2$ and $m = 1$ so that $k + m = 3$. The corresponding instructions are these:

```
        ZAP     X,A         PUT 999 IN A 3-BYTE MULTIPLICAND FIELD
        MP      X,B         MULTIPLY BY 9, A 1-BYTE MULTIPLIER
        ...
A       DC      PL2'999'
B       DC      PL1'9'
X       DS      PL3
```

The product $999 \times 9 = 8991$ is then represented correctly as a 3-byte packed-decimal number, 08991C.

The rules for the divide instruction DP require that the number of bytes in the divisor not exceed 8 and also be less than that of the dividend. We therefore assume that $p \leq 8$, and we must assure that the dividend field satisfies two criteria: (1) it must be more than p bytes long and (2) it must be long enough to contain all the significant digits of the quotient. Both of these criteria will be satisfied if the dividend contains p bytes of leading zeroes.

To continue the example, let us assume that $c = 5$ in a 1-byte field, so that $p = 1$. Since our previous result was $a \cdot b = 8991$ in a 3-byte field, we need to put $a \cdot b$ in a 4-byte field with 1 byte of leading zeroes. The corresponding instructions are these:

```
        ZAP     Y,X         PUT 8991 IN A 4-BYTE DIVIDEND FIELD
        DP      Y,C         DIVIDE BY +5, A 1-BYTE DIVISOR
        ...
X       DC      PL3
Y       DS      PL4
C       DC      PL'5'
```

The result, $8991 \div 5 = 1798\ 1/5$, is correctly represented in the 4-byte dividend field, Y, as two consecutive packed-decimal numbers, a 3-byte quotient and a 1-byte remainder: 01798C1C.

This analysis illustrates that if we had defined XX as a 4-byte field we could have computed $(a \cdot b)/c$ in three instructions:

```
            ZAP       XX,A          PUT 999 IN A 4-BYTE MULTIPLICAND FIELD
            MP        XX,B          MULTIPLY BY 9, A 1-BYTE MULTIPLIER
            DP        XX,C          DIVIDE BY 5, A 1-BYTE DIVISOR
            ...
XX          DS        PL4           RESULT IS 01798C1C
```

12.4 COMPARISONS

Any two packed-decimal numbers can be algebraically compared without changing either number. This is accomplished by means of the Compare Packed (CP) instruction, an SS_2-type instruction. Note that the character compare instructions (CLC, etc.) cannot be used because they do not interpret the sign bits algebraically and do not properly account for operands of unequal length.

If we let

$V_1 =$ the number specified by the address and length
of the first operand D1(L1,B1),
$V_2 =$ the number specified by the address and length
of the second operand D2(L2,B2),

then the instruction

CP   D1(L1,B1),D2(L2,B2)

sets the condition code as follows:

condition	condition code
$V_1 = V_2$	0
$V_1 < V_2$	1
$V_1 > V_2$	2

The comparison is made as though both V_1 and V_2 were equal in length, though they need not be. The only restrictions on length are that both L1 and L2 be less than or equal to sixteen.

As with any other comparison instruction, RX-type conditional branch instructions may be used to determine the result of a comparison:

BE	branches if $V_1 = V_2$
BNE	branches if $V_1 \neq V_2$
BH	branches if $V_1 > V_2$
BNH	branches if $V_1 \leq V_2$
BL	branches if $V_1 < V_2$
BNL	branches if $V_1 \geq V_2$

Alternatively, the RR-type conditional branch instructions, BER, BNER, etc., may be used.

Example 1.

			V1	V2
	CP	V1(2),V2(3)	012C	00345D
		result: $V_1 > V_2$		

Example 2.

			V1	V2
	CP	V1(4),V2(2)	00345C	345C
		result: $V_1 = V_2$		

Example 3.

			V1	V2
CP	V1(4),V2(1)		1234567D	0C
	result: $V_1 < V_2$			

The CP instruction is especially useful when it is necessary to determine if a number is zero prior to using it as a divisor. It can also be used to determine the nature of the result of an MP or DP instruction, by comparing the result to =P'0'. No distinction is made between a positive and a negative zero by the CP instruction.

12.5 DECIMAL POINT ALIGNMENT: SHIFTING ON THE IBM 370

In order to illustrate the problem of decimal point alignment, consider the problem of computing $A*B+C$ for various values of A, B, and C as illustrated in the examples.

Example 1.

Assembly Language			machine language
A	DC	P'+2.5'	025C
B	DC	P'+3.5'	035C
C	DC	P'+1.0'	010C

In machine language, the three numbers are all integers. The position of the decimal point does not affect the machine language representation. In other words, $+2.5$ is represented the same as $+25$ and as $+0.25$.

Consequently, the value $A*B = 8.75$ is represented as 875C; this is indistinguishable from $+0.875$, $+8.75$, and $+87.5$. So the immediate question is, how can we add $+1.0$ to $+8.75$? Since both numbers are treated as integers, we would have

$$
\begin{array}{r}
875C \\
+\ 010C \\
\hline
885C
\end{array}
$$

This is clearly wrong, for the correct answer, $+9.75$, would be represented as 975C.

The resolution of the dilemma is embodied in the concept of *shifting*. To align the implied decimal points so that addition can take place properly, we shift one of the factors right or left. If we shift to the *left,* we cause zeroes to be inserted on the right and a corresponding number of digits to be deleted from the left. If we shift to the *right,* we cause zeroes to be inserted on the left and a corresponding number of digits to be deleted from the right. For example, if we shift P'+1.0' *left* one position, then 010C becomes 100C. The addition in this example can now be performed correctly. We use the caret (∧) to indicate the position of the implied decimal point:

$$
\begin{array}{r}
8_\wedge 7\ 5\ C \\
+\ 1_\wedge 0\ 0\ C \\
\hline
9_\wedge 7\ 5\ C
\end{array}
$$
— zero inserted on right to align implied decimal points

In ordinary arithmetic, we would do exactly the same thing when adding 8.75 and 1.0:

$$
\begin{array}{r}
8.75 \\
+\ 1.00 \\
\hline
9.75
\end{array}
$$
— zero inserted on right to align explicit decimal points

Note that we ordinarily would not consider shifting 8.75 right to align it with 1.0, because to do so would result in a loss of accuracy. In shifting a number to the right, we drop the least significant digits. For example, in a right shift of one position, 8.75 becomes 8.7 (or 8.8, if rounded), so that 8.75 + 1.0 becomes

	8.7	0 8 7 C			8.8	0 8 8 C
either {	+ 1.0	0 1 0 C	or	{	+ 1.0	0 1 0 C
	9.7	0 9 7 C			9.8	0 9 8 C

But despite this loss of accuracy, there are times when a shift to the right is quite appropriate, as the next example illustrates.

Example 2.

	Assembly Language		machine language
A	DC	P'+2.5'	0 2$_\wedge$5 C
B	DC	P'+3.14159'	0 3$_\wedge$1 4 1 5 9 C
C	DC	P'+1.0'	0 1$_\wedge$0 C

Here, the number at B is an approximation to the number $\pi = 3.14159265....$ If the result of calculating $A*B+C$ is desired to two decimal positions, we must shift both $A*B$ and C, as follows:

$$A*B = (0\ 2_\wedge 5\ C) * (0\ 3_\wedge 1\ 4\ 1\ 5\ 9\ C) = 7_\wedge 8\ 5\ 3\ 9\ 7\ 5\ C \rightarrow 7_\wedge 8\ 5\ C$$
$$C = 0\ 1_\wedge 0\ C \longrightarrow 1_\wedge 0\ 0\ C$$
$$A*B+C = \longrightarrow 8_\wedge 8\ 5\ C$$

If the result had been desired to three decimal positions, we would have *rounded* $A*B$ before shifting:

$$A*B = 7_\wedge 8\ 5\ 3\ 9\ 7\ 5\ C \longrightarrow 0\ 7_\wedge 8\ 5\ 4\ C$$
$$C = 0\ 1_\wedge 0\ C \longrightarrow 0\ 1_\wedge 0\ 0\ 0\ C$$
$$A*B+C = \longrightarrow 0\ 8_\wedge 8\ 5\ 4\ C$$

In general, we always round when shifting to the right in order that the resulting number be the best approximation possible for the number of digits that remain after the shift. In the IBM 370 (but *not* the 360), the instruction used to shift and round a packed-decimal number is Shift and Round Packed (SRP). This instruction is discussed below. Instructions needed to accomplish shifting and rounding on the IBM 360, where the SRP is not available, will be described in Section 12.6.

Shift and Round Packed Instruction

The SRP instruction is a modified SS$_1$-type instruction, with the following assembly language and machine language formats:

As indicated, the first operand specifies the packed-decimal number's location in memory and its length in bytes. However, the number computed as the effective address from the second operand, namely,

$$\{\text{displacement D2}\} + \{\text{base-address in Register B2}\}$$

is *not used as an address*. Instead, its low-order 6 bits denote the number of digit positions to be shifted and the direction of the shift: if the low-order 6 bits represent a nonnegative integer n, then the packed-decimal number is shifted n positions to the left; if those 6 bits represent a negative integer $-n$, the number is shifted n positions to the right. The sign of the number is not shifted, and vacated digit positions are filled with zeroes. For right shifts of n digits, the negative integer $-n$ is assumed by the hardware to be in two's complement form. Since the Assembler does not translate $-n$ to its 6-bit two's complement representation, you should, as in the examples below, write $64-n$ rather than $-n$.

Although *rounding occurs only during right shifts,* a valid decimal digit must always be specified for I3, regardless of the shift direction. Before a right shift is completed, the integer specified by the I3 field is added to the left-most digit that is to be shifted out. Therefore, to round while shifting right, the I3 field should be 5; to avoid rounding, it should be 0. (Note that a number is rounded as though it were positive. In a right shift of *n* positions, the rounding factor is added to the *n*th digit from the right, and the resulting carry digit (0 or 1) is added to the $(n+1)$st digit from the right, with further carries (if any) propagated as required by the rules of addition. Then the right shift is performed and the *n*th digit and all lower-order digits are discarded.)

Example 1.

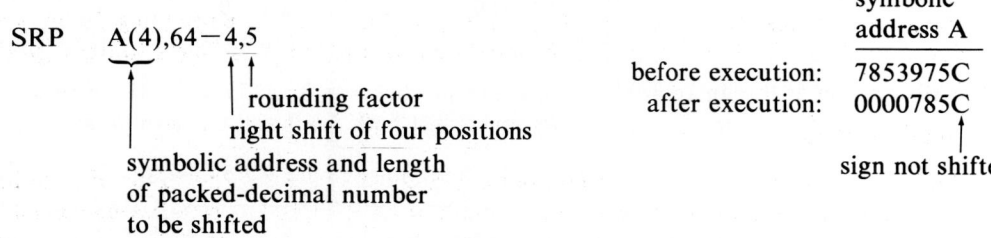

	symbolic address A
before execution:	7853975C
after execution:	0000785C

sign not shifted

SRP   A(4),64 — 4,5

rounding factor
right shift of four positions
symbolic address and length
of packed-decimal number
to be shifted

Example 2.

SRP   A(4),64 — 3,5

	symbolic address A
before execution:	7853975D
after execution*:	0007854D

*Note that the number is rounded as though it were positive.

Example 3.

SRP   B(2),1,5

	symbolic address B
before execution:	010C
after execution:	100C

rounding factor
(present but not used in left shifts)
left shift of one position

Example 4.

SRP   B(2),2,0

	symbolic address B
before execution:	010C
after execution*:	000C

left shift of two positions

*This example generates an *overflow error condition* because a significant digit (i.e., a nonzero digit) has been shifted out during the left shift. When this occurs, condition code 3 is set, and the program may be automatically interrupted and terminated.

Example 5.

SRP   C(5),0(8),5

           ↑ ↑
          │ rounding factor
      amount and direction of shift
      is determined by the low-order
      6 bits in Reg 8

before execution: 031415926C
after execution: 000031416C

In this example, it was assumed that Register 8 contains X'FFFFFFFD', i.e., -3. Thus, the amount of shift is three positions and the direction is to the right, as illustrated. The rounding factor is added to the left-most digit shifted out (the 9 in this example), and the carry is added to the lowest-order digit that remains, thus increasing the 5 to a 6.

Multiplication and Division

The requirements for assuring a sufficient number of significant digits in the result of a multiplication or division were described in Section 12.4 for integer computations. Those same requirements must be met when one or more factors contain implied decimal points, but there is also an additional requirement. *We must assure that a product and quotient contain an appropriate number of significant digits to the left and right of the implied decimal point.*

To illustrate this requirement, consider this multiplication: P'60'∗P'5' = P'300'. Since decimal arithmetic instructions ignore implied decimal points and treat all packed-decimal numbers as integers, then in the computer we also get P'60'∗P'.5' = P'300' and P'6.0'∗P'5' = P'300', whereas obviously 60∗0.5 = 30 and 6.0∗5 = 30. Similarly in divisions: in the computer, P'60' ÷ P'5' = P'12', P'60' ÷ P'.5' = P'12', and P'6.0' ÷ P'5' = P'12', whereas in fact 60 ÷ 0.5 = 120 and 6.0 ÷ 5 = 1.2.

To assure an appropriate number of significant digits to the left and right of the implied decimal point in a product or quotient, we can proceed as follows.

Multiplication: If p and q are the number of digits to the right of the implied decimal point (i.e., the number of fraction digits) in the multiplicand and multiplier, respectively, then the result of a multiply (MP) instruction will always contain $p + q$ fraction digits. Therefore, to assure that there are just k fraction digits in the product, we can shift the MP's result $p + q - k$ digits to the right. For example, if we want no fraction digits in the result of P'60'∗P'.5', then $k = 0$ with $p = 0$ and $q = 1$. Thus we must shift the MP result $p + q - k = 1$ digit to the right:

```
        ZAP     X,=P'60'        CREATE 3-BYTE MULTIPLICAND
        MP      X,=P'.5'        MULTIPLY BY 1-BYTE MULTIPLIER
        SRP     X,64-1,5        SHIFT RESULT RIGHT 1 DIGIT
        ...
X       DC      PL3             CORRECT PRODUCT = 00030C
```

Division: If p and q are the number of fraction digits in the dividend and divisor, respectively, and if $p \geq q$, then the quotient resulting from a divide instruction (DP) always contains $p - q$ fraction digits. If $p < q$, then $q - p$ low-order digits of the quotient will be truncated. To assure that there will be k fraction digits in the quotient, we can shift the *dividend* $q + k$ digits to the left before dividing, and shift the DP's quotient p digits to the right after dividing. For example, if we want one fraction digit in the result of P'6.0' ÷ P'5', then $k = 1$ with $p = 1$ and $q = 0$:

```
        ZAP     X,=P'6.0'       CREATE 4-BYTE DIVIDEND
        SRP     X,1,0           SHIFT DIVIDEND LEFT 1 DIGIT
        DP      X,=P'5'         CREATE DP'S 3-BYTE QUOTIENT
        SRP     X(3),64-1,5     SHIFT QUOTIENT RIGHT 1 DIGIT
        ...
X       DS      PL4             CORRECT RESULT = 00012C0C
```

Since it is imperative to avoid loss of significant digits when shifting left, the dividend should have $q + k$ leading zero digits in addition to what it would require in simple integer division. That is why we created a 4-byte dividend rather than a 3-byte dividend in the above example.

Note: The above general procedures are not necessary if we already know the value of each factor. But they or similar procedures are required when the values of the factors are not known at assembly time. In general we don't know those values, since they are likely to be either input data or the results of other calculations. Therefore, we should always estimate the *maximum* number of significant digits that are expected to occur to the right and left of the implied decimal point in each factor and make the appropriate decisions for space allocation and shifting. As a simple example of this, we can safely estimate that monthly salaries require no more than two digits to the right and five digits to the left of the implied decimal point: P'99999.99', or PL4.

12.6   COPYING A NUMBER—SHIFTING ON THE IBM 360

Although any packed-decimal number can be copied from one main memory location by means of the MVC, MVCL, or ZAP instructions, there are three instructions that are especially designed for certain copying operations intrinsic to packed-decimal numbers. These are

MVO	Move with Offset	(SS$_2$-type)
MVN	Move Numerics	(SS$_1$-type)
MVZ	Move Zones	(SS$_1$-type)

The MVO instruction copies a number from one memory location to another, but the result is *shifted left 4 bits* (half a byte) from what the original number was. This instruction makes it possible to shift a packed-decimal number on the IBM 360.

The MVN instruction copies the *right-most 4 bits* of one or more consecutive bytes. This makes it easy to set or alter the sign bits of a packed-decimal number, for example, to create an absolute value.

The MVZ instruction copies the *left-most 4 bits* of one or more consecutive bytes. It is used primarily to set the sign bits in a number represented in EBCDIC format (so-called zoned-decimal format, to be discussed in Section 12.8).

In each of these three instructions, the field being copied (the source) is specified by the second operand, and the destination is specified by the first operand. The following examples illustrate these concepts. This section concludes with a discussion of shifting packed-decimal numbers on the IBM 360.

Move with Offset

$$\text{MVO} \quad \underbrace{\text{D1(L1,B1)}}_{\text{destination}}, \underbrace{\text{D2(L2,B2)}}_{\text{source}}$$

All bytes of the source field are copied from right to left, but they are all shifted left 4 *bits* and replace the digits, but not the sign, of the destination field. If L2 < L1, the source field is extended left with enough high-order zeroes to fill the destination field. If L2 ≥ L1, the source field is truncated on the left in order to fit into the destination field. The condition code is *not* set if overflow occurs.

Example 1.

			A	B
MVO	A(4),B(4)	before execution:	2468135D	6314159C
		after execution:	314159CD	6314159C

Number copied from B is offset 4 bits to the left, but its leading digit is lost since there is not enough room for it.

Example 2.

			A	B
MVO	A(5),B(2)	before execution:	123456789D ⌐	987C
		after execution:	00000987CD ⌐	987C

Copied number is offset 4 bits to the left, and leading zeroes are inserted to fill the remaining space.

Move Numerics

$$\text{MVN} \quad \underbrace{D1(L,B1)}_{\text{destination}},\underbrace{D2(B2)}_{\text{source}}$$

This is similar to the MVC instruction, except that *only the right-most 4 bits of each source byte are copied.* The left-most 4 bits of each destination byte are not altered.

Example 3.

			A
MVN	A+3(1),=P'−1'	before execution:	0135792C
		after execution:	0135792D

sign copied from =P'−1'

Move Zones

$$\text{MVZ} \quad \underbrace{D1(L,B1)}_{\text{destination}},\underbrace{D2(B2)}_{\text{source}}$$

This is similar to the MVC instruction, except that *only the left-most 4 bits of each source byte are copied.* The right-most 4 bits of each destination byte are not altered.

Example 4.

			A
MVZ	A+3(1),=X'D0'	before execution:	F1F2F3F4
		after execution:	F1F2F3D4

copied from =X'D0'

Shifting Packed-decimal Numbers on the IBM 360

Since the Shift and Round Packed (SRP) instruction is not available on the IBM 360, the problem of aligning the implied decimal point in packed-decimal numbers must be resolved by means of other instructions.

One way to shift a packed-decimal number to the left N digits is to multiply it by 10^N. Similarly, to shift a packed-decimal number *right* N digits, we can divide it by 10^N. Both multiplication and division are fairly time-consuming instructions; the multiply instruction is essentially a sequence of successive additions, the divide a sequence of successive subtractions. Moreover, there is no simple way to round when doing right-shifts by means of a division instruction. Consequently, shifting is usually done as a combination of instructions based on the MVO. There are many ways to do this, and it is suggested that you devise your own methods

Figure 12.2a   Shifting left an odd number of digits. (L is an absolute constant, equal to the length in bytes of the number at location Q.)

```
*  SHIFT 1 DIGIT LEFT        *  SHIFT 3 DIGITS LEFT        *  SHIFT 5 DIGITS LEFT
   ZAP    W(16),Q(L)            ZAP    W(16),Q(L)             ZAP    W(16),Q(L)
   MVN    W+15(1),=X'00'        MVN    W+15(1),=X'00'         MVN    W+15(1),=X'00'
   MVO    Q(L),W(16)            MVO    Q(L),W+1(16)           MVO    Q(L),W+2(16)
   ...                          ...                           ...
W  DC     32X'00'           W  DC     32X'00'             W  DC     32X'00'
```

Figure 12.2b   Shifting left an even number of digits. (L is an absolute constant, equal to the length in bytes of the number at location Q.)

```
*  SHIFT 2 DIGITS LEFT       *  SHIFT 4 DIGITS LEFT        *  SHIFT 6 DIGITS LEFT
   MVO    W(16),Q(L)            MVO    W(16),Q(L)             MVO    W(16),Q(L)
   MVC    W+15(1),=X'00'        MVC    W+15(1),=X'00'         MVC    W+15(1),=X'00'
   MVO    Q(L),W(16)            MVO    Q(L),W+1(16)           MVO    Q(L),W+2(16)
   ...                          ...                           ...
W  DC     32X'00'           W  DC     32X'00'             W  DC     32X'00'
```

Figure 12.2c   Shifting right an odd number of digits—with rounding. (L is an absolute constant, equal to the length in bytes of the number at location Q.)

```
*  SHIFT 1 DIGIT RIGHT       *  SHIFT 3 DIGITS RIGHT       *  SHIFT 5 DIGITS RIGHT
   ZAP    W(16),Q(L)            ZAP    W(16),Q(L)             ZAP    W(16),Q(L)
   MVN    W+15(1),=P'0'         MVN    W+15(1),=P'0'          MVN    W+15(1),=P'0'
   AP     W(16),=P'5'           AP     W(16),=P'500'          AP     W(16),=P'50000'
   MVO    Q(L),W(15)            MVO    Q(L),W(14)             MVO    Q(L),W(13)
   ...                          ...                           ...
W  DC     16X'00'           W  DC     16X'00'             W  DC     16X'00'
```

Figure 12.2d   Shifting right an even number of digits—with rounding. (L is an absolute constant, equal to the length in bytes of the number at location Q.)

```
*  SHIFT 2 DIGITS RIGHT      *  SHIFT 4 DIGITS RIGHT       *  SHIFT 6 DIGITS RIGHT
   MVN    W+15(1),=P'0'         MVN    W+15(1),=P'0'          MVN    W+15(1),=P'0'
   MVO    W(16),Q(L-1)          MVO    W(16),Q(L-1)           MVO    W(16),Q(L-1)
   AP     W(16),=P'5'           AP     W(16),=P'500'          AP     W(16),=P'50000'
   MVO    Q(L),W(15)            MVO    Q(L),W(14)             MVO    Q(L),W(13)
   ...                          ...                           ...
W  DC     16X'00'           W  DC     16X'00'             W  DC     16X'00'
```

as a way of learning how to use the MVO, MVN, MVZ, and ZAP instructions. In addition, you are urged to study figures 12.2a–d, in which solutions to the four main shifting problems are presented: (1) shift left an odd number of digits; (2) shift left an even number of digits; (3) shift right an odd number of digits, with rounding; and (4) shift right an even number of digits, with rounding. In each of the solutions, it is assumed that the packed-decimal number to be shifted is at symbolic location Q, and consists of L bytes, $L \leq 16$. The condition code will not necessarily reflect the result of the shifts.

12.7   APPLYING PACKED-DECIMAL OPERATIONS

To illustrate the use of packed-decimal operations, two small but typical business-oriented problems will now be described and solved.

The first problem is to calculate the amount, A, of interest earned on a principal of P dollars compounded at an annual interest rate, I, for a period of N years:

$$A = P(1 + I)^N - P$$

Figure 12.3 *Computation of* $A = P(1 + I)^N - P$.

```
*  CALCULATION USING PACKED-DECIMAL OPERATIONS
*                   A = P * (1 + I) ** N - P
*
*  P = PRINCIPAL IN DOLLARS AND CENTS              P'XXXXX.XX'
*  I = ANNUAL INTEREST, E.G.:    0.0950  (9.5%)    P'X.XXXX'
*  N = NUMBER OF YEARS                                  P'XX'
*  A = INTEREST EARNED                             P'XXXXXX.XX'
*
*  INITIALIZATION
          ZAP    X(4),I(3)           INITIALLY,
          AP     X(4),=P'10000'          X=1+I = 1.XXXX
          ZAP    Y(8),P(4)               Y=P WITH LEADING ZEROES
          ZAP    CTR(8),N(2)         CTR=N, FOR LOOP-CONTROL
          CVB    5,CTR               CONVERT N TO BINARY INTEGER
*  COMPUTE  Y = ((P*(1+I))*(1+I))*...*(1+I)
LOOP      MP     Y(8),X(4)           GENERATES SIX DECIMAL PLACES
          SRP    Y(8),64-4,0         TRUNCATE TO TWO PLACES
          BCT    5,LOOP              REPEAT N-1   TIMES
*  COMPUTE    A = Y - P
          ZAP    A(5),Y(8)           MOVE Y AND REMOVE LEADING ZEROES
          SP     A(5),P(4)           A = XXXXXX.XX
           .
           .
X         DS     PL4                 1 + I          X.XXXX
Y         DS     PL8                 P*(1+I)**N    XX...XXXX.XX
CTR       DS     D                   N (FOR CVB)    000000XX.
P         DS     PL4                 P              XXXXX.XX
A         DS     PL5                 A              XXXXXX.XX
N         DS     PL2                 N                    XX.
I         DS     PL3                 I              X.XXXX
           .
           .
```

The second problem is to convert a date (given as month/day/year) into its so-called Julian date, namely the number that indicates how many days have elapsed from the beginning of the year to that date.

Computation of Interest

The solution to this problem (fig. 12.3) illustrates the types of decisions that a programmer has to make when doing calculations that involve decimal point positioning. These decisions are: (1) How many digit positions, both to the right and to the left of the decimal point, should be provided for the results of intermediate calculations? and (2) In what order should the calculations be performed?

In deciding how many digit positions should be provided to the *left* of the implied decimal point, simply estimate the largest number that is likely to be calculated, and be certain to allow enough leading zeroes to avoid the possibility of overflow. The descriptions of the MP and DP instructions are helpful in deciding the number of leading zeroes for which to provide space.

In deciding how many digit positions should be provided to the *right* of the implied decimal point, remember that when two numbers are multiplied, the number of digits to the right of the decimal point in the product is the sum of the number of digits to the right of the decimal point in each factor.

Finally, in deciding the order in which calculations are to be performed, you must take care to minimize the possibility of cumulative round-off errors, or errors due to approximations.

In the solution shown in figure 12.3, the following decisions can be seen:

1. In the computation of $P \times (1 + I)$, a total of 16 digit positions were reserved: six to the right of the decimal, since $1 + I$ had four to the right and P had two; and ten to the left in order to take care of the assumed worst-case conditions of $P = \$100,000$, $I = 20\%$, and $N = 25$ years.

2. In the computation of the result, the amount of money on hand *at the end of each year* was truncated (not rounded) to dollars and cents before the calculation for the next year was made. This method is one way to avoid the accumulation of unearned money through round-off.

Note that the CVB instruction in figure 12.3 converts the packed-decimal number N (number of years) to a binary integer for loop control. The CVB is described in the next section.

The following data can be used to trace through the program of figure 12.3 in order to see how the decimal point alignment problem is handled:

$$P = \$10,000.00 \qquad (10000.00)*(1.0850) = 10850.000000$$
$$I = 8.5\% \qquad (10850.00)*(1.0850) = 11772.250000$$
$$N = 5 \text{ years} \qquad (11772.25)*(1.0850) = 12772.891250$$
$$(12772.89)*(1.0850) = 13858.585650$$
$$(13858.58)*(1.0850) = 15036.559300$$

so that $A = \$15,036.55 - \$10,000. = \$5,036.55$.

Calculation of Julian Date

The Julian date of any day of the year is the number that indicates how many days have elapsed from the beginning of the year, up to and including that day. For example, the Julian date of January 1 is 1, that of February 1 is 32, and that of December 31 is 365 (366 in leap years).

The Julian date is useful in cost accounting and related business applications where it is necessary to compute elapsed time in days and/or weeks. It is much simpler to subtract two Julian dates to arrive at the result than it is to subtract two calendar dates. For these types of applications, it is convenient to have an algorithm that converts a calendar date given as month/day/year to its equivalent Julian date. The purpose of this problem is to describe such an algorithm and to show how it might be programmed using the packed-decimal arithmetic instructions.

To convert a calendar date, mm/dd/yy, to its Julian date, the algorithm is as follows:

Let M = mm,   the two-digit number representing the month.
Let D = dd,   the two-digit date of the month.
Let Y = yy,   the last two digits of the year.

Calculate $J_1 = (M-1)*30.57$, and *round it off to an integer*. Then the Julian date J corresponding to the calendar date $M/D/Y$ is given by one of these three expressions:

$$J = J_1 + D \qquad \text{if } M \leq 2$$
$$J = J_1 + D - 1 \qquad \text{if } M > 2 \text{ and } Y \text{ is a leap year}$$
$$J = J_1 + D - 2 \qquad \text{if } M > 2 \text{ and } Y \text{ is not a leap year}$$

In addition to its dependence on the values of M, D, and Y, the algorithm is clearly dependent on the value of the constant 30.57, the concept of rounding, and the calculation that determines whether or not Y is a leap year. Except when $Y = 00$, Y is a leap year if it is exactly divisible by 4. (If $Y = 00$, the full four-digit year must be exactly divisible by 400 in order for it to be a leap year. But since the year 2000 is exactly divisible by both 4 and 400, this case won't be considered in the program solution of fig. 12.4.)

The concept of rounding is quite straightforward in this problem. The product $(M-1)*30.57$ will always have two digits implied to the right of the decimal point, so that a right shift of two positions, with rounding, is all that is required.

The constant 30.57 is, to two decimal places, the average of the ten Julian dates corresponding to March 1, April 1, May 1,..., December 1, when these dates are leap year dates. Thus, the product $(M-1)*30.57$ rounded off to an integer gives the Julian date of the first day of March, April, May,..., December in a leap year. Once these Julian dates are determined, the remaining calculation simply adds the date of the month, and subtracts 2 or 1 depending on whether the year is or is not a leap year.

A program segment to accomplish these calculations is given in figure 12.4. On the IBM 360, the SRP instruction would have to be replaced by the following sequence (see also fig. 12.2d). In this sequence, W would be defined by the DC directive W   DC   16X'00'

```
MVN       W+15(1),=P'0'       INITIALIZE W TO P'+0'
MVO       W(16),JD(2)         TRUNCATE TO 1 DECIMAL PLACE, AND OFFSET
AP        W(16),=P'5'         ROUND BY ADDING 5 TO LOW-ORDER DIGIT
MVO       JD(3),W(15)         TRUNCATE RESULTING LOW-ORDER DIGIT
```

Figure 12.4 Calculation of Julian date.

```
* CALCULATING JULIAN DATE J CORRESPONDING TO CALENDAR DATE M/D/Y:
*                   J = (M-1)*30.57 + D - X
*        WHERE      X = 0  IF M ≤ 2
*                   X = 1  IF M > 2 AND Y IS A LEAP YEAR
*                   X = 2  IF M > 2 AND Y NOT A LEAP YEAR
*
            ZAP    JD(3),M(2)              ADD LEADING ZEROES TO MONTH
            SP     JD(3),=P'1'            M-1
            MP     JD(3),=P'30.57'       (M-1)*30.57
            SRP    JD(3),64-2,5           ROUND OFF TO AN INTEGER
            AP     JD(3),D(2)            (M-1)*30.57 + D
            CP     M(2),=P'2'             IS M > 2 ?
            BNH    DONE                   BRANCH IF EITHER JAN OR FEB
            ZAP    YX(3),Y(2)             ADD LEADING ZEROES TO YEAR,
            DP     YX(3),=P'4'            THEN TEST FOR LEAP YEAR.
            CP     YXR(1),=P'0'           IS REMAINDER ZERO ?
            BE     LEAP                   IF SO, IT'S LEAP YEAR
            SP     JD(3),=P'2'            IF NOT LEAP YEAR, J= (M-1)*30.57+D-2
            B      DONE
LEAP        SP     JD(3),=P'1'            IF LEAP YEAR, J= (M-1)*30.57+D-1
DONE        ZAP    J(2),JD(3)             REMOVE UNNEEDED LEADING ZEROES
              .
              .
M           DS     PL2                    MONTH          XX.
D           DS     PL2                    DAY            XX.
Y           DS     PL2                    YEAR           XX.
J           DS     PL2                    JULIAN         XXX.
JD          DS     PL3                    FOR CALCULATING (M-1)*30.57  XXX.XX
YX          DS     PL3                    FOR CALCULATING Y/4
YXR         EQU    YX+2                   REMAINDER OF Y/4  IS ONE BYTE LONG
              .
              .
```

12.8 CONVERSION TO AND FROM PACKED-DECIMAL FORMAT

Three different methods of representing numbers in the IBM Systems 360 and 370 have been described: (1) EBCDIC format, (2) binary integer format, and (3) packed-decimal format. In addition, as will be shown in chapter 13, there is a fourth method of representation: floating-point format. A natural question arises: Are these formats interchangeable? That is, can we easily change a number from one format to another?

The answer is *yes* for the first three formats and *no* (at least, not easily) for floating-point format. The conversions among EBCDIC, binary integer, and packed-decimal formats are made quite easy by two sets of instructions.

1. Instructions for converting between binary and packed-decimal:

CVD converts binary to packed-decimal
CVB converts packed-decimal to binary

2. Instructions for converting between packed-decimal and EBCDIC:

PACK converts EBCDIC to packed-decimal
UNPK converts packed-decimal to EBCDIC

There is no single instruction for converting from Binary to EBCDIC (or vice versa), but it is a simple matter to do so by using two instructions from the sets just mentioned:

CVD
UNPK   converts binary to EBCDIC in two steps

PACK
CVB   converts EBCDIC to binary in two steps

The methods of using these instructions will now be described. Two important limitations of PACK and UNPK will be discussed at the end of this section.

Packed-decimal/Binary Conversions

opcode	meaning	type
CVD	CONVERT TO DECIMAL Converts a 32-bit binary integer into an 8-byte packed-decimal number.	RX
CVB	CONVERT TO BINARY Converts an 8-byte packed-decimal number into a 32-bit binary integer.	RX

For these two instructions, the following hold true:

1. The RX formats of the CVD and CVB are

$$CVD\ R1,D2(X2,B2)$$
$$CVB\ R1,D2(X2,B2)$$

2. The location of the 32-bit binary integer is specified by the first operand field, which is a register address. Thus, when using CVD, the binary integer must already be in that register; when using CVB, the resulting integer will be placed in that register.

3. The location of the 8-byte packed-decimal number *must be on a double-word boundary in the IBM 360*. Its address is specified by the second operand field.

4. The packed-decimal number that is converted by the CVB cannot be greater than P'2147483647' or less than P'−2147483648'. This is because numbers outside this range cannot be represented as 32-bit signed integers. If an attempt is made to convert a number outside this range, a fixed-point divide exception occurs and the program is interrupted.

CVD and CVB Examples

			Reg 5	memory location A
CVB	5,A	before execution:	any number	00 00 00 00 00 00 01 6C
		after execution:	00 00 00 10	00 00 00 00 00 00 01 6C

			Reg 5	memory location A
CVB	5,A	before execution:	any number	00 00 00 00 00 00 01 6D
		after execution:	FF FF FF F0	00 00 00 00 00 00 01 6D

			Reg 5	memory location A
CVD	5,A	before execution:	7F FF FF FF	any number
		after execution:	7F FF FF FF	00 00 02 14 74 83 64 7C

			Reg 5	memory location A
CVD	5,A	before execution:	80 00 00 00	any number
		after execution:	80 00 00 00	00 00 02 14 74 83 64 8D

Packed-decimal/EBCDIC Conversions

opcode	meaning	type
PACK	Converts numbers from EBCDIC to packed-decimal format.	SS₂
UNPK	Converts packed-decimal numbers to EBCDIC format (see note 3 below).	SS₂

For these two instructions, the following hold true:

1. The first operand specifies the result field, the second the field used to create the result:

$$\text{PACK} \quad \underbrace{\text{D1(L1,B1)}}_{\text{packed-decimal field}}, \underbrace{\text{D2(L2,B2)}}_{\text{EBCDIC field}}$$

$$\text{UNPK} \quad \underbrace{\text{D1(L1,B1)}}_{\text{EBCDIC}}, \underbrace{\text{D2(L2,B2)}}_{\text{packed-decimal}}$$

2. L1 and L2 are *byte* counts; each is required to be less than or equal to 16. The counts need not be equal, but care must be taken to avoid loss of the most significant digits during the conversion process. Such loss will not occur if we use a slightly conservative rule of thumb, namely, that every byte of a packed-decimal number corresponds to 2 bytes of an EBCDIC number. For PACK, this rule leads us to choose $L1 > \frac{1}{2}*L2$; for UNPK, it leads us to choose $L1 \geq 2*L2$.

3. The EBCDIC data format used by these two instructions is a slight but important variation of the standard EBCDIC format. This variation is known as the *zoned-decimal* format. In standard EBCDIC, every digit is represented in 8 bits:

1	1	1	1	BCD digit

|← 4 bits →|← 4 bits →|

The left half of this byte is called the *zone* portion; the right half, the *numeric* portion. In a standard EBCDIC number each zone portion consists of four binary 1's (a hex F), as shown above. In the variation of EBCDIC processed by the PACK and UNPK instructions, *the zone portion of the right-most byte contains the sign of the number:*

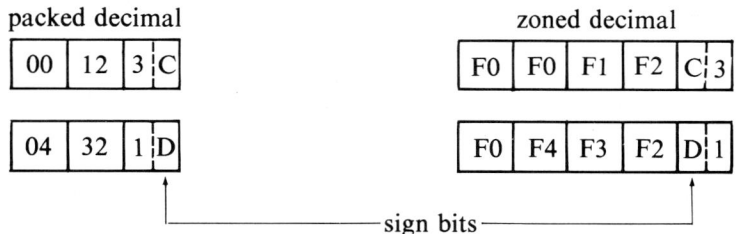

The bits recognized as valid sign bits in zoned-decimal format are the same as those in packed-decimal format: X'A', X'C', X'E', or X'F' for plus; X'B' or X'D' for minus. The UNPK instruction always copies the sign bits unchanged from the low-order 4 bits of the packed-decimal number to the zone bits of the low-order byte in the receiving EBCDIC field. PACK always copies the sign bits unchanged from the low-order EBCDIC byte to the low-order packed-decimal byte, as shown in the diagram. Whether the numbers being converted are positive or negative, there are certain inherent limitations to this treatment of the sign bits. These limitations will be discussed further at the end of this section.

PACK and UNPK Examples

			B	A
PACK	A(4),B(4)	before execution:	F1 F2 F3 C4	any 4 bytes
		after execution:	F1 F2 F3 C4	00 01 23 4C

result   source
field   field

L1=4,L2=4: more than enough space in result field, so leading
BCD zeroes are generated as needed.

			B	A
PACK	A(2),B(4)	before execution:	F1 F2 F3 D4	any 2 bytes
		after execution:	F1 F2 F3 D4	23 4D

L1=2,L2=4: insufficient space in result field to contain entire source
field: one high-order digit is not converted.

			Y	X
UNPK	X(4),Y(4)	before execution:	12 34 56 7C	any 4 bytes
		after execution:	12 34 56 7C	F4 F5 F6 C7

result   source
field   field

L1=L2=4: not enough space in result field to hold all the digits of
source field: three high-order digits are not converted.

			Y	X
UNPK	X(8),Y(4)	before execution:	12 34 56 7D	any 8 bytes
		after execution:	12 34 56 7D	F0 F1 F2 F3 F4 F5 F6 D7

L1=8, L2=4: more than enough space in result field, so leading
EBCDIC zeroes are generated as needed.

Neither PACK nor UNPK sets the condition code, and neither causes an error condition when there is insufficient space in the result field.

Further, in the PACK instruction the low-order 4 bits of each byte are not checked for valid codes; they are simply copied unchanged into their respective positions in the packed-decimal representation. This is also true of the zone bits in the right-most byte of the EBCDIC field. The zone bits of the other EBCDIC bytes are ignored.

Similarly, in the UNPK instruction, neither the digits nor the sign bits of the packed-decimal field are checked for validity. They are copied unchanged into their respective positions in the EBCDIC field.

Limitations of PACK and UNPK

The limitation of the PACK instruction becomes apparent when we wish to convert negative numbers to packed-decimal format. PACK only recognizes the sign coded in the zone bits of the right-most byte. Therefore, a negative number such as −1234 must be represented as 123M in EBCDIC notation, since the hex code for the letter M is X'D4'. In IBM punched-card code, this corresponds to punching the minus sign (an "11-zone" punch) in the same column as the low-order digit. It is an awkward requirement, especially when using a terminal instead of punched cards for input data. Therefore, to convert a negative integer that is entered in the usual way, e.g., as −1234 instead of 123M, we need more than just the PACK instruction. We need a set of instructions to correctly process the minus sign. The sequence of instructions below will convert a twelve-character EBCDIC integer field to its 32-bit two's complement binary representation. The twelve characters can include leading blanks or leading zeroes, with the algebraic sign being one of the twelve characters to the left of the leading digit: plus represented by a blank, minus represented by a hyphen (-). For example,

| | |2|1|4|7|4|8|3|6|4|7| | | |-|2|1|4|7|4|8|3|6|4|8| | | | | | | | | | |-|1|0|0| | | | | | | | | | |0|1|0|0| etc.

```
          PACK    NPACKED,NEBCDIC        CONVERT TO PACKED DECIMAL
          MVN     NPACKED+7(1),=P'-1'    ASSUME IT'S NEGATIVE
          LA      5,LNG                  INITIALIZE LOOP COUNT
          LA      6,NEBCDIC              INITIALIZE FIELD ADDRESS
LOOP      CLI     0(6),C'-'              LOOK FOR MINUS SIGN
          BE      FINIS                  IF FOUND, SEARCH NO MORE
          LA      6,1(6)                 INCREASE ADDRESS TO NEXT BYTE
          BCT     5,LOOP                 REPEAT TILL ALL BYTES EXAMINED
          MVN     NPACKED+7(1),=P'+1'    IF NOT NEGATIVE, THEN POSITIVE
FINIS     CVB     5,NPACKED              CONVERT TO BINARY
          ST      5,NBINARY              STORE RESULT
            .
            .
LNG       EQU     12                     LENGTH OF EBCDIC FIELD
NEBCDIC   DS      CL(LNG)                SPACE FOR EBCDIC FIELD
NPACKED   DS      D                      SPACE FOR PACKED-DECIMAL FIELD
NBINARY   DS      F                      SPACE FOR BINARY RESULT
```

There is a similar limitation to the use of the UNPK instruction: UNPK places the sign in the zone bits of the low-order byte of the EBCDIC field, so that, for example, the packed-decimal number P'−1234' will be converted to an EBCDIC field such as C'123M'. Positive numbers are also inappropriately represented after the conversion. For example, P'+1234' will be converted to an EBCDIC field such as C'123D', since the hex code for the letter D is X'C4'. If we want to print the results of a conversion in a more appropriate form, e.g., as −1234 or 1234, we need more than just the UNPK instruction. This is why, in chapter 4, we introduced the OI instruction: it eliminates the sign code created by UNPK in the low-order byte. In the next section, we will discuss how the Edit (ED) and Edit and Mark (EDMK) instructions can be used to produce an appropriate EBCDIC representation for printed output. See especially Example 6 at the end of the next section.

12.9 CREATING READABLE OUTPUT

The PICTURE clause in COBOL contains a number of editing options for producing readable numeric output on a printed page. Among these options are:

1. Insertion of a decimal point in the appropriate position
2. Replacement of leading zeroes by blank spaces, except after the decimal point
3. Insertion of commas or spaces to make large numbers easier to read
4. Use of a blank space instead of a plus sign for positive numbers
5. Use of either a CR suffix or a minus-sign prefix for negative numbers

COBOL provides these and similar options for obvious reasons; but they would be rather cumbersome to program in Assembly Language were it not for two quite remarkable instructions in the IBM Systems 360 and 370—Edit (ED) and Edit and Mark (EDMK). Each of these instructions converts packed-decimal numbers into EBCDIC code, and *simultaneously* performs a number of other operations designed to achieve the types of editing results just listed.

One concept needs to be emphasized in order to understand the underlying principle of the ED and EDMK instructions. As shown in earlier chapters, a line of printed output is produced by transmitting each line from main memory to the printer device, character by character. This means that each line must be completely set up in main memory—blanks, punctuation marks, digits, etc.—in exactly the form that is to appear on the printed page. This is what the ED and EDMK are designed to do. They do it by means of a concept known as a *pattern*.

Patterns

A few illustrations will serve to indicate the types of results that can be achieved by the ED and EDMK instructions:

packed-decimal number		edited result
00 01 23 45 6C		1,234.56
00 01 23 45 6D		1,234.56—
00 12 34 56 7D	$	12,345.67—
00 12 34 56 7D	$	12,345.67CR
00 09 05 10 0C		$****9,051.00

The variations are numerous. For example, the dollar sign can be *floated* so that it just precedes the first significant digit, and instead of commas we could use spaces. Also, for use in European systems, we can interchange the comma and period and substitute a different currency symbol. How is such flexibility achieved in a single instruction? The answer is that each printed output format must be precisely described by a sequence of bytes called a *pattern*. The pattern contains the punctuation in the desired positions and contains information that dictates where *in the pattern* each significant digit is to be placed.

For example, a pattern that would produce the first edited result shown above would be this:

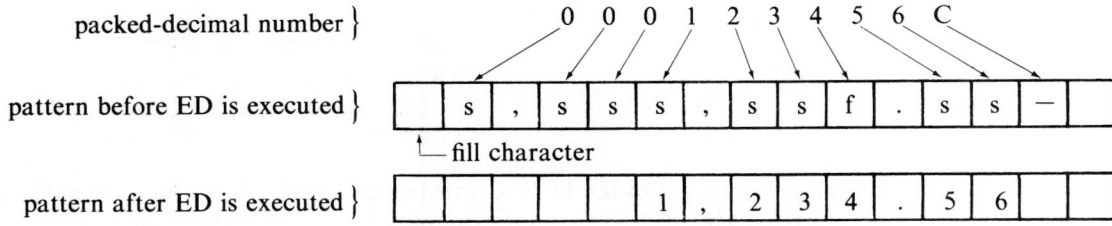

Each byte in a pattern can consist of any 8 bits, but there are three particular 8-bit combinations that have a special purpose when used in a pattern:

$$X'20' = \text{digit selector}$$
$$X'21' = \text{significance starter}$$
$$X'22' = \text{field separator}$$

The *digit selector,* denoted by "s" in the above diagram, causes the current digit to be taken from the packed-decimal number being processed. If that digit is considered to be significant, it replaces the digit selector; if it is not significant, it is discarded and the digit selector is replaced by the fill character.

The *significance starter,* denoted by "f" in the diagram, selects the current digit just as the digit selector does, but, in addition, it *forces all subsequent digits to be considered significant.* If the digit selected by the significance starter was a significant digit, it replaces the significance starter. Otherwise, the significance starter is replaced by the *fill* character.

The *field separator,* used in multiple-field editing, will not be discussed in this text.

Note that the number of digit selectors and significance starters should be equal to the number of digits in the packed-decimal number and that the key concept for understanding how patterns work is that of *significant digit.* Since each packed-decimal number is always considered to be an integer, it should be clear that all of its digits are significant except the leading zeroes. These are all nonsignificant.

The ED and EDMK instructions can detect the difference between significant and nonsignificant digits, i.e., between leading and non-leading zeroes. It is this capacity that allows leading zeroes to be suppressed, currency and/or algebraic signs to be floated, and the other niceties indicated at the beginning of this section.

When a significant digit is detected, or when a significance starter forces significance, an indicator is turned on. Until that event, the indicator remains off. This indicator, known appropriately as the *significance indicator,* is the means by which the ED and EDMK instructions "know" whether a zero is significant or not.

Figure 12.5 *Actions taken during execution of ED and EDMK instructions. (The significance indicator is always off before execution of ED and EDMK.)*

	values being examined		action taken	
	pattern byte	packed-decimal digit	new pattern byte	new state of significance indicator
when the SIGNIFICANCE INDICATOR is *off*	digit selector	0	fill character	off
		1–9	digit (in EBCDIC)	on • ‡
	significance starter	0	fill character	on •
		1–9	digit (in EBCDIC)	on • ‡
	field separator	none	fill character	off
	any other byte	none	fill character	off
when the SIGNIFICANCE INDICATOR is *on*	digit selector	0–9	digit (in EBCDIC)	on •
	significance starter	0–9	digit (in EBCDIC)	on •
	field separator	none	fill character	off
	any other byte	none	pattern byte not changed	on

•If the packed-decimal digit being examined is the right-most digit of the number and if the sign code is plus, the new state of the significance indicator will be *off*. If it is the right-most digit and the sign code is not plus, the new state of the significance indicator will be *on*.

‡When the significance indicator is *off* and detection of a significant digit turns it *on*, the address of that significant digit is placed into bits 8–31 of Register 1 by EDMK.

ED and EDMK Instructions: Format and Meaning

Both ED and EDMK are SS₁-type instructions. Their operands have identical meanings:

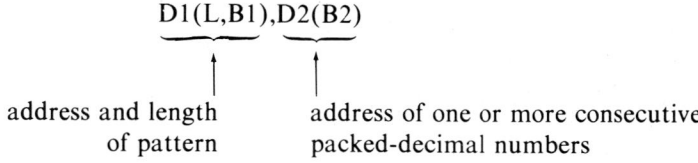

$$D1(L,B1),D2(B2)$$

address and length of pattern   address of one or more consecutive packed-decimal numbers

The only difference between ED and EDMK is that EDMK makes it possible to float a currency and/or algebraic sign, whereas ED does not. In all other aspects, they both work as follows.

The pattern and the packed-decimal number are processed left to right, 1 byte at a time. Each byte of the pattern either is left unchanged or is replaced. If replaced, it is replaced either by the current packed-decimal digit (expanded to EBCDIC format) or by the first character in the pattern, called the *fill character*. The decision as to which of these actions takes place is governed by three factors: (1) the state of the significance indicator (either *on* or *off*), (2) the value of the pattern byte being examined, and (3) the value of the current packed-decimal digit being examined. These factors, and their effect on the pattern byte being examined, are summarized in figure 12.5. *After all digits of a packed-decimal number have been processed, the significance indicator is used to record the sign of the number:*

indicator *off* = sign is positive
indicator *on* = sign is negative

This makes it possible for the negative sign condition to be printed to the *right* of the number, since the remaining pattern bytes will not be changed when the indicator is on (see the ED and EDMK examples).

As shown in figure 12.5, the EDMK instruction causes one other action to take place: when the significance indicator is off and a significant digit is detected, the address of the corresponding *pattern* byte is placed into Register 1. This address can then be used to insert a floating currency and/or algebraic sign into the pattern, as in Example 3. There are, however, two somewhat tedious requirements:

1. The address of the pattern byte immediately following the significance starter should be placed into Register 1 *before* the EDMK instruction is executed. This is because EDMK records the address of the first significant digit only when that digit turns on the significance indicator, not when the significance starter turns on the indicator.

2. *After* EDMK is executed, the address in Register 1 must be reduced by +1 in order for the ensuing MVI instruction to place the floating symbol in the pattern byte preceding the first significant digit.

Both ED and EDMK set the condition code. This allows the conditional branch instructions BZ, BM, BP, etc., to be used following ED or EDMK to determine the algebraic sign (if any) that should be moved into the pattern (see Example 4). The condition code is set to 0 if all source digits are zero; it is set to 1 if the source digits are not all zero and their sign is negative; or it is set to 2. No condition causes the code to be set to 3. But if the pattern has no digit selectors or significance starters, the condition code is set to 0. And if the pattern includes one or more field separators, these rules apply only to the last source field and corresponding pattern bytes. A program's execution will be interrupted by the hardware and terminated by the Operating System if an ED or EDMK instruction encounters an invalid decimal digit or invalid sign code in a packed-decimal field.

ED and EDMK Examples

Note that in the examples given, the pattern bytes are replaced when the ED or EDMK instructions are executed. One way to preserve a pattern for subsequent use with other decimal numbers is to define it via a DC directive and copy it to the area specified as the pattern in the ED and EDMK instruction being executed. This is illustrated in Examples 5 and 6.

Note also that the significance starter X'21' is placed *two* positions to the left of the decimal point, rather than one. This is so that if the integer portion of a number is identically zero, a single zero will appear to the left of the decimal point in the result, as in Example 5. (Recall that the significance starter forces all *subsequent* digits to be considered significant, but does not by itself force the *current* digit to be considered significant.)

Since there are no C-type constants corresponding to X'20',X'21',X'22', we must use X-type constants in a DC directive to generate the desired bytes in patterns. Therefore it helps to become familiar with the following EBCDIC character codes:

$$
\begin{array}{ll}
\text{X'40'} = \text{C' '} & \text{X'4E'} = \text{C'+'} \\
\text{X'4B'} = \text{C'.'} & \text{X'60'} = \text{C'-'} \\
\text{X'5B'} = \text{C'\$'} & \text{X'6C'} = \text{C'\%'} \\
\text{X'6B'} = \text{C','} & \text{X'C3'} = \text{C'C'} \\
\text{X'5C'} = \text{C'*'} & \text{X'D9'} = \text{C'R'}
\end{array}
$$

Example 1.

```
                                          fill character
                                    ┌X:    │       0  1  2  3  4  5  6  C              ┌─────────┐
                   before execution ┤      ↓      / / /  ↓  ↓  ↓  ↓                     ↓         │
                                    └P:   40  20  20/ 6B 20 21 20 4B 20 20 60 40
ED    P(12),X
                                    ┌P:   40  40  F1 6B F2 F3 F4 4B F5 F6 40 40
                    after execution ┤
                                    └              1  ,  2  3  4  .  5  6
```

fill character replaced these pattern
bytes since sign of number is positive

Example 2. **Fixed dollar sign ($) and trailing minus sign (−), if negative**

before execution
{ Y: 0   0   1   2   3   4   5   6   7   D
{ P: 40   20   6B   20   20   20   6B   20   21   20   4B   20   20   60   40

```
ED    P(15),Y
MVI   P,C'$'
```

after execution
{ P: 5B   40   40   40   F1   F2   6B   F3   F4   F5   4B   F6   F7   60   40
      $ 1   2   ,   3   4   5   .   6   7   −

pattern cannot include a fixed or floating sign on left; it must be placed there *after* ED or EDMK

fill character did not replace these, since sign of number is negative

---

Example 3. **Floating dollar sign ($) and trailing CR, if negative**

```
LA    1,P+10        ADDR OF BYTE BEYOND SIGNIF. STARTER
EDMK  P(15),Z       EDIT AND CAPTURE ADDR OF 1ST SIGNIFICANT DIGIT
SH    1,=H'1'       REDUCE ADDR IN REGISTER #1 BY ONE
MVI   0(1),C'$'     PLACE FLOATING SIGN IN FRONT OF 1ST SIGNIF DIGIT
```

before execution
{ Z: 0   0   1   2   3   4   5   6   7   D
{ P: 40   20   6B   20   20   20   6B   20   21   20   4B   20   20   C3   D9

after execution
{ P: 40   40   40   5B   F1   F2   6B   F3   F4   F5   4B   F6   F7   C3   D9
             $ 1   2   ,   3   4   5   .   6   7   C   R

fill character did not replace these, since sign of number is negative

---

Example 4. **Floating minus sign (−), if negative**

```
         LA    1,P+10       ADDR OF BYTE BEYOND SIGNIF. STARTER
         EDMK  P(15),Z      EDIT AND CAPTURE ADDR OF 1ST SIGNIFICANT DIGIT
         BNM   CONTINUE     BRANCH IF EDITED RESULT NOT NEGATIVE
         SH    1,=H'1'      OTHERWISE, REDUCE ADDR IN REG 1 BY +1,
         MVI   0(1),C'-'    AND INSERT FLOATING MINUS SIGN
CONTINUE EQU   *
```

before execution
{ Z: 0   0   1   2   3   4   5   6   7   D
{ P: 40   20   6B   20   20   20   6B   20   21   20   4B   20   20   40   40

after execution
{ P: 40   40   40   60   F1   F2   6B   F3   F4   F5   4B   F6   F7   40   40
             −   1   2   ,   3   4   5   .   6   7

fill character did not replace these, since sign of number is negative

Example 5. Floating asterisk (∗) and trailing minus sign (−), if negative. Fixed dollar sign ($) precedes the asterisks

```
        MVC   P(15),PSAVE     MOVE SAVED PATTERN TO EDITING PATTERN FIELD
        ED    P(15),W         EDIT THE PACKED-DECIMAL NUMBER AT 'W'
        BM    MINUS           BRANCH IF EDITED NUMBER WAS NEGATIVE
        MVC   P+13(2),=C' '   OTHERWISE MOVE BLANK TO COVER UP FILL CHAR.
MINUS   MVI   P,C'$'          THEN MOVE $ INTO 1ST BYTE OR EDITED RESULT
*                     FOLLOWING 15 BYTES ARE A PATTERN THAT CAN BE REUSED
PSAVE   DC    X'5C'           FILL CHARACTER IS C'*'
        DC    X'206B'         ONE DIGIT SELECTOR, ONE COMMA
        DC    X'2020206B'
        DC    X'2020214B'     TWO DIGIT SEL, ONE SIGNIF STARTER, ONE DEC. PT.
        DC    X'2020'         TWO DIGIT SELECTORS
        DC    X'6040'         MINUS AND BLANK, IN CASE NUMBER IS NEGATIVE
W       DC    P'000000.05'    TEST DATA
```

before execution
{
W: 0 0 0 0 0 0 0 0 5 C
P: 5C 20 6B 20 20 20 6B 20 21 20 4B 20 20 60 40
}

after execution
{
P: 5B 5C 5C 5C 5C 5C 5C 5C 5C F0 4B F0 F5 40 40
    $ *   *   *   *   *   *   *   *   0   .   0   5
}

pattern cannot include
a fixed or floating sign
on left; it must be placed
there after ED or EDMK.

these blanks were *not* placed here by ED;
they were placed here by MVC following ED
after testing the condition code to determine that the number's sign was not
negative. Note that since in this example the number wasn't negative, the
ED instruction caused the X'6040' to be
replaced by the fill character. Thus,
the MVC covered up the fill characters.

Example 6. Convert 32-bit binary integer to 12-character EBCDIC, without commas, but with leading zeroes replaced by blanks, and a floating minus sign if the number is negative

```
          L     1,NBINARY        GET BINARY INTEGER
          CVD   1,NPACKED        CONVERT TO PACKED DECIMAL
          MVC   NEBCDIC,PATTERN  MOVE 12-CHAR PATTERN TO RESULT FIELD
          LA    1,NEBCDIC+11     GET ADDR OF BYTE BEYOND SIGNIF STARTER
          EDMK  NEBCDIC,NPACKED+2  EDIT LOW-ORDER 6 BYTES OF PACKED-DECIMAL FIELD
          BNM   CONTINUE         PLUS SIGN REPRESENTED BY BLANK
          SH    1,=H'1'          OTHERWISE, REDUCE ADDR IN REG 1, AND
          MVI   0(1),C'-'          INSERT FLOATING MINUS SIGN
CONTINUE  EQU   *
          .
          .
          .
NEBCDIC   DS    CL12             SPACE FOR RESULT FIELD
NPACKED   DS    D                SPACE FOR PACKED-DECIMAL INTERMED RESULT
NBINARY   DS    F                LOCATION OF 32-BIT BINARY INTEGER
PATTERN   DC    X'402020202020202020202120'  PATTERN FOR INTEGER WITHOUT COMMAS
```

Example 6 points out one further consideration: If n digit positions are specified in the pattern (via X'20' or X'21'), and if the field separator X'22' is not used (as is the case in all the examples of this chapter), then n should be an odd number and the length of the packed-decimal field being edited should be $(n+1)/2$ bytes. For if the length is greater than $(n+1)/2$, then one or more low-order digits will not be matched to any pattern bytes. And if it is less than that, then the CPU will attempt to match some pattern bytes with whatever data follows the packed-decimal field in memory.

That is why the EDMK in Example 6 refers to NPACKED+2 instead of to NPACKED; i.e., since there were $n = 11$ digit positions in the pattern so that $(n+1)/2 = 6$, then we needed to edit the right-most 6 bytes of the 8-byte packed-decimal field.

12.10 SUMMARY

In the packed-decimal format, signed decimal numbers with up to 31 significant digits can be processed using the decimal number system's rules of arithmetic. Each digit of a decimal number is represented in 4-bit binary-coded decimal format: $0_{10} = 0000_2$, $1_{10} = 0001_2$,..., $9_{10} = 1001_2$. The sign is represented by 4 bits to the right of the right-most digit: plus $(+)$ as 1100_2, minus $(-)$ as 1101_2.

Using decimal arithmetic rather than binary arithmetic, results achieved in the computer can be exactly equal to results achievable by hand calculation even when noninteger quantities are involved. This avoids the differences in accuracy that can arise when a fixed number of bits is used to represent noninteger decimal numbers in the binary system. It is especially useful in banking and related business computer applications.

In the IBM 360 and 370 systems, there are instructions to add, subtract, multiply, divide, and compare two numbers represented in packed-decimal format. There are also instructions to affix leading zeroes to a packed-decimal number, to convert between packed-decimal and EBCDIC representation and between packed-decimal and binary representation, and to change a single digit or sign. Shifting left or right—effectively multiplying or dividing by powers of 10 in order to align decimal points—is easily accomplished in the IBM 370 by means of the SRP instruction; in the IBM 360, this can be accomplished by a combination of instructions dependent on MVO. See figure 12.6 for a summary of these instructions.

Unlike the integer arithmetic instructions described in chapter 5 or the floating-point instructions to be described in chapter 13, almost all packed-decimal instructions are either SS_1 or SS_2 format. The only exceptions are CVB and CVD, RX-type instructions for converting to and from binary format. In SS_1- and SS_2-type instructions, the number of bytes to be processed must be specified, explicitly or implicitly. This in turn requires some care to ensure that there have been a sufficient number of bytes allocated for the sum, difference, product, or quotient of two packed-decimal numbers.

In Assembly Language, packed-decimal constants can be generated by means of the data type code P. This can be used in the DC directive and in literals. The P code also can be used in the DS directive to reserve the number of bytes required by a constant; e.g., in the formulation DS P'99.99', three bytes are reserved.

Finally, it was shown that the ED and EDMK instructions provide exceptionally useful mechanisms for translating packed-decimal numbers into formats suitable for printing. There are no comparable instructions for use directly with either binary or floating-point number representations, although binary integers can be converted to packed-decimal representation via the CVD instruction. (Methods for converting floating-point numbers will be discussed in the next chapter.) For conversion from EBCDIC input format to the packed-decimal format, we can use the PACK instruction; to convert from EBCDIC to binary integer, we can use PACK followed by CVB. As discussed in Section 12.8, additional instructions are required to process negative numbers so that the sign can be represented separately from the digits in EBCDIC format.

Figure 12.6 Summary of packed-decimal instructions.

opcode	name	type	section	condition codes	summary of action taken
AP	Add Packed Decimal	SS_2	12.3	0,1,2,3	V_1 is replaced by $V_1 + V_2$
CP	Compare Packed Decimal	SS_2	12.4	0,1,2	V_1 is compared to V_2; the lengths L_1 and L_2 need not be the same
DP	Divide Packed Decimal	SS_2	12.3		V_1 is replaced by $L_1 - L_2$ quotient bytes and L_2 remainder bytes of V_1/V_2; $L_2 < L_1$ and $1 \le L_2 \le 8$
ED	Edit	SS_1	12.9	0,1,2	L-byte V_1 pattern is replaced by edited EBCDIC representation of packed-decimal field V_2
EDMK	Edit and Mark	SS_1	12.9	0,1,2	same as ED, but Reg 1 also gets address of most significant edited digit if that digit is detected while the significance indicator is *off*
MP	Multiply Packed Decimal	SS_2	12.3		V_1 is replaced by $V_1 \times V_2$, with $L_1 < L_2$ and $1 \le L_2 \le 8$
MVN	Move Numerics	SS_1	12.6		the 4 low-order bits of each byte in V_1 are replaced by the 4 low-order bits of corresponding V_2 bytes
MVO	Move with Offset	SS_2	12.6		all except the sign bits of V_1 are replaced by all the bits of V_2, from right to left. If $L_2 < L_1$, the remaining high-order V_1 bits are set to zero; if $L_2 > L_1$, the result is truncated at the high-order end to fit the V_1 field.
MVZ	Move Zones	SS_1	12.6		the 4 high-order bits of each byte in V_1 are replaced by the 4 high-order bits of corresponding V_2 bytes
PACK	Pack	SS_2	12.8		V_1 is replaced by the L_1-byte packed-decimal representation of the L_2-byte EBCDIC field, V_2. If $L_1 > \frac{1}{2}(L_2)$, no truncation can occur.
SP	Subtract Packed Decimal	SS_2	12.3	0,1,2,3	V_1 is replaced by $V_1 - V_2$
SRP	Shift and Round Packed Decimal	SS_1	12.5	0,1,2,3	V_1's digits are shifted n places right or left and rounded during a right shift (see note below)
UNPK	Unpack	SS_2	12.8		V_1 is replaced by the L_1-byte EBCDIC representation of the L_2-byte packed-decimal field, V_2. If $L_1 \ge 2(L_2)$, no truncation can occur.
ZAP	Zero and Add Packed Decimal	SS_2	12.3	0,1,2,3	V_1 is replaced by V_2, with $L_1 - L_2$ bytes of leading zeroes.

Notes: V_1 is the quantity whose address is specified by the first operand, with length L in SS_1 instructions, and L_1 in SS_2 instructions.

V_2's address is specified by the second operand; its length is L in SS_1 instructions, and L_2 in SS_2 instructions.

SRP is a modified SS_1 instruction, with operand $D_1(L_1,B_1),D_2(B_2),I_3$, and $L_1 \le 8$. The rounding factor is given by I_3; the number of positions and direction of shift by the low-order six bits of $D_2(B_2)$: negative (in two's complement notation)=right shift, positive=left shift.

SAMPLE PROBLEM
AND SOLUTION

PROBLEM STATEMENT

Write a program that will read an arbitrary number of input data cards containing student grade records (one card per course, one or more consecutive cards per student), and compute and print each student's grade point average. The input data cards have the following format:

columns	1–20	:	student name	
	21–29	:	student i.d.	
	31–36	:	course i.d.	
	40–45	:	course units	(a nonnegative integer)
	50–52	:	student grade	(in the form of 3.2 on a scale of from 0.0 to 4.0)

SOLUTION PROCEDURE

The procedure will use the well-known formula for computing a grade point average,

$$GPA = \frac{\Sigma U_i G_i}{\Sigma U_i}$$

where U_i is the number of units for course i, and G_i is the numerical grade for that course. (If all the U_i are zero, then the GPA is zero.)

Since all the grade cards for any one student occur consecutively in the input data, the procedure will be to print each student's grade cards as received from the input data stream, and to follow the last card for each student with a line containing the total number of units, ΣU_i, and the grade point average, GPA.

Figure 12.7a   Overview of sample problem solution procedure.

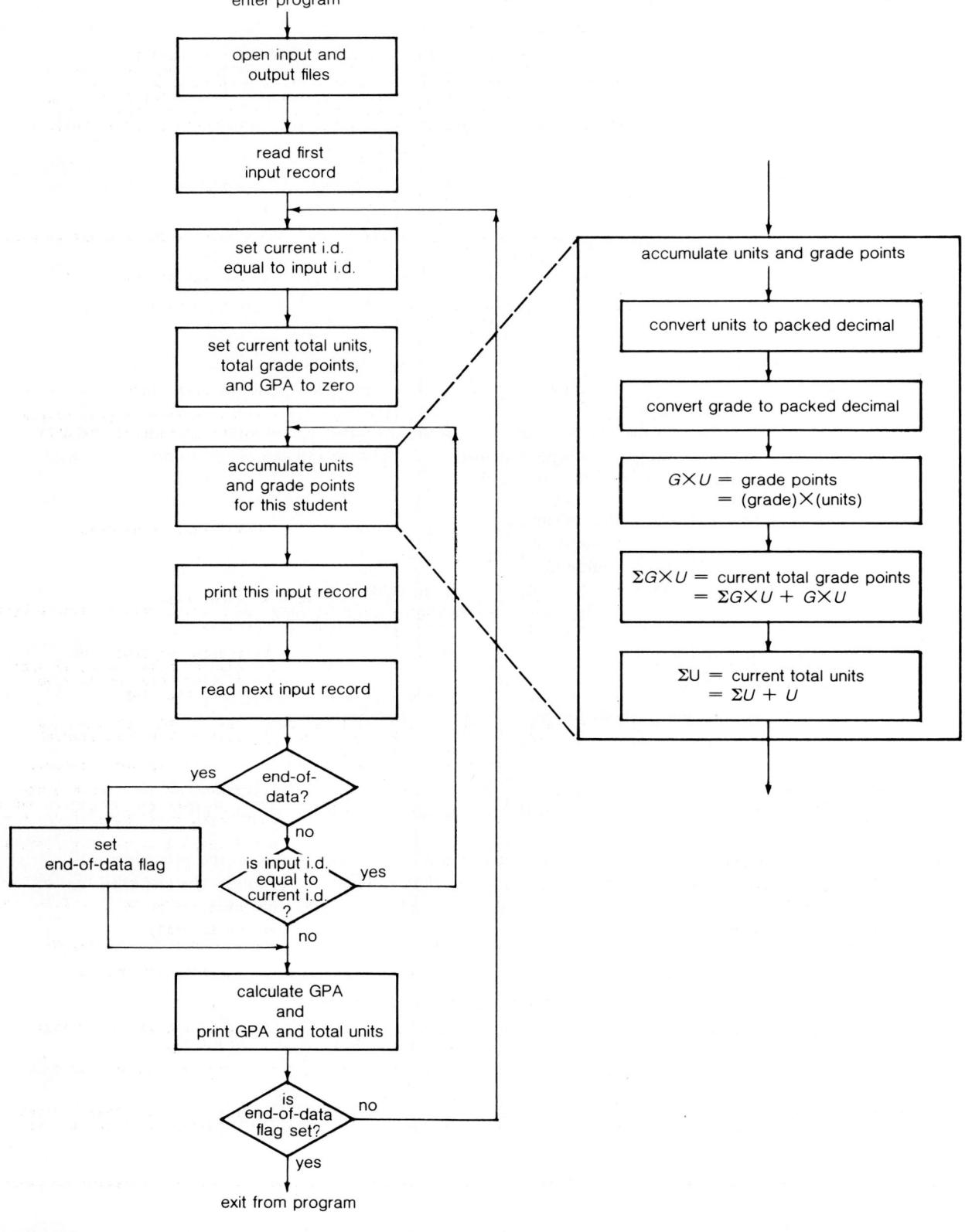

Figure 12.7b   Solution to sample problem.

```
FLAG LOCTN OBJECT CODE     ADDR1  ADDR2  STMNT M SOURCE STATEMENT

       000000                             3      SPCH12   CSECT
                                          4      *
                                          5      * SPCH12  READS INPUT DATA CARDS CONTAINING STUDENT GRADES
                                          6      *   (SOME UNSPECIFIED NUMBER OF CONSECUTIVE CARDS PER STUDENT)
                                          7      *   IN WHICH EACH CARD CONTAINS THE STUDENT'S NAME & I.D.
                                          8      *   AND ONE OF HIS OR HER COURSES TOGETHER WITH THE COURSE I.D.
                                          9      *   AND COURSE UNITS, AND THE GRADE POINTS (0.00-4.00) EARNED
                                         10      *   BY THAT STUDENT IN THAT COURSE.   THE INPUT FORMAT IS THIS...
                                         11      *
                                         12      *          COLS 1-20   STUDENT NAME
                                         13      *              21-29   STUDENT I.D.
                                         14      *              31-36   COURSE I.D.
                                         15      *              40-45   # UNITS        ( U)
                                         16      *              50-53   GRADE POINTS   (GP)
                                         17      *
                                         18      * THE PROGRAM COMPUTES AND PRINTS EACH STUDENT'S GRADE POINT AVERAGE
                                         19      *   (GPA)  USING THIS FORMULA ...
                                         20      *
                                         21      *      GPA = ( SUM OF (GP * U) ) / ( SUM OF (U) )
                                         22      *
       000000 90 EC D00C                 23               STM   14,12,12(13)          STANDARD ENTRY
       000004 05 C0                      24               BALR  12,0
       000006                            25               USING *,12
       000006 50 D0 C4D2        0004D8   26               ST    13,SAVE+4
       00000A 41 D0 C4CE        0004D4   27               LA    13,SAVE
                                         28      *
                                         29      * OPEN INPUT AND OUTPUT FILES, AND READ THE FIRST INPUT CARD
                                         30      *
       00000E                            31               OPEN  (SYSIN,(INPUT))       INPUT IS 'SYSIN' DATA STREAM
       00001A                            37               OPEN  (SYSPRNT,(OUTPUT))    OUTPUT IS 'SYSOUT' PRINTER

                                         43      *  DOS *******
                                         44      *         OPEN  SYSIN
                                         45      *         OPEN  SYSPRNT
                                         46      *************************
       000026                            47               GET   SYSIN,INAREA          READ FIRST INPUT CARD
                                         52      *
                                         53      * MAIN PROCESSING LOOP ...
                                         54      *
                                         55      *  WHEN BEGINNING A NEW STUDENT ...
                                         56      *    SETS CURRENT STUDENT I.D. EQUAL TO INPUT I.D.
                                         57      *    SETS CURRENT TOTAL UNITS (U) AND TOTAL GRADE POINTS (GP) TO ZERO.
                                         58      *    PRINTS A HEADING LINE FOR OUTPUT LISTING
                                         59      *
       000034 D2 08 C18EC1BF 000194 0001C5  60  LOOP     MVC   CSID,SID              SET CURRENT STUDENT I.D.
       00003A F8 10 C197C51A 00019D 000520  61           ZAP   TU,=P'0'              SET CURRENT TOTAL UNITS TO ZERO
       000040 F8 30 C199C51A 00019F 000520  62           ZAP   TGP,=P'0'             SET CURRENT TOTAL GP TO ZERO
       000046                            63               PUT   SYSPRNT,HEADING       PRINT HEADING LINE
                                         68      *
                                         69      *  WHEN THE NEXT INPUT CARD IS STILL FOR THE CURRENT STUDENT ...
                                         70      *    ACCUMULATE UNITS (U) AND GRADE POINTS (GP) FOR THIS STUDENT
                                         71      *    AND PRINT THIS INPUT CARD.
                                         72      *    THEN READ THE NEXT CARD TO SEE IF IT'S FOR THE SAME STUDENT.
                                         73      *
       000054 F2 15 C19DC1D2 0001A3 0001D8  74  REPEAT   PACK  BCDU,SU               CONVT STUDENT UNITS TO PKD-DEC
       00005A F2 30 C19FC1DC 0001A5 0001E2  75           PACK  GP,SGPINT             CONVT INTEGER PART OF GP TO PKD-DEC
       000060 F2 11 C1A3C1DE 0001A9 0001E4  76           PACK  GPDEC,SGPDEC          CONVT FRACTIONAL PART OF GP  "  "
                                         77      *
                                         78      *         SRP   GP,2,0               SHIFT INTEGER GP (MPY BY 100), AND
       000066 F1 F3 C16EC19F 000174 0001A5  79           MVO   XX,GP
       00006C D2 00 C17DC51B 000183 000521  80           MVC   XXS(1),=X'00'
       000072 F1 3F C19FC16E 00019F 000174  81           MVO   GP,XX
       000078 FA 31 C19FC1A3 0001A5 0001A9  82           AP    GP,GPDEC              ADD FRACTIONAL GP TO INTEGER GP.
                                         83      *
       00007E FC 31 C19FC19D 0001A5 0001A3  84           MP    GP,BCDU               MPY GP BY UNITS
       000084 FA 33 C199C19F 00019F 0001A5  85           AP    TGP,GP               AND ADD PRODUCT TO TOTAL GP.
                                         86      *
       00008A FA 11 C197C19D 00019D 0001A3  87           AP    TU,BCDU              ACCUMULATE TOTAL UNITS.
                                         88      *
                                         89      * PRINT STUDENT'S INPUT DATA CARD
                                         90      *
       000090 D2 4F C205C1AB 00020B 0001B1  91           MVC   OUTLINE,INAREA       MOVE CARD TO OUTPUT AREA
       000096                            92               PUT   SYSPRNT,OUTAREA       PRINT IT.
                                         97      *
                                         98      * READ NEXT STUDENT DATA CARD AND SEE IF IT'S FOR CURRENT STUDENT
                                         99      *
       0000A4                          100               GET   SYSIN,INAREA
       0000B2 D5 08 C18EC1BF 000194 0001C5 105           CLC   CSID,SID             IS NEXT STUDENT = CURRENT STUDENT
       0000B8 47 80 C04E        000054 106               BE    REPEAT               IF SO, CONTINUING ACCUMULATIONS.
                                        107      *
```

Figure 12.7b   continued

```
FLAG LOCTN OBJECT CODE     ADDR1  ADDR2  STMNT M SOURCE STATEMENT

                                          108   * WHEN NEXT STUDENT IS DIFFERENT FROM CURRENT STUDENT,
                                          109   * CALCULATE CURRENT STUDENT'S GPA AND PRINT IT WITH TOTAL UNITS.
                                          110   *
      0000BC F8 20 C1A5C51A 0001AB 000520 111   CALC   ZAP   GPAQUO,=P'0'          INITIALIZE GPA TO ZERO
      0000C2 F9 10 C197C51A 00019D 000520 112          CP    TU,=P'0'             IS TOTAL UNITS ZERO
      0000C8 47 80 C0FC        000102     113          BE    CALCX                IF SO, THEN GPA = 0
                                          114   *
      0000CC F8 43 C1A5C199 0001AB 00019F 115          ZAP   GPA,TGP              COPY TOTAL GRADE POINTS TO GPA
                                          116   *      SRP   GPA,1,0              SHIFT LEFT 1 DIGIT PRIOR TO DIVN
      0000D2 F8 F4 C16EC1A5 000174 0001AB 117          ZAP   XX,GPA
      0000D8 D1 00 C17DC51B 000183 000521 118          MVN   XXS(1),=X'00'
      0000DE F1 4F C1A5C16E 0001AB 000174 119          MVO   GPA,XX
                                          120   *
      0000E4 FD 41 C1A5C197 0001AB 00019D 121          DP    GPA,TU               (TOTAL GRADE POINTS) / (TOTAL UNITS)
                                          122   *
                                          123   *      SRP   GPAQUO,64-1,5        ROUND QUOTIENT TO 3 SIGNIF DIGITS
      0000EA F8 F2 C16EC1A5 000174 0001AB 124          ZAP   XX,GPAQUO
      0000F0 D1 00 C17DC51A 000183 000520 125          MVN   XXS(1),=P'0'
      0000F6 FA F0 C16EC51C 000174 000522 126          AP    XX,=P'5'
      0000FC F1 2E C1A5C16E 0001AB 000174 127          MVO   GPAQUO,XX(15)
                                          128   *
      000102 D2 06 C3C1C51D 0003C7 000523 129   CALCX  MVC   PGPA,=X'40202021482020'   GPA PATTERN = XXX.XX
      000108 DE 06 C3C1C1A5 0003C7 0001AB 130          ED    PGPA,GPAQUO
      00010E D2 03 C3BAC524 0003C0 00052A 131          MVC   PUNITS,=X'40202020212020'  UNIT PATTERN = XXXX
      000114 DE 03 C3BAC197 0003C0 00019D 132          ED    PUNITS,TU
                                          133   *
      00011A                              134          PUT   SYSPRNT,BLANKS       PRINT ONE BLANK LINE
      000128                              139          PUT   SYSPRNT,TOTALS       FOLLOWED BY TOTALS
      000136                              144          PUT   SYSPRNT,BLANKS
                                          149   *
                                          150   * DETERMINE WHETHER TO PROCESS NEXT STUDENT OR TO TERMINATE
                                          151   *
      000144 95 FF C1AA        0001B0     152          CLI   EODSW,ON             WAS END-OF-DATA REACHED
      000148 47 70 C02E        000034     153          BNE   LOOP                 IF NOT, GO PROCESS NEXT STUDENT
                                          154   *
                                          155   * END OF JOB PROCESSING
                                          156   *
      00014C                              157          CLOSE (SYSIN)
      000156                              163          CLOSE (SYSPRNT)
      000162 58 D0 C4D2        0004D8     169          L     13,SAVE+4            STANDARD EXIT
      000166 98 EC D00C                   170          LM    14,12,12(13)
      00016A 07 FE                        171          BR    14

                                          172   * DOS *******
                                          173   *      CLOSE SYSIN
                                          174   *      CLOSE SYSPRNT
                                          175   *      EOJ
                                          176   ***************

                                          177   *
                                          178   * END-OF-DATA REQUIRES SETTING A SWITCH SO THAT TOTALS FOR THE
                                          179   * LAST CURRENT STUDENT CAN BE COMPUTED AND PRINTED.
                                          180   *
      00016C 92 FF C1AA        0001B0     181   EOD    MVI   EODSW,ON             SET 'EODSW' TO 'ON' POSITION
      000170 47 F0 C0B6        0000BC     182          B     CALC                 THEN CALCULATE HIS/HER TOTALS
                                          183   *
                                          184   *
                                          185   * CONSTANTS AND DATA AREAS
                                          186   *
      000174 0000000000000000             187   XX     DC    2XL16'00'            TEMPORARY FOR IBM360 SHIFTS
      000183                              188   XXS    EQU   XX+15                16TH BYTE OF XX
      000194                              189   CSID   DS    CL9                  CURRENT STUDENT'S I.D.
      00019D 000C                         190   TU     DC    P'000'               TOTAL UNITS FOR CURRENT STUDENT
      00019F 0000000C                     191   TGP    DC    P'00000.00'          TOTAL GRADE POINTS FOR CUR. STUDENT
      0001A3 000C                         192   BCDU   DC    P'00'                ONE COURSE'S UNITS
      0001A5 0000000 0C                   193   GP     DC    P'0000.00'           ONE COURSE'S GRADE POINTS * UNITS
      0001A9 000C                         194   GPDEC  DC    P'0.00'              ONE COURSE'S GRADE POINTS (FRACTL PART)
      0001AB                              195   GPA    DS    0P'00000.000'        GPA FOR CURRENT STUDENT
      0001AB 00000C                       196   GPAQUO DC    P'00000'             QUOTIENT
      0001AE 000C                         197   GPAREM DC    P'000'               REMAINDER
      0001B0 00                           198   EODSW  DC    X'00'                END-OF-DATA SWITCH, AS FOLLOWS ...
      0000FF                              199   ON     EQU   X'FF'                EODSW = X'FF'  IF AT END-OF-DATA
      000000                              200   OFF    EQU   X'00'                EODSW = X'00'  IF NOT AT END-OF-DATA
                                          201   * INPUT CARD AREA
                                          202   *
      0001B1                              203   INAREA DS    0CL80                DEFINITION OF INPUT AREA ...
      0001B1                              204          DS    CL20                 COLS 1-20  STUDENT NAME
      0001C5                              205   SID    DS    CL9                       21-29  STUDENT I.D.
      0001CE                              206          DS    CL1                       30     UNUSED
      0001CF                              207          DS    CL6                       31-36  COURSE I.D.
      0001D5                              208          DS    CL3                       37-39  UNUSED
      0001D8                              209   SU     DS    CL6                       40-45  # COURSE UNITS
      0001DE                              210          DS    CL4                       46-49  UNUSED
      0001E2                              211   SGP    DS    0CL4                      50-53  GRADE PTS FOR THIS COURSE
                                          212   *
      0001E2                              213   SGPINT DS    CL1                       50     INTEGER PORTION
      0001E3                              214          DS    CL1                       51     DECIMAL POINT
      0001E4                              215   SGPDEC DS    CL2                       52-53  FRACTIONAL PORTION
                                          216   *
      0001E6                              217          DS    CL27                      54-80  UNUSED
```

Figure 12.7b continued

```
FLAG LOCTN OBJECT CODE      ADDR1  ADDR2  STMNT M SOURCE STATEMENT
                                          218   * OUTPUT PRINT AREA
                                          219   *
      000201                              220   OUTAREA  DS    0CL132           DEFINITION OF OUTPUT AREA ...
      000201 4040404040404040            221            DC    CL10' '          COLS 1-10    BLANKS
      00020B                              222   OUTLINE  DS    CL80             11-90        INPUT CARD DATA
      00025B 4040404040404040            223            DC    CL42' '          91-132       BLANKS
                                          224   *
                                          225   * BLANK LINE FOR OUTPUT
                                          226   *
      000285                              227   BLANKS   DS    0CL132
      000285 4040404040404040            228            DC    CL132' '         COLS 1-132   BLANKS
                                          229   *
                                          230   * HEADING LINE FOR OUTPUT
                                          231   *
      000309                              232   HEADING  DS    0CL132           DEFINITION OF HEADING ...
      000309 4040404040404040            233            DC    CL10' '          COLS 1-10    BLANKS
      000313 E2E3E4C4C5D5E340            234            DC    CL20'STUDENT NAME'  11-30      STUDENT NAME
      000327 C94BC44B7B404040            235            DC    CL9'I.D.#'        31-39        STUDENT I.D.
      000330 40                           236            DC    CL1' '           40           BLANKS
      000331 C3D6E4D9E2C5                237            DC    CL6'COURSE'       41-46        COURSE I.D.
      000337 404040                       238            DC    CL3' '           47-49        BLANKS
      00033A E4D5C9E3E240                239            DC    CL6'UNITS'        50-55        # UNITS
      000340 40404040                    240            DC    CL4' '           56-59        BLANKS
      000344 C7D9C1C4C5                  241            DC    CL5'GRADE'        60-64        GRADE POINTS
      000349 4040404040404040            242            DC    CL68' '          65-132       BLANKS
                                          243   *
                                          244   * AREA FOR PRINTED TOTALS
                                          245   *
      00038D                              246   TOTALS   DS    0CL132           DEFINITION OF TOTALS ...
      00038D 4040404040404040            247            DC    CL39' '          COLS 1-39    BLANKS
      0003B4 E2E4D4D4C1D9E840            248            DC    CL12'SUMMARY'     40-51        C'SUMMARY'
      0003C0                              249   PUNITS   DS    CL4              51-55        TOTAL UNITS
      0003C4 404040                       250            DC    CL3' '           56-58        BLANKS
      0003C7                              251   PGPA     DS    CL7              59-65        GPA
      0003CE 4040404040404040            252            DC    CL67' '          66-132       BLANKS
                                          253   *
                                          254   * DCB'S FOR INPUT AND OUTPUT FILES
                                          255   *
      000411                              256   SYSIN    DCB   DSORG=PS,MACRF=(GM),DDNAME=SYSIN,EODAD=EOD,           X
                                          257                  RECFM=FB,LRECL=80,BLKSIZE=4080
                                          309   *
      000474                              310   SYSPRNT  DCB   DSORG=PS,MACRF=(PM),DDNAME=SYSPRINT,                  X
                                          311                  RECFM=FB,LRECL=132,BLKSIZE=4092

                                          363   * DOS *******
                                          364   *SYSIN   DTFCD DEVADDR=SYSIPT,WORKA=YES,IOAREA1=INBUF,EOFADDR=EOD,  X
                                          365                  DEVICE=2540
                                          366   *SYSPRNT DTFPR DEVADDR=SYSLST,WORKA=YES,IOAREA1=OUTBUF,BLKSIZE=132, X
                                          367   *              DEVICE=1403
                                          368   *
                                          369   *INBUF   DS    CL80
                                          370   *OUTBUF  DC    CL132' '
                                          371   ***************

                                          372   *
                                          373   * SAVE AREA
                                          374   *
      0004D4                              375   SAVE     DS    18F

                                          376   * DOS *******
                                          377   *SAVE    DS    9D
                                          378   ***************

                                          379   * LITERALS
      000520 0C                           381                  =P'0'
      000521 00                           382                  =X'00'
      000522 5C                           383                  =P'5'
      000523 402020214B2020              384                  =X'402020214B2020'
      00052A 4020202120                  385                  =X'4020202120'
                                          386            END
```

CROSS-REFERENCE

SYMBOL	LEN	VALUE	DEFN	REFERENCES				
BCDU	00002	0001A3	00192	00074	00084	00087		
BLANKS	00084	000285	00227	00136	00146			
CALC	00006	00008C	00111	00182				
CALCX	00006	000102	00129	00113				
CSID	00009	000194	00189	00060	C0105			
EOD	00004	00016C	00181	00278				
EODSW	00001	0001B0	00198	00152	00181			
GP	00004	0001A5	00193	00075	00079	00081	00082	00084	00085
GPA	00005	0001AB	00195	00115	00117	00119	00121	

Figure 12.7b   continued

GPAQUO	00003	0001AB	00196	00111	00124	00127	00130			
GPAREM	00002	0001AE	00197							
GPDEC	00002	0001A9	00194	00076	00082					
HEADING	00084	000309	00232	00065						
INAREA	00050	0001B1	00203	00049	00091	00102				
LOOP	00006	000034	00060	00153						
OFF	00001	000000	00200							
ON	00001	0000FF	00199	00152	00181					
OUTAREA	00084	000201	00220	00094						
OUTLINE	00050	00020B	00222	00091						
PGPA	00007	0003C7	00251	00129	00130					
PUNITS	00004	0003C0	00249	00131	00132					
REPEAT	00006	000054	00074	00106						
SAVE	00004	0004D4	00375	00026	00027	00169				
SGP	00004	0001E2	00211							
SGPDEC	00002	0001E4	00215	00076						
SGPINT	00001	0001E2	00213	00075						
SID	00009	0001C5	00205	00060	00105					
SPCH12	00001	000000	00003							
SU	00006	0001D8	00209	00074						
SYSIN	00004	000414	00257	00035	00048	00101	00161			
SYSPRNT	.00004	000474	00311	00041	00064	00093	00135	00140	00145	00167
TGP	00004	00019F	00191	00062	00085	00115				
TOTALS	00084	00038D	00246	00141						
TU	00002	00019D	00190	00061	00087	00112	00121	00132		
XX	00010	000174	00187	00079	00081	00117	00119	00124	00126	00127	00188
XXS	00010	000183	00188	00080	00118	00125				

EXERCISES

1. What is the packed-decimal representation of the following constants? (Write your answers in hexadecimal notation.)

   a. P'−10' **d.** P'1000' **g.** P'−99.999'

   b. P'−0.065' **e.** PL4'1' **h.** P'−99,999'

   c. P'+6.5' **f.** PL1'4' **i.** P'999.999'

2. Write the packed-decimal representation (in hexadecimal notation) of the result of each of the following SRP instructions, if each instruction were executed at run time with this number stored at location X:

$$\text{X} \qquad \text{DC} \quad \text{PL5'}-246.75'$$

   a. SRP X,4,0   **c.** SRP X,64−3,5   **e.** SRP X,64−5,5

   b. SRP X,64−4,5   **d.** SRP X,3,5   **f.** SRP X,5,0

3. Suppose that the following statement defines a memory location with symbolic address PD:

$$\text{PD} \qquad \text{DS} \quad \text{PL10}$$

   What packed-decimal number would be stored at PD after each of the following sets of instructions were executed?

   a. ZAP PD,=P'10'
   AP PD,=P'1.0'

   b. ZAP PD,=P'6.25'
   MP PD,=P'2.5'

   c. ZAP PD,=P'+30.57'
   DP PD,=P'−4.3'

   d. ZAP PD,=P'−12345.67890'
   MP PD,=P'+0.0002'

   e. ZAP PD,=P'200'
   AP PD,=P'1'
   MP PD,=P'200'
   DP PD,=P'2'

4. Suppose that a valid packed-decimal number exists at symbolic address R. Write the assembly language statements (not an entire program; just enough statements) needed to accomplish each of the following tasks:

    a. Compute the area of a circle whose radius is given at R.

    b. Compute the volume of a sphere whose radius is given at R.

    c. Calculate the amount $A = (1 + r)^n$, where r is the number at R, and $n = 5$, with $0.000001 \leq r \leq 0.999999$.

    d. Calculate the amount $P = \dfrac{r}{1 - (1 + r)^{-n}}$, where r is the number at R, and $n = 5$, with $0.000001 \leq r \leq 0.999999$.

5. Since there are no instructions explicitly designed to change the sign of a packed-decimal number, to generate its positive absolute value, or to generate its negative absolute value, what instructions can be used to accomplish each of these tasks for an arbitrary packed-decimal number that occupies N bytes at symbolic address Y?

6. Assume that the packed-decimal representation of PL10'149.95' is stored at symbolic memory location Q. Trace the twelve instruction sequences given in figures 12.2a through 12.2d, and show the hexadecimal number that would be produced by the execution of each instruction in each of the twelve sequences. Note that in each sequence, it is assumed that location W initially contains all zeroes.

7. Convert the program statements of figure 12.3 to a subroutine that will compute the amount $A = P(1+I)^N - P$ for arbitrary P, I, and N such that $0 \leq P < 10^5$, $0 < I < 0.20$, and $0 \leq N \leq 25$ (all quantities in packed-decimal format). What changes, if any, would have to be made to your subroutine to extend the permissible range of P to 10^7, and that of N to 40?

8. Convert the program statements of figure 12.4 to a subroutine that will compute the Julian date for any day of the year.

9. Write a subroutine that will compute the elapsed time in hours and minutes between any two clock times that are less than 24 hours apart. For example, if the earlier time is 12:48 P.M. and the later time 01:30 A.M. the next morning, the elapsed time would be 12 hours, 42 minutes.

10. Write a subroutine that will determine the largest value and the smallest value in an array of N packed-decimal numbers. Assume that each number in the array occupies L bytes, with $0 < L \leq 16$. N and L must both be passed to your subroutine. (Hint: You will need to use the execute (EX) instruction discussed in chapter 7.)

11. As was discussed in chapter 11 (Section 11.4) and in Section 12.3, the SPM instruction can be used to prohibit program interruption when a decimal overflow error occurs. Write the instructions (including the SPM) that would prohibit interruption from a decimal overflow error condition. What instructions are required to *remove* the prohibition of a decimal overflow interrupt?

12. What error condition, if any, would be caused by execution of each of the following sets of instructions in which each operand length field is implied?

```
a.      DP      X,N
        ⋮
X       DC      P'5'
N       DC      P'2'

b.      DP      U,V
        ⋮
U       DC      P'5000'
V       DC      P'2'

c.      DP      Z,Y
        ⋮
Y       DC      P'40'
Z       DC      P'0'
```

```
d.        MP       X,=P'128'
          ⋮
   X      DC       P'64'

e.        MP       Q,=P'128'
          ⋮
   Q      DC       P'64'

f.        MP       Q,Q
          ⋮
   Q      DC       PL10'128'

g.        ZAP      Q,P
          AP       Q,X
          ⋮
   Q      DS       PL3
   P      DC       P'54321'
   X      DC       P'12345'

h.        ZAP      R,S
          SRP      R,4,0
          ⋮
   R      DS       PL3
   S      DC       P'97351'
```

13. Based on the set of instructions given near the end of Section 12.8, write a subroutine that will convert an integer from its EBCDIC representation to its packed-decimal representation, under the following conditions:

   a. the EBCDIC representation contains from 1 to 12 bytes, and the sign of the integer immediately precedes the first significant digit (plus represented by a blank, minus by a minus sign C'−');

   b. the address and length of the EBCDIC representation, and the address and length of the resulting packed-decimal representation, are parameters that must be passed to your subroutine.

14. Based on the set of instructions given in Example 6 of Section 12.9, write a subroutine that will convert an integer from its packed-decimal representation to its EBCDIC representation, under the following conditions:

   a. in the resulting EBCDIC representation, leading zeroes should be replaced by blanks, the sign of a positive number should be represented by a blank to the left of the most significant digit, and the sign of a negative number should be represented by a minus sign to the left of the most significant digit;

   b. the address and length of the packed-decimal representation, and the address and length of the resulting EBCDIC representation, are parameters that must be passed to your subroutine.

15. In IBM COBOL, the USAGE clause for numeric items is optional, and if it is omitted then the corresponding numeric data is represented in either zoned-decimal or EBCDIC format, depending on whether or not the picture clause designates an algebraic sign. For example,

COBOL	representation (in hex)
02 X PICTURE 999 VALUE 200.	F2F0F0
02 Y PICTURE S999 VALUE −150.	F1F5D0

Since there are no instructions to do arithmetic on either zoned-decimal or EBCDIC number representations, computations involving such numbers must include conversion to and from a format suitable for computation.

Write a set of instructions and appropriate DC and/or DS directives that will accomplish the same purpose as the following COBOL sentences, if X and Y were defined as above:

> ADD X TO Y.
> MULTIPLY Y BY −1.

16. For each of the packed-decimal numbers given below, define a pattern that could be used by an ED instruction to create the EBCDIC representation shown to the right of the number.

packed-decimal (given)		EBCDIC (desired)	
Assembly	Hexadecimal	Assembly	Hexadecimal
P'999'	999C	C' 999'	4040F9F9F9
P'99.9'	999C	C' 99.9'	40F9F94BF9
P'9.99'	999C	C' 9.99'	40F94BF9F9
P'.999'	999C	C'0.999'	F04BF9F9F9
PL2'9'	009C	C' 9'	40404040F9

17. For each of the packed-decimal numbers given below, define a pattern that could be used by an EDMK instruction to create the EBCDIC representation shown to the right of the number.

packed-decimal (given)		EBCDIC (desired)	
Assembly	Hexadecimal	Assembly	Hexadecimal
P'12345'	12345C	C'+12345'	4EF1F2F3F4F5
P'−123.45'	12345D	C'−123.45'	60F1F2F34BF4F5
PL3'3.87'	00387C	C' 3.87'	404040F34BF8F7
PL4'−19.95'	0001995D	C' −19.95'	4060F1F94BF9F5
PL4'−99999'	0099999D	C'−99,999'	60F9F96BF9F9F9

18. Change the instructions given in Examples 1 through 4 of Section 12.9 so that the patterns given there are reusable.

19. Make whatever changes are necessary to the instructions and directives of Example 6 in Section 12.9 so that the resulting EBCDIC representation will contain an appropriate number of commas, in addition to having leading zeroes replaced by blanks and a floating minus sign if the number is negative.

20. The equation below gives the amount of each monthly payment, $p(r)$, required for an n-year mortgage of d dollars, at a fixed annual interest of $r\%$:

$$p(r) = \frac{d * r/1200}{1 - (1 + r/1200)^{-12n}}$$

For example, if a \$50,000 mortgage is to be paid off in 30 years at 9% annual interest, the monthly payments according to the formula would be

$$p(9) = \frac{50000 * .09/12}{1 - (1 + .09/12)^{-360}} = \$402.31$$

a. Write a subroutine that uses packed-decimal arithmetic to calculate the monthly payments, $p(r_j)$, for any given values of d, n, and r, with $r_j = r + \frac{1}{4}j$ and $j = 0,1,2,3$. Thus, for the above example, your subroutine would calculate these four quantities:

$$p(9) = 402.31, \quad p(9.25) = 411.34, \quad p(9.5) = 420.43, \quad p(9.75) = 429.58$$

b. Write a main program that calls your subroutine for various values of d, n, and r, and prints the results in a suitably edited format.

21. Based on the formula in Exercise 20, write a subroutine that will calculate the total of all monthly payments, $P(r) = 12n*p(r)$, and the ratios, $R(r) = P(r)/d$, for any given d, n, and r. Thus, for $d=50,000$, $n=30$, and $r=9$, your subroutine would calculate $P(r) = 360*402.31 = 144,831.60$ and $R(r) = 2.8966$.

Write a main program that calls your subroutine for various values of d, n, and r and prints the results in a suitably edited format.

13

Floating-point Operations

The concept, format, and use of numbers written in *floating-point* notation is similar to that of numbers written in so-called scientific notation. But, as will be seen, floating-point operations provide an important simplification for the problem of decimal-point alignment; alignment is performed by the hardware during the execution of floating-point instructions.

In scientific notation, a number is written as $\pm D \times 10^N$. N can be a positive or negative integer, or zero, and D is a decimal number, usually between 0 and 10. D is called the *mantissa,* or fraction, N is called the *characteristic,* or exponent, and 10 is the *base*. In order to add or subtract two numbers in scientific notation, we must first adjust their characteristics so that they are equal. For example, to add 2.99776×10^{10} and 3.876×10^6, we can perform the addition only after adjusting the characteristic of the smaller number:

$$
\begin{array}{r}
2.99776 \times 10^{10} \\
+\ 0.0003876 \times 10^{10} \\
\hline
+\ 2.9981476 \times 10^{10}
\end{array}
$$

This adjustment of characteristics is, of course, necessary in order to align the decimal points. In multiplication, the characteristics are added, and in division, they are subtracted:

$$(a \times 10^n) \times (b \times 10^m) = (a \times b) \times 10^{n+m}$$
$$(a \times 10^n) \div (b \times 10^m) = (a \div b) \times 10^{n-m}$$

Through an option available on most models of the IBM 360 and 370 systems, use of scientific notation is emulated by floating-point notation in which a base of sixteen instead of ten is used; and the mantissa is a hexadecimal fraction between 0 and $+1$, rather than a decimal number between 0 and 10.[1] We can therefore write a floating-point number as

$$\pm H \times 16^K$$

where K = a positive or negative integer, or zero, and

$$
\begin{aligned}
H &= 0.h_1 h_2 h_3 h_4 ... \\
&= H_1 \times 16^{-1} + H_2 \times 16^{-2} + H_3 \times 16^{-3} + H_4 \times 16^{-4} + ...
\end{aligned}
$$

(The h_j are hexadecimal digits; the H_j are their decimal representations.)

When adding, subtracting, multiplying, or dividing two floating-point numbers in the IBM Systems 360 and 370, the process of adjusting the characteristics is performed by the hardware. This is one of the major advantages of using floating-point numbers: *decimal-point alignment is a hardware function.*

---

1. Floating-point representation is also used by FORTRAN and COBOL programs. In FORTRAN, "real" variables and constants are in short-format, "double-precision" in long-format. In IBM COBOL, USAGE IS COMPUTATIONAL-1 yields short-format representation, and USAGE IS COMPUTATIONAL-2 yields long-format representation. Both short- and long-format representation are defined in the next section.

It might be instructive to look at the floating-point representations of a few decimal numbers:

decimal system	floating-point, base 16
1.0	0.1×16^1
0.5	0.8×16^0
1.225×10^1	$0.C4 \times 16^1$
2.9976×10^{10}	$0.6FAB576 \times 16^9$

The first two are fairly obvious: 0.1 as a hexadecimal fraction has a value of 1×16^{-1}, or one-sixteenth, so that $0.1 \times 16^1 = (1 \times 16^{-1}) \times 16^1 = 1$; and 0.8 has a value of 8×16^{-1}, or one half. The floating-point representation of the third number is less obvious, though still manageable:

$$0.C4 \times 16^1 = (12 \times 16^{-1} + 4 \times 16^{-2}) \times 16^1$$
$$= 12 + \frac{1}{4}$$
$$= 1.225 \times 10^1$$

The representation of the fourth number, however, is not as obvious. This number is nevertheless accurate to five decimal places, as you can easily verify. Since it is not necessarily a simple matter to convert a number into its hexadecimal floating-point representation, we almost always relegate this chore to a computer program.

At this point we wish to observe a few important properties of floating-point numbers.

1. *Shifting:* Just as moving the decimal point right or left corresponds to multiplying or dividing by *ten,* so moving the hexadecimal point right or left corresponds to multiplication or division by *sixteen.* For example, consider these numbers:

decimal: $1.225 \times 10^1 = 12.25 \times 10^0 = 0.1225 \times 10^2$
hexadecimal: $C.4 \times 16^0 = C4.0 \times 16^{-1} = 0.C4 \times 16^1$

Through these and similar examples, we see that the movement of the hexadecimal or decimal point, which is equivalent to keeping the point fixed while shifting the digits, is always compensated for by a change in the characteristic, and vice versa. This elementary fact is critical to an understanding of floating-point operations.

2. *Normalized form:* As previously mentioned, the mantissa of a floating-point number, $\pm H \times 16^K$, is a hexadecimal fraction less than 1 in magnitude:

$$H = 0.h_1h_2h_3h_4...$$

where each h_j is a hexadecimal digit. A nonzero floating-point number is said to be *normalized* when $h_1 \neq 0$, and *unnormalized* when $h_1 = 0$. An unnormalized number can always be normalized by shifting it to the left and reducing the characteristic by an appropriate amount equal to the number of positions shifted. For example,

unnormalized form	normalized form
$0.00C4 \times 16^3$	$0.C4 \times 16^1$
0.08×16^1	0.8×16^0

In the IBM 360 and 370, and in most other computer systems, floating-point numbers are normalized by the hardware during the execution of most floating-point arithmetic instructions. Although deliberate exceptions to this rule occur in a few floating-point instructions, there are no shifting instructions available for normalization; normalization must be accomplished via other instructions. The advantage of normalized form is that as many significant digits as possible are retained in the available number of bits; in other words, leading zeroes are absorbed into the characteristic. Unnormalized form is useful primarily when converting numbers to and from floating-point format.

3. *Accuracy:* A hexadecimal floating-point number may be only a very good approximation to the decimal number we want to represent. For example, the number 0.1 (one-tenth) is a never-ending fraction in hexadecimal:

$$0.1 \text{ (decimal)} = 0.1999999...\text{(hexadecimal)}$$
$$= 1 \times 16^{-1} + 9 \times 16^{-2} + 9 \times 16^{-3} + 9 \times 16^{-4} + ...$$

No approximation in hexadecimal is exactly one-tenth. For example,

$$
\begin{array}{lll}
0.2 \text{ hex} & = & 2 \times 16^{-1} = 0.125 \text{ decimal} \\
0.1A \text{ hex} & = & 1 \times 16^{-1} + 10 \times 16^{-2} \\
& \approx & 0.10156 \text{ decimal} \\
0.19A \text{ hex} & = & 1 \times 16^{-1} + 9 \times 16^{-2} + 10 \times 16^{-3} \\
& \approx & 0.100098 \text{ decimal}
\end{array}
$$

In other words, the more hexadecimal digits we use, the better the approximation. But it is still an approximation. The same is true for many other rational numbers, such as 1/3, 1/5, 1/7, and 1/9 for which there are no exact floating-point representations.

There are also many *integers* for which no exact floating-point representation exists. For example, the only ones that can be exactly represented in short format are of the form $K \times 16^N$, where $|K| < 16^6 = 16,777,216$ and $0 \le N \le 63$. This range includes all integers whose magnitudes are less than 2^{24} but no *odd* integers and only some *even* integers with magnitudes greater than 2^{24}.

The significance of these limitations is that results obtained via hand calculations or even from binary integer calculations may be slightly different from those obtained via floating-point calculations. To reduce and in some cases eliminate these types of discrepancies, normalized form is almost always used, and long or extended formats may have to be used.

4. *Magnitude:* The approximate magnitude of a floating-point number is essentially independent of the number of bits required to represent the number: magnitude depends primarily on the value of the characteristic. In the IBM Systems 360 and 370, the maximum allowable value for a characteristic is 63 ($=2^6-1$), and the minimum value is -64. Thus the magnitude of normalized floating-point numbers in the 360 and 370 ranges approximately from 16^{-65} to 16^{63} for positive numbers and from about -16^{-65} to -16^{63} for negative numbers. We can translate this into more familiar terms by noting that in the equation

$$16^n = 10^x$$

the value of x corresponding to a known value of n is given by

$$
\begin{aligned}
x & = n \log_{10} 16 \\
& \approx n \, (1.20412)
\end{aligned}
$$

Thus a good approximation is that

$$16^{-65} \approx 10^{-78.2678} \approx 5.4 \times 10^{-79}$$

and

$$16^{63} \approx 10^{75.8596} \approx 7.2 \times 10^{75}$$

In other words, the range of normalized floating-point numbers in the IBM 360 and 370 is from approximately

$$5.4 \times 10^{-79} \quad to \quad 7.2 \times 10^{75}$$

in magnitude. Yet *only 32 bits are used to represent any six-digit number in this range.* Remember that 32 bits limit the maximum value to about 2.1×10^9 in binary integer format, and 32 bits limit the maximum value to about 10^7 in packed-decimal format. Consequently, a far greater range in magnitude is attainable for a given number of bits in floating-point format than in either binary integer or packed-decimal format. This is one of two important reasons for the use of floating-point numbers; the other reason, as previously mentioned, is the hardware's alignment of the decimal point.

The remainder of this chapter will discuss floating-point operations in the following order of topics:

1. The machine language representation of floating-point numbers in the IBM 360 and 370
2. Methods of defining floating-point constants in Assembly Language
3. Overview of floating-point instructions
4. Load and store operations
5. Comparing and testing floating-point numbers
6. Changing the sign of a floating-point number
7. Arithmetic operations
8. Conversion to and from floating-point format

13.1 MACHINE LANGUAGE REPRESENTATION

In the IBM System 370, a floating-point number, $\pm H \times 16^K$, can be represented in three types of fixed-length formats: *short* format, *long* format, and *extended* format. Short and long formats are also available in the IBM 360; extended format is not. In each format, the first bit represents the sign of the floating-point number: 0 for plus, 1 for minus. The next 7 bits represent the characteristic K, coded in what is known as *excess-64 binary notation*. The remaining bits represent the mantissa, H: six hex digits in short format, fourteen in long format, and twenty-eight in extended format. The base (16) is not represented; its value is implied.

short format (single precision)

long format (double precision)

extended format (extended precision)

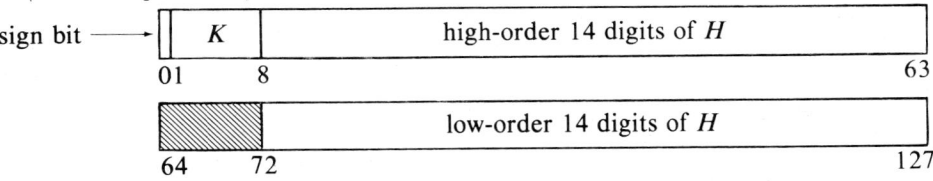

A short-format number occupies 4 bytes, and in the IBM 360 (but not the 370) it must be stored on a full-word boundary. A long-format number occupies 8 bytes; in the 360 it must be stored on a double-word boundary. An extended-format number is stored as two consecutive long-format numbers. The characteristic of the high-order part of an extended-format number is the characteristic of that extended number, and the sign of the high-order part is the sign of the extended number. Thus, bits 64 through 71 are ignored and the mantissa of an extended number is considered to be 28 hex digits, occupying bits 8–63 and 72–127 of the number.

In the representation of the mantissa,

$$H = 0.h_1h_2h_3h_4...$$

The value of H is always less than 1. The hexadecimal point is considered to be between bits 7 and 8 in each of the formats but is not represented; its position is implied. The digit h_1 occupies bits 8–11; h_2, bits 12–15; and so forth. The sign of the mantissa is not represented in the bits occupied by the mantissa's digits. The sign is represented in bit 0 of each format. Thus, we speak of the *sign-magnitude* representation, since it is the absolute value, or magnitude, of the mantissa represented in each of the formats.

As mentioned earlier, the characteristic is represented in excess-64 notation. This means that the true value of characteristic K is represented as a 7-bit binary integer whose value is 64 more than that of K:

true value K (decimal integer)	excess-64 representation of K (7 bits)	hex equivalent of 7-bit excess-64 notation
-64	0000000	00
-63	0000001	01
-62	0000010	02
.	.	.
.	.	.
.	.	.
-1	0111111	3F
0	1000000	40
$+1$	1000001	41
$+2$	1000010	42
.	.	.
.	.	.
$+62$	1111110	7E
$+63$	1111111	7F

The following floating-point representations illustrate these concepts.

decimal number in scientific notation	equivalent number written as hexadecimal fraction times power of 16	representation of decimal number in short format
1.0×10^0	0.1×16^1	0 41 1 0 0 0 0 0
-0.5×10^0	-0.8×16^0	1 40 8 0 0 0 0 0
1.225×10^1	$0.C4 \times 16^1$	0 41 C 4 0 0 0 0
2.9976×10^{10}	$0.6FAB57 \times 16^9$	0 49 6 F A B 5 7
-2.9976×10^{10}	$-0.6FAB57 \times 16^9$	1 49 6 F A B 5 7
1.674×10^{-24}	$0.20613F \times 16^{-19}$	0 2D 2 0 6 1 3 F
-1.674×10^{-24}	$-0.20613F \times 16^{-19}$	1 2D 2 0 6 1 3 F

(sign bit | characteristic (7 bits) | mantissa (24 bits))

In each of the last four numbers, the short-format representation is accurate to six hex digits although it is not the precise value represented by the corresponding decimal number at the left. This loss of accuracy, due to the incommensurability of the decimal and hexadecimal number systems, can become a serious problem when propagated and accumulated in a series of computations. As a partial compensation for this, the long or extended formats can be used. With a greater number of digits in the mantissa, the loss of accuracy can be confined to digits beyond the seventh significant place, sufficient for almost all calculations. The precision provided by the three formats is:

	number of hex digits	maximum number of decimal digits
short format	6	7
long format	14	16
extended format	28	33

Conversion from one format to another is a simple matter since instructions are provided for this purpose. Conversion from decimal notation to floating-point format (and vice versa) requires some calculations that, while straightforward, are usually accomplished by a subroutine. This will be described in Section 13.8.

Figure 13.1 Defining floating-point constants.

Figure 13.1 *Defining floating-point constants.*

```
FLAG LOCTN OBJECT CODE      ADDR1   ADDR2   STMNT M SOURCE STATEMENT

                                            4     * E = SHORT, D = LONG
       000000 41100000                      5            DC      E'1.0'
       000008 4110000000000000              6            DC      D'1.0'
       000010 4019999A                      7            DC      E'0.1'
       000018 401999999999999A              8            DC      D'0.1'

                                            9     * EXPONENT FACTOR GIVES POWER OF 10
       000020 496FAB57                      10           DC      E'2.9976E+10'
       000024 C96FAB57                      11           DC      E'-2.9976E+10'
       000028 496FAB5760000000              12           DC      D'2.9976E+10'

       000030 2020613F                      13           DC      E'1.674E-24'
       000034 A020613F                      14           DC      E'-1.674E-24'

                                            15    * SCALE FACTOR CREATES UN-NORMALIZED NUMBER
       000038 450000C4                       16           DC      ES4'12.25'
       00003C 41C40000                       17           DC      E'12.25'

       000040 4C0006FB                       18           DC      ES3'2.9976E+10'
       000044 496FAB57                       19           DC      E'2.9976E+10'

                                            20    * APPROX SMALLEST AND LARGEST NUMBERS
       000048 001001D1                       21           DC      E'5.4E-79'
       00004C 7FFEB0E4                       22           DC      E'7.2E+75'

                                            23    * MULTIPLE CONSTANTS PERMISSIBLE
       000050 4110000041200000              24           DC      E'1,2,3'        IN SHORT FORMAT
              41300000
       00005C 41100000                       25           DC      E'1',E'2',E'3'
       000060 41200000
       000064 41300000
       000068 41100000                       26           DC      E'1',2E'2,3'
       00006C 4120000041300000
              4120000041300000

       000080 401999999999999A              27           DC      D'0.1,0.2'      IN LONG FORMAT
              4033333333333333
       000090 401999999999999A              28           DC      D'0.1',D'0.2'
       000098 4033333333333333
       0000A0 401999999999999A              29           DC      2D'0.1,0.2'
              4033333333333333
              401999999999999A
              4033333333333333
```

13.2 ASSEMBLY LANGUAGE REPRESENTATION

Corresponding to the three types of machine language representation of floating-point numbers, there are three types of floating-point constants in Assembly Language. These are distinguished by the data type code:

E = short format (single-precision)
D = long format (double-precision)
L = extended format (quadruple-precision).

Examples are shown in figure 13.1. The important things to observe are these: (1) boundary alignment, (2) use of scale and exponent modifiers, Sn and En, to multiply the mantissa by a power of 16 and 10, respectively, and (3) use of the decimal point to distinguish the integer and fractional components of the number.

For the short format, alignment is always on a full-word boundary; for the long and extended formats, on a double-word boundary. Use of the length modifier Ln is not recommended.

The scale modifier Sn is used only when we want to create an unnormalized floating-point number. The value of n is the number of hex zeroes that are to precede the first significant digit in the mantissa. Obviously, the value of n must be positive and consistent with the length of the mantissa.

The exponent modifier En can be used to express the constant in scientific notation. The value of n is the power of 10; the permissible range is from -85 through $+75$.

In addition to defining floating-point constants by means of the DC directive, we also can define the floating-point *literals* in short (E), long (D), and extended (L) format.

To reserve memory space for floating-point data, we can use either the E or the F type codes for short format, since each results in alignment on a full-word boundary. But for long and extended formats, always use the D and L type codes, respectively. For example,

DS   4F ⎱   Each reserves space for four single-precision (short-format)
DS   4E ⎰   floating-point numbers, correctly aligned on full-word boundaries.

DS   30D   Reserves space for 30 double-precision (long-format) floating-point numbers,
                 each on a double-word boundary.

DS   10L   Reserves space for 10 extended-precision floating-point numbers, each on a
                 double-word boundary. (The L type code can only be used for the IBM 370.)

13.3 FLOATING-POINT INSTRUCTIONS: OVERVIEW AND REGISTER USAGE

There are 44 instructions in what is known as the Floating-point Arithmetic Instruction Set of the IBM 360 and 370 and an additional 7 instructions in the Extended-precision Instruction Set of the IBM 370. The 44 instructions are evenly divided into two classes: 22 that process short-format numbers and 22 that process long-format numbers. The remaining 7 instructions are designed for use with extended-precision numbers. All 51 instructions are either RX- or RR-type instructions. We will simply refer to them collectively as *the* floating-point instructions.

The opcodes of these instructions are summarized in figure 13.2. This figure also shows the functional correspondence that exists between the floating-point instructions and the integer arithmetic instructions studied in previous chapters. Notice that in addition to the types of operations familiar from integer arithmetic—load, store, add, subtract, and so forth—there are two types of operations that have no counterpart in the integer arithmetic instructions set: halve and round. Notice also the absence of shift instructions, as has already been mentioned, and the absence of any instructions converting numbers between floating-point and any other format.

The 51 floating-point instructions will be described in the sections that follow. What needs to be pointed out here are the following register usage constraints. In the IBM 360 and 370 systems, all floating-point operations are carried out in a special set of registers, the floating-point registers. There are only four floating-point registers. Each is 64 bits long. Their addresses are 0, 2, 4, and 6. These registers cannot be used for indexing, base registers, or other similar purposes, but only for floating-point operations.

The constraints associated with the use of the floating-point registers are these:

1. *Short-format numbers:* numbers that are represented in the 32-bit short format and processed by the short-format instructions are manipulated in the high-order 32 bits of a floating-point register. Any of the four floating-point registers may be designated.
2. *Long-format numbers:* numbers that are represented in the 64-bit long format and processed by the long-format instructions are manipulated in the entire 64 bits of a floating-point register. Any of the four floating-point registers may be designated.
3. *Extended-format numbers:* numbers that are represented in the 128-bit extended-precision format and processed by the extended-precision instructions are always manipulated in two consecutive floating-point registers; these are always either registers 0 and 2, or registers 4 and 6. When registers 0 and 2 are used, they must be referred to by designating register 0; when registers 4 and 6 are used, they must be referred to by designating register 4.

In RX-type floating-point instructions, the first operand field must designate an appropriate floating-point register address. In RR-type floating-point instructions, both operands must designate appropriate floating-point register addresses. As mentioned, these addresses may be either 0, 2, 4, or 6 in short- or long-format instructions but must be either 0 or 4 in extended-precision instructions. Any other register address will cause a "specification error" to occur, i.e., the program will be interrupted by the hardware and terminated by the Operating System.

13.4 LOAD AND STORE OPERATIONS

Any short- or long-format number can be copied from memory into a floating-point register by means of the Load Short (LE) or Load Long (LD) instructions. Similarly, a short- or long-format number can be copied from a floating-point register to a main memory location by means of the two respective store instructions,

Figure 13.2 Overview of floating-point instructions (with corresponding integer instructions).

	name	type	integer instructions	floating-point instructions		
				short format	long format	extended format
Load into registers	Load	RX	L LH LM	LE	LD	
	Load Registers	RR	LR	LER	LDR	
Store into memory	Store	RX	ST STH STM	STE	STD	
Compare or test	Compare	RX	C CH	CE	CD	
	Compare Registers	RR	CR	CER	CDR	
	Load and Test	RR	LTR	LTER	LTDR	
Sign	Load Complement	RR	LCR	LCER	LCDR	
	Load Negative	RR	LNR	LNER	LNDR	
	Load Positive	RR	LPR	LPER	LPDR	
Arithmetic operations	Add	RX	A AH AL	AE AU	AD AW	
	Add Registers	RR	AR ALR	AER AUR	ADR AWR	AXR
	Subtract	RX	S SH SL	SE SU	SD SW	
	Subtract Registers	RR	SR SLR	SER SUR	SDR SWR	SXR
	Multiply	RX	M MH	ME	MD	MXD
	Multiply Registers	RR	MR	MER	MDR	MXR MXDR
	Divide	RX	D	DE	DD	
	Divide Registers	RR	DR	DER	DDR	
	Halve	RR		HER	HDR	
	Round	RR				LRER LRDR

Store Short (STE) and Store Long (STD). The LE, LD, STE, and STD instructions are all RX-type instructions. No corresponding load or store instructions exist for extended-format numbers; we must use two consecutive LD's or STD's.

To simplify the descriptions of floating-point instructions in this chapter, the following notation will be used:

V_1 = the floating-point number whose address is designated by the *first* operand field in an instruction

V_2 = the floating-point number whose address is designated by the *second* operand field in an instruction

With this notation, the four LOAD and STORE instructions mentioned can be described as follows:

opcode	meaning
LE	LOAD (short) [RX instruction] Copies the short-format number V_2 from memory into the high-order 32 bits of the register designated by the first operand field. The low-order 32 bits of that register are not changed.
LD	LOAD (long) [RX instruction] Copies the long-format number V_2 from memory into the register designated by the first operand.
STE	STORE (short) [RX instruction] Copies the short-format number V_1 from the high-order 32 bits of the register designated by the first operand to the memory location designated by the second operand.
STD	STORE (long) [RX instruction] Copies the long-format number V_1 from the register designated by the first operand to the memory location designated by the second operand.

A short- or long-format number can also be copied from one floating-point register to another by means of RR-type instructions, LER for short format and LDR for long format. There is no corresponding extended-format register-to-register copy instruction; two consecutive LDR's must be used.

opcode	meaning
LER	LOAD REGISTER (short) [RR instruction] Copies the short-format number V_2 into the high-order 32 bits of the register designated by the first operand field. The low-order bits of that register are not changed.
LDR	LOAD REGISTER (long) [RR instruction] Copies the long-format number V_2 into the register designated by the first operand field.

None of the load, load register, or store instructions just described sets the condition code. As mentioned earlier, however, a specification error and program interruption will occur if floating-point register addresses 0, 2, 4, or 6 are not specified in the first operand field of the RX instructions and in both operand fields of the RR instructions. (In the LER and LDR instructions, it is permissible for both operand fields to designate the same register.)

13.5 COMPARING AND TESTING FLOATING-POINT NUMBERS

As in packed-decimal and integer arithmetic, it is often useful to compare two floating-point numbers algebraically without altering either one. One reason for making such a comparison is to determine whether a number is positive, negative, or zero; for example, to determine the nature of a product or quotient or to prevent division by zero. Another reason is to put a set of floating-point numbers into increasing or decreasing numerical sequence, i.e., to sort them.

Two types of instructions for accomplishing these tasks are available in the IBM Systems 360 and 370. One type can be used to compare algebraically any two short- or long-format floating-point numbers, provided at least one of them is in a floating-point register; the other can be used to determine whether a short- or long-format number is greater than, less than, or equal to zero. Both types of instructions set the condition

Figure 13.3 Floating-point Load, Store, Compare, Test, and Sign.

name	Mnemonic opcode	type RX	type RR	condition code set as follows when instruction is executed 0	1	2	3
Single-precision Instructions							
Load	LE	X		---	---	---	---
Load Registers	LER		X	---	---	---	---
Store	STE	X		---	---	---	---
Compare	CE	X		$V_1 = V_2$	$V_1 < V_2$	$V_1 > V_2$	---
Compare Registers	CER		X	$V_1 = V_2$	$V_1 < V_2$	$V_1 > V_2$	---
Load and Test	LTER		X	$V_2 = 0$	$V_2 < 0$	$V_2 > 0$	---
Load Complement	LCER		X	$V_2 = 0$	$V_2 > 0$	$V_2 < 0$	---
Load Negative	LNER		X	$V_2 = 0$	$V_2 \neq 0$	---	---
Load Positive	LPER		X	$V_2 = 0$	---	$V_2 \neq 0$	---
Double-precision Instructions							
Load	LD	X		---	---	---	---
Load Registers	LDR		X	---	---	---	---
Store	STD	X		---	---	---	---
Compare	CD	X		$V_1 = V_2$	$V_1 < V_2$	$V_1 > V_2$	---
Compare Registers	CDR		X	$V_1 = V_2$	$V_1 < V_2$	$V_1 > V_2$	---
Load and Test	LTDR		X	$V_2 = 0$	$V_2 < 0$	$V_2 > 0$	---
Load Complement	LCDR		X	$V_2 = 0$	$V_2 > 0$	$V_2 < 0$	---
Load Negative	LNDR		X	$V_2 = 0$	$V_2 \neq 0$	---	---
Load Positive	LPDR		X	$V_2 = 0$	---	$V_2 \neq 0$	---

Notes:
1. There are no extended-precision instructions for comparing, testing, or performing sign operations on extended-precision numbers.

2. None of these instructions can cause an exponent overflow, exponent underflow, significance exception, or divide exception at run time.

3. V_1 designates the number referred to by the first operand in a floating point instruction, and V_2 designates the number referred to by the second operand in a floating point instruction.

4. In these instructions, V_j ($j = 1$ or 2) is considered to be zero if its mantissa is zero, irrespective of its sign or characteristic.

5. In these instructions, $V_1 = V_2$ if they would be equal when both were in normalized form.

code as noted in the descriptions below, so that a subsequent conditional branch instruction can be used to determine the nature of the result. A summary of the instructions discussed in this section is given in figure 13.3.

To describe these instructions, we once again use the notation

V_1 = the floating-point number whose address is designated by the *first* operand field
V_2 = the floating-point number whose address is designated by the *second* operand field

Compare Instructions: CE, CER, CD, CDR

For comparing two *short*-format numbers:

opcode	meaning	type
CE	Compares V_1 to V_2, where V_1 is in a floating-point register and V_2 is in memory.	RX
CER	Compares V_1 to V_2, where both are in floating-point registers.	RR

For comparing two *long*-format numbers:

opcode	meaning	type
CD	Compares V_1 to V_2, where V_1 is in a floating-point register and V_2 is in memory.	RX
CDR	Compares V_1 to V_2, where both are in floating-point registers.	RR

All four instructions set the condition code:

code	meaning
0	$V_1 = V_2$
1	$V_1 < V_2$
2	$V_1 > V_2$

Therefore, the appropriate conditional branch instructions are:

BER	or	BE	branches if $V_1 = V_2$
BNER	or	BNE	branches if $V_1 \neq V_2$
BHR	or	BH	branches if $V_1 > V_2$
BNHR	or	BNH	branches if $V_1 \leqslant V_2$
BLR	or	BL	branches if $V_1 < V_2$
BNLR	or	BNL	branches if $V_1 \geqslant V_2$

One precaution must be observed when using the CE, CER, CD, or CDR instructions: *a simple comparison of the characteristics of V_1 and V_2 is insufficient to determine which is the larger number.* This is because both numbers are normalized by the hardware during the comparison operation without changing their respective representations in the register or memory location. The examples illustrate this.

Example 1.

		V_1 floating-point register 0	V_2 memory location X
CE	0,X	450000C4	41C40000

result: $V_1 = V_2$, i.e., $12.25 = 12.25$

Example 2.

		V_1 floating-point register 2	V_2 memory location Y
CD	2,Y	AD20613F1B000000	3300000020613F1B

result: $V_1 < V_2$, i.e., $-1.674 \times 10^{-24} < +1.674 \times 10^{-24}$

Example 3.

		V_1 floating-point register 2	V_2 floating-point register 4
CDR	2,4	4F0000006FAB5760	C96FAB5760000000

result: $V_1 > V_2$, i.e., $+2.9976 \times 10^{10} > -2.9976 \times 10^{10}$

Load and Test Instructions: LTER, LTDR

To determine whether a short or long number is positive, negative, or zero, we can use a load-and-test instruction, LTER or LTDR.

opcode	meaning	type
LTER	Tests a *short*-format number V_2, and simultaneously loads it into the register occupied by V_1.	RR
LTDR	Tests a *long*-format number V_2, and simultaneously loads it into the register occupied by V_1.	RR

Both of these set the condition code:

code	meaning
0	the mantissa of V_2 is zero
1	$V_2 < 0$ and its mantissa is not zero
2	$V_2 > 0$ and its mantissa is not zero

Therefore, the appropriate conditional branch instructions to use following either LTER or LTDR are:

BZR	or	BZ	branches if $V_2 = 0$
BNZR	or	BNZ	branches if $V_2 \neq 0$
BMR	or	BM	branches if $V_2 < 0$
BNMR	or	BNM	branches if $V_2 \geqslant 0$
BPR	or	BP	branches if $V_2 > 0$
BNPR	or	BNP	branches if $V_2 \leqslant 0$

There is one precaution to be observed: when using LTER or LTDR V_2 *is considered to be zero if its mantissa is zero;* the characteristic is not examined by the hardware in making the determination.

Example 1.

			floating-point register 0
LTER	0,0	before execution:	41 00 00 00
		after execution:	41 00 00 00

specifies the floating-point register containing V_2

specifies the floating-point register into which V_2 is to be copied

result: $V_2 = 0$, since $0 \times 16^1 = 0$

Example 2.

			floating-point register 0	floating-point register 2
LTER	0,2	before execution:	AB 12 34 56	7F 98 12 AB
		after execution:	7F 98 12 AB	7F 98 12 AB

result: $V_2 > 0$, since sign bit $= 0$, and mantissa $\neq 0$.

Example 3.

			floating-point register 4	floating-point register 6
LTDR	4,6	before execution:	41 10 00 00 00 00 00 00	C1 10 00 00 00 00 00 00
		after execution:	C1 10 00 00 00 00 00 00	C1 10 00 00 00 00 00 00

result: $V_2 < 0$, since sign bit $= 1$, and mantissa $\neq 0$.

13.6 CHANGING SIGNS

It is a particularly simple matter to change the sign of a floating-point number when that number is in memory, for only one bit must be changed. If the number is at location A, we can use simple Boolean instructions to set the sign bit to 0 or 1 or to reverse it:

```
* MAKE SIGN OF A POSITIVE:
     NI   A,X'7F'
* MAKE SIGN OF A NEGATIVE
     OI   A,X'80'
* CHANGE SIGN OF A:
     XI   A,X'80'
```

However, Boolean operations, which apply only to general registers, cannot be used when a number is in a floating-point register. Consequently, three sets of instructions are provided for the three sign operations. All are RR-type load-register instructions, similar to those used with integers in general registers, although designed specifically for short- and long-format floating-point numbers.

To copy the *positive absolute value of V_2* from floating-point register R2 into floating-point register R1 we use

```
     LPER      R1,R2      for short-format numbers
     LPDR      R1,R2      for long-format numbers
```

To copy the *negative absolute value* of V_2 from floating-point register R2 into floating-point register R1 we use

```
     LNER      R1,R2      for short-format numbers
     LNDR      R1,R2      for long-format numbers
```

To copy the *negative* of V_2 from floating-point register R2 into floating-point Register R1 we use

```
     LCER      R1,R2      for short-format numbers
     LCDR      R1,R2      for long-format numbers
```

In each of these instructions, it is of course permissible for R1 and R2 to designate the same register. If that is the case, the instructions simply make the sign of V_2 positive or negative or change it.

Each of the six instructions mentioned sets the condition code so that the conditional branch instructions may be used to determine the nature of the result:

code	meaning
0	mantissa of result is zero
1	sign of result is < 0, and mantissa $\neq 0$
2	sign of result is > 0, and mantissa $\neq 0$

The only precaution to be observed is that although all six instructions *always* set or change the sign, even when the mantissa is zero, the conditional branch instructions cannot be used to distinguish a positive zero from a negative zero. This is because condition code 0 is always set when the mantissa is zero, regardless of the sign of the number.

A summary of the instructions discussed in this section is given in figure 13.3.

13.7 ARITHMETIC OPERATIONS

There are six types of floating-point arithmetic operations: add, subtract, multiply, divide, halve, and round. The assembly language opcodes for these instructions are summarized in figure 13.4. They have the following general properties:

1. All the single-precision instructions operate on short-format numbers. All except the two multiply instructions produce short-format results. Both ME and MER generate double-precision (long-format) products.
2. All the double-precision instructions operate on long-format numbers. These instructions all generate double-precision (long-format) results.

Figure 13.4 Floating-point arithmetic instructions.

Single-precision Instructions

Except for ME and MER, these all operate on short-format numbers and produce short-format results.

	mnemonic opcode	RX	RR	exponent overflow	exponent underflow	significance	divide by zero	specification	condition code
Add normalized	AE	X		X	X	X		X	X
	AER		X	X	X	X		X	X
Add unnormalized	AU	X		X		X		X	X
	AUR		X	X		X		X	X
Subtract normalized	SE	X		X	X	X		X	X
	SER		X	X	X	X		X	X
Subtract unnormalized	SU	X		X		X		X	X
	SUR		X	X		X		X	X
Multiply (short to long format)	ME	X		X	X			X	
(short to long format)	MER		X	X	X			X	
Divide	DE	X		X	X		X	X	
	DER		X	X	X		X	X	
Halve	HER		X		X			X	

Double-precision Instructions

All these operate on long-format numbers and produce long-format results.

	mnemonic opcode	RX	RR	exponent overflow	exponent underflow	significance	divide by zero	specification	condition code
Add normalized	AD	X		X	X	X		X	X
	ADR		X	X	X	X		X	X
Add unnormalized	AW	X		X		X		X	X
	AWR		X	X		X		X	X
Subtract normalized	SD	X		X	X	X		X	X
	SDR		X	X	X	X		X	X
Subtract unnormalized	SW	X		X		X		X	X
	SWR		X	X		X		X	X
Multiply	MD	X		X	X			X	
	MDR		X	X	X			X	
Divide	DD	X		X	X		X	X	
	DDR		X	X	X		X	X	
Halve	HDR		X		X			X	

Extended-precision Instructions

	operand	result	mnemonic	RX	RR	exponent overflow	exponent underflow	significance	divide by zero	specification	condition code
Add	extended	extended	AXR		X	X	X	X		X	X
Subtract	extended	extended	SXR		X	X	X	X		X	X
Multiply	extended	extended	MXR		X	X	X	X		X	
	long	extended	MXD	X		X	X	X		X	
	long	extended	MXDR		X	X	X	X		X	
Round	long	short	LRER		X	X	X			X	
	extended	long	LRDR		X	X	X			X	

Note: The condition code is set by all add and subtract instructions as follows:

0 = mantissa of result is zero
1 = result negative, mantissa ≠ zero
2 = result positive, mantissa ≠ zero

3. Of the extended-precision instructions, AXR, SXR, and MXR operate on extended-precision numbers and produce extended-precision results. MXD and MXDR do not operate on extended-precision numbers; they each multiply two double-precision numbers to produce an extended-precision result. Of the two round instructions, LRER rounds a double-precision number to single-precision format and LRDR rounds an extended-precision number to double-precision format.

The result of any multiply, divide, or halve instruction is always in normalized form, whether or not the factor or factors being operated on are normalized. The same is true of the Add Normalized instructions and the Subtract Normalized instructions. The remaining instructions—the two round instructions and the Add Unnormalized and Subtract Unnormalized instructions—do not force the result to be normalized.

The manner in which these instructions are processed by the hardware is summarized in the following paragraphs. Error conditions that can occur because of the limitations of the floating-point formats are discussed at the end of this section.

The ADD and SUBTRACT Instructions

Addition and subtraction are performed in identical fashion to one another except that in subtraction V_2—the quantity addressed by the second operand field—participates with its sign bit reversed. In all addition and subtraction operations, the sum or difference replaces V_1, and V_2 is left unchanged.

The hardware computes the sum or difference by means of the following sequence of steps:

1. The characteristics of V_1 and V_2 are compared. Denoting their difference by N, the mantissa accompanying the smaller characteristic is shifted right N hexadecimal digits and its characteristic is increased by N. The result of this step is that the two quantities to be added or subtracted have equal characteristics, i.e., the hexadecimal points have been aligned.
2. The left-most digit shifted out during the alignment of Step 1 is retained as an extra low-order digit so that accuracy can be preserved to 6, 14, or 28 digits. The retained digit is called the *guard* digit. The mantissa that was not shifted during Step 1 is extended on the right with one low-order zero digit, and the two 7-, 15-, or 29-digit mantissas are added or subtracted, the sign and magnitude of the result being determined in accordance with the rules of algebra. The result of this step is called the *intermediate* sum or difference. (If the intermediate sum or difference includes a carry out of the high-order digit, one more shift takes place: the mantissa of the intermediate result is shifted *right* one digit, and its characteristic is increased by one.)
3. At this point, normalization takes place in Add Normalized and Subtract Normalized instructions; the characteristic of the intermediate result is decreased by the number of positions shifted. Vacated positions on the right are filled with zeroes, and the normalized result is truncated to 6, 14, or 28 digits, depending on the particular instruction that was executed. (This normalization step does not take place in the Add Unnormalized and Subtract Unnormalized instructions. Instead, the mantissa of the intermediate result computed in Step 2 is simply truncated to 6, 14, or 28 digits.)

The result of Step 3 is the result of the instruction's execution, except when any one of three possible error situations is detected: exponent underflow, exponent overflow, or loss of all significant digits. These error situations will be discussed separately at the end of this section.

The MULTIPLY Instruction

In multiplication, the normalized product of V_1 and V_2 replaces V_1, and V_2 is left unchanged. The length of the product's mantissa is as follows (see fig. 13.4):

opcodes	mantissas of V_1 and V_2	mantissa of $V_1 \times V_2$
ME, MER	6 hex digits (short)	14 hex digits (long)
MD, MDR	14 hex digits (long)	14 hex digits (long)
MXD, MXDR	14 hex digits (long)	28 hex digits (extended)
MXR	28 hex digits (extended)	28 hex digits (extended)

For the instructions in which the product's mantissa is 28 digits (i.e., is in extended format), there is an additional constraint on the use of floating-point registers: V_1—the quantity addressed by the first operand field—must either be in floating-point register 0 or in floating-point register 4.

The hardware computes the product by means of the following sequence of steps, provided V_1 and V_2 are each different from zero (if either is zero, the result is immediately set to zero without further calculation):

1. The numbers V_1 and V_2 are normalized and an intermediate product is computed by multiplying the normalized mantissas and adding their characteristics. Because of the preliminary normalization of V_1 and V_2, the intermediate product is either already in normalized form or requires but one shift left (with compensating decrease in characteristic) to be normalized. If the left shift is required, it is done. The normalized intermediate product is then used as the basis for Step 2.

2. The sum of the characteristics computed in Step 1 is reduced by 64. The mantissa of the normalized intermediate product is adjusted to a length of 14 or 28 digits, depending on the instruction. In ME and MER, the product's mantissa has two low-order zero digits appended, to make 14 digits in all; in MD and MDR, the product's mantissa is truncated to 14 digits; in MXD and MXDR, the product's mantissa is not changed since exactly 28 digits were developed in Step 1; and in MXR, the product's mantissa is truncated to 28 digits.

The result of Step 2 is the result of the instruction's execution, except when either of two possible error situations is detected: exponent underflow or exponent overflow. These error situations will be discussed separately.

The DIVIDE Instruction

In division, the normalized quotient of V_1 divided by V_2 replaces V_1, and V_2 is left unchanged. Unlike integer division and packed-decimal division, *no remainder is preserved in floating-point division*. The quotient has the same number of digits as each of its two factors does, and its sign is determined by the rules of algebra. Referring to the opcodes in figure 13.4, it should be noted that there is no instruction for dividing two extended-precision numbers.

The hardware computes the quotient by means of the following sequence of steps, provided V_1 and V_2 are each different from zero (if $V_1=0$ and $V_2 \neq 0$ the result is immediately set to zero without further calculation):

1. V_1 and V_2 are normalized and an intermediate quotient is computed by dividing the normalized mantissa of V_1 by that of V_2, and subtracting their characteristics. The intermediate quotient is either already in normalized form, or else a right shift of one digit (with compensating increase in characteristic) is necessary to produce a mantissa less than 1 in magnitude. If a right shift is required, it is done.

2. The difference of the characteristics computed in Step 1 is increased by 64, and the mantissa of the intermediate quotient is truncated to 6 or 14 digits (depending on the instruction).

The result of Step 2 is the result of the instruction's execution, except when one of three possible error conditions is detected: exponent underflow, exponent overflow, or a divisor (V_2) of zero. These error situations will be discussed later.

The HALVE Instructions

The two instructions that *halve* a value are equivalent in effect to division by 2: V_2 is effectively divided by 2, and the result replaces V_1. If $V_2=0$, the result is zero without further calculation. The execution time of a halve instruction is appreciably shorter than it would be in a division instruction, since an actual division is not performed: when $V_2 \neq 0$, halving is accomplished by shifting the mantissa right 1 *bit* position (not one digit) and then normalizing the result if necessary. As in addition and subtraction, a guard digit is used to preserve accuracy: the low-order bit that is shifted out becomes the high-order bit of the guard digit (its other bits being zeroes), and this digit participates in the normalization.

The only error condition that can occur is exponent underflow. This will be discussed later.

The ROUND Instructions

The two instructions that *round* are considered to be part of the extended-precision feature. LRDR rounds the number V_2 from extended to long format; LRER rounds V_2 from long to short format. In both cases, the rounded result replaces V_1, which may be in any floating-point register (0, 2, 4, or 6). When using the LRER instruction, V_2 may be in any floating-point register; when using LRDR, V_2 must either be in floating-point register 0 or in floating-point register 4.

The instructions round by adding a hex 8 to the high-order digit of the low-order half of the mantissa of V_2 and propagating the carry to the left. The sign of V_2 is ignored in this addition process.

Normalization does not take place during rounding. But if rounding generates a carry out of the high-order digit of the mantissa, the mantissa is shifted right one digit (with compensating increase in characteristic) so that the mantissa of the result is less than 1 in magnitude.

The only error condition that can occur is exponent overflow. This will be discussed.

Example

To compute $-\frac{1}{2}\pi(a+4)$ where a is a floating-point quantity and $\pi = 3.1415926535897932...$, we can do the following:

```
* FOR SHORT FORMAT                      * FOR LONG FORMAT
      LE    4,EPI        π                    LD    4,DPI
      HER   4,4          ½π                   HDR   4,4
      LE    0,A          a                    LD    0,AA
      AE    0,=E'4'      a+4                  AD    0,=D'4'
      MER   4,0          ½π(a+4)              MDR   4,0
      LCER  4,4          -½π(a+4)             LCDR  4,4
      STE   4,X                               STD   4,XX
      . . .                                   . . .
EPI   DC    E'3.141593'                 DPI   DC    D'3.141592653589793'
A     DC    E'0.740486'                 AA    DC    D'0.740486292941931'
X     DS    E                           XX    DS    D
```

Error Conditions

Four types of error situations can be detected when a floating-point arithmetic instruction is executed:

1. *Exponent overflow:* occurs when the magnitude of a result is equal to or greater than 16^{64}, i.e., its characteristic exceeds 127, and its mantissa is not zero.
2. *Exponent underflow:* occurs when the magnitude of a normalized result is equal to or less than 16^{-65}, i.e., its characteristic is less than zero, and its mantissa is not zero.
3. *Significance exception:* occurs when the *mantissa* of the intermediate sum or difference resulting from any add or subtract operation is zero.
4. *Divide exception:* occurs when the mantissa of a divisor (V_2) in any floating-point divide instruction is zero.

Not all of these situations can occur in all arithmetic operations. The errors detectable in each type of operation are summarized in figure 13.4. When one of these errors is detected during floating-point arithmetic operations, the action taken by the computer hardware depends on two things: (1) the type of error and (2) the provisions specified in the program mask.

The program mask (discussed in chap. 11) can be used to prohibit program interruption when an exponent underflow or significance error occurs. If the appropriate program mask bit is set to 0, then whenever an underflow or significance error occurs, the result of the offending instruction is forced to be a *true zero*, i.e., a number whose mantissa and characteristic are both zero and whose sign is plus. If the appropriate program mask bit is a 1 when an underflow or significance error occurs, the program is interrupted and execution may be terminated by the Operating System.

The program mask cannot be used to prohibit program interruption when an exponent overflow or divide exception error occurs. When either of these errors occurs, the program is interrupted and execution is terminated by the Operating System.

Further details concerning these error conditions can be found in the IBM publications, *Principles of Operation for the IBM System 360* and *Principles of Operation for the IBM System 370*.

13.8 CONVERSION TO AND FROM FLOATING-POINT FORMAT

Two main types of conversions are of interest: (1) that between floating-point and fixed-point integers, and (2) that between floating-point and EBCDIC text in the form $\pm$ x.xxx...E$\pm$n.

The first of these is what is required when floating an integer by means of a FORTRAN statement such as

$$X = \text{FLOAT(I)}$$

or when converting a real number to an integer with a FORTRAN statement such as

$$I = IFIX(X).$$

The second type of conversion is what is needed for input and output. It is somewhat more complex than the first not only because of the I/O format requirements, but also because it can involve conversion of a fraction as well as an integer and conversion of a power of 10 to or from a power of 16.

Single-precision floating-point numbers will be used to illustrate the conversion techniques. This has three consequences:

1. In converting from floating-point to integer format, the value of the integer cannot exceed $2^{31} - 1$, or be less than -2^{31}.
2. In converting from integer to floating-point format, the value of the integer should not exceed $2^{24} - 1$ (16,777,215) since only 24 bits are provided in the short-format mantissa; if the integer value exceeds $2^{24} - 1$, the resulting representation may not be exactly equal to the integer value.
3. In converting to and from text format, only seven significant digits are used since an eight-digit decimal number cannot in general be accurately represented in the six available hex digits.

Conversions that allow for more than seven significant digits and conversions between floating-point and packed-decimal format will not be discussed.

Conversion Between Floating-point and Fixed-point Integer

The essential aspect of the conversion technique is to recognize that an integer can easily be converted in two steps: (1) between short-normalized and long-unnormalized format and (2) between long-unnormalized and fixed-point format. In other words, for any eight-digit integer, the conversion sequence is

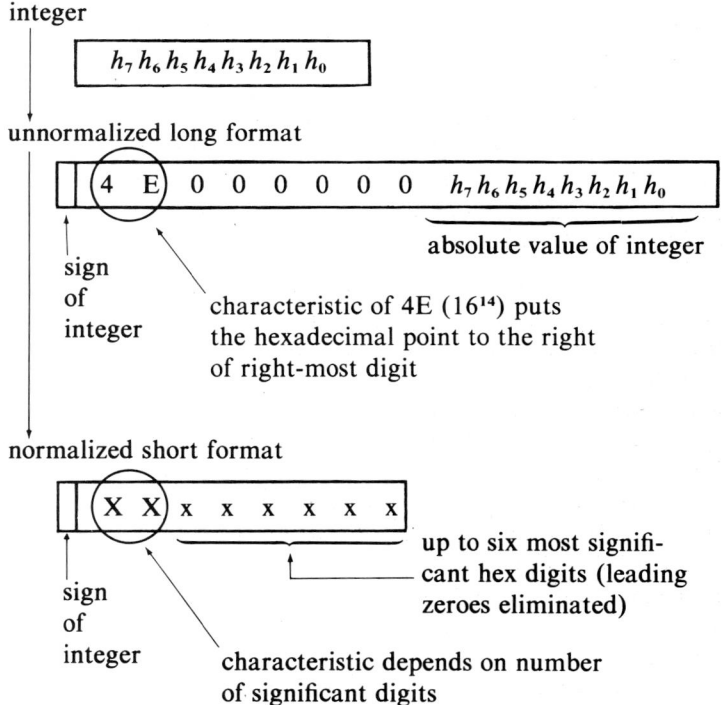

For example, for the integer 100:

hex integer	0	0	0	0	0	0	6	4							
unnormalized	4	E	0	0	0	0	0	0	0	0	0	0	0	0	6	4
normalized	4	2	6	4	0	0	0	0							

Figure 13.5 Convert integer to floating-point format.

```
FLAG LOCTN OBJECT CODE     ADDR1  ADDR2  STMNT M SOURCE STATEMENT

                                          3   * SUBROUTINE XFLOAT(J,X)
                                          4   *    CONVERTS A FULLWORD INTEGER  J  TO NORMLZD SHORT-FORMAT NUMBER  X
                                          5   * PARAMETERS
                                          6   *    1ST PARAMETER = ADDRESS OF J
                                          7   *    2ND PARAMETER = ADDRESS OF X

     000000                               8   XFLOAT  CSECT
     000000 90 EC D00C                    9           STM    14,12,12(13)         STANDARD ENTRY
     000004 05 C0                        10           BALR   12,0
     000006                              11           USING  *,12
     000006 50 D0 C05E         000064    12           ST     13,SAVE+4
     00000A 41 D0 C05A         000060    13           LA     13,SAVE
     00000E 60 00 C04A         000050    14           STD    0,TEMP2              SAVE CONTENTS OF F.P. REG#0

     000012 98 23 1000                   15           LM     2,3,0(1)             GET PARAMETERS
                                         16   *                                  R2 = ADDRESS OF INTEGER J
                                         17   *                                  R3 = ADDRESS OF RESULT X
                                         18   * CREATE UN-NORMALIZED X IN R6,R7 AND STORE IT TEMPORARILY IN 'TEMP1'

     000016 58 22 0000         000000    19           L      2,0(2)              R2 = J
     00001A 10 72                        20           LPR    7,2                 R7 = ABS(J)

     00001C 58 60 C052         000058    21           L      6,FCON              R6 = 0 * (16**14)
     000020 54 20 C056         00005C    22           N      2,SIGN              ISOLATE J'S SIGN BIT, AND
     000024 16 62                        23           OR     6,2                    AFFIX IT TO UN-NORMLZD X
     000026 90 67 C042         000048    24           STM    6,7,TEMP1           STORE UN-NORMLZD LONG-FORMAT X

                                         25   * NORMALIZE BY MULTIPLYING UN-NORMALIZED  X  BY  +1

     00002A 68 00 C042         000048    26           LD     0,TEMP1             FPR#0 = UN-NORMLZD X
     00002E 6C 00 C0A2         0000A8    27           MD     0,=D'1'                * FLO-PT 1
     000032 70 03 0000         000000    28           STE    0,0(3)              STORE NORMLZD SHORT-FRMAT VIA R3

                                         29   * RESTORE REGISTERS AND RETURN TO CALLING PROGRAM

     000036 68 00 C04A         000050    30           LD     0,TEMP2             F.P.REG #0
     00003A 58 D0 C05E         000064    31           L      13,SAVE+4           STANDARD EXIT
     00003E 98 EC D00C                   32           LM     14,12,12(13)
     000042 07 FE                        33           BR     14

     000048                              34   TEMP1   DS     D                    TEMP SPACE FOR UN-NORMLZD VALUE
     000050                              35   TEMP2   DS     D                    TEMP SPACE FOR F.P.REG #0
     000058 4E000000                     36   FCON    DC     X'4E000000'          SHORT FORMAT UN-NORMLZD 0 16**14
     00005C 80000000                     37   SIGN    DC     X'80000000'          SIGN BIT
     000060                              38   SAVE    DS     18F

     0000A8 4110000000000000             39
                                         40           END
```

The subroutine in figure 13.5 converts from integer to floating-point. Any integer greater than 16,777,315 ($=16^6 - 1$) is truncated, resulting in a loss of either 1 or 2 low-order hex digits (maximum value lost is therefore less than one part in 16^5). The subroutine in figure 13.6 converts from floating-point to integer, provided the integer is representable in 32 bits. In both subroutines, provisions for converting negative integers as well as positive ones are included.

Conversion Between Floating-point and EBCDIC Text String

As has already been mentioned, the general format of an EBCDIC floating-point number is

$$\underset{\text{sign}}{\pm} \quad \underset{\substack{\text{integer}\\\text{portion}}}{\underbrace{\text{xxx.....xx}}} . \underset{\substack{\text{fraction}\\\text{portion}}}{\underbrace{\text{xx.....xx}}} \quad \underset{\text{power of ten}}{\underline{\text{E} \pm \text{n}}}$$

It will be assumed that the fraction and integer portions each consist of seven or fewer digits.

When converting from EBCDIC text to floating-point format, the text string is scanned from left to right to determine four things: (1) the sign of the number, (2) the digits in the integer portion, (3) the digits in the fraction portion, and (4) the power of ten, including its sign. The integer portion, fraction portion, and power of ten are each considered to be integers, which we shall denote by J, K, and N, respectively. The

Figure 13.6 *Convert floating-point to integer format.*

```
FLAG LOCTN OBJECT CODE      ADDR1  ADDR2  STMNT M SOURCE STATEMENT

                                            3   * SUBROUTINE  XFIX(X,J)  CONVERTS SHORT FLO-PT  X  TO INTEGER  J
                                            4   * CODE RETURNED IN REGISTER 15
                                            5   *     R15 = 0  IF  X  IS IN RANGE OF FULL-WORD INTEGER VALUES
                                            6   *     R15 = 4  IF  X  NOT IN FULL-WORD INTEGER RANGE
                                            7   *
     000000                                 8   XFIX   CSECT
     000000 90 EC D00C                      9          STM    14,12,12(13)         STANDARD ENTRY
     000004 05 C0                           10         BALR   12,0
     000006                                 11         USING  *,12
     000006 50 D0 C086     00008C           12         ST     13,SAVE+4
     00000A 41 D0 C082     000088           13         LA     13,SAVE
     00000E 60 00 C062     000068           14         STD    0,TEMP2              SAVE F.P.REG #0

                                            15  * GET PARAMETERS FROM CALLING PROGRAM
     000012 98 23 1000                      16         LM     2,3,0(1)             R2= ADDRESS OF SHORT-FORMAT  X
                                            17  *                                 R3= ADDRESS OF RESULT  J
                                            18  * DETERMINE RANGE OF  X
     000016 68 00 C0CA     000000           19         LD     0,=D'0'              LOWER-HALF OF F.P.REG#0 IS 0
     00001A 78 02 0000     000000           20         LE     0,0(2)               UPPER-HALF OF F.P.REG#0 IS X
     00001E 32 00                           21         LTER   0,0                  DETERMINE SIGN OF  X
     000020 47 40 C02A     000030           22         BM     XNEG
     000024 79 00 C07E     000084           23         CE     0,FCONP              IF  X > 0  COMPARE IT TO LARGEST
     000028 47 20 C056     00005C           24         BH     XFIXERR              SHORT-FORMAT INTGR  < 2**31
     00002C 47 F0 C032     000038           25         B      XFIXOK
     000030 79 00 C07A     000080           26  XNEG   CE     0,FCONM              IF  X < 0  COMPARE IT TO -2**31
     000034 47 40 C056     00005C           27         BL     XFIXERR              X < -2**31 NOT CONVERTIBLE

                                            28  * CONVERT X  (ALREADY IN FPR#0)  TO INTEGER FORMAT
     000038 6E 00 C072     000078           29  XFIXOK AW     0,FCON2              UN-NORMLZE, COMPLEMENT IF NEGTVE
     00003C 60 00 C06A     000070           30         STD    0,TEMP1              STORE INTEGER IN 'TEMP1+4'
     000040 D2 03 3000C06E        000074    31         MVC    0(4,3),TEMP1+4       COPY IT TO RESULT J, VIA R3
     000046 48 F0 C0D2     0000D8           32         LH     15,=H'0'             SET RETURN CODE FOR VALID X

                                            33  * NORMAL EXIT
     00004A 68 00 C062     000068           34  XFIXX  LD     0,TEMP2              RESTORE FPR#0
     00004E 58 D0 C086     00008C           35         L      13,SAVE+4
     000052 58 E0 D00C     00000C           36         L      14,12(13)            RESTORE ALL BUT R15
     000056 98 0C D014                      37         LM     0,12,20(13)
     00005A 07 FE                           38         BR     14

                                            39  * SET ERROR CODE IN R15 WHEN  X  NOT IN FULL-WD INTGR RANGE
     00005C 48 F0 C0D4     0000DA           40  XFIXERR LH    15,=H'4'
     000060 47 F0 C044     00004A           41         B      XFIXX

     000068                                 42  TEMP2  DS     D                    TEMP SPACE FOR F.P.REG#0
     000070                                 43  TEMP1  DS     D                    TEMP SPACE FOR UN-NORMLZD INTGR
     000078 4E00000100000000                44  FCON2  DC     X'4E00000100000000'  UN-NORMALIZED 2**32
     000080 C8800000                        45  FCONM  DC     X'C8800000'          NORMALIZED  -2**31
     000084 487FFFFF                        46  FCONP  DC     X'487FFFFF'           NORMALIZED  2**31 - 256
                                            47  * NOTE  2**31 - 256  IS LARGEST SHORT FORMAT INTGR LESS THAN  2**31
     000088                                 48  SAVE   DS     18F
     0000D0 000000000000000000              49
     0000D8 0000
     0000DA 0004

                                            50         END
```

floating-point number represented in EBCDIC format by this scheme can thus be evaluated from the expression

$$\left(J + \frac{K}{10^7}\right) \times 10^N$$

where $N = \pm n$, and $K < 10^7$.

The problem of scanning the text string and converting the three integers to full-word binary format will not be discussed since it does not involve any new concepts or techniques. Consequently the subroutine TXTFP shown in figure 13.7 starts with the assumption that J, K, and N are given as binary integers. The previously mentioned subroutine (XFLOAT, in fig. 13.5) is used to convert J and K to floating-point format, and the floating-point representation of 10^N is determined from tables.

Similarly, for the problem of converting from floating-point to EBCDIC text, the subroutine FPTXT in figure 13.8 computes the integers J, K, and N but does not create the actual text strings. A subsequent conversion (not shown) via the CVD and UNPK, ED, or EDMK instructions is required to produce the EBCDIC text strings once the binary representations of J, K, and N are known. It should be noted that the FPTXT subroutine creates full-word representations of J, K, and N with $-9 \le J \le +9$, $-9999999 \le K \le +9999999$, and $-75 \le N \le +75$.

Figure 13.7 *Convert mixed number to floating-point format.*

```
FLAG LOCTN OBJECT CODE      ADDR1  ADDR2  STMNT M SOURCE STATEMENT

                                            3    * SUBROUTINE TXTFP(J,K,N,X)
                                            4    *
                                            5    * CONVERTS  (J,K,N)  TO SINGLE-PRECISION FLO-PT NUMBER  X
                                            6    *    (J,K,N) CONSISTS OF THREE INTEGERS  J, K, N
                                            7    *    WHICH CORRESPOND TO EXTERNAL FLO-PT FORMAT  J.K*10**N
                                            8    * NO MORE THAN 7 SIGNIFICANT DIGITS ADVISED FOR J AND K
                                            9    *
                                           10    *   CONSTRAINTS ... ABS(N) <= 75,  ABS(K) < 10**7,  J & K SAME SIGN
                                           11    *   RETURN CODE IN REG 15 ... = 0 IF BOTH  N  AND  K  ARE WITHIN LIMITS
                                           12    *                           = 4 IF EITHER  N  OR  K  NOT WITHIN LIMITS

000000                                     13    TXTFP   CSECT
000000 90 EC D00C                          14            STM   14,12,12(13)            STANDARD ENTRY
000004 05 C0                               15            BALR  12,0
000006                                     16            USING *,12
000006 50 D0 C236           00023C         17            ST    13,SAVE+4
00000A 41 D0 C232           000238         18            LA    13,SAVE
00000E 60 00 C202           000208         19            STD   0,TEMP                  SAVE FPR#0

                                           20    * GET CALLING PROGRAM'S PARAMETERS

000012 98 25 1000                          21            LM    2,5,0(1)               R2= ADDR OF J
                                           22    *                                    R3= ADDR OF K
                                           23    *                                    R4= ADDR OF N
                                           24    *                                    R5= ADDR OF RESULT X
000016 45 E0 C0B8           0000BE         25            BAL   14,TXTTEST             SEE IF  K  AND  N  WITHIN LIMITS
00001A 49 F0 C2AE           0002B4         26            CH    15,=H'4'               INVALID IF RETURN CODE = 4
00001E 47 80 C086           00008C         27            BE    TXTFPXX

                                           28    * CONVERT  J  TO SHORT-FORMAT

000022 D2 07 C21A2000       000220         29            MVC   TEMPJ,0(2)             PUT  J  IN TEMP AREA
000028 41 10 C27A           000280         30            LA    1,=A(TEMPJ,XJ)         CALL 'XFLOAT' SUBROUTINE AND
00002C 58 F0 C282           000288         31            L     15,=V(XFLOAT)          HAVE RESULT STORED IN 'XJ'
000030 05 EF                               32            BALR  14,15

                                           33    * CONVERT  K  TO SHORT-FORMAT

000032 D2 07 C2223000       000228         34            MVC   TEMPK,0(3)             PUT  K  IN TEMP AREA
000038 41 10 C286           00028C         35            LA    1,=A(TEMPK,XK)         CALL 'XFLOAT' SUBROUTINE AND
00003C 58 F0 C282           000288         36            L     15,=V(XFLOAT)          HAVE RESULT STORED IN 'XK'
000040 05 EF                               37            BALR  14,15

                                           38    * COMPUTE FLOATING-POINT VALUE  J + ( K / 10**7 )

000042 78 00 C216           00021C         39            LE    0,XK                   TEST  K
000046 79 00 C28E           000294         40            CE    0,=E'0'                IF  K = 0
00004A 47 70 C054           00005A         41            BNE   TXTFP1                     AND
00004E 79 00 C212           000218         42            CE    0,XJ                   IF  J = 0
000052 47 80 C05C           000062         43            BE    TXTFP3                     THEN BYPASS ADDITION
000056 47 F0 C058           00005E         44            B     TXTFP2
00005A 7D 00 C292           000298         45    TXTFP1  DE    0,=E'1E7'              COMPUTE  K / 10**7
00005E 7A 00 C212           000218         46    TXTFP2  AE    0,XJ                   THEN ADD  J
000062 70 00 C22A           000230         47    TXTFP3  STE   0,XTEMP                STORE RESULT TEMPORARILY
                                           48    * COMPUTE  ( J + K/10**7 ) * 10**N

000066 58 44 0000           000000         49            L     4,0(4)                 R4 = N
00006A 12 44                               50            LTR   4,4                    DETERMINE SIGN OF  N
00006C 47 80 C07E           000084         51            BZ    TXTFPX                 IF N = 0, THEN  10**N = 1
000070 41 A0 C296           00029C         52            LA    10,=A(P1,P2)           IF N > 0, USE TABLES  P1,P2
000074 47 20 C076           00007C         53            BP    TXTFP4
000078 41 A0 C29E           0002A4         54            LA    10,=A(M1,M2)           IF N < 0, USE TABLES  M1,M2
00007C 45 E0 C098           00009E         55    TXTFP4  BAL   14,TENN                DETERMINE  10**N  FROM TBLS
000080 7C 00 C22A           000230         56            ME    0,XTEMP        10**N   *  ( J + ( K/10**7 ) )

000084 70 05 0000           000000         57    TXTFPX  STE   0,0(5)                 SAVE SHORT-FORMAT ANSR FOR CALLR
000088 48 F0 C2B0           0002B6         58            LH    15,=H'0'               RETURN CODE = 0 SINCE PARAMS OK

00008C 68 00 C202           000208         59    TXTFPXX LD    0,TEMP                 RESTORE FPR#0
000090 58 00 C236           00023C         60            L     13,SAVE+4             RESTORE GENERAL REGISTERS
000094 58 ED 000C           00000C         61            L     14,12(13)                (BUT NOT REG 15)
000098 98 0C D014                          62            LM    0,12,20(13)
00009C 07 FE                               63            BR    14

                                           64    * INTERNAL SUBROUTINE TO DETERMINE  10**N  FROM TABLES
                                           65    *
                                           66    * UPON ENTRY,    R4 = N
                                           67    *               R10 = ADDR OF TWO TABLE ADDRESSES
                                           68    *                    1ST ADDR IS TABLE #1   P1 IF N>0,  M1 IF N<0
                                           69    *                    2ND ADDR IS TABLE #2   P2 IF N>0,  M2 IF N<0
```

Figure 13.7 continued

```
FLAG LOCTN OBJECT CODE      ADDR1  ADDR2   STMNT M SOURCE STATEMENT

                                             70   *
                                             71   * UPON EXIT,   F.P.REG#0  CONTAINS  10**N
      00009E 98 89 A000                       72   TENN     LM     8,9,0(10)              GET ADDRS FOR TABLES #1 & #2
      0000A2 10 64                            73            LPR    6,4           GET  ABS(N)
      0000A4 8C 60 0003       000003          74            SRDL   6,3                    ABS(N)/8, SAVE REMAINDER IN R7
      0000A8 89 60 0003       000003          75            SLL    6,3                    USE QUOTIENT AS INDEX FOR TBL #2
      0000AC 68 06 9000                       76            LD     0,0(6,9)               GET 10**N1, N1=0,8,16,... OR 72
      0000B0 48 60 C280       0002B6          77            LH     6,=H'0'                CLEAR REG 6
      0000B4 8D 60 0006       000006          78            SLDL   6,6                    USE REMAINDER AS INDEX TO TBL #1
      0000B8 6C 06 8000                       79            MD     0,0(6,8)      10**N = 10**N1 * 10**N2, N2=0,1..OR 7
      0000BC 07 FE                            80   TENNX    BR     14

                                             81   * INTERNAL SUBROUTINE TO DETERMINE IF ABS(N) <= 75  AND  ABS(K) < 10**7
                                             82   *              ENTERED WITH   R3 = ADDR OF  K
                                             83   *                             R4 = ADDR OF  N
                                             84   *              EXIT WITH     R15 = 4  IF EITHER RANGE NOT O.K.
      0000BE 58 84 0000       000000          85   TXTTEST  L      8,0(4)     GET  N
      0000C2 10 88                            86            LPR    8,8        ABS(N)
      0000C4 59 80 C2A6       0002AC          87            C      8,=F'75'
      0000C8 47 20 C0D6       0000DC          88            BH     TXTTESTX            ERROR IF  ABS(N) > 75
      0000CC 58 83 0000       000000          89            L      8,0(3)     GET  K
      0000D0 10 88                            90            LPR    8,8        ABS(K)
      0000D2 59 80 C2AA       0002B0          91            C      8,=F'1E7'
      0000D6 47 B0 C0D6       0000DC          92            BNL    TXTTESTX           ERROR IF  ABS(K) NOT < 10**7
      0000DA 07 FE                            93            BR     14
      0000DC 48 F0 C2AE       0002B4          94   TXTTESTX LH     15,=H'4'
      0000E0 07 FE                            95            BR     14               ERROR CODE IS  R15 = 4
                                             96   * FOLLOWING TWO TABLES --- P1  AND  P2 --- USED WHEN  N > 0

                                             97   * TABLE OF  10**N, FOR N = 0,1,2,3,...,7

      0000E8 4110000000000000                 98   P1       DC     D'1'
      0000F0 41A0000000000000                 99            DC     D'1E1,1E2,1E3,1E4,1E5,1E6,1E7'

                                            100   * TABLE OF  10**N, FOR N = 0,8,16,24,...,72

      000128 4110000000000000                101   P2       DC     D'1,1E8'
      000138 4E2386F26FC10000                102            DC     D'1E16,1E24,1E32,1E40'
      000158 68AF298D050E4396                103            DC     D'1E48,1E56,1E64,1E72'


                                            104   * FOLLOWING TWO TABLES --- M1  AND  M2 --- USED WHEN  N < 0

      000178 4110000000000000                105   M1       DC     D'1E0,1E-1,1E-2,1E-3,1E-4'
      0001A0 3CA7C5AC471B4784                106            DC     D'1E-5,1E-6,1E-7'

      0001B8 4110000000000000                107   M2       DC     D'1E0,1E-8,1E-16,1E-24,1E-32'
      0001E0 1F8B61313BBABCE3                108            DC     D'1E-40,1E-48,1E-56,1E-64,1E-72'

                                            109   * OTHER CONSTANTS AND TEMPORARY AREAS

      000208                                 110   TEMP     DS     D                      FOR  FPR#0
      000210                                 111   TEMP1    DS     D                      FOR  10**ABS(N)
      000218                                 112   XJ       DS     F                      INTEGER J
      00021C                                 113   XK       DS     F                      INTEGER K
      000220                                 114   TEMPJ    DS     D                      FLO-PT J
      000228                                 115   TEMPK    DS     D                      FLO-PT K
      000230                                 116   XTEMP    DS     D                      J + ( K / 10**7 )
      000238                                 117   SAVE     DS     18F                    REGISTER SAVE AREA

      000280 0000022000000218                118
      000288 00000000
      00028C 000002280000021C
      000294 00000000
      000298 46989680
      00029C 000000E800000128
      0002A4 0000017800000188
      0002AC 0000004B
      0002B0 00989680
      0002B4 0004
      0002B6 0000
                                            119            END
```

Figure 13.8 Convert floating-point format to mixed number.

```
FLAG LOCTN OBJECT CODE      ADDR1  ADDR2  STMNT M SOURCE STATEMENT

                                          3    * SUBROUTINE FPTXT (X,J,K,N)
                                          4    *
                                          5    * CONVERTS A SHORT-FORMAT NORMALIZED FLOATING POINT NUMBER X
                                          6    *    INTO THREE INTEGERS J, K, N
                                          7    *    CORRESPONDING TO EXTERNAL FLO-PT FORMAT  J.K*10**N
                                          8    * ABS(J) IS ALWAYS LESS THAN 10.
                                          9    * BOTH J AND K HAVE THE SAME SIGN
                                          10   *    IF NEGATIVE, BOTH ARE IN 2'S COMPLEMENT FORM.
                                          11   *
000000                                    12  FPTXT  CSECT
000000 90 EC D00C                         13         STM   14,12,12(13)           STANDARD ENTRY
000004 05 C0                              14         BALR  12,0
000006                                    15         USING *,12
000006 50 D0 C302       000308            16         ST    13,SAVE+4
00000A 41 D0 C2FE       000304            17         LA    13,SAVE
00000E 60 00 C2BA       0002C0            18         STD   0,FPR0                 SAVE FLO-PT REGS
000012 60 20 C2C2       0002C8            19         STD   2,FPR2
000016 60 40 C2CA       0002D0            20         STD   4,FPR4
00001A 60 60 C2D2       0002D8            21         STD   6,FPR6
00001E D2 0B C2DAC352 0002E0 000358       22         MVC   INT(12),=F'0,0,0'      (J,K,N) = (0,0,0)  INITIALLY
                                          23   *
                                          24   * GET PARAMETERS FROM CALLING PROGRAM
000024 98 25 1000                         25         LM    2,5,0(1)               R2= ADDRESS OF X
                                          26   *                                  R3= ADDR OF J
                                          27   *                                  R4= ADDR OF K
                                          28   *                                  R5= ADDR OF N

                                          29   * DETERMINE WHETHER  X = 0, OR IF  ABS(X) > 1 , < 1 , OR  = 1

000028 68 00 C34A       000350            30         LD    0,=D'0'                CLEAR LOWER-HALF OF FPR#0
00002C 78 02 0000       000000            31         LE    0,0(2)                 PUT  X  IN UPPER-HALF OF FPR#0
000030 20 40                              32         LPDR  4,0                    FPR#4 = ABS(X)
000032 20 60                              33         LPDR  6,0                    FPR#6 = ABS(X)
000034 47 80 C0CC       0000D2            34         BZ    FPTXTX                 IF X=0,  (J,K,N) = (0,0,0)
000038 79 40 C35E       000364            35         CE    4,=E'1'                TEST ABS(X)
00003C 47 40 C048       00004E            36         BL    FPTXT0                 IF < 1, MUST FIND 10**(-N)
000040 47 20 C05C       000062            37         BH    FPTXT1                 IF > 1, MUST FIND 10**(+N)
000044 D2 03 C2DAC362 0002E0 000368       38         MVC   TEMPJ,=F'1'            IF = 1, (J,K,N) = (1,0,0)
00004A 47 F0 C0CC       0000D2            39         B     FPTXTX

                                          40   * ABS(X) < 1

00004E 41 A0 C366       00036C            41  FPTXT0 LA    10,=A(M1,M2,BH)   PARAMS FOR  'PTEN'
000052 45 E0 C0F8       0000FE            42         BAL   14,PTEN                 DETERMINE  N  AND  10**N
000056 11 00                              43         LNR   0,0                    ABS(N)  RETURNED IN  R0
000058 50 00 C2E2       0002E8            44         ST    0,TEMPN                STORE   -N
00005C 2D 40                              45         DDR   4,0                    FLO-PT 10**N RETURNED IN FPR#0
00005E 47 F0 C06A       000070            46         B     FPTXT2                 FPR#4 NOW HAS ABS(X) / 10**N

                                          47   * ABS(X) > 1

000062 41 A0 C372       000378            48  FPTXT1 LA    10,=A(P1,P2,BL)   PARAMS FOR  'PTEN'
000066 45 E0 C0F8       0000FE            49         BAL   14,PTEN                 DETERMINE  N  AND  10**N
00006A 50 00 C2E2       0002E8            50         ST    0,TEMPN                ABS(N)  RETURNED IN R0
00006E 2D 40                              51         DDR   4,0                    FPR#4  =  ABS(X)/10**N
                                          52   *  DETERMINE INTEGER  (J)  AND FRACTIONAL  (K)  COMPONENTS
                                          53   *  OF  ABS(X)/10**N  IN SHORT-FORMAT.
000070 79 40 C35E       000364            54  FPTXT2 CE    4,=E'1'                IF ABS(X)/10**N  < 1 ,
000074 47 40 C088       00008E            55         BL    FPTXT2A                THEN INTEGER 'J' IS ZERO.
000078 70 40 C2DA       0002E0            56         STE   4,TEMPJ                SAVE ABS(X)/10**N  (TEMPORARY)
00007C D4 03 C2DAC2FA 0002E0 000300       57         NC    TEMPJ(4),FCON1         ERASE THE FRACTIONAL 'K' PORTION
                                          58   *                                  LEAVING FLO-PT 'J'
000082 79 40 C2DA       0002E0            59         CE    4,TEMPJ                IF DIFFERENCE IS ZERO
000086 47 80 C0AA       0000B0            60         BE    FPTXT3A                THEN FRACTION IS ZERO.
00008A 7B 40 C2DA       0002E0            61         SE    4,TEMPJ                COMPUTE FRACTIONAL PORTION 'K'
00008E 70 40 C2DE       0002E4            62  FPTXT2A STE   4,TEMPK                SAVE FRACTIONAL PORTION
000092 94 00 C2DE       0002E4            63         NI    TEMPK,X'00'            ERASE CHARACTERISTIC AND SIGN

                                          64   * CONVERT FRACTIONAL PORTION TO FIXED-POINT INTEGER RESULT  K

000096 58 90 C2DE       0002E4            65         L     9,TEMPK                GET FRACTL PORTION AS INTEGER
00009A 5C 80 C37E       000384            66         M     8,=F'1E7'              MULTIPLY BY  10**7
00009E 8F 80 0008       000008            67         SLDA  8,8                    SHIFT PRODUCT INTO R8
0000A2 91 80 2000                         68         TM    0(2),X'80'             TEST SIGN BIT OF  X
0000A6 47 80 C0A6       0000AC            69         BZ    FPTXT3                 IF SIGN BIT 0, K IS POSITIVE
0000AA 11 88                              70         LNR   8,8                    OTHERWISE, MAKE K NEGATIVE
0000AC 50 80 C2DE       0002E4            71  FPTXT3 ST    8,TEMPK                'TEMPK' = K

                                          72   * CREATE FIXED-POINT INTEGER RESULT  J

0000B0 68 00 C34A       000350            73  FPTXT3A LD   0,=D'0'
0000B4 78 00 C2DA       0002E0            74         LE    0,TEMPJ                FPR#0 = J AS FLO-PT NUMBER
0000B8 6E 00 C2F2       0002F8            75         AW    0,FCON2                UN-NORMLZE, COMPLEMENT IF NEGTVE
0000BC 60 00 C2EA       0002F0            76         STD   0,FCON3                LOWER-HALF OF FPR#0 IS J
0000C0 58 90 C2EE       0002F4            77         L     9,FCON3+4              GET INTEGER REPRESENTING J
0000C4 91 80 2000                         78         TM    0(2),X'80'             TEST SIGN OF X
```

Figure 13.8 *continued*

```
FLAG LOCTN OBJECT CODE     ADDR1  ADDR2  STMNT M SOURCE STATEMENT

     0000C8 47 80 C0C8      0000CE        79          BZ    FPTXT4          IF SIGN BIT ZERO,  J IS POSITIVE
     0000CC 11 99                         80          LNR   9,9             OTHERWISE, MAKE J NEGATIVE
     0000CE 50 90 C2DA      0002E0        81   FPTXT4 ST    9,TEMPJ         'TEMPJ' = J

                                          82   * EXIT FROM  'FPTXT'  SUBROUTINE

     0000D2 D2 03 3000C2DA         0002E0 83   FPTXTX MVC   0(4,3),TEMPJ    GIVE RESULTS TO CALLING PROGRAM
     0000D8 D2 03 4000C2DE         0002E4 84          MVC   0(4,4),TEMPK
     0000DE D2 03 5000C2E2         0002E8 85          MVC   0(4,5),TEMPN
     0000E4 68 00 C2BA      0002C0        86          LD    0,FPR0          RESTORE FLO-PT REGISTERS
     0000E8 68 20 C2C2      0002C8        87          LD    2,FPR2
     0000EC 68 40 C2CA      0002D0        88          LD    4,FPR4
     0000F0 68 60 C2D2      0002D8        89          LD    6,FPR6
     0000F4 58 D0 C302      000308        90          L     13,SAVE+4       RESTORE GENERAL REGISTERS
     0000F8 98 EC D00C                    91          LM    14,12,12(13)
     0000FC 07 FE                         92          BR    14
                                          93   * INTERNAL SUBROUTINE TO DETERMINE INTEGER POWER OF 10 CORRESPONDING TO
                                          94   *    CHARACTERISTIC OF VALUE GIVEN IN FPR#6 UPON ENTRY TO THIS ROUTINE
                                          95   *
                                          96   * UPON ENTRY,   F.P.REG #6  = ABS(X)
                                          97   *               GENL REG 10 = ADDR OF PARAMETERS (SEE COMMENTS BELOW)
                                          98   *
                                          99   * UPON EXIT,    F.P.REG #0 = 10**N
                                          100  *               GENL REG 0 = ABS(N)
                                          101  *     WHERE  N  IS THE INTEGER POWER OF 10 THAT WAS TO BE DETERMINED
                                          102  *

     0000FE 98 8A A000                    103  PTEN   LM    8,10,0(10)      R8 = ADDR OF TABLE #1
                                          104  *                           R9 = ADDR OF TABLE #2
                                          105  *                           R10 = ADDR OF CONDTL BRANCH TBL
     000102 48 70 C382      000388        106         LH    7,=H'0'         R7 = INITIAL VALUE OF  N

                                          107  * ASSUME ABS(N) = P + Q, WHERE P AND Q ARE NON-NEG INTGRS &  Q < 10
                                          108  *
                                          109  *  FIRST, DETERMINE VALUE OF P FROM TABLE #1

     000106 69 68 0008      000008        110  PTEN1  CD    6,8(8)          COMPARE ABS(X) TO VALUES IN TBL1
     00010A 44 0A 0000      000000        111         EX    0,0(10)         BRANCH WHEN RANGE FOUND
     00010E 41 88 0008      000008        112         LA    8,8(8)          INCR ADDR TO NEXT ENTRY IN TBL 1
     000112 4A 70 C384      00038A        113         AH    7,=H'10'        INCR VALUE OF  P  BY 10
     000116 47 F0 C100      000106        114         B     PTEN1           CONTINUE SEARCH
     00011A 6D 68 0000      000000        115  PTEN1X DD    6,0(8)          FACTOR OUT  10**P  FROM ABS(X)

                                          116  *  THEN, DETERMINE VALUE OF  Q  FROM TABLE #2

     00011E 69 69 0008      000008        117  PTEN2  CD    6,8(9)          COMPARE  ABS(X)/10**P  TO EACH
     000122 44 0A 0004      000004        118         EX    0,4(10)            VALUE IN TBL 2; BRANCH WHEN
                                          119  *                               RANGE IS FOUND
     000126 41 99 0008      000008        120         LA    9,8(9)          INCR ADDR TO NEXT ENTRY IN TBL 2
     00012A 4A 70 C386      00038C        121         AH    7,=H'1'         INCR VALUE OF  P+Q  BY  1
     00012E 47 F0 C118      00011E        122         B     PTEN2

                                          123  * FINALLY, COMPUTE  10**N

     000132 68 08 0000      000000        124  PTEN2X LD    0,0(8)          GET    10**P
     000136 6C 09 0000      000000        125         MD    0,0(9)          FPR#0 = 10**N = 10**P * 10**Q
     00013A 18 07                         126         LR    0,7             R0 = ABS(N)
     00013C 07 FE                         127         BR    14

                                          128  * CONDITIONAL BRANCH TABLES
                                          129  *     BH  USED WHEN  ABS(X) < 1 I.E.,  N < 0
                                          130  *     BL  USED WHEN  ABS(X) > 1 I.E.,  N > 0

     00013E 47 20 C114      00011A        131  BH     BH    PTEN1X
     000142 47 20 C12C      000132        132         BH    PTEN2X
     000146 47 40 C114      00011A        133  BL     BL    PTEN1X
     00014A 47 40 C12C      000132        134         BL    PTEN2X
                                          135  * FOLLOWING TWO TABLES  --- P1  AND  P2  --- USED WHEN  N  > 0.

                                          136  * TABLE #1  LONG FLO-PT  10**P, P = 0,10,20,30,...,70,80

     000150 4110000000000000              137  P1     DC    D'1E0,1E10,1E20,1E30,1E40,1E50,1E60,1E70'
     000190 7FFFFFFFFFFFFFFF              138         DC    X'7FFFFFFFFFFFFFFF'

                                          139  * TABLE #2  LONG FLO-PT  10**Q, Q = 0,1,2,3,...,8,9,10

     000198 4110000000000000              140  P2     DC    D'1E0,1E1,1E2,1E3,1E4,1E5,1E6,1E7,1E8,1E9,1E10'

                                          141  * FOLLOWING TWO TABLES  --- M1  AND  M2  --- USED WHEN  N < 0.

                                          142  *TABLE #1 FOR NEGATIVE VALUES OF  P  I.E.,
                                          143  *     10**P FOR P  = 0,-10,-20,-30,....,-70

     0001F0                               144  M1     DS    0D
     0001F0 4110000000000000              145         DC    D'1E0,1E-10,1E-20,1E-30,1E-40'
     000218 173BDCF495A9703E              146         DC    D'1E-50,1E-60,1E-70'
     000230 0000000000000000              147         DC    X'0000000000000000'
                                          148  *TABLE #2 FOR NEGATIVE Q ---
                                          149  *     10**Q FOR Q = 0,-1,-2,-3,....,-16
```

Figure 13.8 continued

```
FLAG LOCTN OBJECT CODE     ADDR1 ADDR2  STMNT M SOURCE STATEMENT

     000238 4110000000000000           150  M2       DC    D'1E0,1E-1,1E-2,1E-3,1E-4,1E-5'
     000268 3C1C6F7A0B5ED8D            151           DC    D'1E-6,1E-7,1E-8,1E-9,1E-10'
     000290 37AFEBFF0BCB24AB           152           DC    D'1E-11,1E-12,1E-13,1E-14,1E-15,1E-16'
                                       153  *
                                       154  * CONSTANTS AND TEMPORARY AREAS

     0002C0                            155  FPR0     DS    D                       F.P.REG#0
     0002C8                            156  FPR2     DS    D                       F.P.REG#2
     0002D0                            157  FPR4     DS    D                       F.P.REG#4
     0002D8                            158  FPR6     DS    D                       F.P.REG#6
     0002E0                            159  INT      DS    0F
     0002E0                            160  TEMPJ    DS    F                       INTEGER RESULT J
     0002E4                            161  TEMPK    DS    F                       INTEGER RESULT K
     0002E8                            162  TEMPN    DS    F                       INTEGER RESULT N
     0002F0                            163  FCON3    DS    D                       TEMP SPACE FOR J
     0002F8 4E00000100000000           164  FCON2    DC    X'4E00000100000000'     UNNORMALIZED  2**32
     000300 FFF00000                   165  FCON1    DC    X'FFF00000'             SIGN, CHAR, AND 1ST HEX DIGIT
     000304                            166  SAVE     DS    18F                     GENERAL REGISTERS
     000350 0000000000000000           167
     000358 0000000000000000
     000364 41100000
     000368 00000001
     00036C 000001F000000238
     000378 0000015000000198
     000384 00989680
     000388 0000
     00038A 000A
     00038C 0001

                                       168           END
```

You are urged to study the two subroutines in detail by tracing their execution with a few representative numbers. The method used to convert from powers of 10 to powers of 16 is but one of many possible methods; this is true for the reverse conversions from powers of 16 to powers of 10. Both methods use tables to accomplish the conversions. This has the advantage of relative simplicity over most other methods, but it has two disadvantages: (1) a somewhat longer execution time than might be achieved with more sophisticated methods and (2) a possible loss of accuracy in the least significant digit due to the multiplications and divisions used in achieving the results.

In hand calculations, unlike the method used in the accompanying programs, conversion of a number from decimal scientific notation to hexadecimal floating-point representation consists of three steps. Here, for brevity, we let $P = J + K/10^7$.

Step 1. Convert $P \times 10^N$ to $(P \times 16^W) \times 16^K$,
where $W + K = N/(\log_{10} 16)$, with $|W| < 1$ and $K =$ an integer.

Step 2. Convert $P \times 16^W$ to $0.H_{16} \times 16^M$,
where M is an integer, and $0.H_{16}$ is in normalized form.

Step 3. Combine the results of Steps 1 and 2 to obtain the answer:
$$P \times 10^N = 0.H_{16} \times 16^{M+K}.$$

To illustrate, suppose $P \times 10^N$ is 3.4×10^2.

Then from Step 1 we find that $W + K = 2/1.204120 = 1.660964$, so $K = 1$ and $W = 0.660964$. In other words, $3.4 \times 10^2 = (3.4 \times 16^{0.660964}) \times 16^1$.

Applying Step 2, we find that $3.4 \times 16^{0.660964} = 3.4 \times 6.25 = 21.25_{10} = 15.4_{16} = 0.154_{16} \times 16^2$, so that $0.H_{16} = 0.154_{16}$ and $M = 2$.

From Step 3 the result is then found to be
$$3.4 \times 10^2 = 0.154_{16} \times 16^3.$$

The above procedure is of course valid for any N: positive, negative, or zero. For example, it can be used to show that $3.4 \times 10^{-2} = 0.8B439581..._{16} \times 16^{-1}$, which in hexadecimal short-format notation is 3F8B4396. Similarly, $3.4 \times 10^0 = 0.36666666..._{16} \times 16^1$, i.e., 41366666 in short format.

13.9 SUMMARY

The advantages of using the floating-point instructions and data formats are that (1) the range of numbers that may be represented and operated on is far greater than that attainable with the integer or packed-decimal representations for a given number of bits, and (2) the execution of floating-point instructions frees the programmer from having to align hexadecimal points or other fractional indicators. The range of numbers includes zero and all 6-, 14-, and 28-digit hexadecimal integers as well as mixed numbers whose magnitude is in the approximate range of from 5.4×10^{-79} to 7.2×10^{75}. The instruction set consists of operations analogous to those available for integer arithmetic: loading, storing, and comparing floating-point numbers, testing and/ or changing the sign of floating-point numbers, and adding, multiplying, subtracting, and dividing two floating-point numbers. Supplementing these instructions are two special instructions: *halve* (division by two via shifting) and *round* (transforming from long to short or from extended to long formats with the lowest-order digit of the result rounded).

The short, long, and extended formats all consist of a mantissa, a characteristic, and a sign. The characteristic is expressed in 7-bit, excess-64 notation (X'00' through X'7F') representing the decimal integers -64 through $+63$; this is the power of 16 by which the mantissa is multiplied. The mantissa is the magnitude of a 6-, 14-, or 28-digit hexadecimal number always considered to be less than 1 (6 digits in short format, 14 in long format, and 28 in extended). The sign is a single bit representing the algebraic sign of the mantissa.

When adding, subtracting, multiplying, or dividing two floating-point numbers, and when halving a floating-point number, a nonzero result is always expressed in normalized form unless the unnormalized add or subtract instructions are used. (In normalized form, the leading mantissa digit is nonzero, i.e., X'1' through X'F'.) With the unnormalized add and subtract instructions, the result need not be normalized; its form depends on the relative magnitudes and forms of the numbers being added or subtracted. The result of a load or store operation is in the same form—normalized or unnormalized—as the number that is being loaded or stored. Similarly, no normalization takes place in the round instructions. However, when comparing two floating-point numbers, the comparisons take place as though the numbers were both in normalized form, even though the forms of the numbers are not changed by the comparisons.

All floating-point instructions (fig. 13.9) are of either RR-type or RX-type format. In RR format, both operands designate floating-point registers; in RX format, the first operand designates a floating-point register, the second a main memory address. There are four floating-point registers, each 64 bits long. Their addresses are 0, 2, 4, and 6. The upper half (left-most 32 bits) of each register is used for short-format numbers, the full 64 bits are used for long-format numbers, and the two pairs of registers—0 and 2, and 4 and 6—are used for extended-precision numbers. In the latter case, the address of the first pair is 0, and that of the second is 4. A summary of the instructions that operate on short, long, and extended numbers is given in figures 13.2 through 13.4. The names and mnemonic opcodes of these instructions bear an obvious and useful similarity to those of the integer instruction set described in chapter 5.

Floating-point constants can be generated in Assembly Language with the DC directive and via literals. The E-, D-, and L- data type codes generate the short, long, and extended formats, respectively. However, unlike the provisions for converting numbers between the integer and packed-decimal formats via the CVB and CVD instructions, no comparable instructions exist for converting between integer and floating-point formats, or between packed-decimal and floating-point format. These conversions must be handled via subroutines. Similarly, there are no instructions comparable to PACK, UNPK, ED, or EDMK for converting numeric data between its input or output character representation and its main memory floating-point representation. These operations must be handled via subroutines.

Figure 13.9 Summary of floating-point instructions.

opcode and type RX	RR	instruction name	section	cond code	div-chk	exp-ovfl	exp-und	signif	V_1	V_2	result		
AD	ADR	Add normalized (long)	13.7	X		X	X	X	long	long	long	normalized	$V_1 + V_2$
AE	AER	Add normalized (short)	13.7	X		X	X	X	short	short	short	normalized	$V_1 + V_2$
AU	AUR	Add unnormalized (short)	13.7	X		X		X	short	short	short	unnormalized	$V_1 + V_2$
AW	AWR	Add unnormalized (long)	13.7	X		X		X	long	long	long	unnormalized	$V_1 + V_2$
	AXR	Add normalized (extended)	13.7	X		X	X	X	extended	extended	extended	normalized	$V_1 + V_2$
CD	CDR	Compare (long)	13.5	X					long	long	---	---	V_1 vs. V_2
CE	CER	Compare (short)	13.5	X					short	short	---	---	V_1 vs. V_2
DD	DDR	Divide (long)	13.7	X	X	X	X		long	long	long	normalized	V_1 / V_2
DE	DER	Divide (short)	13.7	X	X	X	X		short	short	short	normalized	V_1 / V_2
	HDR	Halve (long)	13.7				X		---	long	long	normalized	$\frac{1}{2}(V_2)$
	HER	Halve (short)	13.7				X		---	short	short	normalized	$\frac{1}{2}(V_2)$
	LCDR	Load complement (long)	13.7	X					---	long	long	(unchanged)	$-V_2$
	LCER	Load complement (short)	13.7	X					---	short	short	(unchanged)	$-V_2$
LD	LDR	Load (long)	13.4						---	long	long	(unchanged)	V_2
LE	LER	Load (short)	13.4						---	short	short	(unchanged)	V_2
	LNDR	Load negative (long)	13.7	X					---	long	long	(unchanged)	$-\lvert V_2 \rvert$
	LNER	Load negative (short)	13.7	X					---	short	short	(unchanged)	$-\lvert V_2 \rvert$
	LPDR	Load positive (long)	13.7	X					---	long	long	(unchanged)	$+\lvert V_2 \rvert$
	LPER	Load positive (short)	13.7	X					---	short	short	(unchanged)	$+\lvert V_2 \rvert$
	LRDR	Load rounded (ext'd to long)	13.7	X		X			---	extended	long	unnormalized	V_2 rounded
	LRER	Load rounded (long to short)	13.7	X		X			---	long	short	unnormalized	V_2 rounded
	LTDR	Load and test (long)	13.7	X					---	long	long	(unchanged)	V_2
	LTER	Load and test (short)	13.7	X					---	short	short	(unchanged)	V_2
MD	MDR	Multiply (long)	13.7	X		X	X		long	long	long	normalized	$V_1 \times V_2$ truncated
ME	MER	Multiply (short)	13.7	X		X	X		short	short	long	normalized	$V_1 \times V_2$
MXD	MXDR	Multiply (long to extended)	13.7	X		X	X		long	long	extended	normalized	$V_1 \times V_2$
	MXR	Multiply (extended)	13.7	X		X	X		extended	extended	extended	normalized	$V_1 \times V_2$ truncated
SD	SDR	Subtract normalized (long)	13.7	X		X	X	X	long	long	long	normalized	$V_1 - V_2$
SE	SER	Subtract normalized (short)	13.7	X		X	X	X	short	short	short	normalized	$V_1 - V_2$
STD		Store (long)	13.4						long	---	long	(unchanged)	V_2
STE		Store (short)	13.4						short	---	short	(unchanged)	V_2
SU	SUR	Subtract unnormalized (short)	13.7	X		X		X	short	short	short	unnormalized	$V_1 - V_2$
SW	SWR	Subtract unnormalized (long)	13.7	X		X		X	long	long	long	unnormalized	$V_1 - V_2$
	SXR	Subtract normalized (extended)	13.7	X		X	X	X	extended	extended	extended	normalized	$V_1 - V_2$

Notes: V_1 is the floating point number whose address is specified by the first operand.
  V_2 is the floating point number whose address is specified by the second operand.

  A result is considered to be zero if its mantissa is zero, irrespective of its characteristic.

SAMPLE PROBLEM
AND SOLUTION

PROBLEM STATEMENT

Write an assembly language program that will find the real roots (if any) of a quadratic equation with integer coefficients:

$$M x^2 + Nx + P = 0$$

where M, N, and P are arbitrarily given integers.

The three coefficients are given as input data in integer format, as follows:

$$\text{input card columns} \quad 1\text{–}10 : M$$
$$21\text{–}30 : N$$
$$41\text{–}50 : P$$

The results are to be printed on a single line of output for each set of coefficients that are read, with M, N, and P printed in integer format and the two roots X_1 and X_2 printed in external floating-point format. For example, if the equation is $3x^2 - 6x + 2 = 0$, then the results would be printed as

M	N	P	X_1	X_2
3	−6	2	1.57735E 00	0.422650E 00

SOLUTION PROCEDURE

The procedure will use the well-known formulas for finding the real roots of any quadratic equation whose coefficients are as defined above, namely

$$X_1 = \frac{-N + \sqrt{N^2 - 4MP}}{2M} \qquad X_2 = \frac{-N - \sqrt{N^2 - 4MP}}{2M}$$

doing the calculations with short-format numbers and considering these cases separately: $M=N=0$, $M=0$ and $N \neq 0$, $M \neq 0$ and $N=0$, $M \neq 0$ and $N \neq 0$. In the latter two cases, if the discriminant $N^2 - 4MP$ is negative, there are no real roots and a message to that effect will be printed.

We will assume that there exists an external subroutine named SQRT that we can call, with the result being returned in floating-point register 0. We also will assume an arbitrary number of input data cards, each with a set of integer coefficients representing an equation for which the real roots (if any) are to be determined.

And, finally, we assume the existence of external subroutines to convert a number from its external floating-point format to its internal single-precision format, and vice versa.

(Under certain conditions the solution presented here may not give answers with acceptable accuracy. A discussion of the types of conditions for which this may happen may be found in *Computer Methods for Mathematical Computations* by George E. Forsythe et al. [Englewood Cliffs, New Jersey: Prentice-Hall, 1977].)

Figure 13.10a   Overview of sample problem solution procedure.

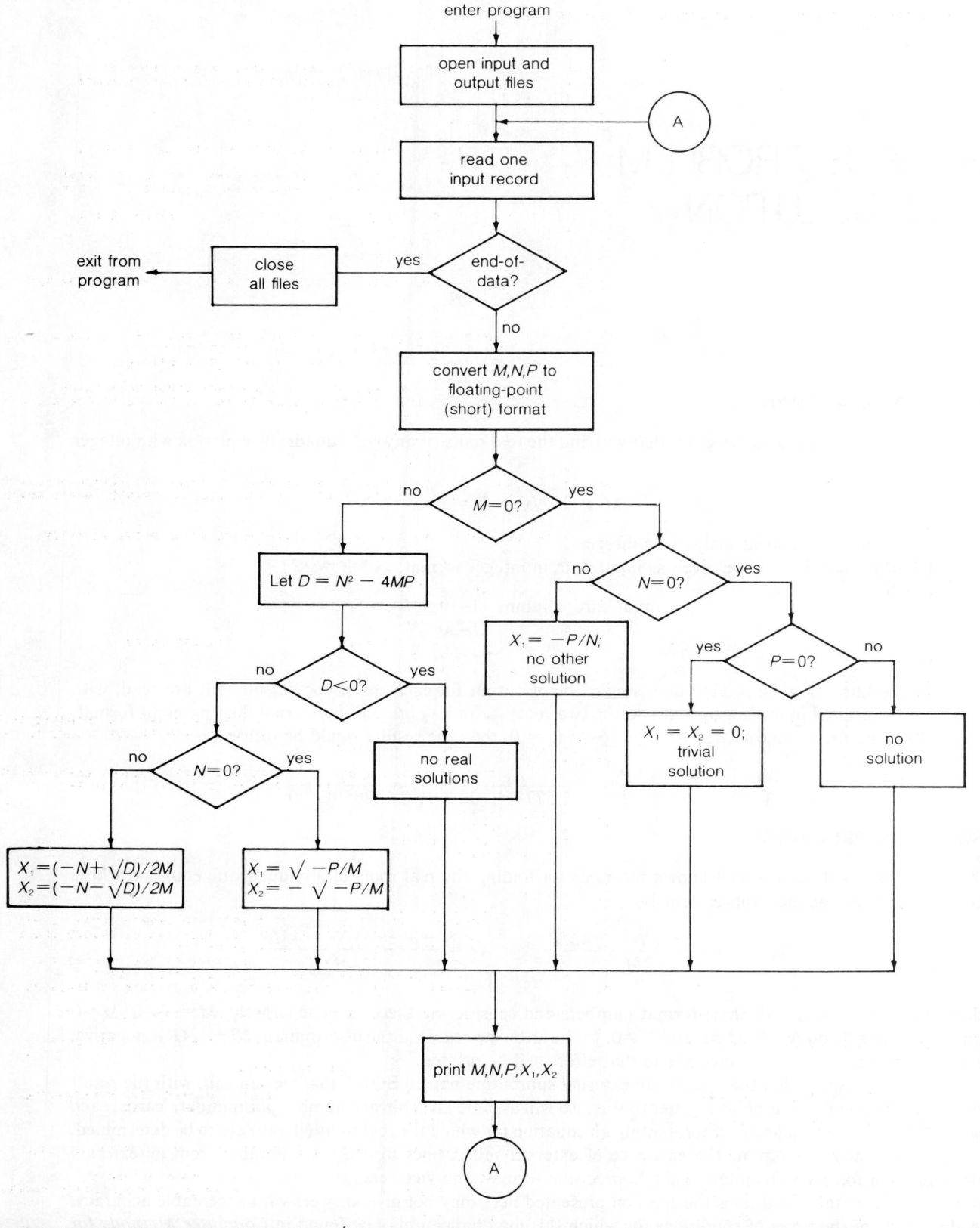

Figure 13.10b Solution to sample problem.

```
FLAG LOCTN OBJECT CODE     ADDR1 ADDR2 STMNT M SOURCE STATEMENT
     000000                                3 SPCH13   CSECT
                                           4 *
                                           5 * SPCH13 USES SHORT-FORMAT FLOATING-POINT ARITHMETIC TO
                                           6 *   FIND THE REAL ROOTS OF A QUADRATIC EQUATION WITH INTEGER
                                           7 *   COEFFICIENTS  M, N, AND P ...
                                           8 *
                                           9 *       M * (X**2)  +  N * X  +  P  =  0
                                          10 *
                                          11 *   IF TWO REAL ROOTS EXIST AND NEITHER  M  NOR  N  IS ZERO,
                                          12 *   THE ROOTS ARE
                                          13 *               X1  =  ( -N  +  (N**2 - 4*M*P)**(1/2) ) / (2*M)
                                          14 *               X2  =  ( -N  -  (N**2 - 4*M*P)**(1/2) ) / (2*M)
                                          15 *
                                          16 *   IF TWO REAL ROOTS EXIST AND  N = 0  BUT  M  IS NOT ZERO,
                                          17 *   THE ROOTS ARE
                                          18 *               X1  =  + ( -P/M )**(1/2)
                                          19 *               X2  =  - ( -P/M )**(1/2)
                                          20 *
                                          21 *   IF ONLY ONE REAL ROOT EXISTS (I.E., IF M=0 AND N IS NOT 0) THEN
                                          22 *   THAT ROOT IS
                                          23 *               X1  =  -P / N
                                          24 *
                                          25 *   OTHERWISE THE ROOTS ARE EITHER TRIVIALLY ZERO  (M = N = P = 0),
                                          26 *   OR DO NOT EXIST  (M = N = 0,  BUT  P  IS NOT 0),
                                          27 *   OR ARE COMPLEX (WHEN  (N**2 - 4*M*P)  IS NEGATIVE).
                                          28 *
                                          29 * THE COEFFICIENTS  M, N, AND P  ARE READ FROM INPUT DATA CARDS
                                          30 *   (ONE CARD PER EQUATION TO BE SOLVED) IN THE FOLLOWING FORMAT...
                                          31 *
                                          32 *       COLS  1-10    M
                                          33 *            21-30    N
                                          34 *            41-50    P
                                          35 *
                                          36 * EACH COEFFICIENT SHOULD BE IN THE RANGE  -2**24  TO  2**24 - 1.
                                          37 * THE COEFFICIENTS AND THE ROOTS (IF ANY) WILL BE PRINTED ON 'SYSOUT'.
                                          38 *
                                          39 *
                                          40 * THE FOLLOWING SYMBOLS ARE USED FOR THE FLOATING POINT REGISTERS
                                          41 *
     000000                               42 FR0      EQU   0         FLO-PT REG #0
     000002                               43 FR2      EQU   2         FLO-PT REG #2
     000004                               44 FR4      EQU   4         FLO-PT REG #4
     000006                               45 FR6      EQU   6         FLO-PT REG #6
                                          46 *
                                          47 *
     000000 90 EC D00C                    48          STM   14,12,12(13)        STANDARD ENTRY
     000004 05 C0                         49          BALR  12,0
     000006                               50          USING *,12
     000006 50 D0 C35A      000360        51          ST    13,SAVE+4
     00000A 41 D0 C356      00035C        52          LA    13,SAVE
                                          53 *
     00000E 58 10 C1BA      0001C0        54          L     1,MASK              SET PROGRAM MASK TO PROHIBIT INT-
     000012 04 10                         55          SPM   1                   ERRUPTS FROM SIGNIF & UNDERFLOWS
                                          56 * OPEN INPUT AND OUTPUT FILES
                                          57 *
     000014                               58          OPEN  (SYSIN,(INPUT))     INPUT IS 'SYSIN' INPUT DATA STREAM
     00001E                               64          OPEN  (SYSPRNT,(OUTPUT))  OUTPUT IS 'SYSOUT' PRINTER

                                          70 *   DOS *******
                                          71 *       OPEN  SYSIN
                                          72 *       OPEN  SYSPRNT
                                          73 ***************

                                          74 *
                                          75 * MAIN PROCESSING LOOP ...
                                          76 *       READS ONE INPUT DATA CARD
                                          77 *       CONVERTS THE THREE INTEGER COEFF'S TO SHORT-FORMAT FLO-PT
                                          78 *       DETERMINES THE NATURE OF THE SOLUTION (AS DESCRIBED ABOVE)
                                          79 *       CALCULATES THE SOLUTION WHEN IT EXISTS
                                          80 *       PRINTS THE COEFF'S AND THE SOLUTION, OR THE COEFF'S AND
                                          81 *       AN APPROPRIATE MESSAGE WHEN NO SOLUTION EXISTS
                                          82 *       REPEATS THE ABOVE PROCEDURE TILL END-OF-DATA IS REACHED.
                                          83 *
     00002A                               84 LOOP     GET   SYSIN,INAREA        GET COEFF'S FROM INPUT DATA
                                          89 *
     000038 45 E0 C152      000158        90          BAL   14,CONVERT          CONVERT THE COEFF'S TO FLO-PT
                                          91 *
                                          92 * SEE IF THERE ARE TWO NON-TRIVIAL ROOTS
                                          93 *
     00003C 78 00 C19E      0001A4        94          LE    FR0,FM              IF  M = 0  THEN TWO NON-TRIVIAL
     000040 32 00                         95          LTER  FR0,FR0             ROOTS DO NOT EXIST.
     000042 47 80 C0D0      0000D6        96          BZ    MZERO
                                          97 *
                                          98 * IF TWO NON-TRIVIAL ROOTS EXIST, SEE IF THEY ARE COMPLEX OR REAL.
                                          99 *
     000046 7C 00 C1A6      0001AC       100          ME    FR0,FP              LET  D = N**2 - 4*M*P
     00004A 7C 00 C3A2      0003A8       101          ME    FR0,=E'4'           D'S SIGN DETERMINES ROOT'S NATURE.
                                         102 *
     00004E 78 20 C1A2      0001A8       103          LE    FR2,FN
```

Figure 13.10b   continued

```
FLAG LOCTN OBJECT CODE     ADDR1  ADDR2  STMNT M SOURCE STATEMENT

     000052 3C 22                         104          MER     FR2,FR2
     000054 3B 20                         105          SER     FR2,FR0             FR2 =  N**2 - 4*M*P
     000056 70 20 C1B2      0001B8        106          STE     FR2,FD        LET D =  N**2 - 4*M*P
                                          107  *
     00005A 32 22                         108          LTER    FR2,FR2             IS  D  NEGATIVE
     00005C 47 B0 C064      00006A        109          BNM     REAL                IF NOT THEN ROOTS ARE REAL
                                          110  *
     000060 D2 27 C21EC3E2  000224 0003E8 111  COMPLEX  MVC    MSG,=CL40'COMPLEX ROOTS'
     000066 47 F0 C11A      000120        112          B       PRINT
                                          113  *
                                          114  * WHEN THE ROOTS ARE REAL AND NON-TRIVIAL, DETERMINE HOW TO FIND THEM.
                                          115  *
     00006A 78 40 C1A2      0001A8        116  REAL     LE     FR4,FN              IF  N = 0 THEN USE SIMPLER FORMULA.
     00006E 32 44                         117          LTER    FR4,FR4
     000070 47 80 C0A6      0000AC        118          BZ      NZERO
                                          119  *  IF NEITHER  M  NOR  N  IS  ZERO, THEN USE STANDARD QUADRATIC FORMULA
                                          120  *
     000074 41 10 C3A6      0003AC        121          LA      1,=A(FD)            COMPUTE  SQRT(D)
     000078 58 F0 C3AA      0003B0        122          L       15,=V(SQRT)
     00007C 05 EF                         123          BALR    14,15
     00007E 70 00 C1B6      0001BC        124          STE     FR0,SQRTFD          RESULT RETURNED IN FLO-PT REG #0
                                          125  *
     000082 7B 00 C1A2      0001A8        126          SE      FR0,FN              COMPUTE  X1 = (-N+SQRT(D))/(2*M)
     000086 7D 00 C19E      0001A4        127          DE      FR0,FM
     00008A 34 00                         128          HER     FR0,FR0
     00008C 70 00 C1AA      0001B0        129          STE     FR0,FX1
     000090 78 00 C1B6      0001BC        130          LE      FR0,SQRTFD          COMPUTE  X2 = (-N-SQRT(D))/(2*M)
     000094 7A 00 C1A2      0001A8        131          AE      FR0,FN
     000098 33 00                         132          LCER    FR0,FR0
     00009A 7D 00 C19E      0001A4        133          DE      FR0,FM
     00009E 34 00                         134          HER     FR0,FR0
     0000A0 70 00 C1AE      0001B4        135          STE     FR0,FX2
     0000A4 45 E0 C17A      000180        136          BAL     14,REVERT           CONVERT  X1 & X2  TO EXTERNAL FORMAT
     0000A8 47 F0 C11A      000120        137          B       PRINT               AND GO PRINT RESULTS.
                                          138  *
                                          139  *   WHEN  M  IS NOT ZERO  BUT  N = 0  THEN USE SIMPLER FORMULA.
                                          140  *
     0000AC 78 00 C1A6      0001AC        141  NZERO    LE     FR0,FP              COMPUTE  -P/M
     0000B0 7D 00 C19E      0001A4        142          DE      FR0,FM
     0000B4 33 00                         143          LCER    FR0,FR0
     0000B6 70 00 C1B2      0001B8        144          STE     FR0,FD
     0000BA 41 10 C3A6      0003AC        145          LA      1,=A(FD)            COMPUTE  SQRT(-P/M)
     0000BE 58 F0 C3AA      0003B0        146          L       15,=V(SQRT)
     0000C2 05 EF                         147          BALR    14,15               RESULT RETURNED IN FLO-PT REG #0
     0000C4 70 00 C1AA      000180        148          STE     FR0,FX1             X1 = + SQRT(-P/M)
     0000C8 33 00                         149          LCER    FR0,FR0
     0000CA 70 00 C1AE      0001B4        150          STE     FR0,FX2             X2 = - SQRT(-P/M)
     0000CE 45 E0 C17A      000180        151          BAL     14,REVERT           CONVERT  X1 & X2  TO EXTERNAL FORMAT
     0000D2 47 F0 C11A      000120        152          B       PRINT               AND GO PRINT RESULTS.
                                          153  *
                                          154  *   WHEN  M = 0  THEN TWO NON-TRIVIAL ROOTS DO NOT EXIST.
                                          155  *
                                          156  *    THERE ARE THREE POSSIBILITIES ...
                                          157  *   (1)  X1 = -P/N   IF  M = 0  AND  N  IS NOT ZERO,
                                          158  *             WITH NO SECOND SOLUTION.
                                          159  *   (2)  X1 = X2 = 0  IF  M = N = P = 0  (THE  TRIVIAL SOL'N).
                                          160  *   (3)  NO SOLUTION   IF  M = N = 0  BUT  P  IS NOT ZERO.
                                          161  *
     0000D6 78 00 C1A2      0001A8        162  MZERO    LE     FR0,FN              IS  N = 0
     0000DA 32 00                         163          LTER    FR0,FR0
     0000DC 47 70 C0F8      0000FE        164          BNZ     CASE1               IF NOT, THEN ONLY ONE ROOT.
                                          165  *
     0000E0 78 00 C1A6      0001AC        166          LE      FR0,FP              IS  N = P = 0
     0000E4 32 00                         167          LTER    FR0,FR0
     0000E6 47 80 C0EE      0000F4        168          BZ      CASE2               IF SO, THEN TRIVIAL SOLUTION.
                                          169  *
     0000EA D2 27 C21EC40A  000224 000410 170  CASE3    MVC    MSG,=CL40'NO SOLUTION'
     0000F0 47 F0 C11A      000120        171          B       PRINT
     0000F4 D2 27 C21EC432  000224 000438 172  CASE2    MVC    MSG,=CL40'TRIVIAL SOLUTION'
     0000FA 47 F0 C11A      000120        173          B       PRINT
     0000FE D2 03 C1AEC3AE  0001B4 0003B4 174  CASE1    MVC    FX2,=E'0'
     000104 78 00 C1A6      0001AC        175          LE      FR0,FP
     000108 7D 00 C1A2      0001A8        176          DE      FR0,FN
     00010C 33 00                         177          LCER    FR0,FR0
     00010E 70 00 C1AA      0001B0        178          STE     FR0,FX1             X1 = -P/N
     000112 45 E0 C17A      000180        179          BAL     14,REVERT           CONVERT  X1  TO EXTERNAL FORMAT
     000116 D2 13 C232C45A  000238 000460 180          MVC    PX2,=CL20'ONLY ONE SOLUTION'
     00011C 47 F0 C11A      000120        181          B       PRINT               GO PRINT RESULTS.
                                          182  *
                                          183  * PRINT THE COEFFICIENTS AND THE ROOTS
                                          184  *
     000120 D2 4F C1CCC246  0001D2 00024C 185  PRINT    MVC    OUTLINE,INAREA      MOVE  M, N, AND P  TO PRINT LINE
                                          186  *
     000126                               187          PUT     SYSPRNT,OUTAREA
                                          192  *
     000134 47 F0 C024      00002A        193          B       LOOP                GO GET NEXT INPUT CARD, IF ANY.
                                          194  *
                                          195  * WHEN END-OF-DATA IS REACHED, TERMINATE THE PROGRAM .
                                          196  *
```

Figure 13.10b continued

```
FLAG LOCTN OBJECT CODE      ADDR1  ADDR2  STMNT M SOURCE STATEMENT

     000138                          197 EOD      CLOSE (SYSIN)
     000142                          203          CLOSE (SYSPRNT)
     00014E 58 D0 C35A       000360  209          L     13,SAVE+4         STANDARD EXIT
     000152 98 EC D00C               210          LM    14,12,12(13)
     000156 07 FE                    211          BR    14

                                     212 *  DOS  *******
                                     213 *         CLOSE SYSIN
                                     214 *         CLOSE SYSPRNT
                                     215 *         EOJ
                                     216 ****************

                                     217 *
                                     218 *   INTERNAL SUBROUTINE ...
                                     219 *
                                     220 *        'CONVERT'      CONVERTS  M, N, P  TO SHORT-FORMAT FLO-PT
                                     221 *
     000158 50 E0 C1BE       0001C4  222 CONVERT  ST    14,CONVTX        SAVE RETURN ADDR
     00015C 41 10 C3B2       0003B8  223          LA    1,=A(M,FM)        CONVERT 1ST COEFF, M
     000160 58 F0 C3BA       0003C0  224          L     15,=V(CONVT)
     000164 05 EF                    225          BALR  14,15
     000166 41 10 C3BE       0003C4  226          LA    1,=A(N,FN)        CONVERT 2ND COEFF, N
     00016A 58 F0 C3BA       0003C0  227          L     15,=V(CONVT)
     00016E 05 EF                    228          BALR  14,15
     000170 41 10 C3C6       0003CC  229          LA    1,=A(P,FP)        CONVERT 3RD COEFF, P
     000174 58 F0 C3BA       0003C0  230          L     15,=V(CONVT)
     000178 05 EF                    231          BALR  14,15
     00017A 58 E0 C1BE       0001C4  232          L     14,CONVTX        RETURN TO CALLER.
     00017E 07 FE                    233          BR    14
                                     234 * INTERNAL SUBROUTINE ...
                                     235 *
                                     236 *        'REVERT'      CONVERTS  X1 & X2  TO EXTERNAL FORMAT
                                     237 *
     000180 50 E0 C1BE       0001C4  238 REVERT   ST    14,CONVTX        SAVE RETURN ADDR
     000184 D2 27 C21EC46E 000224 000474 239       MVC   MSG,=CL40' '     CLEAR THE PRINT AREAS
     00018A 41 10 C3CE       0003D4  240          LA    1,=A(FX1,PX1)     CONVERT 1ST ROOT, X1
     00018E 58 F0 C3D6       0003DC  241          L     15,=V(DECONVT)
     000192 05 EF                    242          BALR  14,15
     000194 41 10 C3DA       0003E0  243          LA    1,=A(FX2,PX2)     CONVERT 2ND ROOT, X2
     000198 58 F0 C3D6       0003DC  244          L     15,=V(DECONVT)
     00019C 05 EF                    245          BALR  14,15
     00019E 58 E0 C1BE       0001C4  246          L     14,CONVTX        RECOVER RETURN ADDR
     0001A2 07 FE                    247          BR    14
                                     248 *
                                     249 *  CONSTANTS  AND  DATA AREAS
                                     250 *
     0001A4                          251 FM       DS    E                SPACE FOR FLO-PT  M
     0001A8                          252 FN       DS    E                SPACE FOR FLO-PT  N
     0001AC                          253 FP       DS    E                SPACE FOR FLO-PT  P
     0001B0                          254 FX1      DS    E                SPACE FOR ROOT  X1
     0001B4                          255 FX2      DS    E                SPACE FOR ROOT  X2
     0001B8                          256 FD       DS    E                SPACE FOR FLO-PT  D = N**2 - 4*M*P
     0001BC                          257 SQRTFD   DS    E                SPACE FOR SQRT(D)
     0001C0                          258          DS    0F
     0001C0 0C000000                 259 MASK     DC    X'0C000000'       MASK FOR SIGNIF AND UNDERFLOW ERRS
     0001C4                          260 CONVTX   DS    F                SAVE AREA FOR REG 14 DURING CONV'N.
                                     261 *
                                     262 * OUTPUT AREA
                                     263 *
     0001C8                          264 OUTAREA  DS    0CL132           DEFINITION OF OUTPUT AREA
     0001C8 4040404040404040         265          DC    CL10' '          COLS 1-10   BLANKS
     0001D2                          266 OUTLINE  DS    CL80             11-90   INPUT DATA CARD
     000222 4040                     267          DC    CL2' '           91-92   BLANKS
     000224                          268 MSG      DS    0CL40            93-132  ROOT MESSAGE AREA
     000224                          269 PX1      DS    CL20             93-112  1ST ROOT AREA
     000238                          270 PX2      DS    CL20             113-132 2ND ROOT AREA
                                     271 *
                                     272 * INPUT AREA
                                     273 *
     00024C                          274 INAREA   DS    0CL80            DEFINITION OF INPUT AREA ...
     00024C                          275 M        DS    CL10             COLS 1-10   1ST COEFF,  M
     000256                          276          DS    CL10             11-20   UNUSED
     000260                          277 N        DS    CL10             21-30   2ND COEFF,  N
     00026A                          278          DS    CL10             31-40   UNUSED
     000274                          279 P        DS    CL10             41-50   3RD COEFF,  P
     00027E                          280          DS    CL30             51-80   UNUSED
                                     281 *
                                     282 * DCB'S FOR INPUT AND OUTPUT FILES
                                     283 *
     00029C                          284 SYSIN    DCB   DSORG=PS,MACRF=(GM),DDNAME=SYSIN,EODAD=EOD,       X
                                     285          RECFM=FB,LRECL=80,BLKSIZE=4080
                                     337 *
     0002FC                          338 SYSPRNT  DCB   DSORG=PS,MACRF=(PM),DDNAME=SYSPRINT,              X
                                     339          RECFM=FB,LRECL=132,BLKSIZE=4092
                                     391 *  DOS  *******
                                     392 *SYSIN   DTFCD DEVADDR=SYSIPT,WORKA=YES,IOAREA1=INBUF,EOFADDR=EOD,   X
                                     393 *              DEVICE=2540
                                     394 *SYSPRNT DTFPR DEVADDR=SYSLST,WORKA=YES,IOAREA1=OUTBUF,BLKSIZE=132,   X
                                     395 *              DEVICE=1403
```

Figure 13.10b   continued

```
FLAG LOCTN OBJECT CODE    ADDR1  ADDR2  STMNT M SOURCE STATEMENT
                                         396   *
                                         397   *INBUF    DS     CL80
                                         398   *OUTBUF   DC     CL132' '
                                         399   ****************

                                         400   *
                                         401   * SAVE AREA
                                         402   *
      00035C                             403   SAVE     DS     18F

                                         404   *  DOS  ******
                                         405   *SAVE     DS     9D
                                         406   ***************

                                         407   * LITERALS
      0003A8 41400000                    409                  =E'4'
      0003AC 000001B8                    410                  =A(FD)
      0003B0 00000000                    411                  =V(SQRT)
      0003B4 00000000                    412                  =E'0'
      0003B8 0000024C000001A4            413                  =A(M,FM)
      0003C0 00000000                    414                  =V(CONVT)
      0003C4 00000260000001A8            415                  =A(N,FN)
      0003CC 000002740000001AC           416                  =A(P,FP)
      0003D4 000001B800000224            417                  =A(FX1,PX1)
      0003DC 00000000                    418                  =V(DECONVT)
      0003E0 000001B400000238            419                  =A(FX2,PX2)
      0003E8 C3D6D4D7D3C5E740            420                  =CL40'COMPLEX ROOTS'
      000410 D5D640E2D6D3E4E3            421                  =CL40'NO SOLUTION'
      000438 E3D9C9E5C9C1D340            422                  =CL40'TRIVIAL SOLUTION'
      000460 D6D5D3E840D6D5C5            423                  =CL20'ONLY ONE SOLUTION'
      000474 4040404040404040            424                  =CL40' '
                                         425            END
```

CROSS-REFERENCE

```
SYMBOL    LEN   VALUE  DEFN    REFERENCES

CASE1    00006 0000FE 00174   00164
CASE2    00006 0000F4 00172   00168
CASE3    00006 0000EA 00170
COMPLEX  00006 000060 00111   00090
CONVERT  00004 000158 00222   00090
CONVT    00004 000000 00414   00224   00227   00230
CONVTX   00004 0001C4 00260   00222   00232   00238   00246
DECONVT  00004 000000 00418   00241   00244
EOD      00004 000138 00199   00306
FD       00004 0001B8 00256   00106   00121   00144   00145   00410
FM       00004 0001A4 00251   00094   00127   00133   00142   00223   00413
FN       00004 0001A8 00252   00103   00116   00126   00131   00162   00176   00226   00415
FP       00004 0001AC 00253   00100   00166   00175   00229   00416
FR0      00001 000000 00042   00094   00095   00095   00100   00101   00105   00124   00126   00127   00128   00128   00129   00130
                             00131   00132   00132   00133   00134   00134   00135   00141   00142   00143   00143   00144   00148
                             00149   00149   00150   00162   00163   00163   00166   00167   00167   00175   00176   00177   00177
                             00178
FR2      00001 000002 00043   00103   00104   00104   00105   00106   00108   00108
FR4      00001 000004 00044   00116   00117   00117
FR6      00001 000006 00045
FX1      00004 0001B0 00254   00129   00148   00178   00240   00417
FX2      00004 0001B4 00255   00135   00150   00174   00243   00419
INAREA   00050 00024C 00274   00086   00185
LOOP     00004 00002A 00085   00193
M        0000A 00024C 00275   00223   00413
MASK     00004 0001C0 00259   00054
MSG      00028 000224 00268   00111   00170   00172   00239
MZERO    00004 000006 00162   00096
N        0000A 000260 00277   00226   00415
NZERO    00004 0000AC 00141   00118
OUTAREA  00084 0001C8 00264   00189
OUTLINE  00050 000102 00266   00185
P        0000A 000274 00279   00229   00416
PRINT    00006 000120 00185   00112   00137   00152   00171   00173   00181
PX1      00014 000224 00269   00240   00417
PX2      00014 000238 00270   00180   00243   00419
REAL     00004 00006A 00116   00109
REVERT   00004 000180 00238   00136   00151   00179
SAVE     00004 00035C 00403   00051   00052   00209
SPCH13   00001 000000 00003
SQRT     00004 000000 00411   00122   00146
SQRTFD   00004 0001BC 00257   00124   00130
SYSIN    00004 00029C 00285   00062   00085   00201
SYSPRNT  00004 0002FC 00339   00068   00188   00207
```

EXERCISES

1. Convert each of the following numbers from its short-format floating-point representation (shown here) to its representation in the decimal system's scientific notation. No more than six significant digits are necessary (e.g., $41100000 = 1.0 \times 10^6$).

   a. 41800000
   b. C1800000
   c. 3F800000
   d. 40400000

   e. 42880000
   f. BE880000
   g. 00000000
   h. 00000001

   i. 4E000001
   j. C8800000
   k. 7FFFFFFF
   l. FFFFFFFF

2. For each of the following questions, assume that W, X, Y, and Z are defined as follows:

W	DC	E'2'	SHORT-FORMAT REPRESENTATION OF DECIMAL 2
X	DS	E	ARBITRARY NUMBER IN SHORT FORMAT
Y	DC	D'0.1'	LONG-FORMAT REPRESENTATION OF DECIMAL 0.1
Z	DS	D	ARBITRARY NUMBER IN LONG FORMAT

   a. Write the floating-point instructions that will add the number at symbolic address W to that at X, and store the result at X.
   b. Write the floating-point instructions that will square the number at symbolic address Y and store the result at Z.
   c. Write the floating-point instructions that will determine whether the number at symbolic address Y is positive, negative, or zero.
   d. Write the floating-point instructions that will determine whether the number at symbolic address Z is greater than 4096.
   e. Write the floating-point instructions that will round the long-format representation of 0.1 to short format, and store the result at X.

3. Suppose that symbolic address R contains a nonnegative short-format floating-point number. Write the instructions (and constants, if necessary) to calculate the following quantities:

   a. The area of a circle whose radius is given at R
   b. The volume of a sphere whose radius is given at R
   c. The amount $A = (1 + r)^n$, where r is the number at R and $n = 5$
   d. The amount of $P = \dfrac{r \times 10^5}{1 - (1 + r)^{-n}}$, where r is the number at R, and $n = 5$

4. Assume that X is the symbolic address of an arbitrary short-format floating-point number. What run-time error conditions would or might occur when each of the following sets of instructions was executed? Why?

a.	LE	0,=E'0'		d.	LE	0,X
	SE	0,X			SE	0,=E'1'
b.	LE	4,X		e.	LE	6,X
	ME	4,=E'16'			HER	6,6
c.	LE	2,=E'1'		f.	LE	4,X
	DE	2,X			MER	4,4

5. Assume that Z is the symbolic address of an arbitrary long-format floating-point number. What run-time error conditions would or might occur when each of the following sets of instructions was executed? Why?

a.	LD	0,=D'10'		d.	LD	4,Z
	AD	0,Z			DDR	4,4
b.	LD	2,Z		e.	LD	4,Z
	LPDR	0,2			LRER	0,4
c.	LD	6,=D'1E10'		f.	LD	6,Z
	DD	6,Z			MER	6,6

6. As discussed in Sections 11.4 and 13.7, the Set Program Mask instruction can be used to prohibit program interruption when an exponent underflow or significance error occurs. Write the instructions (including the SPM) that would prohibit interruption from an exponent underflow error condition, and write the instructions that would prohibit interruption from a significance error condition. What instructions are required to simultaneously prohibit both these error conditions from causing a program interruption? What instructions are required to *remove* the prohibition of interrupts occurring in either of these two error situations?

7. What would be the result if each of the following sets of instructions were executed while interrupts for exponent underflow and significance errors were prohibited? What would be the effect if they were executed while those interrupts were *not* prohibited?

a.	LE	2,=E'1'		c.	LD	2,=D'1'
	SE	2,=E'1'			AD	2,=D'−1'
b.	LD	4,=D'1E-40'		d.	LD	6,=D'1E−40'
	MDR	4,4			DD	6,=D'−1E40'

8. When m and n are integers such that $0 \le m \le n$, then the coefficient B_{mn} of the mth term in the binomial expansion of $(x+a)^n$ is known as the *binomial* coefficient; it is usually written as $\binom{n}{m}$. Thus,

$$(x + a)^n = \sum_{m=0}^{n} B_{mn} x^{n-m} a^m = \sum_{m=0}^{n} \binom{n}{m} x^{n-m} a^m$$

It is known that $B_{mn} = \binom{n}{m} = n!/[(n-m)!m!]$, where $n!$ is the notation for "factorial n," and is evaluated as $n! = n(n-1)(n-2)...(2)(1)$ for positive integers n, with the added definition that $0! = 1$. For example,

$$\binom{2}{0} = \frac{2!}{2!0!} = 1 \; ; \binom{2}{1} = \frac{2!}{1!1!} = 2 \; ; \binom{2}{2} = \frac{2!}{0!2!} = 1 \; .$$

a. Write a subroutine that will calculate the binomial coefficient $\binom{n}{m}$ for arbitrary integers m and n satisfying the relationship $0 \le m \le n \le 20$, assuming that both m and n are passed to your subroutine as short-format floating-point numbers. Do your calculations with single-precision arithmetic instructions.

b. Rewrite your solution to Exercise 8a, this time doing the calculations with double-precision instructions. Compare the results achieved using the two solutions for $\binom{n}{m} = \binom{10}{5}$ and for $\binom{n}{m} = \binom{20}{10}$. Note that both $\binom{10}{5}$ and $\binom{20}{10}$ can be represented *exactly* in short format, since $\binom{10}{5} = 252_{10} = FC_{16}$, and $\binom{20}{10} = 184756_{10} = 2D1B4_{16}$. What accounts for the discrepancy between the two solutions for these quantities?

9. The Newton-Raphson method for finding the real roots of an equation yields an especially simple iterative method for determining the positive square root of any positive real number x. If a_o is a good first approximation to the square root of x, then successively better approximations a_j are given by this recurrence relation:

$$a_{n+1} = \tfrac{1}{2} \left(a_n + \frac{x}{a_n} \right), \text{ for } n = 0,1,2,...$$

Using single-precision floating-point instructions, write a subroutine that will determine the square root of a nonnegative short-format number using this recurrence relation. Stop the iteration at the first value of n such that $|a_{n+1} - a_n| < 10^{-5}$. A simple first approximation is to let $a_o = \frac{1}{2}(x+1)$ when $x > 1$, and $a_o = 1$ when $x < 1$. How many iterations are required when $x = 10$? When $x = 100$? 1000 ? 10,000 ? How might a_0 be chosen so that the number of iterations is not so large when x is large ?

10. The series expansions

$$\sin x = x - \frac{x^3}{3!} + \frac{x^5}{5!} - \frac{x^7}{7!} + \frac{x^9}{9!} - ...$$

$$\cos x = 1 - \frac{x^2}{2!} + \frac{x^4}{4!} - \frac{x^6}{6!} + \frac{x^8}{8!} - ...$$

are useful for computing the trigonometric sine and cosine functions of an angle x given in radians, when $0 \leqslant x < 1$. (x radians $= 180x/\pi$ degrees, where $\pi = 3.1415926...$) When $1 \leqslant x \leqslant \pi/2$, the same series can be used provided x is replaced by $\pi/2 - x$, since $\sin(\pi/2 - x) = \cos x$, and $\cos(\pi/2 - x) = \sin x$.

Using single-precision floating-point instructions, write a subroutine that will compute the sine or cosine function for any x such that $0 \leqslant x \leqslant \pi/2$, with accuracy to at least five decimal digits.

11. Modify the subroutine written for Exercise 10 so that it will compute the sine or cosine for any angle x that is given as a short-format floating-point number. (Hint: Make use of these formulas: $\sin(\pi - x) = \sin x$, $\sin(3\pi/2 - x) = -\cos x$, $\sin(2\pi - x) = -\sin x$, and $\sin(2k\pi + x) = \sin x$ for all integers k.)

12. The sum of the first N positive integers, $1 + 2 + 3 +...+ N$ is $N(N+1)/2$. Derive a formula for the sum of the positive integers M through N: $M + (M+1) + (M+2) +...+ N$, and write a subroutine that will calculate this sum using your formula.

13. For the solution to Exercise 12, you obviously have the choice of using the integer arithmetic instructions of chapter 5, or the short-, long-, or extended-format floating-point instructions. What criteria should govern your choice?

14. One of the more rapidly converging formulas for computing π to an arbitrary number of decimal digits was derived in 1706 by John Machin:

$$\frac{\pi}{4} = 4\left(\frac{1}{5} - \frac{1}{3 \cdot 5^3} + \frac{1}{5 \cdot 5^5} - ...\right) - \left(\frac{1}{239} - \frac{1}{3 \cdot 239^3} + \frac{1}{5 \cdot 239^5} - ...\right)$$

Write a program that uses this formula to compute π with double-precision instructions. What criteria should determine when the calculations should be terminated? (For further information on Machin's formula and other methods of calculating π, see *A History of π* by Petr Beckmann [New York: St. Martin's Press, 1971].)

15. At C cents per gallon, it costs P dollars to purchase an amount of gasoline that is just sufficient to drive 100 miles in an automobile that gets M miles per gallon. What is the equation relating C and M to P? Suppose that 10 different values of C and 10 different values of M are given as short-format floating-point numbers in respective one-dimensional arrays, $C(J)$ and $M(J)$. Write a subroutine that will calculate the 100 values of P and store them in a two-dimensional array, $P(J,K)$. The arrays C, M, and P are to be passed to your subroutine.

16. A simple (though inefficient) sort routine is based on the principle of successively finding the nth smallest number in an array of N numbers, for $n = 1,2,...,N$. The routine is known as an "exchange," or "bubble," sort, and can be represented by this FORTRAN subroutine:

```
            SUBROUTINE XSORT(A,N)
            DIMENSION A(1000)
            M=N−1
            DO 50 J=1,M
            L=J+1
            DO 40 K=L,N
            IF ( A(J) .LE. A(K) ) GO TO 40
            X = A(J)
            A(J) = A(K)
            A(K) = X
    40      CONTINUE
    50      CONTINUE
            RETURN
            END
```

a. Write an assembly language subroutine that will sort N short-format floating-point numbers into ascending sequence, using the bubble sort algorithm described by the above FORTRAN subroutine.

b. Modify your sort subroutine so that it will process long-format numbers instead of short-format numbers.

17. The instructions for processing extended-precision floating-point numbers include the arithmetic operations of add, subtract, multiply, and round, but do not include counterparts of any other single- or double-precision instructions. For each of the following double-precision instructions, write the combination of instructions that will accomplish the same purpose for extended-precision numbers: LD, LDR, STD, LTDR, LCDR, LNDR, LPDR, CD, CDR. (NOTE: In an extended-format number, the low-order 64 bits is formatted like a double-precision number: the first low-order bit is a sign bit, the next 7 bits are the low-order characteristic, and the remaining 56 bits are the low-order mantissa. The sign bit is the same as the sign bit of the full extended-format number, but the characteristic is 14 less than the characteristic contained in the high-order 64 bits. Moreover, if subtracting 14 from the high-order characteristic would cause the low-order characteristic to be negative, then the low-order characteristic is forced (by the hardware) to be 128 more than its correct value.)

18. Provisions for simulating the extended-precision instructions on those IBM 360 and 370 systems that do not have this set as a hardware feature are described in IBM Publication OS/VS1 *Supervisor Services and Macro Instructions* (#GC24-5103). The same publication describes a method for dividing two extended-format numbers using a macro named DXR. Using the DXR macro and whatever other facilities are required, rework Exercise 14 to compute π in extended-precision arithmetic.

PART
FOUR

Directives

14
Cosmetic Directives

Directives that provide control over the appearance of source language statements on the listing, and over certain aspects of the validity of source language statements, will be referred to as *cosmetic directives*. Although the use of this term is not standard terminology, it is introduced here as a way to group the directives in this chapter under an appropriate heading.

Cosmetic directives can be used for the following purposes:

1. To begin a new page at any point on the listing (EJECT)
2. To put a title on each page of the listing (TITLE)
3. To create line spacing that visually separates adjacent bodies of statements on the listing (SPACE)
4. To suppress the printing of selected portions of a listing (PRINT)
5. To define additional mnemonic opcodes in terms of existing ones and to declare mnemonic opcodes to be invalid (OPSYN)
6. To require sequence checking of source language statements (ISEQ)
7. To define a nonstandard statement format (ICTL)

Skillful use of cosmetic directives is an art, and the technique is difficult to verbalize. But a skillful use of these directives in conjunction with comment statements significantly improves the readability and usefulness of a listing. The rules for using these directives are described in this chapter and are summarized in figure 14.2 at the end of the chapter. An example of the use of most of these directives is given in figure 14.1.

14.1 EJECT: BEGIN A NEW PAGE

The EJECT directive causes the line following it to be printed on a new page of the listing. Its format is

opcode	operand
EJECT	blank

An EJECT directive may appear anywhere in the source program and may be used any number of times. It is not printed on the listing. Its purpose is to separate different portions of the listing from one another, thereby enhancing the readability of the listing.

14.2 TITLE: DEFINE A TITLE LINE FOR EACH PAGE

The TITLE directive causes the first line of each page to be printed with a heading, or title, of up to 100 characters. The heading characters are specified in the operand field of the TITLE directive:

opcode	operand
TITLE	a text string of up to 100 characters, enclosed in apostrophes

The text string in the operand field may contain any printable characters, including blanks and punctuation marks. The string is printed beginning at the left margin at the top of each page of the listing. A TITLE directive may appear anywhere and any number of times in the source code, but it is not printed on the listing. For each occurrence of a TITLE directive, the Assembler begins a new page on the listing, using the text string from the operand of that TITLE directive for the heading line. The same heading line is used on each subsequent page until a new TITLE directive is found by the Assembler.

Two points should be noted. First, the TITLE and EJECT directives should not be used in consecutive statements, since each one causes a skip to a new page. And, second, two consecutive apostrophes or ampersands must be used to represent a single apostrophe or ampersand in a TITLE operand. Two consecutive apostrophes are used to distinguish the apostrophe to be printed from the ones that delimit the text string; two consecutive ampersands are used to distinguish the ampersand to be printed from the one that denotes the start of a variable symbol. For example:

source code		printed heading
TITLE	'MAIN PROGRAM'	MAIN PROGRAM
TITLE	' "PUSH" && "POP" ROUTINES'	'PUSH' & 'POP' ROUTINES

14.3 SPACE: INSERT BLANK LINES

The SPACE directive causes one or more blank lines to be inserted in the listing at the point where the SPACE directive exists in the source code. The number of blank lines to be inserted is specified in the operand field either as a self-defining decimal term or as a blank. A blank operand causes one blank line to be inserted. Thus, the format is

opcode	operand
SPACE	a self-defining decimal term
	or blank

A SPACE directive may appear anywhere and any number of times in the source code; it is not printed on the listing. If the operand specifies more blank lines than there is room for on the page to which the SPACE directive pertains, the blank lines are not continued onto the next page.

The SPACE directive is useful for separating minor sections of source code on a listing whenever a page break is not warranted. This greatly enhances the readability of the listing. For example:

source code			printed listing		
SEARCH	CSECT		SEARCH	CSECT	
	STM	14,12,12(13)		STM	14,12,12(13)
	BALR	12,0		BALR	12,0
	USING	*,12		USING	*,12
	ST	13,SAVE+4		ST	13,SAVE+4
	LA	13,SAVE		LA	13,SAVE
	SPACE				
	LM	2,4,0(1)		LM	2,4,0(1)
	L	2,0(2)		L	2,0(2)
	⋮			⋮	

14.4 PRINT: CONTROL THE AMOUNT OF DETAIL PRINTED

The PRINT directive controls the type and amount of detail printed in any portion of the listing. The control information is specified in the operand field by means of certain key words:

opcode	operand
PRINT	one or more key words, separated by
	commas

In the IBM 360 and 370 Assembly Language, there are three levels of detail that can be controlled by the key words. There are, correspondingly, three pairs of key words that can be used in the operand field:

key words	meaning
ON or OFF	whether or not any lines following the PRINT directive are printed on the listing
GEN or NOGEN	whether or not the statements generated in a macro expansion are printed
DATA or NODATA	whether the object code of a constant is printed in its entirety, or whether only the first 8 bytes of each constant's object code are printed

When the Assembler begins to assemble a source-module, it assumes that the ON, GEN, and NO-DATA key words are in effect for the listing. These are known as the *default* values of the key words. Each default remains in effect until explicitly changed by a PRINT directive in the source-module, with these exceptions: the key word OFF overrides the key words GEN and DATA, NOGEN overrides both DATA and NODATA within macro expansions, and both DATA and NODATA apply to macro expansions (as well as to other object-code constants) when GEN is in effect. Further details are given in the following descriptions:

source code	effect on printed listing
PRINT OFF	*No statement following this PRINT directive,* up to and including the next PRINT directive in the source code, *will be printed on the listing.*
PRINT ON	All statements following this PRINT directive, except those affected by NOGEN and NODATA, will be printed on the listing. The previous setting of the other two key word pairs remains in effect.
PRINT GEN	If ON is in effect from a previous PRINT directive or from the default value, macro expansions will be printed on the listing in all statements following this PRINT directive (up to a subsequent PRINT NOGEN, if any).
PRINT NOGEN	If ON is in effect, macro expansions that follow this PRINT directive will not be printed until a subsequent PRINT GEN directive occurs.
PRINT DATA	If ON is in effect, the object code of each constant defined by a DC directive is printed in its entirety up to the point where a subsequent PRINT NODATA directive occurs.
PRINT NODATA	If ON is in effect, only the first 8 object-code bytes of a subsequent DC constant are printed. (NOGEN overrides both DATA and NODATA for macro expansions; but, when GEN is in effect, both DATA and NODATA apply to macro expansions as well as to other object-code constants.)

Key words can be combined in a single PRINT directive. For example,

        PRINT   ON,NOGEN,NODATA

is equivalent to the following three directives, in the order given here:

        PRINT   ON
        PRINT   NOGEN
        PRINT   NODATA

The PRINT directive may appear anywhere and any number of times in a source-module. The occurrence of a key word in a PRINT directive cancels the effect of the opposite key word in that pair that may have occurred in a previous PRINT directive. Thus, PRINT ON cancels a previous PRINT OFF, PRINT GEN cancels a previous PRINT NOGEN, and PRINT DATA cancels a previous PRINT NODATA. To restore a previous setting, the programmer must know what that previous setting was and use the appropriate key word in a PRINT directive. In this way, portions of a listing may be put under control of one key word setting while other portions are under control of its opposite.

To facilitate switching from one key word of a pair to its opposite, the IBM 370 Assembler Language has two other directives, PUSH and POP. (These are available in OS Assembly Language but not in DOS.) The PUSH directive allows the setting of a key word to be temporarily suspended while its opposite is in effect; the POP directive allows the effect of the suspended key word to be restored without having to respecify it. This removes the requirement that a programmer know the settings that are in effect at each point of the source-module and is especially useful in macro definitions. (PUSH and POP can also be used to temporarily suspend and then restore the base register and base address information supplied by USING directives. We will not explore this capability further.)

To suspend the most recently established key words of a PRINT directive, the format of the PUSH directive is simply

opcode	operand
PUSH	PRINT

To restore the key words of the most recently suspended PRINT directive, the format of the POP directive is

POP	PRINT

Between any given PUSH directive and its matching POP directive, the programmer would normally have one or more PRINT directives to institute temporary settings of the key words. Additional PUSH and POP pairs can also be used between other PUSH and POP pairs. Up to four levels of pairs (a limit set by the Assembler) may be nested.

In addition to the PRINT, PUSH, and POP directives in Assembly Language, the job control language contains options that can be used to control the amount of printed detail on a listing. These options are described in the Assembler Programmer's Guide, in the section on Assembler Options, and will not be pursued here.

14.5 OPSYN: DEFINE A NEW MNEMONIC OPCODE

The OPSYN directive establishes a new mnemonic opcode in terms of an existing opcode. It can also be used to remove an existing opcode from the set of allowable opcodes. Its formats are

name field	opcode	operand
a new opcode	OPSYN	an existing opcode
an existing opcode	OPSYN	blank

The first format defines the opcode given in the name field to have all the properties of the opcode given in the operand field. The second format removes the opcode given in the name field from the set of allowable opcodes. The effect of both these formats is of course limited to the source-module in which they occur. For example,

source code	effect
BLE OPSYN BNH	the new opcode Branch if Less than or Equal (BLE) is defined to be equivalent to Branch if Not High (BNH)
ISEQ OPSYN	any subsequent occurrence of the ISEQ directive will be considered invalid

Note that too extensive use of the OPSYN directive would make the program difficult for anyone other than the programmer to understand. For this reason, the OPSYN directive should be used sparingly, if at all, within a program; or it should be used for the same opcodes by everyone in a programming shop so that the newly defined opcodes are available to and understood by all the programmers in that shop.

14.6   ISEQ: SOURCE-STATEMENT SEQUENCE CHECKING

The ISEQ directive is used to cause the Assembler to verify that the statements in a source-module are in the sequence in which they were intended to be. The verification depends upon sequence numbers that the programmer has placed in the identification field of each source statement. Although the identification field normally occupies positions 73 through 80 in standard format, its positions must be specified in the ISEQ directive. This allows nonstandard formats, or fewer than eight positions in standard format, to be sequence-checked.

The ISEQ directive is used in pairs; the first ISEQ of the pair initiates sequence checking, the second terminates it. The format for initiating sequence checking is

opcode	operand
ISEQ	p,q

The format for terminating sequence checking is

opcode	operand
ISEQ	blank

The sequence number of each statement is assumed to begin in position p and end in position q.

While the ISEQ directive is in effect, the Assembler compares the sequence number of each line of code in the source-module, including that of a continuation line, to that of the immediately preceding line of code. If the two sequence numbers are not in increasing sequence, a warning is printed on the listing. A line with only blanks in the identification field is excluded from the sequence-checking operation. For example,

source code	effect
ISEQ 73,80	Sequence checking of source statements begins with the line following this ISEQ directive. The Assembler uses positions 73 through 80 for the identification field.
ISEQ	The blank operand signals the Assembler to terminate sequence checking. Checking may be resumed at a subsequent point in the source-module by a statement of the form ISEQ p,q.

The values of p and q must satisfy the constraint $p \leq q$ or the ISEQ statement is incorrect. Note that if there is no ISEQ directive to terminate sequence checking in a source-module, sequence checking continues to the end of the module.

Other exceptions are discussed in the Assembler Language Reference Manual.

14.7   ICTL: DEFINE NONSTANDARD STATEMENT FORMAT

As mentioned in chapter 2, there are two essentially different statement formats allowable in the IBM 360 and 370 Assembly Language: standard format and nonstandard format. If you wish to use a nonstandard format, the first statement of a source-module must be an ICTL directive (itself in standard format). All statements following will be in the format described by that ICTL directive. No other ICTL directives are permitted in the source-module.

Using the ICTL directive, a programmer can specify the beginning position, the ending position, and the continuing position of the statements appearing in a source-module. Remember that the *beginning* position is the position that is used as the first position of the name field; the *ending* position is the last position of the comment field; and the *continuing* position is the first position that can be used in a continuation line.

Figure 14.1 TITLE, PRINT, and ISEQ.

In standard format, these three positions are defined as

b	=	beginning position	=	position 1
e	=	ending position	=	position 71
c	=	continuing position	=	position 16

To change one or more of these defined positions, the ICTL directive must be written in one of the following three formats:

opcode	operand
ICTL	b
ICTL	b,e
ICTL	b,e,c

In each of these formats, the letters b, e, and c represent decimal integers whose values obey the following constraints: $1 \leq b \leq 40$, $2 \leq c \leq 40$, $41 \leq e \leq 80$ and $b < c < e$, $b + 5 \leq e$.

If the first form—ICTL b—is used, the Assembler assumes that the value of e is 71, as it is in standard format. Moreover, if either the first or the second forms—ICTL b or ICTL b,e—are used, the Assembler assumes that continuation lines are not allowed, regardless of the values of b and e.

If the third form is used, the continuation field—position 72 in standard format—is redefined to be the position immediately following the ending position e. (If $e = 80$, there will be no continuation field and thus no continuation lines.)

Figure 14.2 Summary of cosmetic directives.

statement format	meaning	constraints
EJECT	begins a new page at the point in the listing at which the EJECT directive occurs	operand must be blank
ICTL b,e,c	defines the nonstandard format to be used by all remaining statements in the source module; b identifies the beginning position, e the ending position, and c the continuing position	must be the first statement in source module, with $b<c<e$, $b+5\leq e$, and $1\leq b\leq 40$, $2\leq c\leq 40$, $41\leq e\leq 80$.
ISEQ p,q	specifies that sequence checking of source statements is to begin, using the text string in positions p thru q; if p, q omitted, sequence-checking is terminated	$1\leq p\leq q\leq 80$
a OPSYN b	defines the new opcode a to be equivalent to the existing opcode b, unless b is omitted; if b is omitted, the existing opcode a is defined as invalid	if present, b must be a valid opcode; if b is omitted, a must be a valid opcode.
POP d	restores the PRINT and/or USING directive operands that were saved by the most recently occurring PUSH directive	d must be one of these: PRINT USING PRINT,USING USING,PRINT
PRINT k	the printing of subsequent statements and object code on the listing is controlled by the keyword k until the occurrence of a PRINT or POP directive that overrides k	k must be one of these: GEN or NOGEN DATA or NODATA ON or OFF
PUSH d	causes the Assembler to remember the operands in the most recent PRINT and/or USING directive	same constraints as in POP directive
SPACE n	causes n blank lines to be inserted in the listing at the point at which the SPACE directive occurs; if n omitted, one blank line is inserted	if not omitted, n must be a decimal self-defining term
TITLE '...'	begins a new page on the listing and causes the text string (indicated here by...) to be printed at the top of the new and subsequent pages until another TITLE directive occurs	the text string cannot contain more than 100 characters

Note: PUSH, POP, and OPSYN are available in OS Assembly Language but not in DOS

As Examples 1 and 2 show, an obvious purpose of the ICTL directive is to allow the use of statements in which the identification field occurs first, rather than last, in a line of source code. This facility could be useful if the source code were created with an on-line text editor that placed a line number in the first 8 bytes of each line of code.

Example 1.

source statement: ICTL   9,80,24
effect: $b=9$, $e=80$, $c=24$

Positions 1 through 8 are no longer available for the statement name field. The name field is redefined to begin in position 9. But positions 1 through 8 can be used for the identification field. A subsequent ISEQ directive such as

ISEQ   1,8

could invoke sequence checking using positions 1 through 8 as the identification field.

Note, however, that since $e=80$, there can be no continuation lines in the nonstandard format defined by this example.

Example 2.

$$\text{source statement: ICTL} \quad 9,79,24$$
$$\text{effect:} \quad b=9, \ e=79, \ c=24$$

The effect is the same as in the previous example except that the continuation field position is 80 ($= e+1$) since $e=79$. Thus continuation lines may be used, each beginning in position 24.

14.8 SUMMARY

The directives listed in figure 14.2 provide control over the appearance of the listing, the sequence and format of statements, and the use of opcodes. They have been grouped by the author under the term *cosmetic directives* for pedagogical reasons even though the term is not widely used.

EXERCISES

1. What rules or constraints, if any, exist at your programming center to standardize the use of each of the cosmetic directives mentioned in this chapter?

2. As a general rule of thumb, the directive PRINT ON,GEN,DATA would have the most utility in a source-module that was being debugged or modified, while the PRINT ON,NOGEN,NODATA directive would be more appropriate in a source-module that was a finished product, so to speak. If these rules were followed, would you have to specify all three key word options? Why or why not?

3. What would be the effect of two consecutive TITLE directives in a source-module?

4. What would be the effect of two consecutive EJECT directives in a source-module?

5. What would be the effect of a TITLE directive followed immediately by an EJECT directive or vice versa?

6. What would be the effect of the following TITLE directive:

   TITLE 'MNEMONIC OPCODES FOR IBM'S 360 & 370 SYSTEMS'

7. What would be the effect of the following SPACE directive:

   SPACE 500

8. Formulate and experiment with some rules of thumb concerning use of the SPACE and EJECT directives. Select the one that seems the most effective. Then use your rule in several of your programs, and re-evaluate it at a later date, modifying it if necessary. Compare your rule with the rules used by other programmers.

9. If the OPSYN directive is used in a source-module, it must appear before any assembly language instruction, and may be preceded only by the following directives: ICTL, EJECT, ISEQ, OPSYN, PRINT, SPACE, and TITLE. In view of this, what would be the effect if the following three statements were the first three statements in a source-module:

	ISEQ	73,80
ISEQ	OPSYN	
OPSYN	OPSYN	

10. As mentioned in the text, the ICTL directive makes it possible to have source-modules in which the identification field occurs first, rather than last, in a line of source code. Describe at least two other situations in which the use of the ICTL directive could be of some benefit in writing source code.

15

Pseudo-ops

Pseudo-ops, directives that can affect the value of the memory location counter at assembly time, may be used for the following purposes:

1. To define the beginning of a control section (CSECT, START, DSECT, COM)
2. To specify the end of a source-module (END)
3. To identify the entry points and external references occurring in a source-module (ENTRY, EXTRN)
4. To define constants, reserve data areas, and ensure proper boundary alignments (DC, DS, CNOP)
5. To designate implied base registers (USING, DROP)
6. To change the memory location counter (ORG)
7. To cause the Assembler to assemble the literal constants it has accumulated in the literal pool (LTORG)

In this chapter, descriptions of the CSECT, START, ORG, LTORG, and END pseudo-ops will be given. The others mentioned in the list will not be reviewed, since they were discussed in previous chapters (see fig. 15.5). Since all five pseudo-ops to be discussed at this time are in some way directly dependent on the notion of a control section, we begin with a brief description of the concepts that will be needed.

15.1 CONTROL SECTIONS

Each assembly language source-module consists of one or more relocatable subdivisions known as control sections. There are two types of control sections: *executable* control sections, initiated by CSECT or START directives, and *reference* control sections, initiated by DSECT or COM directives. An executable control section can contain instructions, constants, and data areas. A reference control section contains neither instructions nor constants; it merely describes or reserves memory areas for use by executable control sections at run time.

The use of reference control sections was described briefly in chapter 9, but the use of more than one executable control section has not been discussed. Such use provides an alternative to writing separate source-modules when we wish to segment a large program into separate relocatable sections. Instead of being in separate modules, the executable sections can be within the same source-module. However, since each section is still separately relocatable, it must be written in such a way that control passes properly to another section regardless of the relative physical position of the sections in main memory at run time.

As indicated by figure 15.1, all the control sections of a source-module are assembled into a single object module that is the machine language counterpart of the source-module. Figure 15.1 illustrates a simple situation; there are only three control sections organized in a straightforward manner, although the capability to intermix statements from different sections in somewhat arbitrary fashion exists (as will be shown). Too arbitrary an organization can render a source-module virtually unreadable and difficult to modify, so it is perhaps wisest to employ several simple conventions regarding control section layout and organization.

Figure 15.1 *Relationship of control sections to source and object modules.*

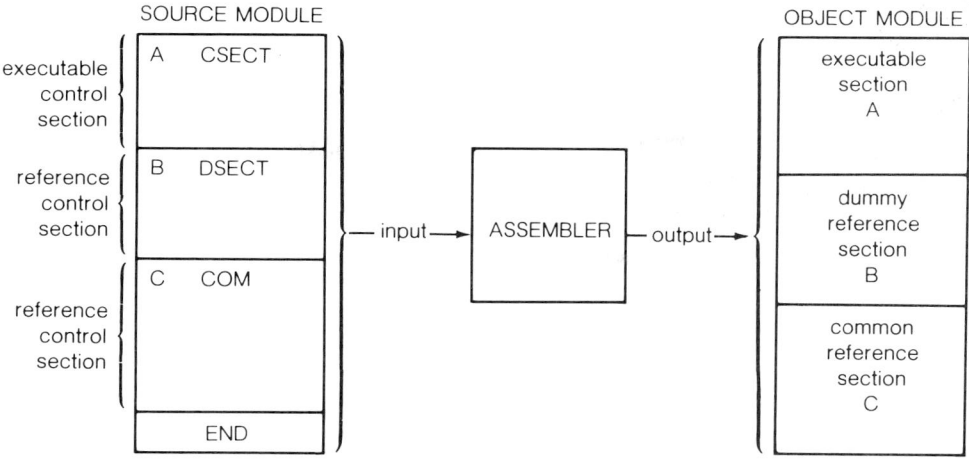

From the standpoint of this chapter, the most important point about control sections is this: *the assembler maintains a separate memory location counter (MLC) for each control section in a source-module.* This means, of course, that the addresses assigned to symbols defined in one control section are independent of the addresses assigned to symbols defined in any other control section. Therefore a separate implied base register (or registers) should be established for each of the control sections of a source-module.

In addition to establishing base registers for the addressability of control sections, a programmer must inform the Assembler on the key issue of which symbols are to be defined in which control sections. The CSECT, START, DSECT, and COM pseudo-ops are the means by which this is done.

15.2 CSECT

The Control Section (CSECT) pseudo-op is used to specify the beginning of an executable control section in a source-module. In those situations where statements from other control sections are intermingled with those of a given control section, CSECT must also be used to indicate the point at which any previously initiated executable control section is to be resumed. Figure 15.2 illustrates a simple case of initiating and continuing an executable control section.

Figure 15.2 *Continuing a control section.*

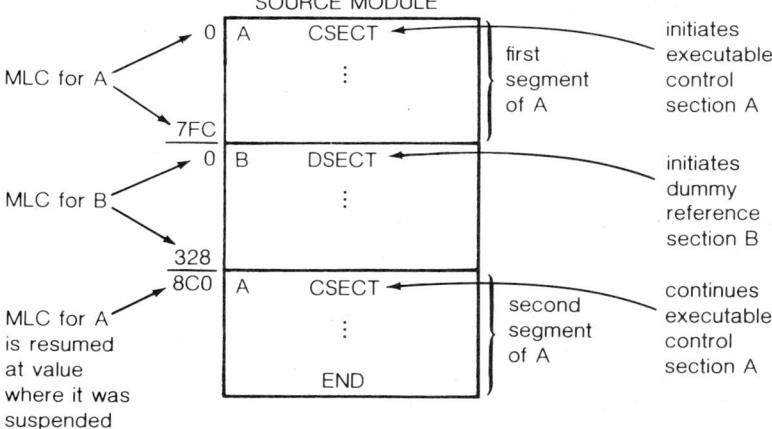

The format of the CSECT pseudo-op is

name field	opcode	operand
{any symbol} {or blank}	CSECT	blank

The symbol (if any) appearing in the name field of a CSECT directive is the name of the control section. This symbol is always considered to be a control section entry point, i.e., it may be referred to as an external symbol from within other source-modules without the necessity of specifying it in an ENTRY directive. If the name field is blank, the control section is said to be unnamed or private. Because unnamed sections cannot be referenced by other control sections, their use is generally not recommended.

In figure 15.2 the reference section named 'B' is placed somewhere in the middle of the source-module rather than at the end. To indicate where dummy section B ends and where executable section A resumes, there is a second CSECT with the same name-field symbol as that which initiated the executable section. When continuing a control section with the CSECT directive, the same symbol must be placed in the name field as that which was used to initiate the section. This identifies which control section is being continued; it does not result in a multiply-defined symbol. Note that when A is suspended by initiating B, the value of the memory location counter for Section A is remembered by the Assembler. Section B is assigned its own memory location counter with initial value zero. When section A is continued, its MLC is resumed by the Assembler at the value where it left off. In figure 15.2, this is assumed to be location 800_x. For another example, see figure 15.4.

15.3 START

The START pseudo-op has only one purpose: to denote the beginning of the *first* executable control section in a source-module. In this respect, it is not as flexible as the CSECT pseudo-op since the CSECT can be used to denote the beginning of *any* executable control section, including the first one. The main advantage of using START instead of CSECT is that START provides a clear-cut indication of where the first executable section begins.

The format of the START pseudo-op is

name field	opcode	operand
{any symbol} {or blank}	START	a self-defining term or blank

The symbol in the name field is the symbolic name of the control section being initiated. It is always considered to be an entry point of the control section. It is permissible to leave the name field blank, as in the CSECT, the result being an unnamed executable section that cannot be referred to from other sections.

The value of the self-defining term in the operand (if present) designates the initial value for the memory location counter of the control section. If the operand is blank, this initial value is zero.

Note that the START pseudo-op cannot be used to resume an executable control section; CSECT must be used for this purpose, even if START was used to initiate the control section.

15.4 ORG

The Origin (ORG) pseudo-op instructs the Assembler to change the value of the memory location counter of the control section in which the ORG occurs. The format of ORG is

name field	opcode	operand
{any symbol} {or blank}	ORG	a relocatable expression or blank

If the operand field contains a relocatable expression, the memory location counter is set to the value of that expression. If the operand field is blank, the counter is set to the smallest address that has not been previously assigned to any constant, data area, or instruction in the control section. In either case, the new value of the memory location counter is assigned to the symbol (if any) that appears in the name field of the ORG directive.

The value of the relocatable expression can be equal to, greater than, or less than the location counter value that it replaces. If it is equal to that value, there is essentially no effect other than to assign the value to the name-field symbol. If it is greater than the current location counter value, the Assembler skips over the intervening addresses and the corresponding bytes are unused.

Perhaps the most frequent use of ORG is to set the location counter back to a previous value in order to redefine an area of memory. The following example illustrates this:

source statement			effect
A	DS	50F	reserves 50 full words for area A
	ORG	A	sets value of location counter to value of A
B	DS	20F	reserves 20 full words for B, beginning at location A
	ORG	A	sets value of location counter to value of A
C	DS	16F	reserves 16 full words for C, beginning at location A
D	ORG		sets location counter to be 1 byte beyond the area reserved for A

The result is that the three reserved areas of memory—A, B, and C—each begin at the same address, as this diagram illustrates:

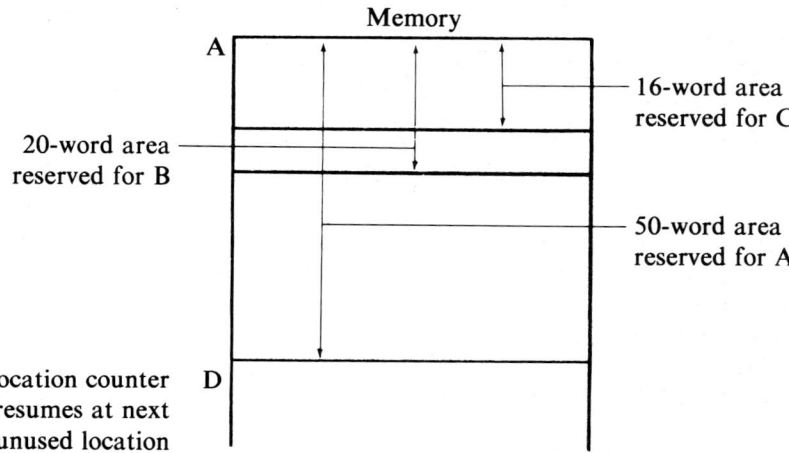

In FORTRAN, a result identical to that depicted in this assembly language example would be achieved by the following two statements:

DIMENSION   A(50),B(20),C(16)
EQUIVALENCE   (A(1),B(1),C(1))

As another example, consider this sequence of statements:

```
DATE     DS     CL6
         ORG    DATE
YEAR     DS     CL2
MONTH    DS     CL2
DAY      DS     CL2
         ORG
```

In this sequence, DATE is a six-character field, and YEAR, MONTH, and DAY are two-character fields superimposed on the DATE field as the next diagram illustrates.

```
DATE|   |   |   |   |   |   |→
     YEAR    MONTH    DAY
```

The same result would be achieved by COBOL data division statements such as

```
02  DATE.
    03      YEAR     PICTURE 99.
    03      MONTH    PICTURE 99.
    03      DAY      PICTURE 99.
```

One final observation: unlike the CSECT and START pseudo-ops (and the LTORG described in the next section), the ORG pseudo-op may be used in reference control sections as well as in executable control sections. It may be used any number of times in a source-module.

15.5 LTORG

The LTORG pseudo-op causes the Assembler to assemble all the literal constants it has accumulated. The phrase "assemble the literal constants" means that each constant in the literal pool is removed from that pool and assigned memory locations in the control section in which the LTORG occurs. The memory location counter for that control section is increased accordingly. (The first literal assembled each time a LTORG is processed is assembled on a double-word boundary.)

Although the LTORG pseudo-op is not required in a source-module, its use is recommended in any source-module containing more than one executable control section, because the Assembler always places all literals (from all the executable control sections in a module) into a single literal pool. If the LTORG is omitted, the Assembler will not assemble the literals until it reaches the end of the first executable control section. When this is allowed to happen, a literal from one executable section may be assembled in a different executable section! To prevent this from happening, these rules should be observed:

1. If there is more than one executable control section in a source-module, there should be a LTORG directive at the end of each of the sections.
2. If statements from different control sections are intermingled in a source-module, i.e., if one or more sections are "continued" as described in Section 15.2, a LTORG directive should occur at the end of each segment of each control section.

Except for these rules, there are no restrictions on the use of the LTORG directive. It may be used whenever you want the literal constants to be assembled in an executable control section.

The format for the LTORG pseudo-op is simply

name field	opcode	operand
{any symbol} {or blank}	LTORG	blank

If there is a symbol in the name field, its value is the address the Assembler would assign to the first literal (if any) that is assembled when the LTORG is processed.

15.6 END

The END directive indicates to the Assembler that there are no more statements to be processed in the source-module. It is, therefore, the physically last statement in the module. The format is

opcode	operand
END	a relocatable expression or blank

The operand is used to designate the first instruction that is to be executed at run time. If the operand is blank, the Assembler assumes that the first instruction to be executed is the first one of the first executable control section in the module. If the operand contains a relocatable expression, the value of that expression is the address of the first instruction to be executed.

When the END directive is processed by the Assembler, all control sections except the first executable section in the source-module are terminated. Any literals remaining in the literal pool are then assembled into the first executable section, and that section is terminated. These concepts are illustrated in figures 15.3 and 15.4.

Figure 15.3 ORG's and DSECT's.

```
FLAG LOCTN OBJECT CODE    ADDR1  ADDR2  STMNT M SOURCE STATEMENT

     000000                               3   MAIN    CSECT
     000000  05 C0                         4           BALR  12,0
     000002                                5           USING *,12
[T1FLD2 and T1FLD1 are in "MAIN," so assembler uses implied base register 12.]
     000002  D2 05 C018C010 00001A 000012  6           MVC   T1FLD2,T1FLD1
     000008  58 B0 C656        000658      7           L     11,=A(TABLE2)
     000000                                8           USING T2,11
     00000C  D2 05 B008B000 000008 000000  9           MVC   T2FLD2,T2FLD1
[At run time, base address is set to "TABLE2," so effective address gives access to fields within TABLE2 area.]
     000012                               10   T1      DS    (50)CL16
[T2FLD2 and T2FLD1 are in dummy "T2," so Assembler uses implied base register 11.]
     000012                               11           ORG   T1
[Implied base reg for dummy section, with displacements computed from base addr specified in USING directive.]
     000012                               12   T1FLD1  DS    CL8
     00001A                               13   T1FLD2  DS    CL6
     000020                               14   T1FLD3  DS    CL2
[ORG directive sets MLC back to T1's value, allowing T1 area to be redefined.]
     000332                               15           ORG
[ORG with blank operand sets MLC to largest previous value in this section.]
     000332                               16   TABLE2  DS    (50)CL16
     (000652)                             17   ENDMAIN EQU   *
[Dummy section has its own MLC, which always begins at 000000.]
     000000                               18   T2      DSECT
     000000                               19   T2FLD1  DS    CL6
     000008                               20   T2FLD2  DS    CL6
     00000E                               21   T2FLD3  DS    CL2
[Literals remaining in literal pool are assembled at end of first executable control section, beginning on double-word boundary.]
     000010                               22   ENDT2   EQU   *
     000658  00000332                     23
                                          24           END
```

Source listing (right panel):

```
         SPACE 2
MAIN     CSECT
         SPACE
         BALR  12,0
         USING *,12
         SPACE 2
         MVC   T1FLD2,T1FLD1
         L     11,=A(TABLE2)
         USING T2,11
         MVC   T2FLD2,T2FLD1
         SPACE
T1       DS    (50)CL16
         SPACE
         ORG   T1
         SPACE
T1FLD1   DS    CL8
T1FLD2   DS    CL6
T1FLD3   DS    CL2
         SPACE
         ORG
         SPACE
TABLE2   DS    (50)CL16
         SPACE
ENDMAIN  EQU   *
         SPACE
T2       DSECT
         SPACE
T2FLD1   DS    CL8
T2FLD2   DS    CL6
T2FLD3   DS    CL2
         SPACE
ENDT2    EQU   *
         END
```

Figure 15.4 CSECT's and LTORG's.

```
FLAG LOCTN OBJECT CODE    ADDR1  ADDR2  STMNT M SOURCE STATEMENT

                                          3   *  "A" IS FIRST EXECUTABLE CONTROL SECTION"
     000000                                4   A       CSECT
     000000  05 C0                         5           BALR  12,0
     000002                                6           USING *,12
[Y is in a different control section, so is not addressable via this section's base reg.]
     000002  58 50 C01E        000020      7           L     5,=F'10'
     000006  50 50 C016        000018      8           ST    5,X
     00000A  50 50 0000        000038      9           ST    5,Y
     000030                               10           USING B,11
     00000E  58 B0 C022        000024      11          L     11,=A(B)
     000012  50 50 B008        000038      12          ST    5,Y
[Y is addressable with dummy base reg and appropriate base address.]
[Can use A-type address constants for all symbols in a source module.]
     000018                               13   X       DS    F
                                          14           LTORG
[Forced assembly of literals for this section before start of new section.]
     000020  0000000A                         
     000024  00000030                         
     (000028)                             15   ENDA    EQU   *
[B's value prints as 000030, but it and the values of all symbols in Section B are controlled by B's MLC, not A's.]
                                          16   *  "B" IS SECOND EXECUTABLE CONTROL SECT
     000030                               17   B       CSECT
     000030  58 60 B010        000040      18          L     6,=F'20'
     000034  50 60 B00C        00003C      19          ST    6,Z
     000038                               20   Y       DS    F
     00003C                               21   Z       DS    F
                                          22           LTORG
[Forced assembly of literals for this section before resumption of previous section.]
     000040  00000014                         
     000028                               23   A       CSECT
[Resumption of Section A reinstates A's MLC, so that W is assembled as part of Section A.]
     000028  C1C2C3C4C5C6C7              24   W       DC    C'ABCDEFG'
                                          25           END
```

Source listing (right panel):

```
*   "A"   SPACE 2
*   "A"   IS FIRST EXECUTABLE CONTROL SECTION"
         SPACE 2
A        CSECT
         SPACE 2
         BALR  12,0
         USING *,12
         SPACE 2
         L     5,=F'10'
         ST    5,X
         ST    5,Y
         SPACE 2
         USING B,11
         L     11,=A(B)
         ST    5,Y
         SPACE 2
X        DS    F
         SPACE 2
         LTORG
         SPACE
ENDA     EQU   *
         SPACE 2
*   "B"  IS SECOND EXECUTABLE CONTROL SECTION
         SPACE 2
B        CSECT
         SPACE 2
         L     6,=F'20'
         ST    6,Z
         SPACE 2
Y        DS    F
Z        DS    F
         SPACE 2
         LTORG
         SPACE
A        CSECT
         SPACE 2
W        DC    C'ABCDEFG'
         SPACE 2
         END
```

Figure 15.5 Summary of psuedo-ops.

name field	opcode	operand	meaning	section
symbol	COM		initiate or continue a common reference control section	9.7
	CNOP	*b,w*	insert RR-type no-ops if necessary to force alignment of MLC to a specific half word within a full or double word	6.4
symbol	CSECT		initiate or continue an executable control section	15.2
symbol	DC	see Section 6.1	define one or more constants for use at run time	6.1
	DROP	r_n	inform the Assembler that one or more registers, r_n, are no longer to be used as implied base registers	9.6
symbol	DS	see section 6.3	reserve one or more memory areas for use at run time	6.3
symbol	DSECT		initiate or continue a dummy reference control section	9.7
	END	*d*	mark the physical end of a source module; *d* optionally specifies address of first instruction to be executed	15.6
	ENTRY	s_n	identify one or more symbols, s_n, that may be referred to from within other source modules	9.7
	EXTRN	s_n	identify one or more symbols, s_n, that are defined in other source modules and may be referenced in this source module	9.7
symbol	LTORG		instruct the Assembler to assemble all literal constants from the literal pool	15.5
symbol	ORG	*e*	force the MLC in this section to be set to *e*; if *e* omitted, force the MLC to be the largest address not previously assigned in the section	15.4
symbol	START	*t*	initiate the first executable control section, and set its MLC to *t*; if *t* omitted, set its MLC to zero	15.3
	USING	e,r_n	inform the Assembler that one or more registers, r_n, are to be used as implied base registers with respective base addresses e, $e+4096, \ldots$	3.5 9.6

NOTE: *symbol* = any valid name-field symbol
b,w = one of these pairs: 0,4; 2,4; 0,8; 2,8; 4,8; 6,8
d = any valid relocatable expression, or blank
e = any valid relocatable or absolute expression, or blank
r_n = a list of valid absolute expressions with values 0–15
s_n = a list of symbols
t = a self-defining term or blank

15.7 SUMMARY

The term *pseudo-op* is used in this text to denote directives that affect or depend on the memory location counter. As indicated in figure 15.5, many of the pseudo-ops described have been covered in previous chapters, and five—CSECT, START, ORG, LTORG, and END—have been discussed in this chapter. Each of these five pseudo-ops is in some way directly related to the concept of a control section.

A control section is a relocatable subdivision of a source-module. Each control section may be given a name that must be unique within the source-module and that constitutes an entry point of that section. CSECT or START may be used to define the beginning of executable control sections, but the use of START is restricted to denoting the beginning of the first executable control section in a source-module. DSECT or COM directives are used to define the beginning of reference control sections, DSECT being used for dummy sections and COM for common sections.

When there is more than one control section in a source-module, each section must begin with the appropriate directive and must be resumed with an appropriate directive if resumption is desired. When resuming a section, its name (if any) must be respecified in the name field of the directive.

Within a control section, the memory location counter may be changed by the ORG directive. The new value is specified by the expression in the ORG's operand field. This capability is especially useful for redefining existing data areas with concurrent but different logical structures and names.

The LTORG directive causes the assembly of all literals existing in the literal pool. Once assembled, a literal is removed from the pool so that it will not be assembled again. Appropriate use of LTORG can assure that literals will be within the range of a particular implied base register. This can prevent literals that are referenced in one control section from being assembled in a separately relocatable section.

The END directive denotes the physical end of a source-module. Its occurrence causes all literals remaining in the literal pool to be assembled. It also can be used to specify the address of the first instruction that is to be executed at run time.

EXERCISES

1. What are the differences between the CSECT and START directives?

2. What are the differences between an executable control section and a dummy control section?

3. Suppose a source-module consists of two control sections, namely an executable control section named MAIN and a dummy control section named DUM. What statements are required in the executable section to allow symbolic references to areas defined within the dummy section?

4. There are three ways in which the end of a control section may be specified in a source-module. One of these is simply to resume, i.e., continue, a previously defined control section with an appropriate directive. What are the two other ways of ending a control section?

5. In the following statements, the first occurrence of the ORG directive sets MLC back to the beginning of the area named TABLE1 in order to redefine the TABLE1 area with symbolically named fields. What is the purpose of the second ORG that occurs? What would be the effect if this second ORG were omitted without changing the other statements?

```
TABLE1    DS     (50)CL16
          ORG    TABLE1
FLD1      DS     CL8
FLD2      DS     CL6
FLD3      DS     CL2
          ORG
TABLE2    DS     (40)CL8
            .
            .
            .
```

6. When data are organized into a table, such as any of the tables discussed in chapter 10, it is often convenient to refer to the fields of any one table entry symbolically. The DSECT directive can be used to define the fields in a typical table entry; suitable instructions in the program can then allow one to symbolically reference any particular table entry. For example, in the preceding exercise, TABLE1 consists of up to 50 16-byte entries. If this table is defined in an executable control section named MAIN, the fields of each entry in the table could be defined by a dummy section as follows:

```
TABLE1    DS     (50)CL16
T1ENTRY   DSECT
FLD1      DS     CL8
FLD2      DS     CL6
FLD3      DS     CL2
MAIN      CSECT
```

What statements are required in the executable section MAIN to permit references via FLD1, FLD2, and FLD3 to the kth entry in TABLE1 for any integer k such that $1 \leq k \leq 50$? How does this technique differ from the use of ORG to define the fields, as in Exercise 5?

7. Write the assembly language statements that would result in memory being reserved in a manner analogous to the effect of these FORTRAN statements:

   a. DIMENSION X(40), Y(40), Z(80)
   EQUIVALENCE (X(1), Y(1), Z(1))

   b. DIMENSION X(5,5), Y(5,5), Z(10,10)
   EQUIVALENCE (X(1,1), Y(1,1), Z(1,1))

   c. DIMENSION X(5,5), Y(5,5), Z(10,10)
   EQUIVALENCE (X(1,1), Y(2,1), Z(5,1))

   d. DIMENSION X(10), Y(20)
   EQUIVALENCE (X(1), Y(10), W)
   (assume that W is a scalar variable; i.e., it is not dimensioned)

8. Write the assembly language statements that would result in memory being reserved in a manner analogous to the effect of these COBOL statements:

   a. 02   STUDENT.
              03 NAME   PICTURE X(40).
              03 I-D   PICTURE (9).

   b. 02   ADDRESS   PICTURE X(80).
        02   MAIL-ADDR REDEFINES ADDRESS.
              03 STREET   PICTURE X(35).
              03 FILLER   PICTURE X(5).
              03 CITY-ST   PICTURE X(30).
              03 FILLER   PICTURE X(5).
              03 ZIP   PICTURE 9(5).

   c. 01   TITLE.
              02 FILLER   PICTURE X(40) VALUE SPACES.
              02 FILLER   PICTURE X(50) VALUE 'STUDENTS ON DEANS LIST'.
              02 FILLER   PICTURE X(5) VALUE 'PAGE'.
              02 PAGE   PICTURE 999.

   d. 02   SALARY   PICTURE 99999 USAGE IS COMPUTATIONAL-3.
        02   SALARY-X   REDEFINES SALARY PICTURE X(3).
              88 NO-SALARY VALUE SPACES.

9. Compare the technique of including more than one executable control section in a source-module to that of placing each executable control section in a separate source-module. What are the advantages of the former over the latter? What are the disadvantages?

10. Under what circumstances could literals be assigned to memory locations whose addresses are beyond the range of all the implied base registers that were specified by USING directives? How could this be avoided without using LTORG? How could it be avoided by means of LTORG?

11. An ORG directive that is used to redefine a previously defined area, as in the solutions to Exercises 7 and 8, can be followed by any valid statements. But you should generally avoid following such an ORG directive with an instruction or with a directive that causes object code to be generated, if that

object code would overlay previously generated object code. For example, what would be assembled into the object module as the result of the following two sets of statements? What problems might this cause at run time?

a.
```
A1      DC      C'ABCD'
        ORG     A1
A2      DC      X'ABCD'
        ORG
```

b.
```
B1      DC      A(B1)
        ORG     B1
B2      DC      F'4'
        ORG
```

12. Prepare a source-module consisting of the following statements and assemble (but do not execute) the module. Note what happens to the address constants. Formulate a rule for address constants that contain symbols defined in dummy sections. Insert other address constants and reassemble the module to verify your rule. Is A(DY-DX) a relocatable or an absolute address constant?

```
A       CSECT
        BALR    12,0
        USING   *,12
        L       1,X
        L       2,Y
X       DC      A(DY)
Y       DC      A(DY-DX)
Z       DC      A(DX+DZ)
B       DSECT
DX      DS      CL3
DY      DS      CL6
DZ      EQU     DY-DX
        END
```

13. When writing a subroutine, one can include DSECT's to describe the parameters that are passed by the calling program, and the fields (if any) within the data areas that the calling program specifies with its parameters. With this in mind, suppose there is a need for a subroutine to compute the batting averages of baseball players, based on information passed via a table. Suppose also that the table is defined in the calling program as follows:

```
PLAYERS    DS     (50)CL22      Space for up to 50 player entries
           ORG    PLAYERS       Typical table entry:
NAME       DS     CL15          BYTES   0–14 player's name (given)
ATBATS     DS     P'+999'               15–16 # times at bat (given)
HITS       DS     P'+999'               17–18 # hits (given)
AVG        DS     P'9.999'              19–21 batting average (computed)
           ORG
```

Write a subroutine that will calculate the batting average of each player in such a table. Define a suitable set of parameters to be passed to your subroutine and define these parameters and the typical table entry by means of DSECT's so that the data can be referred to symbolically from within the subroutine. (Note: by definition, batting average = # hits / # at-bats, with $0 \leq$ # hits $\leq$ # at-bats.)

14. Suppose there is a need for a subroutine that will compute the percentage of *yes* votes and the percentage of *no* votes on each of several ballot propositions in a local election. Suppose that the calling program passes the number of votes cast and space reserved for the percentages, as defined in the following table:

```
VOTES     DS    (30)CL16        Space for up to 30 propositions
          ORG   VOTES           Typical table entry:
PROPNO    DS    CL2             BYTES  0-1 prop. I.D. # (given)
NYES      DS    P'9999999'              2-5 # yes votes (given)
NNO       DS    P'9999999'              6-9 # no votes (given)
PYES      DS    P'999.99'             10-12 % yes votes (computed)
PNO       DS    P'999.99'             13-15 % no votes (computed)
          ORG
```

Write a subroutine that will calculate the percentage of yes and no votes for each proposition in such a table. As in Exercise 13, define a suitable set of parameters to be passed to your subroutine and define these parameters and the typical table entry by means of DSECT's so that the data can be referred to symbolically from within the subroutine.

15. Write a main program (and create suitable test data) to call the subroutine that is written for the solution to Exercise 13. Then change the source-module that contains your main program so that it includes the subroutine of Exercise 13 as a second executable control section.

16. Write a main program (and create suitable test data) to call the subroutine that is written for the solution to Exercise 14. Then change the source-module that contains your main program so that it includes the subroutine of Exercise 14 as a second executable control section.

16

Conditional Assemblies

Although the Assembler normally processes the statements of a source-module in the order in which they exist, this normal processing sequence can be altered by the use of certain directives. Also, instead of being fixed at the time they are written, the content of statements in the source-module can be made to depend on the value of certain variables. If either of these conditions exists during the assembly of a source-module, we have what is known as a *conditional assembly.*

In this book, we will use the term *control directives* to denote the directives used to affect the outcome of conditional assemblies. These directives may be grouped conveniently according to their function:

1. Directives that enable the Assembler to skip over some specific statements in a source-module— AGO, AIF, and ANOP directives
2. Directives that create or modify variables whose values are used by the Assembler to determine whether and/or how to process a statement—GBLx, LCLx, and SETx directives

Before describing the format and purpose of each control directive, we will discuss certain concepts that underlie the use of these directives: sequence symbols, and assembly variables and their scope.

16.1 SEQUENCE SYMBOLS

Like an ordinary symbol, a *sequence symbol* identifies a source-module statement by its appearance in the name field of that statement. But unlike an ordinary symbol, a sequence symbol is not assigned an address when processed by the Assembler. Instead, sequence symbols simply indicate the position of statements in the source-module, so that the AGO and AIF directives can cause the Assembler to skip to certain statements during conditional assemblies and thereby select some for processing and reject others.

In order to distinguish a sequence symbol from an ordinary symbol (and from variable symbols, discussed in the next section), the first character of a sequence symbol must be a period (.). Of the remaining one to seven characters, the first must be a letter and the others, if any, must be either letters or digits. Examples of valid sequence symbols are

```
.A
.B1
.SEQ3
.XY31AB
.W100004
```

The following are invalid sequence symbols for the reasons stated:

B1	first character not a period
.1B	second character not a letter
.SEQUENCE	more than eight characters
.A B C	blanks not allowed
.X(3)	parentheses not allowed

A sequence symbol can appear in the name field of any statement except the following:

> GBLx and LCLx directives
> ISEQ, ICTL, and OPSYN directives
> EQU directives
> ACTR directives (not discussed in this text)
> COPY directives (not discussed in this text)
> DSECT directives in DOS (but not in OS)
> MACRO directives, and the macro prototype statement
>   (see chap. 17)
> Any other statement in which an ordinary symbol or
>   variable symbol already appears in the name field.

16.2   ASSEMBLY VARIABLES AND THEIR SCOPE: GBLx, LCLx, SETx

An *assembly variable* is a symbol whose value can be used by the Assembler to determine whether and/or how to process a statement in the source-module. The value of an assembly variable is not assembled into the object module; it is used only by the Assembler. (In most textbooks and reference manuals, assembly variables are called *SET symbols* because the SETx directive assigns values to them. This terminology is unsatisfactory in the author's opinion. Since we are talking about variables whose values are used by the Assembler while it assembles a source-module, the term *assembly variable* seems more descriptive and useful.)

In Assembly Language, an assembly variable is always represented by a *variable symbol,* which is a string of from two to eight characters, the first of which must be an ampersand (&). Of the remaining one to seven characters, the first must be a letter and the others (if any) must be either letters or digits. Examples of valid variable symbols are

> &A
> &B1
> &VAR3
> &XY31AB
> &W100004

In addition to the rules just mentioned for writing variable symbols, there is one other rule: the first three characters following the ampersand cannot be the letters "SYS." Symbols that begin with the characters &SYS are used as system variables (see Section 16.6). Therefore, examples of invalid variable symbols include

B1	first character not an ampersand
&1B	second character not a letter
&VARIABLE	more than eight characters
&A B C	blanks not allowed
&SYS2	begins with &SYS

There are three distinct types of assembly variables:

1. Arithmetic variables—values must be integers in the range from -2^{31} through $+2^{31} - 1$
2. Boolean variables (also known as logical variables)—values are always either 1 (true) or 0 (false)
3. Character variables—values are strings of from 0 to 255 characters

As will be seen, an assembly variable's type is always specified in the opcode of the directives GBLx, LCLx, and SETx: (1) GBLA, LCLA, SETA for *a*rithmetic assembly variables, (2) GBLB, LCLB, SETB for *b*oolean assembly variables, and (3) GBLC, LCLC, SETC for *c*haracter assembly variables. We will use the generic forms GBLx, LCLx, and SETx when the context is clear, and the specific forms GBLA, GBLB, GBLC, LCLA,..., SETC when it is necessary to make the distinction as to type.

In addition to its type, each assembly variable must be declared as having either global scope or local scope. GBLx directives are used to declare those variables whose scope is global, and LCLx those whose scope is local. Thus, *the declaration via GBLx or LCLx simultaneously determines both the scope and the type of an assembly variable.* No assembly variable can be declared as being both global and local, nor can it be classified as being of more than one type.

The scope of an assembly variable determines the set of source-module statements in which the value of that assembly variable is available to the Assembler. An assembly variable whose scope is *global* is one whose value is available to the Assembler in all statements that follow the first GBLx declaration for that variable. An assembly variable whose scope is *local* is one whose value is available to the Assembler either in the macro definition in which it was declared, or, if it was declared outside all macro definitions, in those statements that are outside macro definitions, i.e., in so-called open code. Since the concept of local scope is directly related to that of macro definitions, we will restrict our discussions and examples in this chapter to global variables. Macros and local variables will be discussed in chapter 17. Nevertheless, the following observations can be made (see fig. 16.1):

Figure 16.1   Global and local scope of assembly variables.

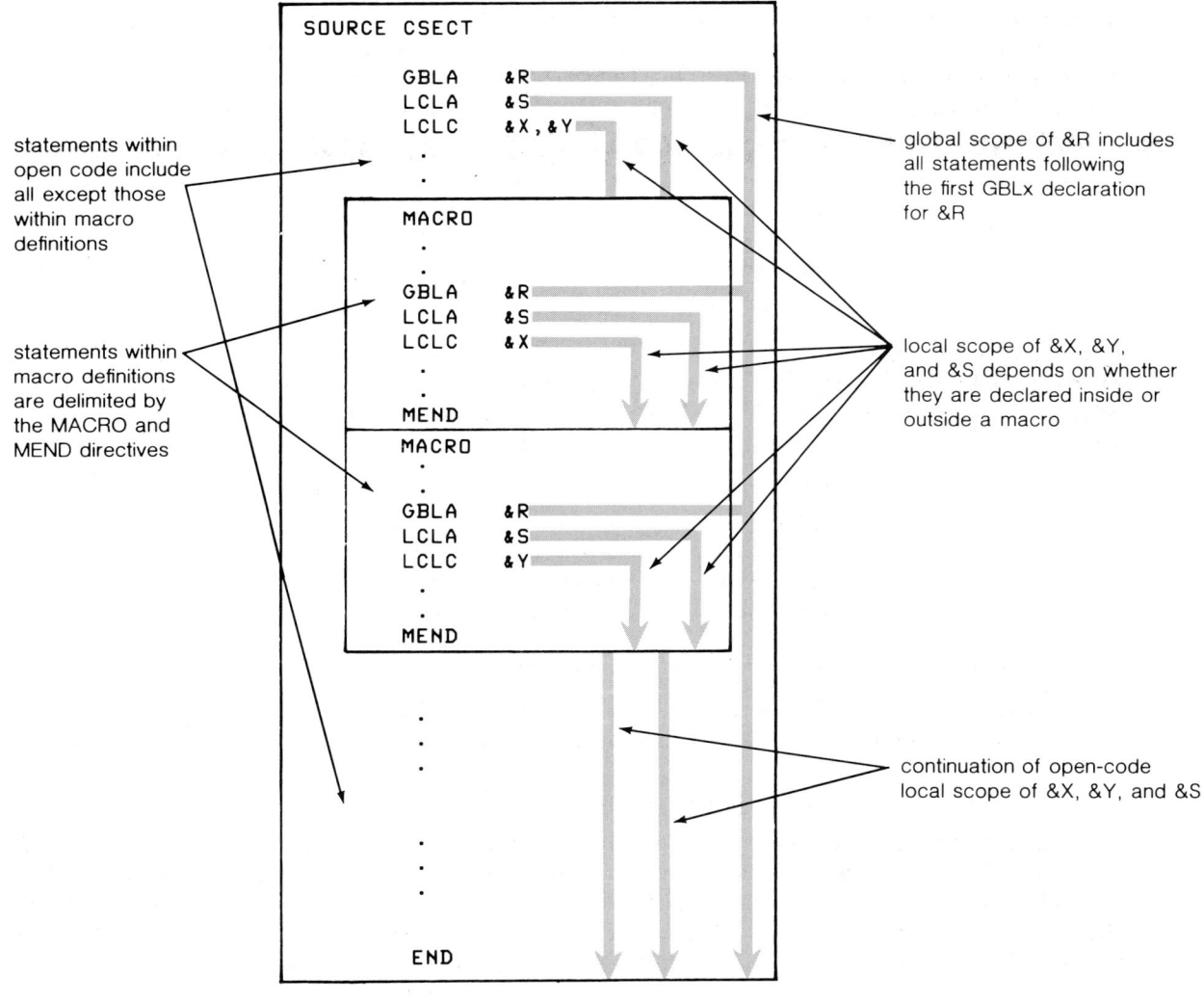

---

1. The initial values of global and local assembly variables are assigned by the Assembler according to the variable's type:

type	initial value
arithmetic	0
boolean	0
character	null string (a string of length zero)

2. The value of a global assembly variable is initialized the *first* time it is declared by a GBLx directive. Thereafter, its value can only be changed by a SETx directive.
3. The value of a local assembly variable is initialized *each* time it is declared by a LCLx directive. It also can be changed by a SETx directive within the variable's scope.
4. In DOS macros and DOS open code, GBLx directives must precede LCLx ones. Moreover, GBLx and LCLx directives in DOS open code must precede the first CSECT or START directive in a source-module.

The formats for the GBLx and LCLx directives are similar to one another:

name field	opcode	operand
blank	{ GBLA GBLB GBLC }	one or more variable symbols separated by commas
blank	{ LCLA LCLB LCLC }	one or more variable symbols separated by commas

For example,

source statement		meaning
GBLA	&X,&Y	declares &X and &Y to be global arithmetic assembly variables, each with initial value 0
LCLC	&UN,&L,&CHAR	declares &UN, &L, and &CHAR to be local character assembly variables, each with initial value null

The formats for the SETx directive are these:

name field	opcode	operand
variable symbol	SETA	an arithmetic expression
variable symbol	SETB	a boolean expression
variable symbol	SETC	a character expression

The opcode must be in agreement with the type of assembly variable identified in the name field. A SETx directive can be used any number of times in a source-module, but only after the corresponding GBLx or LCLx directive has declared the name, scope, and type of the assembly variable identified in the SETx name field. To be valid, a SETx directive must be within the scope of that assembly variable. The following examples illustrate this.

source statement			meaning
&X	SETA	&X+1	The operand is computed to be 1 more than the current value of the variable &X; the resulting sum is the new value of &X. &X must have been previously declared by a GBLA or LCLA directive.
&UN	SETC	'XYZ'	The three-character string XYZ becomes the value of the variable &UN, which must have been declared by a GBLC or LCLC directive.

It might be helpful if we illustrate the use of assembly variables in a simple setting: that in which a single global assembly variable is used to change the content of any number of source-module statements.

Example: Assembly Variables

Let us suppose that we have a source-module in which there are statements containing the name of a university or college. The school's name might, for example, occur in a character string defined by a DC directive such as

SCHOOL	DC	C'UNIVERSITY OF SAN FRANCISCO'

It also might occur in the operand of a TITLE directive

TITLE	'ASSEMBLED AT THE UNIVERSITY OF SAN FRANCISCO'

If we wanted the school name to be a variable instead of a fixed string, so that the name could easily be changed whenever it appeared throughout the source-module, we could define a global character assembly variable to represent the name, as follows:

	GBLC	&UNIV
&UNIV	SETC	'UNIVERSITY OF SAN FRANCISCO'

The GBLC directive declares that we want &UNIV to be a global character assembly variable. The SETC directive assigns the value UNIVERSITY OF SAN FRANCISCO to the variable &UNIV. The Assembler will substitute the value of &UNIV for every occurrence of &UNIV in the source-module. We would therefore write the following statements in place of those given earlier:

SCHOOL	DC	C'&UNIV'
	TITLE	'ASSEMBLED AT THE &UNIV'

Now, whenever we want to change the name of the university in the source-module, all we have to do is change one statement, namely the SETC directive that assigns a value to &UNIV. We would not have to change the DC statement or the TITLE statement or any other statement in which the school's name is represented by the variable symbol &UNIV. In other words, those statements would be assembled *as though* they contained whatever character string we put in the SETC operand.

This extremely simple example should help explain the power of assembly variables: by changing one statement in a source-module, we can cause many statements to be effectively changed. When this capability is combined with that of the AIF and AGO directives, the advantages are increased considerably (see Section 16.3).

16.3 CONDITIONAL ASSEMBLIES: AIF, AGO, ANOP

In addition to being able to substitute the values of assembly variables into statements at the time they are assembled, the Assembler can test the value of an assembly variable and make processing decisions based on the test's outcome. The tests are described in the operand of the Assembler IF (AIF) directive. The decisions are yes-no decisions; either process the statement following the AIF or skip to another statement whose sequence symbol is given in the AIF's operand.

The format for the AIF directive is

name field	opcode	operand
{sequence symbol or blank}	AIF	(logical expression) sequence symbol

The logical expression represents the condition being tested and must be enclosed in parentheses. If the value of the logical expression is true, then the next statement the Assembler processes is the one identified by the sequence symbol in the operand of the AIF directive. If the value of the logical expression is false, the next statement that the Assembler processes is the one immediately following the AIF. Thus, *the AIF directive is used to cause the Assembler to alter its normal statement-by-statement processing sequence, provided that the condition being tested is true.* We can say that the Assembler *conditionally branches* to the statement identified by the sequence symbol in the operand of the AIF directive. Note that it is the Assembler that conditionally branches at assembly time: the AIF directive is not assembled into the object module; therefore, it does not cause the program to branch at run time. Consequently, the logical expression in an AIF directive must contain only terms that can be evaluated at assembly time.

The logical expression states a relationship that will be either true or false. The relationship is a comparison of two expressions to determine whether the value of one of the expressions is equal to, less than, greater than, greater than or equal to, or less than or equal to the value of the other expression. Each of the two expressions can include assembly variables and constants that may be combined arithmetically (+, −, *, /) or logically (AND, OR, AND NOT, OR NOT). The following examples illustrate some of these concepts:

source statement		meaning
AIF	(&X EQ 1).X	If the value of the variable symbol &X is equal to 1, the Assembler branches to the statement identified by the variable symbol .X.
AIF	('&U' NE 'USF').W	If the value of the string represented by the variable symbol &U is not equal to the string USF, the Assembler branches to the statement identified by .W. Note the apostrophes around the assembly variable when it is a character variable.
AIF	((&X EQ 1) AND ('&U' NE 'USF')).T	If both conditions are true—&X = 1 and &U ≠ USF—the Assembler branches to statement .T.

Each of the six arithmetic relations

EQ	(equal)	LT	(less than)	LE	(less than or equal)
NE	(not equal)	GT	(greater than)	GE	(greater than or equal)

must be preceded and followed by a single blank character. Similarly, each of the four logical relations

AND   OR   AND NOT   OR NOT

must be preceded and followed by a single blank character. A blank must also precede the word NOT.

The Assembler GOTO (AGO) directive causes the Assembler to alter its normal processing sequence by directing it to branch to another statement without testing any condition. Its format is

name field	opcode	operand
⎰sequence symbol⎱ ⎱or blank ⎰	AGO	sequence symbol

The sequence symbol in the operand identifies the next statement that the Assembler is to process. For example, the statement

AGO   .V

will cause the Assembler to skip to the statement identified by the sequence symbol .V.

The Assembler No-Op (ANOP) directive provides a means of identifying a statement (and hence a position in the source-module) without causing any action to be taken by the Assembler. Its format is

name field	opcode	operand
{sequence symbol} {or blank}	ANOP	blank

Example: Conditional Assemblies

Suppose that we have an assembly language program that is to be used on several different IBM System 370 computer systems. Suppose that on some of those systems, the high-speed printer prints the symbol $\div$ for the division operator and that on the others it prints the symbol $/$. Also suppose that the EBCDIC codes for these two symbols differ from one another; for the symbol $\div$ it is X'5A', for the symbol $/$ it is X'61'.

One way to guarantee that the program will print the appropriate divide symbol is simply to write two separate source-modules, one for each of the two types of printers. Another way would be to write only one source-module that includes control directives that cause the appropriate divide symbol to be assembled. An outline of how this might be done is shown in figure 16.2.

Figure 16.2 Example of use of AIF, AGO, and ANOP directives.

Note 1: The three statements that include DIV DC X'5A' are processed by the Assembler only if the value of the global character assembly variable &DIVIDE is *not* equal to the one-character string '/'.

Note 2: The three statements that include DIV DC X'61' are processed only if the value of &DIVIDE is equal to '/'.

In figure 16.2, the GBLC &DIVIDE statement declares that the variable symbol &DIVIDE is to be used as a character-type assembly variable throughout the source-module. The GBLC directive also causes the Assembler to assign an initial value of null—a zero-length string—to the &DIVIDE variable. The statement following the GBLC directive

&DIVIDE   SETC   '/'

will be included in the source-module only for those computer systems whose printer prints the symbol /. For the other systems, the above SETC statement is not included in the source-module. The value of the symbol &DIVIDE will therefore be either '/' or '' (null) depending on whether or not the SETC is included. None of the other statements in the source-module have to be changed to accommodate the needs of the printers because of the manner in which the AIF directive is processed.

The AIF directive in figure 16.2 contains the condition that the Assembler will test: whether or not the value of the variable &DIVIDE is equal to the slash character, /. If it is equal to the slash character, the Assembler skips over the three statements that follow the AIF and resumes its processing at the statement whose name field contains the sequence symbol .SLASH. There it will process the statement

DIV   DC   X'61'

which creates the constant needed for the symbol / on the printer. But if the variable &DIVIDE represents the null string instead of the single character /, the AIF condition will be false, and the Assembler will process the statement

DIV   DC   X'5A'

and then skip down to the .DIVX statement. Therefore, only one statement would be assembled with the symbolic address DIV; it would be the statement that defines the appropriate divide symbol.

16.4   SYSTEM VARIABLE SYMBOLS

System variable symbols are variable symbols whose values are assigned by the Assembler. All system variable symbols are character variables; three are global variables, and three are local. A system variable symbol can be used in the operand of any source-module statement in which it is permissible to use a character assembly variable, subject to the restrictions governing use of global and local variables. However, the value of a system variable symbol cannot be changed by a SETx directive.

Global System Variables

The three global system variable symbols are &SYSDATE, &SYSTIME, and &SYSPARM. All are available in OS, but only &SYSPARM is available in DOS.

The value of &SYSDATE is the date on which the source-module in which it appears is assembled. The date is represented by eight characters in the form mm/dd/yy, for example, 03/31/80 for March 31, 1980.

The value of &SYSTIME is the time at which the source-module is assembled. The time is represented by five characters in the form hh.mm, for example, 13.30 for 1:30 P.M., and 01.30 for 1:30 A.M.

The value of &SYSPARM is the character string established by the PARM parameter of the EXEC command in job control language. Its length may be from 0 to 57 characters in OS, and 0 to 8 in DOS. For example, the following JCL

| *in OS:* | //STEP | EXEC | ASMFC,PARM=SYSPARM(SLASH) |
| *in DOS:* | // OPTION | | SYSPARM='SLASH' |

assigns the five-character string SLASH to the system variable &SYSPARM.

To illustrate the use of &SYSDATE and &SYSTIME, suppose that the date and time of assembly were March 31, 1980, at 1:30 P.M. Then the statement

DC   C'ASSEMBLED ON &SYSDATE AT &SYSTIME'

would be assembled as though it were written as

DC   C'ASSEMBLED ON 03/31/80 AT 13.30'

To illustrate the use of &SYSPARM, suppose that the EXEC command were the one given above, namely,

//STEP   EXEC   ASMFC,PARM=SYSPARM(SLASH)

Then the example of figure 16.2 could be simplified by eliminating the GBLC and SETC directives used for &DIVIDE and by replacing the AIF directive by the following directive:

AIF   ('&SYSPARM' EQ 'SLASH').SLASH

The effect would be the same as that previously described for the situation depicted in figure 16.2. The advantage of using &SYSPARM is that the source-module would not have to be changed at all, just reassembled.

Local System Variables

The three local system variable symbols are &SYSECT, &SYSLIST, and &SYSNDX.

The value of &SYSECT is the name of the control section in which &SYSECT is used. Its length is therefore from 0 to 8 characters.

The value of &SYSLIST is the value of a positional parameter in a macro instruction. Its length may be 0, 1, or more characters.

The value of &SYSNDX is a four-digit character string, 0001 through 9999.

The three local system variable symbols can be used only inside macro definitions. Consequently, further discussion will be postponed until chapter 17.

16.5 ARITHMETIC, BOOLEAN, AND CHARACTER EXPRESSIONS

As discussed in the preceding sections, expressions are used in the operands of SETx and AIF directives. There are three distinct types of expressions, each with its own rules of syntax and evaluation. In this section, we describe some of these rules so that somewhat more sophisticated conditional assembly situations can be considered. However, a complete discussion of the rules for forming and evaluating expressions is beyond the scope of this textbook and you are referred to the relevant portions of the *Assembler Language Reference Manual* for further information.

Arithmetic Expressions

An arithmetic expression can contain one or more variable symbols and self-defining terms that are combined by the operations of addition ($+$), subtraction ($-$), multiplication ($*$), and division ($/$). The variable symbols that appear in arithmetic expressions must have been declared in prior statements by the GBLA or LCLA directives. The value of an arithmetic expression is always either a signed integer or zero. Parentheses can be used within the expression to indicate the order in which operations are to be performed. If parentheses are omitted, the operations are performed from left to right, with multiplications and divisions being performed before additions and subtractions. In divisions, the quotient is always truncated to an integer, the fractional portion being dropped.

The following are examples of valid arithmetic expressions:

&X + &Y	the value of this expression is the sum of the values of the variable symbols &X and &Y
&Z*10	the value is ten times the value of &Z
−&Z	the value is the negative of the value of &Z
&A + &B/10	the integer portion of the value of &B/10 is added to the value of &A; the resulting sum is the value of the expression
(&A + &B)/10	the sum of the values of &A and &B is divided by 10; the integer portion of the resulting quotient is the value of the expression

Boolean Expressions

A boolean, or logical, expression can be used to assign a value of 0 or 1 to a boolean assembly variable. But its most frequent use in a source-module is as the condition that is tested in the operand of an AIF directive.

A boolean expression is always enclosed in parentheses, and it always has the value of 1 (true) or 0 (false). Although a boolean expression can be simply a boolean assembly variable, it is more frequently made up of a relation—EQ, NE, GT, LT, LE, or GE—between two arithmetic expressions or two character expressions. It can also consist of one or more logical combinations of such relations.

The following are examples of valid boolean expressions:

(&X NE 100)	if the value of &X is different from 100, the value of this expression will be 1 (true); otherwise it will be 0
('&UNIV' EQ '')	if the value of &UNIV is the null string, the value of this expression is 1; otherwise it is 0
((&X NE 100) OR (&X EQ &Y))	if the value of &X is either different from 100 or equal to the value of &Y, or both, the value of this expression is 1; otherwise it is 0
((&X EQ 100) AND (&X LT &Y))	if the value of &X is equal to 100 and is also less than the value of &Y, the value of this expression will be 1; otherwise it will be 0

Character Expressions

A character expression can have one of two forms. It can be either a string enclosed in apostrophes or it can be the concatenation of two or more strings, each of which is enclosed in apostrophes. In the latter case, the concatenation operator—a period (.)—must be used to separate the apostrophe that ends one string from the apostrophe that begins the next one.

A string in a character expression may contain variable symbols. The Assembler replaces each variable symbol in a character expression with the value of that symbol when it evaluates the expression. The variable symbol may be a character variable, a boolean variable, or an arithmetic variable. In a character expression, the value of a variable symbol is always a character string. Therefore, the value of a boolean variable appearing in a character expression will be either the character '1' or the character '0' and not the number 1 or 0. Similarly, the value of an arithmetic variable appearing in a character expression will be the characters that represent the numeric value of that arithmetic variable (except that the sign and any leading zeroes are not represented).

The value of a character expression is always a character string of from 0 to 255 characters. The examples shown below illustrate this. For these examples, we shall assume that &SYSDATE, &A, &B, and &C have had these values and types assigned to them:

&SYSDATE	=	03/31/80	(character variable)
&A	=	4096	(arithmetic variable)
&B	=	1	(boolean variable)
&C	=	USF	(character variable)

character expression	value of expression	explanation
'USF'	USF	The value of an expression consisting of a character string is just that string.
'&C'	USF	The value of an expression containing a variable symbol is the string that results after the value of that variable has been substituted in the expression.
'&A + 1'	4096 + 1	The value of an expression containing a variable symbol and a string is the string that results after the value of that variable has been substituted in the expression. *Note that no arithmetic is performed.* The value of &A is represented as a string, not as a numeric quantity.
'&A'.' + 1'	4096 + 1	The result of concatenation is a single string, as though both strings were inside the same pair of apostrophes.
'&A.&B' '&A&B'	40961 40961	Concatenation can occur within a pair of apostrophes. The concatenation operator may be omitted if there would be no ambiguity.
'&A..1'	4096.1	The first of the two periods is the concatenation operator; the second is part of the string being concatenated. The result is the same as though it were written as '&A'.1'.
'&A.1'	40961	The concatenation operator is used to avoid ambiguity.
'&C'.'&SYSDATE'	USF03/31/80	The value of the system variable &SYSDATE is substituted before the concatenation takes place.
'&C '.'&SYSDATE' '&C'.' &SYSDATE' '&C &SYSDATE'	USF 03/31/80 USF 03/31/80 USF 03/31/80	When a blank space is desired, it must be explicitly represented. The three expressions shown have the same value.
&A.X	4096X	When a variable symbol is concatenated with an ordinary symbol (X, in this example), the result is the string consisting of the value of that variable symbol immediately followed by the ordinary symbol.
X&A	X4096	The concatenation operator is not used to concatenate an ordinary symbol with a variable symbol.

Figure 16.3   Use of expressions in a conditional assembly.

```
                    .
                    .
                    .
              GBLC    &C
              GBLA    &X
      &C      SETC    'REGS'
                    .
                    .
                    .
              AIF     ('&C' NE 'REGS').REGSX
.REGS         ANOP
R&X           EQU     &X
&X            SETA    &X+1
              AIF     (&X LE 15).REGS
.REGSX        ANOP
                    .
                    .
                    .
```

Some of these aspects of expressions are illustrated in figure 16.3. Other examples will be given in chapter 17.

In figure 16.3, the value of the character variable &C is used to determine whether or not to include the statements that are in the box following the AIF directive. The value of &C is established by the GBLC and SETC directives. The SETC directive would be omitted if the boxed statements were not to be included. (Alternatively, as discussed previously, the system variable &SYSPARM could be used to accomplish the same purpose.) The statements within the box cause the Assembler to generate these 16 consecutive EQU directives:

```
R0      EQU     0
R1      EQU     1
R2      EQU     2
R3      EQU     3
R4      EQU     4
R5      EQU     5
R6      EQU     6
R7      EQU     7
R8      EQU     8
R9      EQU     9
R10     EQU     10
R11     EQU     11
R12     EQU     12
R13     EQU     13
R14     EQU     14
R15     EQU     15
```

Note that the AIF directive within the box causes the Assembler to skip *back* to a statement it has already processed. Since the value of &X is changed before each such skip, a different EQU is generated each time the AIF condition is true. (Remember that the initial value of an arithmetic variable is 0.)

16.6   ADDITIONAL CAPABILITIES

In this section we will mention briefly two other capabilities available in the IBM 360 and 370 Assembly Language: subscripted assembly variables, and the substring notation for character variables.

Subscripted Assembly Variables

Assembly variables can be subscripted, provided they are appropriately dimensioned. The dimension must be declared in the GBLx or LCLx directive. All components of a subscripted assembly variable are of the same type and are assigned the initial value appropriate to that type. For example,

GBLA	&X(10)	Declares that &X is a global subscripted arithmetic assembly variable with up to ten components. The names of the components are &X(1), &X(2),..., &X(10).
LCLB	&Y(5)	Declares that &Y is a local subscripted boolean assembly variable with up to five components named &Y(1),..., &Y(5).
GBLC	&Z(3)	Declares that &Z is a global subscripted character assembly variable with up to three components, &Z(1), &Z(2), and &Z(3).

The dimension in the GBLx and LCLx directives must be an unsigned decimal integer (but not 0). The maximum dimension allowed is 32767 (4095 in DOS). If a variable symbol is dimensioned, it must always be used as a subscripted variable. The subscript can be any valid arithmetic expression whose value is positive but not greater than the dimension size. The following statements illustrate these concepts.

	GBLA	&X(10),&W	declares that &X has ten components, and &W has one
	GBLB	&Y(5)	declares that &Y has five components
	GBLC	&Z(5)	declares that &Z has five components
&X(2)	SETA	3	assigns the value 3 to the second component of &X
&Y(3)	SETB	(&X(2) EQ 3)	assigns the value 1 to the third component of &Y
&Z(5)	SETC	'&X(1)+&X(2)'	assigns the string value 0+3 to the fifth component of &Z
&Z(1)	SETC	'&W.(1)'	assigns the string 0(1) to the first component of &Z

Note that the concatenation operator *must* be used to distinguish subscripting from concatenation.

Substring Notation

One or more consecutive characters within a character string can be referred to by using the substring notation. This notation can be used only in the operand of AIF, SETB, and SETC directives. The notation consists of two arithmetic expressions separated by commas and enclosed in parentheses and is written immediately after the character expression that identifies the string. The first arithmetic expression in parentheses designates the position of the first character in the substring; the second arithmetic expression designates the number of characters in the substring. A substring's length can be from 0 to 255 characters in OS, and from 0 to 8 characters in DOS. For example,

'THIS'(3,2) designates the substring IS

      | substring is two characters long
    substring begins at third position in the string

'&C'(1,1) designates the substring consisting of the first character of the value of &C

      | substring is one character long
    substring begins at first position in the string

'&Z(5)'(2,2) designates the substring consisting of the second and third characters of the string represented by the subscripted variable symbol &Z(5)

Substring notation is particularly useful for selecting and testing characters within a string, as in the following AIF directive:

AIF   ('&C'(1,1) EQ '(').P1

if the first character of the string represented by &C is a left parenthesis, the Assembler skips to the statement identified by the sequence symbol .P1

16.7 SUMMARY

The Assembler's usual processing sequence, in which it processes statements in the order in which they occur in a source-module, can be altered by the use of the AIF and AGO directives. To do this, use sequence symbols to identify statements to which the Assembler is to skip; use assembly variables to specify the conditions (if any) under which the skipping is to occur.

A sequence symbol is a string of from two to eight characters: the first is a period, the second a letter, and the remaining ones (if any) may be letters or digits. When placed in the name field of a statement, the sequence symbol identifies that statement for use by the Assembler at assembly time.

An assembly variable is a symbol whose value can be established and changed by appropriate directives and used by the Assembler at assembly time. It is represented by a variable symbol, a string whose rules of formation are identical to those of a sequence symbol, except that the first character must be an ampersand instead of a period.

There are three distinct types of assembly variables: arithmetic, boolean, and character. Any valid variable symbol can be used for any type of assembly variable, but once an assembly variable's type has been established it cannot be changed within its scope. Both type and scope are established by means of either the GBLx or LCLx directives: GBLx for variables of global scope, and LCLx for those of local scope, where the "x" stands for type—x = A for arithmetic, B for boolean, and C for character variables.

An assembly variable's type determines the manner in which its value is represented and processed. Its value can be changed by appropriate use of a SETx directive of the same type. Its scope determines the set of source-module statements in which its value is available to the Assembler at assembly time.

The Assembler substitutes the value of an assembly variable for that variable before evaluating an expression in which it appears. This capability, together with that of the AIF directive, provides a useful means for varying the object code and/or listing produced by the Assembler with a minimum of changes to the source-module.

Supplementary facilities exist for enhancing the usefulness of these capabilities. For example, the global system variables &SYSDATE, &SYSTIME, and &SYSPARM are character variables whose values are always available at assembly time. &SYSDATE provides the date of assembly, &SYSTIME the time of assembly, and &SYSPARM the string specified in the PARM= parameter of the OS job-control EXEC command or of the SYSPARM= parameter of the DOS OPTION command. Other facilities include subscripting of assembly variables and processing of substrings contained within the values of character assembly variables.

EXERCISES

1. Which of the following are valid sequence symbols? Which are valid variable symbols? Which are valid ordinary symbols?

   a. ABLE
   b. .X3
   c. .3X
   d. .&ABC
   e. &.ABC
   f. &ABLE
   g. .ABLE
   h. ABLE.
   i. ZETA2
   j. &ZETA2

   k. .*
   l. *.
   m. &&X
   n. &L
   o. (&L)
   p. GBLC
   q. &GBLC
   r. .GBLC
   s. .XX
   t. &XX

2. What is the fundamental purpose of sequence symbols? How does this differ from the purpose of ordinary symbols?

3. Which of the following two statements is invalid, and why?

   ```
   .X4    ANOP
   X4     ANOP
   ```

4. The principal differences among arithmetic assembly variables, boolean assembly variables, and character assembly variables are based on the manner in which their values are represented and used by the Assembler. What are the restrictions on the manner in which the values of these three types of assembly variables are represented?

5. What is meant by the term "open code"?

6. What initial values would be assigned to each of the assembly variables occurring in the following statements:

   ```
   GBLC    &A,&B
   LCLA    &XYZ,&ZYX
   LCLC    &STRING,&NUMBER
   GBLB    &EVEN,&ODD
   ```

7. For each of the following AIF directives, determine what values of the arithmetic assembly variable &X will make the logical expression true:

   a. AIF   ((4*(&X/4) NE &X) AND (8*(&X/8) EQ &X)).DA
   b. AIF   (&X/4 LE 4).DB
   c. AIF   (((&X GE 1) AND (&X LT 16)) AND (&X NE 12)).DC

8. Assume that &X is an arithmetic assembly variable and that &B is a boolean assembly variable whose value is determined by the statement

   ```
   &B    SETB    ((&X/2)*2 EQ &X)
   ```

   For what values of &X will the following AIF directive cause the Assembler to branch to .DD?

   ```
   AIF    (&B).DD
   ```

9. What is meant by the term 'null string'? Write a valid SETC directive that will assign the null string to the character variable &C.

10. Write the conditional assembly statements that will generate the following four EQU's:

```
FPR0    EQU    0
FPR2    EQU    2
FPR4    EQU    4
FPR6    EQU    6
```

11. Write the conditional assembly statements that will generate the following table of 256 EBCDIC character codes:

```
EBCDIC     DC     FL1'01'
           DC     FL1'02'
           DC     FL1'03'
            ⋮
           DC     FL1'255'
           DC     FL1'256'
```

12. Suppose there are two subroutines, named PRINT and PUNCH, respectively. Suppose also that a source-module is to be written in such a way that it will call either the PRINT subroutine or the PUNCH subroutine, but not both. Write the conditional assembly statements (and any other statements that are necessary) to enable the module to be assembled with the desired subroutine's name wherever it is needed in the source-module, under the constraint that only one statement need be changed to change the subroutine name in the module.

13. Suppose that a source-module is to be written in such a way that certain floating-point constants are to be either in short format (single precision) or in long format (double precision). How could this be accomplished via conditional assembly statements?

14. In the example given for Section 16.2, the character assembly variable &UNIV was used to specify the name of a university for substitution in statements such as

```
TITLE     'ASSEMBLED AT THE &UNIV'
```

Suppose instead that the TITLE operand is written as follows:

```
TITLE     'ASSEMBLED AT &THE &UNIV'
```

Write the conditional assembly statements that will assign the null string to &THE unless the first seven letters in the value of &UNIV are either UNIVERS or COLLEGE. In the latter cases, assign the string THE to the variable &THE.

15. Suppose that an assembly is initiated by the job control language statement

```
//STEP   EXEC     ASFMC,PARM=SYSPARM(NOSEQ)
```

What would be the effect of the following statements in the source-module:

```
         AIF       ('&SYSPARM' NE 'NOSEQ').OK
ISEQ     OPSYN
.OK      ANOP
```

16. Write the conditional assembly language statements that will generate a table of twelve constants that can be used as patterns with the ED and EDMK instructions to convert packed-decimal numbers to the equivalent of Fortran In format, for $n = 1,2,...,12$. (Patterns are discussed in Section 12.9.)

17
Macros

A *macro* is an opcode that represents a set of one or more assembly language instructions, directives, or other macros. As such, it is a kind of high-level extension of Assembly Language. The set of statements that a macro represents must be defined before the macro can be used in a source-module. Some macros, such as the GET and PUT I/O macros, are defined by system programmers and may be used by any assembly language programmers. Other macros are defined by programmers for use in their own or their colleagues' source-modules. In this chapter, we will describe how to define and use macros. It will be apparent that macros are a significant extension of the concept of conditional assemblies discussed in chapter 16. The use of variable symbols together with the SETx and AIF directives in macro definitions provides capabilities that can make assembly language programming simpler, less error prone, more structured, and more like that in a high-level language without sacrificing the capabilities of Assembly Language.

17.1   A SAMPLE MACRO

Before describing the mechanisms available for defining macros, we will illustrate the use of a macro with a simple example.

Suppose that there is a macro named ADD with the following property: whenever the statement

opcode	operand
ADD	X,Y

is written in a source-module, the effect is equivalent to these three statements:

```
L      5,X
A      5,Y
ST     5,X
```

But more than this, we can write

```
ADD      ALPHA,BETA
```

and get the same effect as if we wrote

```
L      5,ALPHA
A      5,BETA
ST     5,ALPHA
```

In fact, the ADD macro is such that we can write any two valid symbols in place of ALPHA and BETA. All that is required is that we understand three things about the ADD macro:

1. It always causes Register 5 to be used, so that the previous number in that register is replaced by the result of the ADD macro
2. There must be exactly two symbols in the operand, and they must designate full word integers
3. The number whose address is represented by the second symbol is added to the number whose address is represented by the first symbol; the sum is stored at the address represented by the first symbol.

Once these facts are understood, we can write any of the following source-code statements with the knowledge that each will be equivalent to those shown on the right:

source-code statements		equivalent statements	
ADD	X1,X2	L	5,X1
		A	5,X2
		ST	5,X1
ADD	Z,=F'15'	L	5,Z
		A	5,=F'15'
		ST	5,Z
ADD	Y,X	L	5,Y
		A	5,X
		ST	5,Y
ADD	0(4),0(6)	L	5,0(4)
		A	5,0(6)
		ST	5,0(4)

If we were to use the ADD macro in a source-module in any of the ways just illustrated, the Assembler would insert the three equivalent statements at the point where the ADD macro was used. The inserted statements are known as the macro's *expansion*. It is the expansion statements that are executed at run time, not the ADD macro. The ADD macro does not have a corresponding machine language format into which it is translated at assembly time. Instead, the ADD macro represents the expansion statements, and it is these statements that get translated into their corresponding machine language formats.

When the ADD macro or any other macro is used in a source-module, we say that the macro is being *invoked*. This means that the Assembler is called upon to insert the appropriate expansion. This capability is made possible through the mechanism of macro definitions.

17.2 DEFINING MACROS

The definition of a macro can be included in the source-module in which it is invoked, or it can be placed in a separate file that is accessible to the Assembler while it is assembling that source-module. When included in a source module, a macro definition must occur before the first CSECT or START directive in that module and after any ICTL or OPSYN directives. When included in a separate file, the name of the file must be specified in a job control statement. In either case, a macro definition must consist of three types of information:

1. The *name* of the macro—the opcode that will be used to invoke it
2. The format of the operand field of the macro
3. The sequence of instructions, directives, comments, or other macros that the macro opcode represents.

The first statement of a macro definition must be a MACRO directive. This is known as the *header* statement and has the format

name field	opcode	operand
blank	MACRO	blank

The second statement of the definition must describe the name, opcode, and operand fields of the macro. This statement is known as the *prototype* statement, or sometimes as the *model* statement; it defines the syntax to be used when the macro is invoked in a source-module. Its format is

name field	opcode	operand
$\left\{ \begin{array}{l} \text{variable symbol} \\ \text{or blank} \end{array} \right\}$	$\left\{ \begin{array}{l} \text{macro's} \\ \text{name} \end{array} \right\}$	$\left\{ \begin{array}{l} \text{a list of positional parameters} \\ \text{and/or keyword parameters} \end{array} \right\}$

The macro's name must be present in the opcode field of the prototype statement. This name must be different from the names of all mnemonic instructions, directives, and other macros. The name-field symbol and the parameters in the operand are not required; their presence depends on the other statements in the definition. Each *positional* parameter is represented by a variable symbol; each *keyword* parameter is represented by a variable symbol followed immediately by an equal sign (=) and the default value of that symbol. In OS, keyword and positional parameters may be intermixed in the operand. In DOS, all positional operands must precede all keyword ones. In both systems, the parameters must be separated by commas. Blanks are not permitted as separators. The following prototype statements should help clarify these concepts:

Immediately following the prototype statement is a set of one or more statements known as the *body* of the macro definition. The statements in the body of the definition define the manner in which the macro is to be processed by the Assembler when the macro is invoked. The body may include any valid assembly language statement except a MACRO, ICTL, OPSYN, or MEND directive. (In DOS but not OS, one other directive is not permitted: END .)

The last statement of the definition must be an MEND directive. Known as the *trailer* statement, its format is

name field	opcode	operand
sequence symbol or blank	MEND	blank

These concepts are illustrated in figures 17.1 and 17.2. Figure 17.2 shows how the ADD macro described in the preceding section is defined. In addition to the facts that the MACRO directive must occur first, the prototype second, and the MEND last, the following rule is essential: *the variable symbols appearing in the prototype statement represent values that are substituted in the statements of the body when the macro is invoked.*

The variable symbols used in the prototype statement have the following properties:

1. They are character assembly variables whose scope is local, i.e., restricted to the statements in the definition
2. They must be different from all global and other local assembly variables that are declared by GBLx or LCLx statements in the definition
3. Their values are determined when the macro is invoked.

Figure 17.1   Schematic representation of a macro's definition.

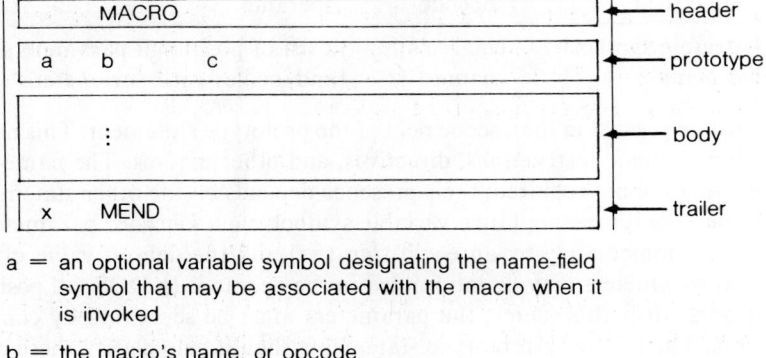

a = an optional variable symbol designating the name-field
symbol that may be associated with the macro when it
is invoked

b = the macro's name, or opcode

c = the specifications of the operand

x = an optional sequence symbol identifying the MEND
statement

Figure 17.2   Definition of ADD macro.

For example, suppose the ADD macro of figure 17.2 is invoked by the statement

         LOOP   ADD   X,Y

Then, at assembly time, the Assembler will compare this statement to the corresponding prototype statement
in the definition of the ADD macro,

         &L   ADD   &A,&B

The Assembler then makes the following assignments of string values.

         &L   =   'LOOP'
         &A   =   'X'
         &B   =   'Y'

It substitutes these values into the statements of the body of the definition, namely,

         &L   L   5,&A
                   A   5,&B
                   ST   5,&A

and thereby produces the expansion

         LOOP   L   5,X
                   A   5,Y
                   ST   5,X

Notice that the relative position of X and Y in the operand of the statement that invokes the ADD macro is of crucial importance. In other words, ADD X,Y would produce a different expansion than ADD Y,X.

Notice also that the variable symbol &L in the name field of the prototype statement allows the programmer to specify a name-field symbol when invoking the macro. The macro definition—statements in the body of the macro—defines the statement of the expansion that is to be associated with the name-field symbol used when the macro is invoked. Thus, we could have other statements that branch to the statement that invokes the macro in our source-module, as in the sequence

```
LOOP      ADD       X,Y
          ---       ---
          ---       ---
          BCT       5,LOOP
```

The manner in which the value of a variable symbol is determined thus depends on whether the symbol is the name-field symbol, a positional parameter, or a keyword parameter. *In all three cases, however, the value is a character string.*

The value of the prototype's name-field symbol is the string that exists in the name field of the statement that invokes the macro. This string consists of from 0 to 8 characters, i.e., it can be null.

The values of the prototype's positional parameters are the strings that occupy the corresponding positions in the operand of the statement that invokes the macro. There is a one-to-one correspondence between the positional parameters in the prototype and the values of these parameters in the invoking statement.

The values of the prototype's keyword parameters (if any) are the strings defined for each keyword parameter in the prototype's operand. These are known as the *default values.* A keyword parameter's default value will be overridden by any value specified for that keyword in the operand of the invoking statement.

It should be noted that *an expansion will be generated whether or not it consists of valid assembly language statements.* Only after it has been generated, not before, will the Assembler flag a statement that is in error.

A few examples should help clarify these concepts. In the prototype statement of figure 17.3, namely,

```
&S        MOVE          &A,&B,&N=
```

the default value of &N is the null string. To override this or any keyword's default value, you must specify that keyword and its desired value, leaving off the ampersand (&). Thus, if the invoking statement is

```
X         MOVE          HERE,THERE,N=10
```

then the value of the keyword parameter &N will be the character string 10. But if the invoking statement is

```
X         MOVE          HERE,THERE
```

the value of the keyword parameter &N will be its default, the null string. And, finally, if the invoking statement is

```
X         MOVE          HERE
```

Figure 17.3   Definition of MOVE macro.

```
          MACRO
&S        MOVE      &A,&B,&N=
          AIF       ('&N' EQ '').M1
&S        MVC       &B.(&N),&A
          AGO       .M2
.M1       ANOP
&S        MVC       &B,&A
.M2       MEND
```

---

not only will the value of &N be null, but so will the value of &B. The expansions generated for these three statements are these:

source statement			expansion statement		
X	MOVE	HERE,THERE,&N=10	X	MVC	THERE(10),HERE
X	MOVE	HERE,THERE	X	MVC	THERE,HERE
X	MOVE	HERE	X	MVC	,HERE

In the third case, the expansion generated is an invalid assembly language statement and will be so flagged by the Assembler.

As another example, consider the prototype statement of figure 17.4. This prototype contains no parameters and no name-field symbol. This means that the only statement that should be used to invoke the REGS macro is one whose opcode contains the macro name REGS and whose name and operand fields are blank. Comparing figure 17.4 to figure 16.3 of the preceding chapter, we see that the REGS macro definition incorporates the statements that generate the 16 consecutive EQU directives discussed in Section 16.5. In other words, the concept of the conditional assembly has been placed inside a macro definition. If the REGS macro is not invoked, its EQU directives will not be generated. If it is invoked, the value of the local arithmetic variable &X will be initialized by the Assembler to be 0 at the time REGS is invoked and the remaining statements in the definition will be processed until the value of &X exceeds 15. For each value of &X less than or equal to 15, the macro definition causes the corresponding EQU directive

$$\text{R\&X} \qquad \text{EQU} \qquad \text{\&X}$$

to be generated.

17.3 USE OF CONTROL DIRECTIVES

The statements in the body of a macro's definition can include any of the control directives—GBLx, LCLx, SETx, AIF, AGO, ANOP. In order to illustrate the additional capabilities in which this results consider the following problem.

Suppose a programmer would like to have a macro to use whenever he or she must write the statements needed to return from a subroutine. The macro would have to represent each of the four standard return sequences (see chap. 9):

```
L      13,SAVE+4
LM     14,12,12(13)        restore all registers
BR     14

L      13,SAVE+4
L      14,12(13)           restore all but R15 and R0
LM     1,12,24(13)
BR     14

L      13,SAVE+4
L      14,12(13)           restore all but R15
LM     0,12,20(13)
BR     14

L      13,SAVE+4
LM     14,15,12(13)        restore all but R0
LM     1,12,24(13)
BR     14
```

One way to accomplish this would simply be to define four separate macros, one for each situation. But the preferable way to accomplish it is by defining one macro that could be used in all four situations. This is preferable because it is easier to understand and easier to use, even though it is more difficult to define.

The problem of designing such a macro has two parts: (1) what the macro prototype should be and how to invoke it, and (2) what statements should be in the body of the definition in order for the Assembler to process the macro as intended when it is invoked.

Figure 17.4   Definition of REGS macro.

```
          MACRO
          REGS
          LCLA    &X
.REGS     ANOP
R&X       EQU     &X
&X        SETA    &X+1
          AIF     (&X LE 15).REGS
          MEND
```

Our choice of prototype is

&L   RETRN   &R1,&R2

(This prototype differs from that of the IBM system macro RETURN, even though both RETRN and RETURN have essentially the same purpose. The IBM macro is more generally useful than the one described here.) The meaning of the RETRN macro is *Return to the calling program after restoring all registers except the registers (if any) designated in the operand.* The exceptions can only be Register 0, Register 15, or both Register 0 and Register 15. Thus, there are four essentially different ways to invoke the RETRN macro:

RETRN		restores all registers
RETRN	0,15	restores all but R15 and R0
RETRN	15	restores all but R15
RETRN	0	restores all but R0

Each of these invoking statements will cause the Assembler to generate the corresponding expansion for the return sequence as given earlier in this section.

Clearly, the definition of the RETRN macro must be able to distinguish among different values of the parameters &R1 and &R2. This is done by using AIF directives in the macro definition. For example, to determine whether any values are present in the operand when RETRN is invoked, a statement such as this AIF can be used:

AIF   ('&R1' EQ '').R1

value of the first operand

null string

sequence symbol of statement to be processed when &R1 is null, i.e., when no values are present in the operand

The other three situations can be similarly tested.

A possible definition of the RETRN macro that always produces the desired expansion is shown in figure 17.5. To understand this definition, you must keep two things clearly in mind:

1. The prototype statement (line 2) identifies the name of the RETRN macro and the variable symbols whose values can be specified when the RETRN macro is invoked.
2. The statements in the body of the definition are processed at assembly time each time the RETRN macro is invoked. It is during this assembly time processing of the definition that the expansion is generated by the Assembler. The expansion is not executed until run time.

In the remainder of this section, we will discuss the definition of the RETRN macro.

Statements 3–7 enable the Assembler to determine the subsequent statements of the definition that should be processed when the macro is invoked and one of the following situations exists: (1) no values are specified in the operand of the invoking statement; (2) one value (either 0 or 15) is specified in the operand; (3) two values are specified in the operand (either 0,15 or 15,0); or (4) one or more unacceptable values are specified in the operand. This is done as follows:

statement number	statement		explanation
3	AIF	('&R1' EQ '').R1	This determines whether the first operand field is present. If not, the Assembler skips to Statement 10, identified by the sequence symbol .R1.
4	AIF	(('&R1' NE '0') AND ('&R1' NE '15')).RERR	When the first operand field is present, this determines whether its value is acceptable.
5	AIF	('&R2' EQ '').R3	When the first operand is present and its value is either 0 or 15, this determines whether the second operand is present. If it is not, the Assembler skips to Statement 25, identified by the sequence symbol .R3.
6	AIF	(('&R2' NE '0') AND ('&R2' NE '15')).RERR	This determines whether the value in the second operand is acceptable.
7	AGO	.R2	When both operands are present and valid, the Assembler skips to Statement 17, identified by the sequence symbol .R2.

Thus, when the condition tested in Statement 3 is true, the only other definition statements processed by the Assembler are

```
10   .R1      ANOP
11   &L       L        13,SAVE+4
12            LM       14,12,12(13)    restore all registers
13            BR       14
14            MEXIT
```

The MEXIT directive instructs the Assembler to stop its assembly-time processing of the RETRN macro. This directive is equivalent to an unconditional skip (AGO) to the MEND directive. Its format is

name field	opcode	operand
{ sequence symbol } { or blank }	MEXIT	blank

When the condition tested in Statement 3 is not true, Statement 4 is processed. If the value of &R1 is neither 0 nor 15, the only other definition statements processed by the Assembler are

```
41   .RERR    ANOP
42            MNOTE    9, '&R1 OR &R2 NOT VALID. EXPANSION NOT GENERATED.'
43   .*
44            MEND
```

The MNOTE directive specifies a message that is printed on the listing and a *severity code* (9, in this case). Its format is

name field	opcode	operand
{ sequence symbol } { or blank }	MNOTE	n,'...'

severity code character string, to be printed on the listing

Figure 17.5   Definition of RETRN macro.

```
 1              MACRO
 2    &L        RETRN       &R1,&R2
 3              AIF         ('&R1' EQ '').R1
 4              AIF         (('&R1' NE '0') AND ('&R1' NE '15')).RERR
 5              AIF         ('&R2' EQ '').R3
 6              AIF         (('&R2' NE '0') AND ('&R2' NE '15')).RERR
 7              AGO         .R2
 8    .*
 9    .*   &R1 NOT PRESENT, THEREFORE &R2 ASSUMED NOT PRESENT
10    .R1       ANOP
11    &L        L           13,SAVE+4
12              LM          14,12,12(13)           RESTORE ALL REGISTERS
13              BR          14
14              MEXIT
15    .*
16    .*   &R1 IS PRESENT, AND &R2 IS PRESENT, AND BOTH ARE VALID
17    .R2       ANOP
18    &L        L           13,SAVE+4
19              L           14,12(13)           RESTORE ALL BUT R15 AND R0
20              LM          1,12,24(13)
21              BR          14
22              MEXIT
23    .*
24    .*   &R1 IS PRESENT, BUT &R2 IS NOT PRESENT
25    .R3       ANOP
26              AIF         ('&R1' EQ '0').R3A
27    &L        L           13,SAVE+4
28              L           14,12(13)           RESTORE ALL BUT R15
29              LM          0,12,20(13)
30              BR          14
31              MEXIT
32    .*
33    .R3A      ANOP
34    &L        L           13,SAVE+4
35              LM          14,15,12(13)           RESTORE ALL BUT R0
36              LM          1,12,24(13)
37              BR          14
38              MEXIT
39    .*
40    .*   INVALID VALUES OF &R1 OR &R2
41    .RERR     ANOP
42              MNOTE       9,'&R1 OR &R2 NOT VALID. EXPANSION NOT GENERATED.'
43    .*
44              MEND
```

A severity code value greater than eight usually causes run time execution to be suppressed. A code less than or equal to eight simply generates a warning message. In either case, the MNOTE directive is printed when it is part of the expansion and its position in the listing is cross-referenced at the end of the listing. The values of any variable symbols appearing in the MNOTE character string are substituted by the Assembler before the string is printed.

Statement 3 (and a few other statements in the definition) begins with the two characters '.*' in positions 1 and 2. This identifies the statement as an *internal macro comment statement*. Such statements are never printed in the expansion; their purpose is to serve as documentation or to provide spacing for readability of the definition on the listing.

When the conditions tested in both Statements 3 and 4 are not true, Statement 5 is processed. This AIF statement determines whether the second operand (the value of &R2) is present when the macro is invoked. If the macro is invoked by either of these two statements:

RETRN   0   ⎫

RETRN   15 ⎭ non-null value for &R1; null value for &R2

the second operand will not be present. When the value of &R2 is null, the Assembler determines which of the two acceptable values of &R1 is present in the invoking statement. It does this via Statement 26. Depending on the value of &R1, either Statements 27–31 or Statements 33–38 are processed. You can verify that these correspond to the cases &R1 = 15 and &R1 = 0, respectively.

Note that when both &R1 and &R2 are present in the operand of the statement that invokes the RETRN macro, the statement can be written as either

$$\text{RETRN} \quad 0,15$$

or

$$\text{RETRN} \quad 15,0$$

In both cases, the correct expansion for restoring all but Registers 0 and 15 is generated; these are generated by Statements 17–22.

In summary, the RETRN macro definition causes the Assembler to generate the correct expansion for a standard subroutine return in each of the four situations shown here:

source statement	expansion generated		
RETRN	L	13,SAVE+4	
	LM	14,12,12(13)	RESTORE ALL REGISTERS
	BR	14	
RETRN 0,15 or RETRN 15,0	L	13,SAVE+4	
	L	14,12(13)	RESTORE ALL BUT R15 AND R0
	LM	1,12,24(13)	
	BR	14	
RETRN 15	L	13,SAVE+4	
	L	14,12(13)	
	LM	0,12,20(13)	RESTORE ALL BUT R15
	BR	14	
RETRN 0	L	13,SAVE+4	
	LM	14,15,12(13)	RESTORE ALL BUT R0
	LM	1,12,24(13)	
	BR	14	

17.4 CONCATENATION: AN EXAMPLE

Corresponding to the RETRN macro of the preceding section, we can define a CALL macro that will generate the standard set of statements required when calling a subroutine. As discussed in chapter 9, this set consists of the statements

```
LA      1,=A(X,Y,...)
LA      13,SAVE
L       15,=V(SUBR)
BALR    14,15
```

Since the statements we have been using to begin an executable control section include LA 13,SAVE, that instruction usually is not needed when calling a subroutine. But if we had not included that instruction when beginning a section, or if the contents of Register 13 had been altered prior to a subroutine call, the instruction would be required in the call.

The definition of the CALL macro in figure 17.6 generates the correct statements for any subroutine name and any number of parameters X,Y,.... It also permits the invoking statement to specify whether or not the address of the register save area should be loaded into Register 13 and, if so, what that address should be. It is a simple definition because it relies on the principle of string concatenation discussed in chapter 16. The definition also illustrates the type of situation in which a keyword parameter is to be preferred over a positional parameter: namely, one in which the default is frequently the value that is desired for the parameter.

The prototype statement in figure 17.6 contains two positional parameters and one keyword parameter. The keyword parameter's default value is used to decide whether or not to generate the instruction that loads

Figure 17.6   *Definition of CALL macro.*

```
1              MACRO
2     &L       CALL      &SUBR,&PARAM,&SAVE=
3     &L       LA        1,=A&PARAM
4              AIF       ('&SAVE' EQ '').C1
5              LA        13,&SAVE
6     .C1      L         15,=V(&SUBR)
7              BALR      14,15
8              MEND
```

Register 13 with the save area address. The first positional parameter is the name of the subroutine to be called; the second is the set of parameters to be used in the call. For example, if this were the statement invoking the CALL macro,

CALL   SQRT,(X)

the expansion generated would be

LA   1,=A(X)
L   15,=V(SQRT)
BALR   14,15

The expansion is generated by the Assembler after it substitutes the following values for the parameters and name-field symbol in the body of the definition:

&L   =   null string
&SUBR   =   SQRT
&PARAM =   (X)
&SAVE   =   null string

Since each of the variable symbols that occurs in a prototype statement is a local character variable, the values given are character strings available to the Assembler only while it generates the expansion for the CALL SQRT,(X) statement. A subsequent CALL statement will cause a possibly different expansion to be generated, depending on the values given in that CALL statement.

There are two important things to note: First, the value of &SAVE that was generated is the default value specified in the prototype. This is because the invoking CALL statement did not specify that the default should be overridden. To override the default, we would have to specify a value for the keyword SAVE as in the statement

CALL   SQRT,(X),SAVE=MAINAREA

If this were done, the expansion would be

LA   1,=A(X)
LA   13,MAINAREA
L   15,=V(SQRT)
BALR   14,15

The second point to note is the manner in which the value of &PARAM is used in the definition. Statement 3 of figure 17.6,

&L   LA   1,=A&PARAM

causes the Assembler to concatenate the string value of &PARAM to the letter A. Thus the second operand in Statement 3,

=A&PARAM

becomes

=A(X)

You can verify that for each of the source statements on the left, the expansion generated is the one given on the right:

source statement			expansion		
LOOP	CALL	SEARCH,(A,N,X)	LOOP	LA	1,=A(A,N,X)
				L	15,=V(SEARCH)
				BALR	14,15
	CALL	CALL,(PARAM),SAVE=SAVE		LA	1,=A(PARAM)
				LA	13,SAVE
				L	15,=V(CALL)
				BALR	14,15
	CALL	HELP		LA	1,=A
				L	15,=V(HELP)
				BALR	14,15

In the expansion for the CALL HELP statement, the Assembler has assigned the null string to the variable symbol &PARAM. This is because no value for &PARAM was specified in the CALL HELP statement. As was indicated earlier, the absence of a string value for *any* positional parameter causes the null string to be assigned as the value for that parameter. The Assembler does not check for inconsistencies or errors of this type unless the macro definition explicitly provides for such checks (via AIF directives). The erroneous statement in the expansion

$$LA \quad 1,=A$$

will be flagged by the Assembler as an error when it tries to assemble that statement.

17.5 USE OF PARAMETER SUBLISTS

A *parameter sublist* is a set of one or more values specified for a positional or keyword parameter when invoking a macro. The values must be separated by commas and enclosed in parentheses. Statements in the body of the definition can refer to any of the values in the sublist by means of subscripts. *The subscript designates the position of the value within the sublist.* The subscript must therefore be greater than or equal to 1.

For example, when invoking the CALL macro that was defined in figure 17.6, the value of the second parameter &PARAM is specified by a parameter sublist. In the CALL SQRT,(X) example discussed earlier, the sublist consisted of only a single value, X, but it is a sublist because it is enclosed in parentheses and represents the value of a macro parameter. In the definition, &PARAM could have been subscripted in the form &PARAM(1) to refer to the value X. The subscript of 1 is used because X is the first value in the sublist. Similarly, for the CALL statement

$$CALL \quad SEARCH,(A,N,X)$$

the value of &PARAM is the string (A,N,X) as before, but &PARAM can also be subscripted to refer to individual values in the sublist:

$$\&PARAM(1) = A$$
$$\&PARAM(2) = N$$
$$\&PARAM(3) = X$$

A subscript greater than the number of values in the sublist corresponds to a value of null. For the above CALL statement, the value of &PARAM(k) for any k greater than 3 is the null string.

We will illustrate the use of sublists by describing the BASE macro defined in figure 17.7. The purpose of the BASE macro is to provide an easy means of establishing *one or more* implied base registers in a source-module. The positional parameter &R in the prototype

$$\&L \qquad BASE \qquad \&R$$

Figure 17.7   Definition of BASE macro.

```
 1              MACRO
 2    &L        BASE       &R
 3              LCLA       &X,&Y              &Y WILL BE MULTIPLE OF 4096
 4    &X        SETA       1                  &X IS SUBSCRIPT FOR SUBLIST VALUES
 5    .*
 6    .*  ESTABLISH FIRST BASE REGISTER VIA 'BALR'
 7    .*
 8    &L        BALR       &R(1),0
 9              USING      *,&R(1)
10    B&SYSNDX  EQU        *
11    .*
12    .*  DETERMINE WHETHER THERE ARE ANY MORE SUBLIST ENTRIES
13    .*
14    .B1       ANOP
15    &X        SETA       &X+1
16              AIF        ('&R(&X)' EQ '').B2
17    .*
18    .*  ESTABLISH ALL BUT FIRST BASE REGISTER VIA 'LA' INSTRUCTIONS
19    .*
20              LA         &R(&X),2048(&R(&X-1))
21              LA         &R(&X),2048(&R(&X))
22    &Y        SETA       4096*&X-4096
23              USING      B&SYSNDX+&Y,&R(&X)
24              AGO        .B1
25    .*
26    .B2       MEND
```

will be specified as a sublist when invoking the BASE macro. For example,

$$\text{BASE} \qquad (12,11)$$

will cause the Assembler to generate an expansion that will establish Register 12 as the first base register and Register 11 as the second. The expansion generated in this case will be

```
          BALR    12,0
          USING   *,12
B0001     EQU     *
          LA      11,2048(12)
          LA      11,2048(11)
          USING   B0001+4096,11
```

The first two statements of this expansion need no explanation, but perhaps the remaining ones do. The second implied base register, Register 11, will be loaded with an address that is 4096 greater than that in the first base register. This address is placed into Register 11 at run time by the combined effect of the two LA instructions. (We cannot write LA 11,4096(12) because the hexadecimal equivalent of 4096_{10} is 1000_{16}, i.e., more than the three hex digits permitted in a displacement.) The Assembler is informed of the base address for Register 11 by the USING B0001+4096,11 directive. The symbol B0001 is generated by the Assembler through the concatenation of the value of &SYSNDX (assumed to be 0001 in this case) with the letter B. The use of the system variable &SYSNDX will be discussed further in Section 17.6.

Statements 3 and 4 in figure 17.7 establish &X and &Y as local arithmetic variables with initial values 1 and 0, respectively. &X will be used as the subscript when referring to a sublist value, e.g., &R(&X). &Y will be used as a multiple of 4096, i.e., 4096, 8192, 12288,..., depending on how many sublist values are specified when the BASE macro is invoked.

Statements 8 and 9 establish the implied base register whose address is given by the first sublist value &R(1) when the macro is invoked. Statement 10 creates a symbol whose value is the base address in Register &R(1); this symbol is created by concatenating the letter B with the value of the system variable &SYSNDX. The value of &SYSNDX is generated by the Assembler; it is a four-digit string that does not change during a macro's expansion but is different for each expansion. For the first macro expanded in a source-module, &SYSNDX is 0001, for the second, it is 0002, and so forth. Thus, if we were to invoke the BASE macro more than once in a source-module, the symbol represented by B&SYSNDX would be different each time BASE was invoked. This avoids the possibility of generating a symbol that would be multiply-defined.

Statement 15 increases the subscript value by 1, and Statement 16 tests the corresponding sublist value to see if it is or is not the null string. If the value of &R(&X) is the null string, this simply means that the end of the sublist has been reached and the expansion is terminated. If &R(&X) is not null, its value is the register address to be used for the next implied base register in the expansion.

Statements 20 and 21 generate the Load Address instructions that will place the appropriate base address into Register &R(&X) at run time, when &X > 1. If we return to our earlier example,

$$\text{BASE} \qquad (12,11)$$

then, when &X = 2, we have, from Statements 20 and 21, the LA instructions

```
                                    sublist value corresponding
                                    to &R(&X) when &X = 2
                                        |
                                        |       sublist value corresponding
                                        |       to &R(&X−1) when &X = 2
                                        ↓           ↓
                 LA        11,2048(12)
                 LA        11,2048(11)
```

Statement 22 computes the current multiple of 4096 to be used in the USING directive, and assigns the computed value to &Y. Statement 23 generates the required USING directive. Continuing the example, we see that with &X = 2,

$$\&Y = 4096*2-4096 = 4096.$$

So, if we assume that &SYSNDX = 0001, the generated USING directive is

$$\text{USING} \qquad \text{B0001}+4096,11$$

The expansion is generated in similar fashion for three or more sublist values. Statement 24 causes the Assembler to skip back to Statement 14, whence it will increase the subscript value and repeat the described processing for the next sublist value, if any. For example, if the BASE macro is invoked by the statement

$$\text{BASE} \qquad (10,11,12)$$

the expansion generated is

```
          BALR     10,0
          USING    *,10
B0002     EQU      *
          LA       11,2048(10)
          LA       11,2048(11)
          USING    B0002+4096,11
          LA       12,2048(11)
          LA       12,2048(12)
          USING    B0002+8192,12
```

If only a single base register is desired, say Register 12, we can write either BASE (12) or BASE 12. In other words, if a sublist contains only one value, the parentheses are not required. In the BASE macro definition, the use of subscripts will work as desired: &R(1) will refer to the first and only sublist value, and &R(2) will refer to the null string. The expansion generated for either BASE (12) or BASE 12 will be

```
                BALR        12,0
                USING       *,12
     B0003      EQU         *
```

The third statement is "wasted," but there is no harm done since B0003 will not be generated again for any macro expansion in that source-module.

17.6   &SYSNDX, &SYSLIST, AND &SYSECT

&SYSNDX, &SYSLIST, and &SYSECT are local system variable symbols whose values are assigned by the Assembler. They may not be declared by GBLx or LCLx directives, and their values may not be changed by SETx directives. They can be used only in macro definitions, not in open code.

&SYSNDX

The value assigned to &SYSNDX is, as discussed, the character string representation of a four-digit decimal integer, from 0001 to 9999. The integer (and hence the string) is not changed during the expansion of a macro but is increased by +1 each time any macro is invoked. This provides an important capability for use in macro definitions for the following reason.

It is often necessary to generate a statement with a name-field symbol so that that statement can be referred to from within the macro expansion. This was done, for example, in the definition of the BASE macro of figure 17.7. But, if a given macro is invoked more than once in a source-module and if that macro's expansion includes a name-field symbol generated by the definition of the macro, it is necessary to find some means of avoiding generation of the *same* name-field symbol each time the macro is invoked. If this were not done, the symbol would be multiply-defined. The &SYSNDX symbol provides the means for avoiding this. In the macro's definition, we simply concatenate &SYSNDX to a string of from one to four characters, the first being a letter, the others being letters or digits, as was done for the BASE macro. Then, each time the macro is invoked the concatenation of the string with the value of &SYSNDX will result in the generation of a symbol that is unique for all expansions of that macro and unique for all expansions of any other macro. (You should, of course, avoid defining symbols in open code that end in four digits.)

&SYSLIST

The &SYSLIST symbol can be used to denote the value of any positional operand. Because &SYSLIST refers to the operands in a statement that invokes the macro, not to the parameters in the prototype, it is not necessary to define corresponding positional parameters in the prototype when &SYSLIST is used in a definition. However, &SYSLIST cannot be used for keyword operands.

When &SYSLIST is used, it must always be subscripted. The subscript indicates the relative position of an operand in the statement that invokes the macro. We could, for example, have defined the ADD macro discussed at the beginning of this chapter as

```
                MACRO
     &L         ADD
     &L         L           5,&SYSLIST(1)
                A           5,&SYSLIST(2)
                ST          5,&SYSLIST(1)
                MEND
```

Had we done so, &SYSLIST(1) would refer to the first operand specified when ADD was invoked and &SYSLIST(2) would refer to the second operand. Not much may have been gained in such a simple example, but suppose we wanted an ADD macro that would add two or more integers, the exact number being determined by the statement that invokes ADD. We could then redefine the ADD macro as

```
        MACRO
&L      ADD
        LCLA    &K
&K      SETA    1
&L      L       5,&SYSLIST(&K)
.A      ANOP
&K      SETA    &K+1
        A       5,&SYSLIST(&K)
        AIF     ('&SYSLIST(&K+1)' NE '').A
        ST      5,&SYSLIST(1)
        MEND
```

We could then invoke the ADD macro to add two integers, or three, or however many we cared to, as the following statements illustrate:

source statement		expansion	
ADD	X,Y,Z	L	5,X
		A	5,Y
		A	5,Z
		ST	5,X

&SYSLIST can also be used to refer to sublist values *within* a positional operand. To do this, two subscripts are used. The first subscript indicates the relative position of the operand; the second indicates the relative position of a sublist value within that operand. Thus, &SYSLIST(m,n) refers to the nth sublist value in the mth positional operand of the statement that invokes a macro. An example will be given in Section 17.7. Note that the subscripts used in &SYSLIST can be any valid arithmetic expressions whose values are positive integers. There are also two special cases: &SYSLIST(0), which refers to the value of the symbol in the name field when a macro is invoked, and &SYSLIST(k,0), which is invalid for all k.

&SYSECT

The value of &SYSECT is the name of the control section in which the macro containing &SYSECT in its definition is invoked. The Assembler substitutes the control section's name for &SYSECT when it generates an expansion. The need for this capability arises in a macro definition that generates a dummy section (DSECT) and then must resume the control section in which that macro is invoked.

Note that the values of all three local system variables are affected by nesting (described in the next section).

17.7   NESTED MACROS

A *nested macro* is a macro instruction that is invoked in the body of a macro definition. It is also known as an inner macro, and its expansion is known as the inner expansion of the macro in which it appears. Correspondingly, a macro definition that includes a nested macro is known as an outer macro. The expansion of the outer macro might or might not invoke the inner expansion, depending on the dictates of AIF directives that appear in the definition.

The definition of the BEGIN macro in figure 17.8 illustrates a simple nesting situation. The REGS macro (defined in fig. 17.4) is nested within the BEGIN macro. When the BEGIN macro is invoked, its expansion will include that of the REGS macro.

The values that are specified in the operand of a nested macro can include any of the parameters specified in the prototype of the outer macro. They also can include any of the variables declared by GBLx or LCLx directives in the outer macro as well as any of the system variables. The parameters or variables of the outer macro are said to be *passed* to the inner macro. In the INIT macro of figure 17.9, the value of &R is passed as a character string from the outer macro to the inner BASE macro. The value of &R used for the expansion of the BASE macro will be the value appearing in the statement that invokes the INIT macro.

Figure 17.8   Definition of BEGIN macro.

```
          MACRO
&L        BEGIN
&L        CSECT
          REGS
          STM     R14,R12,12(R13)
          BALR    R12,0
          USING   *,R12
          ST      R13,SAVE+4
          LA      R13,SAVE
          MEND
```

Figure 17.9   Definition of INIT macro.

```
          MACRO
&L        INIT    &R,&SAVE=SAVE
&L        CSECT
          STM     14,12,12(13)
          BASE    &R
          ST      13,&SAVE+4
          LA      13,&SAVE
          MEND
```

For example, the expansion of the statement:

```
          MAIN        INIT        12
```

consists of these statements:

```
          MAIN        CSECT
                      STM         14,12,12(13)
                      BALR        12,0
                      USING       *,12
          B0001       EQU         *
                      ST          13,SAVE+4
                      LA          13,SAVE
```

(The BASE macro in fig. 17.9 was discussed in the previous section.)

A similar use of nested macros is illustrated by the XSRP macro defined in figure 17.10. XSRP invokes two other macros, Shift Left Packed Decimal (SLPD) and Shift Right Packed Decimal (SRPD). But not only are the prototype parameters passed to the nested macros, the name-field symbol and the value of the local variable &ROUND also are passed. The SLPD macro is defined in figure 17.11; the expansions it generates are equivalent to the code shown in figures 12.2a and 12.2b. The definition of SRPD is left as an exercise.

The prototype of the Shift and Round Packed (XSRP) macro is modeled after the format of the IBM 370 SRP instruction. However, XSRP does not possess the full range of capabilities that SRP does; the number of digits that can be shifted by XSRP must be less than or equal to six and must be specified as a decimal integer, and the rounding factor—also required to be a decimal integer—can be only 0 or 5. Compare these limitations with the capabilities of SRP described in chapter 12; verification is left as an exercise.

The values of the local system variables &SYSLIST, &SYSNDX, and &SYSECT are affected by nested macros in the following manner. &SYSLIST always refers to the positional operands in the macro instruction that invokes a definition containing it. When a macro definition that contains &SYSLIST is invoked as an outer macro, each occurrence of &SYSLIST in that definition refers to the outer macro instruction's positional operands. When invoked as an inner macro, each occurrence of &SYSLIST refers to the operands of the inner macro instruction.

&SYSNDX is assigned a different value for each inner macro that is invoked. The value is not changed during the expansion of an inner macro, but reverts to its previous value when the expansion of the inner macro is completed. Each new value assigned to &SYSNDX is a number that is one more than the previous highest value of &SYSNDX.

&SYSECT always refers to the name of the control section in which a macro containing &SYSECT is invoked. Therefore, the value of &SYSECT can change only if a macro definition contains a START, CSECT, DSECT, or COM directive, or if an open code statement contains one of those directives. When a control section is initiated or continued in open code, the value of &SYSECT is set equal to the name of that

Figure 17.10   Definition of XSRP macro for the IBM 360.

```
              MACRO
&L            XSRP        &X,&N,&R
              LCLC        &ROUND
.*
.* THE XSRP (SHIFT AND ROUND PACKED) MACRO PROVIDES A
.*   LIMITED CAPABILITY FOR SHIFTING PACKED-DECIMAL NUMBERS
.*   ON THE IBM 360.
.*
.*        &X DESIGNATES THE ADDRESS OF THE PACKED-DECIMAL NUMBER.
.*
.*        &N  MUST BE A DECIMAL INTEGER IN THE RANGE -6 TO +6 .
.*            IT REPRESENTS THE NUMBER OF DIGITS TO BE SHIFTED,
.*            AND THE DIRECTION OF SHIFT:
.*                RIGHT SHIFT IF &N IS NEGATIVE
.*                LEFT SHIFT IF &N IS POSITIVE
.*
.*        &R  DETERMINES WHETHER ROUNDING IS TO BE SUPPRESSED
.*            DURING A RIGHT SHIFT:
.*                NO ROUNDING IF  &R = 0
.*                ROUNDING IF &R IS NOT EQUAL TO 0
.*
.*   A RIGHT SHIFT IS ACCOMPLISHED BY INVOKING THE  SRPD  MACRO;
.*   A LEFT SHIFT, BY INVOKING THE  SLPD  MACRO.
.*
.*
.*
.*
              AIF         ('&N'(1,1) EQ '-').SRP2
.*
&L            SLPD        &X,&N
              MEXIT
.*
.SRP2         ANOP
&ROUND        SETC        'YES'
              AIF         ('&R' NE '0').SRP3
&ROUND        SETC        'NO'
.SRP3         ANOP
.*
&L            SRPD        &X,&N,RND=&ROUND
              MEND
```

section. But when a control section is initiated in a macro expansion, the value of &SYSECT continues to be the name of the previous section unless either of two conditions occur. First, if a subsequent macro is invoked as an inner macro in the expansion, then for that inner expansion &SYSECT is the name of the newly initiated control section. Second, if the expansion of the outer macro terminates without resuming the previous control section, &SYSECT becomes the name of the new control section. For example, assume that the macro DUMMY is defined in terms of another macro, DATA, and assume that DATA does not initiate a new control section:

```
                          MACRO
&L                        DUMMY       &A,&B
&L                        DSECT
                          DATA        &A,&B
&SYSECT                   CSECT
                          MEND
```

Figure 17.11   *Definition of SLPD macro for the IBM 360.*

```
                MACRO
&L              SLPD        &P,&D
                LCLA        &A,&B
                LCLB        &EVEN
                LCLC        &W
&B              SETA        &D
&A              SETA        &B/2
&EVEN           SETB        (&A*2 EQ &B)
&W              SETC        'W&SYSNDX'
.*
.*      THE SLPD (SHIFT LEFT PACKED-DECIMAL) MACRO SHIFTS
.*         THE PACKED DECIMAL NUMBER WHOSE ADDRESS IS GIVEN
.*         BY THE VALUE OF    &P   TO THE LEFT   N   DIGITS,
.*         WHERE N   IS GIVEN BY THE VALUE OF &D .
.*
.*         &D   MUST BE WRITTEN AS AN UNSIGNED DECIMAL DIGIT
.*             IN THE RANGE    FROM   1   TO   6 .
.*
.*         (THE POSSIBLE EXPANSIONS ARE SHOWN IN FIGS.12.2A
.*             AND 12.2B .)
.*
                AIF         (&EVEN).EVEN
.*
&L              ZAP         &W.(16),&P
                MVN         &W+15(1),=X'00'
                MVO         &P,&W+&A.(16)
                B           S&SYSNDX
                AGO         .COMMON
.*
.EVEN           ANOP
&A              SETA        &A-1
&L              MVO         &W.(16),&P
                MVC         &W+15(1),=X'00'
                MVO         &P,&W+&A.(16)
                B           S&SYSNDX
.*
.COMMON         ANOP
&W              DC          32X'00'
.*
S&SYSNDX        DS          0H
                MEND
```

During the expansion of the outer macro, DUMMY, the value of &SYSECT will be the name of the control section in which DUMMY is invoked. But during the expansion of the inner macro, DATA, the value of &SYSECT will be the name of the section in which DATA is invoked, represented as &L. When the inner expansion is completed, &SYSECT reverts to its previous value. Thus, the statement

&SYSECT   CSECT

in this example will result in the continuation of the section in which DUMMY was invoked. If no CSECT directive had been included in the definition of DUMMY, then, when the expansion of DUMMY had been completed, the value of &SYSECT would have become the value of &L, i.e., the name of the section initiated by the DSECT within the expansion.

17.8 DATA ATTRIBUTES

Six different attributes, or characteristics, of the data or data areas represented by ordinary symbols and variable symbols can be specified in the operands of SETx and AIF directives. One of the six attributes—the length attribute—also can be specified in the operand of a DC, DS, or EQU directive and in the operand of any instruction.

The attributes are specified with a notation that consists of two characters prefixed to an ordinary or variable symbol. The two characters are a letter followed by an apostrophe ('), as follows:

T'	type attribute
K'	count attribute
S'	scaling attribute
I'	integer attribute
L'	length attribute
N'	number attribute

For example, N'&X denotes the number attribute of the variable symbol &X.

The use of attributes provides additional capabilities in macro definitions and conditional assemblies. We will not illustrate all these capabilities, nor will we discuss all the rules and restrictions pertaining to the use of attributes. What follows is merely a summary of the main uses of attributes and a few illustrative examples. Consult the IBM assembly language reference manual for a complete discussion.

Type Attribute

The value of the type attribute T' of a symbol is a single letter that designates the type of data or data area that the symbol represents. The set of attribute values corresponding to different data types is summarized in figure 17.12. For example, if X were defined by the statement

$$\text{X} \qquad \text{DS} \qquad \text{3CL5}$$

T'X would have the value C, i.e., X represents character data.

Count Attribute

The value of the count attribute K' is an integer that equals the number of characters constituting the value of a variable symbol. (The count attribute cannot be used with ordinary symbols.) For example, if &X is a variable symbol whose value is 100, then K'&X = 3, i.e., three characters are required to represent the value of 100 as a character string. Similarly, if &A is the seven-character string (ALPHA), then K'&A = 7, K'&A–2 = 5, and, using the substring notation introduced in chapter 16, we have

$$\text{'\&A'(2,K'\&A–2)} = \text{ALPHA}.$$

In other words, the count attribute can be used to perform string operations on strings whose length is not known to the programmer.

Scaling Attribute

The scaling attribute S' can be used only with symbols that refer to fixed-point (F,H), floating-point (E,D,L), and decimal (P,Z) constants. For fixed-point and floating-point constants, the value of S' is simply the value of n in the scale modifier Sn used to define the constant. For packed-decimal constants, the value of S' is simply the number of digits to the right of the implied decimal point. The following examples illustrate this:

X	DC	FS2'300'	S'X	=	2
Y	DC	ES1'3.142'	S'Y	=	1
Z	DC	P'3.142'	S'Z	=	3
W	DC	F'10'	S'W	=	0

Figure 17.12   *Type attributes of ordinary symbols.*

If X is an ordinary symbol that is defined in the name field of a DC or DS directive, then the type attribute T'X is a single character whose value depends on the type of data or data area defined by X.

T'X	type of data or data area defined by X
A	A-type address constant
B	Binary constant
C	Character constant
D	Long-format floating-point constant
E	Short-format floating-point constant
F	Full-word binary integer constant
G	Full-word binary integer constant, with explicit length
H	Half-word binary integer constant
K	Any floating-point constant with explicit length
L	Extended-format floating-point constant
P	Packed decimal constant
Q	Q-type address constant
R	A-,S-,Q-,V-, or Y-type address constant with explicit length
S	S-type address constant
V	V-type address constant
X	Hexadecimal constant
Y	Y-type address constant
Z	Zoned decimal constant

Note: For the following type attributes, the length of the defined constant or data area is understood to have been implied, not explicitly given:

A-, S-, Q-, V-, and Y-type address constants
D-, E-, and L-type floating point constants
F- and H-type binary integer constants

If X is an ordinary symbol that is *not* defined in the name field of a DC or DS directive, then the type attribute T'X is a single character whose value depends on the type of statement in which X is defined.

T'X	type of statement in which X is defined
I	assembly language instruction
J	CSECT, DSECT, START, COM directive
M	statement invoking a macro
N	a macro instruction operand that is a self-defining term
O	a macro instruction operand that is omitted (null value)
T	EXTRN
U	LTORG, EQU, and certain other types
W	CCW
$	WXTRN

Integer Attribute

The integer attribute I' can only be used with symbols that refer to fixed-point, floating-point, and decimal constants. The value of I' is the number of positions occupied by the integer portion of such a constant. For fixed-point constants, the word *positions* means bits; for floating-point constants, it means hex digits in the mantissa; and for decimal constants, it means decimal digits. The following examples illustrate this. The formulas at the right show precisely how the integer attribute is calculated, L' being the length attribute.

X	DC	FS2'300'	I'X	=	29	I'	=	$8*L' - 1 - S'$
Y	DC	ES1'3.142'	I'Y	=	5	I'	=	$2*L' - 2 - S'$
Z	DC	P'3.142'	I'Z	=	2	I'	=	$2*L' - 1 - S'$

Length Attribute

The length attribute L' of an ordinary symbol is the number of bytes of memory occupied by the data or data area represented by that symbol. If the symbol represents an instruction, the length attribute of that symbol is the length of that instruction. If the symbol is defined by a DS or DC directive, the length attribute of that symbol is the value n specified by the length modifier, Ln, if any; and, if no length modifier is used in the definition, the length attribute of the symbol is the implied length of the constant or data area. It should be noted that the length attribute is independent of the duplication factor in a DC or DS directive. For example, if V were defined by this statement:

$$V \qquad DC \qquad 3CL8'LENGTH'$$

L'V would have the value 8. Similarly, for the symbols X, Y, and Z defined in the discussion of integer attributes, L'X=4, L'Y=4, and L'Z=3. From its definition, we see that the length attribute of a symbol is an absolute constant, i.e., it is independent of the location of a program in memory at run time.

The length attribute also can be specified for variable symbols, e.g., L'&X. When this is done, the value of that variable symbol must be an ordinary symbol defined by a statement in open code. Otherwise, the Assembler cannot evaluate its length attribute at assembly time. For example, consider this macro definition:

```
        MACRO
&L      MOVER    &A,&B
&L      MVC      &B.(L'&A),&A
        MEND
```

When invoked, the length field in the MVC instruction of the expansion will contain the length attribute of the ordinary symbol designated in the first operand of MOVER. Thus,

$$MOVER \qquad HERE,THERE$$

generates the instruction

$$MVC \qquad THERE(L'HERE),HERE.$$

HERE is the value of the variable symbol &A. For this definition and expansion to be valid, HERE must be the name-field symbol of some open-code statement. Other restrictions on the use of L' with variable symbols will not be discussed.

Number Attribute

The value of the number attribute N' is equal to the number of values in a parameter sublist of a statement that invokes a macro. Note that according to its definition, the number attribute can be specified only inside macro definitions, and can be specified only with variable symbols that represent parameters in a macro's prototype.

Examples. To conclude this brief discussion of attributes, we present two examples of the use of the number attribute, N'. The first example is rather elementary; the second illustrates the power of N' when combined with the system variable &SYSLIST.

According to the definition of the BASE macro of figure 17.7, in order to determine how many sublist values are specified in the operand, we must look for the occurrence of a null sublist value. This concept was embodied in Statement 16 of that definition, namely,

$$AIF \qquad ('\&R(\&X)' \ EQ \ '').B2$$

An alternate way of achieving the same objective would be to use the number attribute N'&R, and rewrite Statement 16 as

$$AIF \qquad (\&X \ GT \ N'\&R).B2$$

With this statement, the Assembler would skip to the statement identified by the sequence symbol .B2 if the value of &X were greater than the number of values specified in the sublist denoted by &R. For example, if the BASE macro were invoked by the statement

$$BASE \qquad (12,11)$$

the value of N'&R would be 2, and the expansion would be terminated after Register 11 had been processed.

Figure 17.13a   HEDIT macro, illustrating use of &SYSLIST(M,N).

```
FLAG LOCTN OBJECT CODE      ADDR1   ADDR2  STMNT M SOURCE STATEMENT

                                       3              MACRO
                                       4    &L        HEDIT    &N,&PN
                                       5    .*  'HEDIT' CONVERTS ONE OR MORE HALF-WORD INTEGERS TO THEIR
                                       6    .*         6-CHARACTER EBCDIC REPRESENTATIONS.  SIX CHARS IS
                                       7    .*         SUFFICIENT SINCE THE RANGE IS -32,768 TO +32,767 .
                                       8    .*
                                       9    .*  IN EACH EBCDIC STRING, THE FIRST CHAR IS THE SIGN (BLANK
                                      10    .*         FOR +) AND THE REMAINING CHARS REPRESENT THE INTEGER
                                      11    .*         WITH LEADING ZEROES REPLACED BY BLANKS.
                                      12    .*
                                      13    .*  THE SYMBOLIC ADDR OF EACH INTEGER AND ITS CORRESPONDING
                                      14    .*         EBCDIC STRING AREA MUST BE SPECIFIED AS THE 1ST AND
                                      15    .*         2ND SUBLIST VALUES OF A POSITIONAL OPERAND.
                                      16    .*
                                      17    .*  FOR EXAMPLE, TO CONVERT 3 HALF-WD INTEGERS WGHOSE SYMBOLIC
                                      18    .*         ADDRS ARE L, M, AND N INTO 6-CHAR EBCDIC STRINGS AT
                                      19    .*         SYMBOLIC ADDRS PL, PM, AND PN, USE 'HEDIT' THIS WAY
                                      20    .*
                                      21    .*              HEDIT    (L,PL),(M,PM),(N,PN)
                                      22    .*
                                      23              LCLA  &K        SUBSCRIPT FOR &SYSLIST
                                      24    &K        SETA  1
                                      25    &L        ST    5,A3&SYSNDX    SAVE REG 5 CONTENTS TEMPORARILY
                                      26    .A0       ANOP
                                      27    .*
                                      28    .*  GET KTH HALF-WD INTEGER AND CONVT TO PACKED DECIMAL
                                      29    .*
                                      30              LH    5,&SYSLIST(&K,1)
                                      31              CVD   5,A2&SYSNDX
                                      32    .*
                                      33    .*  MOVE PATTERN INTO 6-BYTE AREA SPECIFIED BY KTH OPERAND
                                      34    .*         AND EDIT LOW-ORDER 3 BYTES OF PACKED DECIMAL NUMBER
                                      35    .*
                                      36              MVC   &SYSLIST(&K,2).(6),=X'402020202120'
                                      37              ED    &SYSLIST(&K,2).(6),A2&SYSNDX+5
                                      38    .*
                                      39    .*  INSERT MINUS SIGN IF NUMBER WAS NEGATIVE
                                      40    .*
                                      41              BNM   B&K.&SYSNDX
                                      42              MVI   &SYSLIST(&K,2),C'-'
                                      43    B&K.&SYSNDX  EQU  *
                                      44    .*
                                      45    .*  REPEAT CONVERT AND EDIT STEPS FOR EACH OPERAND
                                      46    .*
                                      47    &K        SETA  &K+1
                                      48              AIF   (&K LE N'&SYSLIST).A0
                                      49              B     A4&SYSNDX
                                      50    .*
                                      51    A2&SYSNDX    DS   D        STORAGE FOR PACKED DECIMAL NUMBER
                                      52    A3&SYSNDX    DS   F        STORAGE FOR REG 5 CONTENTS
                                      53    A4&SYSNDX    L    5,A3&SYSNDX   RESTORE REG 5 CONTENTS
                                      54              MEND
```

When used with the system variable &SYSLIST, the number attribute N' is defined as follows: (1) N'&SYSLIST is the number of positional operands specified or specifically omitted when invoking a macro, and (2) N'&SYSLIST*(k)* is the number of sublist values specified or specifically omitted in the *k*th positional operand when invoking a macro. We illustrate the use of &SYSLIST and its number attribute N'&SYSLIST with the macro HEDIT defined in figure 17.13a. In the AIF directive near the end of the definition, namely,

> AIF   (&K LE N'&SYSLIST).A0

N'&SYSLIST will be the number of half-word integers to be converted to EBCDIC representation when HEDIT is invoked. Thus, if HEDIT is invoked by the statement

> HEDIT   (N,PN),(M,PM),(L,PL)

then N'&SYSLIST = 3. You should verify that the definition of figure 17.13a produces the expansions shown in figure 17.13b.

Figure 17.13b Expansions of HEDIT macro (see fig. 17.13a).

```
FLAG LOCTN OBJECT CODE     ADDR1  ADDR2  STMNT M SOURCE STATEMENT

     000000                              56      HEDIT  CSECT
     000000 90 EC D00C                   57             STM    14,12,12(13)
     000004 05 C0                        58             BALR   12,0
     000006                              59             USING  *,12
     000006 50 D0 C12E     000134        60             ST     13,SAVE+4
     00000A 41 D0 C12A     000130        61             LA     13,SAVE
                                         62      *

                                         63             HEDIT  (X,PX)
     00000E 50 50 C03A     000040        64 1           ST     5,A30001    SAVE REG 5 CONTENTS TEMPORARILY
     000012 48 50 C10C     000112        65 1           LH     5,X
     000016 4E 50 C032     000038        66 1           CVD    5,A20001
     00001A D2 05 C112C172 000118 000178 67 1           MVC    PX(6),=X'402020202120'
     000020 DE 05 C112C037 000118 00003D 68 1           ED     PX(6),A20001+5
     000026 47 B0 C028     00002E        69 1           BNM    B10001
     00002A 92 60 C112     000118        70 1           MVI    PX,C'-'
     00002E                              71 1 B10001    EQU    *
     00002E 47 F0 C03E     000044        72 1           B      A40001
     000038                              73 1 A20001    DS     D      STORAGE FOR PACKED DECIMAL NUMBER
     000040                              74 1 A30001    DS     F      STORAGE FOR REG 5 CONTENTS
     000044 58 50 C03A     000040        75 1 A40001    L      5,A30001    RESTORE REG 5 CONTENTS

                                         76             HEDIT  (Y,PY),(Z,PZ)
     000048 50 50 C08A     000090        77 1           ST     5,A30002    SAVE REG 5 CONTENTS TEMPORARILY
     00004C 48 50 C10E     000114        78 1           LH     5,Y
     000050 4E 50 C082     000088        79 1           CVD    5,A20002
     000054 D2 05 C11AC172 000120 000178 80 1           MVC    PY(6),=X'402020202120'
     00005A DE 05 C11AC087 000120 00008D 81 1           ED     PY(6),A20002+5
     000060 47 B0 C062     000068        82 1           BNM    B10002
     000064 92 60 C11A     000120        83 1           MVI    PY,C'-'
     000068                              84 1 B10002    EQU    *
     000068 48 50 C110     000116        85 1           LH     5,Z
     00006C 4E 50 C082     000088        86 1           CVD    5,A20002
     000070 D2 05 C122C172 000128 000178 87 1           MVC    PZ(6),=X'402020202120'
     000076 DE 05 C122C087 000128 00008D 88 1           ED     PZ(6),A20002+5
     00007C 47 B0 C07E     000084        89 1           BNM    B20002
     000080 92 60 C122     000128        90 1           MVI    PZ,C'-'
     000084                              91 1 B20002    EQU    *
     000084 47 F0 C08E     000094        92 1           B      A40002
     000088                              93 1 A20002    DS     D      STORAGE FOR PACKED DECIMAL NUMBER
     000090                              94 1 A30002    DS     F      STORAGE FOR REG 5 CONTENTS
     000094 58 50 C08A     000090        95 1 A40002    L      5,A30002    RESTORE REG 5 CONTENTS
                                         96             HEDIT  (X,PX),(Y,PY),(Z,PZ)
     000098 50 50 C0FA     000100        97 1           ST     5,A30003    SAVE REG 5 CONTENTS TEMPORARILY
     00009C 48 50 C10C     000112        98 1           LH     5,X
     0000A0 4E 50 C0F2     0000F8        99 1           CVD    5,A20003
     0000A4 D2 05 C112C172 000118 000178 100 1          MVC    PX(6),=X'402020202120'
     0000AA DE 05 C112C0F7 000118 0000FD 101 1          ED     PX(6),A20003+5
     0000B0 47 B0 C0B2     0000B8        102 1          BNM    B10003
     0000B4 92 60 C112     000118        103 1          MVI    PX,C'-'
     0000B8                              104 1 B10003    EQU    *
     0000B8 48 50 C10E     000114        105 1          LH     5,Y
     0000BC 4E 50 C0F2     0000F8        106 1          CVD    5,A20003
     0000C0 D2 05 C11AC172 000120 000178 107 1          MVC    PY(6),=X'402020202120'
     0000C6 DE 05 C11AC0F7 000120 0000FD 108 1          ED     PY(6),A20003+5
     0000CC 47 B0 C0CE     0000D4        109 1          BNM    B20003
     0000D0 92 60 C11A     000120        110 1          MVI    PY,C'-'
     0000D4                              111 1 B20003    EQU    *
     0000D4 48 50 C110     000116        112 1          LH     5,Z
     0000D8 4E 50 C0F2     0000F8        113 1          CVD    5,A20003
     0000DC D2 05 C122C172 000128 000178 114 1          MVC    PZ(6),=X'402020202120'
     0000E2 DE 05 C122C0F7 000128 0000FD 115 1          ED     PZ(6),A20003+5
     0000E8 47 B0 C0EA     0000F0        116 1          BNM    B30003
     0000EC 92 60 C122     000128        117 1          MVI    PZ,C'-'
     0000F0                              118 1 B30003    EQU    *
     0000F0 47 F0 C0FE     000104        119 1          B      A40003
     0000F8                              120 1 A20003    DS     D      STORAGE FOR PACKED DECIMAL NUMBER
     000100                              121 1 A30003    DS     F      STORAGE FOR REG 5 CONTENTS
     000104 58 50 C0FA     000100        122 1 A40003    L      5,A30003    RESTORE REG 5 CONTENTS
                                         123     *
     000108 58 D0 C12E     000134        124            L      13,SAVE+4
     00010C 98 EC D00C                   125            LM     14,12,12(13)
     000110 07 FE                        126            BR     14
                                         127     *
     000112 0000                         128     X       DC     H'0'
     000114 8000                         129     Y       DC     H'-32768'
     000116 7FFF                         130     Z       DC     H'+32767'
     000118                              131            DS     0D
     000118                              132     PX      DS     CL6
     000120                              133            DS     0D
     000120                              134     PY      DS     CL6
     000128                              135            DS     0D
     000128                              136     PZ      DS     CL6
     000130                              137     SAVE    DS     18F
     000178 402020202120                 138
                                         139            END
```

416   Directives

17.9 SUMMARY

A macro is an opcode that can be used as a kind of high-level directive to represent a set of one or more instructions, directives, and previously defined macros. The definition of each macro invoked in a source-module must either be included in that source-module or reside in a file accessible to the Assembler when the source-module is being assembled.

Each time a macro is invoked, the Assembler generates an expansion by processing the macro's definition. The statements generated are inserted at the point immediately following the statement invoking the macro and are then assembled as though they were part of the original source-module.

All macro definitions must begin with a header (the MACRO directive), end with a trailer (the MEND directive), and contain a prototype statement as well as one or more statements that constitute the body of the definition. The prototype must immediately follow the header. It defines the macro's name and the parameters whose values may be specified when invoking the macro. The body must immediately follow the prototype. It includes the statements that will be generated and may also include control directives to provide conditional assembly capabilities at the time the expansion is generated.

All parameters included in the prototype are processed as local character assembly variables; their scope is limited to the statements in the definition. The values of these parameters are specified when a macro is invoked and are substituted for the respective prototype parameters during the generation of the expansion at assembly time.

Global assembly variables can be passed from open code to macro definitions, and local assembly variables can be declared within the body of the definition. Appropriate SETx directives can be used in the body to change the values of these variables. The variables also can be used in expressions, e.g., in AIF and SETx operands, to control the processing of the definition. Thus, the statements in the body can specify decisions to be made at assembly time in order to dictate to the Assembler the statements and/or variable values that shall be represented in the expansion.

The examples given in this chapter illustrated the following capabilities that can be used in macro definitions: substitution of values for parameters; decision making during the expansion process, concatenation, sublists, nested macros, substring evaluation, and the use of &SYSNDX, &SYSLIST, MNOTE, MEXIT, and the special comment statement denoted by '.∗' in its first two positions. Also discussed and briefly illustrated was the mechanism of data attributes: T' (type), K' (count), S' (scaling), I' (integer), L' (length), and N' (number). A complete discussion of all the rules relating to the IBM 360 and 370 macro facilities can be found in the *Assembler Reference Manual*.

EXERCISES

1. The assembly language instruction Load and Test Register (LTR) is an RR-type instruction that sets the condition code according as the number that is loaded is zero, negative, or positive. Although there is no comparable RX-type instruction, the macro named Load and Test (LT), defined here, will generate an expansion that in effect would be the RX-type counterpart of LTR.

```
        MACRO
&L      LT          &R,&M
&L      L           &R,&M
        LTR         &R,&R
        MEND
```

Define macros that would in effect be the RX-type counterparts of the LCR, LNR, and LPR assembly language instructions.

2. The assembly language instruction Branch Not High (BNH) is a conditional branch instruction that branches if the condition code is any value except '2'. It would perhaps have been more appropriately named Branch Less than or Equal (BLE). The macro defined here makes the opcode BLE the equivalent of the opcode BNH. Define other macros named BGE, BLT, and BGT that would be equivalent to the instructions BNL, BL, and BH, respectively.

```
        MACRO
&L      BLE         &M
&L      BNH         &M
        MEND
```

3. What is the purpose of the MEXIT directive? If there were no MEXIT directive, how could its purpose be achieved through the use of other directives?

4. A macro's expansion can include constants and storage areas as well as instructions. In the following macro definition, a full word is generated to serve as a temporary storage area for general Register 5 in order that the register can be used to add +1 to an integer stored in memory.

```
            MACRO
&L          BUMP        &M
&L          ST          5,B&SYSNDX
            L           5,&M
            AH          5,=H'1'
            ST          5,&M
            L           5,B&SYSNDX
            B           B&SYSNDX+4
B&SYSNDX DS F
            MEND
```

a. Why is the symbol B&SYSNDX used in the BUMP macro instead of B alone?
b. Why is the instruction   B   B&SYSNDX+4   included in the definition of the BUMP macro?
c. Define a macro named SWAP that will interchange the contents of two full words in memory.

5. One way to copy more than 256 bytes from one memory location to another is to use the MVCL instruction. Another way (often used in the IBM 360, which has no MVCL instruction) is to code consecutive MVC instructions. The following macro definition will cause the required number of MVC instructions to be generated regardless of the number of bytes that are to be copied. The number of bytes to be copied must be specified by the keyword parameter &N or the default of 1 byte will be copied.

```
            MACRO
&L          XMVC        &A,&B,&N=1
            LCLA        &X,&Y
            AIF         ('&L' EQ '').X0
&L          EQU         *
.X0         ANOP
&X          SETA        &N
.X1         AIF         (&X LE 256).X2
            MVC         &A+&Y.(256),&B+&Y
&Y          SETA        &Y+256
&X          SETA        &X-256
            AGO         .X1
.X2         MVC         &A+&Y.(&X),&B+&Y
            MEND
```

Define a macro named XCLC for the IBM 360 that will compare an arbitrary number of bytes at one location in memory to the same number of bytes at another memory location. The condition code must reflect the result of the comparison so that a subsequent conditional branch instruction can be used.

6. Answer the following questions for the XMVC macro defined in Exercise 5:

   a. What expansion would be generated if XMVC were invoked by the statement
      XMVC THERE,HERE,N=800
   b. What is the purpose of the first AIF directive occurring in the definition of XMVC? Why is this directive necessary in the XMVC definition?
   c. Note that &A and &B must be specified as relocatable expressions; they cannot be specified as explicit base-displacement addresses. Why is this so?

7. The HEDIT macro of figure 17.13 converts a half-word binary integer to the EBCDIC form that is suitable for printing. Define a macro named FEDIT that will convert a full-word binary integer to a suitable EBCDIC form. Note that the largest decimal integer that can be represented as a full-word binary integer consists of ten significant digits. (Hint: see Section 12.9.)

8. Define a macro that will convert an integer from its 12-byte EBCDIC representation to its full-word binary representation. (Hint: see Section 12.8.)

9. Complete the definition of the XSRP macro of figure 17.10 by defining an SRPD macro analogous to the SLPD macro of figure 17.11.

10. One of the instructions in the optional extended-precision floating-point instruction set is Load Rounded, Long to Short (LRER). Since this instruction, described in Section 13.7, would be useful even in systems that do not have the extended-precision feature, define a macro, say XLRER, that will duplicate the function of LRER for systems lacking extended-precision hardware.

11. Rewrite the definition of the BASE macro given in figure 17.7 so that it is not necessary to enclose the register addresses within parentheses when invoking the macro, no matter how many registers are specified. Hint: use the system variable &SYSLIST in your definition.

12. Suppose that the BASE macro of figure 17.7 were invoked by the statement

BASE   16

Would an expansion containing the invalid register address be generated? If so, when would the error be detected?

13. Suppose that the REGS macro of figure 17.4 were invoked by the statement

START   REGS   0,15

How would the symbol START be processed by the Assembler? What effect would the operand have on the expansion of the macro?

14. Suppose that the HEDIT macro of figure 17.13a were invoked by the statement

HEDIT   X,PX

Why wouldn't this produce the same expansion as HEDIT (X,PX)? What is the expansion of HEDIT X,PX? What would be the effect at run time?

15. By means of the substring notation introduced in Section 16.6, and used in figure 17.10, it is possible to examine any subset of consecutive characters comprising a macro operand. In particular, a macro operand can be examined one character at a time and thus affect the course of the expansion generated. Using the substring notation, define a macro named PIC that will cause an appropriate editing pattern to be generated for use with the ED and EDMK instructions. For example, if the PIC prototype is

&L   PIC   &P

then the expansion generated for the statement

P1   PIC   999,999.99

should be

P1   DC   X'402121216B2121214B2020'

(Refer to Section 12.9 for definitions and examples of patterns.) This is not a particularly easy problem; you may wish to establish some conditions on the permissible forms of the operand specified when PIC is invoked.

16. The substring notation (see Exercise 15) can be used to allow a revised definition of the CALL macro of figure 17.6. The revision is as follows: instead of requiring the subroutine name and parameter list to be separated by a comma, let the statement invoking the CALL macro be written like a CALL in FORTRAN, e.g. like this:

CALL   SUBR(X,Y,Z)

Write a definition of the CALL macro that will accomplish this.

17. What are the similarities and differences between the use of macros and the use of subroutines? What guidelines, if any, can you formulate to help you decide when to define a macro for a given task and when to write a subroutine for that task? Can you conceive of any tasks for which a macro whose expansion calls a subroutine might be appropriate?

PART
FIVE

Input / Output

18

I/O Hardware Concepts

For a program to be run, it must be in main memory, as must the data on which it operates. Secondary memory is a passive storage device for programs and data not in use. It can store many thousands of times as much information as main memory, yet it is much less costly per unit of information. A major reason for the cost difference is that since programs are not run in secondary memory, access to information stored in secondary memory need not be as uniformly fast as to data and instructions in main memory. Whereas access to information in main memory is accomplished in speeds of the order of one microsecond (10^{-6} seconds) per byte independently of the byte's physical location, access to information in secondary memory is accomplished in speeds of the order of one millisecond (10^{-3} seconds) per byte or more, depending on the physical location of the bytes being accessed. The lower cost of secondary memory per unit of information makes large storage capacities economically feasible. The slower access to information is partly compensated for by a variety of software techniques, many of which will be discussed in the remaining chapters.

Two main classes of secondary memory used by applications programmers are magnetic tapes and magnetic disks. In both, data are stored on magnetized surfaces that move past data-sensing and data-recording mechanisms called *read/write heads*. The amount of data that can be stored on a tape or disk, the data blocksizes that best match the physical characteristics of these devices, and the speed with which data can be transferred between main memory and the devices are all important concerns in input/output programming. These are discussed in the following sections. Other I/O hardware concepts, such as the methods by which the CPU communicates with I/O devices and secondary memory, the role of I/O processors and so-called "channel programming," and the characteristics of magnetic drum memory devices, will not be discussed in this text.

18.1 MAGNETIC TAPES

In a tape device, data can be recorded and sensed only while a magnetized tape surface passes under a stationary read/write head. To position the data that is at point *B,* say, under the read/write head, all the data before point B is reached must also pass under the read/write head. (Tape cassettes used for sound recordings provide a good analogy in this respect.) The tape must be accelerated from rest to its normal processing speed before any data can be sensed, recorded, or skipped over. The acceleration time, known as the *start time,* is of the order of 10 milliseconds. The data-transfer time is of the order of 100,000 to 500,000 bytes per second, or from 2 to 10 microseconds per byte. Data on tape is usually recorded at a density of 800 or 1600 bytes per inch, but both higher-density and lower-density tapes are in use. Whatever the density, the data is recorded in physical blocks that are separated by gaps. When a tape is at rest, a gap (not data) is positioned under the read/write head; thus, a gap allows the tape to accelerate and decelerate without having to sense or record data in the process. These concepts are illustrated in figure 18.1.

The ratio of total gap space to the length of a tape provides a useful measure of the efficiency with which a tape is used to store data. Each gap is approximately one-half inch long. The more blocks there are, the more gaps there are. The number of blocks is determined both by the length of the tape and by the *block*

422

Figure 18.1   Magnetic tape concepts.

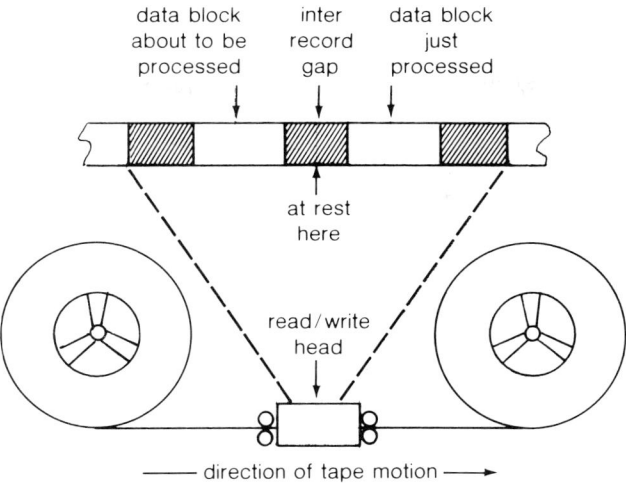

Figure 18.2   Effect of block size on tape capacity (for 3600-foot reel with gap size ½ inch).

blocksize	capacity (no. of bytes)	
	800 BPI	1600 BPI
80	5.76×10^6	6.28×10^6
800	23.0×10^6	34.6×10^6
1600	27.6×10^6	46.1×10^6
3200	30.7×10^6	55.3×10^6
6400	32.5×10^6	61.4×10^6

capacity (in bytes) given by

$$\frac{L \times B}{G + \dfrac{B}{D}}$$

with $L = 3600 \times 12$ inches
$G = $ ½ inch
$D = $ density
$B = $ blocksize

size, i.e., the number of bytes in a block. At 1600 BPI, a 3200-byte physical block (2 inches) results in 20% gap space (i.e., half-inch gaps constitute 20% of the total tape length), and a 6400-byte block results in 10% gap space.

A good approximation to the total number of bytes that can be stored on a reel of magnetic tape in which the size of all data blocks is the same can be calculated from the formula

$$\{\text{tape capacity}\} = \frac{L \times B}{G + \dfrac{B}{D}}$$

where $L = $ tape length in inches
$B = $ blocksize in bytes

$D = $ tape density in bytes per inch
$G = $ gap space in inches

From this formula, it can be seen that the total capacity is dependent on the length, density, and gap size, all of which are given physical characteristics of a tape, and also on the blocksize and on the ratio of blocksize to density. Choice of blocksize is a programmer's option, and the decision should be made with care. In order not to let the gap space dominate the utilization of the tape reel, we should choose B so that B/D is reasonably larger than G. This is illustrated by the data in figure 18.2.

Figure 18.3 *Effect of blocksize on tape transfer time.*

blocksize	transfer time overhead	
	$T = 2 \times 10^{-3}$ ms/byte	$T = 10 \times 10^{-3}$ ms/byte
80	98.4 %	92.6 %
800	86.2 %	55.5 %
1600	75.6 %	38.5 %
3200	60.1 %	23.8 %
6400	43.9 %	13.5 %

overhead percent given by

$$\left(\frac{S}{S + B \times T}\right) \times 100$$

with S = 10 ms start time
T = transfer rate
B = blocksize

There is another reason for careful selection of blocksize. This has to do with the rate at which data is transferred between tape and main memory. We have already mentioned that this rate is usually from 2 to 10 microseconds per byte, after an initial start time of 10 milliseconds. Thus, the total time required to transfer a block of data between tape and main memory is given by the formula

transfer time = start time + (blocksize) (transfer-rate).

The larger the blocksize, the less the effect of start time on total transfer time. If T = transfer rate in milliseconds per byte, and S is start time in milliseconds, then we should choose a blocksize so that the overhead due to start time, as measured by the ratio $S / (S + B \times T)$, is reasonably small. As can be seen from the data in figure 18.3, the choice of blocksize to reduce data-transfer overhead is consistent with that required to reduce total gap space; we want large blocksizes in both cases.

Since it may be necessary to pass over some tape (perhaps a significant amount of tape) in order to reach some desired data record, the total time required to access a data record on tape can be fairly long compared to CPU processing speeds. In the worst case, it may take a few minutes to reach data that is at the end of a 3600-foot reel, if we start our search at the beginning of the tape. This is in sharp contrast to disk devices, discussed in the next section, in which worst-case access times are on the order of a hundred milliseconds.

18.2 MAGNETIC DISKS

In disk packs such as those used in the IBM 3330 disk system, there are a number of continuously rotating coaxial plates called *disks*. Data are stored on the surfaces of the disks in such a way that to access data on any one surface, we need not read past data on other surfaces. Mechanisms allow us to skip directly to the position on a surface where the desired data are stored. As with tape reels, each disk pack can be easily removed from the unit that houses it and be replaced by another pack. When removed, a pack (like a tape reel) is said to be *offline,* i.e., disconnected from the computer system; when placed in the unit and connected to the computer system, it is said to be *online.*

The diagram in figure 18.4 depicts a disk pack of the type used in IBM 3330 systems. In this type of pack, data are stored in concentric circular *tracks* on the surfaces of the disks. Each track of any one surface is vertically aligned with the correspondingly positioned tracks of all other surfaces, thereby forming a cylinder of tracks. Each surface has the same number of tracks, N, so that there are N cylinders. There is usually one read/write head per surface; the head must be positioned to the desired track before data can be sensed or recorded. When an access arm is moved to a track, all the other access arms are simultaneously moved to the tracks of the cylinder to which that track belongs. The positioning motion is called *seeking;* the time required for seeking is called *seek-time.* Once an arm is positioned at a desired track, the read/write head cannot sense or record data at an arbitrary point B on the track until that point has rotated around to a position directly under the head. The time required for this rotation is called *rotational-delay time.* The worst case for seeking occurs when the read/write heads are positioned at the innermost track and the desired data record is positioned in the outermost track (or vice versa). The worst case for rotational delay occurs when the desired data are just past the read/write head, so that a full rotation is required before data can be sensed or recorded. The maximum time required for worst-case seeking and worst-case rotational delay is on the order of a hundred milliseconds.

Figure 18.4 IBM disk pack concepts.

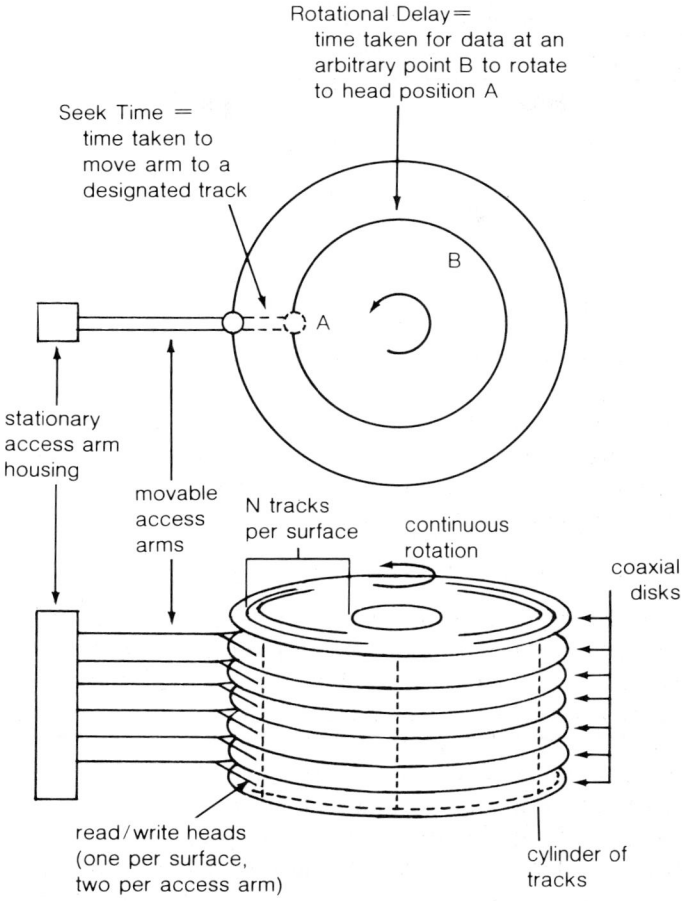

Rotational Delay =
time taken for data at an
arbitrary point B to rotate
to head position A

Seek Time =
time taken to
move arm to a
designated track

B

A

stationary
access arm
housing

movable
access
arms

N tracks
per surface

continuous
rotation

coaxial
disks

read/write heads
(one per surface,
two per access arm)

cylinder of
tracks

Designs other than that depicted in figure 18.4 exist for a number of other manufacturers' disk devices. In some of these, there is one read/write head for each track of a surface, so that seeking is not required. This is called a fixed head or "head-per-track" disk system. In other designs, each access arm can be moved independently of the other arms, so that at different instants different access arms can be positioned at different cylinders. And in still others, the concentric circular track technique is not used; instead, data are stored in discrete sectors of a surface, the number and position of the sectors varying with distance from the center of the surface. Various combinations of these design techniques also exist. However, in the discussions that follow and in those of the remaining chapters, we will be concerned only with the type of disk pack depicted in figure 18.4, since that is the type currently in use on most IBM 360 and 370 systems.

Data on a track are recorded in one or more physical blocks separated by gaps, analogous to inter-record gaps on tape. As with tapes, the more blocks there are on a disk track, the more gaps there are as well. The more gaps, the less room there is for data. Since each track has a fixed circumference and data density, the number of bytes that can be stored on a track depends on the blocksize.

The relationship between blocksize and track capacity is usually determined by consulting tables, such as the one in figure 18.5 for the IBM 3330 disk system. There are two critically important consequences of the data shown in the table:

1. *Blocksizes of less than about 1000 bytes make inefficient use of the available space.* For example, if each block held only one card image (80 bytes), there would be over 60 blocks on the track and over 60% of the available space would be wasted due to the gaps. If each block held 20 card images, there would still be almost 10% wasted space.

Figure 18.5 *Count-Data format: track utilization for IBM 3330 disk system with N = 13165/(135 + B).*
(See also fig. 18.9.)

N = number of data blocks per track	B = maximum possible blocksize for the indicated number of data blocks	maximum number of bytes per track	percent of maximum capacity
1	13030	13030	100 %
2	6447	12894	98.96
3	4253	12759	97.92
4	3156	12624	96.88
5	2498	12490	95.86
6	2059	12354	94.81
7	1745	12215	93.74
8	1510	12080	92.71
9	1327	11943	91.66
10	1181	11810	90.64
15	742	11130	85.42
20	523	10460	80.28
25	391	9775	75.02
30	303	9090	69.76
35	241	8435	64.74
40	194	7760	59.55
45	157	7065	54.22
50	128	6400	49.11
55	104	5720	43.90
60	84	5040	38.68

2. *A blocksize exactly equal to or slightly smaller than one of the blocksizes shown in the table should be chosen.* To do otherwise can result in considerably more wasted space than is shown in the table. For example, if a blocksize of 6450 bytes is chosen instead of 6447, then only one such block would fit on a track. This means that the attained capacity would be $\frac{6450}{13030}$, or approximately 50% of maximum capacity. If the blocksize were 6447, then two such blocks could fit on a track, and the attained capacity would be $\frac{2 \times 6447}{13030}$, i.e., greater than 98.9% of maximum capacity. This concept is illustrated in figure 18.6. The formula at the top of figure 18.5, N = 13165/(135+B), gives the number of data blocks that can fit on an IBM 3330 track for a given blocksize B. The constants represent the space required for gaps and other hardware-dependent information. When using the formula, you must discard the decimal portion of the quotient, since only whole blocks (not portions of blocks) can be stored on a track. For example, if B = 84, then 13165/219 = 60.114..., so N = 60.

The choice of an appropriate blocksize is also important from the standpoint of the time required to transfer data between disk and main memory. As mentioned earlier, two mechanical motions are involved in positioning a desired data block under a read/write head: head positioning and disk rotation. In the IBM 3330 disk storage system, the rotation rate of the disks is about 16.7 milliseconds per revolution so that the average rotational delay (sometimes referred to as average *latency*) is just half this, or 8.4 ms. The seek-time of the 3330 system varies from 0 to 55 ms; it is zero if no seeking is required, 10 ms if seeking to an adjacent cylinder, and 55 ms if seeking from the innermost to the outermost cylinder (or vice versa). The average seek-time cited in IBM publications is 30 ms. The total time required to position a data block under a read/write head is known as the disk *access time;* this is equal to the sum of the rotational delay time and the seek-time. Once positioned, the data is transferred at a rate of 806,000 bytes per second or 1.24 microseconds per byte.

Figure 18.6   Effect of blocksize and gap size on attainable track capacity in IBM 3330.

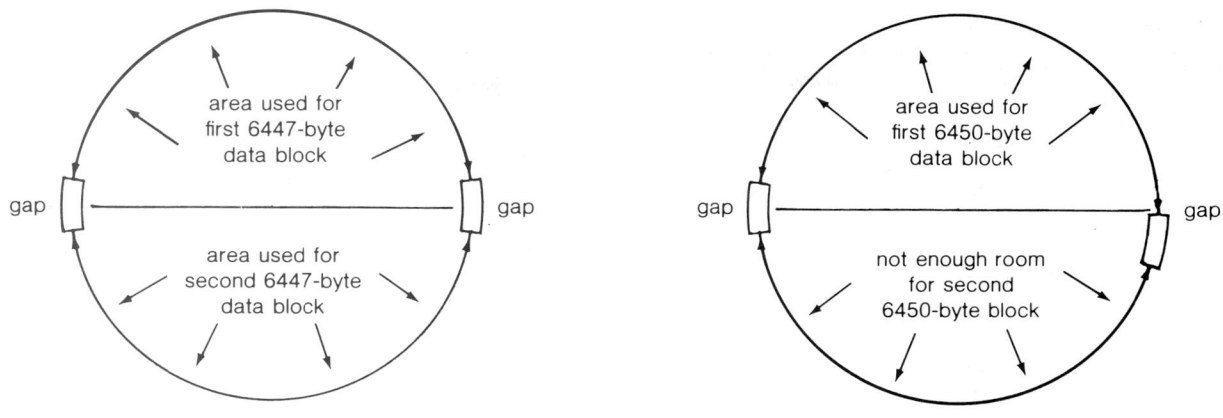

If we define a data-transfer overhead factor, X, as

$$X = \left(\frac{\text{access time}}{(\text{access time}) + (\text{data-transfer time})} \right) (100)$$

where access time is 8.4 plus seek-time (in milliseconds), and data-transfer time is

$$(\text{blocksize}) \, (1.24 \times 10^{-3} \text{ ms})$$

the dependence of X on blocksize for various values of seek-time is as shown in figures 18.7 and 18.8. It should be clear from these figures that a significant reduction in the overhead factor, X, is achieved when the blocksize is greater than about 2000 bytes, and that the best possible reductions are achieved when the seek-time is zero. It also should be clear that the ratio of data-transfer time to access time is quite small except for the largest blocksizes and the smallest seek-times.

The attainable capacity of a track in the IBM 3330 disk system depends not only on blocksize, but also on the method of formatting data on the track. There are two methods that may be used: count-data format and count-key-data format. In *count-data format,* each data block is preceded by a short (12-byte) count block, used by the hardware and Operating System to specify the data blocksize and certain other information. The data block and its count block are separated by a small gap; together they constitute what is known as a *data record:*

←——————— data record ———————→		
(count-data format)		
count block	gap	data block

In *count-key-data format,* each data block is preceded by two blocks: a count block and a key block. The key block contains an alphanumeric character string, called the *key,* that identifies the data block. The count block contains the data-block length, the length of the key, and other information used by the system. Together, the three blocks constitute a data record:

←——————————— data record ———————————→				
(count-key-data format)				
count block	gap	key block	gap	data block

Figure 18.7   Data transfer overhead for IBM 3330 disk system.

| | data transfer overhead | | | |
blocksize (number of bytes)	seek time 0	seek time 10 ms (1 cyl)	seek time 30 ms (pack avg)	seek time 55 ms (worst case)
13030	34.2 %	53.2 %	70.4 %	79.7 %
6447	51.2	69.7	82.8	88.8
4253	61.4	77.7	87.9	92.3
3156	68.2	82.5	90.7	94.2
2498	73.1	85.6	92.5	95.3
1181	85.1	92.6	96.3	97.7
742	90.1	95.2	97.7	98.6
523	92.8	96.6	98.3	99.0
391	94.5	97.4	98.7	99.2
303	95.7	98.0	99.0	99.4
241	96.6	98.4	99.2	99.5

$$\left(\text{Overhead} = \frac{(\text{access time})}{(\text{access time}) + (\text{transfer time})} \times 100\right)$$

Figure 18.8   Data transfer overhead for IBM 3330 disk system.

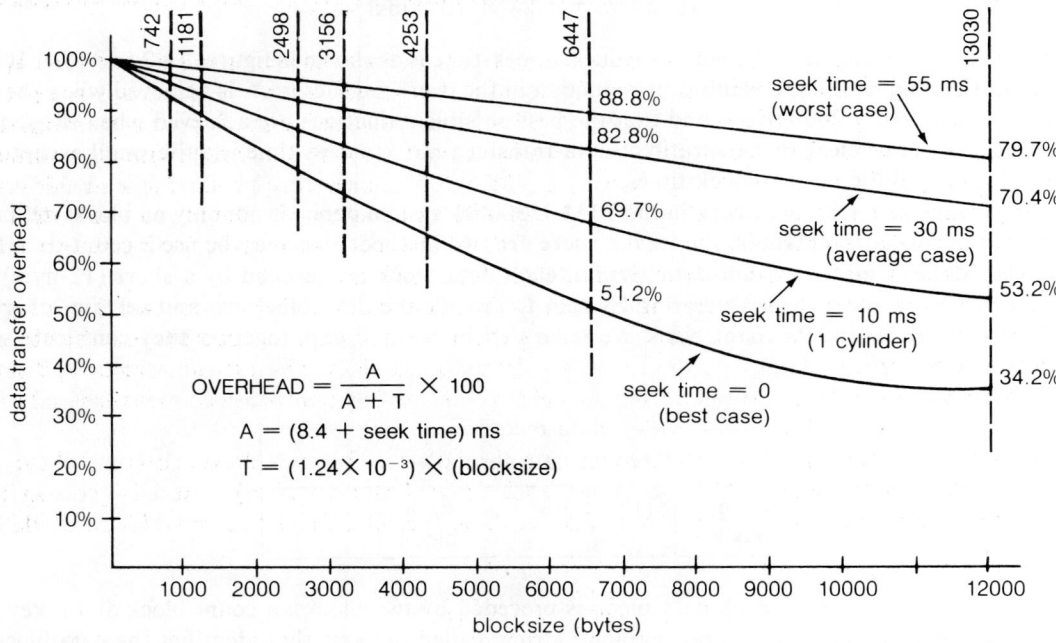

$$\text{OVERHEAD} = \frac{A}{A + T} \times 100$$

$$A = (8.4 + \text{seek time}) \text{ ms}$$

$$T = (1.24 \times 10^{-3}) \times (\text{blocksize})$$

Clearly, the presence of the key block and the accompanying additional gap reduce the amount of space available on a track for data blocks. The track capacities given in figure 18.5 are valid for the count-data format, but not for the count-key-data format. The capacities for count-key-data format are shown in figure 18.9. Comparing these data with those of figure 18.5, it will be noted that the track capacities are systematically less in count-key-data format than in count-data format, the difference becoming progressively worse as more blocks are added to each track. However, the differences are generally small for reasonably large blocksizes, and there is an advantage—the ability to search for data blocks by key rather than by physical position. Count-key-data format is used for indexed sequential files.

Figure 18.9 Count-Key-Data format: track utilization for IBM 3330 disk system with
N = 13165/(191 + DL + KL). (See also fig. 18.5.)

N = number of data blocks per track	maximum possible value of DL+KL (blocksize + key length) for the indicated number of data blocks	maximum number of bytes per track	percent of maximum capacity
1	12974	12974	99.57%
2	6391	12782	98.10
3	4197	12591	96.63
4	3100	12400	95.16
5	2442	12210	93.71
6	2003	12018	92.23
7	1689	11823	90.74
8	1454	11632	89.27
9	1271	11439	87.79
10	1125	11250	86.34
15	686	10290	78.97
20	631	9340	71.68
25	335	8375	64.27
30	247	7410	56.87
35	185	6475	49.69
40	138	5520	42.36
45	101	4545	34.88
50	72	3600	27.63

The main point to note is that the second column in figure 18.9 represents the sum of the key length and the blocksize, not solely the blocksize as in figure 18.5. The larger the key length, the smaller the permissible blocksize for a given entry in the table. Therefore, from the standpoint of space utilization, the data blocksizes chosen for count-key-data format may not be compatible with those for count-data format. For example, if you choose a blocksize of 2000 bytes (i.e., DL=2000), then in count-data format this results in six blocks per track and a utilization ratio of 6×2000/13030, or about 92.1%. But in count-key-data format a DL of 2000 and a key length of 8 amounts to KL+DL=2008; this means only five blocks per track are possible. The space utilization ratio is then 5×2008/13030, or only about 77%.

There are a few other details about track space utilization worth noting. Each track has a beginning and ending point, known as the *index* point. Following the index point are two records used by the system: the "home-address" record (HA), and the track-descriptor record (R0). The user data records, denoted by R1 through Rn, follow the track-descriptor record and may be in either count-data or count-key-data format. This is illustrated in figure 18.10.

The physical position of a data record in a disk pack is denoted by an address consisting of three components: a 2-byte cylinder number (CC), a 2-byte track or head number (HH), and a 1-byte number (R) indicating the relative position of the record on that track. A typical CCHHR record address would be

```
      C C   H H   R
     ⌒⌒   ⌒⌒  ⌒
    ┌────────────────┐
    │ 0064  0011  03 │
    └────────────────┘
     ‾‾‾‾   ‾‾‾‾  ‾‾
    cylinder  track  record
      100      17      3
```

This address is stored in the count block of the third data record on track 17 of cylinder 100. Since programmers do not ordinarily know the address of a data block in the form CCHHR, they must supply some other information that the Operating System can translate into the absolute address. This information is either a relative address that indicates the position of a data block relative to the beginning of a particular collection of data blocks, or the key that uniquely identifies a data block.

Figure 18.10 *Disk track formats (IBM 3330).*

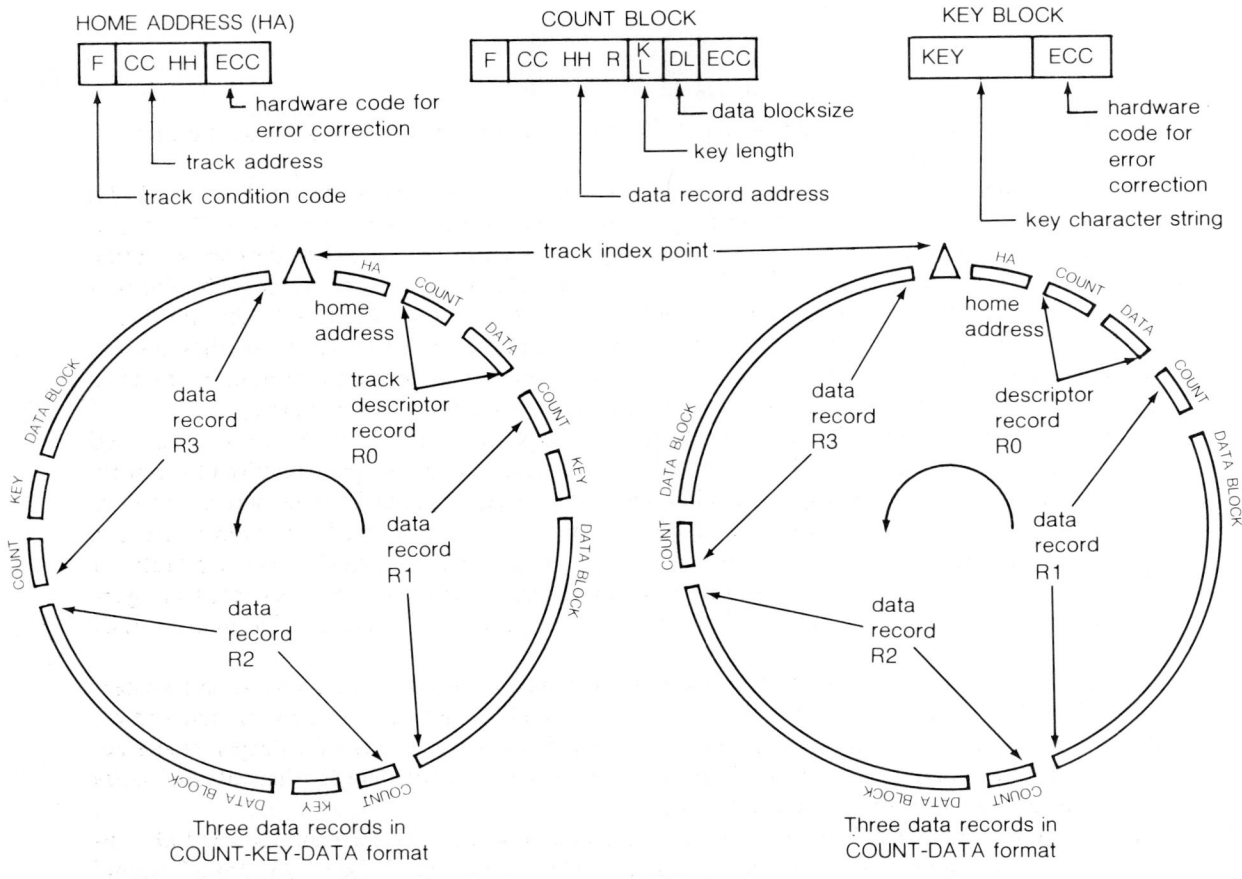

Three data records in
COUNT-KEY-DATA format

Three data records in
COUNT-DATA format

Note that several tracks may be needed to contain a collection of data whose total size exceeds the maximum track capacity. The best arrangement, from the standpoint of minimizing seek-time, would be to store the data on consecutive tracks within a cylinder and to use adjacent cylinders when more than one cylinder was required. This arrangement is known as *contiguous* space utilization. However, due to the competing needs of the many data collections sharing the memory space of a disk pack, contiguous space is not always available for an entire data collection. Therefore, it often happens that only portions of a data collection are stored contiguously, the separate portions being scattered in a somewhat nonregular fashion throughout the disk pack.

18.3 TAPE AND DISK COMPARISON

In the IBM 3330 disk system, there are 19 tracks per cylinder. Thus, the maximum capacity of a cylinder is approximately a quarter of a million bytes: 247,570 bytes if all tracks are formatted in count-data format, and 246,506 bytes if count-key-data format is used. The maximum capacity of a disk pack in the IBM 3330 system depends on the pack model that is used. There are currently two models available: Model 1 contains 404 cylinders and Model 11 contains 808 cylinders. The maximum capacity of a Model 1 pack then is approximately 100 million bytes and that of a Model 11 pack approximately 200 million bytes. For the Model 1, this is roughly equivalent to the capacity of 1.7 tape reels at 1600 BPI (assuming 3600-foot reels and 6400-byte blocks); for the Model 11, it is roughly equivalent to 3.5 such tape reels.

However, it should be clear that the sequence of records on a tape must match the sequence required by programs that process the records. Otherwise, an undue amount of time could be spent moving the tape forward or backward while searching for some desired data record. This would be the case, for example, if tapes were used to store flight information for an airline reservation system. Since the time required to locate an arbitrarily positioned record would be unacceptably long, tapes are not used for such situations. Disks are used instead, because they provide not only the ability to process records sequentially, but also the ability to process records in what is essentially random order. For this reason, the discussions in subsequent chapters will be oriented toward disk input and output.

18.4   SUMMARY

The principal concept discussed in this chapter is that of blocksize and its effect on memory space utilization and data-transfer times in the IBM 3330 disk system.

The choice of blocksize for a given application is usually made by the programmer. For the IBM 3330, reasonably efficient space utilization can be achieved by choosing blocksizes of approximately 2000 bytes or more, the choice being dependent on the data format (count-data or count-key-data) and on the corresponding track capacities shown in figures 18.5 and 18.9. The choice of data format is made indirectly by the programmer when he or she chooses a data-set organization, as will be discussed in chapters 19 through 22.

Blocksizes of 2000 bytes or more are also effective in reducing total data-transfer time, although the principal means of reducing the transfer time is to reduce the seek-time by requesting that data be stored in contiguous fashion (i.e., on consecutive tracks within a cylinder, and on consecutive cylinders).

Blocksize has such a significant effect on space utilization because each disk track's capacity is fixed by the physical characteristics of the disk device: track circumference, data density, space required for control information such as the home address, and space required by gaps between data blocks. The more data blocks there are, the more gaps there will be, and the less space will be available for data. Larger blocksizes can result in fewer blocks, and, therefore, in fewer gaps. This in turn can make more track space available for data. However, to realize these advantages, you must choose a blocksize with care. As illustrated in figure 18.6 and discussed in the text, an uninformed choice of blocksize can result in considerable unused track space.

Blocksize has an effect on the total data-transfer time, because each data-transfer operation transfers an entire data block and is almost invariably preceded by data-transfer delays due to seek motion and rotational positioning of the data. The relative importance of these delays can be reduced if larger blocksizes are used. As will be discussed in the next chapter, blocksizes of sufficient size to achieve the desired efficiencies are obtained by the technique of blocking logical records.

Further information on the IBM 3330 disk system can be found in IBM Publication GA26–1592. Information on other IBM disk systems can be found in publications listed in the IBM System/360 and System/370 Bibliography, Publication GA22–6822.

EXERCISES

1. The data in the first two columns of figure 18.5 for track capacities in count-data format on a disk pack in the IBM 3330 disk system can be derived from the formula

$$N = \frac{13165}{135 + B} = \text{number of blocks per track for blocksize } B.$$

When computing N by this formula, the remainder must be discarded. For example, for blocksize $B = 84$ we have

$$\frac{13165}{135 + 84} = 60.11..., \text{ so } N = 60.$$

Using this formula, compute the maximum number of bytes per track, and the percent of maximum track capacity, corresponding to blocksizes of $B = 80$, $B = 800$, $B = 4000$, and $B = 8000$ in count-data format.

2. Analogous to the formula given in Exercise 1 for count-data format is that for computing track capacities in count-key-data format on a disk pack in the IBM 3330 disk system:

$$N = \frac{13165}{191 + DL + KL} = \text{number of blocks per track for blocksize DL and key length KL.}$$

For example, for $DL = 64$ and $KL = 8$ we have

$$\frac{13165}{191 + 64 + 8} = 50.057..., \text{ so } N = 50.$$

Using this formula, compute the maximum number of bytes per track, and the percent of maximum track capacity, corresponding to blocksizes of $DL = 80$, $DL = 800$, $DL = 4000$, and $DL = 8000$, and $KL = 8$ in count-key-data format.

3. How many 80-byte card-image records can be stored on an IBM 3330 disk system with Model 1 disk packs, under each of the following sets of conditions:

   a. count-data format,   1 record per block
   b. count-data format,   10 records per block
   c. count-data format,   50 records per block
   d. count-data format, 100 records per block

4. How many 80-byte card-image records can be stored on a 3600-foot reel of magnetic tape if the gap size is a half inch, under each of the following sets of conditions:

   a. 800 BPI, 1 record per block
   b. 800 BPI, 10 records per block
   c. 1600 BPI, 1 record per block
   d. 1600 BPI, 10 records per block
   e. 6250 BPI, 1 record per block
   f. 6250 BPI, 10 records per block

5. Suppose that your computer installation were to limit disk blocksizes to a maximum of 4096 bytes. What would be the actual maximum blocksize for 80-byte records? For 132-byte records? For 2500-byte records? In an IBM 3330 disk system, what would be the percent of maximum disk capacity utilized in each of these three cases? Assume that count-data format is used.

6. If your computer installation does not use an IBM 3330 disk system, prepare track capacity tables comparable to those in figures 18.5 and 18.9 for the disk system in use in your installation.

7. Determine the following characteristics of the magnetic tapes used in your computer installation: recording density, gap size, reel length, transfer rate, and start time. If any of these characteristics differ from those given in figures 18.2 and 18.3, determine the effects of blocksize on tape capacity and tape-transfer time for your computer installation's tapes.

8. How many microseconds are required to transfer 1 byte between secondary memory and main memory if the transfer rate of the secondary memory device is 312,000 bytes per second? 192,000 bytes per second? 9600 bytes per second? 30 bytes per second?

9. What is the minimum time required to read all the data stored on a 3600-foot reel of magnetic tape under each of the following sets of conditions. The gap size is one-half inch, the transfer rate 192,000 bytes per second, and the start time 10 milliseconds.
   a. 800 BPI, blocksize = 1600 bytes
   b. 800 BPI, blocksize = 6400 bytes
   c. 1600 BPI, blocksize = 1600 bytes
   d. 1600 BPI, blocksize = 6400 bytes
   e. 6250 BPI, blocksize = 1600 bytes
   f. 6250 BPI, blocksize = 6400 bytes

10. What is the minimum time required to read all the data stored on an IBM 3330 disk system Model 1 disk pack, if the records are stored in count-data format with blocksize = 12000 bytes? Blocksize = 6400 bytes? 1600 bytes? (Hint: Assume that all the tracks of one cylinder are read before those of another cylinder are read, and that the cylinders are read consecutively, i.e., with minimum seek-time between cylinders.)

11. What would be the average time required to read all the data stored on an IBM 3330 disk system Model 1 disk pack, if the records are stored in count-data format with blocksize = 12000 bytes? 6400 bytes? 1600 bytes? (Hint: Compute the average time by assuming that the average access time for each data block is 38.4 milliseconds, i.e., 30 ms seek and 8.4 ms rotational delay.)

12. At 2400 cards per minute, a card reader reads data at the rate of 3200 bytes per second. How long would it take such a card reader to read one box of punched cards (2000 cards)? What is the minimum time to read the same amount of data from an IBM 3330 disk system Model 1 disk pack, if the blocksize were 80 bytes?

19

I/O Software Concepts

In IBM 360 and 370 assembly language programs, all user-program input and output processing is accomplished by means of macro instructions. Most of the macros generate executable statements, including calls to the Operating System; others generate data and/or data areas that are used by the Operating System. Macros such as OPEN, GET, PUT, and CLOSE that generate executable statements are known as *imperative* macros; the others are *declarative* macros.

Though their purpose is generally the same, most macros that are used in OS systems differ in substantial detail from those used in DOS systems. Except for VSAM macros (to be discussed in chap. 22), I/O macros constitute the one major area of Assembly Language where the two versions of IBM 360 and 370 Assembly Language are essentially incompatible. The job control language statements that describe files in each of the two systems are also incompatible, although here too the purpose is generally the same in both systems.

This chapter provides an overview of the main concepts involved in using I/O macros for sequential and indexed-sequential files in both OS and DOS systems. The purpose as well as many of the details of the macros will be described, but programming examples will not be given until chapters 20 and 21. Although most of the concepts to be discussed are needed for an understanding of those chapters, you may wish to read through the present chapter rapidly and return to it when needed. A comprehensive summary at the end of the chapter will help you assimilate the various concepts.

19.1 BLOCKING AND DEBLOCKING

As has been discussed in chapter 18, efficient use of disk and tape storage devices requires reasonably large blocksizes of the order of a few thousand bytes. To achieve such large blocksizes, a technique known as blocking is used. In blocking, a sufficient number of records to be processed by a program, such as 80-byte card data records or 132-byte print-line data records, are positioned end-to-end in a data block. Such records are called *logical records*. If the logical records being processed all have the same length, they are known as *fixed-length records,* and the data blocks which contain them are known as *fixed-length blocks.* If the logical records do not all have the same length (for example, if they represent lines that were typed at a terminal), they are known as *variable-length records,* and the blocks containing them are *variable-length blocks.*

A fixed-length block that contains N fixed-length logical records has the structure shown here:

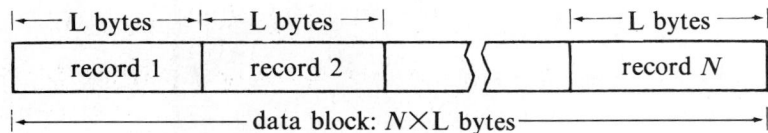

In variable-length blocks, the length of each logical record is placed in a *record descriptor word* (RDW) that is prefixed to that record in the block, and the length of the block is similarly placed in a *block descriptor word* (BDW) that is prefixed to the entire block, as shown here:

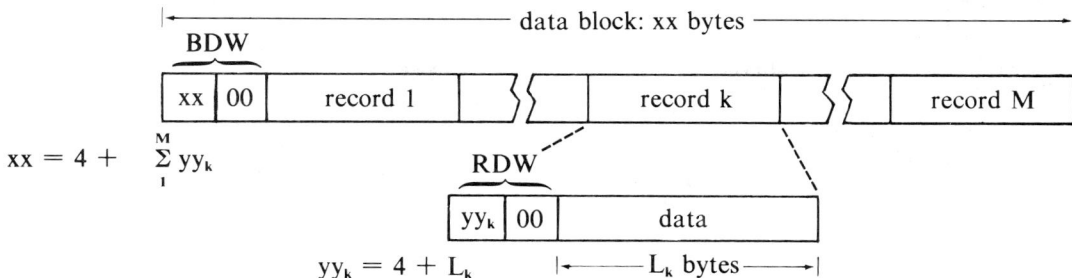

$$xx = 4 + \sum_{1}^{M} yy_k$$

$$yy_k = 4 + L_k$$

As shown, both the RDW and the BDW are 4 bytes; the lengths occupy the first 2 bytes and the remaining 2 bytes are reserved for other system use. The length in each RDW includes the 4 bytes of the RDW itself, and the length in the BDW is the sum of the lengths in each RDW plus the 4 bytes for the BDW. No block can contain both variable and fixed-length records; either one or the other format must be used.

The sequence of the logical records in a data block is the sequence in which they are transferred to or from main memory. When a data block is transferred to main memory, it remains there until all the logical records contained in it are processed or are no longer needed. When a data block is being constructed for output, it is also kept in main memory until it contains all the records that can be fit into it. Then it is written to secondary memory. In this way, each read or write operation benefits from a large blocksize, since the transfer time overhead percentage is less than it would be if logical records were read or written one at a time.

The process of extracting logical records from a data block is known as *deblocking*, that of adding records to a data block is known as *blocking*. These concepts are illustrated in figure 19.1.

Figure 19.1 Blocking and deblocking.

As described in chapter 18, larger blocksizes make more efficient use of disk storage than do smaller ones. But they obviously require more main memory buffer space, and this in turn makes less efficient use of main memory. From the standpoint of CPU processing, the most natural blocksize to use would be 4096 bytes, since this is exactly the amount of main memory that can be covered by a single base register; 4096 bytes is also the unit of space used by some versions of the Operating System when allocating main memory to user programs. Consequently, a compromise between efficient secondary memory utilization and efficient main memory utilization is usually made: blocksizes as near to (but not greater than) 4096 bytes are chosen. In count-data format and in count-key-data format with key lengths not greater than 100 bytes, three 4096-byte data blocks will fit on an IBM 3330 disk track, resulting in about 94% space utilization (see figs. 18.5 and 18.9).

Note that two additional provisions exist in some versions of the IBM 360 and 370 systems for further optimal use of track space. One is known as *track overflow,* an optional hardware feature in which a data block can be continued from one track to the next. The other involves the use of so-called *variable-length spanned records,* an optional software feature that allows variable-length records to be partly in one data block and partly in the next. Neither of these two provisions will be discussed further in this text.

19.2 DATA SET ORGANIZATION

A collection of logical records that have some useful relationship to one another is generally known as a *file* or *data set.* We will use the terms interchangeably. Each data set stored in secondary memory must be assigned a name at the time it is created, and its name must be unique among all names used for data sets on a disk pack. Each data set name (abbreviated as "dsname") must consist of one or more component names, each of from one to eight alphanumeric characters. The components are separated by periods, and the total number of characters in the name, including periods, must not exceed 44. For example: MDK.SOURCE.CREATE might be the name of a source-module used to create other data sets.

There are four methods of organizing the logical records of a data set for processing by a program. These are known as sequential organization, indexed sequential organization, direct organization, and partitioned organization. All four methods are available in OS systems, and all but partitioned organization are available in DOS. In addition, the Virtual Storage Access Method (VSAM)—available in both OS/VS and DOS/VS systems—provides mechanisms for the equivalent of sequential, indexed sequential, and direct organizations. In VSAM these are known as entry-sequenced, key-sequenced, and relative-record data sets. VSAM data sets are described in chapter 22.

In *sequential organization,* the logical records must be processed in the order in which they exist in the data set. The Nth record can only be processed after the $(N-1)$st record has been processed, and before the $(N+1)$st is processed. Sequential organization is probably the simplest of the four organizations for writing programs and provides a relatively efficient means of processing logical records that are in some pre-specified sequence. Sequentially organized data sets are always stored in count-data format.

In *indexed sequential organization,* the logical records can be processed either as though they were sequentially organized or in a random order. To process records randomly, the key of the desired logical record must be specified when requesting input or output from the Operating System. The key—consisting of from 1 to 255 alphanumeric characters—must uniquely identify that record, distinguishing it from all other logical records in the data set. The key must be part of the data in each record. The Operating System maintains an *index* that correlates each logical record key with the data block in which that logical record is located. The index is stored in a separate portion of the data set. Indexed sequential data sets are always stored in count-key-data format.

In *direct organization,* the logical records can be processed either sequentially or in random order, but to process a logical record the relative position of the data block containing it must be specified by the user's program when requesting input or output. The Operating System does not maintain an index; instead, it is the responsibility of the user's program to determine the data block in which a given logical record is stored. Data sets organized by the direct method are stored either in count-data format or in count-key-data format, depending on whether or not the data blocks are to be identified by keys. The two formats cannot be intermixed within a single data set.

In *partitioned organization,* the data set is divided into one or more sequential data sets called *members* of the partitioned data set. Each member is identified by a unique name that is stored in a *directory* that is also part of the partitioned data set. The logical records of each member must be processed sequentially; however, the records of any one member can be processed without having to process the records of any other member. Each member is stored in count-data format; the directory is stored in count-key-data format.

Figure 19.2   Overview of sequential data set format.

blocked fixed-length records:
same length for each logical record;
same length for each block, except
possibly the last.

blocked variable-length records:
each logical record's length given in RDW;
each block's length given in BDW

Each data block and logical record is read or written in the
sequence in which they exist. No index or directory is kept.

Figure 19.3   Overview of indexed sequential data set format.

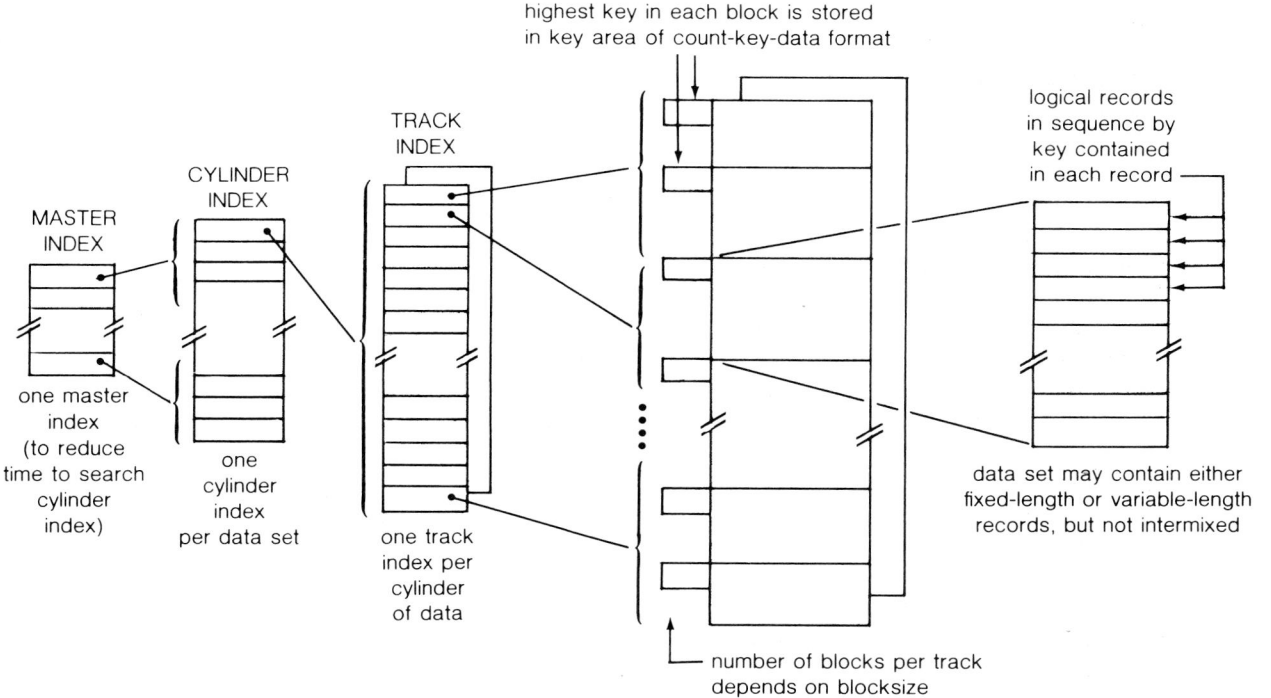

Figure 19.4 Overview of direct data set format.

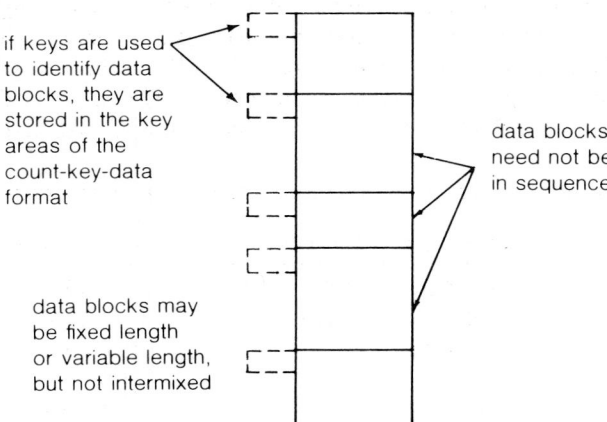

if keys are used to identify data blocks, they are stored in the key areas of the count-key-data format

data blocks need not be in sequence

data blocks may be fixed length or variable length, but not intermixed

Figure 19.5 Overview of partitioned data set format.

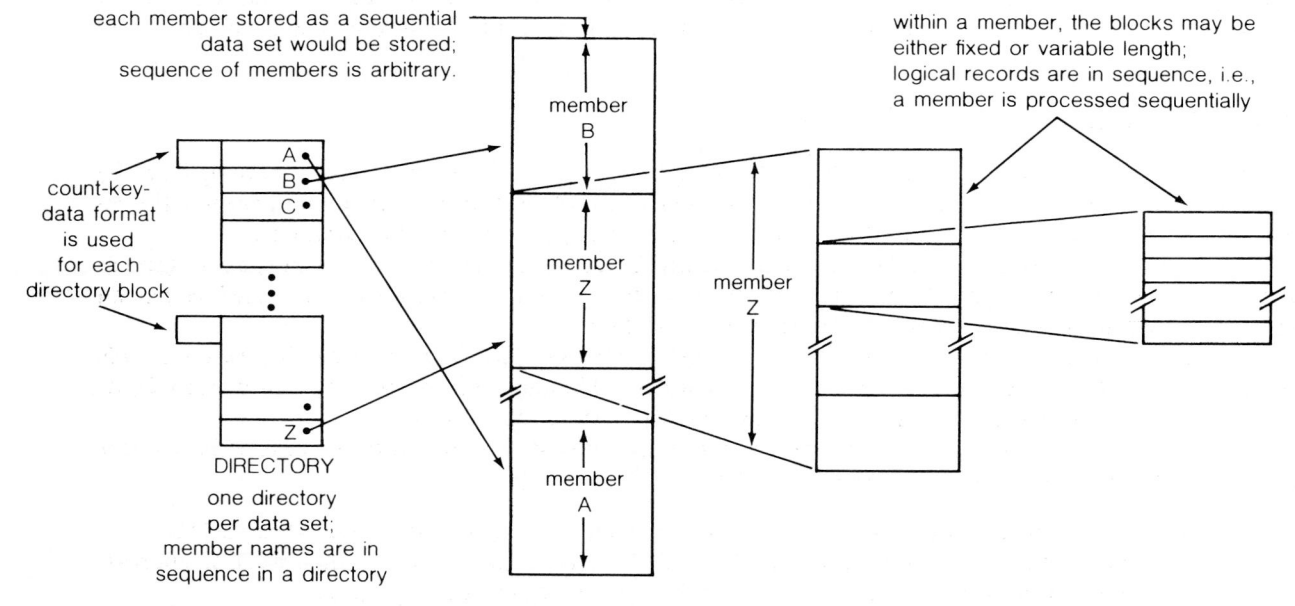

each member stored as a sequential data set would be stored; sequence of members is arbitrary.

within a member, the blocks may be either fixed or variable length; logical records are in sequence, i.e., a member is processed sequentially

count-key-data format is used for each directory block

member B

member Z

member Z

member A

DIRECTORY

one directory per data set; member names are in sequence in a directory

Figures 19.2 through 19.5 illustrate the four different data set organizations in schematic fashion. Neither direct organization nor partitioned organization will be discussed in detail in this text. (Partitioned organization is used extensively for maintaining library files, e.g., source-module libraries, object module libraries, and macro libraries. Direct organization can be used to circumvent some of the constraints associated with indexed sequential organization.)

One essential point should be noted: a file's organization must be defined when the file is first created. Thereafter, its organization cannot be changed.

19.3 ACCESS METHODS

An *access method* is a set of system procedures (programs) that carry out a user program's I/O requests. Some of the programs that constitute each access method reside within the Operating System, and some are system subroutines—also known as logic modules—that are linked to a program at load time or run time.

The access method that is used depends on the organization of the file for which the I/O request is made. It is necessary for the user's program to declare which access method is to be used for each file that it processes, and it is necessary for the I/O macros in the program to conform to the rules of that access method.

In OS systems there are seven access methods; in DOS systems there are four:

file organization	OS access method	DOS access method
sequential	QSAM or BSAM	SAM
indexed sequential	QISAM or BISAM	ISAM
direct	BDAM	DAM
partitioned	BPAM	---
virtual storage	VSAM	VSAM

The letters "AM" above mean simply Access Method; SAM is, for example, Sequential Access Method. In OS, the initial letter Q or B refers to the *technique,* Queued or Basic, which is used with the access method. In queued techniques, the file's records must be processed sequentially, and the access method performs all blocking, deblocking, and I/O synchronization. In basic techniques, the records may but need not be processed sequentially; and with some exceptions, the user's program must perform all blocking, deblocking, and I/O synchronization.

19.4 I/O MACROS

In Assembly Language, every operation that is associated with input and output of files is accomplished by means of macros. The macros can be considered as extensions of Assembly Language that generate the required instructions, constants, and control information needed to perform the I/O operations.

The macros that are used in OS systems differ in detail from those used in DOS systems, but in general both sets of macros are designed for the same purposes. In each system, the macros that are used depend on a file's organization and access method (see figs. 19.6a and 19.6b).

Most of the I/O macros are *executable,* or imperative, macros. That is, at run time they result in calls to the Operating System or to system-supplied subroutines. The other I/O macros are *non-executable,* or declarative, macros which create constants and control information used at run time.

Since executable I/O macros result in calls to system routines, it is important to be aware of the register linkage conventions that are used. These are as follows:

1. Register 13 must contain the address of the user program's register save area when an I/O macro is executed. That is why it is good practice to load Register 13 with the save area address when a program is first entered and not use the register for any other purpose.
2. The contents of Registers 14 and 15 will be changed when an I/O macro is executed. After executing an I/O macro, Register 14 will usually contain the address of the instruction that immediately follows the macro in the source-module, and Register 15 may contain a completion code or error code whose meaning depends on the macro that was executed.
3. The contents of Registers 0 and 1 may also be changed when an I/O macro is executed. These registers are used to pass parameters to and from the user's program.
4. The contents of Registers 2 through 12 are not changed when an I/O macro is executed.

Figure 19.6a I/O macros in OS systems.

macro name	QSAM	BSAM	QISAM	BISAM	BDAM	BPAM	macro function
BLDL						X	build a directory entry list
BSP		X					backspace a physical record
BUILD	X	X	X	X	X	X	build a buffer pool in area reserved at assembly time
BUILDRCD	X						build a buffer pool and a record area
CHECK		X		X	X	X	wait for and test completion of a READ or WRITE
CHKPT	X	X	X	X	X	X	create a checkpoint record
CLOSE	X	X	X	X	X	X	logically disconnect a data set
CNTRL	X	X					control online input/output devices
DCB	X	X	X	X	X	X	construct a data control block
DCBD	X	X	X	X	X	X	create a dummy section for data control blocks
ESETL			X				end sequential retrieval
FEOV	X	X					force end of volume
FIND						X	find the beginning of a BPAM member
FREEBUF		X		X	X	X	return a buffer to a buffer pool
FREEDBUF				X	X		return a dynamically obtained buffer
FREEPOOL	X	X	X	X	X	X	release a buffer pool
GET	X		X				obtain next logical record from input buffer
GETBUF		X		X	X	X	obtain a buffer area from a buffer pool
GETPOOL	X	X	X	X	X	X	build a buffer pool in area acquired at run time
NOTE		X				X	obtain relative position of last block read or written
OPEN	X	X	X	X	X	X	logically connect a data set
PDAB	X						construct a parallel data access block
PDABD	X						create a dummy section for parallel data access blocks
POINT		X				X	establish relative position of block for next read/write
PRTOV	X	X					test for printer carriage overflow
PUT	X		X				move next logical record to output buffer
PUTX	X		X				rewrite updated record or copy an existing record
READ		X		X	X	X	read a block of records
RELEX				X			release exclusive control of data block
RELSE	X		X				release an input buffer
SETL			X				set lower limit for sequential retrieval
SETPRT	X	X					set printer control information
STOW						X	update a BPAM directory
SYNADAF	X	X	X	X	X	X	analyze permanent input/output errors
SYNADRLS	X	X	X	X	X	X	release SYNADAF buffer and save areas
TRUNC	X						truncate an output buffer
WAIT		X		X	X	X	wait for one or more I/O data transfers to be completed
WRITE		X		X	X	X	write a block of records
XLATE	X	X					translate to and from ASCII code

Figure 19.6b   I/O macros in DOS systems.

macro name	card reader	printer	any device	disk (SAM)	ISAM	DAM	macro function
CHECK				X			wait for and test completion of a READ or WRITE
CLOSE	X	X	X	X	X	X	logically disconnect a data set
CNTRL	X	X		X		X	control on-line input-output devices
DTFxx	X	X	X	X	X	X	construct a file control area to define the file
xxMOD	X	X	X	X	X	X	generate an I/O processing module (logic module)
ENDFL				X			terminate file load-mode begun by SETFL
ERET				X			return to access method for error-handling options
ESETL				X			terminate sequential mode begun by SETL
FEOVD				X			force end-of-volume for disk files
GET	X		X	X	X		obtain next logical record from input buffer
LBRET				X		X	return (i.e., exit) from label-handling routines
NOTE				X			obtain address of most recently processed data block
OPEN	X	X	X	X	X	X	logically connect a file to the user's program
POINTx				X			prepare to read or write a specific data block
PRTOV		X					respond to printer carriage overflow
PUT		X	X	X	X		move next logical record to output buffer
READ				X	X	X	read a data block into I/O buffer
RELSE				X			release an input buffer
SETFL				X			initiate load-mode for creating ISAM files
SETL				X			set lower limit to begin ISAM sequential retrieval
TRUNC				X			truncate an output buffer
WAITF					X	X	wait for I/O data transfer completion
WRITE				X	X	X	write a data block from I/O buffer

Note: Device-dependent macros for magnetic tape, paper tape, diskette, optical character readers, and magnetic ink character readers are not shown.

The declarative macros are DTFxx and xxMOD, where xx=CD for cards, PR for printer, DI for device independence, SD for sequential disk files, IS for indexed sequential files, and DA for direct access. All the other macros listed above are imperative (executable).

It is also useful to be aware of the mechanism by which executable I/O macros call the Operating System, since this will appear as part of the assembly listing whenever the PRINT GEN directive is in effect. *The mechanism used is the Supervisor Call (SVC) instruction.* SVC is an RR-type instruction in which the two register address fields are not utilized for register addresses, but instead contain a 1-byte numeric code N that identifies the purpose of the SVC:

Assembly Language	machine language
SVC N	opcode | N
↑decimal integer, from 0 to 255	|—— 2 bytes ——|

The numeric code specified in the operand of the assembly language instruction is represented as an unsigned 8-bit integer in the second byte of the machine language instruction. When SVC is executed, four things happen: (1) control is transferred to a fixed location within the Operating System; (2) the address of the instruction following the SVC is preserved so that the Operating System can return control to the user program following completion of the task being requested; (3) the state of the computer system is set to supervisor mode so that privileged instructions may be executed while the Operating System is performing the task; and (4) the SVC operand is made available to the Operating System through the interruption code field of the program status word. The Operating System determines the purpose of the SVC by examining the SVC operand code and proceeds accordingly.

Figure 19.7a   DCB keyword parameters in OS systems.

DCB keyword	DCB macro parameter	DD subparameter		QSAM	BSAM	QISAM	BISAM	BDAM	BPAM
BFALN	X	X	buffer-boundary alignment	X	X	X	X	X	X
BFTEK	X	X	buffer-processing technique	X	X			X	
BLKSIZE	X	X	physical blocksize	X	X	X		X	X
BUFCB	X		buffer control-block address	X	X	X	X	X	X
BUFL	X	X	buffer length	X	X	X	X	X	X
BUFNO	X	X	number of buffers in buffer pool	X	X	X	X	X	X
BUFOFF	X	X	ASCII-tape block prefix length	X	X				
CODE		X	paper-tape code scheme	X	X				
CYLOFL	X	X	number of tracks in cylinder overflow area			X			
DDNAME	X		name of DD statement	X	X	X	X	X	X
DEN		X	magnetic tape density		X				
DEVD	X		device-dependent parameters	X	X				
DIAGNS		X	trace option for debugging	X	X	X	X	X	X
DSORG	X	X	data set organization	X	X	X	X	X	X
EODAD	X		address of end-of-input-data routine	X	X	X			X
EROPT	X	X	system error option	X					
EXLST	X		address of special processing routine	X	X	X	X	X	X
FRID		X	optical character reader record i.d.		X				
FUNC		X	type of data set for IBM 3525 card punch	X	X				
KEYLEN	X	X	length of record key		X	X		X	X
LIMCT		X	block or track search limit					X	
LRECL	X	X	length of logical record	X	X	X			X
MACRF	X		I/O macro specifications	X	X	X	X	X	X
MODE		X	card reader/punch mode	X	X				
MSHI	X		address of highest-level master index area					X	
MSWA	X		address of work area for new records					X	
NCP	X	X	number of chained channel programs			X		X	X
NTM	X	X	number of tracks for a master index level			X			
OPTCD	X	X	optional processing functions	X	X	X		X	X
PRTSP		X	printer line spacing	X	X				
RECFM	X	X	record format	X	X	X		X	X
RKP	X	X	position of record key			X			
SMSI	X		length of highest-level master index area					X	
SMSW	X		length of MSWA work area					X	
STACK		X	card-punch stacker-bin number	X	X				
SYNAD	X		address of user error-analysis routine	X	X	X	X	X	X
TRTCH		X	seven-track tape recording technique	X	X				

19.5   DECLARATIVE MACROS: DCB AND DTFxx

The Data Control Block (DCB) macro in OS systems and the Define File (DTFxx) macro in DOS systems create a data area containing parameters that describe certain characteristics of a data set. These characteristics are specified by keyword parameters whose names and general purposes are summarized in figures 19.7a and 19.7b. The Operating System and access methods use the information provided by the DCB or DTFxx macros to control the processing of a data set at run time. Therefore there must be one DCB or DTFxx macro in a source-module for each data set that is to be processed.

The Data Definition (DD) statement of OS job control language, and correspondingly the ASSGN, DLBL, and EXTENT statements of DOS job control language, also describe various characteristics of a data set. These supplement the information provided by the DCB and DTFxx macros and provide a means of defining some data set characteristics outside a source-module. These characteristics and the names of the corresponding keyword parameters are briefly summarized in figures 19.8a and 19.8b.

Not all parameters need be specified in any one DCB or DTFxx macro or in any one job control statement. Some are applicable only in certain cases, e.g., for certain types of devices, and for others there are default values that adequately cover most processing needs. The choice of what to specify and how to specify it depends on the keyword, the access method, and the device containing the data set. We will enumerate only those choices we will be using. Descriptions also can be found in the IBM manuals listed at the end of the chapter.

Figure 19.7b DTFxx keyword parameters in DOS systems.

DTF keyword	SAM	ISAM	DAM	keyword function
AFTER=YES			X	formatted WRITE erases a track's unused space
BLKSIZE	XX		XX	physical blocksize
CISIZE	X			control interval size for Fixed Block Architecture (FBA)
CONTROL=YES	X		X	CNTRL macro used for this file
CYLOFL		X		number of tracks in cylinder overflow areas
DELETFL=NO	X			work file labels will not be erased
DEVADDR	X		X	symbolic unit identifier, e.g. SYSxxx
DEVICE	X	X	XX	IBM device i.d., e.g. 3330
DSKXTNT		XX	X	maximum number of disk extents for this file
EOFADDR	XX			name of end-of-input-data routine
ERRBYTE			XX	name of two-byte I/O error indicator area
ERREXT=YES	X	X	X	requests I/O error indicators for non-data transmission
ERROPT	X			IGNORE, SKIP, or process I/O errors via named routine
FEOVD=YES	X		X	read and write disk end-of-volume records
HINDEX		X		i.d. of IBM device (e.g., 3330) containing highest level index
HOLD=YES	X	X	X	track protection via exclusive control during I/O
IDLOC			X	name of area that gets CCHHR of data block
INDAREA		X		name of cylinder index buffer area
INDSKIP=YES		X		bypass unneeded portions of cylinder index
INDSIZE		X		size (in bytes) of cylinder index buffer area
IOAREA1	XX		XX	name of required I/O buffer area
IOAREA2	X	X		name of optional second I/O buffer area
IOAREAL		X		name of I/O buffer area for file creation or extension
IOAREAR		X		name of I/O buffer area for random processing
IOAREAS		X		name of I/O buffer area for sequential processing
IOREG	X	X		locate mode register address (any register 2 thru 12)
IOROUT		XX		LOAD/ADD/RETRVE/ADDRTR designates file processing mode
IOSIZE		X		size (in bytes) of IOAREAL
KEYARG		X	X	name of key field area
KEYLEN		XX	X	length (in bytes) of key field
KEYLOC		X		relative position of key in each logical record
LABADDR	X		X	name of user's label-handling routine
MODNAME	X	X	X	name of xxMOD logic module
MSTIND=YES		X		a master index is used
NRECDS		XX		number of records per block when RECFORM=FIXBLK
NOTEPNT=YES	X			NOTE or POINTx macro will be used
PWRITE=YES	X			data blocks written even if control interval buffer not full
RDONLY=YES	X	X	X	user source module is Read-Only
READID=YES			X	READ macro refers to CCHHR (i.e., to record ID)
READKEY=YES			X	READ macro refers to record KEY
RECFORM	X	XX	X	record format
RECSIZE	X	XX	X	logical record length
RELTYPE			X	DECimal or HEXadecimal record ID in IDLOC and SEEKADR areas
SEEKADR			XX	name of field containing track location of record
SEPASMB=YES	X	X	X	DTFxx assembled into separate module
SRCHM=YES			X	system searches for record on more than one track
TRLBL=YES			X	user standard trailer-label records are read/written
TRUNCS=YES	X			TRUNC macro may be used with this file
TYPEFLE	X	X	XX	file's OPEN mode
UPDATE=YES	X			INPUT or WORK file is to be updated
VARBLD	X			reg. addr. (2–12) for buffer space remaining in locate mode
VERIFY=YES	X	X	X	records are checked for parity error after being written
WLRERR	X			name of user's wrong-length-record error-handling routine
WORKA=YES	X			move mode is used, so GET/PUT specifies I/O record area
WORKL		X		name of I/O record area when creating or extending file
WORKR		X		name of I/O record area when processing randomly
WORKS=YES		X		move mode for sequential processing (like WORKA=YES)
WRITEID=YES			X	WRITE macro refers to CCHHR (i.e., to record ID)
WRITEKY=YES			X	WRITE macro refers to record KEY
XTNTXIT			X	name of user's routine that processes extent labels

Note: XX means the parameter is required, X that it is optional. Some DTFCD and DTFPR parameters are not included in the above list.

Figure 19.8a   DD statement parameters for OS systems.

General Data Set Characteristics

DCB	one or more attributes of the data set, as noted in figure 19.7a
DISP	present and future status of the data set
DSNAME	the name of the data set
LABEL	expiration date, retention period, passwords, and the type of label used
VOLUME	used for data sets on private, multiple, and/or specific volumes

Space Allocation Requests

SPACE	space allocation for one new data set
SPLIT	space allocation for two or more new data sets, sharing cylinders
SUBALLOC	space allocation for two or more new data sets, not sharing cylinders

Input Data Stream

*	input data follows this statement; delimiter is /*, //, or end-of-file
DATA	input data follows this statement; delimiter is /* or end-of-file
DLM	changes the /* delimiter to some other character string

Output Data Stream

HOLD	defers sending the output data set to an output device
OUTLIM	specifies a maximum number of logical records for the output data set
SYSOUT	designates the class of device the output data set is to be sent to

General Hardware-dependent Information

AFF	gives same I/O channel separation as specified by SEP in another DD statement
SEP	separates I/O transmission channel of this data set from those of others
UNIT	specifies types and numbers of devices for the data set

Printer and Punch Characteristics

BURST	printer paper output is to be separated (i.e., 'bursted')
CHARS	identifies character arrangements for IBM 3800 printer subsystem
COPIES	number of copies of the data set that is to be printed
FCB	forms control information
FLASH	forms overlay frame specifications for IBM 3800 printer subsystem
MODIFY	identifies a copy modification module (IBM 3800 printer subsystem)
UCS	identifies character set for printing on an IBM 1403, 3203-4, or 3211

Remote Workstation Specifications

COMPACT	specifies whether and how data sent to a remote workstation is compacted
DEST	specifies a remote workstation for an output data set
TERM	specifies that a remote unit record device is in use

Miscellaneous Capabilities

AMP	program processing attributes for a VSAM data set
CHKPT	requests checkpoints be taken at end-of-volume for QSAM and BSAM data sets
DDNAME	identifies a subsequent DD statement that defines this data set
DSID	specifies the identifier of a data set residing on diskette (IBM 3540)
DUMMY	suppresses I/O, space allocation, and disposition (QSAM or BSAM only)
MSVGP	identifies a group of mass storage volumes on a Mass Storage System device
QNAME	routes teleprocessing messages to an applications program (TCAM only)

NOTE: All the above are optional keyword parameters except *, DATA, and DUMMY. The latter are optional positional parameters. The values and/or subparameters that can be specified by the keyword parameters are described in the JCL manuals referenced at the end of this chapter. Except for DCB, DISP, and SPACE, these will not be discussed in this text.

Figure 19.8b   File parameters in job control statements for DOS systems.

Note: The general formats of the three DOS file JCL statements are:
        / / DLBL   dtfname,'filename',date,xx,DSF,BUFSP=,CAT=,BLKSIZE=,CISIZE=
        / / EXTENT SYSxxx,volser#,type,seq#,track#,space, split
        / / ASSGN SYSxxx,unit,options . . .
For comparison with OS, the following summary parallels figure 19.8a

General File Characteristics			
/ / DLBL	dtfname	identity of user program DTFxx macro	
	filename	the name of the actual file	
	date	expiration date or retention period	
	xx	SD, DA, DU, ISC, ISE, or VSAM	
	DSF	data-secured file	
	BUFSP	VSAM buffer size	
	CAT	name of DLBL statement for VSAM catalog	
	BLKSIZE	block size, for sequential disk files (DTFSD) only	
	CISIZE	control-interval size for DTFSD files on FBA devices	
Space Allocation Requests			
/ / EXTENT	SYSxxx	overrides units specified by DEVADDR= in DTFxx macro	
	volser#	i.d. of volume on which space is requested	
	type	type of extent: data, independent overflow, or index	
	seq#	0 for ISAM master index; *n* for *n*th extent	
	track#	relative CKD track or FBA block where extent begins	
	space	number of tracks or blocks in this extent	
	split	highest track # in each cylinder of a shared CKD extent	
Input Data Stream			
/ / EXTENT	SYSxxx	SYSIPT designates primary input data stream	
Output Data Stream			
/ / EXTENT	SYSxxx	SYSLST designates primary output data stream	
Hardware-dependent Information			
/ / ASSGN	SYSxxx	symbolic unit identified by / / EXTENT or by DEVADDR= in DTFxx	
	unit	cuu: channel and unit address	
		unit is unavailable (UA) or is to be ignored (IGN)	
		SYSyyy: refers to SYSxxx of a previous / / ASSGN	
		class: READER, PRINTER, PUNCH, TAPE, DISK, CKD, FBA, DISKETTE	
		type: IBM model #, e.g. 2560, 1403, 3330, . . .	
	options	TEMP: assignment is temporary	
		PERM: assignment is permanent	
		VOL=: volume serial number if device is tape, disk, or diskette	
		SHR: disk device is shared with other files	
		ss: magnetic tape characteristics, e.g. 9-track vs. 7-track	
		ALT: magnetic tape is alternate unit	
		H1: use card reader input hopper #1	
		H2: use card reader input hopper #2	

OS Systems

As is shown in figure 19.7a, there are 37 DCB keyword parameters: 16 may be specified in either the DCB macro or DD statement, and of the remainder, 11 may be specified only in the DCB macro and 10 may be specified only in the DD statement. When there is a choice, it is preferable to use the DD statement, since more run-time processing flexibility is thereby gained.

The DSORG and MACRF parameters are required in each DCB macro. DSORG specifies the data set's organization. MACRF specifies the type of data-transfer macros that will be used when processing the data set and also specifies certain I/O processing options whose use depends on the access method.

For DSORG, there are only four choices:

DSORG=PS	sequential organization
DSORG=IS	indexed sequential organization
DSORG=DA	direct organization
DSORG=PO	partitioned organization

For MACRF, there are a large number of choices because of the large number of possible I/O processing options. For example, when using QSAM we might write the MACRF= parameter as follows:

dcbname   DCB   DSORG=PS,MACRF=(GM),...   QSAM input via GET macro in MOVE mode

(The MOVE mode used in this form is a buffer processing option that will be discussed later in this chapter.) When using BISAM, we might write the MACRF= parameter as shown here:

dcbname   DCB   DSORG=IS,MACRF=(R),...   BISAM input via READ macro

Note that the combination of codes specified for the DSORG and MACRF parameters defines the access method to be used for processing; organization is specified by DSORG and access technique is implied via MACRF. It is implied because, as can be seen from the I/O macro summary of figure 19.6a, the GET macro can be used only with the queued access technique, whereas the READ macro can be used only with the basic access technique. A similar distinction exists for PUT and PUTX (queued output) and WRITE (basic output).

As can be seen in the above examples, the rules for coding the DCB parameters are designed not only to provide the Operating System with the information it needs to process a data set, but also to serve as abbreviated reminders to the programmer as to the purpose of the parameters.

The RECFM, LRECL, and BLKSIZE parameters designate the record format, logical record length, and data block size, respectively. *Record format* refers to whether the logical records are of fixed or variable length, and whether they are blocked or unblocked. In this text, we will almost always use one of the following two codes for RECFM:

RECFM=FB	each data block contains one or more fixed-length records
RECFM=VB	each data block contains one or more variable-length records

For LRECL and BLKSIZE, the values specified must conform to the following rules:

LRECL=m	where m is the number of bytes in each fixed-length record if RECFM=FB, or the number of bytes in the largest variable-length record if RECFM=VB. For variable-length records, m must include the 4 bytes of the record descriptor word.
BLKSIZE=n	where n is an integral multiple of m for blocks containing fixed-length records, and is equal to (4 + an integral multiple of m) for blocks containing variable-length records.

For example, if the data set consisted of fixed-length 80-byte records, we could write LRECL=80, RECFM=FB, BLKSIZE=4080. This would give 51 records per block. If the data set consisted of variable-length records, the largest of which was 137 bytes (including the record descriptor word), we could write LRECL=137,RECFM=VB,BLKSIZE=3977. This would give 29 records per block, plus a 4-byte block-descriptor word. These blocksize choices are the largest that would contain an integral number of records and still be less than or equal to 4096, as discussed earlier in Section 19.1.

DOS Systems

The DTFxx macro that is used in DOS systems designates either a device or an access method for disk files. The principal DTFxx macros are these:

DTFCD	card reader/punch file
DTFPR	printer file
DTFDI	device-independent file
DTFSD	sequential disk file
DTFIS	indexed sequential file
DTFDA	direct access file

Other DTFxx macros are available for use with specific devices and will not be considered in this text. These include DTFMT (magnetic tape), DTFPT (paper tape), DTFDU (diskette unit), DTFMR (magnetic ink reader), DTFOR (optical reader), and DTFCN (console). Information about these macros can be found in the DOS macro reference manuals listed at the end of this chapter.

The name-field symbol of a DTFxx macro is used in all other I/O macros that refer to the same file as that DTFxx macro. As discussed in the next section, we will use the term "dtfname" when speaking of this name-field symbol. *There is one important constraint to remember:* the dtfname must not be more than seven characters long, because the DTFxx macro expansion includes symbols that consist of the dtfname suffixed with a single letter. For example, if dtfname=CARD, then symbols such as CARDC, CARDS, and CARDL may be created within the CARD DTFxx macro.

Figure 19.8b lists most of the DTFxx parameters for SAM, ISAM, and DAM disk files. Parameters for DTFCD and DTFPR (as well as for DTFSD) will be discussed in chapter 20; those for DTFIS, in chapter 21. Comparison of figure 19.8b with figure 19.8a shows similarities in purpose but differences in detail between OS and DOS systems.

The access method and file organization are specified via the letters *xx* in the DTFxx macro name. A file's processing mode is designated by the TYPEFLE= or IOROUT= parameter, and the record processing mode (*move* mode vs. *locate* mode) is specified, respectively, by the mutually exclusive WORKA= and IOREG= parameters.

Record format, logical record length, and data block size are specified by the RECFORM, RECSIZE, and BLKSIZE parameters. For example:

RECFORM=FIXBLK	each data block contains one or more fixed-length records, BLK meaning "blocked";
RECFORM=VARUNB	each data block contains exactly one variable-length record, UNB meaning "unblocked".
RECSIZE=m	m is the number of bytes in each fixed-length record if RECFORM=FIXBLK or =FIXUNB; and m is the number of bytes, plus 4, in the largest variable-length record if RECFORM= VARBLK or =VARUNB. (The extra 4 bytes is for the record descriptor word that precedes each record.)
BLKSIZE=n	n is an integer multiple of m for blocks containing fixed-length records and is equal to (4 + an integer multiple of m) for blocks containing variable-length records.

19.6 OPEN AND CLOSE

The Operating System maintains the information necessary to characterize a data set while it is being stored or processed. Some of the information is stored on disk in the data set's control block (DSCB), also known as the file's *label,* but most is provided through job control statements and the DCB or DTFxx macros. The information from these sources is merged at run time when a data set is opened via the OPEN macro, as shown in figure 19.9 for OS systems. A similar merge process, not shown here, takes place in DOS systems. Note that the DSCB or label is created by the merge process when a new data set is being created. Thereafter, the DSCB or label is updated.

The connection between a file, job control statements, and DCB or DTFxx macros is established by parameters:

Figure 19.9 *Merging the DSCB, DD, and DCB macro information.*

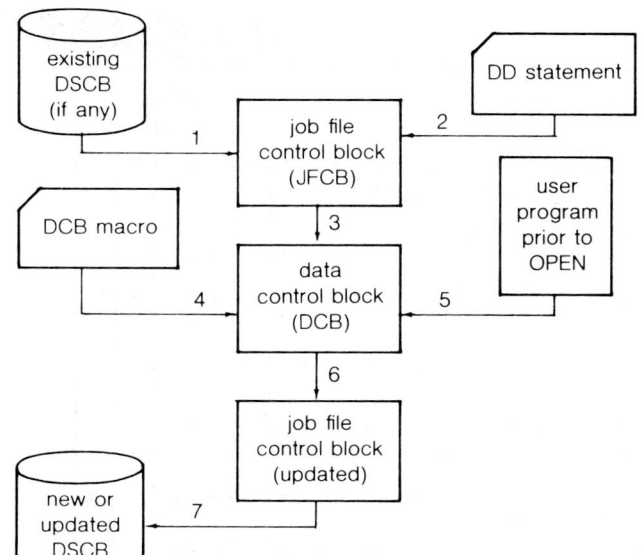

1. The existing data set control block (DSCB), if any, is used to initialize the Job File Control Block.
2. The DD statement supplements and overrides the information that was obtained from the DSCB.
3. The JFCB is used to initialize the data control block (DCB).
4. The DCB macro's information supplements and overrides that which was obtained from the JFCB.
5. Run-time modifications may be made to the DCB by the user program prior to completion of the OPEN process.

   The information contained after completion of Step 5 is the information that is used when any I/O-related macro is invoked. (In a few cases, that information may subsequently be modified by the user's program.)
6. The manner in which the JFCB is updated depends on whether the data set was opened for output or not. If it was opened for output, the DCB information replaces that which was in the JFCB. If it was opened for input or update, no existing JFCB information is replaced, but new information is added.
7. If the data set was opened for output, then the updated JFCB is written as the new DSCB.

Within an assembly language program, all references to a data set are made by references to the *dcbname* or *dtfname*. In OS systems, the DDNAME= parameter of the DCB macro identifies the corresponding DD statement, and the DD statement in turn identifies the actual data set. In DOS systems, the DLBL statement identifies the DTFxx macro. The DLBL also identifies the actual file, as shown above. It should be noted that most books and reference manuals use the term "filename" where we have used "dtfname". The latter is more accurate, since the actual name of a file need not be identical with the dtfname.

The formats for the OPEN and CLOSE macros depend on whether you are using OS or DOS.

OS Systems

To open an OS data set, the address of the DCB macro and one of several possible processing options must be specified in the OPEN macro. Its format is

>   OPEN   (dcb-address,(processing option))

The seven principal processing options are defined in figure 19.10a. The dcb-address may be specified symbolically or may be contained in a register whose address is enclosed in parentheses. For example, to open a data set whose DCB macro's dcbname is TRANS, to be processed for input, we could write

>   OPEN   (TRANS,(INPUT))

Alternatively, if the address of the DCB macro TRANS were in Register 3, we could write

>   OPEN   ((3),(INPUT))

at the time the OPEN were invoked. The latter form is not often used with the OPEN macro, but in the use of some other macros being able to specify a parameter via a general register gives added flexibility to the use of the macro.

When processing of a data set is completed, it must be logically disconnected from the program before the program's execution is terminated. This is called *closing* a data set. It is accomplished by the CLOSE macro, whose simplest form is

>   CLOSE   (dcb-address)

Figure 19.10a Processing options with the OPEN macro in OS systems.

processing option	meaning	QSAM	BSAM	QISAM	BISAM	BDAM	BPAM
EXTEND	An existing data set is to be processed by adding records to its end. No records already in the data set may be changed or deleted, and no records may be inserted at any point in the existing data set.	X	X	X	*		
INPUT	An existing data set is to be used for retrieval of information. No records in the data set will be changed or deleted, and no records will be added or inserted.	X	X	*	*	X	X
INOUT	The data set is first used for INPUT and then without closing or reopening it, for OUTPUT.		X		*		
OUTPUT	A new data set is to be created or the information in an existing data set is to be entirely replaced by new records.	X	X	X	*	X	X
OUTIN	The data set is first used for OUTPUT and then, without closing or reopening it, it is used for INPUT.		X		*		
OUTINX	The data set is processed like an OUTIN data set, except that in the OUTPUT mode processing, the records are added to the end of the data set as in EXTEND.		X		*		
UPDAT	The information in an existing data set is to be used for retrieval and existing logical records may be changed, but records may not be inserted, added, or deleted.	X	X	*	*	X	X

*Note: Except when creating or extending an indexed sequential data set using QISAM, the processing options for indexed sequential data sets are not specified in the OPEN macro for QISAM or BISAM. Instead, they are specified in the MACRF= parameter of the DCB macro.

More than one data set can be closed with a single execution of the CLOSE macro, provided that the dcb-addresses for each data set are listed in the operand, separated by commas:

CLOSE   (dcb-address-1,dcb-address-2,...)

As with the OPEN macro, the dcb-addresses may be contained in general registers. Thus, to close the TRANS data set, we could write CLOSE (TRANS), or, if Register 3 contained the address of the TRANS DCB macro, CLOSE ((3)).

When a data set is closed, the fields of the DCB macro are restored to the setting that existed before the OPEN macro was invoked. Because of this, a data set can be reopened for subsequent processing before program execution is terminated. We might do this, for example, to create a data set in OUTPUT mode and then process it during the same run in INPUT mode.

DOS Systems

To open a DOS file, the address of the DTFxx macro must be specified in the OPEN macro, and one of several processing options must be given by the TYPEFLE= or IOROUT= parameter of the DTFxx macro. The format of OPEN is

OPEN   dtf-address

The dtf-address may be specified symbolically—in which case it is just the dtfname—or it may be contained in a register whose address is enclosed in parentheses. For example, to open a file whose dtfname is TRANS, we could write

OPEN   TRANS

Alternatively, if the address of the TRANS DTFxx macro were in Register 3, we could write

OPEN   (3)

Figure 19.10b   *Processing options with the OPEN macro in DOS systems.*

processing option	meaning	SAM	ISAM	DAM
TYPEFLE=INPUT	For SAM files, an existing file is to be used for retrieval of information; no records in the file can be changed or deleted, and no new records can be added or inserted. For DAM files, label records will be read; data records can be read or written.	X		X
TYPEFLE=INPUT, UPDATE=YES	An existing SAM file is to be used for retrieval of information and for changing (i.e., updating) selected records. No records can be deleted, added, or inserted.	X		
TYPEFLE=OUTPUT	For SAM files, a new file is to be created, or an existing file is to be entirely replaced by new records. For DAM files, label records will be written; data records can be written or read.	X		X
TYPEFLE=WORK	A SAM file is to be used first for output, and then for input or output.	X		
IOROUT=RETRVE, TYPEFLE=x	An existing ISAM file is to be used for retrieval and/or updating. No records in the file can be deleted, and no new records can be added or inserted. x can be RANDOM, SEQNTL, or RANSEQ.		X	
IOROUT=ADDRTR, TYPEFLE=x	An existing ISAM file is to be used for retrieval and updating of existing records and for insertion of new records. x can be RANDOM, SEQNTL, or RANSEQ.		X	
IOROUT=ADD	New records can be inserted into an existing ISAM file.		X	
IOROUT=LOAD	A new ISAM file is to be created (i.e., loaded), or an existing ISAM file is to be extended by adding new records in sequence beyond the end of the file.		X	

The processing options are defined in figure 19.10b. As can be seen, the choice of options depends on the access method (more specifically, on the DTFxx macro). For SAM and DAM disk files, the options are specified by the TYPEFLE= parameter and also (in one case only) by the UPDATE= parameter. For ISAM files, they are specified by the IOROUT= parameter, with TYPEFLE= indicating whether sequential or random processing is to be used.

Each file that has been opened must be closed, i.e., logically disconnected from the program, before terminating run-time execution. This is done by the CLOSE macro. Its format is

CLOSE   dtf-address

More than one file can be closed with a single execution of CLOSE, provided the dtf-addresses for each file are listed in the operand:

CLOSE   dtf-address-1,dtf-address-2,...

As with the OPEN macro, a dtf-address can be specified via a register. For example, to close the TRANS file, we could write either CLOSE TRANS or CLOSE (3). In the latter case, the dtf-address TRANS must be in Register 3. After a file is closed, it can be reopened with the same DTF macro or with a different one.

19.7 GET, PUT, AND PUTX

When processing sequential or indexed-sequential files, logical records are read and written one at a time, in sequence, by means of the GET, PUT, and PUTX macros.[1]

In OS systems, GET reads a logical record, PUT writes a new logical record, and PUTX rewrites a record that was read via GET.

In DOS, GET reads a logical record and PUT writes a new record or rewrites a record that was read via GET. The PUTX macro is not available in DOS.

In both OS and DOS, the rewrite function is used to change, i.e., update, the contents of a logical record; the record that is rewritten *replaces* the record that had been read from disk.

---

1. There is one exception to this. In DOS, it is the WRITE macro rather than the PUT macro which is used to create an ISAM file, even though the records must be written in sequence.

Figure 19.11   Move mode and locate mode.

In *move mode*, a GET or PUT macro causes the logical record to be copied from input buffer to logical record area, or vice versa.

In *locate mode*, the address of the logical record in the input or output buffer is returned in Register 1 following a GET or PUT macro. The logical record is not copied to or from a logical record area in the user's program.

The operand of GET, PUT, and PUTX must specify the name of the file's DCB or DTFxx macro. The operand of GET or PUT (but not PUTX) may also specify the name of the I/O area that is used for the logical record. Whether or not we specify the name of that I/O area depends on whether we are using *move* mode or *locate* mode, as discussed below.

The fundamental concept embodied in the GET, PUT, and PUTX macros—the concept that distinguishes these macros from the READ and WRITE macros to be discussed in the next section—is that *logical records, not data blocks, are being transferred.* The GET macro does not necessarily cause a data block to be read from secondary memory, and the PUT and PUTX macros do not necessarily cause a data block to be written to secondary memory. Instead, with the GET macro the sequentially-next logical record is obtained from the data block that may already have been read into main memory when a previous GET was invoked. This is the process of deblocking discussed earlier. Similarly, with the PUT and PUTX macros, the logical record is placed into a data block that will not be written until it can contain no more records. This is the process of blocking. The processes of blocking and deblocking are performed by the access methods and are transparent to the user's program.

Move Mode vs. Locate Mode

Two main logical record processing modes are available in OS and DOS. In *move mode,* the access method copies a logical record from the input buffer area to the user's logical record area when a GET macro is executed, and copies a logical record from the user's logical record area to the output buffer area when a PUT macro is executed. In *locate mode,* logical records are not copied to or from the buffer area. Instead, the access method gives the user's program the address of the logical record, while the record remains in the buffer area so that the user program can process the record directly from that buffer area. Locate mode can save processing time and memory space; move mode is somewhat simpler to program. Either (but not both) of the modes can be used for a file at run time.

The concepts of move mode and locate mode are depicted in the diagrams of figure 19.11 for OS systems. In these diagrams, it is assumed that a logical record is being copied from a file identified by a DCB macro named DCBY to a file identified by a DCB macro named DCBX. In move mode the logical record areas (RY for input and RX for output) are specified in the GET and PUT macros, respectively. In locate mode, the logical record areas are not specified in the GET and PUT macros; instead, the address of each logical record is in Register 1 (placed there by the access method), and the program uses that address to copy the record from input to output buffer.

In OS, the MACRF= parameter of the DCB macro must specify whether move mode or locate mode is to be used. For example, MACRF=(GM) specifies move mode for the input file, and MACRF=(PM) specifies move mode for the output file. Similarly, MACRF=(GL) and MACRF=(PL) would specify locate mode for input and output files.

In DOS, move mode is specified by WORKA=YES for sequential files, and WORKS=YES for indexed sequential files. Locate mode is specified by IOREG=(n), $2 \leq n \leq 12$, where n is the address of the register in which the access method places the logical record's address. If IOREG= is specified, then neither WORKA= nor WORKS= can be specified, and vice versa. All three, of course, are parameters in the DTFxx macro.

End-of-File

If there are N logical records in a file, the end-of-file condition occurs when a GET macro is executed for the $(N+1)$st time. If this happens, the Operating System does not return control to the instruction following the GET macro. Instead, it returns control to the instruction whose address is specified by the EODAD= parameter of the DCB macro for OS and the EOFADDR= parameter of the DTFxx macro for DOS. If no EODAD= or EOFADDR= parameter is specified and an end-of-file condition occurs, then the user program is terminated. Note that this corresponds to the END= parameter in a FORTRAN READ statement and to the AT END clause in a COBOL READ statement.

19.8   READ AND WRITE

In some situations, input and output must be accomplished by the READ and WRITE macros instead of the GET, PUT, or PUTX macros.

In OS, READ and WRITE must be used with the basic access methods BSAM, BISAM, BDAM, and BPAM. In DOS, they must be used with SAM work files, with all DAM files, and with ISAM files when processing randomly and when adding or inserting new records. The OS formats and other considerations for READ and WRITE are different from those of DOS.

OS Systems

When processing data sets with any of the basic access methods, data-transfer operations are accomplished by means of the READ and WRITE macros:

> READ   reads a data block
> WRITE   writes a data block

The general formats for these macros depend on which access method is being used, as shown in the following representations:

for BSAM and BPAM:

$$\begin{Bmatrix} \text{READ} \\ \text{WRITE} \end{Bmatrix} \text{decb-name,type,dcb-addr,buffer-addr,buffer-length,} \begin{Bmatrix} \text{MF=E} \\ \text{MF=L} \end{Bmatrix}$$

for BISAM:

$$\begin{Bmatrix} \text{READ} \\ \text{WRITE} \end{Bmatrix} \text{decb-name,type,dcb-addr,buffer-addr,buffer-length,key-addr,} \begin{Bmatrix} \text{MF=E} \\ \text{MF=L} \end{Bmatrix}$$

for BDAM:

$$\begin{Bmatrix} \text{READ} \\ \text{WRITE} \end{Bmatrix} \text{decb-name,type,dcb-addr,buffer-addr,buffer-length,key-addr,track-addr,} \begin{Bmatrix} \text{MF=E} \\ \text{MF=L} \end{Bmatrix}$$

The *decb-name* parameter points to an area generated within the expansion of a READ or WRITE macro. This area, known as the *data event control block* (decb), always begins on a full-word boundary within the macro expansion. It is used by the Operating System to store the information given by the macro's parameters and to pass back to the user's program indicators that describe the reasons for the failure, if any, of the I/O operation. These indicators are known as *exception codes*. The format of the data event control block depends on the access method (fig. 19.12a).

Figure 19.12a   Data event control block formats for OS systems.

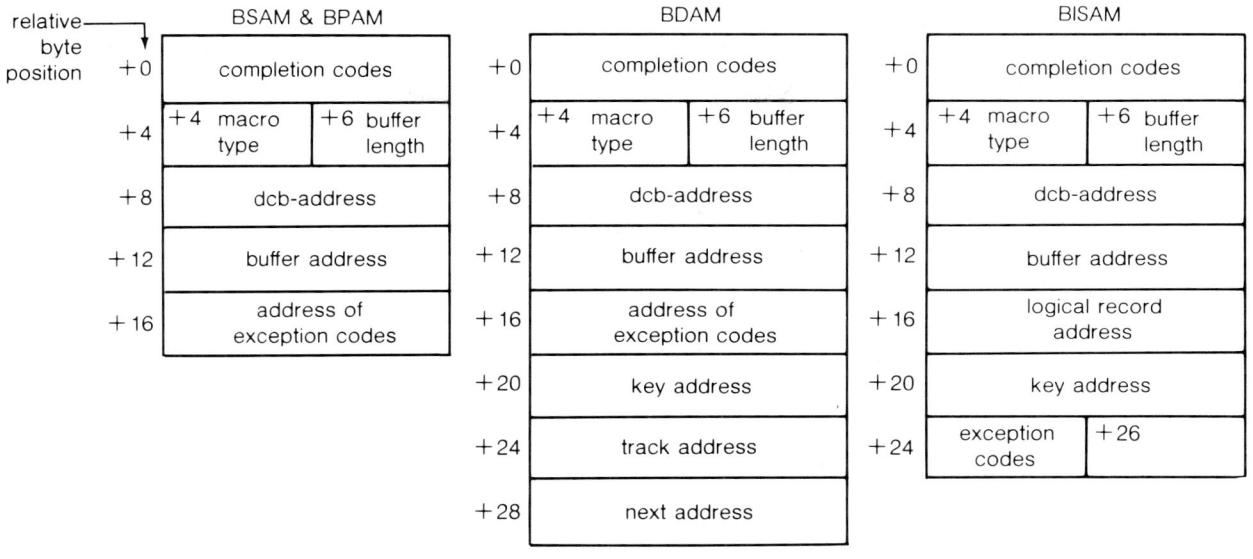

Figure 19.12b   Type parameter codes used in READ and WRITE macros for OS systems. (Note: Not all BDAM codes are shown.)

BSAM/BPAM read

SF read the data set sequentially

SB read a mag tape data set backwards (BSAM only)

BSAM/BPAM write

SF write the data set sequentially

SD write a fixed-length dummy record in count-key-data format (BSAM only)

SZ write a dummy track-descriptor record to fill the track to capacity (BSAM only)

BISAM read

K read a block for retrieval, not for update

KU read a block for possible updating

BISAM write

KN write a new record, or rewrite a variable-length record whose length has been changed

K rewrite a block that has been updated

BDAM read

DI read the data block (and key block, if any) from the track address given with the READ

DK read the data block from the track position identified by the key given with the READ

DIF
DKF same as DI or DK, but also requests the track address of the block that is read

BDAM write

DI write the data block (and key block, if any) at the track address given with the WRITE

DK write the data block into the track position identified by the key given with the WRITE

DIF
DKF same as DI or DK, but also requests the track address of the block that is written

DA write a new data block in the first available track position

DAF same as DA, but also requests the track address of the block that is written

The *type* parameter specifies certain variations of the READ or WRITE macro that characterize the type of processing to be performed. The variations depend on the access method as well as on whether it is a READ or WRITE macro. Most of the codes that can be specified are summarized in figure 19.12b.

The *dcb-addr* parameter identifies the address of the DCB macro that is associated with the READ or WRITE macro being executed. The *buffer-addr* parameter identifies the buffer area to be used, and the *buffer-length* parameter specifies the number of data bytes to be read or written. The *key-addr* parameter points to the memory area that contains the key which identifies data blocks stored in count-key-data format, and the *track-addr* parameter points to the memory area that contains the relative or absolute disk track address of the data block to be read or written.

The need to specify the buffer-address and buffer-length reflects the fact that the Operating System does not perform blocking or deblocking functions. In addition, when processing blocks in random order, the Operating System does not know which block is to be read or where to insert a block that is to be written until the block's position is identified by the user's program. BISAM requires that the position be identified by a key; the key is used to determine the disk track address via the index maintained by the Operating System. BDAM requires that the block's position be identified either by a key or by its track address, or both.

The MF=E and MF=L keyword parameters in the READ and WRITE macros are not always used. When both are omitted, the macro is said to be in *standard form*. MF=E is the *execute form* and MF=L the *list form* of the macro. In the standard and list forms, the macro's expansion includes a data event control block, and the decb-name parameter is the name of that decb. In the execute form, the expansion does not include a decb; instead, the decb-name parameter refers to a decb in some other standard or list form of the macro. There are two major uses for the execute and list forms: (1) the decb in a list-form macro can be shared by two or more execute-form macros, and (2) when a list-form macro is in an eraseable area of memory, execute forms that refer to it can be used for I/O from within reentrant programs or in programs that are executed in a read-only portion of memory. In chapter 21, we will encounter instances in which shared decb's are required for BISAM. We will not, however, have occasion to illustrate reentrant or read-only situations.

DOS Systems

The formats for the READ and WRITE macros in DOS depend on the access method as follows:

for SAM work files:

$$\left\{ \begin{matrix} \text{READ} \\ \text{WRITE} \end{matrix} \right\} \quad \text{dtf-address,type,buffer-address,buffer-length}$$

for ISAM and DAM files:

$$\left\{ \begin{matrix} \text{READ} \\ \text{WRITE} \end{matrix} \right\} \quad \text{dtf-address,type}$$

In all the formats, the *dtf-address* parameter identifies the DTFxx macro for the file that is being read or written, and the *type* parameter specifies certain variations of the macro that characterize the type of processing to be performed as shown in figure 19.13.

For SAM work files, the *buffer-address* and *buffer-length* parameters designate, respectively, the I/O buffer area to be used and the number of bytes to be read or written. The buffer-address must be specified because unlike most of the other DTFxx macros the DTFSD for SAM work files does not permit IOAREA1 or IOAREA2 to designate the buffer. The buffer-length must be specified in the READ or WRITE macro when the record format is undefined, but is not specified there for unblocked record formats. In the latter case, the buffer-length is the value of the BLKSIZE= parameter in the DTFSD.

For DAM files, like SAM work files, the record format must be either unblocked or undefined. However for DAM READ or WRITE macros, the buffer-*address* is specified by the IOAREA1= parameter of the DTFDA macro. The DAM READ macro assumes that the buffer-*length* is the value of the BLKSIZE= parameter, but the WRITE macro requires that for unblocked records the user's program must put the length into the record descriptor word, and for undefined record formats it must put it in the register specified by the RECSIZE= parameter of DTFDA.

For ISAM files, the requirements are as follows. The buffer-length is specified by the IOSIZE= parameter of DTFIS. The buffer-address for a READ is specified by IOAREAR= in DTFIS. The buffer-address for a WRITE is specified by IOAREAL= when creating a new file or adding new records to a file; but it is specified by IOAREAR= when updating existing records, since the records are rewritten from the same area into which they were read.

SAM read		*SAM write*	
SQ	read the file sequentially	SQ	write in count-key-data format
		UPDATE	rewrite a data block but not the count or key blocks
ISAM read		*ISAM write*	
KEY	read the record whose key is in the KEYARG area	KEY	rewrite a record that has been updated
		NEWKEY	write a new record
DAM read		*DAM write*	
ID	read the data block and key block from the track address specified in the SEEKADR field	ID	write the key and data blocks to the track address specified in the SEEKADR field
KEY	read the data block whose key matches that in the KEYARG field	KEY	write the data block to the track position whose key matches the one in the KEYARG field
		AFTER	same as ID, except that a new record is written following the previously last record on the track
		AFTER,EOF	same as AFTER, except that an end-of-file record is written following the last record on the track
		RZERO	erase the track whose address is specified in the SEEKADR field

Further details for ISAM files will be given in chapter 21. DAM files and SAM work files will not be covered in this text. It should be noted however that unlike OS, there is no data event control block associated with a DOS READ or WRITE macro. Consequently, if you are interested in using SAM work files or DAM files, you must be able to process I/O error exception conditions as described in the IBM reference manuals listed at the end of this chapter.

19.9   I/O SYNCHRONIZATION

When a data block is read or written, a certain amount of time will elapse (access time plus data-transfer time) before the data transfer is completed. The user's program must be delayed until that time; otherwise the data in the buffer area may be invalid or incomplete. The process of delaying execution is known as I/O *synchronization.*

OS Systems

In the queued access methods, the delays are performed by the Operating System before it returns control to the user's program following a GET, PUT, or PUTX macro. In the basic access methods, a CHECK or WAIT macro must follow each READ or WRITE in order to cause the requisite delay. CHECK must always be used with BSAM and BPAM operations; either CHECK or WAIT can be used with BISAM and BDAM.

The simplest formats of the CHECK and WAIT macros are

CHECK	decb-address	for BSAM, BPAM, BDAM
CHECK	decb-address, DSORG=IS	for BISAM only
WAIT	ECB=decb-address	for BISAM & BDAM only

The decb-address in the operand of these macros is simply the address of the data event control block used in the corresponding READ or WRITE macro.

The main difference between the CHECK and WAIT macros has to do with the manner in which the Operating System returns control to the user's program upon completion of the I/O operation. Control is always returned to the instruction immediately following the WAIT macro, regardless of whether or not any errors occurred during the I/O operation. Control is returned to the instruction immediately following the CHECK macro only if no errors or end-of-data condition occurred during the I/O operation. If end-of-data was detected, control is returned to the address specified by the EODAD parameter in the DCB macro. If errors were detected, control is returned to the address specified by the synchronization error address (SYNAD) parameter in the DCB macro.

When control is returned to the SYNAD routine or to the instruction following a WAIT macro, the user's program must examine the exception codes (and certain other information provided by the Operating System) to determine the cause of the error, if any, and take appropriate action. In general, the alternatives are to accept the fact that the block was read or written with an error, to skip that block and resume processing at the next data block, or to abnormally terminate the program with an ABEND macro.

A SYNAD routine also can be specified when queued access methods are used. Although neither the CHECK nor WAIT macro is used with queued access methods, the Operating System will return control to the SYNAD routine if a data error is detected during execution of an I/O macro. Since there is no data event control block, the exception codes are made available in one of two ways: (1) with QISAM, they are stored in two bytes within the DCB macro expansion; (2) with QSAM, they are stored in an area whose address is specified in Register 0 upon entry to the SYNAD routine.

With the basic access methods, the user's program is terminated if an error occurs while a CHECK macro is being executed and no SYNAD routine had been specified. With the queued access methods, absence of a SYNAD routine causes user-program termination whenever an error occurs during an I/O operation, except under these two conditions for sequential data sets: (1) Data blocks causing I/O errors on a *printer* data set opened for OUTPUT can be ignored by coding EROPT=ACC in the DCB macro. In this case, each offending data block is written (i.e., "accepted") despite the I/O error. (2) Data blocks causing I/O errors on *any* sequential data set opened either for INPUT or UPDAT can be either accepted or skipped by coding EROPT=ACC or EROPT=SKP, respectively, in the DCB macro. If accepted, each offending block is read (GET) or rewritten (PUTX) despite the error; if skipped, each offending block is bypassed, i.e., not read or rewritten.

DOS Systems

In DOS, the I/O delays are performed by the Operating System before it returns control to the user's program following a GET or PUT macro. But a CHECK or WAITF macro must follow each READ or WRITE in order to cause the requisite delay. CHECK is used only with SAM work files; WAITF is used with ISAM and DAM files.

The formats of the two macros are

| CHECK | dtf-address | for SAM work files only |
| WAITF | dtf-address | for ISAM or DAM files |

The main difference between CHECK and WAITF has to do with the manner in which the Operating System returns control to the user's program upon completion of the I/O operation. Control is always returned to the instruction following the WAITF macro, regardless of whether or not any I/O errors occurred. But control is returned to the instruction immediately following a CHECK macro only if no errors or end-of-file condition occurred. If end-of-file was detected, control is returned to the address specified by the EOFADDR= parameter of the DTFSD macro. If errors were detected, then the option specified in the ERROPT= parameter is processed.

When control is returned to the user's ERROPT routine or to the instruction following a WAITF macro, the user's program must examine the exception codes provided by the Operating System to determine the cause of the error, if any, and take appropriate action. It should be noted, however, that the ERROPT= parameter need not specify the address of an error-processing routine. Instead, it can specify action that the Operating System is to take before it returns control to the instruction that follows a CHECK macro. Thus, for SAM input work files, we can specify ERROPT=IGNORE or ERROPT=SKIP, and an error will either be ignored or the entire block skipped. (For SAM output work files, ERROPT=IGNORE is permissible, but not ERROPT=SKIP.) Similar options exist for card and printer files.

Figure 19.14   Use of two input buffer areas.

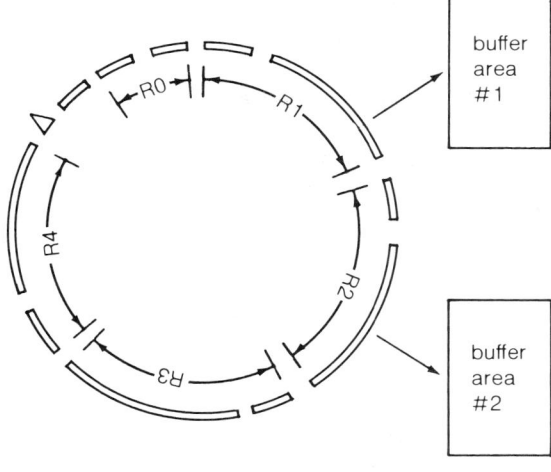

buffer
area
#1

buffer
area
#2

Area #1 will contain
data blocks from
disk data records
R1, R3, R5, . . .
Area #2 will contain
data blocks from
disk data records
R2, R4, R6, . . .
While R1 is being
processed from
Area #1, R2 is read
into Area #2.
While R2 is being
processed, R3 is
read into Area #1.
And so forth, with
processing from
Area #1 while reading
into Area #2,
and vice versa.

19.10   BUFFER AREAS

As has been discussed, data blocks read into main memory are read into buffer areas; data blocks written from main memory are written from buffer areas. Each buffer area must be large enough to contain the largest data block (including BDW and RDW's) that will be processed in the data set for which it is being used.

There may be one or more buffer areas associated with a data set. In the IBM 360 and 370 systems, there are several ways of specifying the size and number of buffer areas, defining the buffer areas, and using the buffer areas during input/output operations. Essentially, the alternatives involve the following two concepts:

1. Buffers may be in memory areas that are either defined at assembly time or are acquired at run time.
2. When more than one buffer area is acquired at run time, it is usually part of a *buffer pool,* a set of contiguous buffer areas.

When processing a data set sequentially, it is advantageous to use two buffers. When processing in random fashion, there is usually little advantage gained from using more than one buffer. The reason for this difference is the following: when processing sequentially, the order in which the data blocks are read or written is determined by the sequence of the logical records in the data set. The Nth block must be processed after the $(N-1)$st block and before the $(N+1)$st block. Therefore, during input operations the $(N+1)$st block can be transferred from secondary memory to main memory while the Nth block is simultaneously being processed by the CPU. Similarly, during output operations the $(N-1)$st block can be transferred from main memory to secondary memory while the Nth block is being processed. This is illustrated in figure 19.14 for input operations on sequential data sets. Note, however, that when processing records randomly, it is not so simple to predict which data block is needed next; the decision depends on the data and on the manner in which it is being processed.

The possibility for simultaneous I/O and CPU processing operations is due to the manner in which the hardware is designed and will not be discussed here. However, it should be clear that because of the relatively long access times and data-transfer times required to copy data blocks to or from secondary memory, simultaneous use of two buffers can reduce the amount of time a program must wait for each data block transfer to be completed.

As may be expected, the methods for acquiring and utilizing buffer areas depend on whether or not we are using OS or DOS systems.

OS Buffer Options in Queued Access Methods

The principal buffer utilization technique used with queued access methods is known as *simple buffering.* Another technique, known as *exchange buffering,* also can be used. This technique, which is more complex and less generally applicable than simple buffering, will not be discussed in this text.

If simple buffering is used, and if the buffer pool area is acquired at the time the data set is opened, a programmer need not be concerned with the details of how the buffers are assigned or utilized. The number of buffers in the pool is automatically set to 2, and the synchronization of the use of the buffers is performed by the Operating System. Each buffer area in the pool is associated with the same opened data set; the pool has the format shown in figure 19.15a.

In addition to being able to automatically create a buffer pool at open time, two other methods are available: (1) by executing a GETPOOL macro prior to opening a data set, or (2) by executing a BUILD macro prior to opening a data set. The BUILD macro creates the pool in an area that had been reserved at assembly time by a DS directive. The GETPOOL macro creates the pool in an area acquired at run time. Except in special processing circumstances, neither BUILD nor GETPOOL need be used. Automatic acquisition of a buffer pool at open time provides sufficient capabilities for most processing needs.

OS Buffer Options in Basic Access Methods

Three buffer utilization procedures are available with basic access methods: dynamic buffering, direct buffering, and user-controlled buffering.

In *dynamic* buffering, the buffer pool area is obtained and structured by the OPEN macro. The number of buffers in the pool is specified by the BUFNO parameter in the DCB macro. A buffer is selected from the pool each time a READ macro is executed, and the same area can be used by a subsequent WRITE macro when updating. Dynamic buffering, which is only available for use with BDAM and BISAM when a data set is opened for input or updating, simplifies I/O programming by placing the responsibility for control of the buffers in the Operating System (see chap. 21).

In *direct* buffering, the buffer pool area may be created by the BUILD, GETPOOL, or OPEN macros as in the queued access methods. The structure of the pool area is the same as that shown in figure 19.15a for the queued methods. But, unlike the queued methods, a buffer area must be selected from the pool before it can be used in a READ or WRITE macro. This is done by executing a GETBUF macro. When no longer needed (for example, when a data set is closed) the buffer area can be returned to the pool by a FREEBUF macro and be used for other purposes.

In *user-controlled* buffering, the user's program is entirely responsible for reserving and using buffer areas. A buffer pool area is not created by the Operating System; instead, buffer areas are reserved at assembly time and utilized by the user's program at run time in whatever way best suits the processing needs.

The three buffering methods are not mutually exclusive; they may all be used with a single data set. It is up to the user's program to designate which buffer area is being used with a given READ or WRITE macro instruction.

DOS Buffer Options

All I/O buffer areas in DOS must be reserved at assembly time. They are part of the user-program's memory area and are not supplied by the Operating System. For sequential processing, either one or two buffers may be reserved. For random processing, only one buffer is reserved.

For SAM files (but not SAM work files), the names of the buffer areas must be specified by the IOAREA1= parameter (and optionally the IOAREA2= parameter) of the DTFSD macro. The areas must be reserved by DS directives. For SAM work files, the buffers must be reserved by DS directives and their addresses specified in READ and WRITE macros.

For DAM files, the name of the buffer area is specified by the IOAREA1= parameter and the buffer area must be reserved by the DS directive.

For ISAM files, two buffers can be used when creating (i.e., loading) a file or when sequentially retrieving from it. The optional second area's name must be specified by the IOAREA2= parameter in the DTFIS, but the required first area's name is specified by IOAREAL= for file creation, and by IOAREAS= for sequential retrieval. Only one buffer is used when randomly processing an ISAM file. Its name is specified by the IOAREAR= parameter in the DTFIS. In all cases, the areas must be reserved by DS directives.

The formats of the I/O areas depend on the access method. In figure 19.15b we show the formats to be used with ISAM files. These and the formats for the other access methods are explained in detail in the *DOS/VS Supervisor and I/O Macros* reference manual, IBM# GC33–5373.

Figure 19.15a   Format of buffer pool area for OS systems.

The beginning of each buffer area in the pool is aligned on a double-word boundary unless BFALN=F is specified in the DCB macro.

BFALN=F causes buffers to be aligned on a full-word boundary that is not also a double-word boundary.

Figure 19.15b   ISAM buffer area formats for DOS systems. (Note: These formats assume that RECFORM=FIXBLK, i.e., fixed-length logical records with two or more records per data block.)

Note: These formats assume that RECFORM=FIXBLK, i.e., fixed-length logical records with two or more records per data block. See also "I/O Areas" in *DOS/VS Supervisor and I/O Macros*, IBM #GC33–5373.

1. Format of the area specified by IOAREAL= and IOAREA2= , with IOROUT=LOAD or IOROUT=ADD.

Used when loading (i.e., creating or extending) an ISAM file, and when inserting new records into an ISAM file.

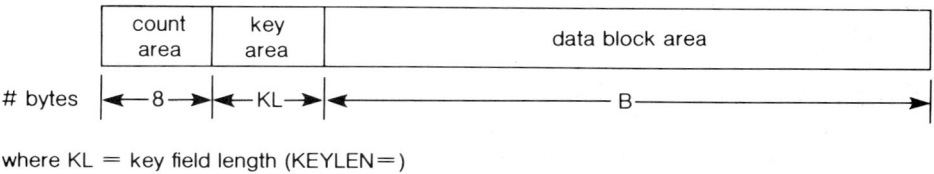

where KL = key field length (KEYLEN=)
and   B   is defined below.

Each logical record in the data block area must contain that record's key.

2. Format of the area specified by IOAREAS= and IOAREA2= , with IOROUT=RETRVE and TYPEFLE=SEQNTL; and by IOAREAR= with IOROUT=RETRVE and TYPEFLE=RANDOM.

Used when processing sequentially or randomly for retrieval and updating of existing records in an ISAM file.

where B = either DL + 10 or R × DL , whichever is larger

and DL = logical record length (RECSIZE=)

R = blocking factor (NRECDS=)

Each logical record in the data block area will contain that record's key.
Note: When a record is retrieved from the ISAM overflow area, the first 10 bytes of the data block area will contain the record's *sequence link* (SL), a system pointer used for maintaining logical sequence of overflow records. There is always only one overflow record per data block, even though RECFORM=FIXBLK.

19.11 SUMMARY

Since the Operating System controls all input/output operations, it is not possible to do I/O without properly describing the data sets and the operations to be performed. Two mechanisms exist for this purpose: job control language (JCL) and assembly language macro instructions.

JCL is used to describe certain characteristics of a data set to be processed at run time. Assembly language macros are used to provide additional information about the data set, to characterize the I/O operations to be performed, and to initiate I/O data transfer and related control operations performed by the Operating System at run time. The JCL statements and macro instructions that are used for sequential and indexed-sequential files in OS systems differ in most details from those used in DOS systems, but their overall purposes are the same in both systems.

Before processing of a data set can begin, it must be opened (i.e., logically connected to the user's program) through execution of the OPEN macro at run time. It is at this time that the descriptions in the JCL statements, the declarative macros (DCB or DTFxx), and the data set's control block or label are merged (see fig. 19.9). Among the characteristics obtained by the Operating System at open time are these: the physical space requirements for the data set in secondary memory, the organization of the data set's records and the method by which they will be accessed, and descriptions of the buffer and record areas. Still other characteristics are passed to the Operating System at the time that an I/O operation is initiated. After all I/O operations have been completed, the data set is logically disconnected from the program by the CLOSE macro. After it has been closed, the data set's future availability is determined by information supplied in JCL statements.

Although these remarks apply to all data sets processed at run time, there are an appreciable number of details that may differ from one data set to another. These details depend primarily on three factors: (1) the type of device on which the data set is stored, (2) the data set's organization, and (3) the I/O access method to be used. The type of device in turn determines the data set organizations that are permitted, and the data set organization determines the access methods that are permitted. For storage devices in which random access is not physically practicable, such as magnetic tape, paper tape, cards, printers, and so forth, only the sequential organization is permitted. For disk and other direct-access storage devices, any of the data set organizations that are supported by the Operating System are permissible.

The organization of a data set must be established at the time the data set is created, and thereafter it cannot be changed. In OS systems organization is specified by the DSORG= parameter in the DCB macro; in DOS systems it is specified by the letters *xx* in the DTFxx macro.

The access method used with a data set at run time is a set of system procedures that carry out the I/O operations requested by the user's program. The access method must be established at the time a data set is opened. In OS, this is done through the combined values of the DSORG= and MACRF= parameters in the DCB macro. In DOS systems, the data-set organization as specified by the DTFxx macro determines the access method. Once an organization and access method are specified in either OS or DOS, the user's program is constrained to use only certain I/O macros and DCB or DTFxx parameters. Perhaps the most important constraint concerns the choice of GET/PUT macros vs. READ/WRITE macros.

In OS, GET must be used for input, and PUT (or PUTX) for output whenever a queued access technique—QSAM or QISAM—is used with a sequential or indexed sequential data set. With the basic access techniques—BSAM, BISAM, BDAM, and BPAM—READ is used for input and WRITE for output.

In DOS, GET and PUT are used for SAM files (other than work files), READ and WRITE for DAM and for SAM work files. ISAM files require GET for sequential retrieval and PUT for updating existing records when processing sequentially; but READ is used for random retrieval, and WRITE is used to add or insert new records into a file.

Among the other concepts presented in this chapter, perhaps the most important are those associated with handling the end-of-data condition, synchronizing I/O with CPU operations, and designating buffer and record areas.

End-of-data

In the OS queued techniques (QSAM and QISAM), and in one of the basic techniques (BSAM), end-of-data will cause the program to be terminated unless the EODAD= parameter in the DCB macro specifies a user routine to handle this condition. In all other basic techniques, end-of-data is not a meaningful concept since the records are being processed randomly.

In DOS, the EOFADDR= parameter in the DTFxx macro plays the same role that EODAD= does in OS.

Synchronization

Synchronization is essentially a delay in program execution whenever this is necessary to ensure that a data-transfer operation has been completed before any further attempt is made to use the buffer associated with that transfer. Moreover, if transmission (or other) errors are detected by the Operating System, synchronization involves action to resolve the errors by terminating the program, by ignoring the errors, or by bypassing the block that caused the errors.

In OS queued techniques, the delays are an inherent part of the execution of the GET, PUT, and PUTX macros; in the basic techniques, the delays must be explicitly requested via the CHECK or WAIT macros following execution of a READ or WRITE macro. For resolution of I/O errors, there are three options from which to choose in the queued techniques and three in the basic techniques. The OS options, which must be specified via the DCB macro at the time a data set is opened, are as follows.

For OS queued access:

1. Let the Operating System terminate the program.
2. If the data set is the printer or is any sequential input data set, let the Operating System bypass the data block or accept it with errors by coding EROPT=SKP or EROPT=ACC, respectively.
3. For any data set, let the user program handle the errors via a subroutine whose entry point is designated in the SYNAD= parameter.

For OS basic access:

1. Use the CHECK macro and let the Operating System terminate the program if errors are detected.
2. Use the CHECK macro and let the user program handle the errors by designating an error subroutine entry point via the SYNAD= parameter.
3. Use the WAIT macro and let the user program handle the errors when the Operating System returns control to the instruction following WAIT.

In DOS, the options available for handling I/O errors depend on whether we are using the GET/PUT macros or the READ/WRITE macros.

For DOS GET/PUT:

1. Let the Operating System terminate the program if an I/O error occurs.
2. Let the Operating System ignore an error or skip past a data block that is in error, by coding ERROPT=IGNORE or ERROPT=SKIP in the DTF macro.
3. Let the user program handle the error by coding the name of the error-handling routine in the ERROPT= parameter.

For DOS READ/WRITE:

1. With SAM work files, use the CHECK macro and let the Operating System handle the error according to the ERROPT= parameter specification (IGNORE, SKIP, or user-routine-address).
2. With ISAM and DAM files, use the WAITF macro and process the error when the Operating System returns control to the instruction that follows WAITF.

Buffers

Buffers are the main memory areas used for transfer of data blocks to and from secondary memory. The methods available for allocating and using buffers depends on which access methods are specified.

In OS, there are two different buffering techniques with queued access methods, "simple" and "exchange".

The simple buffering technique is the default (i.e., it need not be explicitly requested), and may be used with either QSAM or QISAM. The exchange buffering technique must be explicitly requested via the BFTEK parameter in the DCB macro but may be used only with QSAM. In certain cases (primarily those involving input and output of the same logical records) exchange buffering can improve I/O efficiency, but in order to concentrate on more fundamental processes it will not be discussed further in this text.

Simple buffering can take place without executing any buffer-related macros and without specifying any buffer-related DCB parameters. In this approach, a buffer pool consisting of two buffer areas is allocated by the Operating System at open time. Or, you can explicitly request buffer allocation via the GETPOOL macro before opening a data set or request that your own (user program) buffers be used via the BUILD macro. Whichever approach is used, the buffers are properly used by the Operating System whenever a GET, PUT, or PUTX macro is executed.

With OS basic access methods, three buffering techniques are available: "dynamic," "direct," and "user-controlled" buffering. The READ and WRITE macros cause data blocks, not logical records, to be transferred.

Direct buffering is like simple buffering in that the buffer pool may be allocated either at open time or via the GETPOOL or BUILD macros. However, unlike simple buffering, the number of buffer areas in each pool must be designated by the BUFNO= parameter of the DCB macro. A buffer area must also be selected from the pool via the GETBUF macro and its address must be designated in each READ or WRITE macro.

Dynamic buffering is restricted to use with BDAM and BISAM. The buffer pool is allocated at open time by the Operating System and a buffer area is selected by the Operating System each time a READ or WRITE macro is executed. The use of dynamic buffering with BISAM processing will be discussed in chapter 21.

User-controlled buffering requires the user's program to handle all functions related to reserving buffer space and designating buffer-addresses.

In DOS, all buffer areas must be reserved by the user's program at assembly time. Thus, in a sense, the only buffering technique available is akin to the OS "user-controlled" buffering.

Record Areas

The principal methods for designating logical record areas are known as move mode and locate mode. In move mode, each logical record is moved by the Operating System from buffer area to record area (or vice versa) when an input (or output) macro is executed. In locate mode, logical records are not so moved; instead, they are processed directly from their locations in the buffer area. The two modes are mutually exclusive; one or the other must be designated. In OS, the designation is made via the MACRF= parameter; in DOS, move mode is designated by the WORKA= or WORKS= parameters and locate mode by the IOREG= parameter.

Other Considerations

A number of other I/O software concepts and mechanisms are provided for in the IBM 360 and 370 systems in addition to those mentioned. One of the main reasons for such diversity of capabilities is the desire to be able to increase I/O processing efficiency in programs that are run frequently, especially when large data sets are processed. The disparity between I/O access times and data-transfer times on the one hand and main memory access times and processing speeds on the other make such improvements worthwhile. You can pursue these additional topics through the references listed in the next section.

19.12 REFERENCE MANUALS

Further details on the material summarized in this chapter, and information on other I/O processing options not covered, can be found in the reference manuals cited in this section.

For comprehensive discussions and examples of the I/O software facilities:

OS/VS1	*Data Management Services Guide* IBM Publication GC26–3874	DOS/VS	*Data Management Guide* IBM #GC33–5372
OS/VS1	*JCL Services* IBM Publication GC24–5100	DOS/VS	*System Management Guide* IBM #GC33–5371

For detailed explanations of macro and job-control formats:

OS/VS1	*Data Management Macro Instructions* IBM Publication GC26–3872	DOS/VS	*Supervisor and I/O Macros* IBM #GC33–5373
OS/VS1	*JCL Reference* IBM Publication GC24–5099	DOS/VS	*System Control Statements* IBM #GC33–5376

It will also help to be familiar with the types of utility programs available for certain often needed data set operations, such as printing or punching a data set, creating a copy of a data set, and maintaining partitioned data sets. Information about utility programs can be found in

OS/VS1	*Utilities* IBM Publication GC26–3901	DOS/VS	*System Utilities* IBM #GC33–5381

If you are interested in learning about the virtual storage access method (VSAM), these three manuals are extremely useful:

OS/VS	*Virtual Storage Access Method Programmer's Guide* IBM Publication GC26–3813
OS/VS	*Access Method Services* IBM Publication GC26–3840
VSAM	*Primer and Reference Manual* IBM Publication G320–5774

EXERCISES

1. What, if any, rules or restrictions govern the choice of blocksize for data sets stored on disk in your computer installation?

2. What is the purpose of the technique known as *blocking?* What is the purpose of *deblocking?* Under what condition is blocking and deblocking not required?

3. What are the consequences of specifying RECFM=FB in a DCB macro for a data set? What are the consequences of specifying RECFM=VB in a DCB macro for a data set?

4. If a sequential data set consists of no more than N fixed-length logical records, each of length L bytes, determine the maximum value of the BLKSIZE parameter that is less than or equal to 4096, for each of the following values of L: $L = 80$, $L = 132$, $L = 256$, $L = 2500$. (Assume that the data set is to reside on a disk pack in the IBM 3330 disk system.)

   How many tracks would be required to store a sequential data set under each of the above four conditions? (Assume that $N = 10,000$.)

5. If a sequential data set consists of no more than N variable-length logical records, the maximum record length being L bytes, determine the maximum value of the BLKSIZE parameter that is less than or equal to 4096, for each of the following values of L: $L = 80$, $L = 132$, $L = 256$, $L = 2500$. (Assume that the data set is to reside on a disk pack in the IBM 3330 disk system.)

   How many tracks would be required to store a sequential data set under each of the above four conditions? (Assume that $N = 10,000$.)

6. Write an appropriate form of the //EXTENT statement or SPACE= parameter of the JCL DD statement to reserve a sufficient amount of disk space for each of the four situations given in Exercise 4.

7. Write an appropriate form of the //EXTENT statement or SPACE= parameter of the JCL DD statement to reserve a sufficient amount of disk space for each of the four situations given in Exercise 5.

8. Of the four data-set organizations mentioned in this chapter—sequential, indexed sequential, partitioned, and direct—only one can be used for data sets stored on magnetic tape. Which one is it and why are none of the others permitted to be used with tape data sets?

9. Define what is meant by the "end-of-data" condition for sequential data sets. Under what OPEN processing options (defined in fig. 19.10) can the end-of-data condition occur? How is the EODAD= or EOFADDR= parameter used in conjunction with the end-of-data condition? What happens at run time when end-of-data occurs if no EODAD= or EOFADDR= parameter has been specified?

10. Each access method is in a sense a set of subroutines that exist as part of the Operating System. These subroutines are *called* by the SVC instruction that is generated as part of the expansion of each executable I/O macro. What are the similarities between the SVC instruction and the BALR 14,15 instruction used to call user-defined subroutines? What are the differences between the SVC and the BALR 14,15 instructions?

11. As discussed in Section 19.4, Register 13 must contain the address of the user program's register save area each time an I/O macro is executed at run time. What other constraints do the I/O macro register conventions place on user programs? How do these conventions differ from and how are they similar to the conventions that exist for calls to user-defined subroutines?

12. Write a DCB or DTFPR macro for a sequential data set whose contents are to be sent to a high-speed printer. (The length of a printed line can be no more than 132 characters and the number of lines to be printed should be assumed to be no more than 5000.) Explain each DCB or DTFPR parameter that you use and explain the value assigned to that parameter.

13. Write a DCB or DTFxx macro for a sequential input data set whose contents are some arbitrary number of 80-byte card-image records. Explain each parameter that you use and explain the value assigned to that parameter.

14. Write appropriate OPEN and CLOSE macros for each of the data sets described in Exercises 12 and 13.

15. The GET macro obtains the sequentially-next logical record from a data block. If we assume that only one input buffer had been requested, and if either (1) no previous GET macro had been executed or (2) the previous GET had obtained the last logical record from a data block, then execution of a GET macro causes the Operating System to read the next data block (if any) and then obtain the first logical record from that block.

    a. Depict this sequence of events with a flow diagram.

    b. Explain how this sequence of events might be modified to minimize the delay inherent in reading a data block if there were two input buffers instead of one. Depict your explanation with a flow diagram showing the modified sequence of events.

16. The READ macro causes the Operating System to read the sequentially-next data block from secondary memory. It is up to the user's program to obtain the sequentially-next logical record from that data block.

    a. Write a subroutine named DEBLOCK that will obtain the sequentially-next logical record from a data block that had been read via a READ macro. Assume that the records are fixed-length. The parameters that should be passed to your subroutine are these:

    —the address of the input buffer, as had been specified in the READ macro
    —the address of the logical record area into which the sequentially-next logical record should be moved (as in move mode)
    —the address of the logical record length
    —the address of the data blocksize
    —the address of a full-word binary integer N, which is the number that identifies the relative position within the data block of the record to be obtained within that block. ($N = 0,1,2,..., M$, where M identifies the last record in the block. $N=0$ means it is a new data block.)

Your DEBLOCK subroutine must move the entire logical record to the calling program's logical record area, and increase the value of N by $+1$, returning the increased value to the calling program. However, if there were no more logical records in the data block at the time the call to DEBLOCK was made, your subroutine should return a value of $N = 0$.

    b. Write a main program that will test your DEBLOCK subroutine. Your main program need not execute a READ macro; instead, it can simply contain a simulated data block, for example, one that is created by the following set of directives:

BLOCK	DC	CL20'RECD 1'
	DC	CL20'RECD 2'
	DC	CL20'RECD 3'
	DC	CL20'RECD 4'
LRECL	DC	F'20'
BLKSIZE	DC	F'80'
RECDAREA	DC	CL20
N	DC	F'0'

17. In a sequential data set with fixed-length records, every data block except possibly the last one contains the same number of bytes, i.e., the same number of logical records. The last data block may or may not contain the same number of logical records as do the other data blocks.

    a. Since there is no record descriptor word or block descriptor word with fixed-length data blocks, how might the length of the sequentially-last data block be indicated in the data set?

    b. Modify your DEBLOCK subroutine of Exercise 16 to allow for the possibility that the last data block is not as long as the others.

18. Modify your DEBLOCK subroutine of Exercise 16 so that instead of moving the sequentially-next logical record to the calling program's logical record area, it returns the address of that record in Register 1. (This is then analogous to locate mode.)

19. In move mode, the PUT macro places the designated logical record into the next available position in the output buffer, provided that there is room for the record. The data block is not written from the output buffer until either (1) a PUT macro would cause the number of bytes in the data block to exceed the value of BLKSIZE or (2) the data set is closed, whichever occurs first.

   a. Assume that only one output buffer had been requested. Depict the sequence of events that occur when a PUT macro is executed in move mode, as described above.
   b. Explain how this sequence of events might be modified to minimize the delay inherent in writing a data block if there were two output buffers instead of one. Depict your explanation with a flow diagram.

20. The WRITE macro causes the Operating System to write a data block from a designated buffer area to the next available secondary memory location allocated for the data set. It is up to the user's program to move logical records into the buffer area before executing a WRITE macro.

   a. Write a subroutine named BLOCKING that will move a designated logical record into the next available position in a buffer area. Assume that the records are fixed-length. The parameters that should be passed to your subroutine are these:

      —the address of the output buffer, as would be specified in the WRITE macro
      —the address of the logical record area containing the logical record to be moved to the output buffer (as in move mode)
      —the address of the logical record length
      —the address of the data blocksize
      —the address of a full-word binary integer N, which is the number that identifies the relative position within the data block of the logical record that is about to be moved to the data block. ($N = 0,1,2,..., M$, where M identifies the last record in the block, and $N=0$ means that it is a new data block.)

   Your BLOCKING subroutine must move the entire logical record to the appropriate position within the data block and increase the value of N by $+1$, returning the increased value to the calling program. However, if there was no more room in the data block at the time the call to BLOCKING was made, your subroutine should return a value of $N = 0$.

   b. Write a main program that will test your BLOCKING subroutine. Create a simulated set of logical records with DC directives, as in Exercise 16b.

21. Modify your BLOCKING subroutine of Exercise 20 so that instead of moving the logical record to the output buffer, it returns the address of the next position in the buffer in Register 1 and increases N by $+1$. However, if there is no more room in the buffer, your subroutine should return a value of $N = 0$ and the address (in Register 1) of the first position in the buffer. This is then analogous to locate mode.

22. Modify your BLOCKING subroutine of Exercise 20 so that the record that is moved to the buffer area *replaces* the record that had most recently been moved to that area. In this case, your subroutine must not increase the value of N. The new subroutine is analogous to updating records in move mode.

23. What is the purpose of the SYNAD parameter in the DCB macro? How does its use differ for sequential access methods as opposed to basic access methods? (Further information about SYNAD can be found in the descriptions of the DCB macro for each of the access methods in the *Data Management Macro Instructions* reference manual.)

20

Sequential Organization

The processing of sequential data sets always involves at least three distinct phases: an initialization phase, a main processing phase, and an end-of-data phase. In the initialization phase, each data set is opened and perhaps the first record is read. In the main processing phase, each record is processed according to whatever criteria are appropriate to the problem. In the end-of-data phase, the last output record (if any) remaining in main memory has to be written and the data sets must be closed.

We will begin with a discussion of several processing considerations for two of the most frequently used sequential data sets. Following this discussion, the problems of creating, updating, and retrieving information from a sequential data set will be discussed, using as an example a fictitious dormitory-room master file. Note that the topics presented in this chapter build upon the sequential file concepts discussed in chapter 19. Both OS and DOS processing techniques will be covered, but in OS we will consider only QSAM and not BSAM. BSAM is usually reserved for special needs such as creating data sets that are processed via BDAM.

20.1 THE SYSTEM INPUT AND OUTPUT DATA SETS

The system input data set contains what is known as the input data stream. In OS, it is referred to as SYSIN; in DOS, as SYSIPT. The system output data set contains information to be printed. In OS, it is referred to as SYSOUT; in DOS, as SYSLST.

All data read from SYSIN or SYSIPT are in EBCDIC format (C-type data). If the data are to be used for numeric calculations, they must be converted to an appropriate numeric format (e.g., F-, P-, or E-). Similarly, all data written to the SYSOUT or SYSLST files must be in EBCDIC format. Numeric data calculated in a program must be converted to EBCDIC before they are written. Elementary conversion procedures were described in chapter 4; more complete procedures were explained in chapters 12 and 13.

SYSIN and SYSOUT in OS Systems

The SYSIN data set is a sequential data set created by the Operating System. A special form of the DD statement, either DD * or DD DATA, identifies the SYSIN data. Neither SPACE= nor DISP= can be specified for SYSIN, and only a few DCB subparameters—BLKSIZE, LRECL, and BUFNO—are permitted.

Like SYSIN, the SYSOUT data set is a sequential data set created by the Operating System. It is identified on a DD statement by the parameter SYSOUT=. Neither SPACE= nor DISP= can be specified for SYSOUT.

Both SYSIN and SYSOUT data sets are opened and closed in the same way as any other data set, and the DCB macro must be used to designate organization (DSORG), macro format (MACRF), and the DD statement pertaining to it (DDNAME). Examples of opening and closing SYSIN and SYSOUT, together with appropriate DCB macros, are given in figures 20.1 and 20.2. In this text, we will assume that the respective DD statements have the forms

```
for SYSIN:      //SYSIN     DD *
for SYSOUT:     //SYSPRINT  DD SYSOUT=A
```

The corresponding DDNAME parameters for the DCB macro, as shown in figures 20.1 and 20.2, are DDNAME=SYSIN and DDNAME=SYSPRINT.

You can designate the blocksize for SYSIN and SYSOUT, choosing a value consistent with the device characteristics. However, some computer installations use default values of blocksizes for both these data sets. You should determine what blocksizes should be specified at your computer installation. Unless stated otherwise, these values (for the IBM 3330 disk system) will be coded for SYSIN and SYSOUT in this text:

for SYSIN:	RECFM=FB,LRECL=80,BLKSIZE=4080	(51 records per block)
	RECFM=VB,LRECL=84,BLKSIZE=4036	(48 records per block)
for SYSOUT:	RECFM=FB,LRECL=132,BLKSIZE=4092	(31 records per block)
	RECFM=VB,LRECL=136,BLKSIZE=4084	(30 records per block)

SYSIPT and SYSLST in DOS Systems

The SYSIPT data set needs no job control statements unless it is assigned to a device other than the system card reader. When it's the card reader, the data records described by the DTFCD macro simply follow the // EXEC command for the program that reads those data.

Similarly, SYSLST needs no job control statements unless it is assigned to a device other than the system printer. When it's the printer, the output records defined by DTFPR are printed on the system printer.

We will consider only the customary assignments of card reader and system printer.

The simplest form of the DTFCD macro is as follows:

```
dtfname      DTFCD      DEVADDR=SYSIPT,WORKA=YES,IOAREA1=INBUF,        -
                        EOFADDR=EOJ,DEVICE=2540
```

This specifies that SYSIPT data records will be read from an IBM 2540 card reader, with a single I/O buffer named INBUF, and that the name of the user's end-of-file routine is EOJ. Move mode is used due to the WORKA=YES parameter. Several parameters that are important for sequential disk (DTFSD) files are not specified in DTFCD, because they have default values that ordinarily should not be overridden. These include TYPEFLE=INPUT, BLKSIZE=80, RECFORM=FIXUNB; in other words, SYSIPT records are unblocked, of fixed length (80 bytes), and are used for input. Other parameters may be specified, but they depend on properties of the input card reader (e.g., whether it also has a card punch component) and will not be discussed in this text.

The simplest form of the DTFPR macro is as follows:

```
dtfname      DTFPR      DEVADDR=SYSLST,WORKA=YES,IOAREA1=OUTBUF,       -
                        BLKSIZE=132,DEVICE=1403
```

This specifies that SYSLST records will be printed on an IBM 1403 printer, with a single I/O buffer named OUTBUF. Move mode is used due to the WORKA=YES parameter. The BLKSIZE= parameter states that the I/O buffer is 132 characters long. There is no TYPEFLE=OUTPUT parameter permitted; the printer is always an output file. There is no RECFORM= parameter because the default is REC-FORM=FIXUNB, and FIXBLK is not permitted. Other parameters may be specified; some of these depend on the properties of the printer, but a few are important because they determine how the user program will control printer line spacing. The latter include CTLCHR=, CONTROL=, and PRINTOV=. Of these, only the CTLCHR= parameter will be discussed in this text (see Section 20.4). Absence of all three of these parameters, as in the above example, indicates that control of printer line spacing will be done independently of the printer's carriage control mechanism. This was the case in figure 2.5b of chapter 2.

Input/Output Example

To read data from the system input file and write the card-image records on the system output file, the simplest procedure is that shown in figure 20.1, using move mode (see Section 19.7). Each execution of the GET macro causes a card image to be moved from the input buffer into the logical record area named CARD, and each execution of the PUT macro causes the image to be moved from the logical record area named LINE to the output buffer. An MVC instruction moves the image from the CARD area to the LINE area. (This is essentially the procedure that was depicted in fig. 19.11.)

Figure 20.1   Move mode with SYSIN and SYSOUT.

```
EG1         CSECT
*
*    THIS PROGRAM READS RECORDS FROM THE 'SYSIN' DATA SET
*    AND WRITES THEM ONTO THE 'SYSOUT' DATA SET
*
*    QSAM PROCESSING IS USED IN MOVE MODE, WITH FIXED-LENGTH RECORDS
*
            STM      14,12,12(13)       STANDARD ENTRY
            BALR     12,0
            USING    *,12
            ST       13,SAVE+4
            LA       13,SAVE
*
*    THE 'SYSIN' DATA SET IS OPENED FOR INPUT USING THE 'TRANSIN' DCB
*    THE 'SYSOUT' DATA SET IS OPENED FOR OUTPUT USING THE 'TRANSOU' DCB
*
            OPEN     (TRANSIN,(INPUT))
            OPEN     (TRANSOU,(OUTPUT))
*           OPEN     TRANSIN,TRANSOU  OPEN SYSIPT & SYSLST

*    A LOGICAL INPUT RECORD IS MOVED FROM THE SYSTEM'S INPUT BUFFER TO THE
*     PROGRAM'S LOGICAL INPUT RECORD AREA NAMED 'CARD', VIA THE GET MACRO.
*    THEN THE RECORD IS MOVED TO THE LOGICAL OUTPUT RECORD AREA NAMED
*     'LINE' VIA THE   MVC   INSTRUCTION.
*    AND FINALLY IT IS MOVED FROM THE LOGICAL OUTPUT RECORD AREA TO THE
*     SYSTEM'S OUTPUT BUFFER VIA THE   PUT   MACRO.
*
COPYLOOP    GET      TRANSIN,CARD      OBTAIN A LOGICAL INPUT RECORD
            MVC      LINE(80),CARD     MOVE IT TO LOGICAL OUTPUT AREA
            PUT      TRANSOU,LINE      MOVE IT TO SYSTEM OUTPUT BUFFER
            B        COPYLOOP          GO GET NEXT INPUT RECORD
*
*    WHEN THE END-OF-DATA CONDITION IS REACHED ON THE INPUT DATA SET, THE
*    OPERATING SYSTEM TRANSFERS CONTROL TO THE ADDRESS DESIGNATED BY
*    THE EODAD= PARAMETER IN THE DCB MACRO, NAMELY 'EOJ'.
*
EOJ         CLOSE    (TRANSIN)         CLOSE THE 'SYSIN' DATA SET
            CLOSE    (TRANSOU)         CLOSE THE 'SYSOUT' DATA SET
            L        13,SAVE+4         STANDARD EXIT
            LM       14,12,12(13)
            BR       14
*EOJ        CLOSE    TRANSIN,TRANSOU   CLOSE SYSIPT & SYSLST
*           EOJ                        TERMINATE
*
*    'TRANSIN' IS DCB FOR 'SYSIN'; 'TRANSOU' FOR 'SYSOUT'
*    'CARD' IS RECORD AREA FOR 'SYSIN';  'LINE' FOR 'SYSOUT'
*
TRANSIN     DCB      DSORG=PS,MACRF=(GM),DDNAME=SYSIN,EODAD=EOJ,RECFM=FB,  X
                     LRECL=80,BLKSIZE=4080
TRANSOU     DCB      DSORG=PS,MACRF=(PM),DDNAME=SYSPRINT,RECFM=FB,         X
                     LRECL=132,BLKSIZE=4092
*TRANSIN    DTFCD    DEVADDR=SYSIPT,WORKA=YES,IOAREA1=INBUF,EOFADDR=EOJ,   X
*                    DEVICE=2540
*TRANSOU    DTFPR    DEVADDR=SYSLST,WORKA=YES,IOAREA1=OUTBUF,BLKSIZE=132,  X
*                    DEVICE=1403
CARD        DS       CL80              LOGICAL INPUT RECORD AREA
LINE        DC       CL132' '          LOGICAL OUTPUT RECORD AREA
SAVE        DS       18F               REGISTER SAVE AREA
*SAVE       DS       9D
*INBUF      DS       CL80
*OUTBUF     DC       CL132' '
            END
```

Figure 20.2   Locate mode with SYSIN and SYSOUT.

```
EG2         CSECT
*
*   THIS PROGRAM READS RECORDS FROM THE 'SYSIN' DATA SET
*   AND WRITES THEM ONTO THE 'SYSOUT' DATA SET
*
*   QSAM PROCESSING IS USED IN LOCATE MODE, WITH FIXED-LENGTH RECORDS
*
            STM     14,12,12(13)       STANDARD ENTRY
            BALR    12,0
            USING   *,12
            ST      13,SAVE+4
            LA      13,SAVE
*
*   OPEN 'SYSIN' FOR INPUT VIA 'TRANSIN' DCB
*     AND 'SYSOUT' FOR OUTPUT VIA 'TRANSOU' DCB
*
            OPEN    (TRANSIN,(INPUT))
            OPEN    (TRANSOU,(OUTPUT))
*           OPEN    TRANSIN,TRANSOU    OPEN SYSIPT & SYSLST
GREG        EQU     1                  LOCATE MODE RECD ADDR FOR 'GET'
*GREG       EQU     2
PREG        EQU     1                  LOCATE MODE RECD ADDR FOR 'PUT'
*PREG       EQU     2
*
*   OBTAIN ADDRESS OF FIRST LOGICAL RECORD AREA IN OUTPUT BUFFER AREA
*
            PUT     TRANSOU            ADDRESS IS RETURNED IN REG 1
            LR      8,PREG             SAVE IT IN REG 8
*
*   OBTAIN ADDRESS OF LOGICAL RECORD IN INPUT BUFFER,
*     MOVE THE RECORD FROM THE INPUT BUFFER TO THE OUTPUT BUFFER,
*     AND THEN OBTAIN ADDRESS OF NEXT LOGICAL RECORD IN OUTPUT BUFFER.
*
COPYLOOP    GET     TRANSIN            ADDRESS IS RETURNED IN REG 1
            LR      9,GREG             SAVE IT IN REG 9
            MVC     0(80,8),0(9)       MOVE RECORD FROM INPUT TO OUTPUT
            PUT     TRANSOU            AREAS, AND OBTAIN ADDRESS OF NEXT
            LR      8,PREG             OUTPUT RECORD.  SAVE IT IN REG 8,
            B       COPYLOOP           AND THEN GET NEXT INPUT RECD ADDR.
*
*   'SYSIN' END-OF-DATA CONDITION CAUSES CONTROL TO BE TRANSFERRED
*     TO 'EOJ' ROUTINE,  VIA EODAD= PARAMETER IN DCB MACRO
*
EOJ         CLOSE   (TRANSIN)          CLOSE 'SYSIN' DATA SET
            CLOSE   (TRANSOU)          CLOSE 'SYSOUT' DATA SET
            L       13,SAVE+4          STANDARD EXIT
            LM      14,12,12(13)
            BR      14
*EOJ        CLOSE   TRANSIN,TRANSOU    CLOSE SYSIPT & SYSLST
*           EOJ                        TERMINATE
*
*   'TRANSIN' IS DCB FOR 'SYSIN';  'TRANSOU', FOR 'SYSOUT'
*   NO LOGICAL RECORD AREAS ARE DEFINED WHEN USING LOCATE MODE
*
TRANSIN     DCB     DSORG=PS,MACRF=(GL),DDNAME=SYSIN,EODAD=EOJ,RECFM=FB,    X
                    LRECL=80,BLKSIZE=4080
TRANSOU     DCB     DSORG=PS,MACRF=(PL),DDNAME=SYSPRINT,RECFM=FB,           X
                    LRECL=132,BLKSIZE=4092
SAVE        DS      18F
*TRANSIN    DTFCD   DEVADDR=SYSIPT,IOREG=(2),IOAREA1=INBUF,EOFADDR=EOJ,     X
*                   DEVICE=2540
*TRANSOU    DTFPR   DEVADDR=SYSLST,IOREG=(2),IOAREA1=OUTBUF, BLKSIZE=132,   X
*                   DEVICE=1403
*SAVE       DS      9D
*INBUF      DS      CL80
*OUTBUF     DC      CL132'
            END
```

You will see that in figure 20.1 we have written the program to run in an OS system but have shown the substitutions that are required to convert the program to DOS. We will follow this practice throughout the remainder of the text.

Instead of using move mode, it is possible to use locate mode with either or both of the system input/output files. Three important characteristics of locate mode should be noted:

1. The address of the logical record area is not specified in the GET or PUT macro when locate mode is used for input or output, because the logical record areas are not defined in the user's program at assembly time.

2. The address of the logical record obtained via the GET macro is returned in a register following execution of the GET macro. In OS, that address is always returned in Register 1. In DOS, it is always returned in the register whose address n is specified by the IOREG$=(n)$ parameter in the DTFCD macro. The value of n must be in the range 2 through 12.

3. The address of the *next* logical record area to be used by the PUT macro is returned in a register following execution of PUT. As with GET, the register used with PUT in OS is Register 1, and in DOS it is Register n, where n is specified by IOREG$=(n)$ in DTFPR, and $2 \leq n \leq 12$. Since it is the *next* logical record whose address is returned, this means that when PUT is executed, the Operating System has remembered where the *current* logical record area is. It also means that the first execution of PUT in locate mode is in the nature of an initialization procedure; it simply returns the address of the first logical record area, but doesn't assume that there is a record to be processed.

Note that if there are N records to be written, there must be N executions of the PUT macro. But the Kth execution writes the $(K-1)$st record, since the first execution of PUT does not write a record at all. Therefore, since the Nth execution writes the next-to-last record, a natural question is, "When does the last record get written?" The answer is that it gets written by the Operating System when the data set is closed. In effect, the Operating System executes the PUT that is required to write the last record.

These observations are illustrated in the program of figure 20.2. The address returned by the GET macro is used by the source operand of the MVC instruction, and the address returned by the PUT macro is used by the destination operand of that instruction. In this way the logical record is moved from the input buffer to the output buffer. Note that to make the transition between OS and DOS easier, we have used symbolic register addresses GREG and PREG instead of numeric register addresses.

20.2 PROCESSING FIELDS IN A LOGICAL RECORD

To process fields in a record using *move* mode, the logical record area should be subdivided into named areas, each area corresponding in length and relative position to a field of the logical record. For example, consider this card image:

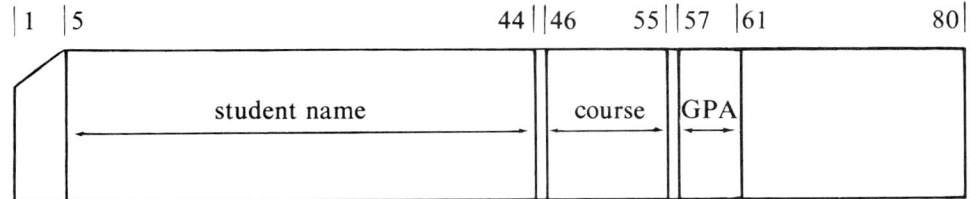

We could define a logical input record area for this record as follows:

```
CARD     DS    CL80    RESERVE 80 POSITIONS FOR CARD IMAGE
         ORG   CARD    SET MEMORY LOCATION COUNTER TO 'CARD'
         DS    CL4     COLUMNS 1- 4   UNUSED
NAME     DS    CL40      "      5-44   FOR STUDENT NAME
         DS    CL1       "      45     UNUSED
COURSE   DS    CL10      "      46-55  FOR COURSE TAKEN
         DS    CL1       "      56     UNUSED
GPA      DS    CL4       "      57-60  FOR GPA (AS 'X.XX')
         ORG           SET MEM LOC CTR TO FIRST BYTE BEYOND 'CARD'
```

With the definition shown, each field of the card image can be referred to in the operand of an instruction or directive. If we wanted to modify the program of figure 20.1 to print the cards for only those students with a GPA of 3.50 or better, we would simply insert these two statements immediately after the GET macro:

```
CLC    GPA,=C'3.50'    COMPARE GPA TO 3.50
BL     COPYLOOP        READ NEXT CARD IF GPA LESS THAN 3.5
```

To process fields within a logical record in *locate* mode, a DSECT defining the logical record fields must be established at assembly time. A dummy base register that points to the beginning of the DSECT area must also be established by means of a USING directive at assembly time, and the logical record address received from the GET macro should be loaded into the dummy base register at run time. For example, the card image shown earlier would be defined like this:

```
CARD      DSECT                   BEGIN DUMMY SECTION NAMED 'CARD'
          DS     CL4
NAME      DS     CL40
          DS     CL1             SAME AS IN ABOVE MOVE MODE DEFINITIONS
COURSE    DS     CL10
          DS     CL1
GPA       DS     CL4
EG2       CSECT                   RESUME CONTROL SECTION NAMED 'EG2'
```

If this dummy-section definition is inserted in the program of figure 20.2, then to print the cards for just those students with a GPA of 3.5 or better, we would add the following three statements (or statements similar to them) immediately following the GET macro:

```
USING     CARD,11
LR        11,GREG
CLC       GPA,=C'3.50'
BL        COPYLOOP
```

Any available register can be used as the dummy base register. The point to be noted is that both the USING directive that establishes the dummy base register and the load instruction that places the appropriate address into that register at run time must designate the same register, and they must both occur before any instruction that refers to fields within the dummy section.

20.3 PROCESSING VARIABLE-LENGTH RECORDS

In figures 20.1 and 20.2, the MVC instruction was used to move a logical record from an input area to an output area. The length of the record was known to be 80 characters, so the length of 80 could be coded in the MVC in the source-module. However, when processing variable-length records, the length of a record is not necessarily known until it is processed at run time. However, the record length can be obtained at run time from the record descriptor word. Once the record length is obtained, the record can be moved with an Execute instruction. We will illustrate this procedure first for move mode and then for locate mode. Although the system input and system output data sets are not likely to contain variable-length records, we will continue to use our example, making whatever changes are necessary to accommodate variable-length records.

The logical record area must be defined to include the record descriptor word (RDW). At the least, the area should begin on a half-word boundary, to make the count field in the RDW accessible to LH and STH instructions. This can be accomplished, of course, by preceding the DS directive that defines the area with a DS 0H directive:

```
          DS     0H
CARD      DS     CL84
```

Note that the definition of the record area now includes 4 bytes for the RDW; it also assumes that the largest variable-length record will be 80 bytes. (Remember that the area reserved must always be large enough to contain both the RDW and the largest variable-length record in the data set.) The modifications to figure 20.1 necessary to process variable-length records in move mode can then be coded like this:

```
COPYLOOP    GET     TRANSIN,CARD        OBTAIN A LOGICAL RECORD
            LH      10,CARD             LOAD RECORD LENGTH FROM RDW
            SH      10,=H'1'            SUBT +1 FOR EXECUTE INSTR
            EX      10,VMVC             MOVE RECORD FROM INPUT TO OUTPUT
            PUT     TRANSOU,LINE          AREAS, AND PUT IT INTO OUTPUT
            B       COPYLOOP              BUFFER. THEN GET NEXT RECORD.
VMVC        MVC     LINE(0),CARD        MVC FOR VAR-LNG MOVE.
             .
             .
             .
TRANSIN     DCB     ...,RECFM=VB,LRECL=84,BLKSIZE=4036
TRANSOU     DCB     ...,RECFM=VB,LRECL=136,BLKSIZE=4084
*TRANSIN    DTFCD   ...,RECFORM=VARUNB,BLKSIZE=84
*TRANSOU    DTFPR   ...,RECFORM=VARUNB,BLKSIZE=136
*INBUF      DS      CL84
*           DS      CL136
            DS      0H
CARD        DS      CL84
            DS      0H
LINE        DC      CL136' '
```

In locate mode, a similar procedure can be followed, but the process of obtaining the record length should be modified: the record length must be obtained from the record descriptor word (RDW) of the logical record, i.e., from the first 2 bytes of the logical record area.

We will show how to do this for the general case of blocked records (RECFM=VB or RECFORM=VARBLK) even though the DOS SYSIPT and SYSLST files do not permit blocked records. The same method can then be used for any file (DOS or OS) in which blocked records are permitted. The method consists of moving the first 2 bytes of the RDW to a temporary area that is aligned on a half-word boundary, so that the LH (Load Half Word) instruction can be used whether we have an IBM 360 or IBM 370. In the IBM 360 this is necessary because LH requires half-word alignment of the data being loaded and because there is no guarantee that the beginning of each logical record in the I/O buffer will be on a half-word boundary. The reason that there is no such guarantee is that even if the first record in a buffer is aligned on a half-word boundary, a subsequent record in the buffer need not be so aligned unless every record's length is a multiple of two. Clearly, with variable-length records, this can not be assumed to be true. Thus the modifications are as follows:

```
COPYLOOP    GET     TRANSIN             OBTAIN ADDRESS OF LOGICAL RECORD
            LR      9,GREG              USE REG 9 TO SAVE INPUT RECD ADDR
            MVC     VRECL,0(9)          GET LENGTH FROM RDW IN I/O BUFFER
            LH      10,VRECL            LOAD RECD LNG FROM HALF-WORD AREA
            SH      10,=H'1'            SUBT +1 FOR EXECUTE INSTR
            EX      10,VMVC             MOVE RECORD FROM INPUT TO OUTPUT
            PUT     TRANSOU               AREAS, AND OBTAIN ADDRESS OF NEXT
            LR      8,PREG                OUTPUT RECORD. SAVE THIS IN REG 8
            B       COPYLOOP              AND THEN GET NEXT INPUT RECD ADDR.
VMVC        MVC     0(0,8),0(9)         MVC FOR VAR-LNG MOVE.
VRECL       DS      H                   HALF WORD FOR RECORD LENGTH
```

20.4 CONTROLLING PRINTER-LINE SPACING

The first character of each logical record written to the system output data set can be used to control printer-line spacing. The most common space-control functions are to single space, double space, triple space, suppress spacing, and skip to a new page. Each of these, and others not to be discussed here, is designated by a control character, which is simply one of the 256 EBCDIC characters. There are two different sets of control characters to choose from: the American National Standards Institute (ANSI) characters and the IBM machine-code characters. In the ANSI set, the spacing action is taken before the line is printed; in the IBM set, the

Figure 20.3 **Control characters for printer line spacing in OS and DOS.**

action taken before line is printed	control character	action taken	control character if action taken after line is printed	control character if action taken without printing the line
single space	X'40' (blank)	single space	X'09'	X'0B'
double space	X'F0' (zero)	double space	X'11'	X'13'
triple space	X'60' (minus)	triple space	X'19'	X'1B'
suppress space	X'4E' (plus)	suppress space	X'01'	(none)
skip to new page	X'F1' (one)	skip to new page	X'89'	X'8B'
ANSI control characters		IBM machine code control characters		

action is taken either after the line is printed or without printing the line at all. The control characters that must be used are shown in figure 20.3.

In OS, the choice of control character set is designated in the RECFM= parameter of the DCB macro. The ANSI set is designated by the letter "A," the IBM set by the letter "M": RECFM=FBA or VBA, or RECFM=FBM or VBM.

In DOS, we must specify CTLCHR= ASA for the ANSI set and CTLCHR= YES for the IBM set. (The CTLCHR= parameter is specified in the DTFPR macro.) Unlike in OS, the record format parameter (RECFORM=) in DOS plays no role in designating the control character set.

Once one of these designations is made, it is the user program's responsibility to place the desired control character into the first character of *each* logical record. (If using variable-length records, the control character is placed in the first position following the record descriptor word.)

To illustrate these concepts, we use the ANSI set and move mode for SYSIN and SYSOUT with fixed-length records. The procedure is readily adaptable to locate mode and/or variable-length records, and to DOS.

The program shown in figure 20.4 reads records from SYSIN and writes them onto SYSOUT. Beginning with the first record, every fiftieth record is written so that it will be printed at the top of a new page. Intervening records are single-spaced in sets of five; every fifth record is double-spaced. Note that since every record that is written must contain a control character, the SYSIN records are moved to the second position of the SYSOUT records, not to the first as in the preceding examples in this chapter. The control character itself is not printed; it simply controls the spacing. Thus, though the length of the record area is 133 characters, the length of the printed line remains at 132 characters. (Note, however, that in order to keep the blocksize within 4096 bytes a 133-byte logical record results in a blocksize of 3990, instead of 4092 as with 132-byte records.)

If a title line with the date of the report and a page number is desired at the top of each page, the following types of modifications must be made:

1. A logical record area must be defined to include the title, space for the date and page number, and the top-of-page control character.
2. The date of the report must be obtained from the Operating System, and it must be suitably formatted for printing.
3. A page-number counter must be maintained and converted to EBCDIC format each time a new page is to be started.
4. The title line must be printed each time the line-number counter reaches the limit established for number of lines per page.

Figure 20.4 *Printer line spacing example.*

```
EG3         CSECT
*
*     THIS PROGRAM READS RECORDS FROM SYSIN AND WRITES THEM TO SYSOUT.
*     EVERY FIFTIETH RECORD IS WRITTEN SO THAT IT WILL BE PRINTED AT
*     THE TOP OF A NEW PAGE.  INTERVENING RECORDS ARE SINGLE-SPACED
*     IN SETS OF FIVE:  EVERY FIFTH RECORD IS DOUBLE-SPACED.
*
*     ANSI PRINTER CONTROL CHARACTERS ARE USED, WITH FIXED-LENGTH
*       RECORDS IN QSAM MOVE MODE.
*
            STM     14,12,12(13)             STANDARD ENTRY
            BALR    12,0
            USING   *,12
            ST      13,SAVE+4
            LA      13,SAVE
*
            OPEN    (TRANSIN,(INPUT))        OPEN 'SYSIN'
            OPEN    (TRANSOU,(OUTPUT))       OPEN 'SYSOUT'
*           OPEN    TRANSIN,TRANSOU          OPEN SYSIPT & SYSLST
*
COPYLOOP    GET     TRANSIN,CARD             MOVE CARD TO RECORD AREA
            BAL     14,SPACING               GO SET UP PRINT CONTROL CHAR
            MVC     PRINT2(80),CARD          MOVE CARD TO OUTPUT LINE AREA
            PUT     TRANSOU,LINE             MOVE PRINT LINE TO OUTPUT BUF-
            B       COPYLOOP                   FER, AND GO GET NEXT CARD RECD
*
EOJ         CLOSE   (TRANSIN)                CLOSE SYSIN
            CLOSE   (TRANSOU)                CLOSE SYSOUT
            L       13,SAVE+4                STANDARD EXIT
            LM      14,12,12(13)
            BR      14
*EOJ        CLOSE   TRANSIN,TRANSOU          CLOSE SYSIPT & SYSLST
*           EOJ                              TERMINATE
*
*     INTERNAL SUBROUTINE TO SET UP PRINT CONTROL CHARACTER BASED ON NUMBER
*     OF LINES THAT HAVE BEEN PRINTED.  CALLED VIA R14, WITH NO PARAMETERS.
*
SPACING     LH      5,SETCTR                 DETERMINE IF FIVE CONSEC LINES
            SH      5,=H'1'                    HAVE BEEN PRINTED.
            BP      SPACE1                   IF NOT, CONTINUE SINGLE-SPACING
            LH      5,LINECTR                DETERMINE IF 50 LINES HAVE
            SH      5,=H'1'                    BEEN PRINTED. IF NOT, JUST
            BP      SPACE2                   SET UP DOUBLE SPACE.
            MVI     PRINT1,NEWPAGE             OTHERWISE, SET CTL CHAR
            MVC     LINECTR,MAXLINE          FOR NEW PAGE, AND RESET
            MVC     SETCTR,MAXSET            LINE COUNTERS.
            B       EXIT
SPACE2      STH     5,LINECTR                WHEN DOUBLE-SPACING, SET CTL
            MVI     PRINT1,DBLSPACE          CHAR AND RESET 5-LINE CTR.
            MVC     SETCTR,MAXSET
            B       EXIT
SPACE1      STH     5,SETCTR                 WHEN SINGLE-SPACING, JUST SET
            MVI     PRINT1,SGLSPACE          CTL CHAR, AND REDUCE LINE CTRS.
            LH      5,LINECTR
            SH      5,=H'1'
            STH     5,LINECTR
EXIT        BR      14
*
*     CONSTANTS AND DATA AREAS FOR PRINTER LINE SPACING EXAMPLE
*
TRANSIN     DCB     DSORG=PS,MACRF=(GM),DDNAME=SYSIN,EODAD=EOJ,RECFM=FB,   X
                    LRECL=80,BLKSIZE=4080
```

Figure 20.4 continued

```
TRANSOU    DCB     DSORG=PS,MACRF=(PM),DDNAME=SYSPRINT,RECFM=FBA,        X
                   LRECL=133,BLKSIZE=3990
*TRANSIN   DTFCD   DEVADDR=SYSIPT,WORKA=YES,IOAREA1=INBUF,EOFADDR=EOJ,   X
*                  DEVICE=2540
*TRANSOU   DTFPR   DEVADDR=SYSLST,WORKA=YES,IOAREA1=OUTBUF,BLKSIZE=133,  X
*                  DEVICE=1403
*
CARD       DS      CL80            CARD INPUT AREA
*
LINE       DS      CL133           PRINTER OUTPUT AREA
           ORG     LINE
PRINT1     DS      CL1             SPACE FOR PRINT CONTROL CHARACTER
PRINT2     DC      CL132' '        PRINT LINE AREA, INITIALLY BLANK
           ORG
*
LINECTR    DC      H'0'            NUMBER OF LINES PRINTED, EACH PAGE
MAXLINE    DC      H'50'           MAX NUMBER OF LINES PER PAGE
*
SETCTR     DC      H'0'            NUMBER OF CONSEC SINGLE-SPACED LINES
MAXSET     DC      H'5'            MAX NUMBER OF CONSEC SGL-SP LINES
*
NEWPAGE    EQU     X'F1'           ANSI CTL CHAR FOR TOP OF NEW PAGE
SGLSPACE   EQU     X'40'           ANSI CTL CHAR FOR SINGLE-SPACING
DBLSPACE   EQU     X'F0'           ANSI CTL CHAR FOR DOUBLE-SPACING
*
SAVE       DS      18F
*SAVE      DS      9D
*INBUF     DS      CL80
*OUTBUF    DC      CL133' '
*
           END
```

The logical record area for the title could be defined as follows:

```
TITLE      DS      CL133           SPACE FOR TITLE LINE
           ORG     TITLE           BEGIN REDEFINITION FOR FIELDS
           DC      X'F1'           ANSI CTL CHAR FOR TOP OF NEW PAGE
           DC      CL14' '         BLANKS TO CENTER THE TITLE
*FOLLOWING IS SOME APPROPRIATE TITLE, WITH TRAILING BLANKS
           DC      CL90'  LISTING OF SYSIN DATA'
MONTH      DS      CL2             SPACE FOR TWO-DIGIT MONTH
           DC      C'/'
DAY        DS      CL2             TWO-DIGIT DAY OF MONTH
           DC      C'/'
YEAR       DS      CL2             TWO-DIGIT YEAR
           DC      CL11' '         SPACING FOR READABILITY
           DC      C'PAGE '
PAGE       DC      CL4' '          UP TO FOUR-DIGIT PAGE NUMBER
           ORG
```

Date and Time in OS: The TIME Macro

To obtain the date and time of the report at run time, the simplest form of the TIME macro that can be used is

opcode	operand
TIME	blanks

(The general format of the TIME macro, and a number of other useful macros, can be obtained from the publication *OS/VS1 Supervisor Services and Macro Instructions,* IBM Publication GC24–5103.) When the TIME macro is invoked, the Operating System returns the date in Register 1 and the time of day in Register 0 in the following formats:

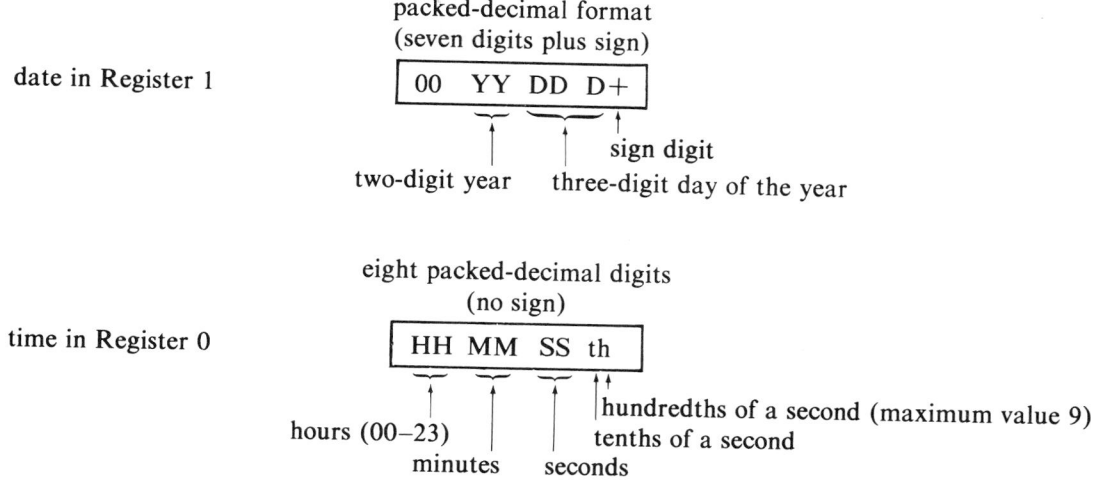

date in Register 1

packed-decimal format
(seven digits plus sign)

00 YY DD D+

two-digit year · three-digit day of the year · sign digit

time in Register 0

eight packed-decimal digits
(no sign)

HH MM SS th

hours (00–23) · minutes · seconds · tenths of a second · hundredths of a second (maximum value 9)

The three-digit day of the year must be converted to month, day, and year in EBCDIC format in order to be printed in the form shown in the TITLE area above. This and the other changes listed are left as exercises.

Date and Time in DOS: The COMRG and GETIME Macros

To obtain the date and time in DOS, two separate macros are required. Each macro returns a result in Register 1. In their simplest forms, the operand field should be blank:

opcode	operand
GETIME	
COMRG	

(Other aspects of these macros, as well as other useful macros, are described in the IBM Publication *DOS/VS Supervisor and I/O Macros,* GC33–5373.)

In the above form, the GETIME macro returns the time-of-day in Register 1 as a signed packed-decimal number, in the following format:

time in Register 1

    0 H H M M S S +

HH is hours (00–23), MM is minutes, and SS is seconds.

The COMRG macro returns the *address* of the date rather than the date itself. The address is returned in Register 1, and the field that it points to is known as the *communication region,* of which the first 8 bytes contain the calendar date in EBCDIC format, stored as mm/dd/yy. Thus it is a simple matter in DOS to put the date in a title line. For example, using the title line definition given earlier, just move the date from communication region to title line as follows:

```
COMRG
MVC      MONTH(8),0(1)
```

To put the time-of-day in the title line, we would first have to convert it from packed decimal to EBCDIC. This and the other changes listed above are left as exercises.

20.5 DORMITORY-ROOM MASTER FILE: PROBLEM STATEMENT

In this and the next chapter, we will illustrate the use of the I/O macros by considering the following problem: *a data set is to be created, maintained, and used to provide information about dormitory-room occupancy on a university campus. The information to be maintained for each dorm room is the dorm identity and room number, and the names of the students (if any) who are assigned to that room.*

Since the data set will contain all the information we want to know and maintain about dorm-room occupancy, it is known as a *master file*. The data set used to create or update the master file records is known as a *transaction file*. We will use the system input data set for the transaction file.

The dorm-room master file, like other master files used in computer data processing, will be assumed to be stored on disk for some indefinite length of time. Whenever new information is to be added to it or existing information is to be changed or deleted, a program to make the additions, changes, and deletions is executed, using the information in the transaction file records as the basis for the adjustments to the master file records. Whenever a report giving room occupancy data is desired, a program that produces the report is executed. Programs that will accomplish these functions are described in the sections that follow.

To process the master file as a sequential data set, we require that its logical records be in some useful sequence and that the logical records of the transaction file be in the same sequence. Since the problem statement is oriented around dormitory rooms rather than students, we will require that the records be in sequence by dorm and room number within dorm. The dorm field in each record is thus referred to as the *major field* for sequencing and the room number field as the *minor field*.

The following assumptions are made about the nature of the data:

1. Each dormitory is identified by a one- to four-character abbreviation, all of which must be letters. If less than four letters are used, the field is padded on the right with blanks. For example,

HH	=	Hayes-Healy Hall
PHE	=	Phelan Hall
INTL	=	International House

2. Each dormitory-room number consists of one to four letters or digits. If less than four letters and digits are used, the field is padded on the left with blanks. For example,

304	=	room number 304
1202	=	room number 1202
2A	=	room number 2A

3. There are no more than two students assigned to a room, but there may be only one student assigned to some rooms, and no students assigned to others.
4. Each student is identified by his or her name in a forty-character field, and by his or her student i.d. number in a nine-character field.

20.6 TRANSACTION RECORD FORMAT

We will assume that each transaction record is a fixed-length, 80-byte card record stored on the system input data set. The format of each record is shown in figure 20.5. The transaction code field (card column 4) identifies the purpose of the transaction in the following manner:

code	meaning
1	Add a record for this dorm and room number to the master file. (No student name or i.d. will appear on records bearing transaction code 1. Its purpose is to add a record for a dorm room to which no student has been assigned.)
2	Add the student identified in this transaction record to the master file record identified by the dorm and room number field given in the transaction.
3	Delete the student identified in this transaction record from the master file record identified by the dorm and room number in the transaction.
4	Delete the master file record that is identified by the dorm and room number in the transaction. (No student name or i.d. will appear on records bearing transaction code 4.)

For a given dorm and room number, it will be assumed that the transaction records are in sequence by transaction code. Thus, the transaction code is a second minor field, subordinate to the room number.

Figure 20.5 Transaction record format.

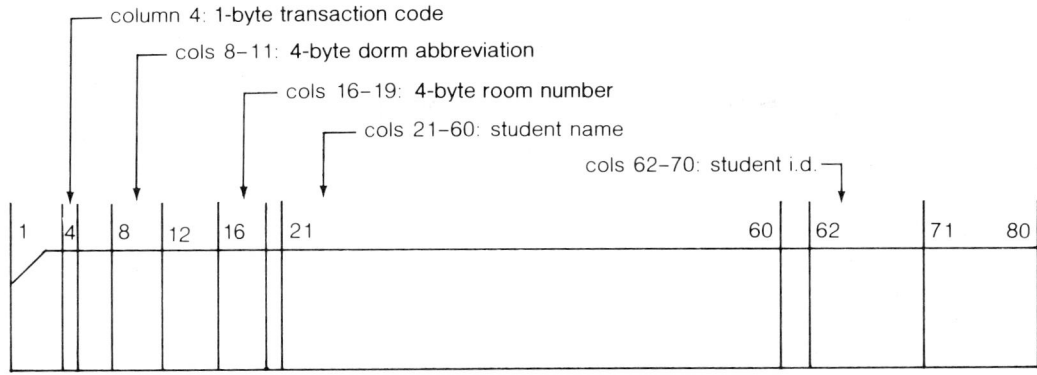

Note that we are assuming "perfect" data in the transaction file. We assume first of all that the records are in proper sequence; second, that every "add" and "delete" request is a correct one in the sense that there is no transaction to add a student or a room if that student or room already exists in the master file and there is no request to delete a student or room if there is no master file record for that student or room; and third, that there are no duplicate records in the transaction file and no records with invalid transaction codes. Although these may seem like reasonable assumptions, in practice mistakes can be made by whoever prepares the transaction data. It is up to the program to detect and reject erroneous data and to produce a printed report describing the errors. But, since the purpose of this example is to demonstrate correct use of I/O macros, handling of data errors will not be dealt with in the discussions that follow. This will be left as an end-of-chapter exercise.

20.7 MASTER FILE RECORD FORMAT

For the master file record format, we will require that there be one record per dorm room. As mentioned earlier, the records will be in sequence by dorm (major) and room number (minor). Each record will contain and be identified by the dorm abbreviation and room number, the values of these two fields thereby serving as each record's *key*.

To simplify the processing descriptions given in the sections that follow, we shall use a fixed-length record format, as shown in figure 20.6a. This requires that space be reserved in each record for the identities of the two students who might be assigned to the room to which that record pertains. If fewer than two students are assigned to a room, space reserved but not used is filled with blanks.

Note that instead of fixed-length records we could choose to use variable-length records, as shown in figure 20.6b. This can result in a saving of storage space at the expense of some additional programming steps required when adding students to a record or deleting students from a record. For, instead of filling unused space with blanks, the unused area simply does not exist in the record; its length is null. When using variable-length records, it is often convenient to have a count of the number of students that are represented in the record. This count can either be derived from the record length stored in the record descriptor word or can be explicitly stored in the record, as shown in figure 20.6b. However, except for the discussion of space allocation in the next section, we will not describe the procedures required for processing the variable-length format.

20.8 MASTER FILE SPACE ALLOCATION

Space allocation for the master file is required only when the file is created. The amount of space requested as primary allocation is acquired at that time; if more space is needed subsequently—because either more students are added or more rooms are added—the space is acquired by the Operating System in amounts equal to the secondary allocation request.

Figure 20.6a   Fixed-length master file record format.

bytes 0–3: four-byte dorm abbreviation
bytes 4–7: four-byte room number

| | | student name (40 bytes) | i.d. (9) | student name (40 bytes) | i.d. (9) |

← ——————————— space used whether needed or not ——————————— →

Figure 20.6b   Variable-length master file record format.

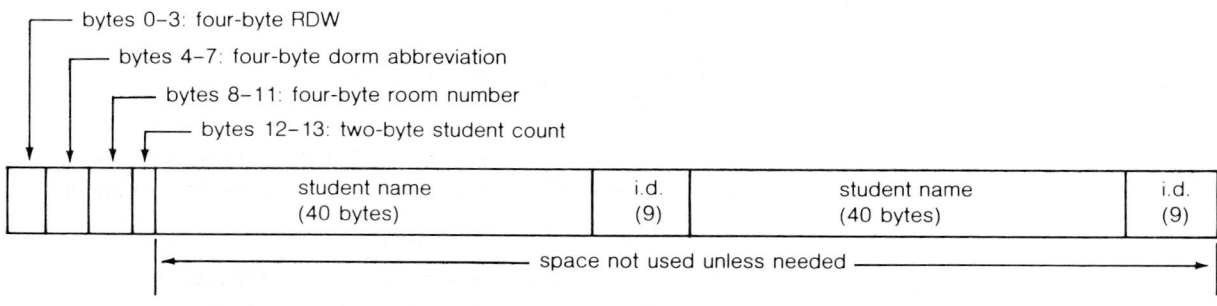

bytes 0–3: four-byte RDW
bytes 4–7: four-byte dorm abbreviation
bytes 8–11: four-byte room number
bytes 12–13: two-byte student count

| | | | | student name (40 bytes) | i.d. (9) | student name (40 bytes) | i.d. (9) |

← ——————————— space not used unless needed ——————————— →

The simplest procedure for determining how much primary space should be requested for a sequential data set is to determine a blocksize, estimate the number of records that will be in the data set, and request space for the number of blocks required to contain the estimated number of records. Since additional space will be granted each time it is required—up to 15 times in all—a secondary allocation of 10% of the primary allocation will usually be ample. If we estimate R records will be in the data set, with S bytes per record, and if we choose a blocksize of B bytes, then the number of blocks that should be requested as a primary allocation is $(R \times S)/B$.

Since sequentially-organized data sets are stored in count-data format, we base the choice of blocksize on the data that was given in figure 18.5. For fixed-length records (106 bytes per record), a blocksize of 4028 bytes will contain 38 records and result in track-space utilization of 92.7%. For variable-length records (maximum record length of 112 bytes per record), a blocksize of 4036 bytes would contain at least 36 records and result in track-space utilization of 92.9%. In the present problem, we can estimate the number of records that will be contained in the master file by estimating the number of dorm rooms. If we assume that there are 5000 dorm rooms, the primary allocation request is determined as follows:

for fixed-length records:

$$
\begin{aligned}
R &= 5000 \text{ records} \\
S &= 106 \text{ bytes per record} \\
B &= 4028 \text{ bytes per block} \\
(R \times S)/B &= 132 \text{ blocks}
\end{aligned}
$$

for variable-length records:

$$
\begin{aligned}
R &= 5000 \text{ records} \\
S &= 112 \text{ bytes per record} \\
B &= 4036 \text{ bytes per block} \\
(R \times S)/B &= 139 \text{ blocks}
\end{aligned}
$$

The number of blocks determined for variable-length record format is an upper limit: it assumes that each variable-length record will contain the identities of two students. (Note that these blocksizes were chosen assuming that the secondary memory device is an IBM 3330 disk system. Appropriate adjustments would have to be made if a different disk system were used or if the computer installation management staff had established other criteria for determining blocksizes.)

20.9   CREATING A SEQUENTIAL DATA SET

One way of creating a sequential data set is simply to copy records, one at a time, from one data set to another. The first data set could be opened for INPUT; the one being created, for OUTPUT. Programs to accomplish this were given in figures 20.1 and 20.2. The sequential data set being created in those programs was the system output file. But a simple change to the job control statements, DCB or DTF macros, and logical record area definitions is all that would be needed to adapt those programs to the problem of creating other sequential data sets.

The cited method, simple as it is, is not sufficient for all problems. The dorm-room master file presents a good example of the need for a different procedure. For instance, if two consecutive transaction records were for the same dorm and room, but for different students, as in this situation,

| HH | 310 | A.H. STONEWOOD | 234567890 |
| HH | 310 | H.A. WHITTAKER | 123456789 |

copying them one at a time to the output data set would create *two* records for that dorm room, not one as required by the problem statement. Therefore, we need a method to create the following record for the above transaction records.

| HH | 310 HA WHITTAKER | 123456789 | A.H. STONEWOOD | 234567890 |

The method needed requires that the master file record be constructed in the logical record area and *not be moved to the output buffer until both student transaction records have been read from the transaction file.* In more general cases, we would have to construct the master file record based on N transaction records. (For example, instead of dorm rooms, we can imagine classrooms with N students for arbitrary N.)

An outline of the program required to create a sequential data set under the general conditions just mentioned is given in figure 20.7. The steps depicted assume that the sequential input file is in the same sequence as that desired for the output file. Because of the nature of sequential files, this must always be the case; if it is not the case, the file that is created will not be of much use for the purposes of making future additions or changes.

As mentioned earlier, the processing steps are organized into three phases: initialization, main processing, and end-of-data. In the main processing phase, the PUT macro needed to move a logical record into the output buffer will not be invoked until a complete logical record has been constructed. For our dorm-room master file, a complete logical record will consist of the dorm abbreviation, the room number, and zero, one, or two sets of student identities. The number of students identified in a logical output record will depend on the number of students assigned to that dorm room. This in turn will depend on the data that exists in the transaction file. Since the transaction records are in sequence by dorm and room number, all records for a given dorm and room will occur consecutively in the transaction file. If fewer than two students are assigned to a room, the master file record area will be padded with blanks before the record is moved to the output buffer.

To determine when all transaction records for a given dorm and room number have been processed, each transaction record must be compared to the previous transaction record that was processed. Or, each transaction record can be compared to the logical record being constructed in the output area. The two records will be considered equal as long as they both refer to the same master file record—in our example, to the same dorm and room number. When the two records are not equal, the processing for the master file record identified in the output record area has been completed and it can be moved to the output buffer via a PUT macro. The construction of a new output record can then begin.

When the end-of-data condition is reached on the transaction file, there will still be one master file record remaining in the output record area. This is because we cannot in general anticipate whether end-of-data or simply another transaction record will be obtained when the GET macro is invoked. Therefore, at end-of-data, the record still remaining in the output record area must be moved to the output buffer before closing the data sets.

Figure 20.7 *Overview of steps to create a sequential data set.*

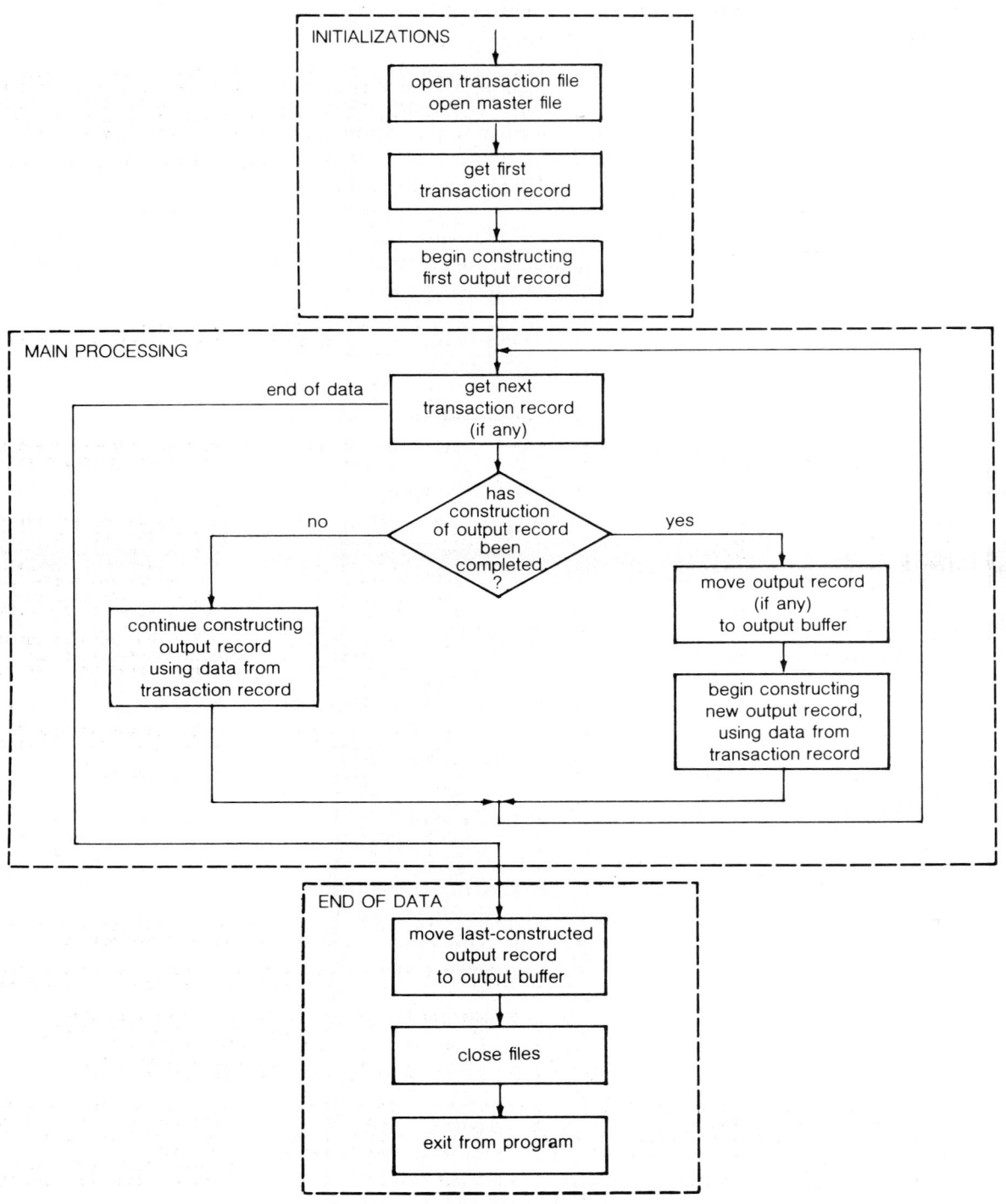

The sequence of processing steps just described, and diagrammed in figure 20.7, is accomplished for the dorm-room master file by the program in figure 20.8. A few typical transaction records and the resulting output master file records are shown in figure 20.9. In studying the program, note that the assumption of "perfect" data eliminates the need to check for duplicate transaction records, or for data that incorrectly assigns more than two students to a room, or for data that is out of sequence. None of these checks is included in the program of figure 20.8.

Figure 20.8   Creating the dorm room master file via QSAM.

```
                                              3   CREATE    CSECT
                                              4   *
                                              5   * THIS PROGRAM CREATES A SEQUENTIAL DATA SET USING QSAM..
                                              6   * TRANSACTION DATA IS IN 'SYSIN' DATA SET, OPENED IN MOVE MODE.
                                              7   *OUTPUT DATA SET CONTAINS ONE RECORD PER DORM ROOM, IN SEQUENCE
                                              8   * BY DORM AND ROOM NUMBER.  EACH RECORD CONTAINS NAMES AND I.D.'S
                                              9   * OF UP TO TWO STUDENTS ASSIGNED TO THE ROOM WHICH THAT RECORD
                                             10   * REPRESENTS.
                                             11   *OUTPUT DATA SET RECORDS ARE FIXED-LENGTH, PROCESSED IN MOVE MODE.
                                             12   *
                                             13             PRINT NODATA,NOGEN
000000 90 EC DO0C                            14             STM   14,12,12(13)      STANDARD ENTRY
000004 05 CO                                 15             BALR  12,0
000006                                       16             USING *,12
000006 50 DO C292              000298        17             ST    13,SAVE+4
00000A 41 DO C28E              000294        18             LA    13,SAVE
                                             19   *
                                             20   * INITIALIZATIONS
                                             21   *
00000E                                       22             OPEN  (MASTER,(OUTPUT)) OPEN MASTER FILE
00001A                                       28             OPEN  (TRANS,(INPUT))   OPEN 'SYSIN' TRANSACTION FILE

                                             34   *  DOS *******
                                             35   *       OPEN  MASTER
                                             36   *       OPEN  TRANS
                                             37   ***************

000026                                       38             GET   TRANS,INAREA      GET FIRST TRANSACTION RECORD
000034 45 EO CO A2            0000A8         43             BAL   14,CONSTRCT       BEGIN CONSTRUCTING FIRST OUTPUT RECD
                                             44   *
                                             45   * MAIN PROCESSING
                                             46   *
000038                                       47   READ      GET   TRANS,INAREA      GET NEXT TRANS RECD (IF ANY)
000046 D5 03 COE9C132 0000EF 000138          52             CLC   TDORM,MDORM       IF THE DORM AND ROOM OF TRANS RECD
00004C 47 70 CO 5C            000062         53             BNE   WRITE             ARE NOT EQUAL TO THAT OF OUTPUT
000050 D5 03 COF1C136 0000F7 00013C          54             CLC   TROOM,MROOM       RECD, THEN MOVE OUTPUT RECD TO OUT-
000056 47 70 CO 5C            000062         55             BNE   WRITE             PUT BUFFER AND BEGIN NEW RECD.
00005A 45 EO COC2             0000C8         56             BAL   14,UPDATING       OTHERWISE, CONTINUE CONSTRUCTING THE
00005E 47 FO CO 32            000038         57             B     READ              OUTPUT RECD VIA 'UPDATING' ROUTINE.
                                             58   *
000062                                       59   WRITE     PUT   MASTER,OUTAREA    MOVE OUTPUT RECD TO OUTPUT BUFFER.
000070 45 EO CO A2            0000A8         64             BAL   14,CONSTRCT       BEGIN CONSTRUCTING NEXT OUTPUT RECD.
000074 47 FO CO 32            000038         65             B     READ              THEN GET NEXT TRANS RECD.
                                             66   *
                                             67   * END-OF-DATA PROCESSING
                                             68   *
000078                                       69   EOJ       PUT   MASTER,OUTAREA    MOVE LAST OUTPUT RECD TO OUTPUT BUF-
000086                                       74             CLOSE (MASTER)          FER, THEN CLOSE ALL FILES.
000092                                       80             CLOSE (TRANS)
00009E 58 DO C292             000298         86             L     13,SAVE+4         STANDARD EXIT.
0000A2 98 EC DO0C                            87             LM    14,12,12(13)
0000A6 07 FE                                 88             BR    14
                                             89   *  DOS *******
                                             90   *       CLOSE MASTER
                                             91   *       CLOSE TRANS
                                             92   *       EOJ
                                             93   ***************


                                             94   * INTERNAL SUBROUTINE WITH TWO ENTRY POINTS, 'CONSTRCT'  &  'UPDATING'
                                             95   * BOTH ENTERED WITH  BAL  14,... WITH NO PARAMETERS.
                                             96   *
                                             97   *'CONSTRCT' BEGINS CONSTRUCTION OF A NEW OUTPUT MASTER RECD.
                                             98   *'UPDATING' CONTINUES CONSTRUCTION OF AN EXISTING OUTPUT MASTER RECD.
                                             99   *
                                            100   * TRANSACTION CODE 'TTYPE' DETERMINES UPDATING ACTION
                                            101   *    TTYPE = C'1' ... ADD A NEW ROOM WITH NO STUDENTS
                                            102   *          = C'2' ... ADD A STUDENT NAME & I.D.
                                            103   *          = C'3' ... DELETE A STUDENT NAME & I.D.
                                            104   *          = C'4' ... DELETE ENTIRE MASTER RECD.
                                            105   *
0000A8 D2 03 C132COE9 000138 0000EF         106   CONSTRCT  MVC   MDORM,TDORM       WHEN CONSTRUCTING A NEW RECD, MOVE
0000AE D2 03 C136COF1 00013C 0000F7         107             MVC   MROOM,TROOM       DORM AND ROOM NUMBER FROM TRANS TO
0000B4 D2 30 C13AC19C 000140 0001A2         108             MVC   MDATA1,BLANKS     OUTPUT AREA, AND BLANK OUT STUDENT
0000BA D2 30 C16BC19C 000171 0001A2         109             MVC   MDATA2,BLANKS     DATA AREAS.
0000CO 95 F2 COE5            0000EB         110             CLI   TTYPE,C'2'        IF TRANS CODE IS '2' INSTEAD OF '1',
0000C4 47 70 CO ED            0000E6         111             BNE   EXIT              CONTINUE CONSTRUCTION. ELSE, EXIT.
                                            112   *
0000C8                                      113   UPDATING  EQU   *
000000                                      114             USING SDAREA,11          SET UP DUMMY BASE REGISTER TO ACCESS
0000C8 41 BO C13A            000140         115             LA    11,MDATA1          FIELDS IN STUDENT DATA AREA BY NAME.
0000CC D5 08 BO28C19C 000028 0001A2         116             CLC   MID,BLANKS         IF FIRST STUDENT AREA IS BLANK, MOVE
0000D2 47 80 CO D4            0000DA         117             BE    ADD1               NAME & I.D. TO THAT AREA.
0000D6 41 BB DO 31            000031         118             LA    11,DATALNG(11)     OTHERWISE, INCR ADDR TO SECOND AREA.
0000DA D2 27 BOOOCOF6 000000 0000FC         119   ADD1      MVC   MNAME,TNAME        MOVE STUDENT NAME & I.D. INTO APPRO-
0000EO D2 08 BO28C11F 000028 000125         120             MVC   MID,TID            PRIATE STUDENT DATA AREA.
0000E6 07 FE                                121   EXIT      BR    14                 THEN EXIT TO CALLING ROUTINE.


                                            122   * TRANSACTION INPUT RECORD AREA
```

Figure 20.8   *continued*

```
FLAG LOCTN OBJECT CODE      ADDR1  ADDR2  STMNT M SOURCE STATEMENT

                                           123   *
       0000E8                              124   INAREA    DS        CL80              RESERVE 80 BYTES FOR CARD IMAGE.
       0000E8              000138          125             ORG       INAREA            BEGIN REDEFINITION OF INPUT AREA.
       0000E8                              126             DS        CL3               COL 1-3    UNUSED
       0000EB                              127   TTYPE     DS        CL1               4          TRANS TYPE CODE
       0000EC                              128             DS        CL3               5-7        UNUSED
       0000EF                              129   TDORM     DS        CL4               8-11       DORM ABBREVIATION
       0000F3                              130             DS        CL4               12-15      UNUSED
       0000F7                              131   TROOM     DS        CL4               16-19      DORM ROOM NUMBER
       0000FB                              132             DS        CL1               20         UNUSED
       0000FC                              133   TNAME     DS        CL40              21-60      STUDENT NAME
       000124                              134             DS        CL1               61         UNUSED
       000125                              135   TID       DS        CL9               62-70      STUDENT I.D.
       000138              00012E          136             ORG
                                           137   * MASTER FILE OUTPUT RECORD AREA
                                           138   *
       000138                              139   OUTAREA   DS        CL106             RESERVE 106 BYTES FOR RECORD.
       000138              0001A2          140             ORG       OUTAREA           BEGIN REDEFINITION OF OUTPUT AREA.
       000138                              141   MDORM     DS        CL4               BYTES 0-3  DORM ABBREVIATION
       00013C                              142   MROOM     DS        CL4                     4-7  DORM ROOM NUMBER
       000140                              143   MDATA1    DS        CL49                    8-56   1ST STUDENT DATA AREA
       000171                              144   MDATA2    DS        CL49                    57-105 2ND STUDENT DATA AREA
       0001A2              0001A2          145             ORG
                                           146   *
                                           147   * DUMMY SECTION FOR PROCESSING FIELDS WITHIN STUDENT DATA AREAS BY NAME
                                           148   *
       000000                              149   SDAREA    DSECT
       000000                              150   MNAME     DS        CL40              NAME FIELD AREA
       000028                              151   MID       DS        CL9               I.D. FIELD AREA
       000031                              152   DATALNG   EQU       *-MNAME           LENGTH OF STUDENT DATA AREA
       0001A2                              153   CREATE    CSECT
                                           154   *
                                           155   * BLANKS USED TO INITIALIZE STUDENT DATA AREAS
                                           156   *
       0001A2 40                           157   BLANKS    DC        (DATALNG)C' '     'DATALNG' IS SIZE OF STUDENT DATA AREA
                                           158   *
                                           159   * DCB'S FOR TRANSACTION FILE AND OUTPUT MASTER FILE
                                           160   *
       0001D3                              161   TRANS     DCB       DSORG=PS,MACRF=(GM),DDNAME=SYSIN,EODAD=EOJ,            X
                                           162                       RECFM=FB,LRECL=80,BLKSIZE=4080
                                           214   *
       000234                              215   MASTER    DCB       DSORG=PS,MACRF=(PM),DDNAME=DORMS,                      X
                                           216                       RECFM=FB,LRECL=106,BLKSIZE=4028

                                           268   *  DOS  *******
                                           269   *TRANS     DTFCD DEVADDR=SYSIPT,WORKA=YES,IOAREA1=INBUF,EOFADDR=EOJ,      X
                                           270   *                DEVICE=2540
                                           271   *INBUF     DS        CL80
                                           272   *
                                           273   *MASTER    DTFSD DEVADDR=SYSO15,DEVICE=3330,TYPEFLE=OUTPUT,WORKA=YES,     X
                                           274   *                RECFORM=FIXBLK,RECSIZE=106,BLKSIZE=4036,IOAREA1=OUTBUF
                                           275   ***************

                                           276   *
                                           277   * REGISTER SAVE AREA
                                           278   *
       000294                              279   SAVE      DS        18F

                                           280   *  DOS  *******
                                           281   *SAVE      DS        9D
                                           282   *         LTORG
                                           283   *         DS        0D
                                           284   *OUTBUF    DS        CL4036
                                           285   ***************

                                           286             END
```

```
            CROSS-REFERENCE


SYMBOL    LEN    VALUE  DEFN    REFERENCES


ADD1      00006  0000DA 00119   00117
BLANKS    00001  0001A2 00157   00108  00109  00116
CONSTRCT  00006  0000A8 00106   00043  00064
CREATE    00001  000000 00153
DATALNG   00001  000031 00152   00118  00157
EOJ       00004  000078 00070   00183
EXIT      00002  0000E6 00121   00111
INAREA    00050  0000E8 00124   00040  00049  00125
MASTER    00004  000234 00216   00026  00060  00070  00078
MDATA1    00031  000140 00143   00108  00115
```

Figure 20.8   continued

```
MDATA2     00031 000171 00144     00109
MDORM      00004 000138 00141     00052  00106
MID        00009 000028 00151     00116  00120
MNAME      00028 000000 00150     00119  00152
MROOM      00004 0001 3C 00142    00054  00107
OUTAREA    0006A 000138 00139     00061  00071  00140
READ       00004 000038 00048     00057  00065
SAVE       00004 000294 00279     00017  00018  00086
SDAREA     00001 000000 00149     00114
TDORM      00004 0000EF 00129     00052  00106
TID        00009 000125 00135     00120
TNAME      00028 0000FC 00133     00119
TRANS      00004 000104 00162     00032  00039  00048  00084
TROOM      00004 0000F7 00131     00054  00107
TTYPE      00001 0000EB 00127     00110
UPDATING   00001 0000C8 00113     00056
WRITE      00004 000062 00060     00053  00055
```

Figure 20.9   Typical transaction data and resulting master file data for dorm file creation.

DOS programmers should note two important aspects of the program in figure 20.8. They both concern the output buffer area. For a sequential disk file this area must include space for an 8-byte field that the Operating System uses for the "count" field when writing the buffer in count-data format. The field occupies the first 8 bytes of the buffer, and its length must be included in the BLKSIZE= parameter of the DTFSD macro. This field is not present in input buffers, only in output buffers.

Moreover, the presence of a large buffer area in the user's program presents an addressability problem when using a single implied base register as we have done. The problem is that memory addresses that are more than 4095 bytes beyond the single implied base address cannot be represented in base-displacement form. This is why we have placed the DOS buffer area at the very end of the source-module and used the LTORG directive before defining the buffer area. As discussed in chapter 15, LTORG causes all literals to be assembled beginning at the point where the LTORG occurs. If there had been any literals used in the program (there weren't) their addresses would have been representable in base-displacement form, since they would have been within the range of the single implied base address. They wouldn't have been within that range if we had allowed the Assembler to place them *after* the buffer area, as it would have done had there been no LTORG.

20.10   UPDATING A SEQUENTIAL DATA SET

The process of updating a sequential data set includes four possible actions:

Action 1: Add records to the end of the data set.

Action 2: Change or delete some of the data in existing records without deleting any records and without changing the length of any records.

Action 3: Insert new records in their proper sequence within the data set, or change the length of one or more existing records by adding new data to them or deleting data from them.

Action 4: Delete one or more existing records from the data set.

In the context of the dorm-room master file example, these four actions could stem from the following situations:

1. Records would be added to the end-of-the-data set if a new dorm, with a four-letter abbreviation that was alphabetically greater than those of existing dormitories, were built. Adding such records to the end of the data set would not alter the sequence of the master file records.

2. Since fixed-length records are used, data in existing records could be changed or deleted without altering the records' lengths, whenever a new student was assigned to a room or a student was transferred from one room to another.

3. New records would be inserted if new rooms became available in existing dorms or if a new dorm with a four-letter abbreviation that was not alphabetically greater than those of existing dormitories were built. (If variable-length records were used, the length of an existing record could be changed by adding or removing a student's name and i.d.)

4. Records would be deleted from the data set if the corresponding rooms were no longer available for some reason or if a mistake had been made in dorm abbreviation or room number when a record was added to the master file.

In the most general case, transaction records representing all four possible actions may exist in the transaction file. In such a case, the entire existing master file must be examined, one record at a time. Records for which no changes are to be made are copied to a new master file. Records for which one or more changes are to be made are copied to the new master file after the changes are made. Records which are to be deleted are not copied. And insertions and additions are written onto the new master file in their proper sequence.

In two special cases, the existing master file need not be copied, thereby saving processing time. In one of these cases, described as Action 1, the transaction records must represent only additions to the end of the data set. In the other case, described as Action 2, the transaction records must represent only changes or deletions to existing records without changing their lengths.

Action 1: EXTEND Mode (OS Only)

To add records to the end of an existing OS sequential data set, the data set can be opened in EXTEND mode. The records may be processed either in move mode or locate mode, and the record format may be either fixed or variable length. The processing steps are the same as those required for creating a sequential data set. Thus, the only change to the program shown in figure 20.8 would be to replace the master file OPEN macro with this macro

OPEN   (MASTER,(EXTEND))

The author knows of no comparable capability in DOS for sequential disk files.

Action 2: UPDAT Mode (Figs. 20.10 and 20.11)

To make changes or deletions in existing records without changing their lengths, and without performing any of the other three updating actions listed earlier, a sequential data set can be opened for updating only. In OS, this is done by specifying UPDAT in the OPEN macro. In DOS, it is done by specifying UPDATE=YES together with TYPEFLE=INPUT in the DTFSD macro.

In the processing steps that are used when a data set is opened for updating, each updated record is rewritten to the same relative position in the data set that it occupied before the updating occurred. For this reason, the process is known as *updating in place*. In OS, it is the PUTX macro (not PUT) that is used to rewrite a record; in DOS, PUT is used.

Figure 20.10 *Overview of UPDAT procedures for sequential data sets.*

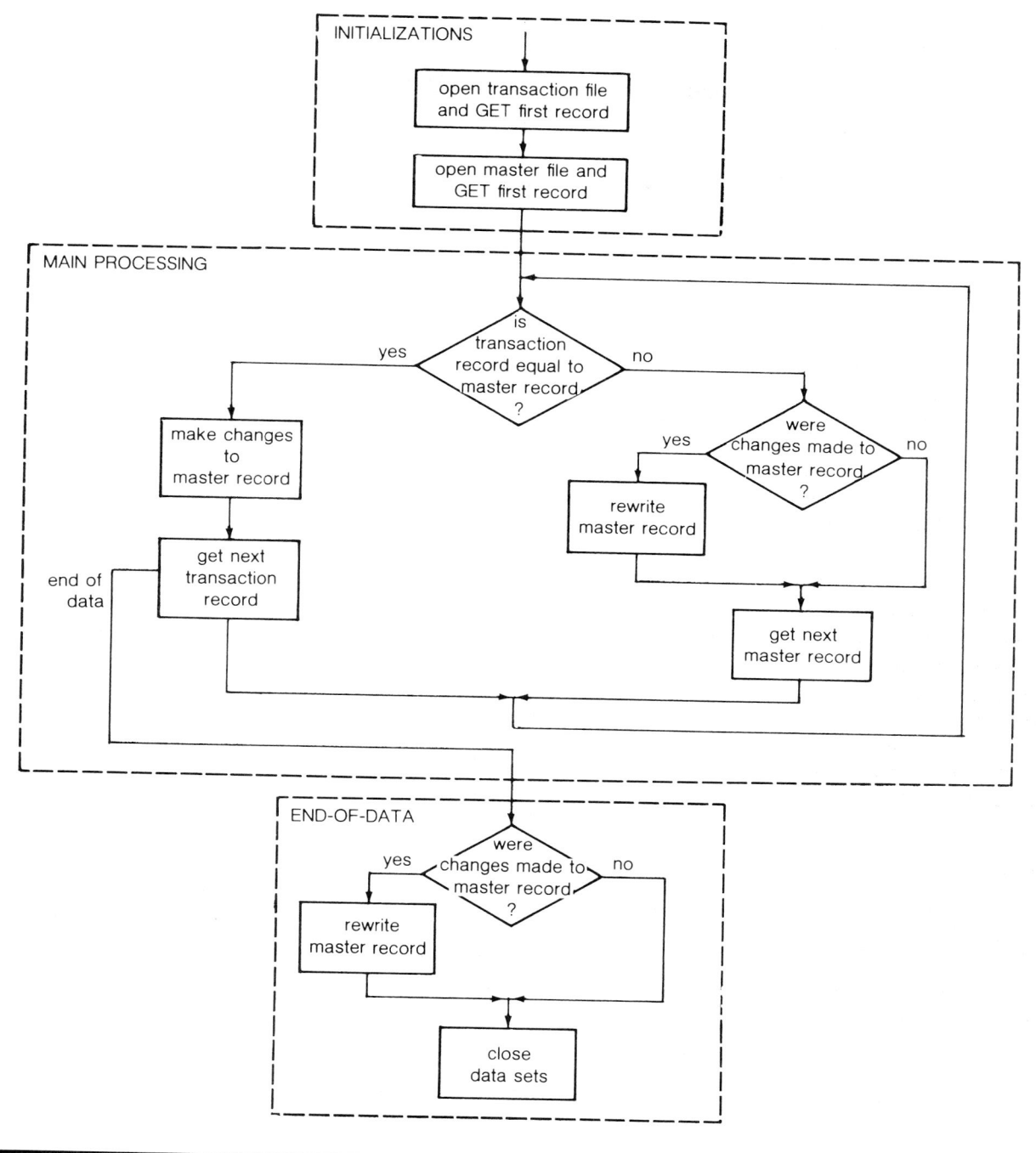

No record can be rewritten unless it is the most recently read record. The GET macro is used in both OS and DOS to read each record. But, as in the process of creating a sequential data set, there may be any number of consecutive transaction records that are used to update a given master record. Accordingly, a master record is not rewritten until all updating changes have been made to it. (It is not rewritten at all if *no* updating changes are made to it since rewriting would only incur an unnecessary waste of processing time.)

When the end-of-data condition is reached on the transaction file, there may still be a master record that was in the process of being updated in main memory. If so, this master record must be rewritten before closing the data sets. The decision of whether or not to rewrite is controlled by a flag, or switch, that is reset each time a new master record is read, and set whenever a change is made to that record.

Figure 20.11   Updating the dorm room master file via QSAM (UPDAT).

```
FLAG LOCTN OBJECT CODE    ADDR1 ADDR2 STMNT M SOURCE STATEMENT

                                        3   UPDAT  CSECT
     000000                             4   *
                                        5   *THIS PROGRAM UPDATES THE DORM ROOM MASTER FILE IN 'UPDAT' MODE,
                                        6   * USING QSAM PROCESSING WITH FIXED-LENGTH RECORDS AND LOCATE-
                                        7   * MODE BUFFERING.
                                        8   *
                                        9   *NO RECORDS ARE ADDED, DELETED, OR INSERTED, BUT EXISTING RECORDS
                                       10   * MAY BE MODIFIED BY THE ADDITION OR DELETION OF STUDENT NAMES AND
                                       11   * I.D.'S.  WHEN A NAME AND I.D. IS DELETED, IT IS SIMPLY REPLACED
                                       12   * BY BLANKS.  WHEN A NAME AND I.D. IS ADDED TO A RECORD, IT IS PUT
                                       13   * INTO THE STUDENT DATA AREA THAT IS BLANK.  IT IS  ASSUMED THAT THE
                                       14   * INPUT TRANSACTION DATA ARE 'PERFECT'   NO ERRORS, NO DUPLICATES,
                                       15   * NO INVALID TRANSACTIONS.
                                       16   *
     000000 90 EC D00C                 17          STM    14,12,12(13)       STANDARD ENTRY.
     000004 05 C0                      18          BALR   12,0
     000006                            19          USING  *,12
     000006 50 D0 C24E        000254   20          ST     13,SAVE+4
     00000A 41 D0 C24A        000250   21          LA     13,SAVE
     000000                            22          USING  OUTAREA,11          DUMMY BASE REG FOR OUTPUT AREA
                                       23   *
     00000E                            24          OPEN   (TRANS,(INPUT))     OPEN 'SYSIN' DATA SET.
     00001A                            30          OPEN   (MASTER,(UPDAT))    OPEN MASTER FILE

                                       36   *  DOS  *******
                                       37   *       OPEN   TRANS
                                       38   *       OPEN   MASTER
                                       39   ***************

     000026                            40          GET    TRANS,INAREA       GET FIRST TRANSACTION RECORD.
     000034 45 E0 C0AE        0000B4   45          BAL    14,GETMSTR         GET FIRST MASTER RECORD
                                       46   *
                                       47   * MAIN PROCESSING PROCEDURES
                                       48   *
     000038 D5 03 C10FB000 000115 000000 49 MAINLOOP CLC  TDORM,MDORM        IF DORM AND ROOM OF TRANS RECD ARE
     00003E 47 70 C05C        000062   50          BNE    REWRITE            NOT EQUAL TO THOSE OF MASTER RECD,
     000042 D5 03 C117B004 00011D 000004 51        CLC    TROOM,MROOM        THEN RE-WRITE MASTER (IF NECESSARY)
     000048 47 70 C05C        000062   52          BNE    REWRITE            AND THEN GET NEXT MASTER RECD.
     00004C 45 E0 C0CA        0000CA   53          BAL    14,UPDATING        OTHERWISE, GO DO UPDATING, AND THEN
     000050                            54          GET    TRANS,INAREA       GET NEXT TRANS RECD AND REPEAT THE
     00005E 47 F0 C032        000038   59          B      MAINLOOP           PROCESS TILL END-OF-DATA.
                                       60   *
     000062 95 FF C189        00018F   61   REWRITE CLI   MFLAG,BYP          MFLAG NOT 'BYP' IF CHANGES HAD BEEN
     000066 47 80 C070        000076   62          BE     BYPASS             MADE TO MASTER RECORD.
     00006A                            63          PUTX   MASTER             WHEN THAT IS THE CASE, RE-WRITE IT.
                                       67   *  DOS  ********
                                       68   *       PUT    MASTER
                                       69   ***************

     000076 45 E0 C0AE        0000B4   70   BYPASS BAL    14,GETMSTR         IN EITHER CASE, GET NEXT MASTER RECD,
     00007A 47 F0 C032        000038   71          B      MAINLOOP           AND CONTINUE PROCESSING.
                                       72   * END-OF-DATA PROCESSING
                                       73   *
     00007E 95 FF C189        00018F   74   EOJ    CLI    MFLAG,BYP          BEFORE CLOSING, SEE IF MASTER RECD
     000082 47 80 C08E        000094   75          BE     EOJX               MUST BE RE-WRITTEN.
     000086                            76          PUTX   MASTER             IF SO, REWRITE IT.
                                       80   *  DOS  ********
                                       81   *       PUT    MASTER
                                       82   ***************

     000092                            83   EOJX   CLOSE  (TRANS)            THEN CLOSE ALL DATA SETS, AND EXIT.
     00009E                            89          CLOSE  (MASTER)
     0000AA 58 D0 C24E        000254   95          L      13,SAVE+4
     0000AE 98 EC D00C                 96          LM     14,12,12(13)
     0000B2 07 FE                      97          BR     14

                                       98   *  DOS  *******
                                       99   *EOJX   CLOSE TRANS
                                      100   *       CLOSE MASTER
                                      101   *       EOJ
                                      102   ***************

                                      103   * INTERNAL SUBROUTINE 'GETMSTR' ENTERED VIA BAL 14,GETMSTR
                                      104   * GETS NEXT MASTER RECD IN LOCATE MODE, AFTER RESETTING RECD-CHGD FLAG.
                                      105   *
     0000B4 18 2E                     106   GETMSTR LR    2,14               SAVE RETURN ADDRESS
     0000B6 92 FF C189        00018F  107          MVI    MFLAG,BYP          RESET RECORD-CHANGED FLAG, TO INDI-
     0000BA                           108          GET    MASTER             CATE NO CHANGES HAVE YET BEEN MADE.
     0000C4 18 B1                     112          LR     11,REGX            SAVE ADDR OF LOGICAL RECD AREA IN
     0000C6 18 E2                     113          LR     14,2               REG 11, THEN RETURN TO CALLER.
     0000C8 07 FE                     114          BR     14
                                      115   *
                                      116   * SYMBOLIC REGISTER ADDRESS FOR LOCATE MODE
                                      117   REGX   EQU    1                  OS SYSTEMS
     000001                           118   *REGX  EQU    9                  DOS SYSTEMS

                                      119   * INTERNAL SUBROUTINE 'UPDATING' ENTERED VIA BAL 14,... WITH
                                      120   * LOGICAL RECORD ADDRESS IN REGISTER 11, FOR DUMMY BASE REGISTER.
                                      121   * ADDS OR DELETES STUDENT NAME & I.D. FROM STUDENT DATA AREA
                                      122   * IN MASTER RECD.  SETS FLAG INDICATING MSTR RECD HAS BEEN CHANGED.
                                      123   *
```

Figure 20.11 continued

```
FLAG LOCTN OBJECT CODE      ADDR1 ADDR2  STMNT M SOURCE STATEMENT

                                          124      * TRANSACTION CODE 'TTYPE' DETERMINES UPDATING ACTION
                                          125      *    TTYPE = C'1' ... ADD A NEW ROOM WITH NO STUDENTS
                                          126      *          = C'2' ... ADD A STUDENT NAME & I.D.
                                          127      *          = C'3' ... DELETE A STUDENT NAME & I.D.
                                          128      *          = C'4' ... DELETE ENTIRE MASTER RECD.
  0000CA                                  129      *
  0000CA 18 AB                            130  UPDATING EQU    *
  0000CC 95 F2 C10B       000111          131           LR     10,11            SAVE LOGICAL RECD AREA ADDR IN REG 10
  0000D0 47 80 C0E6       0000EC          132           CLI    TTYPE,C'2'       TRANS CODE '2' MEANS ADD STUDENT
  0000D4 D5 08 B030C145 000030 00014B     133           BE     ADD
  0000DA 47 80 C0DC       0000E2          134  DEL      CLC    MID,TID          OTHERWISE, ASSUME IT'S CODE '3' AND LOOK
  0000DE 41 BB 00 31      000031          135           BE     DEL1             FOR STUDENT I.D. IN 1ST & 2ND DATA AREAS
  0000E2 D2 30 B008C158 000008 00015E     136           LA     11,DATALNG(11)   IF NOT IN 1ST, MUST BE IN 2ND  INCR ADDR
  0000E8 47 F0 C100       000106          137  DEL1     MVC    MDATA1,BLANKS    REPLACE NAME & I.D. WITH BLANKS WHEN DE-
  0000EC D5 08 B030C158 000030 00015E     138           B      EXIT             LETING.
  0000F2 47 80 C0F4       0000FA          139  ADD      CLC    MID,BLANKS       WHEN ADDING, LOOK FOR VACANT STUDENT DATA
  0000F6 41 BB 00 31      000031          140           BE     ADD1             AREA.  IF NOT 1ST ONE, THEN ASSUME THAT
  0000FA D2 27 B008C11C 000008 000122     141           LA     11,DATALNG(11)   2ND AREA IS VACANT, AND INCR ADDR TO IT.
  000100 D2 08 B030C145 000030 00014B     142  ADD1     MVC    MNAME,TNAME      MOVE NAME & I.D. FROM TRANS RECD TO STU-
  000106 92 00 C189       00018F          143           MVC    MID,TID          DENT DATA AREA.
  00010A 18 BA                            144  EXIT     MVI    MFLAG,REWR       BEFORE RETURNING, SET FLAG TO INDICATE
  00010C 07 FE                            145           LR     11,10            THAT RECD WAS CHGD, AND RESTORE DUMMY
                                          146           BR     14               BASE REG CONTENTS

                                          147      * TRANSACTION INPUT RECORD AREA
                                          148      *
  00010E                                  149  INAREA   DS     CL80             RESERVE 80 BYTES FOR CARD IMAGE.
  00010E              00015E              150           ORG    INAREA           BEGIN REDEFINITION OF INPUT AREA.
  00010E                                  151           DS     CL3              COL 1-3   UNUSED
  000111                                  152  TTYPE    DS     CL1                  4      TRANS TYPE CODE
  000112                                  153           DS     CL3                  5-7    UNUSED
  000115                                  154  TDORM    DS     CL4                  8-11   DORM ABBREVIATION
  000119                                  155           DS     CL4                 12-15   UNUSED
  00011D                                  156  TROOM    DS     CL4                 16-19   DORM ROOM NUMBER
  000121                                  157           DS     CL1                  20     UNUSED
  000122                                  158  TNAME    DS     CL40                21-60   STUDENT NAME
  00014A                                  159           DS     CL1                  61     UNUSED
  00014B                                  160  TID      DS     CL9                 62-70   STUDENT I.D.
  00015E              000154              161           ORG
                                          162      *
                                          163      * MASTER FILE LOGICAL RECORD AREA VIA 'DSECT' (FIXED LENGTH RECDS)
                                          164      *
  000000                                  165  OUTAREA  DSECT
  000000                                  166  MDORM    DS     CL4              BYTES 0-3     DORM ABBREVIATION
  000004                                  167  MROOM    DS     CL4                    4-7     DORM ROOM NUMBER
  000008                                  168  MDATA1   DS     CL49                   8-56    1ST STUDENT DATA AREA
  000039                                  169  MDATA2   DS     CL49                  57-105   2ND STUDENT DATA AREA
  000008              00006A              170           ORG    MDATA1           REDEFINE STUDENT DATA AREA
  000008                                  171  MNAME    DS     CL40                   8-47    STUDENT NAME FIELD
  000030                                  172  MID      DS     CL9                   48-56    STUDENT I.D. FIELD
  000031                                  173  DATALNG  EQU    *-MNAME                         LENGTH OF STUDENT AREA
  00015E                                  174  UPDAT    CSECT
                                          175      *
                                          176      * BLANKS USED TO INITIALIZE STUDENT DATA AREAS
                                          177      * MFLAG INDICATES WHEN A MASTER RECD MUST BE REWRITTEN.
                                          178      *
  00015E 40                               179  BLANKS   DC     (DATALNG)C' '    'DATALNG' IS SIZE OF STUDENT DATA AREA
  00018F FF                               180  MFLAG    DC     X'FF'            X'FF' = DON'T REWRITE; X'00' = REWRITE
  000000                                  181  REWR     EQU    X'00'            REWR = RECORD HAS BEEN CHGD, REWRITE OK
  0000FF                                  182  BYP      EQU    X'FF'            BYP = RECD NOT CHGD, DONT REWRITE
                                          183      * DCB'S FOR TRANSACTION FILE AND OUTPUT MASTER FILE
                                          184      *
  000190                                  185  TRANS    DCB    DSORG=PS,MACRF=(GM),DDNAME=SYSIN,EODAD=EOJ,              X
                                          186                  RECFM=FB,LRECL=80,BLKSIZE=4080
                                          238      *
  0001F0                                  239  MASTER   DCB    DSORG=PS,MACRF=(GL,PL),DDNAME=DORMS,                    X
                                          240                  RECFM=FB,LRECL=106,BLKSIZE=4028

                                          292      * DOS  *******
                                          293      *TRANS  DTFCD DEVADDR=SYSIPT,WORKA=YES,IOAREA1=INBUF,EOFADDR=EOJ,  X
                                          294      *             DEVICE=2540
                                          295      *INBUF  DS    CL80
                                          296      *
                                          297      *MASTER DTFSD DEVADDR=SYS015,DEVICE=3330,TYPEFLE=INPUT,UPDATE=YES, X
                                          298      *             RECFORM=FIXBLK,RECSIZE=106,BLKSIZE=4028,IOAREA1=OUTBUF, X
                                          299      *             IOREG=(REGX)
                                          300      ***************

                                          301      *
                                          302      * REGISTER SAVE AREA
                                          303      *
  000250                                  304  SAVE     DS     18F

                                          305      * DOS  *******
                                          306      *SAVE   DS     9D
                                          307      *       LTORG
                                          308      *       DS     0D
                                          309      *OUTBUF DS     CL4028
                                          310      ***************

                                          311              END
```

Figure 20.11 *continued*

CROSS-REFERENCE

SYMBOL	LEN	VALUE	DEFN	REFERENCES			
ADD	00006	0000EC	00139	00133			
ADD1	00006	0000FA	00142	00140			
BLANKS	00001	00015E	00179	00137	00139		
BYP	00001	0000FF	00182	00061	00074	00107	
BYPASS	00004	000076	00070	00062			
DATALNG	00001	000031	00173	00136	00141	00179	
DEL	00006	0000C4	00134				
DEL1	00006	0000E2	00137	00135			
EOJ	00004	00007E	00074	00207			
EOJX	00004	000094	00085	00075			
EXIT	00004	000106	00144	00138			
GETMSTR	00002	0000B4	00106	00045	00070		
INAREA	00050	00010E	00149	00042	00056	00150	
MAINLOOP	00006	000038	00049	00059	00071		
MASTER	00004	0001F0	00240	00034	00064	00077	00093	00109
MDATA1	00031	000008	00168	00137	00170		
MDATA2	00031	000039	00169				
MDORM	00004	00000D	00166	00049			
MFLAG	00001	00018F	00180	00061	00074	00107	00144
MID	00009	000030	00172	00134	00139	00143	
MNAME	00028	000008	00171	00142	00173		
MROOM	00004	0000C4	00167	00051			
OUTAREA	00001	0000C0	00165	00022			
REGX	00001	000001	00117	00112			
REWR	00001	000000	00181	00144			
REWRITE	00004	000061	00061	00050	00052		
SAVE	00004	000250	00304	00020	00021	00095	
TDORM	00004	000115	00154	00049			
TID	00009	00014B	00160	00134	00143		
TNAME	00028	000122	00158	00142			
TRANS	00004	000190	00186	00028	00041	00055	00087
TROOM	00004	00011D	00156	00051			
TTYPE	00001	000111	00152	00132			
UPDAT	00001	000000	00174				
UPDATING	00001	0000CA	00130	00053			

Figure 20.12a *Overview of general updating procedure for sequential data sets.*

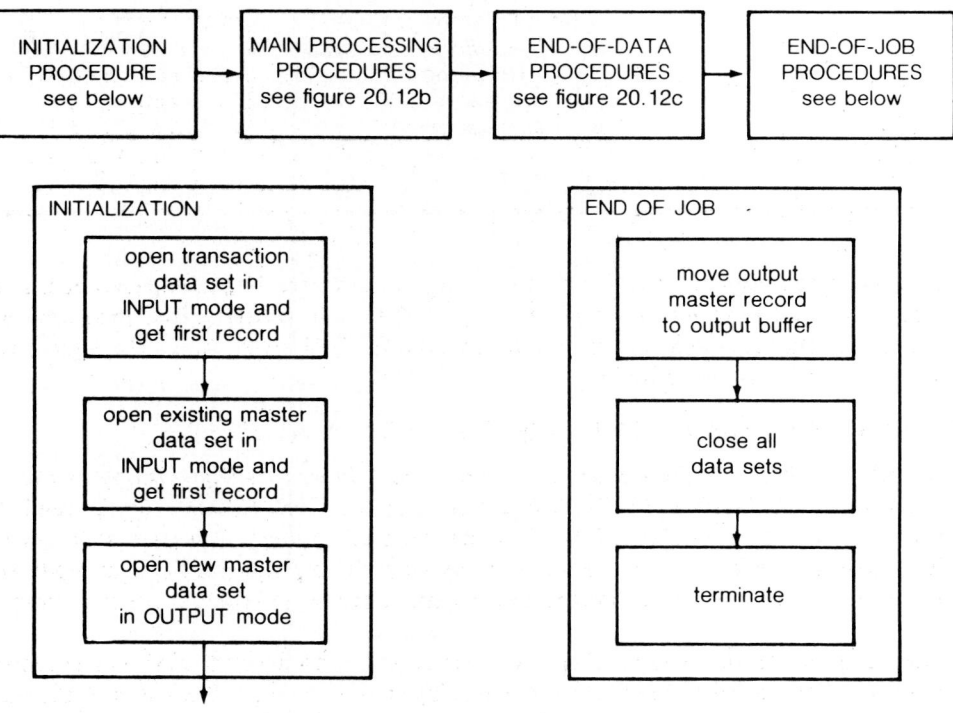

Figure 20.12b   Main processing procedure for updating sequential data sets.

These processing concepts are illustrated in the diagram of figure 20.10. A program that updates the dorm-room master file in UPDAT mode is given in figure 20.11. In studying that program, note that the logical record area for the master record is defined by a DSECT directive, since the logical record is not moved to or from the buffer in locate mode.

Actions 1 through 4: INPUT and OUTPUT Modes (Figs. 20.12a–c and 20.13)

In the general updating situation, the transaction file may contain records representing any of the four updating actions listed earlier. Neither the EXTEND mode nor the UPDAT mode can be used. Instead, the existing sequential master file is opened in INPUT mode and a new sequential master file is opened in OUTPUT mode. The existing master file is not altered in any way; the new master file is an updated version of the existing file, including new records, changed records, and unchanged records, but excluding deleted records.

In this updating procedure, two sets of records are merged to produce the new master records. One set consists of the transaction records; the other, of the existing master records. Each step of the merge process is designed to construct an output master record in its proper sequence. The steps involved are shown in the diagrams of figures 20.12a–20.12c.

Figure 20.12c   End-of-data procedures for updating sequential data sets.

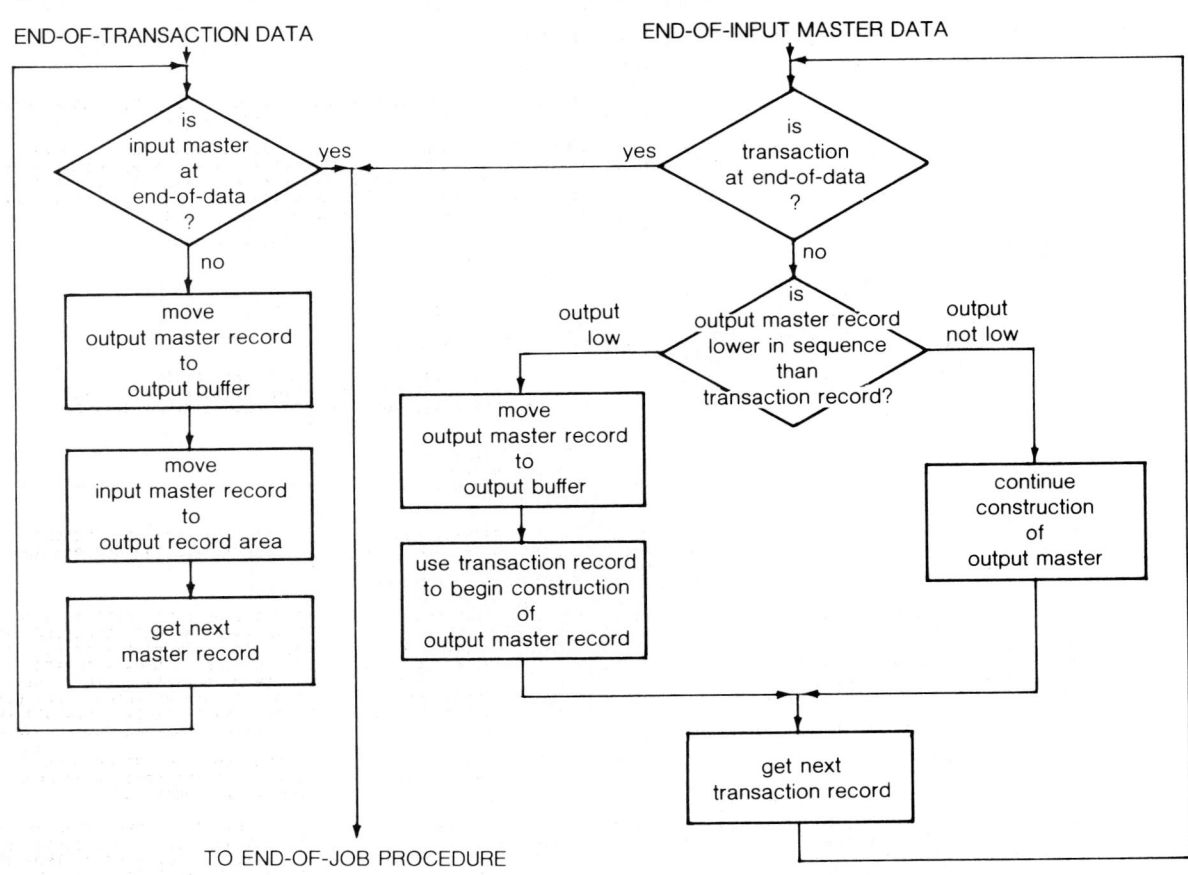

When the construction of an output master record has been completed, the master record is moved to the output buffer and one of the two input records is used to begin construction of the next output master record. Unless the transaction record currently being processed is lower in sequence than the master, the record chosen to begin the construction is the existing master record.

However, while the construction is in progress, one or more transaction records may contain information pertaining to the new master record. Each of these must be processed before the new master record can be moved to the output buffer. If one of the transaction records for the new master record is a 'delete record' transaction, a flag is set so that the new master record will not be moved to the output buffer.

In general, we cannot predict which input data set—transaction or master—will reach end-of-data first. Therefore, the procedure includes provisions for either event. If end-of-data occurs on the transaction data set first, the remaining input master records must be copied to the new output master. If the end-of-data condition occurs on the input master data set first, the remaining transaction records must be processed as though it were in EXTEND mode, i.e., the transaction records are simply added to the end of the new master.

Finer details of the procedure outlined in the preceding paragraphs are given in the program of figure 20.13, which updates the dorm-room master file discussed in preceding sections. As in the previous programs, the updating procedure presented assumes that the input transaction data contain no errors or duplicates and that they are in the same dorm and room number sequence as the existing master data set. In addition, it is assumed that when there is more than one transaction record for a given dorm and room number, these are in sequence by the transaction-code number.

The program shown in figure 20.13 uses move mode for all three data sets. In practice, it would reduce processing time to use locate mode with both the input and output master files, since this would eliminate moving records from the input buffer to the logical record area and from the record area to the output buffer. Use of locate mode is left as an exercise.

Figure 20.13 *Updating the dorm room master file via QSAM.*

```
FLAG LOCTN OBJECT CODE    ADDR1  ADDR2  STMNT M SOURCE STATEMENT
       000000                              3    UPDATE    CSECT
                                           4    *
                                           5    * THIS PROGRAM UPDATES THE DORM ROOM MASTER FILE, USING QSAM PROCESSING
                                           6    *   AND MOVE MODE BUFFERING FOR FIXED-LENGTH RECORDS.
                                           7    *
                                           8    * THE UPDATING PROCEDURE PERMITS ADDITIONS, INSERTIONS, AND DELETIONS
                                           9    *   OF MASTER FILE RECORDS, AND CHANGES TO EXISTING RECORDS.  (RECORD-
                                          10    *   LENGTHS CANNOT BE CHANGED SINCE THEY ARE FIXED-LENGTH RECORDS.)  IT
                                          11    *   IS ASSUMED THAT THE INPUT TRANSACTION DATA ARE 'PERFECT', I.E., NO
                                          12    *   ERRORS, NO DUPLICATES, NO INVALID TRANSACTIONS.
                                          13    *
  000000 90 EC D00C                       14             STM     14,12,12(13)        STANDARD ENTRY
  000004 05 C0                            15             BALR    12,0
  000006                                  16             USING   *,12
  000006 50 D0 C472    000478             17             ST      13,SAVE+4
  00000A 41 D0 C46E    000474             18             LA      13,SAVE
                                          19    *
                                          20    * INITIALIZATION PROCEDURES
                                          21    *
  00000E                                  22             OPEN    (TRANS,(INPUT))     OPEN TRANS FILE
  00001A                                  28             OPEN    (MSTRIN,(INPUT))    OPEN EXISTING MASTER FILE
  000026                                  34             OPEN    (MSTROUT,(OUTPUT))  OPEN NEW OUTPUT MASTER FILE

                                          40    * DOS ******
                                          41    *         OPEN    TRANS
                                          42    *         OPEN    MSTRIN
                                          43    *         OPEN    MSTROUT
                                          44    ****************
  000032                                  45             GET     TRANS,TAREA         GET FIRST TRANSACTION RECORD
  000040                                  50             GET     MSTRIN,OLDAREA      GET FIRST INPUT MASTER RECORD
                                          55    *
                                          56    * MAIN PROCESSING PROCEDURES
                                          57    *
  00004E D5 03 C1FBC244 000201 00024A     58    MAINLOOP CLC     TDORM,OLDMDORM      IF TRANS RECD IS LOWER IN SEQUENCE
  000054 47 40 C078     00007E            59             BL      TRANSLO             THAN INPUT MASTER RECD, USE TRANS
  000058 47 70 C060     000066            60             BNE     MASTERLO            RECD TO BEGIN CONSTR OF OUTPUT RECD.
  00005C D5 03 C203C248 000209 00024E     61             CLC     TROOM,OLDMROOM      IF DORMS ARE EQUAL, THEN TEST ROOM#
  000062 47 40 C078     00007E            62             BL      TRANSLO             USE TRANS IF IT'S LOWER, ELSE ...
  000066 D2 69 C2AEC244 0002B4 00024A     63    MASTERLO MVC     NEWAREA,OLDAREA     BEGIN CONSTR OF OUTPUT RECD USING
  00006C                                  64             GET     MSTRIN,OLDAREA      INPUT MASTER RECD.  THEN GET NEXT
  00007A 47 F0 C08A     000090            69             B       PROCESS             MASTER RECD BEFORE PROCESSING OUTPUT
                                          70    *
  00007E 45 E0 C17A     000180            71    TRANSLO  BAL     14,CONSTRCT         GO CONSTRUCT OUTPUT RECD USING TRANS
  000082                                  72             GET     TRANS,TAREA         RECD, AND GET NEXT TRANS RECD BEFORE
                                          77    *                                   PROCESSING OUTPUT.
                                          78    *
  000090 D5 03 C2AEC1FB 0002B4 000201     79    PROCESS  CLC     NEWMDORM,TDORM      IF OUTPUT MASTER RECD IS LOWER IN SEQ
  000096 47 70 C0B4     0000BA            80             BNE     COMPLETE            THAN TRANS RECD, THEN CONSTR OF OUT-
  00009A D5 03 C2B2C203 0002B8 000209     81             CLC     NEWMROOM,TROOM      PUT RECD HAS BEEN COMPLETED. (IF
  0000A0 47 70 C0B4     0000BA            82             BNE     COMPLETE            HIGHER, TRANS DATA IS OUT OF SEQ )
                                          83    *
  0000A4 45 E0 C19E     0001A4            84             BAL     14,UPDATING         IF OUTPUT MSTR = TRANS RECD ...
  0000A8                                  85             GET     TRANS,TAREA          UPDATE THE RECD, AND THEN
  0000B6 47 F0 C08A     000090            90             B       PROCESS              GET NEXT TRANS RECD.
                                          91    *                                   SEE IF NEXT TRANS = OUTPUT MSTR.
  0000BA 45 E0 C15A     000160            92    COMPLETE BAL     14,PUTMSTR          WHEN CONSTR COMPLETED, MOVE RECD TO
  0000BE 47 F0 C048     00004E            93             B       MAINLOOP            OUTPUT BUFFER, AND GO DETERMINE HOW
                                          94    *                                   TO BEGIN CONSTR OF NEXT OUTPUT RECD.
                                          95    *
                                          96    * END-OF-DATA PROCEDURES
                                          97    *
  0000C2 95 FF C349     00034F            98    ENDTRANS CLI     EODSW,EOF           WHEN END OF TRANSACTION DATA OCCURS
  0000C6 47 80 C12A     000130            99             BE      EOJ                 FIRST, SEE IF MASTER INPUT HAD AL-
  0000CA 92 FF C349     00034F           100             MVI     EODSW,EOF           READY REACHED END-OF-DATA.  IF SO,
  0000CE 45 E0 C15A     000160           101    COPYLOOP BAL     14,PUTMSTR          GO TO 'EOJ'.  OTHERWISE, SET FLAG
  0000D2 D2 69 C2AEC244 0002B4 00024A    102             MVC     NEWAREA,OLDAREA     AND COMMENCE COPYING INPUT MASTER
  0000D8                                 103             GET     MSTRIN,OLDAREA      RECDS TO OUTPUT MASTER FILE, TILL
  0000E6 47 F0 C0C8     0000CE           108             B       COPYLOOP           INPUT MASTER END-OF-DATA IS REACHED
                                         109    *
  0000EA 95 FF C349     00034F           110    ENDMSTR  CLI     EODSW,EOF           WHEN END OF INPUT MASTER OCCURS,
  0000EE 47 80 C12A     000130           111             BE      EOJ                 SEE IF TRANS INPUT HAD ALREADY
  0000F2 92 FF C349     00034F           112             MVI     EODSW,EOF           REACHED END-OF-DATA.  IF SO,
  0000F6 D5 03 C2AEC1FB 0002B4 000201    113    ADDLOOP  CLC     NEWMDORM,TDORM      GO TO 'EOJ'.  OTHERWISE, SET FLAG.
  0000FC 47 40 C110     000116           114             BL      ADDPUT             COMMENCE ADDING TRANS RECDS TO END
  000100 47 70 C108     00010E           115             BNE     ADDLOOPX            OF NEW MASTER.
  000104 D5 03 C2B2C203 0002B8 000209    116             CLC     NEWMROOM,TROOM     WHEN ADDING RECDS, ALLOW FOR MORE
  00010A 47 40 C110     000116           117             BL      ADDPUT             THEN ONE TRANS PER DORM ROOM SO
  00010E 45 E0 C19E     0001A4           118    ADDLOOPX BAL     14,UPDATING        THAT TWO STUDENTS CAN BE ADDED.
  000112 47 F0 C118     00011E           119             B       ADDGET
                                         120    *
  000116 45 E0 C15A     000160           121    ADDPUT   BAL     14,PUTMSTR          WHEN FINISHED CONSTR OF OUTPUT RECD,
  00011A 45 E0 C17A     000180           122             BAL     14,CONSTRCT         MOVE IT TO OUTPUT BUFFR, THEN BEGIN
                                         123    *                                   CONSTR OF NEXT OUTPUT RECD.
  00011E                                 124    ADDGET   GET     TRANS,TAREA        CONTINUE GETTING TRANS RECDS TILL
  00012C 47 F0 C0F0     0000F6           129             B       ADDLOOP            END-OF-DATA REACHED.
                                         130    *
                                         131    *
                                         132    * END-OF-JOB PROCEDURE
                                         133    *
```

Figure 20.13 **continued**

```
FLAG LOCTN OBJECT CODE      ADDR1  ADDR2 STMNT M SOURCE STATEMENT

     000130 45 E0 C15A       000160        134    EOJ      BAL    14,PUTMSTR                MOVE LAST MASTER OUTPUT RECD TO BUF-
     000134                                135             CLOSE  (MSTROUT)                 FER, THEN CLOSE FILES AND TERMINATE
     00013E                                141             CLOSE  (MSTRIN)                  PROGRAM.
     00014A                                147             CLOSE  (TRANS)
     000156 58 D0 C472       000478        153             L      13,SAVE+4
     00015A 98 EC D00C                     154             LM     14,12,12(13)
     00015E 07 FE                          155             BR     14
                                           156    *  DOS  ******
                                           157    *          CLOSE MSTROUT
                                           158    *          CLOSE MSTRIN
                                           159    *          CLOSE TRANS
                                           160    *          EOJ
                                           161    ****************
                                           162    * INTERNAL SUBROUTINE TO MOVE NEW MSTR RECD TO OUTPUT BUFFER,
                                           163    * PROVIDED THAT IT HASN'T BEEN DELETED.
                                           164    *
     000160 95 FF C34A       000350        165    PUTMSTR  CLI    MFLAG,BYP                 DID TRANS RECD DELETE IT
     000164 47 80 C174       00017A        166             BE     BYPASS                    ...YES
     000168 18 2E                          167             LR     2,14                      IF NOT, SAVE RETURN ADDR,
                                           168             PUT    MSTROUT,NEWAREA           AND MOVE RECD TO OUTPUT BUFFER.
     00016A                                                                                 THEN RECOVER RETURN ADDR,
     000178 18 E2                          173             LR     14,2                      RESET DELETE FLAG,
     00017A 92 00 C34A       000350        174    BYPASS   MVI    MFLAG,WR                  AND RETURN TO CALLER.
     00017E 07 FE                          175             BR     14
                                           176    *
                                           177    *
                                           178    * INTERNAL SUBROUTINE WITH TWO ENTRY POINTS, 'CONSTRCT' & 'UPDATING'
                                           179    * BOTH ENTERED WITH BAL 14,... WITH NO PARAMETERS.
                                           180    *
                                           181    * TRANSACTION CODE 'TTYPE' DETERMINES UPDATING ACTION
                                           182    *    TTYPE = C'1'  ...  ADD A NEW ROOM WITH NO STUDENTS
                                           183    *          = C'2'  ...  ADD A STUDENT NAME & I.D.
                                           184    *          = C'3'  ...  DELETE A STUDENT NAME & I.D.
                                           185    *          = C'4'  ...  DELETE ENTIRE MASTER RECD.
                                           186    *
                                           187    *'CONSTRCT' BEGINS CONSTRUCTION OF NEW OUTPUT MASTER RECD USING TRANS
                                           188    * RECD.  'UPDATING' CONTINUES CONSTRUCTION OF NEW OUTPUT MASTER RECD.
                                           189    *
     000180 D2 03 C2AE C1FB 0002B4 000201  190    CONSTRCT MVC    NEWMDORM,TDORM            WHEN CONSTRUCTING A NEW RECD, MOVE
     000186 D2 03 C2B2 C203 0002B8 000209  191             MVC    NEWMROOM,TROOM            DORM AND ROOM NUMBER FROM TRANS
     00018C D2 30 C2B6 C318 0002BC 00031E  192             MVC    NEWDATA1,BLANKS           TO OUTPUT AREA, AND BLANK OUT STU-
     000192 D2 30 C2E7 C318 0002ED 00031E  193             MVC    NEWDATA2,BLANKS           DENT DATA AREAS.
     000198 95 F2 C1F7       0001FD        194             CLI    TTYPE,C'2'                IF TRANS CODE IS '2', INSTEAD OF '1',
     00019C 47 80 C1AE       0001B4        195             BE     OKUPDATE                  CONTINUE CONSTRUCTION.
     0001A0 47 F0 C1F2       0001F8        196             B      EXIT                      OTHERWISE, EXIT.
                                           197    *
     0001A4                                198    UPDATING EQU    *
     0001A4 95 F4 C1F7       0001FD        199             CLI    TTYPE,C'4'                IS THIS A DELETE REQUEST
     0001A8 47 70 C1AE       0001B4        200             BNE    OKUPDATE                  ...IF NOT, GO DO UPDATING.
     0001AC 92 FF C34A       000350        201             MVI    MFLAG,BYP                 IF SO, SET DELETE FLAG TO BY-
     0001B0 47 F0 C1F2       0001F8        202             B      EXIT                      PASS WRITING TO NEW MASTER.
                                           203    *
     0001B4                                204    OKUPDATE EQU    *
     000000                                205             USING  SDAREA,11                 SET UP DUMMY BASE REGISTER TO ACCESS
     0001B4 41 B0 C2B6       0002BC        206             LA     11,NEWDATA1               FIELDS IN STUDENT DATA AREA BY NAME.
     0001B8 95 F2 C1F7       0001FD        207             CLI    TTYPE,C'2'                IF TRANS CODE = '2', THEN ADD STUDENT
     0001BC 47 80 C1D8       0001DE        208             BE     ADD                       NAME AND I.D.
     0001C0 D5 08 B028 C231 000028 000237 209    DEL      CLC    NEWMID,TID                OTHERWISE, ASSUME CODE = '3', AND
     0001C6 47 80 C1C8       0001CE        210             BE     DEL1                      DELETE EITHER 1ST OR 2ND NAME & I.D.
     0001CA 41 B0 D031       000031        211             LA     11,DATALNG(11)            IF NOT 1ST, MUST BE 2ND  INCR ADDR.
     0001CE D2 27 B000 C318 000000 00031E 212    DEL1     MVC    NEWMNAME,BLANKS           DELETE BY REPLACING NAME & I.D. WITH
     0001D4 D2 08 B028 C318 000028 00031E 213             MVC    NEWMID,BLANKS             BLANKS.
     0001DA 47 F0 C1F2       0001F8        214             B      EXIT
     0001DE D5 08 B028 C318 000028 00031E 215    ADD      CLC    NEWMID,BLANKS             WHEN ADDING, SEE WHICH STUDENT DATA
     0001E4 47 80 C1E6       0001EC        216             BE     ADD1                      AREA IS BLANK, AND MOVE NAME & I.D.
     0001E8 41 B0 D031       000031        217             LA     11,DATALNG(11)            INTO THAT AREA.  IF NOT 1ST AREA,
     0001EC D2 27 B000 C208 000000 00020E 218    ADD1     MVC    NEWMNAME,TNAME            THEN ASSUME IT'S 2ND AREA.
     0001F2 D2 08 B028 C231 000028 000237 219             MVC    NEWMID,TID
     0001F8 07 FE                          220    EXIT     BR     14                        EXIT TO CALLING ROUTINE.
                                           221    * TRANSACTION INPUT AREA
                                           222    *
     0001FA                                223    TAREA    DS     CL80                      RESERVE 80 BYTES FOR CARD IMAGE.
     0001FA                 00024A         224             ORG    TAREA                     BEGIN REDEFINITION OF INPUT AREA.
000: 0001FA                                225             DS     CL3                       COL 1-3   UNUSED
000: 0001FD                                226    TTYPE    DS     CL1                            4     TRANS TYPE CODE
000  0001FE                                227             DS     CL3                            5-7   UNUSED
000       000201                           228    TDORM    DS     CL4                            8-11  DORM ABBREVIATION
          000205                           229             DS     CL4                            12-15 UNUSED
000       000209                           230    TROOM    DS     CL4                            16-19 DORM ROOM NUMBER
000       00020D                           231             DS     CL1                            20    UNUSED
000       00020E                           232    TNAME    DS     CL40                           21-60 STUDENT NAME
000       000236                           233             DS     CL1                            61    UNUSED
000       000237                           234    TID      DS     CL9                            62-70 STUDENT I.D.
000       00024A                 000240    235             ORG
000                                        236    *
000                                        237    * INPUT MASTER RECORD AREA
000                                        238    *
000       00024A                           239    OLDAREA  DS     CL106                     RESERVE 106 BYTES  (FIXED-LNG RECDS).
000       00024A                 0002B4    240             ORG    OLDAREA                   BEGIN REDEFINITION OF OUTPUT AREA.
```

Figure 20.13 **continued**

```
FLAG LOCTN OBJECT CODE    ADDR1 ADDR2  STMNT M SOURCE STATEMENT

     00024A                              241   OLDMDORM DS     CL4
     00024E                              242   OLDMROOM DS     CL4        BYTES 0-3  DORM ABBREVIATION
     000252                              243   OLDDATA1 DS     CL49       4-7  DORM ROOM NUMBER
     000283                              244   OLDDATA2 DS     CL49       8-56  1ST STUDENT DATA AREA
     0002B4                       0002B4 245            ORG               57-105  2ND STUDENT DATA AREA
                                         246   *
                                         247   * OUTPUT MASTER RECORD AREA
     0002B4                              248   *
     0002B4                       00031E 249   NEWAREA  DS     CL106      RESERVE 106 BYTES  (FIXED-LNG RECDS).
     0002B4                       NEWAREA 250            ORG               BEGIN REDEFINITION OF OUTPUT AREA.
     0002B8                              251   NEWMDORM DS     CL4        BYTES 0-3  DORM ABBREVIATION
     0002BC                              252   NEWMROOM DS     CL4        4-7  DORM ROOM NUMBER
     0002ED                              253   NEWDATA1 DS     CL49       8-56  1ST STUDENT DATA AREA
     00031E                       00031E 254   NEWDATA2 DS     CL49       57-105  2ND STUDENT DATA AREA
                                         255            ORG
                                         256   *
                                         257   * DSECT TO DEFINE FIELD NAMES WITHIN STUDENT DATA AREAS
     000000                              258   *
     000000                              259   SDAREA   DSECT
     000028                              260   NEWMNAME DS     CL40       BYTES 0-39  STUDENT NAME FIELD
     000031                              261   NEWMID   DS     CL9        40-48  STUDENT I.D. FIELD
     00031E                              262   DATALNG  EQU    *-NEWMNAME LENGTH OF STUDENT DATA AREA
                                         263   UPDATE   CSECT
                                         264   *
                                         265   * BLANKS USED TO INITIALIZE STUDENT DATA AREAS
                                         266   * EODSW USED TO SIGNAL WHEN END-OF-DATA REACHED.
                                         267   * MFLAG USED TO SIGNAL THAT CURRENT MASTER RECD IS DELETED
     00031E 40                           268   *
                                         269   BLANKS   DC     (DATALNG)C' '   'DATALNG' IS SIZE OF STUDENT DATA AREA
     00034F 00                           270   *
     0000FF                              271   EODSW    DC     X'00'     X'00'=NEITHER FILE AT END; X'FF'=ONE AT END.
     000350 00                           272   EOF      EQU    X'FF'     X'FF' = FLAG FOR END-OF-DATA ON EITHER FILE
     000000                              273   MFLAG    DC     X'00'     X'00'=OK TO WRITE;X'FF'=DONT WRITE
     0000FF                              274   WR       EQU    X'00'     X'00' = RECD NOT DELETED, WRITE OK
                                         275   BYP      EQU    X'FF'     X'FF' = RECD DELETED, DONT WRITE IT
                                         276   * DCB'S FOR TRANS FILE, INPUT MASTER FILE, AND OUTPUT MASTER FILE
     000351                              277   *
                                         278   TRANS    DCB    DSORG=PS,MACRF=(GM),DDNAME=SYSIN,EODAD=ENDTRANS,    X
                                         279                   RECFM=FB,LRECL=80,BLKSIZE=4080                      X
     000384                              331   MSTRIN   DCB    DSORG=PS,MACRF=(GM),DDNAME=OLDDORM,EODAD=ENDMSTR,    X
                                         332                   RECFM=FB,LRECL=106,BLKSIZE=4028                     X
                                         333   *
     000414                              385   MSTROUT  DCB    DSORG=PS,MACRF=(PM),DDNAME=NEWDORM,                  X
                                         386                   RECFM=FB,LRECL=106,BLKSIZE=4028                     X
                                         387
                                         439   * DOS ******
                                         440   *TRANS    DTFCD DEVADDR=SYSIPT,WORKA=YES,IOAREA1=INBUF,EOFADDR=ENDTRANS,X
                                         441   *                DEVICE=2540
                                         442   *INBUF    DS     CL80
                                         443   *
                                         444   *MSTRIN   DTFSD DEVADDR=SYS015,DEVICE=3330,TYPEFLE=INPUT,WORKA=YES,  X
                                         445   *                RECFORM=FIXBLK,RECSIZE=106,BLKSIZE=4028,IOAREA1=OLDBUF, X
                                         446   *                EOFADDR=ENDMSTR
                                         447   *
                                         448   *MSTROUT  DTFSD DEVADDR=SYS016,DEVICE=3330,TYPEFLE=OUTPUT,WORKA=YES, X
                                         449   *                RECFORM=FIXBLK,RECSIZE=106,BLKSIZE=4036,IOAREA1=NEWBUF
                                         450   ***************
                                         451   * REGISTER SAVE AREA
     000474                              452   *
                                         453   SAVE     DS     18F
                                         454   * DOS ******
                                         455   *SAVE     DS     9D
                                         456   *         LTORG
                                         457   *         DS     0D
                                         458   *OLDBUF   DS     CL4028
                                         459   *NEWBUF   DS     CL4036
                                         460   ***************
                                         461            END
```

CROSS-REFERENCE

```
SYMBOL     LEN   VALUE  DEFN   REFERENCES

ADD        00006 0001DE 00215  00208
ADDGET     00004 00011E 00125  00119
ADDLOOP    00006 0000F6 00113  00129
ADDLOOPX   00004 0001DE 00118  00115
ADDPUT     00004 000116 00121  00114  00117
ADD1       00006 0001EC 00218  00216
BLANKS     00001 00031E 00269  00192  00193  00212  00213  00215
```

Figure 20.13 **continued**

```
BYP        00001 0000FF 00275   00165 00201
BYPASS     00004 00017A 00174   00166
COMPLETE   00004 0000BA 00092   00080 00082
CONSTRCT   00006 000180 00190   00071 C0122
COPYLOOP   00004 0000CE 00101   00108
DATALNG    00001 000031 00262   00211 00217 00269
DEL        00006 0001C0 00209
DEL1       00006 0001CE 00212   00210
ENDMSTR    00004 0000EA 00110   00354
ENDTRANS   00004 0000C2 00098   00300
EODSW      00001 00034F 00271   00098 00100 00110 00112
EOF        00001 0000FF 00272   00098 00100 00110 00112
EOJ        00004 000130 00134   00099 C0111
EXIT       00002 0001F8 00220   00196 00202 00214
MAINLOOP   00006 00004E 00058   00093
MASTERLO   00006 000066 00063   00060
MFLAG      00001 000350 00273   00165 00174 00201
MSTRIN     00004 0003B4 00333   00032 00051 00065 00104 00145
MSTROUT    00004 000414 00387   00038 00139 00169
NEWAREA    0006A 0002B4 00249   00063 00102 00170 00250
NEWDATA1   00031 0002BC 00253   00192 C0206
NEWDATA2   00031 0002ED 00254   00193
NEWMDORM   00004 0002B4 00251   00079 00113 00190
NEWMID     00009 000028 00261   00209 00213 00215 00219
NEWMNAME   00028 000000 00260   00212 00218 00262
NEWMROOM   00004 0002B8 00252   00081 00116 00191
OKUPDATE   00001 0001B4 00204   00195 C0200
OLDAREA    0006A 00024A 00239   00052 00063 00066 00102 00105 00240
OLDDATA1   00031 000252 00243
OLDDATA2   00031 000283 00244
OLDMDORM   00004 00024A 00241   00058
OLDMROOM   00004 00024E 00242   00061
PROCESS    00006 000090 00079   00069 00090
PUTMSTR    00004 000160 00165   00092 C0101 00121 00134
SAVE       00004 000474 00453   00017 00018 00153
SDAREA     00001 000000 00259   00205
TAREA      00050 0001FA 00223   00047 00074 00087 00126 00224
TDORM      00004 000201 00228   00058 00079 00113 00190
TID        00009 000237 00234   00209 00219
TNAME      00028 00020E 00232   00218
TRANS      00004 000354 00279   00026 00046 00073 00086 00125 00151
TRANSLO    00004 00007E 00071   00059 C0062
TROOM      00004 000209 00230   00061 00081 00116 00191
TTYPE      00001 0001FD 00226   00194 C0199 00207
UPDATE     00001 000000 00263
UPDATING   00001 0001A4 00198   00084 C0118
WR         00001 000000 00274   00174
```

20.11 RETRIEVING FROM A SEQUENTIAL DATA SET

Retrieval, in the context of this section, means extracting data from the records of a data set for the purpose of producing printed reports based on the data. Clearly, whatever data is extracted must be obtained by sequentially reading one logical record at a time. Data need not be extracted from all the records, but each record must be read and examined to see if it meets the criteria governing selection of data.

There are three main types of reports commonly produced:

Type 1: A report listing all or some portion of the data in a data set in the sequence in which the records are read.

Type 2: A report listing all or some portion of the data in a sequence other than that in which the records are read.

Type 3: A report giving some information derived from the data set but not stored as data in that data set.

For our dorm-room master file, the following reports exemplify the cited categories:

1. A report listing the names and i.d.'s of all students in a given dorm in numerical order by room number.
2. A report listing the names and i.d.'s of all students in a given dorm in alphabetical order by student name.
3. A report showing the number and/or percent of rooms that are vacant in a given dorm.

To produce the first type of report, the fields in each record are tested to see if they meet the criteria established for the report and, if so, the desired data are extracted and written to the system output file. Page and line spacing, a title line with date and page number, and column headings are usually inserted in the report to improve readability.

To produce the second type of report, we must extract the desired data from the existing records, but instead of writing the extracted information to the system output file, it is written to a new data set. After all the desired information has been extracted, the new data set is sorted into the sequence needed for the report, and the sorted data set is then processed as when producing a report of the first type.

To produce the third type of report, totals or other derived data must be accumulated until all the records that can contribute data to the report have been read. At that point, the derived data are printed.

To illustrate some of the processes involved, consider the following problem of producing a report based on data in the dorm-room master file: *For a given dorm, the report is to list all the rooms that are unoccupied or have only one student assigned to them. If a student is assigned, his or her name is also to be listed. At the end of the report, the total number of rooms in the dorm, together with the percent of rooms unoccupied, with only one student assigned to them, and fully occupied, is to be printed. The format of the report is to be as shown here.*

DORM OCCUPANCY REPORT			PAGE 3
DORM	ROOM	ROOM OCCUPANT	
HH	320	B.L. CARVER	345678901
HH	330	----	
HH	335	A.A. SAMPEN	235689013
HH	420	X.J. WASHBOURN	098765432

TOTAL NUMBER OF ROOMS	% FULL	% HALF FULL	% EMPTY
225	72.4%	25.6%	2.0%

To designate the dorm for which the report is to be produced, we can use a transaction record similar to the ones used in creating and updating the dorm-room file, but containing no information other than the dorm abbreviation and a transaction code of '5'.

A procedure for producing this report is depicted in the diagram of figures 20.14a and 20.14b. Note that since the dorm identity is the major sequencing field in the dorm-room master file, the records in the master file are read until the first one that matches the given dorm identity is found. From that point on, the desired information is extracted from each master record that is read until either the end-of-data condition is reached on the master, or a record for a different dorm is encountered. In either case, the extraction process is terminated when that point is reached in the master file, and the total number of rooms and percentages is then printed. It is left as an exercise to write the program that will produce the desired report.

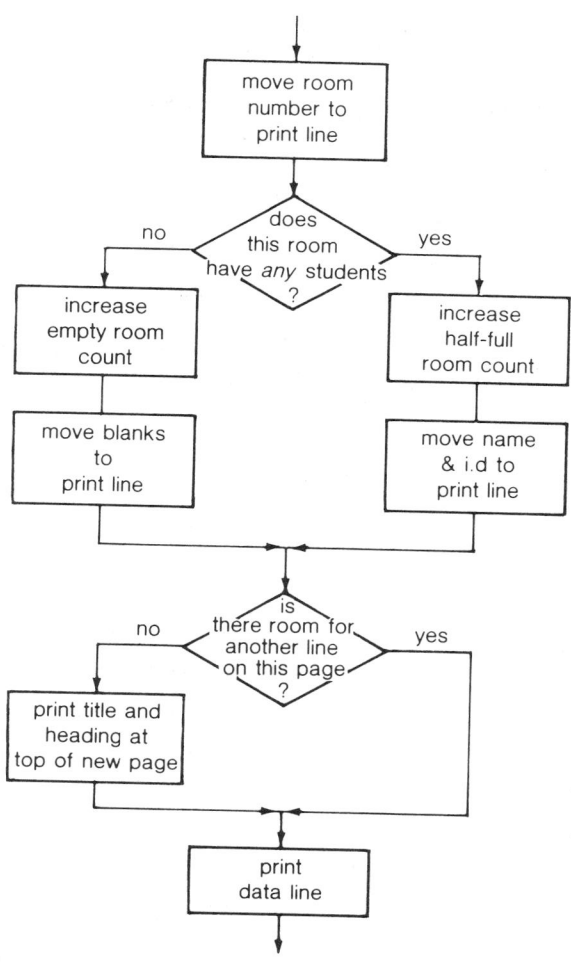

20.12 SUMMARY

To summarize the procedures involved in processing a sequential data set, we have seen that in creating, updating, or retrieving information, we must process the records in the sequence in which they exist. For this reason, the procedures described in this chapter are applicable not only to disk data sets but also to data sets stored on magnetic tapes.

Due to the sequential nature of the data, we ordinarily should not write or rewrite a record until it has been determined that the construction of that record has been completed. In the simplest cases, a single transaction record will suffice to construct a record. But in more general cases, more than one transaction record, occurring consecutively in the transaction file, will be used in the construction process.

There are four possible updating actions and three possible methods for updating a sequential data set. When the only updating action consists of adding records to the end of an existing data set, the data set can be opened in EXTEND mode. None of the existing records of the data set are processed; only new records are added. When the only updating action consists of making changes or deletions in existing records without changing their length, the data set can be opened in UPDAT mode. All the records in the data set, up to and including the last one to be changed, must be read via the GET macro. Only those that are to be changed are rewritten. The records are updated in place.

When any combination of the four updating actions may occur in the transaction file, the existing master data set must be opened in INPUT mode and a new data set, opened in OUTPUT mode, must be created. All the records in the existing data set must be processed, even those for which no changes are to be made. The existing data set is not altered in any way. The new data set is an updated version of the existing set, including new records, changed records, and unchanged records, but excluding deleted records.

When retrieving information from a sequential data set, each record must be examined to see if its data meets the criteria established for retrieval. If the report produced by the retrieval process is to be in a different sequence than that of the records in the data set, the extracted information must be sorted before it can be printed. If the sequence for the report matches that of the data set, the extracted information can be printed after each record has been read.

EXERCISES

1. Determine what conventions and restrictions, if any, exist at your computer installation with regard to the use of SYSIN and SYSOUT, or SYSIPT and SYSLST.

2. What statements in the programs of figures 20.1 and 20.2 would have to be changed if either (a) the input data were other than SYSIN or (b) the output data set were other than SYSOUT? What would the changes be?

3. Compare the programs of figures 20.1 and 20.2. What are the advantages of using locate mode over using move mode? What are the disadvantages?

4. Change the programs of figures 20.1 and 20.2 so that both the input and output data sets contain variable-length records (RECFM=VB in OS, RECFORM=VARUNB in DOS).

5. Suppose that the input data records for the program of figure 20.1 contained the following information:

        columns   5–44 = student name
        columns 46–55 = course identification
        columns 57–60 = course grade points, from 0.00 to 4.00

Write a program that will read an arbitrary number of such input records and compute and print the percentage of records with grade points between n and $n+1$, for $n = 0,1,2,3$.

6. Write a subroutine that will convert the date returned by the TIME macro (as discussed in Section 20.4) to 8-byte EBCDIC format as mm/dd/yy. For example, if the date returned is X'0080038C', the 8-byte EBCDIC representation would be C'02/07/80'.

7. Modify the program given in figure 20.4 so that the first line printed on each page of output contains a title, the page number, and the date on which the program is run. The date should be in the format mm/dd/yy, which can be generated either by the subroutine written for Exercise 6 or by any similar subroutine or macro already existing for this purpose at your computer installation.

8. What are the corresponding assembly language statements and/or DCB or DTFxx macro parameters for each of the following IBM COBOL clauses?

    a. BLOCK CONTAINS 4000 CHARACTERS
    b. RECORD CONTAINS 80 CHARACTERS
    c. RECORDING MODE IS FB
    d. READ filename AT END STOP RUN
    e. WRITE record AFTER ADVANCING 2 LINES
    f. OPEN INPUT filename

9. Prepare suitable test data to create a sequential dorm-room master file in accordance with the specifications given in this chapter. Ensure that your test data covers at least the following situations: no students assigned to a room, one student assigned to a room, two students assigned to the same room. Ensure that the transaction records are in proper sequence by sorting them via the IBM Sort/Merge program (see IBM Publication SC33–4035, *Sort/Merge Programmer's Guide*).

10. Using the test data from Exercise 9 and the program in figure 20.8, create a sample dorm-room master file. To verify that its contents are correct, print the master file via the IBM OS utility program IEBPTPCH (see IBM Publication GC26–3901, *Utilities*) or the corresponding DOS utility program (see Publication GC33–5381).

11. What specific types of possible data errors have been avoided in this chapter by the assumption of 'perfect' data in the transaction file that is input to the program of figure 20.8? Modify the program of figure 20.8 so that it would detect and reject all such errors and print them on the system output data set. Prepare test data that would force your modified program to encounter these errors.

12. Under what conditions can the open-mode processing option known as EXTEND be used to update a sequential data set? What would be the advantage of using this processing option rather than the more general procedures depicted in figures 20.12 and 20.13? Why couldn't the UPDAT mode (as shown in figs. 20.10 and 20.11) be used as an alternative to the EXTEND mode?

13. a. What specific types of possible data errors have been avoided in this chapter by the assumption of "perfect" data in each of the following updating situations: EXTEND mode, UPDAT mode, and the general updating procedures of figure 20.12?
   b. Assume that a transaction file processed by the program of figure 20.13 inadvertently contained records for three different students to be assigned to the same dorm room. What would be the result when these records were processed by the program?
   c. Assume that a transaction file processed by the program of figure 20.13 inadvertently contained a record to delete a student from a dorm room to which he or she had never been assigned. What would be the result when this record was processed by the program?
   d. What changes would have to be made to the program of figure 20.13 to enable it to detect and reject the data errors described in Exercises 13b and 13c?

14. a. What changes would have to be made to the program of figure 20.13 to enable it to process the input transaction file in locate mode rather than move mode?
   b. What changes would have to be made to the program of figure 20.13 to enable it to process both the input and output master files in locate mode rather than move mode?

15. Write a program that will print the entire contents of the dorm-room master file in some suitably readable format. Your program should be written to allow for an arbitrary number of records on the master file with no more than 50 lines printed per page and with an appropriate title line including date and page number on each page.

16. Write a program that will create a sequential file consisting of just those dorm-room master file records containing less than two students per room.

17. Write a program that will produce the dorm-room occupancy report described in Section 20.11, based on the procedures depicted in figures 20.14a and 20.14b.

18. Using the solutions to Exercises 16 and 17, suitably modified if necessary, describe how the dorm-room occupancy report could be produced in such a way that all the rooms to which no students were assigned were printed before all the rooms to which one student was assigned. Implement your solution to this problem. (Hint: You may wish to use the IBM Sort/Merge program described in IBM Publication SC33–4035.)

19. A high school district has decided to convert its teacher-assignment records to a form suitable for computer processing and maintenance. The records presently exist on paper. Each teacher's record contains the teacher's name, the name of the school to which the teacher is currently assigned, from one to three subjects that the teacher is qualified to teach, and the year in which the teacher first was employed by the school district.

   a. Design a transaction record format that can be used to create a sequential master file consisting of all the current manually maintained teacher assignment records, and design a master file format for these records.

b. Design a transaction record format that can be used to update the teacher-assignment master file, with capabilities to add new teachers, delete teachers who have retired or left the district, change any or all of the subjects that a teacher is qualified to teach, and change the school to which the teacher is assigned.

c. Write a program to create the teacher-assignment master file.

d. Write a program to update the teacher-assignment master file, allowing for the possibility of transaction data errors.

e. Write a program (or programs) that will produce each of the following reports:

1. A report giving all the information in the master file, listed in ascending sequence by year of first assignment (so-called "seniority" sequence)

2. A report giving all the information about teachers who are qualified to teach a given subject, the subject being identified by a transaction record that is read by the retrieval program

f. Create appropriate test data to verify that each of the programs in Exercises 19c, 19d, and 19e work correctly.

21
Indexed Sequential Organization

Each record of an indexed sequential data set must be uniquely identified by the value of a key field that is part of the record. The records must be maintained in ascending sequence by key values, i.e., the record with the lowest key must occur first, and the key field of each record must begin in the same relative position and have the same length as the key fields of the other records of the data set.

Use of indexed sequential organization provides one significant advantage over that of sequential organization: not only may the logical records be processed sequentially, but they may also be processed randomly. In OS, the QISAM access method is used for sequential processing, and the BISAM access method for random processing. In DOS, the ISAM access method is used for both sequential and random processing.

To enable random processing to be accomplished without requiring a user's program to determine the position of records within the data set, the Operating System maintains an index that associates each key value with the position of the record identified by that value. In simplest terms, the user program presents a key to the Operating System, and the Operating System finds and reads that record (if it exists) or writes it into its logically correct sequential position.

In this chapter, we will discuss several aspects of indexed sequential processing, beginning with an overview. Space allocation considerations will then be discussed as will the processes of creating, updating, and retrieving from an indexed sequential data set. These processes will be illustrated with the dorm-room master file introduced in chapter 20. You may therefore find it useful to review the concepts presented in chapters 19 and 20, especially figures 19.6 (I/O macros), 19.7 (DCB and DTFIS parameters), and 19.10 (OPEN options).

21.1 INTRODUCTORY CONCEPTS

Although the concepts are essentially the same whether we are using OS or DOS systems, the processing details for indexed sequential data sets are significantly different between the two systems. We have already mentioned one major difference: the use of two access methods (QISAM and BISAM) in OS, but only one (ISAM) in DOS. But there are other major differences. One is the manner in which I/O error conditions are communicated to the user's program from the Operating System. Another is the manner in which buffers are allocated. A third is the way in which buffers are used by the GET, PUT, READ, and WRITE macros. And a fourth, though not strictly an assembly language consideration, is the manner in which space is allocated by the job control language statements. Because of these and other differences, it is probably fair to say that in indexed sequential processing we have the most pronounced instance of incompatibility between OS Assembly Language and DOS Assembly Language.

QISAM

The queued indexed sequential access method (QISAM) must be used to create an indexed sequential data set in OS. It can also be used when updating in place via PUTX in UPDAT mode and when adding records to the end of a data set via PUT in EXTEND mode. It cannot, however, be used to insert new records into an existing data set (see Section 21.4).

The processing steps used with QISAM are similar to those described in the preceding chapter for QSAM. Buffer allocation and I/O synchronization are performed as in QSAM. Records must be read or written in their correct logical key sequence. There are, however, a number of differences between the two access methods, two of them quite significant. One significant difference is that *sequential processing can begin at any arbitrary record in the data set* when updating or retrieving records in an indexed sequential data set using QISAM. The record at which processing begins must be identified by its key and specified in a Set Location (SETL) macro before invoking a GET macro. Any number of SETL macros can be invoked at run time; thus, in effect, we can sequentially process the records in one or more separate sections of an indexed sequential data set without having to process the entire data set. In order to stop retrieval from one section before beginning a new section of the data set, we simply invoke the End SETL (ESETL) macro. This can be done before or after the end-of-data condition is reached.

The other significant difference between QISAM and QSAM processing is that in QISAM *records can be deleted when updating in place.* This is accomplished by using the first byte of each logical record (or the first byte immediately following the record descriptor word if using variable-length records) as a *delete flag.* The user's program must set this byte to X'FF' if the record is to be deleted, and to X'40' (a blank) if it is not to be deleted. Any record flagged for deletion in this manner will not be retrievable via QISAM in subsequent processing. Note that the programmer must declare his or her intention of using the first byte as a delete flag at the time an indexed sequential data set is created; once this is done, the first byte should not be used for any other purpose. (The method of declaring this is to specify OPTCD=L in the DCB macro or DD statement.)

Other differences between QISAM and QSAM processing methods include:

1. The DSORG parameter must always be coded as DSORG=IS for QISAM. The RECFM, LRECL, and BLKSIZE parameters should be coded only when creating the data set, not when updating or retrieving from it.
2. Move mode or locate mode buffering can be used, but the other buffering options available with QSAM processing—data mode, substitute mode, and exchange buffering—are not permitted with QISAM.
3. When retrieving records in INPUT mode, we must specify in the MACRF parameter whether or not the SETL macro will be used by coding MACRF=(GM,SK) or (GL,SK) instead of MACRF=(GM) or (GL). If SETL is not going to be used, sequential retrieval will begin at the first record in the data set and proceed from there as in QSAM processing.
4. When updating records in UPDAT mode, locate mode buffering must be used, but PU rather than PL is coded in the MACRF parameter and use of the SETL macro must be indicated: MACRF=(GL,PU) or (GL,SK,PU).

See Section 21.3 for further details of QISAM.

BISAM

The OS basic indexed sequential access method (BISAM) cannot be used to create an indexed sequential data set, but it can be, and frequently is, used to update or retrieve records. (The use of BISAM corresponds to the clause "access is random" in IBM COBOL, whereas the use of QISAM corresponds to "access is sequential.")

When updating an indexed sequential data set using BISAM, new records may be added or inserted and existing records may be changed or deleted. Deletion is accomplished by the same delete-flag method used in QISAM. However, when using BISAM, it is important to be aware that records that are flagged for deletion—whether by QISAM or by BISAM—may still physically be in the data set. (The reason for this, which has to do with the way the Operating System processes such records, will be discussed in the next section when the concept of prime and overflow areas is described.) Unlike QISAM, the BISAM READ macro ignores the delete flag; it will retrieve a logical record whether it has been flagged for deletion or not, provided it is still physically in the data set. On the other hand, a record flagged for deletion will be physically replaced when BISAM is used to write a new record with the same key as the flagged record. Thus, there will never be two records with the same key in the data set.

Remember that the use of the READ or WRITE macros requires that the user program perform certain buffer related functions. For BISAM, these include I/O synchronization via the CHECK or WAIT macros, buffer allocation via direct or dynamic buffering, and I/O error processing. The principal I/O error that must be processed is known as an *invalid key* condition. An invalid key during a READ would occur if there were no record in the data set corresponding to the record key designated in the READ macro. An invalid key during a WRITE would occur if there were already a record in the data set corresponding to the designated record key when an attempt was being made to write a new record. These conditions can be detected by examining certain control bits in the data event control block after a CHECK or WAIT macro has been invoked.

In addition to these considerations, there are two other points to be noted:

1. The OPEN macro is not used to designate the processing mode when using BISAM. We simply write

OPEN   (dcb-address)

and specify the processing mode via the MACRF parameter.

2. Certain DCB parameters are never specified when using BISAM; among these are BLKSIZE, LRECL, RECFM, KEYLEN, and RKP. The values of these parameters are specified only when an indexed sequential data set is created. Thereafter, they are obtained from the data set control block at open time.

Further details of BISAM will be discussed in Section 21.5.

ISAM

As mentioned earlier, both sequential-mode processing and random-mode processing are accomplished by the same access method, ISAM, in DOS systems. The main differences between the two modes are designated in the DTFIS macro.

To *create* an indexed sequential file in DOS, we must use the WRITE macro with IOAREAL= buffer area and specify IOROUT=LOAD in the DTFIS macro. In addition, we must follow the OPEN macro with a SETFL (Set File Load-Mode) macro and precede the CLOSE macro with an ENDFL (End SETFL) macro. Records must be written in ascending key sequence.

To *extend* an indexed sequential file, i.e., to add records in ascending key sequence beyond the previous last record of the file, we use the same procedures and parameters as when creating the file. The difference between creating and extending is not indicated in the user's program; instead, it is specified in the // DLBL job control statement via a code (ISC or ISE) following the expiration date field, as follows (see also fig. 19.8b):

to create a file: // DLBL dtfname,'filename',date,ISC,...
to extend a file: // DLBL dtfname,'filename',date,ISE,...

To *update* an indexed sequential file, we can use either sequential-mode processing or random-mode processing. In sequential mode, we can choose between updating in place and the general updating procedures. Updating in place is restricted to changing data field contents (but not the key field), and is specified via IOROUT=ADDRTR and TYPEFLE=SEQNTL in the DTFIS macro. It uses the GET macro to retrieve a record and the PUT macro to rewrite a record that has been retrieved. Generalized updating permits all possible changes to a record (except that once again we cannot change the key field), requires that the file to be updated be opened for retrieval (IOROUT=RETRVE), and a new file—the updated file—created as described above. The only way to change a key field in a record is to delete that record and add a new record with the correct key field.

To update in *random mode*, generalized updating is permitted by specifying IOROUT=ADDRTR and TYPEFLE=RANDOM. In this mode, records can be updated in place, and new records can be inserted in their proper key-sequenced position without having to create a new file. However, there is no provision for deleting records in random mode (and none when updating in place in sequential mode). In particular, the delete-flag mechanism of OS does not exist in DOS. The only way to delete a record is via the generalized sequential-mode procedures (i.e., by not copying an input record to the output file), or via a mock delete-flag mechanism which you must program yourself.

In addition to the above considerations, there are several other points to be noted:

1. The logical record format must be either fixed-blocked or fixed-unblocked (RECFORM=FIXBLK or =FIXUNB).

2. When loading or adding new records onto a file, the buffer must include a count area and a key area, as was depicted in figure 19.15b.

Figure 21.1a *Requesting and arranging space for an indexed sequential data set in OS systems.*

DD statements	arrangement of areas	explanation

```
//ddname DD DSNAME=dsname,DISP=(NEW,KEEP),
//          SPACE=(CYL,(p),,CONTIG),DCB=(DSORG=IS),...
```
prime area = p cylinders with index at its end; partially used index cylinders used for independent overflow.

```
//ddname DD DSNAME=dsname,DISP=(NEW,KEEP),
//          SPACE=(CYL,(p,,x),,CONTIG),DCB=DSORG=IS,...
```
prime area = p cylinders with x cylinders as embedded index; partially used index cylinders are independent overflow areas.

```
//ddname DD DSNAME=dsname(PRIME),DISP=(NEW,KEEP),
//          SPACE=(CYL,(p),,CONTIG),DCB=DSORG=IS,...
//       DD DSNAME=dsname(OVFLOW),DISP=(NEW,KEEP),
//          SPACE=(CYL,(w),,CONTIG),DCB=*.ddname,...
```
prime area = p cylinders; independent overflow areas = w cylinders, with index at its end.

```
//ddname DD DSNAME=dsname(PRIME),DISP=(NEW,KEEP),
//          SPACE=(CYL,(p,,x),,CONTIG),DCB=DSORG=IS,...
//       DD DSNAME=dsname(OVFLOW),DISP=(NEW,KEEP),
//          SPACE=(CYL,(w),,CONTIG),DCB=*.ddname,...
```
prime area = p cylinders with x cylinders as embedded index; independent overflow area = w cylinders.

```
//ddname DD DSNAME=dsname(INDEX),DISP=(NEW,KEEP),
//          SPACE=(CYL,(x),,CONTIG),DCB=DSORG=IS,...
//       DD DSNAME=dsname(PRIME),DISP=(NEW,KEEP),
//          SPACE=(CYL,(p),,CONTIG),DCB=*.ddname,...
```
prime area = p cylinders; index area = x cylinders, with partially used index cylinders used as independent overflow area.

```
//ddname DD DSNAME=dsname(INDEX),DISP=(NEW,KEEP),
//          SPACE=(CYL,(x),,CONTIG),DCB=DSORG=IS,...
//       DD DSNAME=dsname(PRIME),DISP=(NEW,KEEP),
//          SPACE=(CYL,(p),,CONTIG),DCB=*.ddname,...
//       DD DSNAME=dsname(OVFLOW),DISP=(NEW,KEEP),
//          SPACE=(CYL,(w),,CONTIG),DCB=*.ddname,...
```
prime area = p cylinders; index area = x cylinders; independent overflow area = w cylinders.

Figure 21.1b *Requesting space for an indexed sequential data set in DOS systems.*

Note: The statements below must be given in the sequence shown here. (See also fig. 19.8b)

```
// DLBL dtfname,'filename',date,ISC
// EXTENT ,,4,0,a,n  — optional master index area
// EXTENT ,,4,1,b,r  — required cylinder index area
// EXTENT ,,1,2,c,s  — required prime data area
// EXTENT ,,2,3,d,t  — optional independent overflow area
```

extent type ——————

extent seq# ——————

relative track number where space allocation begins

number of consecutive tracks in the space allocation

The areas a thru a+n, b thru b+r, c thru c+s, and d thru d+t must not contain any tracks in common with one another.

3. When retrieving or updating an existing record the buffer must be 10 bytes longer than the length of a record in order to accommodate the sequence-link field used in overflow records. This was also depicted in figure 19.15b and will be discussed further in the next section.

4. The SETL (Set Location) and ESETL (End SETL) macros can be used to skip to any desired position in an indexed sequential file before processing subsequent records sequentially.

21.2 SPACE ALLOCATION

Secondary memory space for an indexed sequential data set is generally allocated in three distinct areas: the prime data area, the independent overflow area, and the cylinder index area.

In OS systems, there are a number of ways in which the allocated space can be arranged. These depend on the manner in which the SPACE= parameter of the DD statement is coded, as shown in figure 21.1a. In DOS systems, there is essentially only one way in which the space can be arranged, and this is done by // EXTENT statements as shown in figure 21.1b.

In addition to the prime, overflow, and index areas just mentioned, there are two other areas (both optional) which can be allocated. Of the two the most frequently used is the cylinder overflow area. This area occupies tracks within each cylinder of the prime data area and is allocated through the CYLOFL= parameter of the DCB or DTFIS macro. The other area is the master index area, which is allocated only for exceptionally large files. In OS it is requested by the OPTCD= and NTM= parameters of the DCB macro, and in DOS by the MSTIND=YES parameter of the DTFIS macro together with an // EXTENT statement.

The *prime data area* contains blocks written at the time the data set was created. The data blocks in this area are stored in ascending sequence, sequenced by the highest key of the logical records in each block. The logical records within each data block are also in ascending key sequence. In addition to containing records written by a user program, each cylinder of the prime data area contains a track index written and maintained by the Operating System. The track index contains one pair of entries for each prime data track in the cylinder. Each pair of index entries contains four items: (1) the address of the prime data track to which it refers, (2) the key of the highest record in that track, (3) the address of the lowest overflow record associated with that track, and (4) the key of the highest overflow record associated with that track. These entries are used by the Operating System to determine the track on which a given logical record is or should be stored. The format of the track-index entries is depicted in figure 21.2.

The *independent* and *cylinder overflow areas* are used to contain logical records forced off prime data area tracks when new records are inserted in ascending sequence. The process is illustrated in figure 21.3. Note that when a record flagged for deletion is forced off a prime data track, it is not moved to the overflow area; instead, it is discarded. This is the only way that such records can be physically removed from the data set without recreating the data set. Note also that records in the overflow area are unblocked and are not stored in key sequence; they are stored in the sequence in which they are placed there. The intended processing sequence is maintained in a next-record-address field (sequence link) that is prefixed to each logical record, as shown in figure 21.3. Thus, overflow track space is used inefficiently, both for storage and for searching. The inefficiencies can be eliminated only by recreating the data set, for example, by opening it for sequential input and copying it to a new data set. This process is known as *reorganizing* the data set: in the new data set all records will be blocked and in sequence in the prime data area, and the overflow areas will be empty.

The *index area* of an indexed sequential data set contains a cylinder index and the optional master index. It does not contain the track indexes, which as we have seen, are part of the prime data area. There is only one cylinder index for the data set. Each entry in the cylinder index is associated with one of the cylinders of the prime data area. An entry contains the address of the track index in that prime cylinder and the highest key that is stored in that track index. Cylinder index entries are used by the Operating System to determine the prime data cylinder on which a logical record is, or should be, stored. Once this has been determined, the track index in that prime cylinder is searched to determine the address of the record; this search hierarchy is depicted in figure 21.4. The master index shown in the figure is optional and is used only with large data sets, e.g., those requiring at least 40 cylinders of prime area on an IBM 3330. Each entry in the master index contains the address of a track in the cylinder index together with the highest key stored in that cylinder-index track. Thus, the master index adds another level to the search hierarchy.

To visualize the concepts of prime, index, and overflow areas, it may be helpful to consider the following analogy. Suppose that a multivolume set of encyclopedia is like an indexed sequential data set; the articles in the encyclopedia are data blocks, the pages are tracks, and the volumes are cylinders. If this is the case, the titles printed at the beginning of each article are keys; the set of all keys printed at the top of each page

Figure 21.2 *Record formats in prime data area.*

in a volume together with the page number for each key may be thought of as an index to that volume (a "track" index); and the set of all keys printed on the volume bindings together with the volume numbers may be thought of as a cylinder index.

If we want to find an article, we look first at the cylinder index to find the correct cylinder (i.e., the volume in which the article appears), then at the track index (the titles at the top of each page), and finally at the article titles (the keys) printed at the beginning of each article on the page. If we were the publishers and wanted to add an article to the encyclopedia, we would either have to reprint the volumes in order to maintain alphabetical sequence of articles or we could publish a supplementary volume or volumes. A single supplementary volume containing all new articles would correspond to an independent overflow area; a supplement to each existing volume would correspond to a cylinder overflow area. (The existing volumes themselves correspond to the prime data area.) When the supplements had gotten reasonably fat, we would reprint the encyclopedia, putting everything in its proper sequential position, thereby eliminating the supplements. This corresponds to the process of reorganization of an indexed sequential data set. Finally, we may note that if we had a very large number of volumes, stored in several rooms of a library, we might want to create a short document giving the identity of the highest volume in each room. This corresponds to the master index.

The problem of determining how many cylinders to allocate for an indexed sequential data set can now be seen to depend on how much space is required for each of the following: prime area data blocks, prime area track indexes, prime area cylinder overflow records, index area master and cylinder index entries, and independent overflow records. Since all the data in these various areas is stored in count-key-data format, we should use the information that was given in figure 18.9 for the IBM 3330 disk system (or similar data for whatever storage device is being used). Alternatively, we can use the track-capacity formulas from which

Figure 21.3 Adding records to an indexed sequential data set.

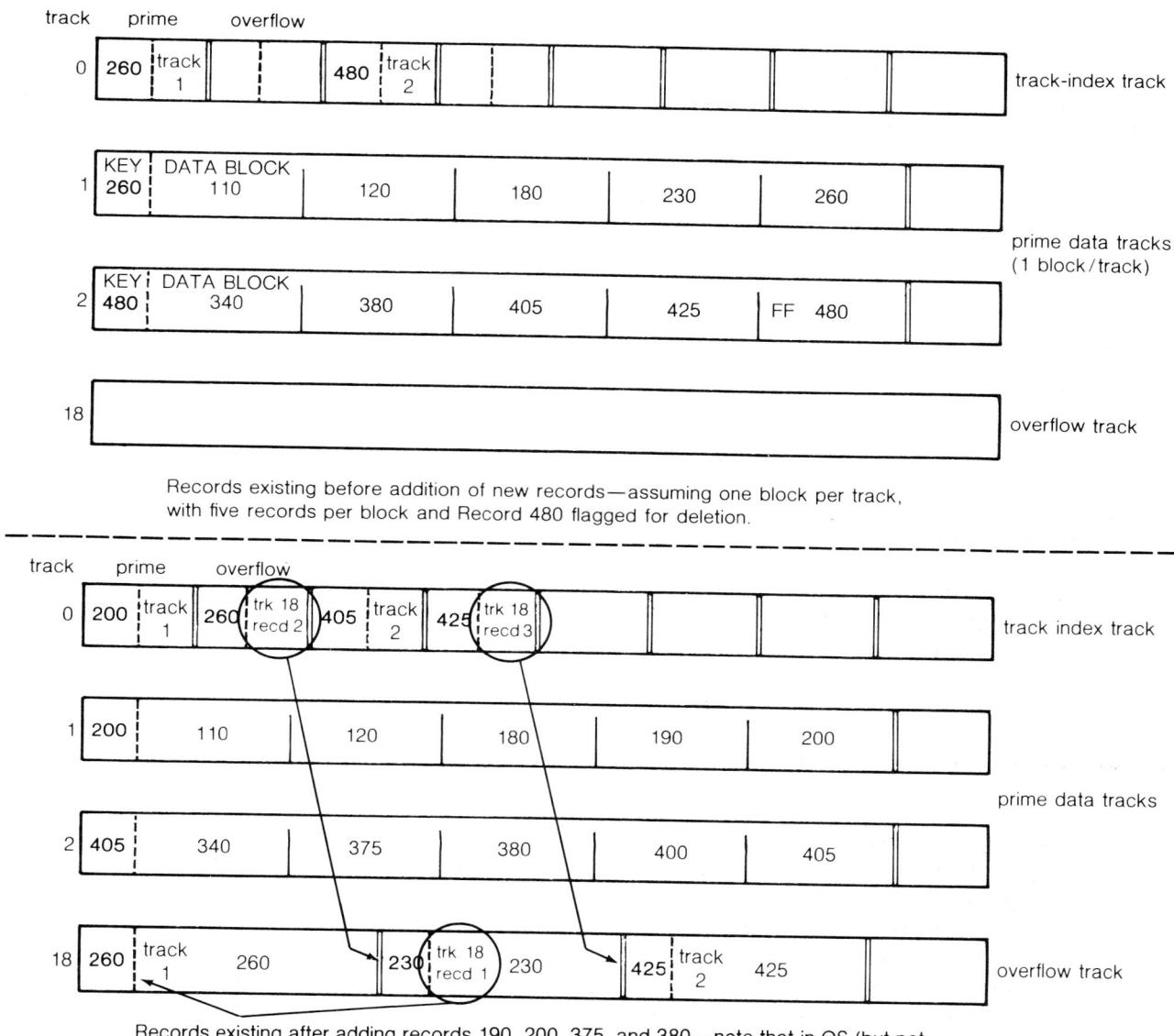

Records existing before addition of new records—assuming one block per track, with five records per block and Record 480 flagged for deletion.

Records existing after adding records 190, 200, 375, and 380—note that in OS (but not DOS) Record 480 was discarded since records flagged for deletion are not moved to the overflow area.

those data are derived, since the formulas allow us to consider various key-lengths and data block lengths more easily. For the IBM 3330 system, the track capacity formula is[1]

$$\left\{ \begin{array}{c} \text{number of blocks} \\ \text{per track} \end{array} \right\} = \frac{13165}{191 + \text{KL} + \text{DL}}$$

1. The numerical factors in this formula include allowances for the home address, the various gap spaces, and other overhead considerations. Capacity formulas for other IBM direct access devices can be found in *OS/VSI Data Management Services Guide,* IBM Publication GC26–3874, in the section on Space Allocation or in *DOS/VS Data Management Guide,* GC33–5372.

Figure 21.4 *Hierarchy of indexes in indexed sequential data set.*

CYLINDER AND MASTER INDEX ENTRY

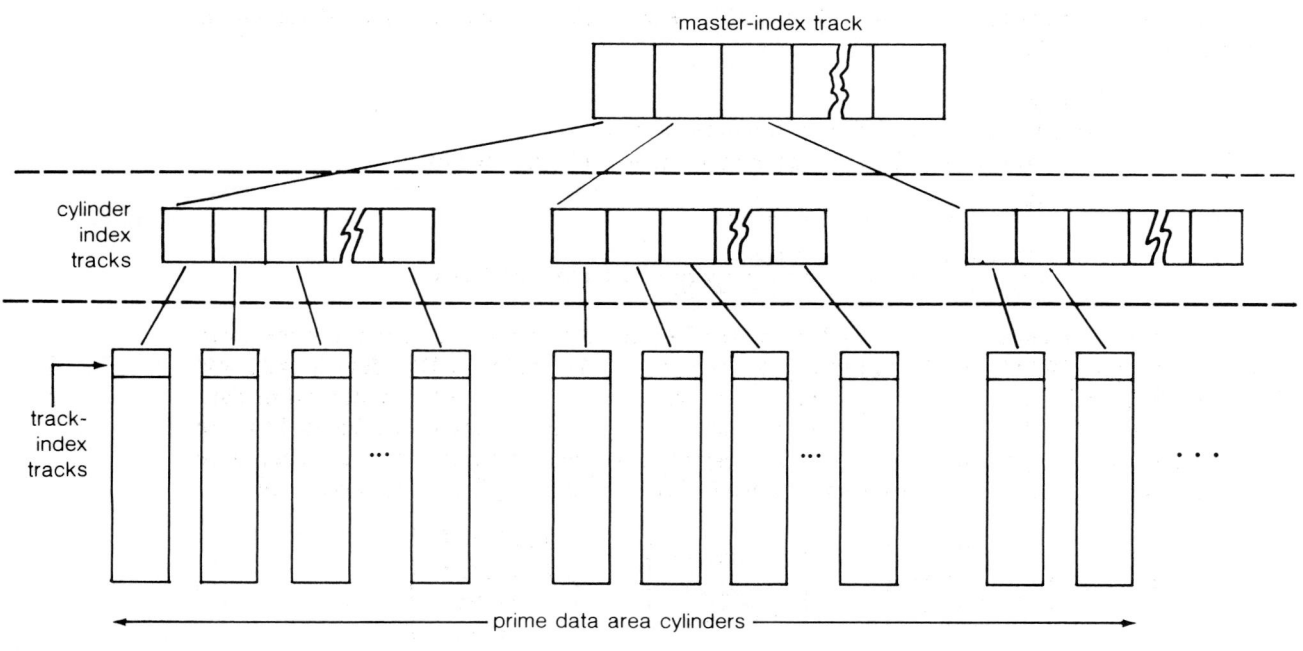

where KL and DL represent the key-length and data block length, respectively. KL is defined by the KEY-LEN= parameter in the DCB or DTFIS macro and is the same for all data in the prime, index, and overflow areas; it is simply the length of the key area in the count-key-data format. The quantity DL depends on whether we are calculating the number of blocks per track in the prime data area, the overflow area, or the track, cylinder, and master indexes. For the prime data area, DL is simply the blocksize. For the overflow areas, DL is 10 plus the logical record length (the factor 10 accounts for the next-record address prefixed to each overflow record; see fig. 21.3). For each of the indexes, DL = 10.

It is fairly easy to obtain an estimate of the amount of space needed for the various indexes. If we assume that key-length KL is less than or equal to 128 bytes (a reasonable assumption), this formula shows that, with DL=10, the number of blocks that can be stored on an index track ranges from 40 for KL=128 to 64 for KL=2. Therefore, since there are only 19 pairs of entries (one pair for each track in a prime data cylinder, or 38 track index entries in each track index), *only one track is needed for each track index.* Similarly, since each track of the cylinder index will account for 40 to 64 prime data area cylinders, a safe estimate is that *only one track of cylinder index is needed for every 10,000,000 bytes of prime data blocks* (remember that, in the IBM 3330 disk system, each cylinder can contain about a quarter of a million bytes). This rationale also shows that a master index is not needed except for unusually large data sets: each track of a master index will account for 40 to 64 tracks of a cylinder index, or 40×40 to 64×64 cylinders of the prime data area. For the IBM 3330 disk system, 1600 cylinders would entail either two or four disk *packs,* depending on whether a Model 11 or a Model 1 pack was being used. It should be stressed that these conclusions are based on the IBM 3330 disk system and the assumption that the key-length does not exceed 128 bytes. For situations other than these, you should make your own calculations.

The remaining task is to determine the amount of space needed for the prime data blocks and for the overflow records. To do this, we must estimate the total size of the data set to be created and estimate the number of overflow records that can be expected to occur. Suppose that the logical record length is denoted by L, the blocksize by B, and the estimated number of logical records in the data set by R. Then, the number of prime data blocks required will be $(L \times R)/B = N$. If the blocksize and key-length permit M blocks per track and if there are P prime data tracks per cylinder, the number of cylinders required for the prime data area will be given by the formula

$$\{\text{number of cylinders for prime data}\} = C = \frac{N}{M \times P} = \frac{L \times R}{B \times M \times P}$$

For example, if the dorm-room master file defined in chapter 20 were to be created as an indexed sequential data set, the calculations would be as follows:

$$L = 106 \text{ bytes per record}$$
$$B = 4028 \text{ bytes per block for fixed-length records}$$
$$R = 5000 \text{ records per data set (estimated number of dorm rooms)}$$
$$N = \frac{L \times R}{B} = 132 \text{ blocks per data set}$$
$$M = \frac{13165}{191 + KL + DL} = \frac{13165}{191 + 8 + 4028} = 3 \text{ blocks per track}$$

In the formula for M, the value chosen for KL, key-length, was 8 bytes, since we would want to use the dorm abbreviation and dorm room (4 bytes each) as the key of each record. The value of DL, data length, was simply the blocksize, B. To calculate the number of cylinders required, we must decide how many prime data tracks are available per cylinder. We have already seen that one of the prime data tracks will be used for the track index. And, as we will suggest below, two of the tracks in each prime data area cylinder should be reserved for cylinder overflow. Therefore, the number of prime data tracks per cylinder, P, is given by

$$P = \left\{ \begin{array}{c} \text{total} \\ \text{number of} \\ \text{tracks per} \\ \text{cylinder} \end{array} \right\} - \left\{ \begin{array}{c} \text{number of} \\ \text{tracks for} \\ \text{track index} \end{array} \right\} - \left\{ \begin{array}{c} \text{number of} \\ \text{tracks for} \\ \text{cylinder} \\ \text{overflow} \end{array} \right\}$$

$$= \{19\} - \{1\} - \{2\}$$
$$= 16 \text{ prime data tracks per IBM 3330 cylinder.}$$

Thus, the number of cylinders required for the dorm-room master file using indexed sequential organization is

$$C = \frac{N}{M \times P} = 3 \text{ cylinders}$$

Since no additional seek-time is required to access a record when it is placed in the cylinder overflow area (the access arm already being positioned at that prime data cylinder), it is good practice to always reserve tracks for cylinder overflow. Independent overflow can also be reserved, should more space be needed. The use of independent overflow has another advantage: in some data sets, the records added after the data set is created are often clustered around some key value. For example, the i.d.'s assigned to new students may be consecutive numbers, the dorm-room numbers in a new dorm will be consecutive, etc. Thus, some cylinders will experience more overflow than others. Rather than reserving more cylinder overflow space—the same number of tracks always being reserved for each cylinder—we should reserve independent overflow space. A common practice is to reserve about 10% of the tracks for cylinder overflow, and, if warranted, about 10% additional space for independent overflow. When these areas are filled (or sooner), the data set should be reorganized.

Dorm-Room Master File in OS

For the dorm-room master file, two tracks for cylinder overflow areas per prime data cylinder and one cylinder for independent overflow area would be ample. If we knew that there was a record for each dorm room in the file and that no new dorms would be built in the near future, no overflow areas would need to be reserved: the Operating System could allocate whatever was needed when it was needed. Thus, when creating the dorm-room master file as an indexed sequential data set, we could code the DD statement as shown below. In both cases, we would also code CYLOFL=2 in the DCB macro. The CYLOFL= parameter must be used to reserve tracks for cylinder overflow; the DD statement SPACE= parameter is not used for this purpose. In addition, we would use the OPTCD= parameter of the DCB macro to designate independent and/or cylinder overflow usage.

1. to request three contiguous cylinders, letting the Operating System subdivide it:

```
//ddname      DD      DSNAME=dsname,DCB=(DSORG=IS),
//                    SPACE=(CYL,(3),,CONTIG),DISP=(NEW,KEEP),...
```

2. to request three contiguous prime area cylinders, and one cylinder for independent overflow:

```
//ddname      DD      DSNAME=dsname(PRIME),DCB=(DSORG=IS),
//                    SPACE=(CYL,(3),,CONTIG),DISP=(NEW,KEEP),...
//            DD      DSNAME=dsname(OVFLOW),DCB=(*.ddname),
//                    SPACE=(CYL,(1)),DISP=(NEW,KEEP),...
```

Dorm-Room Master File in DOS

As in OS, two tracks for cylinder overflow areas per prime data cylinder and one cylinder for independent overflow area is ample. But in DOS, space must be reserved not in units of cylinders but in units of tracks. The IBM 3330 has 19 tracks per cylinder, so it is a simple matter to convert from cylinders back to tracks. The prime and independent overflow areas can be reserved as follows. The cylinder overflow area must be reserved via the CYLOFL= parameter of the DTFIS macro.

```
// DLBL     dtfname,'filename',,ISC
// EXTENT   SYS001,volser#,4,1,190,1     one track for cylinder index
// EXTENT   ,,1,2,133,57                 57 tracks for prime data area
// EXTENT   ,,2,3,209,19                 19 tracks for ind. overflow
```

21.3 CREATING AN INDEXED SEQUENTIAL DATA SET

The processing logic required to create an indexed sequential data set is essentially the same as that for creating a sequential data set, described in Section 20.9 and figures 20.7 and 20.8. However, certain additional parameters must be considered in the DCB and DTFIS macros, and in DOS two additional imperative macros (SETFL and ENDFL) must be executed.

In both OS and DOS, the length and position of the key field must be the same in all logical records of the data set. Moreover, the blocksize must reflect the fact that count-key-data format is used when data blocks are written to the disk storage unit. If we again let DL denote blocksize and KL the key-length, then the track capacity formula for the IBM 3330 disk system in count-key-data format is $13165/(191+KL+DL)$. If we decide that we want three data blocks per track, then from this formula we find the maximum possible blocksize is

$$\begin{aligned} DL &= \frac{13165}{3} - (191 + KL) \\ &= 4388 - 191 - KL \\ &= 4197 - KL \end{aligned}$$

As in sequential data sets, the actual blocksize must be a multiple of the record length for fixed-length records and a multiple of the largest record length, plus 4 bytes for the block descriptor word, when using variable-length records. Before calculating the blocksize for the dorm-room master file, we first discuss the DCB and DTFIS parameters that we will need.

DCB Parameters

Figure 21.5a describes the principal DCB parameters for indexed sequential data sets. The length and position of the key field must be indicated by KEYLEN= and RKP=, respectively. RKP=0 designates the first position in a record. For fixed-length records, RKP can be 0 or greater. For variable-length records, RKP must be 4 or greater, since the record descriptor word occupies bytes 0–3. In either case KEYLEN can be from 1 to 255 bytes. The record length, denoted by LRECL, must include the key-length since the key is

Figure 21.5a *Principal DCB parameters when creating an indexed sequential data set in OS systems.*

parameter	meaning
BLKSIZE=n	blocksize of n bytes, including 4 bytes for the block descriptor word (if any)
CYLOFL=c	c tracks in each prime data cylinder are to be used as cylinder overflow area (see OPTCD=Y below)
DDNAME=ddname	identifies the DD statement that describes the data set
DSORG=IS	specifies that organization is indexed sequential
KEYLEN=k	k bytes is the length of the key field in each logical record (see RKP below)
LRECL=m	m bytes in each logical record, if RECFM=FB; if RECFM=VB, $m = 4 + \{$maximum record length$\}$
MACRF=$\left\{\begin{matrix}\text{(PM)}\\\text{(PL)}\end{matrix}\right\}$	(PM) for PUT macro in move mode, (PL) for PUT macro in locate mode
NTM=t	if the cylinder index requires more than t tracks, then a master index will be created provided that OPTCD=M is specified; if after it is created the master index requires more than t tracks, then a higher level master index will be created; if the higher level requires more than t tracks, then a still higher level master index will be created, but no more than three levels are created.
OPTCD=...	OPTCD=I specifies that independent overflow area is to be used; OPTCD=L, that the delete flag option will be used; OPTCD=M, that a master index is to be created; OPTCD=Y, that cylinder overflow areas are to be used.
RECFM=$\left\{\begin{matrix}\text{FB}\\\text{VB}\end{matrix}\right\}$	FB for blocked fixed-length records, VB for blocked variable-length records
RKP=p	p is the relative position of the first byte in the key field; $p = 0$ designates the first byte position in the record.

NOTE: BLKSIZE, CYLOFL, KEYLEN, LRECL, NTM, OPTCD, RECFM, and RKP *can only be specified when creating an indexed sequential data set. They cannot be specified when updating or retrieving from the data set.*

part of each record; it must include the byte reserved for the delete flag, if any; and if variable-length records are used it must include the 4 bytes reserved for the record descriptor word.

The OPTCD parameter designates certain optional functions that may be requested. The functions are specified by one-letter codes concatenated in any order. The most important of these are I, L, M, and Y.

Note that if OPTCD=I is specified, we must also have requested a space allocation for an independent overflow area in the job control language. If OPTCD=M is specified, we must also use the NTM parameter to define the condition under which a master index is created. If OPTCD=Y is specified, we must also use the CYLOFL parameter to specify the number of tracks to be reserved for cylinder overflow in each prime data area cylinder. And, if OPTCD=L is specified, 1 byte must be reserved for the delete flag in the first position of each fixed-length record and in the fourth position of each variable-length record (i.e., just after the record descriptor word). Moreover, if OPTCD=L is specified, the record key cannot begin in the position used for the delete flag, so that RKP must be 1 or greater for fixed-length records and 5 or greater for variable-length records.

It is generally good practice to specify the delete-flag option unless we know that records are not going to be deleted. For, if OPTCD=L is not specified, the only way to delete a logical record is with the general updating procedures described for sequential files, i.e., the entire data set must be processed in input mode (using QISAM) and a new data set, which does not include the deleted records, would have to be created. Given that the delete-flag option exists, this would be an unnecessarily time-consuming process.

DTFIS Parameters

Figure 21.5b describes the principal DTFIS parameters. The length and position of the key field are given by KEYLEN= and KEYLOC=, respectively. KEYLOC=1 denotes the first position in a record. The key-length can be from 1 to 255 bytes. The record length, denoted by RECSIZE, must include the key-length since the key is part of each record.

There is no parameter for blocksize. Instead, the *blocking factor*, i.e., the number of records per block, is specified by NRECDS=. Thus, blocksize = NRECDS×RECSIZE. Variable-length records are not permitted; either blocked or unblocked fixed-length records must be designated.

To reserve *n* tracks in each prime data area cylinder for the cylinder overflow area, we write CYLOFL=*n*. To indicate that a master index is to be used, we need MSTIND=YES. In addition it is mandatory that the DSKXTNT=*x* parameter specify the total number of extents that are allocated via //EXTENT job control statements. The minimum value of *x* is 2, since there must be at least one prime data extent and one cylinder index extent.

It is also mandatory to specify IOROUT=LOAD and IOAREAL=buffername when creating an indexed sequential file. And, we must specify WORKL=workareaname. Both the buffer and the work area must be reserved via DS directives. The buffer must include space for the count and key fields used in count-key-data format, as was depicted in figure 19.15b. The work area must include space for those count and key fields *only* if the records are *un*blocked.

As mentioned earlier, DOS makes no provision for a delete-flag option. Therefore it is not necessary to reserve a delete-flag byte at the beginning of each logical record. Nevertheless, it is good practice to do so, for two reasons: (1) the file can then be processed in OS systems as well as DOS systems; and (2) the user's program then has an easy-to-use mechanism for marking and recognizing records that are in effect deleted even though they still physically exist in the file.

The Dorm-room Master File in OS Systems

To illustrate these concepts, we will now describe the changes needed to create the dorm-room master file of chapter 20 as an indexed sequential data set. Only a few changes are needed. The record format must be redefined to include the delete-flag byte position, and the DCB macro must be appropriately coded. Figures 21.6a and 21.6b depict the revised record formats. The corresponding logical record area description for the fixed-length format is as shown here:

```
* MASTER FILE RECORD AREA
*
OUTAREA  DS    CL107          RESERVE 107 BYTES FOR THE RECORD
         ORG   OUTAREA        BEGIN REDEFINITION OF RECORD AREA
MDELETE  DC    CL1' '         BYTE 0    DELETE FLAG (INITIALLY BLANK)
MDORM    DS    CL4                1-4   DORM ABBREVIATION
MROOM    DS    CL4                5-8   DORM ROOM
*   NOTE:  BYTES 1-8 CONSTITUTE THE RECORD KEY FIELD
MDATA1   DS    CL49               9-57  1ST STUDENT DATA AREA
MDATA2   DS    CL49               58-106 2ND STUDENT DATA AREA
         ORG
```

This description should be compared to the one given in figure 20.8. The only change is the inclusion of the delete-flag byte position and the corresponding increase in record length from 106 to 107 bytes.

Given this record description, the DCB macro required to create the dorm-room master file as an indexed sequential data set would be written as shown below. The designation OPTCD=ILY assumes that independent overflow may be needed when updating the master file. If not, OPTCD=LY would be sufficient.

```
MASTER  DCB   DSORG=IS,MACRF=(PM),DDNAME=DORMS,                     X
              RECFM=FB,LRECL=107,BLKSIZE=4066,                      X
              KEYLEN=8,RKP=1,CYLOFL=2,OPTCD=ILY
```

The value of BLKSIZE, 4066, is the largest value that is a multiple of 107 (the record length) without being greater than 4096. It accommodates 38 records per block and provides for three blocks per track on the IBM 3330. The track-space utilization is thus $3\times(KL+DL)/13060$, or about 93.8%, in the prime data area. In the overflow areas, however, the track-space utilization is only about 40%, since the overflow records are unblocked 107-byte records.

Figure 21.5b *Principal DTFIS parameters when creating an indexed sequential data set in DOS systems.*

parameter	meaning
CYLOFL=c	c tracks in each prime data cylinder are to be used as cylinder overflow area
DEVICE=device#	device# is the identity assigned by IBM to the unit that contains the *prime data area*. For example, for the IBM 3330 disk system, specify DEVICE=3330
DSKXTNT=x	x extents have been allocated, including all index, overflow, and prime data extents.
HINDEX=device#	device# is the identity assigned by IBM to the unit that contains the *highest level index*. For example, DEVICE—3330 designates the IBM 3330 disk system.
IOAREAL=buffername	name of the I/O buffer area for file creation
KEYLEN=k	k bytes is the length of the key field in each record
KEYLOC=p	p is the relative position of the first byte in the key field; p = 1 designates the first byte position in the record
MSTIND=YES	specifies that a master index is to be used
NRECDS=n	n is the number of records in a data block. If RECFORM=FIXBLK, then n > 1; if RECFORM=FIXUNB, n=1.
RECFORM= $\left\{ \dfrac{\text{FIXBLK}}{\text{FIXUNB}} \right\}$	FIXBLK for blocked fixed-length records FIXUNB for unblocked fixed-length records
RECSIZE=m	m bytes in each logical record, so that blocksize = RECSIZE×NRECDS = m·n
WORKL=workareaname	name of logical record area used for file creation (i.e., move mode is mandatory)

Figure 21.6a *Fixed-length master file record format.*

Figure 21.6b *Variable-length master file record format.*

If these changes are made to the program that was given in figure 20.8, the master file will be created as an indexed sequential data set. No other changes are required in the program. (The DD statements, however, must also be appropriately changed.)

However, it must be stressed that the records written onto the new data set must be in ascending key sequence and no two records can contain the same record key. If the first of these conditions is violated, a "sequence check" error will occur; if the second is violated, a "duplicate record" error condition will occur.

The Dorm-room Master File in DOS Systems

The record area description given above for OS systems is also valid for DOS, provided we decide to use blocked records. That of course is what we will do, since it is a much more efficient way to utilize disk space than unblocked records. The blocksize (4066 bytes) calculated for OS is equally valid for DOS. Given this, plus the fact that we will not use a master index (the file simply not being large enough to warrant that), the DTFIS macro for the dorm-room master file is this:

```
MASTER      DTFIS DSKXTNT=3,IOROUT=LOAD,WORKL=OUTAREA,IOAREAL=MSTBUF,      X
                  RECFORM=FIXBLK,RECSIZE=107,NRECDS=38,HINDEX=3330,        X
                  KEYLEN=8,KEYLOC=2,CYLOFL=2,DEVADDR=SYS001,DEVICE=3330
```

If this DTFIS replaces the DTFSD macro that was used in figure 20.8, and if two other changes are made to the program of figure 20.8, then the master file will be created as an indexed sequential file. (The job control statements must of course also be changed appropriately.) One change that is required in the program of figure 20.8 is the insertion of two macros, SETFL and ENDFL. The SETFL macro establishes that the file is to be processed in "load mode," i.e., for file creation, and must immediately follow the OPEN macro. The ENDFL macro simply ends the load mode and must immediately precede the CLOSE macro. The formats of the two macros are identical:

opcode	operand
SETFL	dtf-address
ENDFL	dtf-address

The other change that is required in the program of figure 20.8 in order to create an indexed sequential file in DOS is to replace the PUT macro with a WRITE macro. Its format is this:

opcode	operand
WRITE	dtf-address,NEWKEY

The second parameter in the operand must be NEWKEY. Of course, before the WRITE macro is executed the logical record must exist in the work area identified by the WORKL= parameter of DTFIS. The access method moves that record to the buffer specified by IOAREAL= when the WRITE macro is executed.

The above changes to figure 20.8 are left as exercises for you. Note that the records that are written to the indexed sequential data set when creating it must be in ascending key sequence and that no two records can contain the same record key. If the first of these conditions is violated, a "sequence-check" error will occur; if the second is violated, a "duplicate-record" error will occur.

21.4 UPDATING IN SEQUENTIAL MODE

The process of updating an indexed sequential data set in sequential mode includes the same four possible updating actions as those listed in Section 20.10 for sequential data sets:

Action 1: Add records to the end of the data set.
Action 2: Change or delete some of the data in existing records without deleting any records and without changing the length of any records.
Action 3: Insert new records in their proper sequence within the data set, or change the length of one or more existing records by adding new data to them or deleting data from them.
Action 4: Delete one or more existing records from the data set.

Because it requires that the entire data set be recreated, Action 3 is not usually performed sequentially unless there is a substantially large number of new records to be inserted. That is, *new records cannot be inserted into an existing data set using sequential mode.* This is because insertion of new records may require that a record be added to an overflow area, and the sequential processing mode is not designed to do this. Instead, random-mode processing must be used. However, sequential-mode processing can be used for Actions 1, 2, and 4.

Sequential Mode in OS Systems

To add records to the end of an indexed sequential data set (Action 1), the processing logic required is almost identical to that used for creating such data sets. There are only two differences: (1) the data set must be opened in EXTEND mode rather than OUTPUT mode and (2) DISP=(MOD,KEEP) must be coded on the DD statement rather than DISP=(NEW,KEEP). The records that are added must be in ascending key sequence and must all have a key that is greater than the highest key in the existing data set. If either condition is violated, a "sequence check" error or a "duplicate record" error will occur. Note that it is prime data area space that is used for the added records, not overflow space. Therefore, if not enough prime space was initially allocated to anticipate the addition of records in EXTEND mode, a "space not found" error condition would occur. To utilize the overflow areas, we would have to add new records in random mode.

For Action 2, the data set is opened without specifying the processing mode in the OPEN macro. Instead, the MACRF parameter is used to indicate that updating is to be performed:

```
        OPEN    (MASTER)
                  .
                  .
                  .
MASTER  DCB     DSORG=IS,MACRF=(GL,PU),DDNAME=DORMS,EODAD=EOJ
```

Note that we must provide for an end-of-data routine, since the data set is to be read sequentially. We must also use PUTX to rewrite records that are being updated and locate mode buffering; PUT cannot be used, and neither can move mode. The processing logic is the same as that depicted in figure 20.10.

If the OS delete-flag option is specified (OPTCD=L), Action 4 can be combined with Action 2. To delete a record, we must move X'FF' into the delete-flag byte position *and rewrite the record*. Otherwise, the processing logic is again the same as that depicted in figure 20.10.

Sequential Mode in DOS Systems

To add records to the end of an indexed sequential data set (Action 1), the processing logic is identical to that used for creating such data sets. There is no difference between a DOS assembly language program that creates an indexed sequential data set and one that extends it. The difference is in the job control statements, specifically in the //DLBL statement, as was described in Section 21.1: To create such a data set we must code ISC in the appropriate //DLBL field; to extend or otherwise update such a data set, we must code ISE in that field.

For Action 2 (updating existing records), there are a number of differences to be aware of. They are almost all confined to the DTFIS macro, as shown below. But in addition, the imperative macros SETFL and ENDFL are not used for updating, and the PUT macro rather than the WRITE macro is used for rewriting an updated record.

The DTFIS macro must be coded as follows for sequential-mode updating:

```
MASTER   DTFIS DSKXTNT=3,IOROUT=ADDRTR,WORKS=OUTAREA,IOAREAS=MSTBUF,   X
               RECFORM=FIXBLK,RECSIZE=107,NRECDS=38,HINDEX=3330,        X
               KEYLEN=8,KEYLOC=2,CYLOFL=2,DEVADDR=SYS001,DEVICE=3330,   X
               TYPEFLE=INPUT,EOFADDR=EOJ
```

In this, we have used the dorm-room file definitions for concreteness. But what is important to note is the inclusion of the TYPEFLE=INPUT parameter, the replacement of IOROUT=LOAD with IOROUT=ADDRTR, and the change from WORKL= to WORKS= and IOAREAL= to IOAREAS=. These changes constitute the mechanism by which the DOS access method is informed that sequential-mode updating is to take place, regardless of whether it's the dorm-room file or any other indexed sequential file.

Finally, it should be noted that Action 4 (deleting existing records) is not supported by DOS access methods. This is because there is no delete-flag option as there is in OS and no other mechanism other than user-program awareness. In other words, a user program can of course put X'FF' into the first byte of a record to flag it for deletion as is done in OS systems, and this is recommended. But any DOS assembly language program which reads that record will have to recognize the X'FF' code and ignore the record.

The SETL Macro in OS and DOS

The speed of the updating process for Actions 2 and 4 can be increased by use of SETL and ESETL, provided these macros are not executed too frequently. SETL enables updating to take place in any arbitrary data block without having to read preceding blocks in sequence. As mentioned in chapter 19, one advantage of sequential access methods is that of being able to use two buffers: one to contain the logical records being processed and the other to allow the next data block to be read or the previous one written while processing of logical records takes place. Too frequent use of SETL and ESETL can negate this advantage. Each execution of SETL may require access to the cylinder and track indexes, and each execution of ESETL may cause the most recently changed data block to be rewritten even if the next transaction is for a record in that same block. One compromise is to use SETL once, at the beginning of execution, and then process the remaining records sequentially.

The format of the ESETL macro is simply

in OS:	ESETL	dcb-address
in DOS:	ESETL	dtf-address

The format of the SETL macro is

in OS:	SETL	dcb-address,option-code,key-address
in DOS:	SETL	dtf-address,option-code

The *key-address* field in the OS SETL macro designates the location of the key field that is to be used to identify the record at which sequential updating is to begin. In DOS, this key-address is specified by the KEYARG= parameter in the DTFIS macro instead of in the SETL macro. The option-code parameter indicates whether the key-address points to a complete record key or to a partial record key, i.e., a *key class,* also known as a *generic* key. It can also be used to indicate that retrieval is to begin at the first non-deleted record in the data set; in the latter case, the key-address parameter is omitted. The codes and their meanings are

DOS option code	OS option code	meaning
KEY	K	start retrieval at the first non-deleted record whose key matches the key given at key-address
---	KH	start retrieval at the first non-deleted record whose key is equal to or greater than the key given at key-address
GKEY	KC	start retrieval at the first non-deleted record whose key class is equal to or greater than the key class given at key-address
BOF	B	start retrieval at the first non-deleted record in the data set

(By *non-deleted record* we mean a record whose delete-flag byte position does not contain X'FF'. However, if using DOS, or if the delete option was not selected when the OS data set was created, all records are considered to be non-deleted.)

The concept of a *key class* can be very useful. A key class is defined by specifying the first n characters of a key, $1 \le n \le$ KEYLEN, and setting the remaining characters to *binary* zeroes. For example, in our dorm-room file, a 4-byte dorm abbreviation could constitute a key class within the 8-byte record key. It could be specified as shown here:

```
        MVC      KEYCLASS,=8X'00'
        GET      TRANS,INAREA
        MVC      KEYCLASS(4),TDORM
        SETL     MASTER,KC,KEYCLASS       OS ONLY
        SETL     MASTER,GKEY              DOS ONLY
        GET      MASTER
         .
         .
         .
KEYCLASS DS      CL8                      8 BYTES NEEDED SINCE KEYLEN=8
```

In OS, the DCB macro indicates that SETL processing is to be used, by the way in which the MACRF= parameter is coded: MACRF=(GL,SK,PU). Otherwise, the DCB is coded the same as for other sequential-mode updating.

In DOS, the DTFIS macro doesn't specifically indicate that SETL processing is to be used, but the KEYARG= parameter must designate the name of the field that will contain the search key when SETL is executed: KEYARG=KEYCLASS in the above example. Given this procedure, if the 4-byte dorm abbreviation in the TDORM field were C'HH   ', processing would begin with the first non-deleted record whose 8-byte key was C'HH   xxxx' or higher, regardless of the value of the room number xxxx.

There is, however, one precaution to observe: *a "record-not-found" error condition will occur if the specified key or key class is higher than any key or key class in the data set, or if there is not a matching key or key class in the data set.*

The processing logic that may be used when updating sequentially in conjunction with the SETL macro is depicted in the diagram of figure 21.7. Except for the inclusion of the SETL step during the initialization procedures, this diagram is identical to that given in figure 20.10 for sequential updating. Thus, as mentioned earlier, SETL is executed only once; thereafter the master file records are processed sequentially. The program of figure 21.8 illustrates how this logic might be applied to the problem of updating the dorm-room master file. As in the preceding chapter, it is assumed that the transaction data are "perfect": no transaction will request that a student be added to a room to which he or she has already been assigned or which is already full, and none will request that a student be deleted from a room to which he or she has not been assigned. In addition, it is assumed that the SETL does not result in a "record-not-found" condition.

21.5 RANDOM-MODE PROCESSING CONSIDERATIONS IN OS SYSTEMS

As mentioned in the opening section of the chapter, BISAM is used for random updating and retrieval of logical records in an existing indexed sequential data set. It cannot be used to create a data set.

We will cover five main aspects of the use of OS macros and buffers: dynamic buffering, the READ and WRITE macro formats, the MACRF parameter, I/O synchronization, and invalid key conditions.

Dynamic Buffering

In dynamic buffering, the Operating System allocates a buffer pool at open time. The DCB macro should include the BUFNO=1 parameter to indicate that only one buffer area is needed in the buffer pool. The Operating System uses this buffer area each time a READ macro is invoked. The user program need not reserve space for the buffer pool or buffer area.

Data blocks are always read into the buffer area and, except in two situations, they are written from the same area. The exceptions occur when a new logical record is to be added to the data set and when the length of an existing variable-length record is to be changed. In both these situations, the user program's WRITE macro must designate the address of an area within the program that contains the logical record to be written.

In the other two possible updating situations—when updating an existing record without changing its length or when deleting an existing record via the delete-flag option—*the record must be changed in the buffer area* and rewritten from that area. This is similar to the use of locate mode in sequential processing. Unlike locate mode, however, the address of the logical record in the buffer area is not returned in Register 1 following a READ macro. Instead, it is stored in the data event control block, as shown in figure 21.9.

READ and WRITE Macros and the MACRF Parameter

When we update an *existing* record in an indexed sequential data set, we must first read the data block containing the desired logical record. The key of that record must be specified by a parameter in a version of the READ macro known as READ KU. After modifying the record, it must be rewritten by a version of the WRITE macro known as WRITE K. When a *new* record is added to the data set, we must use a version of the WRITE macro known as WRITE KN.

The general form of the READ and WRITE macros is as shown below. The *type* parameter is coded as K, KU, or KN to designate the version of the macro being used.

$$\begin{Bmatrix} \text{READ} \\ \text{WRITE} \end{Bmatrix} \text{decb-name,type,dcb-address,buffer-address,buffer-length,key-address,} \begin{Bmatrix} \text{MF=E} \\ \text{MF=L} \end{Bmatrix}$$

Figure 21.7   Overview of sequential-mode updating via SETL.

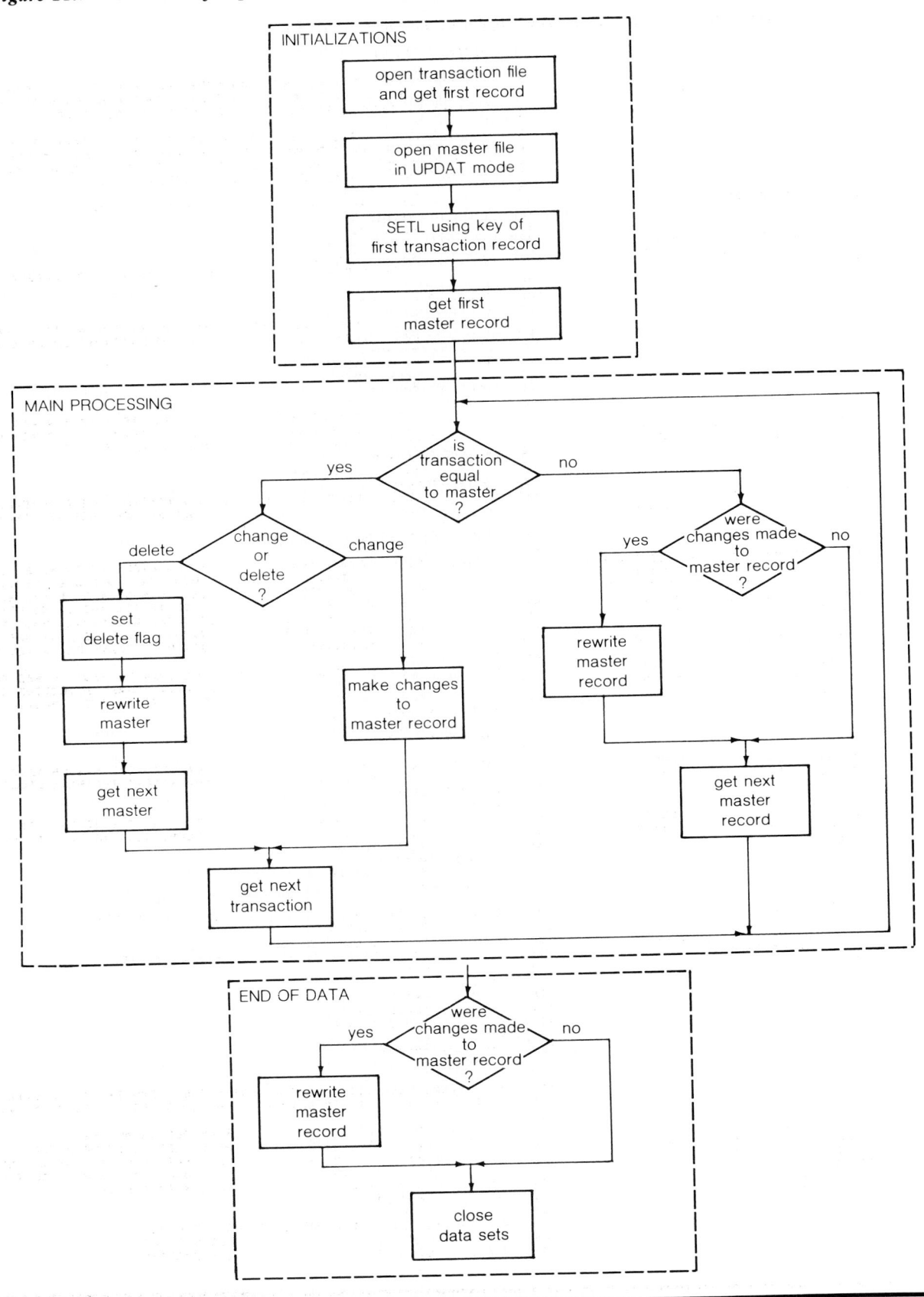

Figure 21.8 Updating the dorm room master file via QISAM and SETL.

```
FLAG LOCTN OBJECT CODE       ADDR1  ADDR2  STMNT M SOURCE STATEMENT

       000000                               3    QISAM    CSECT
                                            4    *
                                            5    * THIS PROGRAM UPDATES THE DORM ROOM MASTER FILE USING QISAM IN
                                            6    *   LOCATE MODE.  TRANSACTIONS ARE IN SEQUENCE BY DORM AND ROOM
                                            7    *   NUMBER, CORRESPONDING TO MASTER FILE KEY SEQUENCE.
                                            8    *
                                            9    * THE FIRST TRANSACTION'S KEY IS USED TO START RETRIEVAL VIA SETL
                                           10    *   MACRO.  THEREAFTER PROCESSING IS DONE AS IN SEQTL FILES, EXCEPT
                                           11    *   THAT RECORDS MAY BE DELETED VIA DELETE FLAG OPTION (OPTCD=L) ES-
                                           12    *   TABLISHED WHEN MASTER FILE WAS CREATED.
                                           13    *
   000000 90 EC D00C                       14             STM    14,12,12(13)      STANDARD ENTRY.
   000004 05 C0                            15             BALR   12,0
   000006                                  16             USING  *,12
   000006 50 D0 C32A          000330       17             ST     13,SAVE+4
   00000A 41 D0 C326          00032C       18             LA     13,SAVE
   000000                                  19             USING  MAREA,11          DUMMY BASE REG FOR LOGICAL RECD
                                           20    *
                                           21    * INITIALIZATIONS
                                           22    *
   00000E                                  23             OPEN   (MASTER,(UPDAT))   OPEN MASTER FOR UPDAT IN LOCATE MODE
   00001A                                  29             OPEN   (TRANS,(INPUT))    OPEN TRANSACTIONS IN MOVE MODE
                                           35    *  DOS  *******
                                           36    *        OPEN   MASTER
                                           37    *        OPEN   TRANS
                                           38    ***************
   000026                                  39             GET    TRANS,TAREA       GET FIRST TRANSACTION RECORD
   000034 D2 03 C19EC155 0001A4 00015B     44             MVC    KDORM,TDORM       MOVE 1ST TRANS KEY TO KEY AREA FOR
   00003A D2 03 C1A2C15D 0001A8 000163     45             MVC    KROOM,TROOM        USE IN 'SETL' MACRO
                                           46    *  DOS  *******
                                           47    *        SETL   MASTER,GKEY
                                           48    ***************
   000040                                  49             SETL   MASTER,K,KAREA    START MASTER FILE RETRIEVAL AT RECD
   000058 45 E0 C0D2          0000D8       57             BAL    14,GETMSTR         WHOSE KEY MATCHES 1ST TRANS KEY.
                                           58    *
                                           59    * MAIN PROCESSING
                                           60    *
   00005C D5 03 B001C155 000001 00015B     61    MAINLOOP CLC    MDORM,TDORM       IF KEY FIELD IN TRANS RECD DIFFERS
   000062 47 70 C080          000086       62             BNE    REWRITE            FROM THAT IN MASTER RECD, THEN GO
   000066 D5 03 B005C15D 000005 000163     63             CLC    MROOM,TROOM        SEE IF MASTER RECD HAS HAD CHANGES
   00006C 47 70 C080          000086       64             BNE    REWRITE            MADE TO IT, AND IF SO REWRITE IT.
   000070 45 E0 C0E8          0000EE       65             BAL    14,UPDATING        IF TRANS KEY EQUALS MASTER KEY, CON-
   000074                                  66             GET    TRANS,TAREA        TINUE TO UPDATE THAT MASTER RECD,
   000082 47 F0 C056          00005C       71             B      MAINLOOP           GET NEXT TRANS RECD, AND REPEAT.
                                           72    *
   000086 95 FF C1D7          0001DD       73    REWRITE  CLI    MFLAG,BYP         WERE CHANGES MADE TO MASTER RECD
   00008A 47 80 C094          00009A       74             BE     BYPASS             IF NOT, BYPASS REWRITING IT.
   00008E                                  75             PUTX   MASTER             IF SO, REWRITE IT (UPDATE IN PLACE).
                                           79    *  DOS  *******
                                           80    *        PUT    MASTER
                                           81    ***************
   00009A 45 E0 C0D2          0000D8       82    BYPASS   BAL    14,GETMSTR        THEN GET NEXT MASTER RECD,
   00009E 47 F0 C056          00005C       83             B      MAINLOOP          AND REPEAT THE MAIN PROCESSING LOOP.
                                           84    * END-OF-DATA
                                           85    *
   0000A2 95 FF C1D7          0001DD       86    EOJ      CLI    MFLAG,BYP         IF CHANGES WERE MADE TO MASTER
   0000A6 47 80 C0B2          0000B8       87             BE     EOJX               RECD, REWRITE IT VIA 'PUTX'.
   0000AA                                  88             PUTX   MASTER
                                           92    *  DOS  *******
                                           93    *        PUT    MASTER
                                           94    ***************
   0000B6                                  95    EOJX     CLOSE  (TRANS)           CLOSE DATA SETS
   0000C2                                 101             CLOSE  (MASTER)
   0000CE 58 D0 C32A          000330      107             L      13,SAVE+4
   0000D2 98 EC D00C                      108             LM     14,12,12(13)      STANDARD EXIT
   0000D6 07 FE                           109             BR     14
                                          110    *  DOS  *******
                                          111    *EOJX     CLOSE  TRANS
                                          112    *         CLOSE  MASTER
                                          113    *         EOJ
                                          114    ***************
                                          115    * INTERNAL SUBROUTINE TO GET NEXT MASTER RECD IN LOCATE MODE.
                                          116    *   ENTERED VIA  BAL 14,GETMSTR . RETURNS ADDR OF RECD IN  R11 .
                                          117    *
   0000D8 18 2E                           118    GETMSTR  LR     2,14              SAVE RETURN ADDRESS
   0000DA 92 FF C1D7          0001DD      119             MVI    MFLAG,BYP         RESET RECORD-CHANGED FLAG.
   0000DE                                 120             GET    MASTER            GET ADDR OF NEXT LOGICAL RECD IN R1.
   0000E8 18 B1                           124             LR     11,REGX           COPY ADR INTO DUMMY BASE REG, R11.
   0000EA 18 E2                           125             LR     14,2              RETURN TO CALLER.
   0000EC 07 FE                           126             BR     14
                                          127    *
                                          128    * SYMBOLIC REGISTER ADDRESS FOR LOCATE MODE
   000001                                 129    REGX     EQU    1                 OS SYSTEMS
                                          130    *REGX     EQU    9                 DOS SYSTEMS
```

Figure 21.8 continued

```
FLAG LOCTN OBJECT CODE     ADDR1  ADDR2  STMNT M SOURCE STATEMENT

                                          131  * INTERNAL SUBROUTINE TO UPDATE AN EXISTING MASTER RECD.
                                          132  *    ENTERED VIA BAL 14,UPDATING  WITH ADDR OF MASTER RECD IN R11.
                                          133  *
                                          134  * TRANSACTION CODE 'TTYPE' DETERMINES UPDATING ACTION
                                          135  *    TTYPE = C'1' ... ADD A NEW ROOM WITH NO STUDENTS
                                          136  *          = C'2' ... ADD A STUDENT NAME & I.D.
                                          137  *          = C'3' ... DELETE A STUDENT NAME & I.D.
                                          138  *          = C'4' ... DELETE ENTIRE MASTER RECD.
                                          139  *
000EE 95 F4 C151           000157          140  UPDATING CLI    TTYPE,C'4'      DETERMINE WHETHER IT'S A DELETE OR A
0000F2 47 70 C10A          000110          141           BNE    CHANGE          CHANGE REQUEST.
0000F6 18 4E                               142           LR     4,14            IF DELETE, SAVE R14 TO ALLOW 'PUTX'
0000F8 92 FF B000          000000          143           MVI    MDELETE,X'FF'   TO REWRITE THE RECD, AFTER FLAGGING
0000FC                                     144           PUTX   MASTER          IT FOR DELETION.
                                          148  *  DOS *******
                                          149  *         PUT    MASTER
                                          150  ***************
000108 45 E0 C0D2          000008          151           BAL    14,GETMSTR      AFTER REWRITING, GET NEXT MASTER RECORD
00010C 18 E4                               152           LR     14,4            THEN RECOVER R14 AND EXIT TO CALLER.
00010E 07 FE                               153           BR     14
                                          154  *
000110 18 AB                               155  CHANGE   LR     10,11           SAVE LOGICAL RECD ADDR IN REG 10.
000112 95 F2 C151          000157          156           CLI    TTYPE,C'2'      ADD A STUDENT IF TTYPE = '2'
000116 47 80 C12C          000132          157           BE     ADD
00011A D5 08 B031C18B      000031 000191   158  DEL      CLC    MID,TID         OTHERWISE ASSUME IT'S CODE '3' AND LOOK
000120 47 80 C122          000128          159           BE     DEL1            FOR I.D. IN 1ST & 2ND DATA AREAS
000124 41 BB 0031          000031          160           LA     11,DATALNG(11)  IF NOT IN 1ST, MUST BE IN 2ND  INCR ADDR
000128 D2 30 B009C1A6      000009 0001AC   161  DEL1     MVC    MDATA1,BLANKS   REPLACE NAME & I.D. WITH BLANKS WHEN
00012E 47 F0 C146          00014C          162           B      EXIT            DELETING A STUDENT.
000132 D5 08 B031C1A6      000031 0001AC   163  ADD      CLC    MID,BLANKS      WHEN ADDING LOOK FOR VACANT STUDENT DATA
000138 47 80 C13A          000140          164           BE     ADD1            AREA.  IF NOT 1ST ONE, THEN ASSUME THAT
00013C 41 BB 0031          000031          165           LA     11,DATALNG(11)  2ND AREA IS VACANT, AND INCR ADDR.
000140 D2 27 B009C162      000009 000168   166  ADD1     MVC    MNAME,TNAME     MOVE NAME & I.D. FROM TRANS RECD TO STU-
000146 D2 08 B031C18B      000031 000191   167           MVC    MID,TID         DENT DATA AREA.
00014C 92 00 C1D7          0001DD          168  EXIT     MVI    MFLAG,REWR      BEFORE RETURNING, SET RECD-CHGD FLAG AND
000150 18 BA                               169           LR     11,10           RESTORE DUMMY BASE REG CONTENTS.
000152 07 FE                               170           BR     14              EXIT TO CALLER.


                                          171  * MASTER FILE LOGICAL RECORD AREA (VIA DUMMY SECTION)
                                          172  *
000000                                     173  MAREA    DSECT
000000                                     174  MDELETE  DS     CL1      BYTES 0     DELETE FLAG
000001                                     175  MDORM    DS     CL4           1-4    DORM ABBREVIATION
000005                                     176  MROOM    DS     CL4           5-8    DORM ROOM
000009                                     177  MDATA1   DS     CL49          9-57   1ST STUDENT DATA AREA
00003A                                     178  MDATA2   DS     CL49          58-106 2ND STUDENT DATA AREA
000009                           00006B    179           ORG    MDATA1 REDEFINE STUDENT DATA AREA
000009                                     180  MNAME    DS     CL40          9-48   STUDENT NAME FIELD
000031                                     181  MID      DS     CL9           49-57  STUDENT I.D. FIELD
000031                                     182  DATALNG  EQU    *-MNAME              LENGTH OF STUDENT AREA
000154                                     183  QISAM    CSECT
                                          184  *
                                          185  *
                                          186  * TRANSACTION INPUT AREA
                                          187  *
000154                                     188  TAREA    DS     CL80     RESERVE 80 BYTES FOR CARD IMAGE
000154                           0001A4    189           ORG    TAREA    BEGIN REDEFINITION OF INPUT AREA
000154                                     190           DS     CL3      COL 1-3     UNUSED
000157                                     191  TTYPE    DS     CL1           4      TRANS TYPE CODE
000158                                     192           DS     CL3           5-7    UNUSED
00015B                                     193  TDORM    DS     CL4           8-11   DORM ABBREVIATION
00015F                                     194           DS     CL4           12-15  UNUSED
000163                                     195  TROOM    DS     CL4           16-19  DORM ROOM NUMBER
000167                                     196           DS     CL1           20     UNUSED
000168                                     197  TNAME    DS     CL40          21-60  STUDENT NAME
000190                                     198           DS     CL1           61     UNUSED
000191                                     199  TID      DS     CL9           62-70  STUDENT I.D.
0001A4                           00019A    200           ORG
                                          201  * KEY AREA, AND OTHER CONSTANTS
                                          202  *
0001A4                                     203  KAREA    DS     CL8      RESERVE 8 BYTES FOR RECORD KEY
0001A4                           0001AC    204           ORG    KAREA
0001A4                                     205  KDORM    DS     CL4      BYTES 0-3   DORM ABBREVIATION
0001A8                                     206  KROOM    DS     CL4           4-7    DORM ROOM NUMBER
0001AC                           0001AC    207           ORG
                                          208  *
0001AC 40                                  209  BLANKS   DC     (DATALNG)C' ' DATALNG IS LENGTH OF STUDENT DATA AREA
0001DD FF                                  210  MFLAG    DC     X'FF'         X'FF'=DON'T REWRITE;X'00'=DO REWRITE.
0000FF                                     211  BYP      EQU    X'FF'         BYP = RECD NOT CHGD, DONT REWRITE IT.
000000                                     212  REWR     EQU    X'00'         REWR = RECD CHGD, REWRITE IT.


                                          213  * DCB'S FOR TRANSACTION FILE ('SYSIN')
                                          214  *   AND MASTER FILE WITH FIXED-LENGTH RECORDS, IN LOCATE MODE.
                                          215  *
0001DE                                     216  TRANS    DCB    DSORG=PS,MACRF=(GM),DDNAME=SYSIN,EODAD=EOJ,        X
                                          217                   RECFM=FB,LRECL=80,BLKSIZE=4080
                                          269  *INBUF    DS     CL80
```

Figure 21.8   continued

```
FLAG LOCTN OBJECT CODE    ADDR1  ADDR2  STMNT M SOURCE STATEMENT

                                        270  *
      000240                            271  MASTER    DCB     DSORG=IS,MACRF=(GL,SK,PU),DDNAME=DORMS,EODAD=EOJ

                                        338  *  DOS  *******
                                        339  *TRANS     DTFCD DEVADDR=SYSIPT,WORKA=YES,IOAREA1=INBUF,EOFADDR=EOJ,          X
                                        340  *                DEVICE=2540
                                        341  *
                                        342  *MASTER   DTFIS DEVADDR=SYS001,DEVICE=3330,DSKXTNT=3,HINDEX=3330,             X
                                        343  *               RECFORM=FIXBLK,RECSIZE=107,NRECDS=38,IOAREAS=MSTBUF,          X
                                        344  *               KEYLEN=8,KEYLOC=2,CYLOFL=2,IOREG=(REGX),                      X
                                        345  *               IOROUT=ADDRTR,TYPEFLE=SEQNTL,EOFADDR=EOJ,KEYARG=KAREA
                                        346  ***************

                                        347  *
                                        348  * REGISTER SAVE AREA
                                        349  *
      00032C                            350  SAVE      DS      18F

                                        351  *  DOS  *******
                                        352  *SAVE      DS      9D
                                        353  *         LTORG
                                        354  *         DS      0D
                                        355  *MSTBUF   DS      CL4066
                                        356  ***************

                                        357            END
```

CROSS-REFERENCE

```
SYMBOL    LEN   VALUE   DEFN   REFERENCES

ADD       00006 000132 00163  00157
ADD1      00006 000140 00166  00164
BLANKS    00001 0001AC 00209  00161  00163
BYP       00001 0000FF 00211  00073  00086  00119
BYPASS    00004 00009A 00082  00074
CHANGE    00002 000110 00155  00141
DATALNG   00001 000031 00182  00160  00165  00209
DEL       00006 00011A 00158
DEL1      00006 000128 00161  00159
EOJ       00004 0000A2 00086  00238  00291
EOJX      00004 0000B8 00097  00087
EXIT      00004 00014C 00168  00162
GETMSTR   00002 0000C8 00118  00057  00082  00151
KAREA     00008 0001A4 00203  00051  00204
KDORM     00004 0001A4 00205  00044
KROOM     00004 0001A8 00206  00045
MAINLOOP  00006 00005C 00061  00071  00083
MAREA     00001 000000 00173  00019
MASTER    00004 000230 00273  00027  00050  00076  00089  00105  00121  00145
MDATA1    00031 000009 00177  00161  00179
MDATA2    00031 00003A 00178
MDELETE   00001 000000 00174  00143
MDORM     00004 000001 00175  00061
MFLAG     00001 0001DD 00210  00073  00086  00119  00168
MID       00009 000031 00181  00158  00163  00167
MNAME     00028 000009 00180  00166  00182
MROOM     00004 000005 00176  00063
QISAM     00001 000000 00183
REGX      00001 0000C1 00129  00124
REWR      00001 000000 00212  00168
REWRITE   00004 000086 00073  00062  00064
SAVE      00004 00032C 00350  00017  00018  00107
TAREA     00050 000154 00188  00041  00068  00189
TDORM     00004 00015B 00193  00044  00061
TID       00009 000151 00199  00158  00167
TNAME     00028 000168 00197  00166
TRANS     00004 0001E0 00217  00033  00040  00067  00099
TROOM     00004 000163 00195  00045  00063
TTYPE     00001 000157 00191  00140  00156
UPDATING  00004 0000EE 00140  00065
```

Figure 21.9 BISAM data event control block format.

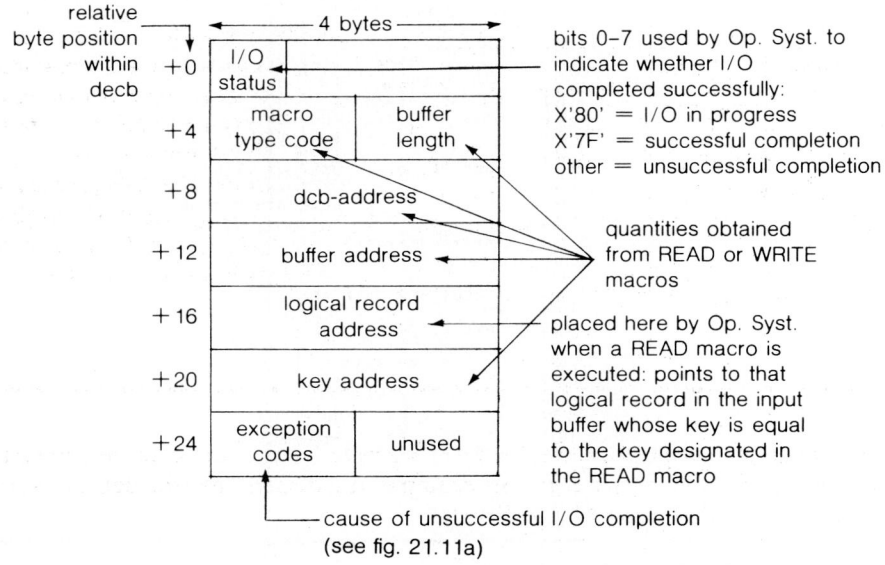

The keyword parameters MF=E and MF=L identify what is known as the *execute* and *list* forms of these macros. The use of the list and execute forms is necessary in order to be able to read and write from the same buffer area using the same data event control block. The list form (MF=L) must be placed in a data area of the source-module, not intermixed among instructions to be executed at run time. The execute form (MF=E) *is* placed among instructions to be executed, just as a GET or PUT or standard READ or WRITE would be. Whenever the execute form is processed at run time, the data event control block created by the macro expansion of the corresponding list form is used *as though it were part of the expansion of the execute form.* The correspondence between the two forms is identified by the decb-name parameter.

As an example of these concepts, consider the following statements.

Figure 21.10   Principal MACRF code combinations for BISAM.

intended processing mode	WAIT macro		CHECK macro		code meaning
	dynamic buffering	direct buffering	dynamic buffering	direct buffering	A new records are to be added (WRITE KN)
input only	(RS)	(R)	(RSC)	(RC)	C CHECK macro is used to test for I/O completion (if C not coded, then WAIT must be used)
output only	----	(WA)	-----	(WAC)	R READ macro is used
updating existing records	(RUS,WU)	(RU,WU)	(RUSC,WUC)	(RUC,WUC)	S dynamic buffering is requested in READ macros
updating, and/or adding new records	(RUS,WUA)	(RU,WUA)	(RUSC,WUAC)	(RUC,WUAC)	U existing records will be updated (when U is combined with R, it must also be combined with W)
					W WRITE macro is used

There are several points to be noted. First, the OPEN macro does not indicate the processing mode; the MACRF parameter is used for this purpose. In this example, it indicates that the dataset will be opened to enable updating using dynamic buffering with BISAM:

$$MACRF=(RUS,WUA)$$

uses READ macro | new records may be added
possible updating | existing records may be updated
dynamic buffering | WRITE macro will be used for output

Other possible MACRF codes are summarized in figure 21.10.

Second, to update existing records, execution of the READ KU macro must be followed by execution of the WRITE K macro; both must refer to the same data event control block by means of the execute form MF=E.

Third, the information in the data event control block named ISAMDECB is initialized by the expansion of the list form of the READ macro. Figure 21.9 indicates the information that is initially placed in that control block: type, dcb-address, buffer-address, buffer-length, and key-address. Thus, the execute forms do not have to respecify these items unless they are to be changed or were changed by another macro. The execute form of the READ macro specifies type KU because the execute form of the WRITE refers to the same data event control block and specifies a different type, K. Since the other parameters are not changed by any macro, they need not be respecified.

Fourth, the area designated by the key-address field must contain the key of the record to be read. This must also be the key of the record that is being updated. The key-address area must be separate from the buffer area.

Fifth, the use of 'S' (enclosed in apostrophes) in the buffer-address and buffer-length fields of the READ and WRITE macros has the following meanings:

with READ macro:
  buffer-address = 'S' means that dynamic buffering is to be used
  buffer-length = 'S' means that the number of bytes to be read is to be taken from the count field of the record (for blocked records, 'S' must be coded)

with WRITE macro:
  buffer-address = 'S' means that the data block is in the same dynamic buffer used in the previous READ KU macro
  buffer-length = 'S' is always specified in a WRITE macro unless a variable-length record is being rewritten with a length different from its previous length

If we were adding new records instead of or in addition to updating existing records, a WRITE KN macro would have to be used to add the new records. To do so, the following rule should be observed: *all records or blocks of records read using a* READ KU *macro with a given data control block macro* (DCB) *must be written back with a* WRITE K *macro before a new record can be added, unless the* READ KU *and the* WRITE KN *that are used to add a record refer to the same data event control block.*

Following this rule, it is most often simplest to let the READ KU, WRITE K, and WRITE KN macros all refer to the same data event control block. However, dynamic buffering (buffer-address = 'S') cannot be specified for the WRITE KN macro because the new record is not in the dynamic buffer: it is in some logical record area within the user's program. The record area must include a 16-byte prefix used by the Operating System. The logical record itself begins in the 17th byte of the area, as shown below. (It is not blocked, since it will either be written onto an overflow track or will replace an existing record in a prime data block.)

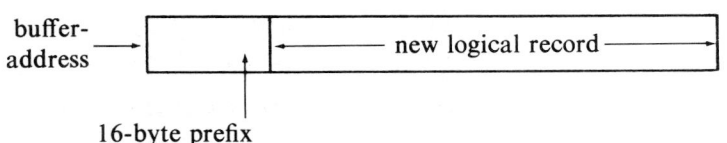

As an illustration of this rule, consider these statements:

```
          OPEN        (MASTER)
          .
          READ        ISAMDECB,KU,,'S',MF=E
          .
          .
          WRITE       ISAMDECB,K,,'S',MF=E
          .
          .
          WRITE       ISAMDECB,KN,,BUFFER,MF=E
MASTER    DCB         DSORG=IS,MACRF=(RUS,WUA),DDNAME=DORMS,BUFNO=1
          READ        ISAMDECB,KU,MASTER,'S','S',KEYADDR,MF=L
KEYADDR   DS          CL8             SPACE FOR RECORD KEY
BUFFER    DS          CL123           SPACE FOR OUTPUT AREA
          ORG         BUFFER
          DS          CL16            16-BYTE SYSTEM PREFIX
NEWRECD   DS          CL107           107-BYTE LOGICAL RECORD
          ORG
```

With these statements, either of the two WRITE macros can be executed following the READ KU macro; the choice depends on processing logic not shown. The important point is that all three macros use the same data event control block. Following the execution of the READ KU macro, either the WRITE K, the WRITE KN, or the READ KU will be the next read or write request executed. This will release the data block that was being held by the Operating System pending possible update, and it will thereby satisfy the requirements of the rule. Note that even when adding a new record the separate key-address area must contain the key of that record.

I/O Synchronization and Invalid Key Conditions

In BISAM processing, as in all basic access methods in the IBM 360 and 370 systems, there must be a provision to delay execution of the user's program until the I/O data transfer has been completed. This is the I/O synchronization function discussed in chapter 19. In addition, there must be a provision for detecting when an invalid key condition has occurred during a READ or WRITE operation. Both of these provisions can be accomplished through the use of the CHECK macro or the WAIT macro.

We cannot intermix the use of CHECK and WAIT with a given data set: the choice must be designated in the MACRF parameter. Use of the CHECK macro also requires that the user program include an internal subroutine whose purpose is to process any invalid key or other error conditions occurring during a READ or WRITE operation. The address of this subroutine must be designated by the SYNAD= parameter in the DCB macro: when an error condition occurs, the Operating System transfers control to the SYNAD sub-

exception code bit position	--- source ---		meaning when bit is set to '1'
	READ	WRITE	
0	X	type K	logical record not found in data set
1	X	X	record length invalid
2		type KN	space not found for new record in overflow areas
3	X	type K	dynamic buffering request invalid or update WRITE request invalid
4	X	X	uncorrectable I/O data transfer error
5	X	X	unreachable block
6	X		record just read was in overflow area
7		type KN	duplicate record detected: the new record to be added has same key as an existing record
8–15			used by Operating System

routine. If no error condition occurs, control is transferred to the instruction immediately following the CHECK macro.

The use of the WAIT macro does not depend on the SYNAD address: control is always transferred to the instruction immediately following the WAIT macro, and it is then up to the user's program to determine what further action should be taken. Since the WAIT macro is simpler to use, we will focus on it and not discuss the CHECK macro further.

The simplest form of the WAIT macro is

WAIT   ECB=decb-name

The name of the data event control block in the operand must be the same as the name in the corresponding READ or WRITE macro. When WAIT is executed, the user's program will be delayed until the I/O data transfer is completed. When control is returned to the instruction following WAIT, the user's program must test the exception code bits in the data event control block to determine the cause of completion: successful or unsuccessful, and, if unsuccessful, why. The exception code bits are stored in byte positions 24 and 25 of the data event control block (see figs. 21.9 and 21.11a) and may be tested with a TM instruction.

If all the exception bits are zero, or if all but bit 6 are zero, the I/O data transfer was completed successfully. (Bit 6 merely records the fact that a record was read from an overflow area and is not, properly speaking, an error condition.) If any of the other bits are not zero, the corresponding error condition indicated in figure 21.11a occurred during the I/O operation and the user program must take some appropriate action. Ordinarily, there is not much that can be done except to terminate the program by means of the abnormal end (ABEND) macro, perhaps preceding that by writing an error message. However, two of the eight exception code bits correspond to invalid key conditions; the user's program need not be terminated when these occur.

If bit 0 (record not found) is on, this may simply have been caused by a transaction request to update a record that does not exist in the data set. The invalid transaction can be written to an error message file and the program can process the next transaction. Similarly, if bit 7 (duplicate record) is on, it may be due to a request to add a new record to the data set when a record with that key already exists in the data set. After writing an appropriate error message, the program can process the next transaction. The processing steps that will accomplish these procedures are presented in Section 21.7.

21.6 RANDOM-MODE PROCESSING CONSIDERATIONS IN DOS SYSTEMS

As mentioned in Section 21.1, the ISAM access method is used for both sequential and random processing in DOS. But as can be expected there are a number of differences between the two processing modes. In this section we will cover five main aspects of DOS random-mode processing: buffering, DTFIS parameters, READ and WRITE macros, I/O synchronization, and invalid key conditions.

Buffering

As in all DOS access methods, the user's program must reserve buffer space via the DS directive and designate the buffer that is to be used by specifying an IOAREAx parameter in the DTFIS macro. In ISAM random-mode processing, there are two different types of buffers that must be reserved: one for adding new records to a file and one for retrieving and updating existing records from the file. In the following discussion, we will assume that the record format is defined as RECFORM=FIXBLK. The considerations for buffering are slightly different if unblocked records are processed and will not be discussed in this text.

The buffer used for adding new records is designated by the IOAREAL= parameter. A work area for new records must be designated by WORKL=, because locate mode is not permitted when adding or inserting new records. The IOAREAL buffer must, just as when creating a file, include space for three consecutive fields: the count and key fields that are used by the access method when writing in count-key-data format, and the data block field:

count area	key area	data block area

#bytes →|← 8 →|← KL →|← NRECDSxRECSIZE →|

The length of the data block area must be at least 10 bytes longer than the length of one logical record, in order to provide space for the 10-byte next-record-address field (sequence link) in records which are added to the overflow area.

The buffer used for retrieving and updating existing records is designated by the IOAREAR= parameter, and the corresponding logical record work area is designated by the WORKR= parameter unless locate mode is used. (Locate mode can be used when retrieving or updating, but we will not consider it. As will be recalled, it is designated by the IOREG=(n) parameter, with $2 \leq n \leq 12$, where n is the address of the register in which the Operating System returns a logical record's address.)

The IOAREAR= buffer must *not* include space for the count and key fields; space is reserved only for the data block. But as with IOAREAL=, the data block area must be at least 10 bytes longer than the length of a logical record to accommodate the sequence link field in overflow records.

Thus, a DTFIS macro for the random-mode updating of the dorm-room master filed would contain at least the following parameters: IOAREAL=, IOAREAR=, WORKL=, WORKR=; and each of the four areas would be defined by suitable DS directives. The program of figure 20.14 shows how this would be done.

DTFIS Parameters

In addition to the buffering parameters mentioned above, and in addition to the parameters mentioned in the section on creating indexed sequential files, the DTFIS macro must also include the following parameters for random-mode processing:

IOROUT=ADDRTR	specifies that retrieval, updating of existing records, and insertion of new records may take place at run time;
TYPEFLE=RANDOM	specifies that the ADDRTR functions will be done via random-mode processing;
KEYARG=*keyfieldname*	specifies the symbolic address of the area in which the key of a record must be placed in order to perform random retrieval or updating.

The KEYARG= parameter is the same one used in sequential-mode processing with the SETL macro. In both that situation and in the present one the Operating System uses the key that is stored in the KEYARG field to search its indexes for the location of the data block which contains the logical record whose key matches the one in the KEYARG field. The user's program must know what that key is; it will usually obtain it from a transaction record. If it doesn't know the key, the record cannot be retrieved or updated.

READ and WRITE Macros

The READ and WRITE macros must be used with random-mode processing; GET and PUT are not permitted. The macros have simple formats:

> *To retrieve existing records*
> READ   dtf-address,KEY
> *To update the most recently retrieved record*
> WRITE   dtf-address,KEY
> *To insert or add a new record*
> WRITE   dtf-address,NEWKEY

The READ KEY and WRITE KEY macros use the IOAREAR buffer area and the WORKR record area. The key of the record that is to be retrieved or updated must be stored in the KEYARG field before a READ KEY or WRITE KEY is executed.

The WRITE NEWKEY macro uses the IOAREAL buffer area and the WORKL record area. The key of the record being written need not be placed in the KEYARG field before executing a WRITE NEWKEY.

Note that a record that is to be updated must first be read via READ KEY, and it must be written via WRITE KEY before another READ or WRITE macro is executed. It is not, however, necessary to update every record that is read. If a record is not to be updated, then the READ KEY macro can be followed by another READ KEY for a different record or by a WRITE NEWKEY for a different record.

All READ and WRITE macros must be immediately followed by a WAITF macro, as described below.

I/O Synchronization and Invalid Key Conditions

The I/O synchronization requirements discussed in chapter 19 are achieved via the WAITF macro, whose format is

opcode	operand
WAITF	dtf-address

Execution of WAITF ensures that the I/O data-transfer operation has either been completed or has been prematurely terminated due to an error condition. The WAITF macro must therefore be executed immediately after each READ or WRITE macro so that further processing is not attempted on an incomplete or nonexistent record.

When the user program regains control following the WAITF macro, it can determine whether or not an error occurred by testing bits stored by the Operating System in the DTFIS macro expansion area. These bits are in a single status byte whose symbolic address is always the dtfname suffixed with the letter C. For example, for our MASTER DTFIS the status byte's name is MASTERC.

The meaning of the bits in the status byte depends on whether or not we are in LOAD mode, because the Operating System uses the same byte to record error status information when in LOAD mode *and* when not in LOAD mode. Thus, there are two sets of bits, as shown in figures 21.11b and 21.11c. We will consider only the IOROUT=ADDRTR case, i.e., figure 21.11b.

If all the bits in the status byte are zero, or if all but bit 7 is zero, the I/O data-transfer operation was completed successfully. If any of the other bits are not zero, the corresponding error condition indicated in figure 21.11b occurred during the I/O operation and the user program must take some appropriate action.

Ordinarily, there is not much that can be done except to terminate the program by means of the abnormal termination macro (CANCEL), perhaps preceding that by writing an error message. However, two of the eight error bits correspond to invalid key conditions; the user's program need not be terminated when these occur.

If bit 3 (record not found) is on, this may simply have been caused by a transaction request to update a record that does not exist on the master file. The invalid transaction can be written to an error message file and the program can process the next transaction. Similarly, if bit 5 (duplicate record) is on, it may be due to a request to add a new record to the file when a record with that key already exists in the file. After writing an appropriate error message, the program can process the next transaction. The processing steps that will accomplish these invalid key procedures are presented in the next section.

error code bit position	meaning when bit is set to '1'
0	an uncorrectable I/O error other than those listed below
1	a wrong length record was detected
2	end of file was detected during sequential retrieval
3	record not found in file
4	record ID (CCHHR) specified in SETL is not in prime area
5	duplicate record detected: the new record to be added has the same record key as an existing record in the file
6	the cylinder or independent overflow area that was to be used for adding a record is full, and the record can't be added
7	the retrieved record is stored in an overflow area

Figure 21.11c   Error code bits if IOROUT=LOAD in DOS. (See also IBM Publication GC33-5373.)

error code bit position	meaning when bit is set to '1'
0	an uncorrectable I/O error other than those listed below
1	a wrong length record was detected
2	prime data area full: new extents must be allocated
3	cylinder index area not large enough: must allocate more
4	master index area not large enough: must allocate more
5	duplicate record detected: the record being added has the same key as the previous one that was added
6	sequence check: the record being added is not in proper sequence
7	prime data area does not have enough space left to write an end-of-file (EOF) record

21.7   UPDATING IN RANDOM MODE

In random-mode update procedures, the transaction records need not be in the same key sequence as the master file records. Nevertheless, it is customary (and it can conserve overall processing time) to place all transaction records for a given key together, in sequence by transaction code. When this is done, there need only be one READ and one WRITE per updated record and only one WRITE per new record.

Note that all four updating actions are possible in random mode: new records can be inserted in their proper sequence or added to the end of the data set, and existing records can be changed or deleted. Remember that in the general updating procedures used for sequential data sets, we have to create a new data set consisting of all the new, changed, and unchanged records of the existing data set, but excluding the deleted records. In that procedure, the existing data set is not altered in any way. In random mode updating, *the existing data set is altered:* it is not copied to a new data set. Records for which there are no update transactions are not read at all.

The updating procedures may be divided into three main phases: initialization, main processing, and end-of-data. This is shown in the diagrams of figures 21.12a–21.12c, to which the following discussion is oriented.

In the initialization phase, the master and transaction files are opened and the first transaction record is read. An error report file (SYSOUT or SYSLST, for example) may also be opened if we intend to list transactions that cause invalid key conditions or uncorrectable errors. The first master record is not read in

Figure 21.12a   Overview of random-mode updating procedure. (See also figs. 21.12b and 21.12c.)

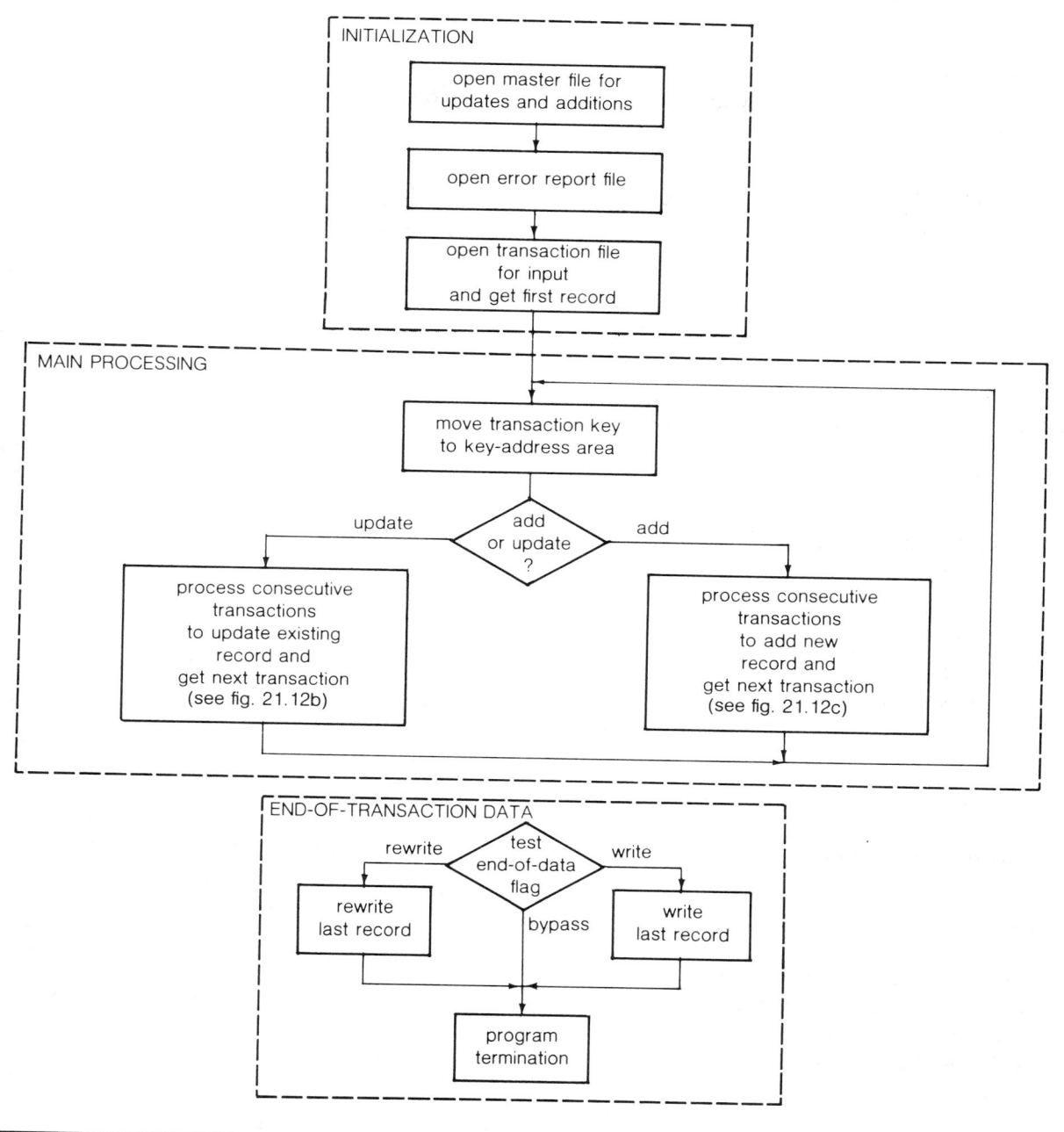

the initialization phase. A master record is read only when it is determined that a record is to be changed or deleted in the main processing phase. That record may then be read without having to read any records that precede it in sequence.

The first step in each iteration of the main processing phase is to move the key of the current transaction record to the area that is designated by the key-address parameter in an OS READ or WRITE macro and by the KEYARG= parameter in a DOS DTFIS macro. The key in the key-address area is used by the Operating System to determine the location in secondary memory of the record that is to be read or written. *When adding a new record,* the data in the transaction record is used to begin construction of the new record in the area reserved for that purpose. Since successive transaction records may contain additional information

Figure 21.12b *Random-mode processing to update existing records.*

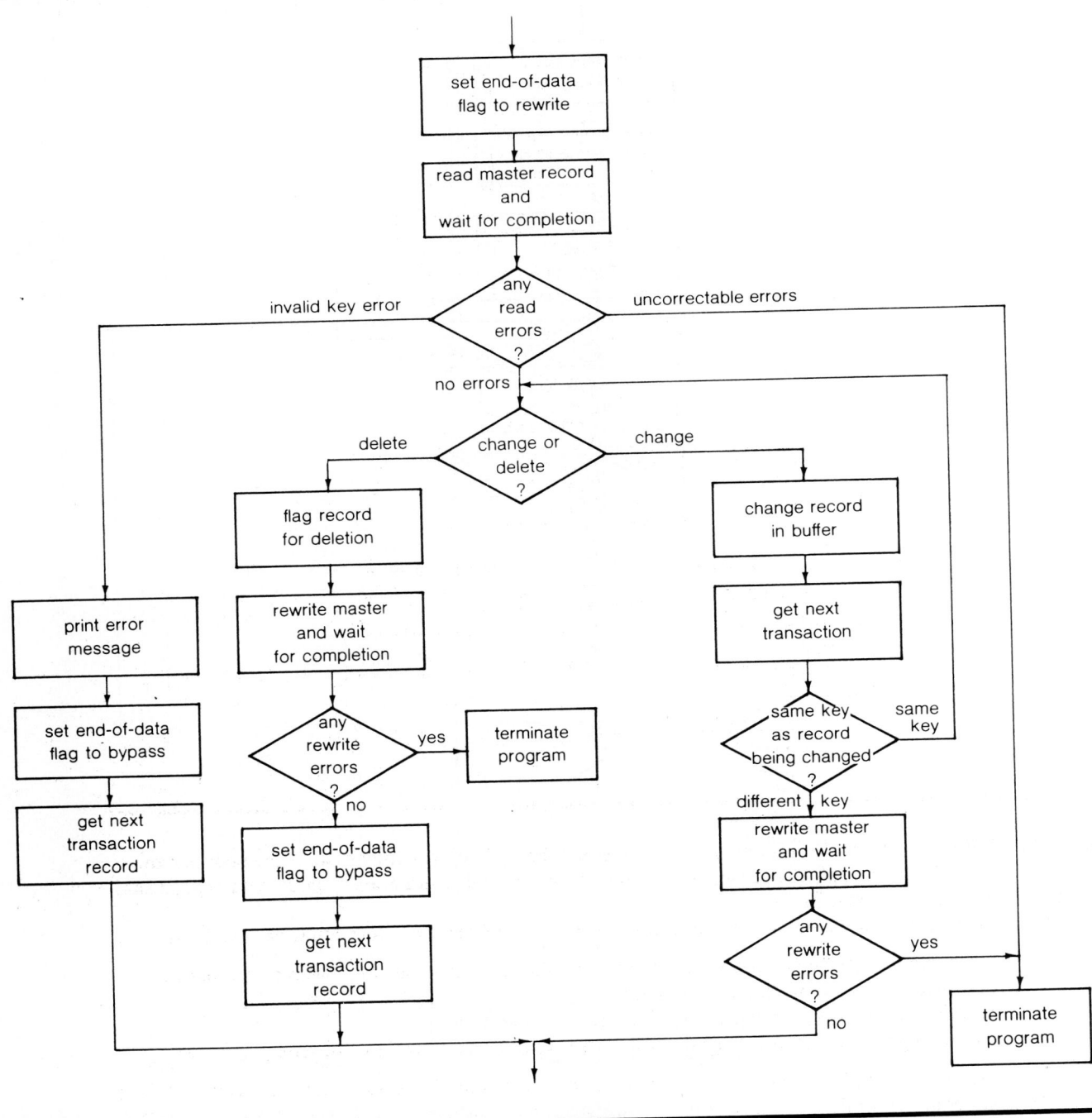

for the same new record, the new record is not written until all consecutive transaction records with that new record's key have been processed. New records are written in OS by the WRITE KN macro and in DOS by the WRITE NEWKEY macro.

When updating an existing record, that record must first be read from the master file by means of the OS READ KU or DOS READ KEY macro. If the update request is to delete the record, the delete flag (X'FF') is moved into the first position of the record, the record is rewritten in OS via WRITE K and in DOS

Figure 21.12c *Random-mode processing to add new records.*

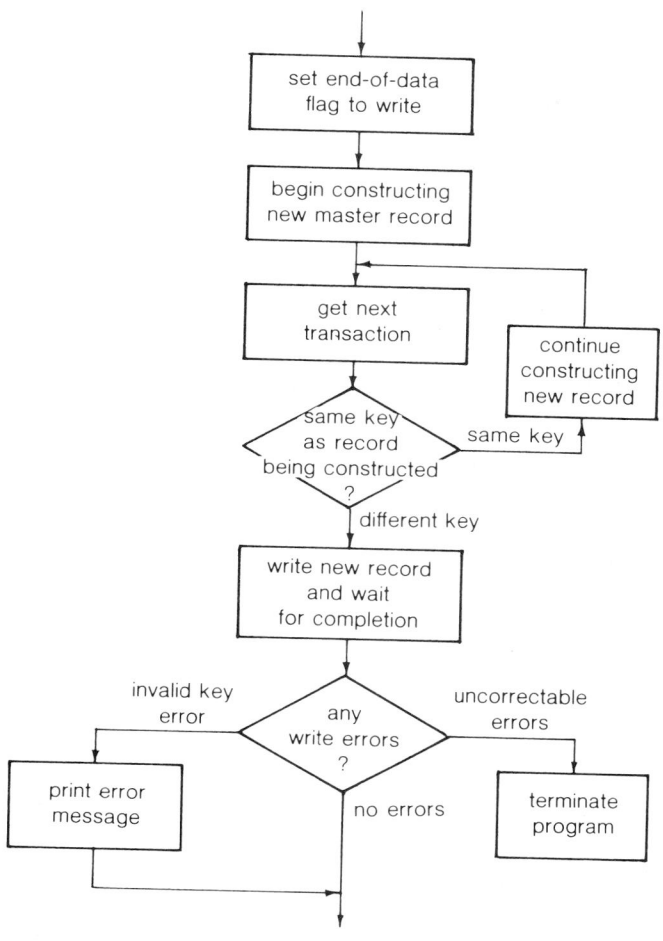

via WRITE KEY, and the next transaction is read to repeat the main processing phase. If the update request is to change an existing record, the record is rewritten only after all transaction records with that master record's key have been processed.

When the transaction file end-of-data condition occurs, one of three possible situations can exist:

1. If a new record was being constructed at the time end-of-data occurred, that record must be written before processing can be terminated.
2. If an existing record was being changed, it must be rewritten.
3. If an existing record had just been deleted, there is no record to write or rewrite.

Note that the master file will never reach an end-of-data condition because records are read from it in random order, not sequentially.

Also note that an invalid key condition can occur when reading or writing a master record, unless it is assumed that the transaction data are "perfect," as was the case for previous discussions in the text. To illustrate how to process these conditions, assume that they may occur as follows: When attempting to read a record that is to be updated, an invalid key condition would occur if that record were not on the master file. If this happens, the transaction causing the error is printed and the next transaction is read. When attempting to write a new record, an invalid key condition would occur if a record with that key were already on the master file. If this happens, the transaction causing the error is printed, and—except during end-of-data processing—the next transaction record is read. When attempting to rewrite an updated record, an invalid key condition can not occur due to a transaction record error. Since an error detected during a rewrite operation will either be due to a hardware malfunction or to a programming error—for example, an unintended alteration of the key or of the data event control block—it will be treated as an uncorrectable error.

The program in figure 21.13 illustrates the BISAM updating procedures for the dorm-room master file, using the transaction record format that was described in figure 20.5. When studying this program, note that a DSECT directive has been used to define the record fields for the master file records. For records that are to be updated, the dummy base register is loaded with the logical record address made available in the data event control block following the READ KU macro. For new records that are to be added, the dummy base register is loaded with the address of the logical record area reserved for new records. Interspersed comment statements show how similar actions would be accomplished in DOS systems.

21.8   RETRIEVAL

To retrieve information from an indexed sequential data set without updating, one of three procedures can be followed:

1. The procedure outlined for sequential data sets in Section 20.11 can be used with sequential-mode processing methods.
2. The procedure outlined for sequential data sets can be used in conjunction with the SETL macro with sequential-mode processing.
3. A random retrieval procedure can be used.

In all three retrieval procedures, the DCB macro parameters—BLKSIZE, CYLOFL, KEYLEN, LRECL, NTM, OPTCD, RECFM, and RKP—are not specified in the DCB macro or DD statement; instead, their values are obtained at open time from the data set control block. There is no similar constraint for DTFIS parameters.

Sequential Retrieval

In strict sequential retrieval, the data set must be opened for input, and either move mode or locate mode buffering can be used. In OS, this is done as follows:

```
        OPEN        (MASTER,(INPUT))
          .
          .
MASTER  DCB         DSORG=IS,MACRF=(GM),DDNAME=DORMS,EODAD=EOJ
```

In DOS, the corresponding DTFIS macro for strict sequential retrieval must designate IOAREAS and WORKS areas and specify sequential retrieval as follows:

```
MASTER  DTFIS       ...,TYPEFLE=SEQNTL,IOROUT=RETRVE,EOFADDR=EOJ,        X
                    IOAREAS=buffername,WORKS=workareaname,...
```

Sequential Retrieval Using SETL

When the SETL macro is to be used, the data set is also opened for input using either move mode or locate mode. In OS, the intention to use SETL must be indicated in the MACRF parameter, as when updating:

```
        OPEN        (MASTER,(INPUT))
          .
          .
MASTER  DCB         DSORG=IS,MACRF=(GM,SK),DDNAME=DORMS,EODAD=EOJ
```

In DOS a DTFIS macro must specify sequential retrieval with IOAREAS and WORKS areas and also must specify the KEYARG field name:

```
MASTER  DTFIS       ...,TYPEFLE=SEQNTL,IOROUT=RETRVE,EOFADDR=EOJ,        X
                    IOAREAS=buffername,WORKS=workareaname,               X
                    KEYARG=keyfieldname,...
```

The processing logic required for this procedure is depicted in figure 21.14. As in the updating procedures, the transaction records may designate either a specific record key or a record key class. Figure 21.14 assumes a record key class is being designated. For example, a request for retrieval of information for an entire dorm would use the key class method.

Figure 21.13 Updating the dorm room master file in BISAM.

```
FLAG LOCTN OBJECT CODE        ADDR1  ADDR2  STMNT M SOURCE STATEMENT

     000000                                    3      BISAM    CSECT
                                                4      *
                                                5      *
                                                6      * THIS PROGRAM UPDATES THE DORM ROOM MASTER FILE,
                                                7      *   IN RANDOM MODE USING  BISAM .
                                                8      *
                                                9      * TRANSACTIONS ARE NOT NECESSARILY IN KEY SEQ, BUT ALL CONSECUTIVE
                                               10      *   TRANS RECORDS FOR A GIVEN KEY ARE PROCESSED BEFORE WRITING THE
                                               11      *   CORRESPONDING MASTER RECORD.
                                               12      *
                                               13      * INVALID KEY ERRORS ARE REPORTED ON 'SYSOUT' WITHOUT TERMINATING
                                               14      *   THE PROGRAM.  THE FIRST UNCORRECTABLE ERROR TO OCCUR CAUSES
                                               15      *   PROGRAM TERMINATION.
                                               16      *
     000000 90 EC D0CC                         17               STM    14,12,12(13)    STANDARD ENTRY
     000004 05 C0                              18               BALR   12,0
     000006                                    19               USING  *,12
     000006 50 D0 C672         000678          20               ST     13,SAVE+4
     00000A 41 D0 C66E         000674          21               LA     13,SAVE
     000000                                    22               USING  MAREA,11         DUMMY BASE REG FOR MASTER RECD AREA
                                               23      * OS ONLY ----------------------------------------------
     000000                                    24               USING  DECBD,9
     00000E 41 90 C2B6         0002BC          25               LA     9,MSTRDECB      DUMMY BASE REG FOR DATA EVENT CTL BLOCK
                                               26      *---------------------------------------------------

                                               27      * INITIALIZATIONS
                                               28      *
     000012                                    29               OPEN   (MASTER)        OPEN MASTER FOR UPDATES & ADDITIONS
     00001E                                    35               OPEN   (REPORT,(OUTPUT))  OPEN ERROR REPORT FILE
     00002A                                    41               OPEN   (TRANS,(INPUT))  OPEN TRANSACTION FILE
                                               47      * DOS ******
                                               48      *         OPEN   MASTER
                                               49      *         OPEN   REPORT
                                               50      *         OPEN   TRANS
                                               51      ***************

     000036                                    52               GET    TRANS,TAREA      GET 1ST TRANS RECD
                                               57      *
                                               58      * MAIN PROCESSING
                                               59      *
     000044 D2 03 C37DC38C     000383 000392   60      MAINLOOP MVC    KDORM,TDORM      MOVE TRANSACTION KEY TO KEY-ADDRESS AREA
     00004A D2 03 C381C394     000387 00039A   61               MVC    KROOM,TROOM
     000050 95 F1 C388         00038E          62               CLI    TTYPE,C'1'       TRANS CODE = '1' MEANS ADD NEW RECORD
     000054 47 80 C09E         0000A4          63               BE     NEWADD
     000058 47 F0 C0E2         0000E8          64               B      UPDATE           OTHERWISE, GO PROCESS UPDATES

                                               65      * END-OF-TRANSACTION-DATA
                                               66      *
                                               67      *   END-OF-DATA FLAG 'EODFLG'  CONTROLS PROCESSING DECISIONS
                                               68      *        IF 'EODFLG' = WR   = X'0F', THEN WRITE LAST MASTER RECORD.
                                               69      *        IF 'EODFLG' = REWR = X'F0', THEN REWRITE LAST MASTER RECORD.
                                               70      *        IF 'EODFLG' = BYP  = X'FF', THEN DON'T WRITE OR REWRITE.
                                               71      *
     00005C 95 FF C4C1         0004C7          72      EOJ      CLI    EODFLG,BYP       EODFLG=BYP IF END-OF-DATA OCCURRED AFTER
     000060 47 80 C072         000078          73               BE     XBYPASS          A MASTER RECD HAD BEEN DELETED.
     000064 95 0F C4C1         0004C7          74               CLI    EODFLG,WR        EODFLG=WR   IF END-OF-DATA OCCURRED WHILE
     000068 47 80 C06E         000074          75               BE     XWRITE           A NEW MASTER RECD WAS BEING CONSTRUCTED.
     00006C 45 E0 C1EC         0001C2          76      XREWRITE BAL    14,REWRITE       EODFLG=REWR IF END-OF-DATA OCCURRED WHILE
     000070 47 F0 C072         000078          77               B      XBYPASS          AN EXISTING MSTR RECD WAS BEING UPDATED.
     000074 45 E0 C1EA         0001F0          78      XWRITE   BAL    14,WRITE

     000078                                    79      XBYPASS  CLOSE  (TRANS)          AFTER HANDLING LAST MASTER RECD, CLOSE
     000082                                    85               CLOSE  (MASTER)         ALL FILES, AND EXIT FROM PROGRAM
     00008E                                    91               CLOSE  (REPORT)
     00009A 58 D0 C672         000678          97               L      13,SAVE+4
     00009E 98 EC D00C                         98               LM     14,12,12(13)
     0000A2 07 FE                              99               BR     14

                                              100      * DOS ******
                                              101      *XBYPASS  CLOSE TRANS
                                              102      *         CLOSE MASTER
                                              103      *         CLOSE REPORT
                                              104      *         EOJ
                                              105      ***************

                                              106      *
                                              107      * ADD NEW RECORD TO MASTER FILE
                                              108      *
     0000A4 92 0F C4C1         0004C7         109      NEWADD   MVI    EODFLG,WR        SET END-OF-DATA FLAG TO WRITE LAST RECD.
     0000A8 41 B0 C312         000318         110               LA     11,NEWRECD       SET DUMMY BASE REG TO NEW-RECD AREA.
                                              111      * DOS ******
                                              112      *         LA     11,RECDL
                                              113      ***************
     0000AC 45 E0 C24C         000252         114               BAL    14,CONSTRCT      GO BEGIN CONSTRUCTION OF NEW RECD.
     0000B0 D2 4F C305C385     0003DB 00038B  115               MVC    ERRTRANS,TAREA   SET ERR MSG FOR POSSIBLE INVALID KEY.
     0000B6
     0000C4 D5 03 C37DC38C     000383 000392  116      ADDLOOP  GET    TRANS,TAREA      GET NEXT TRANS RECD (IF ANY), AND
     0000CA 47 70 C0DA         0000E0         121               CLC    KDORM,TDORM      SEE IF ITS KEY MATCHES THAT OF RECD BE-
     0000CE D5 03 C381C394     000387 00039A  122               BNE    ADDEND           ING CONSTRUCTED.  IF NOT, GO WRITE NEW
                                              123               CLC    KROOM,TROOM      RECD TO MASTER FILE.
```

Figure 21.13   *continued*

```
FLAG LOCTN OBJECT CODE      ADDR1  ADDR2  STMNT M SOURCE STATEMENT

     000004 47 70 CODA      0000E0     124          BNE     ADDEND             OTHERWISE, CONTINUE CONSTRCTING NEW RECD
     0000D8 45 EO C26E      000274     125          BAL     14,UPDATING        USING INFO IN TRANS RECD.
     0000DC 47 FO COBO      0000B6     126          B       ADDLOOP            AFTER WRITING NEW RECD TO MASTER, THEN
     0000E0 45 EO C1EA      0001F0     127  ADDEND  BAL     14,WRITE           DETERMINE WHAT TO DO WITH NEXT TRANS.
     0000E4 47 FO CO3E      000044     128          B       MAINLOOP
                                       129  *
                                       130  *
                                       131  * UPDATE EXISTING RECORD IN MASTER FILE
                                       132  *
     0000E8 92 FO C4C1      0004C7     133  UPDATE  MVI     EODFLG,REWR        SET END-OF-DATA FLG TO REWRITE LAST RECD
     0000EC 45 EO C15E      000164     134          BAL     14,READ            THEN READ MASTER RECD THAT MATCHES KEY IN
     0000F0 12 BB                      135          LTR     11,11              KEY-ADDRESS AREA.  RETURN WITH ADDR OF
     0000F2 47 70 C106      00010C     136          BNZ     VALIDKEY           LOGICAL RECD IN REG 11, UNLESS INVALID
     0000F6 92 FF C4C1      0004C7     137          MVI     EODFLG,BYP         KEY ERROR.  IF INVALID KEY, THEN RESET
     0000FA                            138          GET     TRANS,TAREA        END-OF-DATA FLAG TO BYPASS REWRITE, AND
     000108 47 FO CO3E      000044     143          B       MAINLOOP           GET NEXT TRANS AND GO PROCESS IT.
                                       144  *
     00010C 95 F4 C388      00038E     145  VALIDKEY CLI    TTYPE,C'4'         IF VALID KEY, SEE IF TRANS IS CHANGE OR
     000110 47 80 C140      000146     146          BE      DELETE             DELETE REQUEST.
     000114 45 EO C26E      000274     147  CHANGE  BAL     14,UPDATING        IF CHANGE, THEN GO MAKE CHANGES.
     000118                            148          GET     TRANS,TAREA        THEN GET NEXT TRANS RECD (IF ANY).
     000126 D5 03 C37DC38C 000383 000392 153        CLC     KDORM,TDORM        SEE IF ITS KEY MATCHES THAT OF RECD BE-
     00012C 47 70 C138      00013E     154          BNE     DIFFKEY            ING UPDATED.  IF NOT, GO REWRITE THAT
     000130 D5 03 C381C394 000387 00039A 155        CLC     KROOM,TROOM        RECD BACK TO MASTER FILE.
     000136 47 70 C138      00013E     156          BNE     DIFFKEY
     00013A 47 FO C106      00010C     157          B       VALIDKEY           OTHERWISE, CONTINUE MAKING CHANGES.
     00013E 45 EO C1BC      0001C2     158  DIFFKEY BAL     14,REWRITE         AFTER REWRITING CHANGED RECD, DETERMINE
     000142 47 FO CO3E      000044     159          B       MAINLOOP           WHAT TO DO WITH NEXT TRANSACTION RECD.
                                       160  *
     000146 92 FF B000      000000     161  DELETE  MVI     MDELETE,X'FF'      WHEN THE REQUEST IS TO DELETE THE MASTER
     00014A 45 EO C1BC      0001C2     162          BAL     14,REWRITE         RECD, THEN SET DELETE FLAG AND REWRITE
     00014E 92 FF C4C1      0004C7     163          MVI     EODFLG,BYP         THE RECD.  SET END-OF-DATA FLAG TO BYPASS
     000152                            164          GET     TRANS,TAREA        WRITING OR REWRITING LAST MASTER RECD.
     000160 47 FO CO3E      000044     169          B       MAINLOOP           GET NEXT TRANS RECD AND PROCESS IT.


                                       170  * INTERNAL SUBROUTINES   'READ'    READS FOR UPDATING
                                       171  *                        'REWRITE' WRITES AN UPDATED RECORD
                                       172  *                        'WRITE'   WRITES A NEW RECORD
                                       173  * ALL THREE CALLED VIA  BAL 14,XXX.
                                       174  * OS USES ERROR BYTE NAMED 'EXCODE' IN DECB NAMED 'MSTRDECB'.
                                       175  * DOS USES ERROR BYTE NAMED 'MASTERC' IN DTFIS NAMED 'MASTER'.
                                       176  *
     000164 18 2E                      177  READ    LR      2,14               SAVE RETURN ADDRESS
     000166                            178          READ    MSTRDECB,KU,,'S',MF=E  USE DYNAMIC INPUT BUFFER
     00017C                            185          WAIT    ECB=MSTRDECB       WAIT FOR I/O COMPLETION
     000186 58 BO 9010      000010     189          L       11,RECDADDR        GET ADDR OF LOGICAL RECORD.
     00018A 91 7D 9018      000018     190          TM      EXCODE,X'FF'-OVF-RNF  GIVE ERR MSG IF OTHER THAN
     00018E 47 70 C23C      000242     191          BNZ     ABEND              OVERFLOW OR RECD-NOT-FOUND.
     000192 91 80 9018      000018     192          TM      EXCODE,RNF         IF RECD NOT FOUND, GIVE NON-
     000196 47 70 C19C      0001A2     193          BNZ     RDERR              FATAL MSG.  OTHERWISE,
                                       194  * DOS  ******
                                       195  *       READ    MASTER,KEY
                                       196  *       WAITF   MASTER
                                       197  *       LA      11,RECDR
                                       198  *       TM      MASTERC,X'FF'-OVF-RNF
                                       199  *       BNZ     ABEND
                                       200  *       TM      MASTERC,RNF
                                       201  *       BNZ     RDERR
                                       202  * **************
     00019A 95 FF B000      000000     203          CLI     MDELETE,X'FF'      SEE IF RECORD IS 'DELETED'
     00019E 47 70 C1B8      0001BE     204          BNE     RDEXIT             IF NOT, THEN READ WAS O.K.
     0001A2 D2 33 C425C48D 00042B 000493 205 RDERR  MVC     ERRMSG,NOTFMSG     ELSE, PRINT 'RECD-NOT-FOUND'
     0001A8 D2 4F C3D5C385 0003DB 00038B 206        MVC     ERRTRANS,TAREA     MSG WITH CURRENT TRANSACTION.
     0001AE                            207          PUT     REPORT,ERRLINE
     0001BC 1B BB                      212          SR      11,11              RESET RECD ADDR SINCE IT'S BAD.
     0001BE 18 E2                      213  RDEXIT  LR      14,2               RECOVER RETURN ADDRESS, AND
     0001C0 07 FE                      214          BR      14                 RETURN TO CALLER.
                                       215  *
     0001C2 18 2E                      216  REWRITE LR      2,14               SAVE RETURN ADDRESS
     0001C4                            217          WRITE   MSTRDECB,K,,'S',MF=E  USE INPUT BUFFER FOR OUTPUT.
     0001DA                            224          WAIT    ECB=MSTRDECB       WAIT FOR I/O COMPLETION.
     0001E4 91 FF 9018      000018     228          TM      EXCODE,X'FF'       SEE IF ANY EXCEPTION CODES ON.
     0001E8 47 70 C23C      000242     229          BNZ     ABEND              IF ANY ERRORS, THEN TERMINATE.
                                       230  * DOS  ******
                                       231  *       WRITE   MASTER,KEY
                                       232  *       WAITF   MASTER
                                       233  *       TM      MASTERC,X'FF'
                                       234  *       BNZ     ABEND
                                       235  * **************
     0001EC 18 E2                      236          LR      14,2
     0001EE C7 FE                      237          BR      14                 OTHERWISE, RETURN TO CALLER.
                                       238  *
     0001F0 18 2E                      239  WRITE   LR      2,14               SAVE RETURN ADDRESS
     0001F2                            240          WRITE   MSTRDECB,KN,,NEWBUF,MF=E  USE NEW RECD BUFFER AREA.
     000210                            249          WAIT    ECB=MSTRDECB       WAIT FOR I/O COMPLETION.
     00021A 91 FF 9018      000018     253          TM      EXCODE,X'FF'       SEE IF ANY EXCEPTION CODES ON.
     C0021E 47 80 C238      00023E     254          BZ      WREXIT             IF NONE, THEN NO ERRORS.
     000222 91 FE 9018      000018     255          TM      EXCODE,X'FF'-DUP   IF ANY BUT DUPL-RECD, THEN
```

Figure 21.13 continued

```
FLAG LOCTN OBJECT CODE      ADDR1  ADDR2  STMNT M SOURCE STATEMENT

     000226 47 70 C23C      000242        256           BNZ    ABEND              TERMINATE PROGRAM.
                                          257  *  DOS  *******
                                          258  *           WRITE  MASTER,NEWKEY
                                          259  *           WAITF  MASTER
                                          260  *           TM     MASTERC,X'FF'
                                          261  *           BZ     WREXIT
                                          262  *           TM     MASTERC,X'FF'-DUP
                                          263  *           BNZ    ABEND
                                          264  ***************
     00022A D2 33 C425C459 00042B 00045F  265           MVC    ERRMSG,DUPLMSG     IF DUPL-RECD ONLY, THEN PRINT
     000230                               266           PUT    REPORT,ERRLINE     MSG WITH CURRENT TRANSACTION.
     00023E 18 E2                         271  WREXIT    LR     14,2               RETURN TO CALLER.
     000240 07 FE                         272           BR     14

                                          273  * 'ABEND' ROUTINE IS CALLED WHEN I/O ERROR OTHER THAN INVALID KEY IS
                                          274  *   DETECTED DURING A READ, REWRITE, OR WRITE OPERATION.
                                          275  * 'ABEND' TERMINATES THE PROGRAM AND ITS JOB STEP, VIA 'ABEND' MACRO.
                                          276  *   COMPLETION CODE FOR TERMINAION IS ARBITRARILY CHOSEN AS 4095.

     000242                               277  ABEND     ABEND 4095,DUMP,STEP
                                          284  *
                                          285  *  DOS  ******
                                          286  *ABEND    DUMP
                                          287  ***************
                                          288  *

                                          289  * INTERNAL SUBROUTINE WITH TWO ENTRY POINTS, 'CONSTRCT' & 'UPDATING'
                                          290  * BOTH ENTERED WITH BAL 14,...  WITH NO PARAMETERS.
                                          291  *
                                          292  * TRANSACTION CODE 'TTYPE' DETERMINES UPDATING ACTION
                                          293  *    TTYPE = C'1' ...  ADD A NEW ROOM WITH NO STUDENTS
                                          294  *          = C'2' ...  ADD A STUDENT NAME & I.D.
                                          295  *          = C'3' ...  DELETE A STUDENT NAME & I.D.
                                          296  *          = C'4' ...  DELETE ENTIRE MASTER RECD.
                                          297  *
                                          298  *'CONSTRCT' BEGINS CONSTRUCTION OF NEW OUTPUT MASTER RECD USING TRANS
                                          299  * RECD.  'UPDATING' CONTINUES CONSTRUCTION OF NEW OUTPUT MASTER RECD.
                                          300  *
     000252 D2 03 B001C38C 000001 000392  301  CONSTRCT  MVC    MDORM,TDORM        WHEN CONSTRUCTING A NEW RECD, MOVE
     000258 D2 03 B005C394 000005 00039A  302           MVC    MROOM,TROOM        DORM AND ROOM NUMBER FROM TRANS
     00025E D2 30 B009C2D0 000009 0002D6  303           MVC    MDATA1,BLANKS      TO OUTPUT AREA, AND BLANK OUT STU-
     000264 D2 30 B03AC2D0 00003A 0002D6  304           MVC    MDATA2,BLANKS      DENT DATA AREAS.
     00026A 95 F2 C388     00038E         305           CLI    TTYPE,C'2'         IF TRANS CODE IS '2', INSTEAD OF '1',
     00026E 47 80 C26E     000274         306           BE     UPDATING           CONTINUE CONSTRUCTION.
     000272 07 FE                         307           BR     14                 OTHERWISE, EXIT.
                                          308  *
     000274 18 AB                         309  UPDATING  LR     10,11              SAVE LOGICAL RECD AREA ADDR IN REG 10.
     000276 95 F2 C388     00038E         310           CLI    TTYPE,C'2'         IF TRANS CODE = '2', THEN ADD STUDENT
     00027A 47 80 C296     00029C         311           BE     ADD                NAME AND I.D.
     00027E D5 08 B031C3C2 000031 0003C8  312  DEL       CLC    MID,TID            OTHERWISE, ASSUME CODE = '3', AND
     000284 47 80 C286     00028C         313           BE     DEL1               DELETE EITHER 1ST OR 2ND NAME & I.D.
     000288 41 BB 0D 31    000031         314           LA     11,DATALNG(11)     IF NOT 1ST, MUST BE 2ND  INCR ADDR.
     00028C D2 27 B009C2D0 000009 0002D6  315  DEL1      MVC    MNAME,BLANKS       DELETE BY REPLACING NAME & I.D. WITH
     000292 D2 08 B031C2D0 000031 0002D6  316           MVC    MID,BLANKS         BLANKS.
     000298 47 F0 C2B0     0002B6         317           B      EXIT
     00029C D5 08 B031C2D0 000031 0002D6  318  ADD       CLC    MID,BLANKS         WHEN ADDING, SEE WHICH STUDENT DATA
     0002A2 47 80 C2A4     0002AA         319           BE     ADD1               AREA IS BLANK, AND MOVE NAME & I.D.
     0002A6 41 BB 0D 31    000031         320           LA     11,DATALNG(11)     INTO THAT AREA.  IF NOT 1ST AREA,
     0002AA D2 27 B0C9C399 000009 00039F  321  ADD1      MVC    MNAME,TNAME        THEN ASSUME IT'S 2ND AREA.
     0002B0 D2 08 B031C3C2 000031 0003C8  322           MVC    MID,TID
     0002B6 18 BA                         323  EXIT      LR     11,10              BEFORE EXITING, RESTORE DUMMY BASE
     0002B8 07 FE                         324           BR     14                 REG CONTENTS.

                                          325  *  THE FOLLOWING READ MACRO AND DECBD DSECT ARE FOR  OS  ONLY .
                                          326  *  ---------------------------------------------------------------
                                          327  *
                                          328  * LIST FORM OF READ MACRO TO DEFINE DATA EVENT CONTROL BLOCK AREA
     0002BA                               329           READ   MSTRDECB,KU,MASTER,'S','S',KAREA,MF=L

                                          339  * DUMMY SECTION FOR DATA EVENT CONTROL BLOCK TO DEFINE FIELDS.
     000000                               340  *
     000000                               341  DECBD     DSECT
     000010                               342           DS     4F                 1ST FOUR WORDS NOT REFERRED TO.
     000014                               343  RECDADDR  DS     F                  5TH WORD IS LOGICAL RECORD ADDRESS.
     000018                               344  KEYADDR   DS     F                  6TH IS ADDRESS OF KEY AREA.
     000080                               345  EXCODE    DS     H                  7TH IS EXCEPTION CODES
     000002                               346  RNF       EQU    B'10000000'        BIT 0 = RECD-NOT-FOUND
     000001                               347  OVF       EQU    B'00000010'        BIT 6 = OVERFLOW-RECORD
     0002D6                               348  DUP       EQU    B'00000001'        BIT 7 = DUPLICATE-RECORD
                                          349  BISAM     CSECT
                                          350  *  ---------------------------------------------------------------
                                          351  *
                                          352  * DUMMY SECTION TO DEFINE 107-BYTE MASTER FILE LOGICAL RECORD AREA.
```

Figure 21.13 continued

```
FLAG LOCTN OBJECT CODE    ADDR1 ADDR2 STMNT M SOURCE STATEMENT

                                      353  *
       000000                         354  MAREA    DSECT
       000000                         355  MDELETE  DS    CL1            BYTES 0        DELETE FLAG BYTE
       000001                         356  MDORM    DS    CL4                 1-4       DORM ABBREVIATION
       000005                         357  MROOM    DS    CL4                 5-8       DORM ROOM
       000009                         358  MDATA1   DS    CL49                9-57      1ST STUDENT DATA AREA
       00003A                         359  MDATA2   DS    CL49                58-106    2ND STUDENT DATA AREA
       000009      00006B             360           ORG   MDATA1         REDEFINE STUDENT DATA AREA
       000009                         361  MNAME    DS    CL40                9-48      STUDENT NAME FIELD
       000031                         362  MID      DS    CL9                 49-57     STUDENT I.D. FIELD
       000031                         363  DATALNG  EQU   *-MNAME                       LENGTH OF STUDENT AREA
       0002D6                         364  BISAM    CSECT
                                      365  *
                                      366  * BLANKS USED TO INITIALIZE STUDENT DATA AREAS
       0002D6 40                      367  BLANKS   DC    (DATALNG)C' '   'DATALNG' IS SIZE OF STUDENT DATA AREA
                                      368  *
                                      369  * LOGICAL RECORD AREA FOR NEW ADDITIONS TO MASTER FILE
                                      370  *
       000308                         371           DS    0D             RESERVE 123  BYTES ON DBL-WD BDY
       000308                         372  NEWBUF   DS    CL123
       000308      000383             373           ORG   NEWBUF
       000308                         374           DS    CL16           16-BYTE SYSTEM  AREA
       000318                         375  NEWRECD  DS    CL107          107-BYTE LOGICAL RECD, AS IN 'MAREA'
       000383      000383             376           ORG
                                      377  *
                                      378  * KEY AREA FOR USE WITH READ AND WRITE MACROS
                                      379  *
       000383                         380  KAREA    DS    CL8            8-BYTE KEY
       000383      00038B             381           ORG   KAREA
       000383                         382  KDORM    DS    CL4            1ST 4 BYTES = DORM ABBREVIATION
       000387                         383  KROOM    DS    CL4            2ND 4 BYTES = DORM ROOM NUMBER
       00038B      00038B             384           ORG
                                      385  *

                                      386  * TRANSACTION INPUT AREA
                                      387  *
       00038B                         388  TAREA    DS    CL80           RESERVE 80 BYTES FOR CARD IMAGE.
       00038B      0003DB             389           ORG   TAREA          BEGIN REDEFINITION OF INPUT AREA.
       00038B                         390           DS    CL3            COL 1-3        UNUSED
       00038E                         391  TTYPE    DS    CL1                 4         TRANS TYPE CODE
       00038F                         392           DS    CL3                 5-7       UNUSED
       000392                         393  TDORM    DS    CL4                 8-11      DORM ABBREVIATION
       000396                         394           DS    CL4                 12-15     UNUSED
       00039A                         395  TROOM    DS    CL4                 16-19     DORM ROOM NUMBER
       00039E                         396           DS    CL1                 20        UNUSED
       00039F                         397  TNAME    DS    CL40                21-60     STUDENT NAME
       0003C7                         398           DS    CL1                 61        UNUSED
       0003C8                         399  TID      DS    CL9                 62-70     STUDENT I.D.
       0003DB      0003D1             400           ORG
                                      401  *

                                      402  * LOGICAL RECORD AREA FOR 'SYSOUT' PRINT LINE
                                      403  *
       0003DB                         404  ERRLINE  DS    0CL132         RESERVE 132  BYTES
       0003DB                         405  ERRTRANS DS    CL80           80-BYTE TRANS RECD AREA
       00042B                         406  ERRMSG   DS    CL52           52-BYTE ERR MESSAGE AREA
                                      407  *
 00045F 40C3C1D5E340C1C4             408  DUPLMSG  DC    CL52' CANT ADD   RECD KEY ALREADY EXISTS ON MASTER FILE'
 000493 40C3C1D5E340E4D7             409  NOTFMSG  DC    CL52' CANT UPDATE  RECD KEY DOESNT EXIST ON MASTER FILE'

                                      410  *
                                      411  * EODFLG USED TO CONTROL PROCESSING WHEN AT END OF TRANSACTION FILE.
                                      412  *
       0004C7 FF                      413  EODFLG   DC    X'FF'          END-OF-DATA FLAG  FOR LAST MASTER RECD
       0000FF                         414  BYP      EQU   X'FF'          BYP  = DONT WRITE OR REWRITE WHEN AT END
       00000F                         415  WR       EQU   X'0F'          WR   = WRITE MSTR RECD WHEN AT END
       0000F0                         416  REWR     EQU   X'F0'          REWR = REWRITE MSTR RECD WHEN AT END

                                      417  *
                                      418  * DCB'S FOR TRANS FILE, INPUT MASTER FILE, AND REPORT FILE
                                      419  *
       0004C8                         420  TRANS    DCB   DSORG=PS,MACRF=(GM),DDNAME=SYSIN,EODAD=EOJ,            X
                                      421                 RECFM=FB,LRECL=80,BLKSIZE=4080
                                      473  *
       000528                         474  MASTER   DCB   DSORG=IS,MACRF=(RUS,WUA),DDNAME=DORMS
                                      541  *
       000614                         542  REPORT   DCB   DSORG=PS,MACRF=(PM),DDNAME=SYSPRINT,                  X
                                      543                 RECFM=FB,LRECL=132,BLKSIZE=4092

                                      595  * DOS *******
                                      596  *TRANS   DTFCD DEVADDR=SYSIPT,WORKA=YES,IOAREA1=INBUF,EOFADDR=EOJ,  X
                                      597  *              DEVICE=2540
                                      598  *INBUF   DS    CL80
                                      599  *
                                      600  *REPORT  DTFPR DEVADDR=SYSLST,WORKA=YES,IOAREA1=OUTBUF,BLKSIZE=132, X
                                      601  *              DEVICE=1403
                                      602  *OUTBUF  DC    CL132' '
```

Figure 21.13   continued

```
FLAG LOCTN OBJECT CODE     ADDR1 ADDR2 STMNT M SOURCE STATEMENT

                                      603    *
                                      604    *MASTER   DTFIS DEVADDR=SYS001,DEVICE=3330,DSKXTNT=3,HINDEX=3330,     X
                                      605    *                RECFORM=FIXBLK,RECSIZE=107,NRECDS=38,                 X
                                      606    *                IOAREAR=MSTBUF,WORKR=RECDR,KEYLEN=8,KEYLOC=2,CYLOFL=2, X
                                      607    *                IOAREAL=MSTNBUF,WORKL=RECDL,                          X
                                      608    *                IOROUT=ADDRTR,TYPEFLE=RANDOM,KEYARG=KAREA             X
                                      609    *
                                      610    * ERROR BYTE IN 'MASTER' DTFIS HAS FOLLOWING RELEVANT BITS
                                      611    * RNF      EQU   B'00010000'         BIT 3 = RECD-NOT-FOUND
                                      612    * DUP      EQU   B'00000100'         BIT 5 = DUPLICATE-RECORD
                                      613    * OVF      EQU   B'00000001'         BIT 7 = OVERFLOW-RECORD
                                      614    *
                                      615    *RECDR    DS    CL107
                                      616    *RECDL    DS    CL107
                                      617    ****************
           000674                     618    SAVE     DS    18F          REGISTER SAVE AREA.

                                      619    * DOS *******
                                      620    *SAVE     DS    9D
                                      621    *        LTORG
                                      622    *        DS    0D
                                      623    *MSTBUF   DS    CL4066       DOS ISAM BUFFER FOR RETRIEVAL & UPDATE
                                      624    *KL       EQU   8            KEY LENGTH
                                      625    *MSTNBUF DS     CL(8+KL+4066) DOS ISAM BUFFER FOR NEW RECDS
                                      626    ****************
                                      627             END
```

CROSS-REFERENCE

```
SYMBOL     LEN    VALUE   DEFN    REFERENCES

ABEND      00002 000242  00278    00191   00229   00256
ADD        00006 00029C  00318    00311
ADDEND     00004 0000E0  00127    00122   00124
ADDLOOP    00004 0000B6  00117    00126
ADD1       00006 0002AA  00321    00319
BISAM      00001 000000  00364
BLANKS     00001 0002C6  00367    00303   00304   00315   00316   00318
BYP        00001 0000FF  00414    00072   00137   00163
CHANGE     00004 000114  00147
CONSTRCT   00006 000252  00301    00114
DATALNG    00001 000031  00363    00314   00320   00367
DECBD      00001 000000  00341    00024
DEL        00006 00027E  00312
DELETE     00004 000146  00161    00146
DEL1       00006 00028C  00315    00313
DIFFKEY    00004 00013E  00158    00154   00156
DUP        00001 0000C1  00348    00255
DUPLMSG    00034 00045F  00408    00265
EODFLG     00001 0004C7  00413    00072   00074   00109   00133   00137   00163
EOJ        00004 00005C  00072    00442
ERRLINE    00084 0003CB  00404    00209   00268
ERRMSG     00034 0004 2F 00406    00205   00265
ERRTRANS   00050 0003CB  00405    00115   00206
EXCODE     00002 000018  00345    00190   00192   00228   00253   00255
EXIT       00002 0002B6  00323    00317
KAREA      00008 000383  00380    00337   00381
KDORM      00004 000383  00382    00060   00121   00153
KEYADDR    00004 000014  00344
KROOM      00004 000387  00383    00061   00123   00155
MAINLOOP   00006 000044  00060    00128   00143   00159   00169
MAREA      00001 0000C0  00354    00022
MASTER     00004 000518  00476    00033   00089   00334
MDATA1     00031 000009  00358    00303   00360
MDATA2     00031 00003A  00359    00304
MDELETE    00001 000000  00355    00161   00203
MDORM      00004 000001  00356    00301
MID        00009 000031  00362    00312   00316   00318   00322
MNAME      00028 0000C9  00361    00315   00321   00363
MROOM      00004 000005  00357    00302
MSTRDECB   00004 0002BC  00330    00025   00179   00186   00218   00225   00241   00250
NEWADD     00004 0000A4  00109    00063
NEWBUF     0007B 0003C8  00372    00244   00373
NEWRECD    0006B 000318  00375    00110
NOTFMSG    00034 000493  00409    00205
OVF        00001 000002  00347    00190
RDERR      00006 0001A2  00205    00193
RDEXIT     00002 0001BE  00213    00204
READ       00002 000164  00177    00134
RECDADDR   00004 000010  00343    00189
REPORT     00004 000614  00543    00039   00095   00208   00267
```

Figure 21.13   continued

CROSS-REFERENCE

SYMBOL	LEN	VALUE	DEFN	REFERENCES					
REWR	00001	0000F0	00416	00133					
REWRITE	00002	0001C2	00216	00076	00158	00162			
RNF	00001	000080	00346	00190	00192				
SAVE	00004	000674	00618	00020	00021	00097			
TAREA	00050	00038B	00388	00054	00115	00118	00140	00150	00166	00206	00389
TDORM	00004	000392	00393	00060	00121	00153	00301		
TID	00009	0003C8	00399	00312	00322				
TNAME	00028	00039F	00397	00321					
TRANS	00004	0004C8	00421	00045	00053	00083	00117	00139	00149	00165
TROOM	00004	00039A	00395	00061	00123	00155	00302		
TTYPE	00001	00038E	00391	00062	00145	00305	00310		
UPDATE	00004	0000E8	00133	00064					
UPDATING	00002	000274	00309	00125	00147	00306			
VALIDKEY	00004	0001CC	00145	00136	00157				
WR	00001	00000F	00415	00074	00109				
WREXIT	00002	00023E	00271	00254					
WRITE	00002	0001F0	00239	00078	00127				
XBYPASS	00004	000078	00081	00073	00077				
XREWRITE	00004	00006C	00076						
XWRITE	00004	000074	00078	00075					

Whether the key or key class method is used, there is a possibility that a transaction record will contain a record key or key class not represented in the master file. In such a case, a "record-not-found" error condition will occur when the SETL macro is executed.

Random Retrieval

The processing logic required for random retrieval is probably the simplest of the three methods. The transaction records need not be in key sequence. However, the key class method cannot be used; each transaction must designate a specific record key to identify the record that is to be retrieved. For this reason, the random retrieval method is usually reserved for interactive systems, where the sequence of requests cannot be predicted in advance.

In OS, when using BISAM for retrieval, the READ K instead of the READ KU macro is used. The list and execute forms are usually not required. A dummy section is used to define the record fields, and a dummy base register is established to access those fields beginning at the record address provided in the data event control block. The data set can be opened for input only, using dynamic buffering to retrieve records without updating them. For example, in the dorm-room master file, this could be done as shown here:

```
        OPEN        (MASTER)
        .

        .
        READ        MSTRDECB,K,MASTER,'S','S',KAREA
        WAIT        ECB=MSTRDECB
        .

        .
MASTER  DCB         DSORG=IS,MACRF=(RS),DDNAME=DORMS
```

The key of the desired record must be moved to the area designated by the key-address parameter in the READ macro. In this example, the key-address parameter is KAREA. After the READ operation has been completed, i.e., following the WAIT macro, the exception codes can be tested for "record-not-found" or uncorrectable error situations, and appropriate action can be taken. If there are no errors, the logical record address can be obtained from the data event control block.

In DOS, the DTFIS macro must specify random retrieval, together with the IOAREAR and WORKR areas and the KEYARG field name:

```
MASTER  DTFIS       ...,IOROUT=RETRVE,TYPEFLE=RANDOM,            X
                    IOAREAR=buffername,WORKR=workareaname,       X
                    KEYARG=keyfieldname,...
```

Figure 21.14 *Sequential retrieval using SETL.*

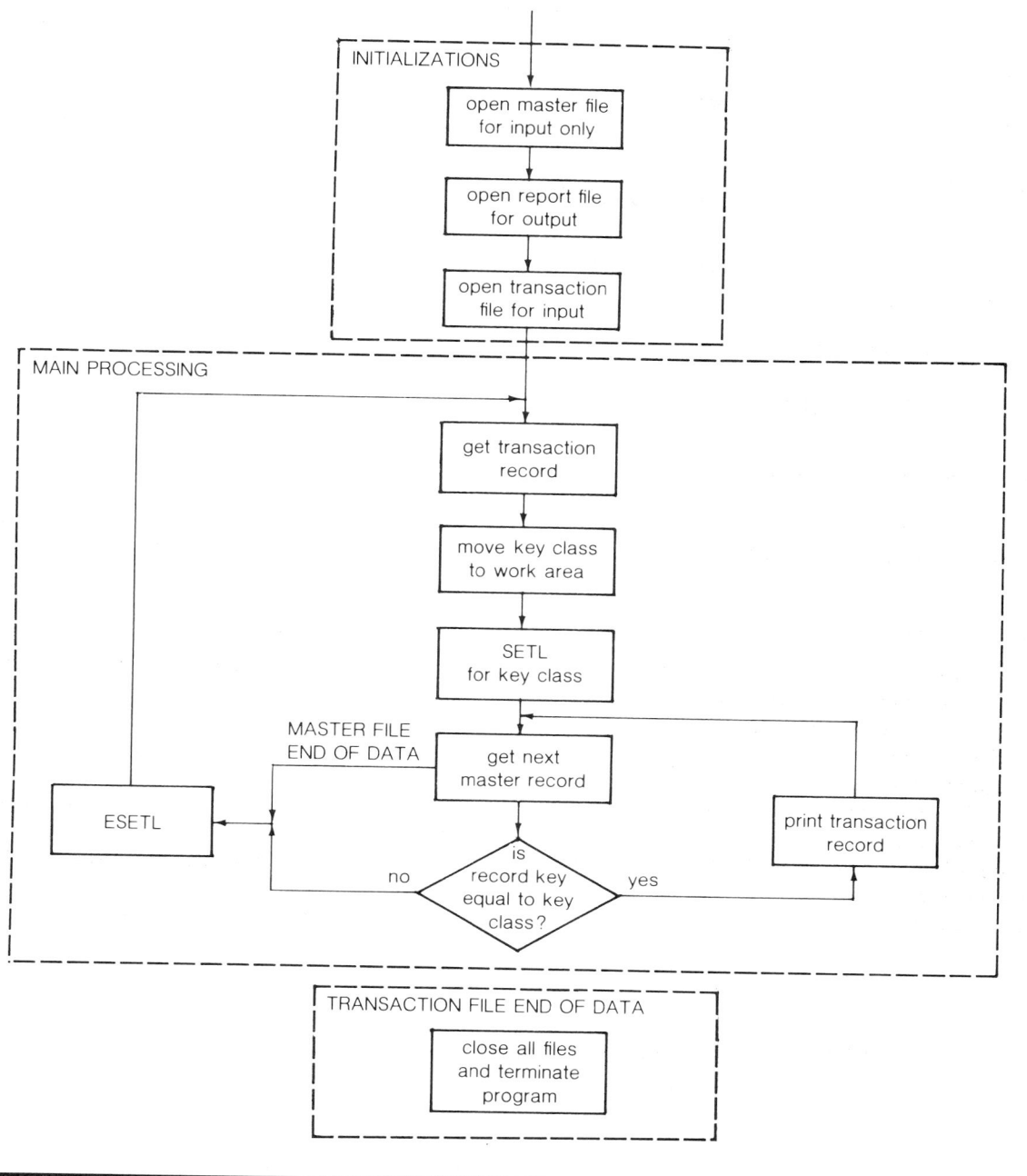

The WAITF macro must immediately follow the READ KEY macro in order to synchronize I/O operations with run-time CPU operations:

```
READ       MASTER,KEY
WAITF      MASTER
```

The error code bits can then be tested for "record-not-found" or other I/O error condition. Of course, any condition except record-not-found would be a fatal error, and the program would normally have to be terminated.

The diagram in figure 21.15 illustrates the principal processing steps required to retrieve records in random order from an indexed sequential data set. The programming required to carry out these processes is left as an exercise for you.

Figure 21.15   Random retrieval.

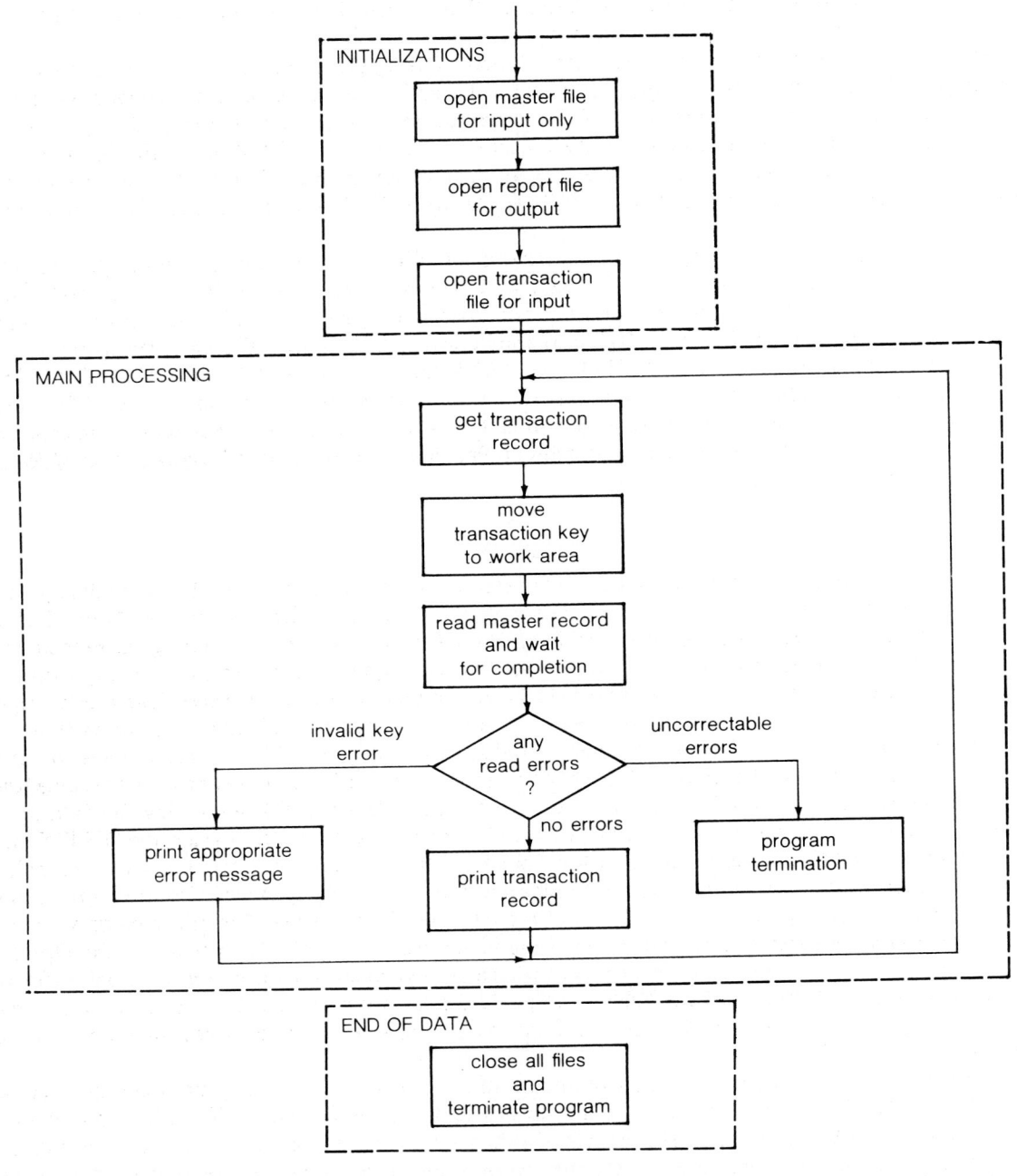

21.9   CONCLUDING REMARKS

Perhaps the most important aspect of using indexed sequential data sets is the choice of an appropriate key by which the records can be sequenced. Once that key is chosen, all further processing logic is essentially dependent on it. For example, in our dorm-room file, having chosen the dorm and room number as the key, a request such as "In what room is John Doe?" would normally have to be answered by processing every record until John Doe's name is found. On the other hand, the dorm and room number key is more natural if the purpose of the data set is to maintain records about room assignments.

Compared to sequential data set processing, the capabilities for updating in random mode, without having to recreate the data set, can provide a significant time and space saving if the number of records in the overflow areas is relatively small compared to the number in the data set. The need to reorganize the data set periodically stems from the decrease in performance that results when more and more records are placed into the poorly utilized overflow areas.

Methods for handling error conditions that can occur during processing deserve more discussion than has been given in this introductory chapter. For such a discussion, the OS assembly language programmer should consult the descriptions of the SYNAD error-processing conventions in the *OS/VS1 Data Management Services Guide* and the descriptions of the exception code bits for BISAM and QISAM in *Appendix A* of the *OS/VS1 Data Management Macro Instructions* reference manual. The DOS programmer should investigate the use of ERREXT=YES by consulting the *DOS/VS Supervisor and I/O Macros* reference manual.

Descriptions of methods for improving the performance of indexed sequential processing procedures not mentioned in this chapter can also be found in the above mentioned manuals. In OS, these methods include improvements to the index handling procedures of the Operating System (via OPTCD=U and the MSHI and SMSI parameters in the BISAM DCB macro) and improvements to the buffering procedures used when adding new records via BISAM (via the MSWA and SMSW parameters in the DCB macro). In DOS, similar improvements can be made by using the INDAREA= and INDSKIP= parameters of the DTFIS macro and by utilizing statistics that the Operating System makes available in the DTFIS macro expansion. These statistics are described in the above referenced manual, Part 4, in the section titled *Organization of Records on DASD: Programming Considerations*.

21.10 SUMMARY

Indexed sequential data sets provide a means of processing records either sequentially or randomly. In sequential-mode processing, most of the concepts that apply to sequential data sets are equally applicable to indexed sequential data sets. This includes blocking and deblocking and double buffering. In random-mode processing, the task of determining the relative and physical positions of a record in secondary memory is performed by the Operating System, which uses the index it maintains for this purpose. The user's program need take little special action other than to provide the key of the record that is to be read or written.

Each record in an indexed sequential data set must be uniquely identified by the contents of its key field. Moreover, the key field of each record must begin in the same relative position and have the same length (from 1 to 255 bytes) as the key fields of all other records in the data set. When creating the data set, the records must be written in increasing key sequence. QISAM must be used in OS systems; the WRITE macro together with the SETFL/ENDFL macros are required in DOS. At the time the data set is created, the Operating System allocates space for the prime, independent overflow, and cylinder index areas (all in count-key-data format) according to the specifications of the job control statements. The new records are written into the prime area and appropriate entries are made in the track and cylinder indexes by the Operating System. A portion of the prime area (one or more tracks per cylinder) is always used for track indexes; it may also be used for cylinder overflow. For very large data sets—for example, those requiring more than t tracks for the cylinder index where t exceeds a cylinder's capacity—we can also request that a master index be created.

Sequential-mode processing can begin at any arbitrary record in an existing indexed sequential data set by using the SETL macro to identify the first record that is to be processed. If SETL is not executed, sequential processing begins at the first record in the data set. It is not necessary to create a new data set when updating in sequential mode, provided that new records are not being inserted and that existing variable-length records are not having their lengths changed. Records can, however, be added to the end of the data set (in the prime area), records can be deleted logically (though not physically), and record contents can be replaced without having to create a new data set. In OS, a record whose delete-flag byte is X'FF' is considered to be deleted and is ignored by all subsequent QISAM I/O requests even though physically it might still be in the prime data area. In DOS, the user's program must check the delete-flag byte to determine whether a record has been flagged for deletion.

In random-mode processing, all four updating actions (described in Section 21.6) are permitted without having to create a new data set. The Operating System uses the prime and/or overflow areas when new records are inserted and when the lengths of variable-length records are changed. However, as more and more records are added to the overflow areas processing efficiency may decrease significantly due to the poor organization of overflow records. For this reason, you should periodically reorganize an indexed sequential data set, for example by using sequential-mode processing to copy the records in sequence from the existing data set to a new one.

Contrary to what happens in sequential processing, the Operating System detects and rejects attempts to read or write records under certain data error conditions. The most common conditions for sequential mode are these:

1. When creating a data set, the key of each record written must be greater than the key of the immediately preceding record. If it is less, an out-of-sequence error condition will occur; if it is equal, a duplicate-key error condition will occur. The same conditions can arise when adding records to the end of a data set in EXTEND mode.
2. If not enough prime space was allocated to anticipate the number of records being added (either when creating or extending a data set), a space-not-found error condition will occur.
3. If there is not a key or key class in the data set that matches the one specified when a SETL macro is executed, a record-not-found error condition will occur (see Section 21.4).

In random mode, the most common conditions are:

1. When attempting to read a record that is to be updated, an invalid-key condition occurs if the key specified by the READ macro does not match the key of any record in the data set.
2. When attempting to insert a new record into the data set, an invalid-key condition occurs if the key specified by the WRITE macro is equal to the key of a record that is already in the data set. (If the matching data set record is flagged for deletion, however, then in OS but not DOS it is simply replaced and no error condition is posted.)

Methods for handling these errors were discussed in Sections 21.5 through 21.7.

EXERCISES

1. If we wish to process an indexed sequential data set with an assembly language program, what factors determine whether we should use QISAM or BISAM?

2. What capabilities exist in QISAM processing mode that do not exist in BISAM processing mode, and vice versa?

3. What capabilities exist both in QISAM processing and in BISAM processing?

4. What is the difference in purpose between the prime data area, the overflow areas, and the index area as specified in a DD statement or EXTENT statements for an indexed sequential data set?

5. What is the difference in purpose between the independent overflow area and the cylinder overflow areas for an indexed sequential data set?

6. Explain why the statement "overflow track space is used inefficiently, both for storage and for searching" is true.

7. What is the reason for designating the delete-flag option (OPTCD=L)? What are the requirements for use of the delete-flag option in QISAM processing? In BISAM processing? In DOS ISAM?

8. Write the SPACE= parameter of the DD statement or the //EXTENT statements required to reserve space for an indexed sequential data set under each of the following sets of conditions (for an IBM 3330 disk system):

   a. Separate prime, index, and independent overflow areas for 100,000 80-byte records with 10-byte keys
   b. Separate prime and independent overflow areas (with the index at the end of the overflow area), for 10,000 200-byte records with 16-byte keys
   c. A prime area subdivided by the Operating System for the index and independent overflow areas, for 10,000 100-byte records with 8-byte keys.

9. Analogous to the formula for the IBM 3330 disk system, the track capacity formula for the IBM 3350 disk system is

$$\text{number of blocks per track} = \frac{19254}{267 + KL + DL} \text{, in count-key-data format.}$$

There are 30 tracks per cylinder and 555 cylinders in a disk pack of the IBM 3350 disk system.

   a. Assuming that $KL + DL = 18987$ (i.e., one data block per track), what is the capacity of a disk pack in the IBM 3350 disk system if all the tracks are recorded in count-key-data format?
   b. Denoting the number of blocks per track as given by the above formula by N, what is the maximum value of $KL+DL$ for each of the values $N = 1,2,3,..., 10$?
   c. Assuming 8-byte keys and 10-byte data blocks in all the index areas, what would be the maximum number of track-index tracks required per cylinder of a disk pack in the IBM 3350 disk system?
   d. Assuming 8-byte keys and 107-byte logical records (e.g., the dorm-room master file), how many logical records could be stored per *track* in the IBM 3350 disk system if the blocksize were 4066 bytes? How many if the blocksize were 2889 bytes? Using the track-capacity formula given above, show that a blocksize of 2889 bytes is the best choice that is less than or equal to 4096 bytes, from the standpoint of track space utilization in the IBM 3350 for the dorm-room master file.
   e. Calculate the number of prime data area cylinders that would be required for a 5000-record dorm-room master file stored in the IBM 3350 disk system; one track per cylinder is used for the track index and two tracks are reserved for cylinder overflow. Assume that $KL=8$, $DL=BLKSIZE=2889$, and $LRECL=107$. What would be the significance of the answer to this problem if prime data space were allocated only in units of whole cylinders?

10. What assembly language statements would be required to accomplish the same purpose as each of the following IBM COBOL clauses:

   a. APPLY CYL-OVERFLOW OF 2 TRACKS ON filename
   b. ACCESS IS RANDOM...OPEN INPUT
   c. ACCESS IS RANDOM...OPEN I/O
   d. ACCESS IS SEQUENTIAL...OPEN OUTPUT

11. What DCB macro parameters are required to describe each of the following situations for an indexed sequential data set for which the record format is fixed block:

   a. A record key that occupies the last 8 bytes of an 80-byte record, the first byte of the record being reserved for the delete flag
   b. Up to three levels of master index, each level consisting of two tracks
   c. Use of both independent and cylinder overflow, the latter consisting of three tracks per cylinder
   d. The data set is opened in QISAM EXTEND mode
   e. The data set is opened for updating in place, using the SETL macro for positioning to the appropriate record

12. Prepare suitable test data to create an indexed sequential dorm-room master file in accordance with the specifications given in this and the preceding chapter. Ensure that your test data covers at least the following situations: no students assigned to a room, one student assigned to a room, two students assigned to the same room. Ensure that the transaction records are in proper sequence by sorting them via the IBM Sort/Merge program (see IBM Publication SC33–4035, *Sort/Merge Programmer's Guide*).

13. Using the test data from Exercise 12, and the program in figure 20.8 (suitably modified for indexed sequential processing), create a sample dorm-room master file. To verify that its contents are correct, print the master file via the OS utility program IEBISAM (see IBM Publication GC26–3901, *Utilities*) or the corresponding DOS utility program (see Publication GC33–5381).

14. Write an assembly language program that could be used to reorganize the dorm-room master file. (Assume that it already existed as an indexed sequential data set, as discussed at the end of Section 21.3.)

15. Write a program that will print the entire contents of the dorm-room master file in some suitably readable format, with the following specifications: your program should be written to allow for an arbitrary number of records on the master file, there should be no more than 50 lines printed per page, each page should begin with an appropriate title line with date and page number on each page, and a new page should be started each time there is a change in dorm building.

16. Write a program in accordance with the same printing specifications as those given in Exercise 15, except that instead of printing the entire contents of the master file only those records containing two students per dorm room should be printed.

17. Write a program that will delete all those records in the dorm-room master file that contain no student names and i.d.'s.

18. Assume that there is a transaction file in which each record contains a dorm building abbreviation in columns 8–11, and a dorm room number in that building in columns 16–19. There is no other information in the transaction file records. Write a program using BISAM to print the dorm-room master file records that correspond to the transaction file records. Hint: see figure 21.15.

19. Assume that there is a transaction file in which each record contains a dorm building abbreviation in columns 8–11. There is no other information in the transaction file records. Write a program using the SETL macro to print all the dorm-room master file records for the dorm building given in each transaction record. Each set of records for a given dorm building should be printed starting on a new page. Hint: see figure 21.14.

20. A government agency has decided to create a computer file that records the name, model year, and average city and highway gas mileage ratings (miles per gallon) of each model of automobile manufactured in the United States since 1975.

   a. Design a transaction record format that can be used to create an indexed sequential master file consisting of all the information mentioned. Design a master file format for these records.
   b. Design a transaction record format that can be used to update the gas-mileage master file, with capability to add or delete records and to correct errors in existing records.
   c. Write a program to create the gas-mileage master file as an indexed sequential data set. Prepare appropriate test data to verify that your program is correct.
   d. Write programs that will update the master file in EXTEND mode, UPDAT mode, and random mode. Prepare appropriate test data to verify that your programs are correct.
   e. Write a program that will produce a report giving all the information in the master file for a given year, listed in ascending sequence by city gas mileage rating (major field) and automobile model name (minor field).

22

VSAM (Virtual Storage Access Method)

The Virtual Storage Access Method has been designed for several purposes; it is intended as a replacement for the OS and DOS indexed sequential access methods (QISAM,BISAM; ISAM). It may also be used instead of the OS and DOS sequential access methods (QSAM,BSAM; SAM). And it can be used in data base management applications such as IBM's Information Management System (IMS). As will be seen, the Access Method Services utility program AMS provides a relatively simple means of creating VSAM data sets, and the VSAM I/O macros provide a variety of processing options.

VSAM must be used with one of the IBM virtual storage Operating Systems, e.g., OS/VS, DOS/VS, and their variations and extensions. In this chapter we will refer to these systems as simply OS and DOS, respectively.

Readers who have studied the preceding three chapters in this text will soon notice conceptual similarities among the sequential, indexed sequential, and virtual storage access methods. However, though very useful as background information, such prior study is not absolutely essential. The I/O macros and associated parameters available in VSAM differ in considerable detail from those of the other access methods; there are a large number of parameters and processing options that have no counterparts in the other access methods. This extensive variety exists in part to provide alternative means of accomplishing a task and in part to provide mechanisms for optimizing VSAM performance and memory space utilization.

Unlike the sequential and indexed sequential access methods, VSAM macros and associated parameters are essentially the same in both OS and DOS systems. Similarly, the use of the Access Method Services program is essentially the same in OS and DOS. Therefore, except for examples involving job control language, there are no separate OS and DOS descriptions of these facilities in this chapter. The differences that do exist between OS and DOS are noted in context.

This chapter is intended as an introduction to VSAM. It is concerned only with its use as a replacement for sequential and indexed sequential access methods. Even in this context, many processing options are either treated very briefly or are omitted. Our purpose is to provide enough information for the beginning VSAM programmer to understand basic concepts, to be able to write programs for elementary applications, and to then be able to progress to more advanced applications with the aid of the IBM reference manuals listed at the end of the chapter. The material is organized as follows:

Section	Content
22.1	Introductory concepts and terminology
22.2	Defining and loading VSAM data sets via AMS
22.3	Basic I/O macros
22.4	Loading a VSAM data set
22.5	Updating an entry-sequenced data set
22.6	Updating a key-sequenced data set
22.7	Alternate indexes
22.8	Topics for further study
22.9	Reference manuals
22.10	Summary

The author is indebted to his former student, Mr. Bruce Barton, for providing invaluable assistance in the formulation of this chapter.

22.1 INTRODUCTORY CONCEPTS

VSAM provides support for three types of data sets, known as Entry-Sequenced Data Sets (ESDS), Key-Sequenced Data Sets (KSDS), and Relative Record Data Sets (RRDS). All three types must be stored on and processed from direct-access storage devices, e.g., disks. ESDS is conceptually similar to sequential organization; KSDS, to indexed sequential organization; and RRDS, to relative organization. We will discuss only ESDS and KSDS in this text.

Physical Organization

The memory space in which a VSAM data set is stored on a direct-access storage device is organized into discrete units known as control intervals. A *control interval* is the unit of information that is read from and written to a storage device by the Operating System. Depending on its size, a control interval can contain one or more fixed-length or variable-length logical records, one or more physical data blocks, and some unused space. It also contains information that defines the length of the records contained in it, as shown in figure 22.1.

The size of a control interval can be independent of a track's capacity, of the physical blocksize, and of the logical record lengths. If data records are larger than the control interval size, it is permissible to specify that they be allowed to extend across (i.e., *span*) control interval boundaries. In many applications, however, use of spanned records is not necessary. Moreover, a suitable choice of control interval size will result in each control interval containing exactly one data block.

Control intervals are grouped by VSAM into regions of storage known as *control areas*. Each area occupies contiguous space (e.g., consecutive tracks) on the storage device. The maximum size of a control area is one cylinder; its minimum size is one track. Every physical space extent of a data set consists of one or more control areas. VSAM data sets therefore always consist of one or more control areas, depending on how much space is allocated.

Logical Organization

ESDS records are stored in a data set in the sequence in which they are presented to the Operating System. They can, but need not, be sorted prior to being presented for storage. In this sense the sequencing of ESDS records is analogous to that of sequential data-set records.

KSDS records are stored in a data set in ascending key sequence. The key field which controls sequencing is known as the *primary key* field. The primary key must be the same length (from 1 to 255 bytes) in each record, must be in the same relative position within each record, and must uniquely identify the record in which it exists. In this sense the primary keys and sequencing of KSDS data records are analogous to those of indexed sequential data-set records.

The relative location of a logical record in a VSAM data set is defined by its *relative byte address* (RBA), a full-word binary integer which specifies the position of the record relative to the beginning of the data set. The RBA of the Nth record is equal to the total number of bytes contained in the preceding N-1 records. For example, the RBA of the first record is zero, and the RBA of the second record is equal to the length (in bytes) of the first record. The record lengths used in calculating RBA's include all control information and unused space stored with each record (see fig. 22.2).

VSAM always uses the RBA to determine a record's location in a data set. But except in certain advanced applications of VSAM, RBA's are not normally needed by user programs to access records. There are other, simpler means available to user programs. If needed, however, RBA's can be obtained at run time via the SHOWCB macro, which will be discussed in Section 22.6.

Data Components, Index Components, and Clusters

VSAM maintains an *index component* (i.e., a set of index records) with each key-sequenced data set. Its function is analogous to that of the index maintained for indexed sequential data sets. Namely, it enables the VSAM modules to translate a primary key of a KSDS record into the RBA of that record. Thus, if a user program presents a primary key to VSAM, that key can be used by VSAM to locate the KSDS record which the key identifies, and thereby make it possible to read or write that record without having to read or write all the preceding records.

Figure 22.1 *Physical space organization.*

A control interval always consists of a whole number of physical blocks.

The size of control intervals depends on the device. It can be chosen when a data set is defined and must be either   512m   with m = 1,2,..., 16 (i.e., 512, 1024, 1536, ..., 8192)
         or 8192 + 2048n , n = 1,2,..., 12 (i.e., 10240, 12288, ..., 32768)

Physical blocksize is chosen by VSAM and is always either 512, 1024, 2048, or 4096.

Example 1:   **CISZ = 12288, BLKSZ = 4096. Device is IBM 3330.**

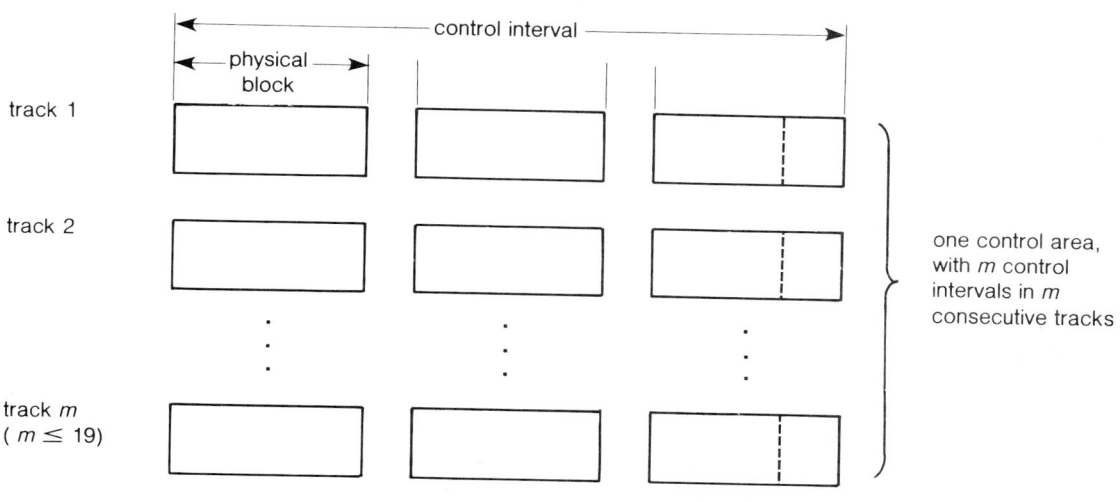

Example 2:   **CISZ = 4096, BLKSZ = 4096. Device is IBM 3330.**

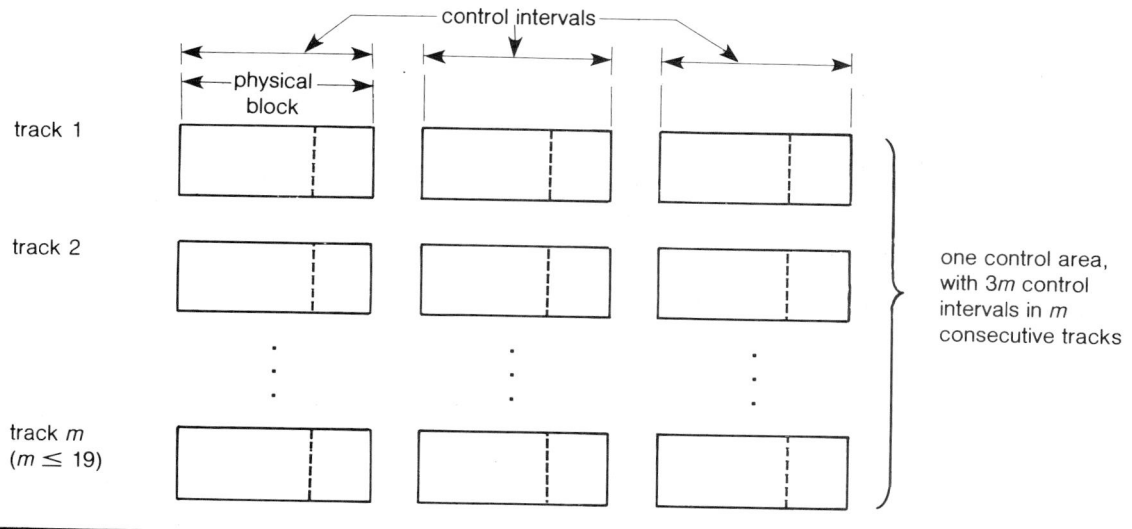

Figure 22.2 RBA's and control interval formats.

Note: The formats shown below apply only to *un*spanned records.

If in both Case 1 and Case 2 we assume that the records are in the Nth control interval (N = 1,2,...), then the RBA of record 1 is $RBA_1 = (N-1)\times CISZ$, and the RBA of record k is $RBA_k = RBA_1 + L_1 + L_2 + ... + L_{k-1}$ for k > 1. For example, if N = 2 and CISZ = 4096, then $RBA_1 = 4096$ and $RBA_3 = 4096 + L_1 + L_2$.

Case 1: No two consecutive records have the same length.

Case 2: *m* consecutive records (*m* > 1) have the same length.

In this case what would have been the *m* RDF's by the above scheme are collapsed into 2 RDF's, thereby saving space in the control interval. The 2 RDF's have the following format:

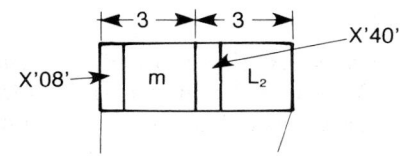

For example, suppose there are n=m+2 records in the control interval, and all but the first and last have same length L_2. Then only 4 RDF's are needed, as shown here:

The term *base cluster* (and sometimes just *cluster*) describes the totality of basic information that VSAM always maintains about a data set. An ESDS cluster consists of one component, namely the *data component*— i.e., the set of all control areas that contain control intervals in which data records are stored. A KSDS cluster consists of two components: the data component and the index component.

The index component is organized by VSAM into a tree structured hierarchy. The lowest level nodes of this tree are known as the *sequence set* of the index. Each node in the sequence set is analogous to a track index of an indexed sequential data set. In all the applications which we will discuss, one sequence set node resides on the first track of each control area. In VSAM this positioning of the sequence set nodes is known as *imbedding* the index.

Each entry in a sequence set node points to one of the control intervals in the corresponding control area. Each entry in a higher level node points to one of the nodes in the next lower level. VSAM always generates as many higher level nodes as are needed for the highest level to fit on one track—the root node of the index tree.

The manner in which index entries are formatted is a topic beyond the scope of this text. But two aspects are worth noting: (1) the entries in any index node are stored in a fixed-length data block known as an *index control interval;* and (2) the size of index control intervals is always either 512 bytes, 1024 bytes, 2048 bytes, or 4096 bytes. The size of an index control interval can be specified when defining a KSDS. The choice of size obviously determines the number of entries that can be stored in a node; for many applications, an appropriate size is 512 bytes.

Alternate Indexes

In addition to the base cluster, an ESDS or KSDS can also optionally consist of one or more alternate indexes. Each alternate index is itself a key-sequenced data set. Its purpose is to permit one or more records in the data component of the base cluster to be identified and accessed by a key other than the primary key. That key is known as an *alternate key*. More than one record of a KSDS or ESDS data component can be identified by a single alternate key value. In other words, unlike the value of a primary key, the value of an alternate key need not uniquely identify a record. The use of alternate keys and alternate key indexes will be discussed in Section 22.7.

Accessing Records

ESDS and KSDS organizations permit both sequential accessing and direct accessing, with or without alternate indexes. *Sequential* accessing means that the Nth record must be accessed before the (N+1)st record can be accessed and only after the (N−1)st record is accessed. *Direct* accessing means that any logical record can be accessed at any time, provided that the record is appropriately identified when the access request is made.

Sequential Access

ESDS records are sequentially accessed in ascending RBA sequence. This mode is known as *addressed sequential* access. VSAM maintains the value of the current record's length and RBA so that it can calculate the RBA of the next record. The user program need not present an RBA in order to access a record in this mode.

Addressed sequential access is always used to create a new ESDS. It can also be used to add new records to the end of an existing data set, and to retrieve, update (without changing record length), and mark existing records for deletion. An ESDS record that is marked for deletion remains in the data set; it is up to the user's program to ignore or to re-use the space of such records during subsequent operations.

KSDS records that are sequentially accessed must be read or written in primary key sequence. In this case the accessing mode is known as *keyed sequential* access. This mode is always used to create a new KSDS, and may also be used to sequentially retrieve, update, and delete records, and to add new records to an existing KSDS. VSAM erases deleted records from a KSDS.

It is possible to begin sequential accessing at any arbitrary record position in an ESDS or KSDS. To do this, the user's program must inform VSAM of the desired beginning record position. For ESDS, this must be done by specifying the RBA of the desired record position as the search argument in a POINT macro. For KSDS, the POINT macro is also used to specify the beginning record position, but instead of the RBA you must specify the primary key of the desired record as the search argument. Use of the POINT macro will be outlined in Section 22.8.

Figure 22.3 Schematic of KSDS index structure.

In these diagrams, only the prime keys are shown. They are assumed to be 3 bytes long. It is also assumed that two sets of higher-level indexes are needed.

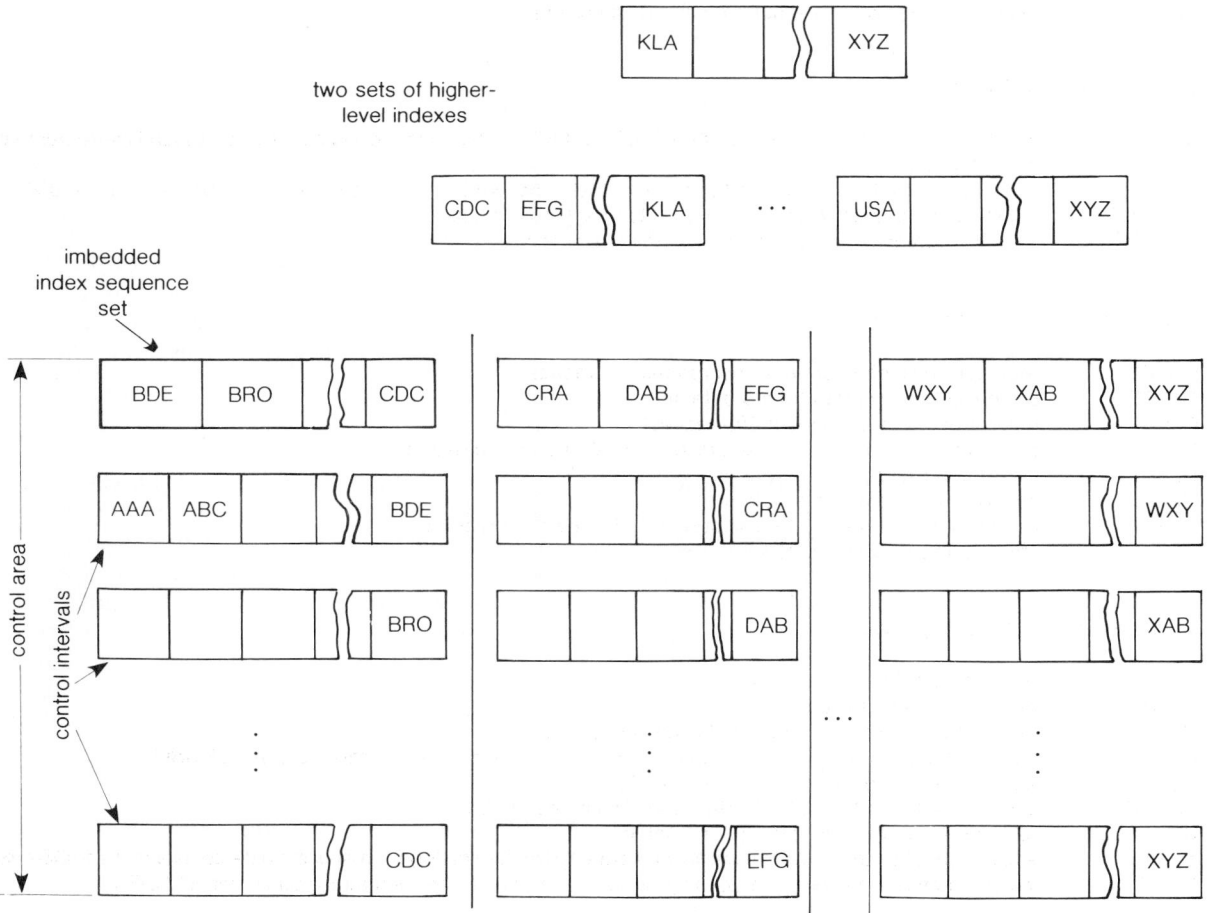

Note: Like the logical records in a control interval, the entries in an index record are stored in ascending prime key sequence.

The imbedded index sequence set (the lowest-level index) contains the highest key and a pointer for each control interval that contains data in the control area that the sequence set pertains to.

Each higher-level index contains the highest key and a pointer for each of the immediately lower-level indexes that it pertains to.

No attempt is made in the above diagrams to account for spanned records or for unused (i.e., free) control intervals.

Direct Access

If alternate keys are not used, there are two modes of direct accessing for KSDS and one for ESDS. We will refer to these modes as *ordinary* direct accessing to distinguish them from direct accessing via alternate keys. (Note: the term "ordinary" is the author's, not IBM's.)

The ESDS mode of ordinary direct accessing is known as *addressed direct* access. This mode requires that the RBA of each desired record be presented to the Operating System in order to read or write a record. As in ESDS sequential processing, this mode permits existing records to be retrieved, updated without changing length, and marked for deletion. However, this mode may not be used to add new records to the data set.

The two KSDS modes of ordinary direct accessing are known as *keyed direct* and *keyed skip-sequential* access. In both modes, the primary key of a record must be presented to the Operating System in order to read or write that record. Existing records can be retrieved, updated, and deleted, and new records can be

552   Input/Output

Figure 22.4 VSAM macro summary.

Nonexecutable Control Block Macros

ACB	generates an access-method control block at assembly time
EXLST	generates a list of exit-routine addresses at assembly time
RPL	generates a request parameter list at assembly time

Executable Control Block Macros

GENCB	generates the same information that an ACB, EXLST, or RPL macro does but does so at run time rather than assembly time
MODCB	modifies the contents of any of the control blocks that were generated by ACB, EXLST, RPL, or GENCB
SHOWCB	obtains the contents of one or more fields of any control block
TESTCB	tests the contents of any one of the fields in a control block

Request Macros for General Use

CHECK	waits for completion of an asynchronous I/O request
CLOSE	disconnects a program from a data set
ENDREQ	terminates an asynchronous I/O request
ERASE	deletes a record from a key-sequenced or relative-record data set
GET	retrieves a record from a data set
OPEN	connects a program to a data set
POINT	positions a data set at a designated record or class of records
PUT	stores a record into a data set

Request Macros for Advanced Applications

BLDVRP	builds a VSAM resource pool
DLVRP	deletes a VSAM resource pool
GETIX	retrieves a specified index control interval (OS only)
MRKBFR	marks a buffer for output, or to release it from exclusive control or shared status (OS only)
PUTIX	stores a specified index control interval (OS only)
SCHBFR	searches a buffer for an RBA within specified ranges (OS only)
SHOWCAT	retrieves information from a VSAM catalog
VERIFY	ensures that the end-of-data information contained in the catalog for a specific data set is accurate (OS only)
WRTBFR	writes a deferred buffer or (in OS only) writes a buffer that was marked for output via MRKBFR

Note: All the request macros are executable macros.

inserted or added. However, whereas records can be processed in any sequence with keyed direct accessing, the keyed skip-sequential mode requires that records be processed in ascending primary key sequence. The method by which VSAM searches the index component results in faster processing for the keyed direct method under some circumstances and in faster processing for keyed skip-sequential under others. Keyed skip-sequential is faster only if there are relatively few records to be processed *and* only if those records have reasonably closely grouped primary key values.

I/O Programming Considerations

VSAM data sets must be defined, and space must be allocated for them, before any records can be stored in them. The process of defining a data set and allocating space for it is accomplished via the Access Method Services program (AMS), and will be described in the next section. The process of storing records into an empty data set, known as *loading* the data set, can be accomplished either via AMS or via a user program. Once an ESDS or KSDS is loaded, it must be closed and reopened before any other processing of that data set can occur.

As in sequential and indexed sequential assembly language I/O programming, VSAM I/O programming is accomplished via macros. There are two types of macros: request macros and control block macros (see fig. 22.4).

Figure 22.5   Relationship of JCL and VSAM macros.

Request macros are designed to be executed at run time. They initiate actions such as opening a data set, and retrieving and updating records.

Some of the control block macros are also designed to be executed. They can, for example, be used to create, modify, obtain, or test selected fields of the control blocks. The control blocks themselves are similar in purpose to the DTFxx areas in DOS and the DCB areas in OS systems. They provide information that is used at run time by the Operating System when it responds to a request macro or to an executable control block macro. That information is generated by the ACB, RPL, and EXLST macros in both DOS and OS systems.

The ACB macro must be referred to when opening and closing a VSAM data set. The basic options specified in an ACB are these: the identity of an OS DD statement or DOS DLBL statement which in turn identifies the VSAM data set to be processed and the anticipated logical record accessing modes. Among the other options that may be specified in an ACB are the buffer space requirements for reading and writing control intervals and the address of the EXLST macro that pertains to this ACB. A password can also be specified, if needed to access the data set. (DOS users should note that unlike the other access methods, DOS VSAM allocates buffer space for use at run time. You can designate how many buffers are to be allocated by VSAM, but you do not reserve space for those buffers at assembly time. The same is true in OS VSAM.)

The RPL macro must be referred to each time any macro other than OPEN or CLOSE (or GENCB) is executed at run time. The basic options specified in an RPL are these: the name of the ACB that the RPL is associated with (see fig. 22.5); the address and length of the I/O record work area; the record accessing mode to be used for a particular request; the address of the search argument for direct accessing and for record positioning; and whether or not the request is for updating a record.

The EXLST macro specifies the symbolic names of user-program routines that are to be executed when certain run-time exceptions (such as end of data or I/O error conditions) occur.

The ACB and RPL macros are required; the EXLST macro is optional. EXLST is used primarily in applications where program execution and I/O operations proceed concurrently. It will not be discussed further until Section 22.8. ACB and RPL are used in all applications. Examples of their use will be given beginning in Section 22.3.

As will be seen from the examples later in this chapter, omitting the EXLST macro requires that compensating action be taken by the program. For when EXLST is omitted, VSAM always puts a code in Register 15 and returns to the instruction following execution of an I/O macro *whether or not an error has occurred!* The Register 15 code is =F'0' if no errors occurred, =F'8' if a logical (software) error occurred, and =F'12' if a physical (hardware) error occurred. It is of critical importance that the program test that code before proceeding; if there is an error and it is not handled by the program in some way, the program will in all likelihood blow up at some later instruction, and tracing the cause of the problem may prove exceedingly difficult at that point.

22.2 ACCESS METHOD SERVICES (AMS)

AMS is the VSAM utility program, executable under the name IDCAMS in both OS and DOS systems. The most important of its functions are:

1. it defines VSAM catalogs and data sets and allocates space for them;
2. it loads VSAM data sets from the input data stream and from other nonVSAM data sets and VSAM data sets;
3. it prints the contents of VSAM catalogs and data sets.

AMS *must* be used to define VSAM catalogs and data sets and to allocate space for them. Its other functions are optional; their use depends on your needs.

Brief definitions of all the AMS commands are given in figure 22.6. A definitive description of the commands is in the AMS manuals noted at the end of this chapter. Here, we will discuss only the elementary aspects of the DEFINE and REPRO commands. This will provide the essential tools needed by beginning VSAM programmers.

Figure 22.6   AMS command summary.

General Usage

DEFINE	creates a catalog entry for a VSAM object
DELETE	deletes one or more VSAM objects and their catalog entries
LISTCAT	lists information contained in a VSAM catalog
PRINT	prints the contents of a VSAM data set or of a sequential or indexed-sequential data set
REPRO	copies a VSAM or sequential or indexed sequential data set into another VSAM or sequential data set, or copies a catalog to another catalog
VERIFY	verifies and corrects certain information about a data set in a catalog

Special Usage

ALTER	changes catalog information about a VSAM object that was previously defined
BLDINDEX	initially loads a newly defined alternate index
CHKLIST	lists tape data sets that were open at the time a checkpoint was taken (OS only)
CNVTCAT	converts OS catalog entries into VSAM catalog entries (OS only)
EXPORT	unloads a VSAM base cluster or alternate index, together with its catalog entry, onto a movable storage volume; alternatively, copies a user catalog onto a movable volume and then disconnects that catalog from the system's master catalog
EXPORTRA	unloads data sets whose catalog entries are damaged, using the information about the data set that is in the catalog recovery area instead of the information in the catalog itself
IMPORT	defines and loads a data set or catalog that had been unloaded via EXPORT
IMPORTRA	reconstructs a data set that had been unloaded via EXPORTRA, by redefining it and reloading it
LISTCRA	lists the contents of a catalog recovery area and (optionally) compares it with the contents of the associated catalog
RESETCAT	adjusts information in a catalog to be consistent with that which is in its associated catalog recovery area and in the VTOC

In general a fairly substantial number of parameters can be specified with each command to indicate the precise nature of the function that is desired. The parameters and their formats are virtually the same in both OS and DOS. In addition, a certain minimal amount of job control language (JCL) must accompany execution of the AMS program. The OS JCL is of course different from the DOS JCL.

There are several considerations of overriding importance when using AMS:

1. Every computer system that supports VSAM must have exactly one master catalog that is created by AMS for the entire system. The master catalog is usually defined by the system administrator and will not be considered here.
2. Every VSAM user data set must be described either in the master catalog or in a user catalog which is created by AMS. For various reasons (e.g., increased processing efficiency and easier transportability to other computer systems), a user catalog should be used for this purpose rather than the master catalog.
3. There can be no more than one user catalog per storage volume (e.g., one per disk pack). Like the master catalog, user catalogs are ordinarily defined by a system administrator rather than by a programmer.
4. No two VSAM data sets that are listed in the same catalog can have the same data-set name. Indeed, no two VSAM *objects* that are listed in the same catalog can have the same name.

In (4) above, the term *object* means any of the following: master catalog, user catalog, data space, cluster (i.e., VSAM data set), nonVSAM data set, alternate index, and path (a path connects an alternate index to a VSAM data set and will be discussed in Section 22.7).

The names of VSAM objects must contain from 1 to 44 characters, of which the first must be a letter (A through Z, and @ $ #) and the others can be letters or digits. Names longer than eight characters must be segmented by periods into groups of 8 or fewer letters and digits (e.g., **VSAM.DATA.SET**). Consecutive periods are not permitted, and the last character of a name cannot be a period. That portion of a name consisting of a period and all characters to the left of that period is known as a *qualifier;* names containing qualifiers are known as *qualified names*. For example, **VSAM.** is a qualifier, as is **VSAM.DATA.,** but **VSAM.DATA.SET** is not a qualifier; it is a qualified name. *Un*qualified names are permitted but not recommended, because just as no two objects in a catalog can have the same name, so also no unqualified name can be the same as the first qualifier in a qualified name. For example, the two names **DATA** and **DATA.SET** cannot both exist in the same catalog.

The DEFINE Command

The AMS *DEFINE* command must be used to create a new catalog and must be used to create an entry in an existing catalog for any VSAM object. There are seven variations of this command, corresponding to the seven VSAM objects:

in full	*abbreviated*
DEFINE MASTERCATALOG	DEF MCAT
DEFINE USERCATALOG	DEF UCAT
DEFINE SPACE	DEF SPC
DEFINE CLUSTER	DEF CL
DEFINE NONVSAM	DEF NVSAM
DEFINE ALTERNATEINDEX	DEF AIX
DEFINE PATH	DEF PATH

A few of the parameters that can be specified with each DEFINE command are required; the others are optional.

Probably the most important consideration in using the DEFINE command is the allocation of storage space for objects. AMS provides several methods by which this can be done. These depend of course on your ability to estimate how much space is required (see below). The methods of space allocation that seem to the author to be appropriate for most applications consist of three steps:

1. use the DEF UCAT command to allocate space for a user catalog
2. use the DEF SPC command to allocate space to be shared by all VSAM clusters and alternate indexes that are defined in that user catalog
3. use the DEF CL command to request space for a cluster and the DEF AIX command to request space for an alternate index.

If these three steps are followed, then the storage space required for all objects (except the catalog itself) is allocated by VSAM from the single DEF SPC data space on an as needed basis. That single space is then known as a *suballocatable* data space.

Whoever supervises the use of VSAM at your computer installation will most likely be responsible for doing steps (1) and (2), i.e., DEF UCAT and DEF SPC. Consequently, here we will discuss only the required parameters and a few of the optional parameters for DEF CLUSTER.

To estimate the space requirements for a cluster, we note that its size is roughly $n \cdot k$ bytes, where n is the approximate number of logical records in the cluster and k is the average record length. Thus, *for a given* n *and* k, *the number of tracks required for the data component depends on the size of a control interval and on the number of control intervals per track.*

Given this, the estimated space requirements can be summarized as in the following table. It should be noted that for KSDS, we have introduced the factor A to account for various control area sizes. You will recall from Section 22.1 that one track of each control area is used by the imbedded index sequence set; thus that track must be subtracted from each KSDS control area in a cylinder to determine the number of tracks available to the data component in that control area (see fig. 22.3).

Estimates of a cluster's space requirements can be determined from the following formulas:

	K = #tracks per data component	Y = #cylinders per data component	J = #tracks per index component
ESDS	$K = (n \cdot k)/(C \cdot S)$	$Y = K / X$	---
KSDS	$K = (n \cdot k)/(C \cdot S)$	$Y = K / (X - A)$	$J = 1 + (A \cdot Y)/B$

where
- n = approximate number of logical records in the cluster
- k = average length of a record in the cluster
- S = number of bytes per data control interval
- C = number of data control intervals per track
- X = number of tracks per cylinder
- A = number of control areas per cylinder
- B = number of entries in an index record

It must be stressed that the above formulas are only approximations. More accurate estimates can be obtained by following the procedures described in the AMS manuals. Whichever method is used, the quantities n and k must be estimated; the quantities S, C, and X are device dependent (see below); $A = 1$ if space is requested in units of cylinders; and B depends on the size of the index control interval.

The data component control interval size S is an important quantity which should be designated in the DEF CLUSTER command. Once its value is chosen, then the value of C is determined by the device characteristics. Recommended values of S, with corresponding values of C and X, are:

	IBM 2314	IBM 3330	IBM 3340	IBM 3350	
S	2048	4096	4096	4096	bytes per CI
C	3	3	2	4	CI's per track
X	20	19	12	30	tracks per cyl.

As mentioned, the quantity B in the formula for J is the number of entries in an index record. B depends on the size of the index control interval. This size should also be designated in the DEF CLUSTER command for KSDS clusters. Recommended values of the index control interval size, with the corresponding approximate values of B, are:

	IBM 2314	IBM 3330	IBM 3340	IBM 3350	
index CI	512	512	512	1024	bytes per index CI
B	60	60	60	120	#entries per record

There are a number of reasons for the above recommendations. They result in good track space utilization. They result in each data control interval being equal in size to one physical data block. And they make reasonably efficient use of the index control intervals. However, there is one important underlying assumption. That is that the length of the primary key in a KSDS is not more than about 10 bytes. If it is longer than this, then the index CI size may have to be doubled or quadrupled (see the AMS manuals and the VSAM Primer noted at the end of the chapter).

Figure 22.7 DEFINE CLUSTER parameters.

Note: Only a small subset of the many possible options are shown here. Consult the AMS manual for restrictions and other options. In the notation below, a long vertical bar separates two choices of which either but not both can be specified. Uppercase represents keywords; lowercase represents values.

General Format
```
DEFINE CLUSTER (cluster options)—
       DATA (data options)—
       INDEX (index options)—
       CATALOG (catalog options)
```

cluster options

NAME (entryname)	specifies the name of the cluster
VOLUME (volser)	identifies the volume where the cluster will reside
CYL (p s) | TRK(p s) | REC(p s)	specifies the amount of space to be allocated; p is the primary allocation, s the secondary
FILE (dname)	identifies the DD or DLBL statement linked to the cluster
NONINDEXED | INDEXED	NONINDEXED means it's an ESDS; INDEXED means it's a KSDS
NOREUSE | REUSE	specifies whether or not it is a "reusable" data set
SUBALLOCATION | UNIQUE	specifies whether the data set shares a suballocatable data space or is allotted its own space
NOIMBED | IMBED	(KSDS only) specifies whether or not to imbed the index sequence set

Note: NONINDEXED, NOREUSE, SUBALLOCATION, and NOIMBED are the defaults.

data options

NAME (entryname)	specifies the name of the data component
RECSZ (avg max)	specifies the average and maximum length of data records
CISZ (size)	specifies the data component control interval size
KEYS (length offset)	for KSDS only, specifies the length of the prime key and its displacement from the beginning of a record
FSPC (ci ca)	for KSDS only, ci specifies the percent of space in each control interval and ca the percent in each control area that is to be left free when the cluster is loaded

index options (for KSDS only)

NAME (entryname)	specifies the name of the index component
CISZ (size)	specifies the index component control interval size

catalog options

catalogname / password	identifies the name of the catalog in which the cluster is to be defined and specifies the password (if any) required to update the catalog; the slash / between catalogname and password must be included if a password is specified

To illustrate the above formulas, we will use the dorm-room master file described in chapters 20 and 21. As you will recall, that file contained approximately 5000 fixed-length records, with a record length of 106 bytes for the sequential version and 107 bytes for the indexed sequential version. For an IBM 3330 disk system, the number of data component tracks for an ESDS version of that file is $K = (5000 \cdot 106)/(4096 \cdot 3) \approx 44$, and for a KSDS version it is also 44 tracks. The number of index component tracks for the KSDS version is (assuming one control area per cylinder) $J = 1 + (1 \cdot Y)/60$, where $Y = 44/18$. Thus $J = 2$. Therefore the total number of tracks required for the KSDS version of the dorm-room file is 46, and the total for the ESDS version is 44. In either case we therefore request an allocation of 3 cylinders for an IBM 3330. (When allocation is in units of cylinders, the control area size is always one cylinder, i.e., $A = 1$ in the formula for J. When allocation is in units of tracks, the control area size will be an integral number of tracks equal to the lesser value of the primary and secondary allocation, but not exceeding one cylinder. In this case A can be greater than or equal to 1.)

Referring to the DEF CLUSTER parameters given in fig. 22.7, it is now a relatively simple matter to define the dorm-room cluster. The definition will specify the cluster's name, space requirements, type (ESDS or KSDS), and the device on which it is stored. It will also specify names and control interval sizes for the data component and (KSDS only) index component. Logical record length and KSDS key length and key position complete the specifications. The requested space will be suballocated from the data space defined by DEF SPC. That is the default, and no special parameter is needed to request this. However, if suballocation were not desired, then the UNIQUE parameter would have to be specified for the cluster and for the data and index components.

The job control language required in OS systems to define an ESDS cluster is the same as that required for a KSDS cluster. Similarly, the DOS job control is the same for ESDS and KSDS clusters. If the name of the cluster is DORM.FILE and the name of the user catalog is SAMPLE.UCAT, then the job control statements can be written as follows:

For OS Systems:

```
//STEP003  EXEC  PGM=IDCAMS
//STEPCAT  DD    DSN=SAMPLE.UCAT,DISP=SHR
//CLDD     DD    VOL=SER=VOLA,DISP=OLD,UNIT=3330
//SYSPRINT DD    SYSOUT=A
//SYSIN    DD    *
```

For DOS Systems:

```
// DLBL    CLDD,'DORM.FILE',,VSAM
// EXTENT  SYS010,VOLA
// ASSGN   SYS010,DISK,VOL=VOLA,SHR
// EXEC    IDCAMS,SIZE=AUTO
```

If DORM.FILE is a KSDS cluster, then the AMS commands which should follow the above job control statements for both OS and DOS are these (recall that the dorm-room file primary key was 8 bytes long and occupied positions 2 through 9 of each record):

```
DEF   CL    (                              -
              NAME (DORM.FILE)             -
              FILE (CLDD)                  -
              VOL (VOLA)                   -
              CYL (3 1)                    -
              INDEXED IMBED                -
              )                            -
      DATA (                              -
              NAME (DORM.FILE.DATA)        -
              RECORDSIZE (107 107)         -
              KEYS (8 1)                   -
              CISZ (4096)                  -
              )                            -
      INDEX (                             -
              NAME (DORM.FILE.INDEX)       -
              CISZ (512)                   -
              )                            -
      CAT (SAMPLE.UCAT/updatepassword)
```

If DORM.FILE is an ESDS cluster instead of a KSDS cluster, then the AMS commands which would follow the above job control statements are:

```
DEF     CL   (                                              -
                 NAME (DORM.FILE)                           -
                 FILE (CLDD)                                -
                 VOL (VOLA)                                 -
                 CYL (3 1)                                  -
                 NONINDEXED                                 -
                 )                                          -
        DATA (                                              -
                 NAME (DORM.FILE.DATA)                      -
                 RECORDSIZE (106 106)                       -
                 CISZ (4096)                                -
                 )                                          -
        CAT (SAMPLE.UCAT/updatepassword)
```

The format for the AMS commands and parameters shown above is recommended for most needs. All information is in columns 2 through 72. One or more blanks can be used to separate command and parameter words and values. The continuation indicator (a hyphen) is, for ease of visual checking, placed in the same column of all lines that are being continued. You should ordinarily avoid continuing a parameter or its value from one line to the next, but if it must be done the continuation character in that case is a plus ($+$) rather than a hyphen ($-$), and the continuation of the parameter or value must begin in column 2. Other aspects of the AMS statement formats are described in the manuals.

The REPRO Command

The AMS *REPRO* command can be used to load a new VSAM data set with records obtained from a nonVSAM data set, or from another VSAM data set. Other important uses of REPRO, such as copying catalogs and clusters, are described in the AMS manuals.

The VSAM data set that is loaded by REPRO must have been previously defined by the DEFINE command. The type of data set that is being loaded does not have to match the type of data set from which the records are obtained. To illustrate this flexibility, the example below assumes that a sequential data set is the input to the REPRO command and that the output is a KSDS cluster. The input data set is the one created in chapter 20—i.e., the sequential dorm-room file. The output data set is the one defined earlier in this section. As can be seen, DOS AMS requires that nonVSAM input data-set characteristics be described; OS AMS doesn't.

Two points are worth noting: (1) the only change required to load an ESDS cluster rather than a KSDS cluster is to change the job control statements which identify the cluster that is being loaded; and (2) the cluster being loaded must be identified in the JCL by its base cluster name, not by its data or index component names.

For OS Systems:

```
//STEP004   EXEC   PGM=IDCAMS
//STEPCAT   DD     DSN=SAMPLE.UCAT.DISP=SHR
//NEWDD     DD     DSN=DORM.FILE,DISP=OLD
//OLDDD     DD     VOL=SER=VOLB,UNIT=3330,DISP=(OLD,KEEP),
//                 DSN=SEQTL.DORM.FILE,DSORG=PS,
//                 DCB=(RECFM=FB,LRECL=106,BLKSIZE=4028)
//SYSPRINT DD      SYSOUT=A
//SYSIN     DD     *
      REPRO                        -
          INFILE (OLDDD)           -
          OUTFILE (NEWDD)
  /*
```

```
// DLBL     OLDDD,'SEQTL.DORM.FILE'
// EXTENT   SYS020,,,,50,130
// ASSGN    SYS020,DISK,VOL=VOLB,SHR
// DLBL     NEWDD,'DORM.FILE',,VSAM
// EXTENT   SYS010,VOLA
// ASSGN    SYS010,DISK,VOL=VOLA,SHR
// EXEC     IDCAMS,SIZE=AUTO
     REPRO
        INFILE (OLDDD                      -
           ENV (RECFM (FB)                 -
                BLKSZ (4028)               -
                RECSZ (106)                -
                PDEV (3330))               -
              )                            -
        OUTFILE (NEWDD)
/&
```

22.3 BASIC I/O MACROS

A VSAM data set which has been defined in a catalog via the AMS program is ready to be processed. The first act of processing the data set must be to load it. This can be done via the AMS *REPRO* command or via a user program. Thereafter, the data set can be updated, copied, printed, or just accessed for retrieval only.

In this section we discuss the basic input/output macros that are used to process VSAM data sets in Assembly Language. These include the two principal control block macros (ACB and RPL) and the five principal request macros (OPEN,CLOSE,GET,PUT,ERASE) which were summarized in figure 22.4. Examples of their use will be given in subsequent sections.

Permission to process a VSAM data set must be requested at run time by an OPEN macro. That macro must in turn specify the address of an ACB macro which describes the anticipated processing requirements. Figure 22.8 summarizes the parameters that can be specified in an ACB macro. A subset of these should always be specified, while the others are applicable only in special processing situations. All the accessing modes which are going to be used while the data set is being processed must be specified in the ACB macro.

When the OPEN macro is executed, VSAM determines whether the data set identified by the ACB macro had been defined via AMS and is currently specified by appropriate job control statements. It also determines whether the access parameters—e.g., password, updating, access modes, etc.—are consistent with what is specified for the data set in the catalog. If all these conditions are met, then the OPEN request is granted, i.e., the data set is then said to be "open" and is available for processing. If any of the conditions are not met, VSAM puts an explanatory error code in the ERROR field of the ACB and puts a nonzero indicator in Register 15 before returning to the user program. If the program finds that Register 15 is not zero, it can take appropriate action after examining the ACB error code via the SHOWCB macro (see Section 22.6).

Once a data set is open, the GET, PUT, and ERASE macros can be used to access logical records. GET is used to retrieve an existing record, and PUT is used to update an existing record and to add or insert a new record. PUT is therefore also used to load a data set. ERASE is used to delete existing KSDS (but not ESDS) records. All three macros have identical operand formats, as shown in figure 22.9a. If any error is detected while VSAM is responding to a GET, PUT, or ERASE request, an error code is placed in the FDBK field of the corresponding RPL macro, and VSAM puts a nonzero indicator in Register 15 before returning to the user program. As with OPEN errors, the user program can use the SHOWCB macro to determine the precise cause of the error.

It is important to note that execution of a PUT macro to update an existing record must be preceded by execution of a GET macro for that same record. The same is true for the ERASE macro: it must be preceded by a GET for the record that is to be erased. In both cases the GET is known as "GET-for-update". The PUT is similarly known as "PUT-for-update". The parameter that specifies the update mode for GET and PUT is one of the RPL's OPTCD parameters, 'UPD' (see p. 564).

Figure 22.8 ACB macro parameters.

General format: acbname ACB keyword$_1$=value$_1$,...,keyword$_n$=value$_n$

Only those keywords that pertain to your processing needs have to be specified. They can be specified in any order.

An asterisk (*) in the left-hand margin denotes keywords and options available in OS/VS but not in DOS/VS. See the OS/VS VSAM Progammer's Guide or the DOS/VS Suervisor and I/O Macros manual for further restrictions and explanations.

keywords commonly used

AM=VSAM	states that the access method is VSAM
DDNAME=dname	dname identifies the associated JCL statement
MACRF=(macrf-options)	specifies options for run-time processing (see below)

keywords for error handling

EXLST=exlstname	identifies this ACB's EXLST macro
MAREA=address	names an area to receive OPEN/CLOSE error messages
MLEN=length	specifies the length of the MAREA area

keywords for buffers

BUFND=n$_1$	n$_1$ = # I/O buffers used for data component CIs
BUFNI=n$_2$	n$_2$ = # I/O buffers used for index component CIs
BUFSP=s	s = maximum number of bytes for all data and index buffers
STRNO=n$_3$	n$_3$ = max number of requests requiring concurrent data-set positioning (such requests are known as *strings*)
* BSTRNO=n$_4$	n$_4$ = # strings accessing the base cluster of a path

Note: Defaults are n$_3$=1, n$_1$=n$_3$+1, n$_2$=n$_3$, n$_4$=n$_3$.
  Default for s is consistent with n$_1$ and n$_2$ and with catalog info.

keywords for catalogs

PASSWD=address	names a field that contains the highest-level password required for the type of access specified in MACRF=
* CATALOG=NO|YES	specifies whether a catalog is being opened as a catalog (YES) or as a data set (NO); default is NO
* CRA=SCRA|UCRA	requests system or user storage be used when processing a catalog recovery area

macrf-options for data set access

KEY|ADR|CNV	keyed, addressed, or control-interval access
SEQ|DIR|SKP	sequential, direct, or skip-sequential access
IN|OUT	IN means retrieval only; OUT means loading or updating
NRM|AIX	NRM means process the object named by DDNAME=; AIX means process the alt index whose path is named by DDNAME=
NRS|RST	NRS: not a reusable data set, or else do not set high-RBA to zero; RST: reset high-RBA of reusable data set to zero

Note: Defaults are KEY, SEQ, IN, NRM, and NRS.

macrf-options for performance improvement

NUB|UBF	whether or not user program manages use of I/O buffers
* NFX|CFX	whether or not buffers and control blocks are swappable
* NCI|ICI	whether or not to use improved control-interval processing
* NIS|SIS	whether or not to split control intervals/areas at the position where a record is inserted

Note: Defaults are NUB, NFX, NCI, and NIS. *N* means *not*.

macrf-options for shared resources

NSR|LSR|GSR	nonshared, locally shared, or globally shared resources
NDF|DFR	nondeferred or deferred writing of shared buffers
* DDN|DSN	shared control blocks are based on ddnames/dsnames

Note: Defaults are DDN, NDF, and NSR. GSR is for OS/VS only.

Figure 22.9a *OPEN, CLOSE, GET, PUT and ERASE macro parameters.*

```
OPEN    (acbname) I (r)

CLOSE   (acbname) I (r)                      OS and DOS close and disconnect

CLOSE   (acbname) I (r), TYPE=T              OS/VS closing without disconnecting
TCLOSE  (acbname) I (r)                      DOS/VS closing without disconnecting

GET     RPL=rplname I (r)
PUT     RPL=rplname I (r)
ERASE   RPL=rplname I (r)
```

Note: acbname and rplname are the name-field symbols that identify the ACB and RPL macros, respectively.
r is the address of a register (2 thru 12, enclosed in parentheses) that contains the address of an ACB or RPL macro.

Figure 22.9b   *RPL macro parameters.*

General format: rplname   RPL   keyword$_1$=value$_1$,...,keyword$_n$=value$_n$

Only those keywords that pertain to your processing needs have to be specified. They can be specified in any order.

An asterisk (`*`) in the left-hand margin denotes keywords and options available in OS/VS but not in DOS/VS. See the OS/VS VSAM Programmer's Guide or the DOS/VS Supervisor and I/O Macros manual for further restrictions and explanations.

---

keywords commonly used

AM=VSAM	states that the access method is VSAM
ACB=acbname	identifies the associated ACB control block
AREA=areaname	identifies the work area for logical records in move mode
AREALEN=m	m is the length of the work area, and should be no less than the length of the longest record to be processed
ARG=fieldname	identifies the field that contains the search key or RBA used in direct and skip-sequential access, and in positioning
KEYLEN=k	k is the length of the generic key used when OPTCD=GEN
RECLEN=r	r is the length of the record that PUT adds or inserts
OPTCD=(optcd-options)	specifies options for run-time processing (see below)

---

keywords for advanced applications

TRANSID=i	i is a number that identifies all the modified buffers associated with a given transaction ($0 \le i \le 31$)
* ECB=address	identifies an event control block used with asynchronous I/O
* MSGAREA=address	names an area to receive physical I/O error messages from VSAM
* MSGLEN=length	specifies the length of the MSGAREA area; must be $\ge$ 128
NXTRPL=address	specifies the address of the next RPL in a chain of RPL's

---

optcd-options

KEY I ADR I CNV	keyed, addressed, or control-interval access
SEQ I DIR I SKP	sequential, direct, or skip-sequential access
MVE I LOC	move mode or locate mode
NUP I UPD I NSP	is not for update, is for update, or note sequential position
KEQ I KGE	with keyed access, find the first record with a key that is either equal to, or greater than or equal to, the search key
FKS I GEN	specifies whether the search key is a full key or a generic key
FWD I BWD	record accessing is either in the forward or the backward direction; if BWD, then KEQ and FKS are assumed
ARD I LRD	ARD: record accessing is as specified in other parameters; LRD: locate or retrieve the last record in the data set (BWD)
* SYN I ASY	synchronous or asynchronous accessing
* NWAITX I WAITX	specifies whether or not to give control to the user's UPAD error-exit routine to synchronize processing of shared resources

Note: Defaults for all optcd-options are specified above as the first choice in each group of two or three options.

Figure 22.9b summarizes the parameters that can be specified in an RPL macro. As with ACB, certain RPL parameters always should be specified, while the others apply only in special cases. Unlike the ACB, in which all anticipated accessing modes must be specified, only one accessing mode can be specified in an RPL macro. It must be the mode for which the GET, PUT, or ERASE is being used.

Regardless of the access mode, and regardless of whether the data set is a KSDS or an ESDS, the input/output processing mode should be specified in the RPL macro as follows:

	with GET	*with PUT*
for retrieval only	OPTCD=(...,NUP,LOC,...) OPTCD=(...,NUP,MVE,...)	-----
for updating	OPTCD=(...,UPD,MVE,...)	OPTCD=(...,UPD,MVE,...)
for adding new records	----	OPTCD=(...,NUP,MVE,...)

GET can be used in either move mode or locate mode, but both PUT and ERASE must always be used in move mode. *Move mode* (OPTCD=MVE) means that VSAM moves a logical record to and from the area specified by the AREA= parameter in the RPL macro. *Locate mode* (OPTCD=LOC) means that for the GET macro VSAM doesn't move the record to the AREA area. Instead it puts its *address* in that area. That address is the location of the record in the VSAM I/O buffer. As is indicated above, the author recommends that except when retrieving without updating, move mode should be used for all but the most performance sensitive situations. The extra processing incurred by move mode will usually be offset by the processing incurred when switching from locate mode to move mode during update operations. It should be noted, however, that move mode requires that the AREA and AREALEN parameters be specified in the RPL macro.

A final point to observe is that when PUT is used to store new records (as when loading a data set), the RPL's RECLEN= parameter must specify the length of each record that is being stored. If the records are all the same length, this is a simple matter; the length can just be coded in the RPL at assembly time. If the records are of varying length, then RECLEN= must be specified via a MODCB macro prior to each execution of a PUT macro (see Section 22.6). RECLEN= is not required for GET or ERASE; the length of existing records is known by VSAM.

22.4   LOADING A VSAM DATA SET

In Section 22.2, we showed how the AMS *REPRO* command could be used to load a key-sequenced data set. The input was a sequential data set, and the example was based on the dorm-room file described in chapter 20.

In this section, we illustrate how to load a VSAM data set via an assembly language program. By writing your own program instead of using REPRO, you are of course better able to interpret and utilize the input records.

We will again base our illustration on the dorm-room master file. For this you should be familiar with Section 20.9 and the program given in figure 20.8 that creates the master file as a sequential data set. There, it will be recalled, we showed how more than one input record could result in a single master file record. That same processing logic will be used here. The only differences between what follows now and what was done in chapter 20 are in the use of the request macros OPEN, GET, PUT, and CLOSE, and in the use of the ACB and RPL control block macros instead of the OS DCB or DOS DTFSD macros.

Figure 22.10 shows the changed portions of the program that was given in figure 20.8. Not changed (and therefore not shown) are the standard program entry and exit sequences, the internal subroutine to construct a master record, the input and output record areas, and the OS DCB (or DOS DTFCD) macros describing the input transaction file.

The output data set in figure 22.10 is being loaded as an entry-sequenced data set (ESDS). From our prior discussions it should be clear that this data set must have already been defined in a VSAM catalog via AMS. In figure 22.10 the ACB MACRF and RPL OPTCD parameters both specify ADR, SEQ (addressed sequential access), because no other accessing mode is permitted when loading an ESDS.

Figure 22.10 *Loading a VSAM data set.*

```
1    CREATE   CSECT
2    *
3    *  THESE PROGRAM SEGMENTS ARE CHANGES TO THE PROGRAM GIVEN
4    *  IN CHAPTER 20, FIG. 20.8. THEY ARE INTENDED TO INDICATE
5    *  HOW TO CODE THE OPEN, PUT, AND CLOSE MACROS AND THE
6    *  ASSOCIATED ACB AND RPL MACROS WHEN LOADING A VSAM
7    *  ENTRY SEQUENCED DATA SET.
8    *
9             ...                     STANDARD ENTRY NOT SHOWN
10   *
11   * INITIALIZATIONS
12   *
13            OPEN    (MASTER)        OPEN VSAM MASTER FILE
14            LTR     15,15           SEE IF OPEN WAS SUCCESSFUL
15            BNZ     STDXIT          IF NOT, TERMINATE.
16            OPEN    (TRANS,(INPUT)) OPEN 'SYSIN' TRANSACTION FILE
17   *  DOS *******
18   *        OPEN    TRANS
19   **************
20   *
21            GET     TRANS,INAREA    GET FIRST TRANSACTION RECORD
22            BAL     14,CONSTRCT     BEGIN CONSTRUCTING FIRST OUTPUT RECD
23   *
24   * MAIN PROCESSING
25   *
26   READ     GET     TRANS,INAREA    GET NEXT TRANS RECD (IF ANY)
27            ...                     PROCESS IT AS IN FIG. 20.8
28   *
29   WRITE    PUT     RPL=LOADIT      MOVE OUTPUT RECD TO OUTPUT BUFFER.
30            LTR     15,15           SEE IF ANY I/O ERRS
31            BNZ     EOJX            IF SO, TERMINATE.
32            BAL     14,CONSTRCT     BEGIN CONSTRUCTING NEXT OUTPUT RECD.
33            B       READ            THEN GET NEXT TRANS RECD.
34   *
35   * END-OF-DATA PROCESSING
36   *
37   EOJ      PUT     RPL=LOADIT      MOVE LAST OUTPUT RECD TO OUTPUT BUF.
38   EOJX     CLOSE   (MASTER)        CLOSE ALL FILES.
39            CLOSE   (TRANS)
40   *  DOS *******
41   *        CLOSE   TRANS
42   **************
43   STDXIT   ...                     STANDARD EXIT NOT SHOWN.
44   *
45   *
46   * INTERNAL SUBRS 'CONSTRCT' AND 'UPDATING' ARE THE SAME AS
47   *  IN FIG.20.8, AND ARE NOT SHOWN HERE.
48   * OS DCB AND DOS DTFCD FOR TRANS FILE ARE ALSO THE SAME,
49   *  AS ARE THE I/O RECORD AREAS FOR THE TRANS AND MASTER FILES.
50   * BUT OS DCB AND DOS DTFSD FOR MASTER FILE ARE REPLACED BY
51   *  THIS VSAM ACB / RPL PAIR.
52   *
53   MASTER   ACB     AM=VSAM,DDNAME=DORMS,MACRF=(ADR,SEQ,OUT)
54   LOADIT   RPL     AM=VSAM,ACB=MASTER,RECLEN=106,               X
55            AREA=OUTAREA,AREALEN=106,OPTCD=(ADR,SEQ,NUP,MVE)
56   *
57   * REGISTER SAVE AREA IS SAME AS IN FIG. 20.8
58            END
```

If the data set had been defined as a KSDS rather than an ESDS, the only changes required in the statements of figure 22.10 would be to code MACRF=(KEY,SEQ,...) and OPTCD=(KEY,SEQ,...) instead of =(ADR,SEQ,...), and to change the record length to 107 instead of 106 by defining one blank to be the first character of the record. The record length change must also be reflected in the RECLEN= parameter of the RPL macro. The extra blank character which is introduced in this way is included only for compatibility with the indexed sequential delete flag (see chap. 21) and is not absolutely necessary. However what *is* necessary is that the KSDS be loaded using keyed sequential access and that the records that are loaded be in ascending prime key sequence.

It is of crucial importance to note that we have not used an EXLST macro in the statements of figure 22.10. As mentioned at the end of Section 22.1, this means that we *must* test the Register 15 code returned by VSAM after each I/O macro is executed. That code will be zero if no error occurred, and nonzero if some error did occur. Failure to test that code and take some appropriate action would most likely result in a subsequent fatal error causing the program to blow up. As can be seen, we have simply terminated the program if a nonzero code is returned in Register 15 by VSAM. (It might have been more appropriate to print a message telling the user why the program terminated, but we leave that for you. The precise nature of the error can be determined by examining the ERROR or FDBK codes supplied by VSAM, as will be described in Section 22.6.)

Finally, it may be noted that the information about record format and blocksize is not coded in an ACB or RPL because VSAM gets that information from the catalog. The same is true of key length and key position for key-sequenced data sets.

22.5 UPDATING AN ENTRY-SEQUENCED DATA SET

There are two principal techniques for updating an entry-sequenced data set. One technique requires the creation of a new data set. The other updates the existing data set in place.

If a new data set is to be created, it must have been previously defined via AMS. The existing data set is opened in input mode (ACB *IN* parameter), and the new data set is opened in output mode (ACB *OUT*). Both are processed with RPL OPTCD=NUP i.e., not an update. The new data set is in effect loaded with all the unchanged and changed records of the old data set, excluding the records that are being deleted. New records (i.e., records not in the existing data set) can also be added to the new data set during processing.

The above method is the same as that used with sequential data sets (see Section 20.10 and the flow diagrams of figure 20.12a–c), except of course for the differences in I/O macros that are required for VSAM. Changes to the sequential update program in chapter 20, figure 20.13, that are similar to those shown in figure 21.10 would serve to update an ESDS dorm-room master file.

The other method of updating an ESDS is akin to the sequential UPDAT mode of OS systems, except that in VSAM the update-in-place can be done either by addressed sequential access or by addressed direct access. Whichever access mode is used, changes to the data set are made by replacing existing records rather than by copying them to a new data set. The lengths of updated records cannot be changed; neither can records be erased. However, a record can be "marked for deletion" to indicate that they are subsequently to be ignored or replaced (see the following).

In this section we will discuss only the addressed sequential access mode. Addressed direct is a more complex process because it requires that the program specify the RBA (relative byte address) of each record that is to be updated. That in turn requires that the program somehow know the RBA *before* it can read a record. In addressed sequential you do not have to specify the RBA because the records are read in the sequence in which they exist in the data set and VSAM therefore can calculate the RBA of each record.

Each data-set record is read one at a time by the GET macro into the work area designated by the RPL AREA= parameter. The GET macro must be a GET-for-update, i.e., with OPTCD=UPD coded in the associated RPL.

When the program's logic determines that a particular record is to be updated, the desired changes are made to the record in the AREA= work area. The record must then be rewritten by the PUT-for-update macro (PUT with OPTCD=UPD) before the next GET-for-update is executed.

If on the other hand the program determines that a record is not to be updated, then it bypasses execution of the PUT-for-update, i.e., the record is not rewritten. Instead, the program just executes the next GET-for-update.

The process continues until all records that were intended to be updated were in fact updated. As we can see, the advantage of updating in place instead of updating by creating a new data set is that computer processing time is not wasted on writing unchanged records. The disadvantage is that there is not as much flexibility: Records cannot be inserted, the lengths of existing records cannot be changed, and deleted records cannot be erased but can only be marked for deletion. Despite these disadvantages, updating in place is often used.

A program that carries out the above procedure for the dorm-room master file is outlined in figure 22.11. It is based on the flow diagram of figure 20.10 and is similar to the program of figure 20.11 that updates sequential data sets in the OS UPDAT mode. The only difference in the procedures is that VSAM update-in-place includes marking records for deletion. This is done by putting a distinguishing code (X'FF' in our program) in the record before rewriting it. By studying figure 22.11, you will see that records previously marked for deletion are either ignored or replaced by new records of the same length after they are read by the program.

Figure 22.11   ESDS updating in place.

```
 1    UPDAT     CSECT
 2    *
 3    *THIS PROGRAM UPDATES THE ESDS DORM ROOM MASTER FILE USING ADDRESSED-
 4    * SEQUENTIAL ACCESSING, WITH FIXED-LENGTH RECORDS AND MOVE MODE.
 5    *
 6    * THE PROGRAM IS SIMILAR TO THE ONE IN FIG. 20.11 FOR UPDATING A SE-
 7    * QUENTIAL DATA SET, EXCEPT FOR THE USE OF MOVE MODE, MARKING RECORDS
 8    * FOR DELETION, AND BYPASSING/REPLACING DELETED RECDS.
 9    *
10    *NO RECORDS ARE ADDED OR INSERTED. RECORDS MAY BE MARKED FOR DELE-
11    * TION OR MODIFIED BY THE ADDITION OR DELETION OF STUDENT NAMES AND
12    * I.D.'S.  WHEN A NAME AND I.D. IS DELETED, IT IS SIMPLY REPLACED
13    * BY BLANKS.  WHEN A NAME AND I.D. IS ADDED TO A RECORD, IT IS PUT
14    * INTO THE STUDENT DATA AREA THAT IS BLANK.  IT IS ASSUMED THAT THE
15    * INPUT TRANSACTION DATA ARE 'PERFECT'   NO ERRORS, NO DUPLICATES,
16    * NO INVALID TRANSACTIONS.
17    *
18              ...                   STD ENTRY NOT SHOWN HERE.
19    *
20              OPEN  (MASTER)        OPEN MASTER FILE
21              LTR   15,15           SEE IF OPEN WAS SUCCESSFUL
22              BNZ   STDXIT          IF NOT, TERMINATE.
23              OPEN  (TRANS,(INPUT)) OPEN 'SYSIN' DATA SET.
24    *  DOS ******
25    *         OPEN  TRANS
26    ***************
27    *
28              GET   TRANS,INAREA    GET FIRST TRANSACTION RECORD.
29              BAL   14,GETMSTR      GET FIRST MASTER RECORD
30    *
31    * MAIN PROCESSING PROCEDURES
32    *
33    MAINLOOP  CLC   TDORM,MDORM     IF DORM AND ROOM OF TRANS RECD ARE
34              BNE   REWRITE         NOT EQUAL TO THOSE OF MASTER RECD,
35              CLC   TROOM,MROOM     THEN RE-WRITE MASTER (IF NECESSARY)
36              BNE   REWRITE         AND THEN GET NEXT MASTER RECORD.
37              BAL   14,UPDATING     OTHERWISE, GO DO UPDATING, AND THEN
38              GET   TRANS,INAREA    GET NEXT TRANS RECD AND REPEAT THE
39              B     MAINLOOP        PROCESS TILL END-OF-DATA.
40    *
41    REWRITE   CLI   MFLAG,BYP       MFLAG NOT 'BYP' IF CHANGES HAD BEEN
42              BE    BYPASS          MADE TO MASTER RECORD.
43              PUT   RPL=UPDIT       WHEN THAT IS THE CASE, RE-WRITE IT.
44              LTR   15,15           IF ANY I/O ERR, TERMINATE.
45              BNZ   EOJX
46    BYPASS    BAL   14,GETMSTR      OTHERWISE, GET NEXT MASTER RECD,
47              B     MAINLOOP        AND CONTINUE PROCESSING.
48    *
49    * END-OF-DATA PROCESSING
50    *
51    EOJ       CLI   MFLAG,BYP       BEFORE CLOSING, SEE IF MASTER RECD
52              BE    EOJX            MUST BE RE-WRITTEN.
53              PUT   RPL=UPDIT       IF SO, REWRITE IT.
54    EOJX      CLOSE (MASTER)        THEN CLOSE ALL DATA SETS, AND EXIT.
55              CLOSE (TRANS)
56    *  DOS ******
57    *         CLOSE TRANS
58    ***************
59    *
60    STDXIT    ...                   STD EXIT NOT SHOWN
61    *
62    * INTERNAL SUBROUTINE 'GETMSTR' ENTERED VIA BAL 14,GETMSTR
63    * GETS NEXT MASTER RECD IN MOVE MODE, AFTER RESETTING RECD-CHGD FLAG.
64    * BYPASSES RECDS MARKED FOR DELETION UNLESS TRANS RECD IS FOR SAME
65    * DORM & ROOM AS MASTER. IF SO, TRANS DATA REPLACES MASTER DATA.
66    *
67    GETMSTR   LR    2,14            SAVE RETURN ADDRESS
68              MVI   MFLAG,BYP       RESET RECORD-CHANGED FLAG, TO INDI-
69    GETMSTRA  GET   RPL=UPDIT       CATE NO CHANGES HAVE YET BEEN MADE.
70              LTR   15,15           IF END-OF-DATA OR I/O ERR,
71              BNZ   EOJX            IGNORE REST OF TRANS FILE.
72              CLI   DELMARK,X'FF'   SEE IF RECD MARKED FOR DELETION.
73              BNE   GETMSTRX        IF NOT, O.K.
74              CLC   TDORM,MDORM     ELSE, SEE IF TRANS RECD IS FOR
75              BNE   GETMSTRA        SAME DORM & ROOM AS MSTR RECD.
76              CLC   TROOM,MROOM     IF NOT, BYPASS MSTR RECD BY
77              BNE   GETMSTRA        READING NEXT MSTR RECD.
78              BAL   14,CONSTRCT     ELSE, REPLACE MSTR WITH TRANS DATA.
79    GETMSTRX  LR    14,2            THEN RETURN TO CALLER.
80              BR    14
81    *
82    * INTERNAL SUBROUTINE 'UPDATING' ENTERED VIA  BAL 14,UPDATING
83    * MARKS RECORDS FOR DELETION IF TRANSACTION CODE IS '4'; ELSE,
84    * ADDS OR DELETES STUDENT NAME & I.D. FROM STUDENT DATA AREA
85    *  IN MASTER RECD.  SETS FLAG INDICATING MSTR RECD HAS BEEN CHANGED.
86    *
87    * TRANSACTION CODE 'TTYPE' DETERMINES UPDATING ACTION
88    *     TTYPE = C'1'  ...  ADD A NEW ROOM WITH NO STUDENTS
89    *           = C'2'  ...  ADD A STUDENT NAME & I.D.
90    *           = C'3'  ...  DELETE A STUDENT NAME & I.D.
91    *           = C'4'  ...  DELETE ENTIRE MASTER RECD.
```

Figure 22.11 **continued**

```
 92   *
 93   UPDATING  EQU    *
 94             USING  SDAREA,11              SET DUMMY BASE REG TO ACCESS
 95             LA     11,MDATA1               STUDENT DATA AREA.
 96             CLI    TTYPE,C'4'      TRANS CODE '4' MEANS DELETE RECD
 97             BE     ERASE
 98             CLI    TTYPE,C'3'      TRANS CODE '3' MEANS DELETE STUDENT
 99             BNE    ADD             OTHERWISE ASSUME IT'S CODE '2' (ADD)
100   DEL       CLC    MID,TID         IF IT'S A DELETE, THEN MUST LOOK
101             BE     DEL1            FOR STUDENT I.D. IN 1ST & 2ND DATA AREAS
102             LA     11,DATALNG(11)  IF NOT IN 1ST, MUST BE IN 2ND  INCR ADDR
103   DEL1      MVC    MDATA1,BLANKS   REPLACE NAME & I.D. WITH BLANKS WHEN DE-
104             B      EXIT             LETING.
105   ADD       CLC    MID,BLANKS      WHEN ADDING, LOOK FOR VACANT STUDENT DATA
106             BE     ADD1            AREA.  IF NOT 1ST ONE, THEN ASSUME THAT
107             LA     11,DATALNG(11)  2ND AREA IS VACANT, AND INCR ADDR TO IT.
108   ADD1      MVC    MNAME,TNAME     MOVE NAME & I.D. FROM TRANS RECD TO STU-
109             MVC    MID,TID          DENT DATA AREA.
110             B      EXIT
111   ERASE     MVC    MDATA1,BLANKS   WHEN "ERASING", BLANK OUT STUDENT
112             MVC    MDATA2,BLANKS    INFO IN MSTR WORK AREA.
113             MVI    DELMARK,X'FF'   THEN MARK RECD FOR DELETION
114   EXIT      MVI    MFLAG,REWR      BEFORE RETURNING, SET FLAG TO INDICATE
115             BR     14               THAT RECD MUST BE REWRITTEN.
116   *
117   * INTERNAL SUBR 'CONSTRCT' ENTERED VIA  BAL  14,CONSTRCT
118   * REPLACES MSTR RECD DATA WITH TRANS DATA.
119   *
120   CONSTRCT  EQU    *
121             USING  SDAREA,11       SET DUMMY BASE REG FOR ACCESS
122             LA     11,MDATA1       TO STUDENT DATA AREA.
123             MVC    MNAME,TNAME     PUT STUDENT NAME & I.D. INTO
124             MVC    MID,TID         1ST STUDENT AREA, AND BLANK OUT
125             MVC    MDATA2,BLANKS   2ND AREA.
126             MVI    MFLAG,REWR      SET FLAG TO REWRITE MSTR RECD.
127             BR     14
128   *
129   * TRANSACTION INPUT RECORD AREA
130   *
131   INAREA    DS     CL80            RESERVE 80 BYTES FOR CARD IMAGE.
132             ORG    INAREA          BEGIN REDEFINITION OF INPUT AREA.
133             DS     CL3             COL 1-3   UNUSED
134   TTYPE     DS     CL1             4         TRANS TYPE CODE
135             DS     CL3             5-7       UNUSED
136   TDORM     DS     CL4             8-11      DORM ABBREVIATION
137             DS     CL4             12-15     UNUSED
138   TROOM     DS     CL4             16-19     DORM ROOM NUMBER
139             DS     CL1             20        UNUSED
140   TNAME     DS     CL40            21-60     STUDENT NAME
141             DS     CL1             61        UNUSED
142   TID       DS     CL9             62-70     STUDENT I.D.
143             ORG
144   *
145   * MASTER FILE LOGICAL RECORD AREA (FIXED LENGTH RECDS)
146   *
147   OUTAREA   DS     OCL106
148   MDORM     DS     CL4             BYTES 0-3    DORM ABBREVIATION
149   MROOM     DS     CL4             4-7          DORM ROOM NUMBER
150   MDATA1    DS     CL49            8-56         1ST STUDENT DATA AREA
151   DELMARK   EQU    MDATA1          8         X'FF' MARKS DELETED RECDS
152   MDATA2    DS     CL49            57-105       2ND STUDENT DATA AREA
153   *
154   * DUMMY SECTION TO ACCESS STUDENT WORK AREA
155   *
156   SDAREA    DSECT
157   MNAME     DS     CL40            8-47      STUDENT NAME FIELD
158   MID       DS     CL9             48-56     STUDENT I.D. FIELD
159   DATALNG   EQU    *-MNAME                   LENGTH OF STUDENT AREA
160   UPDAT     CSECT
161   *
162   * BLANKS USED TO INITIALIZE STUDENT DATA AREAS
163   * MFLAG INDICATES WHEN A MASTER RECD MUST BE REWRITTEN.
164   *
165   BLANKS    DC     (DATALNG)C' '   'DATALNG' IS SIZE OF STUDENT DATA AREA
166   MFLAG     DC     X'FF'           X'FF' = DON'T REWRITE; X'00' = REWRITE
167   REWR      EQU    X'00'           REWR = RECORD HAS BEEN CHGD, REWRITE OK
168   BYP       EQU    X'FF'           BYP = RECD NOT CHGD, DONT REWRITE
169   *
170   *
171   * OS DCB  AND  DOS DTFCD FOR TRANS FILE IS SAME AS IN  FIG.20.11
172   *    AND IS NOT SHOWN HERE.
173   *  BUT DCB / DTFSD  FOR MASTER IS REPLACED BY  VSAM ACB / RPL PAIR
174   *
175   MASTER    ACB    AM=VSAM,DDNAME=DORMS,MACRF=(ADR,SEQ,OUT)
176   UPDIT     RPL    AM=VSAM,ACB=MASTER,                            X
177                    AREA=OUTAREA,AREALEN=106,OPTCD=(ADR,SEQ,UPD,MVE)
178   *
179   * REGISTER SAVE AREA NEEDED BUT NOT SHOWN HERE
180             END
```

22.6 UPDATING A KEY-SEQUENCED DATA SET

As with ESDS updating, there are two principal methods for KSDS updating: either by creating a new data set which is the updated version of an existing data set, or by updating existing records in place. However, we rarely update a KSDS cluster by creating a new data set; the main purpose of using KSDS is to be able to use its capabilities for direct updating and retrieval.

KSDS updating in place can be accomplished by keyed sequential access, keyed direct access, and keyed skip-sequential access. Only one of these can be used with a given request macro, but a program can switch from one mode to another after opening the data set. The MACRF= parameter of an ACB must specify all the access modes that are to be used during updating. Then when a GET, PUT, or ERASE macro is executed, the OPTCD= parameter of the corresponding RPL macro must designate the particular access mode being used: (KEY,SEQ,...), (KEY,DIR,...), or (KEY,SKP,...).

Use of keyed sequential access to update KSDS records in place is similar to updating ESDS records in place, except that the data set can be positioned to any arbitrary point before beginning sequential updating from that point on. The positioning is done with a POINT macro. Either a primary key or a high-order portion of a primary key (the latter being known as a *generic* key) can be used to designate the starting position. This is analogous to the use of the SETL macro when updating indexed sequential data sets.

Use of keyed direct access to update KSDS records in place is similar to random-mode updating of indexed sequential data sets. The only records that have to be read from the master file are those which are to be updated. The program identifies each such record by specifying its prime key when a GET macro is executed. That key must be stored in the work area designated by the ARG= parameter of the RPL macro prior to executing the GET. Alternatively, a generic key can be used instead of the full prime key. The RPL parameter requirements are the same in this case as those for the POINT macro (see Section 22.8) and won't be discussed here.

In on-line applications, keyed direct access is indispensable because records can be read in any sequence from the master file. In batch applications, this mode is also very useful and efficient provided the number of records that need to be updated is not a large proportion of the total number of KSDS records.

Use of keyed skip-sequential access to update KSDS records in place uses essentially the same program processing logic as keyed direct access. The main difference other than the OPTCD parameter is that the keys have to be presented in ascending key sequence. This is because in this mode VSAM does a sequential search of the index sequence sets to determine the location of records, and the search for each prime key that is presented begins where the search for the preceding prime key left off. Since the keys in the sequence sets are in ascending sequence, the keys that are presented by the user program must also be in ascending sequence. In keyed direct access this isn't necessary because in that mode VSAM does a top-down tree search on the entire index for each key that is presented.

A program that uses keyed direct access to update the KSDS dorm-room master file is outlined in figure 22.12. The program uses a sequential data set of transactions to identify the records that are to be updated. It is based on the flow diagram of figures, 21.12a–c, and is similar to the program of figure 21.13 that updates indexed sequential data sets in random mode.

There are several differences between the indexed sequential and VSAM update procedures. These have to do with the manner in which existing records are erased or updated, the manner in which new records are inserted, and the manner in which invalid key conditions are detected.

In VSAM, records that are to be deleted are erased by the ERASE macro. There is no delete-flag mechanism comparable to that of indexed sequential processing. Instead of marking a record for eventual deletion, VSAM removes the record from its control interval when an ERASE macro is executed.

To update a record, the record must be retrieved by a GET-for-update macro and rewritten (after suitable changes have been made to it in the user's work area) by a PUT-for-update macro. The RPL's OPTCD parameter must specify OPTCD=UPD for the GET and for the PUT. Any field in a record can be changed except the prime key field. To change a prime key, you must first erase the record that has the old prime key, and then insert a new record with the new prime key.

To insert a new record, the record must be written by a PUT macro with OPTCD=NUP (not an update). The same output record area can be used for an insertion as is used for an update. As will be seen, rather than having two different RPL's for the two different OPTCD parameters, the program uses the MODCB macro to change the parameter from UPD to NUP (and vice versa) in a single RPL.

The manner in which an invalid key condition is detected also deserves some comment. You will recall from chapter 21 that an invalid key condition is said to exist in either of two situations: (1) when there is no master file record corresponding to the primary key presented by a GET-for-update; and (2) when there

Figure 22.12 KSDS updating in place.

```
 1   KSDSUPD  CSECT
 2   *
 3   * THIS PROGRAM UPDATES THE KSDS DORM ROOM MASTER FILE,
 4   *   USING  KEYED DIRECT  ACCESS.
 5   * IT IS SIMILAR TO THE PROGRAM OF FIG. 21.13 THAT UPDATES AN IN-
 6   * DEXED SEQUENTIAL FILE IN RANDOM MODE, EXCEPT IN CHECKING FOR
 7   *   INVALID KEY VIA 'SHOWCB', AND USING 'ERASE' TO DELETE RECORDS.
 8   *
 9   * TRANSACTIONS ARE NOT NECESSARILY IN KEY SEQ, BUT ALL CONSECUTIVE
10   *   TRANS RECORDS FOR A GIVEN KEY ARE PROCESSED BEFORE WRITING THE
11   *   CORRESPONDING MASTER RECORD.
12   * INVALID KEY ERRORS ARE REPORTED ON 'SYSOUT' WITHOUT TERMINATING
13   *   THE PROGRAM.  THE FIRST UNCORRECTABLE ERROR TO OCCUR CAUSES
14   *   PROGRAM TERMINATION.
15   *
16            ...                   STANDARD ENTRY NOT SHOWN
17   *
18   * INITIALIZATIONS
19   *
20            OPEN   (MASTER)       OPEN MASTER FOR UPDATES & ADDITIONS
21            LTR    15,15          SEE IF OPEN WAS SUCCESSFUL
22            BNZ    STDXIT         IF NOT, TERMINATE.
23            OPEN   (REPORT,(OUTPUT))  OPEN ERROR REPORT FILE
24            OPEN   (TRANS,(INPUT))    OPEN TRANSACTION FILE
25   * DOS ******
26   *        OPEN   REPORT
27   *        OPEN   TRANS
28   ***************
29            GET    TRANS,TAREA    GET 1ST TRANS RECD
30   *
31   * MAIN PROCESSING
32   *
33   MAINLOOP MVC    KDORM,TDORM    MOVE TRANSACTION KEY TO KEY ARGUMENT
34            MVC    KROOM,TROOM      FOR KEYED DIRECT 'GET-FOR-UPDATE'.
35            CLI    TTYPE,C'1'     TRANS CODE = '1' MEANS ADD NEW RECORD
36            BE     NEWADD
37            B      UPDATE         OTHERWISE, GO PROCESS UPDATES
38   *
39   * END-OF-TRANSACTION-DATA
40   *
41   *        END-OF-DATA FLAG 'EODFLG'  CONTROLS PROCESSING DECISIONS
42   *        IF 'EODFLG' = WR   = X'0F', THEN WRITE LAST MASTER RECORD.
43   *        IF 'EODFLG' = REWR = X'F0', THEN REWRITE LAST MASTER RECORD.
44   *        IF 'EODFLG' = BYP  = X'FF', THEN DON'T WRITE OR REWRITE.
45   *
46   EOJ      CLI    EODFLG,BYP     EODFLG=BYP  IF END-OF-DATA OCCURRED AFTER
47            BE     XBYPASS          A MASTER RECD HAD BEEN DELETED.
48            CLI    EODFLG,WR      EODFLG=WR   IF END-OF-DATA OCCURRED WHILE
49            BE     XWRITE           A NEW MASTER RECD WAS BEING CONSTRUCTED.
50   XREWRITE BAL    14,REWRITE     EODFLG=REWR IF END-OF-DATA OCCURRED WHILE
51            B      XBYPASS          AN EXISTING MSTR RECD WAS BEING UPDATED.
52   XWRITE   BAL    14,WRITE
53   XBYPASS  CLOSE  (MASTER)       AFTER HANDLING LAST MASTER RECD, CLOSE
54            CLOSE  (TRANS)          ALL FILES, AND EXIT FROM PROGRAM
55            CLOSE  (REPORT)
56   * DOS ******
57   *        CLOSE  TRANS
58   *        CLOSE  REPORT
59   ***************
60   STDXIT   ...                   STD EXIT NOT SHOWN
61   *
62   * ADD NEW RECORD TO MASTER FILE
63   *
64   NEWADD   MVI    EODFLG,WR      SET END-OF-DATA FLAG TO WRITE LAST RECD.
65            BAL    14,CONSTRCT    GO BEGIN CONSTRUCTION OF NEW RECD.
66            MVC    ERRTRANS,TAREA  SET ERR MSG FOR POSSIBLE INVALID KEY.
67   ADDLOOP  GET    TRANS,TAREA    GET NEXT TRANS RECD (IF ANY), AND
68            CLC    KDORM,TDORM    SEE IF ITS KEY MATCHES THAT OF RECD BE-
69            BNE    ADDEND           ING CONSTRUCTED.  IF NOT, GO WRITE NEW
70            CLC    KROOM,TROOM      RECD TO MASTER FILE.
71            BNE    ADDEND
72            BAL    14,UPDATING    OTHERWISE, CONTINUE CONSTRCTING NEW RECD
73            B      ADDLOOP          USING INFO IN TRANS RECD.
74   ADDEND   BAL    14,WRITE       AFTER WRITING NEW RECD TO MASTER, THEN
75            B      MAINLOOP         DETERMINE WHAT TO DO WITH NEXT TRANS.
76   *
77   * UPDATE EXISTING RECORD IN MASTER FILE
78   *
79   UPDATE   MVI    EODFLG,REWR    SET END-OF-DATA FLG TO REWRITE LAST RECD
80            BAL    14,READ        THEN READ MASTER RECD THAT MATCHES KEY IN
81            LTR    15,15          KEY-ADDRESS AREA.  RETURN WITH CODE IND-
82            BNZ    VALIDKEY       ICATING WHETHER OR NOT IT WAS INVALID
83            MVI    EODFLG,BYP     KEY ERROR.  IF INVALID KEY, THEN RESET
84            GET    TRANS,TAREA    END-OF-DATA FLAG TO BYPASS REWRITE, AND
85            B      MAINLOOP       GET NEXT TRANS AND GO PROCESS IT.
86   *
87   VALIDKEY CLI    TTYPE,C'4'     IF VALID KEY, SEE IF TRANS IS CHANGE OR
88            BE     DELETE           DELETE REQUEST.
89   CHANGE   BAL    14,UPDATING    IF CHANGE, THEN GO MAKE CHANGES.
90            GET    TRANS,TAREA    THEN GET NEXT TRANS RECD (IF ANY).
91            CLC    KDORM,TDORM    SEE IF ITS KEY MATCHES THAT OF RECD BE-
```

Figure 22.12   continued

```
92              BNE      DIFFKEY          ING UPDATED.  IF NOT, GO REWRITE THAT
93              CLC      KROOM,TROOM      RECD BACK TO MASTER FILE.
94              BNE      DIFFKEY
95              B        VALIDKEY         OTHERWISE, CONTINUE MAKING CHANGES.
96      DIFFKEY BAL      14,REWRITE       AFTER REWRITING CHANGED RECD, DETERMINE
97              B        MAINLOOP         WHAT TO DO WITH NEXT TRANSACTION RECD.
98      *
99      DELETE  DS       OH               WHEN THE REQUEST IS TO DELETE THE MASTER
100             BAL      14,ERASE         RECD, THEN SET DELETE FLAG AND REWRITE
101             MVI      EODFLG,BYP       THE RECD. SET END-OF-DATA FLAG TO BYPASS
102             GET      TRANS,TAREA      WRITING OR REWRITING LAST MASTER RECD.
103             B        MAINLOOP         GET NEXT TRANS RECD AND PROCESS IT.
104     *
105     * INTERNAL SUBROUTINES    'READ'      READS FOR UPDATING
106     *                         'REWRITE' WRITES AN UPDATED RECORD
107     *                         'ERASE'   ERASES AN EXISTING RECORD
108     *                         'WRITE'   WRITES A NEW RECORD
109     * ALL FOUR CALLED VIA   BAL 14,....
110     *
111     READ    LR       2,14                    SAVE RETURN ADDRESS
112             MODCB RPL=UPDIT,OPTCD=(UPD)     SET GET-FOR-UPDATE MODE
113             LTR      15,15            SEE IF 'MODCB' WAS O.K.
114             BNZ      ABEND            IF NOT, TERMINATE.
115             GET      RPL=UPDIT        GET RECD VIA SEARCH ARGUMENT
116             LTR      15,15
117             BZ       RDEXIT           BRANCH IF NO I/O ERR.
118             SHOWCB RPL=UPDIT,                                                X
119                     AREA=FDBKAREA,LENGTH=4,FIELDS=(FDBK)
120             LTR      15,15            SEE IF 'SHOWCB' WAS O.K.
121             BNZ      ABEND            IF NOT, TERMINATE.
122             CLI      FDBKCODE,RNF     ELSE, SEE IF RECD-NOT-FOUND
123             BNE      ABEND            IF NOT, THEN I/O ERR IS FATAL.
124     RDERR   MVC      ERRMSG,NOTFMSG   ELSE, PRINT 'RECD-NOT-FOUND'
125             MVC      ERRTRANS,TAREA   MSG WITH CURRENT TRANSACTION.
126             PUT      REPORT,ERRLINE
127             LH       15,=H'-1'        SET ERROR RETURN CODE
128     RDEXIT  LR       14,2             RECOVER RETURN ADDRESS, AND
129             BR       14               RETURN TO CALLER.
130     *
131     REWRITE LR       2,14             SAVE RETURN ADDRESS
132             PUT      RPL=UPDIT        PUT-FOR-UPDATE  REWRITES THE RECD
133             LTR      15,15            SEE IF ANY I/O ERR
134             BNZ      ABEND            IF SO, TERMINATE
135             LR       14,2
136             BR       14               OTHERWISE, RETURN TO CALLER.
137     *
138     ERASE   LR       2,14             SAVE RETURN ADDRESS
139             ERASE RPL=UPDIT           DELETE THE MOST-RECENTLY-READ RECD
140             LTR      15,15            SEE IF ANY ERR
141             BNZ      ABEND            IF SO, IT'S FATAL.
142             LR       14,2             ELSE, RETURN TO CALLER.
143             BR       14
144     *
145     WRITE   LR       2,14                    SAVE RETURN ADDRESS
146             MODCB RPL=UPDIT,OPTCD=(NUP)     SET 'PUT NOT-AN-UPDATE'
147             LTR      15,15            SEE IF 'MODCB' ERR
148             BNZ      ABEND            IF SO, TERMINATE.
149             PUT      RPL=UPDIT        WRITE NEW RECORD.
150             LTR      15,15            SEE IF I/O ERR
151             BZ       WREXIT           IF NOT, O.K.
152             SHOWCB RPL=UPDIT,                                                X
153                     AREA=FDBKAREA,LENGTH=4,FIELDS=(FDBK)
154             LTR      15,15            SEE IF 'SHOWCB' ERR
155             BNZ      ABEND            IF SO, IT'S FATAL.
156             CLI      FDBKCODE,DUP     ELSE SEE IF 'DUPLICATE-RECD'
157             BNE      ABEND            ANY OTHER ERR IS FATAL.
158             MVC      ERRMSG,DUPLMSG   IF DUPL-RECD ONLY, THEN PRINT
159             PUT      REPORT,ERRLINE   MSG WITH CURRENT TRANSACTION.
160     WREXIT  LR       14,2             RETURN TO CALLER.
161             BR       14
162     *
163     *
164     * 'ABEND' ROUTINE IS CALLED WHEN I/O ERROR OTHER THAN INVALID KEY IS
165     *   DETECTED DURING A READ, REWRITE, OR WRITE OPERATION.
166     * 'ABEND' TERMINATES THE PROGRAM AND ITS JOB STEP, VIA 'ABEND' MACRO.
167     * COMPLETION CODE FOR TERMINAION IS ARBITRARILY CHOSEN AS 4095.
168     *
169     ABEND   ABEND 4095,DUMP,STEP
170     *
171     *  DOS ******
172     *ABEND  DUMP
173     *************
174     *
175     * INTERNAL SUBROUTINE WITH TWO ENTRY POINTS, 'CONSTRCT' & 'UPDATING'
176     * BOTH ENTERED WITH BAL 14,...  WITH NO PARAMETERS.
177     *
178     * TRANSACTION CODE 'TTYPE' DETERMINES UPDATING ACTION
179     *     TTYPE = C'1' ...  ADD A NEW ROOM WITH NO STUDENTS
180     *           = C'2' ...  ADD A STUDENT NAME & I.D.
181     *           = C'3' ...  DELETE A STUDENT NAME & I.D.
182     *           = C'4' ...  DELETE ENTIRE MASTER RECD.
```

Figure 22.12   continued

```
183   *
184   *'CONSTRCT' BEGINS CONSTRUCTION OF NEW OUTPUT MASTER RECD USING TRANS
185   *  RECD.  'UPDATING' CONTINUES CONSTRUCTION OF NEW OUTPUT MASTER RECD.
186   *
187   CONSTRCT  MVC   MDORM,TDORM      WHEN CONSTRUCTING A NEW RECD, MOVE
188             MVC   MROOM,TROOM      DORM AND ROOM NUMBER FROM TRANS
189             MVC   MDATA1,BLANKS    TO OUTPUT AREA, AND BLANK OUT STU-
190             MVC   MDATA2,BLANKS    DENT DATA AREAS.
191             CLI   TTYPE,C'2'       IF TRANS CODE IS '2', INSTEAD OF '1',
192             BE    UPDATING         CONTINUE CONSTRUCTION.
193             BR    14               OTHERWISE, EXIT.
194   *
195   UPDATING  LA    11,MDATA1        SET UP DUMMY BASE REG TO ACCESS STUDENT
196             USING SDAREA,11        DATA FIELDS IN MSTR RECD AREA.
197             CLI   TTYPE,C'2'       IF TRANS CODE = '2', THEN ADD STUDENT
198             BE    ADD              NAME AND I.D.
199   DEL       CLC   MID,TID          OTHERWISE, ASSUME CODE = '3', AND
200             BE    DEL1             DELETE EITHER 1ST OR 2ND NAME & I.D.
201             LA    11,DATALNG(11)   IF NOT 1ST, MUST BE 2ND  INCR ADDR.
202   DEL1      MVC   MNAME,BLANKS     DELETE BY REPLACING NAME & I.D. WITH
203             MVC   MID,BLANKS       BLANKS.
204             B     EXIT
205   ADD       CLC   MID,BLANKS       WHEN ADDING, SEE WHICH STUDENT DATA
206             BE    ADD1             AREA IS BLANK, AND MOVE NAME & I.D.
207             LA    11,DATALNG(11)   INTO THAT AREA.  IF NOT 1ST AREA,
208   ADD1      MVC   MNAME,TNAME      THEN ASSUME IT'S 2ND AREA.
209             MVC   MID,TID
210   EXIT      BR    14
211   *
212   *
213   *    MASTER FILE I/O RECORD AREA
214   *
215   MAREA     DS    0CL107
216   MDELETE   DS    CL1       BYTES 0        FOR ISAM COMPATIBILITY ONLY
217   MDORM     DS    CL4             1-4      DORM ABBREVIATION
218   MROOM     DS    CL4             5-8      DORM ROOM
219   MDATA1    DS    CL49            9-57     1ST STUDENT DATA AREA
220   MDATA2    DS    CL49            58-106   2ND STUDENT DATA AREA
221   *
222   *  DUMMY SECTION TO PERMIT ACCESS TO STUDENT DATA FIELDS
223   SDAREA    DSECT
224   MNAME     DS    CL40            9-48     STUDENT NAME FIELD
225   MID       DS    CL9             49-57    STUDENT I.D. FIELD
226   DATALNG   EQU   *-MNAME                  LENGTH OF STUDENT AREA
227   KSDSUPD   CSECT
228   *
229   *  BLANKS USED TO INITIALIZE STUDENT DATA AREAS
230   BLANKS    DC    (DATALNG)C' '    'DATALNG' IS SIZE OF STUDENT DATA AREA
231   *
232   *  KEY AREA FOR USE AS SEARCH ARGUMENT FOR 'GET' AND 'PUT'
233   *
234   KAREA     DS    CL8             8-BYTE KEY
235             ORG   KAREA
236   KDORM     DS    CL4             1ST 4 BYTES = DORM ABBREVIATION
237   KROOM     DS    CL4             2ND 4 BYTES = DORM ROOM NUMBER
238             ORG
239   *
240   *   AREA RESERVED FOR  'SHOWCB'  FDBK CODES
241   FDBKAREA  DS    0F              MUST BE ON FULLWORD BOUNDARY
242             DS    XL1             BYTE 0    UNUSED
243   R15CODE   DS    XL1                  1    R15 RETURN CODE
244   FTNCODE   DS    XL1                  2    FTNCD (FOR ALT INDEXES)
245   FDBKCODE  DS    XL1                  3    FDBK FROM I/O MACROS
246   DUP       EQU   X'08'           DUPLICATE-RECD FDBK CODE
247   RNF       EQU   X'10'           RECD-NOT-FOUND FDBK CODE
248   *
249   *  TRANSACTION INPUT AREA
250   *
251   TAREA     DS    CL80            RESERVE 80 BYTES FOR CARD IMAGE.
252             ORG   TAREA           BEGIN REDEFINITION OF INPUT AREA.
253             DS    CL3             COL 1-3   UNUSED
254   TTYPE     DS    CL1                  4    TRANS TYPE CODE
255             DS    CL3                  5-7  UNUSED
256   TDORM     DS    CL4                  8-11 DORM ABBREVIATION
257             DS    CL4                  12-15 UNUSED
258   TROOM     DS    CL4                  16-19 DORM ROOM NUMBER
259             DS    CL1                  20   UNUSED
260   TNAME     DS    CL40                 21-60 STUDENT NAME
261             DS    CL1                  61   UNUSED
262   TID       DS    CL9                  62-70 STUDENT I.D.
263             ORG
264   *
265   *  LOGICAL RECORD AREA FOR 'SYSOUT' PRINT LINE
266   *
267   ERRLINE   DS    0CL132          RESERVE 132  BYTES
268   ERRTRANS  DS    CL80            80-BYTE TRANS RECD AREA
269   ERRMSG    DS    CL52            52-BYTE ERR MESSAGE AREA
270   *
271   DUPLMSG   DC    CL52' CANT ADD   RECD KEY ALREADY EXISTS ON MASTER FILE'
272   NOTFMSG   DC    CL52' CANT UPDATE  RECD KEY DOESNT EXIST ON MASTER FILE'
```

Figure 22.12   continued

```
273   *
274   * EODFLG USED TO CONTROL PROCESSING WHEN AT END OF TRANSACTION FILE.
275   *
276   EODFLG   DC    X'FF'      END-OF-DATA FLAG  FOR LAST MASTER RECD
277   BYP      EQU   X'FF'       BYP = DONT WRITE OR REWRITE WHEN AT END
278   WR       EQU   X'0F'       WR  = WRITE MSTR RECD WHEN AT END
279   REWR     EQU   X'F0'       REWR = REWRITE MSTR RECD WHEN AT END
280   *
281   *
282   * OS DCB'S  AND  DOS DTF'S  FOR TRANS FILE AND REPORT FILE
283   *   ARE NOT SHOWN HERE.  THEY ARE THE SAME AS IN  FIG.21.13 .
284   *
285   * OS DCB  AND  DOS DTFIS  FOR MASTER FILE  ARE REPLACED BY
286   *   THIS  VSAM  ACB / RPL  PAIR.
287   *
288   *
289   MASTER   ACB   AM=VSAM,DDNAME=DORMS,MACRF=(KEY,DIR,OUT)
290   UPDIT    RPL   AM=VSAM,ACB=MASTER,RECLEN=107,                X
291                  AREA=MAREA,AREALEN=107,ARG=KAREA,             X
292                  OPTCD=(KEY,DIR,SYN,MVE,UPD)
293   *
294   * REGISTER SAVE AREA NEEDED BUT NOT SHOWN.
295            END
```

already exists a master file record with the same primary key as that of a new record that PUT attempts to add to the file. The first situation is known as "record not found"; the second, as "duplicate record".

When an invalid key or other exception condition occurs, VSAM puts an appropriate error code in the FDBK field of the RPL and also puts a code in Register 15. Then it returns to the user program. The code in Register 15 is $=$F'0' if no exception occurred, $=$F'8' if a logical error (including invalid key) occurred, and $=$F'12' if a physical I/O error occurred. The 1-byte FDBK code is stored in the low-order byte of a full-word work area whose address is designated in a SHOWCB macro (see below).

The most important FDBK codes for beginning VSAM programmers are these[1]:

$$X'04' = \text{end-of-data (for ESDS as well as for KSDS)}$$
$$X'08' = \text{duplicate record}$$
$$X'10' = \text{record not found}$$

As can be seen from the program in figure 22.12, a branch is made to an error-handling routine whenever a nonzero code is detected in Register 15 following execution of a GET or PUT macro. That error routine obtains the FDBK code via a SHOWCB macro and then determines whether the error was caused by an invalid key condition. An invalid key is a nonfatal error; the program can just inform the user and then proceed to the next transaction.

It is important to note that underlying the above method of detecting invalid key conditions is the fact that our program is running in synchronous I/O mode. This means that VSAM does not return to the program until it has finished processing a request macro. You will recognize that this is different from indexed sequential random-mode processing. There, a program must issue a WAIT or CHECK macro to synchronize I/O operations with program execution. In VSAM, the program must explicitly request asynchronous operations via OPTCD=ASY; only then is a CHECK macro used to synchronize operations. In our case we haven't designated OPTCD=ASY; instead, we are using the default OPTCD=SYN—i.e., synchronous mode.

The SHOWCB macro used in figure 22.12 copies information from the designated control block into a user work area. The work area address and length are specified by the AREA= and AREALEN= parameters, respectively (see fig. 22.13). In general, the control block from which information is to be copied must be indicated by one of three parameters: ACB=*address,* RPL=*address,* and EXLST=*address.* In each case *address* identifies the location of the control block and can be specified symbolically, or as a relocatable expression, or in register notation. For the FDBK code, the appropriate control block is the request parameter list (RPL).

---

1. Other FDBK codes are listed in the section on "Return Codes" in the VSAM Programmer's Guide. Also to be found there is a description of ACB ERROR codes for OPEN and CLOSE macros.

Figure 22.13   SHOWCB and MODCB macro formats.

There are three separate SHOWCB and three separate MODCB macro operand formats, corresponding to the three separate control blocks ACB, EXLST, and RPL:

$$\text{showname SHOWCB} \begin{Bmatrix} \text{ACB=} \\ \text{RPL=} \\ \text{EXLST=} \end{Bmatrix} \text{address,keyword}_1 \text{=value}_1, ..., \text{keyword}_n \text{=value}_n$$

$$\text{modname MODCB} \begin{Bmatrix} \text{ACB=} \\ \text{RPL=} \\ \text{EXLST=} \end{Bmatrix} \text{address,keyword}_1 \text{=value}_1, ..., \text{keyword}_m \text{=value}_m$$

As can be seen, you must designate the address of the particular control block being referenced in each of the operand formats.

The keyword parameters and values in the SHOWCB operand are different from those in the MODCB operand.

SHOWCB keywords

AREA=address	designates the address of the area that will receive the values corresponding to the options specified in the FIELDS= parameter
LENGTH=m	m is the length of the AREA area
OBJECT=DATA I INDEX	specifies whether the fields that are specified are for the data component or for the index component (used with SHOWCB for ACB only)
FIELDS=(*field options*)	*field options* is a list of one or more mnemonic code words that identify the control block fields whose values are to be received in the AREA area

Note: For definition of the field-option mnemonics, see either the OS/VS VSAM Programmer's Guide, or the DOS/VS Supervisor and I/O Macros manual.

MODCB keywords

The keywords and options in MODCB are (with but a few minor exceptions) the same as those in the respective ACB, RPL, and EXLST macros. For details, see either of the two manuals mentioned above.

The information that is copied into the work area is requested by one or more options specified in the SHOWCB FIELDS= parameter. Values corresponding to those options are placed in the work area in the order in which the options are specified. Each value requires one full word (except those for the DDNAME and STMST options of the SHOWCB for ACB, which require two consecutive full words each). As can be expected, the user work area must begin on a full-word boundary and be long enough to contain all the values requested.

The exact meanings of all the FIELDS= options are explained in the VSAM Programmer's Guide. Those that are probably of most use to beginning VSAM programmers are:

for SHOWCB ACB: FIELDS=ERROR obtains the error code that is placed in the ACB by VSAM after execution of an OPEN or CLOSE macro

for SHOWCB RPL: FIELDS=FDBK obtains the error code that is placed in the RPL by VSAM after execution of a request macro other than OPEN or CLOSE

FIELDS=RBA obtains the relative byte address of the most recently processed logical record

FIELDS=RECLEN obtains the length of the most recently processed logical record

In the program of figure 22.12, we have used only the FIELDS=FDBK option.

The MODCB macro used in figure 22.12 changes the value of one of the OPCTD parameters in the designated RPL control block. In general, MODCB can be used to change values of one or more parameters in an ACB, RPL, or EXLST control block. As can be seen from figure 22.13, its operand format is similar to that of SHOWCB in that the control block must be identified by *address*. Beyond that the similarity breaks down, for MODCB's other operands are identical in format to those of the control block macro whose fields are to be modified.

Any number of valid parameters can be specified in a single MODCB macro. However, there is one precaution: you cannot modify the contents of an ACB that has not been opened by an OPEN macro; you cannot modify the contents of an RPL that is active, i.e. currently being used by VSAM at the same time that MODCB is executed; and you cannot modify an EXLST parameter unless that parameter was specified when the EXLST was generated.

In our case we are safe. We are modifying an RPL which is inactive, i.e., although it is being used in the program it is not being used at the moment that the MODCB is executed. The OPTCD=SYN (synchronous) parameter ensures that the preceding GET, PUT, or ERASE macro has completed its use of the RPL before the MODCB is executed.

22.7 ALTERNATE INDEXES

An alternate index enables records in an ESDS or KSDS base cluster to be identified and accessed by key. That key is known as an alternate key, to distinguish it from the prime key of KSDS clusters. Its value is stored in what is known as an alternate key field of the base cluster records (see figure 22.14).

Figure 22.14   Schematic structure of an alternate index.

An alternate index is a key sequenced data set. The base cluster to which it is related can be an entry sequenced or key sequenced data set.

As an example, we once again consider the dorm-room file as a KSDS cluster. The second through ninth bytes of each record contain a 4-byte dorm identity and a 4-byte room number. Each record identifies the occupants of one room in a dormitory building (see chap. 21). If we select the first two digits of the *room* number as an alternate key field, we can then use the values of that field as an alternate key to access records for a given *floor* of the dorms without having to access all records. In other words, the alternate key gives us access to just those records that contain that alternate key value.

Any field in the base cluster's records can be defined to be an alternate key field, provided it has a fixed length (1 to 255 bytes) and the same fixed position in all records of the cluster. There can be several different alternate key fields in a base cluster record. They can overlap one another, and they can overlap the prime key field if it's a KSDS cluster. For each alternate key field there must be one alternate index.

AMS Considerations

Each alternate index is itself a key-sequenced data set and must be defined by an Access Method Services DEF AIX (Define Alternate Index) command. That definition must allocate space for the alternate index and identify the base cluster to which the index is related. It must also identify the alternate key field's length and position in the base cluster records, and state whether or not the alternate key values should uniquely identify those records. We will illustrate how to do this for the dorm-room master file, using as the alternate key field the first two digits of the room number.

Corresponding to each DEF AIX command there must be a DEF PATH command and a BLDINDEX command. The BLDINDEX command causes AMS to construct the alternate index records. Obviously, it cannot be used until after the base cluster has been loaded, and until after the two DEFINE commands have entered the appropriate alternate index information into a VSAM catalog. The DEF PATH command defines the means by which alternate key access to records in the base cluster is achieved at run time.

All three commands have the same formats in OS and DOS systems. The job control statements in each system must of course identify the alternate index and base cluster data sets, and in DOS the path itself must also be identified by JCL. No distinction is made in either system's job control statements as to whether the base cluster is a key-sequenced or entry-sequenced data set. AMS obtains that information from the catalog.

If the names we choose for the alternate index and path are DORM.FILE.AIX1 and DORM.FILE.PATH1, respectively, and if the names of the base cluster and user catalog are DORM.FILE and SAMPLE.UCAT, respectively, then the job control statements that precede the DEF AIX and DEF PATH commands can be written as follows (see also Section 22.2):

for OS systems:

```
//STEP006  EXEC  PGM=IDCAMS
//STEPCAT  DD    DSN=SAMPLE.UCAT,DISP=SHR
//AIXDD    DD    VOL=SER=VOLA,DISP=OLD,UNIT=3330
//SYSPRINT DD    SYSOUT=A
//SYSIN    DD    *
```

for DOS systems:

```
// DLBL    CLDD,'DORM.FILE',,VSAM
// EXTENT  SYS010,VOLA
// DLBL    AIXDD,'DORM.FILE.AIX1',,VSAM
// EXTENT  SYS010,VOLA
// DLBL    PATHDD,'DORM.FILE.PATH1',,VSAM
// EXTENT  SYS010,VOLA
// ASSGN   SYS010,DISK,VOL=VOLA,SHR
// EXEC    IDCAMS,SIZE=AUTO
```

The AMS commands that can then be used to define the alternate index and path are:

```
DEF AIX      ( NAME (DORM.FILE.AIX1), FILE (AIXDD) -
               RELATE (DORM.FILE), KEYS (2 5)       -
               VOL (VOLA), TRK (4 4)                -
               NONUNIQUEKEY, UPGRADE )              -
       DATA  ( NAME (DORM.FILE.AIX1.DATA)           -
               CISZ (4096) )                        -
      INDEX  ( NAME (DORM.FILE.AIX1.INDEX)          -
               CISZ (512) )                         -
             CAT (SAMPLE.UCAT/updatepassword)
DEF PATH     ( NAME (DORM.FILE.PATH1), FILE (xxx) -
               PATHENTRY (DORM.FILE.AIX1) )         -
             CAT (SAMPLE.UCAT/updatepassword)
```

In the DEF PATH FILE parameter, *xxx* is AIXDD if the above OS job control statements are used and is PATHDD if the DOS ones are used.

As was mentioned earlier, we have used the first two digits of the dormitory-room number as the alternate key field. For the KSDS version of that file, those two digits occupy the sixth and seventh bytes of each record; hence the *offset* of the field from the beginning of each record is 5 bytes, while the length is 2 bytes: KEYS (2 5).

We specified NONUNIQUEKEY meaning that an alternate key value need not uniquely identify a base cluster record. That is certainly the case in our example; since there are several rooms on each dormitory floor, there will be several records with the same first two digits of the room number.

We specified UPGRADE meaning that VSAM is to keep the contents of the alternate index accurate and up-to-date. (In VSAM parlance, the alternate index is then part of the *upgrade set* of alternate indexes.) If we had not specified UPGRADE, then the information in the alternate index would have had to be kept accurate by a user program.

The space allocation TRK (4 4) was determined as discussed in Section 22.2: with a control interval size of 4096 bytes on an IBM 3330, then the number of tracks required for the data component of the alternate index is $(n \cdot k)/(4096 \cdot 3)$, where n = number of records in the alternate index, and k = average length of each record. The number n is easy to estimate, because *there is only one record in the alternate index for each different alternate key value*. Thus if there are no more than 10 floors per dormitory building, then $n = 10$ since there can be no more than ten different values of the first two digits of the room number. Somewhat more difficult to estimate is k, because the length of each alternate index record depends on how many base cluster records contain a given key value (see fig. 22.14).

One simple estimate is to assume that $k = (1/n) \cdot N \cdot L$, where N is the total number of base cluster records and L is the length of each pointer in the alternate index. This estimate assumes that the different key values are fairly evenly distributed over the base cluster records. In our case, N = 5000 so with $n = 10$ we then have $k = 500 \cdot L$ bytes per alternate index record. For an ESDS cluster, the pointers are just the RBA's, so L = 4; for a KSDS cluster, the pointers are the prime keys, so L is the length of a prime key.

For our KSDS dorm-room master file, we therefore have $k = 4000$. The number of tracks required is thus $(10 \cdot 4000)/(4096 \cdot 3) \approx 3$. To this we added one track for the index component of the alternate index. More accurate methods of estimating an alternate index's space requirements can be found in the AMS manuals.

To complete this brief discussion of the AMS commands for alternate indexes, we recall that the BLDINDEX command is required to construct the alternate index records once the definitions have been made. This command is much simpler than the DEF AIX or DEF PATH command. It consists of just one line:

```
BLDINDEX  INFILE (CLDD), OUTFILE (AIXDD)
```

The associated job control statements are almost identical to those given above for DEF AIX and DEF PATH. The differences are that in OS systems you must *insert* this statement prior to the //SYSPRINT :

```
//CLDD     DD     DSN=DORM.FILE,VOL=SER=VOLA,DISP=OLD,UNIT=3330
```

and in DOS systems the //DLBL and //EXTENT statements for PATHDD are not included in the BLDINDEX JCL.

Programming Considerations

Having defined and constructed the alternate index via AMS, we are now able to use it to access the dorm-room master file. The program statements in figure 22.15 show the essential aspects of retrieving base cluster records through an alternate index.

There are several things to notice. First, in order to access records at run time via an alternate key, a program must open the path, *not* the alternate index itself. *Opening the path simultaneously opens the alternate index* and *the base cluster.* (If you open the alternate index itself you just gain access to the records in that index; if you open the cluster, you just gain access to the records in the cluster without benefit of the alternate index. Opening the path is what is required to gain access to the cluster's records through the alternate index.) Therefore the JCL statement identified by the DDNAME= parameter of the ACB macro must refer to the *path* name, not to the base cluster or alternate index name.

Second, once a path is opened at run time, an alternate key is used as the search argument for a GET macro executed with keyed direct access. That GET retrieves the first record in the base cluster which contains the key value. Any other records containing that same key value must then be retrieved by a GET executed with keyed sequential access. Each GET retrieves one record. The program determines whether there is another record with the same alternate key value by examining the FDBK code which is returned by VSAM. Note that this is done when the Register 15 return code is *zero;* i.e., the existence of another record with the same alternate key is not an error condition.

The third thing to notice is that the program must switch access modes from keyed direct to keyed sequential when more than one record with the same alternate key exists. This is done via the MODCB macro, by modifying the RPL's OPTCD=DIR parameter to OPTCD=SEQ. Then when there are no more records for a given alternate key, the program switches back to keyed direct and moves the next alternate key into the search argument field in preparation for the GET which retrieves the first record corresponding to that key.

In the statements of figure 22.15, the ACB macro designates both keyed sequential *and* keyed direct access. This illustrates the rule that when opening a VSAM data set, the ACB must specify all the accessing techniques that might be used during processing. The RPL, on the other hand, designates only one access technique, namely the one that is being used at that moment.

The ACB of figure 22.15 also specifies the *IN* parameter, meaning that the base cluster's records will be retrieved but not updated. If updating were to be done, *OUT* would have been specified instead of *IN*. But when updating via an alternate index, you are not permitted to change the alternate key value. Changing the alternate key value must be done when updating with ordinary direct or sequential access, i.e., opening the base cluster itself rather than going through the alternate index.

Finally, it should be noted that OPTCD=NSP has been specified in the RPL . NSP (Note Sequential Position) means that VSAM will remember the position of the record that is retrieved in keyed direct mode so that the subsequent keyed sequential retrievals can be made without having to specify an RBA or key in the user program. NSP must be used instead of NUP (No Update), because when NUP is specified with keyed direct access, VSAM does not remember the position of the record that is retrieved.

22.8   TOPICS FOR FURTHER STUDY

The following brief list of topics is intended to introduce beginning VSAM programmers to some of the other VSAM processing capabilities not covered in this chapter. Details of these and other capabilities are in the manuals listed in the next section.

EXLST Macro. This macro establishes the addresses of user-program routines that VSAM branches to when logical or physical errors prevent VSAM from successfully processing a request macro. It can also be used to obtain notification of so-called journalizing events, i.e. events that are not necessarily errors but that a user program may wish to know about in order to keep a record, or journal, of their occurrence. An example of such an event is a change in the RBA of a record.

Figure 22.15 Retrieval via alternate index.

```
1    *
2    *  THE FOLLOWING PROGRAM SEGMENTS SHOW THE ESSENTIAL ASPECTS
3    *  OF RETRIEVING LOGICAL RECORDS FROM THE   KSDS  DORM-ROOM
4    *  MASTER FILE THROUGH AN ALTERNATE INDEX.  SEE TEXT FOR ADDI-
5    *  TIONAL COMMENTS.
6    *
7              OPEN   (MASTER)          OPEN FOR RETRIEVAL VIA ALT INDEX
8              LTR    15,15             SEE IF 'OPEN' FAILED
9              BNZ    ABERR             IF SO, TELL USER.
10             ...                      OPEN TRANSACTION FILE
11   *
12   GETNEW    GET    TRANS,TAREA       GET TRANS RECD WITH DESIRED ALT KEY
13             MVC    ALTKEY,TFLOOR     MOVE KEY TO RPL'S  ARG= FIELD
14             MODCB  RPL=ALTRPL,OPTCD=(DIR)   SET KEYED-DIRECT ACCESS
15             LTR    15,15             SEE IF 'MODCB' O.K.
16             BNZ    ABERR             IF NOT, TELL USER
17             GET    RPL=ALTRPL        GET 1ST RECD WITH ALTKEY VALUE
18             LTR    15,15             SEE IF I/O ERRS
19             BNZ    NOGO              IF SO, MAY BE RECD-NOT-FOUND
20   PROCESS   ...                      ELSE, CAN NOW PROCESS THE RECD
21   *
22   *  WHEN PROCESSING IS FINISHED, SEE IF THERE ARE ANY MORE
23   *   RECORDS WITH THE SAME ALT KEY VALUE.
24   *
25   PROCESSX  SHOWCB RPL=ALTRPL,                                            X
26                   AREA=FDBKAREA,LENGTH=4,FIELDS=(FDBK)
27             LTR    15,15             SEE IF 'SHOWCB' O.K.
28             BNZ    ABERR             IF NOT, TELL USER.
29             CLI    FDBKCODE,DUP      ELSE FDBK CODE TELLS IF MORE RECDS
30             BNE    GETNEW            EXIST WITH SAME ALT KEY.
31             MODCB  RPL=ALTRPL,OPTCD=(SEQ)  IF SO, NEED KEYED-SEQTL ACCESS
32             LTR    15,15             SEE IF 'MODCB' O.K.
33             BNZ    ABERR             IF NOT, TELL USER
34             GET    RPL=ALTRPL        ELSE, GET NEXT RECD WITH SAME KEY
35             LTR    15,15             SEE IF 'GET' FAILED
36             BNZ    ABERR             IF SO, TELL USER
37             B      PROCESS           ELSE, GO PROCESS THE RECD.
38   *
39   *  IF 'GET' GAVE NONZERO ERR CODE IN REG 15, MAY BE RECD-NOT-FOUND.
40   *  DETERMINE THAT WITH 'SHOWCB' FOR FDBK CODE.
41   *
42   NOGO      SHOWCB RPL=ALTRPL,                                            X
43                   AREA=FDBKAREA,LENGTH=4,FIELDS=(FDBK)
44             LTR    15,15             SEE IF 'SHOWCB' O.K.
45             BNZ    ABERR             IF NOT, TELL USER.
46             CLI    FDBKCODE,RNF      ELSE SEE IF RECD-NOT-FOUND ERR
47             BNE    ABERR             IF NOT, THEN ERR WAS SERIOUS.
48             ...                      ELSE, CAN WRITE NON-FATAL ERR MSG
49             B      GETNEW            AND THEN GET NEXT TRANSACTION.
50   *
51   *  TAKE REMEDIAL ACTION (E.G., WRITE MSG TO USER) AND/OR TERMINATE.
52   *
53   ABERR     ...
54   *
55   *  TERMINATE WHEN TRANS FILE REACHES END-OF-DATA
56   *
57   EOD       ...                      CLOSE ALL FILES
58             B      STDXIT
59   *
60   STDXIT    ...                      STANDARD EXIT FROM PROGRAM.
61   *
62   *
63   *  TRANSACTION INPUT RECORD AREA
64   TAREA     DS     OCL80             DEFINE 80-BYTE AREA
65             DS     CL15              COL 1-15  UNUSED
66   TFLOOR    DS     CL02              16-17  1ST TWO DIGITS OF ROOM#
67             DS     CL63              18-80  UNUSED
68   *
69   *  MASTER FILE LOGICAL RECORD AREA
70   MAREA     DS     OCL107            DEFINE 107-BYTE AREA FOR KSDS RECORD
71             ...                      SPECIFY OTHER FIELDS FOR PROCESSING
72   *
73   *  SEARCH ARGUMENT AREA FOR 2-BYTE ALTERNATE KEY.
74   ALTKEY    DS     CL2               CONTAINS 1ST TWO DIGITS OF ROOM#
75   *
76   *  FDBK AREA FOR USE WITH 'SHOWCB' MACRO
77   FDBKAREA  DS     OF                MUST BE ON FULLWORD BOUNDARY
78             DS     XL3               BYTES 0-2  UNUSED
79   FDBKCODE  DS     XL1               3     FDBK CODE
80   DUP       EQU    X'08'             DUPLICATE-RECD CODE
81   RNF       EQU    X'10'             RECD-NOT-FOUND CODE
82   *
83   *  ACB/RPL PAIR FOR ACCESS TO KSDS CLUSTER THROUGH ALT INDEX
84   *
85   MASTER    ACB    AM=VSAM,DDNAME=FLPATH,MACRF=(KEY,DIR,SEQ,IN)
86   ALTRPL    RPL    AM=VSAM,ACB=MASTER,                                    X
87                    AREA=MAREA,AREALEN=107,                                X
88                    OPTCD=(KEY,DIR,SYN,MVE,NSP),ARG=ALTKEY,KEYLEN=2
89   *
```

TESTCB Macro. This is similar to the SHOWCB macro, but instead of putting control block information into a user work area as SHOWCB does, TESTCB simply compares the value of a control block field to a value that you supply and sets the condition code to indicate the result of the comparison.

POINT Macro. This positions a VSAM data set for subsequent sequential processing. Positioning can be done by an RBA, a prime key, or a generic key. If done with a generic key (i.e., a high-order portion of a prime key), then the associated RPL macro's OPTCD parameter must specify whether POINT should find a record with the exact generic key (GEN,KEQ) or with a key that is greater than or equal to the generic key (GEN,KGE). Whether an RBA or a full or generic key is used, it must be moved to the field designated by the ARG= parameter before POINT is executed. If a generic key is used, the RPL KEYLEN= parameter must specify the generic key's length.

GENCB Macro. This is an executable macro that creates an access-method control block (ACB), request parameter list (RPL), or list of exception-routine addresses (EXLST) at run time rather than at assembly time. One advantage of using GENCB instead of ACB, RPL, or EXLST is that if VSAM control block formats change in the future, programs assembled with older versions of VSAM may not have to be reassembled to run under the newer versions.

VSAM Processing Statistics. The SHOWCB-ACB macro can obtain a number of statistics that characterize the processing that has occurred on a given data set. The statistics are full-word integers whose names are specified via the FIELDS= parameter in SHOWCB. Most of the names begin with the letter N; for example, NLOGR obtains the number of logical records that exist in the data component of the designated base cluster.

PRINT, LISTCAT, and DELETE Commands in AMS. These Access Method Services commands print the contents of a VSAM data set, list the contents of a VSAM catalog, and delete a data set or other VSAM object. LISTCAT is particularly useful for determining the names of your data sets (in case you've forgotten them) and for determining how much space was actually allocated to each data set.

Reusable Data Sets. Any VSAM data set can be defined as a temporary, i.e., reusable, data set via the DEF CLUSTER *REUSE* parameter. When opening such a data set, you can specify MACRF=(OUT,RST) in the ACB. The RST resets the highest RBA of records in that data set to zero, so that in effect the data set is considered to be empty when it is opened. Alternate indexes cannot be defined for reusable data sets.

FREESPACE Option for KSDS. A portion of the data space that is allocated to a key-sequenced data set can be reserved for use in subsequent record insertions. The reserved space is known as *free* space. The amount that is to be reserved is specified as a percentage of the total allocation of each control interval and/or control area, via the FREESPACE parameter in the DEF CL, ALTER, or DEF AIX commands. If not specified, then no free space is reserved.

Performance Improvements. The VSAM Programmer's Guide contains a number of guidelines on how VSAM processing performance may be improved. These include the use of free space, the choice of control interval size, the allocation of additional buffers, and the use of separate volumes for the data and index components of a key-sequenced data set.

22.9 REFERENCE MANUALS

The IBM reference manuals listed below provide conceptual and detailed information about the use of VSAM facilities. The "Primer" is especially useful for its many detailed examples of the use of Access Method Services (both OS and DOS) and of space allocation calculations.

IBM Publication #	Title of Reference Manual
G320-5774	VSAM Primer and Reference
GC26-3838	OS/VS VSAM Programmer's Guide
GC26-3840	OS/VS1 Access Method Services
GC26-3841	OS/VS2 Access Method Services
GC33-5382	DOS/VS Access Method Services User's Guide
GC33-5371	DOS/VS System Management Guide
GC33-5372	DOS/VS Data Management Guide
GC33-5373	DOS/VS Supervisor & I/O Macros

22.10 SUMMARY

You may find it useful to review VSAM concepts by rereading Section 22.1. Here we simply summarize the principal terms that have been introduced by IBM for VSAM entities discussed in this chapter.

Access Method Services (AMS).   The utility program that must be used to define VSAM objects and can also be used to load, delete, and print the contents of VSAM catalogs and data sets.

Addressed Direct Access.   Retrieval or storage of a data record that is identified by its relative byte address.

Addressed Sequential Access.   Retrieval or storage of the data record that sequentially follows the previously retrieved or stored record.

Alternate Index.   A key-sequenced data set whose records identify and permit access to base cluster records via an alternate key value.

Alternate Key.   From 1 to 255 consecutive characters of a base cluster record that can be used to access that record via an alternate index. An alternate key's length and position must be the same in each record and must be specified in the AMS DEF AIX command which defines the alternate index.

Base Cluster.   A relative-record, key-sequenced, or entry-sequenced data set other than an alternate index.

Control Area.   A set of one or more control intervals, the total size of which does not exceed one cylinder of a direct access storage device.

Control Block.   The memory area in a program that contains information generated by an ACB, EXLST, GENCB, or RPL macro for use by VSAM when it processes a request macro.

Control Interval.   The fixed-length unit of information that is read from or written to a direct access storage device by VSAM when it retrieves or stores records of a data set.

Data Component.   That portion of a data set which contains the logical records.

Entry-Sequenced Data Set (ESDS).   A VSAM data set whose logical records are stored in the sequence in which they are first presented to the Operating System.

Generic Key.   One or more consecutive high-order characters of a key.

Imbedded Index.   The situation which prevails when each sequence set node of a key-sequenced data set's index is stored in the first track of the control area which the node pertains to.

Index Component.   That portion of a key-sequenced data set which contains the index records.

Keyed Direct Access.   Retrieval or storage of a data record that is identified by its key.

Keyed Sequential Access.   Retrieval or storage of the data record whose key sequentially follows that of the previously retrieved or stored data record.

Keyed Skip-Sequential Access.   Retrieval or storage of a data record that is identified by a key whose value is greater than that of the previously retrieved or stored record. Used only with KSDS.

Key-Sequenced Data Set (KSDS).   A VSAM data set whose logical records are stored in ascending prime key sequence, and whose index component records contain the highest prime key and relative byte address of each control interval in the data component.

Loading a Data Set.   The act of storing records in a previously empty data set.

Path.   The VSAM object that connects an alternate index to its associated base cluster.

Prime Key (or Primary Key).   From 1 to 255 consecutive characters of a KSDS logical record, whose value uniquely identifies that record when the data set is stored or retrieved via keyed direct or keyed skip-sequential access. The prime key's length and position must be the same in each record and must be specified in the AMS DEF CLUSTER command which defines the data set.

Relative Byte Address (RBA). A full-word binary integer which specifies the position of a logical record relative to the beginning of a data set.

Reusable Data Set. A data set defined in such a way that its highest RBA can be reset to zero when it is opened, so that the data set is in effect empty immediately after it is opened.

Sequence Set. The lowest level nodes in a KSDS index. Each sequence set node is associated with a control area, and each entry in a sequence set node points to one of the control intervals in the control area.

Suballocatable Data Space. A portion of the memory of a direct access storage device that is reserved by the AMS DEF SPACE command so that it can be allocated among one or more VSAM data sets.

Upgrade Set. Alternate indexes whose contents are kept accurate and up-to-date by VSAM.

VSAM Catalog. A set of records that VSAM uses to keep track of the characteristics of data sets. There is exactly one VSAM master catalog per computer installation, and there can be one or more user catalogs per installation. There can be no more than one user catalog per storage volume.

VSAM Object. The term used to denote any of the following: master catalog, user catalog, VSAM data set, nonVSAM data set, alternate index, path, and data space.

EXERCISES

1. What are the similarities and differences between a control interval and a physical data block? Between a control interval and a control area?

2. What are the similarities and differences between addressed sequential and keyed sequential access? Between keyed direct and keyed skip-sequential access?

3. What parameters of the ACB macro have counterparts in an OS DCB (or DOS DTF) macro? What parameters of the RPL macro have counterparts in an OS DCB (or DOS DTF) macro?

4. What is the difference in purpose between the AREA= and ARG= parameters of an RPL macro? Between the AREALEN= and KEYLEN= parameters? Between the AREALEN= and RECLEN= parameters?

5. What is the difference between a GET and a GET-for-update when used with entry-sequenced data sets? When used with key-sequenced data sets?

6. What is the name and updatepassword of the VSAM user catalog that you will be using when defining data sets at your computer installation? Under what conditions does your installation use suballocatable data spaces? Under what conditions are you permitted to use the UNIQUE parameter when allocating space for a data set at your installation?

7. Suppose that all but two cylinders of a disk pack at your computer installation are available for allocation to a VSAM data set. What is then the largest number of records that can be stored in an entry-sequenced data set on a single disk pack if the record length is 100 bytes? 200 bytes? 500 bytes? 1000 bytes? You can assume that each control area consists of one cylinder.

8. Under the same conditions as in Exercise 7, what is the largest number of records that can be stored in a key-sequenced data set on a single disk pack, assuming that the prime key length is 10 bytes?

9. Which of the statements in figure 22.10 have to be modified, and what must those modifications be, in order to load a key-sequenced data set instead of an entry-sequenced data set?

10. Write a program which will print the contents of the ESDS dorm-room master file. Write the AMS commands that will print the contents of that file (for this you will need to learn about the PRINT command from the AMS manuals).

11. What modifications have to be made to the statements of figure 22.11, and what new statements must be added to those in the figure, in order to process transactions that would add new records to the end of the existing data set?

12. What modifications have to be made to the statements of figure 22.12, and what new statements must be added to those in the figure, in order to process transactions that would change the prime key of an existing record? You can assume that a transaction record with type code '5' (not shown in the figure) contains both the prime key of an existing record and the key which is to replace it.

13. If the student i.d. fields of the KSDS dorm-room master file were to be used as alternate keys, one alternate index would have to be defined for each student i.d. field. Write the AMS commands that would accomplish this. (Note: Neither field can be defined as a UNIQUEKEY because some master file records may contain information about just one student, and some may not contain information about any students. In those cases the i.d. field is blank.)

14. What changes and additions would have to be made to the program statements of figure 22.15 in order to access the KSDS dorm-room master file through the alternate indexes defined in Exercise 13? (Hint: You have to open two paths, not just one.)

APPENDIXES

APPENDIX A. Nonprivileged Instructions

mnemonic code	machine code	type	instruction name	text section	mnemonic code	machine code	type	instruction name	text section
c A	5A	RX	add	5.3	LH	48	RX	load halfword	5.2
c AD	6A	RX	add normalized (long)	13.7	LM	98	RS	load multiple	5.2
c ADR	2A	RR	add normalized (long)	13.7	c LNDR	21	RR	load negative (long)	13.6
c AE	7A	RX	add normalized (short)	13.7	c LNER	31	RR	load negative (short)	13.6
c AER	3A	RR	add normalized (short)	13.7	c LNR	11	RR	load negative	5.6
c AH	4A	RX	add halfword	5.3	c LPDR	20	RR	load positive (long)	13.6
c AL	5E	RX	add logical	5.3	c LPER	30	RR	load positive (short)	13.6
c ALR	1E	RR	add logical	5.3	c LPR	10	RR	load positive	5.6
c AP	FA	SS$_2$	add decimal	12.3	LR	18	RR	load	5.2
c AR	1A	RR	add	5.3	LRDR	25	RR	load rounded (extended to long)	13.7
c AU	7E	RX	add unnormalized (short)	13.7					
c AUR	3E	RR	add unnormalized (short)	13.7	LRER	35	RR	load rounded (long to short)	13.7
c AW	6E	RX	add unnormalized (long)	13.7	c LTDR	22	RR	load and test (long)	13.5
c AWR	2E	RR	add unnormalized (long)	13.7	c LTER	32	RR	load and test (short)	13.5
c AXR	36	RR	add normalized (extended)	13.7	c LTR	12	RR	load and test	5.4
BAL	45	RX	branch and link	9.5	M	5C	RX	multiply	5.3
BALR	05	RR	branch and link	9.3	* MC	AF	SI	monitor call	---
* BAS	4D	RX	branch and save	9.5	MD	6C	RX	multiply (long)	13.7
* BASR	0D	RR	branch and save	9.3	MDR	2C	RR	multiply (long)	13.7
BC	47	RX	branch on condition	8.4	ME	7C	RX	multiply (short)	13.7
BCR	07	RR	branch on condition	8.4	MER	3C	RR	multiply (short)	13.7
BCT	46	RX	branch on count	4.5	MH	4C	RX	multiply halfword	5.3
BCTR	06	RR	branch on count	---	MP	FC	SS$_2$	multiply decimal	12.3
BXH	86	RS	branch on index high	4.6	MR	1C	RR	multiply	5.3
BXLE	87	RS	branch on index low or equal	4.6	MVC	D2	SS$_1$	move characters	7.2
c C	59	RX	compare	5.5	* MVCIN	E8	SS$_1$	move inverse	7.2
c CD	69	RX	compare (long)	13.5	*c MVCL	0E	RR	move characters long	7.8
c CDR	29	RR	compare (long)	13.5	MVI	92	SI	move immediate	7.2
*c CDS	BB	RS	compare double and swap	---	MVN	D1	SS$_1$	move numerics	12.6
c CE	79	RX	compare (short)	13.5	MVO	F1	SS$_2$	move with offset	12.6
c CER	39	RR	compare (short)	13.5	MVZ	D3	SS$_1$	move zones	12.6
c CH	49	RX	compare halfword	5.5	MXD	67	RX	multiply (long to extended)	13.7
c CL	55	RX	compare logical	7.3	MXDR	27	RR	multiply (long to extended)	13.7
c CLC	D5	SS$_1$	compare logical characters	7.3	MXR	26	RR	multiply (extended)	13.7
*c CLCL	0F	RR	compare logical characters long	7.8	c N	54	RX	and	8.2
c CLI	95	SI	compare logical immediate	7.3	c NC	D4	SS$_1$	and characters	8.2
*c CLM	BD	RS	compare logical under mask	7.3	c NI	94	SI	and immediate	8.2
c CLR	15	RR	compare logical	7.3	c NR	14	RR	and	8.2
c CP	F9	SS$_2$	compare decimal	12.4	c O	56	RX	or	8.2
c CR	19	RR	compare	5.5	c OC	D6	SS$_1$	or characters	8.2
*c CS	BA	RS	compare and swap	---	c OI	96	SI	or immediate	8.2
CVB	4F	RX	convert to binary	12.8	c OR	16	RR	or	8.2
CVD	4E	RX	convert to decimal	12.8	PACK	F2	SS$_2$	pack	12.8
D	5D	RX	divide	5.3	c S	5B	RX	subtract	5.3
DD	6D	RX	divide (long)	13.7	c SD	6B	RX	subtract normalized (long)	13.7
DDR	2D	RR	divide (long)	13.7	c SDR	2B	RR	subtract normalized (long)	13.7
DE	7D	RX	divide (short)	13.7	c SE	7B	RX	subtract normalized (short)	13.7
DER	3D	RR	divide (short)	13.7	c SER	3B	RR	subtract normalized (short)	13.7
DP	FD	SS$_2$	divide decimal	12.3	c SH	4B	RX	subtract halfword	5.3
DR	1D	RR	divide	5.3	c SL	5F	RX	subtract logical	5.3
c ED	DE	SS$_1$	edit	12.9	c SLA	8B	RS	shift left single	8.1
c EDMK	DF	SS$_1$	edit and mark	12.9	c SLDA	8F	RS	shift left double	8.1
EX	44	RX	execute	7.7	SLDL	8D	RS	shift left double logical	8.1
HDR	24	RR	halve (long)	13.7	SLL	89	RS	shift left single logical	8.1
HER	34	RR	halve (short)	13.7	c SLR	1F	RR	subtract logical	5.3
IC	43	RX	insert character	7.2	c SP	FB	SS$_2$	subtract decimal	12.3
*c ICM	BF	RS	insert characters under mask	7.2	c SPM	04	RR	set program mask	11.4
L	58	RX	load	5.2	c SR	1B	RR	subtract	5.3
LA	41	RX	load address	4.5	c SRA	8A	RS	shift right single	8.1
c LCDR	23	RR	load complement (long)	13.6	c SRDA	8E	RS	shift right double	8.1
c LCER	33	RR	load complement (short)	13.6	SRDL	8C	RS	shift right double logical	8.1
c LCR	13	RR	load complement	5.6	SRL	88	RS	shift right single logical	8.1
LD	68	RX	load (long)	13.4	*c SRP	F0	SS$_1$	shift and round decimal	12.5
LDR	28	RR	load (long)	13.4	ST	50	RX	store	5.2
LE	78	RX	load (short)	13.4	STC	42	RX	store character	7.2
LER	38	RR	load (short)	13.4					

c = condition code is set   * = IBM System 370

mnemonic code	machine code	type	instruction name	text section
* STCK	B205	S	store clock	---
* STCM	BE	RS	store characters under mask	7.2
STD	60	RX	store (long)	13.4
STE	70	RX	store (short)	13.4
STH	40	RX	store halfword	5.2
STM	90	RS	store multiple	5.2
c SU	7F	RX	subtract unnormalized (short)	13.7
c SUR	3F	RR	subtract unnormalized (short)	13.7
SVC	0A	RR	supervisor call	19.4
c SW	6F	RX	subtract unnormalized (long)	13.7

mnemonic code	machine code	type	instruction name	text section
c SWR	2F	RR	subtract unnormalized (long)	13.7
c SXR	37	RR	subtract normalized (extended)	13.7
c TM	91	SI	test under mask	8.3
TR	DC	SS$_1$	translate	7.9
c TRT	DD	SS$_1$	translate and test	7.9
c TS	93	S	test and set	8.3
UNPK	F3	SS$_2$	unpack	12.8
c X	57	RX	exclusive or	8.2
c XC	D7	SS$_1$	exclusive or characters	8.2
c XI	97	SI	exclusive or immediate	8.2
c XR	17	RR	exclusive or	8.2
c ZAP	F8	SS$_2$	zero and add decimal	12.3

c = condition code is set   * = IBM System 370

Instruction Format Summary

type	machine language instruction formats		assembly language operand formats		Notes
RR	op, R1, R2 (bits 0, 8, 12)		explicit	R1,R2	
RX	op, R1, X2, B2, D2 (bits 0, 8, 12, 16, 20, 31)		explicit	R1,D2(X2,B2) / R1,D2(,B2) / R1,D2(X2) / R1,D2	1
			implicit	R1,S2(X2) / R1,S2	
RS	op, R1, R2, B3, D3 (bits 0, 8, 12, 16, 20, 31)		explicit	R1,R2,D3(B3)	2
			implicit	R1,R2,S3	
SI	op, I2, B1, D1 (bits 0, 8, 16, 20, 31)		explicit	D1(B1),I2	3
			implicit	S1,I2	
S	op, B1, D1 (bits 0, 16, 20, 31)		explicit	D1(B1)	
			implicit	S1	
SS$_1$	op, L, B1, D1, B2, D2 (bits 0, 8, 16, 20, 32, 36, 47)		explicit	D1(L,B1),D2(B2)	4,5
			implicit	S1,S2	
			mixed	D1(L,B1),S2 / S1(L),D2(B2) / S1(L),S2 / S1,D2(B2)	
SS$_2$	op, L1, L2, B1, D1, B2, D2 (bits 0, 8, 12, 16, 20, 32, 36, 47)		explicit	D1(L1,B1),D2(L2,B2)	5,6
			implicit	S1,S2	
			mixed	D1(L1,B1),S2(L2) / D1(L1,B1),S2 / S1(L1),S2(L2) / S1(L1),S2 / S1,S2(L2) / S1(L1),D2(L2,B2) / S1,D2(L2,B2)	

NOTES:
1. RX: When the index field X2 is omitted, it is assumed to be 0. An X2 field of 0 means no indexing.
2. RS: IBM manuals give R1,R3,D2(B2) where we have given R1,R2,D3(B3)
3. SI: The I2 field is 1 byte, used as immediate data.
4. SS$_1$:   In machine language, the length field L is represented by a number that is one less than that used in Assembly Language.
5. SS$_1$, SS$_2$:   Any of the length fields can be omitted in Assembly Language when a symbolic address is used. If so omitted, the Assembler uses the length-attribute of the corresponding symbol.
6. SS$_2$:   In machine language the length fields L1 and L2 are represented by numbers that are one less than those used in the corresponding assembly language fields.

APPENDIX B. Extended Mnemonic Codes for BC and BCR Instructions.

	RX-type instructions					RR-type instructions		
extended mnemonic code	mnemonic code	machine code	instruction name			extended mnemonic code	mnemonic code	machine code
B	BC 15,	47F	unconditional branch			BR	BCR 15,	07F
NOP	BC 0,	470	unconditional no operation			NOPR	BCR 0,	070
			used after compare instructions					
BE	BC 8,	478	branch if equal			BER	BCR 8,	078
BL	BC 4,	474	branch if low			BLR	BCR 4,	074
BH	BC 2,	472	branch if high			BHR	BCR 2,	072
BNE	BC 7,	477	branch if not equal			BNER	BCR 7,	077
BNL	BC 11,	47B	branch if not low			BNLR	BCR 11,	07B
BNH	BC 13,	47D	branch if not high			BNHR	BCR 13,	07D
			used after arithmetic instructions					
BZ	BC 8,	478	branch if zero			BZR	BCR 8,	078
BM	BC 4,	474	branch if minus			BMR	BCR 4,	074
BP	BC 2,	472	branch if plus			BPR	BCR 2,	072
BO	BC 1,	471	branch if overflow			BOR	BCR 1,	071
BNZ	BC 7,	477	branch if not zero			BNZR	BCR 7,	077
BNM	BC 11,	47B	branch if not minus			BNMR	BCR 11,	07B
BNP	BC 13,	47D	branch if not plus			BNPR	BCR 13,	07D
BNO	BC 14,	47E	branch if not overflow			BNOR	BCR 14,	07E
			used after test under mask instructions					
BZ	BC 8,	478	branch if zeroes			BZR	BCR 8,	078
BO	BC 1,	471	branch if ones			BOR	BCR 1,	071
BM	BC 4,	474	branch if mixed			BMR	BCR 4,	074

APPENDIX C. Condition Code Settings for Nonprivileged Instructions

	instruction		condition code 0	condition code 1	condition code 2	condition code 3
INTEGER OPERATIONS	add subtract	A, AR, AH S, SR, SH	result is zero	result is negative	result is positive	operation generated an overflow
	add subtract	AL, ALR SL, SLR	result is zero, with no carry (AL, ALR only)	result is not zero, with no carry	result is zero, with carry	result is not zero, with carry
	compare	C, CR, CH	both operands are equal	first operand less than second	first operand greater than second	---
	load	LCR	result is zero	result is negative	result is positive	overflow generated
		LNR	result is zero	result is negative	---	---
		LPR	result is zero	---	result is positive	overflow generated
		LTR	result is zero	result is negative	result is positive	---
	shift	SLA, SLDA	result is zero	result is negative	result is positive	overflow generated
		SRA, SRDA	result is zero	result is negative	result is positive	---
BYTE OPERATIONS	insert	ICM	all inserted bits 0, or all mask bits 0	1st inserted bit is 1	1st inserted bit is 0, but not all are 0	---
	compare	CL, CLR CLC, CLI	both operands are equal	first operand less than second	first operand greater than second	---
		CLCL	operands are equal, or have zero lengths	first operand less than second	first operand greater than second	---
		CLM	bytes selected are equal or mask bits are all 0	first operand field less than second	first operand field greater than second	---
	copy	MVCL	first operand's length equals second operand's	first operand's length less than second's	first operand's length greater than second's	destructive overlap (no bytes copied)
	translate	TRT	all argument bytes tested; all function bytes zero	one or more argument bytes not tested	search stopped on last argument byte	---

	instruction		condition code 0	condition code 1	condition code 2	condition code 3
BIT OPERATIONS	AND OR EXCL-OR	N, NC, NI, NR O, OC, OI, OR X, XC, XI, XR	result is zero result is zero result is zero	result is not zero result is not zero result is not zero	--- --- ---	--- --- ---
	test	TM	all selected bits 0, or all mask bits 0	some selected bits are 0, and some are 1	---	all selected bits are 1's
		TS	left-most bit of tested byte is 0	left-most bit of tested byte is 1	---	---
DECIMAL	add subtract	AP, ZAP SP	result is zero	result is negative	result is positive	operation generated an overflow
	compare	CP	both operands are equal	first operand less than second	first operand greater than second	---
	shift	SRP	result is zero	result is negative	result is positive	overflow generated
FLOATING POINT	add	AE, AER, AD, ADR, AU, AUR, AW, AWR, AXR	mantissa of result is zero	result is negative	result is positive	---
	subtract	SE, SER, SD, SDR, SU, SUR, SW, SWR, SXR	mantissa of result is zero	result is negative (mantissa not zero)	result is positive (mantissa not zero)	---
	load	LCER, LCDR LNER, LNDR LPER, LPDR LTER, LTDR	result mantissa is zero result mantissa is zero result mantissa is zero result mantissa is zero	result is negative result is negative --- result is negative	result is positive --- result is positive result is positive	--- --- --- ---
	compare	CE, CER CD, CDR	both operands are equal	first operand less than second	first operand greater than second	---
MISCELLANEOUS	compare and swap	CS, CDS	compared operands equal, second one is replaced	compared operands not equal, first is replaced	---	---
	set program mask	SPM	(the condition code is set to the value of bits 2 and 3 of the designated register)			
	store clock	STCK	clock in set state	clock in not-set state	clock in error state	clock in stopped state or not-operational
	editing	ED, EDMK	last edited field is zero	last edited field is negative	last edited field is positive	---

APPENDIX D.
Summary of Possible Run-time Error Exception Conditions in Problem Mode Programs

	name of exception	cause of exception	instructions in which exceptions can occur
binary integer arithmetic instructions	Fixed-point Overflow*	Occurs when there is a carry out of the high-order numeric bit position different from the carry out of the sign-bit position	A, AR, AH, S, SR, SH, LCR, LPR, SLA, SLDA
	Fixed-point Divide	Occurs when the divisor is zero or when the quotient or the result of a CVB instruction is greater than $2^{31} - 1$ or less than -2^{31}	D, DR, CVB
	Specification	Occurs when the first operand does not specify an even-numbered register address	D, DR, M, MR, SLDA, SRDA, SLDL, SRDL
decimal arithmetic instructions	Decimal Overflow*	Occurs when one or more significant high-order digits are lost because the destination field is too small to contain the result	AP, SP, ZAP, SRP
	Decimal Divide	Occurs when the divisor is zero or when the quotient exceeds the specified data-field size	DP
	Specification	Occurs when the multiplier or divisor exceeds fifteen digits and sign, or when the first operand field is not longer than the second operand field in a multiplication or division	DP, MP
	Data	Occurs when any of the following conditions occur 1. The sign or digit codes of operand fields in any packed-decimal or CVB instruction are invalid	AP, CP, DP, MP, SP, SRP, ZAP, ED, EDMK, CVB
		2. The first operand field in an MP instruction has an insufficient number of high-order zeroes	MP
		3. The operand fields in AP, CP, DP, MP, and SP overlap in a way other than with coincident right-most bytes	AP, CP, DP, MP, SP
		4. The operand fields in ZAP overlap, and the right-most byte of the second operand is to the right of the right-most byte of the first operand	ZAP
floating-point arithmetic instructions	Exponent Overflow	Occurs when the result characteristic exceeds 127 and the result mantissa is not zero	All floating-point Add, Subtract, Multiply, Divide, and Round instructions
	Exponent Underflow*	Occurs when the result characteristic is less than zero and the result mantissa is not zero	All floating-point Add Normalized, Subtract Normalized, Multiply, Divide, and Halve instructions
	Significance*	Occurs when the result mantissa in floating-point addition or subtraction is zero	All floating-point Add and Subtract instructions
	Floating-point Divide	Occurs when the mantissa of the divisor is zero.	DD, DDR, DE, DER
	Specification	Occurs when an invalid floating-point register address is specified in a floating-point instruction	All floating-point instructions
non-privileged instructions in general	Specification	Occurs under any of the following conditions 1. An instruction address does not designate a location on an even-byte boundary	All branch instructions, and the EX instruction
		2. An operand address does not designate a half-, full-, or double-word boundary in an instruction requiring such a boundary designation	Various instructions**
		3. Even-numbered register addresses are not specified in the CLCL or MVCL instructions	CLCL, MVCL
		4. Bit positions 8–11 of an MC instruction do not contain all zeroes	MC
	Execute	Occurs when the target instruction of an EX instruction is another EX instruction	EX
	Privileged	Occurs when a privileged instruction is executed in problem mode	All privileged instructions
	Operation	Occurs when an attempt is made to execute an instruction that has an invalid opcode.	All invalid opcodes
	Access	Occurs under a variety of conditions, perhaps best summarized as follows: whenever an attempt is made to obtain or store information in an area of memory to which the program is not allowed to have access, this exception occurs. These errors are separately categorized as protection, addressing, segment-translation, page-translation, and translation-specification exceptions. The reader is referred to the *Principles of Operation* manual for the IBM System 360 or 370, for explanatory details.	All instructions that require access to a main memory location in order to complete their execution cycle

Footnotes to Run-time Error Exceptions

*NOTE: Through appropriate execution of the SPM instruction (see Section 11.4), program interruption may be prohibited for fixed-point overflow, floating-point overflow, exponent underflow, and significance error exceptions. All other exceptions always cause program interruption.

**Specification errors occur when operand addresses are not aligned as follows:

	IBM 360	IBM 370
on half word	EX and all branch instructions AH, CH, LH, MH, SH, STH	EX and all branch instructions
on full word	A, AL, C, CL, D, L, LM, M, S, SL, ST, STM AE, AU, CE, DE, LE, ME, SE, STE, SU N, O, X	CS
on double word	AD, AW, CD, DD, LD, MD, MXD, SD, STD, SW, CVB, CVD	CDS

APPENDIX E.   Assembler Directives

name field[1]

b	o	v	s	opcode[7]	operand[2]	meaning	summary of action taken by Assembler	text section
X				ACTR	arithm-expr	assembler counter	sets maximum number of AIF and AGO branches permitted within a macro or open code	none
X			X	AGO	sequence-symbol	assembler go to	skips to statement identified by sequence-symbol in operand	16.3
X			X	AIF	(logic-expr)sequence-symbol	assembler if	skips to statement identified by sequence-symbol in operand, provided logical-expression is true	16.3
X			X	ANOP		assembler no-op	identifies statement by sequence-symbol (if any) in name field, but takes no other action	16.3
X	X	X	X	CNOP	b,w	conditional no-op	generates zero or more RR-type no-op instructions (NOPR) for alignment on half-, full-, or double-word body	6.4
X	X	X	X	COM		common section	defines beginning or continuation of common reference control section	9.7
X				COPY	library member name	copy library statements	copies pre-defined source statements from a library file, and inserts them into source module	none
X	X	X	X	CSECT		control section	defines beginning or continuation of an executable control section	15.2
X	X	X	X	CXD		constant for external dummy section	reserves a full word for total length of memory required by external dummy sections	none
X	X	X	X	DC	dupl type modf const	define constant	generates one or more constants in accordance with specifications given in operand	6.1
X			X	DROP	base-reg-list	drop base registers	removes registers from list established by USING directives	9.6
X	X	X	X	DS	dupl type modf const	define storage	reserves memory space in accordance with specifications given in operand	6.3
X	X	X	X	DSECT		dummy section	defines beginning or continuation of dummy reference control section	9.7
	X	X		DXD	dupl type modf const	external dummy section	describes memory areas to be reserved for external dummy section	none
X			X	EJECT		page eject	continues listing on following page	14.1
X			X	END	relo-expr, or blank	end of module	terminates Pass 1 and Pass 2 processing, and uses operand to identify first run-time instruction	15.6
X			X	ENTRY	list of symbols	entry point	identifies symbols defined in the source-module but which may be referred to in another module	9.7
	X	X		EQU	relo-expr or abs-expr	equivalence constant	assigns integer specified by operand to symbol in name field	6.2
X			X	EXTRN	list of symbols	external symbol	identifies symbols referred to in source-module but defined in another source-module	9.7
X				GBLx	list of assembly vars.	global variable, of type "x"	defines one or more assembly variables with global scope, and type "x"	16.2
X				ICTL	b or b,e or b,e,c	control source statement format	define the beginning, ending, and/or continuing positions of all following statements	14.7
X				ISEQ	l,r or blank	sequence-check source statements	initiate or terminate sequence-checking of source-module statements	14.6
X				LCLx	list of assembly vars.	local variable, of type "x"	defines one or more assembly variables with local scope, and type "x"	16.2
X	X	X	X	LTORG		literal origin	assigns addresses to all literals referenced since last occurrence of LTORG	15.5
X				MACRO		macro header	prepares to accept definition of a macro, beginning with following statement	17.2
X			X	MEND		macro trailer	terminates definition of a macro	17.2

b	o	v	s	opcode[7]	operand[2]	meaning	summary of action taken by Assembler	text section
X			X	MEXIT		macro exit	skips to the MEND directive in the macro definition in which MEXIT occurs	17.3
X			X	MNOTE	n,'text-string'	macro note	prints text-string on listing, and identifies it in cross-reference	17.3
	opcode			OPSYN	opcode, or blank	opcode synonym	makes name-field opcode synonymous with operand opcode, or invalidates it	14.5
X	X	X	X	ORG	relo-expr, or blank	MLC origin	sets MLC equal to value of operand's relocatable expression, or to its previous highest value	15.4
X			X	POP	4	recover status from push-down list	restores status of PRINT and/or USING directives saved by most recent PUSH directive	14.4
X			X	PRINT	5	control printing details	controls amount of detail on listing, in accordance with specifications in operand	14.4
X			X	PUNCH	"text-string"	produce punched card output	punches one card, whose contents are the text-string given in operand	none
X			X	PUSH	4	save status in push-down list	saves status of most recent PRINT and/or USING directive	14.4
X			X	REPRO		produce punched card output	punches one card, whose contents are given in the statement line following the REPRO directive	none
		X		SETx	3, 6	assign value to assembly variable	assigns value specified by operand to assembly variable identified in name field	16.2
X			X	SPACE	n, or blank	line spacing	inserts n lines in listing (if operand blank, $n = 1$)	14.3
X	X	X	X	START	self-defining term, or blank	control section	defines the beginning of the first executable control section in a source module	15.3
X			X	TITLE	'text-string'	page title	prints text string at top of each page until subsequent TITLE processed	14.2
X			X	USING	base-addr,base-reg-list	specifies implied base registers & base addresses	determines base-displacement form of address corresponding to implicit operand, using base register whose base address gives smallest displacement	3.5 9.6
X			X	WXTRN	list of symbols	weak external symbol	same as EXTRN, except that automatic search of libraries is suppressed	none

Footnotes to Assembler Directives

1. The name field for each directive will either be a blank (b), an ordinary symbol (o), a variable symbol (v), or a sequence symbol (s). Whichever of these is permitted for a given directive is indicated by an X in the appropriate column of the name-field heading. Absence of an X means that that type of name field is not permitted in that directive. For example, in the END directive, the name field can only be blank *or* a sequence symbol.

2. The following abbreviations are used:

abs-expr	absolute expression	dupl	duplicator
arithm-expr	arithmetic expression	logic-expr	logical expression
base-addr	base address	MLC	memory location counter
base-reg-list	base register list	modf	modifier
const	constant	relo-expr	relocatable expression
		vars	variables

3. In the GBLx, LCLx, and SETx directives, the letter "x" stands for either A, B, or C, indicating, respectively, an arithmetic assembly variable, a boolean assembly variable, or a character assembly variable.

4. The operands of the PUSH and POP directives must be one of the following four strings:

   PRINT
   PRINT,USING
   USING,PRINT
   USING

5. The operand of the PRINT directive must contain one or more of the following keywords, separated by commas: ON, OFF, GEN, NOGEN, DATA, NODATA

6. The operand of a SETx directive must be an arithmetic expression, a boolean expression, or a character expression, whichever is appropriate for the assembly variable identified in the SETx name field.

7. The following directives are not available in DOS/VS: CXD, DXD, OPSYN, POP, PUSH.

APPENDIX F. EBCDIC and ASCII Schemes.

EBCDIC

bits 0,1,2,3 → columns; bits 4,5,6,7 → rows

bits 0123 →	0000	0001	0010	0011	0100	0101	0110	0111	1000	1001	1010	1011	1100	1101	1110	1111	bits 4567
	NUL	DLE	DS		SP	&	-						{	}	\	0	0000
	SOH	DC1	SOS			/			a	j	~		A	J		1	0001
	STX	DC2	FS	SYN					b	k	s		B	K	S	2	0010
	ETX	DC3	WUS	IR					c	l	t		C	L	T	3	0011
	SEL	RES	BYP	PP					d	m	u		D	M	U	4	0100
	HT	NL	LF	TRN					e	n	v		E	N	V	5	0101
	RNL	BS	ETB	NBS					f	o	w		F	O	W	6	0110
	DEL	POC	ESC	EOT					g	p	x		G	P	X	7	0111
	GE	CAN	SA	SBS					h	q	y		H	Q	Y	8	1000
	SPS	EM		IT				`	i	r	z		I	R	Z	9	1001
	RPT	UBS	SM	REF	¢	!	¦	:								|	1010
	VT	CU1	CSP	CU3	.	$	,	#									1011
	FF	IFS	MFA	DC4	<	*	%	@					♪		⊓		1100
	CR	IGS	ENQ	NAK	(	)	_	'									1101
	SO	IRS	ACK		+	;	>	=					⊤				1110
	SI	IUS	BEL	SUB	|	¬	?	"							EO		1111

ASCII

bits 1,2,3 → columns; bits 4,5,6,7 → rows

bits 123 →	000	001	010	011	100	101	110	111	bits 4567
	NUL	DLE	SP	0	@	P	`	p	0000
	SOH	DC1	!	1	A	Q	a	q	0001
	STX	DC2	"	2	B	R	b	r	0010
	ETX	DC3	#	3	C	S	c	s	0011
	EOT	DC4	$	4	D	T	d	t	0100
	ENQ	NAK	%	5	E	U	e	u	0101
	ACK	SYN	&	6	F	V	f	v	0110
	BEL	ETB	'	7	G	W	g	w	0111
	BS	CAN	(	8	H	X	h	x	1000
	HT	EM	)	9	I	Y	i	y	1001
	LF	SUB	*	:	J	Z	j	z	1010
	VT	ESC	+	;	K	[	k	{	1011
	FF	FS	,	<	L	\	l	|	1100
	CR	GS	-	=	M	]	m	}	1101
	SO	RS	.	>	N	^	n	~	1110
	SI	US	/	?	O	_	o	DEL	1111

NOTE: The seven ASCII bits are numbered so as to enable direct comparison with EBCDIC. For example, the letter J is

1001010 in ASCII
11010001 in EBCDIC

The control character mnemonics are defined below. Note that SP is the space, or blank, character.

Sources: IBM Publications GA22–7000, *System 370 Principles of Operation* and GX20–1850, *System/370 Reference Booklet.*

* ACK	Acknowledge		DS	Digit Select		IT	Indent Tab	SA	Set Attribute
* BEL	Bell	* EM	End of Medium		IUS/	Interchange Unit Separator/	SBS	Subscript
* BS	Backspace	* ENQ	Enquiry		ITB	Intermed. Transmission Block	SEL	Select
BYP/	Bypass/		EO	Eight Ones	* LF	Line Feed	* SI	Shift In
INP	Inhibit Presentation	* EOT	End of Transmission		MFA	Modify Field Attribute	SM/	Set Mode/
* CAN	Cancel	* ESC	Escape	* NAK	Negative Acknowledge	SW	Switch
* CR	Carriage Return	* ETB	End of Transmission Block	NBS	Numeric Backspace	* SO	Shift Out
CSP	Control Sequence Prefix	* ETX	End of Text	* NL	New Line	* SOH	Start of Heading
CU1	Customer Use 1	* FF	Form Feed	* NUL	Null	SOS	Start of Significance
CU2	Customer Use 2	* FS	Field Separator	POC	Program-Operator Communication	* SP	Space
CU3	Customer Use 3	GE	Graphic Escape	PP	Presentation Position	SPS	Superscript
* DC1	Device Control 1	* GS	Group Separator	RES/	Restore/	* STX	Start of Text
* DC2	Device Control 2	* HT	Horizontal Tab	ENP	Enable Presentation	* SUB	Substitute
* DC3	Device Control 3	IFS	Interchange File Separator	RFF	Required Form Feed	* SYN	Synchronous Idle
* DC4	Device Control 4	IGS	Interchange Group Separator	RNL	Required New Line	UBS	Unit Backspace
* DEL	Delete	IR	Index Return	RPT	Repeat	* US	Unit Separator
* DLE	Data Link Escape	IRS	Interchange Record Separator	* RS	Record Separator	* VT	Vertical Tab
								WUS	Word Underscore

* Indicates that definitions of purpose may be found in the *American National Dictionary for Information Processing,* Technical Report X3/TR–1–77, September 1977, published by the Computers and Business Equipment Manufacturers Association, 1828 L Street NW, Washington, DC 20036. Definitions for the remaining control characters may be found in the various IBM reference manuals describing individual device characteristics.

APPENDIX G.   References

Abel, Peter. *Programming Assembler Language*. Reston, Virginia: Reston Publishing Co., 1979.

ANDIP: American National Dictionary for Information Processing. American National Standards Committee X3 Technical Report X3/TR–1–77. Computers and Business Equipment Manufacturers Association, 1977.

Brearley, Harrington C., Jr. *Introduction to Assembler Language Programming for the IBM System 360–70*. New York: Macmillan, 1974.

Brown, Gary DeWard. *System/370 Job Control Language*. New York: Wiley, 1977.

Burian, Barbara J. *A Simplified Approach to S/370 Assembly Language Programming*. Englewood Cliffs, N.J.: Prentice-Hall, 1977.

Campbell-Kelly, M. *An Introduction to Macros*. Elsevier, 1973.

Cashman, Thomas J., and Shelly, Gary B. *IBM 360 and Assembler Language Work Book*. Anaheim, Calif.: Anaheim Publishing Co, 1973.

Chapin, Ned. *Three-Sixty—Three-Seventy Programming in Assembly Language*. New York: McGraw-Hill, 1973.

Computing Surveys (Special Issue). *Programming*. December 1974.
    Brown, P.J., "Programming and Documenting Software Projects," 213–20.
    Kernighan, B.W. and Plauger, P.J., "Programming Style: Examples and Counterexamples," 303–19.
    Knuth, D.E., "Structured Programming with Go To Statements," 261–301.
    Wirth, N., "On the Composition of Well-Structured Programs," 247–59.
    Yohe, J.M., "An Overview of Programming Practices," 221–45.

Dahl, O.-J., Dijkstra, E.W., and Hoare, C.A.R. *Structured Programming*. Academic Press, 1972.

Denning, P.J. *"A Hard Look at Structured Programming."* In *Structured Programming*, D. Bates, editor. pp. 183–202. Infotech International Ltd., 1976.

Feingold, Carl. *Introduction to Assembler Language Programming*. Dubuque, Iowa: Wm. C. Brown Company Publishers, 1978.

Flores, Ivan. *Job Control Language and File Definition*. Englewood Cliffs, N.J.: Prentice-Hall, 1971.

Freeman, Peter, and Wasserman, Anthony. *Tutorial on Software Design Techniques*. IEEE Computer Society, 1976.

Hannula, Reino. *Computers and Programming: A System 360–370 Assembler Language Approach*. Boston: Houghton Mifflin, 1974.

Johnson, David L. *Structured Assembly Language for IBM Computers*. Palo Alto, Calif.: Mayfield Publishing Co., 1982.

Katzan, Harry, Jr. *Computer Systems Organization and Programming*. Chicago: Science Research Associates, 1976.

Kent, W. "Assembler-Language Macroprogramming: A Tutorial Oriented Toward the IBM 360." In *Computing Surveys*, pp. 183–96. December 1969.

Knuth, Donald E. *The Art of Computer Programming*. Addison Wesley.
    Vol. 1: *Fundamental Algorithms*, 2d Ed. 1973
    Vol. 2: *Semi-Numerical Algorithms*, 2d ed. 1981
    Vol. 3: *Sorting and Searching*, 1973

Kuo, Shan Sun. *Assembler Language for Fortran, Cobol, and PL/1 Programmers IBM 360/370*. Addison Wesley.

McQuillen, Kevin. *System/360–70 Assembler Language (DOS)*. M. Murach & Associates, 1974.

Peterson, James L. *Computer Organization and Assembly Language Programming*. New York: Academic Press, 1978.

Presser, L., and White, J.R. "Linkers and Loaders." In *Computing Surveys,* pp. 149–67. September 1972.

Rindfleisch, Daniel H. *Debugging System 360/370 Programs Using OS and VS Storage Dumps*. Englewood Cliffs, N.J.: Prentice Hall, 1976.

Rindfleisch, Daniel H. *Utilizing System 360/370 OS and VS Job Control Language and Utility Programs*. Englewood Cliffs, N.J.: Prentice-Hall, 1979.

Rudd, Walter G. *Assembly Language Programming and the IBM 360 & 370 Computers*. Englewood Cliffs, N.J.: Prentice Hall, 1976.

Shelly, Gary B., and Cashman, Thomas J. *IBM 360 Assembler Language Disk-Tape Advanced Concepts*. Anaheim, Calif.: Anaheim Publishing Co., 1978.

Shelly, Gary B., and Cashman, Thomas J. *DOS Job Control for Assembler Programmers*. Anaheim, Calif.: Anaheim Publishing Co., 1972.

Silver, Gerald A. *Computer Algorithms and Flowcharting*. New York: McGraw-Hill, 1975.

Stark, Richard, and Dearholt, Donald M. *Computer Concepts and Assembler Programming: 360/370 Systems*. Academic Press, 1975.

Stern, Nancy; Sager, Alden; and Stern, Robert A. *370/360 Assembler Language Programming*. New York: Wiley, 1979.

Struble, George W. *Assembler Language Programming: The IBM System/360 and 370,* 2d edition. Addison Wesley, 1975.

Tuggle, Sharon K. *Assembler Language Programming: Systems/360 and 370*. Chicago: Science Research Associates, 1975.

Turski, W.M. *Computer Programming Methodology*. Heyden and Sons, Ltd., 1978.

Weik, Martin H. *Standard Dictionary of Computers and Information Processing,* revised 2d edition. Hayden, 1977.

Yarmish, Rina, and Yarmish, Joshua. *Assembly Language Fundamentals 360/370 OS/VS DOS/VS*. Addison Wesley, 1979.

IBM Reference Manuals:
A22–6821 *System/360 Principles of Operation*
GA22–7000 *System/370 Principles of Operation*
GC20–1699 *Data Processing Glossary*
GC24–5093 *OS/VS1 Debugging Guide*
GC24–5099 *OS/VS1 JCL Reference*
GC24–5100 *OS/VS1 JCL Services*
GC24–5103 *OS/VS1 Supervisor Services and Macro Instructions*
GC26–3813 *OS/VS Linkage Editor and Loader*
GC26–3872 *OS/VS1 Data Management Macro Instructions*
GC26–3874 *OS/VS1 Data Management Services Guide*
GC26–3901 *OS/VS1 Utilities*
GC33–4010 *OS/VS-DOS/VS-VM/370 Assembler Language*
GC33–4021 *OS/VS-VM/370 Assembler Programmer's Guide*
GC38–1001 *OS/VS1 Message Library: System Messages*
GC33–5371 *DOS/VS System Management Guide*
GC33–5372 *DOS/VS Data Management Guide*
GC33–5373 *DOS/VS Supervisor and I/O Macros*
GC33–5376 *DOS/VS System Control Statements*
GC33–5380 *DOS/VS Serviceability Aids and Debugging Procedures*
GC33–5381 *DOS/VS System Utilities*
G320–5774 *VSAM Primer and Reference*

INDEX